Imperial Measurements

Theoretically, both the United Kingdom and Canada use the metric system, but older recipes rely on the "imperial" measurement system, which differs from standard U.S. measurements in its liquid ("fluid") measurements:

¼ cup = 2.5 ounces
½ cup ("gill") = 5 ounces
1 cup = 10 ounces
1 pint = 20 ounces
1 quart = 40 ounces

Measurement Conversions

Note that volume (i.e., cup) measures and weight (i.e., ounce) measures convert perfectly for liquids only. Solids are a different story; 1 cup of flour weighs only 4 or 5 ounces.

Dash or pinch = less than ¼ teaspoon
3 teaspoons = 1 tablespoon
2 tablespoons = 1 fluid ounce
4 tablespoons = ¼ cup = 2 fluid ounces
16 tablespoons = 1 cup = 8 fluid ounces
2 cups = 1 pint
2 pints = 1 quart
4 quarts = 1 gallon

Some Useful Substitutions

1 tablespoon baking powder = 2 teaspoons
    baking soda + 1 teaspoon cream of tartar
1 cup brown sugar = 1 cup white sugar
    + 2 tablespoons molasses
1 cup cake flour = ⅞ cup all-purpose flour
    + ⅛ cup cornstarch
1 cup buttermilk = 1 scant cup milk at room
    temperature + 1 tablespoon white vinegar
1 cup sour cream = 1 cup yogurt
    (preferably full fat)

Imperial vs. Metric

These are approximate, but are fine for all uses.

1 ounce = 28 grams
1 pound = 500 grams or ½ kilo
2.2 pounds = 1 kilo
1 teaspoon = 5 milliliters (ml)
1 tablespoon = 15 milliliters
1 cup = ¼ liter
1 quart = 1 liter

How to Cook
Everything
Vegetarian

Other Books by Mark Bittman:

How to Cook Everything

The Best Recipes in the World

Fish: The Complete Guide to Buying and Cooking

How to Cook Everything: The Basics

How to Cook Everything: Bittman Takes on America's Chefs

Mark Bittman's Quick and Easy Recipes from The New York Times

How to Cook *Everything* Vegetarian

Simple Meatless Recipes for Great Food

Mark Bittman

Illustrations by Alan Witschonke

John Wiley & Sons, Inc.

Copyright © 2007 Double B Publishing, Inc.

Illustrations copyright © Alan Witschonke

Published by Wiley Publishing, Inc., Hoboken, New Jersey
Published simultaneously in Canada

For general information about our other products and services, please contact our Customer Care Department within the United States at (800) 762-2974, outside the United States at (317) 572-3993 or fax (317) 572-4002.

Wiley also publishes its books in a variety of electronic formats. Some content that appears in print may not be available in electronic books. For more information about Wiley products, visit our web site at www.wiley.com.

Library of Congress Cataloging-in-Publication Data

Bittman, Mark.
How to cook everything vegetarian : simple meatless recipes for great food / Mark Bittman ;
Illustrations by Alan Witschonke.
p. cm.
Includes index.
ISBN: 978-0-7645-2483-7 (cloth)
1. Vegetarian cookery.   I. Title.
TX837.B5284 2007
641.5'636—dc22   2006036937

Printed in the United States of America

10 9 8 7 6 5 4

Designed by Nick Anderson
Wiley Bicentennial Logo: Richard J. Pacifico

Layout by North Market Street Graphics

Contents

Acknowledgments   vii

Introduction   ix

The best meatless meals are the ones you cook yourself. Start now, here.

Ingredients   1

Terrific vegetarian food begins with simple, everyday ingredients.

Equipment   7

You don't have to spend a fortune on equipment to cook well. All you need are the essential tools, and suggestions for expanding based on how you *really* cook.

Techniques   17

Start with basic knife skills, measuring, and food safety. Then move on to the essential cooking techniques and build confidence to improvise.

Salads   33

Salads can be a light side dish or a full meal. Here are many refreshing green salads, plus vegetable, bean, and grain salads. Pickles, too.

Soups   99

Soups are among the easiest dishes to cook, yet produce results everyone loves. Here's a wide range of vegetarian soups from around the world, from basic to complex.

Eggs, Dairy, and Cheese   161

Eggs go way beyond breakfast. After exploring boiling, scrambling, frying, and so on, try easy but sophisticated egg dishes, or the recipes for cooking with cheese—and even how to make your own.

Produce: Vegetables and Fruits   233

A-to-Z details on every major vegetable and fruit, as well as techniques and recipes for preparing them in every way imaginable.

Pasta, Noodles, and Dumplings   439

The worldwide favorites in vegetarian style, including noodles from scratch, classics from Europe and Asia, and inspiration for endless variations.

Grains   499

Rice dishes—like quick risotto and sushi—are only part of the story. Versatile whole grains—like barley, bulgur, and quinoa—are quick-cooking and easy to master.

Legumes   575

Beans, along with lentils and peas, are a vegetarian staple, and a delicious one, especially with a full collection of dishes that includes skillet beans, stews, purées, classic and innovative baked beans, crunchy fritters, and cakes.

Tofu, Vegetable Burgers, and Other High-Protein Foods   637

From grilled tofu to juicy veggie burgers, this is the place for high-protein vegetarian dishes.

Breads, Pizzas, Sandwiches, and Wraps   679

The basics of quick breads and muffins, flatbreads and crackers, super yeast breads and pizzas, as well as ideas for filling all kinds of sandwiches, tacos, and wraps.

Sauces, Condiments, Herbs, and Spices   749

A staggering array of sauces, salsas, rubs, marinades, and more, plus the fundamentals about herbs and spices, oils and vinegars, and chiles.

Desserts   833

Creative, great-tasting, easy to make, and imaginative cookies and bars, cakes, pies, ice cream, puddings, and candy.

Menus   909

Recipes by Icon   915

Sources   931

List of Illustrations   933

Index   935

Acknowledgments

Maybe novels are written alone, but no cookbook is, especially one as comprehensive in its goals as this one. Like *How to Cook Everything,* its predecessor, *How to Cook Everything Vegetarian* was a massive undertaking for which I needed and received a great deal of help.

Unlike its older sibling, however, this book benefited from the daily presence of a super-collaborator, Kerri Conan. Kerri, an old friend, came along just as I was beginning to put the book together, and has given it all her energy, intelligence, devotion, and cooking and writing skills. This book is as much her baby as it is mine, and it scares me to death to think about how much it would have suffered had she not joined me in working on it.

So, she joins me in thanking a number of other people. Chief among them is Amanda McDougall, who worked with us on a near-daily basis for well over a year. Amanda brought not only cooking and recipe-writing skills but a freshness and creativity to the project that Kerri and I, both old-timers, sorely needed. Equally important was Chris Benton, who helped us shape a rough gem—we hope—into something far more polished.

Other people who played important roles were Kate Bittman, Peter Meehan, Linda Funk, Thom Leonard, Susan Hughes, Genevieve Ko, Rita Powell, Alice Kearney, Julia Turshen, Carl Karush, Michael Chessa, Mark Fitzgerald, and Alan Richman. We'd also like to thank Sean Santoro, for his willingness to eat everything.

At Wiley, we're especially grateful to Linda Ingroia, Todd Fries, Natalie Chapman, Michael Friedberg, Adam Kowit, Charleen Barila, and Rob Garber. Michael Olivo worked furiously to smooth the production process. Jeff Faust brought the cover to its current wonderful state. Nick Anderson is responsible for the interior design. Gypsy Lovett and Carrie Bachman handled publicity.

On a more personal level, I'm thankful that I'm able to mention more-or-less the same people I have for the last 20 years: agent extraordinaire Angela Miller and my dear friend John H. Willoughby, as well as Charles L. Pinsky, John Ringwald, David Paskin, Pamela Hort, Semeon Tsalbins, Shari and Harry Suchecki, Serene Jones, and my oldest friends, Mitch Orfuss, Mark Roth, and especially Sherry Slade and Fred Zolna.

Finally, there are my fabulous daughters, Kate and Emma, whose support has been unwavering and invaluable, and my beloved parents and most loyal fans, Murray and Gertrude Bittman. I'm blessed by their presence.

Introduction

My cooking and eating life has changed greatly in the three years since I began working on *How to Cook Everything Vegetarian*. I wasn't a vegetarian then, and I'm not one now. But I'm a lot closer, for two reasons: one, I have a far greater appreciation for the noncarnivorous world. And two, the world is changing in a way that is going to push all of us, reluctantly or not, towards being at least semivegetarian; our current rate of meat and fish consumption simply cannot be justified, and that's not going away.

I'm not trying to convince you to become a vegetarian, however. For starters, it's not that easy to define what the word means, even if you're one of the millions of Americans who call themselves "vegetarians." Many eat fish; some eat chicken; almost all of them eat animal products of some kind.

The difference between vegetarians and omnivores—people who eat everything, or almost everything—is shrinking, and will continue to do so. Omnivores have vegetarian meals and days, whether intentionally or just because the options have increased dramatically; and some vegetarians continue to eat fish, poultry, and even meat occasionally, because they like it, because they want an occasional shot of its nutritive values, or because it's offered to them and they see no value in being dogmatic.

Increasingly, Americans are becoming "flexitarians," a recently invented word that describes both vegetarians who aren't that strict and meat-eaters who are striving for a more health-conscious, planet-friendly diet. It's likely that by the time *How to Cook Everything Vegetarian* is printed more than 50 percent of us will meet that description, though fewer than 10 percent of us describe ourselves as vegetarians (and far fewer as vegans, who refrain from eating any animal products, even dairy and honey). What flexitarians and vegetarians have in common is the willingness to base meals exclusively on vegetables.

Much of this long-term trend is about health, but there are also the desire to treat animals more fairly, an interest in treating the earth more intelligently, a growing awareness that supreme self-indulgence may lead to long-term disaster, and a recognition of the benefits of a more varied diet, one that can't be described as meat-and-potatoes. Because there are so many reasons, eating vegetarian can quickly become a complicated tangle of personal and political issues.

But the health and nutrition factor *isn't* complicated, and it can be summed up like this: *A diet that's high in vegetables, fruits, whole grains, and legumes is a healthier diet than one that isn't.* The evidence to support this hasn't changed much over the years, except to become more compelling, as it will continue to do.

Dairy, fish, and meat can be added or not, but fewer and fewer impartial nutritionists would argue that any animal products are essential, and certainly no one believes that eating over half a pound of animal protein a day on average—yep, that's the American diet—is good for us.

Unfortunately, it's still difficult to eat good vegetarian meals unless you cook them yourself. The reason is simple and somewhat cynical: There's little money to be made by getting Americans to eat better. (This is also why government agencies directly and indirectly subsidize meat-eating to a phenomenal extent.) The restaurant world is okay with your eating a salad instead of a burger, though they'd rather you put some meat on it and have a fries and Coke too. The supermarket world is fine with offering you a variety of vegetables, but it'll somehow manage to persuade you to buy tons of processed and prepared foods along with them.

Why? Because raw, more-or-less unadulterated vegetables, fruits, grains, and beans are among the least profitable items restaurants and supermarkets can sell. The

real money is made on so-called "value-added" products, which means, essentially, that profits come from the cheap labor it takes to process and preserve the food. A head of romaine lettuce might weigh a pound and cost two dollars. Chop it up and toss in some shredded cabbage and carrots, however, and you can sell a quarter pound for three or four dollars. Stick a piece of cooked chicken on top, along with some bad dressing, and it's eight dollars. Maybe twelve. You get the idea.

The fact that you are holding this book and reading these pages demonstrates that you're interested in increasing your consumption of nonanimal products, and it shows something equally important: You're willing to cook like a vegetarian, at least some of the time. I wrote this book to increase your ability and options for doing so.

How to Cook Everything Vegetarian looks at the non–meat-eating world from the ground up: an approach that builds on basics of cooking in a twenty-first-century American kitchen. We've got everything we need to cook well at our fingertips. Despite their faults, our supermarkets are an efficient food-delivery system; if that weren't enough, we can order food on-line. There are no excuses: We can all get a variety of nonmeat products easily.

What most Americans do not have is experience in putting vegetarian meals together. We've become accustomed (some would say addicted) to eating out, ordering in, and buying preprepared foods, which revolve almost exclusively around meat. And few would argue that this is in our best interests from both a health and a flavor perspective. Even those people who do cook at home reckon that the easiest way to anchor a meal is to throw a steak or a chicken breast on the grill or under the broiler and scatter a few nominal vegetables around it.

If you know how to successfully build a meal without that steak or chicken—at least sometimes—you have the beginning of a much more sensible diet, from every perspective. As I said at the start, I'm not here to convince you to become a vegetarian. I wrote this book to help you (and, to be sure, me) increase the *proportion* of nonmeat products in your diet. And the only way to do that is to make vegetarian meals both appealing and satisfying, whether you choose them once in a while or every day.

How to Cook Everything Vegetarian contains just about everything you need to know to cook every vegetable, fruit, grain, legume, and dairy product you can readily find (and some that are harder to find) in the United States today. It offers the absolute basics of cooking everything from plain white rice to things you may never have heard of, like seitan. It shows you how to make a simple green salad and also a seaweed salad. There are soups, stews, desserts, casseroles, grilled food, pasta dishes, rice, beans, salads . . . not literally everything, but everything I could think of that will be useful to the beginning and experienced American home cook who wants to eat a diet that's less meat-dependent or entirely meat-free.

And this is all done from a perspective of simplicity. I'm not a chef, but a self-taught home cook who has been preparing food daily (sometimes twice daily or more) for almost forty years and writing about it for almost thirty. This book is a follow-up to the best-selling *How to Cook Everything* (which might now be thought of as *How to Cook Everything for Omnivores*) and, like that, is intended to offer the same level of comprehensive guidance and delicious recipes.

That's what this book is about: simple, straightforward, good-tasting cooking. It just happens to exclude meat, poultry, and fish.

Planning Vegetarian Meals

Although the trend is changing, at least among the health-conscious, meat-based meals tend to be centered on the meat, with all the other dishes dismissively called "sides." Vegetarian meals can follow the same pattern. You can, for example, use a lasagne or a quiche as a substitute for the center-of-the-plate meat, and the meal will feel much like a meat-based meal.

But a vegetarian meal is more commonly a table with a few dishes on it, all of them of equal importance. (That's why there's no "appetizer" chapter in this book; almost all of the recipes can serve as appetizers or "main" courses.) The grain is not less valuable than the cooked vegetable, the salad, or the bread; they're all there to complement one another. Pickles you made yourself, a nice piece of cheese, or a bowl of nuts—all are valid courses in the vegetarian meal. Most full-time vegetarians find they need to eat more bulk than they did when they were meat-eaters (they still wind up losing weight), because vegetarian food generally contains less fat and less protein—both of which we get plenty of, even on a strict vegetarian diet. And because of what's known as *palate satiety*—our tendency to get tired of each individual dish as we eat more and more of it (notice how the first bite is often the "best"?)—you might need a dish or two more in a vegetarian meal to relish everything fully.

That doesn't mean extra work, really, especially if you begin to ignore the linear way we were taught to think about home-cooked food: one meal, followed by another meal, and so on, as if they were independent, unconnected activities. (This wasn't the case 150 years ago, when almost everyone grew up on a farm or at least with a full-time homemaker. But none of us was cooking back then. We've all learned how to cook, if at all, as an independent activity, not as part of the pattern of life.)

But if you can start to think more in terms of the big picture, you will have the building blocks for potential meals at all times—in your fridge, freezer, and pantry. You might have a container of cooked grains (there's no reason not to double a recipe; they keep for days). Another of beans (same thing; and beans freeze perfectly). A bin full of fresh vegetables. Some vinaigrette you proudly made. A jar of refrigerator pickles. Plenty of flour, cheese, nuts, and eggs. Maybe a pile of tortillas or a loaf of bread, home baked or bought.

What you might once have thought of as leftovers are now seen as staples: You take the "leftover" grains and heat them up in some olive oil, maybe with a little garlic and a "leftover" vegetable; suddenly, you realize you're making something like fried rice. The beans, maybe with some carrots and onions, become soup, refried beans, or bean cakes. A vegetable gets steamed, or even served raw, with a little vinaigrette. The pickles get thrown on the table; why not? At this point you might not even need the bread and cheese. (See, too, "How to Use Leftovers Intuitively," page 30.)

I knew I was a successful vegetarian cook when I made dinner for a family of friends in Oklahoma during the summer of 2006. The night before, we'd eaten a big-time meat meal: slow-cooked brisket, a lot of it, with some not-especially-interesting sides. Breakfast had centered on bacon and sausage; lunch was leftover brisket, augmented by a little salami. You know the scene.

But to me, summer means vegetables galore. So I went to the store and bought freshly shelled beans, beautiful melons and peaches, a bushel of corn, some tiny new potatoes, some pickling cukes, and not much else. Not surprisingly, given the previous twenty-four hours, I steered clear of meat. I grilled corn and watermelon (check it out; see page 430), made a peach salsa and a bean salad, quick-pickled the cukes, and boiled the potatoes and threw butter on them. The whole thing might have taken me an hour and a half, but I was cooking for fifteen (I also had some help). And we got to the ice cream (which I'd bought; we all have our indulgences), and the chronic meat-eaters realized they'd gone *a whole meal* without meat . . . and enjoyed it like an1y other great meal.

How to Use This Book

A cookbook is useful only if you can find what you're looking for and head to the kitchen (or at least the market). Though I like to think *How to Cook Everything Vegetarian* is also readable, it has a handful of features designed to help you use it immediately, no matter how you like to cook.

Recipe Titles: All are in English or familiar terms, like tacos, burritos, and risotto. If they originated outside the United States, a translation appears as well.

Servings and Portions: The majority of recipes make four servings. The notable exceptions are desserts,

legume dishes (because I encourage you to cook from scratch and store leftovers), and sauces and seasonings. Because vegetarian meals are not necessarily centered on one main dish, several chapter introductions include additional guidelines for figuring portion sizes.

Time: Each recipe includes an estimation of how long it takes to prepare from start to finish and notes how much of that time requires your active attention. Obviously, this will vary based on your experience, but you don't have to be an expert cook to meet the time estimates here.

Icons: There are three symbols: ⓕ, ⓜ, and ⓥ. ⓕ tells you that the recipe is fast, taking less than 30 minutes to prepare. ⓜ indicates that the dish can be made ahead—either in full or to a certain point—and stored for finishing or serving later. (These are excellent dishes when entertaining.) ⓥ means the dish or some of its variations are vegan, or very nearly so with minor adjustments. To learn more about how to make those substitutions, see "The Basics of Vegan Cooking" on page 29.

Variations, Lists, and Charts: Hassle-free cooking is all about options, so nearly all of my recipes include variations. The ones that involve changing a technique or substituting several ingredients appear after the main recipe and are also listed in the Index. Any lists and charts that follow will build on the variations, with more ideas for combining ingredients and flavor profiles. Feel free to use these suggestions verbatim or as a way to explore and improvise on your own.

The Lexicons: These are the rundowns of key ingredients in the vegetarian kitchen, like rice, grains, legumes, chiles, and oil. They always appear in the sections of the book where they are most relevant. The "Produce: Vegetables and Fruits" chapter is essentially one long lexicon, with lots of charts full of information on varieties of an individual fruit or vegetable, followed by the recipes that feature each particular food.

The Index: As comprehensive as it can be and the fastest way to search for what you need.

Ingredients

In all cooking, it makes sense to start with ingredients. You need equipment, you need technique, and you need time and—for most people—recipes. But you can't eat anything without food, so it makes sense to start here.

When you plan a vegetarian meal, you narrow your options, but not much. When you think about all the food that's already in your kitchen, you'll readily realize that meat, poultry, and fish don't make up much of it. The food you need to cook vegetarian meals—indeed, to become a vegetarian if you choose to do so—is already there.

One could argue that eliminating animals from your diet means you must make sure that those foods you do eat are of higher quality; I won't argue that. In fact, I'd argue that no matter what ingredients comprise your diet, they should be of the highest quality that makes sense to you (and, of course, that falls within your budget).

For example, I can usually tell the difference, blindfolded, between estate-bottled, super-high-quality extra virgin olive oil from Liguria, Italy (where my favorites are from), and the commodity stuff that comes from somewhere or other. The first, however, usually costs $30 a liter or more; the second costs about $8 a liter. To me, the difference usually isn't worth it. There are times I might use the better stuff, and when I have it I save it for those occasions, but I'm never distraught when I'm forced to use less-fabulous olive oil. (In fact, the cheap extra virgin olive oil that's available today is better than 99 percent of the olive oil you could buy at any price just fifteen or twenty years ago.)

Artisanal pasta? Yogurt made from biodynamically produced milk? Organically grown heirloom beans? Locally picked ripe white peaches? English farmhouse cheddar? Sure, when I feel like it. And when I don't, good pasta, local yogurt, supermarket beans, Georgia peaches, decent Vermont cheddar—they're fine with me. It's all a judgment call and part of the compromise of everyday cooking.

I draw the line at junk (usually; like everyone else, I make exceptions), at food that really makes a difference, or at ingredients that are really badly made. You can, for example, buy soy sauce that takes a day to produce and is basically salty brown liquid; you can just as easily, and without spending much more, buy real fermented soy sauce, a complex and delicious product that will add life to almost anything. That's an easy choice.

When does it matter? It matters when it matters to you. But here's what matters to me.

8 Ingredients That Must Be Genuine

1. Extra virgin olive oil. As long as it's extra virgin, it's good.
2. Parmigiano-Reggiano. The real thing is the king of cheese.
3. Real soy sauce. The label should say "brewed" or "fermented." Ingredients should be soy, wheat, salt, water, and bacteria. Nothing else, and certainly not TVP (textured vegetable protein) or caramel coloring.
4. Yogurt. I want whole milk, I want active cultures, and I want no thickeners. But use low-fat or even nonfat if you must.
5. Dry pasta. Americans still can't make it; it's gotta come from Italy. Most of the Italian brands are good. None of the American brands are.
6. Basmati rice. A lot of good rices are produced outside of their original regions, but basmati from India is still the best.
7. Salt. It doesn't have to be sea salt; kosher is fine. Just so long as it's not iodized or mixed with other additives.
8. Black peppercorns. You really should grind your own right before every use or nearly every use.

What About Organic?

You can't start talking about vegetarianism, or even about a healthy diet, without being assaulted with questions about whether you buy "organic." Unfortunately, this is a political rather than a cooking question, an extremely complicated one, and one that cannot be answered fully here (or anywhere, for that matter, though the book *The Omnivore's Dilemma* by Michael Pollan carefully addresses the current state of food production in the United States).

But, since this is my book, and people ask me this question all the time (and because writing a book about vegetarian cooking makes you think hard about this issue), it seems fitting to say what I think about this question. I don't routinely buy organic food, and I rarely go out of my way to buy organic food. It's not that I'm against it; when I had a large garden, which I did for about ten years, it was nearly organic: we composted, didn't rely much on chemical fertilizers, and avoided pesticides religiously.

But that's small time, and in a way that's my point: I would rather buy local vegetables from a conscientious gardener or farmer than so-called organic vegetables from a multinational corporation. I think buying local is more important and has more impact than supporting organic.

The reason this is such a difficult question to answer is that my preference here is an impractical one. I don't have the time or energy to seek out local produce on a regular basis; I do most of my shopping in a supermarket, just like almost everyone else in this country. And in supermarkets, organic food doesn't have much of an advantage over conventional food. For the most part, they're both industrially produced in far-away places. I'd rather buy sort of local conventional milk than ultrapasteurized organic milk from hundreds if not thousands of miles away. But would I rather buy organic broccoli from California (I live on the east coast) than conventional broccoli from New Mexico? Sure. Am I convinced it matters much? No. I'm not even convinced that industrially produced "organic" food is any healthier or more sustainable than industrially produced "conventional" food.

It's obviously a complicated question that's constantly evolving. My quick advice, for what it's worth, is: Buy local when you can. Buy the best food you can find when you can't find local. In general, I'd say, be flexible; there may be times when the best vegetable you can find is not only not local and not organic but not even fresh. There are times it might be frozen.

It's worth mentioning here, as I did in "How to Use this Book" (page xiv), that if you run into an ingredient you're not familiar with—or you just want comprehensive info on a category of ingredients, like legumes—please consult the index, which is as comprehensive as I could make it.

The Bottom Line: What You Really Need

The list of ingredients you need to cook can be short or as long as you want. (While writing this book, I was fine in a cabin in the woods for a few days with just some grains, beans, canned goods, soy sauce, and olive oil, along with milk and a few veggies picked up at a farmstand.) I like to strike a balance between having a wide variety of things on hand, so I can expand my choices at will, and having so much food that it starts to go bad. (I also have a policy of trying to run my pantry dry once a year, usually in summer, to make sure everything, even dried goods and spices, maintains at least a semblance of freshness.) But if you were going to stock a vegetarian pantry from the start and throw a few things into the fridge as well, without going overboard, here's what I would recommend:

21 Ingredients You Really Need

1. Olive oil. Extra virgin, as noted earlier. And some decent neutral oil, like grapeseed or corn.
2. Vinegar. See page 759.
3. Soy sauce. As noted earlier.
4. Rice. See page 501. Start with a long-grain and a short-grain, white and brown.
5. Pasta. Italian, as noted earlier. Rice noodles are good to have around also (see page 464).

6. Beans. Dried and canned, and frozen if you can find them. You won't always have time to soak and cook, and canned beans are better than nothing.
7. Spices. From chiles to curry powder to peppercorns. Buy only as much as you will use in a year, if possible.
8. Flours. All-purpose at a minimum. Whole wheat is a good second choice. You'll want cornmeal too. Store them all in the fridge or freezer if you have room.
9. Canned tomatoes. I like to get whole and chop, process, or purée them myself.
10. Aromatic vegetables. Onions, garlic, shallots, celery, and carrots.
11. Baking soda, baking powder, cornstarch, and the like. Yeast if you're going to bake bread.
12. Dried mushrooms. Especially cèpes (porcini) and shiitakes. See page 313.
13. Eggs.
14. Milk and yogurt, and buttermilk for baking.
15. Parmesan. As noted earlier, and on page 209.
16. Nuts and seeds. Sesame seeds for a start, but you can go nuts here (sorry). Many of these have a short shelf life, though, so store in the freezer or buy in small quantities.
17. Lemons and limes. Add freshness to almost anything; in many cases much nicer than vinegar.
18. Butter. Unless you have a problem with it, it's one of the greatest of all ingredients.
19. Sugar and other sweeteners.
20. Long-lasting vegetables and fruits, like potatoes, apples, and oranges. What a boon that you can keep these for weeks or months.
21. Standard condiments like ketchup, mustard, and mayonnaise.

16 More Ingredients That Are Really Nice to Have on Hand

1. Capers. Packed in vinegar or salt. The anchovies of the vegetable world.

2. Seaweed, or sea greens. Really a valuable pantry item; see page 355.

3. Miso. See page 151. Truly one of the world's great ingredients.

4. Sesame oil. Dark. Refrigerate, please; see page 755.

5. Bread crumbs. Best made fresh, but, you know . . . that's not always possible. The best premade are panko, the Japanese kind, which are quite crunchy.

6. Fresh scallions, chiles, and ginger. Strong ingredients that keep for days, if not longer.

7. Coconut milk. I'd put it in my top twenty-one, but not everyone cooks with it as much as I do. Still, the cans keep forever, so it's worth buying.

8. Hot sauce, hoisin sauce, tamarind paste, curry paste, horseradish, and other slightly exotic condiments and seasonings.

9. Mirin and sake. Great for Japanese foods.

10. Fermented black beans. These keep forever and will add something special to any stir-fry.

11. Dried fruit. For both snacking and cooking.

12. Frozen vegetables. Look, life isn't ideal. Better these than nothing. See page 235.

13. Tahini and/or peanut butter. The second, for many of us, is essential, but both are useful.

14. Cream and/or sour cream. If you have it, you'll use it, and you'll love it.

15. Parsley (especially) and other fresh herbs. Underrated and wonderful.

16. Red and white wine. You can cook without them, but if you drink you should cook with them.

Time

What can I say? There isn't enough of it. If you garden, make your own pickles and jams, and freeze tomato sauce from fresh tomatoes for the winter, more power to you. But for most people, it's a terrific scramble just to set aside enough time to cook a couple or a few times a week. That's the sad truth.

We all must eat, yet in this country few people must cook to do so. I will argue, however, that you must cook to eat well. Take-out, prepared food, and restaurant food is fine—at least some of it is—but it's rarely fresh, and you have no control over what goes into it. None. When you cook your own food, you will not add ingredients you've never heard of or chemicals or tons of fat; you just won't do it.

That's not about time; that's just one of the arguments for cooking yourself. It's also far less expensive, and it can be fun (see "The Zen of Cooking?" below). Both of these have an obvious impact on your judgments about whether cooking is "worth the time" it takes. If it's less expensive, you might not need to work as much; if it's fun, well, that's what you're saving your time for, isn't it? (And if it's healthier, you'll have more time in the form of a longer life.)

But those arguments rarely carry much weight with the people who complain to me that they "never have the time" to cook from scratch. To those people I simply say: The thirty to sixty minutes it takes to get a decent meal on the table—if you get your mate and/or your kids and/or your guests to help, even that time can be shortened—is not that much more than the time it takes to reheat the stuff you bought at the supermarket or even to call a pizza delivery service. In fact, if your house is well stocked (and it will be after you undergo the shopping trip recommended in the ingredients section) and you know how to cook (and you will if you practice, even if you know nothing right now), cooking a decent meal is about twice as fast as organizing the family, driving to a restaurant, ordering, waiting, and eating.

I can't argue that cooking is faster than microwaving a frozen dinner. Only that even in the hands of a novice cook, it's infinitely better, cheaper, and healthier.

The Zen of Cooking?

One final point about time. There is a state that experienced cooks enter, and it's not necessarily one of inebriation (though that's possible too, given that the wine is always handy). Being close to real food, peeling, chopping, browning, stirring, tasting . . . these elemental, routine tasks become second nature with practice. You don't have to think a tremendous amount to cook, but you do have to be in one place, calm and concentrated. And when you do that enough, you find yourself comfortable, you find yourself enjoying it, the way you might a drive on an untrafficked road or even the time spent mowing the lawn or watching mindless television. Some people even use cooking as a creative expression or at the very least a relaxing break in their day. As the Zen saying might go, "When you're washing the dishes, wash the dishes." Which means simply this: If you get into cooking, you'll love it and find it meaningful work. And then you won't question the time spent at all.

Equipment

If you're new to cooking, try living with the bare necessities—a couple of basic pans, good knives, some measuring utensils, and stovetop tools like spoons and spatulas—until you get an idea of the kinds of foods you like to make. Then let your cooking style dictate how to expand your collection. You might not need a baking stone and pizza wheel, a stockpot, or a lot of cake pans. Then again you might; but you'll know it's time to get a specific tool, appliance, or pan when you're making something often enough to realize you could do with better tools—which is exactly what these things are. In the meantime, take a minimalist approach and don't buy kitchen equipment until you know you need it.

When you do buy new equipment, choose quality and function over appearance. Hold hand tools to get a feel for them, check the movement on electric appliances (and ideally turn them on in the store so you can check out the noise and vibration levels), and compare the weights of different pans. Since the ultimate goal is to buy pieces you will actually use, try to make sure you'll be comfortable with your equipment before taking it home.

Good cookware need not be expensive: There are real bargains to be had, even with first-rate products. Look for tools—and tableware—at tag sales and thrift stores or hit up your family and friends for their hand-me-downs. Some of the most useful utensils are old-school anyway.

Because vegetable-oriented diets depend more on breads, soups, and salads than meat-based cooking, the equipment needs shift just a bit. Here's a rundown of what I consider the essential equipment for vegetarian or flexitarian cooking, loosely in order of importance.

The Basics of Knives

You can't cook without knives, and a good knife is worth the investment. Note that I didn't say an expensive knife; just a good one. There are now so many good knives sold in so many places that there's really no excuse for buying junk. Inspect knives in person before you buy them and hold them to make sure the fit, weight, and balance are right. (If you wind up going the mail-order route, be sure there's a full-refund policy.)

One piece of my former advice hasn't changed: Carbon-steel alloy blades are *the* knives of choice for beginners, and for most veterans as well. You'll see knives made from old-fashioned steel (which require frequent sharpening and discolor easily), stainless (too flimsy and hard to sharpen), and even ceramic (beautiful, but definitely not for most cooks), but resist the urge, no matter what the ads say. It doesn't matter as much whether the handle is plastic, wood, or recycled rubber, as long as the blade is a good one, the handle feels good when you hold it, and it doesn't move much in your hand. The grip is almost as important as the blade, and only you can judge whether it's a comfortable fit. (For the specifics of actually using knives, see pages 18 to 23.)

The Three Knives You Must Have

- **Chef's knife:** An eight-inch blade is what most home cooks like; go to ten inches if you have especially big hands and like the feel or six inches if your hands are smaller. You'll use this for almost all kitchen tasks.
- **Paring knife:** You can buy expensive paring knives or pretty good ones that are so cheap you can almost consider them disposable. It's nice to have a couple of slightly varying styles. Use for peeling, trimming, and other precise tasks.
- **Long serrated knife or bread knife:** A must for bread and other baked foods, for cutting lasagne into servings, and for splitting cakes into layers.

Also very helpful for ripe tomatoes and large fruits or vegetables like melons or squash.

Washing and Storing Knives

Though you can put many knives in the dishwasher—especially plastic-handled ones—I don't. It's too easy for them—or you—to get nicked. Carefully sponge them (including handles) clean with soapy water, rinse, dry, then store. Don't leave knives in dish racks and other places where they might hurt someone.

Kitchen drawers are not the safest place for knives, so I recommend a knife holder to keep the blades from chipping and to protect their edges and your hands. Wood blocks with slots sit on the countertop; magnetic racks—my choice, though some people find looking at exposed blades unnerving—hang on the wall or cabinet and suspend your knives from the blades.

Sharpening

Dull knives are dangerous. They slip off the food you're cutting and right onto the closest surface, which may be your finger. Although you must be extremely careful with sharp knives—casual contact will lead to a real cut—at least they go where you want them to. Respect your knives: Start with good ones and keep them sharp.

An electric sharpener is the best, easiest, and most expensive way to keep knife blades sharp. And the convenience of sharpening them whenever they need it is tough to beat. Even moderately serious cooks should consider this a worthwhile investment. The alternative is to learn to use a whetstone (not that difficult and very effective but time-consuming) or to take your knives to a hardware or kitchen supply store for sharpening.

A steel is a handy tool for maintaining the edge of knives between sharpenings. It's nothing more than a sturdy rod stuck in a handle, but it takes some practice (see page 18). To use, hold the knife in your cutting hand and the steel in the other. Hold the steel upright or lay it flat on a countertop. Now put the knife blade edge against the inside top of the steel, at a fifteen- to twenty-degree angle, and pull it toward you, down and across the steel several times. To do the other edge on the countertop, turn the knife over and put it on the outside of the steel. Repeat a few times.

The Basics of Pots and Pans

Once you get excited about cooking, it's tempting to buy a full set of shiny new pots and pans. But again, your choices should be dictated by how you cook, not what a manufacturer can fit into a box. The exception is a small set of, say, three pots and a couple of lids, which may get novices off to an easy start.

Choosing a Type of Pan

Arguably, copper pots and pans are best. They conduct heat perfectly, last forever, and look incredible. But they're prohibitively expensive and difficult to maintain.

Fortunately, there are good second choices. Cast iron conducts heat nearly as well at a fraction of the cost, and is pretty much nonstick to boot. With the growing concerns about nonstick coatings (see right), I now cook almost everything in well-seasoned cast-iron cookware. However, the downsides are worth noting: Cast iron weighs a ton (so for large pieces, make sure there are handles on both sides); it requires a certain amount of important (but easy) maintenance; and the iron itself can cause some foods—acidic ones in particular—to discolor or taste slightly tinny. (This reaction won't hurt you or the pot; in fact it adds a little iron to your diet. But it can be annoying.) Just make sure you buy pure iron and not an alloy.

Stainless steel is a decent choice, though more expensive, because you must buy high-quality; inexpensive stainless is simply too thin. The bottoms of the best pots and pans are made by wrapping relatively thick stainless steel around a core of aluminum and/or copper; the combination conducts heat evenly, prevents warping, and minimizes burning. These pans should be fairly heavy. If not, keep looking.

Durable and attractive, stainless steel is a "neutral" metal, meaning you can cook anything in it without worrying about pitting or reacting (see the sidebar on page 11). It's great for stockpots and saucepans, where you're working with mostly liquids. Sauté pans and skillets are excellent, too, as long as you accept the fact that food will stick to their surfaces unless you use at least a thin coating of butter or oil and properly heat the pan (see page 25). And you can heat them up as hot as you like.

Aluminum is another popular material for cookware, provided it has been "anodized," a process that hardens the metal and makes it more durable and less reactive (again, see the sidebar on page 11). Even though various cookware lines might look similar, quality and prices can range wildly, so be sure the metal is nice and thick, especially on the bottom. It pays to read and compare the product information carefully so you know exactly what you're getting and whatever special attention the new pans may require.

Ceramic cookware is great for oven-braising, gratins, and baking, but with rare exceptions you can't use it on the stove. Don't even bother with glass pots and pans. They break when you least expect it, and they're worthless for anything but boiling water. (Glass and ceramic bakeware is a different matter; see page 12.)

A word about nonstick coatings: Until recently I did all sorts of high-heat cooking (from pan-frying to roasting) in assorted chemically coated nonstick pans. But like most people, I've become convinced that concerns about their safety at both moderately high and high temperatures are warranted. So I now limit their use almost exclusively to sautéing and egg cooking and always with a generous amount of liquid or fat in the pan. And I no longer use nonstick for browning when I feel I would need to preheat a dry pan—which releases harmful fumes—before adding food or liquid. Finally, I don't buy them any more; cast iron, believe it or not, really does just about as good a job, once you've been using it for a while.

Handles and Lids

Good pots and pans have their handles attached by rivets, and those handles are made of metal; wood and plastic are functional enough as long as you know the pan will *never* go in the oven or broiler. Some cookware has synthetic handles, made of silicone or high-tech plastic. I still think metal is best; just keep plenty of pot holders or towels handy.

The more pans you have with lids, the better. And though the material isn't that important, once again, metal is best. The best pans should have a sunken lip for the lid to ride inside the pan and form a good seal.

Using, Cleaning, and Storing Cookware

You can improve the performance and nonstick capabilities of virtually all cookware by doing two simple things before frying or sautéing: Heat the empty pan slowly over the desired temperature; don't start the stove on heat that's too high only to knock it back down. (Don't do this with nonstick pans.) And, ideally, don't add really cold ingredients to the pan; room temperature, or close to it, is best—if you think ahead you can remove things from the refrigerator beforehand.

You can use metal cooking utensils with stainless, cast-iron, or most other all-metal pans, but you might cause some scratching, especially when deglazing the pan and scraping up browned bits. So as a general rule, I favor wooden spoons and spatulas. With nonstick coatings, of course, you must use nonmetal utensils.

With the exception of some stainless steel, I don't put pots and pans in the dishwasher (they take up too much room anyway). Cast iron requires a little bit different treatment (see the sidebar at right), but for everything else it's best to use your regular dish soap, a nonabrasive sponge or nylon scrubbie, and a little elbow grease. For stubborn messes, soak; for really hard stuff, boil some water in the pan while scraping the bottom with a wooden spoon. Some pans can even take a sprinkle of mildly abrasive cleanser.

Seasoning and Cleaning Cast-Iron Pans

Like aluminum, cast iron is porous and rough, and until the pan is used and "seasoned" with a combination of heat and fat, food will stick to it. Enter the seasoning process—simple to initiate, even simpler to maintain. You can now buy preseasoned cast iron, but it's good to have some control and to know how to do it.

First, wash the new pan well, then dry it. Set the oven to 350°F and set the pan on the stove; turn the heat to low. Use a brush or paper towel to spread a tablespoon or so of neutral oil, like grapeseed or corn, around the inside of the pan—sides and all. There should be no excess, but the entire surface should be shiny. Put the pan in the oven and bake for about an hour, then turn off the oven and leave it inside to cool.

To maintain newly seasoned cast iron, it helps if you use the pan for sautéing or frying the first few times you cook in it. That way the pan is guaranteed to absorb more oil and seal its surfaces.

Once the pan is seasoned, you can use a mildly abrasive scouring pad to wash it. You might hear that soap will tear off the seasoning, but I've never found that to be true; a little mild soap and hot water is fine. Every few uses—especially after braising in liquids that break down the seasoning, like tomato sauce or wine—I dry my cast-iron skillet over low heat. When the water begins to evaporate, I wipe it out with a towel and use a paper towel to smear around a little oil, let it sit over the heat for a few more minutes, then wipe it out again.

Besides the rare instance of cracking (which will render the pot or pan useless), the worst that can happen to cast iron is that the pan will lose its seasoning or rust; both are fixed by reseasoning. In the case of rust, scour the pan out well with steel wool or a wire brush before heating and oiling. As the pan ages with use (assuming you care for it properly) it will darken and become increasingly smooth, beautiful, and nonstick.

5 Crucial Pots and Pans

If you cook a lot, you will add to this list; you may want a smaller skillet and saucepan or an additional stockpot or Dutch oven, especially one made of clay or other ceramic. But in terms of types of pans you need for vegetarian cooking, this pretty much covers everything:

1. **Deep 12-inch skillet with lid:** When you see *large* or *large, deep* skillet in a recipe, this is what I mean. It will definitely look huge in the store, but you need a fair amount of surface area to sauté, stir-fry, and pan-roast food properly without crowding. You don't want it too deep, just about 2 to 3 inches high; curved sides are better than straight for most uses.

2. **Large stockpot with lid:** At least 2 gallons. For making stock; shocking, parboiling, or steaming vegetables; and boiling pasta, noodles, or dumplings. If you can find one with a steamer basket, all the better, though it's easy enough to fit one with an inexpensive expandable basket that sits in the bottom of the pot.

3. **Medium skillet:** 8 to 10 inches (eventually you'll probably have both), preferably with lid; the lid from your stockpot may fit this: Make this your cast-iron skillet if your large skillet is stainless or aluminum. This is for small-batch sautéing, frying, cooking eggs, and the like.

4. **Large Dutch oven or saucepan with lid:** Sometimes this is referred to as a "casserole," though it should be both stoveproof and ovenproof (so you can sauté aromatics and other vegetables, then add liquid) and hold at least 3 quarts. You'll use this for soups, stews, sauces, and deep frying. I like enameled cast iron or some other nonreactive interior. But especially for braising, it's important that the lid fit well and that the pot conduct heat evenly and slowly.

5. **Small or medium saucepan with lid:** Something in the 1-quart range. Use this for boiling eggs, warming and reheating small amounts of food, or doing tasks that require small quantities of solids or liquids.

The Basics of Ovenware

You have three dependable ways to go for ovenware—metal (including pans coated in enamel), glass, or ceramic. There's nothing glamorous about taking plain metal pans to the table, but if you're utterly new to cooking, that's where I suggest you start, since they will be the most versatile and economical. You can always add to your collection, and you undoubtedly will.

Any metal pan except uncoated aluminum is fine for baking. Again, my concerns about nonstick lining limit the choice somewhat, especially for roasting pans and baking sheets, the most likely to be super-heated without liquid. But these days you can find good, heavy, professional-style metal pans, even in discount stores, and they're virtually indestructible. You can even heat them on top of the stove to deglaze the bottom or melt butter. When you're using glass or ceramic ovenware, you must be careful not to change temperature too rapidly; you can't add cold liquid to a hot baking dish or the other way around, nor can you use it on the stove. And of course these pans can both can chip and break. In general, I prefer ceramic over glass, but my specific reservations follow.

4 Essential Pans for the Oven

These are pans you'll always use, and for the rest of your life. Start with these, then move on to the next list as needed.

1. **Rectangular roasting pan, preferably metal:** The standard measurement is 9 × 13 inches. Make sure it's at least 2 inches deep so it holds at least 12 cups of food or liquid. The large surface area makes it perfect for roasting mixed vegetables, and you'll use it for all sorts of sweet and savory baking.

2. **Large rimmed baking sheet:** You might as well buy two. Also known as *jelly-roll pans,* these are more versatile than baking sheets and work great for cookies, as well as crisp-roasting vegetables and baking and warming things like veggie burgers, fritters, and savory cakes.

3. **Eight- or 9-inch square pan:** Universally useful, but essential for quick breads, brownies, cobblers, cakes, and the like.

4. **Large gratin dish:** Not quite as big or as deep as your main roasting pan. It can be oval, round, or rectangular and made of glass, ceramic, or metal. Ideally it will hold about 8 cups. With it, you can make virtually all of the gratins in this book.

10 More Pans for the Oven

Not everyone will want all of these, but devoted cooks will. Get 'em as you need 'em.

1. **Standard loaf pan:** One notch down from a commercial sandwich-size loaf (technically measuring $8^1/_2 \times 4^1/_2 \times 3$ inches). Avoid glass loaf pans; bread may not rise or bake as evenly in them. You'll need this pan not only for bread but also for "meat" loaves, many seitan dishes, and more.

2. **Nine-inch pie plate:** For pies, tarts, and quiches. Plus, almost anything you can make in an 8-inch square pan you can make in a pie plate; just cut it into wedges instead of squares. This is the one place where glass is really nice.

3. **Nine-inch springform pan:** This is the one where the bottom drops out and the sides are held together with a big clip. It's essential for cheesecake, though you'll be surprised by how many other sweet and savory things you'll make in it. Good quality is important here to prevent leaking.

4. **Custard cups or ramekins:** The 6-ounce size is standard (in glass or ceramic). Buy eight. Beyond their intended purpose for making individual desserts, they're great for holding small amounts of ingredients while you cook.

5. **Two 9-inch cake pans:** When you want to bake a layer cake. Otherwise, you don't need them. Nonstick is nice here.

6. **Muffin tins:** To some people these are more important than cake pans. Remember, though, every muffin can be baked as a quick bread. Here you might consider nonstick; otherwise use cast iron.

7. **Tube or bundt pan:** For cake enthusiasts. The tube pan is deep and flat sided; the bundt is rounder and indented for a more decorative effect. One or the other generally does it, though the tube pan is much more versatile, because you can also bake savory breads and molds in it. You can bake any recipe for a two-layer cake in one of these pans; increase the cooking time by 10 to 15 minutes.

8. **Soufflé dish:** 2-quart is the standard size, and ceramic is the standard material. You can use it for more than soufflés of course (it's essentially a bowl), but you can't make a soufflé without one of these.

9. **Cookie sheets:** If you bake a lot of cookies, rimless baking sheets are more convenient than rimmed pans. And you'll be able to keep them cleaner.

10. **Nine-inch fluted tart pan:** Metal ones have removable bottoms, but ceramic ones are easier to clean and look great on the table.

The Basics of Small Utensils

Sometimes you need more than a knife and wooden spoon. A variety of hand-held, manual tools, accessories, and gadgets can make kitchen tasks easier. Like me and most cooks, eventually you'll probably acquire as many as your cabinets can hold. Here are three lists to help you prioritize a bit.

Must-Have Kitchen Tools

These are the ones you can't do without. They're in no particular order because you really do need them all.

- **Mixing bowls:** Small, medium, and large to start, preferably stainless steel—the most basic and functional—and this is one thing that's practical to buy in a set. (Stainless even looks okay on the table, but if you want nice-looking serving bowls, buy them separately.) You will definitely collect more bowls as your needs grow.
- **Cutting boards:** One is enough if it's a big one, but I prefer having a few of different sizes so at least one is always dry. (And remember, you should be washing them between tasks; see "How to Handle Food Safely" on page 30.) Wood or plastic, your choice. Wooden ones can be sanded clean, plastic can go in the dishwasher (but get rid of them as soon as they start to peel). To keep cutting boards from sliding around on the countertop while you work, lay a damp towel underneath them.
- **Wooden and stainless spoons, spatulas, and whatnot:** These are the goodies you keep right by the stove: A few wooden spoons, a couple of wide and narrow spatulas, a ladle, and at least one slotted spoon. If you have nonstick pans, you may need some plastic or silicone utensils; otherwise wood and stainless steel are all you need.
- **Tongs:** Get spring-loaded rather than scissorlike or tension kinds. Stainless steel or aluminum are best, though a wooden set (when you can find them; usually at Asian groceries) is kind of nice also.
- **Pot holders (or mitts) and kitchen towels:** It doesn't matter what they look like; what's important is that pot holders and mitts protect your hands and towels be absorbent, all cotton, and washable.
- **Measuring cups—liquid and dry measure—and measuring spoons:** It sounds silly, but you really shouldn't use liquid and dry measuring utensils interchangeably. One you pour from (it looks like a pitcher with writing on it), and the others are different-size cups you level off with a knife (see "The Basics of Measuring" on page 22). A glass 2-cup liquid measuring cup is a good place to start; buy a 4-cup as the second if possible. Dry-measure cups and spoons generally come in sets. Be sure to buy a set that's practical. They're relatively inexpensive, so if you can, get two of everything so one is likely to be clean.
- **Colanders and strainers:** The family of bowl- or basketlike devices with holes in them for draining. You need a colander immediately, and soon you will want at least one fine-mesh strainer for fine foods or to make purées.
- **Cheese grater:** An old-fashioned box grater is fine, but get stainless if you can afford it or be willing to throw out cheaper models at the first sign of rust. The new ultrasharp hand-helds ("Microplanes") are very good and easy to use.
- **Timer:** We all need to be reminded when it's time to check something, at least some of the time. Electronic ones are more precise, but they also break more easily than old fashioned dial-around types. You might have one on your microwave or oven, in which case you just saved ten bucks!
- **Vegetable peeler:** The sharpness and the handle grip are more important than the shape, though I lean toward the U-shaped ones.
- **Instant-read thermometer:** Very handy for making sure foods are done, especially if you're an inexperienced cook. I absolutely depend on one when baking bread.
- **Salad spinner:** A lot of people skip this because it takes up a chunk of space, but small ones are now available. And you can use the spinner to store

washed greens in the fridge and prolong their life by days; having a spinner means you can always have washed greens ready to eat. (See "The Basics of Preparing Salad Greens" on page 36.)

More Kitchen Tools You'll Probably Want
You might call these necessary luxuries.

- **Balloon whisk:** Especially if you don't have any other rotary or electric mixer. You'll probably end up with a couple different sizes, but start with a medium-big one that feels comfortable in your hand.
- **Rolling pin:** If you're buying only one, get a straight wooden pin without ball bearings; you'll have more control, and it won't break. But those with ball bearings are kind of fun, and work nicely.
- **Wire racks:** Mostly for cooling baked foods, but also for roasting. Get at least a couple and make sure one fits in your main roasting pan. (Round ones are handy too.)
- **Funnel:** It's a shame—and also usually a big mess—not to have one when you need one. Plastic is fine.
- **Citrus reamer:** Or some sort of tool to easily extract citrus juice from its fruit.
- **Skewers:** Wooden ones are fine, especially for odd jobs like poking and testing food for doneness. But for grilling they need to be soaked in warm water before use or they'll burn. Metal skewers are for serious grillers; I prefer nonround ones because food doesn't slide around.
- **Wooden salad bowl and servers:** If you eat a lot of salads, this is the most convenient way to assemble, dress, toss, and serve them.
- **Barbecue utensils:** They're the ones with really long handles. If you grill a lot, they'll make the whole experience a lot more enjoyable. So will a long-armed oven mitt.
- **Asian skimmers and "spiders":** Even more useful than a slotted spoon for deep frying. They look like

baskets on wooden sticks and come in all different sizes. Great for taking mushrooms out of their soaking water or for fishing shocked vegetables out of ice water.
- **A huge mixing bowl:** For shocking vegetables, icing wine and drinks at a party, or serving punch. You can use a stockpot for some of these tasks, provided it's not already in use, but it's not the most attractive serving piece.
- **Kitchen scissors:** Snipping is often easier—and safer—than chopping, especially for herbs, bean threads and other long noodles, cutting string, and opening packages (give your teeth a break).
- **Brushes:** For spreading melted butter, oil, or water on top of something in an even layer. The new silicone ones are cool because they don't leave nylon bristles behind. Whatever you get, be sure it's food grade and not just from the hardware store.
- **Kitchen scale:** Not essential, but as you get more interested in cooking you will reach for it frequently. (For starters, you'll know exactly what "1 pound apples" means.) Spring-loaded are fine; you don't need an expensive electronic scale unless you want it. Be sure you can easily adjust to "zero" to compensate for the tare (the weight of the container holding your ingredient).

Nice-to-Have Kitchen Tools
Cherry-pick from this list, depending on where your cooking enthusiasms lie. But remember, everything can be made from the tools on the preceding lists. My little rule of thumb to help distinguish want from need: If you make something more than once or twice a year—and think you'll tackle it more with the right stuff—then a new gadget is worth the money and space.

- **Steaming basket:** They expand to fit different-size pots. You can use an inverted plate or shallow bowl, but this is more convenient and not expensive. If you steam dumplings a lot (or other foods that require a large surface area), consider getting a bamboo steaming basket; you'll find them in all different sizes at Asian markets or department stores.

- **Mandoline:** Thank goodness Japanese (and Japanese-style) mandolines are now all over the place for less than $40. There's really no reason to buy the expensive stainless steel French model unless you're a professional. You might think you're pretty good with a knife, but once you see the pile of paper-thin potatoes you just cut in about five seconds flat with a mandoline, you'll be hooked. Note, however, that it's also way too easy to hook a finger on its super-sharp blade, so be extra careful around this tool; use the guard and, if you like a little wine when you cook, be sure to tackle the mandoline while you're still on your first glass.

- **Zester:** Easier than peeling and mincing with a paring knife, but not as easy as a Microplane. However, if you want long strands, this is the only way to get them.

- **Garlic press:** You'll notice I rarely do anything more than mince garlic (really I just chop; I don't mind large pieces), but some people really love garlic squeezed through one of these.

- **Melon baller:** Sure, you can cube melon or use a spoon, but this way makes all sorts of stuff look so cool. Good for coring pears, too.

- **Offset spatula:** For frosting cakes and lifting things directly up from the bottom without disturbing them too much.

- **Manual pasta machine:** If you have any interest at all in making pasta, or have tried and failed to roll it out by hand, this simple machine is worth the money.

- **Food mill:** Basically a strainer on steroids, with a hand-crank paddle wheel to push foods through the holes while they're straining. Essential if you make a lot of tomato sauce.

- **Baking stone, peel, and pizza wheel:** The best way to bake bread and pizza at home. (See "The Basics of Yeast Bread" on page 701.)

- **Ricer:** You can't beat this for fluffy mashed potatoes, and that means a ricer improves anything you make with mashed potatoes, like gnocchi (page 486).

- **Silicone mat:** A flexible rubbery mat used for lining baking sheets in place of butter and flour; it helps insulate heat so whatever you're baking doesn't burn or stick. Good for delicate cookies.

The Basics of Appliances and Electric Gadgets

This is the stuff that's not quite as big-ticket as a new stove and fridge but requires a paid electric bill and a working plug. Let's assume you have a toaster. And I'm going to take a guess that you have neither the desire nor the space to buy every kitchen appliance on the market. So here is some discussion about the electric gadgets you *might* need to cook from this book with a little more ease. I say *might* because, again, you can do everything by hand that these machines can do; but I also know that when cooking at home is enjoyable and convenient you're likely to do it a lot more often.

What and how you cook should dictate what you end up owning. Not for me. But this list will give you an idea of what I consider priorities. Note that if something isn't here, I don't think it's even worth considering.

- **Food processor:** Hands down the most important electric tool in the kitchen. It can grate massive amounts of almost anything in seconds; it can make bread dough, pie dough, even some cookie batters, in a minute; it can purée vegetables, slice potatoes, and whip up spreads and dips. If you have one, use it. (I rely on it heavily, although not exclusively, in my recipes.) If you don't, make the investment as soon as you can; there are very good ones available for less than $200, and if you cook a lot you will use it daily. The small ones are valuable in their own right (not the "mini-choppers," but the 3- to 4-cup full-fledged food processors), but start with a large one, a model that can handle at least 8 (and preferably 12) cups of batter or dough.

Other than the instructions that come with the machine, there's only one thing you need to know to use a food processor: Don't overprocess. If you want a purée, turn the machine on and walk away. But if you want to mince, use the "pulse" button, turning the machine on and off as many times as is necessary to get the texture you need. These are very powerful machines, capable of puréeing almost anything within seconds.

- **Electric mixer:** If you bake a lot, you will probably want both a powerful standing mixer and a small hand-held mixer. If you bake occasionally, you will want one or the other. If you never bake, then you might be perfectly happy with a whisk.
- **Blender:** Crucial if you want creamy soups, dips, or sauces. An immersion blender, which you stick into a pot or a bowl and work with your hands, is helpful but not as versatile or powerful. A blender is also good for perfect vinaigrettes.
- **Electric knife sharpener:** It spares you from having to go to the hardware store with your knives every couple of months. Maybe not urgent, but great for someone to give to you on your next birthday.
- **Electric juicer:** Handier than you think, especially for vegetarians. Having one on the counter opens up a whole world of beverages, stocks, sauces, vinaigrettes, granitas, gels, and sorbets.
- **Coffee/spice grinder:** Coffee drinkers probably already have one, but that doesn't count for spice grinding, since you need a separate one for that task. With an electric grinder you can happily spend a rainy afternoon toasting and blending your own mixes. Leave it on the counter and you can easily grind spices for any meal. The difference in flavor is remarkable.

- **Ice cream maker:** I really like ice cream and sorbet, and I'm not alone in this. There is a range of models, prices, and features, and if you're not an enthusiast—or willing to jump in with both feet—you might want to start with an inexpensive manual model with a container you freeze. At the other end of the spectrum are the top-end electric models with self-contained refrigeration and a price tag of at least $200. If you're going to make that kind of investment, do your homework and make sure you get one that has a powerful compressor and motor for reliability and ease.
- **Pressure cooker:** Pressure cookers can be the gateway to daily freshly made beans, soups, and stews. So if you have one, by all means use it. If you don't, first try some of the make-ahead techniques in these recipes. Or get in the habit of making extra and setting some aside, because then you'll probably never miss a pressure cooker. If you do want one, buy it new—they're safer and easier to use than they were even ten years ago.
- **Microwave:** The only place in this book I give the microwave serious consideration is at the beginning of the "Vegetables and Fruits" chapter as an option for steaming vegetables. Granted, it is good for reheating, melting butter, and taking the chill off foods. But that's hardly a reason to buy one. That said, if you tend to sock away extra meals and components in the freezer—and if you didn't have a quick way to thaw and reheat them you probably wouldn't do so—then a microwave really is a convenience that helps you eat better. You probably have one anyway, but if you don't, there are lots of other things I'd recommend buying first.
- **Bread machine:** There was a time when I recommended these with reservation. Now I don't at all. The bread-making techniques on pages 702 to 706 result in a loaf that's nearly as easy as with a bread machine and infinitely better. So I guess what I'm saying is: Don't bother.

Techniques

If you're an experienced cook, you can probably skip this entire section. For novices, however, it's an important one: It contains the nuts and bolts of the cooking techniques used throughout this book (and, for that matter, most other cookbooks).

You don't have to master technique to prepare terrific meals at home. All you need is the basic instruction you'll find here and a little practice. Executing great recipes is pretty easy and not nearly as intimidating as TV chefs might lead you to believe.

On the surface, vegetarian cooking appears easier than working with meat, fish, and poultry. But that's true only if you're content with the most basic steaming, stir-frying, and baking techniques or you're happy eating a lot of pasta. Good, varied meals based on vegetables, dairy, or eggs present their own challenges. Good kitchen skills will instantly expand your recipe repertoire by making you more comfortable trying new dishes and,

even more important, giving you the confidence to improvise.

Perhaps the best thing about learning to cook is that the process is rarely painful. Once in a while you might make a blunder that renders something inedible, but for the most part everything you prepare at home—even while you're "practicing"—will be better than what you get from take-out. And if it makes you feel any better, every cook I know, from my colleagues in the press to the world's great restaurant chefs, flubs a dish now and then. That's the benefit of working in the kitchen: not only do you learn from your mistakes; they never last long enough to haunt you. (And usually you can eat them anyway.)

Preparing Food for Cooking

First things first: The way you prepare food has a direct impact on how it cooks. So here's an overview of the tasks required before you subject anything to heat—roughly in order of how you might tackle them.

Washing, Peeling, and Trimming

All vegetables should be washed before cooking. Generally speaking (specific differences are discussed throughout the book), you can submerge uncut and unpeeled vegetables in a tub of cold water or run them under cold running water. (Even though it might defy common sense, don't wash produce immediately after purchasing, because you'll shorten its shelf life.) Wash away visible dirt and, we hope, you'll also be washing away pesticide residue, bacteria, fungi, and the by-products of picking, packing, shipping, and handling. If it makes you more secure, use a few drops of liquid soap, but be sure to rinse it off thoroughly.

Anything that grows underground—potatoes, sweet potatoes, turnips, and the like—should be scrubbed with a brush a bit to remove any remaining soil. You might need a brush or some soap to remove the "protective" wax or oil from some fruits and vegetables, but a better solution is simply to avoid coated produce.

I also like to run bricks of firm tofu under running water to rinse away its packing water, and some people wash their eggs before cracking. Other foods outside the category of fresh produce—cheese, tempeh, and, of course, dried fruit and vegetables—are better off left alone. Before cooking, it's usually best to dry the food, unless you're planning to steam, boil, or shock it. Damp or wet food will never brown properly.

You can trim and peel produce at any point during washing. Do what's most efficient. Use a paring knife to remove stems, blossom ends, cores, and any blemishes or bruises. A peeler or a paring knife will handle thin and medium skins (from carrots to potatoes, apples, and turnips). For the toughest, thickest skins, you'll need to work (cutting away from you, please) on a cutting board, usually with a chef's knife. A spoon works best for scooping out seeds and other interior fibers. Once this tidying up is done, you're ready to cut.

The Basics of Cutting

Cut food is easier to handle, cooks faster, and is convenient to serve and eat; it adds textural contrast and visual interest. And evenly cut food also cooks more evenly.

USING A STEEL

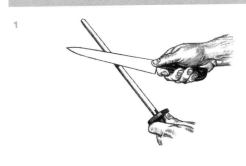

Using a steel is easy and effective at keeping knives sharp. The important thing is the angle, which should be between 15 and 20 degrees. (STEP 1) Pull one side of the knife toward you across the top of the steel, simultaneously sliding it from base to tip (your pulling hand will move in a diagonal motion); then (STEP 2) repeat with the other side across the bottom of the steel, always pulling toward you and trying to maintain a consistent angle.

(STEP 1) You can choose to hold a knife with your hand completely on the handle or with your first finger or two wrapping around the blade. In either case, the position should be comfortable. (STEP 2) To finely chop herbs or small vegetables, put the tip of the blade on the cutting surface and rock the knife up and down; use your other hand to hold the food on the cutting board, curling your fingers and thumb a bit so your knuckles act as a bumper or guide, keeping the tips of your fingers out of harm's way. (STEP 3) When the pieces become very small and stable, you won't have to hold them anymore, so you can put your free hand over the point of the blade for greater stability; use a rocking motion to finely chop or mince the food further.

So you've got your (sharp) chef's, paring, and serrated knives (see "The Basics of Knives" on page 8). Now it's time to put them to use; a few simple knife skills and even a little knife theory will make your food both tastier and more attractive.

Hold your knives however you feel most comfortable and secure. Some people sort of shake hands with their chef's knife, the knife you'll use for three-quarters of your cutting. But the way to hold one for maximum stability and flexibility is to grip the handle as close to the blade as is comfortable and put your thumb on the inside, against the hilt, with your other fingers wrapped around the other side. You can even stretch your forefinger up the blade a little bit for more control. When you work with a chef's knife, use your other hand to hold the food on the cutting board, curling the fingers and thumb a bit so your knuckles act as a bumper or guide, keeping the tips of your fingers out of harm's way. Almost all cutting skills with a chef's knife are basically variations on a rocking motion, with the tip held steady on the cutting board while you maneuver the handle up and down—sort of how a paper cutter works. If this is new to you, try practicing without any food first and

hold your curled fingers against the blade so you feel how they work as a guide.

You don't have to be a fanatic, but when a particular food is the star of the dish, you should pay at least moderate attention to consistency while you cut or it won't cook evenly. Whether you're chopping an onion, mincing a clove of garlic, or slicing big planks out of a potato to throw on the grill, you want all pieces to be approximately the same size and thickness. Generally, my recipes tell you how big to cut things—when it's important—but it's okay if the exact measurement isn't spot on as long as you cut everything in pretty much the same way.

Once you get comfortable, you may want to experiment with different shapes, and your dishes will be more interesting for it. All you need is some common sense: Consider the food itself and whether it's mushy or solid. Then factor in the ultimate use for the food—raw in salads, for example, or cooked relatively soft in a stew? And finally, will you eat the dish with your fingers or chopsticks? It seems like a lot to think about, which is why you have recipes. With time, though, it will become second nature.

The Specific Cuts

Chopping

This most basic cut results in three sizes: roughly chopped, "chopped," and mince. For all of these, you can forget super-even cutting; truly equal size is unimportant. For all of these you're just trying to get the job done. You generally chop foods that play a supporting role in the dish—like onions or other aromatics—or things that are going to cook so long they almost melt away.

Roughly Chopped: Chunks that are somewhat uneven, bite-sized, or even bigger; you're just passing the food under the knife blade, without worrying much. Use this cut before puréeing or mashing or when the texture of the dish is intended to be rustic and chunky. Pieces can be as big as an inch in any dimension.

Chopped: Pieces $^1/_4$ inch to $^1/_2$ inch in size. Onions, bell peppers, and celery are the most common vegetables to get this treatment, though you might want firm tofu or cabbage cut this way for some dishes. In recipes where I don't specify size and just say "chopped," this is what I mean.

Minced: The tiniest bits you can manage: Once you get things finely chopped, it's just a final burst of short, quick chops to get food to this stage. (Sometimes it helps to steady the tip of the knife blade while you mince, to keep it anchored to the cutting board.) Mince when you want to add lots of flavor, in an almost invisible, textureless way, with foods like garlic, ginger, shallots, or chiles.

Slicing

To slice with a chef's knife, you still press down, just with a little more precision, and cut into thick or thin slices of fairly uniform size. You can cut crosswise, lengthwise, or on the diagonal. The diagonal slice is probably most attractive and gives you the largest surface area for crisping (it's nice to use in stir-fries). To slice with a serrated knife—for bread, cake, and the like—grip the handle comfortably and use a gentle sawing motion to work your way through the food. Be sure to hang on to the food in such a way that your hands stay clear but your grip remains in control. A mandoline (see page 15) is handy for getting even slices and for other tasks too; I can't recommend one highly enough.

Julienne

Translation: Cut into sticks. They can be big like French fries or small like matchsticks. I don't call for julienne often (I don't do it often), but it's an impressive cut and really not that tough (especially if you use a food processor or mandoline). By hand, first make round foods—let's

Cutting vegetables—or any food—into small pieces is best done in a series of steps. (STEP 1) First, cut the food into manageable and somewhat even-size chunks. (STEP 2) Then chop it into smaller pieces. (STEP 3) Finally, if necessary, mince, using a rocking motion; the knife must be sharp.

There are many ways of slicing, though they all require you to keep your nonknife fingers out of the way (some people call this position "the claw"). (1) For round vegetables like cucumbers or zucchini, you can just cut across. (2) Or you can cut into long strips or (3) on an angle, for attractive ovals. (4) To slice bread, use a serrated knife (a "bread knife") and a sawing motion. (5) For any vegetable that will fit, and for which you want even, ultra-thin slices, a mandoline (like this inexpensive Japanese tool) is the best bet; be sure to watch your fingers (or use a guard) as you run the food up and down over the blade.

use zucchini as an example—stable on the cutting board by slicing off one side. Slice the food crosswise into whatever length you want the final julienne, then slice the food lengthwise. Stack the pieces into piles of three or so layers, then slice them through lengthwise into the same thickness as your first slices. (See illustration on page 22.)

Dicing

Obviously dice is a perfect cube, but stray geometry isn't going to wreck a dish. To get to dice, start with julienne, then cut the sticks crosswise into dice. (See illustration on page 23.)

Roll Cut (Oblique Cut)

These look sort of like round triangles or diagonally cut chunks. (You may have seen vegetables cut like this in stir-fries.) The roll cut works best on round, narrow vegetables like zucchini, carrots, and Japanese eggplant. Here's how: Slice one end diagonally, then roll the rest of the vegetable a quarter turn and slice on the same angle. Your knife never changes position; you just keep rolling the vegetable. Try it; you'll like it.

Chiffonade

Another translation: Cut into strands or ribbons. Use the chiffonade cut on big leafy vegetables like kale or small herbs like basil; the technique is the same regardless of the size. Simply make a pile of washed leaves (not too high), roll them from end to end, and slice the roll as thickly or thinly as you like. (See illustration on page 22.)

MAKING JULIENNE

(STEP 1) The easiest way to cut even strips from a vegetable with rounded sides is to square it off first by removing thin slices. (STEP 2) Then it will sit flat so you can cut it first crosswise to the desired length, then stack and slice into strips.

MAKING CHIFFONADE

This works for large leaves, such as kale, as well as smaller ones, like basil. (STEP 1) Roll the leaf up from bottom to top. (STEP 2) Cut slices of the leaf off from top to bottom.

Paring, Coring, Peeling, and Other Special Tasks

These are the paring knife skills where you hold manageable pieces of food in one hand, the knife in the other, and work in a controlled way without a cutting board; you might be coring and peeling an apple, for example, or trimming the eyes from a potato. Often these jobs involve pulling the paring knife toward you, using the thumb on the hand holding the food as the safety guide. If you're not confident working this way, then stick to putting the food on a board and cutting away from you. You can use the paring knife that way too, especially when handling smaller pieces of food.

The Basics of Measuring

All of the recipes in this book can be measured with cups and spoons, though I sometimes offer weights, especially for bulk ingredients where it might be easier. Many experienced cooks eyeball everything (except when baking) and though I wouldn't advocate ignoring the recipes, with a lot of practice you'll get there. Think about this for starters: Does it matter whether your stir-fry has a heaping cup or a shy cup of chopped carrots?

When measurement matters, however, it really matters, so you should learn the right way to do it. Whenever you bake breads, make desserts, or work with eggs in cus-

tards, soufflés, and the like, you must measure carefully. It's relatively important to accurately measure grains and beans to be cooked, mostly because I think you'll be surprised by how little a cup really is. And liquids are often critically important to measure.

To measure properly you need a liquid measuring cup, a set of flat-topped dry-measure cups, a set of measuring spoons, and a flat-sided knife or narrow spatula. (See "13 Must-Have Kitchen Tools" on page 13.) To measure liquids, set the cup on the counter and fill it to where you think the correct marking is. Then get down at eye level to the cup and double-check. Surface tension causes the liquid to look a little like a concave bubble, and the bottom "line" of that bubble should be even with the line on the cup. Add or pour off some liquid until it is. This sounds ridiculously obsessive, but after you do it a couple times, it will become second nature.

To measure dry ingredients, use a spoon to put them in the cup, heaping them a bit over the top. Then rest the flat side of the knife or spatula on the rim and swipe the excess off the top. (Resist the urge to shortcut by simply dipping the cup in the ingredients; it *does* make a difference.) For measuring spoons, either fill them to capacity with liquid or fill them with dry ingredients and use the same swiping technique to level them off.

MAKING DICE

To make dicing easier, first square off the vegetable by removing thin slices, then cut into even-size sticks (see "Making Julienne," page 22). Then cut the sticks crosswise into dice.

USING A PARING KNIFE

Before there were vegetable peelers, there were paring knives; as long as you're careful—peel toward you, using your thumb to counter the pressure of the knife—they work perfectly.

MEASURING DRY INGREDIENTS

To measure flour accurately, use a spoon to overfill the measuring cup, then sweep the top evenly with the flat side of a knife.

The Importance of Heat

Cooking is all about harnessing heat. So despite whatever your instincts might tell you, high heat does not automatically lead to burned food. Quite the opposite: Often, unless the pan, oven, pot of water, or barbecue is hot enough, the food won't cook properly. This holds true for both dry- and moist-heat techniques. Though a few beginning cooks veer toward the other extreme, most are understandably too timid with heat. Or simply too impatient.

If you can master heat, you can become a great cook. Food responds best—meaning it develops a flavorful brown crust or boils up tender, not mushy—when it suddenly comes into contact with something hot. You almost never want to start with cold ingredients in a cold pan or a cold oven or a cold pot of water. (There are a few exceptions, yes: Boiling potatoes, cooking dried foods like beans or grains, and gently warming scorchable foods like milk or chocolate.) Otherwise, give heat a chance to build up before putting it to work.

Whether you cook with gas or electric doesn't matter; the only difference is that electric stoves take longer to heat up and cool down. So you need to accommodate the way they respond by working two burners at the same time or planning ahead, making adjustments a little before they're needed. No big deal. What counts most is your ability to trust your senses, especially smell. Heat has its own aroma, as does food as it's cooking—and burning. You should also listen for the sound of food cooking vigorously and learn to visually recognize signs of doneness, like crisping around the edges, dryness, and releasing from the pan or grill. Being observant puts you in control and gives you the confidence to use heat more assertively. And your cooking will instantly improve.

The Ten Essential Cooking Techniques

You're probably familiar with these terms and maybe the concepts behind them (and all are described in more detail within the specific chapters), but here's an overview of cooking techniques, with special emphasis on how they apply to vegetarian cooking.

Boiling

Few things are more straightforward than this most fundamental of moist-heat cooking methods. You put water in a pot (usually to about two-thirds full), turn the heat to high, and bring it to a rolling boil. Then toss in a large pinch of salt and add the food. Boiling works best for dried ingredients like pasta, rice, or legumes, where the food must absorb water as it cooks. Many fresh vegetables are also great boiled, and of course boiling is absolutely necessary for stocks and soups. But boiling can leave some foods bland and leeched of nutrients, especially if you overcook; whenever you boil, check the food frequently so it doesn't turn to mush.

Parboiling would be better described as preboiling and refers to a brief boiling before draining and using another cooking technique to finish the cooking. I frequently use this method in conjunction with shocking (see page 241) to prepare vegetables for stir-frying, but it's handy any time you want to partially prepare ingredients in advance.

Simmering is when liquids bubble gently, just below the point of a rolling boil. In recipes, this is the level I mean when I refer to letting something *bubble away*.

Steaming

Since steam is as hot as boiling water, it's an excellent moist-heat method for vegetables, dumplings, tofu, and custards. The idea is to suspend the food above the boiling water so the steam keeps everything from drying out without becoming waterlogged. The pot should be large enough to hold the food comfortably and allow the steam to circulate freely. I often choose steaming over boiling because it's almost as fast (faster, in a way, because you don't have to bring a big pot of water to a boil) and the color and texture are so much better. As with boiling, check the food frequently so it doesn't overcook and check the pot to make sure it doesn't run dry.

1

2

There are many ways to make a steamer. (1) You can just buy a collapsible metal steaming insert, which will work in any pot. (2) Or you can use a heatproof plate, slightly smaller than the pot; to raise it off the bottom of the pot, use an upside-down plate, a couple of small ramekins, a "raft" of sticks, or whatever else is heatproof and stable.

You can steam with an inexpensive folding metal basket, sold almost everywhere you can buy kitchen equipment. They're adjustable and convenient, though most have an annoying piece of metal sticking up in the center, so you have to work around that. Simply open the basket to fit the desired pot, fill with water to just below the basket base, add your food, cover, and steam. (If you're steaming for a long time, you'll still need to check the water level occasionally.)

Bamboo steamers—you buy these in Chinatown or a similar place—can be fun, but they're not always easy to use. Better, usually, is to rig your own steamer: Turn an ovenproof plate, shallow bowl, two or three ramekins, or

a pie plate upside down in a large pot with a tight-fitting lid and put a plate right side up on top; make sure it's stable. Fill the pot with enough water so that it doesn't touch the right-side-up vessel. Put the food in, cover, and turn the heat to high. Once it starts boiling, lower the heat so it bubbles steadily.

Sautéing

Like chiffonade, the French word *sauté* (it means "jump") describes something so specific no other word will do. It's the method for cooking food in oil or butter: Put a large skillet on the stove and add the butter or oil. Turn the heat to medium-high and let the fat heat up so it bubbles (in the case of butter) or shimmers (in the case of oil). You can dredge the pieces of food in flour, bread crumbs, or seasonings before sautéing, but it isn't necessary.

The idea is to sizzle the food (some say you "surprise" it), to create a crust around it, so that it's lightly browned (caramelized, therefore tasty) outside and tender and moist inside. You must follow a few rules to get there: Make sure the fat is hot, almost smoking, before you add the food. And don't crowd the pan or the food will steam and never brown. (An inch or so between big pieces is fine; smaller pieces require less elbow room.) Once everything starts cooking, don't mess with anything until the pieces start to brown and release easily from the pan. You should be able to hear the food sputtering as it cooks and see the fat bubbling around the edges as they brown. You can adjust the heat and gently swirl the fat around if you like, but let the food itself be.

The related panfrying, also called *shallow frying*—it's sautéing but with more fat, halfway between sautéing and deep frying—works best for flat or cutletlike vegetables, fruits, batters, or fritters, when you want some serious crisping but don't want to deep-fry (see page 26). As with sautéing, you can bread, batter, dredge, or do nothing to it before panfrying, depending on whether you want a coating. Put about $1/2$ inch of oil in a large deep skillet. Follow the directions above for heating and testing the oil. When it's hot, add the food. Since the food isn't submerged, you've got to turn it to cook the other side, but because there's more fat than with sautéing, the crust develops better.

There are a couple of other techniques that are not sautéing but use the same kind of pan and a small amount of fat. *Sweating,* for example, almost exclusively refers to cooking aromatics like garlic or onions or supermoist foods like mushrooms. All you do is lower the heat a bit, causing the food to first release its water, then dry out without any browning. And you can always put a lid on the pan during sautéing, lower the heat, and let the moisture in the ingredients create their own steam; this is sometimes helpful with thick pieces of food that require more cooking time. However, you won't get the same browned crust.

Stir-Frying

Stir-frying is a lot like sautéing except for one crucial thing: The stirring. Instead of letting food sit in the pan and brown, you keep things moving. If you don't have a special burner for woks, it's better to use a large skillet for stir-frying. As with sautéing, you start by putting the pan on the stove, adding some fat—in this case almost always oil—and letting it get very hot over medium-high heat. Then you add the food and stir. For more details about the different ways to precook, add, or remove ingredients, see "The Basics of Stir-Frying Vegetables" on page 242.

Deep Frying

Like sautéing and stir-frying, deep frying uses hot oil to cook and brown food. You just use a lot more of it, so the oil surrounds the food. The result is either the crispest, most ethereal delights you can imagine or a soggy, greasy mess. It all depends on having enough good oil at the right temperature, which is almost always between 350°F and 375°F.

Deep frying is sort of special-occasion cooking, because it's a bit of a hassle. But the rewards are worth the work, especially for vegetarian meals, since the texture and flavor are rich and satisfying, with results unlike those from any other cooking method. Nearly everyone loves fried food, and it's especially good at home.

2 Ways to Deep-Fry

1. Use a Dutch oven or large saucepan, or a medium saucepan if you want to use less oil and don't mind working in batches. The pot should be deep, with straight sides. A deep-frying or candy thermometer is handy too. I use grapeseed, corn, or peanut oil for deep frying, though plain supermarket vegetable oil (which is made from soybeans and designed for high-heat cooking) is okay too; olive oil is useful under special circumstances.

   Put at least 2 inches of oil in the pot. It should fill the pot only partially, with several inches of room left to allow the food and the oil to rise safely without overflowing. Since it's a lot easier—and safer—to raise the heat of the oil than try to lower it, turn the heat on the burner to medium and wait several minutes before checking the temperature the first time. (Meanwhile, you can prepare the food and the draining setup. I usually use paper towels on a plate, but you can also try wire racks or clean brown paper bags.) If you have a thermometer, use it; all deep-frying recipes give you a specific temperature (or should). If not, put a piece of plain bread in the oil. It should bubble, float immediately to the top of the oil, and soon turn golden brown. If it sinks and soaks up oil, jack up the heat a notch. If it turns brown quickly, lower the heat a bit; give the oil a few minutes to readjust, then test again.

   It's very important not to overheat the oil because it can spontaneously catch fire (though, honestly, I've never seen this happen). If you see the oil start to smoke, turn off the heat or carefully move it to a cool burner. If the oil catches fire, do not put water on it and do not try to move it. If you can, slip a lid over the pan and turn off the heat. Or use a kitchen fire extinguisher or smother it with a cup or two of baking soda, flour, or sand.

   To start cooking, carefully put the food into the hot oil with metal tongs or a slotted spoon.

Crowding the food will lower the temperature of the oil and prevent it from cooking properly. Gently turn the food as it cooks so it browns evenly. Then if you're new to deep frying, you might want to take a piece out when it looks done and cut it open. There should be a nice crisp crust surrounding tender, just-done insides. Remove the cooked food to drain and you're ready to fry another batch. If you need to add more oil to the pot, be sure to let it heat thoroughly before proceeding.

2. Use a countertop electric deep-fryer. Undeniably the easiest method, but really worth the expense and space only if you deep-fry a lot. Follow the manufacturer's directions.

Braising

This is the most common combined cooking method, where you sear the ingredients first in a little hot butter or oil until they're nicely browned (essentially, you're sautéing them), then add liquid to the pot, cover, and simmer. As the dish cooks, both the cooking liquid and the solid ingredients develop lots of flavor and a luxurious texture. Since the results are often called *stews,* sometimes people call braising *stewing,* though if you want to be super-technical, you don't necessarily sear the food first when you stew.

Braising is frequently used to slow-cook tough pieces of meat, but you can make delicious braised vegetable dishes, and of course it's a great way to cook meat substitutes like tofu, tempeh, and seitan. The cooking time is shorter than for meat braises, but that's not a bad thing either.

Roasting

Oven heat does all the work here; roasting takes dry heat, in a confined environment, and uses it to crust food on the outside while cooking it through on the inside. All you need is a big shallow pan and a little melted butter or oil to coat the food. Two crucial points: The oven must be very hot, almost always over 400°F. The roasting pan can't be too crowded either; the heat must be able to circulate so any moisture in the food can easily evaporate.

Otherwise, you're doing little more than steaming, and you can forget about browning or crispness. You can use seasonings and even a little extra liquid, usually after the food is finished roasting, to make a little pan sauce (see "What's Deglazing?" on page 28).

Baking

Like roasting, but usually with moisture and at lower heat. Most food that's baked is either a semiliquid or a fairly wet solid when it goes in the oven; think of cake batter, custard, or bread dough. There may be sauce, water, or other liquid surrounding solids, as in gratins, casseroles, or lasagne. As the dry heat from the oven warms whatever's in the pan, it causes the moisture to steam and jump-starts all the other chemical reactions needed to raise the dough, melt the cheese, brown the crust, and so on. Delicate items like cakes are usually baked at a lower temperature, like 325°F or 350°F. Breads, pizza, and other sturdy dishes can take higher heat. It's a good idea to have an oven thermometer, because even a glitch of 10 or 15 degrees can make a big difference when you bake.

Grilling

Cooking over an open flame was our ancestors' original method and is still one of our favorite ways to prepare food, especially in summer. There's direct-heat grilling, where you put the food on a grate set right over a hot gas or charcoal fire to crisp, darken, and cook through foods quickly. Or you can grill with indirect heat, with the food off to the side of the fire and the lid on, so the grill works like an oven and cooks foods more slowly. Thick foods are better off with indirect grilling, so the outsides don't burn before the insides get done. Anything that's an inch or less thick is a good candidate for direct-heat grilling. (Barbecuing isn't grilling, but actually slow cooking with smoke. You can also call anything *barbecue* if it's been treated with a barbecue sauce.)

As long as I'm myth-bashing: Unless you grill with a wood fire or add soaked wood chips right before cooking, you're not getting much more flavor than you would out of a broiler. And you generally don't want the flames lapping up to kiss the grill grates periodically, unless you like the flavor of burned food. Grilling can dry out food—even vegetables—so it's important not to overcook them, and it's also nice to serve them with dressings, glazes, or dipping sauces.

If you've got a gas grill, all you have to do is turn it on and wait for the grates to heat up. If you want to use indirect heat on a gas grill, simply turn a burner or two off and use that side for the food. For charcoal grills, I like to use lump charcoal and a chimney to get the fire going, but use briquettes if you like, or an electric starter. Just stay away from the lighter fluid; I think you can still taste

What's Deglazing?

Deglazing is more of a saucing technique than a cooking technique. After panfrying, roasting, or sautéing, you make a sauce out of tasty browned bits that remain in the pan. Here's how: First transfer the cooked food to another plate or bowl and pour all but a tablespoon or two of fat from the pan. Set the pan on a burner—or two if it's a big roasting pan—turn the heat to medium, and add enough liquid to just cover the bottom. You can use water, stock, juice, wine, beer, or liquor. Now stir with a wooden spoon or spatula, scraping up the food and stirring to dissolve it a bit. Add more liquid and adjust the heat as needed; it should be bubbling vigorously.

When all the browned bits of food are removed from the bottom, keep stirring and cooking until the sauce thickens a bit. Taste and adjust the seasoning if necessary, adding herbs or spices as you like or enriching the sauce with some cold butter or cream. Then you have three choices: Return the food to the pan and toss to coat in the sauce and rewarm. Put the food on a serving platter and pour the sauce on top. (You can strain it if you like a less rustic sauce.) Or serve the sauce on the side (strained or unstrained).

it, even after it burns off. Once the charcoal is going, spread it out for direct grilling or leave it in a pile on one side for indirect grilling. Build a two-tiered fire—one that has both hot and low heat sources—by spreading a thin layer of charcoal on one side of the grill and spreading a thicker layer of coals on the other side.

Generally, you want to wait until the coals are covered with ash before you start grilling. You're ready to sear when you can hold your hand right above the rack for only a couple of seconds. For less intense grilling, you want to be able to hold your hand above the heat for about four seconds or so. So adjust the distance of the rack from the fire if you can or spread out the coals a bit. Or just wait.

Most vegetables and nonanimal protein like tofu can be grilled over direct heat, unless they're more than an inch or two thick, or left whole. To ensure everything cooks fairly evenly, try to cut the pieces evenly, especially when using skewers. Cooking on the grill requires a little more attention than stovetop cooking. You'll be flipping and moving food around almost constantly, but that's part of the fun.

Broiling

If you don't have a grill or don't feel like messing with the one you have, broiling is the next best thing. All you have to do is turn it on and, while it heats up, prepare the food and put it on a broiler pan or other rimmed baking sheet.

You'll end up broiling food anywhere from 2 to 6 inches away from the heat source. It all depends on your broiler, the thickness or density of the food, and the toppings or seasonings (sugar and honey, for example, burn faster than oil or vinegar). The recipes give you a starting point. But generally, when the food browns and cooks on one side, take the food out and flip it over. Adjust the distance to the broiler as needed; just like with grilling, you want browned, crisp outsides and moist, tender insides. Since the heat source is on top, you'll get browning and even charring like you do on a grill, but you won't get the smoky flavor or the grill marks. Check your manufacturer's instructions; some electric broilers require that the door be open during use. If that's the case, try heating the oven up to its highest setting with the door closed, then switch to broil and open the door a crack.

The Basics of Vegan Cooking

There are many delicious dishes that are naturally vegan—meaning they contain no animal products at all, like dairy, eggs, or honey. Others might seem tough to adjust with good results, but in reality only a few are actually impossible. In fact, most of the recipes in this book can be prepared successfully with vegan ingredients. The key is to first recognize that some things—pizza, for example—will never be the same as their nonvegan counterparts. But different doesn't necessarily mean worse, provided you also adjust your expectations. Here are some common substitutions for animal-based foods and when they work best.

For Milk

Almost every nondairy milk works in almost every case, though they have their differences. None is as white as cow's milk, though that doesn't bother me much. The biggest problem is separation during heating, but that's also a problem with cow's milk (which is why cream was once so popular in sauces); the solids and the water or whey have a hard time staying coagulated.

Generally, nut milks are excellent in desserts, grain dishes, or thick soups, where their slightly nutty flavor is most welcome, especially in place of cream. Oat milk is the most neutral tasting, with a nice golden color. Rice milk is also neutral tasting but almost as thin as water and slightly sweet. Soy milk is high in protein but also very strong tasting. (It separates a little less than the others during heating, though.) Coconut milk is delicious and thick and heats well, but it has a very distinctive flavor and is almost all fat; I love it, but it's not for every dish.

For Butter

Any oil can be used in place of butter, but there are flavor differences. Grapeseed or corn oil works best in baking or any time you don't want the distinctive taste of olive oil, because their flavors are quite neutral (as long as they're fresh; see page 755). Nut oils often work well in baking too, and they lend a subtle nuttiness.

The only vegan solid fats are coconut oil and the new nonhydrogenated vegetable shortenings, but these can taste greasy and be high in saturated fats. I'd rather take olive or grapeseed oil and stick it in the freezer or refrigerator for a while to produce a spreadable fat that also works well for creaming with sugar in baking recipes. You can even make compound oil as a substitute for Compound Butter (page 801), simply by whipping the oil up with the seasonings and other ingredients using an electric mixer or in the blender and then chilling until it's solid.

For Honey

I like using maple syrup for honey in almost every case. If you're going to use granulated sugar instead, try a brown sugar for a little more flavor. And if you get really ambitious, melt the sugar in a small pan with a few drops of water to make a liquid caramel.

For Eggs

You'll never be able to make fried, hard-cooked, scrambled, or baked eggs with anything other than eggs. Nor can you make omelets, soufflés, or custards (though you can make gelled desserts using agar; see page 882). But in many cases where an egg or two is an ingredient, as in baking, you can come up with a reasonable substitute.

Try this: For every egg, mix 2 tablespoons of water or other liquid with 1 tablespoon of oil and 1 teaspoon of cornstarch. Stir until smooth. In most cases, you'll want a neutral oil like grapeseed or corn; use olive oil if you want a more pronounced flavor. You can also try using 3 tablespoons of silken tofu.

For Cheese

Cheese is tough; I'm not a fan of the commercial vegan substitutes. Though the texture and flavor are completely different, ground nuts or bread crumbs work well on both counts in many recipes in place of cheese, especially gratins and pastas, since what you're usually looking for is an accent or contrast. You might have to increase the liquid a little bit or toss them with a little oil. In recipes where you're looking for the smooth texture of melted cheese, try silken tofu or crumbled firm tofu.

How to Handle Food Safely

Banishing meat, poultry, and fish from your kitchen (as I expect some of you have) doesn't mean you can't get sick from foodborne bacteria. Fruits and vegetables, nuts, eggs and cheese, even dried foods can still make you sick. But as long as you keep a clean kitchen, wash food before cooking, and pay some attention to temperature, you shouldn't have much to worry about.

Start with good kitchen hygiene: Keep your hands, countertops, utensils, appliances, and tables perfectly clean. Soap and hot water is fine. (You can use antibacterial products if you like, but there is some indication that their overuse might actually lower your immunity to infection.) Keep a supply of kitchen towels on hand and change the one you use often (I sometimes go through several a day). And don't let your sponges and dishrags get too dirty, or you'll just spread gunk around your clean kitchen. I boil my sponges for a few minutes every couple of days or toss them in the washing machine, dishwasher, or microwave. When they get past their prime, I replace them.

All fruits and vegetables should be rinsed well before trimming (see "Preparing Food for Cooking" on page 18.) If you really want to be careful, wash your cutting boards and knives after every task before you cut with them again. If there's any remaining dirt or bacteria, this keeps it from spreading.

Your refrigerator should run below 40°F (35°F is ideal), and your freezer should stay below 0°F. Cooked food runs into trouble when it's neither hot enough nor cold enough—in a range of temperature known as "the danger zone" between 40°F and 140°F—so be sure you don't let food hang around at room temperature for more than an hour or so. That means you should cool food down quickly if it's not going to be eaten within an hour and store it in the refrigerator or freezer. Also be sure to reheat leftovers fully. (When in doubt, stick in an instant-read thermometer to see what's what; you might be surprised.) Food is generally considered safe when its internal temperature reaches 165°F. Thaw foods in the refrigerator or under cold running water. And never put cooked food on a plate that previously held raw food.

Once vegetables and grains are cooked, they are the safest foods, provided there's no egg or dairy in the dish. Cheese is best eaten at room temperature, but again, you don't want to leave it there for more than an hour or so. Eggs are a special case; see "Are Runny Egg Yolks Safe?" on page 163.

If you or someone you cook for is at greater risk of serious foodborne illness—this includes children, pregnant women, the elderly, and people with compromised immune systems (from AIDS or cancer)—you should take every precaution possible, which probably means hard-cooking eggs and cooking all food thoroughly. But this is a cookbook, not a prescriptive book; if you have any questions at all about your personal food safety, speak with a doctor and a nutritionist.

How to Use Leftovers Intuitively

In restaurants, chefs call using leftovers "repurposing," because they don't just heat up whatever wasn't served last night. Instead the dish might become something totally different, or the components used to create it are assembled differently to make something else altogether.

25 Great Ideas for Using Leftovers

- Rice Porridge (Jook, page 140)
- Essential Bean Salad (page 72)
- World of Rice Salads (page 79)
- Fried Rice (page 519)
- Grain Griddlecakes (page 569)
- Sushi Rice, Bowls, Rolls, and Nigiri Sushi (pages 527–531)
- Bean Croquettes (page 627)
- Bean Griddlecakes (page 630)
- Pasta with Lentils or Other Legumes (page 454)
- 39 Vegetable and Legume Dishes That Can Be Tossed with Pasta (page 456)
- Improvising Asian-Style Noodle Bowls (page 468)
- 26 Dishes That Make Great Fresh Pasta Filling (page 485)
- Dumpling Combos (page 496)
- 19 Things to Serve Under Poached Eggs (page 170)
- Omelet and Ideas for Filling Omelets (pages 171–173)
- Frittata (pages 182–185)
- 10 Great Leftovers to Turn into Quiche Filling (page 188)
- The Basics of Pizza (page 721)
- Cold Sandwiches, Hot Sandwiches, and Wraps (pages 731–736)
- Bruschetta (page 735)
- The Basics of Tacos and Burritos (pages 737)
- Egg Rolls (page 741)
- Summer Rolls (page 743)
- Using Leftovers to Make Vegetable Purées (page 391)
- Turning Leftover Purées into Griddle Cakes (page 393)

You can learn this approach, too. In fact, you can even plan to have leftovers, by cooking extra of some ingredients or doubling or tripling recipes. Throughout the book, I try to provide some specific ideas for how you might do this. But you'll come up with even more on your own once you start thinking in terms of components.

Take grilled vegetables, for example. It's a lot of work to light the grill, so you may as well make use of the fire and cook a big batch. What's left over can fuel meals for days, since they're so versatile. Legumes are another versatile food. And so are grains. Once you get in the habit of keeping extra already cooked and on hand, the only trick is to know how to use them. The list on this page, which contains not only recipes but also other lists, should get you started.

Reheating

Throughout this book I encourage you to make extra food for future use and leftovers, and to make all or part of dishes hours or even days ahead. This approach to cooking is undeniably efficient and convenient. But until it becomes second nature (and trust me , it will), you might need some tips for reheating.

In general, it's best to reheat food gently, but there are exceptions. You can use a microwave, an oven, or the stovetop. Direct heat, as on a burner, should generally be low; in a microwave or an oven you can often blast away. How long something takes to reheat will depend on how much you've got, how dense it is, and the method you choose, so until you have some experience, check frequently. But generally, hands off: Too much stirring, turning, or fussing will inevitably turn everything to mush.

You can start with frozen food too; it'll just take longer. If you have time, move what you want to reheat to the fridge for a day or so to let it thaw. To take the chill off before reheating, set it out on the counter for up to an hour. (For safety reasons, don't combine these two suggestions and let frozen food sit out on the counter until it thaws.) Or thaw in the microware or during reheating on the stove or in the oven.

The best foods for reheating are high in moisture, like soups, sauces, stews, and beans. Crunchy foods usually don't reheat very well but can be finessed into decent left-overs if you heat them covered in the oven, then spread them out on foil or a cookie sheet to dry out a bit and crisp. Remember, too, that not everything must be reheated—many vegetables, pastas, and grains are best just eaten at room temperature, in salads, or added to another dish in the last minute of cooking.

Salads

Salads are easy, fast, widely adored, and a staple of vegetarians (and meat-eaters too) everywhere. If you can imagine a salad, you can probably make it, especially once you can prepare a vinaigrette, the basic dressing that can turn almost anything, cooked or raw, into something you can call a salad.

Perhaps even more than with most other dishes, the best salads start with the best ingredients, especially since they're often served raw. And it's tough to beat a few slices of fresh-from-the-garden tomato drizzled with oil and sprinkled with salt. But unless you're a fanatic, you're going to have to compromise from time to time. Fortunately, even at a salad's most basic level, you can take ordinary supermarket ingredients—iceberg lettuce, packaged carrots and celery, a few radishes—and, with the help of a little extra virgin olive oil and lemon juice or decent vinegar, turn them into something delicious.

Recently a big fuss has been made about raw foods, as if they were going to save the human race. And although there's undoubtedly something to be said for including uncooked foods in our diets, it's worth remembering that a salad can include cooked vegetables as well and that the salad bowl is a perfect place for leftovers or vegetables you cook in advance, knowing that you're going to serve them at room temperature or cold—which is just about all that distinguishes many salads from "vegetable dishes."

A salad is, in fact, one of the most difficult things to define. A few leaves or a sliced fruit with a minimum of dressing, something refreshing at the beginning or end of a meal, or a bowlful of vegetables that is the meal's centerpiece? Both, either, and everything in between—and I offer many of them here.

As with other chapters in the book, within each section I begin with the most familiar and friendly recipes in terms of time and ingredients, though no salad is particularly difficult or challenging.

A Lexicon of Salad Greens

The simple green salad is just that, but because it has so few ingredients the difference between good and great is subtle. You should, of course, have some delicious extra virgin olive oil (see page 755) on hand—it's easy enough to come by—as well as decent vinegar (see page 760) or a couple of lemons. No matter how good these ingredients are, however, if you toss them with ice-cold iceberg lettuce, you're not going to taste much.

The options for greens in supermarkets have grown tremendously in the last twenty years, and even a little salad of Boston and romaine lettuces mixed together is considerably better than one of either alone. And, in many ways, the more greens the merrier.

There are hundreds of edible greens, each with its own personality. They range from hot mustard greens to sweet chard to bitter radicchio to spicy arugula; and then of course there are lettuces, most of which are far more flavorful than iceberg. The fact that now you can buy mixes of these, prewashed and even precut, makes building a "green" salad easier than ever before.

Though in many instances I find myself buying mixtures of greens—it's just so *easy*—it's still worth understanding the differences among them. So here's a quick primer:

Lettuces

There are four basic types:

- Iceberg: a light green ball of crisp, super-moist but not especially flavorful leaves
- Romaine: long, crunchy leaves, still moist but with some bitterness
- Boston (or butterhead): soft but well-defined heads with tender, only slightly bitter leaves
- Loose-leaf, bunching, or cutting lettuce, like green and red leaf: the biggest category of lettuces and the ones that tend to be the most bitter.

Storing: Iceberg and romaine keep literally for weeks, because their tight heads keep the inner leaves moist. Boston and loose-leaf lettuces don't keep for more than a few days.

Using: Romaine and Boston lettuces are fine by themselves, though better in mixes because they're so mild. Iceberg needs even more help, though it's good in combination with other vegetables, as in Chopped Salad (page 38), or broken into big wedges and used as a vehicle to show off dressing, like Real Ranch or Blue Cheese Dressing (page 772 or 212). Loose-leaf lettuce varies so much in taste and quality that it's hard to generalize. Lettuce can also be braised (see page 238) or thrown into soups.

This variety of texture and flavors is exactly why lettuces are almost always better in combination than alone. The bland tenderness of Boston-style lettuce, for example, mingles nicely with some bitter loose-leaf or radicchio and a few pieces of super-crisp romaine.

Chicory and Endive

The flavor, texture, color, and versatility of this huge group of greens—which includes radicchio, Belgian endive, curly endive, escarole, frisée, and more obscure greens like treviso radicchio and puntarella—is unmatched.

They're all forms of chicory: Sharp, crunchy vegetables that vary wildly in appearance but less so in taste and texture. Tight-headed bright red radicchio; long, leafy radicchio (also called *endive*); lettuce-looking, thick-ribbed escarole; the smooth oval Belgian endive; and lacy, frilly frisée all feature a stark bitterness that is readily tamed by cooking or smoothed by olive oil. All are bitter, most are super-crunchy, some are very expensive. (Yet if you can tell the difference with your eyes closed between $5-a-pound radicchio and $1-a-pound escarole, you have a better palate than I.)

Storing: Keep in plastic, in the vegetable bin, and

Ⓕ Fast   Ⓜ Make Ahead   Ⓥ Vegan

count on at least a few days before you see browning or wilting. Still, the sooner you eat these greens, the better.

Using: Other than endive and frisée, these are almost too bitter to use alone in salads but are great mixed with other greens. Endive can be served like celery, drizzled with olive oil or spread with cream cheese. All of these are delicious braised (try, for example, using them in the recipe for Braised and Glazed Brussels Sprouts on page 272), stir-fried as described in Stir-Fried Vegetables (page 242), or brushed with olive oil, sprinkled with salt, and grilled (page 253).

Arugula, Watercress, and Dandelion

These greens are unrelated except for all being dark green and intensely flavorful. Dandelion greens have the distinction of being among the most vitamin-packed foods on the planet; when young, dandelion is mild flavored; when mature, it is the most bitter of greens. Arugula (also called *rocket* or *rucola*) is the most strangely flavored of all the greens, possessing a distinctive hot muddiness that may be an acquired taste, but an easily acquired one. (The now widely available baby arugula is much milder, so much so that real arugula fans find it insipid.) And super-peppery watercress (there are other cresses, too, and they're all similar) is unjustly used more as a garnish than as a food.

Traditionally these are best in spring and fall, but, like almost everything else, they are now available year-round.

Storing: As strong tasting as these greens are, they're fairly fragile. Buy and use quickly or risk their rotting. If you're desperate to store one for more than a couple of days, dunk the stem end in a glass half full of water and wrap the whole thing, glass and all, in a plastic bag. Store this cool tropical mini-environment in the refrigerator.

Using: Arugula is one of the best salad greens there is; lightly dressed with oil and lemon juice, it's a real treat. It is also great as a bed for grilled vegetables (especially when it wilts a little and absorbs some grilling juices) or in a salad with tomatoes. Watercress makes a fine addition to salads but is also good on sandwiches and in soups—cook with potatoes, in broth or water, and purée to make a vichyssoiselike soup. Dandelions can be eaten in salads when young but quickly become too bitter to eat raw and are then best steamed or stir-fried with soy sauce or garlic and lemon. For this and other recipes for cooking these greens, see pages 300–301.

Salad Mixes (Mesclun)

Mesclun, from the Niçoise dialect for "mixture," is a word originally used to describe a mixture of a dozen or more wild and cultivated greens, herbs, and edible flowers. Now it has come to mean any mix of greens.

Supermarket mesclun may not be as interesting as mesclun you make yourself (especially if you're a gardener), but it sure is easy to use. It's become a year-round staple, sometimes available for as little as $3 a pound, an incredible bargain when you consider that a pound of greens will serve a substantial side salad to at least six people and probably more like eight.

These mixes are often packaged in plastic, with a special process (*Modified Atmosphere Packaging,* it's called, or *MAP*) that keeps them fresh for a week or longer. (The same is true of other prepackaged salads containing less exotic greens, like romaine and iceberg.) Once opened, however—or if you buy your mesclun in bulk—use it within a couple of days, before it starts to turn even the slightest bit funky.

All of these are (theoretically) prewashed, but I wash them anyway, and I recommend you do too.

The "Other" Greens

These are the leafy salad greens that don't easily fall into any of the preceding categories. Some, like spinach (see page 359), are available everywhere in many forms. Some, like mizuna and tatsoi (a small-leafed member of the bok choy family) are traditional Asian greens now going mainstream in America. Others, like mâche, lamb's tongue, and their relatives, are quite tender and fragile, with a small window of freshness.

If you frequent farmer's markets or specialty grocers, you'll run into all of these and more. I encourage you to experiment. It's no big deal; just treat them as you would any other lettuce or salad green. And swap them out for "any mixed salad greens" in the recipes. Almost all may also be lightly cooked— steamed, boiled and shocked, or stir-fried—though when they're young, fresh, and tender, the best way to eat them is raw.

The Basics of Preparing Salad Greens

You can wash salad greens up to a day or two in advance. (STEP 1) Plunge them into a salad spinner filled with water (or a colander set in a large pot or bowl); swirl the greens around, then lift the insert or colander and change the water, repeating as many times as necessary to remove all traces of grit. (STEP 2) If you have a salad spinner, spin the greens dry; otherwise, dry them in a towel. (STEP 3) Store, wrapped loosely in cloth or paper towels, in a semiclosed zippered bag.

Vinaigrette and Other Salad Dressings

Generally vinaigrette is light enough to toss directly with salad greens, but to prevent sogginess I suggest topping mixed greens with creamy dressings right before serving. Here is where you'll find them:

1. Vinaigrette (page 762)
2. Real Ranch Dressing (page 772)
3. Blue Cheese Dressing (page 212)
4. Creamy Bistro Dressing or Sauce (page 799)
5. The Simplest Yogurt Sauce (page 774)

Trimming: For head and whole loose-leaf lettuces, first scoop or cut out the core. (If the head is tight, you'll probably have to use a knife.) Trim away the outer round of leaves and any browned or wilted stems. Tear or cut into smaller pieces if you like and wash.

Washing: *Don't skip this process even if the mixture or single variety comes in a bag labeled "prewashed."* It's fast and easy and a necessary precaution. Put the greens into a salad spinner or in a colander inside a large pot. Fill the container with water and swirl the greens around. Now lift the colander or salad spinner insert out of the water. Pour out the water and repeat as necessary until the water contains no traces of sand. Then spin the greens or pat them dry with towels.

Storing: Washed, dried salad greens are good to have on hand and keep pretty well. If you have a salad spinner with a bowl, pour the water out of it after spinning and pop it in the fridge, greens and all. The remaining moisture and ventilated basket provide a good environment for keeping greens fresh for a couple days or more. If you don't have a salad spinner, line a small plastic bag with clean cloth or paper towels, put the washed greens inside (careful not to pack them too tightly), loosely tie the top, and store in the crisper if possible. Greens should always be kept in a cool part of the refrigerator, but not somewhere cold enough to freeze them.

The Basics of Dressing and Serving Salads

Few dishes are as pretty as salads (as long as you don't dress them too early or too heavily and end up with wilted greens). But there's no law that says salad must be served in a large wooden bowl with a wooden fork and spoon. Here are some other options:

Tossed Salad: Most of the recipes here call for the leaves to be a manageable size, tossed in dressing. Individual preferences aside, as a general rule $^1/_2$ cup dressing is about right to dress 4 cups of dense vegetables, beans, or grains or 6 to 8 cups of salad greens. Once the salad is tossed, you decide whether to divvy it up or serve it from one plate, platter, or bowl at the table. Unless the occasion is formal, I take the whole salad to the table—nobody seems to eat salad at the same time during the meal and, besides, salads make a nice centerpiece.

Drizzled with Dressing: Thick, chunky, or rich dressings don't always work very well, especially if the vegetables are tender, cooked, or left in large leaves, pieces, or slices. Simply arrange the salad and pour a couple tablespoons of dressing around the top. In cases where the dressing is thick enough to use a spoon, serve it on top or a little to the side of the greens.

The Wedge: Retro, but making a comeback, only this time with better dressings. Whether you cut a neat pie-shaped slice from a head of iceberg or roughly break into the heart of a romaine, the lettuce must be crackling crisp. Then just top it with a spoonful of dressing and maybe a sprinkle of something crunchy (see the sidebar at left). This is the time to go for thick, creamy dressings like Real Ranch, Vegetarian Caesar, or Blue Cheese (see pages 772, 773, and 212).

Green Salads

This is what comes to mind when you say "salad": something predominantly green, with a lot of leaves. To me the basic green salad is one or more greens, drizzled with oil and a little lemon juice or vinegar and sprinkled with some salt and pepper, but, as detailed on pages 34–36, the greens may vary considerably, as may the dressing.

There are plenty of different directions to go in, and I offer some of them here. To shortcut the recipes, be sure to look at "15 Ideas for Simple Green Salad" (page 38). A few hints in advance: Try to add some crunch, as per the sidebar at left (the tofu croutons are pretty great). Jazz up your dressing with mustard, roasted garlic, or a fresh herb—but don't overdo it. Toss in leftover cooked vegetables, rinsed with hot water if any of last night's dressing is clinging to them.

Simple Green Salad

MAKES: 4 servings
TIME: 10 minutes

The basic green salad remains a staple because it's fresh, basic, quick, easy, even healthy. You don't even have to make a vinaigrette, though of course using one won't hurt.

6 cups torn assorted greens, like mesclun, or any lettuce

About $^1/_3$ cup extra virgin olive oil

About 2 tablespoons sherry vinegar or balsamic vinegar

Salt and freshly ground black pepper

1 Put the greens in a bowl and toss them with oil, vinegar, a pinch of salt, and some pepper. Taste, adjust the seasoning, and serve immediately.

Greek Salad. The classic, simplified: Add about $^1/_4$ cup chopped fresh mint or parsley (or both); about $^1/_3$ cup crumbled feta cheese; and about $^1/_4$ cup pitted and roughly chopped black olives. Use lemon juice in place of vinegar.

Lyonnaise Salad. Very hearty: Use strong-flavored greens, like frisée, arugula, dandelions, radicchio, etc., alone or in combination. Top with 2 Poached Eggs (page 169) or Peeled Medium-Boiled Eggs (page 165).

Endive Salad. Elegant and delicious: Combine endive with radicchio, watercress, and other strong-flavored greens. Toss in about $^1/_2$ cup toasted walnuts or hazelnuts (see page 40) and use nut oil if you have it.

15 Ideas for Simple Green Salad

1. Omit the oil or minimize the vinegar (either way, it'll still be good).
2. Substitute any flavorful oil, like walnut, hazelnut, or sesame. (Use less at first, because these are stronger than olive oil.)
3. Add freshly grated Parmesan. This is probably the easiest "upgrade" you can make to this salad (and many others).
4. Add chopped vegetables (see Chopped Salad, below).
5. Add chopped pitted olives.
6. Add herbs, in small or large quantities (see Parsley and Herb Salad, page 42).
7. Add tomatoes, cut into quarters or eighths; you might want to remove their seeds first (see page 373), but it isn't essential. Best with balsamic vinegar.
8. Add minced shallot, onion, or scallion; or chopped leek; or minced garlic (just a little bit).
9. Add chopped Hard-Cooked Egg (see page 166) or top with one or more Poached Eggs (page 169) or peeled Medium-Boiled Eggs (page 165).
10. Add crumbled blue or other cheese.
11. Add nuts or seeds, crumbled or chopped if necessary.
12. Add sliced pears, apples, oranges, or other fruit.
13. Add seaweed, about a quarter of the amount in Simple Seaweed Salad (page 53), soaked and drained as in that recipe. Or add nori (laver), toasted briefly over a hot flame and crumbled as on page 357.
14. Add diced Roasted Red (or yellow) Peppers (page 333), capers, or anchovies.
15. Use more intensely flavored greens: Arugula, watercress, endive, radicchio, frisée, escarole, etc.

Chopped Salad

MAKES: 6 servings
TIME: 30 minutes

The most popular nonrecipe in the salad world, chopped salad is a mix of whatever crunchy fresh vegetables you

F Fast   **M** Make Ahead   **V** Vegan

Lettuce leaves can serve as wrappers that turn other dishes into something you can eat with your hands as party food or appetizers. Iceberg, Bibb or Boston, and radicchio are naturally cupped to hold fillings; broad and sturdy green and red leaf lettuces are better for folding and wrapping like burritos.

The preparation is a snap: Cut the core out of the head of lettuce and pull the leaves off, being careful not to tear them. Keep the leaves crisp for a day or two by stacking them, wrapping in damp paper towels, and then wrapping in plastic or enclosing in a plastic bag.

I usually let guests make their own wraps or cups, serving a plate piled high next to a bowl of whatever goes inside. But if you're doing the assembly, save the task for the last minute to keep the cups or wraps fresh.

Small diced or chopped foods make the best fillings (large pieces can crush or tear the lettuce and are unwieldy). Warm, hot, or heavily sauced food will wilt the lettuce, but that's not a bad thing. With those caveats in mind, consider the following as fillings:

- Stir-fried vegetables (pages 242)
- Roasted Cauliflower with Raisins and Vinaigrette (page 282)
- Spicy No-Mayo Coleslaw (page 49)
- Green Beans Tossed with Walnut-Miso Sauce (page 305)
- Baked Mixed Vegetables with Olive Oil (page 380)
- Kimchi Rice (page 512)
- Pineapple Fried Rice (page 521)
- Edamame with Tomatoes and Cilantro (page 583)
- Fresh Favas with Eggs and Croutons (page 591)
- Braised Lentils, Spanish Style (page 598)
- Falafel (page 625), crumbled
- Pressed Tofu Salad (page 652)
- Marinated Tofu (page 652)
- Tofu Escabeche (page 653)

And don't neglect the garnishes: chopped scallions, fresh herbs, olives, capers, or nuts; seeds; crumbled or grated cheese; a dollop of sour cream, yogurt, Guacamole (page 236), or any salsa or chutney (pages 750, 753, and 783–789.

have on hand, dressed with whatever vinaigrette you like. It can be so big and hearty and flavorful you need nothing else for dinner. This recipe will get you started, but the accompanying list will show you the real possibilities.

2 celery stalks (preferably from the heart), chopped

2 carrots, chopped

1 small to medium red onion, minced

1 cucumber, peeled if waxed, seeded, and chopped

1 red or yellow bell pepper, cored, seeded, and chopped

4 cups chopped romaine lettuce

Salt and freshly ground black pepper

$1/2$ cup or more Vinaigrette (made with a small clove garlic instead of shallot) or one of the variations (page 762)

❶ Combine the vegetables and lettuce in a bowl; sprinkle lightly with salt and pepper and toss.

❷ Drizzle with the vinaigrette, toss again, taste and adjust the seasoning, and serve immediately.

10 Additions to Chopped Salad

1. Fennel, $1/2$ bulb or so, trimmed and chopped
2. Avocado—not too ripe—peeled, pitted, and chopped
3. Cabbage, about 1 cup, shredded or chopped

4. Haricots verts or other green beans, about 1 cup, cooked briefly and shocked (page 241)
5. Fresh peas, snow peas, or snap peas, about 1 cup, very lightly cooked and shocked (page 241)
6. Cheese, like Parmesan, blue, or feta—$1/2$ cup grated or crumbled
7. Radishes, $1/2$ cup chopped
8. New potatoes, steamed and cut into small chunks—about 1 cup
9. Chickpeas, $1/2$ cup (or more) cooked or lightly rinsed canned
10. Nuts, like almonds, pistachios, or peanuts, $1/2$ cup chopped into large pieces

Greens with Fruit, Cheese, and Nuts

MAKES: 4 servings
TIME: 20 to 30 minutes

The classic combination here, a restaurant standard from the nineties, is pears, Gorgonzola, and walnuts. But all sorts of trios are possible, ranging from an all-American mix of apples, cheddar, and hazelnuts to the borderline wildness of cherries, goat cheese, and pistachios and the other combos in the list at right. Generally, I like the strong flavor of blues and other aged varieties here, but feta and Parmesan are reasonable choices too. When it comes to the nuts, go with flavors and textures that complement the fruit and the cheese.

About 1 pound fresh fruit or 1 cup dried

1 tablespoon freshly squeezed lemon juice

4 ounces Gorgonzola or other creamy blue cheese

$3/4$ cup shelled walnuts or other nuts

6 cups mixed greens, like mesclun, washed, dried, and torn into bite-sized pieces

About $1/2$ cup Vinaigrette (page 762), made with extra virgin olive oil and balsamic vinegar

1. Peel and core the fruit if necessary and remove any seeds or pits. If large, cut the fruit into $1/2$-inch chunks. Toss the fruit with the lemon juice. Cover and refrigerate for up to 2 hours.

2. Crumble the cheese into small bits; cover and refrigerate until needed. Place the nuts in a dry skillet, turn the heat to medium, and toast them, shaking the pan frequently until they are aromatic and beginning to darken in color, 3 to 5 minutes.

3. When you're ready to serve, toss the pears, cheese, and greens together with as much of the dressing as you like. Chop the nuts coarsely, sprinkle them over all, and serve.

10 Good Fruit, Cheese, and Nut Combinations

1. Grapes, Parmesan, pine nuts
2. Oranges, manchego, almonds
3. Apricots, goat cheese, pecans
4. Dried apricots, blue cheese, walnuts
5. Cantaloupe or honeydew, cotija, pepitas
6. Blueberries, Asiago, pistachios
7. Dried plums, feta, hazelnuts
8. Dried pineapple, Brie, cashews
9. Peaches, ricotta salata, pecans
10. Plums, fontina, almonds

Spinach Salad with Warm Dressing and Tofu Croutons

MAKES: 4 to 6 servings
TIME: About 45 minutes, including making the croutons

There's no reason to shun this favorite American salad just because you want to skip the bacon. Tofu croutons have a crisp appeal all their own, while the slightly sweet, soy-based dressing is rich and satisfying. There is also no

Ⓕ Fast   Ⓜ Make Ahead   Ⓥ Vegan

reason to stop at spinach and tofu; see the list below for add-on ideas.

1 pound fresh spinach leaves

$1/4$ cup peanut oil or neutral oil, like grapeseed or corn

1 tablespoon peeled, minced fresh ginger

1 tablespoon minced garlic

$1/2$ cup sliced scallion

1 tablespoon sugar

2 tablespoons rice wine vinegar

1 tablespoon soy sauce

2 teaspoons dark sesame oil

Hot red pepper flakes to taste

Freshly ground black pepper

1 pound (about $1^{1}/2$ cups) Tofu Croutons (page 656)

Salt, if needed

1 Put the spinach in a bowl large enough to comfortably toss the salad quickly.

2 Put the peanut oil in a medium skillet over medium-high heat. When hot, add the ginger and garlic and cook, stirring constantly, until just soft, about a minute. Add the scallion and cook for another minute. Stir in the sugar, vinegar, and 2 tablespoons water. When the mixture begins to bubble, turn the heat down to medium-low and cook, stirring occasionally, until it becomes a little syrupy, 2 to 3 minutes.

3 Stir in the soy sauce and sesame oil. Season with the red pepper flakes and black pepper. (The dressing may be made to this point up to an hour or so in advance. Just remove it from the heat until ready to serve, then gently rewarm it.) While the dressing is still warm, pour it over the spinach and toss immediately until well coated. Add the croutons and toss again. Taste and adjust the seasoning, adding a little salt if necessary. Serve.

5 Great Ways to Vary Wilted Spinach Salad

1. Garnish with a couple tablespoons of sesame seeds, toasted (see page 784), or sunflower seeds.

2. Add $1/2$ cup finely chopped tomato to the dressing while heating it.

3. Add 2 tablespoons fermented black beans to the dressing while heating it.

4. Toss the finished salad with $1/2$ cup or more edamame (see page 585).

5. Add 2 ounces bean thread noodles, soaked and cut (see page 464), or 2 cups cooked rice vermicelli (see page 464).

Spinach Salad with Feta and Nutmeg

MAKES: 4 to 6 servings

TIME: 15 minutes

Feta in a salad makes us think "Greek," but here you'll find no tomatoes, olives, or romaine. Instead, nutmeg and yogurt complement the cheese and spinach.

1 tablespoon sherry vinegar or freshly squeezed lemon juice

2 ounces feta cheese, crumbled (about $1/2$ cup)

$1/8$ to $1/4$ teaspoon freshly grated nutmeg, plus a little more for garnish

Freshly ground black pepper

3 tablespoons extra virgin olive oil

1 pound fresh spinach leaves

Salt, if needed

$1/2$ cup yogurt

1 Put the vinegar in a large bowl with the feta. Use a fork to mash the cheese a little and stir them together. Add the nutmeg and a sprinkle of black pepper and stir again. Keep stirring while you slowly pour in the olive oil.

2 Chop the spinach leaves into small pieces, add to the bowl, and toss to coat with the dressing. Taste and adjust the seasoning, adding salt if necessary. Divide among salad bowls, top each with a dollop of yogurt and a dusting of nutmeg, and serve.

Cooked Spinach Salad with Feta and Nutmeg. Cook and shock the spinach (see page 241), squeeze as much water out of it as possible, and roughly chop. Substitute for the raw spinach.

Balsamic Strawberries with Arugula

MAKES: 4 to 6 servings
TIME: 15 minutes

In the original *How to Cook Everything*, I featured these strawberries as a peppery, slightly sweet compote in the fruit chapter. In Italy, where balsamic vinegar originated, strawberries with balsamic are served as a dessert. But the combination is equally fantastic in a savory salad.

3 cups strawberries, hulled and halved or quartered

1 tablespoon balsamic vinegar, or more to taste

Freshly ground black pepper

4 cups arugula leaves

Salt

1 tablespoon extra virgin olive oil

1 Toss the strawberries with the vinegar and black pepper in a large salad bowl and let sit for 10 minutes.

2 Add the arugula, sprinkle with salt, and toss again. Drizzle with olive oil and toss gently one last time. Taste, adjust the seasoning, and serve.

Balsamic Strawberries with Arugula and Goat Cheese. Before the final toss in Step 2, crumble 4 ounces of goat cheese over the salad.

Bitter Greens and Herbs

Strong-flavored greens make great salads, and there's a long tradition of using bitter greens, herbs, and flowers as accompaniments to blander foods. The recipes here build on that concept by combining these pungent powerhouses with other ingredients. The results are delicious salads that you can eat by the bowlful.

Parsley and Herb Salad

MAKES: 4 servings
TIME: About 20 minutes

The standard Tabbouleh (page 43) is really a parsley salad with bulgur rather than the other way around, but this is an herb salad in which parsley plays the leading role. I don't agree that flat-leaf (Italian) parsley tastes better than the curly variety, but don't make too big a deal about it—it is easier to handle and feels better in the mouth.

You can omit the honey if you like—which will make it a vegan salad— but many people like the way it smooths the parsley's bitterness.

1 teaspoon fresh thyme leaves

4 cups chopped parsley (or leave flat leaves whole)

$1/4$ cup minced chives, shallot, or scallion

1 fresh tarragon leaf, minced, or a pinch of dried

Juice of 2 lemons, or to taste

$1/3$ cup extra virgin olive oil, or to taste

1 teaspoon honey, or to taste

Salt and freshly ground black pepper

1 Toss the thyme, parsley, chives, and tarragon together in a bowl. Combine the lemon juice, oil, honey, and salt and pepper in a small bowl and whisk to blend.

Dress the salad, then taste and adjust the seasoning as you like. Serve immediately; this salad will not keep.

Lettuce Salad with Parsley. A more familiar but almost equally flavorful version: Use 4 cups mixed tender greens (mesclun or the like) and reduce the parsley to 1 cup. You may need a little more dressing.

Lettuce Salad with Mixed Herbs. With dill, mint, or basil, this is milder and sweeter than the all-parsley version: Use 4 cups of mixed tender greens (mesclun or the like) and, for the parsley, substitute a cup (more or less) of dill, mint, basil, or any combination of those and parsley.

Tabbouleh

MAKES: 4 servings
TIME: 40 minutes

Tabbouleh is all about herbs. The grain may be the traditional bulgur or quinoa, millet, or even rice (which, because it is starchier, may require a bit more dressing). But you must include fresh herbs, and lots of them, to make good tabbouleh, which is why it's a great midsummer dish and a great accompaniment for grilled food.

You can prepare the bulgur ahead of time and toss in the herbs right before serving.

$1/2$ cup fine-grind (#1) or medium-grind (#2) bulgur

$1/3$ cup extra virgin olive oil, or more as needed

$1/4$ cup freshly squeezed lemon juice, or to taste

Salt and freshly ground black pepper

2 cups roughly chopped parsley, leaves and small stems only

1 cup roughly chopped fresh mint leaves

$1/2$ cup chopped scallion

4 medium tomatoes, cored, seeded, and chopped (optional)

 Soak the bulgur in hot water to cover until tender, 15 to 30 minutes. Drain well, squeezing out as much water as possible. Toss the bulgur with the oil and lemon juice and season with pepper.

 Just before you're ready to eat, add the parsley, mint, scallion, and tomatoes and toss gently; taste, adjust the seasoning, and serve.

Green Salad with Caramelized Onion-Thyme Dressing

MAKES: 4 servings
TIME: About 1 hour

The sweetness of the slow-cooked onions, accentuated by a bit of honey and offset by the perfumed bitterness of thyme and olives, perfectly complements a mound of bitter greens. The onion and olives provide substance too.

3 tablespoons extra virgin olive oil

2 large white or yellow onions, thinly sliced

1 large red onion, thinly sliced

Salt and freshly ground black pepper

2 tablespoons honey

2 teaspoons fresh thyme leaves

1 cup black olives, preferably oil cured, pitted

Vinaigrette or Honey-Garlic Vinaigrette (page 762), as needed (about $1/2$ cup)

4 cups mixed greens, like mesclun

2 cups chopped bitter greens, like radicchio or Belgian endive

$1/2$ cup chopped parsley leaves

 Put the oil in a large skillet over medium-low heat. When hot, add the onions, a large pinch of salt, a sprinkling of pepper, the honey, and the thyme. Raise the heat a bit until the mixture sizzles, then adjust the heat so the onions cook steadily without browning. Add the olives and cook, stirring occasionally, until very soft, at least 30 minutes and probably more. (You can prepare the recipe up to this point and let it sit at room temperature for up to a few hours or refrigerate for longer, then reheat gently.)

2 Cool the mixture to lukewarm or room temperature. Toss the vinaigrette with the greens, then top with the onion mixture and the parsley and serve.

Lettuce and Chive Salad, Korean Style

MAKES: 4 servings
TIME: 15 minutes

In Korea, the chives would be served alone, as a side dish. And you can certainly do that. But I love tossing them and their distinctive dressing on top of a mound of greens. It's a great salad to serve with many East Asian dishes.

    2 tablespoons dark sesame oil

    ¹/₂ teaspoon hot red pepper flakes, or to taste

    2 tablespoons soy sauce

    1 tablespoon rice or other mild vinegar

    ¹/₂ teaspoon minced garlic

    1 teaspoon sugar

    8 ounces (2 large bunches) chives

    4 cups any tender lettuce or mixed lettuces

    About 1 tablespoon toasted sesame seeds (see page 321)

1 Make the dressing by combining the sesame oil with the red pepper flakes, soy sauce, vinegar, garlic, sugar, and about 1 tablespoon water.

2 Wash and dry the chives, then cut them into 1- or 2-inch lengths. Toss with the lettuce, then pour the dressing over all and toss again. Garnish with the sesame seeds and serve immediately.

Seasoned Perilla or Shiso Leaves. Great on salads or as a garnish: Instead of the chives, use 1 bunch of perilla leaves (see page 767). If you have time, layer the leaves with the dressing in an airtight container and let them marinate in the refrigerator for a few days. Or to eat immediately, steam the leaves first, shock in ice water, drain, and dress.

Endive and Roquefort Salad

MAKES: 4 servings
TIME: 15 minutes

I like a salad you can eat with your fingers, and this is a beaut because the endive serves as both an ingredient and a spoon (you can even eat it standing up). Each of the major ingredients can be swapped for something else, too, and the flavors of the salad can be varied in many ways (see "6 ideas for Endive Salad," below).

    16 to 24 Belgian endive leaves (about 2 endives)

    4 ounces enoki mushrooms, left whole, or other mushrooms, thinly sliced

    ¹/₂ cup crumbled Roquefort or other blue cheese

    ¹/₃ cup Vinaigrette (page 762), more or less

1 Arrange the endive leaves on a plate and lay a few mushroom pieces on each one. Sprinkle with the Roquefort.

2 Use a spoon to drizzle with vinaigrette and serve.

6 Ideas for Endive Salad

1. For the enokis, substitute matchstick-shaped pieces of regular button mushrooms.

2. For the endive, substitute the small inner leaves of romaine or leaves of radicchio.

3. For the Roquefort, use any blue cheese you like: Stilton, Maytag, Gorgonzola, or any of the creamy French blues. Or substitute freshly grated Parmesan or other hard cheese.

4. For the dressing, use Honey-Garlic Vinaigrette (page 763).

5. Sprinkle the top of the endives with toasted walnuts or hazelnuts (see page 321) and use any Vinaigrette (page 762).

6. Add a small pile of fresh grated radish to the top of each leaf.

Raw Vegetable Salads

The raw form of a few vegetables—beets, carrots, artichokes, celery (and celery root), mushrooms, and so on—makes fantastic salads. With many, the crunch is unsurpassed, while others are sublimely tender. The flavors are sometimes subtle, sometimes stark; they can stand up to a range of bold dressings, which provide contrast and emphasis. So from beet salad with vinaigrette to new versions of coleslaw, from old favorites like Waldorf salad to newer creations like a salad with sunchokes (Jerusalem artichokes), the recipes here are uniformly quick and interesting.

Carrot or Celery Salad

MAKES: 4 servings
TIME: 20 minutes

This is so easy it barely qualifies as a salad, yet celery and carrots are so readily overlooked, and this is so good. Consider using this ultra-basic lemon juice–olive oil dressing—just as you would a vinaigrette—with lightly steamed and cooled broccoli, cauliflower, and other vegetables too. It'll keep well, refrigerated, for up to a day after you make it, though it's best served not-too-cold.

4 medium carrots or 6 medium celery stalks

Salt and freshly ground black pepper

Juice of 1 lemon, or to taste

2 tablespoons extra virgin olive oil, or to taste

1 To prepare the carrots, trim, peel, and cut into coins. To prepare the celery, trim the ends and "string" it (see page 284); then chop it into bite-sized pieces.

2 Toss in a bowl with the salt and pepper, lemon juice, and olive oil. Taste, adjust the seasoning, and serve.

Carrot and Celery Salad. Use half as much of each and toss together.

Carrot or Celery Salad "Rémoulade." Dress as you would Celery Rémoulade (page 47).

Carrot Salad with Cumin

MAKES: 4 servings
TIME: 15 minutes

Here's a simple salad in a typically North African style that features the sweetness of fresh oranges offset nicely by the tang of ground cumin. You can also combine carrot and celeriac, jícama, or sunchokes (Jerusalem artichokes), using the same dressing. It'll keep well, refrigerated, for up to a day after you make it, though it's best served not-too-cold.

1^1/$_2$ pounds carrots

Juice of 2 oranges

Juice of 1 lemon

2 tablespoons extra virgin olive oil

Salt and freshly ground black pepper

1 teaspoon ground cumin, or more to taste

1 Use the julienne cutter of a food processor to cut the carrots into fine shreds, or cut into ^{1}/$_8$-inch-thick slices.

The word *salad* comes from the ancient word for "salt," so it's no surprise that the two concepts go hand in hand. We're not talking about pickles here, but maximizing crispness and flavor in watery vegetables. When vegetables with a high water content come into contact with salt—exactly what happens when you dress them—they release their water. This both dilutes the dressing and prevents the greens from absorbing its flavors.

If, however, you salt these vegetables *before* they go into salad, you can extract some of their water beforehand and make them firmer, crisper, and more flavorful. Specifically:

Cabbage: When slaws are made with salted cabbage, they are noticeably less watery and stay crisp and fresh a few days longer. Just put sliced cabbage in a colander, sprinkle with salt (about a tablespoon for 6 cups of cabbage), and set aside to drain. After about an hour, rinse, gently squeeze dry and drain, then proceed with the recipe.

Cucumbers: Ordinary cukes benefit greatly from salting. First peel, seed, and slice them (see page 293). Then use the same procedure as for cabbage. For extra crispness, rinse, then wring dry in a towel after salting; otherwise, just pat them dry after rinsing.

Radishes: Sliced radishes may be salted like cabbage and cucumbers—they become milder and crisper—but only for an absolute maximum of 45 minutes, or they will become limp.

Onions: As with radishes, you can make onions milder and crisper by salting them, either directly or in a salt-water bath (about 1 tablespoon of salt per quart of water). Let sit for a half hour or longer, then rinse dry before using.

Tomatoes: Lightly salting tomatoes always improves their flavor and tightens their flesh, but they are fragile. Use less salt (about 1 teaspoon per pound of tomatoes) and leave them for only 15 minutes or so. Put salted chopped tomatoes in a colander (and set a bowl under it if you want to trap the tomato water for another use, like that on page 112). Salted, sliced, and wedged tomatoes work best put directly on towels or spread out on wire racks.

Lettuces and Greens: Don't salt (or dress) lettuce or greens until right before serving. They wilt fast and never recover.

---

② Blend the citrus juices, oil, salt and pepper, and cumin and pour the dressing over the carrots. Toss and serve.

Chinese Marinated Celery

MAKES: 4 servings
TIME: 15 minutes, plus 3 hours to marinate

Ⓜ Ⓥ

A little something to snack on before dinner, a great side dish, or a unique addition to a picnic spread. Ten times better than you could imagine. Try it with carrots too.

1 pound celery stalks

1 teaspoon salt

4 teaspoons sugar

3 tablespoons dark sesame oil

1 tablespoon soy sauce

2 teaspoons rice or cider vinegar

$1/2$ teaspoon minced garlic

1 teaspoon chili oil (optional)

① Cut the celery into 2-inch lengths. Mix with the salt and 1 teaspoon of the sugar and set aside for 10 minutes while you whisk together the remaining tablespoon of sugar, the sesame oil, soy sauce, vinegar, garlic, and chili oil.

Ⓕ Fast   Ⓜ Make Ahead   Ⓥ Vegan

❷ Rinse, drain, and pat the celery dry, then toss with the dressing. Let stand in the refrigerator for at least 3 hours and up to a day. Serve chilled.

Ginger-Marinated Celery. With ginger, the celery can cross over to nearly any Asian cuisine: Substitute 1 teaspoon minced or finely julienned peeled ginger for the garlic.

Scallion-Marinated Cucumbers. A bit more work, but with delicious results: Substitute 3 trimmed scallions for the garlic; blanch and shock them, then chop and purée in a food processor or blender with the sesame oil, soy sauce, and vinegar.

Celery Rémoulade

MAKES: 4 to 6 servings
TIME: 20 minutes

The basis for this salad is the rémoulade dressing of tangy, mustardy, homemade mayonnaise, one that can make practically anything taste good. The classic French-bistro preparation is for celery root (page 285), but thinly sliced celery works well too. So do a few other hearty vegetables, listed in the variations.

$^1/_2$ cup Rémoulade Sauce (page 771), plus more to taste

1 medium celery root (about 1 pound), or 1 pound celery stalks

Freshly squeezed lemon juice, to taste

Salt and freshly ground black pepper

2 tablespoons minced parsley leaves for garnish

❶ Have the Rémoulade Sauce ready in a medium bowl.

❷ Peel and trim the celery root (see page 285) or trim and string the celery stalks (see page 284). Use the food processor (or work by hand) to either grate the celery root or slice it into fine julienne. If you're using celery stalks, cut them crosswise into paper-thin slices.

❸ Toss the celery root or celery slices with the rémoulade until coated. Taste and add lemon juice, salt, or pepper as needed. Serve, sprinkled with minced parsley.

Chayote (Mirliton) Rémoulade. A nice way to use raw chayotes: Peel, trim, and pit 2 medium chayotes instead of the celery root or stalks.

Potato Rémoulade. Perhaps the best traditional potato salad you can make: Steam 1 pound of waxy potatoes, like new potatoes, fingerlings, or other small heirloom potatoes. Be sure not to overcook them. Cut them into halves or quarters before dressing.

Waldorf Salad

MAKES: 4 servings
TIME: 15 minutes

This should be a peppery blend of apples, celery, and mayonnaise. Nuts are optional, as are raisins, a bit of honey, and grated carrots, any of which may appeal to you but none of which is essential.

Try using half yogurt and half mayo, which, though not traditional, makes a tart and (I think) better balanced salad.

3 large or 4 medium Granny Smith or other tart apples

3 celery stalks, trimmed and stringed (see page 284)

About $^1/_2$ cup mayonnaise (to make your own, see page 771)

Salt and freshly ground black pepper

$^1/_2$ cup walnuts, roughly chopped (optional)

Freshly squeezed lemon juice, to taste

❶ Peel and core the apples; cut them into $^1/_2$-inch dice. Chop the celery into $^1/_2$-inch dice. Toss them together and add just enough mayonnaise to make the mixture slightly creamy.

② Add salt, lots of pepper, and walnuts if you're using them; toss. Add some lemon juice, then taste and add more salt, pepper, or lemon juice as needed.

Cucumber Salad with Sour Cream or Yogurt

MAKES: 4 servings

TIME: 30 minutes, largely unattended

If you use real garden cucumbers or the long, skinny "European" or "English" cucumbers, you can skip the salting (you may even be able to skip the seeding). But conventional cucumbers, with their thick skins and chewy seeds, really benefit from a brief salting, which draws out excess water and crisps them up (see page 46).

1 to 1$^1/_2$ pounds (about 3 medium) cucumbers

$^1/_2$ cup sour cream or yogurt

2 tablespoons freshly squeezed lemon juice or white wine vinegar

Pinch cayenne or 1 teaspoon good paprika

Salt and freshly ground black pepper

$^1/_4$ cup chopped fresh dill or parsley, or more to taste, plus a few sprigs for garnish

① If you're using really good cucumbers, just slice them and proceed to Step 3.

② If you're using conventional supermarket cucumbers, peel them. Cut them in half lengthwise, then scoop out the seeds with a spoon. Slice, salt, and put in a colander; let drain (over a bowl or in the sink) for 10 to 20 minutes. Rinse, drain, and spin or pat dry. (If you want super-crunchy cucumbers, wring dry in a towel.)

③ Combine the sour cream and lemon juice, then whisk in the cayenne. When the cucumbers are ready, toss them with the dressing. Season with salt and pep-

per, garnish with the dill, and serve or refrigerate for up to an hour.

Cucumber Salad with Tomatoes and Peppers. A mini chopped salad: Add $^1/_2$ cup chopped tomato (seeded and salted to drain excess liquid; see page 46) and $^1/_2$ cup chopped red or yellow bell pepper to the cucumbers.

Cucumber Salad with Soy and Ginger

MAKES: 4 servings

TIME: 30 minutes, largely unattended

This is likely different from most cucumber salads you've ever tasted, but nondairy, easy, and delicious.

1 to 1$^1/_2$ pounds (about 3 medium) cucumbers

Salt and freshly ground black pepper

2 tablespoons rice vinegar, or white vinegar mixed with a little water

A 1-inch piece fresh ginger, peeled and minced or grated

1 teaspoon sugar

2 tablespoons soy sauce, or to taste

Fine sprigs fresh cilantro for garnish

① If you're using really good cucumbers, just slice them and proceed to Step 2. If you're using conventional supermarket cucumbers, peel them, cut in half lengthwise, then scoop out the seeds with a spoon. Slice, salt, and put in a colander; let drain (over a bowl or in the sink) for 10 to 20 minutes. Rinse, drain, and spin or pat dry. (If you want super-crunchy cucumbers, wring dry in a towel.)

② Toss the cucumbers with the salt (if you haven't salted them already), pepper, vinegar, ginger, sugar, and soy sauce, then taste and adjust the seasoning. Garnish and serve.

Cucumber Salad, Korean Style. Like most Korean food, quite strong: Add $1/2$ teaspoon or more minced fresh chile (like serrano, jalapeño, or Thai) and 1 teaspoon minced garlic. Along with the cilantro, garnish with 1 teaspoon sesame oil and 1 tablespoon toasted sesame seeds (page 321).

Spicy No-Mayo Coleslaw

MAKES: 8 servings
TIME: 30 minutes

If you want restaurant-style coleslaw, you combine shredded cabbage with mayo and maybe a little lemon juice. This version is far more flavorful with far less fat. I like cabbage salad (which is what coleslaw amounts to) on the spicy side, so I use plenty of Dijon, along with a little garlic and chile (you could substitute cayenne for the chile or just omit it if you prefer) and scallions.

2 tablespoons Dijon mustard, or to taste

2 tablespoons sherry vinegar, red wine vinegar, or freshly squeezed lemon juice

1 small clove garlic, minced

1 tablespoon minced fresh chile (jalapeño, Thai, serrano, or habanero), or to taste (optional)

$1/4$ cup peanut or extra virgin olive oil

6 cups cored and shredded Napa, Savoy, green, and/or red cabbage

1 large red or yellow bell yellow pepper, roasted and peeled if you like (see page 333), seeded, and diced or shredded

$1/3$ cup diced scallion, more or less

Salt and freshly ground black pepper

$1/4$ cup minced parsley leaves

1 Whisk the mustard, vinegar, garlic, and chile together in a small bowl. Add the oil a little at a time, whisking all the while.

2 Combine the cabbage, peppers, and scallion and toss with the dressing. Season with salt and pepper and refrigerate until ready to serve. (It's best to let this rest for an hour or so before serving to allow the flavors to mellow; the cabbage will also soften a bit and exude some juice. Or let it sit for up to 24 hours if you like. Drain the slaw before continuing.) Just before serving, toss with the parsley.

Cabbage and Carrot Slaw, Mexican Style. Equally good: Substitute 2 medium carrots, grated, for the bell pepper. Use lime juice in place of the vinegar. Finish with cilantro instead of parsley if you like.

Apple Slaw. A little sweeter: Use carrots instead of bell pepper, as in the preceding variation. Use 1 medium onion, grated, in place of the scallion. Shred or grate 2 medium or 1 large Granny Smith or other tart, crisp apples and include them in the mix. Lemon juice or cider vinegar is the best choice for the acid here.

Raw Beet Salad

MAKES: 4 servings
TIME: 20 minutes

Beets, like carrots, can be eaten raw. And they're delicious that way, crunchy and sweet. So sweet, in fact, that they need a strongly acidic dressing like this one for balance.

1 to $1 1/2$ pounds beets, preferably small

2 large shallots

Salt and freshly ground black pepper

2 teaspoons Dijon mustard, or to taste

1 tablespoon extra virgin olive oil

2 tablespoons sherry or other good strong vinegar

1 sprig fresh tarragon, minced, if available

$1/4$ cup chopped parsley leaves

1 Peel the beets and shallots. Combine them in a food processor and pulse carefully until the beets are shredded; do not purée. (Or grate the beets by hand and mince the shallots, then combine.) Scrape into a bowl.

② Toss with the salt, pepper, mustard, oil and vinegar. Taste and adjust the seasoning. Toss in the herbs and serve.

Raw Beet Salad with Cabbage and Orange. Quite nice-looking: Use equal parts beet and cabbage, about 8 ounces of each. Shred the beets (with the shallot) as directed; shred the cabbage by hand or by using the slicing disk of the food processor. Add 1 navel orange (including its juice), peeled and roughly chopped.

Raw Beet Salad with Carrot and Ginger. Ginger and beets are killer together: Use equal parts beet and carrot, about 8 ounces of each. Treat the carrots as you do the beets (you can process them together), adding about a tablespoon of minced peeled ginger to the mix; omit the tarragon. Substitute peanut for olive oil, lime juice for sherry vinegar, and cilantro for parsley.

Raw Beet Salad with Yogurt Dressing. Creamy: Replace the olive oil and one of the tablespoons of vinegar with 2 tablespoons plain yogurt, preferably whole-milk or low-fat.

Jícama Salad with Pineapple and Mint

MAKES: 4 servings
TIME: 20 minutes

You can use jícama, standard radishes, or daikon here; all are equally good. The combination of any of these crisp, slightly sharp roots with sweet fruit (pineapple here, orange in the variation) and a fresh herb-scented dressing is really quite compelling.

    1 medium jícama, peeled and chopped, or 16
        radishes, chopped, or 1 medium daikon, peeled
        and chopped

    2 tablespoons freshly squeezed lime juice

    ½ teaspoon minced fresh chile (jalapeño, Thai,
        serrano, or habanero), or to taste

    Salt

    1 cup small fresh pineapple chunks with juice

    ½ cup chopped scallion or white onion

    ¼ cup chopped fresh mint leaves

① In a bowl, combine the jícama, lime juice, chile, salt, and pineapple. Taste and adjust the seasoning.
② Toss in half the scallion and mint, then garnish with the remainder and serve.

Jícama and Orange Salad. Unquestionably more convenient: Substitute 1 large or 2 small oranges, peeled, segmented, and roughly chopped, for the pineapple. Substitute cilantro for the mint.

Shaved Artichoke Salad

MAKES: 4 servings
TIME: 30 minutes

Ultra-thin slicing is handy for making salads from intensely flavored vegetables because the pieces are tender yet crisp and easier to eat. Cooked or marinated artichoke hearts (page 259) are a great prepared addition to almost any salad, but for a real treat, one that is four-star-restaurant delicious, you must try this salad of shaved baby artichokes layered with Parmesan. Unbelievable.

Almost as good, considerably easier, and cheaper, is virtually the same salad made with button mushrooms or barely cooked sunchokes (Jerusalem artichokes); see the variations.

    1 lemon, plus 1 for garnish (optional)

    8 baby artichokes, cleaned (see page 257)

    Parmesan cheese, as needed

    3 tablespoons extra virgin olive oil, or more as needed

    Salt and freshly ground black pepper

    Chopped parsley or fresh basil leaves for garnish

1 Squeeze the juice of a lemon into a bowl of ice water. Slice the artichoke hearts (and bottoms, if they're tender enough) as thinly as possible; as you slice them, drop them into the water (this will keep them from browning).

2 Thinly slice the Parmesan; you want about as many pieces as you have artichoke slices, and about the same size. Zest the second lemon if you're using it. Remove the artichoke slices from the water and dry, then toss with the olive oil and 1 tablespoon of juice from the remaining lemon. Sprinkle with a little salt and a fair amount of pepper, then layer with the Parmesan. Taste and add more olive oil, lemon juice, salt, or pepper as needed, then garnish with herbs, and zest if you like, and serve immediately.

Sunchoke (Jerusalem Artichoke) Salad. The tougher sunchokes must be parboiled: Scrub and trim about a pound of sunchokes, then put them in a small pan with salted water to cover; bring to a boil and cook just until barely tender, 7 to 10 minutes (they turn mushy fast). Plunge into the bowl of ice water with lemon juice, then cut into thin slices and proceed as directed.

Shaved Mushroom Salad. Really simple: Instead of using raw artichokes, use 1 pound button mushrooms sliced as thinly as possible. Proceed with the recipe, except there is no need to drop the mushroom slices in lemony water.

Avocado Salad with Ginger and Peanuts

MAKES: 4 servings
TIME: 2 hours, largely unattended

Avocado is so rich and creamy that all it needs is a little acidity to become a "salad." This sweet and sour dressing, almost a ginger syrup, really does the trick. Serve this salad with Eggless Vegetable Tempura (page 249) or

Crisp-Fried Noodle Cake (page 469) for a bright, refreshing counterpoint. And for a more substantial salad, eliminate the cilantro sprigs and put the avocados on a bed of watercress before dressing.

$^1/_3$ cup rice vinegar

$^1/_4$ cup sugar

Salt

2 tablespoons minced or grated peeled fresh ginger

Several sprigs cilantro for garnish

2 medium or large avocados, pitted, peeled, and sliced

$^1/_4$ cup chopped roasted peanuts, salted or unsalted for garnish

1 Put the vinegar, sugar, a pinch of salt, and 2 tablespoons water in a small saucepan over medium heat. Cook, stirring, until the sugar dissolves. Add the ginger and continue cooking, stirring occasionally, as the dressing bubbles gently and thickens, about 5 minutes. When it gets noticeably syrupy, remove from the heat, cool, cover tightly or put in a jar, and refrigerate until very cold, at least an hour or so. (The dressing may be made ahead to this point and used up to 2 days later.)

2 To serve, put a few cilantro sprigs on individual salad plates or a small platter. Overlap the avocado slices on top. Drizzle each with the ginger dressing and garnish with a sprinkle of peanuts and salt if you like.

Five-Layer Avocado Salad

MAKES: 4 to 6 servings
TIME: 20 minutes

Serve this festive salad family style, as part of a Mexican buffet, with Naked Tamales with Chile Cheese Filling (page 547), or as the centerpiece of a light lunch. Whenever you serve it, you'll enjoy the alternating, contrasting layers of soft and sweet fruit—avocado and tomato—and

The Intuitive Architecture of Raw Vegetable Salads

Virtually any raw vegetable can become a salad, with or without dressing or other ingredients. All it takes is a willingness to appreciate the flavor of vegetables in their basic, pure form and an understanding of how to put things together.

What works raw: Beyond the obvious lettuces and the like, try almost anything young, small, and sweet or—if older—chopped small. Consider some of the less obvious vegetables like kohlrabi, turnips, fennel, snap and snow peas, even raw mushrooms. There's no reason not to integrate cooked leftovers.

How you slice it: The way you cut a raw vegetable affects its appeal and even its taste. Almost no one would bite into a raw beet, for example, because its deep earthiness is a little overwhelming. But grating, cutting into shoestrings, or slicing ultra-thin—"shaving" as chefs like to say—reveals an alluring woodsiness. Couple that with a crisp texture and gorgeous color, and suddenly raw beets with a drizzle of olive oil and a squeeze of fresh orange juice start to sound pretty good. Similarly, you can slice zucchini—or even seedless cukes—the long way, which makes them a lot more attractive. These various cutting techniques can all be mastered in seconds, with the help of a food processor or an inexpensive mandoline.

Simple dressings: There was a time when a dollop of mayonnaise counted as salad dressing. Though fewer people do that, it remains a sound concept. Mayo, after all, has all the components of a modern dressing rolled into one: Fat, a small bit of acidity, a touch of seasoning, and an attractive creaminess, especially when thinned with a bit of milk, sour cream, yogurt, lemon juice, or even water.

Mostly, we prefer that fat come in the form of lighter oils: Extra virgin olive oil, light or dark sesame oil, and walnut oil are all good choices. But there's nothing stopping you from using any kind of fresh or sour cream (including unsweetened whipped cream) or yogurt to dress raw vegetables. (Vegans, of course, use nondairy versions of these.)

The acidity can come from vinegar or from fresh citrus and other fruit juices, wine, or even spirits. Salt and freshly ground black pepper usually suffice, though a sprinkling of minced fresh herbs is a bonus.

No assembly required: This is the easy part. Put some greens in a bowl or on a platter and top with grated, chopped, sliced, or shaved vegetables. Sprinkle with a little salt and a few drops of something acidic. Drizzle with oil or cream or dollop with yogurt. Finish with a few grinds of black pepper and a handful of herbs if you've got them. Toss if you like or just reach for your fork.

---

crisp and powerful vegetables. If you can easily find Mexican crema, substitute that for the mayonnaise and sour cream.

$1/4$ cup mayonnaise (to make your own, see page 771)

$1/4$ cup sour cream

2 tablespoons olive oil

3 limes

1 or 2 fresh serrano chiles, minced, or to taste

Salt and freshly ground black pepper

2 large ripe tomatoes, cored and cut crosswise into 4 thick slices

$1/4$ pound jícama, daikon or other radishes, Asian pear, or Granny Smith apple, peeled if necessary, grated or finely chopped (about $3/4$ cup)

3 small oranges, preferably blood oranges, peeled of skin and pith and thinly sliced crosswise

1 small red onion, halved and sliced paper-thin

2 medium avocados, pitted, peeled, and sliced

$1/2$ cup chopped fresh cilantro for garnish

F Fast   **M** Make Ahead   **V** Vegan

❶ Whisk together the mayonnaise, sour cream, and olive oil. Add the juice of two of the limes and the chiles and sprinkle with salt and pepper. Put in a small pitcher or serving bowl.

❷ Arrange the tomatoes in one layer on a large, deep platter or bowl. Spread the jícama on top, followed by orange and then onion slices. Top with the avocado slices. Drizzle the salad with about 1/4 cup of the dressing, garnish with cilantro and wedges of the remaining lime, and serve, passing the remaining dressing at the table.

Six-Layer Avocado Salad with Mangoes. More is better: Peel, pit, and cube 1 medium mango. Add it to the salad on top of the onions and before the avocado.

Six-Layer Avocado Salad with Queso Fresco. A little more savory but no longer vegan: Crumble 4 ounces (about 1/2 cup) queso fresco. Add it to the salad between the onions and avocado.

Sea Green (Seaweed) Salads

Sea vegetables or sea greens—calling them "weeds" shows no respect, though everyone (including me) still does—come in a wide variety of shapes, sizes, and colors (see page 355). All taste a lot like the ocean, which is wonderful, especially for people who don't eat fish. They work best when used in relatively small quantities to add depth, brininess, and complexity to a wide range of other ingredients—not just the expected Asian ones, but European, American, and even Latin flavors too. The results are approachable, familiar salads with an unexpected twist.

While seaweed salad has become a popular staple in America's Japanese restaurants, many home cooks remain intimidated. Which is kind of understandable: It's an odd ingredient, after all, and if not treated right can be a bit slimy; people also imagine that sea greens are overpoweringly salty.

But the acid and oil in salads virtually eliminate any sliminess, and the salt thing is just plain myth; a serving of most types of sea greens has about 5 percent of the government's recommended daily sodium allowance. (Wakame is the most notable exception, with up to about a quarter of the daily maximum.) In fact, sea greens are high in calcium and many trace minerals picked up from the ocean in which they grow. (Some varieties even contain a little protein.)

The delicate, vibrant, bright green leaves we see at Japanese restaurants are a particular variety of seaweed—nori or green laver—that is tough to find commercially in this country. Instant wakame (see page 356) comes the closest to that shade without food coloring. Generally, rehydrated dried seaweed is brown to olive green and sometimes almost black.

Though occasionally you will see sea greens fresh or frozen, in vacuum-sealed packages, they're most commonly sold dried. To rehydrate, just soak in warm water. Within a few minutes, they'll expand—as much as 40 percent—and lighten in color. When the leaves are pliable, you just them rinse in cold water, chop them up if necessary, and use 'em.

Simple Seaweed Salad

MAKES: 4 servings
TIME: 20 minutes

The easiest way to produce this salad is to buy a small package of mixed seaweeds (your local natural foods store may sell this, and your local Japanese store certainly does) and proceed from there. But once you get more familiar with seaweed, you can use wakame, kelp, hijiki, or others, alone or in any combination you like.

1 ounce assorted dried seaweeds or wakame

1/4 cup minced shallot, scallion, or red onion

2 tablespoons soy sauce, or to taste

1 tablespoon rice wine or other light vinegar, or to taste

1 tablespoon mirin or 1 teaspoon sugar, or to taste

$^1/_2$ tablespoon dark sesame oil, or to taste

Pinch cayenne, or to taste

Salt, if necessary

1 tablespoon toasted sesame seeds (optional; see page 321)

1 Rinse the seaweed once and soak it in at least 10 times its volume of water. When tender, about 5 minutes later, drain and gently squeeze the mixture to remove excess water. Pick through the seaweed to sort out any hard bits (there may be none) and chop or cut up (you may find it easier to use scissors) if the pieces are large. Put in a bowl.

2 Toss with the shallot, soy sauce, vinegar, mirin, sesame oil, cayenne, and salt. Taste and add salt or other seasonings as necessary. Serve garnished with the sesame seeds.

7 Additions to Simple Seaweed Salad

You can add these singly or in combination. I love radishes and cucumber combined here, for example.

1. $^1/_2$ to 1 pound cucumber, peeled and seeded if necessary (see page 293), thinly sliced, then salted and squeezed to remove excess water (see page 46)

2. Several radishes or a piece of daikon, peeled if necessary, thinly sliced, then salted and squeezed to remove excess water (see page 46)

3. A tablespoon or two of Kombu Dashi (page 103), for extra juiciness and flavor

4. Grated peeled fresh ginger to taste, about a tablespoon

5. Chopped seeded and peeled tomato, about 1 medium

6. $^1/_2$ to 1 cup peeled and chopped Asian pear or Granny Smith apple

7. $^1/_2$ cup chopped nuts, like walnuts, almonds, cashews, or pecans

Arame and Bean Thread Noodles with Ponzu Dipping Sauce

MAKES: 4 servings

TIME: 30 minutes, plus about 2 hours to chill

The fine, noodlelike texture of arame and its mild grassy flavor make this the perfect introduction to the world of seaweed salads. (It doesn't hurt that this is dead easy to make.) The Ponzu Sauce has a bright citrus taste, but if you don't have the right ingredients handy, use Soy Vinaigrette (page 763) instead. Serve this salad cold, with Grilled or Broiled Tofu (page 642) or as a light meal on a bed of mixed greens.

One 2-ounce bundle bean thread noodles

1 ounce dried arame (about 2 cups loosely packed)

1 recipe (about $^3/_4$ cup) Ponzu Sauce (page 780)

$^1/_2$ cup finely chopped toasted walnuts (optional; see page 40)

$^1/_2$ cup sliced scallion for garnish

1 Put the bean threads in a large bowl and cover with boiling water. Soak for about 10 minutes, until soft and clear. Use kitchen scissors or a sharp knife and a fork to cut the threads into 2- to 3-inch pieces. (This shouldn't take more than a few cuts.)

2 Add the arame to the bowl with the bean threads and stir gently to combine. Soak for another 10 to 15 minutes. The bean threads will take on the color of the seaweed, only lighter. Drain in a strainer for a few minutes, then toss with $^1/_4$ cup of the Ponzu Sauce. Cover and refrigerate until very cold. (The salad may be made in advance to this point and kept in the refrigerator for a day or two.)

3 To serve, divide the remaining Ponzu Sauce among 4 small individual dipping bowls so diners can use chopsticks or a fork to dip each bite into the sauce. Toss the salad with walnuts if you're using them, garnish, and serve.

Arame and Bean Thread Noodles with Fermented Black Beans. Substitute Soy Vinaigrette for the Ponzu. In Step 2, add ¹/₄ cup fermented black beans to the salad. Sprinkle with hot red pepper flakes to taste. To serve, toss with more dressing if you like and garnish with chopped fresh cilantro in addition to the scallion.

Bean Thread Noodles With Arame. Increase the amount of bean thread noodles to two 2-ounce bundles. Reduce the amount of arame to ¹/₂ ounce (about 1 cup loosely packed).

Spicy Dulse and Daikon Salad

MAKES: 4 servings

TIME: 20 minutes

Dulse is unlike other sea greens: The texture is soft and chewy, the color is a deep black-green, and the flavor is salty, sweet, and fruity. It tastes a little like raisins. That's why it works in this salad, which is not unlike the classic raisin-carrot combo. A quick squeeze of lime and a drizzle of good oil keeps everything bright and lively.

1 pound daikon, peeled

1 cup chopped dried dulse (about ¹/₂ ounce)

1 tablespoon minced fresh hot chile, like serrano, Thai, or jalapeño

1 lime, plus more to taste

Salt and freshly ground black pepper

2 tablespoons peanut oil or extra virgin olive oil

1 Use the large holes on a box grater or a food processor fitted with a large-holed grater to get as coarse a cut on the daikon as possible. Put the grated daikon in a medium bowl. Toss in the dulse and chile. Let rest for a few minutes to soften the seaweed a bit, but not long enough to discolor the daikon.

2 Squeeze the juice from the lime over the salad, sprinkle with salt and pepper, and toss to coat. Drizzle with peanut oil and toss again. Taste and adjust the seasoning, adding more lime or chile if you like. Serve.

Spicy Dulse and Carrot Salad. Even more familiar: Substitute a pound of carrots for the daikon. (Or use ¹/₂ pound of each.)

Spicy Dulse and Celery Salad. The celery's bitterness is lovely here: Substitute a pound of celery, thinly sliced, for the daikon. Chop up some of the tender celery leaves for a final garnish if you like.

Spicy Dulse and Bean Sprout Salad. Use 3 cups blanched bean sprouts instead of the daikon. Use light or dark sesame oil in place of peanut or olive if you have it.

Sea Slaw

MAKES: 4 to 6 servings

TIME: 20 minutes, plus time to rest if you like

This is the most colorful slaw you've ever seen. The seaweed will quickly absorb some of the dressing and plump up a bit but still remain chewy. You can use any type of seaweed you like, but if you want a really vibrant green the key is instant wakame, an ultra-purified Japanese product available at natural and Asian food stores.

Serve this with any vegetable burger (pages 657–668), or as part of an Asian small-plate feast. Toss a cup or two with chilled cooked noodles and you've got yourself a crunchy pasta salad. Use Vegannaise, and it's a vegan salad.

¹/₄ cup mayonnaise or Vegannaise (page 772)

2 tablespoons rice vinegar

1 tablespoon soy sauce

1 teaspoon sugar

$1/_2$ cup chopped peanuts, salted or unsalted

$1/_4$ cup instant wakame or other dried seaweed

2 cups chopped cabbage (about $1/_2$ pound), preferably Napa

$1/_2$ medium cucumber, peeled, seeded (see page 293), and thinly sliced

$1/_2$ red, orange, or yellow bell pepper, cored, seeded, and thinly sliced

1 cup fresh cilantro leaves

Salt and freshly ground black pepper

Hot red pepper flakes to taste (optional)

1 Whisk the mayonnaise, rice vinegar, soy sauce, sugar, and peanuts together in a large bowl.

2 Add the wakame, cabbage, cucumber, and bell pepper. Toss to coat in the dressing. If possible, refrigerate the salad for an hour or so before serving to let the flavors mellow. (Or cover and keep in the fridge for up to 24 hours.) To serve, add the cilantro, salt, and pepper and toss again. Then taste and adjust the seasoning, adding some hot red pepper if you like.

Seaweed Romaine Salad

MAKES: 4 servings
TIME: 30 minutes

Ⓕ   Ⓜ

We tend to think of seaweed only as an Asian food, but the people of the United Kingdom (and Canada's Maritimes) are also longtime seaweed eaters. And why not? It grows all over the world. This Mediterranean-flavored salad will give you an idea of how well seaweed takes to the flavors of any cuisine.

$1/_2$ cup sun-dried tomatoes (about $1/_2$ ounce)

1 cup dried fine seaweed, like arame, instant wakame, or chopped dulse (about $1/_2$ ounce)

2 tablespoons olive oil

1 tablespoon red wine vinegar

2 tablespoons toasted pine nuts (see page 321)

1 clove garlic, minced or pressed

$1/_2$ cup chopped Roasted Red Peppers (page 333; or use good store-bought roasted peppers)

3 cups torn romaine leaves, plus a few small whole leaves for garnish

$1/_2$ cup chopped fresh basil leaves

$1/_4$ cup freshly grated Romano, Parmesan, or ricotta salata cheese, plus more for the table

Salt and freshly ground black pepper

1 Put the tomatoes in a small bowl and pour on enough boiling water just to cover. Soak for 5 to 8 minutes, until they are pliable but not mushy. Remove with a slotted spoon and drain.

2 Add the seaweed to the hot tomato-soaking water and soak for about 5 minutes. Coarsely chop the tomatoes and put them in a salad bowl. Add the olive oil, vine-

Dried Seaweed Sprinkles in Salads

A sprinkling of dried seaweed provides a crunchy counterpoint in any salad. The texture is lighter than seeds or nuts, less cumbersome than croutons, and of course as healthy as can be. Think of it as a cross between a dried herb and a fresh herb, with a subtle, slightly salty, oceanic taste. When left to marinate in a tossed salad for a few minutes, the seaweed will expand and soften, but just a bit.

You can use arame, hijiki, or instant wakame straight from the package, since they are already in wispy threads; cut dulse and kombu into strips with kitchen scissors. (Try to use a knife and watch bits of seaweed fly all over the kitchen.) Or drop a handful into a spice grinder, coffee mill, or food processor. Just pulse a few times until you get small pieces; be careful not to pulverize.

Another solution is to always keep a jar of Nori "Shake" (page 817) on hand.

Ⓕ Fast   Ⓜ Make Ahead   Ⓥ Vegan

gar, pine nuts, garlic, and roasted bell pepper to the bowl and stir to combine.

❸ Drain the seaweed, reserving the flavorful liquid for another use if you like. Add it to the bowl and stir to coat in the dressing. (The salad may be made up to this point, covered, and refrigerated for up to 2 days.) To serve, toss the romaine and basil into the salad. Sprinkle with the cheese and toss again. Taste and add salt if necessary and lots of black pepper. Garnish with the reserved romaine leaves and pass the extra cheese at the table.

Balsamic Seaweed Romaine. For a slightly sweeter, deeper taste: Use 2 tablespoons balsamic vinegar instead of the red wine vinegar.

High-Flavor Seaweed Romaine. Make either the main recipe or the balsamic variation. When you stir the dressing, add ¹/₂ cup chopped pitted black or green olives, 2 tablespoons capers, and 2 tablespoons minced red onion or shallot. Proceed with Step 3.

Tomato Salads

Tomatoes of all kinds now show up at farmstands and farmer's markets, but supermarket tomatoes haven't changed much over the years (though they've gotten more expensive!). Cherry or grape tomatoes (these are an improvement), roma (plum) tomatoes, and some sort of "beefsteak" or slicer are the norm, and the same rules apply to all: see if you can find tomatoes with *some* sort of tomatoey aroma and give when you gently squeeze one, let them ripen at room temperature until they are soft and deeply colored, and never refrigerate (this makes them mealy).

If you've just come from the farmer's market with a bagful of beauties, then you have a couple of options. Cut some into wedges and some into slices, then arrange them on a platter and drizzle with a good extra virgin olive oil or any simple vinaigrette (page 262). Garnish with fresh herbs and sprinkle with salt and freshly ground black pepper. For something more substantial, try Heirloom Tomato Salad with Hard-Cooked Eggs (page 59).

Less-than-stellar tomatoes call for a little work. Cooking is one way to improve an imperfect tomato, so you'll see recipes here that broil, grill, and pan-sear them before turning them into salad. But the biggest surprise here is probably my use of soy sauce. It's a tomato's unsung hero, lending deep flavor and sheen that works well with both Asian and American dishes.

Cherry Tomato Salad with Soy Sauce

MAKES: 4 servings
TIME: 15 to 30 minutes

The combination of soy sauce and tomatoes is fantastic, and because cherry and grape tomatoes are among the few supermarket fruits that are actually worth eating in winter, this dish can help quench your cravings until the summertime slicers are back.

If you have time, let this salad sit at room temperature for up to 15 minutes to release some of the juice from the tomatoes. The dressing tints them with a deeply flavored mahogany glaze.

2 tablespoons soy sauce, plus more to taste

Pinch sugar

2 teaspoons dark sesame oil

4 cups cherry or grape tomatoes, halved crosswise

¹/₂ cup fresh basil leaves, preferably Thai basil

Freshly ground black pepper

❶ Combine the soy sauce, sugar, and oil in a large bowl. Add the tomatoes and basil and sprinkle liberally with pepper. Stir gently to coat the tomatoes with the dressing.

❷ Let stand at room temperature for up to 15 minutes, stirring once or twice. Taste, add more soy sauce and black pepper if you like, and serve.

Tomato Salad, Ethiopian Style

MAKES: 4 servings

TIME: 15 minutes, plus time to chill

If you have time to chop tomatoes, you have time to make this salad, which also works as a relish to eat with sandwiches and salads.

The light, fresh-tasting, oil-free dressing features turmeric, which turns the salad a lovely sunset color. You can use almost any spice mix you like here instead.

3 tablespoons freshly squeezed lemon juice

1/4 cup minced red onion

1 tablespoon minced jalapeño chile, or more or less to taste

1 teaspoon ground turmeric (optional)

Salt and freshly ground black pepper

4 large tomatoes, cored and coarsely chopped

1. Put the lemon juice, onion, jalapeño, and turmeric, if you're using it, into a medium serving bowl. Sprinkle with salt and pepper and stir to combine. Add the tomatoes and toss to coat.

2. Chill for up to 30 minutes, then taste and adjust the seasoning and serve.

Broiled Tomato and Blue Cheese Salad

MAKES: 4 servings

TIME: About 30 minutes

Though fresh plum tomatoes are acceptable even in the off-season, they're decidedly improved by being broiled for a couple minutes. Add blue cheese (or virtually any other kind of grated or crumbled cheese, like Parmesan, feta, queso fresco, Gruyère, or goat cheese) and you have

a classy, restaurant-style presentation. And the recipe is so easy you might even want to gussy it up a little more; see the variations that follow.

Extra virgin olive oil, for brushing or spraying

6 plum tomatoes, cored and halved lengthwise

Salt and freshly ground black pepper

6 ounces blue cheese, like Roquefort, Maytag blue, Gorgonzola, or Stilton

1 large head Bibb or Boston lettuce, leaves pulled from the core intact

1/4 cup Vinaigrette (page 762)

1/4 cup chopped fresh chives or parsley for garnish

1. Preheat the broiler and adjust the oven rack so it's about 4 inches from the heat source. Brush or spray a baking sheet with olive oil. Put the tomatoes—cut sides up—on the baking sheet. If they won't lie flat, use a spatula or your hand to press them gently until stable. Sprinkle with salt and pepper.

2. Crumble the blue cheese into large pieces, flatten them a bit with your fingers, and put the pieces on top of the tomatoes. Broil for 2 to 3 minutes, until the cheese is golden and bubbly. Remove from the oven and let tomatoes cool down in the pan for a bit to set.

3. Divide the lettuce leaves among the serving plates. Top each with 3 tomato halves, drizzle with the dressing, garnish, and serve. (Or arrange everything on one platter and serve family style.)

Broiled Tomato and Blue Cheese Salad with Fried Sage Leaves. Glorious: Instead of the chives or parsley, use whole sage leaves. Before broiling the tomatoes, put 2 tablespoons extra virgin olive oil in a small skillet or saucepan and turn the heat to medium-high. Fry sage leaves for several minutes, stirring carefully, until crisp and golden. Drain on paper towels. Use them to garnish salad.

Broiled Tomato and Feta Salad with Tapenade. Straight from the Mediterranean: Substitute feta for the blue cheese. Before putting the cheese on top of the tomatoes, smear each half with a little Tapenade (page 326 or good-quality store-bought); $^1/_2$ cup ought to do the trick. Then top with the cheese and proceed with the recipe.

Broiled Tomato and Mozzarella Salad with Pesto. Summery: Substitute fresh mozzarella for the blue cheese. Before putting the cheese on top of the tomatoes, smear each half with a little Traditional Pesto (page 768); $^1/_2$ cup should work fine. Then top with the cheese and proceed with the recipe.

Broiled Tomato and Cheddar Salad with Onions. Good with a few chopped onions sprinkled in there: Substitute thin slices of cheddar for the blue cheese. Use Mustard Vinaigrette (page 763) instead of Balsamic Vinaigrette if you like.

Broiled Tomato and Brie Salad with Almonds. Practically a main course: Substitute small slices of ripe Brie for the blue cheese. After topping the tomatoes with cheese, press a sprinkling of chopped almonds into each slice; $^1/_2$ cup ought to be enough. Then top with the cheese. Use Vinaigrette (page 762) with sherry vinegar instead of wine vinegar if you like.

Heirloom Tomato Salad with Hard-Cooked Eggs

MAKES: 4 servings
TIME: 20 minutes

This straightforward chopped salad with tomato wedges is wonderfully complex, especially if you use a mixture of heirloom tomatoes at the peak of summer. Hard-cooked eggs add a nice chew and heft, but I also like the variations, when the runny yolks mingle with the dressing and coat everything with a rich creaminess.

4 large eggs

2 shallots, thinly sliced

4 cups mixed greens, like mesclun, or bitter greens, like dandelion or frisée

$^1/_4$ cup Mustard Vinaigrette (page 763), plus more for drizzling

Salt and freshly ground black pepper

5 to 6 tomatoes, preferably a colorful variety of heirlooms, cored, seeded, and cut into wedges

2 cups croutons, preferably homemade (page 806)

1 Hard-cook the eggs according to the directions on page 166. When the eggs have cooled to room temperature, peel and cut lengthwise into $^1/_4$-inch slices.

2 Put the shallots and lettuce in a large mixing bowl and toss with $^1/_4$ cup of the dressing. Taste and adjust the seasoning. Arrange on individual serving plates or a platter. Top with the tomato wedges, egg slices, and croutons. Drizzle with a little extra dressing and serve.

Heirloom Tomato Salad with Poached Eggs. Dreamy: Prepare the salad first and arrange it on individual serving plates or shallow bowls. Poach the eggs according to the recipe on page 169. Remove the eggs with a slotted spoon and drain on paper towels. Top each prepared salad plate with an egg.

Heirloom Tomato Salad with Fried Eggs. Hot and cold: Prepare the salad first and arrange it on individual serving plates or shallow bowls. Fry the eggs according to the recipe on page 168. Top each prepared salad plate with an egg.

Pan-Seared Tomato Salad

MAKES: 4 servings
TIME: 20 minutes

Searing tomatoes in a really hot skillet—it takes only 5 minutes—not only tenderizes them but also brings out their sweetness. This little stir-fry makes an unusual room-temperature salad: The juices released from the

tomatoes make a slightly acidic "dressing" that works perfectly with many Asian dishes.

3 tablespoons neutral oil, like grapeseed or corn

1 bunch scallions, trimmed and cut diagonally into 2-inch lengths

6 medium tomatoes, cored and quartered lengthwise

1 tablespoon sugar

2 teaspoons soy sauce, plus more to taste

2 teaspoons dark sesame oil, plus more to taste

Salt and freshly ground black pepper to taste

1 Set a large skillet or wok over high heat for 3 minutes. Add 1 tablespoon of the oil and heat until almost smoking. Add the scallions and cook, stirring constantly, until bright green and fragrant, about 3 minutes. Use a slotted spoon to transfer the scallions to a large serving plate.

2 Wipe the skillet out with a paper towel and add the remaining oil. When the oil is almost smoking, add the tomatoes. Cook, undisturbed, until they are nicely browned and slightly softened, about 2 minutes. Turn, sprinkle with the sugar, and cook for another 2 minutes.

3 Arrange the tomatoes on top of the scallions and drizzle with their pan juices. Sprinkle with the soy sauce and sesame oil. Cool to room temperature, then taste and adjust the seasoning with soy sauce, sesame oil, salt, or pepper as needed and serve.

Pan-Seared Tomato Salad with Corn. Extra chew and flavor: Add 1 cup fresh corn kernels to the skillet with the scallions. If you use frozen corn kernels, cook for an additional minute.

Cooked Vegetable Salads

Salads are not necessarily raw; if you apply the general vegetable-cooking rules (pages 235–239), anything you like has salad potential. And cooked vegetable salads are among the ultimate conveniences: All may be made ahead and chilled, ready to pull from the fridge and dress whenever you feel like it. You also control how hot they are: still warm, room temperature, or chilled. Generally I prefer cooked salads at room temperature. (This is not a food-safety problem; just don't leave anything out on the counter for more than an hour or so.)

Obviously these salads are also a great way to give leftovers a second life. Grilled, roasted, sautéed, and fried vegetables all qualify (see "How to Grill Vegetables," pages 249–256). If they were cooked or served with a little oil the first time around, they might need only a squeeze of fresh citrus or a splash of vinegar and a handful of fresh herbs to become salad. But I encourage you to get in the habit of cooking a little extra and leaving them as plain as possible so you have even more options.

Corn Salad

MAKES: 4 servings
TIME: 30 minutes

Commercial corn salads and salsas are usually made with frozen corn. I'm not against frozen, but if corn is going to be the star, you gotta go fresh. Here you have three choices for preparing the corn: If it's just picked and really good, leave it raw; just shave the kernels from the ears and toss them with the rest of the ingredients.

That's not usually the case, though, and almost as good is to roast the kernels from good corn in a skillet with a little oil, as here. Or use the kernels from already steamed corn, which—if the corn was good in the first place—is an excellent way to take care of the leftovers.

2 tablespoons corn oil

2 to 3 cups corn kernels (from 4 to 6 ears)

1 small red onion, chopped

$1/2$ red bell pepper, cored, seeded, and chopped

1 teaspoon mild chili powder, like ancho, or the equivalent

Salt and freshly ground black pepper

1 medium tomato, peeled if you like, cored, seeded, and chopped

1 medium ripe avocado, peeled, pitted, and chopped

Juice of 2 limes, or more to taste

1/2 cup fresh chopped cilantro leaves, more or less

1 Put the oil in a large skillet (cast iron is good here, but anything will do) and turn the heat to high. When the oil is very hot but not smoking, toss in the corn. Let it sit for a minute or so, then stir or shake the pan. Brown the corn a bit, 5 minutes or less, then turn off the heat and stir in the onion, pepper, chili powder, salt, and pepper.

2 Cool for a few minutes, then toss with the tomato, avocado, lime juice, and cilantro. Taste, adjust the seasoning, and serve.

Curried Corn Salad. The Spice Route: Instead of the chili powder, use Hot or Fragrant Curry Powder (page 815 or 816). Substitute 1 cup cooked shelled peas, cooked potato cubes, chopped cauliflower, or more corn for the avocado.

Corn Salad with Tomatoes, Feta, and Mint

MAKES: 4 servings

TIME: 30 minutes, including cooking the corn

As in the basic Corn Salad recipe, fresh raw corn shucked from the cob is ideal here. The juice from the tomatoes delivers just the right amount of acidity, so there's no need for vinegar. Eat this by the bowl as is or toss it with cooked rice or beans for a more filling salad (add oil and

vinegar accordingly). In midsummer, with a couple of thick tomato slices, there is nothing better.

2 to 3 cups raw or cooked corn kernels (from 4 to 6 ears)

1 large or 2 medium ripe tomatoes, cut into fairly small pieces

4 ounces feta cheese, crumbled (about 1 cup)

3 tablespoons extra virgin olive oil

1/2 cup chopped fresh mint leaves

Salt and freshly ground black pepper

1 Put the corn, tomatoes, and cheese in a medium salad bowl. Drizzle with the olive oil and toss.

2 Add the mint leaves and toss again. Taste and add salt and pepper. Serve.

Pea Salad with Tomatoes, Feta, and Mint. If the peas are garden-fresh, use them raw: Simply substitute peas for the corn.

Cauliflower Salad with Olives and Bread Crumbs

MAKES: 4 servings

TIME: 45 minutes, including cooking the cauliflower

Bread crumbs give this crunchy dish, which is common in southern Italy, enough body to stand on its own; I like to serve it family style, passing more bread crumbs at the table. Or try a spoonful next to Panfried Eggplant (page 244) or grilled zucchini (page 255), then grate some Parmesan over all.

1 medium cauliflower (1 1/2 to 2 pounds), steamed and shocked (see page 241)

1/2 small red onion, very thinly sliced

1/2 cup oil-cured or other good black olives, pitted and coarsely chopped

2 tablespoons extra virgin olive oil

2 tablespoons red wine vinegar

Salt and freshly ground black pepper

1 cup Fried Bread Crumbs (page 805)

1/4 cup minced parsley leaves

 Break cauliflower into relatively small florets and put them in a medium bowl along with the onion and olives. Drizzle with the oil and vinegar and sprinkle with just a little salt and lots of pepper. Toss and set aside. (The salad may be made ahead to this point, covered, and refrigerated for up to a day. Return it to room temperature, tossing occasionally to coat well with the dressing, before proceeding.)

② Mix the bread crumbs with the parsley and sprinkle the top of the cauliflower with half of the crumb mixture. Serve, passing the rest at the table.

Cauliflower Salad with Capers and Bread Crumbs. Instead of the olives, use 1/4 cup capers, preferably salt-cured.

Mushroom Salad, Italian-American Style

MAKES: 4 servings

TIME: About 1 hour

A vinegary, almost pickled mushroom dish that can be used as a garnish or condiment as well as a salad. It's also good tossed with chopped Belgian endive (use 2 heads for this amount of mushrooms) or other bitter greens.

1/4 cup extra virgin olive oil

1 pound button or other mushrooms, trimmed and quartered

Salt and freshly ground black pepper

1/4 cup minced onion

1 tablespoon slivered garlic

1/3 cup red wine vinegar

1/2 cup chopped parsley leaves for garnish

① Put 3 tablespoons of the oil in a wide skillet over medium heat. When hot, add the mushrooms, and cook, stirring occasionally and sprinkling with salt and pepper, until they give up their liquid and begin to brown, about 10 minutes. Lower the heat a bit and add the onion, then cook until the onion softens, another 5 minutes or so. Add the garlic and cook, stirring occasionally, about 2 minutes more. Turn off the heat.

② Transfer the mushrooms to a bowl and stir in the vinegar and remaining tablespoon of oil. Let cool to room temperature for at least 30 minutes. Garnish and serve or let sit at room temperature for another hour or two before serving.

Steamed Mushroom Salad with Coriander

MAKES: 4 servings

TIME: 30 minutes

Steamed mushrooms are really kind of special: They retain much of their raw flavor and texture but gain enough body to hold together when dressed lightly. This is a favorite, whether served on a pile of greens or a mound of cold noodles.

1 pound button or other assorted mushrooms, trimmed and quartered if large

5 tablespoons extra virgin olive oil

1/4 cup chopped shallot

1 teaspoon minced garlic

1 teaspoon coriander seeds, cracked (or use ground coriander)

Salt and freshly ground black pepper

2 tablespoons sherry, balsamic, or cider vinegar

Chopped fresh cilantro leaves for garnish

① Set up a steamer (page 25) and steam the mushrooms until firm, less than 5 minutes. Remove, toss with $^1/_4$ cup of the olive oil, the shallots, and the garlic, and cool to room temperature. (You can prepare the recipe up to this point and leave it at room temperature for up to 2 hours.)

② Toss the mushroom mixture with the coriander, salt, pepper, vinegar, and remaining tablespoon of oil. Taste and adjust the seasoning, then garnish with the cilantro and serve.

Asian-Style Steamed Mushroom Salad. The sesame oil–ginger combo is killer here: For the olive oil, substitute 2 tablespoons peanut oil and 3 tablespoons dark sesame oil. Instead of the shallot, use chopped scallion. Add 1 teaspoon minced peeled ginger. Use rice wine vinegar instead of the other choices and use both soy sauce and a little salt for the final seasoning

Grilled Shiitake or Portobello Salad with Soy Vinaigrette

MAKES: 4 servings
TIME: 40 minutes, including heating the grill

This salad is as simple as can be. You might double the number of mushrooms (a mix is nice) and serve it as a main course.

8 large or 16 small shiitake caps (reserve the stems for stock or discard), left whole, or 2 portobello caps, quartered

Peanut or neutral oil, like grapeseed or corn, as needed, about $^1/_4$ cup

Salt and freshly ground black pepper

6 cups mixed greens, like mesclun

$^1/_2$ cup Soy Vinaigrette (page 763), more or less

① Heat a charcoal or gas grill or a broiler to medium heat and place the rack 4 to 6 inches from the heat source. Toss the mushrooms with enough oil to coat them, then sprinkle them liberally with salt and pepper. Skewer the mushrooms if they're so small they might fall through the grates and grill for just 2 or 3 minutes per side, until lightly browned and slightly crisp.

② Toss the greens with enough of the dressing to coat them lightly, then put the hot mushrooms on top of them; drizzle with a little more of the dressing and serve.

Eggplant Salad with Miso

MAKES: 4 servings
TIME: About 30 minutes

The typical way to prepare this traditional Japanese salad is to boil the eggplant, and I give directions for doing it that way. But if you have the time and energy, sauté the cubes in a little peanut oil, as in Ratatouille Salad, which follows. And grilled eggplant slices (page 252) are great with the sesame soy variation.

About 1 pound eggplant

Salt

$^1/_3$ cup white or other miso, or to taste

1 tablespoon soy sauce

1 tablespoon mirin or brown sugar

1 tablespoon rice vinegar or freshly squeezed lemon juice

Cayenne

$^1/_4$ cup chopped walnuts (optional)

① Trim the eggplant and cut it into 1-inch cubes. (If the eggplant are large, soft, or especially seedy, sprinkle the cubes with salt, put them in a colander, and let them sit for at least 30 minutes, preferably 60. Rinse, drain, and pat dry.)

② Bring a large pot of water to a boil and salt it. Immerse the eggplant in the boiling water and cook until tender, about 5 minutes. Drain well and set in a colander to cool. (You can refrigerate the eggplant, covered, for up to 24 hours at this point. Bring it back to room temperature before proceeding.)

❸ Dry the eggplant with paper towels. Whisk together the miso, soy, mirin, and vinegar in a serving bowl. Thin with a tablespoon of water if necessary. Add the eggplant, sprinkle with salt and cayenne, then toss. Taste and adjust the seasoning. Serve topped with the walnuts if you like.

Eggplant Salad with Miso and Tofu. All you need for dinner: Replace half of the eggplant with $1/2$ pound raw or Baked Tofu (page 641) cut into cubes, ideally the same size as the eggplant.

Eggplant Salad with Soy Vinaigrette. What to do if you don't have miso: Make either the main recipe or the tofu variation, only instead of mixing the miso dressing, use $1/4$ to $1/2$ cup Soy Vinaigrette (page 763). Garnish with 1 tablespoon sesame seeds if you like.

Ratatouille Salad

MAKES: 4 servings
TIME: 30 minutes

Eggplant, zucchini, peppers, onions, and tomatoes are a familiar Mediterranean combination, especially in summer. Too often, however, they're overcooked and mushy. Enter the ratatouille salad, where the vegetables remain distinct and a hint of acidity keeps things fresh tasting, even though the ingredients are cooked.

Eat this alone or on a bed of greens. For a heartier salad, toss in cooked rice, white beans, or the pasta of your choice and drizzle with a little more olive oil. A grating of Parmesan or ricotta salata is a welcome addition.

1 medium or 2 small eggplants (about 8 ounces)

$1/4$ cup extra virgin olive oil

Salt and freshly ground black pepper

1 medium zucchini, roughly chopped

1 small onion, roughly chopped

1 tablespoon minced garlic

1 medium tomato, cored and roughly chopped

1 tablespoon fresh thyme leaves

1 tablespoon freshly squeezed lemon juice

$1/4$ cup minced parsley leaves for garnish

❶ Trim the eggplant and cut it into 1-inch cubes. (If the eggplant is large, soft, or especially seedy, sprinkle the cubes with salt, put them in a colander, and let them sit for at least 30 minutes, preferably 60. Rinse, drain, and pat dry.)

❷ Put 2 tablespoons of the oil in a large skillet over medium heat. When hot, add the eggplant, sprinkle with salt and pepper, and cook, stirring occasionally, until soft and golden, about 10 minutes. Remove from the pan and drain on paper towels.

❸ Put the remaining 2 tablespoons oil in the pan and add the zucchini. Cook, stirring occasionally, until just starting to wilt, about 2 minutes. Add the onion and garlic and cook and stir for another minute or two, until soft. Add the tomato and thyme and cook for another minute, until the tomato just starts to wilt and release its juice. Remove from the heat, stir in the lemon juice, and sprinkle with salt and pepper.

❹ Put the eggplant in a salad bowl and add the vegetables and dressing from the pan. Stir to combine. Cool to room temperature, taste and adjust the seasoning, garnish, and serve. (Or prepare the salad to this point, cover, and refrigerate for up to 2 days; garnish just before serving either cold or at room temperature.)

Eggplant and Zucchini Salad with Cinnamon. Just slightly exotic: Instead of the garlic, use 1 tablespoon minced fresh chile (jalapeño, Thai, serrano, or habanero), or to taste. Instead of the thyme, use 1 teaspoon ground cinnamon. Garnish with minced fresh mint leaves instead of the parsley.

Grilled Eggplant Salad with Garlic and Saffron Mayonnaise

MAKES: 4 servings

TIME: 45 minutes, plus time to chill

Many grilled vegetables are terrific in salads, but eggplant may be the king of them all—meaty, flavorful, and somehow intrinsically smoky. You can understand why Middle Eastern cuisines rely so heavily on it.

Here the eggplants are grilled whole, peeled, cooled, then roughly chopped. But you can also use grilled slices of eggplant (page 252) for a more intense smoky flavor and crisp texture.

1 pound eggplant, preferably small ones

3 cloves garlic, minced

1 tablespoon extra virgin olive oil

Salt and freshly ground black pepper

$^1/_2$ cup mayonnaise, preferably homemade (page 771)

1 large pinch saffron

Lemon wedges for garnish

$^1/_4$ cup chopped parsley leaves for garnish (optional)

❶ Heat a charcoal or gas grill or a broiler and set the rack about 4 inches from the heat source. Cut the eggplants in half lengthwise up to the stem, but do not cut through. Spread the garlic in between the eggplant halves and press the halves back together.

❷ Grill the eggplants, turning once or twice, until they are blackened and soft, 10 to 15 minutes. Let the eggplants cool a bit, then peel off the skins and let cool further. Roughly chop them into relatively large pieces, reserving any juices, and put them in a bowl. Drizzle with olive oil, sprinkle with salt and pepper, and toss to coat.

❸ Stir the mayonnaise and saffron together in a small bowl. (The salad may be prepared ahead to this point; cover the bowls and refrigerate for up to a day. Serve cold or return the eggplant to room temperature.) When ready to serve, mound the eggplant on salad plates or a small platter, with the lemon wedges and a spoonful of saffron aïoli on the side. Sprinkle the eggplant with parsley if you like.

Grilled Eggplant Salad with Yogurt. Faster, easier, and lighter (and not vegan): Instead of serving with saffron aïoli, drizzle the eggplant with $^1/_2$ cup Simplest Yogurt Sauce (page 774), garnish, and serve.

Roasted Onion Salad

MAKES: 4 to 8 servings

TIME: At least 1 hour, largely unattended

As in Green Salad with Caramelized Onion-Thyme Dressing on page 43, the cooked onions here are so sweet you have to add something strong tasting. Vinegar is an obvious choice, of course, but also nice is a bed of arugula (you could use another bitter green, like watercress) with a touch of raw garlic. And don't forget the salt!

You can use any member of the allium family here (onions, leeks, shallots, or garlic) or just a single type. But a combination is kind of cool.

2 medium to large red onions, peeled, roots left on, and halved vertically

2 medium to large white onions, peeled, roots left on, and halved vertically

8 scallions, trimmed

8 shallots, peeled, roots left on

8 large cloves garlic, peeled

Several sprigs fresh thyme

$^1/_4$ cup plus 2 tablespoons extra virgin olive oil

Salt and freshly ground black pepper

$^1/_4$ teaspoon minced garlic

4 cups arugula or watercress

2 tablespoons good balsamic or other vinegar

 Preheat the oven to 375°F. Combine the onions, scallions, shallots, whole garlic, and thyme in a roasting pan or casserole. Toss with $\frac{1}{4}$ cup of the oil and some salt and pepper. Cover with foil (or a lid) and roast, shaking the pan occasionally, until the vegetables are quite tender, at least 30 minutes. Uncover and raise the heat to 425°F, then continue to roast, stirring and shaking, until the vegetables are very tender and beginning to brown, at least 15 minutes more. Cool to room temperature. (You can prepare the recipe in advance up to this point; cover, and refrigerate for up to 2 days, but bring it back to room temperature before proceeding.)

2 Toss the cooked vegetables with the raw garlic and place them, in a mound, on the arugula. Drizzle with the remaining 2 tablespoons olive oil and the vinegar and toss lightly. Taste, adjust the seasoning, and serve.

Beet and Avocado Salad

MAKES: 4 servings

TIME: 20 minutes, with precooked beets

I'd use canned beets in a pinch here; they're not at all bad. But when I buy beets, I try to roast them right away (though they're occasionally great raw; see page 49) so I can use them easily in recipes like this one.

If you can get golden beets or any of the other nicely colored varieties, they're gorgeous mixed with standard red beets here as their juices blend a bit.

3 or 4 medium beets (about 1 pound), roasted (page 267) or boiled (page 266), cooled, peeled, and sliced

2 ripe but firm avocados, peeled, pitted, and sliced

1 small red onion, minced

$\frac{1}{2}$ cup Lemon Vinaigrette (page 763)

1 fresh tarragon leaf, minced, or a pinch dried

Salt and freshly ground black pepper

1 Arrange the beets and avocados in alternating layers in a dish or shallow bowl. Mix together the onion, vinaigrette, and tarragon and spoon over the beets and avocados. Taste and add salt and pepper; serve immediately.

Beet and Avocado Salad with Citrus. A lovely winter salad: Add a grapefruit, segmented (page 431) to the mix. Add about $\frac{1}{2}$ teaspoon chopped orange zest to the vinaigrette. Garnish, if you like, with a bit of chopped fresh mint or parsley.

Beet Salad with Yogurt Sauce. Gorgeous color: Instead of Lemon Vinaigrette, dress the salad with Simplest Yogurt Sauce (page 774). Use tarragon, mint, dill, or parsley.

Greek-Style Cooked Greens

Horta

MAKES: 4 servings

TIME: 20 minutes or longer, plus time to chill if you like

This is a standard Mediterranean preparation for greens. They can be wild, picked off the mountainside (as they are in my overly romanticized image of Greece), grown in your garden, or (most likely) cultivated, harvested by you from the supermarket or farmstand. And they can be almost any green you like, from chard and beet greens to kale, collards, spinach, turnip or mustard greens, even watercress or arugula. A mixture is great too.

This recipe—which is hardly a recipe because there's virtually nothing involved—is perfect for leftovers.

Salt and freshly ground black pepper

1 to 2 pounds dark leafy greens, like collards, kale, or spinach

Several tablespoons extra virgin olive oil

2 lemons, halved, for serving

 Bring a large pot of water to a boil and salt it. Trim the greens of any stems thicker than $^1/_4$ inch; discard them. Wash the greens well. Poach the greens until tender, just a minute or two for spinach, up to 10 minutes or even longer for older, tougher greens. Drain them well and cool them quickly by running them under cold water. Squeeze the greens dry and chop them. (You may prepare them in advance up to this point, cover, and refrigerate for up to a day. Bring to room temperature before proceeding.)

 Toss with the olive oil, salt, and pepper and serve with lemon halves.

Crisp Okra Salad

MAKES: 4 servings

TIME: 25 minutes

This recipe was created by my friend Suvir Saran, an Americanized and creative chef who grew up in India. Although his palate has become quite international, this fantastic dish—while probably not traditional—is purely Indian. It's sour, crisp, and unbelievably delicious. If you think you don't like okra, try this.

Neutral oil, like grapeseed or corn, for deep frying

1 pound okra, stemmed and julienned lengthwise

$^1/_2$ small red onion, thinly sliced

2 small or 1 medium tomato, cored, seeded, and julienned

$^1/_4$ cup chopped fresh cilantro leaves for garnish

$^1/_2$ lemon, or more as needed

1 $^1/_2$ teaspoons Chaat Masala (page 814), or more to taste

$^1/_2$ teaspoon salt, or more to taste

 Put at least 2 inches of oil in a countertop deep-fryer or in a deep pan on the stove over medium-high heat. Bring to 350°F (see "Deep Frying," page 26). Make sure the other ingredients are all ready to go.

 Fry the julienned okra in batches small enough not to crowd your pan or fryer and be sure to let the oil return to 350°F between batches. Fry it until crisp, 5 to 7 minutes—the seeds will swell, and it will be deeply colored at the edges—then transfer to paper towels to drain.

 Toss the okra with the onion, tomato, and cilantro. Squeeze the lemon juice over all, season to taste with chaat masala and salt, and serve.

Marinated Garden Vegetables

MAKES: about 8 servings

TIME: About 45 minutes

You can serve these crunchy, tangy, Italian-American-style vegetables from a bowl, with toothpicks; on top of greens or tossed with salads (using the brine as the dressing, which works nicely); on top of grilled vegetables; as a pickle alongside sandwiches; or tossed with pasta or grains for a quick salad.

1 cup red wine vinegar

2 tablespoons salt

2 sprigs fresh oregano or 2 teaspoons dried

2 bay leaves

2 cloves garlic

$^3/_4$ cup extra virgin olive oil

1 head broccoli, cut into florets

1 small head cauliflower, cut into florets

2 medium zucchini or summer squash, sliced crosswise

2 medium carrots, cut into $^1/_2$-inch-thick slices or sticks

1 red bell pepper, cored, seeded, and sliced

1 onion, cut into eighths

$1/2$ cup green or black olives, pitted if you like (optional)

Freshly ground black pepper

1 Put the vinegar, salt, oregano, bay leaves, garlic, olive oil, and 1 quart water in a large pot and bring to a boil. Add the broccoli and cauliflower and cook for a minute, then add the zucchini, carrots, bell pepper, onion, and olives; cover and turn off the heat.

2 Let cool to room temperature in the pot. Serve at room temperature or chilled, drizzled with some of the liquid and olive oil and sprinkled with lots of black pepper. Keep the mixture in its liquid in a covered plastic or glass container in the refrigerator for a month or more.

Marinated Artichokes. You've got to use fresh artichoke hearts (or tender baby artichokes) here; they're fantastic in salads, sandwiches, and on pizza: Substitute 12 or more cleaned raw artichoke hearts (see page 257) for the vegetables. Add the hearts to the boiling liquid in Step 1 and cook for about 10 minutes, then cover and turn off the heat. Proceed with the recipe.

Marinated Fennel or Artichoke Hearts with Preserved Lemons. Substitute white for the red wine vinegar; 1 tablespoon each coriander and cumin seeds for the oregano; and 4 large fennel bulbs, trimmed and cut into $1/4$-inch-thick slices, or 6 large or 12 small cleaned raw artichoke hearts (see page 257) for the vegetables. Add $1/2$ cup Preserved Lemon slices (page 427). Add the fennel or artichoke hearts to the boiling liquid in Step 1, then add the preserved lemon and turn off the heat. Proceed with the recipe.

Potato Salads

If you're looking for classic potato salad, look no further than the Potato Rémoulade on page 47. This is a group of generally lighter, less-mayonnaise-laden potato salads, the kind I like best. (Though I also love Potato Salad with Cream Cheese Dressing (page 70), which is far from light.)

To me, the basic potato salad is made of just-boiled potatoes dressed in good Mustard Vinaigrette (page 763). To that, you can add any of the suggestions from the list on page 69. Sweet potatoes make a good salad also; they're especially great when grilled first, as in the variation on page 69.

Potato Salad

MAKES: 4 servings
TIME: 30 minutes, plus time to cool

Ⓜ Ⓥ

If you're in a hurry, whisk the vinaigrette ingredients together in a bowl, then just add the potatoes. The real key is to do this while the potatoes are still warm, so they absorb some of the dressing. Then, ideally, serve at room temperature.

$1 \, 1/2$ pounds potatoes, like red new potatoes, fingerling, Yukon Gold, or even russet baking potatoes

Salt and freshly ground black pepper

$1/2$ cup minced parsley leaves

$1/4$ cup minced onion, like scallion, red, or yellow

$1/2$ cup Mustard Vinaigrette (page 763) or any vinaigrette, plus more to taste

1 Peel the potatoes if you like (or wash and scrub them well), then cut them into bite-sized pieces. Put them in a pot with enough water to cover them and add a large pinch of salt. Bring to a boil, then lower the heat so the water bubbles gently. Cook the potatoes until tender but still firm and not all mushy, 15 minutes or so, depending on the potato. Drain, rinse in cold water for a minute, then drain again.

❷ Toss the still-warm potatoes with the parsley and onion. Add the vinaigrette until the mixture is as dressed as you like. Taste and adjust the seasoning. Serve as is, or refrigerate for an hour or so to cool the salad down. (The salad may be prepared in advance up to this point; cover and refrigerate for up to a day.)

Grilled Potato Salad. Great in summer: Instead of boiling the potatoes, grill them according to the directions on page 254. While they are still warm, proceed with Step 2.

10 Simple Additions to Potato Salad

You will probably need to add more dressing, depending on the ingredient.

1. Chopped fresh herbs, like chives, chervil, dill, oregano, rosemary, or sage to taste
2. Chopped sweet pickle
3. Chopped celery or fennel
4. Chopped red bell pepper, fresh or roasted (page 333 or store-bought pimientos)
5. Capers or roughly chopped pitted olives
6. Chopped shallot, raw or lightly cooked in olive oil
7. Cooked fresh peas
8. Chopped hard-cooked egg (page 166)
9. Cayenne or minced fresh chile (jalapeño, Thai, serrano, or habanero)
10. Fragrant or Hot Curry Powder (pages 816 or 815) or other spice mixtures (start with a teaspoon)

Roasted Sweet Potato Salad with Red Pepper Vinaigrette

MAKES: 4 servings

TIME: About 45 minutes

Here is another potato-vinaigrette combo: The red pepper dressing is tart, sweet, and spicy, with a touch of cumin. This is best served warm or at room temperature, though of course you can refrigerate and serve it up to a day later, as long as you take it out of the refrigerator beforehand to take the chill off.

4 large sweet potatoes

$^1\!/_2$ cup extra virgin olive oil

Salt and freshly ground black pepper

$^1\!/_4$ cup red wine vinegar or sherry vinegar

1 medium red bell pepper, cored, seeded, and quartered

2 teaspoons ground cumin

1 tablespoon grated orange zest (optional)

$^1\!/_2$ cup sliced scallion

$^1\!/_2$ cup minced fresh mint or parsley leaves

1 or 2 fresh minced chiles (jalapeño, Thai, serrano, or habanero), or to taste

$^1\!/_4$ cup raisins (optional)

❶ Preheat the oven to 400°F. Peel the sweet potatoes and cut them into bite-sized pieces. Put them on a baking sheet, drizzle with 2 tablespoons of the oil, and toss to coat. Sprinkle with salt and pepper and roast, turning occasionally, until crisp and brown outside and just tender inside, about 30 minutes. Remove and keep on the pan until ready to dress.

❷ Make the dressing while the potatoes cook. Put the remaining 6 tablespoons oil in a blender, along with the vinegar, bell pepper, cumin, and zest if you're using it. Sprinkle with a little salt and pepper. Purée until smooth.

❸ Toss the warm potatoes with the scallion, mint, chiles, and raisins if you're using them. Add $^1\!/_2$ cup of the dressing and toss to coat, adding more if necessary. Taste and adjust the seasoning. Serve immediately or at room temperature.

Grilled Sweet Potato Salad with Red Pepper Vinaigrette. Instead of roasting the sweet potatoes, grill them according to the directions on page 255.

Crisp Shredded Hash Brown Salad with Red Pepper Vinaigrette. Prepare Oven-Roasted Hash Browns (page 345) and be careful not to overseason with salt and pepper. While still warm, proceed with Step 2.

Potato Salad with Cream Cheese Dressing

MAKES: 4 servings

TIME: 25 minutes, plus time to chill

An intense potato salad that rates about a 10 on the decadence scale and whose origins are in Peru, the land of many potato dishes. When served as part of an all-grilled meal, its rich creaminess works perfectly with grilled Corn on the Cob (page 290), The Simplest Bean Burgers (page 660), and anything green.

1½ pounds potatoes, like red new potatoes, fingerling, Yukon Gold, or even russet baking potatoes

Salt and freshly ground black pepper

6 ounces cream cheese

½ cup cream

1 tablespoon freshly squeezed lemon juice

¼ minced fresh chives, parsley, or dill

Which Potato for Salads?

I'm going to hedge my bets here: Generally speaking, you want a low-starch "waxy" potato for salad. Waxy potatoes, often referred to as "new"—even when they're not freshly dug— have thin skins and may be red or tan (tans ones are called "white," though they're not even close). You might even see purple ones, which make for stunning salads.

But—at least once—you might like to try using starchy ("baking") potatoes, like Idaho or other russets. The decomposition of their starches gives the salad a little extra creaminess (you might call it gumminess or sliminess, but it's all a matter of taste) that can be interesting. In addition, their mealiness (which is what makes them such a good choice for French fries) is not a bad attribute in salads.

Or you can use a so-called all-purpose potato, like Yukon Gold, which will give you a firm potato whose exterior decomposes just a little.

Sweet potatoes (which aren't really in the same family) also make great potato salads, though they don't require as much cooking and break apart more easily than potatoes when overdone.

For more about types of potatoes, see page 337.

1. Peel the potatoes if you like (or wash and scrub them well), then cut them into bite-sized pieces. Put them in a pot with enough water to cover them and add a large pinch of salt. Bring to a boil, then lower the heat so the water bubbles gently. Cook the potatoes until tender but still firm and not all mushy, 15 minutes or so, depending on the potato. Drain, rinse in cold water for a minute, then drain again.

2. While the potatoes are boiling, put the cream cheese and cream in a small saucepan over medium-low heat. Heat, stirring occasionally, until the cheese is melted and the dressing thickens. Remove from the heat,

whisk in the lemon juice, and sprinkle with salt and pepper. Let the dressing cool a bit.

3. When the potatoes and dressing are still slightly warm but not hot, pour the dressing on the potatoes, sprinkle with chives, and carefully fold the mixture together. Cover and refrigerate until thoroughly cold (or up to a day). Before serving, taste and adjust the seasoning.

Potato Salad with Cheddar Dressing. A tad sharper: Replace 3 ounces of the cream cheese with 4 ounces of cheddar cheese, grated.

Ⓕ Fast   Ⓜ Make Ahead   Ⓥ Vegan

Many salads are actually better made hours or even a day in advance. This makes them perfect for entertaining and picnics or just keeping handy in the fridge. Here are the ones with little or no loss of quality and no last-minute fuss.

1. Spinach Salad with Feta and Nutmeg (page 41)
2. Raw Beet Salad and its variations (page 49)
3. Carrot or Celery Salad and its variations (page 45)
4. Celery Rémoulade and its variations (page 47)
5. Simple Radish or Jícama Salad (page 50)
6. Spicy No-Mayo Coleslaw and its variations (page 49)
7. Carrot Salad with Cumin (but not its substitutions) (page 45)
8. Simple Seaweed Salad (page 53)
9. Arame and Bean Thread Noodles with Ponzu Dipping Sauce (page 54)
10. Sea Slaw (page 55)
11. Kombu Kimchi (page 96)—actually gets better after it mellows for a few days.
12. Eggplant Salad with Miso (page 63)
13. Ratatouille Salad (page 64)
14. Greek-Style Cooked Greens (page 66)
15. Roasted Cauliflower with Raisins and Vinaigrette (page 282)
16. Corn Salad and its variation (page 60)
17. Mushroom Salad, Italian-American Style (page 62)
18. Grilled Shiitake or Portobello Salad with Soy Vinaigrette (page 63)
19. Potato Salad and its variations (page 68)
20. Roasted Sweet Potato Salad with Red Pepper Vinaigrette (page 69)
21. Any of the Essential Bean Salads (page 72), except the few that include fresh greens
22. Black Bean and Pan-Roasted Corn Salad (page 74)
23. Broiled Three-Bean Salad and its variations (page 74)
24. Lemony Lentil Salad and its variation (page 75)
25. Edamame Salad with Seaweed "Mayo" (page 76)
26. Anything in The World of Rice Salads (page 79)
27. Quinoa Salad with Tempeh (page 84)
28. Sweet Potato and Quinoa Salad and its variation (page 84)
29. Wheat Berry or Other Whole Grain Salad with Cabbage and Coarse Mustard (page 85)
30. Wheat Berry or Other Whole Grain Salad with Peanuts and Fresh and Dried Fruit (page 85)
31. Wheat Berry or Other Whole Grain Salad with Roasted Peppers, and its variation (page 87)
32. Whole Grain Bread Salad (page 89)

Potato Salad with Blue Cheese Dressing. Stronger still: Replace 3 ounces of the cream cheese with 4 ounces of blue cheese, crumbled.

Bean Salads

Few salads benefit from being made ahead and soaking in their juices, but these do, so you might get in the habit of doubling the recipes so you have a bean salad to pull out whenever you want it.

You can also use a spoonful or two as a relish to serve with grilled or roasted vegetables or rice bowls or even for topping soup. Mash slightly or pulse in the food processor and you have an instant, high-flavored sandwich spread. Or toss $1/2$ cup or so with leftover pasta or grains, and you create a portable meal to eat on your lunch hour or, better still, on a picnic blanket.

Undercooking the beans—just slightly, so they are barely tender inside and their skins remain intact—is the key to great bean salads. That and dressing them while still warm so they absorb the flavors around them.

Essential Bean Salad

MAKES: 6 to 8 servings

TIME: 1¹/₂ to 3 hours (depending on the bean), largely unattended

This is a master recipe, something you can rely on forever. The idea of marinating warm beans remains the same whether you use lentils, big white gigante beans, or anything in between. What changes are your choice of seasonings and the cooking time. Note that I say "cooking time" and not "opening-the-can time." Though you can certainly use canned beans here, if you try this recipe once from scratch you will be hooked. (For details about selecting, cooking, and storing dried beans, see pages 576–581.)

The amount in this recipe is big enough to woo a small crowd or to keep some in the fridge to eat over the course of several days. You can also cook a whole batch of beans, freeze half for another use, and cut the recipe down by half.

2 cups dried beans, split peas, or lentils, sorted and cooked (pages 581–582), or 4 to 5 cups precooked or canned

1 tablespoon red wine vinegar, other good vinegar, or freshly squeezed lemon juice, or to taste

2 to 4 tablespoons minced red onion or shallot

Salt and freshly ground black pepper

¹/₄ cup extra virgin olive oil, plus more to taste

¹/₄ to ¹/₂ cup chopped parsley

❶ While the beans are cooking, stir the vinegar and onion together in a large bowl. Sprinkle with salt and pepper. Stir in the olive oil.

❷ Continue cooking the beans until just tender but before their skins split and they become mushy. The exact time will vary depending on the bean variety and the beans' age. Drain the beans and add them to the bowl with the dressing while they are still hot. Toss gently until the beans are coated with dressing, adding more olive oil if you like.

❸ Let cool to room temperature (or refrigerate), stirring once or twice to distribute the dressing. Stir in the parsley just before serving, then taste and adjust the seasoning.

Easiest Essential Bean Salad. A stripped-down version: Prepare Vinaigrette or any of its variations (page 762). Cook any kind of bean until just tender (pages 581–582). Drain and dress the beans in the vinaigrette while still warm.

Essential Bean Salad, Italian Style. A little stronger: Use cannellini or cranberry beans. Season the vinegar with 1 tablespoon minced garlic and 1 teaspoon minced fresh rosemary in addition to the onion. If you'd like a slightly milder taste, use white wine vinegar. If you have fresh basil, and you'll be serving the salad right away, use ¹/₄ cup or so of that in place of the rosemary.

Essential Bean Salad, French Style. Lovely, especially with flageolets: Use lentils (preferably Le Puy, page 599) or flageolet beans. Use sherry vinegar instead of the red wine vinegar. Replace the red onion with thinly sliced shallot. Instead of the parsley, stir in 2 tablespoons minced fresh tarragon right before serving.

Essential Bean Salad, Greek Style. Possibly my favorite: Use dried fava or gigante beans. Substitute fresh lemon juice for the vinegar. Add 1 tablespoon minced garlic to the vinegar along with the onion. Instead of parsley, finish with ¹/₄ cup chopped fresh mint.

Essential Bean Salad, Japanese Style. A teaspoon of soy sauce is nice here too: Use edamame or adzuki beans. Substitute rice wine vinegar for the red wine vinegar and a neutral oil, like grapeseed or corn, for the olive oil. Instead of parsley, finish with 1 sheet nori, toasted and crumbled (see page 357.)

Essential Bean Salad, Chinese Style. The ginger changes everything: Use dried soybeans (black or white) or mung beans. Instead of red wine vinegar, use Chinese black vinegar or rice wine vinegar. Instead of red onion, use 1 tablespoon each of minced peeled ginger

F Fast   **M** Make Ahead   **V** Vegan

and garlic. Replace olive oil with 2 tablespoons dark sesame oil and 2 tablespoons neutral oil, like grapeseed or corn. Use soy sauce instead of salt for final seasoning and toss with $^1/_4$ cup chopped scallion instead of the parsley.

Essential Bean Salad, Indian Style. Allow a little more time for the chickpeas: Use chickpeas. Use rice wine vinegar and 2 to 4 tablespoons of minced or grated peeled fresh ginger (to taste) instead of the red onion or shallot. Instead of olive oil, use 2 tablespoons peanut oil and 2 tablespoons coconut milk, either made from scratch (page 423) or canned (use 1 can, slightly less than 2 cups, with a little water). Use cilantro instead of parsley.

6 Simple Last-Minute Additions to Essential Bean Salads

Depending on the ingredient, you may need more oil and vinegar or lemon juice. Here's a simple formula: For every tablespoon of oil, add a teaspoon of acidity. You will also probably want to add a dash more salt or soy sauce, pepper, and fresh herbs as well.

1. Cheese: Grate or shave Parmesan cheese on the Italian style variation; crumble blue cheese on the French style; or crumble feta on the Greek style.
2. Chopped tomatoes: Spread the beans out on a platter, top with the finishing herb, seaweed, or scallion, according to the recipe or variation, then top with 1 cup chopped fresh tomato. Drizzle with a little more oil and serve.
3. Chopped nuts or seeds: Stir in $^1/_2$ cup. Some specific ideas: Hazelnuts with white beans in the Italian Style Bean Salad; almonds in the French style; walnuts in the Greek style; sesame seeds in the Japanese style; and peanuts in the Chinese style.
4. Bean sprouts: Add 1 cup mung bean sprouts to either the Japanese style or Chinese style variation.
5. Cooked greens: For a more substantial dish, toss the finished salad with any kind of cooked hearty green, like kale, cabbage, escarole, or spinach.

6. Salad greens: Toss the finished salad with 4 cups bite-sized pieces of romaine leaves, or arugula, mesclun, frisée, mizuna, or tatsoi.

Warm Chickpea Salad with Arugula

MAKES: 4 side- or 2 main-dish servings
TIME: 20 minutes with precooked beans

Chickpeas frequently get the salad treatment throughout the Mediterranean and Middle East. My version is a panorama of these recipes that includes ginger, garlic, and cumin. After the seasonings are cooked and the beans warmed, the dressing is finished in the pan and tossed with arugula leaves, which wilts them just slightly. Serve small portions as a side salad or appetizer or add the optional hard-cooked egg and make this a light meal.

3 tablespoons extra virgin olive oil

1 tablespoon minced peeled fresh ginger

1 tablespoon minced garlic

$^1/_2$ teaspoon cumin seeds

Salt and freshly ground black pepper

1 $^1/_2$ cups cooked (see pages 581–582) or drained canned chickpeas

1 tablespoon rice wine vinegar

1 teaspoon honey

4 cups arugula leaves

1 small red onion, halved and thinly sliced

4 hard-cooked eggs, quartered (optional)

1 Put the olive oil in a deep skillet over medium heat. When hot, add the ginger, garlic, and cumin and cook, stirring constantly, until fragrant and the ginger and garlic are soft, 1 to 2 minutes. Sprinkle with salt and pepper, then stir in the chickpeas until hot and coated in the oil and seasonings, about 3 minutes more.

Remove from heat and with a fork, stir in the vinegar, honey, and 1 tablespoon water. Mash a few of the chickpeas as you stir to add texture to the dressing. Put the arugula and red onion in a large bowl and toss with the warm chickpea dressing. Taste and adjust the seasoning. Serve immediately, garnished with hard-cooked eggs if you like.

Black Bean and Pan-Roasted Corn Salad

MAKES: 4 servings

TIME: 20 minutes with precooked black beans

Ⓕ Ⓜ

Black beans are almost smoky, and roasted corn emphasizes that taste while adding an element of sweetness; acidity and heat balance this nicely. There's nothing left to do but enrich the salad with the creaminess of cheese and avocado if you like (skip the cheese and you have a vegan dish), then use it to fill burritos or tacos, serve as a dip to be scooped with chips, or spoon into a bowl to eat as is.

2 tablespoons extra virgin olive oil

Kernels from 4 ears corn

Salt and freshly ground black pepper

1 clove garlic, minced

1 1/2 cups cooked or canned black beans (see pages 581–582), at room temperature

1 ripe tomato, cored and diced (optional)

1 teaspoon minced jalapeño or other small chile

2 tablespoons freshly squeezed lime juice

1 cup chopped fresh cilantro leaves for garnish

1 medium avocado, peeled, pitted, and chopped for garnish (optional)

1/2 cup crumbled queso fresco for garnish (optional)

❶ Put the oil in a large nonstick skillet over high heat. Add the corn, along with a large pinch of salt and some pepper, and cook, shaking the pan or stirring, but only occasionally, until the corn is lightly charred, 5 to 10 minutes. Add the garlic and cook, stirring, for 1 minute more.

 Combine the corn with the beans, tomato, jalapeño, and lime juice. Taste and adjust the seasoning, garnish with cilantro, and avocado and cheese if you like, and serve; or cover and refrigerate for up to a couple of hours. (Bring back to room temperature and garnish right before serving.)

Broiled Three-Bean Salad

MAKES: 4 servings

TIME: 30 minutes with precooked beans

Ⓕ Ⓜ Ⓥ

Traditional three-bean salad is a timeless idea that has been sullied by years of the "whatever" attitude of restaurants, delis, and supermarkets. Yet the combination of chickpeas, kidney beans, and green beans is a real winner, as long as you pay some attention to the dressing. Here I go a little further, broiling the beans to give them a tender yet crisp texture that warms them and releases their flavor.

1 small red onion, thinly sliced

1 clove garlic, minced

One 1-inch piece of ginger, peeled and minced

1 teaspoon sugar

2 teaspoons Fragrant Curry Powder (page 816)

Salt and freshly ground black pepper

2 tablespoons white or cider vinegar

1 pound green beans, cut into 2-inch pieces (about 3 1/2 cups)

Up to 1/4 cup neutral oil, like grapeseed or corn, as needed

1 cup cooked (see pages 581–582) or drained canned chickpeas

1 cup cooked (pages 581–582) or drained canned kidney beans

1/2 cup chopped fresh cilantro for garnish

1 Heat the broiler and adjust the rack so the pan is 4 to 5 inches from the heat source.

2 Put the onion, garlic, and ginger in a large heatproof bowl and sprinkle with sugar, curry powder, and a little salt and pepper. Drizzle on the vinegar and toss gently to coat.

3 Spread the green beans on a rimmed baking sheet or pan and drizzle with 2 tablespoons of the oil. Toss to coat. Broil, watching them carefully and shaking the pan as need until they release their water and begin to blister, 5 to 7 minutes. Add them to the bowl with the onion mixture and toss to coat.

4 Spread the chickpeas and kidney beans on the same baking sheet and drizzle with enough additional oil to coat them. Broil, watching them carefully and shaking the pan as need until they get brown and the chickpeas are crunchy, about 5 minutes. Add them to the bowl and toss to coat. (The salad may be made ahead to this point; just cool it down a bit and refrigerate for up to 2 days.) Before serving, taste and adjust the seasoning and garnish.

Broiled Three-Bean Salad, Italian Style. Closer to the familiar: Eliminate the ginger and curry powder. Add 1 cup chopped tomatoes to the bowl. Instead of white or cider vinegar, use balsamic. Use white beans instead of the kidney beans if you like and replace the neutral oil with extra virgin olive oil. Garnish with shredded or chopped fresh basil instead of cilantro.

Broiled Three-Bean Salad, Spanish Style. With almonds, and very nice: Replace the red onion with one large shallot, thinly sliced. Eliminate the ginger and the curry powder. Add 1/4 cup chopped toasted almonds (see page 321) to the bowl. Instead of white or cider vinegar, use sherry vinegar. Replace the neutral oil with extra virgin olive oil. Eliminate the cilantro and garnish with 2 tablespoons fresh thyme leaves or 2 teaspoons dried.

Lemony Lentil Salad

MAKES: 4 servings
TIME: About 45 minutes

Small French, dark green, almost black lentils—often named after the village where they were first grown, Le Puy—are my first choice for this bistro-style salad. But use whatever lentils you have handy: Plenty of places are growing Le Puy–style lentils now, and the more common brown lentils work well here, as do split peas for that matter.

Whatever you use, avoid overcooking and dress the lentils while they are still hot, then serve the salad warm or at room temperature. If you decide to make it ahead, bring it back to room temperature before serving for maximum flavor. And while you're at it, double the recipe so there are plenty of leftovers; this keeps well for several days.

1 cup dried lentils, preferably lentilles du Puy, sorted and rinsed

1 bay leaf

2 cloves garlic

2 lemons

2 tablespoons olive oil

1 tablespoon capers

1/4 cup minced fresh chives, shallot, or red onion

Salt and freshly ground black pepper

1 Put the lentils in a medium pot and cover with water by 1 inch. Add the bay leaf and garlic and bring to a boil. Cover and lower the heat so the lentils bubble gently. Cook until just tender but not burst, 20 to 30 minutes, checking occasionally to make sure there is always enough water at the bottom of the pan to keep the lentils from burning.

2 Squeeze the juice from one of the lemons into a large bowl. Peel the other lemon and chop the segments roughly into small pieces, taking care to remove the seeds. Add the segments to the bowl along with the olive

oil, capers, and chives. Sprinkle with a little salt and pepper and stir.

③ Drain whatever water remains from the lentils and stir them into the dressing while still hot. Let rest, stirring occasionally to distribute the dressing, until they cool for a few minutes. Taste and adjust the seasoning and serve warm or refrigerate for up to several days.

Tangerine Lentil Salad. Quite seductive: Instead of lemons, use 2 small tangerines.

Edamame Salad with Seaweed "Mayo"

MAKES: 4 servings
TIME: 30 minutes, including making the dressing

Ⓕ Ⓜ Ⓥ

Whether you use fresh or frozen here, edamame (young soybeans; see page 585) need to cook for only a couple of minutes. The result is a crisp, fresh-tasting bean with a texture somewhere between limas and favas, perfect for salads.

Here I dress them simply, in a briny and richly colored vegan "mayonnaise" based on seaweed. To make a cold rice bowl meal, serve this with Citrus Rice Salad (page 82) or with plain Sushi Rice (page 527) and either Pan-Seared Tomato Salad (page 59) or Cherry Tomato Salad with Soy Sauce (page 57).

Salt

2 cups shelled edamame, fresh or frozen

$1/2$ medium red or yellow bell pepper, cored, seeded, and finely chopped

$1/4$ cup Seaweed "Mayo" (page 773) or regular mayo, or more to taste

Freshly ground black pepper

1 tablespoon white or black sesame seeds for garnish (optional)

① Put a few inches of water in a medium saucepan, salt it, and bring to a boil. Cook the edamame, stirring occasionally, for 2 to 3 minutes, until heated through and bright green. Drain and run under cold water until cool.

② Toss the edamame with the bell pepper and mayo. Taste and adjust the seasoning, garnish with sesame seeds if serving immediately, or refrigerate for up to 3 days and garnish just before serving.

Two-Mung Salad

MAKES: 4 servings
TIME: About 30 minutes

Ⓕ Ⓜ Ⓥ

Glassy-clear bean threads make beautiful salads. Here their silky, slippery texture is paired with the crisp crunch of bean sprouts and dressed, as sprout salads commonly are in Korea.

Both ingredients come from mung beans, with the first made from the bean's starch and the second by sprouting them. Bean sprout salads are usually served as a side dish or an appetizer, but though this version is also terrific as part of a larger meal, it's substantial enough to eat alone.

Salt

1 tablespoon soy sauce

1 tablespoon dark sesame oil

1 tablespoon neutral oil, like grapeseed or corn

1 teaspoon minced garlic

1 teaspoon sugar

$1/2$ pound mung or soybean sprouts, trimmed if you like (see page 78)

2 ounces bean thread noodles, soaked, cut, and drained (see page 464)

2 scallions, minced

1 teaspoon toasted sesame seeds (see page 321)

Ⓕ Fast   Ⓜ Make Ahead   Ⓥ Vegan

① Set a medium pot of water to boil and add a generous pinch of salt. Meanwhile, stir together the soy sauce, oils, garlic, and sugar in a large serving bowl.

② When the water comes to a boil, poach the sprouts for about 1 minute; drain and immediately toss with the mixture in the bowl. Add the bean thread noodles. Sprinkle with scallions and sesame seeds and toss again. Taste and adjust the seasoning, adding salt or more soy sauce or sesame oil if you like. Let the dish cool to room temperature and serve immediately or refrigerate for up to a few hours and serve cold.

Fava Bean and Mint Salad with Asparagus

MAKES: 4 servings

TIME: About 1 hour for beans in the shell, less for frozen or precooked

Fava beans and mint are a quintessential springtime combination, found throughout Europe; they're often combined with artichokes or asparagus. And though this salad is at its best when these key ingredients are fresh and in season, if you swap out any or all of them, this can become a year-round dish. Try fresh or frozen edamame or peas instead of the fava beans. Parsley or basil is a reliable substitute for the mint. And though asparagus is almost always available, green beans or wedges of artichokes are also nice.

To make this dish ahead, prepare the fava beans and cook the asparagus according to Step 1, below; assemble at the last minute.

Salt

1 pound asparagus, cut diagonally into 2-inch pieces (about 3 1/2 cups)

2 tablespoons extra virgin olive oil

2 teaspoons freshly squeezed lemon or orange juice

1/2 teaspoon sugar

2 pounds fresh fava beans, shucked, blanched, and peeled (about 2 cups; see page 589), or frozen fava beans, edamame, peas, or lima beans

1 cup fresh mint leaves

Freshly ground black pepper

1 tablespoon grated lemon or orange zest for garnish (optional)

① Bring a large pot of water to boil and salt it. Cook the asparagus for about a minute or two, then drain and run under cold water or plunge into a bowl of ice water to stop the cooking. When cold, drain.

② Whisk together the olive oil, lemon juice, and sugar in a large bowl until the sugar is dissolved. Add the fava beans, asparagus, and mint and toss to coat. Taste and add more salt if needed, plus a sprinkle of pepper. Serve garnished with lemon zest if you like.

Sprouts

MAKES: about 2 cups

TIME: 1 week, largely unattended

The most common sprouts are made from mung beans—they're the familiar ones with the pale heads (sometimes sheathed in green) and longish tails—but you can sprout almost any bean or seed, from alfalfa to radish to wheat to lentil. Even herb seeds like basil will sprout, and they're delicious.

Using this method (or another, if you like), you can also combine sprouts of different types in the same container. All it takes is time and a little daily routine.

1/2 cup mung beans or other beans, seeds, or whole grains

① Put the beans in a quart jar—like a mayonnaise jar. Rinse once with water and drain, then cover with water

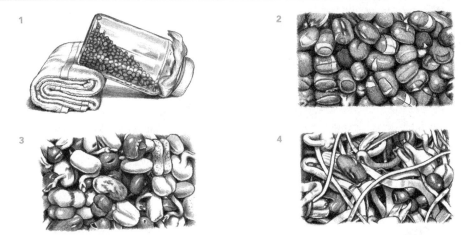

You'll need a clean jar and some kind of mesh top: cheesecloth, a piece of screen, or even a coarse kitchen towel. Rinse the beans (these are mung beans) or seeds well, then put them in the jar, cover with water and let soak for six to twelve hours. (1) Drain, rinse, cover with your top, and prop the jar up as shown. Shield from the light (you can just cover it with a towel). Continue rinsing and draining, at least twice a day but preferably three or four times. (2) After a day or so, the seeds will open. (3) A day or two later, they'll start to sprout. (4) And after (about) three days, the seeds will have fully sprouted. When the sprouts are the length you want them (generally, the bigger the seed, the longer the sprout), rinse one more time and expose to the light for a few hours; this will turn the sprouts green.

and let soak for 6 to 12 hours. Loosely cover the jar with cheesecloth, an old (clean) piece of screen, or a very coarse napkin or piece of towel.

② Drain. Rinse the seeds and drain them again; prop the jar up so that it is on its side with the mouth tilted down. Shield from the light (you can just cover the jar with a towel).

③ Continue rinsing and draining, at least twice a day but preferably 3 or 4 times. After a few days, you'll see that the seeds have sprouted. When the sprouts are the length you want them (generally, the bigger the seed, the longer the sprout), rinse one more time and expose to the light for a few hours; this will turn the sprouts green.

④ Store in the refrigerator and eat within a few days.

Grain Salads

Grain salads are delicious and filling; they also provide some protein, especially when eaten with beans, cheese, or tofu. You can eat them alone, serve them on a pile of greens, or combine them with many of the other salads in this chapter for satisfying and complete meals. They make great side dishes and are terrific for both daily fare and entertaining, because just about all of them can be made way ahead of time.

Various cooking techniques for grains are described on pages 533 to 537, but for salads, I rely mostly on Cooking Grains, the Easy Way (page 537), rinsing after cooking to remove some of the starch and keep the grains

Ⓕ Fast   Ⓜ Make Ahead   Ⓥ Vegan

separate. As with beans, it's important not to overcook to avoid mushiness.

Ideally you'd cook the grains when you want to prepare a salad so you could dress them warm and allow them to absorb flavor as they cool. But you and I both know that if those were the hard-and-fast rules, you wouldn't be eating grain salads very often. But the real-life approach planning for leftovers whenever you cook a pot of grains, doubling the recipe if necessary, will ensure that you always have the ingredients for big-time, last-minute salads at your fingertips.

The World of Rice Salads

MAKES: 4 servings

TIME: About 30 minutes

There are so many kinds of rice to choose from (see pages 502–505 and so many ways to use them that there's no reason to eat the same rice salad twice. This starting point offers enough variations to give you the hang of the way ingredients come together in different cuisines, making rice salad an easy way to experiment with traditional or even cross-cultural combinations. But there are also ideas here for simple, almost single-ingredient rice salads. Many of the salads are also vegan.

The master recipe here will work for virtually any type of rice. Though I make suggestions for the specific variations, ultimately you should use whatever you like and whatever you have handy. Feel free to try other grains here too.

In my opinion, rice salads should never be eaten directly out of the refrigerator (unless, of course, you're desperately hungry), because the starches in the rice need some time to soften up. This slight disadvantage also places them among the ultimate make-ahead dishes. If the salad is assembled a few hours in advance, the rice has a chance to soak up flavors, whether in the fridge or out (you usually don't have to refrigerate if it's going to be

only a couple of hours). Before serving, just pull the salad out and leave it covered on the counter for a half hour or so to take the chill off.

3 to 4 cups cooked rice, cooled

$^{1}/_{4}$ cup chopped scallion

1 small or $^{1}/_{2}$ large red or yellow bell pepper, cored, seeded, and chopped

$^{1}/_{2}$ cup chopped celery

$^{1}/_{2}$ cup chopped carrot

$^{1}/_{4}$ to $^{1}/_{2}$ cup Vinaigrette (page 762), made with extra virgin olive oil and red wine vinegar, plus more as needed

$^{1}/_{2}$ cup chopped fresh parsley

Salt and freshly ground black pepper

1 Put the rice and all the vegetables in a large bowl. Drizzle with vinaigrette and use 2 big forks to combine, fluffing the rice and tossing gently to separate the grains.

2 Stir in the parsley, taste, and adjust the seasoning or moisten with a little more dressing. Serve at room temperature or refrigerate for up to a day, bringing the salad back to room temperature before serving.

Rice Salad, Japanese Style. Use brown or white short-grain rice. Halve the amount of celery and carrot and finely chop them or shred them on a grater. Add 1 cup cubed firm tofu (preferably baked, page 641). Instead of the vinaigrette, toss with $^{1}/_{4}$ cup or so of Simple Miso Dipping Sauce (page 781). Instead of the parsley, crumble 2 sheets of nori over the rice salad and sprinkle with 2 tablespoons black or white sesame seeds.

Rice Salad, Mexican Style. Long-grain or medium-grain, white or brown, all work well here: When blending the vinaigrette, add 1 tablespoon Chili Powder (page 814) and 2 tablespoons Mexican crema or mayonnaise (or substitute, page 772). Instead of celery and carrot, add 1 cup chopped fresh tomato. Substitute chopped fresh cilantro for the parsley and, at the

MORE RICE SALAD VARIATIONS

To make the huge number of variations on rice salad more accessible, I've put them in chart form, where they're broken down by the main recipe's basic components (rice, aromatics and vegetables, dressing, and herbs and garnishes), with changes written as usual. (Descriptions of the rice varieties are on pages 502–505.) Just follow the directions in each column for that variation, referring to the main rice salad recipe.

VARIATION	RICE	AROMATICS & VEGETABLES	DRESSING	HERBS & GARNISHES
Herbed	Use any kind of rice.	Leave out.	Add 1 cup any fresh herbs, alone or in combination, to the blender.	None needed
With Olives	Use any kind of rice.	Instead of bell pepper, celery, and carrot, add 1/2 cup pitted and chopped olives, either alone or in combination.	Vinaigrette	Add 1/2 cup chopped walnuts or hazelnuts if you like.
Hippie	Use brown rice.	Substitute 1 cup cooked and shocked broccoli florets (page 241) for the celery and carrot.	Vinaigrette	Add 1/4 cup toasted sunflower seeds.
Italian Style	Best with Arborio	Add 1 tablespoon minced garlic; substitute thinly sliced red onion for the scallion and 1 cup chopped roma or cherry tomatoes for the pepper, celery, and carrot.	Vinaigrette	Add 1 teaspoon chopped rosemary leaves (or 1/2 teaspoon crumbled dried) and 1/2 cup grated Parmesan.
Pesto	Arborio if possible (page 504).	Leave out.	Use 1/4 cup Traditional Pesto (page 768) with 1 tablespoon red wine vinegar.	A drizzle of extra virgin olive oil and a fresh grating of Parmesan; wonderful served with sliced tomatoes and fresh mozzarella
With Fermented Black Beans	Use jasmine rice (page 503) if you have it.		Replace with Soy Vinaigrette (page 763); add 1 tablespoon minced ginger and 2 tablespoons fermented black beans.	Substitute cilantro, and serve with large lettuce leaves. Just spoon in a little rice salad, fold, and eat.

VARIATION	RICE	AROMATICS & VEGETABLES	DRESSING	HERBS & GARNISHES
French Style	Use long-grain white rice.	Instead of scallion, use 2 tablespoons minced shallot. Substitute sliced radish for the bell pepper and 1 cup chopped cooked green beans (preferably haricots verts) for the celery and carrot.	Make the vinaigrette with white wine vinegar or sherry vinegar and add 2 tablespoons fresh tarragon.	None needed.
Spanish Style (what a paella salad might be like)	Use medium-grain or Arborio rice.	Instead of celery, use 1/2 cup cooked green peas (frozen are fine).	Use sherry vinegar instead of red wine vinegar and add a generous pinch of saffron if you have it.	Garnish with sliced almonds if you like.
Cuban Style	Use long-grain white rice.	Substitute thinly sliced red onion for the scallion and add 1 tablespoon minced garlic. Instead of the celery and carrot, use 1 cup cooked or canned black beans.	Vinaigrette	None needed.None needed.
Persian Style	Use brown or white basmati or jasmine rice.	Instead of the bell pepper, celery, and carrot, add 1/2 cup chopped cashews and 1 cup chopped dates.	Use lemon juice instead of the red wine vinegar and add 1 teaspoon ground cinnamon and 2 teaspoons cumin seeds to the blender.	Use parsley or chopped fresh mint.
Tropical	Use white or brown jasmine or basmati rice.	Instead of bell pepper, celery, and carrot, use 1/2 cup each cubed fresh pineapple and mango and chopped macadamia nuts.	Use rice wine vinegar and neutral oil, like grapeseed or corn.	Use chopped fresh mint and garnish with 1/4 cup toasted coconut if you like.
Wild Rice	Use wild rice.	Instead of bell pepper, celery, and carrots, use 1/2 cup each dried blueberries, cranberries or cherries, and chopped almonds.	Use Lemon Vinaigrette (page 763).	Use fresh mint instead of parsley if you like.

same time, add 2 chopped hard-cooked eggs and chopped jalapeño chiles if you like. Serve with lime wedges.

Rice Salad, Indian Style. Use brown or white basmati rice. When making the vinaigrette, use rice wine vinegar, replace the oil with coconut milk, and add 1 tablespoon Fragrant Curry Powder (page 816), or more to taste. Instead of the bell pepper, celery, and carrot, add ¹/₂ cup each cubed cooked potato, cooked cauliflower florets, and green peas (cooked frozen are fine). Substitute cilantro for the parsley.

Citrus Rice Salad. Use any rice. Instead of red wine vinegar, make the vinaigrette with freshly squeezed citrus juice: Choose from lemon, lime, orange, blood orange, tangerine, pink grapefruit, or a combination. Whatever you use, add 2 tablespoons of the grated zest and 1 tablespoon of sugar or honey to the blender. Do not include the scallion or the vegetables. (You might want to use a little less dressing.) Instead of the parsley, use mint if you like. A handful of chopped almonds or pecans make a nice addition.

Tomato Rice Salad. Use any kind of brown or white rice. When making the vinaigrette, eliminate the vinegar and add 1 medium tomato to the blender. Instead of the scallion and other vegetables, add 2 cups chopped fresh tomato (a mixture of heirloom varieties is nice). Instead of the parsley, use chopped fresh basil or mint, or ¹/₄ cup chopped fresh chives, chervil, dill, or about a tablespoon of fresh thyme leaves.

Barley Salad with Cucumber and Yogurt-Dill Dressing

MAKES: 4 servings
TIME: 40 minutes

Cool, crunchy, and chewy, this is a perfect summer salad. Whole grains of any type will work well here, but you'll need fast-cooking pearled barley (see page 534)—or rice,

of course—if you want to make this from scratch and still serve it within an hour.

1 cup pearled barley

Salt

1 English (long) cucumber, 6 Kirby (pickling) cucumbers, or 2 or 3 medium cucumbers

3 or 4 scallions, chopped

Freshly ground black pepper

2 tablespoons freshly squeezed lemon juice, or more to taste

2 tablespoons extra virgin olive oil

1 cup yogurt

¹/₂ cup fresh chopped dill, mint, or parsley leaves, or a combination

❶ Rinse the barley and put it in a saucepan with water to cover by at least 2 inches. Add a large pinch of salt and cook over medium-high heat, stirring occasionally, until the barley is tender, about 20 minutes from the time the water boils. Drain and spread on a plate to cool (if you're in a hurry, you can rinse under cold water for a minute or so).

❷ Meanwhile, if you're using an English cucumber (or other good cucumber), simply cut it into small, bite-sized chunks. If you're using a regular cucumber, peel it, then cut it in half the long way and scoop out the seeds with a spoon. Cut it into chunks, put in a colander or strainer, and sprinkle with about a tablespoon of salt. Let sit for 20 minutes or so, then rinse and drain well.

❸ Toss together the barley, cucumber, and scallions in a salad bowl; sprinkle with pepper. Whisk together the lemon juice, oil, and yogurt. Toss this dressing with the cucumber mixture, then taste and adjust the seasoning. Add the herb(s), toss all together, and serve.

Barley Pea Salad. A tad more colorful: Instead of the cucumber, use 1 ¹/₂ cups cooked and shocked fresh or frozen peas (page 241). Fresh sugar snap peas are a rare seasonal treat in this salad too.

Barley Cucumber Salad with Walnuts. Some crunch: In Step 3, toss $^1/_2$ cup chopped walnuts into the salad bowl.

Wild Rice Salad with Cucumber and Yogurt. Smoother: Instead of the barley, use wild rice and double the cooking time. (Or use cooked wild rice, page 537.)

Bulgur and Tomato Salad

MAKES: 4 to 6 servings

TIME: 15 to 30 minutes, depending on bulgur

I've taken a hearty Greek dish of tomatoes cooked with cracked wheat and turned it into a much lighter, faster salad, one that features bulgur. When you first read the recipe, it might remind you of Tabbouleh (page 43), but tomatoes are the star here.

> 1 cup fine-grind (#1) or medium-grind (#2) bulgur
>
> 3 cups chopped tomato or quartered cherry tomatoes
>
> 1 small red onion, diced
>
> 2 ounces feta cheese, crumbled
>
> 2 tablespoons red wine vinegar, plus more to taste
>
> $^1/_4$ cup extra virgin olive oil, plus more to taste
>
> 2 tablespoons chopped fresh oregano leaves or 2 teaspoons dried
>
> 1 teaspoon hot red pepper flakes
>
> Salt and freshly ground black pepper

1 Soak the bulgur in hot water to cover until tender, 15 to 30 minutes. Put the tomato, onion, feta, vinegar, olive oil, oregano, and red pepper if you like in a large salad bowl and stir with a fork to combine. Sprinkle with a little salt (remember the feta can be salty) and lots of pepper.

2 When the bulgur is tender but not mushy, drain it in a strainer, pressing down to squeeze out any excess liq-

uid. Put it in the bowl while it's still warm and fluff with a large fork to stir in the other ingredients. Taste and adjust the seasonings, adding more oil or vinegar as needed Serve the salad at room temperature or cool it down and refrigerate it for a couple hours or so.

Tomato and Cracked Wheat Salad. This is heartier and more like the Greek version: Substitute 2 cups cooked cracked wheat (see page 537) for the prepared bulgur.

Tomato and Rice Salad. Substitute 2 cups plain cooked rice (see page 505) for the prepared bulgur.

Tomato, Bulgur, and Chickpea Salad. More substantial: Add 2 cups canned or cooked chickpeas (see pages 579–580) to the salad bowl before adding the bulgur. You will probably want to add a little more vinegar and oil too.

Quinoa Salad with Lemon, Spinach, and Poppy Seeds

MAKES: 4 servings

TIME: 30 minutes

A quick and unusual salad that is light, quite tart, and refreshing.

> $2^1/_2$ cups cooked quinoa or other small-kernel grain (see page 534) or 1 cup raw
>
> About 10 ounces fresh spinach
>
> 1 lemon
>
> Salt and freshly ground black pepper
>
> About $^1/_2$ cup Lemon Vinaigrette (page 763), made with 1 teaspoon honey or sugar added
>
> $^1/_4$ cup poppy seeds for garnish

1 If you haven't already, cook the quinoa or other grain according to the directions on page 537. Drain in a strainer and rinse. Meanwhile, roughly chop the spinach, removing any thick stems (those over, say, $^1/_8$ inch); wash it well, dry it (a salad spinner is best), and put it in a salad bowl.

2 Segment the lemon as you would a grapefruit—it need not be neat, but get as much of the flesh as you can—and toss the segments with the spinach. Sprinkle with salt and pepper.

3 Toss the drained quinoa with the spinach and lemon, then spoon on Lemon Vinaigrette to taste. Garnish with the poppy seeds and serve.

Quinoa Salad with Tempeh

MAKES: 4 to 6 servings

TIME: 30 minutes

You'll love the crispness tempeh (see page 673) contributes to this full-bodied salad. You can make this dish both prettier and tastier by adding bean sprouts (make your own according to the simple directions on page 77) and/or chopped tomato.

2 $^1/_2$ cups cooked quinoa or other small-kernel grain (see page 537) or 1 cup raw

3 tablespoons peanut oil or neutral oil, like grapeseed or corn

4 ounces tempeh, crumbled (about 1 cup)

1 tablespoon minced peeled fresh ginger

1 tablespoon slivered garlic

1 cup mung bean sprouts (optional)

1 cup chopped tomatoes (optional)

2 tablespoons rice wine vinegar

1 tablespoon dark sesame oil

1 tablespoon soy sauce, or to taste

Salt and freshly ground black pepper

$^1/_2$ cup chopped scallion for garnish

$^1/_4$ cup chopped fresh cilantro leaves for garnish

1 If you haven't already, cook the quinoa or other grain according to the directions on page 537. Drain in a strainer and rinse. Meanwhile, put the oil in a skillet over medium-high heat. When hot, add the tempeh and cook, stirring occasionally, until crisp, about 10 minutes. Stir in the ginger and garlic and cook for another minute or two, then add the bean sprouts and tomatoes if you're using them, stir, and turn off the heat. Stir in the vinegar, sesame oil, and soy sauce and transfer to a bowl.

2 When the quinoa is dry and cooled, toss it with the tempeh mixture. Taste and add salt if necessary and a healthy sprinkling of black pepper. (At this point, the salad can rest for an hour or so before being served.) Garnish with the scallion and cilantro and serve.

Sweet Potato and Quinoa Salad

MAKES: 4 servings

TIME: 40 minutes

For a range of colors, flavors, and textures, this pretty little salad is a tough one to beat. If you have leftover sweet potatoes and quinoa, you can whip it up in no time, but even if you start from scratch it isn't much work. As is often the case, you can substitute millet for the quinoa if you like; the golden color is lovely.

2 $^1/_2$ cups cooked quinoa or other small-kernel grain (see page 537) or 1 cup raw

1 large or 2 medium (about 1 pound) sweet potatoes

Salt

1 red bell pepper, cored, seeded, and diced

$^1/_4$ cup minced red onion or shallot

Freshly ground black pepper

$^1/_4$ cup extra virgin olive oil

2 tablespoons balsamic, sherry, or red wine vinegar

$^1/_4$ cup minced fresh chives or parsley leaves

If you haven't already, cook the quinoa or other grain according to the directions on page 537. Drain in a strainer and rinse. Meanwhile, peel the sweet potato and dice it into $1/2$-inch or smaller pieces. Cook it in boiling salted water to cover until tender, about 15 minutes; drain well.

Toss together the potato, quinoa, bell pepper, and onion; sprinkle with salt and pepper. Whisk the oil and vinegar together and toss the salad with about half of this mixture; add all or some of the rest to taste. Taste and adjust the seasoning, garnish with the chives and serve.

Southwestern Sweet Potato and Quinoa Salad. A little more guts: Add 1 avocado, peeled, pitted, and diced, to the mix, along with the sweet potato and quinoa; add $1/4$ teaspoon cayenne, chili powder, or hot red pepper flakes. Add $1/4$ cup toasted pepitas (pumpkin seeds; see page 321). Use freshly squeezed lime juice in place of the vinegar and cilantro in place of the chives.

Wheat Berry or Other Whole Grain Salad with Cabbage and Coarse Mustard

MAKES: 4 to 6 servings
TIME: 20 minutes with cooked grains

The sweet, earthy flavor of wheat berries is combined here with a couple of sharp counterpoints. The result is a hearty salad with pronounced flavors. Try substituting store-bought horseradish (or, for that matter, freshly grated horseradish) for the mustard if you like; start with just a couple of teaspoons, though, until you see how strong it is.

A cup of chopped apple or celery (or both) adds a delightful note of sweetness.

4 cups finely chopped or shredded Savoy or white cabbage

2 cups cooked whole wheat or any of the other grains listed on pages 534–537

$1/2$ large or 1 medium red onion, halved, thinly sliced, and separated into rings

2 tablespoons coarse mustard (like Moutarde de Meaux), or to taste

$1/3$ cup extra virgin olive oil, or as needed

2 tablespoons red wine or other vinegar

Salt and freshly ground black pepper

Toss the cabbage, wheat, and onion together in a salad bowl.

Whisk the mustard, oil, and vinegar together; add a little salt (mustard is quite salty, so you won't need much) and a lot of coarsely ground black pepper—$1/2$ teaspoon at least.

Toss the dressing with the salad, taste and adjust the seasoning, and serve.

Wheat Berry or Other Whole Grain Salad with Peanuts and Fresh and Dried Fruit

MAKES: 4 servings
TIME: 20 minutes with cooked grains

This terrific combination is the basis for a number of variations. Grapes, cut in half, make a wonderful addition to (or substitution for) the oranges. You can add other citrus or, really, almost any other fruit—ripe peaches, in late summer, are awesome.

Any nuts can stand in for the peanuts; pistachios or candied walnuts or pecans are especially nice. (You can, of course, eliminate the nuts entirely.) And use any dried fruit you like: apricots (cut them up with scissors), dates (pit and mince them), and so on.

1 navel orange, peeled and separated into sections

1 teaspoon fresh thyme leaves, chopped fresh sage, or chopped fresh rosemary or $1/4$ teaspoon dried

23 Salads That Make Great Meals

Almost any of the salads here can be made more filling with the addition of protein or other ingredients. Cooked beans, cheese, hard-cooked eggs, and nuts or seeds are the obvious solutions.

I also urge you to try some form of cooked tofu—Grilled Tofu (page 642), Baked Tofu (page 641), or Tofu Croutons (page 656)—instead of plain raw bread cubes. Crunchy Crumbled Tempeh (page 674) and seitan (page 688) are also good options, and remember that there's not only great flavor but a fair amount of protein in sea greens (pages 355–357), cooked whole grains (page 537), whole grain croutons (page 806), and nuts. Pasta—or any noodles—and croutons made from pita or white bread (page 806) provide flavor, bulk, and sometimes crunch.

Another way to expand a salad into a meal is to toss some of the salad with a bowlful of cooked beans, noodles, or grains. All of the recipes in the "Cooked Vegetable Salads" section (page 60), and many of the other all-vegetable salads here, work great with this technique. Just moisten with a little more vinaigrette, dressing, or oil and vinegar.

Other salads in this chapter are hearty enough to make a meal exactly as they are, especially the ones made from beans, grains, and pasta or noodles; you may want to increase the portion size a bit. Here's where to find them:

1. Greens with Fruit, Cheese, and Nuts (page 40)
2. Spinach Salad with Warm Dressing and Tofu Croutons (page 40)
3. Spinach Salad with Feta and Nutmeg and its variation (page 41)
4. Endive and Roquefort Salad (page 44)
5. Arame and Bean Thread Noodles with Ponzu Dipping Sauce and its variations (page 54)
6. Broiled Tomato and Blue Cheese Salad and its variations (page 58)
7. Heirloom Tomato Salad with Hard-Cooked Eggs and its variations (page 59)
8. Essential Bean Salad and its variations (page 72)
9. Warm Chickpea Salad with Arugula (page 73)
10. Black Bean and Pan-Roasted Corn Salad (page 74)
11. Broiled Three-Bean Salad and its variations (page 74)
12. Fava Bean and Mint Salad with Asparagus (page 77)
13. The World of Rice Salads (page 79)
14. Barley Salad with Cucumber and Yogurt-Dill Dressing and its variations (page 82)
15. Bulgur and Tomato Salad and its variation (page 83)
16. Quinoa Salad with Lemon, Spinach, and Poppy Seeds (page 83)
17. Quinoa Salad with Tempeh (page 84)
18. Sweet Potato and Quinoa Salad (page 84)
19. Wheat Berry or Other Whole Grain Salad with Cabbage and Coarse Mustard (page 85)
20. Wheat Berry or Other Whole Grain Salad with Peanuts and Fresh and Dried Fruit (page 85)
21. Wheat Berry or Other Whole Grain Salad with Roasted Peppers and its variations (page 87)
22. Any of the three bread salads (pages 87–89)
23. Summertime Pasta Salad, Japanese Style (page 90)

$1/4$ cup peanut or extra virgin olive oil, or as needed

2 tablespoons red wine or other vinegar

Salt and freshly ground black pepper

2 cups cooked whole wheat or any of the other grains listed on page 534–537

$1/2$ large or 1 medium red onion, halved, thinly sliced, and separated into rings

$1/2$ cup or more dried cranberries or cherries

$1/2$ cup or more roasted peanuts, salted or unsalted

❶ Cut the orange segments in half over your salad bowl so the juices fall into the bowl. Whisk in the herb, oil, and vinegar, along with some salt and pepper.

Ⓕ Fast   Ⓜ Make Ahead   Ⓥ Vegan

2 Add the wheat and onion, along with half the fruit and nuts. Toss, then taste and adjust the seasoning.

3 Garnish with the remaining fruit and nuts and serve.

Wheat Berry or Other Whole Grain Salad with Roasted Peppers

MAKES: 4 servings

TIME: 20 minutes with cooked grains and roasted peppers

This mild, rich salad is not only delicious but also gorgeous, especially if you use red and yellow peppers you've roasted yourself (see page 333). Store-bought roasted peppers, piquillo peppers, or even bottled pimientos are decent substitutes.

Admittedly, there's a lot of precooking to do here—not only the peppers but also the grain and the garlic—but if you think a couple of days ahead, it's a snap to put together. And you'll find plenty of other uses for the peppers and garlic.

¼ cup pine nuts

2 or 3 roasted or grilled peppers (page 252), preferably a mix of red and yellow, peeled, seeded, and torn or cut into strips

2 cups cooked whole wheat or any of the other grains listed on pages 534–537

1 head Roasted Garlic (page 304), the pulp squeezed from the skins

1 cup shredded fresh basil

¼ cup extra virgin olive oil, or as needed

3 tablespoons red wine or other vinegar

Salt and freshly ground black pepper

1 Toast the pine nuts in a small, dry skillet over medium heat, shaking the pan occasionally, until lightly browned. Set aside.

2 Toss together the pepper strips, whole wheat, garlic, and about half the basil in a salad bowl. Whisk the oil and vinegar together, along with some salt and pepper. Toss the dressing with the salad, then taste and adjust the seasoning as necessary.

3 Garnish with the pine nuts and remaining basil and serve.

Wheat Berry or Other Whole Grain Salad with Roasted Peppers and Zucchini. If you're grilling the peppers for this (or another dish), grill 2 or 3 small to medium zucchini at the same time (see page 255 for more specific directions). Cut the zucchini into chunks or slices and toss with the other ingredients in Step 2.

Crouton Salad

MAKES: 4 to 6 servings

TIME: 30 minutes

Because the bread here is toasted, the croutons absorb the tomatoes' juices but stay crunchy. Eat this alone, on a bed of greens, or alongside a generous slice of fresh mozzarella. It also makes a nice side dish for Broiled Eggplant with Peppers, Onions, and Yogurt (page 298) or Mushroom Pâté (page 316).

About 8 ounces crusty bread (stale is fine) or about 8 ounces Croutons (page 806)

¼ cup extra virgin olive oil

2 tablespoons red wine vinegar or freshly squeezed lemon juice

2 ripe tomatoes, cored and roughly chopped

1 small red onion, halved and thinly sliced

1 clove garlic, minced or pressed

Salt and freshly ground black pepper

¼ cup or more roughly chopped basil or parsley

1 Preheat the oven to 400°F. Cut the bread into large cubes and spread on a baking sheet. Bake, turning the cubes once or twice, until golden, about 15 to 20 minutes. Remove from the oven and set aside to cool. (The croutons may be made to this point and kept tightly covered for up to 2 days.)

2 Put the oil, vinegar, tomatoes, onion, and garlic in a large salad bowl. Sprinkle with salt and lots of pepper and toss to coat. Add the croutons and the basil. Taste and adjust the seasoning and serve.

Grilled Bread Salad. If you have the grill going . . . : Instead of cutting the bread and oven-toasting it, heat a charcoal or gas grill to medium-high heat and set the rack 4 inches from the heat source. Grill the bread briefly on both sides, 3 to 5 minutes total. Let cool a bit, then cut roughly into large cubes. Proceed with Step 2.

Bread Salad with Greens. The winter version: Instead of the tomatoes, use 2 cups cooked chopped greens, like escarole, kale, or spinach. Add $^1/_2$ cup currants or raisins and $^1/_4$ cup toasted pine nuts (page 321). You may want to add more olive oil and lemon juice too.

Corn Bread Salad. The southwestern twist: Use Corn Bread (page 687) instead of plain bread croutons. In Step 2, add 1 teaspoon Chili Powder (page 814) to the tomato mixture and substitute $^1/_2$ cup sliced scallion for the red onion if you like. Use cilantro instead of basil or parsley.

Bread Salad, Lebanese Style

Fattoush

> **MAKES:** 4 servings
> **TIME:** 30 minutes

The trick to fattoush is to toast the pita until nice and crisp. To turn the salad into a meal, just spread a layer of Braised Lentils, Moroccan Style (page 598) on a plate

Crudités

Crudités—essentially cut-up raw vegetables—are quick and easy to throw together, and cutting vegetables for crudités is pretty simple: Keep the pieces large enough to pick up easily and dip without dipping your fingers (very small pieces are annoying) or breaking the vegetable, but small or slender enough to pop into your mouth or bite easily; usually about $^1/_2$ inch wide is just right. Broccoli and cauliflower florets work best with about an inch or so of stem to hold onto; core and seed bell peppers and slice into $^1/_2$-inch-or-so-wide sticks, cutting the curved ends off (chop them and use in a rice salad, with pasta, stir-fried vegetables, or fried rice) if you like.

You can prepare all the components of a crudité platter, including the dip, in advance. Just store the raw vegetables in ice water to keep them crisp and the lightly cooked vegetables in airtight containers; both will hold for a day or so. Drain the raw vegetables well and put them on a kitchen towel or a few layers of paper towels to dry off (dip doesn't stick to wet vegetables); bring the cooked vegetables to room temperature.

1. Baby carrots (not the nubby kind sold in bags) with the green tops, tops trimmed to 1 inch and carrots peeled
2. Asparagus spears, trimmed and very lightly steamed (still crunchy and bright green)
3. Green or wax beans, steamed or boiled until crisp-tender
4. Sugarsnap peas, raw if very fresh or very lightly steamed
5. Belgian endive leaves
6. Jícama, peeled and cut into sticks
7. Purple potatoes, steamed until just tender and cut into long wedges
8. Small "new" potatoes, steamed whole
9. Red or white radishes, whole or cut in half

Nearly any salad dressing works fine, as do bean dips.

1. Traditional Pesto (page 768)
2. Parsley "Pesto," or Parsley Purée (page 768)
3. Garlic Mayonnaise or any flavored mayonnaise or Vegannaise (pages 771–772)
4. Real Ranch Dressing (page 772)
5. The Simplest Yogurt Sauce (page 774)
6. Blue Cheese Dressing (page 212)
7. Ginger-Scallion Sauce (page 779)
8. Creamy Cilantro-Mint Chutney (page 784)
9. Simple Miso Dipping Sauce (page 781)
10. Nutty Miso Sauce (page 782)
11. Peanut Sauce, Six Ways (page 794)
12. Tahini Sauce (page 796)
13. Creamy Bistro Dressing or Sauce (page 799)
14. Hummus (page 614)
15. Blue Cheese Dip (page 212)
16. Any bean dip (pages 612–617)
17. Any well-seasoned vegetable purée (page 387)

and put a mound of Fattoush on top; crumbled feta cheese makes a nice garnish. Or just serve the fattoush alone or tossed with greens.

Four 6-inch pita breads

$1/2$ cup minced fresh mint, parsley, or basil leaves

$1/4$ cup minced parsley leaves

1 large or 2 medium ripe tomatoes, cored and roughly chopped

1 medium cucumber, peeled, seeded if you like (see page 293), and roughly chopped

1 red or yellow bell pepper, cored, seeded, and roughly chopped

About $1/2$ cup Vinaigrette (page 762) or extra virgin olive oil mixed with freshly squeezed lemon juice

① Preheat the oven to 350°F. Cut the pitas like pies, into 8 wedges each, put the pieces on a baking sheet, and toast in the oven, turning once or twice, until both sides are crisp and golden, about 15 minutes. Let cool. (The pita croutons may be made to this point and kept tightly covered for up to 2 days.)

② While the bread is toasting, combine the mint, parsley, tomatoes, cucumber, and bell pepper together in a large salad bowl, adding either vinaigrette or olive oil and lemon juice to taste. Toss several times to coat. Add the pita wedges and toss gently again. Taste, adjust the seasoning, and serve.

Whole Grain Bread Salad

MAKES: 4 to 6 servings

TIME: About 45 minutes

This salad is like stuffing, only fresher and brighter. A good multigrain loaf, cut into thick slices, is best, but supermarket bread will work; get the 7- or 9-grain sandwich kind and use 8 regular slices instead of 4 thick ones. Great with Roasted Squash Pieces in the Shell (page 366) or any frittata/flat omelet (pages 182–185). Or serve with Grilled Mushrooms (page 316) or a cup of Chile Bisque (page 131.) Also great for lunch with a slice of strong cheese on the side.

8 ounces whole grain bread (stale is fine), preferably thickly sliced

8 ounces kale, cooked, squeezed dry, and chopped (about 1 cup packed; page 239)

$1/4$ cup extra virgin olive oil

2 tablespoons balsamic vinegar

$1/2$ cup chopped dried figs (10 to 12, depending on the type)

$1/4$ cup chopped pitted dates (about 4)

1 shallot, minced

1 tablespoon minced fresh sage, or 1 teaspoon dried

Salt and freshly ground black pepper

¼ cup chopped toasted hazelnuts (page 40) for garnish

1. Preheat the oven to 400°F. Put the bread on a baking sheet and toast, turning once or twice, until golden and dry, 10 to 20 minutes, depending on the thickness of the slices. Remove from the oven and cool.

2. While the bread is toasting, put the kale, oil, vinegar, figs, dates, shallot, and sage in a large salad bowl. Sprinkle with salt and lots of pepper and toss to coat.

3. Fill a bowl with water and soak the bread for about 3 minutes. Gently squeeze a slice dry, wringing it like a cloth, and use your fingers to crumble it into the salad bowl. Repeat with the remaining slices. Toss well to combine the salad and let sit for 15 to 20 minutes or up to an hour, tossing occasionally. Taste and adjust the seasoning, garnish, and serve.

Hearty Bread Salad with Fresh Figs. If you've got 'em, use 'em: Instead of the dried figs and dates, use 1 cup chopped fresh figs (about 5 or 6 whole figs, depending on the type).

Pasta and Noodle Salads

Over the years I've found that American-style pasta salads—the pseudo-Italian kinds you see at supermarket deli counters and unfortunately too many potluck dinners—almost always disappoint. You often end up with something that's neither salad nor pasta, suffering from muddy flavors, too much acidity, or utter blandness. (I'd just as soon eat the real deal at room temperature—see 8 Pastas and Noodles that are Delicious at Room Temperature at right.) So to make delicious cold dishes with noodles or macaroni as the main ingredient, you really have to tap the ingredients and techniques of other countries.

And then follow these two rules:

Do not refrigerate: The notion that you can make pasta salad the night before, throw it in the fridge, then pull it out at any time is, well, wrong, the worst kind of kitchen expediency, one that—in the name of ease—leaves you with a congealed, flavor-muted dish. Like most salads, those based on pasta do not improve with age, though a couple hours at room temperature does no harm. Basically, make and eat.

Generally, it's best to avoid greens in pasta salad: Pasta is heavy and durable, and most greens are light and fragile (kale, collards, and dandelion are among the few exceptions). If you must use greens, stick to sturdy specimens like hearts of romaine and toss them in just before serving or, even better, add herb leaves—basil is almost always perfect—since they add not only freshness but also great flavor.

8 Pastas or Noodles that are Delicious at Room Temperature

1. Pasta with Garlic and Oil (page 443)
2. Pasta with any version of Fast Tomato Sauce (page 445)
3. Linguini with Raw Tomato Sauce (page 446)
4. Pasta with Broccoli, Cauliflower, or Broccoli Raab (page 452)
5. Pasta with Caramelized Onions (page 453)
6. Pasta with Mushrooms (page 454)
7. Crisp-Fried Noodle Cake (page 469)
8. Stir-Fried Wide Rice Noodles with Pickled Vegetables (page 472)

Japanese-Style Summertime Pasta Salad

Hiyashi Chuka

Serves 4
Time: 30 minutes

A Japanese summertime staple, easy to make and adapt to what you have on hand or find at the market. Essen-

Ⓕ Fast   Ⓜ Make Ahead   Ⓥ Vegan

tially it's little more than a plate of cold noodles, a couple of things stirred into them, with a sweet, brothy dressing that pulls everything together. This version is on the lean side, but I've had this salad with all sorts of delicious toppings; see the list that follows for some ideas. Leave out the eggs (from the recipe or the topping ideas in the list) and you have a vegan dish.

Ramen noodles are traditionally used here, though you can substitute soba, somen, even spaghetti, as long as you adjust the cooking time.

Salt

12 ounces dried ramen noodles

$1/2$ cup Kombu Dashi (page 103) or water

3 tablespoons soy sauce, or more to taste

3 tablespoons rice wine vinegar

1 tablespoon sugar, preferably superfine

1 teaspoon dark sesame oil

1 teaspoon grated or minced peeled fresh ginger

2 tablespoons neutral oil, like grapeseed or corn

3 eggs, lightly beaten

1 cucumber, peeled if waxed, seeded, and julienned

$1/2$ cup loosely packed shredded nori (see page 356)

$1/4$ cup Pickled Ginger (page 821)

2 tablespoons sesame seeds, toasted (see page 321)

$1/4$ cup thinly sliced scallion

Wasabi to taste (optional)

1 Put a large pot of water on to boil and salt it. Drop in the ramen and cook, stirring occasionally, until tender. Rinse in a colander under cold running water.

2 Meanwhile, stir together the dashi, soy sauce, vinegar, sugar, sesame oil, and grated ginger. Taste, add more soy sauce if necessary, and set aside.

3 Put 2 tablespoons of the neutral oil in a wok or large skillet, preferably nonstick, over medium heat. When hot, add the eggs and swirl the pan so they form the thinnest possible layer; you're aiming for a thin egg crêpe of sorts. Cook just until set and transfer the crêpe to a cutting board. Cut into $1/4$-inch strips and set aside.

4 Divide the noodles among 4 serving bowls, then divide the egg, julienned cucumber, nori, and pickled ginger among them. (In Japan, these ingredients are usually either nested in individual piles on top of or around the noodles, though you can just scatter the toppings over the noodles if that seems too fussy.) Top each salad with a pinch of the toasted sesame seeds and the thinly sliced scallion.

5 Serve the noodles with a small bowl of the dressing on the side and let your guests dress and toss the salad at the table. Pass wasabi to season the noodles with if you like.

10 Toppings for Japanese-Style Summertime Pasta Salad

1. Grilled or sautéed shiitake mushrooms (pages 253 or 314)
2. Rehydrated chopped dried tomatoes
3. A spoonful or two of Simple Seaweed Salad (page 53)
4. Spicy Pickles, Asian Style, (page 95, or use store-bought)
5. Individual Poached Eggs (page 169) instead of scrambled eggs
6. Chopped Hard-Cooked Eggs (page 166) instead of scrambled eggs
7. A handful of bean sprouts
8. Crunchy Crumbled Tempeh (page 674)
9. A spoonful or two of silken tofu
10. Cooked black or white soybeans ($1/4$ cup or so per serving)

Israeli Couscous Salad

SERVES 4 to 6

TIME: About 30 minutes

Both Israeli and "regular" couscous are actually forms of pasta; the only difference is size. Regular couscous is tiny; Israeli couscous is about the size of plump peppercorns, which makes it better for salads. (See page 534 for more information.)

The trick to this salad is balancing the strong flavors that go into it: the funkiness of capers and preserved lemon shouldn't dominate the sweetness of the cinnamon and raisins; the blandness of the pasta and the chickpeas shouldn't overwhelm the sprightly raw onion, parsley, and tomato. Taste as you go and adjust as necessary.

Salt

1 pound Israeli couscous

$^1/_4$ cup extra virgin olive oil

2 tablespoons sherry vinegar or freshly squeezed lemon juice

$^1/_2$ teaspoon ground cumin

$^1/_8$ teaspoon ground cinnamon

1 Preserved Lemon (page 427), skin only, sliced as thinly as possible (optional), or 1 tablespoon minced lemon zest

$^1/_2$ small red onion, thinly sliced

$^1/_4$ cup currants or golden raisins

$^1/_2$ cup cooked or drained canned chickpeas

2 tablespoons capers

$^1/_2$ cup pine nuts, toasted (see page 87)

1 pint cherry or grape tomatoes, halved if large

$^1/_2$ cup chopped parsley leaves

1 Bring a large pot of water to a boil and salt it. Cook the couscous, stirring occasionally, until tender but not mushy. When it is ready, drain it well, rinse it very briefly with cold water, drain again, and transfer it to a large mixing bowl.

2 Dress the couscous with the olive oil, vinegar, ground spices, and a pinch of salt and toss it vigorously to ensure the spices are well distributed throughout the pasta. Taste and add more acid or salt as necessary.

3 Add the preserved lemon, onion, currants, chickpeas, capers, pine nuts, tomatoes, and parsley to the couscous, toss them through once or twice, and, if possi-

ble, let the salad rest at room temperature for an hour before serving.

Whole Grain Salad with Preserved Lemon. Heartier (and a little slower to prepare): Instead of the couscous, use about 5 cups cooked whole grain, like farro, barley, or wheat or rye berries.

Couscous Salad with Fennel and Raisins

MAKES: 4 servings

TIME: 30 minutes, including cooking the couscous

F V

Couscous makes a great salad, and it's so quick cooking it can be considered almost last minute. Here it's combined with juicy raisins and crunchy fennel; the Lemon Vinaigrette pulls it all together.

2 $^1/_2$ cups cooked couscous, regular, whole wheat, or "Israeli," or other quick-cooking medium grain (page 537) or 1 cup uncooked

$^1/_2$ cup raisins

$^1/_2$ cup port or red wine

1 fennel bulb

1 teaspoon fennel seed, ground

Salt and freshly ground black pepper

Lemon Vinaigrette (page 763)

1 If you haven't already, cook the couscous according to the directions on page 537. Meanwhile, soak the raisins in the port. Drain the grains in a strainer and rinse.

2 Trim the fennel and cut it into small bite-sized pieces. Reserve a few of the feathery fronds for garnish. Toss the couscous, raisins and port, fennel, ground fennel seed, and salt and pepper together (at this point you can let the salad sit for up to an hour), then spoon about $^1/_4$ cup vinaigrette over all and toss again. Taste and adjust

the seasoning, add more vinaigrette as you like, and, if possible, let the salad rest at room temperature for at least a few minutes—and up to an hour—before serving.

Couscous Salad with Hazelnuts. Crunchy: Put 1 tablespoon extra virgin olive oil in a small skillet over medium heat and, when hot, add $^1/_2$ cup hazelnuts. Toast, shaking the pan occasionally and sprinkling with salt and pepper, until lightly browned. Let sit for 10 minutes, then toss with the salad.

Couscous Salad with Olives. Omit the raisins and soaking wine; substitute $^1/_2$ cup chopped pitted black olives, preferably marinated.

Orzo Salad, Greek Style

Serves 4

Time: About 25 minutes

Orzo (a small rice-shaped pasta) is among the best pastas for salad; it doesn't become soggy or mushy, at least not easily. Here it's married with the classic ingredients of a Greek country salad—orzo is of Greek origin, after all—plus an amped-up quantity of herbs to give it freshness and zing. Using 2 or more herbs in the mix will give the salad real complexity; but if you have only one, that's fine too—add to taste.

Whole wheat orzo. if you can find it, is also great here, as are other small whole wheat pasta shapes, like tiny shells.

Salt

8 ounces (about 1 $^1/_2$ cups) orzo

$^1/_4$ cup plus 2 tablespoons olive oil

Juice of 1 lemon

Freshly ground black pepper

1 $^1/_2$ cups chopped ripe tomato

3 scallions, thinly sliced

$^1/_2$ cup black olives, pitted and roughly chopped

1 cup mixed fresh herbs, like basil, parsley, mint or oregano, stemmed and chopped

$^1/_2$ cup grated aged (firm) feta cheese or ricotta salata

1 Put a large pot of water on to boil and salt it. Drop in the orzo and cook until tender, then rinse in a colander under cold running water. Transfer the cooked and cooled orzo to a large mixing bowl.

2 Dress the orzo with the olive oil, lemon juice, salt, and pepper and toss it to coat the pasta. Taste and add more acid or salt as necessary.

3 Add the tomato, scallions, olives, and herbs to the dressed orzo; toss them through once or twice. If possible, let the salad rest at room temperature for an hour before serving. Just before serving, sprinkle the grated cheese over the salad.

Jean-Georges's Rice Noodle Salad with Grapefruit and Peanuts

MAKES: 4 to 6 servings

TIME: About 30 minutes

This is an adaptation of a recipe from my first book with Jean-Georges Vongerichten, *Cooking at Home with A Four-Star Chef.* Here cold rice noodles are spiked with grapefruit, peanuts, vegetables, herbs, and spices to make a flavor-packed salad in which the whole is greater than the sum of its parts but individual flavors remain distinct.

Use a couple of oranges, tangerines, or even peeled and sliced fresh plums or peaches in place of the grapefruit if you like.

1 or 2 small fresh chiles, minced, or about 1 teaspoon hot red pepper flakes, or to taste

1 clove garlic, finely minced

1 tablespoon packed brown sugar

About 1/4 cup freshly squeezed lime juice

2 tablespoons soy sauce

8 ounces rice vermicelli

1 stalk lemongrass

1 large grapefruit, peeled, sectioned, and chopped

1/2 cup chopped roasted peanuts

1 medium to large ripe tomato, peeled, cored, seeded, and chopped

3 scallions, minced

1/3 cup coarsely chopped fresh mint leaves

1/2 cup coarsely chopped fresh cilantro leaves

1 In a small bowl, combine the chiles, garlic, sugar, lime juice, and soy sauce. Taste and adjust the seasoning. (This dressing may be prepared a day or two in advance; if anything, its flavor will improve.)

2 Soak the rice noodles in fairly hot water (about 120°F, just too hot to touch) for 10 to 20 minutes, or until soft. Meanwhile, set a large pot of water to boil. Trim the stalk of lemongrass (see page 767) and peel off enough layers to expose its tender core. Finely mince enough to make about 1 tablespoon.

3 Mix the grapefruit, 1/3 cup of the peanuts, the tomato, scallions, mint, 1/3 cup of the cilantro, and the lemongrass together in a large bowl.

4 Drain the noodles and plunge them into the boiling water. When the water returns to a boil, drain the noodles and rinse in a colander under cold running water until cooled. Drain well, then toss in the large bowl with the grapefruit mixture and the dressing.

5 Divide the salad among serving bowls, garnish with the remaining cilantro and peanuts, and serve.

The Basics of Pickling Fruits and Vegetables

Pickling is a process that's been around for thousands of years, sustaining people through winters, expeditions, wars, and famine. Every cuisine has at least a handful of pickled things, and pickling isn't simply a means of food preservation anymore; with its variety of salty, sour, sweet, and hot flavors, pickled food is almost universally appealing. We're most familiar with cucumbers, specifically the small and nubby Kirby cucumbers, as pickles, so much so that the word *pickle* almost inherently means a pickled cucumber. But really almost anything—from cabbage to peppers to watermelon rind to hard-cooked eggs—can be pickled.

Simply put, pickling is the introduction of acid to a food that prevents the growth of harmful microbes. There are two basic methods for getting this acid into foods: by using vinegar (an acid) or by salting (using straight salt or a saltwater brine). Through osmosis, the vinegar penetrates by replacing the natural water in the food. Salting is a slightly less direct and more complex process where the salt draws out the food's natural water and allows just enough bacterial growth to produce lactic acid, which then ferments or pickles the food. Cabbage Kimchi (page 96) is a perfect example of this salt-pickling process, as are Kosher Pickles (page 97). Salt is also used when pickling with vinegar to draw out water to crisp the vegetables and to keep the vinegar that seeps into the vegetable or fruit undiluted.

Though vinegar and salt help flavor pickles, often extra seasonings—spices, herbs, garlic, onions, and other aromatics—are added as well. Dill is a favorite seasoning for cucumber pickles in the United States, as are garlic, mustard, black peppercorns, and chiles or hot red pepper flakes. But you can use any spice or herb you like; create an Asian-flavored pickle with ginger, Sichuan peppercorns, or Five-Spice Powder (page 816); a Caribbean flavor by using Jerk Seasoning (page 818); and so on. The options are virtually endless.

There are only a few guidelines to keep in mind when choosing your items to be pickled: The first is freshness. Use the freshest foods for pickling; food that has blemishes or soft spots will start with more of the harmful microbes you want to avoid. Also, consider the size and

F Fast   **M** Make Ahead   **V** Vegan

density of the fruit or vegetable; smaller and softer pieces pickle more quickly than larger pieces.

You also want to think about timing; the pickle recipes here can take anywhere from twenty minutes to several days to cure. If you want your pickles right away, go with the Quick-Pickled Vegetables (below) or Spicy Pickles, Asian Style (below). The Three-Day and Kosher Pickles (pages 96 and 97) take two to three days, and Miso-Cured one to two days.

Quick-Pickled Vegetables

MAKES: 4 servings

TIME: 1 hour or less

Salting vegetables, even for just 15 minutes, really changes their texture and flavor; they become both pliable and crunchy. Of course, the thinner you slice the vegetables, the more quickly they will pickle. Shredding is also a good option to shave off a few minutes of salting and pickling time.

Other vegetables to use in this recipe: shredded or sliced carrots, radish, jícama, or kohlrabi; thinly sliced celery, fennel, cabbage, or onion.

    1 pound cucumber, zucchini, summer squash, or
        eggplant

    1 tablespoon salt

    1/2 teaspoon sugar

    1 tablespoon minced fresh dill or 1 teaspoon dried

    2 teaspoons vinegar

1 Wash the vegetables well, peel them if you like, and slice them as thinly as possible (a mandoline is perfect for this). Put the vegetables in a colander and sprinkle them with the salt; toss well. Gently rub the salt into the vegetables with your hands for a minute.

2 Let sit in the sink or in a bowl for 15 to 30 minutes (cucumbers take less time than eggplant), tossing and

squeezing every few minutes. When little or no more liquid comes out of the vegetable, rinse well in cold water. Put in a bowl.

3 Toss with the sugar, dill, and vinegar and serve immediately; this does not keep well.

Quick-Pickled Vegetables, Mexican Style. This makes a spicy garnish for tacos, rice, beans, and more: Use an assortment of thinly sliced radishes, jícama, cucumber, and red onion. Substitute cilantro for the dill; add a thinly sliced jalapeño if you like (or habanero if you like it mouth-searing); and use red wine vinegar.

Quick-Pickled Mango or Papaya. A perfect use for underripe mangoes or papaya, and it easily moves between Indian, Southeast Asian, Latin, and Caribbean cuisines: Substitute thinly sliced or julienned still-firm mango or papaya for the vegetables and cilantro, mint, or ginger for the dill.

Spicy Pickles, Asian Style

MAKES: 4 servings

TIME: At least 1 hour

Spicy East Asian pickles that are traditionally served in small portions with an assortment of other pickled or fermented items along with meals. I love them for their hot, salty, and slightly sweet flavors.

Other vegetables to use in this recipe: radish, jícama, celery, cabbage, kohlrabi, cauliflower, turnips, or summer squash.

    1 pound Kirby cucumbers

    1 tablespoon salt

    3 to 4 tablespoons Chile-Garlic Paste (page 830) or
        store-bought (try Asian markets)

    1 teaspoon sugar

    2 tablespoons dark sesame oil

    2 tablespoons soy sauce

❶ Wash the cucumbers well, scrub them if they're spiny, and cut into $1/4$-inch-thick slices. Put them in a colander and sprinkle them with the salt; toss well. Gently rub the salt into the cucumbers with your hands for a minute.

❷ Lay a plate over the vegetable mixture while it is still in the colander and weight the plate with whatever is handy: a few cans, your teakettle filled with water, or a brick, for example. Let rest for about 30 minutes; 1 hour is fine. Rinse the cucumbers and then pat dry with paper towels; put in a bowl.

❸ Toss with the chile-garlic paste, sugar, sesame oil, and soy sauce and let sit for at least 30 minutes. Serve immediately or transfer to an airtight container, packing the cucumbers down into the container so the liquid comes to the surface, cover, and refrigerate for up to 3 weeks.

Salted Cabbage with Sichuan Peppercorns. A sweet and hot quick pickling: Substitute 6 cups shredded green or Napa cabbage for the cucumbers and use 1 tablespoon each salt, mirin, soy sauce, and Sichuan peppercorns, reducing the sesame oil to 1 teaspoon. Skip Step 1. Instead mix all the ingredients together in a bowl (toss very well) then press in the bowl with a weighted plate (see Step 2); do not rinse the cabbage. Remove the weight, toss again, and serve or cover and refrigerate; it will keep for 5 days or so.

Kimchi

Spicy Korean-Style Cabbage

MAKES: 12 servings
TIME: About 2 hours, largely unattended

Ⓜ Ⓥ

The best-known pickled cabbage in the Unites States is sauerkraut, but rapidly gaining in popularity is kimchi, the super-spicy Korean version. You can buy kimchi in jars at many Asian (and especially Korean) markets, but making it yourself is neither difficult nor especially time consuming and gives you far more control over the level of spiciness. Kept refrigerated, this will keep for about a week.

Other vegetables that work: scallions (use about 50, total, split in half lengthwise) or 2 to 3 pounds of daikon, black radish, or turnip, peeled and shredded.

1 medium head (about 2 pounds) white, Savoy, or Napa cabbage, separated into leaves

$1/2$ cup coarse salt, more or less

20 scallions, including most of the green, trimmed and roughly chopped

1 tablespoon hot red pepper flakes, or to taste

$1/4$ cup soy sauce

$1/4$ cup minced garlic

$1/4$ cup sugar

❶ Layer the cabbage leaves in a colander, sprinkling a little salt between layers. Let sit over a bowl for at least 2 hours. When the cabbage is wilted, rinse and dry.

❷ Mix the scallions, red pepper flakes, soy sauce, garlic, and sugar together in a bowl. Roughly chop the cabbage and toss with the spice mixture. Serve immediately or refrigerate for up to a week; it will become stronger every day.

Three-Day Pickles

MAKES: about 30 pickle quarters or 15 halves
TIME: 3 days

Ⓜ Ⓥ

These sweet-and-sour pickles are certainly not the usual dill or bread-and-butter pickle. Technically a "refrigerator pickle" (since the curing must be done in the refrigerator), this recipe uses salt, sugar, and vinegar to add sweet-and-sour flavor. And the Pickling Spice adds layers of flavors that are warm (hot even, if you add more chiles) and quite exotic.

Other vegetables and fruit to use in this recipe: carrots, radishes, celery, fennel, kohlrabi, pearl onions, cauliflower, peppers, turnips, summer squash, eggplant, peaches, watermelon rind, spaghetti squash, or beets.

2 pounds Kirby cucumbers

6 tablespoons salt

2 cups white or white wine vinegar

$^1\!/_4$ cup sugar

$^1\!/_4$ cup Pickling Spice (page 819)

❶ Wash the cucumbers well, scrub them if they're spiny, and cut lengthwise into halves or quarters or slice. Put the cucumbers in a colander and sprinkle them with 2 tablespoons of the salt; toss well.

❷ Let sit in the sink or in a bowl for about 2 hours. Rinse the cucumbers and then pat dry with paper towels; put in a nonmetal bowl.

❸ Put the remaining $^1\!/_4$ cup salt, the vinegar, sugar, and pickling spice, along with 2 cups water, in a pot over high heat. Bring to a boil, then let cool for about 5 minutes. Pour the mixture over the cucumbers and let cool to room temperature. (Add more vinegar or water if the cucumbers are not covered.)

❹ Transfer the cucumbers and pickling liquid to airtight jars or containers; store in the refrigerator for at least 3 days or longer for stronger pickles. They will keep in their pickling liquid for up to 3 weeks.

Pickled Peaches, Afghan Style (Tershi). Used like a condiment (great with rice dishes), these potent tangy-sweet pickles can be anything from peaches to tomatoes to eggplant: Substitute peeled and sliced peaches for the cucumbers. Reduce the salt and sugar by half and use just cider vinegar (no water) to cover. Substitute 4 crushed cloves garlic, 2 teaspoons dried mint, 2 teaspoons coriander seeds, and 1 tablespoon hot red pepper flakes for the pickling spice. Skip Steps 1 and 2; proceed with the recipe. These pickles will keep indefinitely.

Kosher Pickles, the Right Way

MAKES: about 30 pickle quarters or 15 halves
TIME: 1 to 2 days

No vinegar here, so these don't keep very long (about a week) but they'll be eaten quickly enough that you won't ever see one go bad.

$^1\!/_3$ cup kosher salt

1 cup boiling water

2 pounds Kirby cucumbers, washed (scrub if spiny) and cut lengthwise into halves or quarters

At least 5 cloves garlic, crushed

1 large bunch dill, preferably fresh and with flowers, or 2 tablespoons dried dill and 1 teaspoon dill seeds or 1 tablespoon coriander seeds

❶ Combine the salt and boiling water in a large bowl; stir to dissolve the salt. Add a handful of ice cubes to cool the mixture, then add all the remaining ingredients.

❷ Add cold water to cover. Use a plate slightly smaller than the diameter of the bowl and a small weight to keep the cucumbers immersed. Set aside at room temperature.

❸ Begin sampling the cucumbers after 4 hours if you've quartered them, 8 hours if you've cut them in half. In either case, it will probably take from 12 to 24 or even 48 hours for them to taste pickly enough to suit your taste.

❹ When they are ready, refrigerate them, still in the brine. The pickles will continue to ferment as they sit, more quickly at room temperature, more slowly in the refrigerator. They will keep well for up to a week.

Miso-Cured Vegetables

MAKES: 4 servings
TIME: 1 or 2 days

A through-and-through Japanese pickle. You can use any type of miso, from the milder white to the robust red; the vegetables pick up the subtle flavors of the miso, and saltier misos pickle more quickly.

Other vegetables to use in this recipe: radish, jícama, celery, kohlrabi, or summer squash.

1 pound turnips, carrots, eggplant, zucchini, or a mixture

At least 2 cups any type of miso

❶ Peel the vegetables and cut them into slices $^1/_4$ inch thick or thinner (a mandoline is perfect for this).

❷ Spread the miso in a bowl, an inch or two deep, and bury the vegetable slices in the miso. Cover with plastic wrap and let stand at room temperature.

❸ After 24 hours, fish out one of the slices, rinse it off, and sample it; depending on the vegetable and the thickness of the slice, it may require another 24 hours.

❹ To serve, rinse the slices and cut them into small pieces. Refrigerate the miso, which may be reused several times to make pickles, or for any other recipe requiring it. These keep for a few days, but they're really at their best right when they're ready.

Soups

Soup making is among the most basic cooking tasks; in fact you can think of it as a one-pot course on fundamental cooking techniques. A single recipe can demonstrate how to manipulate different seasonings,

vegetables, and other ingredients both alone and in combination. You practice timing, controlling temperature, and recognizing doneness, all in a comfortable manner, because no other type of dish is as forgiving as soup. Make a mistake—short of burning the pan—and the results are usually delicious anyway, in large part because, unlike for many other dishes, every bit of flavor remains in what you eat.

But—and this is a real *but*—although soup is a terrific way to use imperfect produce and leftovers like grains or beans, the old saying "junk in, junk out" also applies to the pan on the stove. You must stick to the basic principle of using good, honest ingredients.

Having said that, don't let anyone tell you that soup

is difficult or time consuming; it's only rarely either. Nearly every recipe in this chapter takes less than thirty minutes to prepare; if it takes longer, most of the cooking time is unattended. And almost every stock and soup can be made ahead and reheated; some can even be served cold.

All of this makes soup an ideal first course for entertaining or weeknight suppers or an easy course to build a meal around.

Every soup is best when it begins with stock, so if at all possible, begin with one of the stocks on pages 101–103; the body and extra flavor provided by this base will improve any soup. If you cannot, though, just begin with water (read "Why Not Use Water?" on page 100), but add an extra dose of aromatic vegetables—carrot, celery, and onion are the basics—to compensate.

The Basics of Making Stock

I once thought that roasting vegetables in olive oil was essential when preparing a stock with no meat or fish. And while I still believe the best vegetable stock begins that way, the extensive testing I (and others) performed while putting together this book demonstrated to me that you can make quite a decent vegetarian stock in less than forty minutes. You can make an even better vegetarian stock in an hour and a half (more time than that yields no further improvement), and the process remains simple.

Omnivores may argue that there is no stock like those based on chicken, veal, or beef, and to some extent that's true; one can never duplicate the unctuous texture that comes from glycerin, a protein found largely in bones. But vegetable stocks do have body, and, just as in meat stocks, that body can be enhanced by reducing, or boiling out some of the cooking liquid. Furthermore, one could easily argue that vegetarian stocks have a cleaner, fresher taste than many meat stocks.

To open this section, I'm offering three recipes for straightforward vegetable stock, each a bit more work, a bit more flavorful, and a bit more time consuming than its predecessor. When you want to mimic the flavor of meat stock, try the mushroom stock recipe that follows them. I have also listed a few suggestions for easily varying these stocks. (I'd hoped to include an appraisal of store-bought vegetable stocks but, to date, none is consistently good enough to recommend. You're better off with water simmered for twenty minutes with an onion, a carrot, and a celery stalk—really.)

On Storing Stock

The problem with homemade stock is that it's so good that you eventually run out and have to make it again. This argues for cooking larger quantities at once. Fortu-

Why Not Use Water?

Stock is the liquid that results from simmering solids in water. The solids may be vegetables, meat, fish, poultry, herbs, spices, or any combination.

Although it is usually made in advance and strained, stock is only rarely served clear, as a consommé or broth (which, essentially, is stock with nothing, or very little, added to it). Far more often, it's combined with fresh vegetables or other ingredients—noodles, rice, eggs, cheese, and so on—to make a flavorful soup.

It pays to remember, though, that ultimately all stocks are based on water and that they're created by combining water and solids. So it stands to reason that you can begin any soup with water instead of stock, as long as you add sufficient vegetables and other flavorings and cook the mixture long enough for a flavorful liquid to develop.

In other words, stock is flavoring for soups and sauces that you can make in advance. But it is not the only way of flavoring them. If you don't have stock, start with water; add some wine, some extra vegetables, or some herbs. But don't make the mistake of thinking that there is no soup without stock.

nately, making big batches isn't much more difficult than making small ones. Then it just becomes a question of storing.

If you store it in the refrigerator and bring it back to a boil every second or third day, stock will keep more or less indefinitely. Freezing, of course, is more efficient.

Here you have a couple of options: One is to simply ladle or pour the stock into convenient-size containers—quarts are usually good. (You can recycle yogurt or similar containers.) Cover and freeze.

If you want to save space, boil the stock down to about half its original volume. Now you have concentrate. Just remember to add water when you start cooking it.

 Fast   Make Ahead   Ⓥ Vegan

Frozen stock will keep for weeks or months, though it does deteriorate somewhat in flavor over time. If you remember you have it, however, it's unlikely to last that long. And the cycle will begin again.

Simple, Easy, and Fast Vegetable Stock

MAKES: about 1 quart
TIME: 40 minutes, somewhat unattended

Within reason, any stock you make is going to add more flavor to your soups and sauces than water. If you don't have all the ingredients listed here—it's a pretty minimal list, but you might not have celery or potatoes, for example—do without. And if you don't have a half hour for simmering, give it fifteen minutes. It'll still be worth it.

If, however, you have some flexibility, move on to the next recipe (or the one after that), add some of the ingredients from the sidebar on page 103, or simmer the vegetables for as long as an hour, adding a little more water if necessary.

Double the quantities here if you want to make enough stock to freeze.

2 carrots, cut into chunks

1 onion, quartered (don't bother to peel)

1 potato, cut into chunks

1 celery stalk, chopped

2 or 3 cloves garlic (don't bother to peel)

10 or 20 parsley stems or stems with leaves

2 tablespoons extra virgin olive oil

Salt and freshly ground black pepper

1 Combine everything in a saucepan or small stockpot with 6 cups water, using a pinch of salt and a bit of pepper. Bring to a boil, then adjust the heat so the mix-ture simmers steadily but gently and cook for about 30 minutes, or until the vegetables are tender. (Longer is better if you have the time.)

2 Strain, then taste and adjust the seasoning before using or storing.

One-Hour Vegetable Stock

MAKES: about 1 quart
TIME: 1 hour, somewhat unattended

There are a few differences between this and the preceding recipe: here you cut the vegetables into smaller pieces, which extracts greater flavor; you pan-cook them first, which browns them at least a bit and makes the flavor more complex; and you add a couple more ingredients (the mushrooms make a difference, as you'll quickly see, as does the soy sauce). Simmering time remains about the same, but if you have more time, use it.

Double the quantities here if you want to make enough stock to freeze.

2 tablespoons extra virgin olive oil

2 carrots, sliced

1 onion, quartered (don't bother to peel)

1 potato, sliced

1 celery stalk, chopped

2 or 3 cloves garlic (don't bother to peel)

5 to 10 white mushrooms, halved or sliced

10 to 20 parsley stems or stems with leaves

2 tablespoons soy sauce

Salt and freshly ground black pepper

1 Put the oil in a deep skillet or broad saucepan or casserole over medium-high heat. When hot, add the carrots, onion, potato, celery, garlic, and mushrooms. Cook without stirring for about 5 minutes, then stir once or twice and cook until the vegetables begin to brown. (If

you have more time, brown them well, stirring only infrequently.)

2 Add the parsley, 6 cups water, the soy sauce, and some pepper. Bring to a boil, then adjust the heat so the mixture simmers steadily but gently. Cook for about 30 minutes, or until the vegetables are very tender. (Longer is better if you have the time.)

3 Strain, then taste and adjust the seasoning, adding more soy sauce or a bit of salt, before using or storing.

Roasted Vegetable Stock

MAKES: 3 quarts
TIME: About 2 hours, largely unattended

Roasting the vegetables first to brown them well adds a complex family of flavors that you don't get otherwise. And if you use leeks in place of onions and add a few other ingredients not included in the preceding recipes, you wind up with something really fine. Because this is significantly more work than the other stocks, I double the quantity; it's not something you're likely to make at the last minute, so you might as well make enough for a couple of occasions. You can, of course, halve the quantities if you like.

$1/3$ cup extra virgin olive oil

2 well-washed leeks (see page 310), cut into chunks, or 2 large onions, quartered (don't bother to peel)

4 carrots, cut into chunks

2 celery stalks, cut into chunks

1 parsnip, cut into chunks (optional)

2 potatoes, quartered

6 cloves garlic

15 to 20 white mushrooms, halved or sliced

A small bunch of parsley leaves, plus 10 sprigs 2 or 3 sprigs fresh thyme

$1/4$ cup soy sauce, or more to taste

10 black peppercorns

$1/2$ cup white wine

Salt and freshly ground black pepper

1 Preheat the oven to 450°F. Combine the oil, leeks, carrots, celery, parsnip, potatoes, garlic, and mushrooms in a large roasting pan; stir to coat all the vegetables with oil. Put the pan in the oven and roast, shaking the pan occasionally and turning the ingredients once or twice, until everything is nicely browned. This will take about 45 minutes; don't rush it.

2 Use a slotted spoon to scoop the roasted vegetables into a stockpot; add the herbs, $1/4$ cup soy sauce, peppercorns, wine, salt to taste, and 2 quarts water. Turn the heat to high. Meanwhile, put the roasting pan over a burner on high heat and add 2 to 4 cups water, depending on the depth of the pan. Bring it to a boil and cook, scraping off all the bits of food that have stuck to the bottom. Pour this mixture into the stockpot (along with 2 more cups water if you used only 2 cups for deglazing).

3 Bring to a boil, then partially cover and adjust the heat so the mixture sends up a few bubbles at a time. Cook until the vegetables are very soft, 30 to 45 minutes. Strain, pressing on the vegetables to extract as much juice as possible. Taste and add more soy sauce, salt, or ground pepper if necessary before using or storing.

Mushroom Stock

MAKES: about 6 cups
TIME: About 1 hour

Mushroom stock has a pronounced mushroom flavor that might compete with other ingredients; for most of the soups in this chapter, you will probably want to use one of the preceding three vegetable stocks or plain water. But when there are mushrooms in the soup, or if you plan to use the stock as the foundation for a richly flavored sauce, this is the recipe to turn to.

2 tablespoons neutral oil, like grapeseed or corn

1 small onion, 2 shallots, or 1 leek, well washed and sliced

2 carrots, chopped

2 celery stalks, chopped

Salt and freshly ground black pepper

1 pound white mushrooms, chopped into small pieces

1 ounce dried shiitake, porcini, or Chinese mushrooms or a combination

10 to 20 parsley stems or stems with leaves

2 bay leaves (optional)

1 Put half the oil in a large pan over medium-high heat. When hot, add the onion and cook, stirring occasionally, until soft, about 3 minutes. Add the carrots and celery and sprinkle with salt and pepper. Cook, stirring frequently, until tender, another 10 minutes or so. Remove with a slotted spoon.

2 Put the remaining oil in the pan, turn the heat to high, and when the oil is hot, add the white mushrooms. Cook, stirring, until they give up their juices and begin to brown well, about 10 minutes. Sprinkle with salt, then add the dried mushrooms and cooked vegetables and stir.

3 Stir in 2 quarts water, along with the parsley and bay leaves if you're using them. Bring to a boil, then reduce the heat so that the stock bubbles vigorously. Cook, stirring once or twice, until the vegetables are very soft and the stock has reduced slightly, about 30 minutes. Strain and use or store.

Kombu Dashi

MAKES: about 2 quarts
TIME: 15 minutes

Dashi is the building block of Japanese cuisine and usually flavored with dried bonito (a tunalike fish). But this variation is just as traditional. It may have roots in Japan's Buddhist vegetarian tradition, but I think it's far more likely that home cooks in Japan know that any stock is better than no stock, and if you didn't have dried tuna around, or didn't have the money to buy it, this was the next best thing.

I add ginger to my kombu dashi because I usually have it handy and it adds a nice secondary flavor. Feel free to omit it.

1 piece dried kelp (kombu), 4 to 6 inches long
2 or 3 nickel-sized slices ginger (don't bother to peel)

1 Combine the kelp, ginger, and 2 quarts water in a medium saucepan over medium heat. Do not allow the mixture to come to a boil; as soon as it is about to, turn off the heat and remove the kelp. (You can use it as a vegetable at this point; see page 356 for some ideas).

2 Let the ginger sit in the stock for a couple of minutes as it cools, then strain. Use the dashi immediately or refrigerate for up to 2 days.

No-Cook Dashi. Many Japanese cooks believe this to be a superior version (and it saves you time), but it requires some advance planning: Immerse the dried kelp in 2 quarts of cold water in a bowl on your way out the door in the morning. It will infuse the water with its flavor in 6 to 8 hours. Strain and use as you would cooked dashi.

8 Simple Additions to Any Stock

Stock can be made more complex by the addition of any of these ingredients. Be careful not to add so many, however, that the flavor becomes muddied.

1. A whole head of garlic, left intact, will lend a distinctive but mellow flavor.

2. A 3- or 4-inch piece of seaweed, especially kelp or arame, will give a pleasant brininess (see Kombu Dashi, left). Do not boil the stock after adding the seaweed; just heat gently for 10 minutes or so.

3. Just about any vegetable, or the trimmings of any vegetable, will add flavor. You're almost always safe with members of the onion family (including their peels and other trimmings), tomatoes, and the

milder, sweeter root vegetables. But beware that some vegetables will add unwanted flavors (do you want your stock to taste like broccoli?) and others will change the color. Be cautious: the stockpot is not a garbage can.

4. Stems of light herbs like parsley, dill, or chervil, or small amounts of other herbs, like thyme or tarragon, will add brightness and depth.

5. White wine will add acid, fruit, and complexity.

6. Whole spices, fresh or dried, like ginger, galangal, juniper berries, allspice, cloves, and so on, will surely add character. But use judiciously.

7. Any mushrooms, including dried porcini, again in small to moderate quantities, will add a distinctive but almost always welcome flavor. Also good are the stems of shiitakes, which are too tough to eat but add flavor to stocks.

8. Soy sauce performs wonders. A tablespoon or more in almost any stock will make you think you're brilliant.

Single-Vegetable Soups (or Nearly So)

The clarity of flavor that comes in a bowl of soup made from just one vegetable—or perhaps two—can be an eye opener. They're easy too, and they provide an instructive introduction to the world of soup making, while demonstrating the concept of letting your ingredients determine what you are going to cook. (You might call this being "ingredient-driven," as some chefs do.) An all-vegetable soup will be exactly as good as the quality of the featured vegetable. Forgotten cauliflower from the back of the refrigerator, for example, may make a serviceable Cauliflower Soup, Italian Style (page 105), but the ideal time to prepare that recipe is the day you bring a fresh head home from a garden or farmer's market.

Soups are varied, and when you focus on just one vegetable it's easier to experiment with trading like for like. Because, for example, many root vegetables are inter-

changeable, Glazed Carrot Soup (recipe follows) can easily be converted to a soup based on turnips, celery root, parsnips, or beets, depending on what's available and what you like. I always try to point out these options, but with only a little practice you'll generate your own ideas.

These recipes also demonstrate the principle that precooking vegetables, and many other foods, in a little oil

Ⓕ Fast   Ⓜ Make Ahead   Ⓥ Vegan

coaxes maximum flavor from them. Most of the time this happens in a pan, though a couple of the soups here highlight the benefits of oven roasting or even broiling.

Glazed Carrot Soup

MAKES: 4 servings

TIME: 45 minutes

You can glaze any vegetable that's starchy and sweet enough to convert a little cooking liquid into a syrupy coating, and nothing works better than carrots. Other root vegetables, like turnips, parsnips, rutabagas, or celery root, will give you a stronger flavor treated this way.

The idea is to lightly caramelize the vegetables as they become tender, using a little fat and some water, stock, or juice. The result is a wonderful creaminess.

Use the oil instead of butter and the soup becomes vegan.

A bonus: These kinds of soups are good chilled.

$1^{1}/_{2}$ pounds carrots, sliced

2 tablespoons butter or 1 tablespoon neutral oil, like grapeseed or corn

1 teaspoon sugar, maple syrup, or honey

Salt and freshly ground black pepper

6 cups vegetable stock (pages 101–102) or water

2 tablespoons minced fresh chervil or parsley for garnish

① Put the carrots, butter, $^{3}/_{4}$ cup water, and the sugar in a large skillet or saucepan and turn the heat to high. Sprinkle with salt and pepper, then bring the mixture to a boil. Cover, turn the heat to medium-low, and cook for about 5 minutes.

② Uncover and raise the heat a bit. Cook, stirring occasionally, until the liquid has evaporated and the carrots are cooking in the butter. Lower the heat and continue to cook, stirring occasionally, until the carrots are very tender, about 10 minutes more. If they start to stick or brown, add a tablespoon or so of stock.

③ Add the stock and turn the heat to high. Bring to a boil, stirring to dissolve the syrup at the bottom of the pan. Lower the heat so that the stock gently bubbles and cook, stirring occasionally, until it thickens slightly, about 10 minutes more.

④ Use an immersion blender to purée the soup in the pan or cool the mixture slightly, pour into a blender container, and carefully purée. (The soup may be made ahead to this point, cooled, and refrigerated. Serve cold or gently reheated.) Taste and adjust the seasoning if necessary. Serve, garnished with a sprinkle of chervil.

Glazed Carrots with Orange and Ginger. In Step 1, add 1 tablespoon peeled and minced ginger and 1 tablespoon grated orange zest to the carrot mixture and use orange juice instead of water.

Glazed Carrots with Garlic, Tequila, and Lime. In Step 1, add 1 tablespoon minced garlic and 1 teaspoon grated lime zest to the carrot mixture. Instead of water, use a mixture of $^{1}/_{4}$ cup fresh lime juice, $^{1}/_{4}$ cup tequila, and $^{1}/_{4}$ cup water. Instead of chervil or parsley, garnish with chopped cilantro.

Mustard-Glazed Carrot Soup. In Step 1, add 1 tablespoon Dijon mustard to the carrot mixture.

Cauliflower Soup, Italian Style

MAKES: 4 servings

TIME: 40 minutes

This is how many people cook vegetables in Italy, a technique that can then turn the vegetable into a soup—or pasta sauce—in a sec. Garlic, pepper, and oil are the distinguishing characteristics, and the technique is consistent and simple. Try this with broccoli, celery, cabbage, or Brussels sprouts. Garnish with grated Parmesan, pecorino Romano, or other hard sheep's-milk cheese, chopped hard-cooked eggs, or chopped fresh parsley.

$^1/_3$ cup extra virgin olive oil

1 onion, chopped

1 tablespoon minced garlic

$^1/_2$ teaspoon hot red pepper flakes, or to taste

1 medium head cauliflower, broken or cut into small florets

Salt and freshly ground black pepper

1 quart vegetable stock (pages 101–102)

4 Croutons, made with olive oil (page 806)

1 Put about half the oil in a saucepan or broad, deep casserole over medium heat. When hot, add the onion and cook, stirring occasionally, until it softens and just begins to brown, about 10 minutes. Stir in the garlic, red pepper, cauliflower, and some salt and black pepper and continue to cook, stirring, until the cauliflower glistens, 3 to 5 minutes. Add the stock and stir. Bring to a boil over high heat, then adjust the heat so the mixture simmers. Cook until the cauliflower is tender but not falling apart, 10 to 15 minutes.

2 Taste and adjust the seasoning, then stir in the remaining oil. Serve immediately, over the croutons.

Potato and Leek Soup

MAKES: 4 servings
TIME: 30 minutes

Leek-and-potato soup was once peasant food, but it's not surprising that the combination is the basis for more elegant soups: both vegetables are available year-round, easy to handle, and flavorful. Here, then, is the simplest potato and leek soup, a recipe that strikes me as medieval. It can warm you on a cold winter day or—if you make it in advance—cool you down in the middle of summer. The variations are all a little richer and more elaborate, but not much more difficult. Use the oil instead of butter to make this vegan.

13 Great Soups with Croutons

A garnish can be anything you add to soup at the last minute, from herbs to dumplings. But for crunch the best thing has got to be toasted bread. Croutons come to mind first, but bread crumbs are another, more subtle, option. Here's a list of soups that are killer with croutons.

1. Black Bean Soup or its variations (page 115)
2. Chickpea Soup with Saffron and Almonds or its variations (page 117)
3. Classic Lentil Soup or its variations (page 115)
4. Creamy Carrot Soup or its variations (page 129)
5. Creamy Cauliflower (or Broccoli) Soup (page 130)
6. Creamy Watercress, Spinach, or Sorrel Soup (page 132)
7. Farro Soup (page 141)
8. Onion Soup or its variations (page 108)
9. Rich Zucchini Soup (page 156)
10. Simplest Split Pea Soup (page 118)
11. Tomato Soup and its variations (page 112)
12. White Bean Soup (page 119)
13. Wintertime Tomato Soup and its variations (page 113)

2 tablespoons butter or extra virgin olive oil

3 medium potatoes, any type, peeled and cut into small cubes

3 leeks, white and light green parts only, well washed and sliced into thin rings

Salt and freshly ground black pepper

1 quart vegetable stock (pages 101–102) or water, preferably warmed

1 Put the butter or oil in a large, deep saucepan or casserole over medium heat. When the butter melts or the oil is hot, add the vegetables. Sprinkle with salt and pepper and cook, stirring, for 2 or 3 minutes.

2 Add the stock and cook until the vegetables are very tender, about 20 minutes. (You may prepare the

F Fast   **M** Make Ahead   **V** Vegan

Soup is among the most basic of cooked foods and can be as simple as Jook (page 140)—essentially rice boiled in water—or as complex as a whole-meal Minestrone (page 123). In between, there are as many soups as there are combinations of ingredients, and many are completely intuitive.

Some basic rules are scattered throughout these pages, but if you bear in mind that not everything works, that some items must be added at or near the last minute (especially starchy foods like rice and pasta), and that foods should be added according to their cooking time to keep them fresh (for example, you want to cook carrots much longer than you cook peas), you'll do well. Soup is, after all, the most flexible and forgiving thing you can cook.

Just follow these five steps and you'll be improvising soup before you know it.

1. Start with a little fat and a lot of flavor. Cooking one or two aromatic vegetables, like garlic, ginger, onions, and shallots, in a little vegetable oil or butter takes only a few minutes and gives a soup backbone.

2. Add seasonings. This can be as basic as salt and freshly ground black pepper or as complex as spice blends or citrus zest. Lightly heat them until you can smell their fragrance.

3. Stir in the liquid. Use stock, water, juice, wine, beer, or whatever combination you think best complements the other ingredients.

4. Add your main ingredients in order of the longest cooking time to the shortest. Two examples: First beans, then uncooked rice, then tomatoes, finally spinach; or first mushrooms, then carrots, then bok choy, finally cooked rice noodles. If you want vegetables to melt away into the soup, add them early; for a fresh, crisp taste, add them at the last minute. When using cooked leftovers, add them at the very end.

5. Taste as you go along. Dip your spoon into the pot frequently. Rethink your ingredients and adjust the seasonings. It's only soup.

soup in advance up to this point. Cover, refrigerate for up to 2 days, and reheat before proceeding.) Adjust the seasoning and serve.

Puréed Potato Soup with Leeks. Carefully purée the soup in a blender (or with an immersion blender), then return it to the pot. Stir in $1/2$ to 1 cup cream, sour cream, or yogurt and reheat gently; do not let it boil if you use yogurt. Add salt and pepper as needed, garnish with minced chives, and serve.

Vichyssoise. Make the preceding variation, but do not reheat. Instead, chill thoroughly before garnishing with minced chives.

Vegan Vichyssoise. A variation inspired by the South American habit of making soups creamy with the addition of avocado. Let the puréed soup cool slightly in the blender, then stir in the coarsely chopped flesh of 1 to 2 avocados. Chill thoroughly before garnishing with minced chives.

Korean-Style Potato and Leek Soup. Skip Step 1; start with the potatoes, 1 quart water, and 2 tablespoons Chile and Black Bean Paste (see page 830) or soy sauce in a deep saucepan or casserole. Bring the mixture to a boil, stirring until the paste is completely dissolved, then lower the heat to produce a simmer; cook until the potatoes are tender, about 20 minutes. Just before serving, heat 2 tablespoons of neutral oil, like corn or grapeseed (in place of the butter or olive oil), over heat high heat in a wide skillet and, when it's hot, add the leeks. Cook, stirring or tossing almost constantly, until the leeks are lightly browned at the edges and softened, just a few minutes. Divide the soup among serving bowls, add the stir-fried leeks to each serving, and serve.

4 More Ideas for Potato and Leek Soup

1. Cook about a cup of shredded carrots or cabbage along with the potatoes and leeks (increase the stock proportionally, or the soup will become too thick).
2. Finish the soup with a topping of other fresh herbs, like parsley, basil, or chervil.
3. Grate a little Parmesan over all.
4. Add another vegetable—asparagus is good, as are peas—in place of a portion of the potatoes.

Onion Soup

MAKES: 4 servings

TIME: About 1 hour

Ⓜ Ⓥ

People think of onion soup as fancy, but the most "exotic" ingredients you need here are fresh parsley and thyme. Even without those, an onion soup made with just pantry stalwarts—onions, bay leaves, garlic, and oil (for a vegan version) or butter—is a worthwhile venture.

If you don't have stock on hand, don't fret: simmer the soup 10 to 15 minutes longer and add another bay leaf (and a whole stalk of celery and/or a whole carrot if you have them, discarding them just before you serve the soup). Or see the Charred Onion Soup variation that follows.

$1/4$ cup extra virgin olive oil or 4 tablespoons ($1/2$ stick) butter

4 large onions, thinly sliced (about 6 cups)

Leaves of 2 or 3 sprigs fresh thyme or $1/4$ teaspoon dried

1 bay leaf

1 whole head garlic, cut crosswise through the equator

Salt and freshly ground black pepper

5 cups vegetable stock (pages 101–102)

2 tablespoons cognac, Armagnac, or brandy (optional)

2 tablespoons parsley leaves, or more to taste, for garnish (optional)

❶ Put the oil or butter in a large, deep saucepan or casserole over medium heat. When the oil is hot or the butter is melted, add the onions and cook, stirring occasionally, until very soft and beginning to brown. This will take 30 to 45 minutes; don't rush it.

❷ Add the thyme, bay leaf, garlic, and salt and pepper to taste and cook with the onions for a minute before adding the stock and cognac (if you have parsley, add a few sprigs to the soup at this point; fish them out before serving). Bring to a boil, then turn the heat to medium-low and cook for 15 minutes, with bubbles occasionally breaking the surface. (You may prepare the soup in advance up to this point; cover and refrigerate for up to 2 days, then reheat before proceeding.)

❸ Divide the soup among bowls, scatter the top of each with fresh parsley if you're using it, and serve hot.

More Classic Onion Soup. A thin coating of good cheese—rather than the more common gobs of an inferior variety—makes this light and incredibly deep in flavor. Preheat the oven to 400°F. Cut 4 thick slices of crusty bread, rub them with a clove of garlic on each side, and toast them in the oven, in a toaster oven, or in a pan with olive oil (see Croutons, page 806). Put a crouton in each of 4 ovenproof bowls. Add a portion of soup and top each with at least $1/4$ cup of freshly grated Parmesan cheese. Place the bowls in a roasting pan or on a sturdy cookie sheet and bake for 10 minutes, or until the cheese melts. Serve immediately.

Charred Onion Soup. Charring the onions adds a tremendous amount of color to the soup, rendering it close to classic French onion soup. Preheat the broiler and cut the onions in half through the root end instead of slicing them. Place the onions cut side up on a baking sheet, rub each with a little good olive oil, and cook them under the broiler, until charred and slightly tender, 5 to 10 minutes. When they're cool enough to handle, slice them thinly and proceed with either the master recipe or the preceding variation with cheese.

Spanish Onion Soup with Almonds. Subtly and nicely different: When the soup is done, combine about $1/2$ cup blanched almonds and $1/2$ teaspoon ground cumin in a blender and turn the machine on. Slowly and carefully add some of the broth, a little bit at a time, until the mixture is perfectly smooth. Stir this back into the soup and serve, garnished with chopped parsley.

Roasted Beet Borscht

MAKES: 4 servings

TIME: About 1 hour, plus time to chill if desired; largely unattended

Roasting the beets concentrates their sweet, earthy flavor and turns the soup a deep purple. No, it's not the way my grandmother made hers, but I know she would approve because it tastes so good. She wouldn't have used golden beets either (she probably never saw them), but feel free; their sunny color is awesome.

This soup is good either hot or cold.

$2^1/_2$ to 3 pounds beets, any kind, peeled and quartered

$1/4$ cup neutral oil, like grapeseed or corn

Salt and freshly ground black pepper

1 large white onion, finely chopped

1 bunch fresh dill

Freshly squeezed lemon juice to taste

4 hard-cooked eggs, peeled and quartered (optional)

4 medium red or white "new" (waxy), potatoes, boiled until tender and kept hot for garnish (optional)

Sour cream or yogurt for garnish

1 Preheat the oven to 375°F. Put the beets in a roasting pan, drizzle with 2 tablespoons of the oil, and sprinkle with salt and lots of pepper. Toss to distribute the oil. Roast, turning once or twice until a thin-bladed knife pierces a piece with little resistance, 30 to 40 minutes. (The recipe may be made ahead to this point, the beets cooled, covered tightly, and refrigerated for up to 2 days.) When cool enough to handle, roughly chop the beets as finely as possible.

2 Put the remaining 2 tablespoons of oil in a deep skillet or medium saucepan and turn the heat to medium-high. Add the onion and cook, stirring occasionally, until soft, about 3 minutes. Turn the heat to medium-low and continue cooking, stirring occasionally, until golden and very tender, 10 to 15 minutes more.

3 Add the beets, along with the stems of the dill (tie them in a bundle) and water to cover, about 6 cups. Turn the heat back up to medium-high and bring the soup to a boil, then reduce the heat to medium-low, cover, and cook, stirring occasionally, until the soup is well colored and the beets are starting to melt away, about 10 minutes.

④ Snip or chop the remaining dill. Remove the dill stems from the soup and add the lemon juice. Taste and adjust the seasoning if necessary. Serve the borscht in bowls, with the dill and any of the garnishes you like, and pass the sour cream at the table.

Roasted Mushroom Borscht. Even deeper in flavor: Start with 1 pound of beets and 2 pounds of any mushrooms, like shiitake, cremini, portobello, white, or a mixture of these. Prepare the beets as in Step 1 and trim the mushrooms but leave them whole. When the beets and mushrooms are ready, chop them all as finely as possible and proceed to Step 2.

Cold Roasted Beet or Mushroom Borscht. Quite refreshing: Prepare either the master recipe or the preceding variation through Step 3. Cool and refrigerate, covered, until well chilled or for up to 2 days. When ready to serve, proceed to Step 4.

Borscht Consommé. An elegant and unusual starter: Replace the water with about 6 cups any vegetable or mushroom stock (pages 101–102), along with a bay leaf. When very tender, strain; discard the beets (and the mushrooms if you're making the above variation). To the liquid, add lemon juice, salt, and pepper to taste. Reheat and serve hot, garnished with dill or chives, with or without sour cream.

Sauerkraut Soup

MAKES: 4 servings

TIME: About 1 hour, mostly unattended

Surprising things happen when you base a soup on sauerkraut: it instantly creates a complex broth that mellows its distinct sourness and emphasizes its crisp texture and bright flavor.

The first thing to do is start with good sauerkraut, which is never canned (plastic, refrigerated packages are pretty good if you don't have the option of buying it in bulk) and contains nothing but cabbage and salt. Here I balance the sharp taste with sweet ingredients like caramelized onion, green apples, and floral spices. The little bit of grain in this recipe helps bring all these flavors together and give the soup some body.

2 tablespoons neutral oil, like grapeseed or corn

1 onion, chopped

2 Granny Smith or other tart apples, peeled, cored, and chopped

Salt and freshly ground black pepper

1 pound sauerkraut (about 2 cups), drained and rinsed

6 cups vegetable stock (pages 101–102) or water

2 tablespoons millet or fine-grind bulgur (optional)

2 bay leaves

6 cloves

5 or 6 juniper berries (optional)

① Put the oil in a deep skillet or medium saucepan over medium-high heat. When hot, add the onion and cook, stirring occasionally, until wilted, about 3 minutes. Add the apples, sprinkle with a little salt and lots of pepper, and continue cooking and stirring until they start to release their liquid, about 3 minutes more. Turn the heat down to low and cook, stirring occasionally, until the onions and apples are very tender and golden, about 15 to 20 minutes.

② Raise the heat to medium-high and add the sauerkraut. Keep cooking and stirring until the mixture is dry and starts to stick to the bottom of the pan, 10 to 15 minutes. Stir in the stock, scraping up any little bits that may have stuck to the bottom.

③ Add the millet if you like, the bay leaves and cloves, and the juniper berries if you wish, and bring to a boil. Then lower the heat so that the soup bubbles gently; cover and cook until the sauerkraut and grains are very tender, 20 to 25 minutes. Fish out the bay leaves, cloves, and juniper berries if you used them. Taste and adjust the seasoning, then serve. (You can make this soup in advance, then cover and refrigerate for a day or two. Reheat gently before serving.)

Creamy Sauerkraut Soup. Omit the millet or bulgur. Five minutes before the soup is ready, add 1 cup half-and-half, turn up the heat a little, and cook without boiling until the soup has thickened slightly, about 5 minutes more.

Cherry Sauerkraut Soup. Wonderful in summer: Instead of the apples, use 1 cup pitted sweet cherries (frozen are fine).

Mushroom Sauerkraut Soup. More substantial: Instead of the apples, use $^1/_2$ pound sliced button, cremini, or shiitake mushrooms.

Spanish-Style Plantain Stew

MAKES: 4 servings
TIME: 45 minutes

I call this stew "Spanish style" not because I've ever eaten anything like it in Spain but because it harnesses the flavors of two of Spain's most distinctive ingredients: saffron and smoked paprika.

Cutting the onions, peppers, carrots, and plantains into pieces that are about the same size will produce the best-textured stew, and they'll all cook at about the same rate. If you can't find plantains (or can find only yellow-black or black ripe plantains, which are too sweet here but perfect for Sautéed Ripe Plantains, page 336, substitute 2 large waxy (or "new") potatoes.

$^1/_4$ cup extra virgin olive oil

1 small onion, chopped

2 frying (Anaheim or cubanelle) peppers or 1 green bell pepper, chopped

1 large or 2 medium carrots, chopped

2 cloves garlic, finely chopped

Salt and freshly ground black pepper

1 teaspoon smoked paprika (see page 828)

Pinch saffron

2 green or green-yellow plantains, peeled (see page 336) and cut into chunks

6 cups vegetable stock (pages 101–102) or water

1 bay leaf

Lime wedges and chopped fresh cilantro, for serving (optional)

❶ Put the oil in a large, deep saucepan or casserole over medium-high heat. When hot, add the onion, peppers, carrot, and garlic. Season with salt and pepper and cook, stirring, for 2 or 3 minutes, then sprinkle the smoked paprika over the pan, add the saffron, and cook, stirring, for another minute.

❷ Add the plantains, stock, and bay leaf and bring to a boil. Turn the heat down to low and simmer until the plantains are very soft, about 30 minutes. Fish out the bay leaf and discard.

❸ Taste, adjust the seasoning, and serve, passing the chopped cilantro and lime wedges at the table.

Tomato Soups

Maybe canned tomato soup has made us a wee bit lazy, or at least implanted a preconceived idea of what tomato soup must be: ultra-smooth, creamy, and uniformly rosy pink. The truth, of course, is that tomato soup comes in a variety of forms, all from cooking real tomatoes.

Of course, "real" tomatoes take many forms, from farmstand to supermarket to canned and dried. And all are capable of creating delicious soups. I suggest you let your mood, rather than some commercial tomato soup convention, dictate the way you make tomato soup. Chunks of tomato suspended in broth, or bits of bread mixed with tomatoes, can be just as satisfying as a soup you took the time to blend and enrich with cream.

Tomato and Bread Soup

Pappa al Pomodoro

MAKES: 4 to 6 servings
TIME: 30 minutes

Ⓜ Ⓥ

Pappa, in Italian, in case you couldn't guess, is related to pap—in other words, mush. This is the best possible mush, a Tuscan dish of ripe tomatoes, good bread, and flavorful oil. When made with good ingredients, including aromatic basil, it's fabulous.

$\frac{1}{4}$ cup extra virgin olive oil, plus a drizzle for garnish

1 large onion, sliced

2 cloves garlic, chopped

1 dried red chile (optional)

Salt and freshly ground black pepper

3 cups peeled, cored, seeded, and chopped tomato (canned outside of prime tomato season)

1 to 2 cups vegetable stock (pages 101–102), preferably warmed, water, or the liquid from the tomatoes if you're using canned

$\frac{1}{2}$ a loaf (or more) day-old French or Italian bread, cut into cubes

$\frac{1}{4}$ cup fresh basil leaves, torn (optional but very nice)

❶ Put the oil in a large, deep saucepan or casserole over medium heat. When hot, add the onion, garlic, and dried chile if you're using it. Season with salt and pepper and cook, stirring, until the garlic is fragrant and golden and the onion begins to soften, about 5 minutes.

❷ Add the tomato and cook, stirring occasionally, until the pieces break up, 10 to 15 minutes. Add the stock, stir in the bread, and simmer for another minute.

❸ Take the pot off the heat, check the seasoning, and let it sit until the bread is saturated with the soup, about 10 minutes. (You may prepare the soup in advance up to this point. Cover, refrigerate for up to 2 days, and reheat before proceeding.)

❹ Check the seasoning again, stir in the basil, divide the soup among bowls, and garnish with a drizzle of oil and more freshly ground black pepper.

Tomato Soup

MAKES: 4 servings
TIME: 30 minutes

Ⓕ Ⓜ Ⓥ

Except for those made with the best of late-summer tomatoes, many tomato soups are simply not tomatoey enough. One way to circumvent this problem is to add tomato paste; it adds the depth that even good fresh tomatoes sometimes lack. If there are no good tomatoes around—which is the case about nine months of the year—use good-quality canned tomatoes.

2 tablespoons extra virgin olive oil

2 tablespoons tomato paste

1 large onion, sliced

1 carrot, diced

Salt and freshly ground black pepper

3 cups peeled, cored, seeded, and chopped tomato (canned are fine; include their juice)

1 teaspoon fresh thyme leaves or $\frac{1}{2}$ teaspoon dried or 1 tablespoon minced fresh basil leaves

2 to 3 cups vegetable stock (pages 101–102), preferably warmed, tomato water (see page 46), or water, or more as needed

1 teaspoon sugar (optional)

Minced fresh parsley or basil leaves for garnish (optional)

❶ Put the oil in a large, deep saucepan or casserole over medium heat. When hot, add the tomato paste and let it cook for a minute, then add the onion and carrot. Sprinkle with salt and pepper and cook, stirring, until the onion begins to soften, about 5 minutes.

You can hardly go wrong adding tomatoes to soup; they contribute body, color, flavor, acidity, freshness—the works. And few additions are easier.

The most elegant (and time-consuming) way is to peel and seed the tomatoes first (see page 373). I rarely bother with that, though; usually I just chop up a couple and stir them in (the seeds are a little bitter, but a little bitterness isn't a bad thing). Here's how to use whatever type you have handy:

Supermarket Tomatoes: Unless they're good ones—a rarity—you may as well use canned. But soup is the perfect use for real but overripe tomatoes. If you want them to dissolve into the background, add them to whatever vegetables are cooking in the pan before you pour in the stock or water. For a fresher, meatier taste, stir them in toward the end of cooking.

Fresh Roma (Plum) Tomatoes: These will give you a caramelized and concentrated tomato-paste-like flavor, especially when added before any liquid.

Fresh Heirloom Tomatoes: It doesn't make sense to cook these special tomatoes down to pulp, unless you're featuring them in a fresh tomato soup (page 112). But served raw, either chopped or wedged, they make a delicious and beautiful garnish for many cold soups.

Cherry or Grape Tomatoes: These are best cooked very little or not at all. Either way, I usually cut them in half first.

Canned Tomatoes: The all-purpose workhorse. Already peeled, often seeded and chopped, canned tomatoes are a fine substitute for fresh in almost every soup. Usually you might as well include some of their juice.

Dried Tomatoes (often called *sun-dried*): The slightly sweet, chewy character makes adding dried tomatoes almost like adding tomato paste, only with more texture. Remember that they take several minutes to soften and that a little goes a long way.

Frozen Tomatoes: If time allows, let them thaw out a bit, then slip the skins off and cut them into pieces or wedges.

---

2 Add the tomato and the herb and cook, stirring occasionally, until the tomato pieces break up, 10 to 15 minutes. Add the stock, stir, and taste. (You may prepare the soup in advance up to this point. Cover, refrigerate for up to 2 days, and reheat before proceeding.) Adjust the seasoning; if the soup is flat tasting, stir in the sugar. If the mixture is too thick, add a little more stock or water. Garnish and serve.

Puréed Tomato Soup. The stuff of your childhood, or close to it: Increase the tomato to 4 cups and reduce the stock to 1 cup. When the soup is done, purée it carefully in a blender or with an immersion blender or pass it through a food mill. Reheat, garnish, and serve, preferably with Croutons (page 806).

Cream of Tomato Soup. Substitute butter for olive oil and use the proportions in the preceding variation, substituting 1 cup cream or half-and-half (or alternative milk) for the stock, added just before puréeing. No longer vegan, of course.

Wintertime Tomato Soup

MAKES: 4 servings

TIME: About 1 1/2 hours, mostly unattended

When you crave tomato soup during the deep, dark days of January, it makes sense to prepare a seasonally appropriate version, using canned and dried tomatoes. The combination is powerfully flavorful, especially after you roast the canned tomatoes, which intensifies the taste and improves their texture.

This rustic soup makes a perfect base for stew: Try adding cooked potatoes, pasta, beans, or vegetables after the tomatoes have melted into the broth, or try the rice-based variation.

1 cup loosely packed (about 2 ounces) dried tomatoes (preferably not packed in oil)

1 (28-ounce) can whole peeled tomatoes

1/4 cup extra virgin olive oil

1 tablespoon fresh thyme leaves (optional)

1 tablespoon minced garlic

1 medium carrot, finely diced

1 small red onion, halved and thinly sliced

Salt and freshly ground black pepper

2 tablespoons honey

1 quart vegetable stock (page 102) or water

1/4 cup chopped parsley

1 Preheat the oven to 375°F. Put the dried tomatoes in a heatproof bowl and cover with 2 cups boiling water. Drain the canned tomatoes and reserve the liquid. Halve them and put in a shallow roasting pan; drizzle with 2 tablespoons of the olive oil and sprinkle with the thyme if you're using it. Roast, turning once or twice, until the tomatoes are dried and lightly browned, about 30 minutes.

2 When the tomatoes are done, drain the dried tomatoes and pour their soaking liquid into the roasting pan. Use a wooden spoon to scrape up all the browned bits from the bottom of the pan, breaking up the roasted tomatoes at the same time. Roughly chop the dried tomatoes and add them to the roasting pan.

3 Put the remaining olive oil in a deep skillet or medium saucepan over medium-high heat. When hot, add the garlic and cook just until it begins to color, a minute or so. Add the carrot and onion and cook until

they start to release their liquid, about 3 minutes more. Sprinkle with salt and pepper, then add the honey and stir until it melts, just a few seconds.

4 Add the reserved liquid from the canned tomatoes and continue stirring until the liquid dries out and darkens, about 5 minutes. Stir in the stock, along with the contents of the roasting pan. Turn the heat to high and bring the soup to a boil, then lower the heat so it bubbles gently. Cover and cook until the vegetables are very tender, about 30 minutes. Garnish with the parsley and serve.

Wintertime Tomato and Rice Soup. More substantial: Add 1 cup short-grain rice, like Arborio, to the pan in Step 4, just after the reserved canned tomato liquid has cooked. Increase the stock to 6 cups.

Elegant Wintertime Tomato Soup. Use an immersion blender to purée the finished soup in the pan; or cool the soup to room temperature, carefully purée in a blender, and return to the pan to reheat. Stir in 1 cup heavy cream, sour cream, or any milk and heat gently.

10 Tomato-Friendly Soups

All of these soups can be easily varied by the addition of tomatoes during cooking.

1. Cauliflower Soup, Italian Style (page 105)
2. Classic Lentil Soup and its variations (page 115)
3. Mung Bean Soup (page 121)
4. White Bean Soup and its variations (page 119)
5. Bread Soup (page 121)
6. Vegetable Soup, Thai Style (page 127)
7. Chile Bisque (page 131)
8. Corn Chowder and its variations (page 135)
9. Garlic Fideo Soup (page 144)
10. Rich Zucchini Soup (page 156)

Bean Soups

If there was ever a category of soups that can be successfully made from water and one other ingredient, this is it.

F Fast   **M** Make Ahead   **V** Vegan

Legumes serve many functions in soup. They work as a thickener (see "Giving Soups More Body," page 136), they add distinct textures and tastes, and, whether they're featured or added (see "19 Beans in 10 Soups," page 122), they are certainly filling. (And, as everyone knows, beans are high in both protein and fiber.)

Some of the soups here call for cooking raw beans in the soup pot, so their broth is integral to the soup; this is the most nutritious and flavorful option. Other recipes use already-cooked beans. Most recipes and variations explain how to make the soup using either method.

I'm not a fan of super-thick bean soups. The texture overrides the flavor, and a cup leaves you too full for the rest of your meal. But if it's thick soup you're after, either decrease the amount of stock or water in these recipes by $1/2$ cup or so or toss in another handful or two of beans.

Black Bean Soup

MAKES: 4 servings

TIME: 30 minutes with cooked beans

This works best when you purée some of the sturdy black beans and stir them back in, for a smooth-chunky effect. But in many Latin American versions the beans are left whole, with chunks of sweet potato, squash, or even mango added toward the end of cooking. A little alcohol is sometimes added to the finished soup to help cut the richness of the beans; orange juice and/or zest is another fine addition (see the variation). Omit the dairy garnish for a vegan soup.

2 tablespoons neutral oil, like grapeseed or corn

1 large or 2 medium onions, chopped

1 tablespoon minced garlic

1 tablespoon Chili Powder (page 814)

1 tablespoon ground cumin

2 tablespoons sherry or dark rum (optional)

3 cups cooked black beans (page 581), drained

1 quart vegetable stock (pages 101–102) or water

Salt and freshly ground black pepper

2 teaspoons freshly squeezed lime juice, or to taste

Sour cream or plain yogurt for garnish

Minced fresh cilantro leaves for garnish

1 Put the oil in a deep skillet or medium saucepan over medium heat. When hot, add the onion and cook, stirring, until softened, about 5 minutes. Stir in the garlic, chile powder, and cumin and cook, stirring, for another minute.

2 Stir in the sherry if you're using it, then cook for a minute and add the beans, stock, and some salt and pepper. Turn the heat up to medium-high and bring the soup to a boil, then turn the heat down to medium-low and cook, stirring occasionally, for about 10 minutes. Turn off the heat.

3 Use an immersion blender to purée some of the soup in the pan. Or cool the mixture slightly, pour about half of the soup into a blender, and carefully purée. (The soup may be made ahead to this point, cooled, and refrigerated for up to 2 days. Reheat gently before proceeding.)

4 Add the lime juice and stir; taste and adjust the seasoning. Serve garnished with sour cream and minced cilantro.

Brazilian-Style Black Bean Soup. In Step 2, replace 2 cups of the stock with 2 cups orange juice (preferably freshly squeezed). Add 2 teaspoons minced or julienned orange zest in the last couple of minutes of cooking.

Classic Lentil Soup

MAKES: 4 servings

TIME: About 1 hour

This recipe is about as easy as cooking can be, especially for a dish so filling and nutritious. Unlike the overly thick versions that put so many people off, this lentil soup is nicely balanced.

1 cup dried lentils, washed and picked over

1 bay leaf

Several sprigs fresh thyme or a few pinches dried

1 carrot, cut into $1/2$-inch dice

1 celery stalk, cut into $1/2$-inch dice

6 cups vegetable stock (pages 101–102) or water, or more as needed

Salt and freshly ground black pepper

2 tablespoons extra virgin olive oil

1 onion, chopped

1 teaspoon minced garlic

1 Put the lentils, bay leaf, thyme, carrot, celery, and stock in a deep skillet or medium saucepan. Sprinkle with salt and pepper. Bring to a boil, then turn the heat down to low and cook, stirring occasionally, until the lentils are tender, about 30 minutes.

2 Meanwhile, put the olive oil in a small skillet over medium heat. Add the onion and cook, stirring, until it softens, about 5 minutes. Add the garlic and stir, then cook for 1 minute more and turn off the heat.

3 When the lentils are tender, fish out the bay leaf and thyme sprigs and stir the onion mixture into the soup. (The soup may be made ahead to this point, cooled, and refrigerated for up to 2 days. Reheat gently.) Add more stock if the soup is too thick, then taste, adjust the seasoning, and serve.

French-Style Lentil Soup with Sorrel or Spinach. Best with Lentilles du Puy (see page 599). Wash and chop $1/4$ pound sorrel or spinach. In Step 2, instead of olive oil use 3 tablespoons butter. After the onions have cooked, stir in the sorrel or spinach and 1 teaspoon sugar. Finish the soup as directed, but if you're using spinach, add a squeeze of lemon.

Elegant Lentil Soup. Start with the basic recipe or the preceding variation. Let the soup cool if you have time, then use an immersion blender to purée the soup in the pan. Or cool the mixture slightly, pour it into a blender, and purée carefully. Return the soup to the pan and reheat gently before serving.

Italian-Style Lentil Soup with Rice. Approaching wholemeal status. Increase the amount of stock to 2 quarts. Prepare the soup through Step 1 and start cooking the onions and garlic in Step 2. After the lentils have been cooking for about 15 minutes, stir in $1/2$ cup shortgrain rice, preferably Arborio. Add 1 cup chopped tomatoes (canned are fine) to the pan with the onion. Pass freshly grated Parmesan cheese and extra virgin olive oil for drizzling at the table.

Lentil Soup with Coconut

MAKES: 4 servings

TIME: $1^1/_2$ hours, largely unattended

I use regular brown lentils here, but you can use red lentils (see page 599), which actually cook faster, or the more traditional split pigeon peas, also known as *tavoor dal* (available at most Asian and Indian markets); they're all good. The lentils melt into the background, with soft vegetables and shreds of coconut left swirling in the complex golden broth.

Use whatever vegetables you love, in any combination, from cooked winter squashes, turnips, or sweet potato to cauliflower, spinach, eggplant, or green beans.

3 tablespoons peanut or other neutral oil, like grapeseed or corn

1 medium onion, roughly chopped

1 tablespoon minced garlic

1 tablespoon minced peeled fresh ginger

Salt and freshly ground black pepper

1 teaspoon ground turmeric

3 tablespoons curry powder (to make your own, see page 816) or Sambar Powder (page 816)

1 cup chopped tomato (canned is fine)

1/4 cup sliced or shredded coconut

1 cup sliced okra

1 small zucchini, roughly chopped

1/2 cup dried lentils or split pigeon peas (tavoor dal), washed and picked over

1 quart vegetable stock (pages 101–102) or water

2 cups homemade coconut milk (page 423) or 1 can, slightly less than 2 cups, with a little water

12 fresh curry leaves, if available, or fresh basil leaves

1 Put the oil in a deep skillet or medium saucepan over medium-high heat. When hot, add the onion and cook, stirring occasionally, until soft and translucent, 3 to 5 minutes. Add the garlic and ginger and cook for another minute. Sprinkle with salt and pepper. Turn the heat down to medium-low and cook, stirring occasionally, until the vegetables are golden and beginning to melt together, about 20 minutes.

2 Turn the heat back up to medium-high and add the turmeric and curry powder. Cook, stirring frequently, until darkened and fragrant, about 5 minutes. Stir in the tomato, coconut, okra, zucchini, and lentils. Add the stock and coconut milk, then bring to a boil; turn the heat down to medium-low so that the soup bubbles gently.

3 Cook, stirring occasionally, until the lentils and vegetables break apart, 30 to 40 minutes; add water as necessary to keep the mixture brothy. Stir in the curry leaves, stir once or twice, then taste, adjust the seasoning, and serve.

Chickpea Soup with Saffron and Almonds

MAKES: 4 servings

TIME: At least 2 hours (much less with cooked or canned chickpeas)

The combination of chickpeas, almonds, and saffron is found throughout the Mediterranean, but especially in Spain. Both intense flavor and a range of textures are at play here, with the nuttiness of the beans and almonds tempered by subtle seasoning. If you have a chunk of manchego or other good semihard cheese handy, set it on the table with a grater to add a little last-minute richness.

3/4 cup roasted almonds

1/2 pound dried chickpeas, washed and picked over, or about 2 cups cooked

1/4 cup extra virgin olive oil

1 large onion, chopped

1 teaspoon minced garlic

Salt and freshly ground black pepper

1/4 teaspoon crumbled saffron, or more if you have it

6 cups vegetable stock (pages 101–102) or water

1/4 cup chopped parsley leaves for garnish

1 Use the flat side of a wide knife or cleaver or a small food processor to break the almonds into large pieces.

2 If time allows, soak the chickpeas for several hours or overnight in water to cover. (If it does not, boil them for 2 minutes, then soak for 2 hours; or just start cooking them, unsoaked.) Put in a pot with fresh water to cover by at least 2 inches. Bring to a boil, turn down the heat, and simmer, covered, for at least 1 hour, or until tender.

3 Put half the oil in a deep skillet or a medium saucepan over medium-high heat. When hot, add the onion, garlic, a large pinch of salt, and some pepper and cook, stirring occasionally, until the onion softens and begin to brown, about 10 minutes. Stir in the almonds and the saffron. Turn off the heat.

4 When the chickpeas are tender, remove them from the heat and drain them, reserving their cooking water. Add the chickpeas, along with about 1 cup of their cooking water and the stock, to the almond mixture. Mash with a potato masher or spoon until some or most of the peas are crushed (the final texture is a matter of taste). Cook over medium-high heat, stirring occasionally, until hot. Taste, adjust the seasoning, garnish, and serve.

Chickpea Soup with Olives and Oranges. A terrific mix of flavors: Omit the almonds and saffron. Coarsely chop $^1/_2$ cup pitted green olives and peel, seed, and roughly chop 1 orange. In Step 2, after cooking the onions, stir in the olives and orange pieces and cook, stirring occasionally for another minute or two. Turn off the heat and proceed with the recipe.

Chickpea Soup with Spinach. The bitterness of the spinach is perfect here: Omit the almonds and saffron. In Step 2, after cooking the onions, stir in 1 pound fresh spinach, washed, trimmed, and coarsely chopped. You might also stir in $^1/_4$ cup each of raisins and toasted pine nuts. Cook, stirring occasionally, until the spinach wilts, then turn off the heat and proceed with the recipe.

Smooth Chickpea Soup

MAKES: 4 servings

TIME: 3 to 4 hours, largely unattended

Starting with dried chickpeas is important here, because their cooking water becomes an essential ingredient. The basic idea is to extract as much flavor as possible from the beans, strain them, then enrich the thick broth with tahini, the smooth paste made from sesame seeds. Finely ground almond, cashew, or peanut butter can easily be substituted, with terrific results.

2 cups dried chickpeas, washed and picked over

$^1/_4$ to $^1/_2$ cup tahini or smooth almond, cashew, or peanut butter (including a bit of the accompanying oil if there is any)

1 tablespoon freshly squeezed lemon juice, or more to taste

Salt and freshly ground black pepper

2 teaspoons ground cumin or minced fresh oregano leaves for garnish (optional)

4 thin lemon slices for garnish (optional)

1 If time allows, soak the chickpeas according to the directions on pages 579–580. Drain and discard the soaking water before proceeding. Put the chickpeas in a pot with about 2 quarts of water and turn the heat to medium-high. Bring to a boil, then turn the heat down so that the water bubbles gently. Cover and cook, stirring occasionally, until the chickpeas are very tender, 1 to 2 hours.

2 Reserving the liquid, purée the chickpeas in a food processor (add a little of the liquid if necessary for the machine to do its work) or force through a strainer with a big spoon or a potato masher. Incorporate the purée back into the strained cooking liquid. (If you used a strainer, discard the solids remaining in it.)

3 Adjust the heat so that the soup bubbles gently, adding a little water if necessary (or turn the heat to high and boil the liquid down a bit to reduce it). Stir in the tahini and lemon juice and use a whisk to stir until the soup is smooth. Continue cooking, stirring occasionally, until thickened, 3 to 5 minutes more. Taste and sprinkle with salt and pepper. (The soup may be made ahead to this point, cooled, and refrigerated for up to 2 days. Serve cold or gently reheated. Taste again and adjust the seasoning or add more lemon.) If you like, serve garnished with a sprinkle of cumin or float a slice of lemon on top.

Simplest Split Pea Soup

MAKES: 4 servings

TIME: About 1$^1/_2$ hours

Meat-eaters automatically associate split peas with ham bones, so many vegetarian versions of split pea soup add a smoky taste through smoked chiles like dried chipotle or ancho. Tossing a piece of toasted seaweed into the pot is another way to add a "meaty" dimension. The truth is you don't need either. Why muddle that distinctive pea flavor?

Split peas fall apart quickly, and it's easy to end up with a soup that's too thick, so watch it (you can always stir in more water to thin it out). If you want something more filling, finish each bowl with a handful of Croutons (page 806) or a scoop of cooked rice, barley, or cracked wheat. Or try the vegetable-loaded Caribbean variation.

2 cups dried green split peas, washed and picked over

6 cups vegetable stock (pages 101–102) or water

Salt and freshly ground black pepper

1 Put the split peas and stock in a medium saucepan and bring to a boil over medium-high heat. Turn the heat down to low, cover partially, and cook, stirring occasionally, until the peas are very soft, 45 to 60 minutes.

2 Mash the mixture with a fork or potato masher. (For an ultra-smooth soup, use an immersion blender or cool the mixture slightly, pour into a blender container, and purée carefully.) Reheat the soup, adding more stock or water if it's too thick. Taste, adjust the seasoning, and serve.

Yellow Split Pea Soup with Pantry Vegetables. Here's how it's done in much of the Caribbean: Start by chopping 1 onion, 1 carrot, and 1 celery stalk into $1/2$-inch pieces. Put 2 tablespoons neutral oil, like grapeseed or corn, into a deep skillet or medium saucepan over medium-high heat. When hot, add the vegetables and cook, stirring occasionally, until softened, about 5 minutes; sprinkle with salt and pepper. Substitute $1^1/_2$ cups yellow split peas for the green; add them and the stock to the pan. After cooking for about 20 minutes, add 2 cups peeled and coarsely chopped sweet potato or yam, green plantains, pumpkin, taro root, or cassava or any combination of these. Continue cooking until all the vegetables are soft, another 25 to 40 minutes. Taste and adjust the seasoning; you can leave the soup chunky or mash it a little if you like. Serve with a sprinkle of cayenne pepper and a squeeze of lime.

White Bean Soup

MAKES: 4 servings
TIME: At least 1 hour

You can make soup out of any bean you like, of course, but small white beans cook more quickly than most. (Even without soaking, you need as little as an hour, though for various reasons—see page 580—I can't guarantee that.) They also purée beautifully and have a mild but still beany flavor that most people like. There are many directions to go here, and they're all easy; see "10 Ideas for White Bean Soup," page 120.

$1^1/_2$ cups small white beans, washed, picked over, and soaked if time allows (see page 581)

6 cups vegetable stock (pages 101–102) or water, or more as needed

1 medium onion, chopped

1 medium to large carrot, chopped

1 celery stalk, chopped

2 bay leaves

Pinch dried thyme or 1 teaspoon fresh thyme leaves

Salt and freshly ground black pepper

Chopped parsley leaves for garnish (optional)

1 Drain the beans if you've soaked them, then combine them in a saucepan with the stock, onion, carrot, celery, bay leaves, and thyme. Bring to a boil over medium-high heat, then turn the heat down so the mixture simmers steadily. Cook, stirring occasionally, until the beans are very soft, at least 1 hour; add more liquid as necessary so the mixture remains soupy.

2 When the beans are very tender, season to taste with salt and pepper. If you like, you can purée the soup at this point: put an immersion blender in the pot and semipurée it, leaving it a bit chunky, or put all or some of it in a blender (carefully, and after it's cooled a bit) and purée until smooth. (You may prepare the soup in advance up to this point. Cover, refrigerate for up to 2 days, and reheat before proceeding.) Serve garnished with the parsley.

10 Ideas for White Bean Soup

As good as basic bean soup is, it can be made gloriously delicious with a few simple additions. Try any of these, alone or in combination:

1. Tomato paste (about $^1/_4$ cup) or canned (or, of course, fresh) tomatoes (a cup or two) added at the beginning of cooking

2. Mild chiles, like anchos (1 or 2, stemmed and seeded) added at the beginning of cooking

3. Nori seaweed, toasted (see page 357) and minced, added at the beginning of cooking (about $^1/_4$ cup) and again as a garnish (a sprinkling)

4. Chopped fresh vegetables (1 to 2 cups)—carrots, celery, potatoes, shallots, turnips, or whatever you like—added about 20 minutes before the end of cooking

5. Any whole grain, like brown rice, barley, or peeled wheat ($^1/_2$ cup or so, with the beans reduced by the same amount, added at the beginning of cooking); or quick-cooking grains, like white rice, pearled barley, or bulgur, added during the last 15 to 20 minutes of cooking

6. Minced garlic, at least 1 teaspoon, added about 5 minutes before the end of cooking.

7. Chopped greens, like kale or collards (1 to 2 cups), added during the last 5 minutes of cooking

8. Butter, about 2 tablespoons, stirred in at the end of cooking

22 Whole-Meal Soups

To make these soups a main course, just increase the portion size. And for ideas about how to make soups heartier, see the sidebars and lists about adding body (page 136), beans (page 122), tofu (page 151), cheese (page 142), eggs (page 153), and noodles (pages 142–143). But even that's not always necessary: These chunky soups become stews just by being cooked a little longer, thereby reducing the ratio of liquid to solid.

1. Black Bean Soup and its variations (page 115)
2. Classic Lentil Soup and its variations (page 115)
3. Chickpea Soup with Saffron and Almonds and its variations (page 117)
4. Lentil Soup with Coconut (page 116)
5. Mung Bean Soup (page 121)
6. Simplest Split Pea Soup and its variations (page 118)
7. White Bean Soup and its variations (page 119)
8. Bread Soup and its variation (page 121)
9. Minestrone and its variations, (page 123)
10. Peanut Soup, Senegalese Style, and its variations (page 124)
11. Barley Soup with Seasonal Vegetables and its variations (page 138)
12. Jook (page 140)
13. Farro Soup and its variation (page 141)
14. Mushroom Barley Soup (page 139)
15. Faux Pho (page 143)
16. Persian Noodle Soup, (page 144)
17. Green Tea Broth with Udon Noodles and its variations (page 145)
18. Whole Wheat Noodles in Curry Broth (page 147)
19. Kimchi Soup with Tofu (page 148)
20. Tofu Skins in Hot Pot (page 149)
21. Tofu and Bok Choy "Goulash" and its variations (page 150)
22. Egg "Noodle" Soup and its variations (page 153)

F Fast   M Make Ahead   V Vegan

9. Extra virgin olive oil, about 1 tablespoon per serving, added at the last minute

10. 4 to 8 Garlic Croutons (page 806), 1 or 2 added to the bottom of each soup bowl before serving.

Mung Bean Soup

MAKES: 4 servings

TIME: 30 to 60 minutes, depending on the type of mung bean

Recipes for all kinds of dishes often begin with a base of aromatic vegetables and spices cooked in oil or butter, a process that activates the aromatics' essential oils and releases flavor. But the same technique can be an effective way to finish a dish. In India the common name for such after-flavoring is *tarka*, and it's often used with legumes and grains, either stirred in at the end of cooking or passed at the table.

Mung beans come whole or split and hulled in both green and yellow varieties (see page 579), and the form you use will affect the cooking time and, to a lesser degree, the color, texture, and taste. But really, you can't go wrong.

1 cup mung beans, split or whole, washed and picked over

6 cups vegetable stock (pages 101–102) or water

Salt and freshly ground black pepper

3 tablespoons peanut or neutral oil, like grapeseed or corn

1 tablespoon minced garlic

1 tablespoon peeled and minced fresh ginger

1 teaspoon whole cumin seeds

4 small dried red chiles, or more or less to taste

1/2 teaspoon whole fenugreek seeds (optional)

1/2 cup chopped scallion

2 tablespoons freshly squeezed lemon juice

① Put the mung beans and stock into a medium to large saucepan and bring to a boil over medium-high heat. Lower the heat so that the soup just bubbles, cover, and cook, stirring occasionally, until the beans are tender, an hour or so for whole beans, 40 to 50 minutes for split beans. Sprinkle with salt and pepper and keep hot. (The soup may be made ahead to this point, cooled, and refrigerated for up to 2 days. Reheat gently before proceeding.)

② To make the tarka, put the oil in a small skillet over medium-high heat. When hot, add the garlic and ginger and cook, stirring constantly, until deep golden and slightly crisp, 5 to 8 minutes. Stir in the cumin, chiles, and fenugreek if you're using it. Keep stirring until the spice seeds are fragrant. Add the scallion and cook until soft, about 1 minute more.

③ Remove the soup from the heat and stir in the lemon juice. Remove the chiles, then taste and adjust the seasoning. Add the tarka to the soup in the pot or, if you like, garnish each bowl with a small spoonful and serve.

Bread Soup

Zuppa di Pane

MAKES: 4 servings

TIME: At least 1 hour

Not literally bread soup but bean and vegetable soup with bread. When I first ate this in Tuscany, it was served with 2 condiments—extra virgin olive oil and chopped onion—and I've made it that way ever since. It's traditionally prepared with fresh borlotti or other shell beans, and if you find these (and in fall you often can), your cooking time will be substantially shorter and the flavor somewhat more intense. But almost any dried pink or spotted bean will do nicely.

1 1/2 cups pinto, cranberry, or other pink or spotted beans, washed, picked over, and soaked if time allows (see page 581)

6 cups vegetable stock (pages 101–102) or water, or more as needed

2 medium onions, chopped

1 teaspoon fresh thyme leaves or ½ teaspoon dried

2 cups shredded Savoy cabbage, spinach, kale, or collards

Salt and freshly ground black pepper

Large Cubed Croutons (page 806)

Chopped parsley leaves for garnish

Extra virgin olive oil for serving

① Drain the beans if you've soaked them, then combine them in a saucepan with the stock, half the onions, and the thyme. Bring to a boil over medium-high heat, then turn the heat down so the mixture simmers steadily. Cook, stirring occasionally, until the beans are very soft, at least 1 hour; add more liquid as necessary so the mixture remains soupy. (You may prepare the soup in advance up to this point. Cover, refrigerate for up to 2 days, and reheat gently before proceeding.)

② Add whatever greens you're using, along with some salt and pepper, and continue to cook until tender, from 5 minutes for spinach to about 15 for kale. Stir in the croutons, then garnish with the parsley. Serve with olive oil and the remaining onion.

Chestnut-Bean Soup. A wonderful way to integrate chestnuts, which are in season from fall through early winter: When the beans begin to get tender, add 1 cup or more peeled chestnuts (see page 287), whole or halved. Proceed with the recipe, omitting the croutons.

15 Beans in 8 Soups

Use these suggestions as a starting point for adding beans to soups, then try your own combinations. The easiest way is to stir ½ to 1 cup of precooked beans into the pot at the very end of cooking and heat through before serving.

Cooking beans in the soup—rather than adding precooked beans—benefits both flavor and nutrition, but you will have to make adjustments. First you must compensate for the liquid they will absorb with extra water or stock; since beans are an added, not featured, ingredient here, I use only about ½ cup uncooked beans and about 1 cup extra liquid. You'll also have to cook the soup longer, sometimes considerably so. (See pages 576–583 for what you need to know about selecting beans, soaking them if you want, and approximate cooking times.) Generally you will want to wait until the beans are almost cooked before adding the final vegetables.

Those are the general guidelines. But here are some specific ideas for adding beans to some of the soups in this chapter:

1. Cannellini, cranberry, or fresh fava beans in Cauliflower Soup, Italian Style (page 105)
2. Chickpeas or black beans in Onion Soup and its variations (page 108)
3. White, canellini, or borlotti beans in Tomato Soup and its variations (page 112)
4. Chickpeas or lentils in Mixed Vegetable Soup, Spanish Style (page 124)
5. Black-eyed peas in Peanut Soup, Senegalese Style (page 124)
6. Black beans in Tortilla Soup (page 126)
7. White or gigante beans in Barley Soup with Seasonal Vegetables (page 138)
8. Lima beans in the Barley Soup variation with Summer Vegetables (page 139)

Mixed Vegetable Soups

Knowing your options makes cooking far more convenient, because instead of running out to the store for a specific ingredient you gain confidence in using whatever's handy. This is especially true with soups, where the easiest, most easily varied, and perhaps best soups might be those based on a combination of stock and fresh vegetables. You start with a flavorful base and add the best produce you have on hand: How can you go wrong?

F Fast   **M** Make Ahead   **V** Vegan

Combining many vegetables creates a complex broth that may never be quite the same the next time you make it—and that's okay too.

I've built many choices into the following recipes. Since this is the chapter's most international section, you can also see how mixed vegetable soups are commonly treated in different cuisines and how simple it is to go from one continent to the next just by adjusting seasonings and ingredients.

Minestrone

MAKES: 4 to 6 servings
TIME: 45 to 60 minutes
Ⓜ

The Italian take on what-have-you vegetable soup and, like most others, infinitely and easily varied. A mix of vegetables, always with tomato, is all you're looking for, though combining "hard" and "soft" vegetables improves the results. If you have an old piece of Parmesan lying around, cut the rind into small pieces and add it along with the first batch of vegetables; it'll become chewy during cooking and is not only edible but (not surprisingly) delicious.

$1/4$ cup extra virgin olive oil

1 medium onion, chopped

1 carrot, chopped

1 celery stalk, chopped

$1^1/_2$ to 2 cups hard vegetables, like potatoes, winter squash, parsnips, or turnips, peeled if necessary and cut into smaller than $^1/_2$-inch dice

Salt and freshly ground black pepper

6 cups vegetable stock (pages 101–102) or water

1 cup cored, peeled, seeded, and chopped tomato (canned is fine; include the juice)

$1^1/_2$ to 2 cups soft vegetables, like green beans, cooked dried beans, zucchini or summer squash, or

dark, leafy greens like kale or collards, peeled if necessary and cut into smaller than $^1/_2$-inch dice

$^1/_2$ cup chopped parsley leaves

Freshly grated Parmesan cheese for serving (optional)

❶ Put 3 tablespoons of the oil in a large, deep saucepan or casserole over medium heat. When hot, add the onion, carrot, and celery. Cook, stirring, until the onion softens, about 5 minutes.

❷ Add the hard vegetables and sprinkle with salt and pepper. Cook, stirring, for a minute or two, then add the stock and the tomato; bring to a boil, then adjust the heat so the mixture bubbles gently. Cook, stirring every now and then, until the vegetables are fairly soft and the tomatoes broken up, about 15 minutes. (You may prepare the soup in advance up to this point. Cover, refrigerate for up to 2 days, and reheat before proceeding.)

❸ Add the soft vegetables and the parsley and adjust the heat once again so the mixture simmers. Cook until all the vegetables are very tender, about 15 minutes. Taste and adjust the seasoning, add the remaining olive oil, and serve, passing the cheese at the table if you like.

Pistou. Traditionally you'd use pesto with a lot of garlic here: Stir in $^1/_2$ cup or more freshly made Traditional Pesto or any of its variations (page 768).

Pasta e Fagioli (Pasta and Bean Soup). One of the best bean soups: Use whatever vegetables you like (about half as much) and add 2 cups cooked beans—kidney, white, borlotti, chickpeas, canellini, or a mixture—with the soft vegetables. At the same time, add $^1/_2$ to 1 cup small pasta, like tubetti, or larger pasta broken into bits. About 5 minutes before serving, stir in a teaspoon (or more, to taste) of minced garlic.

Herbed Minestrone. Again, use what you have on hand and to taste; but, for example: In Step 1, add the leaves from a fresh sprig of oregano, marjoram, or rosemary. In Step 3, finish with a few more leaves. Or finish with $^1/_2$ cup or so shredded fresh basil.

Mixed Vegetable Soup, Spanish Style

MAKES: 4 to 6 servings

TIME: 1 hour

 Ⓜ Ⓥ

In Spain, a soup similar to minestrone is likely to begin with roasting the vegetables, which yields a more robust flavor (and takes a little more time).

1 large onion, roughly chopped

1 head garlic, separated into cloves and peeled

1 medium eggplant, peeled and roughly chopped

2 medium zucchini or summer squash, peeled and roughly chopped

1 potato, peeled and roughly chopped

2 large tomatoes, cored and roughly chopped, juices reserved

$1/2$ cup extra virgin olive oil

Salt and freshly ground black pepper

1 teaspoon ground cumin

6 cups vegetable stock (pages 101–102) or water

$1/2$ cup chopped parsley leaves

❶ Preheat the oven to 450°F. In a roasting pan or oven-proof and stovetop-safe casserole, combine the onion, garlic, eggplant, zucchini, potato, tomatoes, all but a table-spoon of the olive oil, a large pinch of salt, some pepper, and the cumin. Toss so that all the vegetables are coated with the oil and roast, shaking or stirring occasionally, until the vegetables are nicely browned, about 45 minutes.

❷ Carefully move the pan to the top of the stove and add the stock and reserved tomato juice. Cook, stirring occasionally, until the vegetables are very soft, another 15 minutes or so. (You may prepare the soup in advance up to this point. Cover, refrigerate for up to 2 days, and reheat before proceeding.) Taste and adjust the seasoning.

❸ At this point you have two options: cool slightly and purée about half the soup, then reheat, add the pars-ley and remaining olive oil, and serve. Or do not purée; simply add the parsley and oil and serve.

Peanut Soup, Senegalese Style

MAKES: 4 servings

TIME: About 45 minutes

Ⓥ

This soup is based on the colorful, chunky peanut ("groundnut") dishes of West Africa. It's filled with veg-etables, and a bowlful topped with a scoop of simply cooked millet (see page 537), or almost any other grain, easily makes a meal. If you'd prefer something creamy, try the variation that follows or the cream-thickened Virgin-ian Peanut Soup, a southern classic, on page 134.

$3/4$ cup roasted and shelled peanuts

2 tablespoons peanut or neutral oil, like grapeseed or corn

1 medium red onion, halved and thinly sliced

1 tablespoon peeled and minced fresh ginger

1 tablespoon minced garlic

Pinch cayenne or more or less to taste

Salt and freshly ground black pepper

6 cups vegetable stock (pages 101–102) or water

2 (about 1 pound) sweet potatoes or yams, peeled and cut into thick slices

8 to 12 plum tomatoes, cored and halved (canned are fine; drain and reserve liquid for another use)

$1/2$ pound collards or kale, washed thoroughly and cut into wide ribbons

$1/4$ cup chunky peanut butter

❶ Use the flat side of a wide knife or cleaver or a small food processor to break the peanuts into large pieces.

❷ Put the oil in a deep skillet or medium saucepan over medium-high heat. When hot, add the onion, ginger, and garlic and cook, stirring occasionally, until the vegeta-bles are soft, 3 to 5 minutes. Add $1/2$ cup of the peanuts

Ⓕ Fast   Ⓜ Make Ahead   Ⓥ Vegan

and the cayenne and sprinkle with salt and pepper. Stir in the stock and the sweet potatoes, bring to a boil, and turn the heat down to medium-low so that the soup bubbles gently. Partially cover the pan and cook, stirring occasionally, until the potatoes are just tender, about 10 minutes.

3 Stir in the tomatoes, collards, and peanut butter. Cover and cook until the collards are tender, 5 to 8 minutes. Taste, adjust the seasoning, and serve, garnished with the remaining peanuts.

Creamy Peanut Soup. Like velvet, but peanutty velvet: Omit the collards or kale. In Step 3, along with the peanut butter, stir in 1 cup heavy cream, rice milk, or coconut milk, either made from scratch (page 423) or canned (use $1/2$ can, slightly less than 1 cup, with a little water). Use an immersion blender to purée the soup in the pan. Or cool the mixture slightly, pour into a blender, and purée carefully. Gently reheat the soup, taste and adjust the seasoning, and garnish with the remaining peanuts.

Southwestern Mixed Vegetable Soup

MAKES: 4 servings
TIME: 40 minutes

Another vegetable soup with wide-ranging possibilities: you can make it fiery hot or mild, increase the amount of corn or black beans or omit either or both, use chayote in place of (or in addition to) the zucchini, omit the tomatillos, add a few strips of roasted poblano, and so on. But the basic recipe is pretty terrific.

2 tablespoons neutral oil, like grapeseed or corn

1 large onion, roughly chopped

1 tablespoon minced garlic

1 dried chipotle chile (optional)

1 tablespoon ground cumin

I've defended frozen vegetables elsewhere (page 235),

Frozen Vegetables in Soup

I've defended frozen vegetables elsewhere (page 235), so I won't go into all their advantages here. But as soup is among the most forgiving things you can cook, it allows the use of frozen vegetables more than most other dishes. In fact it's almost impossible to overstate the value of frozen vegetables in soups. Ones that I would almost never eat solo, or as the main ingredient in a dish, like broccoli or spinach, can work quite well in soups. Others, like corn and peas, are soup staples.

So stock a few bags of frozen veggies in your freezer, supplement them with fresh if possible, and you can put together something brilliant with little time and effort. The rules for buying frozen vegetables in general are described on page 234. There are two good ways to use them in soup. If you're in a hurry, just dump 'em in, straight from the bag. Just remember this will cool off your soup fast, so it's going to take longer to cook.

The second method, and it's better—if you have the time—is to brown the vegetables lightly in oil to defrost them. This will add flavor to both the vegetables and the broth.

1 tablespoon fresh oregano or epazote leaves

Salt and freshly ground black pepper

1 large potato, peeled and roughly chopped

1 cup corn kernels (frozen are acceptable; don't bother to thaw)

1 cup cooked black beans

3 tomatillos, husked and cut into chunks (or use canned tomatillos, drained)

1 medium tomato, cored and roughly chopped

1 medium or 2 small zucchini or summer squash, roughly chopped

6 cups vegetable stock (pages 101–102) or water

$1/4$ cup or more chopped fresh cilantro leaves

① Put the oil in a large saucepan or casserole over medium heat. When hot, add the onion and cook, stirring occasionally, until it begins to brown, about 10 minutes. Add the garlic, chipotle, cumin, oregano, and some salt and pepper and cook, stirring, for about 30 seconds. Add the vegetables along with some more salt and pepper and cook, stirring occasionally, until they are shiny, just a minute or so.

② Add the stock, bring to a boil, and adjust the heat so the mixture bubbles gently. Cook until the vegetables are very tender (the potato will take the longest), 15 to 20 minutes. Taste, adjust the seasoning, and serve, garnished with the cilantro.

Southwestern Mixed Vegetable Soup with Avocado. Hot and cool, really nice: Peel, pit, and slice 2 large avocados and divide the flesh among 4 bowls. Ladle the soup over them. Garnish with cilantro and a squeeze of fresh lime juice.

Tortilla Soup

MAKES: 4 servings
TIME: 1 hour
Ⓜ

Usually cobbled together from leftovers, and truly one of the best uses for stale tortillas, this is delicious and fortifying enough to warrant the limelight. The most important thing to keep in mind is that the soup is at its best 5 or 10 minutes after you add the crisp fried tortillas, when they're pliable but not yet soft. At this point, they have an inimitable, almost meaty texture.

You could substitute one 28-ounce can of tomatoes for the fresh tomatoes and skip Step 3; out of season it's probably your best option. The garnishes, you'll note, are all optional; it's nice to have all of them, but none is essential . . .

1/2 cup peanut or neutral oil, like grapeseed or corn

6 corn tortillas (stale are fine), cut into 1/2-inch strips

Salt

2 fresh chiles, preferably poblano, or 2 dried ancho chiles

3 cloves garlic, sliced

1 large onion, sliced

1 1/2 pounds tomatoes

Freshly ground black pepper

Pinch dried oregano or epazote

1 quart water or vegetable stock (pages 101–102)

1 lime, cut into wedges

1 cup fresh cilantro leaves, chopped for garnish (optional)

1 cup queso fresco or Monterey Jack, cubed for garnish (optional)

1 ripe avocado, peeled, pitted, and sliced for garnish (optional)

1 or 2 radishes, thinly sliced for garnish (optional)

1/2 carrot, grated on the biggest holes of a box grater for garnish (optional)

① Heat the broiler. Heat the oil in a saucepan over medium-high heat. When the oil is hot (about 350°F), begin to fry the tortilla strips in batches until golden brown and crisp, turning after a minute or two, for a total of 2 to 4 minutes. Drain on paper towels, season each batch with a pinch of salt, and set aside. Wait a minute between batches to let the oil return to 350°. (If you're using ancho chiles in the soup, fry them for 30 seconds each in this oil before proceeding to the next step.)

② Discard all but 2 tablespoons of the oil. Turn the heat to medium and cook the garlic and onion, stirring occasionally, until golden and softened, about 10 minutes.

③ Meanwhile, arrange the tomatoes and poblano chiles in a single layer on a rimmed baking sheet and broil a few inches from the heat until charred on one side, then flip them over with tongs and char the other side, about 5 to 8 minutes total. Skin, stem, and seed the chiles (see page 828).

Ⓕ Fast   Ⓜ Make Ahead   Ⓥ Vegan

④ Add the tomatoes and chiles to the pan with the onion and garlic and crush the tomatoes with the back of a wooden spoon. Season with salt, pepper, and a pinch of oregano; add the water and adjust the heat so the mixture simmers gently. Cook for 20 to 30 minutes, crushing the tomatoes from time to time. (You can prepare the soup up to this point in advance, then let it sit for a few hours or cover and refrigerate for up to a day before proceeding. Store the tortilla chips in an airtight container if you're waiting more than 4 or 5 hours.)

⑤ Cool the soup slightly. Using an immersion blender or an upright blender (be careful to avoid spattering), purée the mixture until smooth. Return to the stove over medium heat, stir in the fried tortillas, and simmer for another 3 to 5 minutes. Season to taste with lime juice, salt, and pepper. Garnish with any or all of the garnishes and serve.

Vegetable Soup, Thai Style

MAKES: 4 servings
TIME: 30 minutes

This style of Thai soup tends to be thin, almost meager, but extremely flavorful, laced with lime, chile, and lemongrass. The selection of vegetables here is pretty traditional, but you can substitute freely.

6 cups vegetable stock (pages 101–102), Mushroom Stock (page 102), or water

3 stalks lemongrass

2 tablespoons soy sauce, or more to taste

1 lime leaf, minced, or the grated zest of a lime

1 small hot fresh chile, preferably Thai, stemmed, seeded, and minced, or more to taste

Freshly ground black pepper

1 teaspoon sugar

1/2 cup sliced button or oyster mushrooms

1/2 cup snow peas, trimmed, or shelled peas (frozen are fine)

1/2 cup finely chopped carrots

Juice of 1 lime, or more to taste

Chopped fresh cilantro leaves for garnish

① Put the stock in a saucepan over medium-high heat. Mince the core of one of the lemongrass stalks (see page 767) and add it; trim and bruise the other 2 lemongrass stalks, cut them into 2- or 3-inch lengths, and add them to the pot along with the soy sauce, lime leaf, chile, pepper, and sugar. Stir, then add the vegetables.

② Simmer for about 15 minutes, or until the vegetables are tender but not mushy. Add the lime juice, then taste and adjust the seasoning, adding more soy, lime, chile, or pepper as you like. Garnish with the cilantro and serve.

Mixed Vegetable Soup, Korean Style

MAKES: 4 servings
TIME: 40 minutes

One of the simplest and fastest of mixed vegetable soups but, flavor-wise, the equal of anything, thanks to sesame oil and seeds, soy sauce, and plenty of garlic. The fresh red peppers called for here—sold at all Korean and many other Asian markets—are not super-fiery, but they will add some heat as well as substance. If you can't find them, just add a single dried red chile along with the garlic.

3 tablespoons dark sesame oil

2 tablespoons minced garlic

4 long Korean red peppers, if available, stemmed, seeded, and diced

1 carrot, roughly chopped

You can make a decent soup from nothing more than cabbage, water, and salt, and many people did so for centuries, in Asia, the Mediterranean, and later the New World. So imagine what the complexity and body of this vegetable can add to some of your favorite soups. The trick is to know which type to add when and how much is enough.

For flavor: Choose the regular green (sometimes called *white*) variety, cut the leaves into wide ribbons, and add a couple of handfuls during the last few minutes of cooking time. If you want to tone down the effect, use the milder Napa or Savoy cabbage, make the pieces smaller, use less (a single handful is a good start), or add the cabbage earlier in the cooking process.

For heft: Cabbage is nearly all water, so it doesn't absorb liquid during cooking. It doesn't break down quickly either, so a moderate amount—say 2 cups cut into large or small pieces—can instantly turn any of the soups here into a stew.

For texture: When cabbage does start to break down, it lends a silkiness that acts as a thickener. This is especially true with the long-leafed Napa variety. It doesn't take much—no more than a cup or so. Chop into small pieces or very thin shreds or grate on the large holes of a box grater. Add early in the recipe to allow time for the cabbage to literally melt away.

For color: The only time to use red-leaf cabbage is to enhance an already red or dark soup. None of the green-leaf types will have much impact on color.

1 celery stalk, roughly chopped

1 cup peeled and diced daikon radish or white turnip

2 cups shredded Napa or other cabbage

6 cups vegetable stock (pages 101–102) or water

2 tablespoons soy sauce

Salt and freshly ground black pepper, if necessary

$^1/_2$ cup chopped scallion

1 tablespoon sesame seeds, toasted (see page 321)

1 Put 2 tablespoons of the oil in a large saucepan or casserole over medium heat. When hot, add the garlic. As soon as it begins to sizzle, add the peppers, carrot, celery, daikon, and cabbage. Cook, stirring occasionally, for a couple of minutes, or until the vegetables are coated with oil. Add the stock and soy sauce and bring to a boil.

2 Adjust the heat so the mixture bubbles gently and cook until all the vegetables are tender, about 30 minutes. Taste and adjust the seasoning, then ladle into bowls. Sprinkle with the scallion and sesame seeds, drizzle with the remaining sesame oil, and serve.

Creamy Soups

Many people think that for every bowl of smooth, creamy soup on the table there's a worn-out cook in the kitchen—cream soups are so impressive they must be difficult, right?

Wrong. Actually, this family of soups is easy to make in advance, which makes them perfect for entertaining. In fact, because they're mostly puréed, it's better to make them in advance. Since creaminess often comes from a simple addition, it's really no big deal, and there is no denying their elegance.

There are vegan and low-fat options here, too, from flour and cornstarch to nondairy milks (vegans will obviously want to use some kind of vegetable oil instead of the butter too). And before you just reach for the soy milk, see "Creaminess Without Dairy" on page 132.

Every soup in this section is creamy, but not all are puréed. For those that are completely smooth, always be careful puréeing hot soup. It's important to let it cool down a bit before putting it in a blender and somewhat safer to do so with an immersion blender or a food mill.

F Fast   **M** Make Ahead   **V** Vegan

Creamy Carrot Soup

MAKES: 4 servings
TIME: 45 minutes

This classic French soup can be varied in several ways and can also be produced in a completely different fashion, as in the Glazed Carrot Soup on page 105 and the Thai version at right.

Puréed carrot soup is thick and smooth even without dairy or a substitute—which is why I've made those optional—but their addition produces a rich, filling, and delicious version. And you can follow the same technique with almost any root vegetable—turnips, potatoes, or celeriac, for example. The soup is especially flavorful with parsnips, which are sweet beyond belief.

    3 tablespoons butter or extra virgin olive oil

    1 small onion, sliced

    1 pound carrots, roughly chopped

    1 large starchy potato, peeled and roughly chopped

    Salt and freshly ground black pepper

    5 cups vegetable stock (pages 101–102) or water

    2 teaspoons sugar, or to taste (optional)

    1/2 cup cream or sour cream (optional)

    1/4 cup chopped parsley leaves for garnish

1 Put the butter or oil in a large, deep saucepan or casserole over medium heat. When the butter melts or the oil is hot, add the vegetables. Season with salt and pepper and cook, stirring occasionally, for about 15 minutes, until the carrots soften a bit. Add the stock and cook until the vegetables are very tender, 15 to 20 minutes.

2 Use an immersion blender to purée the soup in the pan. Or cool the mixture slightly (hot soup is dangerous), pass it through a food mill or pour it into a blender, and purée carefully until smooth, working in batches if necessary. (You may prepare the soup in advance up to this point. Cover, refrigerate for up to 2 days, and reheat before proceeding.) Adjust the seasoning; if the soup tastes flat, stir in the sugar to play up the carrot flavor.

3 If you're serving the soup hot, reheat it in the saucepan. If you're serving it cold, refrigerate, covered, for at least 2 hours. Either way, stir in the cream if you're using it, then garnish and serve.

Creamy Fennel Soup. A shot of Pernod, Ricard, or other anise-flavored liqueur added with the vegetable stock will boost the flavor even further. Substitute fennel for carrots; reserve the fennel fronds for garnish and use them in place of the parsley.

Creamy Celery Soup. Substitute celery for the carrots; reserve the celery leaves for garnish if they're green and fresh; otherwise use parsley or dill for garnish.

Thai-Style Carrot Soup

MAKES: 4 servings
TIME: 40 minutes

If you think of carrot soup as creamy and French (and there's no reason not to; see left), this will expand the concept for you. It's still creamy, but decidedly unFrench, with classic Southeast Asian flavors and even a little heat.

    2 tablespoons peanut or neutral oil, like grapeseed or corn

    3 stalks lemongrass, trimmed and bruised (see page 767), then cut into 2-inch lengths

    10 nickel-sized slices peeled ginger

    2 cloves garlic, peeled

    8 to 10 medium carrots (about 1 pound), cut into 1-inch pieces

    Salt and cayenne pepper, to taste

    1 quart homemade coconut milk (page 423) or 2 cans, slightly less than 1 quart, with a little water

    1/4 cup chopped fresh cilantro leaves for garnish, plus their stems

1 teaspoon sugar, if necessary

1 lime, quartered, for serving

1 Put the oil in a medium saucepan over medium heat. When hot, add the lemongrass, ginger, and garlic and cook, stirring and turning occasionally, until the garlic is golden, about 5 minutes.

2 Add the carrots, a large pinch of salt, and $1/4$ teaspoon or so of cayenne. Cook for a minute, then add the coconut milk and 2 cups water. Add the cilantro stems. Bring the mixture to a boil, then lower the heat to medium-low and simmer the soup for 15 minutes—bubbles should break the surface only occasionally—or until the carrots are tender. (You may prepare the soup in advance up to this point. Cover and refrigerate for up to 2 days before puréeing.)

3 Fish out the cilantro stems. Then use an immersion blender to purée the soup in the pan. Or cool the mixture slightly (hot soup is dangerous), pass it through a food mill or pour it into a blender, and purée carefully. Reheat as necessary, then taste and adjust the seasoning, adding salt, cayenne, and sugar if you think the soup needs it. Divide the soup into bowls, garnish with cilantro, and serve with lime wedges.

Creamy Cauliflower (or Broccoli) Soup

MAKES: 4 servings

TIME: About 30 minutes

Ⓕ Ⓜ

Creamy cauliflower soup is simple and comforting; I like to make a double batch in the winter and have it ready to go in the refrigerator, since its mild, uncomplicated flavor makes it a suitable starter before just about anything (especially given that it's easy enough to change its soul from European to Indian; see the variation). It's delicious with a grilled cheese sandwich for a light but satisfying meal.

2 tablespoons butter or olive oil

1 large onion, sliced

1 head cauliflower or 1 pound broccoli, florets separated, stems chopped

2 cloves garlic, chopped

Salt and freshly ground black pepper

$1/2$ cup white wine

3 cups vegetable stock (pages 101–102)

1 cup cream or sour cream

1 Put the butter or oil in a large, deep saucepan over medium heat. When the butter is melted or the oil is hot, add the onion, cauliflower, garlic, a large pinch of salt, and some pepper. Cook until the onion is softened, 5 to 10 minutes. Add the white wine, cook for 1 minute, then add the stock and cook until the cauliflower is very tender, 10 to 15 minutes.

2 Use an immersion blender to purée the soup in the pan. Or cool the mixture slightly (hot soup is dangerous), pass it through a food mill or pour it into a blender, and purée carefully until smooth, working in batches if necessary. (You may prepare the soup in advance up to this point. Cover, refrigerate for up to 2 days, and reheat before proceeding.)

3 Stir in the cream, taste and adjust the seasoning, and serve.

Indian Cauliflower Soup. Only a little more work, but a lot different: Substitute neutral or mustard oil for the olive oil or butter. Add 1 teaspoon each cumin seed and garam masala to the hot oil 30 seconds before adding the vegetables. Substitute yogurt for the cream in the final step. If you like, garnish the soup with chopped cilantro, a scattering of brown mustard seeds (about $1/2$ teaspoon per serving) toasted in a dry pan for a minute, or both.

Creamy Jerusalem Artichoke Soup. You don't see Jerusalem artichokes (sunchokes; see page 369) that often, but when you do, grab them. Substitute about

1 pound, trimmed of hard or discolored spots but not peeled, for the cauliflower.

Chile Bisque

MAKES: 4 servings

TIME: About 1½ hours, largely unattended

This is one of those pure and simple soups flavored by a single ingredient. Well, almost. The only other things between you and the complex taste of mild dried chile are a touch of garlic and a hint of bay. You can change the heat level by using 2 or 3 chiles or none instead of 1; in fact, this soup is a terrific way to experiment with the characteristics of different dried and fresh chiles.

5 or 6 (about 3 ounces) dried ancho chiles

1 chipotle chile, dried or canned (don't use too much of the adobo if you use canned; optional)

2 tablespoons extra virgin olive oil

1 tablespoon minced garlic

¼ cup medium- or long- grain rice

Salt and freshly ground black pepper

1 quart vegetable stock (pages 101– 102) or water

2 bay leaves

1 cup cream

❶ Put a skillet, preferably cast iron, over medium-high heat. Toast the dried chiles until darkened slightly and fragrant, about 2 minutes per side. If you're using canned chipotle, set it aside for later. Put the dried chiles in a bowl and cover with boiling water. Use a plate to keep them submerged if necessary. Let the chiles soak until soft, an hour or so.

❷ After the chiles have been soaking for about 30 minutes, put the oil in a deep skillet or medium saucepan over medium-high heat. When hot, add the garlic and cook, stirring constantly, until soft, about a minute. Add the canned chipotle, if you're using it, and the rice and sprinkle

with salt and pepper. Continue cooking and stirring until the rice starts to turn translucent, about 2 minutes more.

❸ Add the stock and the bay leaves and bring to a boil. Lower the heat so that soup bubbles gently, cover, and cook undisturbed until the rice is very tender, about 20 minutes. Turn off the heat.

❹ When the chiles are soft, drain them, carefully remove their stems and seeds, and add them to the soup pot. Fish out the bay leaves. Use an immersion blender to purée the soup in the pan. Or cool the mixture slightly (hot soup is dangerous), pass it through a food mill or pour it into a blender, and purée carefully. (The soup may be made ahead to this point, cooled, and refrigerated for up to 2 days. Serve cold or reheat it gently.) Add the cream and turn the heat under the pot to medium. Gently reheat the soup until hot but not boiling. Cook, uncovered, for another 3 to 5 minutes, until slightly thickened (if it's too thick, add a little water or stock). Taste, adjust the seasoning, then serve.

6 Unusual Condiments for Almost Any Soup

1. Parsley "Pesto" or Parsley Purée (page 768)
2. Crunchy Nut Chutney (page 784)
3. Balsamic Syrup (page 798)
4. Compound Butter (page 801)
5. Citrus Sprinkle (page 818)
6. Chile Paste, Eight Ways (page 828)

Cream of Parsley Soup

MAKES: 4 servings

TIME: 30 minutes

This brings the green, fresh taste of parsley to soup. Be sure to wash the parsley very, very well (use a salad spinner, repeatedly, until the water is perfectly clear): The tiniest bit of sand can ruin your enjoyment of this soup.

    3 tablespoons butter or extra virgin olive oil

    3 or 4 shallots or 1 medium to large onion, chopped

    4 cups well-washed parsley

    1 quart vegetable stock, (pages 101–102)

    2 cups cream or half-and-half

    Salt and freshly ground black pepper

① Put 2 tablespoons of the butter or oil in a large saucepan or wide casserole over medium-high heat. When the butter is melted or the oil is hot, add the shallots and cook, stirring occasionally, until translucent and soft, about 5 minutes. Add the parsley and cook, stirring occasionally, until it wilts, 3 to 5 minutes. Stir in about half the stock and turn off the heat.

② Use an immersion blender to purée the soup in the pan. Or cool the mixture slightly (hot soup is dangerous), pass it through a food mill or pour it into a blender, and purée carefully. Return to the skillet with the remaining stock and the cream. Heat through, then season to taste. Stir in the remaining butter or oil and serve.

Gratinéed Cream of Parsley Soup. Extra luxury: Put the soup in heatproof individual bowls and top each with a generous grating of Parmesan. Run under the broiler for a minute or two to brown the cheese and serve, warning your guests that the bowls are hot.

Creamy Watercress, Spinach, or Sorrel Soup

MAKES: 4 servings
TIME: About 30 minutes

Ⓕ Ⓜ

Watercress is among my favorite greens; I find its assertively peppery, herbaceous flavor irresistible. Using

it as a soup base tames its spiciness somewhat but without sublimating its flavor. If you can't find cress, feel free to use spinach, arugula, or sorrel.

    2 tablespoons butter or extra virgin olive oil

    4 cups coarsely chopped watercress, well washed and trimmed of thick stems

    2 cups vegetable stock (pages 101–102), warmed, or water

    2 cups cream or milk

    Salt and freshly ground black pepper

① Put the butter or oil in a large, deep saucepan or casserole over medium heat. When the butter is melted or the oil is hot, add the watercress and cook, stirring, until it wilts, about 5 minutes.

Creaminess Without Dairy

Soups can be made creamy without cream, of course: Just use any of the nondairy "milks" discussed on page 29. Soy, almond, and coconut have the most pronounced flavor; rice and oat milks are more neutral (and more watery). Like cow's milk and yogurt, all will tend to separate if boiled. That means vegan milks work best in the company of thoroughly cooked potatoes or beans, and really shine in puréed soups, where there are enough other solids to help control the separation.

Because cream is mostly fat, and vegetable-based milks (and dairy milk and yogurt) are quite lean, it's nearly impossible to duplicate the same mild, silky texture. You can, however, incorporate a tablespoon or two of additional oil into the recipe to enrich it; this is best done either at the very beginning, while cooking the onions, garlic, or ginger; during puréeing (if the soup is going to be puréed); or by passing a full-flavored oil like extra virgin olive or dark sesame at the table, as a last-minute drizzle.

 Fast   Make Ahead   Ⓥ Vegan

② Add the stock, bring almost to a boil, lower the heat, and cook briefly, until the watercress is tender.

③ Use an immersion blender to purée the soup in the pan. Or cool the mixture slightly (hot soup is dangerous), pass it through a food mill or pour it into a blender, and purée carefully. (You may prepare the soup in advance up to this point. Cover, refrigerate for up to 2 days, and reheat before proceeding.) Return to the heat and add the cream or milk. Sprinkle with salt and pepper, reheat gently—do not boil—and serve.

Watercress Soup with Potatoes and Pears. Watercress and pears get along perfectly in salads, and that affinity carries over to soup: In Step 1, before sautéing the greens, add 1 coarsely chopped baking (starchy) potato and 1 coarsely chopped onion to the melted butter. Cover and cook over medium-low heat, stirring occasionally, until the onion and potato are nearly tender, about 15 minutes. Add the watercress and 2 peeled, cored, and chopped pears—they can be slightly underripe—and proceed with the recipe.

Pumpkin (or Winter Squash) Soup

MAKES: 4 servings

TIME: About 1 hour, mostly unattended

I call this pumpkin soup but encourage you to experiment with some of the other members of the hard-skinned squash family (see page 363), especially butternut squash. Any (except the oversized pumpkins used for jack-o'-lanterns) will give you incredibly smooth texture when puréed, with or without cream. And the variations will take you around the world; because winter squashes are easy to grow and the vines are prolific, this is a soup that's popular almost everywhere, as you'll see from the variations.

3 tablespoons butter or neutral oil, like grapeseed or corn

3 pounds sugar pumpkin or any winter squash (1 medium squash), like acorn, butternut, calabaza, Hubbard, kabocha, or turban, peeled, seeded, and cut into 1- to 2-inch cubes

1 medium onion, roughly chopped

1 tablespoon chopped fresh sage or 1 teaspoon chopped fresh rosemary

Salt and freshly ground black pepper

5 cups any vegetable stock (pages 101–102) or water

1 cup cream or half-and-half

① Put the butter or oil in a deep skillet or medium saucepan over medium-high heat. When the butter is melted or the oil is hot, add the pumpkin and onion and cook, stirring occasionally, until the onion softens, about 5 minutes. Add the herb, sprinkle with salt and pepper, and continue cooking until fragrant, another minute or so. Add the stock and bring to a boil, then lower the heat so the soup bubbles gently. Partially cover and cook, stirring occasionally, until the pumpkin starts to fall apart, about 30 minutes.

② Use an immersion blender to purée the soup in the pan. Or cool the mixture slightly (hot soup is dangerous), pass it through a food mill or pour it into a blender container, and purée carefully. (The soup may be made ahead to this point, cooled, and refrigerated for up to 2 days. Serve cold or reheat it gently.)

③ Heat the puréed soup until almost boiling. Stir in the cream and heat through, but do not boil. Taste, adjust the seasoning, and serve garnished with an extra grinding of black pepper if you like.

Pumpkin Soup with Chipotle. A little bit of fire: In Step 1, add 1 tablespoon minced garlic to the pumpkin mixture. When the soup is done, gently heat $1/2$ cup Smoky and Hot Salsa Roja (page 788). After serving, garnish each bowl (or the soup terrine) by putting a dollop of chipotle sauce in the center and swirling it through the soup with a knife.

Indian-Style Pumpkin Soup. Lovely, especially with coconut milk: Omit the sage or rosemary. In Step 1, add 1 tablespoon minced garlic, 1 tablespoon minced peeled fresh ginger, and 1 tablespoon curry powder (page 816) to the pumpkin mixture. Substitute 1 cup coconut milk (page 423 or canned) for the cream or half-and-half. If you like, garnish with $1/4$ cup each of chopped fresh cilantro and chopped scallion.

Rustic Pumpkin Soup. Easier: Use any of the seasoning combinations described in the main recipe or variations. In Step 1, add 1 cup roughly chopped tomato (canned is fine) to the pumpkin mixture. Increase the stock to 6 cups. Don't bother to purée the soup, and omit the cream or half-and-half.

Bread-and-Water Pumpkin Soup. A super-basic recipe, but still delicious: Pare down the ingredient list so that it includes only the pumpkin, salt and pepper, and 6 cups water. In Step 1, add 6 cloves peeled garlic. After the pumpkin cooks, stir in 4 or 5 slices of crustless stale French or Italian bread. Purée as directed in Step 2 and serve.

Argentinean Pumpkin Soup. Much closer to a whole meal: Along with the pumpkin and onion, add 1 bell pepper, preferably red, stemmed, seeded, and chopped, and 2 or 3 medium waxy potatoes, peeled and cubed. Along with the stock, add 2 or 3 chopped tomatoes (canned are fine) and about a cup of dried apricots. Add more stock or water if necessary if the mixture becomes too thick. Do not purée the soup, but, during the last few minutes of cooking, add a cup of corn kernels, preferably freshly stripped from the cob (or frozen). Cream is optional.

Virginian Peanut Soup

MAKES: 4 servings

TIME: 45 minutes

Where Peanut Soup, Senegalese Style (page 124), is rustic and loaded with vegetables, this classic American peanut soup is subtle and refined. Traditionally, a smooth, roux-thickened peanut soup signals the beginning of a heavy southern meal, but I've replaced the roux with fresh cream and a potato and added chunky peanut butter. Smooth peanut butter is a product that often contains extra sugars and fats that mask the true flavor of peanuts, though, of course, "real" smooth peanut butter exists, and if you prefer that, go ahead and use it. But I like the crunch.

2 tablespoons butter

$1/4$ cup minced onion

2 celery stalks, chopped

2 carrots, chopped

Salt and freshly ground black pepper

1 large russet potato, peeled and cut into chunks

2 bay leaves

5 cups vegetable stock (pages 101–102) or water

1 cup heavy or light cream, or half-and-half

$1/2$ cup chunky peanut butter

2 tablespoons chopped roasted peanuts for garnish

1 Put the butter in a deep skillet or medium saucepan over medium-high heat. When melted, add the onion and cook, stirring occasionally, until it softens, about 3 minutes. Stir in the celery and carrots, sprinkle with salt and pepper, and cook until the vegetables begin to release their liquid, 3 to 5 minutes.

2 Add the potato, bay leaves, and stock. Bring to a boil, then reduce the heat so the soup bubbles gently. Cover and cook, stirring occasionally, until the vegetables are very soft, 25 to 30 minutes. Carefully push the soup through a strainer with a big spoon or a potato masher so that some of it comes out the other side puréed. Use a spoon or a rubber spatula to scrape that vegetable puree back into the strained soup. Discard the remaining solids in the strainer.

F Fast   M Make Ahead   V Vegan

③ Bring the soup back to a gentle bubble. Stir in the cream and peanut butter and cook, without boiling, until slightly thickened, about 3 minutes. Garnish with the peanuts and serve.

Vegan Virginian Peanut Soup. Instead of butter, start with 2 tablespoons peanut oil. Omit the cream and use 1 cup soy milk.

Corn Chowder

MAKES: 4 servings

TIME: About 1 hour

This chowder celebrates the bounty of a single summertime crop—corn. And since you will probably make it only once or twice a year, I would opt for the richer half-and-half option, though the leaner version has a purity of flavor I also love.

Kernels from 6 ears fresh corn, cobs reserved

Salt and freshly ground black pepper

4 tablespoons ($1/2$ stick) butter or neutral oil, like grapeseed or corn

$1/2$ cup chopped scallion

$1/2$ teaspoon sugar

$1/4$ cup flour

1 quart milk or half-and-half

Corn Bread Croutons (page 806) for garnish (optional)

① Put the corn cobs and 2 cups water in a pan with a tight-fitting lid over medium-high heat. Sprinkle with salt and pepper. Bring to a boil, then lower the heat so the water bubbles gently, cover, and cook, checking occasionally, for about 30 minutes. Leave the cobs in the pot until you're ready to make the soup, then remove them and save the broth.

② Put the butter or oil in a deep skillet or medium saucepan over medium-high heat. When the butter is melted or the oil is hot, add the scallion and sugar and cook, stirring occasionally, until the scallion is soft, about 1 minute. Turn the heat down to medium and stir in the flour. Cook, stirring constantly with a whisk or a wooden spoon, until the mixture starts to turn golden and the flour no longer smells raw, 5 to 10 minutes. Add the milk and the reserved broth and turn the heat up to medium-high. Stir or whisk constantly until the flour is dissolved and the soup starts to thicken, about 2 minutes.

③ Stir in the corn kernels and bring to a boil, then lower the heat so that the soup bubbles gently. Cook, stirring occasionally, until the corn is tender and the soup has thickened, 10 to 15 minutes. Taste, adjust the seasoning, garnish, and serve.

Thicker Corn Chowder. Peel 1 large baking potato and cut into small ($1/2$-inch) dice. Add the potato to the pot along with the corn in Step 3. After bringing the soup to a boil, cook covered, instead of uncovered, stirring occasionally. Proceed with the recipe.

Roasted Corn Chowder. Heat the oven to 400°F. Rub a little extra virgin olive oil over each husked corn cob before slicing off the kernels. Sprinkle with salt and pepper and put on a rimmed baking sheet. Roast the corn, turning frequently, until the kernels start to brown, 15 to 25 minutes. When the corn is cool enough to handle, shuck the kernels (see page 288) and follow the recipe from the beginning of Step 1.

Corn Chowder with Tomatoes. Canned tomatoes work just fine here. Coarsely chop 3 roma (plum) tomatoes. (If you're using fresh, you may peel and seed them first, but it's not necessary.) In Step 3, add them to the pot with the corn and proceed with the recipe.

Cheesy Corn Chowder. Prepare either the main recipe or one of the variations through Step 2. In Step 3, along with the corn, add $1/2$ cup grated cheese, like Parmesan, sharp cheddar, or hard goat cheese. Proceed with the recipe.

I'd rather eat a bowl of fresh-tasting, broth-based soup than one that has been gratuitously thickened with raw flour or cornstarch. But for those times when you want something a little heartier and maybe more filling, here are the ingredients that will make a good soup thicker while also adding flavor *and* nutrients:

Potato: The starch in an all-purpose or russet ("baking") potato adds heft to soup, along with a little flavor. (Waxy potatoes, like "new" potatoes, have a different effect.) If you're going to purée the soup after cooking, just peel and dice a potato and add it at the same time as the broth or water. If you want to thicken a chunky bean or vegetable soup, a spoonful or two of leftover mashed potatoes will do the trick. A few minutes before serving, stir them into the pot until completely dissolved and heat until almost boiling.

Grains: Grains—especially whole grains like cracked wheat, brown rice, or millet—are more flavorful than potatoes in soup. Adding a scoop of cooked grains to the finished soup is one thing. But if you want to increase body and richness, add a small quantity of grain at the beginning of the recipe; cook until it's falling apart, then purée. (Chile Bisque, page 131, is one example of how this works.) Other models for inspiration: Try sprinkling 1/4 cup of couscous grains over the cooking carrots in Glazed Carrot Soup (page 105) or add 1/2 cup of millet to Step 1 of the "Smooth Chickpea Soup" (page 118).

Pasta: Cooking noodles in soup has definite advantages. The noodles absorb the flavors of the stock while releasing starches—wheat or rice, depending on the noodle—that thicken the soup and add a subtle nuttiness. Be sure you have a little extra liquid and room in the pot to accommodate the noodles as they swell and then serve the soup immediately: All noodles turn to mush quickly. (If your soup is done before you're ready to add the noodles, turn off the heat. Bring the soup back to a boil a while before you're ready to eat, then stir in the noodles.)

Legumes: Of all the ingredients that thicken soups, beans are among the most flavorful. White beans tend to be the most neutral and versatile and lend a creaminess rivaled only by butter or cream, especially when puréed. Like grains, cooked legumes can be added to already-made soups as an afterthought or cooked along with the other ingredients until tender, then puréed or mashed.

Nut and Seed Butters or Pastes: These deliver loads of flavor; use them judiciously so they won't compete with other ingredients. Because they have more fat than beans, they also make the soup richer, with more body. A good example of nuts as a thickener is Peanut Soup, Senegalese Style (pages 124–125).

Bread: A couple of soups, like Zuppa di Pane (page 121) and Tomato and Bread Soup (page 112), include bread as a key ingredient. If possible, use stale, days-old bread, which absorbs broth without disintegrating. Croutons are the most obvious way to enhance soup with bread, but bread crumbs work well too. And few things are simpler or more satisfying than slipping a piece of toast into a bowl and pouring a ladleful of soup over it.

Butter: For an unsurpassed velvety texture and heightened flavor, cut up some cold butter, from a teaspoon or two to a couple of tablespoons. When the soup is ready to serve, turn off the heat, add to the pot, and stir until melted.

Dairy and Nondairy Creams and Milks: This category includes cream, half-and-half, sour cream, milk, yogurt, Mexican crema, and crème fraîche as well as vegan milks, like coconut, soy, almond, and rice. All have some thickening power, though some tend to separate when heated to a boil. See the introduction to the Cream Soups section on page 128 and "Creaminess Without Dairy" on page 132.

 Fast   Make Ahead   Ⓥ Vegan

Mushroom Stew

MAKES: 4 servings

TIME: 45 minutes

I don't often use flour to thicken soups because there are more flavorful and nutritious ways to give them body (see page 136). But there are exceptions, like the Corn Chowder on page 135 and this Louisiana-inspired mushroom stew. In both cases the flour is cooked, here in a moderately toasted roux, in which the flour takes on a lovely nuttiness. For extra richness, substitute a cup of cream for a cup of stock.

4 tablespoons (¹/₂ stick) butter or neutral oil, like grapeseed or corn

¹/₄ cup flour

1¹/₂ pounds shiitake, portobello, cremini, or button mushrooms or a mixture, thickly sliced

Salt and freshly ground black pepper

¹/₄ cup minced onion

¹/₄ cup minced celery

¹/₄ cup minced green bell pepper

2 or 3 sprigs fresh thyme, plus (optional) 2 tablespoons leaves for garnish

6 cups Mushroom Stock (page 103), vegetable stock (pages 101–102), or water

¹/₄ cup dry sherry for garnish (optional)

1 Put the butter or oil and the flour in a deep skillet or medium saucepan over medium heat. As the mixture warms, stir constantly with a wooden spoon or a whisk. The roux should bubble along at first, then start to take on a golden color. If it is smoking, or darkening too fast, lower the heat a little. Continue cooking and stirring until the roux turns the color of coffee with cream, 10 to 15 minutes.

2 Turn the heat up to medium-high and add the mushrooms. Sprinkle with salt and pepper. Cook, stirring constantly, until they are coated in the roux and start to release their liquid. Turn the heat down to medium-low and cook, stirring occasionally, until they begin to brown, 5 to 8 minutes. Stir in the onion, celery, bell pepper, and thyme and cook, stirring occasionally, until the vegetables are soft, about 3 minutes.

3 Stir in the stock, turn the heat up to medium-high, and bring to a boil. Lower the heat so the soup bubbles gently, cover, and cook, stirring occasionally, until the soup has thickened and the vegetables are very tender, about 10 minutes. Fish out the sprigs of thyme. Taste, adjust the seasoning, then serve and, if you like, garnish each bowl by pouring a tablespoon of sherry into the middle and sprinkling the top with thyme leaves.

Mushroom Stew with Green Beans. Trim ¹/₂ pound green beans and cut them into 1-inch pieces. In Step 3, right after you add the stock, stir in the beans, then proceed with the recipe.

Curried Coconut Soup with Lemongrass

MAKES: 4 servings

TIME: 40 minutes

 Ⓥ

A Thai-style soup that becomes quite substantial when you add fried tofu (or try Crunchy Crumbled Tempeh, page 674). This soup is also wonderful with a couple of spoonfuls of Steamed Sticky Rice or a cup or two of soaked and cut mung bean threads (see page 464) stirred in at the last minute.

2 tablespoons neutral oil, like grapeseed or corn

1 large onion, chopped

1 teaspoon minced garlic

1 tablespoon peeled and minced fresh ginger

1 small fresh chile, preferably Thai, stemmed, seeded, and minced (optional)

3 stalks lemongrass, peeled, trimmed, and minced (see page 767)

1 tablespoon Curry Powder (pages 815–816)

1 cup sliced shiitake mushroom caps (reserve stems for stock or discard)

1 quart vegetable stock (pages 101–102)

2 cups homemade coconut milk (page 423) or one 13-ounce can unsweetened coconut milk

2 tablespoons soy sauce, or to taste

Salt and freshly ground black pepper

Freshly squeezed lime juice, to taste

$1/2$ cup minced scallion, for garnish

$1/4$ cup minced fresh cilantro, for garnish

① Put the oil in a deep skillet or medium saucepan over medium-high heat. When hot, add the onion. Cook, stirring occasionally, until it begins to brown, about 10 minutes, then lower the heat a bit and cook for 5 minutes more, until it is very, very tender. Add the garlic, ginger, chile, lemongrass, and curry powder and cook, stirring, for about a minute. Add the mushrooms and cook for another minute, stirring.

② Add the stock and bring to a boil, then adjust the heat so the mixture simmers and cook for about 10 minutes. Stir in the coconut milk and cook about 5 minutes more. Add the soy sauce, then taste and add more soy sauce or some salt and pepper if necessary. Stir in a couple of tablespoons of lime juice, then taste and add more if you like. Garnish and serve.

Grain Soups

Whole grains work brilliantly in soup, rarely dominating but always contributing. Unlike beans, they're neutral enough to provide a backdrop for other ingredients, but they bring their own special flavors and textures.

All the grains here are cooked directly in the stock or water, which adds body to the soup. But precooked grains are a valuable last-minute addition to many soups. If you cook extra whenever you make a pot of grains, you'll always have some handy when inspiration strikes.

Barley Soup with Seasonal Vegetables

MAKES: 4 servings
TIME: 45 minutes

It's tempting to think of barley soup as quintessential winter fare. But when you let the season dictate your choice of vegetables, the heartiness changes dramatically. Start with the basic recipe here, which calls for root vegetables, augmented by the warm flavor of sage. The combination is just what you want on a cold winter day.

Now fast-forward to the summer variation that follows and base your soup on a sampling of tomatoes, corn, zucchini or other summer squash, peas, okra, and eggplant. Garnish it with fresh basil, and suddenly barley soup doesn't seem quite so wintry.

2 tablespoons neutral oil, like grapeseed or corn

1 medium onion, chopped

1 tablespoon minced garlic

Salt and freshly ground black pepper

1 cup pearled barley

6 cups vegetable stock (pages 101–102) or water

About 2 pounds root vegetables—turnips, parsnips, rutabagas, carrots, celery root, waxy potatoes like Yukon Gold or fingerling, alone or in combination—peeled and cut into $1/2$-inch dice

1 tablespoon chopped fresh sage leaves or 1 teaspoon dried rubbed sage

① Put the oil in a deep skillet or medium saucepan over medium-high heat. When hot, add the onion and cook, stirring occasionally, until soft, about 3 minutes. Stir in the garlic, sprinkle with salt and pepper, and cook for 1 minute more. Add the barley and cook, stirring constantly, until the barley starts to toast and stick, about 5 minutes. Stir in the stock and bring to a boil. Then

Ⓕ Fast   Ⓜ Make Ahead   Ⓥ Vegan

lower the heat so the liquid simmers, cover, and cook until the barley begins to soften, 10 to 15 minutes.

2 Turn the heat up to medium-high and add the root vegetables. Bring to a boil, then lower the heat to simmer again, cover, and cook until the vegetables and barley are very tender, another 15 to 20 minutes. Stir in the sage and cook for another minute or two. Taste, adjust the seasoning, and serve.

Barley Soup with Summer Vegetables. No limit to what you can use here, instead of or along with root vegetables: Use tomatoes, corn, zucchini or other summer squash, peas, okra, or eggplant, either alone or in combination. Substitute 1 cup torn fresh basil leaves for the sage, adding half with the vegetables and using the rest as a garnish.

Barley Soup with Roasted Seasonal Vegetables. More work, but more sophisticated and flavorful too: Heat the oven to 450°F. Peel and chop the sampling of root or summer vegetables. Put them in a roasting pan, drizzle with $^1/_4$ cup extra virgin olive oil, sprinkle with salt and pepper, and roast, turning once or twice, until browned and tender, about 30 minutes. Meanwhile, cook the soup as directed, simmering the barley until just tender, 20 to 30 minutes. Add the roasted vegetables, taste, and adjust the seasoning.

Mushroom Barley Soup

MAKES: 4 servings

TIME: 45 minutes

Taking an untraditional approach to the classic Eastern European "grandmother" soup (where the ingredients are usually put in a pot with some beef and boiled), this delivers real heartiness and a depth of flavor—without the meat. As discussed on page 313, the key ingredient for making the most of many mushroom dishes is dried

porcini (unless you can find fresh ones!), so here they figure prominently, along with their soaking liquid. But perhaps most important is the browning step, where the sugars in the carrots promote the caramelization of the fresh mushrooms. This technique elevates their flavor and makes the soup more complex, as does the utterly unorthodox touch of soy sauce.

1 ounce (about 1 cup) dried porcini mushrooms

2 tablespoons extra virgin olive oil

1 pound fresh shiitake, cremini, portobello, or button mushrooms, stemmed and roughly chopped

3 medium carrots, sliced

1 cup pearled barley

Salt and freshly ground black pepper

1 bay leaf

3 cups Mushroom Stock (page 102) or water

1 tablespoon soy sauce

1 Soak the porcini in 3 cups very hot water. Put the olive oil in a deep skillet or medium saucepan over high heat. When hot, add the fresh mushrooms and carrots and cook, stirring occasionally, until they begin to brown. Add the barley and continue to cook, stirring frequently, until it begins to brown, 5 to 10 minutes. Sprinkle with a little salt and plenty of pepper and turn off the heat.

2 When the porcini are soft, strain them through a strainer and reserve the soaking liquid. Sort through and discard hard bits, if any, then coarsely chop the mushrooms.

3 Turn the heat to medium-high, add the porcini to the pot, and cook, stirring, for about a minute. Add the bay leaf, the mushroom soaking water, and the stock. Bring to a boil, then lower the heat to simmer the soup; cover and cook until the barley is very tender, 20 to 30 minutes. Add the soy sauce, then taste, adjust the seasoning, and serve.

Jook

MAKES: 6 servings
TIME: about 2¹/₂ hours

Jook—also called *congee* or *rice gruel*—is a Chinese "porridge" (it's thinner than most), a breakfast item that's also terrific served as a soup in the afternoon or evening. It is truly astonishing how much flavor a cup of rice can impart to six times its volume of water, but it's the garnishes that really make jook delicious. To me, soy sauce, sesame oil, and scallions are essential, but cilantro and peanuts are terrific additions.

1 cup short-grain rice, rinsed

1 teaspoon salt, or to taste

2 inches fresh ginger, peeled

10 shiitake mushrooms, fresh or dried

Soy sauce, to taste (optional)

Dark sesame oil, to taste (optional)

¹/₂ cup chopped scallion for garnish (optional)

¹/₂ cup fresh cilantro leaves for garnish (optional)

¹/₂ cup chopped roasted peanuts for garnish (optional)

1 Wash the rice and put it in a large pot with 6 cups of water and the salt. Bring to a boil over high heat, then turn the heat to low; the mixture should simmer, but only gently. Slice half the ginger and add it to the pot; mince the remaining ginger and set aside. If you're using fresh shiitakes, stem them (discard the stems or reserve for stock), slice the caps, and add them to the pot. If you're using dried shiitakes, cover them with boiling water and soak until pliable; slice and add to the pot.

2 Partially cover the pot and simmer for about 2 hours, stirring occasionally to make sure the rice is not sticking to the bottom. The jook should have a porridge-like consistency, so if it becomes very thick too quickly, turn down the heat and stir in more water. When it is done, the jook will be soupy and creamy. Add the minced

ginger and, if you're using them, soy sauce and/or sesame oil, along with more salt if necessary. Serve with whatever garnishes you choose.

Jook with Vegetables. You can boost jook nicely with more vegetables: Add, for example, during the last 30 minutes of cooking, 2 cups chopped Savoy, Napa, or other cabbage, or iceberg or romaine lettuce, or spinach; 1 cup chopped carrot; 1 cup fresh or frozen peas; or any combination of these. Be sure to add more water to keep the mixture soupy.

North African Couscous Soup

MAKES: 4 servings
TIME: About 20 minutes

The texture of couscous in broth is extremely comforting, so if you have couscous and tomato paste in your pantry, a bowl of this soup should be in your very near future. If you have no fennel or celery, substitute carrots, zucchini, green beans, or even chopped greens in the same quantity.

If you have already-cooked couscous, use 3 cups of it instead of raw, stirring it in after the soup comes to a boil and reducing the cooking time to 1 minute. The texture will be somewhat thinner, however, and the wheat flavor won't be quite as pronounced.

3 tablespoons extra virgin olive oil

1 small red onion, minced

¹/₂ cup finely chopped celery or fennel, including some leaves or fronds

1 tablespoon Za'atar (page 818) or 2 teaspoons ground cumin

Salt and freshly ground black pepper

1 cup couscous, preferably whole wheat

3 tablespoons tomato paste

2 quarts vegetable stock (pages 101–102) or water

1 Put the olive oil in a large saucepan with a tight-fitting lid over medium-high heat. When hot, add the onion and celery and cook, stirring occasionally, until soft, about 2 minutes. Add the za'atar and sprinkle with salt and pepper. Stir constantly to keep the spices from burning and cook until just fragrant, about a minute. Add the couscous and continue stirring and cooking until the couscous begins to toast and darken, 2 to 3 minutes. Stir in the tomato paste until it is evenly distributed and begins to color, another minute or two; then add the stock and stir to dissolve the tomato paste.

2 Bring the soup to a boil, then turn the heat down to low, cover, and cook without disturbing until the couscous is plump and tender, 5 to 10 minutes. Taste, adjust the seasoning, and serve.

Farro Soup

MAKES: 4 to 6 servings

Total **TIME:** 1¹/₂ hours or more, largely unattended

Farro (see page 536) is an ancient grain, a form of wheat that has enjoyed a popular revival in the last couple of decades thanks to our quest for "new" ingredients and the popularity of classic regional Italian cooking. It's a grain that is most closely associated with Tuscany, and indeed this recipe is from Lucca, a spot that's famous for its olive oil. It captures all the rustic, full-flavored country cooking of Tuscany in a soup bowl.

Be sure to have an ample amount of grated Parmesan (at least a cup) at the table to stir into the soup (skip it if you're serving vegans). A bottle of good red wine isn't a bad idea either.

¹/₄ cup extra virgin olive oil

1 large onion, sliced

2 celery stalks, chopped

2 carrots, chopped

Salt and freshly ground black pepper

1 tablespoon minced garlic

1 cup farro, spelt, peeled wheat, or barley

1 cup dried white beans, preferably soaked for several hours or overnight

2 cups chopped tomato (canned is fine; don't bother to drain)

6 cups water or vegetable stock (pages 101–102), or more as needed

¹/₄ cup chopped parsley leaves

¹/₄ cup chopped fresh basil, if available

Freshly grated Parmesan for serving

1 Put the oil in a large, deep saucepan over medium heat. When hot, add the onion, celery, carrots, a large pinch of salt, and some pepper. Cook until the vegetables are glossy and the onion softened, 5 to 10 minutes. Add the garlic and stir; add the farro, beans, tomato, and stock and stir.

2 Bring to a boil, then adjust the heat so the mixture simmers steadily. Cook until the farro and beans are tender, at least an hour, adding stock or water as necessary if the mixture becomes too thick. (You may prepare the soup in advance up to this point; cover and refrigerate for up to 2 days, then reheat before proceeding. If the beans and farro soak up all the liquid in the soup, add water to thin it out, simmer for 5 minutes, and season to taste with salt before proceeding.)

3 Stir in the parsley and basil, then cook for another 5 minutes. Taste, adjust the seasoning, and serve with lots of Parmesan.

Farro-Mushroom Soup. This soup becomes significantly richer with the addition of reconstituted porcini or morel mushrooms: Soak a handful of dried mushrooms in a cup of hot water (piping-hot tap water is fine) for the time it takes to cook the carrots, onion, and celery, then add the mushrooms and their soaking liquid (strain it first if it seems sandy) with the farro, beans, and stock at the end of Step 1. Reduce the water or stock to 5 cups.

When you use it as a last-minute enrichment or garnish, the flavor of cheese remains in the foreground and the cheese doesn't have a chance to separate or become greasy. A handful of recipes and variations in this chapter call for specific cheeses. But here is a rundown of what you need to know about adding cheese to soup:

- The flavor of both cheese and soup will determine whether they'll make a good match. Try to combine mild with mild, for example, or use aged cheese to season sturdy soups that can stand up to more assertive flavors.
- Cheese is almost never an appetizing addition to Chinese, Thai, or Vietnamese soups. In rare cases, a fresh cheese like paneer is appropriate in Indian soups.
- Beware of adding cheese to bean soups. It doesn't take much before the cheese will bind the beans together like glue.
- Soft cheeses, like Brie, boursin, double- and triple-creams, as well as lighter goat and fresh cheeses, work particularly well as a last-minute garnish for cream soups, because they melt away so quickly. Try putting a small spoonful in each bowl and ladle the steaming soup around it. Again, be prudent.
- Salty, sharp, hard grating cheeses—Parmesan is the king—are terrific in many soups but can clump up if cooked too long. So they're best used at serving time.
- The rinds from hard cheeses, when added to the soup early during cooking, enhance both richness and flavor. You can fish them out before serving or chomp on them at the table (a wonderful thing).
- Use smoked cheeses—judiciously—for meatiness.
- Crumbling cheeses, like queso fresco, feta, and blue cheeses, take a long time to melt in soup, which make them good if you're looking to create some contrast.
- To add both cheese and crunch to brothy soups, spread or melt a small amount of cheese on a large crouton and float it on top of each bowl. Or pass a plate of them at the table.
- When in doubt, go with Parmesan. It's buttery. It's nutty. It's creamy. And it works in practically everything.

Noodle Soups

Usually, the best way to make noodle soup is to add cooked noodles to cooked soup just before serving. This maintains the integrity of each and keeps everything from turning into an undifferentiated, starchy mess. Cook the noodles as usual, but undercook them slightly (they should be quite firm when you bite into them), so they don't turn to mush in the hot soup. You can even cook them ahead if you like, then rinse them in cold water to stop the cooking and set them aside in a bowl of tap water (or toss with oil). Then add to the soup during the last couple minutes of cooking. Or just use leftover noodles straight from the refrigerator (if they were heavily sauced, rinse the sauce off first—unless, of course, you want that sauce to be a part of the soup). Warm them in the soup right before serving.

Some particularly good soup-noodle marriages are in the list that follows, but don't be afraid to experiment with others.

Of course every rule has exceptions, and several of the recipes in this section cook the noodles right in the soup. The body-building and flavor benefits are simply too good to ignore altogether. It's true that soups made this way have only a narrow window of time before the noodles start to break down, but I have tried to leave that window open as long possible by calling for using the sturdiest noodles or frying them first to make them a little less soluble.

9 Noodle-Loving Soups

You can add noodles to dozens of soups, but these seem to be made for the purpose. I've made suggestions for the type of noodles, but you can use whatever you like:

 Fast   Make Ahead   Ⓥ Vegan

1. Cauliflower Soup, Italian Style (page 105): Small pasta, like shells, orzo, orecchiette, or rotini, or lightly cooked angel hair.

2. Tomato Soup (page 112): Any of the ideas above will work with the basic recipe (but not the variations).

3. Chickpea Soup with Saffron and Almonds (page 117): Add broken fideo or capellini (see Garlic Fideo Soup, page 144) during the last 8 to 10 minutes of cooking. If you don't want the soup to become too thick, stir in extra water or broth.

4. Vegetable Soup, Thai Style (page 127): any kind of rice noodles, thin or wide, presoaked (see page 464) but not precooked.

5. Kimchi Soup with Tofu (page 148): Mung bean threads, presoaked (see page 464).

6. Tofu Skins in Hot Pot (page 149): Rice vermicelli or mung bean threads, presoaked.

7. Any stock (pages 101–104) or broth made from any miso (page 152) with Tofu Croutons (page 656). Try soba or udon or use any Asian-style rice or wheat noodle.

8. Tofu and Bok Choy "Goulash" (page 150): Rice vermicelli, presoaked.

9. Egg Drop Soup, Eight Ways (page 154), but only these variations: Small or tubular pasta in Egg Drop Soup, Italian Style; or thick rice noodles in Egg Drop Soup with Seaweed.

Faux Pho

MAKES: 4 appetizer or 2 lunch servings

TIME: About 1 hour, depending on garnishes

The Vietnamese meal-in-a-bowl soup known as *pho* is always tricky for vegetarians because fish and meat are normally included, and prominently. But there are vegetarian options, chief among them a broth made from soy sauce and spices like anise, cloves, coriander seeds, bay leaves, cinnamon, or nutmeg.

Rice vermicelli remains the noodle of choice here, and the raw garnishes—especially the traditional fresh herbs and bean sprouts—add the essential fresh-tasting finish. Beyond that the soup's main ingredients can be whatever you have handy.

8 ounces thin dried rice vermicelli

2 tablespoons peanut or neutral oil, like grapeseed or corn

2 tablespoons minced garlic

1 tablespoon peeled and minced fresh ginger

1/2 teaspoon ground anise or coriander seeds

1/2 teaspoon ground cloves, cinnamon, or nutmeg

1/4 to 1/2 cup soy sauce

2 bay leaves (optional)

4 stems fresh cilantro for garnish

4 stems fresh basil, preferably Thai, or mint for garnish

1 fresh chile, preferably Thai, stemmed, seeded, and minced for garnish

2 scallions, chopped for garnish

2 limes, cut into wedges for garnish

1 cup fresh mung bean sprouts (see page 77 to make your own), rinsed for garnish

1 pound (about 4 cups) sliced fresh vegetables, like bok choy, Napa cabbage, mustard greens, broccoli or broccoli raab, carrots, green beans, summer squash, or a combination

1 cup diced tofu or cooked, shelled edamame (see page 585; optional)

Salt and freshly ground black pepper

① Cook the rice vermicelli in boiling salted water until just tender, 2 to 4 minutes; drain, rinse in cold water, and set aside.

② Put the oil in a deep skillet or medium saucepan over medium-high heat. When hot, add the garlic and ginger and cook, stirring frequently, until soft, about a minute. Add the spices and stir until warm and fragrant, about 1 minute more. Stir in 6 cups of water, the soy sauce, and the bay leaves if you're using them. Bring to a boil, lower the heat so that soup bubbles gently, and partially cover while you prepare the toppings and garnishes.

 Arrange the garnishes in bowls or on platters. Add the vegetables and the tofu to the simmering soup if you like, turn the heat to medium-high, cover, and cook until the vegetables are just tender, 3 to 5 minutes. Stir in the rice vermicelli, taste, and sprinkle with salt and pepper if necessary. Serve in big bowls, passing the garnishes at the table.

Garlic Fideo Soup

MAKES: 4 servings

TIME: 30 minutes

Ⓕ Ⓥ

Browned noodles are a real treat; one classic example is Garlicky Vermicelli or Fideo (page 450), the paellalike dish where broken strands of thin noodles are panfried before liquid and the other ingredients are added. Here I turn the same fideo noodles (you can use any ultra-thin pasta, like capellini) into a robust soup, based on the simple garlic-and-bread concoction eaten throughout Spain.

1 pound fideo, capellini, or other very thin pasta

$1/4$ cup extra virgin olive oil

1 small head garlic, cloves peeled and minced (about $1/4$ cup)

Salt and freshly ground black pepper

2 teaspoons sweet paprika (preferably pimentón)

$1/4$ cup chopped fresh parsley, cilantro, or epazote leaves, plus 2 tablespoons for garnish

6 $1/2$ cups vegetable stock (pages 101–102) or water

$1/2$ cup Fresh Bread Crumbs (page 804)

1 Put the noodles in a sturdy bag and whack them with a rolling pin or the back of a knife, breaking them into 1- to 2-inch pieces.

2 Put the olive oil in a deep skillet or medium saucepan over medium-low heat. When hot, add the garlic and cook, stirring frequently, until soft and beginning to color, 5 to 8 minutes.

3 Turn the heat up to medium-high. Add the noodles, sprinkle with salt and pepper, and cook, stirring almost constantly, until they darken, a minute or two. They will probably not cook perfectly evenly—some will become darker than others—but try to avoid letting more than a few pieces blacken.

4 Add the paprika and the $1/4$ cup of herbs and stir for a minute to coat the noodles. Add the stock, being careful to loosen any noodles and garlic that have stuck to the bottom of the pan. Cook, stirring occasionally, until the pasta is just tender, 8 to 10 minutes. Taste, adjust the seasoning,, and serve, garnished with a sprinkle of the remaining herbs and the bread crumbs.

Persian Noodle Soup

Reshteh

MAKES: 4 servings

TIME: About 2 hours, largely unattended

Ⓜ

The traditional version of this Iranian noodle and bean soup calls for a couple hard-to-find ingredients: *kashk*, a cheese made by drying yogurt and *reshteh*, the long, thick noodles that give the dish its Persian name. Not to worry. Sour cream or yogurt and egg noodles or fettuccine taste just as delicious. The real key is to use fresh herbs, not dried.

1 cup chopped parsley

1 cup chopped fresh herbs, like dill, parsley, cilantro, chervil, or mint (use at least two kinds)

$1/2$ cup chopped scallion

3 tablespoons extra virgin olive oil

1 medium onion, roughly chopped

Ⓕ Fast   Ⓜ Make Ahead   Ⓥ Vegan

$^{3}/_{4}$ cup dried black-eyed peas, washed, picked over, and soaked if time allows (see page 581)

2 quarts vegetable stock (pages 101–102) or water

Salt and freshly ground black pepper

$^{1}/_{2}$ pound thick egg noodles—or fettuccine broken into large pieces

$^{1}/_{2}$ cup sour cream or yogurt for garnish

❶ Combine the parsley, herbs, and scallion in a small bowl and measure out $1^{1}/_{2}$ cups. Cover the rest of the herb mixture with a damp towel and refrigerate until needed.

❷ Put the olive oil in a large saucepan with a tight-fitting lid over medium-high heat. Add the onion and cook, stirring occasionally, until soft and turning golden, about 3 minutes. Stir in the $1^{1}/_{2}$ cups of herb and scallion mixture. Add the peas and stock bring to a boil. Turn the heat down so the soup bubbles gently, cover, and cook, stirring occasionally, until the beans are just tender, 1 to $1^{1}/_{2}$ hours. Sprinkle with salt and pepper.

❸ Bring the soup to a boil. If it looks too thick to cook the noodles, add a little extra stock or water. Stir in the noodles and cook, stirring occasionally, until the noodles are just tender, 7 to 10 minutes. Watch the pot to make sure it doesn't bubble over, turning the heat down a little if necessary. Taste, adjust the seasoning, and serve, garnished with a spoonful of sour cream and a generous sprinkling of the reserved herb mixture.

Green Tea Broth with Udon Noodles

MAKES: 4 first-course or 2 lunch servings

TIME: 15 minutes

Ⓕ Ⓥ

In Japan, one often eats udon noodles with the liquid they were cooked in to enjoy both the flavor and the nutrition left behind by the noodles. Sometimes the starting point is water, sometimes stock or broth; often vegetables are cooked in the broth before the noodles are added, so it becomes even tastier.

And sometimes the starting "broth" is green tea. With its somewhat savory taste, the resulting soup is elegant in both simplicity and speed; and the list that follows shows the way to embellish and intensify the flavor.

$^{1}/_{4}$ cup green tea leaves

Salt

8 ounces udon noodles

Freshly ground black pepper

1 tablespoon mirin or sugar (optional)

❶ Put 7 cups water in a large pot with a tight-fitting lid and bring to a boil. Remove from the heat and let rest for a couple minutes. Stir in the tea leaves (or use a tea ball, cheesecloth, or some other mesh contraption), cover, and steep until fragrant and richly colored, 5 to 10 minutes. Strain the "tea broth" through a strainer and put the tea in a large saucepan. Discard the tea leaves.

❷ Bring the tea broth to a boil and sprinkle with salt. Stir in the udon. When the broth returns to a boil, add 2 cups of cold water. When the liquid returns to a boil, turn the heat down so that it bubbles gently without overflowing. Cook, stirring occasionally, until noodles are just tender, 5 to 7 minutes. Taste and add more salt, a few grinds of pepper, and the mirin or sugar, if you like, and serve.

17 Additions to Green Tea Broth with Udon

Some of these are garnishes to serve over the noodles; others are cooked in the broth to give it more character. And some can go either way:

1. 1 cup finely chopped tomato, added to the broth as it simmers
2. A pinch or two of cayenne or other ground chile, added to the broth as it simmers
3. $^{1}/_{2}$ cup cubed tofu, added to the broth when the noodles are nearly finished cooking

4. 1 cup precooked small beans, like soybeans, adzuki, edamame, or mung, added to the broth when the noodles are nearly finished cooking

5. 4 scrambled eggs, added to the broth when the noodles are nearly finished cooking

6. 1 tablespoon grated peeled fresh ginger, added to the broth as it simmers

7. 2 sheets nori, lightly toasted and cut into 1-inch strips (see page 357), for garnish

8. 1 tablespoon white or black sesame seeds, used as a garnish

9. 1 teaspoon black mustard seeds for garnish

10. 2 tablespoons nuts, like pistachios, cashews, or hazelnuts, toasted (see page 321) used as a garnish

11. $\frac{1}{4}$ cup Nori "Shake" (page 817) for garnish

12. A dab of wasabi paste for garnish

13. A thinly sliced onion, added to the broth as it simmers or as a garnish

14. A handful of julienned cucumber, added to the broth as it simmers or as a garnish

15. A cup or two of shredded lettuce or cabbage, added to the broth as it simmers or as a garnish

16. 1 cup mung bean sprouts (see page 77 to make your own), added to the broth as it simmers or used as a garnish

17. 2 tablespoons candied ginger (omit the mirin or sugar), added to the broth as it simmers or as a garnish

Spaetzle Soup the Easy Way

MAKES: 4 servings
TIME: 30 minutes

Ⓕ

To me, homemade pasta in broth is the ultimate comfort food. But say "homemade" and everyone seems to run for the hills, assuming that the challenge will be overwhelming. Spaetzle—free-form mini-dumplings that cook like noodles—require no rolling or cutting and so are easier to make than mashed potatoes.

2 tablespoons butter or extra virgin olive oil

1 large shallot, minced

2 quarts vegetable stock (pages 101–102)

2 cups all-purpose flour

Salt and freshly ground black pepper,

3 eggs

1 cup milk, plus more if needed

Chopped parsley or chives for garnish

Freshly grated Parmesan cheese for serving (optional)

❶ Put the butter or oil in a large saucepan over medium-high heat. When the butter is melted or the oil is hot, add the shallot and cook, stirring occasionally, until soft and golden, a minute or two. Add the stock and bring it to a boil.

❷ Meanwhile, combine the flour with a large pinch of salt and several grinds of pepper in a bowl. Lightly beat the eggs and milk together in another bowl and add to the flour, stirring. If necessary, add a little more milk until the mixture has the consistency of thick pancake batter.

❸ Keep the stock at a steady but not violent boil. Scoop a tablespoon or so of batter and drop it into the stock; small pieces may break off, but the batter should remain largely intact and form a disk. Repeat, using about one-third to one-fourth of the batter to avoid crowding the spaetzle. When the spaetzle rise to the top a couple of minutes later (you may have to loosen them from the bottom, but they will pop right up), they will be done. As they finish, use a slotted spoon to transfer them to serving bowls.

❹ Continue cooking the spaetzle until all the batter is used up. Then ladle the broth over them. Taste the broth and adjust the seasoning, then sprinkle with parsley and serve immediately, passing Parmesan at the table.

Ⓕ Fast   Ⓜ Make Ahead   Ⓥ Vegan

Whole Wheat Noodles in Curry Broth

MAKES: 4 first-course or 2 main-dish servings

TIME: 45 minutes

Ⓥ

American curries from the sixties and seventies often included chopped apples, sweetened coconut, raisins, nuts, and other assorted accompaniments. With a little updating, the concept still makes an appealing, immensely satisfying, and contemporary soup, even though it hardly resembles the curries of Asia.

3 tablespoons neutral oil, like grapeseed or corn

1 small onion, chopped

2 tablespoons minced garlic

1 tablespoon peeled and minced fresh ginger

2 tablespoons curry powder (to make your own, see page 816)

Salt and freshly ground black pepper

2 quarts vegetable stock (pages 101–102) or water

1 pound whole wheat spaghetti

1 medium green apple, peeled, cored, and chopped

1/4 cup raisins

1/2 cup chopped pistachios, cashews, or pumpkin seeds

1/2 cup chopped fresh cilantro for garnish

1/4 cup coconut, lightly toasted in a dry skillet for garnish

❶ Put the oil in a large saucepan over medium-high heat. When hot, add the onion and cook, stirring occasionally, until soft, about 3 minutes. Stir in the garlic and ginger and cook for another minute or so. Add the curry powder, sprinkle with salt and pepper, and cook, stirring constantly, until fragrant, about 1 minute. Add the stock and bring to a boil.

❷ Add the spaghetti and cook, stirring occasionally, until just tender, 8 to 10 minutes. Be careful not to let

the pot boil over. When the pasta is done, turn off the heat and stir in the apple, raisins, and nuts. Cover and let rest for 2 to 3 minutes. Taste and adjust the seasoning, give the soup a good stir, and serve, garnishing each bowl with a sprinkle of cilantro and coconut.

Soups with Tofu

There are two ways to add tofu to soups. The first is to simply add cubes or slices of tofu—pressed, frozen, cooked, or straight from the package—after the soup is made. When heated gently, they become a high-protein, mildly flavorful garnish. See the list on page 151 for ideas about where this works best.

The second way is to feature tofu as a key ingredient. Because tofu soaks up seasonings like a sponge, it's perfect for adding heft, texture, and protein to soup without changing the flavor much.

It's worth experimenting with different types of tofu. Silken varieties have a smooth, custard-like texture that can literally melt into the soup, while firm cubes provide a little something more to chew. Tofu skins (see page 840) work like a cross between noodles and eggs. The recipes here illustrate these differences.

Tofu that has been frozen, baked, or fried is sturdier and often more interesting than tofu right out of the container. Here are a few other guidelines:

Firm Tofu, Crumbled, Cubed, or Sliced: Right out of the package, this is the easy way. And firm tofu stands up well to longer cooking times. But what you get tastes like tofu right out of the package, only warm.

Firm Tofu, Baked, Then Cubed or Sliced: Baking draws a lot of moisture out of the tofu so it can absorb more flavor from the soup. The time in the oven also intensifies the flavor of tofu a bit, like roasted soy nuts.

Firm Tofu, Frozen, Then Crumbled, Cubed, or Sliced: With its spongelike texture and lower moisture content, frozen tofu quickly absorbs flavor from the soup. Plan ahead, though, because tofu needs to a day or so in the freezer, and a couple hours to thaw in warm water before being ready for use.

Firm Tofu, Thinly Sliced and Fried: Whether you oven-fry the slices or panfry them the results are crisp, nutty wafers that are like super-nutritious croutons.

Silken (or Soft) Tofu, Whole, Cubed, or Broken into Pieces: When the soup features crunchy ingredients, as does Kimchi Soup with Tofu (below), the creamy texture of silken tofu is a nice foil. In this case, the tofu also helps balance the heat of the spicy cabbage.

Kimchi Soup with Tofu

MAKES: 4 servings
TIME: 25 minutes

If you're the type of person who gets wildly overambitious at Asian markets, loading up your cart with more kimchi, Korean chile paste, and miso than the average Korean family goes through in a month, this simple, delicious soup will help you use up what you've bought, and it's quick enough to make for lunch. It's even better if you start with homemade cabbage Kimchi (page 96).

Feel free to add a tablespoon of miso instead of the soy or to toss a handful of bean sprouts into the soup just before serving.

3 tablespoons dark sesame oil

6 scallions, cut into 2-inch lengths

1¹/₂ cups cabbage kimchi, either homemade (page 96) or prepared, roughly chopped

8 ounces silken tofu, cut into ¹/₂-inch cubes

1 tablespoon go chu jang (Korean red pepper paste)

6 cups water or vegetable stock (pages 101–102)

1 tablespoon rice vinegar or other mild vinegar

1 tablespoon soy sauce, or more to taste

¹/₂ cup short-grain white rice

Freshly ground black pepper

① Put 2 tablespoons of the sesame oil in a large, deep skillet or medium saucepan over medium-high heat. When hot, add the scallions and cook, stirring, for about a minute. Add the kimchi, tofu, and red pepper paste and cook, stirring, for just a few seconds more. Add the water, vinegar, and soy sauce and bring to a boil. Then adjust the heat so the mixture simmers steadily. (You can prepare the recipe in advance up to this point; cover and let sit at room temperature for an hour or two or refrigerate overnight before proceeding.)

② Add the rice, stir, and once again adjust the heat so the mixture simmers. Cook for 15 to 20 minutes, or until the rice is tender. Taste and adjust the seasoning if necessary, adding more soy if necessary along with some black pepper and the remaining sesame oil. Serve at once.

Korean Mushroom Soup

MAKES: 4 servings
TIME: 30 minutes or a little longer

Korean mushroom soup can be as simple as precooked mushrooms, water, sesame oil, and soy sauce. This is a little more complex, substantial, and flavorful, but not much more work.

¹/₂ ounce dried shiitake or porcini mushrooms

3 tablespoons dark sesame oil

8 ounces fresh button or shiitake mushrooms (shiitake stems discarded or reserved for stock), trimmed and sliced

1 tablespoon minced garlic

³/₄ cup chopped scallion

About 6 cups vegetable or mushroom stock (pages 101–102) or water

8 ounces silken tofu, cut into small pieces (optional)

2 tablespoons soy sauce, or to taste

Salt and freshly ground black pepper

1 If you're using dried shiitakes, put them in a bowl and cover with boiling water; soak for about 30 minutes, or until soft. Porcini or other dried mushrooms can be soaked in hot tap water to cover and will soften more quickly.

2 Put 2 tablespoons of the oil in a deep skillet or medium saucepan over medium-high heat. When hot, add the fresh mushrooms and cook, stirring occasionally, until they give up their liquid, about 10 minutes. Drain the dried mushrooms, reserving the soaking liquid, trim and slice as necessary, and add them to the pan. Cook until they brown nicely, about 10 minutes more, then add the garlic and half the scallion and cook for another minute.

3 Strain the mushroom-soaking liquid and measure it. Add enough stock or water to make 6 cups, then pour this over the sautéed mushrooms. Cook, stirring occasionally, until simmering. (You can prepare the recipe in advance up to this point; cover and let sit at room temperature for an hour or two or refrigerate overnight before reheating.) Add the tofu if you're using it and cook for another minute. Add the soy sauce, salt, and plenty of black pepper. Garnish with the remaining sesame oil and scallion and serve hot.

Tofu Skins in Hot Pot

MAKES: 4 to 6 servings
TIME: About 1 hour

A tropical combo of hot, sweet, sour, and salty flavors makes this Vietnamese-inspired hot pot work perfectly even in warm weather, especially when you factor in the featured ingredient: tofu skins. Also known as *tofu wrappers*, *yuba*, or *bean curd skins* (see page 840), these are sold fresh or, more commonly, dried, at natural foods and Asian food stores and even some supermarkets. (If you can't find them, make this recipe with cubed or sliced tofu instead.) You must soak dried skins briefly to make them pliable for use; briefly frying them, as I do here, brings out their nutty flavor and returns some of the body they lose during soaking.

It's nice to serve this in traditional hot pot style, where the seasoned broth is poured into a special clay pot or a fondue pan and kept hot in the center of the table, along with small bowls of the vegetables and tofu. Then it's up to everyone to finish cooking and serving the soup themselves. But it's more than acceptable to simply follow the recipe here and assemble the soup in the kitchen.

$1/_2$ ounce dried shiitake, straw, or black mushrooms

6 ounces dried tofu skins (usually 1 package)

$1/_4$ cup peanut or neutral oil like grapeseed or corn, plus a little more if needed

2 tablespoons dark sesame oil

Salt and freshly ground black pepper

8 small fresh chiles, preferably Thai or serrano

One (1-inch) piece ginger, peeled and cut crosswise into thin coins

2 tablespoons minced garlic

1 stalk lemongrass, trimmed and minced (see page 767)

$3/_4$ cup chopped scallion

2 quarts vegetable stock (pages 101–102), or water

2 medium sweet potatoes (about 1 pound), peeled and cut crosswise into quarters

2 ears fresh corn, cut crosswise into quarters

2 large ripe tomatoes, cored and quartered

$1/_4$ medium pineapple, cored and cut into eighths

2 tablespoons freshly squeezed lime juice, or to taste

1 small bunch fresh cilantro, trimmed and chopped

1 small bunch fresh mint, trimmed and chopped

1 cup mung bean sprouts

2 limes, cut into wedges

1 Put the mushrooms in a bowl and cover with boiling water; soak for about 30 minutes, or until soft. Meanwhile, put the tofu skins in another bowl, cover with warm water, and soak until just pliable, anywhere from 10 to 30 minutes, depending on how dry they were to begin with. When ready, drain and pat dry with paper towels. Slice into noodlelike ribbons.

2 Put the peanut oil in a large saucepan over medium-high heat. When hot, add the tofu skins and stir to coat with oil. Cook, stirring occasionally, until fragrant, browned, and slightly dry, about 5 minutes. Remove from the pan and drain on paper towels.

3 There should be about 1 tablespoon of oil left in the pan; add a little more or remove some as needed. Add 1 tablespoon of the sesame oil and return the pan to the heat. Drain the mushrooms, then trim and leave them whole or slice. Add them to the pan, sprinkle with a little salt and pepper, and cook, stirring occasionally, until nicely browned, about 10 minutes. Stem, seed, and mince 2 of the chiles (thinly slice the other 6 and set aside for garnish), then stir them into the mix, along with the ginger, garlic, lemongrass, and half the scallion. Cook, stirring, until fragrant, about a minute.

4 Add the stock and the sweet potatoes, then turn the heat up and bring to a boil; adjust the heat so the mixture bubbles gently and cover the pan. Cook until the sweet potatoes are barely tender, about 10 minutes. Add the corn and tomatoes, cover again, and cook for about 5 minutes more.

5 Stir in the pineapple, along with the reserved tofu skins, remaining sesame oil, and remaining scallion. Turn the heat up so that the soup returns to a gentle bubble. Cook long enough to just heat through, another minute or two, then add lime juice to taste. Serve immediately, passing the sliced chiles, herbs, bean sprouts, and lime at the table.

Tofu and Bok Choy "Goulash"

MAKES: 4 servings

TIME: 30 minutes

Any hearty, piquant soup with bits of ground or chopped beef could fairly be called a goulash. This all-vegetable spin achieves a similar texture and flavor with fried crumbled firm tofu, along with ginger, garlic, chiles, and fermented black beans. If you don't have time to freeze or press the tofu, use it straight from the package; the texture will be a little less meaty, but cooking will help the extra moisture evaporate. For a more traditional take on the classic Eastern European goulash, see the variation.

One 12-ounce package firm tofu, pressed (see page 640), frozen (see page 640), or directly from the package

3 tablespoons neutral oil, like grapeseed or corn

1 tablespoon minced garlic

1 tablespoon peeled and minced fresh ginger

1 teaspoon hot red pepper flakes, or to taste

2 tablespoons fermented black beans

6 cups vegetable stock (pages 101–102) or water

1 head (about 1 pound) bok choy

Salt and freshly ground black pepper

1 Using your hands or a fork, crumble the tofu in a small bowl until the pieces are small and uniform. You should have about 2 cups.

2 Put the oil in a deep skillet or a medium saucepan over medium-high heat. Add the garlic and ginger and cook, stirring occasionally, until softened and just beginning to color, about 3 minutes. Stir in the tofu, then let the mixture sit for a moment or two and stir again. Repeat several times, scraping any browned bits off the bottom of the pan with a wooden spoon, until the tofu, garlic, and ginger are golden and dry.

F Fast   M Make Ahead   V Vegan

❸ Add the pepper flakes and black beans and stir until fragrant, mashing the beans slightly into the tofu mixture. Stir in the stock, then scrape up any tofu and seasonings stuck on the bottom of the pan. Bring to a boil, then lower the heat so that soup is just bubbling. Cover the pan and let the soup simmer for about 5 minutes.

❹ Meanwhile, cut the bok choy stalks first in half lengthwise, then crosswise into ribbons about $1/2$-inch wide; coarsely chop the leaves. Add to the soup, then raise the heat a little to continue simmering, and cover again. Cook until the bok choy is barely tender, another 3 to 5 minutes or so. Taste, add salt and pepper, and serve.

More Traditional Goulash Soup with Tofu. Delete the ginger, red pepper flakes, and black beans. Instead, cook $1/4$ cup minced onion with the garlic and season the tofu as it cooks with 1 tablespoon paprika, followed by 2 tablespoons tomato paste. When you add the stock, also add 1 cup diced tomato (canned is fine). Use 1 pound chopped green cabbage (about 4 cups) instead of bok choy. Serve with Boiled Potatoes (page 340).

Tempeh "Goulash." If you like the stronger flavor of tempeh, replace any or all of the tofu with Crunchy Crumbled Tempeh (page 674).

Adding Tofu to 10 Soups

Tofu is best added to soups at the last minute before serving—so it heats through without becoming waterlogged or falling apart. If you're using silken tofu, try to add it whole and let it break naturally as you stir. For firm tofu, press it first if you have time (see page 640) so it absorbs more flavor from the soup.

1. Silken tofu in Korean-Style Potato and Leek Soup (page 107)
2. Firm tofu in Lentil Soup with Coconut (page 116)
3. Firm or silken tofu in Mung Bean Soup (page 121)
4. Firm tofu in Peanut Soup, Senegalese Style (page 124)
5. Firm or silken tofu in Vegetable Soup, Thai Style (page 127)
6. Firm tofu (preferably fried, page 642) in Tortilla Soup (page 126)
7. Firm or silken tofu in Mixed Vegetable Soup, Korean Style (page 127)
8. Silken tofu in Mushroom Barley Soup (page 139)
9. Firm or silken tofu, or tofu skins in Faux Pho (page 143)
10. Silken tofu in Egg Drop Soup with Sea Greens (page 155)

The Basics of Miso

Miso has been used in Japan for centuries, but, like so much else, it probably originated in China. The base is created from soybeans (or other beans), grain (usually rice or barley), and salt. To activate fermentation a *koji* (starter) is added, often one that includes a mold called *Aspergillus orzyae*. High-quality, naturally made miso may go through a cycle of fermentation and aging that lasts as long as three years, sometimes in wood barrels, which add flavor (just as they do in winemaking). With more industrial or "quick" miso, this process is hurried and usually includes pasteurization, which super-heats the miso.

Buying and Storing: Like good yogurt, good miso is a "living" food, full of enzymes, micronutrients, and active cultures potentially beneficial to health. Since pasteurization kills any beneficial microorganisms along with undesirable ones, and at least some of the taste, it's best to buy unpasteurized miso whenever possible. Organic, traditionally made Japanese misos are ideal and worth the money; but there are domestic misos made in that style too.

Today fine misos are available even at supermarkets, though you will find a larger selection at Asian markets and natural foods stores. They are usually sold in plastic tubs in the refrigerated case or in jars or vacuum-sealed packages on the regular shelves. Miso must be stored refrigerated, where it will keep for months. To keep it from spoiling, always use a clean spoon when you remove some from the container.

There are literally dozens of subcategories of miso, but most fall into three categories, depending on the main ingredients:

When soybeans are fermented with white or brown rice the result is **kome-miso.** The paste is usually white or light beige in color and smooth in texture, with a hint of sweetness. You may also see it labeled *mellow miso, white miso,* or *sweet white miso.* These are best used in dressings, light sauces, and as a dairy substitutes.

Mugi-miso is made from barley and soybeans and is often referred to as *yellow, medium,* or *mild* miso. It is usually smooth textured and ranges from golden to reddish brown. Likewise the flavor varies a bit but is best described as "earthy." Consider this an all-purpose miso, not as mild as those made with rice, yet not as intense as soybean misos.

Hatcho miso (for the location where Japanese miso originated) contains all soybeans. Also known as *mame-miso,* this category includes the richest, darkest, and deepest-flavored pastes. Since they're made without grain, they have a higher proportion of protein to carbohydrates. Some are chunky; some are smooth. Either way, this is the best type of miso for heartier soups and stews, full-bodied sauces, and glazes.

Miso is also sometimes identified by color, regardless of ingredients. Shiroy describes the lightest white and yellow ones, while Aka includes the family of red and brown misos. When in doubt, the ingredient section of the label will reveal what's what.

Cooking with Miso: Unless you are a miso aficionado, you will probably be like me and have just one miso in the fridge at a time. It may not be traditional, but all may be used interchangeably in recipes calling for miso. There is one rule, however, that should not be broken: Do not overheat it. You will not only deactivate the beneficial cultures, but you will dramatically alter miso's complex flavors—connoisseurs would say you'll ruin them, and they're not wrong.

Miso Soup

MAKES: 4 servings
TIME: About 15 minutes

At its simplest, miso soup is really just tea—miso mixed with water (which you can do in a cup, with a little whisk). This recipe is slightly more complicated, flavorful, and substantial. Almost needless to say, you can add many different vegetables to miso soup—carrots, peas, beans, and so on—but since the general idea is light and simple, you may choose to keep it that way. Several ideas for additions are listed below.

Hatcho miso is probably best here, because it's so dark and flavorful, but any good miso will make a lovely soup.

1 quart Kombu Dashi (page 103) or water

1/3 cup hatcho or other miso

8 ounces silken tofu, cut into 1/2-inch cubes

1/4 cup minced scallion

1 Heat the dashi or water until steaming (do not boil) in a medium saucepan. Turn the heat to low, then mix about 1/2 cup of the liquid with the miso in a bowl or blender; whisk or blend until smooth. (If you have an immersion blender, the fastest and easiest tool here, carry out this operation in a tall measuring cup.)

2 Pour the miso mixture back into the hot water and add the tofu; stir once or twice and let sit for a minute, just long enough to heat the tofu through. Add the scallion and serve.

7 Additions to Miso Soup

1. Add seaweed, either the kombu from making the dashi (chopped), or a little steamed hijiki.
2. Add sliced shiitake mushroom caps, either fresh (and simmered briefly in Step 1) or dried, soaked (see page 317). Or, for extra flavor, sauté the sliced mushrooms in neutral oil or butter.

3. Add thinly sliced or minced daikon (or other radish), simmered briefly in Step 1.
4. Add a clove of garlic in Step 1.
5. Add about $1/2$ package of soaked and cut bean thread noodles (see page 464).
6. Add about 1 cup of cooked and chopped greens, like collards or spinach, along with the tofu.
7. Garnish with peeled and grated ginger.

Egg Soups

You can add eggs to soup raw or cooked, but even within those categories there are many subtle differences.

In general, when you add raw eggs to soup, you add richness, texture, and flavor, significantly boosting its body and elegance. If you "scramble" the eggs into simmering stock, as in Egg Drop Soup recipes that follow, the result is thin, tender wisps. (You can use this technique in almost any soup to which you want to add egg.)

If you don't want the obvious egg strands in your soup, simply "temper" the eggs—mix them with a little hot broth—before adding them, as in Rich Zucchini Soup (page 156). You must be careful not to boil the soup and curdle the eggs, but as they heat gently, the soup will naturally thicken. (Again, this is a useful technique you can employ elsewhere.)

Or carefully slip whole eggs into the pot—you will be rewarded with a flavorful poached egg in every bowl. When that yolk is broken, the soup is transformed. This is a technique I love; you'll see it here in Poached Egg Soup (page 155), but, again, it's useful in many other instances.

Of course, nothing is easier than topping soup with already-cooked eggs, whether they're fried, scrambled, or hard-boiled. See the list at right for the most basic ideas. Or try the Egg "Noodle" recipe (page 176) for something a little fancier.

9 Ways to Use Eggs In Soups

Cooked eggs are a nice way to quickly fortify and finish soups, because you can cook the eggs while the soup simmers and have them ready to add as you serve. See pages 165 to 170 for all the basic egg-cooking recipes.

1. Stir scrambled eggs into Cauliflower Soup, Italian Style (page 105).
2. Garnish Puréed Potato Soup with Leeks (page 107), with sliced hard-cooked eggs.
3. Set a fried egg atop each bowl of Onion Soup and its variations (page 108).
4. Set a fried egg atop each bowl of Tomato and Bread Soup (page 112).
5. Garnish Creamy Watercress, Spinach, or Sorrel Soup (page 132) with chopped hard-cooked eggs.
6. Stir scrambled eggs into North African Couscous Soup (page 140).
7. Set a fried egg atop each bowl of Farro Soup (page 141).
8. Stir scrambled eggs into Faux Pho (page 143).
9. Set a fried egg atop each bowl of Spaetzle Soup—the Easy Way (page 146).

Egg "Noodle" Soup with Mushrooms

MAKES: 4 servings
TIME: About 45 minutes
Ⓜ

The "noodles" in this soup are made entirely of beaten eggs, which are cooked in a thin layer just until set (you can do this ahead of time or while the soup is simmering). Once the sheet of egg cools down a bit and becomes pliable, you simply roll it up and slice it crosswise into coils of egg "noodles." It may be surprising that these tender ribbons hold up so well in soups, but they do, adding both texture and substance. This recipe features them prominently rather than as a garnish.

This is an easy way to add eggs to all sorts of dishes, from salads and sandwiches to rice and pasta, especially since the "noodles" can be made ahead and refrigerated.

2 tablespoons neutral oil, like grapeseed or corn

8 ounces shiitake mushrooms, thinly sliced, stems discarded or reserved for stock (optional)

Salt and freshly ground black pepper

1 tablespoon minced garlic

4 scallions, thinly sliced on the diagonal

1 tablespoon sesame seeds

2 tablespoons soy sauce

2 teaspoons dark sesame oil

6 cups vegetable stock (pages 101–102) or water

1 recipe Egg "Noodles" (page 176)

4 thick slices firm tofu, cut into small cubes (optional)

$1/_2$ cup chopped fresh cilantro (optional)

❶ Put the oil in a large saucepan over medium-high heat. When hot, add the mushrooms, a large pinch of salt, and plenty of black pepper. Cook, stirring occasionally, until the mushrooms start to release their liquid, about 10 minutes. Lower the heat to medium and cook, stirring occasionally, until nicely browned, about 10 minutes more.

❷ Stir in the garlic and cook until softened, about 3 minutes. Add the scallions and sesame seeds, stirring constantly until fragrant, 2 to 3 minutes. Add the soy sauce, sesame oil, and stock, scraping with a wooden spoon to loosen any bits that might have stuck to the bottom of the pan. Raise the heat to high, bring to a boil, then lower the heat so the soup bubbles gently.

❸ Gently stir in the egg "noodles" and the tofu if you're using it. Serve immediately, garnished with cilantro if you like.

Egg "Noodle" Soup with Rice Cake. More substantial: Slice one (8-inch) rice cake or presliced rice cake (page 473) crosswise on the diagonal into ovals about $1/_8$ inch thick. Increase the oil to $1/_4$ cup and fry the rice cakes, turning once, until browned and crisp on both sides, about 10 minutes total. (Work in batches if necessary to avoid overcrowding.) When finished, pour off all but 2 tablespoons of the oil, proceed through Step 2, then return the rice cakes to the bubbling soup. Cook until the cakes are tender, about 15 minutes, before adding the egg "noodles," along with the tofu and cilantro if you're using them.

Egg "Noodle" Soup with Bean Thread. Two unusual "noodles," combined: Before starting the soup, soak 2 bundles (about 4 ounces) of bean thread noodles in warm tap water until transparent and pliable (see page 464). Keep in the water until ready to use, then drain and cut with scissors into manageable pieces. Stir into soup just before adding the egg "noodles."

Egg Drop Soup, Eight Ways

MAKES: 4 servings

TIME: 15 to 30 minutes, depending on variation

Ⓕ

The idea of scrambling eggs into a pot of simmering liquid is not unique to Chinese restaurants or even to China. In fact, my starting point is a Colombian dish, enriched with milk and seasoned with cilantro. But if you explore the variations, you'll see how global the notion is and how valuable: Whenever you do it, you transform a humble soup into a more substantial first course or a light meal in a bowl.

1 tablespoon extra virgin olive oil

1 tablespoon minced garlic

1 quart vegetable stock (pages 101–102) or water

Salt and freshly ground black pepper

2 cups milk

4 eggs, beaten

$^1/_2$ cup chopped fresh cilantro leaves

2 scallions, sliced

① Put the oil in a deep skillet or medium saucepan over medium-high heat. Add the garlic and cook, stirring occasionally, until soft and golden, about 3 minutes. Add the stock along with a pinch of salt and pepper. Raise the heat to high and bring to a boil. Add the milk and heat until it boils, then lower the heat so that the soup continues bubbling, but not furiously.

② Add the eggs to the soup in a steady stream, stirring constantly. You want the eggs to scramble, not just thicken the soup, but you don't want them to clump, so keep stirring until eggs are cooked, just a couple of minutes.

③ Taste and adjust the seasoning, then serve, garnished with cilantro and scallions.

Egg Drop Soup, Mexican Style. With cheese and chile: Add 1 teaspoon ancho or other mild chili powder to the garlic. Delete the milk and increase the quantity of stock to 6 cups. Stir $^1/_2$ cup of crumbled queso fresco or grated cheddar or Jack cheese into the beaten eggs.

Egg Drop Soup, Italian Style. Parmesan makes this superb: After cooking the garlic, add $^1/_2$ cup chopped tomato (canned is fine) to the pan and heat through. Delete the milk and increase the quantity of stock to 6 cups. Stir $^1/_2$ cup of grated Parmesan cheese into the beaten eggs. Substitute basil or parsley leaves for the cilantro; delete the scallions.

Egg Drop Soup with Spinach. More substantial: Increase the olive oil to 2 tablespoons. After cooking the garlic, add 1 pound chopped cooked spinach (see page 359). Stir $^1/_2$ cup of grated Parmesan cheese into the beaten eggs. Delete the cilantro and scallions. Delete the milk and increase the quantity of stock to 6 cups. Garnish with additional cheese if you like.

Egg Drop Soup with Sea Greens. A lovely Japanese soup, especially with poached egg (see below), or like this:

Replace the olive oil with peanut or neutral oil, like grapeseed or corn, and substitute 1 tablespoon minced peeled fresh ginger for the garlic. Delete the milk and instead add 6 cups of dashi (page 103) to the pan. Toast 2 sheets of nori (see page 357) and slice into thin 1-inch ribbons. Stir into beaten eggs and proceed with the recipe; delete the cilantro.

Curry Egg Drop Soup. Some guts here: Use neutral oil, like grapeseed or corn, or butter instead of olive oil and increase it to 2 tablespoons. Add 1 tablespoon minced peeled fresh ginger and 2 tablespoons of any curry powder (pages 815–816) to the garlic. Replace the milk with coconut milk, either made from scratch (page 423) or canned (use 1 can, slightly less than 2 cups, with a little water). Proceed with the recipe.

Poached Egg Soup. A little more work, but *so* wonderful: Choose any of the variations. Bring the soup to the bubbling point. Instead of scrambling eggs, carefully crack 4 eggs, one at a time, into a small saucer or bowl and slip each into the soup without breaking the yolk. Don't stir. Cover the pan and cook the eggs until the whites are set. Carefully scoop the poached eggs into bowls and gently ladle in the soup. Top with garnishes—and cheese if you're using it—and serve.

8 More Ideas for Egg Drop Soup

To make the soup in its sparest form, pare the ingredients down to 6 cups of any stock, salt and freshly ground black pepper, and the eggs. Start by heating the stock to bubbling and proceed with the recipe. Enjoy as is, or . . .

1. Before adding the eggs, add 2 cups cooked brown or white rice to the bubbling stock.

2. Before adding the eggs, add any leftover cooked potato to the broth, like Crisp Panfried Potatoes (Home Fries) (page 343), Oven-Roasted Hash Browns (page 345), or even chunks of baked potato (page 339).

3. After adding the eggs, stir in 2 cups plain cooked pasta or Asian noodles.

4. After the eggs cook, stir in $\frac{1}{2}$ to 1 cup minced tender and mild but flavorful herbs: chervil, parsley, chives, basil, dill, and/or fennel leaves.

5. Finish the soup with 2 tablespoons chopped olives or Tapenade (page 326).

6. Put a slice of your favorite toasted bread (buttered or brushed with olive oil if you like) in the bottom of each bowl. Pour the soup on top.

7. Stir $\frac{1}{2}$ cup chopped oven-roasted tomatoes (page 375) into the soup pot before serving.

8. Stir in a pat of butter or a tablespoon or two of olive oil just before serving.

Rich Zucchini Soup

MAKES: 4 servings

TIME: 45 minutes

Eggs, a handful of raw rice, and grated zucchini instantly turn a simple broth into a luxurious soup, much like the silky soups and sauces of Greece and Italy. The idea is not to see the eggs but to use them for thickening and subtle flavoring. It's a technique that you can use over and over and one that may seem slightly challenging at first but is basically foolproof.

You can also use other vegetables to similar effect here; in fact, this dish is a perfect showcase for whatever's around, since the vegetables remain colorful and brightly flavored. Try freshly shucked corn kernels, shredded green cabbage, thinly sliced leeks, grated carrots, grated sweet potato, or grated winter squash.

3 tablespoons extra virgin olive oil

2 tablespoons minced onion

1 tablespoon minced garlic

$\frac{1}{4}$ cup short-grain rice

1 pound (about 2 medium) zucchini or other summer squash, grated

Salt and freshly ground black pepper

6 cups vegetable stock (pages 101–102) or water

2 eggs, at room temperature

1 tablespoon freshly squeezed lemon juice

$\frac{1}{4}$ cup chopped parsley for garnish

$\frac{1}{2}$ cup freshly grated Parmesan cheese for garnish (optional)

1. Put the oil in a deep skillet or a medium saucepan over medium-high heat. When hot, add the onion and cook, stirring occasionally, until soft, 2 or 3 minutes. Stir in the garlic and cook for another minute or so. Add the rice and stir to coat with oil, then continue cooking, stirring occasionally, until fragrant, about 2 minutes.

2. Add the zucchini, along with a light sprinkle of salt and a few grinds of pepper. Stir constantly for a couple of minutes, until the zucchini starts to wilt and release its liquid. When the mixture starts to stick to the bottom of the pan, stir in the stock, bring the soup to a boil, and reduce the heat so the mixture simmers steadily. Cover and cook for 20 to 30 minutes, until the rice is tender and the vegetables are starting to melt into the soup.

3. In a large heatproof bowl, beat the eggs with a whisk until creamy, then whisk in the lemon juice. Take a ladle of broth from the pot (be careful not to include too many vegetables) and slowly add the broth to the eggs, a few drops at a time at first, whisking constantly so the eggs don't curdle. Repeat once or twice more, until the egg mixture is thick, smooth, and very warm.

4. Make sure the soup is not boiling, but bubbling gently. Slowly add the egg mixture, stirring constantly. Taste and adjust the seasoning. Serve immediately, garnished with parsley and, if you like, the cheese.

Cold Soups

Many cold soups are puréed and dairy based, like smoothies in a bowl, but there are alternatives: cold soups can also resemble their warm counterparts, including chopped as well as puréed ingredients, savory seasonings, and even the occasional noodles or nuts.

Obviously, summer is the best time to enjoy cold

soups, when vegetables like tomatoes, cucumbers, and radishes are in season. But there are options here designed for year-round eating too. You can consider chilling hot soups; see the list on page 159.

Ultra-Fast Avocado Soup

MAKES: 4 servings

TIME: 10 minutes, plus time to chill

This lovely, celadon-colored soup is about as simple as it gets; the subtle, rich flavors of avocado and milk benefit from a hit of acidity, so I add orange or lime juice at the end, but that's about it. You can, however, dress it up for company in a hurry: A couple of brightly colored cherry tomatoes tossed with oil, salt, and pepper and nestled in the middle of the soup are handsome additions. Even a few cilantro leaves arranged in the middle of the bowl would take this soup from everyday to elegant.

3 or 4 ripe avocados, peeled, pitted, and chopped (about 2 cups)

3 cups milk, preferably whole milk

Salt and cayenne pepper to taste

2 tablespoons freshly squeezed orange or lime juice, or to taste (optional)

① Put the chopped avocado in a blender. Add half the milk, a large pinch of salt, and a small pinch of cayenne, and process to a purée. Beat in the remaining milk, then chill for up to 6 hours if you have time (press a piece of plastic wrap to the surface of the soup so it doesn't discolor).

② Taste and adjust the seasoning if necessary, add the citrus juice if you're using it, and serve—in chilled bowls if you want to be precise.

Chestnut Soup. More work, especially if you start with fresh chestnuts, but still quite straightforward: Frozen chestnuts (see Sources on page 929) are the easiest way to go here. Substitute $1^1/_2$ pounds fresh chestnuts, peeled (see page 287), or 2 cups thawed frozen or reconstituted dried chestnuts (see page 286), drained and rinsed, for the avocados. Boil the chestnuts in water or stock for up to about 30 minutes, or until tender, and drain. Proceed with the recipe.

Gazpacho

MAKES: 4 servings

TIME: About 20 minutes

No one can definitively say what gazpacho is—you see it with grapes, with almonds, even with melon. This basic recipe is what you probably expect when you hear the word *gazpacho*, but, as the variations show, you can take it in a number of different directions.

2 pounds tomatoes, roughly chopped, or one 28-ounce can tomatoes (don't bother to drain)

1 medium cucumber, peeled and diced

2 or 3 slices bread, a day or two old, crusts removed, torn into small pieces

$^1/_4$ cup extra virgin olive oil, plus more for garnish

2 tablespoons sherry vinegar or red wine vinegar, or more to taste

1 teaspoon minced garlic

Salt and freshly ground black pepper

① Combine the tomatoes, cucumber, bread, oil, vinegar, and garlic with 1 cup water in a blender; process until smooth. If the gazpacho seems too thick, thin with additional water.

② Taste and add salt and black pepper as necessary. Serve immediately or refrigerate and serve within a couple of hours, garnished with a drizzle of olive oil.

Spicy Gazpacho. Even gutsier: Omit the vinegar. Garnish the finished soup with $^1/_2$ red or yellow bell pepper, stemmed, seeded, and minced; 2 scallions or shallots, or ½ red onion, minced; ½ fresh jalapeño or serrano chile (or to taste), stemmed, seeded, and very finely minced. Add freshly squeezed lemon or lime juice to taste and serve.

Cold Tomato Soup. Think Frenchified gazpacho, a somewhat more luxurious blend: Substitute an additional pound of tomatoes for the cucumber and substitute freshly squeezed lemon juice for the vinegar. Add a teaspoon of chopped fresh rosemary or tarragon or a tablespoon of chopped fresh chervil, parsley, or dill to the blender (or you can use a variety of herbs, to taste) and process as in Step 1. Garnish with additional freshly ground black pepper in lieu of the olive oil, or with a dollop of sour cream, and with a little more chopped herb.

Cold Tomato Soup with Thai Flavors. Fresh-tasting, extra-refreshing, and extremely low in fat: Add 1 stalk of peeled, chopped lemongrass (see page 767) to the preceding variation, using cilantro as the herb and lime juice instead of lemon juice. Omit the oil. Garnish with a lime wedge and cilantro leaves.

Cool Yogurt Soup with Nuts

MAKES: 4 servings
TIME: 4 hours, largely unattended

Ⓜ

There is nothing easier than turning a couple cups of yogurt, some herbs, and a handful of cut-up vegetables—or fruit, for that matter—into a quick chilled soup, but this is a little different: The produce marinates in a little citrus juice or dressing before being topped with flavor-infused yogurt and crunchy nuts. Now you can enjoy each component distinctly, together in the same bowl.

The basic recipe calls for melon, a close relative of the cucumber, but everything changes when you simply swap the nuts, mint, melon, curry, and citrus juice with other fruits, vegetables, acids, or seasonings; see the variations.

¼ cup shelled roasted pistachios or toasted pumpkin seeds

2 cups yogurt

¼ cup milk

1 cup chopped fresh mint leaves , plus sprigs for garnish

Salt

1 small melon, like honeydew, cantaloupe, or casaba, peeled, seeded, and grated, shredded, julienned, or finely chopped (about 2 cups)

2 tablespoons freshly squeezed orange or lime juice

1 teaspoon chili powder (to make your own, see page 814) or a pinch cayenne

Freshly ground black pepper

❶ Use the flat side of a wide knife or cleaver or a small food processor to break the pistachios or pumpkin seeds into large pieces.

❷ Vigorously stir the yogurt, milk, and chopped mint together in a bowl for a minute or two, until you smell the mint. Stir in a sprinkle of salt and push the mixture through a strainer. Discard the mint and refrigerate the yogurt.

❸ In another bowl, combine the melon, juice, and chili powder. Sprinkle with salt and pepper. Refrigerate for at least 2 hours, stirring occasionally (the fruit will release liquid, which will become part of the soup). To serve, taste both the yogurt and the fruit mixtures and adjust the seasoning if necessary, then spoon some of the melon into chilled soup bowls; top with the yogurt and a sprinkling of pistachios.

Yogurt Soup with Cucumber. A bit more savory: Keep the pistachios and mint, but use shredded cucumber and lemon juice instead of the melon and orange or lime juice. Omit the chili powder or cayenne and use 1 teaspoon Fragrant Curry Powder (page 816) or prepared curry powder.

Yogurt Soup with Tomato. Smacking of summer: Replace the pistachios with toasted pine nuts. Instead of the mint, use fresh basil leaves. Peel, seed, and finely chop 4 medium tomatoes, saving as much juice as possible. You should have about 2 cups to replace the melon.

Toss the tomatoes with orange juice or a crisp white wine. Replace the chili powder or cayenne with fresh thyme leaves.

Yogurt Soup with Radish. More bite: Instead of the pistachios, use toasted hazelnuts and replace the mint with fresh parsley. Coarsely chop 2 cups radishes and toss with 1 tablespoon white wine vinegar and 2 tablespoons extra virgin olive oil instead of the citrus juice. Omit the chili powder or cayenne.

Yogurt Soup with Fresh Peas. Lovely and delicious: Instead of the pistachios, use cashews and replace the mint with $1/4$ cup fresh tarragon leaves. Blanch and cool 2 cups fresh peas and toss with 1 teaspoon sugar, 2 tablespoons extra virgin olive oil, and 1 tablespoon rice wine vinegar or other mild vinegar. Omit the chili powder or cayenne.

Yogurt Soup with Strawberry. Not quite dessert, but wonderful in a brunch setting: Replace the pistachios with toasted almonds. Use 2 cups sliced strawberries and balsamic vinegar instead of the melon and citrus. Omit the chili powder or cayenne and add a few extra grinds of black pepper.

Yogurt Soup with Pineapple. A fine starter for grilled Asian food: Use toasted coconut instead of the nuts. Shred 2 cups fresh pineapple, saving as much juice as possible. Substitute 1 teaspoon Fragrant Curry Powder (page 816) or prepared curry powder for the chili powder or cayenne.

Cold Cucumber and Seaweed Soup

MAKES: 4 servings
TIME: 20 minutes

Japanese and Koreans make good use of both cucumbers and seaweed, and this is an example of how the two combine with their love of cold soups. Add a little shredded

12 Soups You Can Also Serve Cold

Chilled soups are ideal in hot weather, but also make a perfect start to a spicy meal in any season. They're ideal for entertaining, of course, because they're always made ahead and usually served straight from the refrigerator.

In every case, when you make the soup, let it cool a bit, then transfer it to a covered container and put it in the fridge until cold. This usually takes at least a couple of hours.

1. Glazed Carrot Soup (page 105)
2. Roasted Beet Borscht (page 109)
3. Tomato and Bread Soup (page 112)
4. Tomato Soup and its variations (page 112)
5. Smooth Chickpea Soup (page 118)
6. Chile Bisque (page 131)
7. Creamy Carrot Soup and its variations (page 129)
8. Cream of Parsley Soup, but not the variation (page 131)
9. Creamy Watercress, Spinach, or Sorrel Soup and its variation (page 132)
10. Curried Coconut Soup with Lemongrass (page 137)
11. Thai-Style Carrot Soup (page 129)
12. Virginian Peanut Soup and its variation (page 134)

daikon or thinly sliced red radish along with the cucumber if you like; this is also good with about $1^1/_2$ cups cubed soft tofu. All in all, a lovely summer meal starter, simple but very flavorful.

2 cups Kombu Dashi (page 103), chilled

$1/3$ cup soy sauce, or to taste

2 tablespoons mirin or 1 tablespoon honey

2 tablespoons light or dark brown sugar

2 cucumbers, peeled and seeded (see page 293)

3 ounces wakame seaweed, broken into bits and soaked in cold water until soft (page 356)

$1/4$ cup dark sesame oil

2 scallions, chopped

1 tablespoon sesame seeds

Japanese Seven-Spice Mix (page 817) or hot red
   pepper flakes to taste

1 Combine the dashi, soy sauce, mirin, and sugar in small mixing bowl. Stir until the sugar dissolves. Slice the cucumbers lengthwise as thinly as possible; ideally they will look like long, thin noodles. (If you have the time, toss the sliced cucumber with a pinch of salt and put it in a colander to drain for 10 or 15 minutes, then rinse and squeeze dry.)

2 Divide the softened seaweed among 4 serving bowls. Nestle the cucumbers (if you want to get fancy, twist them into little "nests") into the seaweed. Top each portion with a tablespoon of sesame oil, then scatter with the scallions, sesame seeds, and spice mix; pour the soup base over the cucumber noodles at the table.

Eggs, Dairy, and Cheese

We think of eggs as breakfast food, and not incorrectly. But they can be an important part of any meal, especially for vegetarians. As their reputation as a sound, healthy, inexpensive source of both protein and flavor

recovers from the (largely unwarranted) cholesterol scares, they are becoming once again a solid foundation for a good diet. And most of us love eggs in a way we feel about few other foods.

In this chapter, I provide the basics of egg cooking; some more unusual ways to cook eggs for breakfast; a broad look at waffles, pancakes, and the like; and a variety of eggs-for-dinner (or lunch, or brunch, or whatever) dishes that are either new or have sadly been forgotten in the last generation or so.

Cheese—dairy in general, for here I look at milk, yogurt, and some other products that straddle the line between milk and cheese—is a category some people worship (as they do wine) and others take for granted (as they do milk). Indeed, you can find cheese that is worthy

of praise and eat it with nothing more than bread and fruit; that's fine, but this behavior does not fall within the bailiwick of this cookbook. What does, however, is using good cheese in great recipes, to produce mostly savory dishes that can be eaten at any time of day. That's what I do here. I also provide instructions for making your own cheese, which is, as long as you're not terribly ambitious, easier than making bread. Really. Please read on.

Eggs

The egg, a metaphor for life and possibilities, is a culinary miracle: With little effort or expertise, it can become the feature of a meal, a vehicle for transforming leftovers, or a quick way to change a side dish into a dish that graces the center of the table. And perfectly poached, fried, baked, or scrambled eggs are among the most satisfying, beloved, and easiest dishes there are, not only for breakfast but for convenient and super-quick lunches and late-night dinners. (None of this even considers the egg's role in desserts and pastries, which is impossible to overstate.)

Slow and Low or Fast and High?

Eggs are so tolerant of a wide range of conditions that in many cases you can cook them in a hurry or quite leisurely; the only real rule is to avoid overcooking or they will toughen. For example, for years I made my favorite scrambled eggs lovingly and leisurely, taking 40 minutes to do so (see The Best Scrambled Eggs, page 167). Then I discovered I could get just about the same texture by cooking them quickly, stirring constantly, and removing them from the heat the instant they threaten to overcook (see Everyday Scrambled Eggs, page 166). Both ways work fine; the first requires more patience, the second more attention.

Eggs should never become completely hard; even "hard-boiled" eggs should have yolks that remain somewhat creamy. And, often it's easier to avoid toughening when you use low heat. Fried eggs stay tender and become evenly firm over medium to low heat; boiled and poached eggs develop better texture and are less like to be damaged in water that bubbles gently. But you can cook quickly and keep eggs tender and soft, as in real omelets (page 171); again, it just takes attention.

In the following pages are the basic egg recipes in order of simplest to trickiest, though no cooking method is truly difficult. Even poached eggs can be conquered after a few tries.

Eggs at a Glance

Eggs are a near-ideal source of protein, minerals, and vitamins, critically important for many vegetarians. In fact, the egg's protein quality is rated second only to mother's milk, the wonder child to which all other proteins are compared. And the egg is also one of only a handful of foods with naturally occurring vitamin D.

Although in the past eggs have been vilified for their high cholesterol content (an egg contains around 200 mg of cholesterol, about the same as almost 2 cups of grated cheddar), recent studies have questioned the link between dietary cholesterol (that found in food) and blood cholesterol (the cholesterol already in your blood, which is now thought to derive from the saturated fats we consume), putting eggs back on the menu for most people. (Of course, if your cholesterol level is high and your doctor advises you against high-cholesterol food, stick with your doctor's recommendation.)

The Anatomy of an Egg

For the purpose of this book, there are three main components to an egg: the shell, the white, and the yolk. The hard shell is made up of calcium carbonate and varies in color depending on the breed of hen. The largest part of the egg is the white—or albumen—which comprises about two-thirds of the egg and over half of the egg's protein and minerals. The yolk makes up the remaining third of the egg and contains all of the fat and zinc, the majority of the vitamins (including all of the vitamins A, D, and E), and the remaining protein and minerals. Attached to the yolk are the chalazae, the cordlike white coils found at one or both sides of the yolk, which help stabilize and balance the yolk in the white. If you see a small blood spot in the yolk, it's not harmful (and not a fertilized egg); it's just a small vein rupture, and it actually indicates a fresher egg (the older the egg gets, the more diluted the blood spot will be). If it bothers you, remove it with the tip of a knife.

The Facts About Egg Labels

Probably the most important thing you can know about buying eggs is this: If you can get those produced by a local farmer, do. Otherwise, there are so many meaningless and misleading claims that trying to know your way around buying eggs has become more than a little tricky. In fact, much of the information that has always been on egg packages is standard and can often be mostly ignored; sadly, much of the new labeling is equally useless.

First of all, eggs are categorized into grades and sizes

Ⓕ Fast   Ⓜ Make Ahead   Ⓥ Vegan

Concern about the possibility of getting sick from salmonella—a bacterium sometimes found in chicken, eggs, and other foods—from eating raw or undercooked eggs remains widespread. And yet everyone knows the perfect egg is soft and tender with a liquid yolk. Is this flirting with danger?

Not much; salmonella isn't as prevalent in eggs as it was in the 1990s, and it wasn't even that bad back then. It's true, though, that although the risk of eating an infected egg may be small, it is not zero. So if you or the people you cook for are very old, very young, or have a compromised immune system—or if you are worried about eggs for any reason—you should take the following precautions:

Store eggs properly: Buy only refrigerated eggs and keep them in the coldest part of your refrigerator (not the door).

Rinse eggs before using: This is especially true if you buy eggs from small farms where the shells might not have been commercially washed.

Cook eggs thoroughly: Salmonella is killed in eggs if their temperature is maintained at 160°F for 1 minute or 140°F for 5 minutes. At 160°F, egg yolks are firm; at 140°F, they're not.

Precook eggs in recipes that call for raw eggs: This can be a little tricky, but it works for things like mayonnaise. Put the eggs in a small bowl set over a pot of bubbling water on the stove. You don't want the water to touch the bottom of the bowl. Use a whisk to stir the eggs constantly as they warm up and an instant-read thermometer to monitor their temperature. When they reach 140°F, adjust the heat on the burner to maintain that temperature and keep stirring for 15 minutes. (This completely changes the flavor and texture, of course, so you might as well skip semicooked eggs entirely and make Vegannaise, page 772.)

Hold poached eggs in a water bath: If you want to kill salmonella and still have poached eggs with runny yolks, you must keep the cooked eggs in 150°F water for 15 minutes. See the headnote in the Poached Eggs recipe (page 169) for the details.

Use pasteurized eggs: Available both in their shells and out of them, pasteurized eggs have been treated with heat and pressure to kill any bacteria. I'm not a fan of these products in general, but if you are at all concerned about using raw egg whites in mousses or meringues, then dried egg whites will give you peace of mind with only a little sacrifice in flavor and performance. To use, you simply mix the powder with water (the proportions are on the package) and beat as you would fresh egg whites.

(which are technically determined by weight). The U.S. Department of Agriculture has regulations for these two categories, but often state regulations—which must be equivalent or better—override the federal regulations. So egg producers using USDA federal regulations use the USDA Grade stamp on the package; but the lack of such a stamp doesn't mean it's of a different quality or standard from those without the stamp, making the stamp itself worthless.

The grades, AA, A, and B, are based on the appearance, character, and shape of yolk, white, and shell. The thicker and less runny the white, the rounder and "taller" the yolks, and the less blemished and more properly shaped the shell, the higher the grade. AA and A are the most commonly available grades (B grade is most often used in commercial or institutional kitchens), and there is little difference between them. So: Another aspect of buying you can pretty much ignore.

Size grades are based on weight per dozen and include jumbo, extra-large, large, medium, small, and peewee. Extra large and large eggs are most common, and most recipes, including mine, assume large eggs, though you can freely substitute extra-large with no ill consequences. In fact, in general, unless you're using an extraordinary number of eggs in a single recipe (say a dozen or more), extra large and large eggs are largely equivalent.

Some egg labels matter, as they're becoming more specific and complicated. Most of them have been in use for only a few years and fall into two categories: those associated with specific regulated programs and others used without oversight or enforcement. It's worth noting that *no chickens are (legally) raised using hormones;* it's against USDA regulations, so the label "raised without hormones" is meaningless for eggs—they all are, or at least they're supposed to be.

There are also labels that can be used by any egg producer with no official program or regulatory agency inspecting or guaranteeing the claims. In other words, you have to trust the word of the producer.

Free-Range (AKA Free-Roaming): Implies that the birds are not kept in cages and sometimes have outdoor access, though it can be just a door open at some point in the day. "Free-range" as defined by the USDA applies only to chickens used for meat, and not egg layers, so there are no USDA standards for so-called "free-range" eggs. Buyer beware.

Cage-Free: The birds are not kept in cages, but no outdoor access is guaranteed.

Natural: Probably the most abused and misunderstood label for eggs (and many other foods). In fact there are no standards for "natural" eggs. This label essentially means nothing, certainly not that the eggs were laid in an organic, sustainable, or humane environment.

Omega-3 Enriched: Sometimes called "designer eggs," these have nearly six times the amount of omega-3 fatty acids than standard eggs but look, cook, and taste no different. The hen's feed is supplemented with a mix of vitamins and omega-3 fatty acids derived from flax seeds, fish oil, and/or bioengineered algae; these in turn act as a nutritional supplement for the people who eat them. I'd recommend getting your omega-3s elsewhere, but these are hardly harmful.

Vegetarian Fed: No animal by-products are included in the feed. If it were true, "100% Vegetarian-Fed" would be a more secure assurance of feed quality, but unfortunately it's not regulated or enforced.

There are also some labels that are associated with a specific set of voluntary rules and regulations and monitored by third-party auditors.

Organic (Certified Organic): If you see the USDA Certified Organic stamp, it means the hens are raised without cages and with access to the outdoors; are fed organic, all-vegetarian diets; and are raised without antibiotics, pesticides, and insecticides; it also means the eggs aren't irradiated. "Certified Organic" is the only way to guarantee that your eggs were raised without antibiotics. A new term, "Beyond Organic," is gaining recognition (though it isn't USDA regulated) as being stricter than the USDA Certified Organic standards.

Certified Humane, Free Farmed, and Animal Care Certified: Technically, these are separate certifications, but they all refer to the animals' living conditions and treatment; guaranteeing a minimum amount of space; access to fresh air, water, and food; and limited stress and/or noise, among other things. Each certification is overseen by independent associations whose inspection regulations are approved by the USDA, but they are not part of a USDA regulatory program. Participation is voluntary.

Buying and Storing Eggs

Aside from the pack date, there are four sure signs of a fresh egg. Unfortunately, you have to crack open the egg to find out—not something you can do in a supermarket before purchasing.

- The whites are thick and don't spread out.
- The whites are a bit cloudy; this means that the naturally occurring carbon dioxide hasn't had time to fully escape from the egg after hatching.
- The yolk is firm and stands tall.
- The chalazae (the coiled cordlike attachments to the yolk) are prominent.

And before buying, take a quick peek inside the carton to make sure all the eggs are sound.

Eggs should always be kept in the refrigerator, which keeps them fresh and minimizes the growth of harmful bacteria like salmonella. If eggs are refrigerated properly (not in the door of the fridge, where it's often too warm), they can keep for as long as four to five weeks beyond the pack date. Store them in their carton and away from strong-smelling foods; though hard, the shells are porous and the eggs easily absorb odors.

The Basics of Cooking Eggs

Here is everything (I hope) you need to know about cooking eggs. Beginning cooks can use this as a reference; those with experience may find some helpful tips here (my method of hard-cooking eggs, for example, is a little different, and it's changed over the years). Please, if you do nothing else, try baking eggs (page 169), a technique that works perfectly for a crowd and is pure luxury.

Really, boiled eggs should be called "poached," because the water should never be at a real boil; all boiling does is bounce the eggs around the pot and crack the shells. The degree of doneness is only a matter of timing, but room-temperature eggs will cook in about a minute less than those straight from the refrigerator.

If you're cooking more than one egg, make sure you use a saucepan big enough for the water to circulate freely. You'll also need to extend the cooking time to the maximum in each of the following recipes.

Soft-Boiled Egg

MAKES: 1 serving
TIME: Less than 10 minutes

The egg-lover's way to eat eggs, barely cooked, but warm and comforting. Soft-boiled eggs are also great stirred into a bowl of reheated leftover brown rice or a cup of broth.

1 egg

Salt and freshly ground black pepper

1 Fill a saucepan about two-thirds full with water and bring it to a gentle boil.

2 Use a spoon or some other handy tool to lower the egg into the gently boiling water. Adjust the heat so the mixture barely simmers, then cook for 3 to 4 minutes, the lower time if you want the yolk completely runny and the white still slightly liquid, the latter if you want the white very soft but set.

3 Run the egg briefly under cold water, crack the shell, and scoop out the egg. Sprinkle with salt and pepper if you like and serve.

Medium-Boiled Egg

MAKES: 1 serving
TIME: About 10 minutes

These are easier than poached eggs and about the same texture; when done, the white is firm and the yolk runny. You can even reheat them after shelling by dipping them in simmering water for about 30 seconds.

1 egg

Salt and freshly ground black pepper

1 Fill a saucepan about two-thirds full with water and bring it to a gentle boil.

2 Use a spoon or some other handy tool to lower the egg into the gently boiling water. Adjust the heat so the mixture barely simmers, then cook for 6 to 7 minutes; the shorter time guarantees a cooked but runny yolk, but there may be some undercooked white. With the longer time, the white will be fully cooked, but some of the yolk may have hardened. Try it both ways and see which you prefer.

❸ To remove the shell, plunge into cold running water for about 30 seconds, then crack and peel gently, as you would a hard-cooked egg (but more carefully). Sprinkle with salt and pepper if you like and serve.

Hard-Cooked (Hard-Boiled) Egg

MAKES: 1 serving
TIME: About 15 minutes

Hard-cooked eggs are so convenient and versatile you may want to keep a few ready in the fridge at all times (they keep for a week). They're used in recipes throughout this book, from appetizers to hearty dinnertime dishes. I think they're best when just slightly undercooked and still creamy, not chalky.

Easy Peeling

Ironically, older eggs peel more easily after boiling than fresh eggs. What helps enormously—since you're not going to deliberately age your eggs to facilitate peeling—is to immediately run boiled eggs under cold tap water or plunge them into a bowl of ice-cold water (this also cools them down for handling, which is convenient). If you like, leave them in long enough to cool thoroughly—5 minutes or so—then store them in the fridge. They'll be even easier to peel after they come back out, another good reason for making extra.

If you don't want a cold boiled egg, cool them down fast in cold water so the outside cools enough to separate from the shell but the inside stays warm.

If the yolk has a greenish color, it's due to a small and harmless amount of sulfur in the egg and not cooling the egg quickly enough. To prevent or minimize it, be sure to immerse the eggs in an ice-water bath as soon as possible after they've finished cooking.

1 egg
Salt and freshly ground black pepper

❶ Fill a saucepan about two-thirds full with water and add the egg. Bring to a boil, then turn off the heat and cover. The average large to extra-large egg will be ready 9 minutes later.

❷ Plunge into cold running water for a minute or so, then refrigerate or crack and peel. Sprinkle with salt and pepper if you like and serve.

Scrambled Eggs

Here are recipes for the fast way and the patient way to cook scrambled eggs; they're both great. In either case, lightly beat the raw eggs with a fork or a whisk, just until the yolks and whites are combined; overbeating will make them tough and watery.

Everyday Scrambled Eggs

MAKES: 2 servings
TIME: 10 minutes

Very good scrambled eggs can be had in a hurry, provided you don't overcook them. Adding a little extra liquid helps prevent overcooking (if that liquid is cream, of course, it also lends a luxurious texture). A tiny squeeze of lemon will make them even more tender. But this technique—starting in a cold pan, and making sure that the curds stay small—is the single best way to make creamy, delicious scrambled eggs.

See "12 Simple Additions to Scrambled Eggs" (page 167).

4 or 5 eggs

1 or 2 tablespoons butter or extra virgin olive oil

Salt and freshly ground black pepper

1 to 2 tablespoons milk; cream; rice, soy, oat, or nut milk; freshly squeezed lemon juice; or water (optional)

❶ Beat the eggs lightly and combine in a medium skillet, preferably nonstick, with the remaining ingredients. Turn the heat to medium-high and cook, stirring frequently and scraping the sides of the pan (a heatproof rubber spatula is a good tool here).

❷ As the eggs begin to curdle, you may notice that some parts are drying out; whenever you see that, remove the pan from the heat and continue to stir until the cooking slows down a bit. Then return to the heat and continue cooking. The eggs are done when creamy, soft, and still a bit runny; do not overcook unless, of course, you intend to. Serve immediately.

Scrambled Eggs with Cheese. Use virtually any kind of cheese you like except for the ones that don't melt easily—like feta or queso fresco: As the eggs begin to set, stir in $1/2$ cup grated cheese.

The Best Scrambled Eggs

MAKES: 2 servings

TIME: 40 minutes

Perfect for dinner or a lazy weekend brunch, because these are easily cooked while you prepare other ingredients.

4 or 5 eggs

Salt and freshly ground black pepper

2 tablespoons cream

2 tablespoons butter or extra virgin olive oil

❶ Crack the eggs into a bowl and beat them just until the yolks and whites are combined. Season with salt and pepper and beat in the cream.

❷ Put a medium skillet, preferably nonstick, over medium heat for about 1 minute. Add the butter and swirl it around the pan. After the butter melts, but before it foams, turn the heat to low.

❸ Add the eggs to the skillet and cook over low heat, stirring occasionally with a wooden spoon. At first nothing will happen; after 10 minutes or so, the eggs will begin to form curds. Do not lose patience: Keep stirring, breaking up the curds as they form, until the mixture is a mass of soft curds. This will take 30 minutes or more. Serve immediately.

11 Simple Additions to Scrambled Eggs

As in making a flat omelet (page 183) or frittata (page 184), you can add almost anything you want to the beaten uncooked eggs before scrambling. Try any of these with either Everyday Scrambled Eggs or The Best Scrambled Eggs:

1. Minced pickled jalapeños to taste
2. Sautéed mushrooms, onions, spinach, or other cooked vegetables, cut into small dice, about $1/2$ cup
3. Chopped fresh herbs, 1 teaspoon (stronger herbs like oregano, tarragon, and thyme) to 1 tablespoon (milder ones like parsley, chive, chervil, basil, and mint)
4. Sour cream, cream cheese (cut into bits), or goat cheese (crumbled or grated), about $1^2/3$ cups.
5. Any chile (pages 826 to 828) or any cooked beans, about $1/2$ cup
6. Cooked and lightly buttered grains, especially farro, pearled barley, bulgur, or millet
7. Any cooked salsa (page 787), up to $1/2$ cup, drained if it's quite moist
8. Peeled, seeded, and diced tomato, up to 1 cup; or $1/4$ cup reconstituted sun-dried tomato (or, even better, $1/2$ cup Oven-Dried Tomatoes, page 377)
9. Tabasco; Worcestershire, Hold the Anchovies (page 799); soy sauce; or other store-bought sauces to taste
10. Minced scallion, up to $1/2$ cup
11. Chopped Roasted Red Peppers (page 333), up to $1/2$ cup

Fried Eggs, Sunny-Side Up or Over Easy

MAKES: 1 or 2 servings
TIME: 10 minutes

F

Correctly cooked, fried eggs are neither tough nor rubbery, but nearly as delicate as poached, with tender whites and a barely cooked yolk. Low heat is the easiest way to achieve this, but with practice you'll be able to use higher heat and get the same results. If you use the smaller amount of fat here, you'll sacrifice some flavor and will have to take more care to prevent the eggs from sticking to the pan (unless you use a nonstick pan).

Butter, of course, is the most luxurious medium for cooking eggs and often the most delicious. But it's hardly the only choice; extra virgin olive oil lends a delicious flavor (and, if you have not, you should try frying eggs in it, perhaps with a few sage leaves, finishing with a grating of Parmesan), and dark sesame oil is interesting, especially if you're frying an egg to put on top of Jook (page 140). Grapeseed or corn oil is also acceptable.

1 teaspoon to 1 tablespoon butter or oil

2 eggs

Salt and freshly ground black pepper

1 Put a medium skillet, preferably nonstick, over medium heat for about 1 minute. Add the butter and swirl it around the pan. When its foam subsides, about a minute later, crack the eggs into the skillet. As soon as the whites lose their translucence—this takes only a minute—turn the heat to low and sprinkle with salt and pepper.

2 Cook the eggs until the whites are completely firm; the last place for this to happen is just around the yolk. If the egg has set up high, rather than spread out thin, there are two techniques to encourage it to finish cooking: The first is to cut right through the uncooked parts with a small knife; this allows some of the still-liquid white to sink through the cooked white and hit the surface of the pan, where it will cook immediately. The second is to cover the skillet for a minute or two longer to encourage the white to finish cooking. Alternatively, of course, you can flip the eggs over when they're solid enough to be lifted by a spatula. When the eggs are cooked, after about 5 minutes, remove them from the pan and eat immediately.

Fried Eggs with Cheese. Because sometimes you just feel like it: When the eggs just start to set up, sprinkle a tablespoon or two of grated cheddar, Monterey Jack, Swiss, Gruyère, or Parmesan on top of each egg.

Eggs in the Nest—or Eggs in the Hole. In any case, eggs and toast all in one: For each egg, butter a slice of any sandwich bread and use a biscuit cutter or drinking glass to cut a big hole out of the middle of each. (There should be little more than crust remaining.) After the butter melts in Step 1, put the bread slices and the circles—butter side up—in the pan and crack the eggs into the holes. When the eggs start to firm up, carefully flip the slices and the circles over and cook the other side for a few more seconds, then serve.

5 Simple Ideas for Fried Eggs

1. As the butter or oil heats, season it with a few leaves of fresh herbs or a smashed clove of garlic.
2. Fry some thinly sliced pieces of smoked tofu (see page 639) in the pan (in a little butter or oil) before cooking the eggs.
3. As the white sets, use a butter knife to fold its edges over the yolk, making a little package and further protecting the yolk from overcooking.
4. Add Worcestershire Sauce, Hold the Anchovies (page 799), or other liquid seasoning, like soy or hot sauce, to the white before it sets.
5. Cook $1/_2$-inch-thick tomato slices—either ripe or green tomatoes—alongside the eggs (increase the amount of butter slightly).

F Fast   **M** Make Ahead   **V** Vegan

Baked ("Shirred") Eggs

MAKES: 1 or 2 servings
TIME: 30 minutes

This is one of the best ways to cook eggs for a crowd, and there's something about the texture of baked eggs that cannot be duplicated by any other method. Before baking, you can top baked eggs with bread crumbs, grated cheese, minced fresh herbs, or a sprinkle of your favorite spice blend—alone or in combination.

You can put all sorts of raw or cooked vegetables, grains, or legumes into the cup before adding the egg, which makes this an easy way to use up leftovers. Try chopped tomatoes, scallions, or herbs; rice pilaf or fried rice; Caramelized Onions (page 329); or cooked mushrooms or greens. You may need to cook the eggs a couple minutes more, depending on the addition.

Butter or oil, as needed

About 1 tablespoon cream (optional)

2 eggs

Salt and freshly ground black pepper

① Heat the oven to 375°F. Smear a bit of butter or oil in 2 custard cups or small ramekins. If you like, put a couple teaspoons of cream in the bottom of each (a nice touch). Break 1 egg into each of the cups, then put the cups on a baking sheet.

② Bake for 10 to 15 minutes, or until the eggs are just set and the whites solidified. Because of the heat retained by the cups, these will continue to cook after you remove them from the oven, so it's best to undercook them slightly (the precise time, in a good oven on a middle rack, is 12 minutes). Sprinkle with salt and pepper if you like and serve.

Oven-Poached Eggs. A little more work that results in ultra-tender eggs: Instead of putting the custard cups or ramekins on a baking sheet, put them in a deep ovenproof pan. Fill the pan with about an inch of boiling water and cover with foil. Carefully put the pan in the preheated oven and bake to desired doneness, between 15 and 30 minutes.

Poached Eggs

MAKES: 2 servings
TIME: 10 minutes

Making a poached egg that looks perfect takes a little practice. If you really care, you'll trim away the (inevitably) ragged edges of the whites with kitchen scissors. I don't bother anymore, since a poached egg in its natural form has its own appeal.

If you want to make more than two eggs, simply use a bigger pan, and be careful to avoid crowding. It's tricky to make poached eggs in multiple batches, but if you are up for the challenge, the best way is to keep a large pot of water warm over very low heat. Use an instant-read thermometer to make sure the temperature hovers between 145°F and 150°F and adjust the heat accordingly. As the eggs are cooked, move them to the second pot of water and cover. Fish them out with a slotted spoon when you're ready to serve.

1 teaspoon salt

1 teaspoon white vinegar

2 eggs

① Bring about an inch of water to a boil in a small, deep skillet, add the salt and vinegar, and lower the heat to the point where the liquid barely bubbles (if you were to measure it with an instant-read thermometer, the temperature would be just under 200°F). One at a time, break the eggs into a shallow bowl and slip them into the water.

② Cook for 3 to 5 minutes, just until the white is set and the yolk has filmed over. Remove with a slotted spoon and allow the water to drain off for a couple seconds. If you are eating the eggs right away, put them directly on the toast or what have you. If you like, drain them briefly on paper towels before serving. Poached eggs are delicate, so be careful handling them.

5 Flavorful Liquids for Poaching Eggs

Not something you might do intuitively, but quite clever, and lovely. You can also boost the flavor of these poaching liquids (or of water) by adding sprigs of fresh herbs (tarragon, parsley, dill, basil, rosemary, thyme, or cilantro); throwing in a chile or a couple cloves of smashed garlic; or simmering a cup or so of chopped or sliced vegetables, like onions, leeks, carrots, celery, fennel, parsnips, or mushrooms in the liquid.

1. Vegetable stock: Replace the poaching liquid with any vegetable stock (pages 101–102).
2. Juice: Replace some or all of the poaching liquid with vegetable juice, like tomato, carrot, spinach, or celery.
3. Wine: Replace half of the poaching liquid with white or red wine (the red wine will dye the eggs a pretty burgundy color).
4. Cream: For a super-rich poached egg.
5. Tea: subtle flavor and subtle color added to the eggs; replace some or all of the poaching liquid with freshly brewed tea (strain out the leaves first).

6 Great Sauces for Poaching Eggs

You can poach eggs in thicker liquids like sauces, though the technique is slightly different from the one described in the recipe. Make sure the sauce is at least an inch deep in the pan and heat it only to the gentlest bubble so it doesn't scorch. After all the eggs have been slipped in, cover the pan tightly to steam the eggs. When you're done, you have a delicious sauce to pour over the eggs. To make a full meal, simply serve with vegetables and some pasta, rice, grains, noodles, or potatoes alongside.

1. Fast Tomato Sauce or any of its variations (page 445)
2. Salsa Roja or any of its variations (page 787)
3. Mushroom Ketchup (page 791)
4. Smooth Green Chile Sauce, Indian Style, or any of its variations (page 792)
5. Cooked Tomatillo Salsa or any of its variations (page 788)
6. Spicy Indian Tomato Sauce (page 793)

19 Things to Serve Under Poached Eggs

1. Toasted or grilled bread
2. Any waffle (pages 203–206)
3. Corn Bread (page 687)
4. Biscuits (page 694)
5. Virtually any grain, legume, or vegetable pancake or griddlecake
6. Baked circles or squares of Savory Pie Crust (page 867)
7. Tortillas (soft or fried)
8. Any Mashed Potatoes (page 341), Curried Stir-Fried Potatoes (page 348), or any Oven-Roasted Potatoes (page 344)
9. Any cooked rice, grain, pasta, or noodle, especially with butter, extra virgin olive oil, or sauce
10. Baked Mixed Vegetables with Olive Oil (page 380)
11. Braised Lentils, Spanish Style (page 598)
12. Sautéed spinach (page 359), or other cooked greens, like kale, collards, or chard (page 239)
13. Fried Eggplant (or Any Other Vegetable) (page 244)
14. Any corn dish, like Pan-Grilled Corn with Chile or Tomatoes (page 290), any Creamed Corn (page 290), or Corn Pancakes, Thai Style (page 291)
15. Sautéed Mushrooms (page 314)
16. Creamed Onions or its variations (page 330)
17. Paprika Peppers (page 335)
18. Panfried Pumpkin with Tomato Sauce (page 366)
19. Most Vegetable Purées (pages 387–391)

F Fast   M Make Ahead   V Vegan

The Basics of Omelets

The classic French omelet is a prime example of taking an elemental ingredient—the egg—and turning it into an elegant centerpiece. Omelets can be thick or thin and filled with almost anything: cheese, vegetables, grains, fresh herbs, salsas, sauces, and more.

Making a beautiful omelet takes some practice, but making a very good omelet is dead easy. Just keep these simple guidelines in mind: Use a nonstick or well-seasoned pan and a plastic spatula (metal will damage the nonstick surface, but even if you're not using nonstick plastic is a good option because of its flexibility); use hot butter or oil and keep the heat fairly high (this helps to keep the egg from sticking and creates a thin layer of egg that protects the rest of the egg from direct heat); don't overstuff or you'll never be able to roll it up, and you might even have trouble folding. You can roll or fold—in half or in thirds—whichever is easiest for you. Or just make a Flat Omelet (page 182) and avoid rolling or folding altogether.

FOLDING AN OMELET IN THIRDS

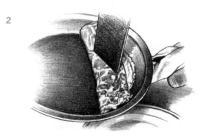

(STEP 1) Using a large spatula, loosen one edge of the omelet; lift and fold about a third of it toward the center. (STEP 2) Now slide the spatula under the center of the omelet; lift and fold it over the opposite edge.

FOLDING AN OMELET IN HALF

(STEP 1) First, hold the pan at a 45-degree angle so that half of the omelet slides onto the plate, then (STEP 2) gently increase the angle of the pan over the plate, allowing the omelet in the pan to fold over onto the first half.

Simplest Omelet

MAKES: 2 servings
TIME: 15 minutes

Omelets are, of course, great breakfast and brunch dishes, but they are also fine at dinner. This recipe is for a really basic omelet, but it can be filled with almost anything. The variations range from classic (and usually simple), to a bit more complex; some are practically all-in-one meals.

See "10 Ideas for Filling Omelets" (page 172).

4 or 5 eggs

2 tablespoons milk or cream (optional)

Salt and freshly ground black pepper

2 tablespoons plus 1 teaspoon butter or extra virgin olive oil

1 Beat the eggs, milk if you're using it, and some salt and pepper together in a bowl. Have a clean plate ready near the stove.

2 Put a 10-inch nonstick skillet over medium-high heat and wait a minute. Add 2 tablespoons of the butter; when it melts, swirl it around the pan until its foam subsides, then pour in the egg mixture. Cook, undisturbed, for about 30 seconds, then use a rubber spatula to push the edges of the eggs toward the center. As you do this, tip the pan to allow the uncooked eggs in the center to reach the perimeter.

3 Continue this process until the omelet is mostly cooked but still quite runny in the center, a total of about 3 minutes (you can cook until the center firms up if you prefer).

4 Hold the pan at a 45-degree angle so that half of the omelet slides onto the plate, then gently increase the angle of the pan over the plate, allowing the omelet in the pan to fold over onto the first half. Alternatively, you can fold the omelet into thirds (like a letter) using a large spatula, and then slide it out of the pan.

5 Rub the top of the omelet with the remaining teaspoon of butter and serve.

Cheese Omelet. Use any grated, crumbled, or soft cheese: Add $^{1}/_{2}$ to $^{3}/_{4}$ cup cheese to the eggs—in a line along the axis on which you will fold or roll—about a minute before finishing the omelet.

Spanish Omelet. A classic combination of onions and tomatoes: Before cooking the omelet, cook 2 tablespoons chopped scallion or onion in 1 tablespoon butter in a small saucepan over medium heat for 30 seconds. Stir in 1 cup chopped tomato, cook for about 2 minutes, season with salt and pepper, and keep warm. Add the tomato mixture, with a sprin-

kling of smoked paprika if you like, to the eggs as in the preceding variation.

Mashed Potato Omelet. A great way to use leftover mashed potatoes or mashed sweet potatoes, celery root, parsnips, or other vegetables: Add about $^{3}/_{4}$ cup, heated and thinned a bit with milk or cream if necessary, and some grated cheese if you like. Add to the eggs as in the first variation.

Cheese and Apple Omelet. This omelet can be savory (with the blue cheese) or sweet—omit the blue cheese and add a bit of sugar and cinnamon to the apples: Add 3 tablespoons cream cheese, cut or pulled into pieces, 3 tablespoons crumbled blue cheese (optional), and $^{1}/_{2}$ Granny Smith apple, cored and chopped. Cook the apple in some butter or olive oil if you like or leave it raw for more crunch. Add the cheese(s) and apple to the eggs—as in the first variation.

Fresh Cheese and Spinach Omelet, Indian Style. Make the cheese—called *paneer* in India—yourself for a really special omelet; but the omelet is still fabulous even without it: Heat $^{1}/_{4}$ cup yogurt over medium-low heat and add 1 cup fresh spinach leaves, $^{1}/_{2}$ teaspoon Garam Masala (page 815), and a sprinkle of salt and pepper; cook until the spinach is wilted. Add $^{1}/_{4}$ cup Fresh Cheese, the Easy Way (page 230), cut into small cubes, and the yogurt mixture to the eggs as in the first variation.

10 Ideas for Filling Omelets

You can fill an omelet with just about anything, just as you would a crêpe or a dumpling. Here are two lists, the first for more traditional fillings, the second for more substantial fillings, those that will make your omelet a centerpiece.

Cooked fillings, such as vegetables or grains, should be warm; raw fillings, such as cheese, should be finely grated so they melt or at least heat up quickly. Mix and match any of the fillings, but keep the quantity to about 1 cup.

F Fast   M Make Ahead   V Vegan

Classic omelet fillings:

1. Grated cheese—virtually any kind. Figure about 2 tablespoons per egg.
2. Chopped fresh herbs, 1 teaspoon (stronger herbs like oregano, tarragon, or thyme) to 1 tablespoon (milder ones like parsley, chive, chervil, basil, or mint).
3. Cored, peeled, seeded, and diced tomato, drained of excess moisture if necessary.
4. Sautéed mushrooms, onions, spinach, or other cooked vegetables, cut into small dice, about ¹/₂ cup.

Omelet fillings that make a meal:

1. Refried beans, or any beans, mashed, puréed, or not, with cheese (served with salsa).
2. Cooked grains, bulgur, quinoa, barley, kasha, wheat berries, or farro, with cooked mushrooms, and 2 or 3 slices soft cheese (like Brie or even cream cheese) or any cheese.
3. Cooked asparagus and/or Roasted Red Peppers (page 333) with goat cheese.
4. Ricotta cheese mixed with Traditional Pesto (page 768).
5. Cooked spinach or other greens, like kale, chard, or collards (squeezed of excess water), with diced smoked tofu (see page 639).
6. Roasted corn (see page 290) sautéed with scallion or sliced onion and fresh chiles, with crumbled queso fresco.

Folded Omelet

MAKES: 2 servings
TIME: 15 minutes

These individual omelets are pressed and folded so they make two sealed egg packages—you can even eat them on the run. It's important to use thinly sliced or grated fillings in smaller quantities than the traditional omelet so the omelet properly seals.

14 Egg or Cheese Dishes for Hearty Breakfasts

Real stick-to-your-ribs breakfast dishes:

1. Simplest Omelet (page 171)
2. Pasta Frittata (page 184)
3. Flat Omelet with Rutabaga (page 183)
4. Chilaquiles with lots of garnishes (page 176)
5. Huevos Rancheros (page 174)
6. Eggs au Gratin (page 194)
7. Egg Hash (page 178)
8. Savory Bread Pudding (page 192)
9. Swiss-Style Cheese Bake (page 220)
10. Fresh Cheese Scramble (page 218)
11. Cottage Cheese Patties (page 226)
12. Cheese Blintzes (page 198)
13. Baked Sweet Omelet (page 179)
14. Breakfast Burritos (page 174)

4 eggs

Salt and freshly ground black pepper

2 tablespoons butter or neutral oil, like grapeseed or corn

³/₄ cup finely grated or crumbled cheese

❶ Beat together the eggs and some salt and pepper in a bowl.

❷ Put an 8-inch nonstick skillet over medium-high heat and wait a minute. Add the butter or oil; when the butter melts, swirl it around the pan until its foam subsides, then pour in half of the egg mixture to cover the bottom of the pan.

❸ Sprinkle half the cheese evenly over top and cook until just the sides are firm, then use a rubber spatula to fold over one edge about 2 inches. Press down on the folded edge and continue to roll and press; cook the roll until the omelet is "sealed" and will not unroll, just a minute or two. Repeat with the remaining egg mixture.

Folded Omelet with Grated Vegetables. Use any finely sliced or grated vegetables, like onion, potato, carrots, mushrooms, zucchini, or summer squash: Add about $^{3}/_{4}$ cup thinly sliced or grated vegetables. Cook the vegetables in butter or oil until tender and sprinkle over the egg immediately after it's poured into the pan.

Egg Dishes for Breakfast

Of course you can eat these egg dishes at any time of the day or night, but they're traditionally what we think of as breakfast or brunch foods.

Huevos Rancheros

MAKES: 2 servings
TIME: 35 minutes

Ⓜ

If you have the basic components on hand, Huevos Rancheros are just a matter of assembly, and since the recipe is easily multiplied, they're perfect for entertaining. They also make a satisfying brunch, lunch, or even dinner, especially when served with salsa (page 751), extra beans, or a mound of avocado slices, shredded lettuce, and limes. A pitcher of Mexican crema on the side is really nice.

$^{1}/_{4}$ cup neutral oil, like grapeseed or corn, plus more as needed

Four 5-inch corn tortillas

$^{1}/_{4}$ cup Twice-Cooked (Refried) Beans (page 592) or any soft, well-seasoned beans

4 eggs

Salt and freshly ground black pepper

$^{1}/_{2}$ cup Salsa Roja or Cooked Tomatillo Salsa (pages 787–788) or store-bought salsa

$^{1}/_{4}$ cup queso fresco or grated Monterey Jack or cheddar cheese

$^{1}/_{4}$ cup chopped fresh cilantro or parsley for garnish

❶ Preheat the oven to 350°F. Heat the oil in a small skillet over medium heat. When hot but not smoking, fry the tortillas one at a time until softened and heated through, about 3 seconds per side. Make sure they do not crisp. Drain on paper towels.

❷ Spread 1 tablespoon of the beans in the center of each tortilla and set aside. (You can prepare the dish to this point up to an hour or so in advance.)

❸ Use a little more oil to fry the eggs sunny side up (in a nonstick skillet if you like), sprinkling with salt and pepper as they cook and following the directions for Fried Eggs on page 168. Put an egg in the center of each tortilla, then top with 2 tablespoons salsa and 1 tablespoon cheese.

❹ Carefully transfer the tortillas to a baking dish that holds them snugly. Bake until the cheese is melted, about 5 minutes, then serve immediately.

Simplest Huevos Rancheros. Omit the tortillas and beans. Scramble the eggs in oil; as they are beginning to set in the pan, stir in the salsa and cheese. Sprinkle with a little salt and pepper and serve.

Huevos Rancheros with Red Mole. A luxury, but a must if you have leftover sauce: Instead of the salsa, use the Red Mole sauce from the Cheese Enchiladas recipe on page 223. Garnish with chopped tomatoes and scallions if you like.

Breakfast Burritos

MAKES: 4 servings
TIME: 20 minutes with cooked beans

Ⓕ

Just about every fast-food joint now sells breakfast burritos, but few will be as good as yours. Fill them as you would tacos, with ingredients like chopped fresh tomatoes, cilantro, black olives, or scallions; minced fresh chiles; avocado slices or chunks; or small cubes of Crisp Panfried Potatoes (Home Fries), page 343.

If you're really addicted to a hot and hearty meal on the run, double or triple the recipe, wrap the burritos well in plastic or foil, and tuck them away in your freezer. Reheat foil-wrapped burritos in a 350°F oven for 20 minutes or so; or remove the wrapping, drape each burrito with a paper towel, and reheat in the microwave for a couple of minutes. Then away you go.

> 2 cups Twice-Cooked (Refried) Beans (page 592), Chili non Carne (page 607), or plain cooked or drained canned pinto or black beans
>
> 4 large flour tortillas
>
> 6 eggs
>
> 2 tablespoons butter or extra virgin olive oil
>
> 1 cup crumbled Fresh Cheese (page 230) or queso fresco or grated cheddar or Jack cheese

1 Warm the beans or chili in a small pot. To warm the tortillas, wrap them in foil and put in a 300°F oven for about 10 minutes or stack them between 2 damp paper towels and microwave for 30 to 60 seconds.

2 Beat and cook the eggs in the oil according to the directions for Everyday Scrambled Eggs on page 166. (You will have to use a large skillet.)

3 When the eggs are nearly done, remove them from the heat and assemble the burritos. Spread the cheese on each tortilla and top with $1/2$ cup or so of beans. Add the eggs and any sauces or garnishes you like. Roll up and serve.

Vegan Breakfast Burritos. Nice texture: Omit scrambling the eggs in oil in Step 2. Instead, prepare 1 recipe Basic Scrambled Tofu (page 655) and use that to fill the burritos. Instead of the cheese, use $1/2$ cup chopped nuts like cashews or hazelnuts. Proceed with the recipe and garnish or sauce according to the lists that follow.

9 Sauces for Breakfast Burritos

1. Salsa Roja (page 787)
2. Cooked Tomatillo Salsa (page 788)
3. Fresh Tomato Salsa (page 750)
4. Pico de Verde (page 751)
5. Papaya and Other Fruit Salsas (page 751)
6. Radish Salsa (page 752)
7. Lighter Cilantro "Pesto" (page 769)
8. Bottled hot sauce
9. Mexican crema

Japanese Egg Crêpes

Tamago

MAKES: 5 or 6 crêpes
TIME: 15 minutes

F **M**

These egg crêpes are simple, delicious, and downright cute. They're ideal for Sushi Bowls (page 527) and Sushi Rolls (page 528) but could also make a delicate crêpe for filling with Spiced Stir-Fried Bean Sprouts (page 265) or Stir-Fried Vegetables (page 242).

To flip the crêpe, use a spatula to pull one edge from the side of the pan, gently pull up that edge with your fingers, pull up another side with your other hand, and gently flip the crêpe over. Expect to fail on the first crêpe (consider it an experiment); it takes a little bit of practice to get the hang of it.

> 4 eggs
>
> 2 teaspoons soy sauce
>
> 1 teaspoon sugar
>
> Pinch salt
>
> 1 tablespoon neutral oil, like grapeseed or corn

1 Put the first four ingredients in a bowl and whisk until the sugar and salt are dissolved. Put a small non-stick pan over medium heat. Pour a small amount of oil into the pan, then spread it evenly over the pan using a brush or paper towel. Pour a small amount of the egg mixture into the pan, tilting it from side to side so the egg mixture completely covers the bottom. The crêpe should be very thin. Cook until the top is firm, about a minute or less; carefully flip it over and cook for another 15 seconds or so.

② Pile the finished crêpes on a cutting board. Let cool to room temperature, then cut the crepes lengthwise into thirds and cut into thin strips. Serve or store, covered in the refrigerator, for up to several hours (bring back to room temperature before serving).

Japanese Egg Crêpes with Nori. The thin strips of nori add nice subtle flavor and look pretty: Toast 1 or 2 sheets of nori by using tongs to hold the sheets, one at a time, over a medium-high flame for a few seconds, until they change color. If you have an electric stove, run them under the broiler for 15 seconds to a minute on each side. Cut (using scissors) into 4 or 5 strips, stack, and cut crosswise into thin strips. Sprinkle each crêpe with some of the nori strips before the egg mixture sets. Proceed with the recipe.

Japanese Egg Rolls. Called *Dashimaki Tamago*, the crêpes are cooked and rolled together: Add 2 more eggs and ¼ cup Kombu Dashi (page 103). In Step 1, make the crêpe a bit thicker; when just the edges are firm, roll the crêpe from the front of the pan to the back of the pan. Brush more oil onto the empty part of the pan and pour in more egg mixture. Roll the first rolled crêpe in the opposite direction, from the back to the front of the pan, rolling the second crêpe along with it. Repeat one more time and transfer the rolled crêpes to a cutting board. Repeat this process with the remaining egg mixture. Slice the egg rolls into pieces, as thick or as thin as you like. Serve with White Rice (page 505), Sushi Rice (page 527), or as Nigiri Sushi (page 530).

Egg "Noodles." Simpler, with a neutral flavor that goes with anything: Omit the soy sauce and sugar and beat the eggs with 2 teaspoons water instead.

Chilaquiles
Scrambled Tortillas

MAKES: 2 servings
TIME: 30 minutes

Chilaquiles is an authentic Mexican dish that can be prepared many different ways, but in all cases they contain fried tortilla strips softened a bit in eggs or sauce. You can enjoy them simply with a little salsa or sprinkle with garnishes like avocado, chopped tomatoes or scallions, cilantro, sour cream, or queso fresco or Jack cheese—alone or in combination.

6 small corn tortillas (stale are fine)
½ cup extra virgin olive oil or corn oil
4 eggs
2 tablespoons cream or milk
Salt and freshly ground black pepper

① Cut the tortillas in half and then into strips about 1 inch wide. Put the oil in a deep skillet over medium-high heat. When hot but not smoking, fry the tortilla strips, turning frequently, until golden brown and crisp on both sides, about 3 minutes. Work in two batches to avoid crowding if necessary. Use a slotted spoon to transfer them to paper towels. Set the pan with the oil aside.

② Beat the eggs with the cream and sprinkle with salt and pepper.

③ Pour off all but a tablespoon or so of the oil and turn the heat down to medium. Add the eggs and the tortilla strips to the pan and cook, stirring frequently until the eggs are done how you like them, between 4 and 6 minutes. Taste, adjust the seasoning, and serve.

Scrambled Tortillas with Scallions and Chiles. Sharp and spicy: In Step 3, after pouring off the extra oil and heating the pan, add ½ cup sliced scallion and 1 minced fresh chile (like jalapeño or Thai), or to taste, or hot red pepper flakes or cayenne to taste. Stir and cook for a minute or two to soften the vegetables, then add the tortillas and eggs and proceed with the recipe.

Matzo Brei. Substitute 2 sheets of matzo for the tortillas; soak them briefly in water to cover, until semisoft. Crumble into the egg-milk mixture (do not fry). Cook in 2 or 3 tablespoons butter. Serve with salt or sugar.

French Toast

MAKES: 4 servings

TIME: 20 minutes

Ⓕ Ⓜ

Originally a way to bring new life to stale bread (it's called *pain perdu* —lost bread—in France), French toast can be made with virtually any fresh or stale bread, including quick breads and even tortillas. European-style loaves require a bit more soaking to soften the crust, while hearty whole grain breads make more substantial slices. My favorite are soft thick slices of brioche or challah, which make a truly decadent French toast.

You can easily vary this basic recipe: Use any nut, grain, or soy milk instead of dairy milk; or enrich the soaking liquid by using half-and-half or cream. Season it with ground cardamom, cloves, allspice, nutmeg, or almond extract instead of the cinnamon or vanilla extract. To make an eggier French toast, increase the eggs and decrease the milk by a couple tablespoons per added egg.

2 eggs

1 cup milk

Dash salt

1 tablespoon sugar (optional)

1 teaspoon vanilla extract or ground cinnamon (optional)

Butter or neutral oil, like grapeseed or corn, as needed

8 slices bread

❶ Put a large griddle or skillet over medium-low heat while you prepare the egg mixture. Preheat the oven to 200°F.

❷ Beat the eggs lightly in a broad bowl and stir in the milk, the salt, and the sugar and vanilla if you're using them.

❸ Put about 1 teaspoon of butter or oil on the griddle or in the skillet. When the butter is melted or the oil is hot, dip each slice of bread in the batter; good bread or stale bread can soak up more batter than packaged white bread, as you'll see. Turn once or twice in the batter, then put it on the griddle. Cook until nicely browned on each side, turning once after 3 to 5 minutes (you may find that you can raise the heat a bit). Serve immediately or put in the oven to keep it warm for up to 30 minutes.

Crispy French Toast. There are two ways to give French toast a bit of a crust: Stir $^1/_2$ cup flour into the batter or dip the bread in the batter, then dredge it in sweetened bread crumbs or crushed cornflakes. In either case, cook as directed.

Nut-Crusted French Toast. Add another egg and decrease the milk to $^3/_4$ cup. Spread about 1 cup sliced almonds or any finely chopped nuts on a plate; after dipping the bread in the egg mixture, put the slice on the nuts and press gently to make the nuts stick; flip it over to coat the other side. Proceed with the recipe, taking care not to burn the nut coating.

Caramelized French Toast. A sugar coating melts and creates a lightly crunchy coating: Sprinkle or dredge the dipped bread with sugar. Proceed with the recipe and serve as directed.

5 Toppings for French Toast

Aside from or in addition to the obvious maple syrup:

1. Soft whipped cream (see page 856)
2. Any fruit purée
3. Sautéed apples, pears, bananas, or other fruit or any fruit compote

4. Not-Too-Sweet Maple Buttercream Frosting (page 860)

5. Creamy Nut Sauce, made with almonds (page 797)

Egg Hash

MAKES: 4 servings

TIME: 45 minutes

Usually eggs are served on hash. Here hard-cooked eggs *are* the hash. The secret is patience: To get the best browning and the least crumbling, you've got to let the potatoes and later the eggs do their thing in the pan, without too much stirring. A cast-iron pan really helps.

4 tablespoons ($^1/_2$ stick) butter or $^1/_4$ cup extra virgin olive oil, or a combination

2 or 3 large white potatoes, peeled if you like and cut into small dice

Salt and freshly ground black pepper

6 Hard-Cooked Eggs (page 166), peeled

1 tablespoon minced garlic

$^1/_2$ cup chopped scallion

$^1/_4$ cup minced parsley for garnish

❶ Put 2 tablespoons of the butter and/or oil in a large skillet, preferably nonstick, over medium-high heat. When the butter is melted or the oil is hot, add the potatoes, sprinkle with salt and pepper, and cook undisturbed, until the edges brown and they release easily from the pan, about 5 minutes. Toss the potatoes gently, scraping up any bits from the bottom of the pan, and turn the heat down to medium. Cook, stirring occasionally, until they are crisp and golden on all sides and tender inside, about 10 to 15 minutes more. Add a spoonful or two of water to the pan and stir to remove any browned bits. Transfer them to a plate.

❷ Cut the eggs in half. Put the yolks in a small bowl and mash them lightly with a fork. Chop the whites into large pieces.

❸ Put the remaining butter or oil in the pan and turn the heat back up to medium-high. When the butter is melted or the oil is hot, add the egg whites and cook undisturbed until they start to sizzle and crisp, about 3 minutes. Then sprinkle them with salt and pepper and toss them gently, scraping up any bits from the bottom of the pan. Turn the heat down to medium again and add the garlic. Cook, stirring occasionally, until the garlic is soft and the eggs are golden all over, another 2 or 3 minutes.

❹ Return the potatoes to the pan along with the scallions and toss to combine. Turn the heat down to medium-low and cook, stirring occasionally, until the hash is piping hot, 3 minutes or so. Gently stir in the egg yolks. Taste, adjust the seasoning, and serve immediately, sprinkled with parsley.

Egg Hash with Curry and Coconut Milk. A little creamier: Omit the parsley and mince $^1/_2$ cup of cilantro instead. Chop $^1/_4$ cup pistachios if you like. In Step 3 when you add the garlic, also stir in 2 tablespoons Hot or Fragrant Curry Powder (pages 815–816). In Step 4, stir in $^1/_2$ cup coconut milk and cook for another couple of minutes to heat through. Proceed with the recipe. Garnish with cilantro and pistachios. Serve with lime wedges.

Egg Hash with Celery and Pickles. Sort of like a warm potato salad: in Step 4, when you add the egg yolks, stir in $^1/_2$ cup minced celery, $^1/_4$ cup minced sweet or dill pickles, and 1 tablespoon Dijon mustard. Proceed with the recipe.

Chipotle Egg Hash. Hot and smoky: Omit the parsley and mince $^1/_2$ cup of cilantro instead. In Step 4, when you add the egg yolks, stir in 2 or 3 (or to taste) chopped canned chipotle chiles and a spoonful of their adobo. Proceed with the recipe. Garnish with cilantro and serve with a dollop of sour cream if you like.

Egg Hash with Rice. A great quick supper, especially if you have leftover rice: Omit the potatoes. In Step 1, start the hash by cooking 3 to 4 cups cooked long-

❺ Fast   Ⓜ Make Ahead   Ⓥ Vegan

grain white or brown rice in the butter and/or oil. Stir the rice only when it starts to brown. Instead of taking 15 minutes, the rice will be golden in 5 to 8. Transfer to a plate and proceed with the recipe.

Baked Sweet Omelet

MAKES: 2 servings
TIME: About 30 minutes

The sweet omelet isn't something we see often, but really does make sense in the way pancakes, crêpes, and other dessert-y breakfasts do. Plus, think of all the egg-based desserts, like custards and flans. Serve hot or at room temperature, sprinkled with confectioners' sugar and a selection of marmalade, jam, jelly, or Macerated Fruit (page 417) and whipped cream, crème fraîche, or yogurt.

  4 eggs
  $1/2$ cup milk or cream
  1 tablespoon all-purpose flour
  Pinch salt
  2 tablespoons sugar
  2 tablespoons butter

  ① Preheat the oven to 350°F.
  ② Separate the eggs (see page 898). Beat the yolks with the milk, flour, salt, and sugar. Beat the whites until stiff but not dry.
  ③ Put the butter into a large ovenproof skillet, preferably nonstick, over medium heat. When it melts, gently fold the egg whites into the yolk mixture. Pour into the skillet and cook for 2 minutes, then transfer to the oven. Bake until puffy and browned on top, 10 to 20 minutes.

Baked Almond or Hazelnut Omelet. Substitute almond or hazelnut flour (or grind some almonds or hazelnuts in a spice grinder until finely chopped but not a paste)

for the regular flour and add $1/4$ cup chopped almonds or hazelnuts. Mix the flour and chopped nuts with the eggs; proceed with the recipe.

Baked Sweet Omelet with Dried Fruit. Use any chopped dried fruit: Add 3 tablespoons or so chopped dried fruit and about 2 tablespoons sesame seeds, if you like. Mix the dried fruit and sesame seeds with the egg mixture; proceed with the recipe.

Baked Cherry Omelet. Raspberries, blueberries, halved apricots, and slices of peach or nectarine work nicely too: Add $1/2$ cup pitted cherries (frozen and defrosted are okay), substitute crème fraîche or sour cream for milk or cream, and add a pinch of ground cinnamon if you like. Mix the cherries and crème fraîche with the egg mixture; proceed with the recipe.

Eggs, Not Necessarily for Breakfast

You might call these savory egg dishes, but what's more savory than a fried egg? What these have in common is a certain level of, for want of a better term, nonbreakfast-ness. You can, of course, eat anything for breakfast (including cold leftover pizza, as I'm sure you know); but these are somewhat more substantial dishes, suitable for family dinners and company.

Egg Salad

MAKES: 4 servings
TIME: 15 minutes with hard-cooked eggs

At its simplest, egg salad is chopped eggs bound with some mayo, but it's better with a squeeze of fresh lemon juice, a bit of chopped pickles, or some chopped fresh herbs stirred in. It's better still with homemade mayonnaise or one of the variations (page 771). Additionally, any Deviled Eggs (see right) recipe can be made into an egg salad—just add more mayonnaise or the equivalent—and vice versa. Use tofu instead of eggs (see the variations) and it's even vegan.

6 Hard-Cooked Eggs (page 166), peeled and diced

$^1/_4$ cup mayonnaise, preferably homemade (page 771), or Vegannaise (page 772), plus more if needed

1 tablespoon freshly squeezed lemon juice

3 tablespoons finely chopped gherkin or dill pickle (optional)

3 tablespoons chopped fresh dill

Salt and freshly ground black pepper

Combine all the ingredients; add more mayonnaise if you like. Taste, adjust the seasoning, and serve immediately or cover and refrigerate for up to 2 days.

Waldorf Egg Salad. Great with a bowl of salad greens: Omit the gherkins and dill; add $^1/_4$ cup chopped walnuts, $^1/_2$ Granny Smith apple, cored and diced, and $^1/_2$ celery stalk, diced. Proceed with the recipe.

Egg Salad with Roasted Red Peppers or Sun-Dried Tomatoes. Almost rich; spread it on bread for a lovely sandwich: Add $^1/_2$ cup or so chopped Roasted Red Pepper (page 333) or soaked chopped sun-dried tomato. Substitute 1 teaspoon minced garlic for the gherkins and basil or parsley for the dill.

Tofu "Egg" Salad. Totally vegan, though you wouldn't know it: Substitute $1^1/_2$ cups finely diced medium or firm tofu for the eggs and use the Vegannaise.

Egg or Tofu "Pâté." Nice for serving at parties or sliced and garnished and served as a plated appetizer: Prepare the egg salad or one of its variations. Line a small bowl, mold, gratin dish, or loaf pan with plastic wrap. Put the salad in the vessel, pressing well to pack it in and mash it a bit. Refrigerate for at least an hour. Invert on a serving plate and garnish with lettuce leaves, radish slices, cucumber spears, or olives.

Deviled (or Stuffed) Eggs

MAKES: 4 servings
TIME: 5 minutes with hard-cooked eggs

The difference between a stuffed egg and a deviled egg? Cayenne, mustard, or anything that provides a bit of bite makes it deviled. With or without cayenne, these eggs are dead-easy to make, a real crowd pleaser, and the variations are almost limitless.

4 Hard-Cooked Eggs (page 166), peeled

Salt

2 tablespoons mayonnaise, preferably homemade (page 771)

1 teaspoon Dijon mustard, or to taste

$^1/_4$ teaspoon cayenne, or to taste

Paprika or minced parsley leaves for garnish

1 Cut the eggs in half lengthwise and carefully remove the yolks.

2 Mash the yolks with the salt, mayonnaise, mustard, and cayenne. Taste and adjust the seasoning. Spoon the filling back into the whites. (If you are making a lot of deviled eggs and want them to be especially attractive, use a pastry bag to pipe them back into the whites.)

3 Sprinkle with paprika and serve or cover and chill, well wrapped, for up to 1 day before serving.

Curried Deviled Eggs. Subtly spiced: Substitute yogurt for the mayonnaise if you like and Fragrant Curry Powder (page 816) for the Dijon. Use cilantro leaves for garnish.

Jalapeño Deviled Eggs. Make these as spicy as you like: Substitute sour cream for the mayonnaise, 2 teaspoons or more minced jalapeño for the Dijon, and $^1/_8$ teaspoon ground cumin for the cayenne. Use cilantro leaves for garnish.

Miso-Stuffed Eggs. A mild miso, like white or yellow, is best here: Substitute 1 heaping teaspoon miso for the Dijon and 2 tablespoons minced scallion for the cayenne. Garnish with Japanese Seven-Spice Mix (page 817) or Nori "Shake" (page 817).

Spring Vegetable–Stuffed Eggs. The key is mincing the vegetables to just the right size so they don't look too chunky but provide a nice texture: Add 1 tablespoon each minced radish, snow pea, and scallion. Garnish with a cooked asparagus tip, sliced in half lengthwise, or a sprig of chervil.

Sea Greens–Stuffed Eggs. Not the usual stuffed egg, but it's delicious: Omit the Dijon and cayenne, and substitute Seaweed "Mayo" (page 773) for the regular mayo, if you like. Add 1 tablespoon minced scallions and 2 or 3 tablespoons soaked and chopped hijiki, dulse, or wakame (page 356). Garnish with Nori "Shake" (page 817) or toasted sesame seeds.

Feta and Olive–Stuffed Eggs. Greek style: Substitute finely crumbled feta cheese for the mayonnaise, 2 tablespoons finely chopped black olives for the Dijon, and a large pinch of minced oregano leaves for the cayenne. Drizzle in a bit of good extra virgin olive oil if the yolk mixture is dry. Garnish with the parsley or a couple slivers of olive.

15 Ways to Flavor Egg Salad or Deviled Eggs

Stir any of these ingredients into the yolk mixture in Deviled Eggs (page 180) or use to season Egg Salad (page 180).

1. Traditional Pesto (page 768)
2. Real Ranch Dressing (page 772)
3. Creamy Bistro Dressing or Sauce (page 799)
4. Raw Onion Chutney (page 783)
5. Crunchy Nut Chutney (page 784)
6. Grainy Mustard, Many Ways (page 776)
7. Blue cheese
8. Goat cheese
9. Wasabi
10. Horseradish
11. Minced fresh herbs, like chives, mint, chervil, parsley, or cilantro
12. Minced garlic
13. Chopped capers
14. Chopped olives
15. Chopped gherkins

Pickled Eggs

MAKES: 6 eggs

TIME: 1 1/2 hours, plus 1 day to marinate, largely unattended

Ⓜ

There's nothing old-fashioned about the flavors in this classic bar snack, and pickled eggs are a great ingredient or garnish for other dishes, because you can use them virtually anywhere you use plain hard-cooked eggs. Do check out the variations; this could be a whole new standard for your snack, side dish, or garnish options.

6 Hard-Cooked Eggs (page 166), peeled

1 1/2 cups cider vinegar

1/4 cup pickling spice (to make your own, see page 819)

2 teaspoons salt

1 tablespoon sugar

1 large onion, halved and thinly sliced

❶ Put the eggs in a roomy glass or crockery bowl or jar (preferably one with a tight-fitting lid).

❷ Put the vinegar, spice, salt, sugar, and onion in a nonreactive pot with 1 1/2 cups water and bring to a boil. Turn the heat down so the mixture bubbles gently and cook until the onion is soft and the spices are fragrant, about 10 minutes.

❸ Carefully pour the hot mixture over the eggs and let sit at room temperature for an hour or so, until cool. Cover tightly and refrigerate for at least 24 hours before eating. The eggs will keep in the fridge for about a week.

Pickled Eggs with Oranges and Warm Spices. Great during the holidays: Omit the pickling spice. Halve 2 oranges and slice them thinly (with the skin). In Step 2, add the oranges to the pot, along with a tablespoon each of whole cloves and coriander seeds and a cinnamon stick. Proceed with the recipe.

Soy Sauce–Pickled Eggs. Perfect with all sorts of Asian dishes or alone: Omit the pickling spice and reduce the salt to 1 teaspoon. In Step 2, add $1/4$ cup soy sauce to the pot. Proceed with the recipe. If you like, to garnish sliced eggs, drizzle with a few drops of dark sesame oil and sprinkle with some minced chives and sesame seeds.

Five Spice–Pickled Eggs with Soy. A little more sophisticated with the seasoning: Follow the preceding variation, only add 2 tablespoons Five-Spice Powder (page 816) to the vinegar mixture before boiling.

Pickled Eggs with Beets and Horseradish. Brightly colored and sharply flavored: Omit the pickling spice. Peel and grate 2 medium beets. In Step 2, add the beets to the pot along with $1/4$ cup freshly grated horseradish (or 2 tablespoons prepared), or more or less to taste.

Pickled Eggs with Jalapeños and Carrots. A more substantial version of the Mexican table condiment: Peel 2 or 3 carrots and slice them crosswise into coins. Slice as many fresh jalapeños as you can stand (probably 3 or 4). In Step 2, add the carrots and jalapeños to the pot.

Pickled Eggs with Sun-Dried Tomatoes and Garlic. Piquant and richly colored: Omit the pickling spice. Peel a head of garlic and lightly crush the cloves according to the directions on page 303. In Step 2, add the garlic to the pot, along with $1/4$ cup sun-dried tomato halves or slices, 2 bay leaves, and 1 tablespoon black peppercorns, and a teaspoon of hot red pepper flakes if you like. Proceed with the recipe. If you like, to garnish sliced eggs, drizzle with a few drops of extra virgin olive oil and a sprinkle of chopped fresh basil.

13 Egg Dishes Suitable for Dinner or Supper

Most of these dishes cook in less than 30 minutes; add a salad or a side of vegetables or legumes and you've got yourself a fast, well-rounded meal.

1. Poached Eggs (page 169) (see "6 Great Sauces for Poaching Eggs," page 170, and "19 Things to Serve Under Poached Eggs," page 170)
2. Simplest Omelet (page 171)
3. Pasta Frittata (page 184)
4. Flat Omelet with Rutabaga (page 183)
5. Chilaquiles with lots of garnishes (page 176)
6. Huevos Rancheros (page 174)
7. Hard-Cooked Eggs in Quick Tomato Curry Sauce (page 194)
8. Egg Hash with Curry and Coconut Milk (page 178)
9. Egg Hash with Rice (page 178)
10. Eggs au Gratin (page 194)
11. Cheese or Onion Quiche (pages 187–188)
12. Savory Bread Pudding (page 192)
13. Cheese or Pea Soufflé (pages 185–186)

The Basics of Frittate and Other Flat "Omelets"

Flat omelets—the paradigm is the frittata—are simply unfolded, open-face omelets. They're almost always quite savory, and though they're fine for breakfast I think of them as all-purpose; I've made them for lunch, supper, brunch, and appetizers. They're good entertaining dishes because you can also make them a bit in advance—they're just as good at room temperature as they are warm—and can easily be cut into wedges or squares.

Flat omelets can be as thick or as thin as you like and can be filled with just about any vegetable (fresh, frozen, or leftover), herb, cheese, pasta, grain, or tofu.

F Fast   M Make Ahead   V Vegan

In Spain a flat omelet is called a *tortilla* and is most often made with potatoes and onions; the Italian frittata is made in countless different ways.

The technique is consistent; only the ingredients vary. Traditionally, they're all quite simple, but don't let that get in the way of your coming up with new filling combinations; see "7 Great Fillings for Flat Omelets" (page 184) for some suggestions. This is one of those standbys—like simple pasta dishes or stir-fries—that you can learn and then rely on in a pinch forever.

Furthermore, they're the easiest omelets to make as there is no folding. To finish cooking, you set the pan in the oven for a bit to set the top (or you can run it under the broiler, though you must be careful not to toughen the egg).

Flat Omelet with Cauliflower or Broccoli

MAKES: 4 servings
TIME: 30 minutes

All sorts of vegetables can be used here, including fresh, frozen, and left over.

> 3 tablespoons extra virgin olive oil
>
> 1^1/$_2$ cups chopped cauliflower or broccoli
>
> ^{1}/$_2$ onion, peeled and sliced
>
> 1 tablespoon minced garlic (optional)
>
> Salt and freshly ground black pepper
>
> 4 or 5 eggs
>
> Freshly grated Parmesan for garnish

1 Put 2 tablespoons of the olive oil in an 8- or 10-inch nonstick or well-seasoned pan over high heat. Add the cauliflower and about ^{1}/$_3$ cup water, cover, and cook, stirring occasionally, until the cauliflower is soft

and the water evaporated. If you're using precooked vegetables, skip adding the water and cook over medium-high heat until heated through.

2 Add the remaining olive oil and then the onion and the garlic if you're using it; continue to cook, sprinkling with salt and pepper, until the onion is soft, about 5 minutes more. Turn the heat to low.

3 Beat the eggs with some salt and pepper. Pour the eggs over the cauliflower, using a spoon if necessary to evenly distribute the vegetable. Cook, undisturbed, until the eggs are barely set, 5 to 10 minutes. Grate Parmesan over the top and serve hot, warm, or at room temperature.

Cheesy Flat Omelet. You can make this with or without the vegetables and just sprinkle grating or crumbling cheese on top at the end, then melt it in the oven or under the broiler if you prefer. Or: In Step 3, add ^{3}/$_4$ cup cheese, like cottage cheese, goat cheese, ricotta, crumbled blue cheese, grated Jack, or cheddar, to the beaten eggs. Proceed with the recipe.

Flat Omelet with (Frozen) Rutabaga. The rutabaga gives a nice, sweet, cabbagey flavor, and you can perform this magic with almost any frozen vegetable: Substitute frozen diced rutabaga, straight from the bag, for the cauliflower and omit the onion and garlic. In Step 1, cook the rutabaga until the pieces separate and are soft; continue to cook, sprinkling with salt and pepper, until they begin to brown. Proceed with the recipe.

Flat Omelet with Rhubarb and Cottage Cheese. Substitute chopped rhubarb (page 284) for the cauliflower. Omit the onion, garlic, and Parmesan. Add ^{1}/$_2$ cup cottage cheese to the egg mixture. Proceed with the recipe.

Flat Omelet, Mexican Style. A great filling for tacos and enchiladas as well: In Step 1, substitute 3 chopped scallions and about a tablespoon minced jalapeño for the cauliflower and onion (cook for just a minute, with no water). In Step 3, add ^{1}/$_2$ cup crumbled queso fresco and ^{1}/$_4$ cup chopped cilantro leaves to the eggs and omit the Parmesan. Proceed with the recipe. Serve with salsa and a stack of warm tortillas.

Flat Omelet, Greek Style. Skip Step 1 and omit the onion, garlic, and Parmesan; add to the beaten eggs $^1/_2$ cup chopped Roasted Red Pepper (page 333), $^1/_2$ cup or so crumbled feta cheese, and 1 teaspoon chopped fresh oregano leaves (or $^1/_2$ teaspoon dried). Proceed with the recipe.

Pasta Frittata

MAKES: 4 servings

TIME: 40 minutes, including cooking the pasta

This is a perfect way to use leftover pasta, instantly lovable and easily varied; add whatever fresh herbs you like or use grains, bread, or potatoes instead of pasta (see the variations). And you don't even have to use long pasta; try this with rigatoni for more chew.

$^1/_4$ pound spaghetti, linguine, fettuccine, or other long pasta or about $^1/_2$ pound cooked pasta

Salt

4 tablespoons ($^1/_2$ stick) butter or extra virgin olive oil

5 eggs

Freshly ground black pepper

1 cup grated Parmesan cheese

$^1/_4$ cup chopped parsley or fresh basil leaves (optional)

1 If you're using dried pasta, bring a large pot of water to a boil and salt it. Cook the pasta until barely tender, somewhat short of where you would normally cook it. Drain and immediately toss it in a wide bowl with half the butter or oil. Cool it a bit.

2 Preheat the oven to 400°F. Put the remaining butter or oil in a large ovenproof nonstick skillet over medium-high heat.

3 Beat the eggs with some salt and pepper in a large bowl, then stir in the pasta with half of the Parmesan and the herb if you're using it. Pour the egg mixture into the skillet and immediately turn the heat down to medium-

low. Use a spoon if necessary to even out the top of the frittata. Cook, undisturbed, until the mixture firms up on the bottom, 10 to 15 minutes, then transfer to the oven. Bake until the top is just cooked, about 10 minutes more. Remove and serve hot or at room temperature with the remaining Parmesan.

Basic Frittata. As easy as it gets: Omit the pasta, add one more egg, and add all the Parmesan in Step 3.

Frittata with Grains. Substitute $1^1/_2$ cups or so cooked grains, like farro, wheat berries, rye berries, quinoa, bulgur, or buckwheat, for the pasta.

Bread Frittata. Poor people's food, obviously, but good: Substitute $1^1/_2$ cups or so cubed or torn day-old crusty bread for the pasta.

Potato Tortilla. Cut into slices and serve as a Spanish tapa or a terrific sandwich filling. The large amount of olive oil isn't a typo; most is poured off, and it can be used in sautéing or stir-frying (store in the fridge): Substitute 3 or 4 medium potatoes, peeled and thinly sliced, for the pasta and add a medium thinly sliced onion. Use 1 cup olive oil and add one more egg. Omit the Parmesan. In Step 1, heat the oil in the pan over medium heat; add the potatoes and onion when a slice of potato bubbles in the oil. Sprinkle with some salt and pepper, adjust the heat so the oil bubbles slowly (you don't want to brown the potatoes), and cook the potato mixture, turning every few minutes, until tender when pierced, about 20 minutes. Drain the potato mixture in a colander, reserving the oil. Proceed with the recipe, using 2 tablespoons of the reserved oil to cook the tortilla. Serve warm (not hot) or at room temperature.

7 Great Fillings for Flat Omelets

Just about any vegetable, herb, or cheese can be used in flat omelets, alone or in combination. About $1^1/_2$ cups vegetables, $^3/_4$ cup cheese, or 1 cup vegetable and $^1/_2$ cup cheese combined are good starting points.

If you're using leftover cooked vegetables: Let them come to room temperature or give them a quick flash in the pan with some oil or butter, then add the beaten eggs

🅕 Fast   🅜 Make Ahead   🅥 Vegan

and cook as directed in either of the frittata recipes on pages 183–184.

If you're using fresh or frozen vegetables: For fresh vegetables, cut or slice the vegetable into bite-sized pieces and cook in the pan with a tablespoon or two of oil or butter until tender (adding a little water, as in Flat Omelet with Cauliflower or Broccoli, page 183) or boil in salted water until tender and drain very well. For frozen vegetables, defrost them at room temperature or in the pan (see Flat Omelet with Rutabaga, page 183).

1. Caramelized Onions (page 329) and blue cheese
2. Asparagus, goat cheese, and basil
3. Summer squash, wheat berries, and cottage cheese
4. Spinach and ricotta
5. Artichoke hearts, whole wheat or regular pasta, and parsley
6. Sliced potatoes and rosemary (see Crisp Panfried Potatoes [Home Fries], page 343)
7. Green beans and smoked tofu (see page 639)

The Basics of Soufflés

If you can get past the fear of soufflés, you'll find they aren't as difficult as you think. In fact, they're easy, as long as you attend to a couple of key points.

The first is beating the egg whites correctly. It's vital to use a clean metal or glass bowl; plastic can retain traces of fats and oils that will prevent the egg whites from foaming. For the same reason, no trace of yolk can be in the whites; their fat will keep the whites flat.

Whip the whites until they are shiny and can hold real peaks, but ones whose tips fold over a bit. If the whites become stiff, clumpy, and watery, they're overwhipped; you'll have to start over, but it's a mistake you are unlikely to make more than once. (See "Beating Egg Whites," page 899.)

Mixing the egg whites into the soufflé base is also important: You want to fully incorporate them while maintaining their airiness. (*Soufflé* has the same root as the word for breath; this is all about air.) First, fold in about one-third of the egg whites to lighten the base. Use

your hand or a wide spatula to scoop the mixture from the bottom and fold it over the top, and don't worry too much about deflating the whites at this point. Then add the rest of the egg whites, using the same folding technique but a little more gently; incorporate well, but if light streaks of egg white remain, that's okay. If the mixture goes flat, it's overmixed and your soufflé won't rise much.

Keep in mind that soufflés with cheese and vegetable purées won't rise as much as those without but also won't fall as much either; in other words, they're more stable.

Cheese Soufflé

MAKES: 4 to 6 servings
TIME: About 1 hour

An easy but impressive and delicious dish. Make one large soufflé or make 4 to 6 individual soufflés in $1^1/_2$- to 2-cup ramekins; the cooking time may be reduced by as much as half with the smaller dishes.

4 tablespoons ($^1/_2$ stick) butter

$^1/_4$ cup all-purpose flour

$1^1/_2$ cups milk, warmed until hot to the touch (about a minute in an average microwave)

6 eggs, separated

Salt and freshly ground black pepper

Dash cayenne or $^1/_2$ teaspoon dry mustard

$^1/_2$ cup freshly grated Parmesan cheese

$^1/_2$ cup grated or crumbled cheddar, Jack, Roquefort, Emmental, and/or other cheese

1 Use a bit of the butter to grease a 2-quart soufflé or other deep baking dish. (Hold off on this step if you're going to delay baking the soufflés until later.)

2 Put the remaining butter in a small saucepan over medium-low heat. When the foam subsides, stir in the flour and cook, stirring, until the mixture darkens, about 3 minutes. Turn the heat down to low and whisk in the milk, a bit at a time, until the mixture is thick. Let cool for

a few minutes, then beat in the egg yolks, salt, pepper, cayenne, and cheeses. (You can prepare this base a few hours in advance of cooking; cover tightly and refrigerate; bring back to room temperature before continuing.)

❸ About an hour before you're ready to cook, preheat the oven to 375°F. Use an electric or hand mixer or a whisk to beat the egg whites until fairly stiff. Stir about a third into the base to lighten it, then gently—and not overthoroughly—fold in the remaining whites, using a rubber spatula or your hand. Transfer to the prepared dish and bake until the top is brown, the sides are firm, and the center is still quite moist, about 30 minutes. Use a thin skewer to check the interior; if it is still quite wet, bake for another 5 minutes. If it is just a bit moist, the soufflé is done. Serve immediately.

Herb and Cheese Soufflé. Add chopped fresh herbs, 1 teaspoon (stronger herbs like marjoram, oregano, tarragon, and thyme) to 2 tablespoons (milder ones like parsley, chive, chervil, basil, dill, and mint); sprinkle into the yolk mixture just before folding in the egg whites.

Pesto Soufflé. Substitute Traditional Pesto (page 768) for half of the grated or crumbled cheese.

Goat Cheese and Dried Apricot Soufflé. Tangy and slightly sweet—a great brunch dish: Substitute half goat cheese and half grated pecorino or Parmesan for the cheeses. Add $1/4$ cup each finely chopped dried apricots and pistachios along with the yolks in Step 2.

Pea or Other Vegetable Soufflé

MAKES: 4 to 6 servings
TIME: About 1 hour

Ⓜ

A lovely springtime dish, especially with fresh peas. Purée the peas or simply mash them well for a more rustic soufflé. Just about any vegetable will work in this soufflé—see "10 Vegetables to Use for a Soufflé," page 187.

Salt

$1^1/4$ cups fresh or thawed frozen peas

$1^1/2$ cups milk, warmed until hot to the touch (about a minute in an average microwave)

4 tablespoons ($1/2$ stick) butter

$1/4$ cup all-purpose flour

6 eggs, separated

Freshly ground black pepper

Dash cayenne or $1/2$ teaspoon dry mustard

$1/2$ cup freshly grated Parmesan cheese

2 tablespoons minced fresh mint leaves (optional)

❶ Bring a small pot of salted water to boil; blanch the peas for 2 to 3 minutes, until bright green and tender. Drain the peas and drop into a bowl of ice water to stop the cooking for a minute; drain again and purée using a food processor or blender (add a tablespoon or two of the milk if necessary). Meanwhile, use a bit of the butter to grease a 2-quart soufflé or other deep baking dish. (Hold off on this step if you're going to delay baking the soufflés until later.)

❷ Put the remaining butter in another small saucepan over medium-low heat. When the foam subsides, stir in the flour and cook, stirring, until the mixture darkens, about 3 minutes. Turn the heat to low and whisk in the milk, a bit at a time, until the mixture is thick. Let cool for a few minutes, then beat in the egg yolks, some salt and pepper, the cayenne, Parmesan, mint, and pea purée. (You can prepare this base a few hours in advance of cooking; cover tightly and refrigerate; bring back to room temperature before continuing.)

❸ About an hour before you're ready to cook, heat the oven to 375°F. Use an electric or hand mixer or a whisk to beat the egg whites until fairly stiff. Stir about a third into the base to lighten it, then gently—and not overthoroughly—fold in the remaining whites, using a rubber spatula or your hand. Transfer to the prepared dish and bake until the top is brown, the sides are firm, and the center is still quite moist, about 30 minutes. Use a thin skewer to check the interior; if it is still quite wet, bake for another 5 minutes. If it is just a bit moist, the soufflé is done. Serve immediately.

Spinach Soufflé. A classic: Substitute 2 tablespoons minced onion and 1 cup cooked, drained, and chopped spinach for the peas. Omit the mint leaves and add a grating of nutmeg if you like along with the yolks in Step 2.

Chestnut Soufflé. A special-occasion dish; use fresh chestnuts if you can (canned or jarred just aren't the same): Substitute about $^1/_2$ pound prepared chestnuts (see page 287) for the peas and omit the mint. Purée the chestnuts in a food processor or blender, adding some of the milk as needed; add along with the yolks in Step 2.

Polenta or Millet Soufflé. Not as light and fluffy as a traditional soufflé, but really delicious: Substitute 1 cup Polenta (page 543) or Millet Mash (page 565) for the grated or crumbled cheese, reduce the milk by $^1/_2$ cup, and, if you like, add 4 or so cloves Roasted Garlic (page 304), mashed, along with the yolks in Step 2.

Ten Vegetables to Use for a Soufflé

Use about a cup of cooked, drained, and chopped or puréed vegetable, alone or in combination.

1. Fresh fava or lima beans
2. Eggplant
3. Cauliflower
4. Corn
5. Roasted Red Peppers (page 333)
6. Carrots
7. Sweet potato
8. Parsnips
9. Butternut or other winter squash
10. Mushrooms

The Basics of Quiche

Egg-based pies are nearly universal, though we associate them most closely with northern (especially northeastern) France. Still, rich, savory custards with a flaky bottom crust are made throughout Western Europe and elsewhere in the world as well. In most, egg and cream or milk are the main components of the custard; cheese is the best-known other filling, but many vegetables and herbs play a part and vary widely. The quiche is also a great vehicle for using leftovers.

The crust—for many the hardest part to get right—is basically an unsweetened pie or tart crust. (Some people use puff pastry for an even richer quiche.) To get that perfectly flaky, crunchy crust, you must precook it in a hot oven before adding the custard mixture.

Serve quiche with a salad for brunch, lunch, or dinner. It's also great for parties, because you can make it the day before; reheat in a 350°F oven or serve at room temperature.

Cheese Quiche

MAKES: 4 to 8 servings

TIME: About 1$^1/_2$ hours, somewhat unattended; less with a premade crust

Use just about any cheese; if it's soft, like goat cheese, ricotta, or cottage cheese, reduce the cream by $^1/_2$ cup or so, depending on how wet the soft cheese is. Fresh herbs are a simple way to add flavor: Add $^1/_4$ cup chopped basil, parsley, chives, chervil, cilantro, or dill; 1 teaspoon or so chopped tarragon, thyme, rosemary; or about 1 tablespoon chopped marjoram or oregano.

> 1 recipe Savory Piecrust (page 867) or Savory Tart Crust (page 868), chilled
>
> 6 eggs, at room temperature
>
> 2 cups grated Emmental, Gruyère, Cantal, cheddar, or other flavorful cheese
>
> 2 cups cream, half-and-half, or milk, heated just until warm
>
> $^1/_2$ teaspoon salt
>
> $^1/_4$ teaspoon cayenne or to taste

❶ Preheat the oven to 425°F and set the rack in the middle. Bake the chilled crust for 10 to 12 minutes, or until the crust begins to brown. Remove and cool on a rack while you prepare the filling. Reduce the oven temperature to 325°F.

② Combine the eggs, cheese, cream, salt, and cayenne and beat until well blended.

③ Put the partially cooked shell on a baking sheet and pour in the egg mixture. Bake for 30 to 40 minutes, or until almost firm (it should still jiggle just a little in the middle) and lightly browned on top; reduce the oven heat if the shell's edges are darkening too quickly. Cool on a rack; serve warm or at room temperature.

Ricotta and Parmesan Quiche. Rich and sharp: Substitute 1 cup ricotta and 1 cup freshly grated Parmesan for the Emmental and decrease the cream to 1 cup.

Pesto Quiche. Great in summer: Substitute $^3/_4$ cup Traditional Pesto (page 768) for $^1/_2$ cup each cheese and cream.

Quiche "Lorraine." The deep flavor of the caramelized onion and smokiness of the tofu take the place of the traditional bacon: Add 3 cups sliced onion and $^1/_2$ cup or so chopped smoked tofu (see page 639). Caramelize the onion (see Step 2 in the Onion Quiche recipe that follows) and add the tofu in the last few minutes. Combine the onion mixture with the eggs and proceed with the recipe.

Onion Quiche

MAKES: 4 to 8 servings

TIME: About 1$^1/_2$ hours, somewhat unattended; less with a premade crust

Ⓜ

You can substitute nearly any vegetable you like for the onions here (see "How to Use Other Vegetables in Quiche," page 189), though onion quiche is an absolute classic and—when the onions are cooked until almost creamy, as they are here—really lovely.

1 recipe Savory Piecrust (page 867) or Savory Tart Crust (page 868) in a 10-inch tart pan or 9-inch deep-dish pie pan, chilled

4 tablespoons ($^1/_2$ stick) butter or olive oil

6 cups thinly sliced onion

Salt and freshly ground black pepper

1 teaspoon fresh thyme leaves or $^1/_2$ teaspoon dried thyme

6 eggs, at room temperature

2 cups cream, half-and-half, or milk, heated just until warm

① Preheat the oven to 425°F and set the rack in the middle. Bake the chilled crust for 10 to 12 minutes, or until the crust begins to brown. Remove and cool on a rack while you prepare the filling. Reduce the oven temperature to 325°F.

② Put the butter or oil in a large, deep skillet over medium heat. When the butter is melted or the oil is hot, add the onion and some salt and pepper. Turn the heat up to medium-high and cook, stirring frequently, until the onion is very soft and lightly browned, at least 20 minutes and probably longer; adjust the heat so it doesn't brown too much or crisp up, but just cooks until practically melted. Add the thyme, stir, turn off the heat, and cool slightly. Combine the eggs and cream in a bowl and then add the onion mixture.

③ Put the partially cooked shell on a baking sheet and pour in the egg mixture. Bake for 30 to 40 minutes, or until almost firm (it should still jiggle just a little in the middle) and lightly browned on top; reduce the oven heat if the shell's edges are darkening too quickly. Cool on a wire rack; serve warm or at room temperature.

Leek and Herb Quiche. The leeks have a milder onion flavor but are just as delicious: Substitute chopped leek for the onion and $^1/_4$ cup mixed fresh herbs, like parsley, chives, chervil, or basil, for the thyme.

Mushroom Quiche. Fresh or dried mushrooms are equally delicious; soak dried mushrooms in hot water or some of the cream, heated, until soft (squeeze a bit if soaked in water; no need to squeeze if soaked in the cream):

There are two ways to prepare vegetables before adding them to the egg mixture for quiches. The first is to cook them in the pan with butter or olive oil and season with salt and pepper, like the onions in the Onion Quiche (page 188). Most vegetables won't take as long as onions; use your judgment, keeping in mind that they will cook a little more as the quiche bakes.

Other vegetables work best in quiches after they have been cooked briefly in boiling salted water, drained well, then combined with the egg mixture.

In either case, cool all vegetables slightly before adding them to the eggs. And limit the total quantity of extra ingredients—vegetables, cheese, nuts, whatever—to 2 cups. Here are some specific ideas and guidelines to get you started:

- Broccoli or cauliflower, chopped into small florets: Boil for a minute or two.
- Asparagus: Cook in butter or oil—or boil—until just tender. Great with goat cheese.

- Artichoke hearts: Boil for a couple minutes. Combine with ricotta and basil.
- Potatoes: Boil until you can pierce easily with a fork. Season with rosemary or dill.
- Eggplant: Peel if you like and cut into small cubes. Cook in butter or oil until browned and tender, 5 minutes or so. Good with olives, a little tomatoes, and Parmesan.
- Bell peppers: Cook until just tender in a little butter or olive oil.
- Spinach or greens, like kale, chard, collards (squeezed of excess liquid).
- Tomatoes: Start with no more than 2 cups chopped fresh or drained canned tomatoes. Cook in butter or oil until quite dry.
- Greens—kale, spinach, watercress, and the like: Follow the directions for boiling and shocking greens on page 241. Squeeze out as much water as possible, then coarsely chop them.

Substitute 4 cups sliced fresh mushrooms or 2 cups soaked and sliced dried mushrooms for the onions. In Step 2, cook the mushrooms until just tender, then proceed with the recipe.

10 Great Leftovers to Turn into Quiche Filling

Using either of the basic recipes as a guide, use 2 cups leftovers or 1 cup leftovers combined with 1 cup cheese.

1. Quinoa with Caramelized Onions (page 559) or Kasha with Golden Brown Onions (page 562)
2. Any cooked grain (see Cooking Grains the Easy Way, page 537)
3. Beans and Mushrooms (page 596), drained, or any cooked or canned beans, drained
4. Red Cabbage with Apples (page 277)
5. Roasted or Grilled Asparagus (page 261)
6. Cauliflower, Broccoli, or Just About Anything Else, Roman Style (page 271)
7. Pan-Grilled Corn with Chile (page 289)
8. Eggplant Slices with Garlic and Parsley (page 297)
9. Anything-Scented Peas (page 333)
10. Any Mashed Potatoes (page 341)

The Basics of Savory Custard, Flan, and Bread Pudding

Dessert comes to mind when you think of custard and its relatives flan and bread pudding (and rightly so; see pages 885–887). But they also make great savory dishes.

Just to be clear: Custard and flan are essentially identical, except that flan is turned out of its container and typically has a caramel sauce cooked with it (you'll see a variation on that theme in the savory flan recipe in this section); bread pudding is no more than a custard containing bread.

Making custard that's perfectly smooth and creamy is part technique, part timing, and part courage. Cooking the custards in a hot water bath really does make a difference, especially if you're using one large dish (individual ramekins or custard cups are a bit less sensitive). Water baths help to regulate the heat around the dish and ensure even cooking, which is helpful when you're cooking eggs. The custards I've cooked using a water bath turn out uniformly smooth and ultra-creamy from the inside to the outside. Without the water bath they cook more quickly but sometimes unevenly; the sides may curdle and exude water, and the interior may remain runny. They still have a good flavor, but it's a gamble; so, lazy as I am, I've come to think a water bath is worth the extra bit of work.

Knowing when to pull the custard out of the oven is also key. The custard should still jiggle a good amount and offer only slight resistance when touched, but not be liquid; remember, it will continue to cook after it's pulled out of the oven. This is the part that takes courage: You *must* remove the custard before you think it's done; after you overcook them once or twice, this will become second nature. (The water bath makes knowing when to take the custard out of the oven easier because the whole custard is at the same point of doneness; without the water bath, the sides will be firm while the center is still liquid.)

Baked Savory Custard

MAKES: 4 to 6 servings
TIME: 45 minutes

Ⓜ

This custard is as basic as you can get. Toss in a bit of cheese, fresh herbs, or some cooked chopped vegetables to add flavor.

Tips for Cooking with Hot Water Baths

- Always use water that's just under the boiling point.
- Use a low rack under the dish(es), which will allow the water bath to circulate underneath as well (this is not essential, but it helps).
- Put the larger pan that will hold the water bath in the oven, then put your dish(es) in the center, then pour in the boiling water. This is much easier and safer than carrying a big pan filled with boiling water.
- Add water to within an inch or so of the top of the dish(es).
- When finished baking, take the dish(es) out of the water bath, then let the hot water bath pan cool a bit before removing; if it's very full of water, ladle some out first.

2 cups cream, half-and-half, or milk

1 sprig fresh thyme (optional)

2 eggs, plus 2 yolks

Pinch cayenne

1/2 teaspoon salt

❶ Put the cream in a small pot with the thyme if you're using it. Cook just until it begins to steam.

❷ Preheat the oven to 300°F and put a kettle of water on to boil. Put the eggs, cayenne, and salt in a medium bowl and whisk or beat until blended. Remove the thyme and add the cream gradually to the egg mixture while whisking constantly. Pour the mixture into a 1-quart dish or into 4 to 6 small ramekins or custard cups.

❸ Put the dish or ramekins in a baking pan and pour hot water into the pan to within about 1 inch of the top of the dish or ramekins. Bake until the mixture is not quite set—it should jiggle a bit in the middle—30 to 40 minutes for ramekins, somewhat longer for a baking dish. Use your judgment; cream sets faster than milk. Serve warm, at room temperature, or cold within a few hours of baking.

Baked Cheesy Custard. A cheese that melts easily is best here: Add $1/2$ cup finely grated Parmesan, Emmental, Gruyère, cheddar, Jack, or goat cheese; stir into the heated cream until melted.

Baked Roasted Garlic Custard. Subtle and sweet: Add 4 to 8 cloves Roasted Garlic (page 304), peeled and smashed into a paste, to the egg mixture.

Baked Spinach Custard. Any cooked green works nicely; be sure to squeeze out the excess water: Add $1/2$ cup chopped cooked spinach to the egg mixture, with a sprinkling of nutmeg if you like.

Poblano Custard

MAKES: 6 to 8 servings

TIME: 45 minutes

Ⓜ

Using purées to flavor custards is easy. Here poblano chiles add some mild heat and a pretty green hue to the custard. But you can substitute another vegetable purée if you like: see the variations and "14 Vegetables to Use for Savory Custards and Flans" (page 192) for ideas.

4 medium poblano or other mild fresh chiles, roasted and cleaned (page 828)

2 cups cream, half-and-half, or milk

$1/2$ cup grated queso fresco or Jack cheese (optional)

3 eggs, plus 3 yolks

$1/4$ cup chopped fresh cilantro leaves

$1/2$ teaspoon salt

① Finely chop 2 tablespoons of the chiles and set aside. Combine the remaining chiles and the cream in a pot and use an immersion blender to purée; or pour into a blender and purée. Cook the chile mixture just until it begins to steam. Add the cheese, if you're using it and stir until it melts.

② Preheat the oven to 300°F and put a kettle of water on to boil. Put the eggs, cilantro, and salt in a medium bowl and whisk or beat until blended. Gradually add the chile mixture to the egg mixture, whisking constantly, then add the reserved chopped chile. Pour the mixture into a 1-quart dish or into four 4-ounce ramekins or custard cups.

③ Put the dish or ramekins in a baking pan and pour hot water into the pan to within about 1 inch of the top of the dish or ramekins. Bake until the mixture is not quite set—it should jiggle a bit in the middle—30 to 40 minutes for ramekins, somewhat longer for a baking dish. Use your judgment; cream sets faster than milk. Serve warm, at room temperature, or cold within a few hours of baking.

Mushroom Custard. If you're using cremini or portobello mushrooms, scrape out the dark gills from the undersides to keep the custard from turning an unattractive gray; soak dried mushrooms in the cream: Substitute 3 cups chopped fresh mushrooms or 3 ounces dried mushrooms for the chiles; Parmesan, Emmental, or Manchego cheese for the queso fresco; 2 sprigs fresh thyme or 1 sprig rosemary for the cilantro. Reduce the cream by $1/4$ cup. Steep the thyme or rosemary in the cream, then remove it before adding to the eggs in Step 2.

Green Pea and Parmesan Custard. A pretty, pale green custard: Substitute 2 cups fresh or thawed frozen green peas for the chiles; Parmesan for the queso fresco; 2 tablespoons chopped fresh mint leaves for the cilantro. Set aside $1/4$ cup of the peas to add to the mixture in Step 2.

On those rare occasions when I really want to wow someone, I use barely cooked vegetables to wrap custards, creating pretty little packages. The wrapping isn't simply ornamental either; it adds flavor to the dish as well as color and, needless to say, a wow factor. You can also add small amounts—a tablespoon or two for each package—of cooked and diced vegetables, chopped olives or capers, chopped fresh herbs, nuts, or crumbled or grated cheese, for more flavor and texture. And for an even more elaborate presentation, you can wilt chives in hot water and use them to tie the wrapped custards.

Wrapping with lettuce or leafy greens: Romaine, butter, or Boston lettuce and chard, escarole, or spinach leaves all work well here. Dip the lettuce or green leaves into salted boiling water for about 10 seconds (for lettuces) to 30 seconds for tougher greens. Remove the leaves and immediately plunge them into a bowl of ice water; drain and blot dry. Grease the insides of the ramekins or custard cups with butter or oil and line with the leaves, leaving overhanging pieces; pour in the custard mixture, fold the overhanging pieces over the top, and cook as usual.

Wrapping with other vegetables, like eggplant, zucchini, summer squash, or roasted peppers or chiles: Cut the eggplant, zucchini, or summer squash into ¼-inch-thick slices; the long way usually works best (use a mandoline if you have one). Brush the eggplant, with some oil and roast in a 350°F oven until soft but not falling apart. Roast the zucchini or squash like the eggplant, or blanch it in boiling salted water for about 20 seconds and then immediately plunge it into a bowl of ice water; drain and blot dry. Roast and clean peppers or chiles as directed (page 828). Grease the insides of the ramekins or custard cups with butter or oil and line with overlapping slices of vegetable, leaving overhanging pieces; pour in the custard mixture, fold the overhanging pieces over the top, and cook as directed.

14 Vegetable Options for Savory Custards and Flans

Substitute about 2 cups of any of these cooked and puréed vegetables for the poblano chiles or butternut squash in the flan recipes.

1. Asparagus
2. Spinach or other greens (squeezed of excess water)
3. Green peas
4. Tomato
5. Zucchini or summer squash
6. Mushrooms
7. Roasted Red (or yellow) Pepper (page 333)
8. Eggplant
9. Corn
10. Leeks
11. Onions
12. Fennel
13. Roasted Garlic (page 304)
14. Chestnuts

Savory Bread Pudding

MAKES: 6 to 8 servings

TIME: About 1 hour, largely unattended

A terrific use for not only day-old bread but also leftover vegetables. And you can prepare this up to Step 3 a day ahead or even bake it a day or two ahead of time and reheat it before serving.

Ⓕ Fast   Ⓜ Make Ahead   Ⓥ Vegan

To dry out fresh bread, cut or tear it into pieces and put it on a baking sheet in a single layer. Bake it in a 250°F oven until dried out but not browned. If the bread starts to brown, reduce your oven to the lowest temperature or turn the heat off entirely.

3 cups milk

4 tablespoons ($^1/_2$ stick) unsalted butter, plus butter for the pan

$^1/_4$ cup chopped mixed fresh herbs, like parsley, chives, thyme, and sage

Salt and freshly ground black pepper

8 thick slices day-old dark rye or other bread, crusts removed if very thick

3 eggs

2 cups grated Gruyère, Emmental, cheddar, or Jack cheese

① Preheat the oven to 350°F. Warm the milk, butter, herbs, and a good sprinkling of salt and pepper in a small saucepan over low heat just until the butter melts. Meanwhile, butter a $1^1/_2$-quart or 8-inch square baking dish (glass is nice) and cut or tear the bread into bite-sized pieces—not too small.

② Put the bread in the baking dish and pour the warm milk over it. Let it sit for a few minutes, occasionally submerging any pieces of bread that rise to the top. Beat the eggs briefly and stir them into the bread mixture along with the cheese. Set the baking dish in a larger baking pan and pour hot water into the pan to within about an inch of the top of the dish.

③ Bake for 45 to 60 minutes, or until a thin knife inserted in the center comes out clean or nearly so; the center should be just a little wobbly. Run under the broiler for about 30 seconds if you like, to brown the top a bit. Serve hot or store, covered, in the refrigerator for up to 2 days. Cover with foil and reheat in a 325°F oven for about 15 minutes; remove the foil and heat for another 5 minutes or so for a crisper crust.

Bread Pudding with Brussels Sprouts. Mushrooms, asparagus, and cubes of eggplant also work nicely here: Increase the milk to $3^1/_2$ cups and add 1 large onion, sliced, 2 cups trimmed and halved Brussels sprouts, and 1 cup diced smoked tofu (see page 639). Put 2 tablespoons butter in a pan over medium-high heat. Add the onions and cook until soft, about 5 minutes. Mix in the onions, Brussels sprouts, and tofu along with the eggs. Proceed with the recipe.

Bread Pudding with Sun-Dried Tomatoes and Mozzarella. Use a good white or semolina bread: Add 1 cup chopped sun-dried tomatoes and $^1/_4$ cup pitted and chopped black olives. Substitute chopped fresh basil leaves for the herbs and slices of fresh mozzarella for the grated cheese. In Step 1, add the tomatoes to the milk when heating.

Multigrain Bread Pudding with Winter Squash. Toss in handful of cooked wheat, farro, rye, or other chewy grain for added texture: Increase the milk to $3^1/_2$ cups and add about 3 cups peeled and cubed winter squash or pumpkin. Substitute 3 tablespoons chopped fresh sage leaves for the mixed herbs. Coat the squash in oil and roast in a 350°F until just tender. Proceed with the recipe.

6 Ideas for Savory Bread Puddings

By changing the type of bread, herbs, vegetables, and/or cheese, you can make bread pudding part of your standard repertoire. Here are some combinations I like; you'll find others:

1. Caramelized Onions (page 329) and smoked Gouda with dark multigrain bread
2. Asparagus and goat cheese
3. Blue cheese and walnuts or hazelnuts with whole wheat bread
4. Eggplant, raisins, and pine nuts with parsley
5. Kale and Roasted Garlic (page 304) with dark or marbled rye
6. Roasted Red (or yellow) Peppers (page 333) with ricotta and basil

Eggs au Gratin

MAKES: 4 servings

TIME: 30 minutes

Since all the ingredients in this dish are cooked before assembly, a quick broiling to melt the cheese and make everything hot and bubbly is all that's left for the last minute. (The variations will take a little longer.) This requires nothing more than a vinegary green salad on the side and a crusty baguette. For entertaining, simply double or even triple the recipe and use a bigger baking dish.

> 1 tablespoon butter
>
> 1 recipe Béchamel (page 803), made up to 2 days in advance if you like
>
> Milk, up to 1/2 cup, for thinning the sauce
>
> 2 tablespoons Dijon mustard
>
> Salt and freshly ground black pepper
>
> 8 Hard-Cooked Eggs (page 166)
>
> 1 cup grated Gruyère or Swiss cheese
>
> 1/4 cup minced parsley for garnish
>
> Sprinkle of paprika (optional)

1 Preheat the broiler and make sure the rack is about 4 inches from the heat source. Use the butter to grease a medium shallow baking pan or gratin dish, one that will just hold the eggs in one layer.

2 Put the béchamel in a small saucepan and add 2 tablespoons of the milk and the mustard. Turn the heat to medium and warm the sauce, stirring frequently to prevent scorching. (If your béchamel is freshly made, you'll just be adding the mustard and thinning it a bit.) Add enough milk so that the sauce is thicker than soup but thin enough to pour. Taste and add salt and pepper if necessary.

3 Pour half of the hot béchamel into the bottom of the prepared pan or dish and spread it around evenly. Carefully cut the eggs in half lengthwise and nestle them into the sauce, cut side up; it should be a fairly tight fit.

Spoon the remaining sauce over the eggs. Sprinkle the cheese over all.

4 Broil for 3 to 5 minutes, until the cheese is melted and golden and the sauce is bubbling. Sprinkle with a few more grinds of pepper, the parsley, and the paprika if you like and serve.

Eggs au Gratin with Caramelized Onions and Olives. Very bistrolike: Prepare Caramelized Onions (page 329). In Step 3, after you spread the béchamel around the dish, put the onions on top; then nestle in the eggs. Proceed with the recipe. When you take the baking pan or dish out of the broiler, sprinkle up to 1/2 cup pitted and chopped black olives on top along with the parsley and serve.

Eggs au Gratin with Spinach. A cross between the classic eggs Florentine and a spinach eggs Benedict, only with hard-cooked eggs: While the béchamel is warming in Step 2, wilt a pound of fresh spinach leaves in 2 tablespoons of butter or olive oil. Sprinkle with salt and pepper. In Step 2, put the spinach into the prepared pan or dish first, then top with half the béchamel and the eggs. Proceed with the recipe.

Eggs au Gratin with Fennel. Easy yet very sophisticated: Omit the mustard. Trim and thinly slice 1 medium fennel bulb. While the béchamel is warming in Step 2, cook the fennel in 2 tablespoons butter or olive oil. Sprinkle with salt and pepper. In Step 2, put the fennel into the prepared pan or dish first, then top with half the béchamel and the eggs. Proceed with the recipe.

Hard-Cooked Eggs in Quick Tomato Curry Sauce

MAKES: 4 servings

TIME: 30 minutes with cooked eggs

This is a smart, delicious recipe, but it's also a concept that can quickly turn almost any sauce into a meal; see the list below for more ideas. To bulk this up a bit, add 2 to 3 cups of chopped mixed vegetables, like carrots, green beans, potatoes, zucchini, cauliflower, and/or eggplant, along with $1/2$ cup water to the sauce; simmer until the vegetables are almost done, then add the hard-cooked eggs.

Serve with White Rice (page 505), Simpler-than-Pilaf Baked Rice (page 515), or Stuck-Pot Rice with Potato Crust (page 526).

8 Hard-Cooked Eggs (page 166)

2 tablespoons neutral oil, like grapeseed or corn

1 cup sliced scallion

2 tablespoons curry powder (to make your own, see page 815)

Salt and freshly ground black pepper

2 cups chopped ripe tomato (about 1 pound whole), preferably peeled and seeded, or drained chopped canned

1 cup homemade coconut milk (page 423) or about $1/2$ of a (13-ounce) can

Chopped fresh cilantro leaves for garnish

① Peel the eggs and set them aside to come to room temperature.

② Put the oil in a large deep skillet over medium-high heat. Add the scallion and cook, stirring frequently, until soft, about a minute. Stir in the curry powder and sprinkle with salt and pepper. When the spices are fragrant, add the tomato and coconut milk. Bring the mixture to a boil, then lower the heat so that it bubbles assertively and cook, stirring occasionally, until the sauce is thickened, about 20 minutes.

③ When the sauce is ready, add the eggs and cook, stirring once or twice, for another 5 minutes or so. Taste and adjust the seasoning, garnish, and serve.

Hard-Cooked Eggs in Red Curry Stew. For a Thai flavor that's great with Sticky Rice (page 507): Substitute $1/4$ cup Red Curry Paste for the scallion, curry powder, and tomato. Add 2 cups coconut milk instead of 1 and 3 or so cups of chopped mixed vegetables, like

red or yellow bell peppers, green beans, carrots, eggplant, or potatoes, if you like. Put a pan over medium-high heat, add about 2 tablespoons oil, and cook the vegetables until just tender. Add the curry paste, stir well, then add the coconut milk. Proceed with the recipe.

Poached Eggs in Tomato Curry Sauce. Use this technique for any of the sauces in this recipe: When the sauce is ready, add another $1/2$ cup of water or stock and adjust the heat so that the mixture bubbles gently, carefully crack each of the eggs into a saucer, and slide it into the sauce. When all the eggs are in, cover the pan tightly and cook until the eggs are done to your liking, anywhere from 3 to 7 minutes. To serve, scoop each egg out with a little of the sauce.

11 Sauces for Stewing Hard-Cooked Eggs

Instead of cooking the quick pan sauce in the main recipe, put any of the following sauces in the pan and add about $1/4$ cup water to thin it a bit. Heat until bubbling, then proceed with the recipe from Step 3.

1. Smooth Green Chile Sauce, Indian Style (page 792)
2. Tomato Chutney (page 785); you'll need to add a full cup of water
3. Nutty Miso Sauce (page 782)
4. Creamy Nut Sauce (page 797)
5. Béchamel or any of its variations (page 803); garnish with chopped parsley, if you like
6. Creamy Bistro Dressing or Sauce (page 799)
7. Any cooked salsa, like Salsa Roja (page 787) or Cooked Tomatillo Salsa (page 788)
8. Simplest Dal (page 600) or other any dal recipe (see pages 600–604)
9. Peanut Sauce, Six Ways or any of its variations (page 794); garnish with cilantro if you like
10. Fast Tomato Sauce or any of its variations (page 445); garnish with chopped fresh basil or parsley
11. Spicy Indian Tomato Sauce (page 793)

The Basics of Crêpes and Blintzes

Crêpes and blintzes are closely related, thin pancakes that can have sweet or savory fillings. Crêpes are French, have much less filling, and are more about dough with flavoring than blintzes, which you might think of as the Eastern European version of cannelloni. In either case, making a crêpe or blintz sweet or savory is as simple as adding sugar (as in the crêpes), using a different flour, and/or using a sweet or savory filling. Savory crêpes are often made with buckwheat flour and folded, whereas sweet ones rely on white flour and are rolled (though white ones can be filled with savory ingredients too, and the folding/rolling option is your call).

Though the quantity makes them somewhat time consuming, the process of making crêpes and blintzes is easy: Use a nonstick pan to make flipping almost effortless. The easiest way to flip a crêpe or blintz is to lift the edges with a spatula and use your fingers to pull it up off the pan, then flip it to the other side. It takes just one or two tries (the first crêpes almost never work, even for professionals), and there's batter to make up for the loss.

When filling, remember that crêpes are more delicate and intended to have little filling so you can taste the crêpe. Blintzes are sturdier and can hold more filling, but still need to have space to fold nicely and make sealed packages for sautéing or baking.

Crêpes

MAKES: 12 to 16 crêpes; enough for 4 to 8 servings
TIME: 40 minutes

Ⓜ

Crêpes are perfect for breakfast, brunch, lunch, light supper, or dessert. The batter can be made a day ahead, and even the crêpes can be made ahead, refrigerated, and then wrapped in foil and reheated in a 325°F oven.

Change the flavor of the wrapper itself by substituting cornmeal, whole wheat, rye, or teff flour—all of which lend a slightly different flavor—for half of the flour. A splash of flavored brandy, amaretto, kirsch, or rose water is a nice addition to sweet crêpe batter too.

1 cup all-purpose flour

Pinch salt

1 tablespoon sugar (optional)

1 1/4 cups milk, plus more if needed

2 eggs

2 tablespoons butter, melted and cooled, plus butter for cooking

① Whisk together all the ingredients except the butter for cooking until smooth; you can do this in a blender. If the mixture isn't quite pourable, add a little more milk. If time allows, let the batter rest in the refrigerator for an hour or up to 24 hours.

② Put an 8- or 10-inch nonstick skillet over medium heat and wait a couple of minutes; add a small pat of butter. Stir the batter and use a large spoon or ladle to pour a couple of tablespoons of the batter into the skillet. Swirl it around so that it forms a thin layer on the bottom of the pan.

③ When the top of the crêpe is dry, after about a minute, turn and cook the other side for 15 to 30 seconds. (The crêpe should brown only very slightly and not become at all crisp.) Bear in mind that the first crêpe almost never works, even for professionals, so discard it if necessary; there is plenty of batter.

④ Stack the crepes on a plate as you make them, and keep them warm in a low oven while you make the remaining crepes. Even better, fill each crêpe while it's still in the pan, putting the filling in the center of the bottom third of the crêpe. If you want your filling warmed, keep the pan over low heat for a few minutes. Either roll the crêpe starting at the end with the filling or fold the bottom third over the filling, fold in the sides, then fold the crêpe from the bottom up. Slide it onto a plate and serve. Repeat the process, adding butter to the skillet and adjusting the heat as needed, until all the batter is used up.

Spoon some filling across the lower third of the crêpe.

Lift the bottom edge and roll it up.

A filled crêpe.

Buckwheat Crêpes. Resting this batter for an hour does make a difference, but if you're in a real hurry, it can be reduced or skipped: Substitute buckwheat flour for the white flour and add ¹/₄ cup white flour. Reduce the milk to ¹/₂ cup and add 1 cup water. Let the batter rest for at least an hour. Proceed with the recipe.

Garlic Crêpes. A simple addition but a great way to add lots of flavor: Add 2 teaspoons finely minced garlic to the batter and proceed with the recipe.

Coconut Crêpes. These are great both savory and sweet: Substitute coconut milk for the regular milk and add the sugar if you're making a sweet crêpe.

Almond Crêpes. Delicious with a splash of amaretto added: Substitute almond flour or any nut flour for half the white flour and almond milk for the regular milk. Add 2 tablespoons amaretto if you like and use the sugar.

Chocolate Crêpes. Perfect for bananas quickly cooked with some butter and brown sugar: Add ¹/₄ cup cocoa powder and use the sugar.

5 Fillings for Sweet Crêpes

As simple as sugar and lemon juice or any of these:

1. Any jam, jelly, marmalade, or Macerated Fruit (page 417)
2. Nutella, any nut butter, or peanut butter
3. Any peeled, seeded (or pitted or cored) fresh fruit, cooked briefly with sugar to taste, some butter if you like, and a little rum or cinnamon
4. Crème fraîche, sour cream, or yogurt (sweetened if you like)
5. Any sweet Compound Butter (page 801) or Brown Butter (page 801), sprinkled with cinnamon, cardamom, and/or cloves

6 Fillings for Savory Crêpes

Often savory crêpes are filled with cheese and vegetables, but neither is required.

1. Any grated or thinly sliced cheese: Gruyère, Brie, goat, mozzarella, cheddar, or Fresh Cheese (page 230)
2. Cooked, drained, and chopped green vegetables, reheated in butter or oil as described on page 240 (don't bother to chop vegetables whose shape is naturally suited to crêpes, like asparagus spears)

3. Sautéed mushrooms, onions, or leeks
4. Roasted Red Peppers (page 333), chiles, winter squash, or eggplant
5. Baked Savory Custard (page 190), spooned into the crêpe after baking
6. Cooked beans or lentils

Cheese Blintzes

MAKES: 4 servings

TIME: About 1 hour

Eggier and sturdier than crêpes, blintzes are traditionally filled with cottage cheese, mashed potatoes, or fruit, then sautéed or baked with butter. Because they are folded into little packages, they can be filled with more than the more delicate French-style crêpes. And as with crêpes, any other grain flour can be used for a portion of the regular flour to change the flavor.

$^3/_4$ cup all-purpose flour

Salt

1 cup milk

3 eggs

2 tablespoons butter, melted and cooled, or neutral oil, like grapeseed or corn, plus more butter or oil for cooking

1$^1/_2$ cups Fresh Cottage Cheese (page 230) or store-bought cottage cheese, drained if very moist

$^1/_2$ cup sour cream or thick yogurt

1 tablespoon sugar, or to taste

1 teaspoon ground cinnamon, or to taste

① Whisk together the flour, a pinch of salt, and the milk until smooth; you can do this in a blender. Beat in the eggs and stir in the 2 tablespoons melted and cooled butter or oil. If time allows, let rest in the refrigerator for an hour or up to 24 hours and beat again.

② Put an 8- or 10-inch nonstick skillet over medium heat and wait a couple minutes; add a small pat of butter. Stir the batter and use a large spoon or ladle to pour a couple of tablespoons of the batter into the skillet. Swirl it around so that it forms a thin layer on the bottom of the pan.

③ When the top of the blintz is dry, about a minute, turn and cook the other side for 15 to 30 seconds. (The blintz should brown only very slightly and not become at all crisp.) Bear in mind that the first blintz almost never works, even for professionals, so discard it if necessary; there is plenty of batter. Stack the finished blintzes on a plate; you will usually reheat them before serving.

④ Combine the cottage cheese, sour cream, another pinch of salt, the sugar, and the cinnamon. Put about 2 tablespoons of the filling in the center of the blintz about a third of the way from the bottom. Fold the bottom third over the filling, then fold in the sides, then roll from the bottom up to create a package. When they are all done, you have two choices:

• Arrange them on a greased (preferably buttered) ovenproof platter. Dot with butter and sprinkle with sugar and cinnamon if you like. Bake in a pre-heated 400°F oven for 10 minutes, then serve.

• Sauté several at a time in about 2 tablespoons butter until brown and crisp on both sides, a total of about 5 minutes.

Mashed Potato Blintzes. Totally traditional: Substitute well-seasoned Mashed Potatoes (page 341) or other mashed vegetables for the cheese filling.

Vegetable and Cheese Blintzes. Lots of possibilities here: Substitute about a cup of chopped or sliced cooked vegetables (like mushrooms, spinach, asparagus, peas, onions, cauliflower, or broccoli) and $^1/_2$ cup grated, crumbled, or soft cheese for the cheese filling. Toss in a tablespoon or so chopped fresh herbs if you like.

Fruit Blintzes. Fabulous with a dollop of crème fraîche or sour cream: Substitute any peeled, seeded (or pitted or cored) fresh fruit—apples, pears, cherries, berries, and bananas to name a few—cooked briefly with sugar to taste, some butter if you like, and a little rum or cinnamon for the cheese filling.

 Fast   Make Ahead   Ⓥ Vegan

Broiled Crêpes or Blintzes

MAKES: 4 to 6 servings

TIME: 15 minutes with cooked crêpes

Crêpes, sweet or savory: The main recipe is best at breakfast, brunch, or dessert, while the savory variation is perfect for brunch, lunch, or a light dinner. You can use unfilled blintzes here in place of the crêpes.

3 tablespoons butter

2 cups sliced apple or pear (peeled and cored), banana, or strawberries, or whole raspberries or blueberries

12 or so cooked and unfilled crêpes (page 196) or blintzes (page 198)

1 cup cream cheese, cottage cheese, or goat cheese

$1/4$ cup cream

$1/3$ cup sugar

① Put 2 tablespoons of the butter in a pan over medium-high heat. Add the fruit and cook until slightly soft, about 3 minutes (skip this step for the berries if you like).

② Grease a baking dish with the remaining butter and lay a crêpe or blintz at one end. Smear a tablespoon of the cheese down the third of the crêpe closest to the middle of the dish, then spoon on a portion of the fruit; roll the crêpe to the end of the dish. Repeat with the remaining crêpes, placing the filled crêpes side by side in the dish. Brush the tops of the crêpes with the cream and then sprinkle with the sugar.

③ Put the dish under the broiler until the sugar caramelizes, about 5 minutes, watching carefully. Serve immediately.

Baked Mushroom Crêpes. Buckwheat crêpes are great here; any mushroom will work, as will asparagus, spinach, or mashed peas: Substitute 3 cups sliced mushrooms for the fruit and grated Gruyère, fontina, or Jack for the cream cheese. Omit the cream and sugar. Proceed with Step 1 and add some salt and pepper; in Step 2, fill the crêpes with the mushrooms and sprinkle the cheese over the top. Proceed with the recipe.

(STEP 1) Spoon some filling about a third of the way from the bottom of the blintz. (STEP 2) Fold the bottom third over the filling. (STEP 3) Fold in the sides. (STEP 4) Roll from the bottom up.

The Basics of Pancakes

Pancakes are made of a simple batter of eggs, flour, and liquid, usually with a bit of baking powder for leavening. It's a forgiving batter with lots of room for improvising: beat the egg whites and/or use cottage cheese for light and airy pancakes; switch the type of flour; add fruit, peanut butter, chocolate chips, or spices. If you like thick pancakes, reduce the liquid; add more liquid for thinner pancakes.

The Everyday Pancake batter whips up in no time and can be stored in the fridge for a couple of days, which makes it great for weekdays. You can also mix the dry ingredients to store indefinitely (this, essentially, is Bisquick); just add the eggs and milk when you're ready to cook.

Everyday Pancakes

MAKES: 4 to 6 servings

TIME: 20 minutes

It's amazing how quickly you can whip up this batter. Store it, covered, in the refrigerator for up to 2 days. Adjust the consistency of the batter with either more milk or more flour as necessary.

2 cups all-purpose flour

2 teaspoons baking powder

$1/4$ teaspoon salt

1 tablespoon sugar (optional)

2 eggs

$1^1/_2$ to 2 cups milk

2 tablespoons butter, melted and cooled (optional), plus butter or neutral oil, like grapeseed or corn, for cooking

❶ Heat a griddle or large skillet over medium-low heat while you make the batter.

❷ Mix the dry ingredients together. Beat the eggs into $1^1/_2$ cups of the milk, then stir in the 2 tablespoons melted cooled butter if you're using it. Gently stir this mixture into the dry ingredients, mixing only enough to moisten the flour; don't worry about a few lumps. The batter should pourable, or nearly so; if it's too thick, add a little more milk.

❸ If your skillet or griddle is nonstick, you can cook the pancakes without any butter. Otherwise, use a teaspoon or two of butter or oil each time you add batter. When the butter foam subsides or the oil shimmers, ladle batter onto the griddle or skillet, making any size pancakes you like. Adjust the heat as necessary; usually the first batch will require higher heat than subsequent batches. The idea is to brown the bottom in 2 to 4 minutes without burning it. Flip when bubbles rise to the surface of the pancakes and the bottoms are cooked; they won't hold together well until they're ready.

Ⓕ Fast   Ⓜ Make Ahead   Ⓥ Vegan

④ Cook until the second side is lightly browned and serve or hold on an ovenproof plate in a 200°F oven for up to 15 minutes.

Vegan Pancakes. Omit the eggs and substitute a soy, grain, or nut milk for the regular and oil, like a nut or neutral oil, for the melted butter. Proceed with the recipe. Optional ideas for flavor: Replace half of the all-purpose flour with a whole grain or substitute $^3/_4$ cup pecans, walnuts, or blanched almonds for $^1/_2$ cup of the all-purpose flour if you like; grind it into a flour (not too long or it will turn into a paste).

Sourdough Pancakes. This requires a sourdough starter, but if you have one this is a good place to take advantage of your foresight: Substitute 1 cup sourdough starter (see page 710) for half the flour, reduce the milk and salt by half and the baking powder to $^1/_2$ teaspoon, and use only 1 egg. Mix the starter, flour, and $^1/_2$ cup of the milk to a medium-thin batter; let sit for an hour. Just before cooking, stir in the salt, sugar, and baking powder; then beat in the egg. Proceed with the recipe.

Light and Fluffy Pancakes

MAKES: 4 servings

TIME: 20 minutes

Here the egg whites are whipped into a foam and folded into the batter, creating a cross between pancake and soufflé.

1 cup milk

4 eggs, separated

1 cup all-purpose flour

Dash salt

1 tablespoon sugar

1$^1/_2$ teaspoons baking powder

Butter or neutral oil, like grapeseed or corn, as needed

① Heat a griddle or large skillet over medium-low heat while you make the batter.

② Beat the milk and egg yolks together. Mix the dry ingredients together. Beat the egg whites with a whisk or electric mixer until fairly stiff.

③ Combine the dry ingredients and milk-yolk mixture, stirring to blend. Gently fold in the beaten egg whites; they should remain somewhat distinct in the batter.

④ Add about 1 teaspoon of the butter or oil to the griddle or skillet. When the butter is melted or the oil is hot, add the batter by the heaping tablespoon, making sure you include some of the egg whites in each spoonful. Cook until lightly browned on the bottom, 3 to 5 minutes, then turn and cook until the second side is brown. Serve or hold in a 200°F oven for up to 15 minutes.

10 Other Ideas for Pancakes

1. Add up to 1 cup peeled and grated, finely chopped, or sliced fresh fruit or chopped dried fruit (see Blueberry or Banana Pancakes, page 202).

2. Add 1$^1/_2$ cups mashed or puréed fruit (like bananas, apricots, apples, strawberries, or pumpkin); reduce the flour by $^1/_2$ cup and add another egg.

3. Stir in up to 1 cup cooked grains, like any rice, millet, wheat or rye berries, couscous, barley, quinoa, or wild rice; or any rolled or flaked grains, like oats, quinoa, millet, kamut, or brown rice.

4. Add $^1/_4$ cup unsweetened cocoa powder and/or a handful of chocolate chips; thin with a little milk or buttermilk if necessary.

5. Substitute orange juice for the milk and add 1 teaspoon grated orange zest if you like.

6. Substitute coconut milk for the regular milk and/or add up to $^1/_2$ cup shredded coconut.

7. Substitute $^1/_2$ cup nut flour for $^1/_2$ cup of the all-purpose flour and/or use nut milk for the milk.

8. Add up to 2 teaspoons peeled and minced fresh or ground ginger or 2 tablespoons chopped crystallized ginger.

9. Add about 2 teaspoons minced or grated orange or lemon zest.

10. Add up to 1 cup chopped nuts or, even better, Crunchy Granola (page 573).

Cottage Cheese and Sour Cream Pancakes

MAKES: 3 to 4 servings

TIME: 20 minutes

F

With cottage cheese and sour cream (or yogurt) as their main ingredients, these are quite different from traditional pancakes—light, creamy, and completely delicious.

1 cup cottage cheese

1 cup sour cream or yogurt

3 eggs, separated

$\frac{1}{4}$ teaspoon baking soda

1 cup all-purpose flour

Dash salt

1 tablespoon sugar

Butter or neutral oil, like grapeseed or corn, as needed

1 Heat a griddle or large skillet over medium-low heat while you make the batter.

2 Beat the cottage cheese, sour cream, and egg yolks together. Combine the dry ingredients. Beat the egg whites until fairly stiff but not dry.

Pancake Variations

Use any of these variations with either Everyday or Light and Fluffy Pancakes.

Buttermilk, Yogurt, or Sour Milk Pancakes: See the Dairy Lexicon on page 206 for a quick way to make your own, then substitute it or yogurt for the milk in Everyday or Light and Fluffy Pancakes; use $\frac{1}{2}$ teaspoon baking soda in place of the baking powder and proceed with the recipe. If necessary (it probably will be with sour cream or thick yogurt), thin the batter with a little milk.

Blueberry or Banana Pancakes: Use fresh or frozen (not thawed) blueberries; overripe bananas are great here: Just before cooking, stir the blueberries into the batter. For the bananas, slice them and press into the surface of the cooking pancakes. Cook the pancakes a little more slowly than you would other pancakes as they burn more easily.

Whole Grain Pancakes: A bit denser in texture but great grain flavor: Substitute whole wheat, quinoa, amaranth, or teff flour or cornmeal, rolled oats, or a combination for up to 1 cup of the flour.

Wheatless Pancakes: A fine substitution: Use rice flour instead of wheat flour. Proceed with the recipe.

Gingerbread Pancakes: Perfect served with a dollop of whipped cream: Substitute $\frac{1}{2}$ cup molasses for the sugar; add along with the milk. Add 2 teaspoons peeled and minced fresh or ground ginger or 2 to 3 tablespoons minced crystallized ginger, 1 teaspoon ground cinnamon, and a pinch ground cloves.

Nut Butter Pancakes: Cook these more slowly than other pancakes, as they burn easily: Add up to $\frac{1}{4}$ cup nut butter or tahini and $\frac{1}{4}$ cup chopped nuts (ideally the same nuts as the nut butter) or sesame seeds; add with the milk.

Lemon–Poppy Seed Pancakes: An especially good variation of the Light and Fluffy Pancakes: Substitute $\frac{1}{2}$ teaspoon baking soda for the baking powder. Add 2 tablespoons freshly squeezed lemon juice, 2 teaspoons grated lemon zest, and 2 tablespoons poppy seeds; add with the milk.

F Fast   **M** Make Ahead   **V** Vegan

3 Stir the flour mixture into the cottage cheese mixture, blending well but not beating. Gently fold in the beaten egg whites; they should remain somewhat distinct in the batter.

4 Add about 1 teaspoon butter or oil to the griddle or skillet. When the butter is melted or the oil is hot, add the batter by the heaping tablespoon, making sure you include some of the egg whites in each spoonful. Cook until lightly browned on the bottom, 3 to 5 minutes, then turn and cook until the second side is brown. Serve immediately; these will not hold.

Lemon-Ricotta Pancakes. Substitute ricotta (you can make your own if you have time; see page 230) for the cottage cheese, increase the baking soda to $^1/_2$ teaspoon, and add 2 tablespoons freshly squeezed lemon juice and 2 teaspoons grated lemon zest.

The Basics of Waffles

Waffles, as the variations demonstrate, are great for lunch, supper, or even dinner (topped with a rich vegetable stew), as well as desserts (topped with ice cream) and snacks. And breakfast of course.

The best waffles are super-crisp outside and creamy inside. To me, their texture is even more important than what you put in them or on them, so it's crucial to get waffles out of the iron and onto the table quickly. You can keep them warm in the oven for a little while if you absolutely must, but it sort of defeats the whole purpose: Waffles are meant to be eaten immediately.

Raised waffles, made with yeast, are absolutely unbeatable, and—as long as you remember to start a batch the night before—they're just as easy to make. Buttermilk waffles are almost as good and much more spontaneous. Even the simplest, pancakelike waffles, which tend to be thin and crunchy, have their place. A handful of guidelines applies to all:

- The iron must be hot. Almost all have lights that let you know when they're ready for baking.
- The iron should be clean and lightly oiled (even if it's nonstick). Before turning it on, brush the iron

lightly with grapeseed or other neutral oil (or use an oil-soaked paper towel). When it's good and hot, open the iron for a minute to let any smoke escape; close it until it reheats a bit, then start cooking.

- If you have an extra 5 minutes, separate the eggs and beat the whites by themselves (see page 898), then fold them into the remaining batter right before cooking. You'll be amazed at the fluffiness.
- Be patient and don't underbake waffles. After pouring or spreading the batter over the bottom plate, close the top and leave it alone for at least two minutes. Gently pull up on the top of the iron. If the lid resists, give it another minute or two. Don't automatically trust the indicator light and don't rely on the myth about waffles being ready when there's no more steam wafting. If you want your waffle crisp, you're probably going to have to wait an extra minute or so after the light goes on (or off, depending on your machine), then do the little tug test.
- Serve waffles straight from the iron. If you must hold them for a few minutes—5, tops—put them on a rack in a 200°F oven.
- During those couple of minutes spent waiting for the waffles to bake, melt the butter and warm the syrup. I use the microwave set on low.

Everyday Buttermilk Waffles

MAKES: 4 to 6 servings

TIME: 10 minutes, plus time to bake

If you've got buttermilk, sour cream, or yogurt, these are the most tender, spontaneous waffles you can make. Plain milk works too; see the first variation.

2 cups all-purpose flour

$^1/_2$ teaspoon salt

2 tablespoons sugar

$1^1/_2$ teaspoons baking soda

$1^3/_4$ cups buttermilk or $1^1/_2$ cups sour cream or yogurt thinned with $^1/_4$ cup milk

2 eggs, separated

4 tablespoons ($^{1}/_{2}$ stick) butter, melted and cooled

$^{1}/_{2}$ teaspoon vanilla extract (optional)

Neutral oil, like grapeseed or corn, for brushing the waffle iron

① Combine the flour, salt, sugar, and baking soda in a large bowl. In another bowl, whisk the buttermilk and egg yolks together. Stir in the butter and the vanilla if you're using it.

② Brush the waffle iron lightly with oil and heat it. Stir the wet ingredients into the dry. Beat the egg whites with a clean whisk or electric mixer until they hold soft peaks. Fold them gently into the batter.

③ Spread a ladleful or so of batter onto the waffle iron and bake until the waffle is done, usually 3 to 5 minutes, depending on your iron. Serve immediately or keep warm for a few minutes in a low oven.

The Quickest, Easiest Waffles. Less air, more crisp, but still very good: Instead of the baking soda, use 2 teaspoons baking powder. Use $1^{1}/_{2}$ cups milk instead of the buttermilk. Don't bother to separate the eggs; just whisk them in whole with the buttermilk in Step 1. Proceed with the recipe.

Whole Grain Waffles. Heartier and a little denser, but with more fiber, this formula works for both the main recipe and the preceding variation: Substitute up to 1 cup whole wheat flour, cornmeal, rolled oats, or a combination for the white flour.

Wheatless Waffles. They won't be as fluffy, but they will crisp up nicely and have a pleasant grittiness: Use rice flour instead of wheat flour in either the main recipe or the first variation.

10 Things You Can Stir into Any Waffle Batter

1. Ground cinnamon or any curry powder (pages 815–816), up to 2 teaspoons per batch of batter
2. Molasses, substituted for $^{1}/_{2}$ cup milk (excellent with cornmeal)
3. Minced or grated orange or lemon zest, about 2 teaspoons
4. Grated cheese, like Emmental (Swiss), cheddar, or Jack; about 1 cup
5. Grated Parmesan cheese; up to $^{1}/_{2}$ cup
6. Chopped (not minced) nuts, Crunchy Granola (page 573), or shredded sweetened or unsweetened coconut, up to 1 cup
7. Freshly minced or ground ginger, up to 2 teaspoons
8. Fresh fruit, like blueberries, raspberries, apples, or other fruit cut into $^{1}/_{4}$- to $^{1}/_{2}$-inch dice
9. Dried fruit, like apricots, cherries, cranberries, or raisins—up to $^{1}/_{2}$ cup coarsely chopped
10. Cooked grains, like any rice, millet, wheat or rye berries, couscous, barley, quinoa, or wild rice—up to 1 cup

Overnight Waffles

MAKES: 4 to 6 servings

TIME: 8 hours or more, largely unattended

Eat these traditionally with butter and syrup for breakfast or use them as a "bread" to serve with virtually any meal. With a distinctive yeasty flavor and a fluffy but chewy texture, they're that good.

$^{1}/_{2}$ teaspoon active dry yeast

2 cups all-purpose flour

1 tablespoon sugar

$^{1}/_{2}$ teaspoon salt

2 cups milk

8 tablespoons (1 stick) butter, melted and cooled

$^{1}/_{2}$ teaspoon vanilla extract (optional)

Neutral oil, like grapeseed or corn, for brushing the waffle iron

2 eggs

The difference between real maple syrup and the colored and flavored sugar syrup sold at most supermarkets is equivalent to the difference between butter and margarine: one is a natural, wholesome product, and the other is a nutritionally useless, not-very-good-tasting, unnatural substitute.

The label will tell you all you need to know: ingredients (it should say "pure maple syrup" and nothing else); where the syrup is from (Canada produces the bulk, while Vermont and other New England states produce some); and the grade.

Maple syrup is made by boiling and evaporating the sap from a specific kind of maple tree. It takes about 40 gallons of sap to make just 1 gallon of syrup, so it's not inexpensive. But as luck would have it, my favorite maple syrup (and, according to many aficionados, the best)—Grade B—happens to be the cheapest. Here's a rundown of what each grade is like.

Grade A Light Amber: It has the mildest, most delicate maple flavor, considered best for candy and maple cream.

Grade A Medium Amber: This is the most popular pure syrup, slightly darker and with a more pronounced flavor.

Grade A Dark Amber: The flavor gets stronger as the syrups get darker, so this is the deepest of the Grade As.

Grade B: This syrup has the strongest maple flavor with a distinct caramel or cooked sugar taste. I use it as both a table and cooking syrup. Unless you prefer a milder flavor, there's no reason to buy anything else.

1 The night before you want to serve the waffles, combine the yeast, flour, sugar, and salt in a large bowl. Stir in the milk, then the melted butter and vanilla. The mixture will be creamy and loose. Cover with plastic wrap and set aside overnight at room temperature. (Of course you can do this in the morning if you want waffles for supper.)

2 To start baking, brush the waffle iron lightly with oil and heat it. Separate the eggs and stir the yolks into the batter. Beat the whites until they hold soft peaks. Fold them gently into the batter.

3 Spread a ladleful or so of batter onto the waffle iron and bake until the waffle is done, usually 3 to 5 minutes, depending on your iron. Serve immediately or keep warm for a few minutes in a low oven.

Pumpkin Waffles with Maple Cream Cheese Sauce

MAKES: 4 to 6 servings

TIME: 20 minutes with cooked or canned pumpkin, plus time to bake

Perfect on cold winter mornings. Or skip the sauce and serve underneath Curried Eggplant with Coconut Milk (page 296) or Mushroom Stew with Green Beans (page 137). If you're short on time, don't separate the eggs; just whisk them into the milk whole in Step 3.

$1/2$ cup cream cheese, at room temperature

$1/2$ cup maple syrup

$1^1/2$ cups cooked or 1 cup canned pumpkin or winter squash

$1^3/4$ cups all-purpose flour

2 teaspoons baking powder

1 teaspoon sugar

$1/2$ teaspoon salt

$1^1/2$ cups milk, preferably whole, plus milk for thinning as needed

3 eggs, separated

4 tablespoons (¹/₂ stick) butter, melted and cooled

Neutral oil, like grapeseed or corn, for brushing the waffle iron

¹/₂ cup chopped hazelnuts or walnuts for garnish (optional)

1 Whisk the cream cheese and maple syrup together until completely blended. Put in a small pitcher.

2 If you're using cooked pumpkin, put it in a small pot and turn the heat to medium. Cook, stirring frequently and mashing with a fork, until it is very dry and starting to stick to the pan, about 5 minutes. Remove from the heat and continue mashing and stirring until very smooth.

3 Combine the dry ingredients in a large bowl. In another bowl, whisk the milk and egg yolks together. Stir in the melted butter and the cooked or canned pumpkin.

4 Brush the waffle iron lightly with oil and heat it. Stir the wet ingredients into the dry. Beat the egg whites with a clean whisk or electric mixer until they hold soft peaks. Fold them gently into the batter and thin with a spoonful or two of milk if necessary.

5 Spread a ladleful or so of batter onto the waffle iron and bake until the waffle is done, usually 3 to 5 minutes, depending on your iron. Serve immediately or keep warm for a few minutes in a low oven. Pass the Maple Cream Cheese Sauce, and the nuts if you like, at the table.

Baked Potato Waffles. Great for using leftovers: Omit the pumpkin and rice or mash enough baked potatoes to make 1 cup. Add them to the wet ingredients in Step 3. Proceed with the recipe. Serve sweet with the Maple Cream Cheese Sauce or top with Mornay Sauce (page 804) or Mushroom Ketchup (page 791) for savory waffles.

Sweet Potato Waffles. Brightly colored and fluffy: Omit the pumpkin and mash enough cooked sweet potatoes to make 1 cup. Add them to the wet ingredients in Step 3. Proceed with the recipe. Serve sweet with the Maple Cream Cheese Sauce or pass some sour cream and a bowl full of Fresh Tomato Salsa (page 750), Pico de Verde (page 751), Citrus Salsa (page 752), or Chipotle-Cherry Salsa (page 752).

Dairy

The best-tasting dairy may be cheese (so flavorful that I've devoted a whole section to it, starting on page 208), the most versatile butter, the healthiest yogurt, but almost all dairy products have great value, from every point of view.

First, a few words about how to store them: Refrigerate dairy products in their original (or clean glass) containers, ideally at 40°F or a little colder. Pour off what you need, then immediately return the rest to the fridge; never put unused milk or cream back in the carton or jug, or it's likely to spoil faster. To avoid off flavors, keep milk tightly sealed and away from bright light. When stored properly, a dairy product should stay good for a couple days after its "sell by" date. You can freeze unsalted butter for a month or so without noticeably affecting its flavor (and salted butter somewhat longer), but don't freeze milk or cream.

If you can't tolerate milk or milk products (or if you're a vegan), you still have options. But don't expect to duplicate the richness of whole milk, cream, or butter. See the section on alternative milks in "The Basics of Vegan Cooking" (page 29).

The Dairy Lexicon

Milk: Whole (3.25 percent fat), reduced fat (2 percent fat); low-fat (1 percent fat); fat free, skim, or nonfat (no fat): Unless otherwise noted, you can use reduced-fat, low-fat (not fat-free), or whole milk in the recipes in this book, though I always cook with at least 2 percent.

Buttermilk: This tangy, thick, and sometimes lumpy liquid isn't at all what it used to be, which was the liquid that remained after churning butter. Now it's made from milk of any fat content, cultured with lactic acid–producing bacteria. It's more like thin yogurt than anything else, though the flavor is slightly different. It is usually labeled "cultured buttermilk" or "cultured low-fat buttermilk." Use it for baking, flavoring mashed potatoes, or making cold sauces, dips, and dressings.

For a quick substitute, you can "sour" regular milk: Let $1^3/_4$ cups of milk come to room temperature (or microwave it for 30 seconds or so). Stir in 2 tablespoons white vinegar and let the mixture sit until clabbered—thick and lumpy—about 10 minutes (you'll know). Use as much as you need in any recipe that calls for buttermilk.

Cream: You'll see all sorts of confusing labels for cream, but the kind you want is heavy—not whipping—cream, without any additives or emulsifiers, and not ultrapasteurized (this takes longer to whip and has a distinctive, definitely cooked, flavor). Figure 1 cup of cream whips up to about 2 cups. The fat content of whipping cream ranges from 30 percent to 36 percent; heavy cream is 36 percent fat or more.

Half-and-Half: Just like the name implies, this is half milk and half cream, with a fat content that can range anywhere from 10.5 percent to 18 percent. It's nice in soups or sauces when you don't need quite the richness of heavy cream, and it's certainly easy enough to blend your own.

Sour Cream: Cream that has been cultured by adding lactic acid bacteria, to make it thick and produce its characteristic tangy flavor. Sour cream can be tricky to cook with because it can curdle—though not so quickly as yogurt—so add it to other ingredients over very low heat. If you want to use reduced-fat sour creams, find one without a lot of added ingredients and stabilizers; it will probably be thinner but will taste better.

Crème Fraîche: Like sour cream, this is thick, rich, tangy, and almost decadent. But it can be hard to find and expensive. So here's how to make your own: Put a cup of cream in a small glass bowl and stir in 2 tablespoons of buttermilk or yogurt. Let the mixture sit at room temperature until thickened, anywhere from 12 to 24 hours. Cover tightly, refrigerate, and use within a week or so.

Yogurt: Cultured milk, made with different bacteria from buttermilk and sour cream, which produce its unique flavor and texture. Look for "live, active cultures"—or similar terminology—on the label and avoid any with gelatins, gums, or stabilizers. Yogurt is available in whole, low-fat, and nonfat versions, as well as all sorts of crazy flavors. But why bother? Just flavor plain yogurt yourself (page 208; you can also make it yourself, see below). It can be warmed gently but not super-heated, or it will curdle. In recipes, whole-milk yogurt always gives the richest results.

Butter: Butter is fat and water, so higher fat is better; the supermarket standard is 80 percent, which means 20 percent is water. But it doesn't matter much except for when you're baking delicate cookies or cakes (though higher-fat butter also tends to be higher quality and better tasting). Always buy unsalted butter (also called sweet butter) but know that it doesn't keep quite as long as the salted kind. (Store extra sticks in the freezer, not the fridge.) Never use whipped butter in recipes; its volume isn't the same as that of stick butter.

UHT Milk: Short for ultra-high-temperature milk, this is the nonrefrigerated stuff you see in aseptic (sterilized and vacuum-sealed) boxes on supermarket shelves. UHT milk keeps for three months after packaging and is always dated. It's great to have some in the pantry for emergencies.

Yogurt

MAKES: 1 quart
TIME: Overnight or longer, largely unattended

Though many excellent-quality yogurts are sold in stores, there is nothing quite like the slightly sweet flavor of homemade. And though yogurt is a little trickier to make than fresh cheese (page 230)—mostly because the temperature must be controlled for a long time while it processes—it's easy enough to get the hang of.

Whole milk makes the richest yogurt, though you can use any kind of milk you like. You can even start with reconstituted nonfat dry milk; just mix it about twice as thick as the package directs.

1 quart milk

1/2 cup natural plain yogurt ("with active cultures"), ideally at room temperature

1 Put the milk in a small to medium saucepan and bring it just to a boil; turn off the heat and cool to 110°F to 115°F (use an instant-read thermometer).

2 Whisk the milk and yogurt together. Put in a yogurt maker, a prewarmed thermos, or a heated bowl wrapped in a towel or blanket and set in a warm place. The idea is to keep the mixture at about 100°F.

3 Do not disturb the mixture at all for at least 6 hours. Then carefully check by tilting the container to see whether the milk has become yogurt. If not, leave it alone for another 6 hours. When the yogurt is done, refrigerate and use within 1 week.

Yogurt Cheese. You can make this with store-bought yogurt too. There are even filters available specifically for this purpose: Instead of refrigerating the yogurt, put it in a jelly bag or several layers of cheesecloth and suspend it over the sink or a large bowl. Let drain for at least 6 hours, preferably longer, until the yogurt has a cream cheese–like consistency. Use exactly as you would cream cheese.

10 Ideas for Flavoring Plain Yogurt

Some of these—honey, maple syrup, or jam, for example—can be added to a whole batch. Some can be used in combination. Some are best used to make raitas and other like mixtures (page 775). Add to taste.

1. Honey
2. Maple syrup
3. Vanilla extract, with or without sugar
4. Chopped nuts
5. Preserves or jam
6. Chutneys (pages 783–787)
7. Spice blends (pages 810–819)
8. Traditional Pesto (page 768)
9. Any pickles, finely chopped
10. Minced fresh or dried chiles

Cheese

There's no question that cheese is a good source of protein, even though a large percentage of its calories comes from saturated fat and it doesn't have the fiber found in grain- or legume-based proteins. On the other hand, it's high in calcium and other nutrients that can't be found anywhere else, and from the perspectives of flavor and texture there's nothing else like it. The variety of cheeses available now is staggering, perhaps slightly overwhelming at times, but capable of greatly improving our experiences around the table.

There are literally thousands of types of cheese available from all corners of the globe. They may be made from cow's, sheep's, or goat's (or, for that matter, yak's) milk; they may be eaten fresh or aged. They might be fresh or aged from as little as three months to as long as several years. Of the best, virtually no two are identical. This all makes learning about them either daunting or thrilling. You can increase your knowledge by finding a good cheese shop. (Some upscale supermarkets have well-stocked cheese counters too.) Have comparison tastings at home or try new kinds whenever you're in cheese-friendly restaurants. You'll quickly develop a repertoire.

For most of us, cooking with cheese is far more common than eating a cheese course. And the principles that determine which cheese works best in which dishes—strength of flavor, firmness, graininess, the ability to crumble or melt—quickly transfer to the concept of eating cheese plain. So your favorite cooking cheeses can introduce you to similar varieties and styles to try on cheese plates.

F Fast   **M** Make Ahead   **V** Vegan

If you want to become an expert, up the ante of tastings and start reading. There are some good, classic cheese books and I suggest some suppliers in "Sources" (page 929) Cheese is best bought in small quantities (with the exception of hard cheeses like Parmesan, which keep for months); you can't eat much at one sitting, and chances are you'll get sick of a given cheese, no matter how good, before you finish a large piece. Equally likely is that its quality will degrade; soft, fresh cheeses especially don't keep too long, unless they're mass produced, in which case they're probably not worth eating.

Unless you have a specific cheese storage device or plan to eat the cheese that day, you must keep it in the fridge. You have several wrapping options. My first choice is a plastic or glass container with a tight-fitting lid. This lets the cheese breathe a bit without drying out. Wax or butcher paper, foil, and plastic wrap are all acceptable, with the exception of goat's milk cheeses, which really don't fare very well wrapped in plastic. Generally, the harder the cheese, the longer it will last; and a bit of mold doesn't even mean cheese is bad; you can just trim it off.

Most cheese is best eaten at room temperature, so let the piece you plan to use sit out, covered with a cloth or dome, for long enough to take the chill off.

The Basics of Cooking with Cheese

Here's a simple guide for cooking with the cheeses used in this book, listed in order of my preferences:

The Ultimate All-Purpose Cheese

Parmesan: I cannot emphasize how important it is to spring for the real thing—Parmigiano-Reggiano—which is imported from Italy (and only Italy) and sold virtually everywhere. Look for irregularly sized chunks with a waxy rind marked with the name in pinhole-punched lettering. With a complex nutty flavor and a slightly grainy but almost buttery texture, Parmesan is the cheese you will reach for most often, whether you're cooking Italian food or not. You can blend it into batters and doughs before baking, stir it into sauces and soups, melt it on virtually anything, and pass a bowlful at the table as a last-minute condiment. (Even the rinds are great for seasoning soups, stews, and—especially—risotto. Cook chunks of them for 15 minutes or longer and they'll become soft enough to eat; their flavor is incredible.) Grate finely or coarsely, "shave" with a vegetable peeler, or break a wedge into chunks with a dull knife. Great for snacking too.

Melting Cheeses

The best melting cheeses melt smoothly without leaving behind a rubbery, stringy, or greasy mess. It's best to grate these cheeses or slice them thinly for cooking.

The Swiss-Style Cheeses—"Swiss," Gruyère, Fontina, Emmental, Comté: Though each of these is unique, I'm

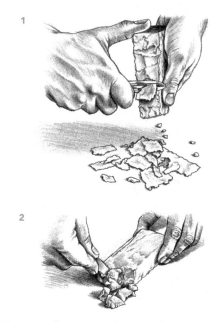

Real Parmesan has a granular, irregular texture; it's almost never sliced like other cheeses. Two easy ways to serve it are (1) to shave it, using an ordinary vegetable peeler and (2) to use a small, not-too-sharp knife or other tool to break off chunks.

grouping them together here because they share a velvety texture when melted and a complex, nutty taste that makes them good choices for combining with other ingredients.

Monterey Jack or Mexican-Style Cotija: Mild, milky, semisoft, with good body when melted, these rindless cheeses are perfect for Mexican food as a creamy counterpoint to assertive seasoning.

Cheddar: I prefer sharp cheddar cheeses, with at least a little bit of age on them, because these are more flavorful and melt better. Cheddars are also good stand-alone cheeses for snacking, especially when combined with apples, dried fruit, nuts, and whole grain toast. If you can't get your hands on a true English cheddar, look for a high-quality cheddar made near where you live; some are really great and not that expensive.

Mozzarella: Freshly made mozzarella (which often comes packed in water or sometimes oil) is quite different from the drier, slightly aged brick kind available at supermarkets and delis. In fact, I rarely use the latter unless I must. Fresh mozzarella tastes like milk, only with a little tang, and should never be rubbery or stringy. It's a great cheese to eat raw in salads or sandwiches.

Cheeses That Keep Their Shape During Cooking or Baking

These are the cheeses that give you the best of both worlds: they're great uncooked, and when heated they retain most of their original flavor and texture but soften slightly rather than melt. Crumble them with your fingers or a fork or cut into cubes or thick slices.

Fresh Cheese, the Easy Way (page 230): Mild, versatile, fresh, and delicious. I can't say it enough; you've just got to try it.

Ricotta Salata: White, milky, buttery, and slightly nutty. Usually made from sheep's milk, this dense cheese is generally more complex and less salty than feta.

Feta: Though many feta cheeses are now packed in airtight plastic, I prefer to buy cheese stored in brine. The flavor is fresh and milky with salty rather than sharp notes, and the texture is dry and crumbly. If the feta you buy is too salty for you, try another variety (some are quite mild) or rinse the cheese and pat it dry before using it.

Queso Fresco (Queso Blanco): The ultimate Mexican garnish, this snow-white fresh cheese crumbles into relatively fine, milky-tasting bits.

Farmer's Cheese: Old-fashioned cheese that can still be found at most supermarkets. It's good in a pinch if you can't find any of the other cheeses in this section.

Sandwich Cheeses

In addition to cheddars, Swiss cheeses, mozzarella, and Jack, try provolone—at its best, the flavor is somewhat reminiscent of Parmesan, only milder—or a semihard pecorino (sheep's milk cheese) from Italy. All of these work either melted or raw. Use a sharp knife or a cheese-slicing tool for the thinnest pieces possible.

Cheeses for Garnishing or Snacking

I'm no fan of gratuitous garnishing, especially when it comes to something as potentially powerful as cheese. That said, a sharp, somewhat salty cheese—used judiciously—makes a terrific last-minute seasoning for croutons, hearty salads, broths and soups, pasta, grain and bean dishes, or even thick slices of toasted bread.

Blue Cheeses: Gorgonzola, Roquefort, Cabrales, and other European blues and American blue cheese like Maytag: For many, blue-veined cheeses (which intentionally cultivate harmless but flavorful molds) are an acquired taste, but I love them. Though they sometimes turn an unattractive grayish color when cooked, it's worth it. Try sprinkling some strong blue on plain cooked vegetables, sprinkling with Fresh Bread Crumbs (page 804), and running under the broiler; there are few better ways to jazz up vegetables.

Grating Cheeses: Beyond Parmesan, there's pecorino Romano, manchego, Grana Padano, dry Jack, aged goat cheeses, and myzithra (from Greece). Each has its own texture, color, and degree of sharpness. (Romano is probably the saltiest in this group.) Grating cheeses are fun, because they're easy to use and have a powerful impact. You can hardly go wrong.

Creamy Cheeses for Dips, Spreads, and Enrichment

Generally these are best eaten uncooked or barely cooked in some kind of breading or crust. In rare cases you might

Ⓕ Fast   Ⓜ Make Ahead   Ⓥ Vegan

melt some into soups or sauces as a flavorful substitute for cream. They work great in combination with other dairy ingredients—and other, stronger cheeses for that matter—for making dips and spreads. And they are all commonly used for dessert. Those with rinds can be sliced with a dull knife; the others are usually scooped or spread.

Fresh Goat Cheeses (Chèvres): This tangy cheese has become increasingly popular, and you can spend a little or a lot for an array of shapes and sizes. My suggestion: Cook with the inexpensive varieties and save the farmstead goat cheeses for nibbling.

Cream Cheese: If you have access to anything other than the overprocessed supermarket varieties, you know the potential of cream cheese. (See "The Basics of Making Fresh Cheese," page 228.) The best ones are slightly crumbly, a little tangy, and leave a rich, creamy coating in your mouth.

Mascarpone: Perhaps my favorite of the creamy cheeses, with a mild, slightly sweet flavor. Try some as a sandwich spread or mix with a little confectioners' sugar or honey and serve a dollop with fruit.

Brie, Camembert, and Toma: The first two are of French origin, while the third is Italian, but versions of all are now made in the United States, and some are good. They're all soft-ripened cow's milk cheeses with a thick, slightly fuzzy edible rind. You won't cook with them often, though they can be good melted on sandwiches or in sauces and soups and in pasta dishes with nuts, bitter greens, or whole wheat noodles.

Spice-Marinated Feta

MAKES: 4 to 6 servings

TIME: 3 days

Ⓜ

Marinated feta is great stuff, delicious served as an appetizer with pita or other bread, with a green salad, in a sandwich, or melted on a pizza. The oil, which is also infused with the flavor of the spices, herbs, and aromatics,

is wonderful for salad dressings and drizzling over just about anything you would drizzle regular olive oil on.

This takes a few days for the flavors to really meld, but it's worth the wait. If you don't have the time, check out the first variation, which can be made and served within an hour.

You can use other cheese here, of course, like Fresh Cheese, the Easy Way (page 230), goat cheese, yogurt cheese, blue cheese, ricotta salata, or queso fresco. If the cheese is already soft, like goat cheese, you can omit the cream cheese and increase the quantity to 12 ounces.

8 ounces feta cheese

4 ounces cream cheese or yogurt cheese, softened

1 tablespoon Za'atar (page 818) or a blend of toasted sesame seeds, ground cumin and coriander, and grated lemon zest

2 cloves garlic, smashed

2 sprigs fresh thyme

$1/2$ cup extra virgin olive oil, plus more if necessary

❶ Put the feta and cream cheese in a food processor and blend until fairly smooth (some chunks of feta are fine).

❷ Lay a 12-inch piece of plastic wrap on a flat surface and transfer the cheese mixture to it, making a fat log shape about 3 inches from the short edge. Roll the edge of the plastic and use it to shape the cheese into a log or disk; use a spatula to help keep the cheese in shape. Refrigerate it until it firms up just a bit, about 15 minutes.

❸ Unwrap the cheese and cut it to fit into a clean glass jar; sprinkle it with the spices. Put the cheese in the jar, add the garlic and thyme, then pour in the olive oil to cover. Cover and refrigerate for at least 3 days and up to 2 weeks.

Quick Spice-Marinated Feta Patties. The garlic and spices are blended with the cheese for a quick "marination": Add 1 clove garlic and the spices when blending the cheese, then form into small patties or balls. Drizzle with half of the olive oil and let marinate until ready to serve. (These will keep, covered and refrigerated, for about 3 days.)

Herb-Marinated Cheese. Feta, goat, fresh mozzarella, Fresh Cheese, the Easy Way (page 230), and ricotta salata are all great here: Increase the cheese to 8 ounces and omit the cream cheese and spices. Add 2 to 4 sprigs or the leaves of any herb, mixed or single. Skip to Step 3 and proceed with the recipe.

Zesty Marinated Cheese. Use the feta and cream cheese blend or any of the cheeses in the previous variation: Substitute 2 teaspoons grated lemon, orange, and lime zest for the spices; 1 teaspoon cracked black or pink peppercorns for the garlic; and 1 teaspoon or more hot red pepper flakes for the thyme. Proceed with the recipe (skipping Steps 1 and 2 if you're using whole cheese).

Blue Cheese Dip or Spread

MAKES: about 6 servings
TIME: 15 minutes

Ⓕ Ⓜ

This recipe forms the basis for all kinds of cheese dips and spreads: blue cheese, goat cheese, or cream cheese—just about any soft cheese can be used here. And you can adjust the texture however you like: for a dip, thin with sour cream or plain yogurt; for a thick spread, use cream cheese or yogurt cheese.

> 1 cup crumbled blue cheese
>
> 1 cup sour cream or cream cheese
>
> 2 tablespoons minced shallot or scallion
>
> 2 teaspoons minced fresh sage
>
> 2 tablespoons freshly squeezed lemon juice
>
> Salt and freshly ground black pepper

Combine all the ingredients and mash with a fork or potato masher or whirl in a food processor. Taste and adjust the seasoning, adding salt, pepper, and lemon juice if necessary. (Thin the mixture with milk or cream if it's too thick.) Serve immediately or cover and refrigerate for up to 2 days.

Tofu Dip or Spread. Vegan, but creamy: Omit the blue cheese and substitute 8 ounces soft silken (for a dip) or firm (for a spread) tofu for the sour cream or cream cheese. Use any of the flavorings in the main recipe, in the variations, or in the following list. Purée until very smooth in a food processor; add small amounts of soy milk to thin it if necessary.

13 Flavorings to Stir or Blend into Any Cheese Dip or Spread

A single ingredient can add loads of flavor, but don't go overboard.

1. Any herbs, fresh or dried
2. Lemon zest, grated
3. Lemon juice
4. Sun-dried or Oven-Dried Tomatoes (page 377)
5. Fresh chile or pepper, minced
6. Chipotle chiles in adobo sauce, chopped
7. Spinach, cooked, squeezed dry, and chopped
8. Mushrooms, minced and cooked (see page 314)
9. Caramelized Onions (page 329)
10. Roasted Garlic (page 304)
11. Chile powder (page 814) or Fragrant Curry Powder (page 816)
12. Za'atar (page 818)
13. Citrus Sprinkle (page 818)

Cheese Balls

MAKES: 4 to 6 servings
TIME: 10 minutes

Ⓕ Ⓜ

Is there anything so retro as serving cheese balls at a party? But whether passé or hip, cheese balls are among the quickest and most effortless hors d'oeuvres you can

 Ⓕ Fast   Ⓜ Make Ahead   Ⓥ Vegan

4 MORE CHEESE DIP OR SPREAD IDEAS

Use the sour cream, plain yogurt, or cream as a thinner to make a dip or cream cheese as a binder to make a spread.

CHEESE	THINNER OR BINDER		AROMATICS	SEASONINGS
1 cup feta	1 cup sour cream or plain yogurt	1 cup cream cheese	2 tablespoons minced scallion; 1 teaspoon minced garlic	1 teaspoon chopped fresh marjoram leaves
1 cup goat cheese	1 cup sour cream	1 cup cream cheese	2 tablespoons minced shallot	1/4 cup chopped mixed fresh herb leaves (like parsley, chives, chervil, and thyme)
1 1/2 cups finely grated Parmesan	1 cup sour cream	1 cup cream cheese	1 teaspoon finely grated lemon zest	Lots of freshly ground black pepper
3/4 cup cream cheese	1 cup cream	(increase cream cheese to 2 cups)	2 tablespoons minced scallion	1/2 cup watercress sprigs (use a food processor to blend)

throw together for a last-minute get-together or as a snack. Make them bite-sized or shape into one or two large balls for a cheese platter (flattened into a disk shape so it doesn't roll around).

Nearly any cheese will work in this recipe; soft cheese will just blend into the cream cheese, and harder ones must be grated. Also, change the texture and look of the cheese balls by rolling them in anything from chopped fresh herbs to toasted bread crumbs, chopped nuts or seeds, crushed chips or crackers, or even chopped dried fruit. Also see "4 More Cheese Dip or Spread Ideas" (above) for more ideas on how to flavor cheese balls.

8 ounces cream cheese, softened

2 tablespoons butter, softened

1 tablespoon freshly squeezed lemon juice

1/2 teaspoon cayenne (optional)

Salt and freshly ground black pepper

8 ounces goat cheese, blue cheese, or finely grated sharp cheddar

1/2 cup finely chopped parsley and chives

1 Put the cream cheese, butter, lemon juice, cayenne, and a pinch of salt and pepper in the bowl of an electric mixer and beat until combined. Stir in the cheese.

2 Form into small balls, about an inch in diameter, or shape into 1 or 2 large balls. Roll the balls in the chopped herbs; flatten the large balls into a disk shape (it's easier to cut into). Wrap in plastic and refrigerate to set up firmly if you like. Serve the small balls with toothpicks and the large ones on a platter with crackers or bread.

The Basics of Cooking Cheese

Cooking cheese by itself, or nearly so, is a revelation, and there isn't much mystery to it; just use a firm cheese that doesn't melt too easily but isn't too hard either. The cheeses that work best are pliable, meaning a slice will bend without breaking—think Fresh Cheese (page 230), mozzarella, provolone, paneer, kasseri, queso blanco or fresco, and some of the softer fetas. Refrigerate your prepared cheese for about an hour; chilling it will help it keep its shape during cooking. Bear in mind that cooking cheese—whether you're frying, grilling, or broiling—must be quick. There's no need to cook the cheese; you just want to give it a quick flash of heat to brown the exterior or cook the coating.

Pan- and Deep-Frying Cheese

The goal is a crunchy exterior with a soft center. Deep-frying will achieve a crunchier outside and more even cooking, but panfrying yields good results too and uses a lot less oil. See Panfried Cheese (right) for cooking instructions. For deep frying, put an inch or two of oil in a deep pot and heat it to 350°F; submerge the cheese and fry until it's golden brown and crisp.)

There are three good methods of coating; from most to least crunchy, they are:

1. Flour-egg-crumbs: Dredge the cheese cubes or sticks first in flour, then coat with beaten egg, and finally with bread crumbs, panko, or cornmeal.
2. Quick and simple: Press the cheese directly into bread crumbs, panko, cornmeal, ground lentils, ground rice (page 682), or plain flour. This will work for all moist cheeses, those to which a coating will stick; it's best for panfrying.
3. Batter coating: a simple mixture of water and chickpea or other flour or meal; see Fried Fresh Cheese (page 215).

Grilling and Broiling Cheese

Finding a good grilling cheese can be tricky; you want one that won't melt or crumble into the grill (in any case, you need to cut it quite thick, $1/4$ inch or more). Fresh Cheese, the Easy Way (page 230), works nicely, as do mozzarella, feta, or store-bought paneer. Broiling cheese allows far more flexibility, but you still want cheese that holds its shape; otherwise it becomes a molten mass.

You can marinate the cheese before grilling, as in Grilled Fresh Cheese (page 216); barbecue sauce (like Fast, Down-Home Barbecue Sauce on page 789) is nice (though the sauce will char a bit, so cook this over low heat); or use something as simple as olive oil with smashed garlic cloves or onion slices.

See Grilled Fresh Cheese (page 216) for grilling directions. To broil, put the cheese in a gratin dish and broil until the surface is bubbling and golden brown.

11 Sauces to Serve with Fried, Grilled, or Broiled Cheese

Serve the sauce as a dip or put a spoonful over the top or underneath.

1. Fast Tomato Sauce (page 445)
2. Traditional Pesto or Parsley "Pesto" (page 768)
3. Spicy Indian Tomato Sauce (page 793)
4. Smooth Green Chile Sauce, Indian Style (page 792)
5. Real Ranch Dressing (page 772)
6. Any raw or cooked salsa (pages 750–752 and 787–788)
7. Caramelized Onion Chutney (page 786)
8. Homemade Ketchup (page 790)
9. Mushroom Ketchup (page 791)
10. Creamy Bistro Dressing or Sauce (page 799)
11. Teriyaki Sauce (page 779)

Panfried Cheese

MAKES: 4 servings

TIME: 20 minutes

Panfried cheese is universally popular, with the technique remaining much the same and the cheese changing. The Spanish version, made with paprika and sheep's milk cheese, is my favorite. But Gouda, provolone, mozzarella, kasseri, and feta all work nicely. Softer cheeses hold their shape better during cooking if they're well chilled to begin with, so coat and refrigerate if possible.

3 tablespoons all-purpose flour

1 teaspoon paprika

8 ounces mild soft sheep's milk or other cheese, cut into $1/2$-inch slices

2 eggs, beaten

$1/2$ cup fine bread crumbs, preferably fresh (page 804)

Extra virgin olive oil for frying

Ⓕ Fast   Ⓜ Make Ahead   Ⓥ Vegan

① Mix the flour and paprika together. Dredge the cheese slices in the flour, then the beaten egg and, finally the bread crumbs. If time allows, put the cheese on wax paper and refrigerate for an hour or longer.

② Put at least $1/8$ inch oil in a heavy skillet over medium-high heat. When the oil is hot—it will shimmer—fry the cheese slices until golden brown, about 30 seconds, then turn and brown the other side. Drain on paper towels and serve as soon as possible.

Fried Fresh Cheese

MAKES: 4 to 6 servings
TIME: 15 minutes with premade cheese

Battered and quickly fried cheese makes a super appetizer or snack, especially in India. If you use chickpea flour or any of the ground dals for the batter, this dish is known as *paneer pakora*. Try it with some typical accompaniments, like Smooth Green Chile Sauce, Indian Style (page 792), any chutney (see pages 783–787), or Raita (page 774). The cubes are also fantastic in dishes like Simplest Dal (page 600), Brussels Sprouts in Coconut Milk (page 274), or Saag Paneer (page 360). If you use cornmeal, try serving the cheese with any tomato-based sauce or salsa.

2 tablespoons chickpea flour, ground masoor or channa dal (page 577), or cornmeal, or more as needed

Salt and freshly ground black pepper

Neutral oil, like grapeseed or corn, for frying

1 recipe Fresh Cheese, the Easy Way (page 230) or store-bought paneer, queso fresco, or fresh mozzarella

① Put the chickpea flour and 6 tablespoons water in a small bowl and whisk until combined. Sprinkle with salt and pepper. The consistency should be like a pancake bat-ter; add chickpea flour or water as necessary and adjust the seasoning.

② Put $1/2$ to 1 inch oil in a large, deep skillet, preferably nonstick, over medium or medium-high heat and heat until the oil is very hot but not smoking.

③ Cut the cheese into bite-sized cubes and toss several pieces in the chickpea batter until well coated. Carefully put batches of the cheese in the hot oil, gently rotating them for even cooking and browning on all sides, 5 to 7 minutes. Drain on paper towels and immediately sprinkle with salt and pepper. Serve hot or at room temperature.

Spiced Fried Fresh Cheese. A pinch of cayenne for heat and any other ground spice or spice mixture you like: Add $1/2$ teaspoon or so Garam Masala (page 815), Fragrant Curry Powder (page 816), or Chile Powder (pages 814–816) with a pinch of cayenne; mix the spice(s) into the chickpea batter and proceed with the recipe.

Coconut Fried Fresh Cheese. Make the chickpea batter just slightly thicker than pancake batter so it really coats the cheese cubes; roll the battered cubes in finely shredded coconut. Proceed with the recipe.

Fresh Cheese and Vegetable Pakora. The Indian version of tempura: In Step 1, double the amount of batter by doubling the chickpea flour and the water. Use a little more salt and pepper too. Add assorted vegetables, cut into chunks, slices, or rings: potato, onion, eggplant, winter squash or sweet potatoes, bell pepper, cauliflower, even leaves of spinach or chard. Proceed with the recipe.

Fried Fresh Cheese with Spiced Yogurt. A lovely dish; excellent served with basmati rice and Cilantro-Mint Chutney (page 783) or Tamarind-Date Chutney (page 785): Add 1 large onion, peeled and sliced, 1 tablespoon minced garlic, 1 tablespoon Garam Masala (page 815) or Fragrant Curry Powder (page 816), and 2 cups yogurt. Cook the onion in some neutral oil until golden brown; add the garlic and spices and cook for another minute. Stir in the yogurt, fried cheese cubes, and some salt and pepper; heat until barely bubbling. Adjust the seasoning and serve immediately.

10 Dishes or Sauces for Fried Fresh Cheese
Stir the fried cheese cubes into the sauce or dish about 5 or 10 minutes before it has finished cooking to heat it through and allow it to absorb the flavors without falling apart.

1. Spicy Indian Tomato Sauce (page 793)
2. Smooth Green Chile Sauce, Indian Style (page 792)
3. Spiced Tomato Sauce (page 449)
4. Simplest Dal (page 600) or any dal recipe (pages 600–604)
5. Sautéed Eggplant or any of its variations (page 295)
6. Spinach with Fresh Cheese and Yogurt (page 360)
7. Leeks Braised in Oil or Butter or any of its variations (page 310)
8. Stovetop Mixed Vegetables with Olive Oil (page 381)
9. Biryani (page 512)
10. Spicy Red Beans, Indian Style (page 593)

Grilled Fresh Cheese

Paneer Tikka

MAKES: 4 servings

TIME: 40 minutes with premade cheese, largely unattended

Ⓜ

Ideally you'd use a tandoori oven for this Indian dish, but that's an option only for restaurants. Fortunately, a grill works just fine, and broiling is also another possibility. The spiced yogurt marinade adds loads of flavor to the fresh cheese, and both cheese and marinade can be made a day ahead.

You can also grill or broil the cheese alone, without the skewers. Just cut it into thick strips instead of cubes.

1/2 cup yogurt

1 teaspoon minced garlic

1 teaspoon minced peeled fresh ginger

1/2 teaspoon ground cumin

1 teaspoon ground coriander

1/4 teaspoon cayenne

1 tablespoon freshly squeezed lemon juice

Salt

1 recipe Fresh Cheese, the Easy Way (page 230), or about a pound store-bought mozzarella or paneer, cut into 1 1/2-inch cubes

2 small red or yellow onions, peeled and quartered

2 medium tomatoes, cored and quartered

1 medium bell pepper, any color, cored, seeded, and cut into 1 1/2-inch pieces

2 tablespoons melted butter or olive oil

Chopped fresh cilantro leaves for garnish

❶ Combine the yogurt, garlic, ginger, spices, and lemon juice, sprinkling with some salt; add the cheese cubes and let marinate while you heat the grill or refrigerate for up to 1 hour.

❷ Heat a charcoal or gas grill to medium heat; put the rack 4 to 6 inches from the heat source. If you're using wooden skewers, soak them for a few minutes. Thread the fresh cheese cubes, onions, tomatoes, and bell pepper onto the skewers, leaving a little bit of space between pieces. Brush the vegetables with the butter or olive oil.

❸ Grill until the cheese is lightly browned and the vegetables are tender, 8 to 10 minutes. Sprinkle with the cilantro and serve.

Grilled Tofu Tikka. Substitute firm tofu for the fresh cheese.

Fresh Cheese Patties. These make a great Indian-style "burger"; sandwich the patties between bread with lettuce and tomato and spread with a chutney (pages

Ⓕ Fast   Ⓜ Make Ahead   Ⓥ Vegan

783–787): Reduce the yogurt to 3 tablespoons, omit the tomatoes and bell pepper, and use 1 onion, finely chopped it. Add about $^1/_4$ cup flour. Crumble the cheese and mix with the yogurt, garlic, ginger, spices, lemon juice, onion, and some chopped cilantro leaves. Shape into small patties and coat lightly with flour. Heat the butter or oil in a nonstick pan and cook the patties until browned on both sides, 5 or 6 minutes total.

Baked Goat Cheese

MAKES: 4 servings
TIME: 15 minutes

A restaurant staple that is surprisingly fast and easy to make at home; terrific on top of a green salad, as an appetizer (especially the tomato and phyllo variations below), or as a side dish.

To make ahead of time, prepare Step 1 up until the bread crumbs. The cheese can "marinate" in the olive oil and herbs in the fridge for a day or two.

> One 6-ounce goat cheese log, cut into 8 slices or molded into 8 patties
>
> $^1/_4$ cup extra virgin olive oil
>
> Salt and freshly ground black pepper
>
> $^1/_4$ cup mixed chopped fresh herbs, like basil, chives, parsley, chervil, tarragon, or thyme
>
> $^1/_2$ cup bread crumbs, preferably fresh (page 804)

1 Preheat the oven to 350°F. Brush the cheese slices with the olive oil and sprinkle with salt, pepper, and the mixed herbs, then coat with the bread crumbs.

2 Put on a baking sheet and bake the cheese until it's golden brown and soft, about 10 minutes. Let rest for just a couple minutes and serve warm.

Baked Goat Cheese with Tomato Sauce or Tomatoes. Also great with tomato-based salsas, including Salsa Fresca (page 750): Put the goat cheese slices (with or without the bread crumbs) in a gratin dish and spoon about a cup or so of Fast Tomato Sauce (page 445) over the top; or top thick, seasoned tomato slices with one or two slices of goat cheese. Bake until the tomato sauce is bubbling or the goat cheese and tomato slices are soft. Sprinkle with fresh herbs and/or chopped black olives and serve.

Baked Goat Cheese with Nuts. Substitute finely chopped pine nuts, almonds, walnuts, or hazelnuts for the bread crumbs. Press the goat cheese into the chopped nuts so that the nuts form a kind of crust. Proceed with the recipe.

Baked Goat Cheese with Quinoa. These are also excellent molded into patties and cooked in a pan with some olive oil until golden brown on both sides. And they're great with a tomato sauce: Add 2 cups cooked quinoa, sprinkle with salt and pepper, and mix it in with the goat cheese and herbs. Form into balls, patties, or logs or put in a ramekin and sprinkle with bread crumbs. Proceed with the recipe.

Curried Fresh Cheese

Paneer Masala

MAKES: 4 servings
TIME: 25 minutes with premade cheese

The most familiar paneer-based dish to Americans is *Saag Paneer*, Spinach with Fresh Cheese and Yogurt (see page 360). But fresh cheese, like tofu (which it resembles), is a wonderful mild yet rich main ingredient for curries and Indian-style stir-fries. It browns beautifully and holds its shape well when cooked.

> 6 tablespoons butter or neutral oil, like grapeseed or corn
>
> 1 recipe Fresh Cheese, the Easy Way (page 230), or about a pound store-bought mozzarella, paneer, or queso fresco, cut into bite-sized cubes

1 large onion, finely chopped

2 tablespoons minced garlic

2 tablespoons peeled and minced fresh ginger

1 tablespoon garam masala (to make your own, see page 815) or any curry powder (to make your own, see pages 815–816)

2 cups (about 1 pound) chopped ripe tomato (canned is fine; don't bother to drain)

Salt and freshly ground black pepper

$\frac{1}{2}$ cup cream, coconut milk—homemade (page 423) or canned—or yogurt

$\frac{1}{2}$ cup chopped fresh cilantro leaves (optional)

① Put half the butter or oil in a large pan over medium-high heat. When the butter is melted or the oil is hot, add the cheese and cook until golden brown on all sides, a total of 6 to 10 minutes; remove from the pan and set aside.

② Put the remaining butter or oil in the same pan over medium-high heat. When the butter is melted or the oil is hot, add the onion and cook, stirring occasionally, until the onion is soft, about 5 minutes. Add the garlic, ginger, and garam masala; cook for another minute. Add the tomato, sprinkle with some salt and pepper, stir, and cook until slightly thickened, about 10 minutes.

③ Add the cheese to the tomato mixture along with the cream and bring to a slow bubble; cook for about 5 minutes. Adjust the seasoning, garnish with the cilantro, and serve.

Fresh Cheese with Fresh Tomatoes and Mint. Think of tomatoes and mozzarella with basil, only warm: Substitute mint leaves for the cilantro and omit the cream. Omit the garam masala. Use peeled, seeded, and chopped fresh tomato. In Step 2, add the tomato with the garlic and ginger, cook for a minute or two, then add the cheese. Stir in the mint just before serving.

Fresh Cheese with Chile Paste. Make this as hot as you like; for a less mouth-searing dish, mellow out the chile paste with a little tomato paste thinned with water, or Homemade Ketchup (page 790): Substitute $\frac{1}{4}$ cup or so Indian-Style Chile Paste (page 829), or whatever chile paste you have on hand with a pinch of garam masala or Fragrant Curry Powder (page 816) stirred in, for the onion, garlic, ginger, garam masala, tomatoes, and cream. In Step 1, once the cheese has browned add the chile paste and stir until the chile paste is well distributed in the pan. Cook for just a minute, adding a splash of water if it gets too dry. Garnish with cilantro and serve.

Fresh Cheese with Chiles. Toss in some roasted cashews or peanuts for crunch: Substitute 2 cups chopped mild green fresh chile (page 826) for the tomato. Omit the cream. In Step 2, add the chile with the onion and cook with the garlic and ginger for just 2 more minutes before adding the cheese.

Fresh Cheese Scramble

MAKES: 4 servings

TIME: 15 minutes with premade cheese

Crumbling fresh cheese for a stir-fry makes a quick, easy dish, but—more important—the mild flavor of the cheese goes well with just about any vegetable and can be spiced as much or as little as you like. Serve this with The Simplest Indian-Style Flatbread (page 698), Flaky Indian-Style Flatbread (page 699), over basmati rice, or just toast.

1 tablespoon neutral oil, like grapeseed or corn

1 small onion or 1 scallion, chopped

1 tablespoon minced garlic

F Fast   **M** Make Ahead   **V** Vegan

1 teaspoon garam masala (to make your own, see page 815) or Fragrant Curry Powder (page 816)

$1/2$ cup fresh or thawed frozen peas or cooked edamame (page 585)

1 recipe Fresh Cheese, the Easy Way (page 230), or about a pound store-bought farmer cheese, paneer, or queso fresco, crumbled

Salt and freshly ground black pepper

Chopped fresh cilantro leaves for garnish (optional)

1 Put the oil in a large skillet over medium-high heat. When hot, add the onion and garlic and cook, stirring occasionally, until the onion is soft, about 3 minutes. Add the spices and stir; cook for another 2 minutes.

2 Stir in the peas and crumbled cheese and sprinkle with salt and pepper. Cook, stirring often, until heated through, 2 to 3 minutes. Add a tablespoon or two of water if the cheese begins to stick to the pan. Taste and adjust the seasoning, sprinkle with cilantro if you're using it, and serve.

Fresh Cheese Scramble with Chiles. Use any kind of fresh chile you like (see "The Basics of Chiles and Peppers," page 822): Add 1 or 2 (or as many as you like) fresh chiles (like jalapeño, serrano, or Anaheim), cored, seeded and sliced, or 1 tablespoon hot red pepper flakes. Add with the onions in Step 1.

Fresh Cheese Scramble with Tomatoes. Add 1 cup chopped ripe tomato (about $1/2$ pound whole), preferably peeled and seeded, or chopped drained canned with the spices in Step 1.

Fresh Cheese Scramble with Eggs. Chopped Hard-Cooked Eggs (page 166) are also great here: Add 3 eggs, lightly beaten, in Step 2; stir often, cooking until the eggs are cooked but still moist and soft. Proceed with the recipe.

Cheese Crisp with Onions

MAKES: 4 servings
TIME: 20 minutes

These crispy cheese patties—called *frico* in their home, Italy's Friuli region—are great served with polenta or simply eaten as a snack or appetizer. (They're usually made with local cheese called Montasio, which is nearly impossible to find here, but the cheeses listed are good substitutes.)

You can make one large frico or several small crisps. For the small crisps, remove the onions from the pan, make small piles of the cheese (a couple tablespoons each, evenly spaced) in the pan, let the cheese melt a bit, add some of the onions on top, sprinkle with another layer of cheese, and then flip the crisps when the bottom is golden brown.

2 tablespoons extra virgin olive oil

2 medium onions, julienned

Freshly ground black pepper

2 cups freshly grated Parmesan, Grana Padano, or Asiago

1 Put the olive oil in a nonstick pan over medium-high heat. When hot, add the onions and cook until golden brown, stirring, about 10 minutes. Sprinkle with a good amount of black pepper and stir.

2 Use a rubber spatula to distribute the onions evenly over the bottom of the pan; evenly distribute the cheese over the top. Cook until the cheese is melted and golden brown on the bottom, about 5 minutes.

3 Use the spatula to slide the crisp onto a plate; put another plate on top of the crisp. Put one hand firmly in the center of the bottom plate and other hand the same way on the top plate; flip the crisp over and then use the spatula to slide it back into the pan and continue cooking until golden brown, about 5 minutes. Serve immediately.

Cheese Crisp with Potato. Like a cheesy hash brown: Substitute 1 medium russet potato, julienned or grated, for the onion; increase cooking time in Step 1 to about 15 minutes.

Simple Cheese Crisps. These can be shaped into little cups or cones when they're still warm (just press them into a ramekin and they'll harden as a cup) and filled with seasoned rice or vegetables, for a nice appetizer: Omit the onions. Preheat the oven to 350°F. Make small circular piles of cheese (about 3 to 4 tablespoons each, evenly spaced) on a parchment-lined (or Silpat, if you have it) baking sheet. Cook until the cheese is melted and golden in color. Let cool on the baking sheet or remove and mold into a shape, then let cool. These crisps will keep for several days in an airtight container, separated by parchment or wax paper.

Nutty Cheese Crisps. Add a sprinkling of chopped herbs and spices as you like: See the preceding variation and add about 1 or 2 teaspoons chopped nuts to the cheese piles.

Cheese "Burger"

MAKES: 4 servings
TIME: 20 minutes
Ⓕ Ⓜ

You can always slip one between two slices of toasted bread or a hamburger bun, but I think these decadent cheese patties are much better served as an entrée with Fast Tomato Sauce (page 445). Or make them smaller and serve them as croutons for any tossed green salad. In the winter, they're great in a shallow bowl with a ladle or two of Roasted Vegetable Stock (page 102).

2 cups freshly grated Parmesan cheese

1 cup chopped parsley

1 cup bread crumbs, preferably fresh (page 804)

2 eggs

2 tablespoons extra virgin olive oil

Salt and freshly ground black pepper

❶ Combine the cheese, parsley, and bread crumbs in a medium bowl. Add the eggs and use a fork to gently beat the eggs and blend everything into a semisolid mixture. The "dough" should be about the consistency of dumpling or biscuit dough. Carefully shape the mixture into 4 patties and set them on a plate or wax paper.

❷ Put the olive oil in a large skillet over medium-high heat. When the oil is hot but not smoking, add the patties (it's not so bad if you crowd them a bit). Cook without disturbing until they start to look crisp around the edges, about 5 minutes. Then carefully flip and cook the other side for 3 to 5 minutes. Drain briefly on paper towels. Sprinkle lightly with salt and heavily with pepper and serve.

Couscous and Cheese "Burger." This is especially nice with whole wheat couscous: Instead of the bread crumbs, use 1 cup cooked couscous.

Pesto Cheese "Burger." More substantial and nuttier: Use chopped fresh basil instead of the parsley and use 3 eggs instead of 2. In Step 1, add $1/_2$ cup finely chopped pine nuts or walnuts to the egg mixture. Proceed with the recipe.

Baked Cheese "Burgers." Multiply the recipe and they're perfect for a crowd: Instead of cooking the burgers in a skillet, preheat the oven to 375°F at the beginning of Step 1. Line a baking sheet with parchment paper or grease well with olive oil and set the prepared patties on the sheet. Bake until crisp and golden, about 15 minutes.

Swiss-Style Cheese Bake

MAKES: 4 to 6 servings
TIME: 45 minutes
Ⓜ

When you don't have time for full-on fondue (page 221) or want to have something ready to pop into the oven after a day outside in the cold, this dish—essentially

Ⓕ Fast   Ⓜ Make Ahead   Ⓥ Vegan

melted cheese with potatoes and vegetables—is perfect. Like fondue, it originally hails from the Alps.

Try layering the ingredients into small individual crocks if you have them—the kind you would use for onion soup. And consider that you can use virtually any kind of cooked vegetables for layering here, which makes it a great use for leftovers.

Butter or extra virgin olive oil for greasing the baking dish(es)

2 cups grated fontina, Emmental, Gruyère, Cantal, cheddar, or Jack cheese

1 tablespoon cornstarch

3 cups cooked potato cubes (boiled or roasted, peeled or not)

Salt and freshly ground black pepper

2 cups roughly chopped cooked asparagus, broccoli, or Brussels sprouts

$1/4$ cup chopped walnuts (optional)

$1/4$ cup freshly grated Parmesan cheese

Chopped parsley leaves for garnish (optional)

1 If you're baking immediately, preheat the oven to 375°F. Grease an 8-inch square baking pan with a little butter or olive oil. Toss the grated cheese with the cornstarch until the cheese is coated evenly.

2 Spread the potatoes evenly in the bottom of the pan. Sprinkle with salt and pepper and half of the cheese mixture. Top with the vegetable, a little more salt and pepper, and the remaining cheese mixture. Sprinkle with the walnuts if you like and the Parmesan. Cover the pan tightly with foil. (The dish may be assembled to this point and refrigerated for up to a day. Bring to room temperature and preheat the oven before proceeding.)

3 Put the pan in the oven and bake, covered, until the cheese melts and the vegetables are hot, 15 to 20 minutes. Remove the foil and continue baking until the cheese is golden and bubbly, another 10 minutes or so. Sprinkle with parsley if you're using it and let rest for a few minutes before serving.

Layered Mozzarella with Roasted Peppers and Olives. Think of a submarine sandwich, only in a casserole: Use grated mozzarella for the main cheese and 1 cup Roasted Red Peppers (page 333) and $1/4$ cup chopped black olives instead of the asparagus, broccoli, or Brussels sprouts. In Step 2, instead of the potatoes, line the bottom of the baking pan with several thick slices of French or Italian bread (stale is fine). Layer with the mozzarella, followed by the peppers, then more mozzarella. Use pine nuts instead of walnuts if you like and proceed with the recipe.

Cheese Fondue

MAKES: 8 to 10 servings

TIME: 25 minutes

If you live in a cold climate, and you produce cheese and wine, you might want to combine them with heat, and that's exactly what happened in Switzerland, the home of fondue. Thus using Swiss cheeses—like Gruyère, Emmental (the original "Swiss"), Appenzeller, Fribourg, or Vacherin, for example—is traditional, but any good melting cheese works equally well (cheddar, Jack, Comté, or fontina, to name just a few). Dry and acidic white wines are good for balancing the heaviness of the cheese, but beer, dry ciders, and red wine are also nice; see the variations.

If you don't have a fondue pot, use any enamel or ceramic-lined pot; or start the process in any pot at all, then transfer the finished fondue to an oven-safe ceramic dish that you can set over a tea light.

Serve with cubes of crusty bread, firm tofu, and cut fruit and vegetables. Many vegetables can be used raw, but some—potatoes, eggplant, and artichokes, for example—should be cooked first. Other vegetables, like green beans, asparagus, broccoli, and cauliflower, are best when lightly cooked, until barely tender. In any case, be sure the vegetables are completely dry, or the fondue will not stick to them.

2 cups dry white wine, or a little more as needed

1 large clove garlic, peeled and crushed (optional)

2 tablespoons cornstarch

1 pound Gruyère, shredded (about 4 cups)

1 pound Emmental, shredded (about 4 cups)

① Combine the wine with the garlic if you're using it in a large saucepan over medium heat and bring to a slow bubble. Whisk the cornstarch and 1 tablespoon cold water together; set aside.

② Lower the heat, then gradually stir in the cheese until it's melted and creamy; do not let the fondue boil. Whisk the cornstarch slurry again and then add to the fondue while stirring; cook for another 5 minutes, until thick and creamy. If the fondue is too thick, add a little more wine and cook for another 3 minutes or so. Serve immediately, with cubes of bread and vegetables.

Blue Cheese Fondue. Blue cheese gives fondue a great flavor. But using only blue is overwhelming (and the color becomes an unappealing gray), so a combination is best: Substitute 1 cup water and 1 cup apple brandy for the wine (or just add a tablespoon or two of brandy), and blue cheese, crumbled, for either the Gruyère or the Emmental. Proceed with the recipe.

Mustard-Cheese Fondue. Great with a hearty, dark bread, like pumpernickel or seedy whole grain: Substitute dry cider for the wine. Add $1/4$ cup any Dijon-style mustard or Grainy Mustard (page 776) or 2 to 3 tablespoons yellow mustard seeds with the cheese in Step 2. Proceed with the recipe.

Smoked Cheese Fondue with Beer. A pinch of cayenne or a minced jalapeño wouldn't be inappropriate: Substitute beer—dark porter or stout is really great—for the white wine and smoked Gouda or cheddar for the Gruyère and Emmental. Proceed with the recipe.

Fontina and Porcini Fondue. An Italian-style fondue; the mild fontina cheese really lets the porcini flavor shine: Use 2 pounds grated fontina and 1 cup dried porcini. Soak the porcini in hot water until soft, squeeze out the excess water, chop finely, and stir in with the cheese in Step 2; substitute the porcini soaking water (strain it first if it's sandy) for some or all of the wine. Proceed with the recipe.

Tomato and Chile Cheese Fondue. Far from traditional but fun and delicious: Substitute $1^1/2$ cups beer for the wine, a mild or medium cheddar or Jack for the cheeses, and add a tablespoon or two of tequila. Add 1 cup cored, peeled, seeded, and chopped tomatoes and 1 medium poblano or other mild fresh chile, roasted, cleaned, and finely chopped (page 828) with the beer in Step 1. Proceed with the recipe.

Sharp Cheddar Fondue with Red Wine. Use an orange-colored cheddar for the best color: Substitute a fruity red wine for the white, grated sharp cheddar for the Gruyère, and grated mild or medium cheddar for the Emmental. Proceed with the recipe.

12 Great Additions to Fondue

It's easy to add subtle—or not so subtle—flavors to your fondue. Some ideas:

1. 1 cup cored, peeled, seeded, and chopped tomato
2. 1 tablespoon minced chipotles in adobo sauce, or to taste
3. 1 tablespoon minced jalapeño
4. 1 or 2 tablespoons horseradish
5. $1/4$ cup or so any store-bought mustard or 2 to 3 tablespoons mustard seeds
6. Pinch cayenne
7. Large pinch smoked paprika
8. Splash or two Worcestershire Sauce, Hold the Anchovies (page 799)
9. 1 cup finely chopped Caramelized Onions (page 329)
10. 4 to 8 cloves Roasted Garlic (page 304)
11. $1/4$ cup Traditional Pesto (page 768), stirred in at the last minute

Ⓕ Fast   Ⓜ Make Ahead   Ⓥ Vegan

12. 2 to 3 ounces rehydrated dried mushrooms (page 317) or 1 cup finely chopped fresh, lightly sautéed

Cheese Enchiladas with Red Mole

MAKES: 8 servings

TIME: about 3 hours, largely unattended

A wonderful holiday or special-occasion dish. (If you're looking for everyday enchiladas, see the first variation.) It's based on mole, a group of classic slow-cooked Mexican sauces that get their rich, deep flavor from a long list of ingredients (making the sauce isn't *that* time-consuming once everything is assembled). This mole is loaded with nuts, and I've purposefully kept the cheese filling to a minimum so the sauce remains the star.

Serve these enchiladas with a selection of garnishes like sliced white or red radishes, sliced avocado, chopped fresh tomatoes or tomatillos, shredded lettuce, sour cream or crema, chopped peaches or nectarines, or chopped Hard-Cooked Eggs (page 166). For side dishes, try Minimalist Guacamole (page 264), Radish Salsa (page 752), Red or Green Rice Pilaf (page 511), Mexican Rice with Vegetables (page 512), Beer-Glazed Black Beans (page 585), or Twice-Cooked (Refried) Beans (page 592).

12 to 15 mild to medium dried chiles, like New Mexico, mulatto, pasilla, guajillo, or ancho (or a combination), toasted, soaked, and cleaned (see page 827)

2 cups assorted nuts, like peanuts, almonds, pecans, walnuts, pine nuts, and hazelnuts

$^1/_4$ cup tahini or sesame seeds

$^1/_4$ cup cocoa powder or chopped unsweetened chocolate

1 large onion, roughly chopped

1 head garlic, peeled

4 plum tomatoes, cored (canned are fine)

2 thick slices white bread (stale is fine)

1 quart vegetable stock (pages 101–102) or water, plus more as needed

$^1/_4$ cup neutral oil, like grapeseed or corn, plus more for frying

3 or 4 bay leaves

1 cinnamon stick

2 tablespoons ground cumin

1 tablespoon ground allspice

2 teaspoons anise seeds

Salt and freshly ground black pepper

Brown sugar as needed (optional)

24 small corn tortillas, plus more if any break

3 cups shredded Monterey Jack or cotija cheese

$^1/_2$ cup crumbled queso fresco for garnish

$^1/_2$ cup chopped red onion or scallion for garnish

$^1/_2$ cup chopped fresh cilantro for garnish

Lime wedges for garnish

1 Put the chiles, nuts, tahini, cocoa, onion, garlic, tomatoes, and bread in a blender with just enough stock to get the machine running. (You may have to work in 2 batches.)

2 Put $^1/_4$ cup of the oil in a large, deep pot over medium heat. Add the puréed mixture and all of the spices. Sprinkle with salt and pepper. Cook, stirring frequently and scraping the bottom of the pan, until it begins to color and become fragrant, 3 to 5 minutes. Turn the heat to low and continue cooking, stirring occasionally, until the mixture is deeply colored, softened, and nearly dry, another 15 to 20 minutes.

3 Turn the heat back up to medium-high and slowly stir in the remaining stock. Bring the pot to a boil, then lower the heat so the sauce barely bubbles. Cook, stirring occasionally and adding more liquid as needed, for an hour or so, until the sauce is thick and smooth. Taste and adjust the seasoning and add a tablespoon or so of brown sugar if you like. (The mole may be made ahead to this point, cooled, and refrigerated for up to 3 days. Gently reheat before proceeding.) Remove the cinnamon stick and bay leaves and keep the sauce warm.

④ Preheat the oven to 350°F. Spoon a thin layer of the mole into the bottom of a 9 x 12-inch baking dish. Put about 1/2 inch of the oil in a large, deep skillet over medium-high heat. When hot but not smoking, cook the tortillas, one at a time, until softened and pliable, about 10 seconds. Add more oil to the pan as needed. Drain on paper towels.

⑤ Sprinkle about 2 tablespoons of the Monterey Jack in the center of each tortilla, roll tightly, and put the enchiladas in the prepared dish, seam side down. The rolls should be packed in snugly against one another. Cover the top with some more mole and bake for 25 minutes. When the enchiladas come out of the oven, sprinkle them with the queso fresco, onion, and cilantro. Serve with lime wedges on the side and pass the remaining mole at the table.

Simple Cheese Enchiladas. Definitely easier: Instead of making the mole, prepare a double recipe of Red Enchilada Sauce (page 788). Proceed with the recipe from Step 4, substituting this sauce for the mole.

Cheese Enchiladas with Green Enchilada Sauce. Also known as Enchiladas Suisas: Instead of making the mole sauce, prepare a double recipe of Green Enchilada Sauce (page 788). Increase the amount of Monterey Jack to 5 cups and fill the tortillas with a bit more than a tablespoon each. Use any remaining cheese to sprinkle on top of the enchiladas before baking.

Scrambled Egg and Cheese Enchiladas. Great with either mole or Red Enchilada Sauce (page 788): Just before you're ready to assemble the enchiladas in Step 4, scramble 4 or 5 eggs according to the recipe on page 166. Stop cooking when the eggs are just holding together but still rather loose. Proceed with the recipe, using a spoonful of scrambled eggs along with the cheese to fill each enchilada.

Hard-Cooked Egg and Cheese Enchiladas. For terrific texture, especially with the mole: Up to several days in advance, hard-cook 6 eggs according to the recipe on page 166. When you're ready to assemble the enchiladas in Step 4, peel the eggs and mash them roughly with a fork. Proceed with the recipe, using a sprinkling of the eggs along with the cheese to fill each enchilada.

Squash Enchiladas. Made with pumpkin, acorn, butternut, or any of the winter squashes listed on page 363: Instead of the Monterey Jack cheese, use 4 cups cooked, mashed, and seasoned winter squash to fill the tortillas in Step 5, then proceed with the recipe.

Sweet Potato Enchiladas. Colorful and slightly sweet: Instead of the Monterey Jack cheese, use 4 cups cooked, mashed, and seasoned sweet potatoes to fill the tortillas in Step 5. Proceed with the recipe.

Tofu Enchiladas with Red Mole. Vegan and delicious: Make the sauce and tortillas as directed. Omit all the cheeses in the recipe and prepare a double recipe of Basic Scrambled Tofu (page 655). Use this to fill the enchiladas and proceed with the recipe.

Cheese Dumplings

MAKES: 4 servings
TIME: About 40 minutes

A delicate, flavorful cheese dumpling that can be added to soups, sauces, or a variety of other dishes (see page 226) or simply tossed with butter or oil and served alone. Add fresh herbs, chopped nuts, or cooked or finely grated veggies and they become even more interesting.

Salt

2 cups crumbled Fresh Cheese, the Easy Way (page 230), or store-bought farmer cheese or queso fresco

2 eggs

1/4 cup minced scallion (optional)

1/4 cup chopped parsley leaves (optional)

Freshly ground black pepper

3/4 cup all-purpose flour

Ⓕ Fast   Ⓜ Make Ahead   Ⓥ Vegan

① Bring a large pot of salted water to a boil.

② Combine the cheese, the eggs, and the scallion and parsley if you're using them in a bowl. Add some salt and pepper and stir well. Add about $^1/_2$ cup of the flour and stir; add more flour until the mixture forms a dough you can handle. Knead for a minute or so on a lightly floured surface. Pinch off a piece of the dough and boil it to make sure it will hold its shape; if it does not, knead in a bit more flour.

③ Roll small pieces of the dough into balls and put them on a sheet of wax paper; do not allow them to touch.

④ A few at a time, add the dumplings to the boiling water and stir. A minute after they rise to the surface, the dumplings are done; remove with a slotted spoon. Serve the dumplings immediately—see "11 Ways to Serve Cheese Dumplings" (page 226).

Fluffy Cheese Dumplings. Lighter and airier with only a bit more effort: Add another egg and separate the whites. Reduce the flour to $^1/_4$ cup and add $^1/_2$ teaspoon baking powder. In Step 2, combine the cheese, scallions, and parsley with the egg yolks and baking powder, along with some salt and pepper; stir in the flour. Whip the egg whites to fairly stiff peaks, then fold about a third of the egg whites into the cheese mixture; gently fold in the remaining egg whites. Use spoons to scoop out dumplings and drop them into the boiling water to cook.

Goat Cheese Dumplings. Lovely with a mix of chopped fresh herbs: Substitute goat cheese for the Fresh Cheese and add some chopped chives, tarragon, and thyme to the parsley.

Ricotta Dumplings

MAKES: 4 to 6 servings

TIME: About 1 hour

Basic cheese dumplings, Mediterranean style. The bread binds the dough while keeping it light and fluffy; the Parmesan guarantees good flavor.

$1^1/_2$ cups Ricotta Cheese, preferably homemade (page 230) or store-bought

$^1/_2$ cup milk or cream

2 cups torn or chopped day-old bread or 1 cup bread crumbs, preferably fresh (page 804)

Salt

1 cup freshly grated Parmesan cheese

4 eggs

$^1/_2$ cup finely chopped reconstituted sun-dried tomatoes or Roasted Red Peppers (page 333), patted dry with paper towels before chopping

$^1/_4$ cup finely chopped pitted black olives (optional)

$^1/_4$ cup chopped fresh basil leaves (optional)

① Combine the ricotta, milk, and bread; mix well and let soak for at least 30 minutes or until the bread is completely wet and soft (skip the soaking if you're using bread crumbs).

② Meanwhile, bring a large pot of salted water to a boil. Add the cheese, eggs, tomatoes, and olives and basil if you're using them to the dough and stir well; you want a wet dough that you can still handle. If the dough is too wet to handle, add some bread crumbs.

③ Work in small batches, forming the dough into balls and immediately adding them to the boiling water. They're done when they rise to the surface; remove with a slotted spoon. Serve immediately (see "11 Ways to Serve Cheese Dumplings, page 226).

Panfried Ricotta Dumplings. Flattening out the dumplings a bit ensures that they cook through: Proceed with the recipe up to Step 3; don't bother boiling the water. Form the dough into slightly flattened balls and then coat in bread crumbs. Put extra virgin olive oil in a large skillet over medium-high heat; working in batches, cook the dumplings until browned on both sides, about 5 minutes total. Delicious served with Fast Tomato Sauce (page 445).

Ricotta Dumplings with Quinoa or Millet. A great way to use leftover cooked grains or to make the dumplings more substantial: Substitute 1 cup cooked quinoa or millet for the bread; no need to soak the grains in Step 1. Proceed with the recipe.

Pesto-Ricotta Dumplings. Really delicious: Substitute $3/4$ cup Traditional Pesto (page 768) for the sun-dried tomatoes, olives, and basil. Proceed with the recipe.

11 Ways to Serve Cheese Dumplings

These cheese dumplings can play a main or supporting role in a dish. Add the dumplings alone or with vegetables to:

1. Any flavorful broth or soup
2. Fast Tomato Sauce (page 445) or nearly any of its variations
3. Traditional Pesto (page 768)
4. Smooth Green Chile Sauce, Indian Style (page 792)
5. Spicy Indian Tomato Sauce (page 793)
6. Rustic Pine Nut Sauce (page 796)
7. Brown Butter (page 801)—sauté the dumplings with the butter until they brown
8. Lentils and Potatoes with Curry (page 600)
9. Simplest Dal (page 600)
10. Spicy Red Beans, Indian Style (page 593)
11. Chili non Carne (page 607)

Cottage Cheese Patties

MAKES: 4 servings
TIME: 30 minutes

Ⓕ Ⓜ

Something between a savory pancake and a gnocchi (page 486), these little patties are ideal, either warm or at room temperature, for brunch or lunch. They're great with eggs and toast, with a green salad, or sweet (see the variation), with a fruit salad.

2 cups cottage cheese

4 tablespoons ($1/2$ stick) butter or $1/4$ cup extra virgin olive oil

1 small onion, finely chopped

Salt and freshly ground black pepper

1 egg

$1/4$ cup chopped parsley leaves

① Put the cottage cheese in the center of a doubled sheet of cheesecloth or a clean dish towel; pull up the ends of the cloth and twist the cottage cheese into a ball, squeezing out as much liquid as you can. Or, if you have time, line a strainer with the cheesecloth and put over a bowl with about an inch between the bottom of the bowl and the strainer; add the cottage cheese to the strainer and let drain for several hours or overnight in the fridge.

② Meanwhile, put 1 tablespoon of the butter or oil in a skillet and turn the heat to medium-high. Add the onion, sprinkle with salt and pepper, and cook, stirring frequently, until the onion is soft and turning color, about 2 minutes. Remove from the heat and set aside.

③ Combine all of the ingredients, along with the onion, in a bowl with a sprinkling of salt and pepper, and mix until well blended. Form the cottage cheese mixture into patties (any larger than about 3 inches across and they break too easily).

④ In the same skillet as before, put the remaining butter or olive oil in and turn the heat to medium-high. When a drop of water skids across the skillet before evaporating, it's ready. Add as many patties at once as will fit comfortably, turning them when they are brown, after a couple of minutes. Total cooking time will run between 5 and 8 minutes. Serve warm or room temperature.

Herbed Cottage Cheese Patties. Add chopped fresh herbs, 1 teaspoon (stronger herbs like oregano, tarragon, or thyme) to 2 tablespoons (milder ones like parsley, chive, chervil, basil, dill, or mint); add in Step 3 with other ingredients.

Cottage Cheese Patties with Nuts. For a great contrast of textures: Add $1/2$ cup chopped nuts, like walnuts, almonds, pine nuts, or cashews, and reduce the cottage cheese by $1/2$ cup.

Cottage Cheese Patties with Quinoa. The grains add a soft crunch: Add $3/4$ cup cooked quinoa (see page 537)

Ⓕ Fast   Ⓜ Make Ahead   Ⓥ Vegan

and a teaspoon or so minced garlic if you like and reduce the cottage cheese by $\frac{1}{2}$ cup.

Sweet Cottage Cheese Patties. A subtle sweetness; great for breakfast: Add 1 teaspoon grated lemon zest, 2 tablespoons freshly squeezed lemon juice, 2 tablespoons sugar, and 1 teaspoon ground cinnamon. Omit the onion and the parsley and use butter.

Baked Phyllo-Wrapped Goat Cheese

MAKES: 4 servings
TIME: 30 minutes

Wrap individual slices of goat cheese to make phyllo packages or wrap the whole log and slice it upon serving. For extra flavor, toss chopped nuts, roasted garlic, chopped Roasted Red Peppers (page 333), or a dollop of Traditional Pesto (page 768) or Tapenade (page 326) into the phyllo packages.

One 6-ounce goat cheese log

$\frac{1}{2}$ cup extra virgin olive oil or 8 tablespoons (1 stick) butter, melted

Salt and freshly ground black pepper

$\frac{1}{4}$ cup mixed chopped fresh herbs, like basil, chives, parsley, chervil, tarragon, or thyme

8 to 12 sheets phyllo dough, thawed

1 Heat the oven to 350°F. Cut the cheese into 8 slices or keep it whole. Brush the cheese with the olive oil and sprinkle with salt, pepper, and the mixed herbs; set aside.

2 Keep the phyllo sheets covered with a piece of plastic wrap and a damp towel over the top to keep them from drying out. Remove one sheet at a time and quickly brush it with the olive oil or melted butter. To fold a slice of goat cheese in the phyllo, put the cheese on the lower third of the piece of phyllo and do not overstuff. Fold over one corner as shown in the illustration, then continue to fold in triangles. Or just roll the phyllo up. For wrapping the whole log, stack the phyllo (each brushed with the oil or butter) and roll the log with the sheets; tuck in the ends of the phyllo.

3 Brush the packages or roll with more olive oil or butter and put on a baking sheet; bake until golden brown, 10 to 15 minutes. Let rest for just a couple minutes and serve warm.

10 Things to Serve with Baked Goat Cheese
Serve baked goat cheese with any of these items or layer one or two of them with the goat cheese in a ramekin or dish to create little hot pots.

1. Roasted Red Peppers (page 333)
2. Dry-Pan Eggplant (page 294)
3. Sautéed Mushrooms (page 314)
4. Cooked spinach
5. Tomato slices
6. Fast Tomato Sauce (page 445)
7. Chopped olives or Tapenade (page 326)
8. Traditional Pesto (page 768)
9. Chopped nuts
10. Parsley and Herb Salad (page 42)

Goat Cheese and Mushroom Tart with Potato Crust

MAKES: 6 to 12 servings
TIME: 45 minutes, largely unattended

Potato crust? Amazing, delicious, and dead-easy, as is the filling for this little four-star tart. Add some finely grated

Parmesan or sprinkle in some chopped herbs for an even more flavorful crust or choose a more traditional crust, like Savory Piecrust (page 867) or Savory Tart Crust (page 868).

3 tablespoons butter or extra virgin olive oil

1 large russet potato, peeled

Salt and freshly ground black pepper

2 cups chopped mushrooms, like shiitake, cremini, button, or wild

1 tablespoon chopped fresh tarragon, sage, thyme, or rosemary leaves

$1^{1}/_{2}$ cups crumbled goat cheese

$^{3}/_{4}$ cup heavy cream or half-and-half

1 egg, plus 1 yolk

1 Preheat the oven to 400°F. Liberally grease a 9- or 10-inch pie or tart pan with 2 tablespoons of the butter or some of the olive oil. Grate the potato; sprinkle with salt and pepper. Toss together, then squeeze out the excess water. Press the potato mixture into the bottom of the pan to form a thin crust. Bake the crust until golden brown and crisp, 30 to 40 minutes. Remove from the oven and set aside. Lower the oven temperature to 375°F.

2 Meanwhile, put the remaining butter or olive oil in a pan over medium-high heat. When the butter is melted or the oil is hot, add the mushrooms and cook and stir for a couple minutes, then add the herbs and continue cooking until soft and almost dry, about 5 minutes. Stir together the cheese, cream, and egg; sprinkle in a bit of salt and pepper and then stir in the mushrooms.

3 Put the goat cheese mixture into the prepared crust. Bake until set but still slightly jiggly in the middle, 20 to 30 minutes. Remove from the oven and cool it on a rack for a few minutes. Slice and serve warm or at room temperature.

Ricotta Cheese and Zucchini Tart with Potato Crust. Stir in a spoonful or two of Traditional Pesto (page 768) or Fast Tomato Sauce (page 445) for added flavor: Substitute 2 small or 1 medium zucchini or summer squash, sliced, for the mushrooms; $^{1}/_{4}$ cup chopped fresh basil leaves for the tarragon, and ricotta for the goat cheese.

Cheese and Tomato Tart. For real cheese lovers; use any grated cheese here: Substitute Savory Tart Crust (page 868) for the potato crust and 2 medium tomatoes, sliced, for the mushrooms. Use $^{3}/_{4}$ cup goat cheese, ricotta, quark, or any soft fresh cheese and add $^{3}/_{4}$ cup grated cheese of your choosing. Stir the grated cheese into the soft cheese mixture, then layer the cheese mixture with the tomato slices in the tart pan, ending with a few tomato slices on top; sprinkle with some extra grated cheese if you like.

Blue Cheese and Pecan Tart. Use the potato or cheese crust from the main recipe and the variation, respectively: Substitute sliced onions for the mushrooms; $^{1}/_{4}$ cup chopped parsley leaves for the herbs; $^{3}/_{4}$ cup crumbled blue cheese and $^{3}/_{4}$ cup ricotta or soft fresh cheese for the goat cheese. Add $^{3}/_{4}$ cup toasted pecans. Caramelize the onions by cooking them as you would the mushrooms in Step 2 and stir them into the cheese mixture along with the pecans. Proceed with the recipe.

The Basics of Making Fresh Cheese

Yes, you can make cheese, and I strongly urge you to give it a try. It's almost as easy as boiling milk, and everything you need is available at the supermarket. The best thing is that this recipe requires virtually no practice; your very first batch will be better than anything you can buy. Really. And you'll find that it has so many uses—delicious eaten on its own, a wonderful enrichment for a variety of other dishes, as you'll see in the lists on page 229—in the vegetarian kitchen.

F Fast   **M** Make Ahead   **V** Vegan

All cheese begins by separating curds (milk solids) and whey (watery liquid). Most commercially made cheeses rely on rennet, a special enzyme, to cause this chemical reaction (known as *curdling* or *coagulating*). But fortunately there are a couple easy ways for the home cook to curdle milk. Some include using a harsh acid like vinegar or lemon juice, though buttermilk, which acts as a mild-tasting but effective coagulant, is even nicer. The result is tender cheese with a pure milky flavor, akin to the Indian staple paneer; true queso fresco, the fresh white cheese common in Mexico; the fromage blanc of France; and a dozen other products made worldwide. (See the list of possible stir-in flavors on page 231 for some ideas for making less traditional fresh cheeses.)

To use fresh cheese, just cut it into slices or cubes or gently crumble it by hand or with two forks (it's too soft to grate). Fresh cheese will keep for three or four days in the fridge, though you may freeze it (tightly wrapped) for up to three months. The recipe makes a small batch, so you probably won't have any left anyway.

5 Simple Ways to Eat Fresh Cheese

1. Crumble as a garnish on tacos, green salads, sandwiches, or pizza.
2. Toss crumbled fresh cheese, including cottage cheese or ricotta, on hot pasta right before serving, either alone or in combination with freshly grated Parmesan. With a little tomato sauce, this makes a nice "pink" pasta.
3. Use cottage cheese or ricotta as the basis for dips, spreads, or sauces by whirring a cup or so in a food processor for a few minutes with enough milk, cream, or yogurt to reach the desired consistency.
4. Serve a few slices drizzled with honey and sprinkled with toasted nuts.
5. Drizzle a few slices with extra virgin olive oil and sprinkle with salt and freshly ground black pepper.

1. Pour the coagulated, lumpy mix into a cheesecloth-lined strainer.
2. Twist and squeeze out excess moisture.
3. Hang from a wooden spoon or other implement over the sink or a colander or strainer set over a bowl.

9 Dishes or Sauces That Work Great with Fresh Cheese

Stir cubes of fresh cheese into the following dishes during the last few minutes of cooking, to heat the cheese through and allow it to absorb the flavors without falling apart. It doesn't melt but might get a little soft.

1. Curried Eggplant with Coconut Milk (page 296)
2. Spinach with Fresh Cheese and Yogurt (page 360)
3. Simplest Dal (page 600 or any dal recipe (see pages 600 to 604)
4. Lentil Soup with Coconut (page 116)
5. Spicy Indian Tomato Sauce (page 793)
6. Smooth Green Chile Sauce, Indian Style (page 792)
7. Spiced Tomato Sauce (page 449)
8. Bulgur Chili (page 557)
9. Fast Tomato Sauce (page 445)

Fresh Cheese, the Easy Way

MAKES: about a pound

TIME: 2 hours, largely unattended

Ⓜ

The recipe—and all the variations—work with 1 percent, 2 percent, or whole milk, which makes the richest cheeses. If you live near a farm and can find raw whole milk, you'll get the best flavor.

$1/2$ gallon milk

1 quart buttermilk

Salt (optional)

❶ Put the milk in a large, heavy-bottomed pot over medium-high heat. Cook, stirring occasionally to keep it from scorching, until the milk bubbles up the sides of the pot, 10 to 15 minutes.

❷ Line a strainer with 3 layers of cheesecloth or a piece of undyed cotton muslin. Have a long piece of twine ready.

❸ Add the buttermilk to the boiling milk all at once and stir constantly until the mixture separates into curds and whey. It will look like cooked egg whites suspended in a slightly thick yellowish liquid. Remove from the heat and stir in a large pinch of salt if you like.

❹ Carefully pour the mixture through the cloth and strainer so that the curds collect in the bottom and the whey drains off. Gather up the corners of the cloth and twist the top to start working the curds into a ball. Run the bundle under cold water until you can handle it. Keep twisting and squeezing out the whey until the bundle feels firm and dry. Don't worry about handling it roughly; it can take it. (See page 229.)

❺ Tie the string around the top to hold it tight, then tie the string around a long spoon or stick to suspend the cheese over the sink or a colander or strainer set over a bowl to drain. Let it rest, undisturbed, until cool and set, about $1^1/_2$ hours. Remove the cloth and serve immediately or wrap in plastic and refrigerate for up to 3 days. Or freeze the cheese for up to 3 months.

Fresh Cottage Cheese. Incredible stuff; drain as dry or as moist as you like: In Step 4, after you pour the curds and whey through the cheesecloth, simply leave the curds loose in the strainer until they've drained the amount of moisture you desire, anywhere from 30 to 60 minutes or so. Then scoop the curds into a container and store in the refrigerator.

Fresh Ricotta. Also unbelievable, especially with top-quality milk: Reduce the amount of buttermilk to 2 cups and proceed with the recipe through Step 3. The mixture will look like thickened buttermilk. In Step 4, after you pour it through the cheesecloth, simply leave the ricotta in the strainer until it reaches the texture you like, anywhere from 30 to 60 minutes. Then scoop the ricotta into a container and store in the refrigerator. To make the ricotta smooth, beat or whisk it after draining.

Brined Fresh Cheese. Like a mild feta: After the cheese is set, mix a brine of 2 tablespoons salt and 2 cups water in a jar or plastic container. Submerge the cheese in the brine and refrigerate for at least 24 hours before eating.

7 Ways to Flavor Fresh Cheese

In Step 4 of the recipe for making fresh cheese, after pouring the curds and whey into the cloth-lined strainer, immediately stir any of the following ingredients into the curds and proceed with the recipe.

1. Up to $^1/_4$ cup Traditional Pesto (page 768) or any of the herb pastes on pages 768–770
2. Up to $^1/_4$ cup of any of the Chile Pastes on pages 828–830
3. Up to $^1/_4$ cup finely chopped nuts, like walnuts, almonds, or hazelnuts
4. Up to 2 tablespoons curry powder (to make your own, see pages 815–816), chaat masala (to make your own, see page 814), or garam masala (to make your own, see page 815)
5. Up to 1 tablespoon coarsely ground fresh black or green peppercorns
6. Up to $^1/_4$ cup finely chopped Roasted Red Peppers (page 333; or roasted pimientos or piquillos) or olives
7. Up to 1 tablespoon of any finely grated citrus zest

Produce: Vegetables and Fruits

There is not a healthy person on earth who does not eat fruits and vegetables, and obviously they take on increased importance for vegetarians. So this chapter is the longest in the book and probably the most useful.

I've included fruits and vegetables in the same chapter because they are all "produce" and all in the same supermarket aisle. The distinction between the two is also blurry, at least in the kitchen: We treat a lot of what are technically fruits as vegetables, and they're among the most important ones—tomatoes, eggplant, winter and summer squashes, cucumbers, even corn.

Still, we don't often cook with the plants we think of as fruits (stone fruit, apples, bananas, and so on), and we think of what we call fruits as sweet and vegetables as savory, so I've separated the two within the chapter. (You will, of course, find many sweet fruit recipes in the dessert chapter.)

Here what you're going to find is a complete lexicon of vegetables, followed by a complete lexicon of fruits,

with details about shopping, storing, and basic cooking, as well as a couple hundred (slightly) more advanced recipes. The chapter is a primer for dealing with the most important building blocks of daily eating. Following the lexicons are recipes that pull a lot of this bounty together into single dishes—the mixed vegetable creations like stir-fries, gratins and pies, and so on.

Though most Americans buy groceries in supermarkets, where the number of available vegetables and fruits has grown dramatically over the last thirty years or so—some say by a factor of twelve—it isn't always the best place to find these basic ingredients. Supermarkets are often more expensive than the alternatives, and the selection is still not as good as it may be elsewhere.

Furthermore, shopping at a conventional supermarket may almost guarantee that you're getting those fruits and vegetables that have been bred for their ability to travel long distances and remain visually appealing for days and weeks, rather than those bred for flavor. You may have better choices: In those parts of the country with serious winters, these choices are more limited of course. In summer, look for farmer's markets. In winter, a health food store may give you better options; you might occasionally find that frozen vegetables are preferable to what your supermarket is offering in the so-called fresh section.

If you live in the southern half of the country, especially Florida or the Southwest, you've got good fresh vegetable and fruit options throughout the year. Incredibly, though, the large supermarket chains in those regions carry many of the same items that are shipped to supermarkets in the North; for good locally grown produce you are better off looking in independent supermarkets, small chains, health food stores, and year-round farmer's markets.

Having said all that, it's worth returning to reality and mentioning that most of us, most of the time, buy our vegetables and fruits in the supermarket and that both the general and the specific information in this chapter will help you buy the best-quality produce possible and treat it as well as you can.

The Basics of Buying and Handling Fresh Produce

The quality of the produce you select is just about as important as how you cook it, though my feelings about what to buy have evolved over the years. And, therefore, so have my rules:

Buying

Don't think "fresh or nothing": Some frozen vegetables and even fruits are not only good enough to eat; they're sometimes better than what passes for fresh (see "Don't Freeze Out Frozen" on page 235). This is especially true in the winter. And frozen vegetables and fruits have undeniable convenience, which may encourage you to eat a greater quantity of them; washing, preparing, and cooking are all easier. I'm not saying you should uniformly opt for frozen produce, but I am saying it's a good option.

When you do buy fresh produce, be picky: Maybe you know the drill: Most vegetables should be slightly firm and most fruits slightly soft. Check for damage or rotten spots and make sure the color is close to ideal. Pay attention to the little stickers to see where the produce came from, keeping in mind that miles traveled are a good indication of when fruits and vegetables were harvested. (Unless it was flown, that broccoli that traveled three thousand miles is at least a week old.) After a while, you'll naturally gravitate to what's seasonal, since that's what's both freshest and grown closer to home. This is easy enough in the summer or if you live in the South. But elsewhere it means turning more frequently to root vegetables in the winter months, as did many of our ancestors.

Be flexible: If you go to the store, and something you'd planned on doesn't look too fresh, reach for an alternative or head to the freezer case. In almost every recipe in this chapter I offer substitutions for the main vegetable to help you cook with the freshest produce you can find.

Consider the season: In these days of high-tech shipping and storage, virtually all fresh produce is available year-round. But since well-traveled fruits and vegetables aren't necessarily the best, seasonal selections almost always guarantee the best quality (and naturally match the kind of cooking you're doing). Because of the many climates in the United States, Americans don't have a "national season" for everything. So throughout the year, try to tune in to what's available closest to where you live.

Consider the source: If you're concerned about the impact of mainstream farming methods on your health and the environment—and who isn't?—you might think

F Fast   M Make Ahead   V Vegan

about buying organic fruits and vegetables (see "What About Organic?" on page 2). But my feeling is that it's even more important to seek out locally or regionally grown fresh produce—if it's organic, so much the better—because you'll be getting the best fruits and vegetables available and supporting the people who raise them.

Storing and Preparing

Don't wash vegetables and fruits until you're ready to use them, because washing rinses away their natural defenses against rotting. Plus storing moist produce can promote mold or bacteria growth. And remember that not all fruits and vegetables benefit from refrigeration; check the individual listings in this chapter for more details.

I like to wash almost all fresh vegetables and fruits before cooking or eating, even when they'll be peeled. Any bacteria or dirt on the outside will spread to the inside with handling.

A soft brush is great for potatoes you don't want to peel, cucumbers with little spines, and other, more rigorous jobs. (You can also use one of those mildly abrasive dishwashing pads.) Washing greens and other vegetables couldn't be easier:

1. Put them in a salad spinner (or a colander inside a large pot).
2. Fill it with water.
3. Swish the veggies around.
4. Lift the colander out of the water.
5. Drain.

The Basics of Cooking Vegetables

The main reason to cook a vegetable (the main reason to cook *any* food, really) is to make it tender and tastier and to release nutrients that aren't available in raw food.

But *how* you cook a particular vegetable can completely change its taste and texture and, for that matter, its nutritional profile. Some cooking methods deepen fla-

vor by caramelizing the natural sugar or starches in vegetables—usually with a fat like butter or oil—while other techniques brighten both their taste and their color with water, steam, or the small amount of moisture contained in the vegetables themselves.

Regardless of the cooking method, it's important to leave a little elbow room in the pot whenever you cook vegetables. A pot of boiling water will take a long time to return to a boil if you load it with too many vegetables—bad news because they'll tend to get mushy and overcooked. In the microwave, overcrowding keeps vegetables from cooking evenly. Crowding during sautéing or frying is also problematic, since the vegetables will soak up extra oil and never brown properly. Bottom line: Have a little patience and work in batches if you must.

Virtually all vegetables can be cooked according to any of the general methods explained here. There are, however, a few exceptions; you'll find them noted in the individual vegetable descriptions that begin on page 256. My goal is to help you grow more comfortable cooking vegetables spontaneously and experimenting with your own favorite flavors and techniques. The recipes throughout this chapter provide a great place for beginners to start and a great reference for more experienced cooks.

Vegetables and Nutrition

Despite what enthusiasts of raw diets contend, most vegetables are actually more nutritious when cooked. For example, the starch in potatoes, and to some extent broccoli and cauliflower, will not be absorbed by the stomach (and can cause gastric distress) unless it's cooked until just about soft. And anything with even a moderate amount of fiber or protein requires at least some heat (or juicing, which also breaks down the fibers) for the body to absorb them during digestion. Generally, cooking increases the bioavailability of the nutrients in vegetables.

At the same time it's true that cooking vegetables in water (or broth, wine, or whatever) can rob them of nutrients, since most vitamins, minerals, and other nutrients migrate out of the vegetables and into the surrounding liquid. Submerging vegetables for a long time in boiling water is the least nutritious way to cook them; steaming is a slightly better alternative, especially if the vegetables remain above the boiling liquid or you incorporate the steaming liquid into the dish.

To get the most out of your vegetables, cook them al dente, just enough to unlock the nutrients but not long enough to allow the bulk of them to escape. If you want the vegetables cooked beyond al dente, for puréeing, mashing, or blending into soups or sauces, you might consider cooking them in a way that uses little or no water—roasting, stir-frying, or microwaving—or include the cooking liquid in the finished dish. And if you really love boiled vegetables, consider saving the cooking water and using it for soups or beverages. Or—and this is a very valid alternative—don't worry too much about the nutritional profile!

Recognizing Doneness

The preceding discussion implies that there's only a small window of ideal doneness. And to a certain degree that's true: It doesn't take more than a few minutes for most vegetables to turn from raw to mushy (though mushy vegetables can offer their own pleasures).

Here's a handful of tools to help you recognize when vegetables reach their ideal stage of doneness:

Harder, starchier vegetables take longer to cook: That time can always be decreased by cutting the vegetable into smaller pieces, of course. Once your veggies are prepared, try bending a piece to get an idea of how long it might take to cook. Spinach requires virtually no heat to wilt. Likewise thin asparagus tips or matchsticks of carrots. But thick asparagus stalks or chunks of carrots will take much longer. Things you can't bend at all—like potatoes and other root vegetables—are going to take quite a bit longer.

Remember that vegetables, like other foods, continue to cook as they cool down: Remove them from the heat just before they reach the stage of doneness you want. (This will come easily with practice, trust me.)

Watch for the color to brighten: Vegetables cooked al dente are even more vibrant than when raw. But they quickly peak and begin to look washed out as they start to soften. (That's why overcooked potatoes look a little gray.) You've got to pay attention, because in vegetables that don't take long to cook, this will happen in an instant.

Check vegetables frequently as they cook: There's no shame in poking around with a knife tip, toothpick, or skewer. Every once in a while, grab a piece and taste. It's the only way you'll ever know for sure. Eventually you'll be able to do this by sight, smell, and a poke of your finger.

Take control of doneness by learning to "shock" vegetables: This technique gets them ready ahead of time for finishing to perfect doneness at the last minute. (See the sidebar on page 241.)

Microwaving Vegetables

The microwave is ideal for steaming veggies with hardly any water at all, providing you know your machine well enough to yank them out before they overcook. Put vegetables on a plate or in a shallow bowl and sprinkle them with a few drops of water, then cover them loosely with a vented microwave cooking lid, a paper towel, or a heavy fitted lid (be careful when you open it; the steam will be very hot). Then set the timer and press the button.

Steaming Vegetables

Cooking vegetables above—not in—a small amount of simmering water is fast and efficient and preserves much of the vitamin content. This method is great for plain vegetables you want to eat right away or marinate in a vinaigrette (page 762) and cool down for salad. (For a specific example, see Basic Steamed Cauliflower on page 281.)

You can buy fancy vegetable steamers, but one of those fold-up baskets that you set into the bottom of a covered pot works fine, as does a colander or even, in a pinch, a bowl that will fit in the pot (see "Ways to Rig a Steamer," page 25). Fill the basket or bowl with vegetables, set it over an inch or so of water, cover, and turn the heat to high. Turn the heat down enough to keep the water bubbling steadily. Check frequently to prevent overcooking and make sure there's still water in the bottom of the pot. If you want to stop cooking immediately to hold the vegetables for future use, shock them according to the directions on page 241.

Boiling and Parboiling Vegetables

Simple and straightforward: Bring a large pot of water to a boil, salt it generously, and toss in whole or cut vegetables. (See Boiled or Steamed Greens and variations on page 239.) When the vegetables begin to get tender, drain them, either by fishing them out with a strainer or slotted spoon or pouring the water and the vegetables into a colander. The term *parboiling* really means noth-

ing more than "preboiling," where vegetables are intentionally underdone because they'll be cooked again by another method.

Boiling or parboiling is handy if you have several different vegetables to cook and each requires a different cooking time; you simply keep the water rolling and work in batches. But because fully boiled vegetables tend to leave both color and nutrients behind in the water, I often boil vegetables only briefly, then shock them (see page 241) and reheat just before serving.

Blanching Vegetables

When you want to make a sharp-tasting vegetable—like garlic, onions, or shallots—milder before further cooking, you can blanch it in a pot of bubbling—not fully boiling—liquid for a few minutes. (For a specific example, see Creamed Onions, page 330.) Water is the simplest, though you can also use milk, wine, beer, or juice. The idea isn't to make them soft, just to cook them long enough to take the bite out. Three to five minutes will do. It's worth noting that the same technique, with the time reduced to 30 seconds or less, makes almost all fruits and vegetables—from garlic to tomatoes to peaches—easy to peel.

Sautéing Vegetables

I wish there were another word for this technique, since it sounds much more intimidating than it is: nothing more than cooking food quickly in hot fat. (Stir-frying is a subset of sautéing.) Start with a deep, broad skillet, set it over medium to medium-high heat, and add some oil or butter—about 1 or 2 tablespoons per pound (more if you like). When the oil or butter gets hot, stir or toss the vegetables around in the pan until they're cooked, seasoning as needed. (For a specific example, see Sautéed Mushrooms, page 314.)

The only downside is that sautéing raw vegetables takes a little practice to keep them from burning before they're cooked through; you must check them frequently. A good alternative is to use the basic techniques of parboiling and shocking (page 241), then proceed to Precooked Vegetables in Butter or Oil (page 240). This combination is an excellent one.

Braising Vegetables

A combination of sautéing and simmering, braising allows you to cook vegetables until they're fully tender and take advantage of all their flavor. Root vegetables, cabbages, sturdy winter greens, and alliums (garlic, shallots, leeks, and onions) are all good candidates for braising because they benefit from the extra time. (For a specific example, see Braised Potatoes, Nine Ways, page 346.)

Begin by sautéing as just described. After the vegetables have been softened a little and coated in hot oil, add enough liquid—stock, milk, juice, wine, or water—to come about halfway up the vegetables. Bring to a boil, then lower the heat so the mixture bubbles gently or put the pot in a moderate oven. You can cover the vegetables during braising or leave them uncovered, adding more liquid as needed to keep everything from drying out.

Braising and Glazing Vegetables

This valuable technique is less straightforward than the others, but you can master it easily. The idea is to combine the benefits of steaming—speed and moisture—with the power of sautéing, caramelization, and crispness, all in one pot. As an added benefit, when you braise and glaze vegetables, their nutrients don't get left behind in a pot of water. (For a specific example, see Braised and Glazed Brussels Sprouts on page 272.)

Here's how it works: Put some oil or butter in a deep skillet and turn the heat to medium. Sauté some garlic, onion, shallot, and/or ginger if you like—just for 30 seconds or so—then add your vegetable (like carrots, broccoli, cauliflower, asparagus, or any root vegetable, sliced or chopped as you will) with a little water and a sprinkle of salt. The longer the vegetables need to cook, the more water you'll need, but generally just $1/4$ to $1/2$ cup will do.

Now cover the pan. Cook, uncovering only often enough to stir and check the water level, until the vegetables are just tender, 5 to 15 minutes, depending on the vegetable and how large the pieces are. The goal is to keep just enough water in the pan to steam the vegetables until they're cooked without letting the pan go dry. To glaze, uncover and raise the heat to cook out virtually all of the remaining water; the combination of the fat and the starches and sugars from the vegetables will create a glossy coating.

Frying Vegetables

Messy, with a lot of added fat, but a favorite. When it comes to frying vegetables, you've got a few choices, starting with the decision to coat or not coat (see Pan-Fried Eggplant on page 244, and Battered and Fried Vegetables, Three Ways, on page 245). Whether you coat the vegetables or not, you can either panfry them in shallow oil ($1/2$ inch deep or so) or deep-fry in enough oil to submerge them (2 or 3 inches of oil in a deep pot).

To panfry: Set a deep skillet over medium to medium-high heat and pour in the oil. It should be hot but not smoking before you add the vegetables (test a small piece first; the vegetable should immediately sizzle vigorously).

To deep-fry: The oil should reach a temperature between 350°F and 375°F. (See "Deep Frying," page 26, and Battered and Fried Vegetables, Three Ways, page 245.) Be careful to allow enough room at the top of the pot for the vegetables to displace the oil and cause it to rise. And be careful not to overload the pot or the vegetables will become soggy.

Roasting Vegetables

The dry heat of roasting in a relatively hot oven intensifies the flavor of vegetables by driving out their internal water. The results range from slightly chewy to completely tender on the inside to crisped on the outside, with good color and nutrition. Roasting is a great method for entertaining, because the results can be served right out of the oven or at room temperature. (For a specific example, see Winter Squash Slices, Roasted, page 366.)

F Fast   M Make Ahead   V Vegan

In general, tender vegetables roast well at 375°F, and sturdier, slower-cooking vegetables (like potatoes and root vegetables) can cook at 400°F or higher. Cut the vegetables about the same size to promote even roasting, toss them in oil or melted butter (1 to 2 tablespoons per pound of vegetables) then spread them out in a large roasting pan or rimmed baking sheet. Sprinkle with salt and freshly ground black pepper and pop them in the oven.

When the vegetables start to brown and release from the pan, shake the pan or use a spatula to toss them around a bit so they brown on all sides, being careful not to break the pieces apart. Roasting takes a little longer than other cooking methods, anywhere from 15 minutes for asparagus to an hour for potatoes. But it's easy enough to peek in on them every now and then.

Grilling or Broiling Vegetables

This is the ultimate crisp-tender cooking method, ideal for "meaty" large pieces or slices. It might sound obvious but when you expose the surface of vegetables to intense heat, the outsides will cook much faster than the insides. So ideally you get browning (or charring) *and* tenderness, with the added bonus of a smoky flavor. (For a specific example, see Grilled or Broiled Eggplant, page 295.)

Sturdier vegetables—eggplant, onions, mushrooms, squash, corn on the cob, and potatoes—are the most obvious candidates to grill or boil, though tomatoes, green beans, and asparagus work great too. You can thread smaller pieces on skewers or use a grilling basket. Coat everything lightly with a little oil—or a marinade—and grill or broil about 4 inches away from the heat source.

Essential Vegetable Recipes

I can provide you with all the vegetable recipes you could ever handle (and am close to doing that here), but as a veteran home cook I know as well as anyone that the basics are the most important. If you know how to han-

dle a vegetable simply and quickly and make it taste good, you're likely to cook it and eat it more often, and those are the recipes you're going to turn to most.

Here they are: the basics of steaming, boiling, stir-frying, reheating, saucing, and more—the fast, easy, everyday ways to make vegetable dishes a standard part of life.

Boiled or Steamed Greens

MAKES: 4 servings
TIME: 10 to 30 minutes

This is the basic method for cooking any greens (or, as you'll see from the variation, just about any vegetable at all). Boiling gives you a little more control, but steaming is faster; both work just fine. Read "The Basics of Cooking Vegetables" (page 235) for more detail, and see Precooked Vegetables in Oil or Butter (page 240), for the best ways to make this simple preparation more elaborate.

A word about tender greens versus sturdy: If the leaves and stems are pliable and can be eaten raw—as with spinach, arugula, or watercress—it's a tender green. If the stems are as crisp as celery and the leaves a little

It doesn't take a brilliant chef to figure out that a finely chopped carrot cooks more quickly than a whole one. The science behind this phenomenon is simple: cutting vegetables—or any food—creates more surface area, and a higher proportion of surface area to interior means quicker cooking.

So if you're using a fast cooking method, like stir-frying, it makes sense to cut your vegetables into small pieces, like a julienne (see "The Basics of Cutting," page 18). But for a stew or slow braise, large chunks (a rough chop, large dice, or roll cut; see pages 20–21) are ideal so the vegetable cooks slowly with the other ingredients.

When you're mixing vegetables that cook at different times—say carrots and asparagus—you can either stagger the cooking times (add the carrots first) or simply cut the carrot into small or thin enough pieces so that it will have roughly the same cooking time as the asparagus.

tough or rubbery—as in bok choy, chard, kale, or collards—it's best to separate the leaves from the stems (see the illustration on page 308) and give the stems a little head start.

Other vegetables you can use: any greens at all, except sorrel (which will dissolve).

Salt

1 to 2 pounds greens, like spinach, kale, or chard, washed and trimmed

Freshly squeezed lemon juice, extra virgin olive oil, butter, or any of the "13 Ways to Jazz Up Precooked Vegetables" (page 241)

① Prepare a steamer (see page 25) or put a pot of water on to boil and salt it. If the greens have very thick stems (over $^1/_8$ inch or so), separate them from the leaves.

② Add the stems or the stems and leaves to the pot or the steaming vessel and cook until bright green and tender, from 3 minutes (for spinach) to 10 (for kale and collards). (If you held back the leaves, add them when the stems are just about tender.)

③ Drain, then serve, drizzled or topped with whatever you like. Or shock in ice or cold water (page 241), drain again, and set aside.

Boiled or Steamed Tender Vegetables. The only differences are preparation and time; this will work for broccoli, cauliflower, green beans, asparagus, peas of any type, even eggplant (be careful not to overcook): Cook until the vegetable is just tender, which will vary from about 3 minutes (peas) to 7 (broccoli florets) to 10 or 12 (broccoli stems, some green beans) and up to 25 (for a large whole head of cauliflower). Proceed from Step 3.

Boiled or Steamed Root Vegetables or Tubers. Not quite so simple; in many ways it's best to follow individual recipes given in this chapter, especially for potatoes and sweet potatoes. But as a general rule, this will work; use for beets, turnips, radishes, winter squash, and so on: Peel the vegetable or not, as you prefer; leave whole if possible to prevent waterlogging. Cook until the vegetable is quite tender and can be pierced easily with a thin-bladed knife, from 10 minutes (radishes, for example) to nearly an hour (larger potatoes). Proceed from Step 3.

Precooked Vegetables in Butter or Oil

This is the one indispensable vegetable recipe. It won't work for every single vegetable, but it can be used with the vast majority and has very real advantages. It allows you to prepare the vegetable so that it can be taken to the table within 5 minutes, and it can be brought to that point as long as a day or two in advance. This means you can start and finish the vegetable as you're taking other

Ⓕ Fast   Ⓜ Make Ahead   Ⓥ Vegan

With just a little effort, a bowl, and some ice, you can guarantee that many vegetables will be perfectly done and beautifully colored. The technique is called *shocking* because after a brief boil (called *parboiling,* which is basically just preboiling), you shock the vegetables by immediately plunging them in a bath of ice water. The idea is to precook the vegetables just enough to tenderize them, then rapidly stop the cooking by cooling them down.

It works brilliantly for many green vegetables, like asparagus and green beans, and also for carrots, cauliflower, turnips, and many others.

Shocking is a great method when you're cooking vegetables for a crowd, leaving only a quick warming in butter or oil for the last minute (see "Precooked Vegetables in Butter or Oil," page 240). It's also the best way to prepare multiple vegetables of differing cooking times for stir-fries, salads, or other dishes where some lingering crispness is desirable. And shocking cooked greens—spinach, kale, escarole, and the like—gives you both great color and the opportunity to squeeze out extra moisture.

Here's how it works: Bring a large pot of water to a rolling boil and salt it well. Set up a large bowl of water with lots of ice cubes. Drop the vegetable into the boiling water. After about 30 seconds (shorter for spinach, longer

for most other things; of course the size of your pieces will affect matters greatly), start testing—you can poke with a thin-bladed knife or taste; you're looking for the vegetable to be almost done, nearly tender, but not quite. When that happens, immediately fish the vegetables out with a large strainer, tongs, or a slotted spoon and put them in the bowl of ice water for a minute or two. When they've cooled down, remove from the ice bath and drain in a colander.

Squeeze drained greens tightly to remove as much water as possible, then chop, slice, or cook according to the recipe. Work in batches if you're shocking more than one type of vegetable, simply moving them through the process until you're done; there's no need to change the water. (If you're doing a lot of vegetables, the cooking water effectively becomes stock.)

You can store shocked and drained vegetables—covered tightly and refrigerated—for up to a day before proceeding. Or use them immediately.

You can save a bit of work by shocking small amounts of boiled vegetables under or in a bowl of cold tap water, which will slow (but not dramatically halt) cooking. This works best, of course, if your tap water is really cold, which is not always the case.

dishes to the table or just before. It's also useful with leftover simmered or steamed vegetables (first rinse them with boiling water to remove any prior seasoning if necessary).

① Trim, wash, peel, or otherwise prepare the vegetable for cooking.

② Steam or boil it as detailed in Boiled or Steamed Greens and variations (page 239), just until tender.

③ Drain it, then shock it as described above. Drain it again.

④ Set aside or cover and refrigerate for a day or two.

When you want to eat:

⑤ Put a tablespoon or two of butter or olive oil (enough to cover the bottom) in a skillet over medium heat. When the butter is melted or the oil is hot, add the vegetables, raise the heat to medium-high, and cook, stirring, until hot, just a couple of minutes. Season and serve.

13 Ways to Jazz Up Precooked Vegetables

Saucing, of course, is an excellent way to give a boost to your vegetables; browse through the sauces and condiments chapter for dozens of ideas. But for something quick or not so obvious, try one of these ideas:

1. Freshly squeezed lemon or lime juice
2. Chopped herbs
3. Grated citrus zest
4. Chopped nuts
5. Toasted bread crumbs
6. Nut or seed oil, like sesame, walnut, hazelnut, or pumpkin seed oil
7. Any Croutons (page 806)
8. Chopped Hard-Cooked Egg (page 166)
9. Crunchy Crumbled Tempeh (page 674), Tofu Croutons (page 656), or any of the crumbles on page 805
10. Vinaigrette (pages 762–763)
11. Compound Butter (page 801)
12. Any flavored oil (pages 756–758)
13. Spice blends—especially Za'atar (page 818), Citrus Sprinkle (page 818), chaat masala (to make your own, see page 814), Japanese Seven-Spice Mix (page 818), and Nori "Shake" (page 817)

The Basics of Stir-Frying Vegetables

Stir-frying is one of the best, easiest, and fastest ways to get an entire meal on the table. You can stir-fry just about any vegetable and most other things as well (see, for example, Stir-Fried Tofu with Scallions, page 645). The procedure is this: You chop your ingredients into more-or-less bite-sized pieces. You start rice, if you want it, and set the table, because the stir-frying itself is usually the last thing you do. In the last ten minutes or so before you eat, you stir-fry. During those ten minutes, you'll be as busy as a chef, but up to that point it's all completely relaxed and can happen at whatever pace you like.

You'll find more detail on stir-frying on page 646, but for a short or refresher course, here are the basics:

1. Remember that the smaller you cut your pieces, the faster they will cook and, to some extent, the more flavor you will get (more browning on more surfaces equal more flavor, up to a point).

2. You can add all the ingredients you like—there are many options, as you can see from the lists on pages 243 and 244—but too many slow you down and muddy the flavor.

3. Use a flat-bottomed skillet—better than a wok for home-cooked stir-fries—the larger the better. Nonstick or well-seasoned cast-iron is best, and high heat is essential.

4. Don't stir too much; you need to encourage browning, and if you move things around they won't brown at all. (True stir-frying can take place only over the kind of heat you can't produce on a home stove.)

5. You may need to parboil and shock those vegetables that won't become tender through direct stir-frying, even if you cut them small: broccoli stems, thick asparagus, and turnips are good examples. If you don't have time for that, cut them small and stir-fry them first. (For the most control this way, remove them from the pan when they're almost done, cook the other vegetables, and return the first batch to the mix for final warming.)

6. You need a little liquid in stir-fries. That liquid can be water or something with more flavor. Add a little with the vegetables to encourage them to cook more quickly and a little at the end, if necessary, to keep the soy sauce from burning.

Stir-Fried Vegetables

MAKES: 4 servings
TIME: 15 minutes

Ⓕ Ⓥ

Stir-fries are quick, easy, and a fantastic way to use those single carrots, celery stalks, and handful of other vegeta-

Ⓕ Fast   Ⓜ Make Ahead   Ⓥ Vegan

bles sitting in your fridge. One key to a fast stir-fry is the size in which you cut your vegetables: The smaller you cut them, the quicker they will cook.

2 tablespoons neutral oil, like grapeseed or corn

1 tablespoon minced garlic

1 tablespoon peeled and minced fresh ginger

1/2 cup chopped scallion or onion

1 large carrot, cut into pieces, sliced, or julienned

2 stalks celery, cut into pieces, sliced, or julienned

1 pound snow or snap peas, trimmed (defrosted frozen are fine)

1/4 cup any stock or water, or a little more

2 tablespoons soy sauce

1 teaspoon dark sesame oil

1 Heat a large, deep skillet over medium-high heat for 3 or 4 minutes. Add the oil and, almost immediately, the garlic, ginger, and scallion. Cook, stirring, for about 15 seconds, then add the carrot, celery, snow peas, and stock and raise the heat to high.

2 Cook, stirring constantly, until the vegetables are tender, about 7 minutes. If the mixture is completely dry, add a couple tablespoons more liquid, then the soy sauce and sesame oil; stir and turn off the heat. Serve or store, covered, in the refrigerator for up to a day.

18 Additions to Stir-Fried Vegetables

Generally, you can add about 1 to 2 cups of any vegetable, total, to the basic stir-fry. If you keep the scallion, carrot, and celery in the basic recipe, you can substitute for the snow or snap peas or reduce that amount and compensate with any of the following. Or you can build a bigger stir-fry by using one or more of these in combination with the vegetables in the basic recipe; all you'll need to do is add a bit more liquid.

1. Bamboo shoots, added at the last minute
2. Water chestnuts, added at the last minute
3. Tofu, squeezed or fried and cubed (but see Stir-Fried Tofu with Scallions, page 645), added with about 2 minutes cooking to go
4. Tofu skin, frozen or dried and reconstituted (page 640), added with about 2 minutes cooking to go
5. Green beans, preferably parboiled and shocked (see page 241), added with the peas
6. Spinach, trimmed, added with about a minute to go
7. Watercress, trimmed, added at the last minute
8. Leeks, trimmed, washed, and chopped, instead of the scallion or onion but in greater quantity if you like
9. Mushrooms, fresh or dried and reconstituted (Chinese black mushrooms, a form of shiitake, are especially good), trimmed and sliced or chopped, added with the peas
10. Daikon, trimmed and julienned or shredded, added with about a minute to go
11. Corn kernels, added with about a minute to go
12. Cabbage or bok choy, trimmed and shredded, added with the onion
13. Asparagus, blanched (see page 237), added with the peas
14. Zucchini or summer squash, cut into slices or chunks, added with the onion
15. Any color bell pepper, cored, seeded, and sliced, added with the onion
16. Soy or mung bean sprouts, added at the last minute
17. Broccoli or cauliflower, blanched (see page 237), added with the peas
18. 1 medium to large tomato, halved and seeded (see page 373), then chopped, added with the scallions

7 Seasonings or Crunchy Bits to Add to Stir-Fried Vegetables

Add the following in quantities to taste. You'll want more nuts—up to a cup—than black beans (just a couple tablespoons), but the quantity of any of these can be adjusted in any direction you like.

1. Walnuts, peanuts, or cashews, stirred in during the last minute of cooking (you can precook the nuts earlier to brown if you like, but be careful not to burn them)
2. Fermented black beans, about 2 tablespoons, soaked for about 10 minutes in $^1/_4$ cup of Shaoxing wine, sherry, or water and added with about a minute to go
3. Dried chiles, as many as you like, left whole, or 1 or 2 small fresh chiles, stemmed, seeded, and minced, added at the beginning of cooking
4. $^1/_2$ cup (or to taste) Crunchy Crumbled Tempeh (page 674), added with the soy sauce
5. 1 tablespoon (or to taste) any Chile Paste (page 829), or hoisin sauce, added along with the soy sauce
6. 1 tablespoon sugar (or to taste), honey, or other sweetener, along with the stock or water
7. Tofu Croutons (page 656), added with the soy sauce

Panfried Eggplant (or Any Other Vegetable)

MAKES: 4 servings

TIME: 1 hour

This is the model for frying vegetables so they're crunchy and tender, like the zucchini sticks you get in chain restaurants, only better. Eggplant produces a very substantial "cutlet" when handled this way, but so do many of the other vegetables in the chart on page 246. And the variety of toppings and dipping sauces you can use is huge, though I always seem to come back to lemon juice, maybe with a little hot sauce.

Like deep-fried food, panfried vegetables are at their crispest immediately after cooking. When done, drain the pieces briefly on paper towels and serve. If you must hold fried vegetables for a bit—no longer than 10 or 15 minutes please—drain them briefly, then immediately transfer them to a warm oven as directed. A wire rack set over a rimmed baking pan is ideal, but any ovenproof platter will work.

4 or 5 small or 2 large eggplant, about 2 pounds total, trimmed

Salt

1 cup all-purpose flour for dredging

3 cups plain bread crumbs for dredging

3 eggs, beaten

Freshly ground black pepper

3 tablespoons butter plus 3 tablespoons olive oil, or all oil or all clarified butter, plus more as needed

Chopped parsley leaves for garnish

Lemon wedges

1 Cut the eggplant into $^1/_2$-inch-thick slices; salt them (see page 46) if large and time allows. Preheat the oven to 200°F. Set out the flour, bread crumbs, and beaten eggs on plates or shallow bowls next to each other on your counter and have a stack of parchment or wax paper ready. Season the eggs liberally with salt and pepper.

2 Rinse and dry the eggplant. Dredge the slices, one at a time, in the flour, then dip in the egg, then dredge in the bread crumbs. Stack the breaded cutlets between layers of wax paper and then transfer the stack to chill in the refrigerator for at least 10 minutes and up to 3 hours.

3 Put the oil and/or butter in a deep pan on the stove and turn the heat to medium-high; when the oil is ready—about 350°F—a pinch of flour will sizzle in it. Put in a few of the eggplant slices; cook in batches as necessary, being sure not to crowd the pan, adding additional oil to the pan as necessary.

F Fast   M Make Ahead   V Vegan

④ Turn the eggplant slices as soon as they're browned, then cook the other side. The total cooking time should be 5 minutes or less. As each piece is done, transfer it first to paper towels to drain briefly, then to an ovenproof platter, and transfer the platter to the oven.

⑤ Serve as soon as all the pieces are cooked, garnished with the parsley, with the lemon wedges on the side.

Celery Root "Schnitzel." The history of vegetarianism in central Europe led to the mainstreaming of this dish, which is terrific: Substitute celery root (or potato, beet, or rutabaga) for the eggplant, cutting it into $1/4$-inch-thick slices and cooking for about 10 minutes total. Proceed with the recipe.

Sesame-Fried Eggplant. An Asian-style variation that's great with any soy-based dipping sauce (pages 777–780): Use 2 cups of bread crumbs and 1 cup of sesame seeds for the final dredging. Replace some of the oil or butter (2 to 3 tablespoons) with sesame oil.

Coconut-Fried Plantains. A totally tropical appetizer, side dish, or dessert: Substitute 4 or 5 yellow to yellow-black plantains for the eggplant; peel and cut straight or diagonal into about $1/4$-inch-thick slices. Use $1^1/2$ cups bread crumbs and $1^1/2$ cups shredded coconut for the final dredging.

Grain-Fried Butternut Squash. Replacing part or all of the bread crumbs with ground grains adds a nutty flavor: Substitute about 2 pounds peeled and sliced butternut squash for the eggplant. Use 3 cups ground oats or barley instead of the bread crumbs for the final dredging.

Fried Onion Rings, Streamlined. A simple coating of flour makes for a slightly less crunchy and really simple onion ring; these make a fantastic garnish too: Substitute 2 thinly sliced onions for the eggplant. Omit the bread crumbs and eggs; dredge the onion rings in just flour and fry until golden brown.

3 Ways to Vary Any Fried Vegetable

1. Change the breading: For the bread crumbs, try using panko crumbs, shredded coconut, finely chopped nuts or seeds, or pulverized raw whole grains, like rice, rolled oats or barley, or kasha (pulse in the food processor to grind any of these); or grated Parmesan (mixed with bread crumbs).

2. Streamline the process: Omit the eggs and bread crumbs and simply dredge the vegetables in flour before frying. Note that this works best for vegetables with a decent amount of moisture for the flour to stick to; hard vegetables like carrots or winter squash won't have the same flour coating as onions or zucchini.

3. Make Vegan Fried Vegetables: Instead of the egg, use soy, grain, or nut milk. For frying, always use all oil.

Battered and Fried Vegetables, Three Ways

MAKES: 4 servings
TIME: 30 minutes

Ⓕ

There are infinite ways to batter and deep-fry vegetables, but these are my favorites, three easy batters that share the same technique and can be used on nearly any vegetable. Their accompanying sauces can be anything from a squeeze of lemon or lime juice to a soy sauce dip to a chutney (see 25 Dipping Sauces for Battered and Fried Vegetables, page 249).

The Batters

The European-style batter is most frequently found in Italy and Spain and feels even more Mediterranean when you serve it with Garlic Mayonnaise (Aïoli), page 771. Use an assortment of vegetables and you've got yourself a wonderful *fritto misto* (Italian for "fried mix") to serve as

BREADING AND FRYING OTHER VEGETABLES

Here's a primer on the best vegetables to bread and fry. You can panfry or deep-fry (page 238) most vegetables; the exceptions are noted. A squeeze of lemon or lime juice is always nice on breaded and fried vegetables, and a sprinkle of salt and pepper is a must. Season the food immediately after removing it from the oil; otherwise the seasoning won't stick. Use salt, pepper, cayenne, or any spice mixture (pages 810–819).

Note that the sauce suggestions are exactly that: suggestions. Serve any fried vegetables with any sauce you like.

VEGETABLE	PREPARATION	HOW TO FRY	SUGGESTED ACCOMPANIMENTS
Artichoke Hearts	Parcook until tender; remove leaves and choke and trim base (see page 258); cut in half or leave whole (depending on size); dredge as directed.	Deep frying at about 350°F is best for even browning; cook until the breading is golden brown since the vegetable is already cooked.	Garlic Mayonnaise (Aïoli) (page 771); Cold Mustard Sauce (page 771); Spicy Yogurt Sauce (page 774)
Bananas and Plantains	Use yellow to yellow-black plantains; peel and cut into bite-sized chunks or diagonal slices for plantains; add shredded coconut to bread crumbs if you like.	Frying at lower heat (about 350°F) will cook the fruit more, resulting in a gooier interior, while frying at a higher heat (375°F) will just brown the breading, leaving the fruit more raw.	Sweet or savory is equally good: Coconut Chutney (page 784); Crunchy Nut Chutney (page 784); Sweet Yogurt Sauce (page 774): Cooked Tomatillo Salsa (page 788); Southern-Style Peanut Sauce (page 796)
Carrots and Parsnips	Peel and cut into bite-sized chunks or 1/4-inch-thick sticks; parcook thick chunks until tender; dredge as directed.	Fry at about 350°F until golden brown on both sides, about 5 minutes total.	Peanut Sauce, Six Ways (page 794); Tahini Sauce (page 796); Dill Purée (page 769); Cilantro-Mint Chutney (page 783)
Celery Root	Peel and cut into 1/4-inch-thick slices; dredge as directed.	Fry at about 350°F until golden brown on both sides, about 5 minutes total.	Parsley "Pesto" or Parsley Purée (page 768); Smooth Green Chile Sauce, Indian Style (page 792)
Fennel	Trim and cut crosswise into 1/4-inch-thick slices; dredge as directed.	Fry at about 350°F until golden brown on both sides, about 5 minutes total.	Mint or Dill "Pesto" (page 768); Herbed Yogurt Sauce (page 774)
Mushrooms	Small whole button, cremini, and shiitake caps work best; clean and trim; dredge as directed.	Deep frying at about 350°F is best for even browning; cook until the breading is golden brown (the interior cooks quickly).	Seaweed "Mayo" (page 773); Basil Dipping Sauce (page 777); Simple Miso Dipping Sauce (page 781)
Onions	Trim the onions and cut crosswise into 1/2-inch-thick slices; separate the slices into rings; dredge in flour, egg, and bread crumbs or just flour as directed.	Deep frying is certainly more efficient for onion rings, but panfrying small quantities is fine. Thinner slices cook more quickly of course; fry at about 375°F until golden brown, about 3 minutes total.	Fast, Down-Home Barbecue Sauce (page 789); Chipotle-Cherry Salsa (page 752); Blue Cheese Dressing (page 212)

 Fast   Make Ahead   Ⓥ Vegan

VEGETABLE	PREPARATION	HOW TO FRY	SUGGESTED ACCOMPANIMENTS
Potatoes	Peeling is optional; cut lengthwise into wedges (no more than $1/2$ inch at thickest part) or into $1/4$-inch-thick slices; dredge as directed.	Fry at about 350°F so the potato has time to cook before the exterior gets too dark; flip the pieces when one side is golden brown, about 8 minutes total.	Ketchup (to make your own, see page 790); Roasted Pepper Mayonnaise (page 771); Simple Miso Soy Dipping Sauce (page 781); Spicy Indian Tomato Sauce (page 793)
Squash Blossoms	Leave whole; dredge as directed.	These need very little cooking, so fry at high heat—375°F—just enough to get the exterior golden brown, about 4 minutes total.	Chile Pico de Verde (page 751); Avocado Yogurt Sauce (page 774)
Sweet Potatoes and Yams	Peeling is optional; cut lengthwise into wedges (no more than $1/2$ inch at thickest part) or into $1/4$-inch-thick slices; dredge as directed.	Fry at about 350°F so the potato has time to cook before the exterior gets too dark; flip the pieces when one side is golden brown, about 8 minutes total.	Jamaican Jerk Ketchup (page 790); Ponzu Sauce (page 780); Black Bean Ketchup (page 791)
Tomatoes	Green and not-quite-ripe tomatoes are best; cut into $1/4$- to $1/2$-inch-thick slices; dredge as directed.	Shallow-frying is best — especially for red tomatoes—as the pan provides "support" for the tomato slices; flip the slices when one side is golden brown, about 5 minutes total.	Fresh Tomato Salsa (page 750); Lighter Cilantro (or Other Herb) "Pesto" (page 769)
Tropical Tubers	Peeling is optional; cut lengthwise into wedges (no more than $1/2$ inch at thickest part) or into $1/4$-inch-thick slices; dredge as directed.	Fry at about 350°F so the tubers have time to cook before the exterior gets too dark; flip the pieces when one side is golden brown, about 8 minutes total.	Salsa Roja (page 787); Green Olive Mojo (page 769); Nutty Miso Sauce (page 782)
Winter Squash	Peel and cut into $1/4$-inch-thick slices; dredge as directed.	Fry at about 350°F so the potato has time to cook before the exterior gets too dark; flip the pieces when one side is golden brown, about 8 minutes total.	Traditional Pesto (page 768); Curry Ranch Dressing (page 772)
Zucchini and Yellow Squash	Cut into bite-sized chunks or diagonal slices; dredge as directed.	Fry at about 375°F until golden brown on both sides (the interior cooks quickly), about 5 minutes total.	Salsa Cruda (page 751); Real Ranch Dressing (page 772); Chile-Yogurt Sauce (page 793)

an appetizer or part of a meal. If you don't want to cook with beer—but still want the light and fluffy results—try the sparkling water option.

Tempura, which is Japanese, is nearly foolproof and creates a coating that's light and crisp. Combined with vegetables and a soy-based dipping sauce, it's a delight. Be sure to use ice-cold water for the lightest batter; warm batter will absorb more oil and become soggy. To chill the water properly, combine 2 cups water and 2 cups ice just before you're ready to cook; let sit for a minute, then measure the water from this, straining out the ice cubes.

The Indian-style batter is as simple as you can get. The chickpea flour is starchy enough that it needs no egg, and the flavor is nutty and delicious. Serve it with almost any chutney and it will be a hit.

The Vegetables

As with all deep-fried foods, hard vegetables should be thinly sliced, $1/4$ inch thick or less; tender ones, like zucchini and eggplant, can be cut thicker, up to $1/2$ inch or so. Items like mushrooms and green beans can be left whole.

Nearly any vegetable can be battered and fried, but especially zucchini, eggplant, winter squash, sweet potatoes, mushrooms, bell pepper, green beans, broccoli, cauliflower, asparagus tips, onion rings, fennel, beets, or carrots.

The Technique

As is almost always the case with deep frying, these vegetables must be cooked in batches to avoid overcrowding the pot (see "Deep Frying," page 26). You want the pieces to be able to swim around in the oil a bit and not stick together. Generally, you want a neutral oil, like grapeseed or corn oil, but olive oil is not out of place for a *fritto misto*.

Usually the best way to serve battered and fried vegetables is as a casual kitchen appetizer, the moment the morsels come out of the oil and are drained. But if you want to serve them as part of a sit-down meal, keep them warm for a few minutes in a low oven (ideally on a rack). Tempura is the most fragile and with even just a

couple minutes in the oven will lose some of its light crispness.

Neutral oil, like grapeseed or corn, for deep frying

Batter, European Style

1 cup all-purpose flour, plus 1 cup for dredging

1 teaspoon baking powder

1 teaspoon salt

Freshly ground black pepper

1 egg

$3/4$ cup beer or sparkling water

Coarse salt for finishing

Batter, Japanese Style (Tempura)

3 egg yolks

$1 1/2$ cups all-purpose flour or rice all-purpose flour, plus 1 cup for dredging

2 cups ice-cold water

Batter, Indian Style (Pakora)

$1/4$ cup chickpea all-purpose flour, ground masoor or channa dal (page 577), or cornmeal, plus 1 cup for dredging

$3/4$ to 1 cup water

Pinch cayenne (optional)

Salt and freshly ground black pepper

1 Put at least 2 inches oil in a countertop deep-fryer or in a deep pan on the stove and turn the heat to medium-high; bring to 350°F (see "Deep Frying," page 26). While the oil is heating, prepare the vegetables and the dipping sauce.

2 Mix the batter ingredients until just combined; it's okay to leave some lumps (you don't want to overmix). The European-style batter should be the consistency of pancake batter; the Japanese- and Indian-style batters should be quite thin.

③ Dredge each piece of food lightly in the remaining flour, then dip into the batter and add to the oil. Do not crowd the vegetables; you will have to cook in batches. Cook, turning once if needed, until golden all over, just a few minutes. Drain on a rack or paper towels and serve immediately, with the dipping sauce or lemon wedges.

Battered Apple "Fries." Make these with European-style beer batter for a savory version, or with sparkling water and a sprinkle of confectioners' sugar for a sweet version: Use 2 or 3 apples, like Golden Delicious, Granny Smith, or any all-purpose apple (see page 418). Peel the apple if you like. Cut the apples "lengthwise" (from stem end to flower end) into roughly $1/4$-inch-thick slices, then cut the slices into sticks (resembling fries).

Beer-Battered Squash Blossoms. A summertime treat, these large, tender flowers are lovely battered and fried; use European-style batter: Use 12 to 16 (or more) whole squash blossoms.

Eggless Vegetable Tempura. The sparkling water adds airiness to this two-ingredient batter; use rice flour if you prefer: Start with the Japanese-style recipe. Omit the egg yolks and substitute well-chilled sparkling water for the ice water.

25 Dipping Sauces for Battered and Fried Vegetables

There are dozens of sauces that go great with any of these three batters, but here are some that really stand out.

With the European-Style Batter:

1. Garlic Mayonnaise (Aïoli) (page 771)
2. Chilean Salsa (page 750)
3. Salsa Cruda (page 751)
4. Green Tomato Pico de Verde (page 751)
5. Traditional Pesto (page 768)
6. Cilantro, Dill, Basil, or Mint Purée (page 769)
7. Real Ranch Dressing (page 772)
8. Salsa Sofrito (page 788)

With the Japanese-Style Batter:

1. Dashi Dipping Sauce (page 780)
2. Basil Dipping Sauce (page 777)
3. Soy and Sesame Dipping Sauce and Marinade, Korean Style (page 778)
4. Ponzu Sauce (page 780)
5. Simple Miso Dipping Sauce (page 781)
6. Cilantro "Pesto" with Ginger and Chile (page 770)
7. Mayonnaise (to make your own, see page 771) with wasabi
8. A mixture of soy sauce and rice vinegar

With the Indian-Style Batter:

1. Cilantro-Mint Chutney (page 783)
2. Pineapple Chutney (page 785)
3. Tomato Chutney (page 785)
4. Curry Ranch Dressing (page 772)
5. The Simplest Yogurt Sauce (page 774)
6. Raita (page 774)
7. Ginger Yogurt Sauce (page 774)
8. Smooth Green Chile Sauce, Indian Style (page 792)
9. Spicy Indian Tomato Sauce (page 793)

How to Grill Vegetables

Grilled vegetables are quick, effortless, and delicious. And, since almost all vegetables can be grilled, there are plenty of options.

You can serve grilled vegetables—hot or at room temperature—with almost anything: grain dishes, burgers baked, grilled, or broiled tofu, or more simply with cheese, a green salad or almost any soup, sprinkled with chopped fresh herbs, or drizzled with extra virgin olive oil or a flavored oil (see page 758). Assemble small grilled vegetable skewers for an appetizer and serve with a dipping sauce or make larger skewers for a buffet.

Grilling Tips

Here are a few pointers to perfect your vegetable and fruit grilling technique.

- To prevent sticking, use 2 to 3 tablespoons of oil per pound of vegetables.
- Cut your vegetable or fruit into large pieces so they won't fall between the grill grates. More fragile foods, like peaches or radicchio, are best cut into halves or quarters. For many items, like potatoes, squash, eggplant, or apples, slices are fine; they should be between $1/4$ and $1/2$ inch thick (lengthwise or on a diagonal for smaller items like zucchini). Generally, you want slices thin enough to cook through without burning on the outside but thick enough not to slip through the grill. Skewer or use a grilling basket for very small foods.
- Soak wood skewers in water before using to keep them from burning. (If you can get it, use a rosemary branch as a skewer; it will flavor the items nicely, and as long as it's fresh, no soaking is necessary.)
- Use a clean grill; your vegetables and fruit will be less likely to stick.
- For the most part, use direct heat; you generally don't want too hot a fire or the fruit or vegetables will char. Use indirect heat for large or dense items like a whole sweet potato or winter squash; this allows the interior to cook without drying out too much or the exterior charring. Until you get the hang of grilling, watch them and move them to a cooler part of the grill if necessary.
- If you're grilling a variety of vegetables, be sure to start with the ones that take the longest to cook and add them incrementally, saving the quickest-cooking ones for last. Because grilled vegetables are also great at room temperature, it's okay to pull them off as they are done while the rest catch up.
- Apply barbecue or other sweet sauce or coating toward the end of cooking so it has time to glaze but not burn.

25 Dishes in Which to Use Grilled Vegetables

Here are recipes to which you can add grilled veggies or in which you can grill the vegetables instead of using the cooking method called for.

1. Stir-Fried Tofu with Scallions (page 645)
2. Smoky Scrambled Tofu with Onions (page 655)
3. Barley "Succotash," (page 541)
4. Polenta "Pizza" (page 547)
5. Kasha with Radicchio or Escarole (page 563)
6. Summer Vegetable Stew with Wheat Berries (page 564)
7. Braised Lentils with Roasted Winter Squash (page 598)
8. Flageolets with Fennel (page 605)
9. Simplest Omelet (page 171)
10. Pasta Frittata (page 184)
11. Squash Enchiladas (page 224)
12. Sweet Potato Enchiladas (page 224)
13. Beet and Avocado Salad (page 66)
14. Eggplant Salad with Miso and Tofu (page 64)
15. Ratatouille Salad (page 64)
16. Roasted Onion Salad (page 65)
17. Corn Salad (page 60)
18. Potato Salad (page 68)
19. Broiled Three-Bean Salad (page 74)
20. Fava Bean and Mint Salad with Asparagus (page 77)
21. Crouton Salad (page 87)
22. Couscous Salad with Fennel and Raisins (page 92)
23. Caramelized Onion Chutney (page 786)
24. Tomato Chutney (page 785)
25. Any cooked tomato sauce (pages 448–449)

 Fast   Make Ahead   Ⓥ Vegan

GRILLING EVERYDAY VEGETABLES

VEGETABLE	PREPARATION	FLAVORING IDEAS	HOW TO GRILL	HOW TO SAUCE OR SEASON	SERVING SUGGESTIONS
Artichokes	Use whole (halved and chokes removed), baby, or hearts (see page 257); parboil in salted water until just tender and shock (see page 241); skewer baby and hearts; brush with oil.	Use flavored oil (pages 755–758) or sprinkle with Citrus Sprinkle (page 818). Or after shocking, marinate in any vinaigrette for at least an hour; pat dry before grilling.	Cook over direct heat, turning occasionally, until browned and tender when pierced with a skewer or knife tip, about 10 minutes.	Garlic (or any other flavored) Mayonnaise (page 771) for dipping, or top with Traditional Pesto (page 768) (or any other; pages 768–770).	Serve with Simple Risotto (page 517) or Kidney Beans with Apples and Sherry (page 786).
Asparagus	Trim (see page 261) and leave whole; brush or toss with oil.	Use Herb- or Aromatic-Flavored Oil (page 758), coat with Sweet Miso Glaze (page 782), or sprinkle with Citrus Sprinkle (page 818).	Cook over direct heat, turning occasionally, just until the thick part of the stalks can be pierced with a skewer or knife tip, 6 to 12 minutes, depending on thickness.	Top with Compound Butter (page 801) or sprinkle with Citrus Sprinkle (page 818).	Serve with Parsley and Herb Salad (page 42) or Tofu, Provençal Style (page 649).
Avocado	Peel and slice; brush with lemon or lime juice; oil is optional.	Marinate in any vinaigrette for a few minutes; pat dry before grilling.	Cook over direct heat, turning occasionally, until lightly browned on both sides, about 5 minutes.	Top with Citrus Salsa (page 752) or Miso Carrot Sauce with Ginger (page 781).	Serve with Espresso Black Bean Chili (page 608).
Broccoli or Cauliflower	Trim (page 270) and leave whole or cut into large florets; brush with extra virgin olive oil for Mediterranean dishes, sesame or neutral oil for Asian.	Sprinkle with salt and pepper.	Cook over direct heat, turning occasionally, until lightly browned on all sides, then move to indirect heat until just tender, no more than 10 minutes total.	Top with grated Parmesan cheese, or soy sauce; or serve at room temperature with a vinaigrette for dipping.	Use in pasta, noodle, or rice dishes; or to toss with salad. Serve as a simple vegetable side dish.
Chayote	Peel and remove the pit, then halve, quarter, cut into thick slices, or cube and skewer; brush with oil.	Sprinkle with chili powder (to make your own, see page 814) or Jerk Seasoning (page 818) or coat with Sweet Miso Glaze (page 782).	Cook over direct heat, turning occasionally, until browned and tender when pierced with a skewer or knife tip, 10 to 15 minutes.	Top with Smooth Green Chile Sauce, Indian Style (page 792).	Serve with Mexican Rice with Vegetables (page 512), Baked Pinto Beans Enchilada Style (page 621), or use to fill tacos or burritos.

VEGETABLE	PREPARATION	FLAVORING IDEAS	HOW TO GRILL	HOW TO SAUCE OR SEASON	SERVING SUGGESTIONS
Chestnuts	Score the flat side with a sharp knife, making an X (page 287).		Cook over direct heat with the cover down, turning occasionally, until you can remove the shells easily, about 15 minutes. After cooking, remove both outer shell and inner skin.	Top with any Compound Butter (page 801) or sprinkle with five-spice powder, curry powder, or garam masala (to make your own, see page 815).	Eat warm, out of hand, or sauté with Brussels sprouts or some cream or butter or mash with mashed potatoes.
Chiles and Peppers	Core and seed; halve or cut into squares and skewer; oil is optional.	Stuff whole chiles before grilling: Cut a slit down one side and remove the core and seeds but leave the stem intact if you can. Fill cavity with cheese, cooked grains or legumes, or a combination.	Cook over direct heat, turning occasionally, until the skin is blistered, dark brown, and tender, 10 to 15 minutes.	Top with Mint or Dill "Pesto" (page 769), The Simplest (or nearly any) Yogurt Sauce (page 774), or Creamy Cilantro-Mint Chutney (page 783).	Serve with Tabbouleh (page 43), Stewed Fava Beans with Tahini (page 604), or Baked Brazilian Black Beans (page 619).
Corn	Remove silks; keep in husks or remove them; oil is optional when husks are removed.	Use any flavored oil (pages 756–758) or sesame oil or coat with Sweet Miso Glaze (page 782) or sprinkle with chili powder (to make your own, see page 814) or Jerk Seasoning (page 818).	Cook over direct heat, turning occasionally, until some of the kernels char a bit and others are lightly browned, 15 to 20 minutes with husks on; less than half that with husks off.	Top with nearly any Compound Butter (page 801), or Ginger-Scallion Sauce (page 779); sprinkle with sumac (page 821).	Cut off the cob and use in any dish that calls for cooked corn.
Eggplant	Peel the skin if you like; cut into $1/4$ to $1/2$-inch-thick slices or $1^1/_2$-inch cubes and skewer; brush with oil.	Sprinkle with curry powder (to make your own Hot or Fragrant Curry Powder, see page 815 or 816), garam masala (to make your own, see page 815), or coat with Soy and Sesame Dipping Sauce and Marinade, Korean Style (page 778)	Cook over direct heat, turning occasionally, until browned and tender, 5 to 20 minutes, depending on thickness.	Top with Nutty Miso Sauce (page 782), Peanut Sauce, Six Ways (page 794), or Basil Dipping Sauce (page 777) or sprinkle with Japanese Seven-Spice Mix (page 817).	Serve with Braised Tofu in Caramel Sauce (page 650), Tofu Pancakes, Six Ways (page 654), or Chickpea Fondue (page 615).

F Fast   M Make Ahead   V Vegan

VEGETABLE	PREPARATION	FLAVORING IDEAS	HOW TO GRILL	HOW TO SAUCE OR SEASON	SERVING SUGGESTIONS
Endive or Radicchio	Halve or quarter; brush with oil.	Use any flavored oil (pages 756–758), or sprinkle with Za'atar (page 818).	Cook over direct heat, turning occasionally, until browned and tender when pierced with a skewer or knife tip, 10 to 15 minutes.	Top with Traditional Pesto (page 768) (or any other; pages 768–770), or any vinaigrette (pages 762–763).	Serve with Risotto with Dried and Fresh Mushrooms (page 518) or Braised Lentils, Spanish Style (page 598).
Fennel	Trim; halve (if small) or quarter; brush with oil.	Use any flavored oil (pages 756–758), or sprinkle with curry powder (to make your own Hot or Fragrant Curry Powder, see page 815 or 816) or garam masala (to make your own, see page 815).	Cook over direct heat, turning occasionally, until browned and tender when pierced with a skewer or knife tip, 10 to 15 minutes.	Sprinkle with Citrus Sprinkle (page 818).	Serve with Black Beans with Orange Juice (page 606) or Lemony Lentil Salad (page 75).
Green Beans	Trim; leave whole and put in a grilling basket if you have one; toss in oil.	Use Aromatic-Flavored Oil (page 758) or sesame oil or coat with Soy and Sesame Dipping Sauce and Marinade, Korean Style (page 778) or Sweet Miso Glaze (page 782).	Cook over direct heat, turning occasionally, until lightly browned and tender, about 10 minutes.	Top with Ginger-Scallion Sauce (page 779) or Cilantro "Pesto" with Ginger and Chile (page 770).	Serve with Broiled Three-Bean Salad (page 74) or Spinach Salad with Warm Dressing and Tofu Croutons (page 40).
Jicama	Trim, peel, and cut into $1/2$-inch slices. Brush with oil.	Use extra virgin olive oil seasoned with minced fresh rosemary leaves; or sesame oil.	Cook over direct heat, turning occasionally, until lightly browned and tender, about 10 minutes.	Top with Traditional Pesto (page 768).	Serve the rosemary version with Eggplant Parmesan (page 299); the sesame version with Sea Slaw (page 55).
Leeks	Trim; halve lengthwise; brush with oil.	Use Spice-Flavored Oil (page 758).	Cook over direct heat, turning once, until very tender, 10 to 15 minutes.	Top with Balsamic Syrup (page 798) or Creamy Nut Sauce (page 797).	Serve with Raw Beet Salad (page 49).
Mushrooms	Remove stems from portobello or shiitakes; trim small mushrooms; grill whole, slice thickly, or cut into cubes. If small, skewer. Brush with oil.	Use any flavored oil (pages 756–758) or simply minced garlic in oil or coat with Soy and Sesame Dipping Sauce and Marinade, Korean Style (page 778) or Sweet Miso Glaze (page 782).	Cook over direct heat, turning occasionally, until browned, juicy, and tender, 15 to 20 minutes.	Serve Simple Miso Dipping Sauce (page 781) for dipping or top with Rustic Pine Nut Sauce (page 796) or marinate in any vinaigrette after grilling.	Serve with Marinated Tofu (page 652) or Grilled or Broiled Seitan (page 672).

VEGETABLE	PREPARATION	FLAVORING IDEAS	HOW TO GRILL	HOW TO SAUCE OR SEASON	SERVING SUGGESTIONS
Okra	Trim; leave whole and skewer or put in a grilling basket if you have one; toss in oil.	Use Aromatic-Flavored Oil (page 758) or sprinkle with Jerk Seasoning (page 818) or curry powder (to make your own Hot or Fragrant Curry Powder, see page 815 or 816).	Cook over direct heat, turning occasionally, until browned and tender when pierced with a skewer or knife tip, 5 to 10 minutes, depending on size.	Top with Tomato Chutney (page 785) or Seaweed "Mayo" (page 773).	Serve with Beer-Glazed Black Beans (page 785).
Onion	Halve through the root end without peeling or peel and cut into wedges or $1/2$-inch slices; brush with oil.	Use any flavored oil (pages 756–758) or sprinkle with any spice mixture (pages 810–819) or coat with Soy and Sesame Dipping Sauce and Marinade, Korean Style (page 778) or Sweet Miso Glaze (page 782).	Cook over direct heat, turning once (use a spatula to keep together), until nicely browned and tender, about 15 minutes.	Top with almost any Fresh or Cooked Salsa (pages 750–753 and 787–789), or Teriyaki Sauce (page 779).	Serve with Tofu Escabeche (page 653) or Braised Tempeh with Soy and Tomato Sauce (page 675).
Plantain	Use plantains that are yellow with some black; cut off each end; slice in half lengthwise or peel and cut into 1-inch-thick slices; brush with oil.	Use Spice- or Aromatic-Flavored Oil (page 758) or coat with Chipotle Paste (page 829) or sprinkle with chili powder (page 814) or Jerk Seasoning (page 818).	Cook over direct heat, turning occasionally, until browned, 3 to 7 minutes, depending on ripeness.	Top with Bean Salsa (page 751), Chile Pico de Verde (page 751), or Green Olive Mojo (page 769).	Serve with Baked Brazilian Black Beans (page 619) or Naked Tamales with Chile Cheese Filling (page 547).
Potatoes	Use waxy red or white potatoes; parboil in salted water until just tender; cut into long wedges or $1/2$-inch-thick slices; brush with oil.	Use any flavored oil (pages 756–758) or sprinkle with any spice mixture (pages 810–819) or coat with barbecue sauce (pages 789–790), or Sweet Miso Glaze (page 782).	Cook over direct heat, turning occasionally, until browned and tender, 15 to 20 minutes.	Serve Simple Miso Dipping Sauce (page 781) for dipping or top with Fresh Tomato Salsa (page 750), or Fast, Down-Home Barbecue Sauce (page 789).	Serve with Spicy Ketchup-Braised Tofu (page 651).
Scallions	Trim; leave whole; oil is optional.	Coat with Soy and Sesame Dipping Sauce and Marinade, Korean Style (page 778), or Sweet Miso Glaze (page 782).	Cook over direct heat, turning occasionally, until browned and tender, about 10 minutes.	Serve Ponzu Sauce (page 780) for dipping or top with Tahini Soy Sauce (page 778).	Serve with Naked Tamales with Chile Cheese Filling (page 547) or Bulgur Chili (page 557).

 Fast   Make Ahead   Ⓥ Vegan

VEGETABLE	PREPARATION	FLAVORING IDEAS	HOW TO GRILL	HOW TO SAUCE OR SEASON	SERVING SUGGESTIONS
Squash or Zucchini	Trim; cut into $1/2$-inch lengthwise slices or long diagonal slices; brush with oil.	Use Herb- or Aromatic-Flavored Oil (page 758) or sprinkle with Citrus Sprinkle (page 818) or curry powder (to make your own Hot or Fragrant Curry Powder, see page 815 or 816).	Cook over direct heat, turning occasionally, until browned and tender, 10 to 15 minutes.	Top with Cilantro Purée, Dill Purée, Basil Purée, or Mint Purée (page 769).	Serve with Parmesan Rice Cakes (page 569) or Polenta "Pizza" (page 547).
Sweet Potatoes	Halve or cut into long wedges or $1/2$-inch slices; brush with oil.	Use Spice- or Aromatic-Flavored Oil (page 758) or sprinkle with any of the spice mixtures (pages 810–819) or coat with barbecue sauce (pages 789–790), or Sweet Miso Glaze (page 782).	Cook over indirect heat, turning occasionally, until the flesh is very tender all the way through and the outsides are golden, 20 to 25 minutes.	Top with nearly any Compound Butter (page 801) or Simple Miso Dipping Sauce (page 781).	Serve with White Rice and Black Beans (page 510).
Tomatoes	Use slightly green or not fully ripe tomatoes; halve, cut into $1/2$-inch slices or leave whole if small and skewer; brush with oil if cut.	Use any flavored oil (pages 756–758) or sprinkle with any spice mixture (pages 810–819).	Cook over direct heat, turning once, until browned but not falling apart, 5 to 10 minutes.	Top with Traditional Pesto (page 768) or any other; (see pages 768–770).	Serve with White Beans, Tuscan Style (page 594), Parsley and Herb Salad (page 42), or Bulgur and Tomato Salad (page 83).
Winter Squash	Use butternut, acorn, or pumpkin; peel and seed; cut into $1/2$-inch slices or $1 1/2$-inch cubes and skewer; brush with oil.	Use any flavored oil (pages 756–758) or sprinkle with Jerk Seasoning (page 818), curry powder (to make your own Hot or Fragrant Curry Powder, see page 815 or 816), or garam masala (to make your own, see page 815) or coat with Sweet Miso Glaze (page 782).	Cook over indirect heat, turning occasionally, until the flesh is very tender all the way through, about 20 to 25 minutes; finish by browning over direct heat if you like.	Top with Brown Butter (page 801).	Serve with Barley Pilaf (page 539) or Biryani (page 512).

The Vegetable Lexicon

Here, arranged alphabetically, is everything you need to know about the most common vegetables. In each entry, the basic information points you to the ideal cooking method and then is followed by recipes that feature that particular fresh produce.

But don't let the structure fool you. The entire section is designed to foster flexibility, with a line in each recipe and vegetable suggesting possible substitutions. If you think of this section as a mini-dictionary, the world of fruits and vegetables will become a lot more accessible than you might expect.

Beyond the substitution lines, you can also apply what you learn in each lexicon to the Essential Vegetable recipes that begin on page 239. This will expand your repertoire of vegetable dishes exponentially and lay the groundwork for developing your own variations and accompaniments.

Artichokes and Cardoons

Artichokes are the flower buds of a domesticated thistle plant. The petals (we call them "leaves") are green, tough, and spiked and surround the choke. The prized heart is at the base of the bud and is attached to the thick stem, which is also edible.

Round, bulbous globe artichokes are the most common. So-called baby artichokes have more tender leaves and no chokes, so they can be eaten whole. But there's a catch: Not all small artichokes are "baby" artichokes. The best are fully mature artichokes that grow at the base of the plant; unless you shop close to the source or they're marked accurately, what you see most often are small artichokes that grow on side branches and are labeled "baby." These are not as tender and have a semideveloped choke that must still be removed. They're really good; but they're not the same thing.

Whole artichokes can be boiled, but I prefer steaming because they don't become as waterlogged (the problem is you have to make sure not to burn the pot dry during the long cooking time). Eating the leaves is fun: scrape off the flavorful "meat" using your front teeth. The closer you get to the center, the more tender the leaves, which can be eaten in bunches, but avoid the furry needlelike choke (it got its name for a reason!). To cut to the chase, trim away the leaves and scrape away the choke with a spoon to get to the delicious heart. Hearts and baby artichokes can be sautéed, braised, fried, roasted, or grilled whole, halved, or sliced. Canned, jarred, or frozen artichokes are fine but really don't taste much like fresh ones.

Cardoons, a relative of artichokes, are hard to find in the United States outside of farmer's markets. They are more popular in Italy, France, Spain, and parts of South America. To cook them you strip the dark green leaves from the white to pale green ribbed stalks, then cook and eat the stalks; the flavor is a cross between artichokes and celery.

Buying and storing: Artichokes are usually available throughout the year but are abundant and cheaper in the spring. They come in an array of sizes, but you're looking for those that are heavy for their size, don't look withered or dried out (the outer leaves should snap off), and make a squeaking sound when you squeeze them. Store wrapped loosely in plastic in the refrigerator.

Cardoons should have firm stems and dark green leaves. Store wrapped loosely in plastic in the refrigerator.

Preparing: For whole artichokes, cut off the pointed tips of the leaves with scissors or cut off the whole top third or so; sometimes using a large serrated knife will help you get through the tough leaves, but any heavy knife will do the job. Use a paring knife to peel around the base and cut off the bottom $1/4$ inch; pull off the toughest exterior leaves. To remove the choke before cooking, halve or quarter the artichoke and scrape it out or cut off the tops of the leaves, pry open the central leaves, and pull and then scrape out the choke with a spoon.

For artichoke hearts: Cut off as much of the tops of the leaves as possible or halve the artichoke length-

Ⓕ Fast   Ⓜ Make Ahead   Ⓥ Vegan

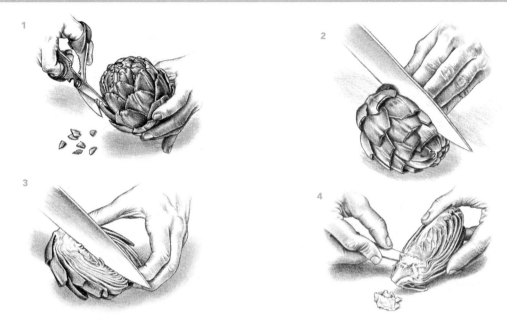

(STEP 1) Use scissors or a sharp knife to cut the pointed tips from the tops of the artichokes. (STEP 2) Cut the artichoke in half. (STEP 3) Then cut it into quarters. (STEP 4) Scrape the fuzzy choke out from each of the quarters.

wise. Use a paring knife to trim and peel the base; scrape out the choke with a spoon.

For small or baby artichokes: If tender enough, they can be eaten whole, but sometimes they benefit from the tops of the leaves and the exterior leaves being trimmed. Otherwise, halve, quarter, or slice lengthwise. Remove the choke if necessary.

Most canned and jarred artichokes are already cooked and can be added whole or chopped or sliced in the last few minutes of cooking; heavily marinated or brined ones can be rinsed to wash away some of the liquid's flavor. Thaw frozen artichokes and use as you would fresh, but cutting the cooking time roughly in half since they are already partially cooked. None of these substitutes comes close in flavor or texture to a fresh artichoke.

For cardoons, strip the stems of leaves and discard them; use a knife to remove the tough fibers that run down the vegetable lengthwise (like celery) and then cut into 2-inch pieces.

Due to a natural enzyme, raw artichokes and cardoons discolor very quickly when cut and darken quite a bit when cooked; rub with half a lemon or dip in water with a couple tablespoons of lemon juice or vinegar immediately after cutting to minimize darkening.

Best cooking methods: Steaming (for whole, hearts, or cardoons), sautéing (only for baby artichokes and

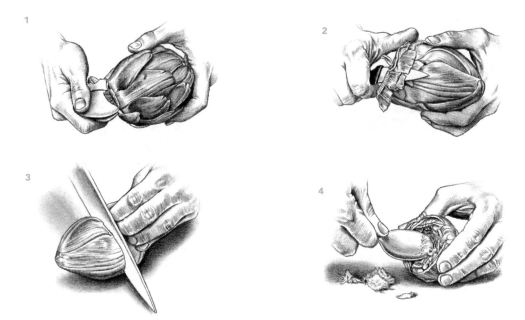

(STEP 1) Peel off tough outer leaves. (STEP 2) Trim around the bottom of the artichoke. (STEP 3) If you want to cook only the bottom, cut off the top half of the leaves. (STEP 4) Then scoop out the choke. If you want to leave the artichoke whole but remove the choke, leave it whole and force the top leaves open, then use a long spoon to scrape out the choke. (This will take a little while to do completely but isn't difficult.)

hearts), and braising (only for baby artichokes and hearts or cardoons).

When are they done? For whole artichokes, when the outer leaves pull off easily. Taste one: If the meat comes off easily and is tender, the artichoke is done. For artichoke hearts, when very tender; pierce with a skewer or thin-bladed knife to check, then taste to be sure. For cardoons, when tender enough to be pierced easily with a skewer or thin-bladed knife.

Other vegetables to substitute: In terms of flavor, artichokes and cardoons are somewhat interchangeable. There is no real substitute for artichoke hearts in recipes.

Steamed Artichokes

MAKES: 4 servings
TIME: 45 minutes

The best way to cook artichokes simply is to steam them, because you don't have to wait for a big pot of water to boil and, more important, they don't become soggy. Just make sure the pot doesn't boil dry. Serve the artichokes hot, warm, at room temperature, or cold; they're good any way at all.

You can add some gentle seasonings to the pot if you

 Fast   Make Ahead   Vegan

like: tarragon or thyme, onion or garlic, lemon juice or vinegar.

4 large or 12 small artichokes

1. With scissors or a large knife, trim the top $^1/_2$ inch or so from the artichokes. Using a paring knife, peel around the base and cut off the bottom $^1/_4$ inch. Break off the roughest of the exterior leaves.

2. Put the artichokes bottom up in a steamer. Cover and cook for 20 to 40 minutes. Sample an outer leaf; when it pulls away easily and its meat is tender, they're done.

3. Drain them upside down for a minute or two longer before serving hot; store upside down if you plan to serve them later. If you like, scoop out the chokes with a teaspoon (see the illustration on page 258). Serve hot with melted butter, at room temperature with vinaigrette, or cold with mayonnaise. Or serve at any temperature with lemon and/or olive oil and salt.

Braised Artichoke Hearts

MAKES: 4 servings
TIME: 45 minutes

This dish is just as good at room temperature as it is hot, and you'll probably want to double it to be sure you have leftovers for tossing with pasta or rice, topping pizzas, or mixing into frittatas. You can speed things up considerably by using frozen artichoke hearts, though the results may be disappointing.

Other vegetables you can use: any winter squash, which will make things easier (and probably less expensive).

$^1/_2$ cup freshly squeezed lemon juice (from 3 or 4 lemons)

Salt and freshly ground black pepper

6 large artichokes or about 3 cups frozen artichoke hearts

3 tablespoons extra virgin olive oil

1 tablespoon minced garlic

Chopped parsley leaves for garnish

1. Put the lemon juice in a bowl with $^1/_2$ cup water and sprinkle with a little salt and pepper.

2. Cut the bottom off the artichokes and save the leaves for another use (don't bother to remove the choke from them now). Trim the bottoms to reveal the heart (see page 257). As you finish each artichoke, cut the heart into thick slices and toss them with the lemon water.

3. Put the oil in a large, deep skillet over medium heat. When hot, add the garlic and cook, stirring frequently, until it softens, about a minute. Use a slotted spoon or tongs to transfer the artichokes to the pan, saving the liquid in the bowl. Cook, stirring occasionally, until the slices begin to soften a bit, about 5 minutes. Add the reserved liquid, bring to a boil, and cover. Reduce the heat to medium-low and cook for about 10 minutes, shaking the pan every now and then to toss the artichokes. Check for tenderness. If not quite ready, cover and cook until done, another minute or so.

4. Taste and adjust the seasoning, then serve hot or at room temperature, garnishing just before serving.

Roasted Artichoke Hearts. Crisp, with a haunting flavor: Preheat the oven to 425°F. In Step 3, increase the oil to $^1/_4$ cup, put it in a large ovenproof skillet or roasting pan, and set it in the oven. When the oil gets hot, transfer the artichoke slices and garlic to the pan and toss to coat in the oil. (Save the lemon water.) Roast until the slices release from the pan, 10 minutes or so, then turn them and continue roasting until tender, another 10 minutes. Transfer the artichokes from the pan to a serving platter and set the pan over medium-high heat. Add about a cup of the lemon water and stir up any brown bits from the bottom of the pan. Cook for a few minutes, until the mixture thickens a bit, stir in the parsley, then taste and adjust the seasoning. Pour the sauce over the artichokes and serve immediately or at room temperature.

Vinegar-Braised Artichoke Hearts. I like this best with sherry vinegar, but you can also use white wine or even balsamic vinegar: Simply use vinegar instead of the lemon juice in either the main recipe or any of the variations.

Braised Artichoke Hearts with Potatoes. The potatoes will soak up most of the liquid, leaving you with a thick vegetable stew: Peel and steam or boil 2 large waxy potatoes (or use leftovers). Cut them into large chunks. Increase the extra virgin olive oil to $1/4$ cup and the minced garlic to 2 tablespoons. In Step 3, when you lift the lid to check the artichokes, fold in the potatoes. Cover the pan and proceed with the recipe, cooking just long enough for the potatoes to reheat.

Braised Artichoke Hearts with Lots of Roasted Garlic. Two great mellow flavors in one dish: Roast and peel 2 or 3 heads of garlic (see page 304). In Step 3, when you lift the lid to check the artichokes, fold in the garlic. Cover the pan and proceed with the recipe.

10 Great Stir-Ins for Braised Artichoke Hearts

1. Pitted green or black olives
2. Dried fruit, especially golden raisins, currants, cherries, or apricots
3. Nuts, especially walnuts, almonds, or hazelnuts
4. Different herbs: especially chives, basil, tarragon, mint, or chervil
5. Arugula or spinach leaves
6. Dried tomato bits
7. Chopped fresh tomatoes
8. Candied ginger
9. Virtually any Crouton (page 806)
10. Grated or crumbled cheese, especially Parmesan, feta, blue, or fresh cheese

Asparagus

Asparagus is a member of the lily family whose long, usually green spears can be delicate and thin to thick and stubby. Once a springtime favorite that's now available year-round at supermarkets, the best remains local and freshly picked. Check out farmer's markets from as early as February in the South through May or June in the North.

There are also white and purple varieties that are more common in Europe but are occasionally seen here. White asparagus is grown underground or under cover to prevent greening and can be quite expensive; it's more delicate in texture and has a subtle nutty flavor that distinguishes it from the green and purple varieties.

Easy to prepare and quick cooking, asparagus is classically steamed, but roasted or grilled is equally wonderful. In any case, be sure not to cook it until it's completely soft and soggy. Asparagus is delicious hot, at room temperature, or cold. And leftovers are great with eggs or added to salads.

PREPARING ASPARAGUS

Snap off the bottom of each stalk; they will usually separate naturally right where the woody part ends.

All but the thinnest asparagus are best when peeled.

 F Fast   **M** Make Ahead   **V** Vegan

Buying and storing: Any color and really any size asparagus is good; it simply comes down to a matter of personal preference and what's available. Look for plump, unshriveled spears with undamaged tips and avoid spears that look woody. Often markets store them stem down in cold water, which is fine, but not entirely necessary. Store wrapped loosely in plastic in the refrigerator; use as soon as possible.

Preparing: Snap off the bottom of each spear; it will usually break naturally where you want it to. I recommend peeling asparagus (use a vegetable peeler) to remove the fibrous skin from just below the tip to the base; this step isn't necessary if the spears are pencil thin.

Best cooking methods: Steaming is basic, but sautéing, roasting, and grilling are all great.

When is it done? Asparagus is done when you can easily insert a skewer or thin-bladed knife into the thickest part of the stalk. Undercooked asparagus is crisp; overcooked asparagus is mushy.

Other vegetables to substitute: Green or wax beans, sugar snap peas, or broccoli raab.

Asparagus Done Simply

MAKES: 4 servings
TIME: 15 minutes

You can cook asparagus almost any way you like, and it'll be just fine. The simplest ways to go are boiling (or simmering or poaching; you can call it whatever you like), steaming, or microwaving. This recipe includes all three.

1½ to 2 pounds asparagus, trimmed and peeled

Salt

To boil: Lay them in a skillet that can hold the spears without crowding, cover with salted water, cover the skillet, and turn the heat to high. Cook just until the thick part of the stalks can be pierced with a knife.

To steam: Stand them up in a pot with an inch of salted water on the bottom (it's nice, but hardly essential, to tie them in a bundle first). Cover and turn the heat to high. Cook just until the thick part of the stalks can be pierced with a knife.

To microwave: Lay them in a microwave-safe plate or shallow bowl with about 2 tablespoons of salted water; cover with a lid. Microwave on high for 3 minutes, shake the container, and continue to microwave at 1-minute intervals, just until the thick part of the stalks can be pierced with a knife.

Roasted or Grilled Asparagus

MAKES: 4 servings
TIME: 30 minutes

Asparagus are terrific when blasted with high heat; if you haven't had them browned, you're in for a new treat.

If you have a grill going, you should really try grilling them; thick spears, especially, are wonderful this way (thin ones are good too, but you have to be especially careful not to let them fall through the grill grates).

If the grill is not on, roast them. They're amazing this way, especially with butter.

1½ to 2 pounds asparagus, trimmed and peeled

1 to 2 tablespoons extra virgin olive oil or butter (melted if you're grilling)

Salt

Lemon wedges for serving

❶ Preheat the oven to 450°F or heat a charcoal or gas grill to medium-high heat. If you're roasting, put the asparagus in a roasting pan, drizzle with a tablespoon or two of oil or dot with butter, and sprinkle with salt. If you're grilling, brush the asparagus with oil or butter and sprinkle with salt. Put the asparagus in the oven or on the grill (you might want to skewer thin asparagus in little bunches to make turning easier and keep them from falling through the grates or just be sure to lay them crosswise).

2 Roast or grill, turning the spears once or twice, just until the thick part of the stalks can be pierced with a knife, 10 to 15 minutes. Serve immediately, with lemon.

5 Classic Ways to Serve Cooked Asparagus

Cooked asparagus can be served immediately in any of these ways or first shocked (if cooked using a "wet" method) and refrigerated, covered, for up to 2 days, then cooked according to the directions for Precooked Vegetables in Butter or Oil (page 240). Many of these are good in combination, as you'll quickly discover.

1. Drizzle with extra virgin olive oil or melted butter (Brown Butter, page 801, is super). Any Compound Butter (page 801) or Flavored Oil (page 758) is also good.

2. Squeeze lemon or lime juice over it or drizzle with vinegar.

3. Douse with any Vinaigrette (pages 762–763).

4. Top with mayonnaise (to make your own, see page 771) or Hollandaise Sauce (page 802), both classics.

5. Top with minced or finely crumbled hard-cooked eggs (page 166).

Stir-Fried Asparagus

MAKES: 4 servings

TIME: 20 minutes

F **V**

Among the simplest and most straightforward of stir-fries and one of the best made with only one vegetable.

1$^1/_2$ to 2 pounds asparagus, trimmed and peeled, then cut into 2-inch lengths

2 tablespoons peanut or neutral oil, like grapeseed or corn

1 tablespoon minced garlic

2 dried chiles (optional)

1 tablespoon soy sauce

1 teaspoon dark sesame oil (optional)

Salt

1 If the asparagus is thick, follow the directions for Asparagus Done Simply (page 261), undercooking the asparagus a bit and shocking it (see page 241), then draining and drying. If it's thin, no precooking is necessary.

2 When you're ready to cook, heat a wok or large skillet over high heat for 3 or 4 minutes. Add the oil, wait a few seconds, then add the asparagus. Cook, stirring, for a minute, then stir in the garlic and the chiles if you're using them. Cook until the asparagus is dry, hot, and beginning to brown, about 5 minutes.

3 Add 2 tablespoons water and the soy sauce and continue to cook until the asparagus is tender, another 3 to 5 minutes. Add the sesame oil if you're using it and salt if necessary and serve.

5 Ideas for Stir-Fried Asparagus

As with any stir-fry, this one has infinite variations. Some of my favorites:

1. Add 1 tablespoon fermented black beans, soaked for a few minutes in dry sherry, Shaoxing wine, or water to cover, along with the soy sauce.

2. Add 2 tablespoons minced peeled fresh ginger along with the garlic.

3. Cook the asparagus with about $^1/_2$ cup chopped onion and/or sliced red or yellow bell pepper.

4. Cook the asparagus with 4 to 6 peeled and halved shallots.

5. During the final minute of stir-frying, sprinkle with about $^1/_4$ cup chopped nuts, like peanuts, hazelnuts, cashews, or almonds.

Avocados

Technically a fruit, the avocado floats between vegetable and fruit status; it's almost always used in a savory manner like a vegetable, but is rarely cooked, so it's treated more like a fruit. And while it is loaded with fat, that fat is mostly monounsaturated (and it's cholesterol free). Avocado flesh is a pretty light green, ultra-smooth, and creamy, with a rich and subtle flavor. It's perfectly complemented by acid in citrus fruit or that of a mild vinegar, but easily overwhelmed by other flavors.

There are many varieties— from tiny to melon size— but it's mostly Hass and Fuerte that we see here. Hass are pear shaped and have a dark green to black leathery, wrinkled, and bumpy skin; they're great for eating straight, spreading, or mashing. Fuerte are usually larger and have smooth green skin and firmer flesh that's not as well suited to spreading or mashing but is good for slicing.

Buying and storing: Avocados ripen nicely at room temperature, so they are often sold nearly rock hard. Give them a gentle squeeze before buying: you don't want mushy spots or bruises; when one is ripe, it will yield to pressure. To ripen avocados more quickly, put them in a paper bag at room temperature for a couple days or longer. Store ripe avocados in the refrigerator for up to a week.

Preparing: Slice avocados lengthwise around the seed; peel off the skin or scoop out the flesh with a spoon. If you want to store half, wrap it with the pit intact and refrigerate—the pit helps keep it from turning brown.

Avocados discolor very quickly when cut; sprinkle with lemon or lime juice immediately after cutting to minimize darkening.

Best cooking method: Best eaten raw (sliced, mashed, or puréed), at most they can be grilled quickly. Delicious simply spread on bread and sprinkled with lemon or lime juice or a mild vinegar and salt.

When is it done? Avocado needs no cooking. Grilled avocado is done when lightly browned.

Other fruits or vegetables to substitute: Really, there is no substitute.

Crunchy Corn Guacamole

MAKES: 4 servings
TIME: 15 minutes

A new twist on the traditional guacamole (which you can find in the form of the first variation). The fresh corn kernels add texture and flavor without taking away from that of the avocado.

1 lime

1 cup corn kernels, preferably just stripped from the cobs (see page 288), but thawed frozen is acceptable

$\frac{1}{2}$ teaspoon minced garlic

$\frac{1}{2}$ cup chopped scallion

1 serrano or jalapeño chile, stemmed, seeded, and minced (optional)

PREPARING AVOCADOS

Pitting and peeling an avocado is easy. (STEP 1) Cut through the skin and flesh lengthwise to the pit, then rotate the avocado to cut all the way around it. Twist the halves apart. (STEP 2) A careful, swift, and not-too-forceful strike of the knife will implant it in the pit, which will then lift out easily. (STEP 3) Finally, scoop out the flesh with a spoon.

Salt

2 tablespoons chopped fresh cilantro leaves

$^1/_4$ cup roughly chopped toasted pumpkin seeds (see page 321)

3 medium ripe avocados, preferably Hass

① Grate the lime zest (or use a zester to make long strands) and reserve; cut the lime into wedges. Put the lime zest, corn, and garlic in a food processor; squeeze in half of the lime wedges and pulse to make a chunky purée.

② Put the corn mixture along with the scallion, chile, and a large pinch of salt into a medium bowl and mash until the mixture is well combined. Add the cilantro and pumpkin seeds and mash a few more times.

③ Cut the avocados in half and reserve the pits if you will not be serving the guacamole right away. Scoop the flesh into the bowl and mash, leaving a few chunks of avocado. Squeeze in lime juice from the reserved lime wedges to taste.

④ Season with salt to taste and serve or tuck the pits back into the mixture and cover the surface with plastic wrap (this will help keep the guacamole from turning brown), then refrigerate for up to 4 hours. Remove the pits before serving.

Minimalist Guacamole. More traditional: Omit the corn kernels and pumpkin seeds. Add the zest and garlic to the scallion in Step 2 and proceed with the recipe.

"Guacasalsa." Based on a Venezuelan condiment called *guasacaca*, it's traditionally used as a marinade or a spread, but this version is mild enough to be used as a dip: Substitute Fresh Tomato Salsa (page 750) or Fresh Tomatillo Salsa (page 751) for everything but the avocado. Skip Steps 1 and 2 and proceed with the recipe, using the juice of $^1/_2$ lime in Step 3.

Guacamole with Tomatillos. The tomatillos add a nice hit of acidity: Substitute $^1/_2$ cup chopped tomatillo for the corn and pumpkins seeds if you like. Skip Step 1 and add the tomatillos to Step 2.

Avocado and Dried Tomato Spread or Dip. Substitute $^1/_2$ cup chopped Oven-Roasted Fresh Plum Tomatoes (page 375), Oven-Dried Tomatoes (page 377), or store-bought sun-dried tomatoes for the corn, cilantro, and pumpkin seeds (soak hard, dried tomatoes for a few minutes in hot water first). Skip Step 1.

Avocado and Goat Cheese Spread or Dip. Spread this on bread and layer with grilled vegetables for a fantastic sandwich: Omit the garlic, chile, cilantro, and pumpkin seeds. Substitute lemon for the lime and $^3/_4$ cup goat cheese for the corn. Put everything in a food processor if you want a smooth spread; for a chunkier spread, just use a potato masher or fork.

Pea Spread or Dip. Great on Crostini (page 737): Instead of the corn and the avocados, use 1 pound lightly steamed fresh or frozen peas. Omit the chile and pumpkin seeds. Use lemon instead of lime and process all the peas as you would the corn in Step 1. Substitute fresh mint leaves for the cilantro. If you like, thin the consistency a bit by adding a little cream, yogurt, or silken tofu.

Asparagus Spread or Dip. A great low-calorie alternative to traditional guacamole: Follow the variation for Pea Spread or Dip, but use 1 pound lightly steamed asparagus instead of the peas. Pat it dry, slice it into manageable pieces, and proceed with the recipe.

Bamboo Shoots

The tender emerging shoots of an edible bamboo plant, this vegetable is not commonly seen fresh in the United States (you might try Asian markets; I've found them there occasionally), but they're readily available canned at nearly every supermarket. Canned bamboo shoots are yellowish tan in color, have a nice crunchy texture, and are quite bland.

Buying and storing: No guesswork in buying canned bamboo shoots; they're either already cut into strips or a

Ⓕ Fast   Ⓜ Make Ahead   Ⓥ Vegan

whole piece that must be cut. Once opened, store any unused portion in its water in the refrigerator; use as soon as possible.

Preparing: Chop or slice as necessary.

Best cooking method: Stir-frying, added at the last minute.

When are they done? When just heated through and still crunchy.

Other vegetables to substitute: Water chestnuts, daikon, or jícama.

Bean Sprouts

Just about every bean, seed, or grain can be sprouted (see page 77), but we most commonly see mung and soybean sprouts. Mung bean sprouts have pale yellow or green heads with fairly long, semitranslucent plump tails. They are available fresh in bags or bulk (also canned, but these aren't worth the tin they're in).

Soybean sprouts—also sold in bags or loose—are larger; their heads are a yellow-colored split soybean, and the white crunchy tails are about 2 inches long. Soybean sprouts are often used in Korean dishes and offer a more substantial crunch than mung beans.

Buying and storing: Look for plump, crisp, fresh-smelling sprouts. Of course, avoid those that are slimy or off-smelling. If they're prepackaged in bags, inspect as best you can. Look for bean sprouts in Asian markets if they're not at your supermarket. Store wrapped loosely in plastic or in the store's packaging in the refrigerator; use as soon as possible—they turn to mush quickly.

Preparing: Some people like to trim the tails, but it's hardly necessary. Rinse and drain the sprouts well.

Best cooking methods: Stir-frying, added at the last minute.

When are they done? When just heated through and still crunchy.

Other vegetables to substitute: There is no substitute for bean sprouts, but if it's bland crunch you're after, try bamboo shoots or water chestnuts.

Spiced Stir-Fried Bean Sprouts

MAKES: 4 servings

TIME: 10 minutes

One of the quickest things you can get on the table and endlessly versatile too. Serve it with Steamed Sticky Rice (page 507) or crisp outer leaves of romaine or iceberg lettuce for wrapping the beans into crunchy little bundles.

Other vegetables you can use: shredded or julienned zucchini; kale or collards cut into ribbons.

> 2 tablespoons peanut or neutral oil, like grapeseed or corn
>
> 1 pound (about 4 cups) bean sprouts, trimmed if you like
>
> 1 tablespoon peeled and minced fresh ginger or garlic
>
> 2 tablespoons any spice blend, like Chinese five-spice powder or curry powder (to make your own, see pages 815–816)
>
> Salt and freshly ground black pepper

1 Put the oil in a deep skillet or wok over medium-high heat. When hot, add the bean sprouts and the ginger, raise the heat to high, and toss a few times to coat.

2 Let the vegetables cook for a couple minutes, until they begin to sputter, then stir them around a bit. Sprinkle with the spice blend and salt and pepper and stir again, adding a few drops of water if they're starting to stick to the pan. Stir once or twice more. The bean sprouts are ready when barely tender and the spices are fragrant, which just takes a couple minutes. Taste, adjust the seasoning, and serve hot or at room temperature.

Beet Greens

These are the leafy greens usually attached to the beet root. They are closely related to chard and often mistaken for it; you can treat them identically. Both the stems and the leaves are edible; young and very tender ones can be tossed into salads, while tougher leaves and stems must be cooked.

Buying and storing: Most often beet greens are available only when attached to the root (it's two vegetables in one!). Choose greens that are fresh looking, vibrantly colored, and unwilted. Remove the greens from the root and store wrapped loosely in plastic in the refrigerator; use as soon as possible.

Preparing: Wash well. Leave small leaves whole and chop or tear larger ones into strips or pieces.

Best cooking methods: Steaming and braising.

When are they done? When wilted and tender.

Other vegetables to substitute: Chard or turnip greens.

Beets

Beets come in a beautiful array of colors and sizes, from dark red to golden yellow to striped, and shapes—from the familiar round to long and thin, to tiny. They're all good. The beet's sweet and earthy flavor is wonderful and just as good served cold or at room temperature as it is hot. Additionally, raw beets keep for weeks in the fridge and also keep for several days once cooked.

If staining from the vibrantly colored juices is the only thing keeping you from cooking beets, check out the preparation tips that follow and Beets Baked in Foil (page 267) for a nearly stain-free beet experience.

Buying and storing: Unlike most root vegetables, size doesn't matter when it comes to beets; large ones are almost always just as good as small, and they're easier to handle. One sure sign of freshness is the presence of the greens (which are edible and lovely; see "Chard" on page 285 and "Beet Greens," page 265); if they're fresh looking, the roots are fresh too. Beets should be nearly rock hard when you buy them; avoid any that are soft. Remove all but an inch of the greens (cook the greens as soon as you can) and store the roots wrapped loosely in plastic in the refrigerator. They keep for weeks.

Preparing: Scrub well; leave on an inch or so of the greens to minimize bleeding. (Peel the beets after they've cooked.)

Best cooking methods: Baking, roasting, and braising and glazing.

When are they done? When tender all the way through; pierce with a skewer or thin-bladed knife to check. Slight overcooking is usually preferable to undercooking.

Other vegetables to substitute: Turnips, rutabagas, carrots, or parsnips.

Beets Done Simply

MAKES: 4 servings
TIME: About 45 minutes
Ⓜ Ⓥ

Faster than Beets Baked in Foil (page 267) and almost as convenient, but a little messier—or at least potentially so.

Other vegetables you can use: turnips, rutabagas, daikon, or parsnips.

Salt
4 large or 8 medium beets, about 1¹/₂ to 2 pounds, with about 1 inch of their tops still on

To boil: Bring a large pot of water to a boil; salt it. Put the beets in the water, cover the pot, and turn the heat to medium-low. Simmer until the beets can be pierced with a thin-bladed knife, 30 to 45 minutes. Drain and drop into ice water; drain again and peel.

To steam: Put the beets in a steamer above an inch or two of salted water. Cover and cook over steadily bubbling water for about 30 to 45 minutes, until they can be pierced with a thin-bladed knife. Drain and drop into ice water; drain and peel.

To microwave: Put the beets in a microwave-safe plate or shallow bowl with about 2 tablespoons of salted water; cover with a lid. Microwave on high for 6 minutes, shake the container, and continue to microwave at 2-minute intervals, just until they can be pierced with a thin-bladed knife. Drain and drop into ice water; drain and peel.

Use these in Precooked Vegetables with Butter or Oil (page 240) or any other recipe that calls for cooked beets; or store, refrigerated, for a couple of days before using in any recipe for cooked beets.

Beets Baked in Foil

MAKES: 4 servings
TIME: About 1 hour

This is the single best method for cooking beets. It produces beets that are firm and not at all waterlogged. Better, perhaps, is that it's easy, neat, and convenient: once cooked, you can eat them or store them without further handling until you're ready to eat.

At that point you unwrap and peel them, then slice them and heat in butter or oil, eat them cold, or proceed with any other beet recipe. Since large beets will take much longer to cook than small ones, try to buy beets that are roughly equal in size.

You don't have to roast them individually wrapped. If you're planning to use them all at once, right away, just put in a roasting pan or heavy skillet, cover, and proceed as directed.

Other vegetables you can use: turnips or rutabagas or other root vegetables.

4 large or 8 medium beets, about 1½ to 2 pounds

① Preheat the oven to 400°F. Wash the beets well. Wrap them individually in foil and put them on a cookie sheet or roasting pan.

② Cook, undisturbed, for 45 to 90 minutes, until a thin-bladed knife pierces one with little resistance (they may cook at different rates; remove each one when it is done). Use in Precooked Vegetables with Butter or Oil (page 240) or any other recipe that calls for cooked beets; or store, refrigerated, for a couple of days before using.

Beet Crisps

MAKES: 4 servings
TIME: 30 minutes

You can deep-fry virtually any ultra-thinly-sliced root vegetable and get homemade chips (see page 352), but you can also crisp slightly thicker pieces in the oven, with a lot less oil and a lot less mess. Beets are especially great this way because of their bright color and naturally sweet flavor.

Other vegetables you can use: carrots, parsnips, rutabagas, kohlrabi, sweet potatoes, or turnips.

1 pound beets, trimmed and peeled

3 to 4 tablespoons neutral oil, like grapeseed or corn

Salt and freshly ground black pepper

① Preheat the oven to 400°F. Lightly grease a couple of baking sheets or line them with parchment if you like.

② Cut the beets in half and then crosswise into thin slices (⅛ inch or so). You can use a mandoline for this; just don't set it too thin. (And if the beets are small, simply cut them crosswise.) Toss them in the oil and spread the slices out on the baking sheets. (It's okay if they're close, but don't let them overlap.)

③ Roast the beet slices until they're beginning to brown on the bottom, 10 to 12 minutes. Flip them over and sprinkle with salt and pepper. Keep roasting until they're well browned, another 10 minutes or so. Serve immediately.

8 Ways to Season Beet and Other Vegetable Crisps

When you sprinkle with salt and pepper, dust the crisps with any of the following seasonings:

1. Curry powder (to make your own, see pages 815–816)
2. Chaat masala (to make your own, see page 814)
3. Garam masala (to make your own, see page 815)

4. Chili powder (to make your own, see page 814)
5. Jerk seasoning (to make your own, see page 818)
6. Five-spice powder (to make your own, see page 816)
7. Japanese Seven-Spice Mix (page 817)
8. Za'atar (to make your own, see page 818)

Beets with Pistachio Butter

MAKES: 4 servings
TIME: about 1 hour

The color combination is striking here and the flavors fantastic. The beets are sweet and earthy, and the pistachio butter adds a rich, nutty roasted flavor.

Both components can be made ahead (up to 4 days for the beets; a week or more for the pistachio butter), and the pistachio butter can be used on just about any roasted or grilled vegetable or tossed with pasta and fresh herbs.

Other vegetables you can use: turnips, rutabagas, carrots, or parsnips.

4 large or 8 medium beets (about 1¹/₂ pounds), trimmed

¹/₂ cup neutral oil, like grapeseed or corn, or pistachio oil

4 cloves garlic, smashed and peeled

1 cup shelled pistachios

Salt and freshly ground black pepper

Chopped pistachios for garnish

1 Bake the beets in foil (see page 267). Meanwhile, put half the oil in a skillet over medium heat. When hot, add the garlic and cook for about a minute, then add the pistachios; cook, stirring often, for about 3 minutes.

2 Remove from the heat, let cool a bit, and transfer to a food processor. Purée until smooth, adding more oil

as necessary; the consistency should be thinner than that of peanut butter, just pourable. Taste and adjust the seasoning. The pistachio butter can be covered and refrigerated for up to 2 weeks.

3 Slip the skins off the beets and cut them into large chunks. Sprinkle with salt and pepper. Put the beets in a serving dish and spoon the pistachio butter over the top; garnish with the chopped pistachios. Serve hot or at room temperature.

Carrots with Walnut Butter. The caramelized sweetness of roasted carrots works beautifully with walnut butter: Substitute carrots, cut into chunks, for the beets, and walnuts for the pistachios. Toss the carrots in some oil, sprinkle with salt and pepper, and roast in a 375°F oven until tender. Proceed with the recipe.

Parsnips with Hazelnut Butter. Peel the hazelnuts, if you have the patience, to reduce bitterness: Substitute parsnips, cut into chunks, for the beets and hazelnuts for the pistachios. Toss the parsnips in some oil, sprinkle with salt and pepper, and roast in a 375°F oven until tender. Proceed with the recipe.

Bok Choy and Other Asian Greens

The word *choy* in Cantonese basically means "greens," and there are a whole slew of choy to choose from, especially in Asian markets. To keep things simple, only the most common are included here, but don't let that stop you from trying more; almost all can be prepared and cooked the same way.

Bok choy (also called *pak choi* or *Chinese white cabbage*) is certainly the most common Asian green, found in many restaurant stir-fries. It grows in large, loose heads with wide, crisp white stalks and dark green flat leaves. Its flavor is mildly cabbagey and fresh, and the stalks take on a marvelous, almost creamy texture once

F Fast   **M** Make Ahead   **V** Vegan

cooked. The miniature jade-green variety—called *Shanghai* or *baby bok choy*—is equally delicious, tender, and cute.

Gai lan (aka *Chinese broccoli, kale,* or *mustard greens*) is not often found at supermarkets but is abundant in Asian markets. It looks similar to broccoli raab; the long, narrow stalks are smooth, thick, and green with dark green leaves and small clusters of flower buds. The stems retain a lovely crispness when cooked, and the leaves wilt similarly to kale; the flavor is a cross between broccoli and mustard greens but milder than either.

Two other Asian greens look and cook very similar to gai lan: choy sum (aka *white flowering cabbage*) and yao choy (aka *green flowering cabbage*). They can be distinguished from gai lan by their lighter green leaves and yellow flowers, but they are so similar to gai lan they are virtually interchangeable.

Tatsoi (also called *spoon cabbage*) is often found in various spring or mesclun lettuce mixes and is good both raw and quickly cooked. The leaves are small (about 2 inches across), dark green, and round, with a delicate, light green stem—looking rather like a spoon. The flavor is mild with a hint of mustard, and the texture is tender but with a slight bite.

Buying and storing: The leaves and stems should be fresh looking and crisp; avoid any with yellowing on the leaves. Bok choy's stems should be unbroken and bright white. Look for unopened flowers on gai lan, choy sum, or yao choy, but a few open buds are okay. Store wrapped loosely in plastic in the refrigerator.

Preparing: Wash and remove any damaged or yellowing leaves.

Bok choy: Cut off the root end and the inch or so above it and slice or chop it as you like. If the stems are thick, separate them from the leaves and start by cooking them a couple minutes before the leaves. Shanghai bok choy can remain whole.

Gai lan: Trim any dried-out or tough stems, and separate the leaves from the stems (the stems need longer to cook).

Tatsoi: Cut the stems from the root end if they are still attached.

Best cooking methods: Steaming and sautéing or stir-frying.

When is it done? When the stems are tender but still crisp (especially for gai lan) and the leaves are wilted.

Other vegetables to substitute: Cabbage, kale, or broccoli can replace any of the Asian greens.

Quick-Cooked Bok Choy

MAKES: 4 servings
TIME: 30 minutes

Ⓕ Ⓥ

Bok choy is, dare I say it, unique. Not the greens; they're about the same as those of many other cabbages. But its fat, thick stems become creamy and tender during cooking in a way that you cannot duplicate with other greens. This makes the basic, simple version of this recipe just wonderful; the slightly more complicated variations are even better.

Other vegetables you can use: Napa or other Chinese cabbages, white chard (probably the closest in texture, but with different flavor), or broccoli raab.

1 head bok choy, about 1$^1/_2$ pounds

3 tablespoons peanut or neutral oil, like grapeseed or corn

Salt and freshly ground black pepper

① Cut the leaves from the stems of the bok choy. Trim the stems as necessary, then cut them into roughly 1-inch pieces; rinse everything well. Put the oil in a large skillet over medium-high heat. When hot, add the stems and cook, stirring occasionally, until they just lose their crunch, about 3 minutes. Add the greens and about $^1/_2$ cup water (or vegetable stock, pages 101–102, if you prefer).

② Cook, stirring occasionally, until the liquid evaporates and the stems become very tender, about 10 minutes more; add a little more water if necessary. Sprinkle with salt and pepper and serve immediately.

Bok Choy, Mediterranean Style. Quite classy: In Step 1, use extra virgin olive oil. In Step 2, when the greens are tender, stir in 2 tablespoons drained capers, $^1/_4$ to $^1/_2$ cup chopped pitted olives (preferably oil-cured; see page 326), and 1 tablespoon minced garlic. Cook for another minute or so, stirring, then add lemon juice or balsamic vinegar to taste (start with 1 tablespoon). Cook for another 5 seconds and serve.

Bok Choy with Black Beans. Add some Baked or Deep-Fried Tofu (page 641 or 643) along with the greens for extra heft: While cooking the stems in Step 1, soak 1 tablespoon fermented black beans in 2 tablespoons sherry, Shaoxing wine, or water. In Step 2, when the greens are tender, stir in the beans and their liquid, along with 2 teaspoons minced garlic and 1 teaspoon minced ginger. Cook for another minute or so, stirring, then add 1 tablespoon soy sauce, or to taste. Cook for another 5 seconds and serve.

Broccoli

A member of the *very* large *Brassica* genus that includes cabbage, mustard, turnips, and more, and a longtime regular in Italian cuisine, broccoli was barely known in the United States until the 1920s. These days broccoli is available year-round at every grocery store (there's no reason to buy frozen). But its popularity is warranted: it's flavorful, easy to prepare and cook, inexpensive, and nutritious.

We're most familiar with the dark green type, but some can have a bit of purple coloring in the buds. Broccoli can be prepared in a variety of ways, which makes it a great standby vegetable to have on hand in the fridge. Serve it raw, lightly cooked, or completely cooked; steamed, boiled, sautéed, stir-fried, or braised.

Buying and storing: Look for tightly packed florets with no yellowing, on top of a crisp stem. Store wrapped loosely in plastic in the refrigerator; it will keep for several days.

Preparing: Strip the stalk of leaves, if any (these are perfectly edible; cook along with the tops, if you like). Cut off the dried-out end of the stalk and peel (with a vegetable peeler or paring knife) the tough outer skin as best you can without going crazy. (To peel with a paring knife, hold the broccoli upside down; grasp a bit of the skin right at the bottom, between the paring knife and your thumb. Pull down to remove a strip of the skin.) If you like, cut the stalk into equal-length pieces and break the head into florets.

Best cooking methods: Steaming, microwaving, braising and glazing, and stir-frying are great. Regardless of the method, it often makes sense to cook the stalks longer than the florets; just start them a minute or two earlier.

When is it done? It's a matter of taste. When bright green, it's still crisp and quite chewy, and some people like it that way. Cook it for another couple of minutes and it becomes tender; overcook it and it becomes mushy and begins to fall apart. Try cooking until a skewer or thin-bladed knife can easily pierce the stalk.

Other vegetables to substitute: Broccoli and cauliflower are almost always interchangeable; or substitute "broccoflower," Romanesco, (page 280) or broccoli raab (page 272).

Stir-Fried Broccoli

MAKES: 4 servings
TIME: 30 minutes

Broccoli is made for stir-fry: you get some crunch from the stems (cut them fairly thin so they'll cook quickly) and tenderness from the florets, and no precooking is needed. And you can use broccoli as a main ingredient in just about any recipe in this book.

If you have leftover cooked broccoli, by all means use it. Just keep the cooking time to a minimum, no longer than it takes to heat the broccoli through.

2 tablespoons peanut or neutral oil, like grapeseed or corn

About 1$^1/_2$ pounds broccoli, trimmed, the stems cut into pieces no more than $^1/_8$ inch thick

Salt

1 teaspoon sugar

1 cup vegetable stock (pages 101–102) or water

2 tablespoons soy sauce

① Put the oil in a wok or large, deep skillet over medium-high heat. When hot, add the broccoli, raise the heat to high, and cook, stirring, until it becomes bright green and glossy and begins to brown, about 5 minutes.

② Add salt to taste, the sugar, and the stock. Stir and continue to cook until almost all of the liquid evaporates and the broccoli is tender, about 5 minutes more. Stir in the soy sauce, taste and adjust the seasoning, and serve.

Stir-Fried Broccoli with Dried Shiitakes. Now you're adding chewiness and more flavor: Soak about $^1/_4$ cup dried black (shiitake) mushrooms in 1 cup very hot water until tender, changing the water if necessary. Drain them, reserving the liquid, trim them, and cut them up. In Step 1, add the mushrooms along with the broccoli. In Step 2, add 1 teaspoon minced garlic and 1 teaspoon minced peeled fresh ginger along with the salt and sugar. Stir for 15 seconds before adding the strained mushroom soaking liquid in place of the stock. Finish as directed.

Broccoli, Cauliflower, or Just About Anything Else, Roman Style

MAKES: 4 servings

TIME: 30 minutes

Ⓕ Ⓜ Ⓥ

If there's a more versatile way to cook vegetables, it's boiling, and this is much more interesting. You see almost everything done this way in Rome, and it's always good. The variation is a little simpler, but it requires more judgment; prepared correctly, it will be just as good.

Other vegetables you can use: almost anything—dark, leafy greens, like collards and kale; green beans; carrots; potatoes; turnips; or beets, for example.

3 to 4 tablespoons extra virgin olive oil

1 tablespoon minced garlic

2 dried chiles (optional)

Salt and freshly ground black pepper

1 pound broccoli or cauliflower (about 1 medium head), trimmed, broken into florets of any size, parboiled, shocked (see page 241), and dried

Zest and juice of 1 lemon

Chopped parsley leaves for garnish

① Put 2 tablespoons of the olive oil in a large skillet over medium heat. When hot, add the garlic, with the chiles if you're using them, and cook, stirring occasionally, until the garlic is golden, a minute or two. Add the drained vegetable and raise the heat to high. Cook, stirring only when necessary—you don't want the vegetable to fall apart—until it begins to brown; add the lemon zest and cook for another minute or two.

② Serve hot or at room temperature. Just before serving, stir in the lemon juice, drizzle with some more oil, garnish with the parsley, and serve.

Braised and Glazed Broccoli, Cauliflower, or Just about Anything Else. No precooking needed: In Step 1, start with $^1/_4$ cup of olive oil. Thirty seconds after adding the garlic, add the broccoli or cauliflower and $^1/_4$ cup of water. Cover the pan. Cook, uncovering and stirring occasionally, until the broccoli or cauliflower is just tender, 10 to 15 minutes. Uncover, raise the heat, and cook out all but a little of the remaining water (by then the vegetables should be turning golden). Proceed with the recipe from Step 2.

Broccoli Raab

Broccoli Rape, Rabe, or Rapini

Whether a slender and bitter cousin of broccoli, or more closely related to the turnip (which apparently is the reality), broccoli raab is one great vegetable: strongly and deliciously flavored and easy to prepare and cook. It has elongated stems with small flower heads surrounded by variously sized spiky leaves.

Buying and storing: Look for bright green color, crisp stems, and unwilted leaves. Avoid those with more than a few tiny yellow flowers blooming; they'll be too bitter. Store wrapped loosely in plastic in the refrigerator; use as soon as possible.

Preparing: Trim the dry ends of the stems and pull off any yellowing or wilted leaves. Parboil and shock (see page 241) to preserve the green color or for quicker final cooking.

Best cooking methods: Boiling, steaming, microwaving, or braising.

When is it done? When you can insert a skewer or thin-bladed knife into the thickest part of the stalk. Undercooked broccoli raab is too crisp; overcooked broccoli raab is mushy.

Other vegetables to substitute: Broccoli, asparagus, gai lan (page 269), or turnip or mustard greens.

Brussels Sprouts

Believed to have been developed in Belgium (hence the name), these miniature cabbages are among my favorites when cooked properly. The tiny heads grow in vertical rows on long, thick stalks; occasionally they're sold still on the stalk, which isn't necessarily a sign of freshness.

Buying and storing: Brussels sprouts are a winter vegetable and are best from early fall through early spring. Smaller is better; reject any with yellow or loose leaves or those that are soft or not tightly packed. Store wrapped loosely in plastic in the refrigerator.

Preparing: Trim the hard edge of the stem and remove any loose leaves. Cut, slice, or leave whole.

Best cooking method: Roasted, sautéed, or simmered.

When are they done? When just tender enough to be pierced easily by a skewer or a thin-bladed knife. Do not overcook.

Other vegetables to substitute: Any cabbage.

Braised and Glazed Brussels Sprouts

MAKES: 4 servings

TIME: 30 minutes

Sometimes I like to brown Brussels sprouts a bit, which is why this braise-and-glaze technique is a little different from the general description on page 271 and deserves a special recipe. I also like to leave the Brussels sprouts whole because there is less of a tendency for them to overcook and they look great. If you use the oil instead of butter, this is vegan.

Other vegetables you can use: shredded green or red cabbage, broccoli, or cauliflower.

3 tablespoons butter or extra virgin olive oil

1 pound Brussels sprouts, trimmed

1/2 cup or more vegetable stock (pages 101–102), white wine, or water, or more as needed

Salt and freshly ground black pepper

1 Combine the butter, Brussels sprouts, and stock in a deep skillet with a tight-fitting lid, sprinkle with salt and pepper, and bring to a boil. Cover and adjust the heat so the mixture simmers; cook until the sprouts are just tender, 5 to 10 minutes, checking once or twice and adding liquid as needed.

2 Uncover and raise the heat to boil off all the liquid so that the vegetables become glazed and eventually browned. Resist the urge to stir them frequently; just let them sizzle until golden and crisp, then shake the pan and loosen them to roll over. It's okay if some sides are more well done than others. Taste and adjust the seasoning, then serve hot or at room temperature.

Roasted Brussels Sprouts with Garlic

MAKES: 4 servings
TIME: 45 minutes

Brussels sprouts must be cooked thoroughly, but not until they're mushy; they're best when the insides are tender but not soft. And they're ideal, I think, when the exterior is crisp. This combination of sautéing and roasting does the trick nicely, and these sprouts are good when very, very dark brown, almost burned.

Other vegetables you can use: red cabbage (I like it cut into wide ribbons) or wedges of radicchio.

1 pound Brussels sprouts

$^1/_4$ cup extra virgin olive oil

5 cloves peeled garlic, or more to taste

Salt and freshly ground black pepper

1 tablespoon balsamic vinegar

❶ Preheat the oven to 450°F. Trim the hard edge of the stem from the Brussels sprouts, then cut each in half through its axis. Put the oil in a large ovenproof skillet over medium-high heat. When it shimmers, arrange the sprouts in one layer, cut side down. Toss in the garlic and sprinkle with salt and pepper.

❷ Cook, undisturbed, until the sprouts begin to brown, 5 to 10 minutes, then transfer to the oven. Cook, shaking the pan occasionally, until the sprouts are quite brown and tender, about 30 minutes.

❸ Taste and adjust the seasoning; drizzle with the balsamic vinegar, stir, and serve hot or warm.

Sautéed Brussels Sprouts with Hazelnuts

MAKES: 4 servings
TIME: 30 minutes

These are lovely with mint or dill, but parsley does fine. Use the oil and this is vegan.

Other vegetables you can use: cabbage (shredded), snow peas, snap peas, green or wax beans, iceberg lettuce (shredded), or chicory or its relatives (see page 300).

1 pound Brussels sprouts

$^1/_4$ cup extra virgin olive oil or 4 tablespoons ($^1/_2$ stick) butter

Salt and freshly ground black pepper

$^1/_2$ cup chopped hazelnuts

1 tablespoon balsamic vinegar or freshly squeezed lemon juice

$^1/_4$ cup shredded fresh mint, dill, or parsley leaves

❶ Trim the hard edge of the stem from the Brussels sprouts, then cut each one into thin slices or shreds; you can do this on a mandoline, with the blade side of a box grater, or with a knife. Put half the oil or butter in a large skillet over medium-high heat. When the oil is hot or the butter is melted, add the sprouts and $^1/_4$ cup water; sprinkle with salt and pepper, turn the heat to medium, and cover. Cook, undisturbed, for about 5 minutes, or until nearly tender.

❷ Meanwhile, heat the remaining oil or melt the remaining butter in a small skillet over medium heat. Add the nuts and cook, stirring almost constantly, until fragrant but just barely browned, about 5 minutes.

❸ When the sprouts are ready, uncover and raise the heat back to medium-high. Cook, stirring occasionally, until any remaining water evaporates and the sprouts are fully tender, another 5 to 10 minutes. Stir in the vinegar, garnish with the nuts and their butter or oil and the herb, and serve.

Brussels Sprouts in Coconut Milk

MAKES: 4 servings
TIME: 30 minutes

You can give Brussels sprouts—or any kind of cabbage, for that matter—an Indian-style treatment as simply as cooking it in butter or oil with a sprinkling of curry powder. But this is a more sophisticated treatment, creamy and delicious.

Other vegetables you can use: any shredded cabbage, cubed potatoes, parsnips, turnips, or kohlrabi.

> 3 tablespoons neutral oil, like grapeseed or corn
>
> 1 tablespoon yellow or black mustard seeds
>
> 2 dried chiles
>
> 1 tablespoon garam masala or curry powder (to make your own, see page 815 or 816) or any similar spice blend
>
> 1 to 1 1/2 pounds Brussels sprouts, trimmed and cut in half
>
> Salt and freshly ground black pepper
>
> 1 cup coconut milk (to make your own, see page 423)
>
> Chopped fresh cilantro leaves for garnish (optional)

1 Put the oil in a heavy skillet with a lid over medium heat. When hot, add the mustard seeds, chiles, and spice mix and cook, stirring, for about 30 seconds. Add the Brussels sprouts, cut side down, along with a good pinch of salt and a liberal sprinkling of pepper. Cook, undisturbed, for 5 minutes.

2 Stir, then add the coconut milk and, if it's very thick, about 1/4 cup water. Bring to a gentle boil, then cover and cook until the Brussels sprouts are tender, about 10 minutes. Uncover and, if necessary, raise the heat to high to thicken the mixture a bit. Taste and adjust the seasoning, then garnish if you like and serve.

Burdock

Gobo

The root of a thistle plant (and related to artichokes), burdock is not often used in the United States, though that may be changing. Known as *gobo* in Japan, it's often braised with carrots or other vegetables and is prized for its sweet, earthy flavor. You're most likely to find the long, slender, and fibrous roots still covered in dirt and anywhere from 1 to 3 feet long; look in Asian markets.

Buying and storing: Look for dirt-coated pieces (it helps keep them fresh) that are firm and no more than an inch or so thick. Store (with the dirt on) wrapped loosely in plastic in the refrigerator; use as soon as possible.

Preparing: Scrub the dirt off the root just before using; peeling is not necessary. Trim the ends and crush and/or chop, slice, or shred as you like.

Due to a natural enzyme—again, like artichoke—raw burdock discolors very quickly when cut; rub with half a lemon or dip in water with a couple tablespoons of lemon juice or vinegar immediately after cutting to minimize darkening.

Best cooking methods: Braising and stir-frying.
When is it done? When it's tender but still crisp.
Other vegetables to substitute: Artichoke hearts and cardoons are similar in flavor; carrots or celery are similar in texture.

Quick-Braised Burdock and Carrots

Kinpira Gobo

MAKES: 4 servings
TIME: 15 minutes

If you've never tried burdock, this traditional Japanese dish is a nice introduction. The textures and colors are great. Serve with plain white or brown rice or, for a less

F Fast   **M** Make Ahead   **V** Vegan

authentic—though delicious—approach, try tossing the finished dish with warm soba noodles.

Other vegetables you can use: in virtually any combination, potatoes, kohlrabi, parsnips, turnips, beets, winter squash.

About 8 ounces burdock, peeled and julienned

2 teaspoons dark sesame oil

1 medium carrot, julienned

2 tablespoons soy sauce

1½ tablespoons mirin

1½ tablespoons sake

2 teaspoons sugar

2 teaspoons toasted sesame seeds (see page 321)

① Immerse the burdock in a bowl of water with a squeeze of lemon juice or splash of vinegar so it doesn't turn dark. Drain just before adding to the pan.

② Put the sesame oil in a small pan over medium-high heat. Add the burdock and cook for about 2 minutes. Add the carrot and cook until the burdock and carrot are just tender, about 10 minutes. Pour in the soy, mirin, sake, sugar, and sesame seeds and cook until about half of the liquid remains, about 5 minutes. Turn off the heat and cool to room temperature or store, covered, in the refrigerator for up to 2 days.

Cabbage

Green Cabbage, Red Cabbage, Savoy Cabbage, and Napa Cabbage (for Chinese Cabbage, see Bok Choy)

A member of the large *Brassica* genus (along with broccoli, cauliflower, kale, and more), cabbage comes in many forms and flavors, but here we're talking about head cabbage. The best of the lot is Savoy, which has tender, crinkly, light green leaves. The elongated, mostly white, and ruffled-leaved Napa is also tender and lovely used raw. The smooth-leaf green and red varieties are decent, the red offering a great color, but they tend to be tougher and more strongly flavored than either Savoy or Napa.

By and large, cabbage has a bad reputation for being a rather unpleasant-tasting vegetable, and when overcooked it can be. So if you think you hate it, try it raw or quickly cooked, like in a stir-fry or very lightly poached, before making a final judgment; you will be pleasantly surprised.

Buying and storing: Look for tightly packed heads that are heavy for their size; avoid any with yellowing or loose leaves. Size is irrelevant in terms of flavor, but how much will you actually use? Rare is the occasion that you'll need a 4-pound head unless you're making coleslaw or sauerkraut for a crew. Cabbage is available year-round, so there's no reason to buy canned or frozen. Store fresh in the refrigerator; it'll last a couple weeks.

Preparing: Remove the first layer or two of exterior leaves and then remove the core. Use a thin-bladed knife to cut a cone-shaped section wider than the area of the core out of the stem end. To shred it, cut the cabbage into quarters (or eighths, depending on size) and cut crosswise into thin strips or use a mandoline. Napa cabbage can be cut crosswise whole to shred it.

Best cooking methods: Sautéing, stir-frying, and braising. Also, see Kimchi (page 96).

When is it done? When crisp-tender to soft but not mushy.

Other vegetables to substitute: Brussels sprouts, collards, or bok choy (especially for stir-frying).

Buttered Cabbage

MAKES: 4 servings
TIME: 20 minutes

For a two-ingredient vegetable dish, this is pretty great, especially when you consider cabbage is a vegetable that

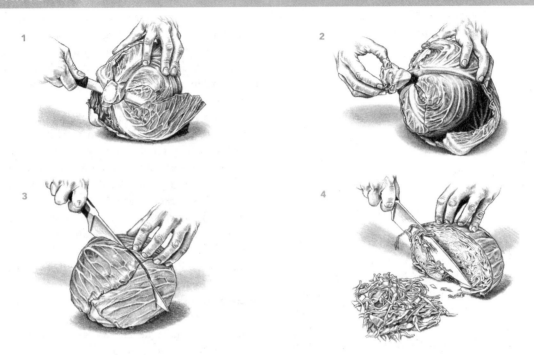

(STEPS 1–2) The easiest way to core a head cabbage is to cut a cone-shaped section from the bottom. (STEP 3) To shred head cabbage, first cut it into manageable pieces. (STEP 4) Cut thin sections across the head; they'll naturally fall into shreds. (You can also use a mandoline for this; see page 21). If the shreds are too long, just cut across them.

everyone pooh-poohs. But even with ordinary white cabbage, this is simply delicious (it's a tad better with Savoy, I'll admit), largely because you don't overcook the cabbage. For extra flavor, melt the butter with a clove of garlic, some minced shallot, or a little good paprika.

Serve this as a side dish or combined with other relatively plain dishes, like Boiled Potatoes (page 340), Fresh Egg Noodles with Scallions and Paprika (page 497), or Chickpeas in Their Own Broth, with Crisp Bread Crumbs (page 805).

Other vegetables you can use: Of course this is a basic vegetable preparation, but to keep it in the same spirit, think collards, kale, bok choy, and the like.

Salt

2 to 4 tablespoons butter

About 20 cabbage leaves

❶ Put a medium to large pot of water on to boil and salt it well. Put the butter in a small saucepan over medium-low heat and melt it; if you let it brown a little bit, so much the better, but don't burn it.

Ⓕ Fast   Ⓜ Make Ahead   Ⓥ Vegan

2 When the water boils, add the cabbage and cook, stirring every now and then, until it becomes tender, about 5 minutes. Remove with tongs or a slotted spoon and drain well; toss gently with the melted butter and serve.

Cabbage with Tomatoes and Sour Cream

MAKES: 4 servings

TIME: 40 minutes

A substantial dish from Russia, very good in winter, when canned tomatoes will do just fine. I like it with cumin seeds, though caraway seeds are a bit more traditional.

Other vegetables you can use: about 2 pounds kohlrabi or waxy potatoes, cut into wedges.

    2 tablespoons butter

    1 medium onion, chopped

    1 tablespoon minced garlic

    6 cups shredded cabbage, preferably Savoy (about
        1 small head)

    Salt and freshly ground black pepper

    2 cups chopped tomatoes (drained canned are fine)

    1 tablespoon caraway or cumin seeds (optional)

    $^1/_2$ cup sour cream

1 Put the butter in a large, deep skillet over medium heat. When it melts, add the onion and garlic and cook, stirring occasionally, until the onion softens, about 5 minutes. Add the cabbage and raise the heat a bit. Cook, stirring occasionally and adjusting the heat so the cabbage cooks without browning, until it softens, about 10 minutes. Sprinkle with salt and pepper.

2 Add the tomatoes, with the seeds if you're using them, and cook over lively heat, stirring occasionally, until the mixture becomes saucy but thick, 10 to 15 minutes. Lower the heat to a minimum, then taste and adjust

the seasoning. Stir in the sour cream and cook for another couple minutes, stirring; serve hot.

Red Cabbage with Apples

MAKES: 4 servings

TIME: About 45 minutes

A pretty sweet-and-sour dish, best served alongside a rich stew like Flageolets, French Style (page 604), or Kasha with Golden Brown Onions (page 562). You can use butter instead of oil if you prefer, but then it won't be vegan.

Other vegetables you can use: any cabbage.

Other fruit you can use: pears, pitted cherries, or 1 cup pitted and halved prunes.

    2 tablespoons neutral oil, like grapeseed or corn

    2 pounds red cabbage, trimmed and shredded

    3 cloves

    1$^1/_2$ pounds Granny Smith or other apples, peeled,
        cored, and cut into chunks

    Salt and freshly ground black pepper

    $^1/_2$ cup vegetable stock (pages 101–102), not-too-dry
        white wine, apple cider, or water, plus more if
        needed

    1 tablespoon freshly squeezed lemon juice or cider or
        other vinegar, or to taste

1 Put the oil in a large, deep skillet or saucepan over medium heat. When hot, add the cabbage and the cloves and cook, stirring, until the cabbage becomes quite soft, about 20 minutes; adjust the heat so the cabbage doesn't brown. Add the apples, sprinkle with salt and pepper, and cook, stirring occasionally, for a minute or two.

2 Add the stock, turn the heat to medium-low, and cook, stirring occasionally, until the cabbage is very tender and the apples are also quite soft but not yet falling apart, 10 to 15 minutes. Add more liquid if necessary.

❸ Add the lemon juice, taste and adjust the seasoning, discard the cloves, and serve.

Carrots

The most common of all root vegetables, carrots are cheap, versatile, and available year-round. We take them for granted when we shouldn't: They taste good, and they're sweet; you can eat them raw or cook them almost any way you like.

Beyond the usual orange, carrots come in a variety of colors, including purple, maroon, yellow, and white. The differences in flavor are subtle. Visit a farmer's market for the widest selection (late summer through early winter is the official season). But keep in mind that although they are pretty raw, the color will fade (sometimes completely) when they're cooked.

Buying and storing: Bagged carrots are a no-brainer—as long as they're hard and crisp. Carrots with the tops should be very fresh: the tops should be bright green, crisp, and unwilted. But remove the tops before storing, as they draw moisture and nutrients from the carrot itself. Avoid any carrot that is soft, flabby, cracked, or growing new leaves. I don't usually buy the so-called baby carrots (they're actually cut and peeled regular carrots); even though they're convenient, they dry out too quickly. Store wrapped loosely in plastic in the refrigerator. They keep for at least a couple weeks but eventually dry out and crack and lose a lot of their nutrients.

Preparing: Peel with a vegetable peeler, then trim off both ends. Chop, slice, or grate as you like.

Best cooking methods: Steaming, braising, braising and glazing, or roasting.

When are they done? When tender but not soft. Taste and you'll know.

Other vegetables to substitute: Parsnips, beets, turnips, or celery root.

(STEP 1) To dice a carrot, cut it in half lengthwise, then into quarters or, if necessary, smaller sections. (STEP 2) Cut across the sections, as small as you like.

Quick-Glazed Carrots

MAKES: 4 servings
TIME: 30 minutes
F **M**

One of the most useful recipes ever and, sadly, one that is often overlooked. Carrots cooked this way are terrific hot, warm, or at room temperature (use oil instead of butter if you plan to serve them less than hot—which also makes them vegan) and take to a wide variety of herbs and other simple treatments. If you can find real baby carrots—the very thin ones—just trim them quickly (don't even bother to peel them); they'll be super.

Use oil instead of butter and the carrots are vegan.

Other vegetables you can use: parsnips or turnips.

1 pound carrots, more or less, cut into coins
or sticks

2 tablespoons butter or extra virgin olive oil

Salt and freshly ground black pepper

1 teaspoon freshly squeezed lemon juice (optional)

Chopped fresh parsley, dill, mint, basil, or chervil
leaves for garnish (optional)

1 Combine all the ingredients except the garnish in a saucepan no more than 6 inches across; add about $^1/_3$ cup water (or white wine or stock). Bring to a boil, then cover and adjust the heat so the mixture simmers.

2 Cook, more or less undisturbed, until the carrots are tender and the liquid is pretty much gone, 10 to 20 minutes. Uncover and boil off the remaining liquid, then add the lemon juice if you're using it. Taste and adjust the seasoning; serve hot, or within an hour or two, garnished with the herb if you like.

Quick-Glazed Carrots with Orange and Ginger. Not much more work but sexier and far more impressive: Add 1 tablespoon minced or grated peeled fresh ginger to the initial mix; use freshly squeezed orange juice in place of water. Garnish with a teaspoon or more of grated orange and/or lemon zest.

Balsamic-Glazed Carrots with Garlic. Another variation that doesn't take much but is amazing: Use balsamic vinegar in place of the water and add 5 to 10 whole cloves of peeled garlic along with the carrots. Proceed as above, adding water if the mixture dries out before the carrots are done.

5 Ways to Jazz Up Quick-Glazed Carrots

1. Add $^1/_2$ cup or so of chopped onion, shallot, scallion, or leeks.
2. Add $^1/_2$ cup or so of chopped pitted dates, raisins, dried currants, or dried tomatoes.
3. Whisk together 1 tablespoon soy sauce and 1 tablespoon miso, then stir this into the carrots just as they're done. (Use sake as the glazing liquid instead of the water if you have it.)

4. Add 1 cup or so peas, snow peas, or snap peas along with the carrots (thawed frozen are fine).
5. Add a tablespoon or so of any mild chile paste (one made with ancho chiles would be ideal).

Carrots with Dates and Raisins

MAKES: 4 servings
TIME: 20 minutes

  ⓥ

Another quick vegetable dish that works well at room temperature, this is perfect for a Middle Eastern–style meal with Stuck-Pot Rice and Lentils with Pita Crust (page 525) and a dollop of yogurt. Or serve it as part of a table filled with salads, spreads, and breads.

Other vegetables you can use: parsnips or kohlrabi.

2 tablespoons extra virgin olive oil

1 small yellow onion, halved and thinly sliced

$^1/_2$ cup chopped pitted dates

$^1/_4$ cup raisins, preferably golden

Large pinch saffron (optional)

Salt and freshly ground black pepper

1 pound carrots, peeled and cut into $^1/_4$-inch-thick
slices or roll-cut (see page 21)

$^1/_2$ cup chopped pistachios, almonds, or walnuts for
garnish (optional)

Minced fresh mint leaves for garnish

1 Put the oil in a deep skillet with a tight-fitting lid over medium heat. Add the onion and stir until soft, 3 minutes or so, then add the dates, the raisins, and the saffron if you're using it, sprinkle with salt and pepper, and stir until fragrant, about a minute.

2 Stir in the carrots and $^1/_4$ cup water, bring to a boil, cover the pan, and turn the heat down to medium-low. Cook, undisturbed, for 5 minutes.

3 Uncover and raise the heat a bit. Cook, stirring occasionally, until the liquid has evaporated and the carrots are cooking in the oil, 5 to 10 minutes. Lower the heat and continue to cook, stirring occasionally, until tender, just a minute or two more. Taste and adjust the seasoning, then garnish and serve.

Carrots with Dried Apricots and Chipotle. Sweet, smoky, and hot: Soak 1 or 2 dried chipotle chiles in warm water to cover until soft and pliable, about 20 minutes. Drain well, remove the stem and seeds, and mince the flesh as finely as you can. Omit the raisins and the saffron. Instead of the dates, use chopped dried apricots. Proceed with the recipe, adding the chile in Step 1, along with the dried apricots.

Cauliflower

Another member of the *Brassica* genus (along with cabbage, broccoli, kale, collard greens, Brussels sprouts, and much more); with its ivory-colored florets, cauliflower is arguably the most striking in terms of appearance. Even cooler are the chartreuse-colored "broccoflower" and the outlandishly spiky, lime-green Romanesco, both of which are hard to identify as either cauliflower or broccoli; the broccoflower is a hybrid of the two, and Romanesco is a less-common cousin of cauliflower. A more recently developed type (read: genetically modified) is a peachy-colored, vitamin A–rich (like twenty-five times the amount of white) orange cauliflower; there are purple cauliflowers too. Like broccoli, all of them can be prepared in a variety of ways; serve them raw, lightly cooked, or completely cooked; steamed, boiled, roasted, sautéed, stir-fried, or braised.

Buying and storing: It should be heavy, beautifully white with no gray or brown spots, and crisp. Ideally, you want one with the leaves still wrapped around the flower. Store wrapped loosely in plastic in the refrigerator and use within a week or so.

Preparing: Remove the outer leaves and, if necessary, scrape off any gray or brown spots. You can cook it whole or separate it into florets before cooking. To separate into florets, begin at the base of the head and cut

(STEP 1) First remove all outer leaves.

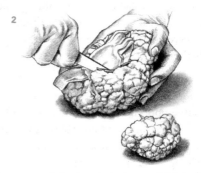

(STEP 2) You can cook the head whole or cut it into florets.

florets from the core, one after the other. The florets may in turn be broken or cut into smaller pieces if you like.

Best cooking methods: Steaming, braising and glazing, and roasting.

When is it done? When just tender enough to pierce with a skewer or thin-bladed knife. Overcooking is not as disastrous as it is with other members of the cabbage family, but, naturally, it's not desirable.

Other vegetables to substitute: Broccoli and cauliflower are almost always interchangeable; or substitute broccoflower or Romanesco.

           Fast   Ⓜ Make Ahead   Ⓥ Vegan

Basic Steamed Cauliflower

MAKES: 4 servings

TIME: About 30 minutes

You can speed the cooking of cauliflower by cutting it up before cooking, but because it crumbles easily, you'll lose some of it in the process. It's best to allow enough time to cook the thing whole. And steaming is better than simmering, not only because it's faster but also because it won't leave the cauliflower waterlogged. Serve hot cauliflower with butter, extra virgin olive oil, and/or lemon juice; garnish with parsley. Or shock (see page 241), put in a covered container, and refrigerate for up to 2 days. Then break into florets and cook according to the directions for Precooked Vegetables in Butter or Oil (page 240) or use in other recipes.

> 1 head cauliflower, about 1½ pounds, trimmed of green parts
>
> Chopped parsley leaves for garnish

Put the cauliflower in a steamer above an inch or two of salted water. Cover and cook over steadily bubbling water until it is just tender enough to be pierced to the core with a thin-bladed knife and no longer. (Because it's large, the cauliflower will retain quite a bit of heat after cooking, so it should still be ever-so-slightly chewy when you remove it from the steamer.) Total cooking time will be 12 to 25 minutes, depending on the size of the head.

Breaded Sautéed Cauliflower

MAKES: 4 servings

TIME: 30 minutes (less with cooked cauliflower)

There are many ways to sauté vegetables with bread crumbs (or nuts; see the variation) for a little added crunch, and they're all good. Whether the bread crumbs stick to the vegetable is not all that important, because you'll get the crunch anyway, but for the prettiest presentation, use the egg. To make this vegan, leave out the egg and use the oil.

Other vegetables you can use: broccoli, for sure, though it won't look as nice; whole green beans, Brussels sprouts.

> 1 pound cauliflower (about 1 medium head), cored, trimmed, broken into florets of any size, parboiled, shocked (see page 241), and dried
>
> All-purpose flour for dredging (optional)
>
> 2 or 3 eggs, lightly beaten in a bowl (optional)
>
> 1 cup bread crumbs, preferably fresh (page 804), for dredging
>
> 4 tablespoons (½ stick) butter or ¼ cup extra virgin olive oil
>
> Salt and freshly ground black pepper
>
> Chopped parsley leaves for garnish
>
> Lemon wedges for serving (optional)

1 If you're using the egg, roll each piece of cauliflower in the flour, dip in the egg, then in the bread crumbs. If you're not using the egg, just roll the pieces in the bread crumbs, patting to help them adhere.

2 Put the butter or oil in a large skillet and turn the heat to medium. When the butter melts or the oil is hot, begin to add the cauliflower. Cook the cauliflower pieces, adjusting the heat so the bread crumbs brown without burning on all sides and sprinkling with salt and pepper as they cook.

3 When the cauliflower is browned and tender, anywhere from 8 to 12 minutes, garnish and serve, with lemon wedges if you like.

Sautéed Cauliflower with Onion and Olives. The glossy olives and red pepper flakes give this kick and color: Use olive oil; before cooking the cauliflower, add 1 cup chopped onion (red is nice); cook, stirring occasionally, until the onion softens, 3 to 5 minutes. Proceed as directed, adding ½ to 1 cup pitted black olives (oil-cured are good here, though you can use whatever you like) and ½ teaspoon hot red pepper flakes, or to taste.

Sautéed Cauliflower with Garlic, Vinegar, and Capers. Quintessentially Mediterranean: Use olive oil; add 1 tablespoon chopped garlic along with the cauliflower. Just before it's done, add 1 tablespoon red wine, sherry, or other vinegar and about a tablespoon of capers.

Sautéed Cauliflower with Feta and Mint. Perfect with sliced tomatoes on the side: Instead of the parsley, chop about $1/2$ cup of fresh mint leaves. In Step 3, when the cauliflower is ready, stir in $1/2$ cup finely crumbled feta cheese and the mint.

Sautéed Cauliflower with Almonds, Raisins, and Saffron. Golden raisins are particularly nice-looking here: In Step 3, when the cauliflower is just beginning to turn golden, stir in a pinch of saffron, $1/4$ cup chopped almonds, and $1/4$ cup raisins. Proceed with the recipe, cooking and stirring until everything is browned.

Roasted Cauliflower with Raisins and Vinaigrette

MAKES: 4 or more servings
TIME: 45 minutes, largely unattended

Roasting toughens cauliflower and dries it out a bit; with many foods, this description might not sound that appealing, but because cauliflower is often mushy and watery, these are good things. I like to get it nice and brown, and cooking it with a bit of the dressing deepens its flavor. The remaining vinaigrette is tossed with the cauliflower at the last minute, along with the raisins, whose sweetness counters the vinegar beautifully.

Other vegetables you can use: broccoli spears or any root vegetable, cut into cubes and roasted.

1 large head cauliflower, cored, trimmed, and
    separated into florets

$1/2$ cup extra virgin olive oil

Salt and freshly ground black pepper

2 tablespoons sherry vinegar or balsamic vinegar, or
    to taste

$1/2$ cup raisins

$1/2$ cup chopped parsley leaves

1 Preheat the oven to 400°F. Put the cauliflower in a roasting pan, drizzle with 3 tablespoons of the oil, sprinkle with salt and pepper, and toss to distribute. Roast, turning once or twice, for 15 minutes or so, until the cauliflower just starts to soften.

2 Meanwhile, combine the remaining oil with the vinegar and a little salt and pepper; taste and adjust the seasoning. Remove the pan from the oven, drizzle the cauliflower with 2 tablespoons of the vinaigrette, and toss to coat. Roast again, turning once more, until a thin-bladed knife pierces a piece with little resistance, another 15 minutes. (The recipe may be made ahead to this point, cooled, covered tightly, and refrigerated for up to 2 days. Return to room temperature before proceeding.)

3 When you're ready to serve, put the cauliflower in a large salad bowl and add the raisins and parsley. Add the remaining dressing and toss. Taste and sprinkle with more salt if needed and lots of pepper, then serve hot, warm, or at room temperature.

Mashed Cauliflower with Cheese

MAKES: 4 servings
TIME: 30 minutes

This is one dish that came out of the low-carb diet craze that is actually worth making. The diet set touted this dish as a mashed potato substitute because of the fluffy, creamy texture. But I think it's great as a vegetarian main dish, with other vegetables—and, yes, some bread or cooked grains!—on the side. Use any good melting cheese (see page 209) you like here or all Parmesan for a less creamy, fluffier version.

Other vegetables you can use: broccoli.

Salt

1 large head cauliflower, cored, trimmed, and separated into florets

1 cup milk or cream, plus more as needed

2 tablespoons butter

2 cups grated white melting cheese, like cheddar, Asiago, or Gruyère

Freshly ground black pepper

$1/4$ teaspoon freshly grated nutmeg

Chopped parsley leaves for garnish

1 Fill a large pot with water, put it on to boil, and salt it. Boil the cauliflower until very tender, about 15 minutes. Drain, reserving about a cup of the cooking water. Wipe the pot dry.

2 Put the milk, butter, and cheese in the pot over medium-low heat. Sprinkle with salt and pepper and the nutmeg. Cook, stirring occasionally to keep the mixture from sticking, until the cheese and butter start to melt, 3 to 5 minutes. Stir in the cauliflower and mash with a fork or potato masher; stir well to combine. The mixture should be the consistency you like in mashed potatoes. If it's not creamy enough, add a little of the cauliflower cooking water or more milk or cream until it is. Taste and adjust the seasoning, garnish, and serve.

Manchurian-Style Cauliflower

MAKES: 4 to 6 servings
TIME: 30 minutes
F

This recipe comes courtesy of my friend Suvir Saran, one of this country's best and most consistent Indian chefs;

he reports it's a dish that's closely associated with the Chinatown in Calcutta, where it's sold on the street, to be eaten off toothpicks. But whatever the case, it drives people nuts—it's just that good. It's a bit of work, a two-step process that includes deep frying, but the work goes quickly, and the dish will be the centerpiece of any table on which you put it.

Other vegetables you can use: broccoli.

Neutral oil, like grapeseed or corn, for deep frying

3 eggs

$2/3$ cup cornstarch

1 teaspoon freshly ground black pepper

1 teaspoon salt, for the batter, plus salt for the sauce

1 large or 2 small heads cauliflower, cored, trimmed, and separated into florets

2 teaspoons finely minced garlic

1 cup ketchup (to make your own, see page 790)

$1/2$ teaspoon cayenne, or to taste

1 Put at least 2 inches oil in a countertop deep fryer or in a deep pan on the stove and turn the heat to medium-high; bring to 350°F (see "Deep Frying," page 26).

2 Beat the eggs and cornstarch together until well blended in a bowl large enough to hold the cauliflower. Season the batter with pepper and salt, then add the cauliflower. Use your hands to toss until the florets are coated evenly.

3 Fry the cauliflower in batches small enough not to crowd your pan or fryer and be sure to let the oil return to temperature (350°F) between batches. Fry until the florets take on a pale, sandy color, with a little brown mottling, about 5 minutes; transfer to paper towels to drain.

4 Warm 1 tablespoon oil in a large nonstick pan or wok over medium heat and immediately add the minced garlic. Cook the garlic for a minute or two, until fragrant but not colored, then add the ketchup. Cook, stirring, for about 5 minutes, until the sauce bubbles, thickens, and starts to caramelize around the edges of the pan. Add the cayenne; taste and add salt as necessary. Toss the cauliflower in the sauce until coated evenly and serve.

Roasted Cauliflower, Manchurian Style. Easier, but without the batter: Reduce the amount of oil to 3 tablespoons. Omit the eggs and cornstarch. Preheat the oven to 400°F. Put the cauliflower in a large baking pan or rimmed baking sheet, drizzle with 2 tablespoons of the oil, and sprinkle with 1 teaspoon each of the pepper and salt. Toss until well coated. Roast for about 30 minutes, stirring once or twice, until the cauliflower is tender and golden. During the last 5 minutes or so of roasting, begin preparing the sauce as described in Step 4 and proceed with the recipe.

Celery

Celery is a standby vegetable for most of us, used raw in crudités or chopped up and cooked in soups, stews, and stir-fries, but it's rarely used alone, which is a shame because it's wonderful when cooked: The flavor and texture of celery mellows, making it a mildly—but still uniquely—flavored vegetable.

Buying and storing: Celery should be crisp, bright pale green, and tightly packed—I like celery with its leaves as they're great used like a fresh herb. Avoid rubbery, wilted, or yellow celery. Store wrapped loosely in plastic in the refrigerator; celery keeps for about two weeks.

Preparing: Trim the leaves from the celery (and reserve it for use as a garnish if you like) and cut off the bottom core or remove as many stalks as you need. String the celery if it's tough and very fibrous, or just cut it into whatever size pieces you need.

Best cooking methods: Braising, hands down.

When is it done? When good and tender; taste a piece.

Other vegetables to substitute: Celery and fennel are almost always interchangeable.

Celery is usually best when its "strings" are removed. Simply grasp the end of the stalk between your thumb and a paring knife and pull the strings down the length of the stalk.

Oven-Braised Celery

MAKES: 4 servings
TIME: 30 minutes

You can cook celery using the basic braise-and-glaze method (see page 238), but, because it's more fibrous than most other vegetables, it benefits from slightly longer cooking in somewhat more liquid. Cooked this way, celery becomes downright tender and quite mellow.

Other vegetables you can use: fennel, which takes quite well to this treatment.

1½ pounds celery, more or less, trimmed
2 tablespoons extra virgin olive oil or butter

 Fast   Make Ahead   V Vegan

Salt and freshly ground black pepper

1 cup vegetable stock (pages 101–102) or water

Chopped parsley or fresh dill leaves for garnish

① Preheat the oven to 375°F. Cut the celery into pieces about 2 inches long. Put the oil or butter in a large, deep ovenproof skillet or flameproof gratin dish over medium heat. When the oil is hot or the butter is melted, add the celery and cook, stirring occasionally, for about 2 minutes. Sprinkle with salt and pepper and add the stock; bring to a boil and put in the oven.

② Cook until the celery is very tender, about 15 minutes. If much liquid remains, cook a little longer (in the unlikely event that it dries out before the celery becomes tender, add a little more liquid). Garnish and serve hot or warm.

Celery Root
Celeriac, Celery Knob

The large, brown, often oddly shaped, bulbous and knotty root of a type of celery grown only for its root; its flavor is distinctively celery, but the creamy and soft texture mellows it a bit when it's cooked. It's often used raw in salads (like in Celery Rémoulade, page 47), but it's also delicious boiled, sautéed, or roasted, and especially puréed and blended with mashed potatoes.

Buying and storing: Look for firm, heavy specimens with no soft spots; the smoother the skin, the easier to peel. Don't mind the dirt that often covers them. As with most root vegetables, celery root keeps for a long time, but its flavor is most intense when it is firm and crisp; don't wait until it becomes flabby to eat it. Store wrapped loosely in plastic in the refrigerator.

Preparing: It must be peeled before being used; use a sharp knife rather than a vegetable peeler and acknowledge from the outset that you will lose a good portion of the flesh. If more than a few minutes will pass between peeling the celery root and using it, you might drop it into acidulated water (1 tablespoon lemon juice or vinegar per cup of water) to keep it from discoloring.

Best cooking methods: Boiled, sautéed, braised and glazed, and roasted.

When is it done? When it's soft.

Other vegetables to substitute: Parsnips or turnips.

Chard
Swiss Chard

Chard is beautiful, with dark green and sometimes ruffled leaves and stems that may be brightly colored crimson red, orange, yellow, or stark white. It's related to the beet, whose greens (see page 265) can be used just like chard. But chard, which is available year-round, has no edible root.

Its flavor is that associated with oxalic acid, the same as what is found in spinach and rhubarb, but compounded by sweetness. This makes chard lovely in omelets and quiches and on its own. Young and very tender stems and leaves can be tossed into salads, while tougher ones must be cooked. Unfortunately, quite a bit of the vibrant color seeps out of the stems and veins when they're cooked.

Buying and storing: Chard can be either thick or thin stemmed; both are good. Look for undamaged stems and deeply colored, unwilted leaves. Store wrapped loosely in plastic in the refrigerator; it will last several days.

Preparing: Wash it well and tear or chop the leaves. If the stems are very thick, strip the leaves from them before proceeding so you can cook the stems a couple minutes longer.

Best cooking methods: Steaming, braising, and sautéing. Regardless of the method, it often makes sense to cook thick stems longer than the leaves; just start them a minute or two earlier.

When is it done? When wilted and tender.

Other vegetables to substitute: Chard and beet greens are almost always interchangeable; or substitute dandelion, turnip greens, or spinach.

Chard with Oranges and Shallots

MAKES: 4 servings

TIME: 25 minutes

A perfect dish for winter, this warm salad has both vibrant color and a tangy sweet-sour flavor. Plus, you can make it an hour or so ahead to serve at room temperature. The skin of the orange or tangerine becomes almost candied and provides a nice chew, but if you'd rather not eat it, simply peel the orange before chopping.

Other vegetables you can use: any chard, bok choy, kale, or any cabbage. For the citrus, use kumquats (quartered) if they are available.

1 pound white, red, or rainbow chard, washed and trimmed

2 tablespoons extra virgin olive oil

2 shallots, thinly sliced

2 tablespoons sugar

1 small unpeeled orange or tangerine, seeded and coarsely chopped

2 tablespoons sherry vinegar

Salt and freshly ground black pepper

1 Cut the stems out of the chard leaves. Cut the leaves into wide ribbons and slice the stems (on the diagonal if you like); keep the leaves and stems separate.

2 Put the oil in a large skillet with a lid over medium heat. When hot, add the shallots and sugar and cook for a minute, then stir in the orange or tangerine bits and lower the heat to low. Cook, stirring frequently, until everything is caramelized, about 10 minutes. Stir in the vinegar.

3 Return the heat to medium and stir in the chard stems. Cook, stirring occasionally, until they soften a bit, just a minute or two. Add the chard ribbons, cover, and turn off the heat. Let the chard steam for 2 or 3 minutes, then stir and re-cover the pan for another couple of min-

utes. Sprinkle with salt and lots of pepper and serve immediately, or within an hour or two at room temperature.

Chestnuts

Native to southern Europe and the eastern United States (and entirely unrelated to water chestnuts), chestnuts were once an abundant crop in the States until blight wiped out nearly all the chestnut trees in the early twentieth century. Now Americans get chestnuts from Europe and China.

Sweet and fairly soft (for nuts), chestnuts are starchy and mealy; the shells are smooth, dark brown, and rounded with a flattened side. They have the least amount of protein and the highest starch content of all the nuts and are usually roasted or boiled and used like a vegetable. They are sold fresh in their shells (the best way to get them) in the fall and early winter. Frozen chestnuts are a good substitute when fresh are out of season, but canned or jarred ones are usually soggy and break apart easily; they're fine for puréeing or mashing but not much else.

Buying and storing: Fresh and in-season are the best. Look for heavy, big, full, unblemished nuts; they dry out as they age and begin to rattle around in their shells. Store wrapped in damp paper towels in a plastic bag in the refrigerator for up to two weeks, but use as quickly as you can.

Preparing: Chestnuts must be precooked and their shells and skins removed. The easiest way to precook and peel is to make a shallow cut on the flat end, using a sharp paring knife. Then simmer in water to cover or bake at about 350°F until the shells curl and can be peeled off. (You can also roast or deep-fry to take off the shells, always making the shallow cut first.) Remove the inner skin as well, using a paring knife. (See page 287 for preparation instructions.) If the process becomes difficult, reheat the chestnuts.

Best cooking methods: Boiling is best if you're going to mash or purée; roasting or grilling is ideal for eating out of hand or sautéing.

 Fast   Make Ahead   Ⓥ Vegan

(STEP 1) Before cooking a chestnut, score the flat side with a sharp knife, making an X.

(STEP 2) After cooking, remove both outer shell and inner skin. If the peeling becomes difficult, reheat.

When are they done? They're ready to eat when the shell is easily removed, or they can be cooked a little longer if you want to purée them.

Other vegetables to substitute: None, really.

Boiled, Grilled, or Roasted Chestnuts

MAKES: 1 pound; 4 to 6 servings
TIME: About 30 minutes

Boiled chestnuts are great for puréeing, mashing, or using in recipes. For eating out of hand or sautéing, grilling or roasting is better.

The odd thing about peeling chestnuts is that it must be done while they're still warm; so use a thin towel to protect your fingers as much as you can. They need not be sizzling hot for the skins to slip off, but as you'll see, the hotter the better. If they start to cool, and the skins start to stick a bit, reheat and start again.

1 pound chestnuts, a shallow cut made in the flat side

To boil: Put the chestnuts in a pot with lightly salted water to cover and bring to a boil. Turn off the heat after 3 or 4 minutes. Remove a few chestnuts at a time from the water and use a sharp knife to cut off the outer and inner skins. Purée, mash, or use in other recipes.

To grill or roast: Start a charcoal or wood fire, preheat a gas grill, or turn the oven to 450°F. Put the chestnuts directly on the grill or on a sheet of aluminum foil with holes poked in it or on a baking sheet. Grill (preferably with the cover down) or roast, turning occasionally, until you can remove the shells easily, about 15 minutes. Eat warm, out of hand, sauté in olive oil or butter, or use in other recipes.

Collard Greens (*see* Kale and Collard Greens, page 308)

Corn
Maize

One of America's favorite vegetables, as it should be—it's indigenous to the Americas and has been cultivated for thousands of years. When fresh, it's used as a vegetable, but it takes many forms and has many uses (see "The Maize Maze," page 542). The fresher you can get it, generally the better it tastes. It used to be that immediately after picking the natural sugars quickly turned to starch, but the new breeds of corn retain their sweetness incredibly well, sometimes for several days. The two common varieties available these days are the robustly flavored yellow corn and the sweet and mild white corn; cobs mixed with white and yellow kernels are a hybrid.

Buying and storing: Corn is the quintessential summertime food, at its best freshly picked, so buy it at a farmer's market or farmstand if you can. Look for ears that are tightly wrapped in their husks, which should be green and fresh looking, not overly dried out. The silks should be supple and golden or golden brown. The kernels should be tightly packed and plump and should come to the tip of the cob. Store corn, still in its husk, in the refrigerator; it will not go bad but will decline in sweetness as it ages. Frozen corn is fine to cook with but isn't nearly as good as fresh corn; I don't recommend canned corn, nor any kind of prepared creamed corn, except your own (see page 290).

Preparing: Shuck the corn just before cooking it. Always remove the silk from cobs before cooking it— even if you're cooking in the husk: just peel back the husk, remove the silk, and fold the husk back over the corn; the silk burns easily and is harder to remove after than before cooking. If you want kernels only, cut or scrape them from the cob with a knife.

Best cooking methods: Steaming, roasting, and grilling. Stir-fried is also nice (see "The Basics of Stir-Frying Vegetables," page 242), and salsa made with corn is delicious (see Corn Salsa, page 751).

When is it done? When it's hot; there's no point in cooking it any further.

Other vegetables to substitute: Really, there is no substitute for corn on the cob. For corn kernels, green peas, green or wax beans, or (for raw corn kernels), diced jícama).

PREPARING CORN

(STEP 1) The "silk" is usually removed from corn before cooking. You can remove the husk or simply peel it back and take out the silk, then fold the husk back over the corn. This works well for grilling; for steaming or boiling, remove the husk entirely.

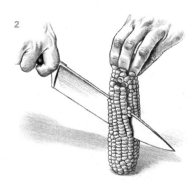

(STEP 2) When you want kernels only, use a sharp knife to scrape them from the cob.

Steamed Corn on the Cob

MAKES: 4 servings

TIME: 20 minutes or less

Keep corn cool, shuck it at the last minute, cook it just long enough to heat it up, and you'll get the most out of it. There is no reason at all to boil corn: Steaming does a perfect job, and you avoid the hassle of bringing a huge

 Fast   Make Ahead   Ⓥ Vegan

quantity of water to a boil. You can keep the corn warm over the boiling water for a while without a problem; this is not to say you should overcook it, or cook it in advance, but that you can eat four ears while holding the other four in the pot.

8 ears fresh corn, shucked

Salt and freshly ground black pepper

Butter (optional)

❶ Put the corn in a pot with an inch or two of salted water; it's okay if some of the corn sits in the water and some above it. Cover and cook over high heat until it is just hot, 10 minutes or less (if the water is already boiling when you add the corn, and/or the corn is very fresh, and your stove is powerful enough to keep the water boiling, the cooking time could be as little as 3 minutes).

❷ Serve the corn with salt, pepper, and, if you like, butter.

Milk-Steamed Corn on the Cob. Tender and sweet, especially good with less-than-ideal corn: Use milk instead of water to steam the corn.

10 Flavorings for Hot Corn

Add either alone or in combination:

1. Grated Parmesan cheese
2. Lemon or lime juice (especially with a few dashes of hot sauce)
3. Hot red pepper flakes or cayenne pepper
4. Any spice blend, especially chaat masala or chili powder (to make your own, see page 814)
5. Finely chopped pumpkin, sunflower, or sesame seeds
6. Finely chopped nuts, like hazelnuts, almonds, cashews, or peanuts
7. Minced fresh herbs, like parsley, mint, chervil, or chives
8. Mashed Roasted Garlic (page 304)
9. Nori "Shake" (page 817)
10. More butter!

Pan-Grilled Corn with Chile

MAKES: 4 servings
TIME: 20 minutes

At some point in the summer, you may get sick of plain corn on the cob or even grilled corn (page 290); at times such as those, this is the recipe to turn to. It's fast, it's easy, and it's completely different; when browned like this, corn takes on a brand-new flavor. This is also great used in the salads on pages 60–61.

Other vegetables you can use: peas.

6 ears fresh corn, shucked

1 tablespoon neutral oil, like grapeseed or corn

1 teaspoon minced fresh chile (like jalapeño or Thai), or to taste, or hot red pepper flakes or cayenne to taste

1 teaspoon minced garlic or 1 tablespoon minced shallot or white or red onion

Salt and freshly ground black pepper

Chopped fresh cilantro leaves for garnish

Lime wedges (optional)

❶ Use a knife to strip the kernels from the corn (page 288). It's easiest if you stand the corn up in a shallow bowl and just cut down the length of each ear as many times as is necessary; you'll quickly get the hang of it.

❷ Put the oil in a large skillet over high heat. When hot, add the corn, chile, and garlic; let sit for a moment. As the corn browns, shake the pan to distribute it so each kernel is deeply browned on at least one surface.

3 Remove from the heat, then add salt and pepper to taste. If you're serving immediately, stir in the cilantro and squeeze a little lime juice over the top (pass some more lime at the table); or use in any of the corn salad recipes on pages 60–61.

Pan-Grilled Corn with Tomatoes. This becomes a little stewy: In Step 2, cook the corn and chile until brown, omitting the garlic. Once the corn browns, add 2 more tablespoons oil and 1 chopped large onion; cook until the onion softens, 5 to 10 minutes. Add 2 cups chopped tomato (preferably, way preferably, fresh and good, but canned will do in a pinch) and cook, stirring occasionally, until the tomato breaks down. Proceed from Step 3.

Corn on the Cob, Grilled or Roasted

MAKES: 4 servings
TIME: 20 minutes

Grilled corn is unbeatable; I like to prepare it this way, but you can also peel down the husk, remove the inner silks, and smooth the husks back in place; this will give you bright yellow corn with attractive, nicely charred husks. But I like to blacken the kernels a bit.

Grilled corn is nice sprinkled with a little chili powder (to make your own, see page 814) too. Skip the butter to make this vegan.

Other vegetables you can use: None are quite the same, but you can grill whole zucchini.

    8 ears fresh corn, shucked
    Salt and freshly ground black pepper
    Butter (optional)

Heat a gas or charcoal grill until moderately hot; put the rack about 4 inches from the heat source. Or turn the

oven to 500°F. Grill or roast the corn, turning occasionally, for 10 to 20 minutes, or until some of the kernels char a bit and others are lightly browned. Serve with salt, pepper, and, if you like, butter.

Creamed Corn

MAKES: 4 servings
TIME: 20 minutes

All I can say is, if you've never made this yourself, especially with fresh-shucked corn, you may pass out with pleasure. The cornstarch, which will thicken the mixture and make it more like the canned cream corn most of us grew up with, is entirely optional.

    6 ears fresh corn (or 3 cups frozen corn kernels)
    3 tablespoons butter
    1½ to 2 cups cream or half-and-half
    Salt and freshly ground black pepper
    Cayenne to taste (optional)
    Sugar if necessary
    1 tablespoon cornstarch (optional)
    Chopped parsley leaves for garnish

1 Shuck the corn and strip the kernels from it into a bowl (see page 288) to save the liquid. Put the butter in a skillet or broad saucepan over medium heat. When the butter foams, add the corn and cook, stirring, for a minute or two. Add 1½ cups cream and bring to a gentle simmer; add a good pinch of salt, some pepper, and a pinch of cayenne if you like. Simmer for about 10 minutes, or until the corn is tender.

2 Taste and add a little sugar if you like. Continue to cook until the mixture is thick, another few minutes, adding a little more cream if necessary. If you'd like it thicker, combine the cornstarch with a tablespoon of cold water and stir it into the corn; the mixture will thicken almost immediately. Taste and adjust the seasoning, garnish, and serve.

Creamed Corn with Onion. Sweeter, if anything, with a bit of crunch: Before adding the corn to the butter, cook about 1/2 cup chopped onion, stirring frequently, until quite tender but not browned, about 10 minutes.

Creamed Corn with Cheese. Richer: Instead of cornstarch, thicken with about a cup of grated semihard cheese, like cheddar. If you like, finish this with a sprinkling of Parmesan and run under the broiler for a minute or two.

Vegan Creamed Corn with Chile. In Step 1, use neutral oil, like grapeseed or corn, in place of the butter. Cook 1 teaspoon minced fresh chile (like jalapeño or Thai), or to taste, for about a minute, before adding the corn (or use good chili powder—or see page 814 to make your own—to taste, along with the corn). Use coconut or almond milk in place of the cream and proceed as directed.

Corn Pancakes, Thai Style

MAKES: 4 servings

TIME: 30 minutes

🄵

I have made corn fritters twenty different ways over the years, and I do think these are the best: barely bound fresh corn, seasoned with soy and chile, bound by eggs, cooked in butter. The two recipes that follow are great, and different, but if I had to choose one, it would be this.

Other vegetables you can use: peas, preferably fresh.

2 eggs, separated

Salt and freshly ground black pepper

1/2 cup chopped scallion

1 teaspoon minced fresh chile (like jalapeño or Thai, page 826), or to taste, or hot red pepper flakes or cayenne to taste

2 cups corn, preferably just stripped from the cobs (see page 288), but thawed frozen is acceptable

1 tablespoon soy sauce

1/4 cup all-purpose flour

3 to 4 tablespoons butter, peanut oil, or neutral oil, like grapeseed or corn, as needed

① In a large bowl, combine the egg yolks, a pinch of salt, a good 1/2 teaspoon or more black pepper, the scallion, chile, corn, soy sauce, and flour; mix well.

② Beat the egg whites until stiff. Put the butter or oil in a large skillet (cast-iron or nonstick is best) over medium-high heat. Fold the egg whites into the corn mixture. When the butter foam subsides or the oil is hot, spoon pancake-sized dollops into the pan, 4 to 6 at a time.

③ Cook until nicely browned on one side, 3 to 5 minutes, then turn and brown the other side. Keep warm in a low oven if necessary while you cook the remaining pancakes, adding additional butter or oil as necessary. Serve immediately.

8 Sauces for Corn Pancakes, Thai Style, and Corn Fritters

You can serve any of the Thai-style pancakes naked or with a bit of lime and perhaps some minced chile and chopped basil on top, and they're great that way. Less traditional, more adventurous ideas for side or dipping sauces to accompany any corn pancake here include:

1. Fresh Tomato Salsa (page 750)
2. Fresh Tomatillo Salsa (page 751)
3. Cilantro Purée or Chimichurri (page 769)
4. Cilantro "Pesto" (page 769)
5. Any Raita (page 774)
6. Basil Dipping Sauce (page 777)
7. Ginger-Scallion Sauce (page 779)
8. Maple syrup

Corn Fritters

MAKES: 4 servings
TIME: 30 minutes

These are super-crisp, really good, and among the easiest things to fry.

Neutral oil, like grapeseed or corn, as needed

$3/4$ cup cornmeal, the fresher the better

$1/2$ cup all-purpose flour

2 teaspoons baking powder

Salt and freshly ground black pepper

$3/4$ cup milk, plus more if needed

1 egg

2 cups corn, preferably just stripped from the cobs (see page 288), but thawed frozen is acceptable

❶ Put at least 2 inches of oil in a countertop deep-fryer or in a deep pan on the stove and turn the heat to medium-high; bring to 350°F (see "Deep Frying," page 26).
❷ Combine the dry ingredients in a large bowl. Beat together the milk and egg, then pour the mixture into the dry ingredients, adding a few tablespoons more milk if needed to make a thick, smooth batter. Stir in the corn.
❸ Drop the fritters by the $1/4$ cup or large spoonful into the hot oil; you'll probably need to raise the heat to maintain temperature. Cook the fritters in batches, turning once, until nicely browned on all sides, a total of about 4 or 5 minutes per batch. Drain the fritters on paper towels, then eat them as they are done or keep them warm in the oven until they are all done.

Arepas. A South American staple, made with cheese: Omit the flour, baking powder, and egg. Increase the amount of cornmeal to 1 cup, and reduce the amount of corn kernels to $1/2$ cup. Add $1/2$ cup grated cheese, like cheddar, to the mix, along with a little more milk, 1 cup total, to make a slightly thinner, pancakelike batter and cook in a shallow skillet with just a few tablespoons of butter or oil, as you would pancakes.

Buttered Popcorn

MAKES: 4 to 6 servings
TIME: About 10 minutes

Forget, please, microwave popcorn, except in an "emergency." Traditional buttered popcorn doesn't take much more time or effort and contains no weird ingredients. Add butter, sugar, nori, Parmesan, or chopped herbs (see the variations) and it's incredible. Use a compound butter or a good extra virgin olive oil to add flavor or cut down on saturated fat. (The oil instead of butter makes the popcorn vegan.)

2 tablespoons neutral oil, like grapeseed or corn

$1/2$ cup popping corn

4 tablespoons ($1/2$ stick) butter or good extra virgin olive oil (optional)

Salt

❶ Put the neutral oil in a large, deep saucepan (6 quarts or so) with a lid over medium heat. Add 3 kernels of corn and cover.
❷ When the 3 kernels pop, remove the cover and add the remaining corn. Cover and shake the pot, holding the lid on as you do so. Cook, shaking the pot occasionally, until the popping sound stops, about 5 minutes. Meanwhile, melt the butter if you choose to use it.
❸ Turn the popcorn into a large bowl; drizzle with the butter and sprinkle with salt while tossing the popcorn. Serve immediately if possible; popcorn is best when hot.

Salty-Sweet Popcorn. You will crave this, and it's great with or without the butter: Sprinkle the popcorn with salt and superfine sugar as soon as it's done, tossing for even coverage. Taste and add more seasoning as needed.

Parmesan Popcorn. Grate the Parmesan as finely as possible: Add $1/4$ cup finely grated Parmesan and toss with the hot popcorn.

Herb Popcorn. Lovely with either butter or olive oil: Add $1/4$ cup minced fresh herbs. Make sure the leaves aren't wet before chopping; press between paper towels to absorb excess moisture. Sprinkle on the herbs as you drizzle the butter or olive oil.

9 Things to Sprinkle on Popcorn or Roasted Nuts

Some are more potent than others (like the cayenne), so be careful with quantity and toss thoroughly to ensure an even coating.

1. Za'atar (to make your own, see page 818)
2. Citrus Sprinkle (page 818)
3. Chaat masala (to make your own, see page 814)
4. Japanese Seven-Spice Mix (page 817)
5. Nori "Shake" (page 817)
6. Ground sumac (page 821)
7. Smoked paprika
8. Cayenne or hot red pepper flakes
9. Brewer's yeast

Cucumbers

Ubiquitous in salads or—pickled—on burgers, cucumbers are actually a fruit and a member of the gourd family. We're most familiar with three varieties: the common cucumber with dark green, often waxed skin that we see in every grocery store; the long, slender, and almost always plastic-wrapped hothouse or English cucumber; and the small, striped, nubby-skinned Kirby, most often used to make pickles (see page 97).

Cucumbers are rarely cooked, but a simple and very quick sauté in a hot pan is actually quite nice.

Buying and storing: Look for firm, unshriveled, and preferably unwaxed cucumbers. Generally, more narrow specimens have fewer and less bitter seeds. Store unwrapped in the refrigerator for up to a week, but use as soon as possible.

Preparing: Always peel waxed cucumbers; otherwise peeling is optional. Halve the cucumber lengthwise and

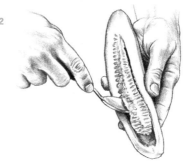

Thick cucumbers should almost always be seeded. It takes almost no time at all. (STEP 1) First cut the cucumber in half the long way. (STEP 2) Then scrape out the seeds with a spoon.

use a spoon to remove the seeds if there are a lot of them. And consider salting (see page 46) to remove excess water if you're looking for extra crispness or less bitterness or if you're cooking it.

Best cooking method: Best raw or pickled (see pages 96–97).

When is it done? I rarely cook cucumber.

Other vegetables to substitute: Celery, jícama, or water chestnuts.

Dandelion Greens

The leaves of the plant many consider a noxious weed, dandelion greens are incredibly nutrient rich. They're loaded with protein, fiber, calcium, and potassium (more than any other green), in addition to tons of beta-carotene. They're used much more extensively in Europe, where several varieties are cultivated, but are available only sporadically here; look at specialty or farmer's markets. If you're picking wild dandelions, pick them as early as possible in the spring and, of course, from a place where no sprays have been used.

Buying and storing: In the early spring or even fall in some places, look for small (less than 6 inches long), unwilted green leaves; larger leaves are bitter, though that may not bother you. The crown—the white part at the base of the leaves—is prized for its tenderness and flavor. If you're picking your own, the unopened, embryonic flowers are incredibly delicious; you'll know them when you see them. Store wrapped loosely in plastic in the refrigerator.

Preparing: Wash well to eliminate sand. Leave small leaves whole and chop or tear larger ones into strips or pieces.

Best cooking methods: Steaming and sautéing.

When are they done? When wilted and tender.

Other vegetables to substitute: Turnip, mustard, or beet greens.

Eggplant

There are literally dozens of varieties of eggplant, though in most supermarkets we see only the large, oblong, dark purple eggplant. Reliably better, if you can find it, is the slender lavender variety, usually sold in Asian markets but sometimes in Italian ones as well.

Other varieties are green, white, striped, or speckled; long and skinny, round and fat, oblong, or oval; and they range in size from 2 inches to 12 in length. And if you've ever seen the white egg-shaped variety, you understand how this fruit got its name. Check out a summer farmer's market for the best and widest variety of eggplants.

Of course, each type offers a variation in texture and flavor; some are sweeter, some more bitter, and some have a more delicate flesh or tougher skin. The size and shape may also influence what type of eggplant you want

to use. For instance, the long and slender type slices up nicely for stir-fries, while the large type is great when you want large chunks or slices for grilling. If you have the option of choosing different types, then by all means do so, but if the usual dark purple variety is all you can get, then use it—it has fine flavor.

Buying and storing: In general, smaller eggplant contain fewer seeds and are less likely to be bitter (I love the golf ball–sized ones, which do not require any trimming or cleaning). But firmness is the most important aspect when buying an eggplant. Look for undamaged specimens with no brown spots that are heavy for their size. The color of the stems also indicates freshness; the greener and fresher looking they are, the fresher the eggplant. Store in the refrigerator and use eggplant as soon as possible; although the outside will not look much different, the inside will become soft and bitter within a few days.

Preparing: Trim the stem end and peel eggplant if the skin is tough and/or bitter; otherwise leave it on. Slice it crosswise or lengthwise, $1/2$ inch to 1 inch thick, or cube it any size. Salting eggplant (see page 46) to remove bitterness is optional. If the eggplant is fresh and firm, chances are it will taste pretty good without salting, regardless of the variety.

Best cooking methods: Roasting, grilling, broiling, sautéing, and stir-frying.

When is it done? When it's tender—almost creamy—and there are no dry spots.

Other vegetables to substitute: Really, there is no substitute.

Dry-Pan Eggplant

MAKES: 4 servings
TIME: 30 minutes

A great way to cook eggplant for later use, especially stir-fries and Stuffed Eggplant, page 397). It uses no fat, it turns the skin into a thin, crunchy, smoky delight, and it makes the flesh creamy and tasty. A real winner and easy to boot.

>   3 or 4 small to medium eggplant, preferably slender ones (about 1¼ to 1½ pounds total)
>
>   Salt and freshly ground pepper (optional)
>
>   Extra virgin olive oil to taste (optional)
>
>   Freshly squeezed lemon juice to taste (optional)

1 Put the eggplant in a dry, heavy skillet, preferably cast-iron, over medium heat. Cook, turning the eggplant as they blacken on each side and adjusting the heat so the skin darkens without burning, until the skin is blistered and black all over and the flesh collapses (you'll know when it happens).

2 Transfer (the stems won't be hot, so you can just pick them up that way) to a cutting board and slit them lengthwise. Let cool until you can handle them, then chop or purée for other recipes or season with salt and pepper, drizzle with olive oil and lemon, and serve.

Grilled or Broiled Eggplant

MAKES: 4 servings

TIME: 30 minutes; longer if you salt the eggplant

Among the fastest, easiest ways to prepare eggplant. It's so reliably good it almost makes sense to prepare it whenever you've got the grill going, especially since it's great at room temperature.

>   2 medium or 1 large eggplant (1½ to 2 pounds)
>
>   1 teaspoon minced garlic (optional)
>
>   4 to 6 tablespoons extra virgin olive oil
>
>   Salt and freshly ground black pepper
>
>   Chopped parsley leaves for garnish

1 Peel the eggplant if the skin is thick or the eggplant is less than perfectly firm; cut it into ½-inch-thick

slices and, if time allows, salt it (see page 46). Heat a charcoal or gas grill or the broiler to moderately high heat and put the grill rack about 4 inches from the heat source or the broiler rack 4 to 6 inches from the heat source.

2 If you like, stir the garlic into the olive oil, then brush one side of the eggplant slices with the oil. Place, oiled side down, on a baking sheet or directly on the grill. Sprinkle with salt (unless you salted the eggplant) and pepper, then brush with more oil.

3 Broil or grill until browned on both sides, turning once or twice, brushing with more oil if the eggplant looks dry and adjusting the heat or position as necessary to keep the eggplant cooking steadily without burning, usually less than 10 minutes. Serve hot or at room temperature, garnished with parsley.

Sautéed Eggplant

MAKES: 4 servings

TIME: About 30 minutes; longer if you salt the eggplant

It takes a while to cook eggplant on top of the stove, and it usually takes a fair amount of oil, but the results are worth it: creamy and flavorful, like no other vegetable.

Other vegetables you can use: zucchini or summer squash, but the results will not be as satisfying.

>   1½ to 2 pounds eggplant, preferably small
>
>   Salt
>
>   ⅓ cup extra virgin olive oil, more or less
>
>   1 tablespoon minced garlic
>
>   Freshly ground black pepper
>
>   Chopped parsley leaves for garnish

1 Peel the eggplant if the skin is thick or the eggplant is less than perfectly firm; cut it into ½-inch cubes and salt them (see page 46) if the eggplant is large and time allows.

2 Put the olive oil and all but 1 teaspoon of the garlic in a large, deep skillet, preferably nonstick or cast-iron, over medium heat. Two minutes later, add the eggplant. Stir and toss almost constantly until, after 5 or 10 minutes, the eggplant begins to release some of the oil it has absorbed.

3 Continue cooking, stirring frequently, until the eggplant is very tender, about 30 minutes (this can vary greatly). About 5 minutes before it is done, add the remaining garlic.

4 Sprinkle with pepper and additional salt if necessary; garnish and serve.

Curried Eggplant with Coconut Milk. Easier, if anything; quite good with about a third of the eggplant replaced by small cubes of new potato. A spectacular dish to serve over rice: Step 1 remains the same. In Step 2, use 2 tablespoons neutral oil, like grapeseed or corn, and, along with the garlic, add 2 teaspoons minced peeled fresh ginger and 1 teaspoon curry paste, curry powder, or garam masala (to make your own spice blend, see pages 815–816). After the eggplant begins to get tender, stir in about a cup of coconut milk and cook until very soft, about 15 minutes more. Taste and adjust the seasoning, garnish with cilantro, and serve.

Sautéed Eggplant with Tomatoes. A simple ratatouille (pages 380–381): Step 1 remains the same. In Step 2, add 1 medium or 1/2 large onion, chopped, along with the garlic. In Step 3, as the eggplant become tender, stir in about 2 cups chopped tomato (ripe fresh ones are best, but canned are acceptable). Cook for about 10 more minutes, stirring occasionally, until the tomato breaks up, then add the garlic and proceed with the recipe.

Sautéed Eggplant with Onions and Honey. Not sweet, but complex: Steps 1 through 3 remain the same. When the eggplant is done, transfer it to a bowl and add 1/4 cup extra virgin olive oil to the pan. Cook 1 large onion, chopped, and 1 red or yellow bell pepper, cored, seeded, and chopped, in the oil until soft-

ened, about 10 minutes. Return the eggplant to the mix, along with salt, pepper, and lemon juice to taste and about 2 tablespoons honey. Cook for another minute or two, then taste and adjust the seasoning; garnish with parsley and serve.

Sautéed Eggplant with Greens. Use about a pound of spinach, arugula, kale, collards, or any fresh green you find at the farmer's market: If you've got greens with sturdy stems, separate them from the leaves and roughly chop everything. You want 3 to 4 cups total. In Step 3, add the greens to the pan toward the end of cooking. Stems (if you've got them) should go in after the eggplant has cooked for about 15 minutes; sturdy leaves after about 20 minutes. Tender greens like spinach should go in during the last 5 minutes of cooking the eggplant. Add enough olive oil to keep the mixture moist but not greasy. When everything is tender, stir in 1/2 cup grated Parmesan if you like. Taste and adjust the seasoning and serve hot or at room temperature.

Many Additions to Sautéed Eggplant

Eggplant is so distinctive it can stand up to many different flavors. And a lot of these can be used in combination.

1. Make the dish creamy with the addition of yogurt, which goes especially well with spices (you can use it in place of the coconut milk in the curried variation, for example).

2. Make it more substantial by adding sliced bell pepper, lots of onion, zucchini or other summer squash, cubed potato (which will take at least as long as the eggplant to cook), cauliflower, whole shallots, and so on.

3. Make the dish crunchy by adding, near the end of cooking, some Fresh Bread Crumbs (page 804) or a handful of toasted pine nuts, sunflower seeds, or any toasted nuts.

4. Make it more fragrant with the addition of basil, mint, cilantro, or other strong fresh herbs.

Ⓕ Fast   Ⓜ Make Ahead   Ⓥ Vegan

5. Make it sharper by increasing the amount of garlic or adding chiles, chile powder, or chile paste; capers or olives; or chopped scallion, shallot, or onion toward the end of cooking.

Steamed Eggplant

MAKES: 4 servings

TIME: 30 minutes

Almost no one steams eggplant in Europe, so most Americans—latecomers that we are to this prince of vegetables—don't know about this technique. But in Asia it's as old as the steamer itself, and it's widely used and beloved. For good reason: It's simple, it takes advantage of the great flavor of eggplant, it doesn't add a lot of fat (how much oil did you use the last time you sautéed eggplant?), and it produces an extremely tender texture. You'll need a steamer and not much else. Start with the smaller and lighter-colored Asian eggplants if you can find them (of course, that's always my recommendation, as they're generally not as bitter).

You can treat Steamed Eggplant as simply as this: Toss with soy, sesame oil, and a bit of rice vinegar. But the dipping sauce I suggest here is more flavorful and not at all difficult.

Serve this as a side dish or at room temperature or cold as a salad; it's good either way.

4 to 6 small, long eggplant (about 1 1/2 pounds)

1 red bell pepper, halved and cored (optional)

Salt

Soy and Sesame Dipping Sauce and Marinade, Korean Style (page 778)

Chopped fresh cilantro leaves for garnish (optional)

1 Set up a steamer (see page 25). Trim the eggplant and halve lengthwise. Arrange in the steamer with the pepper if you like and sprinkle with a little salt. Steam until the eggplant is very tender, about 15 minutes. Cool until you can handle it (you can set it aside for an hour or so if you're not ready to eat).

2 Shred the eggplant with your fingers or a knife; thinly slice the pepper. Toss with enough of the dipping sauce to flavor and moisten, then taste and adjust the seasoning. Garnish and serve hot, warm, or at room temperature.

11 Sauces to Serve with Steamed Eggplant

Steamed Eggplant doesn't even have to be Asian style; the last three sauces here are Middle Eastern or even more Western.

1. Fishless Fish Sauce (page 778)
2. Ginger-Scallion Sauce (page 779)
3. Dashi Dipping Sauce (page 780)
4. Ponzu Sauce (page 780)
5. Simple Miso Dipping Sauce (page 781)
6. Tahini Sauce (page 796)
7. Ginger Yogurt Sauce (page 774)
8. Grainy Mustard (page 776) thinned with a little soy sauce
9. Any Vinaigrette (pages 762–763)
10. Any mayonnaise (to make your own, page 771)
11. Traditional Pesto or any herb paste or sauce (pages 768–770)

Eggplant Slices with Garlic and Parsley

MAKES: 4 servings

TIME: About 45 minutes; longer if you salt the eggplant

Generally speaking, large eggplant are less desirable than small ones: they have more seeds, the skin is tougher, and they are usually more bitter. But sometimes they're all you can get, and this recipe makes their size an attribute (it does help, though, to salt them). The results are beautifully creamy and savory.

2 medium or 1 large eggplant (1 $\frac{1}{2}$ to 2 pounds total)

Salt

$\frac{1}{4}$ cup extra virgin olive oil

1 tablespoon minced garlic

$\frac{1}{2}$ cup minced parsley leaves, plus more for garnish

Freshly ground black pepper

1 Peel the eggplant if the skin is thick or the eggplant is less than perfectly firm; cut it into 1-inch-thick slices and salt it (see page 46) if time allows.

2 Preheat the oven to 400°F. Smear a baking sheet with half the oil. Cut several slits on one side of each of the eggplant slices and lay them on the baking sheet, cut side up. Mix together the remaining oil, the garlic, and the $\frac{1}{2}$ cup minced parsley and sprinkle with salt (if you did not salt the eggplant) and pepper. Spread this mixture on the eggplant slices, pushing it into the slits.

3 Bake without turning until the eggplant is soft, 40 minutes or more. Garnish and serve hot or at room temperature.

Spicy Mashed Eggplant with Yogurt and Mint. Great at room temperature as a side dish or served like a thick sauce: Instead of the parsley, chop about $\frac{1}{2}$ cup fresh mint leaves. Proceed with the recipe through Step 3. Make sure the eggplant is roasted until very tender, then put the slices in a large bowl and mash with a fork or a potato masher (it's fine to leave the skin on; it will break into small bits). Stir in 1 cup yogurt, 2 tablespoons lemon juice, a pinch of hot red pepper flakes, and the mint. Taste and adjust the seasoning and serve, drizzled with additional olive oil if you like.

Mashed Eggplant with Honey and Lemon. For an extra-smooth purée, whirl the whole thing in a food processor or blender: Proceed with the recipe through Step 3. Make sure the eggplant is roasted until very tender, then put the slices in a large bowl and mash with a

fork or a potato masher (it's fine to leave the skin on; it will break into small bits). Stir in $\frac{1}{4}$ cup each of honey and lemon juice, along with 2 additional tablespoons of olive oil. Taste and adjust the seasoning. If puréeing the mixture, stir in the parsley by hand or serve the eggplant from a shallow bowl and sprinkle the top with parsley.

Broiled Eggplant with Peppers, Onions, and Yogurt

MAKES: 4 servings

TIME: 40 minutes

There are a fair number of ingredients here, and some attention and work are necessary. But the results justify it: it's a big-flavored, really hearty dish. For the best flavor, be patient, be sure to brown each vegetable well, and nearly blacken the top at the end.

3 or 4 small or 1 or 2 large eggplant (about 1$\frac{1}{2}$ pounds), trimmed

6 tablespoons extra virgin olive oil

Salt and freshly ground black pepper

3 red or yellow bell peppers, cored, seeded, and cut into strips

2 or 3 fresh Anaheim or other mild chiles, cored, seeded, and cut into strips

1 onion, peeled and halved

2 tomatoes

1 teaspoon fresh thyme leaves or a pinch dried

2 cups yogurt

Lemon wedges

1 Cut the eggplant into $\frac{1}{2}$-inch-thick slices; salt them (see page 46) if the eggplant are large and time allows. Preheat the broiler. Rinse and dry the eggplant. Put $\frac{1}{4}$ cup of the oil in an ovenproof skillet or roasting pan and turn the eggplant in it; sprinkle with salt, more or less depending on whether you salted the eggplant,

F Fast   M Make Ahead   V Vegan

and pepper. Broil or grill until well browned on both sides and fairly tender, turning once or twice, about 3 to 5 minutes per side.

② Transfer the eggplant to a bowl and put the peppers, chiles, and onion, cut sides down, in the same pan; drizzle with the remaining oil and broil, turning occasionally. The onion will blacken quickly; remove it and, when it cools slightly, separate into rings and add to the bowl. When the peppers are blackened and beginning to collapse, after a total of 10 to 15 minutes, remove them from the pan and add to the bowl.

③ Cut the tomatoes in half through their equator, and, over a sink, squeeze and shake them to extract the seeds (see the illustration on page 373). Put the tomatoes, cut side down, in the skillet and char them; this will take 3 to 5 minutes; roughly chop the tomatoes and add to the bowl.

④ Sprinkle the vegetables with the thyme and stir in the yogurt; taste and add salt and pepper if necessary. Return to the roasting pan and broil until charred on top, just a few minutes, then serve over pitas or rice, with the lemon wedges.

Eggplant Parmesan

MAKES: 6 servings

TIME: About 1 hour; longer if you salt the eggplant

Though this is really a dish in which the eggplant loses some of its identity, it's gooey and as filling as lasagne (though it's equally good without the mozzarella) and more flavorful. If you use Grilled or Broiled Eggplant (page 295) here, you don't have to sauté the eggplant.

Other vegetables you can use: zucchini (cut lengthwise).

2 medium to large eggplant (2 to 3 pounds total)

Salt

Extra virgin olive oil as needed

All-purpose flour for dredging

Freshly ground black pepper

2 cups Fast Tomato Sauce (page 445)

8 ounces grated mozzarella cheese (about 2 cups; optional)

1 cup freshly grated Parmesan cheese, plus more if you omit the mozzarella

About 30 fresh basil leaves

① Peel the eggplant if the skin is thick or the eggplant is less than perfectly firm. Cut it into $1/2$-inch-thick slices and salt it (see page 46) if you like.

② When you're ready to cook, preheat the oven to 350°F. Put about 3 tablespoons of olive oil in a large skillet over medium heat. When hot (a pinch of flour will sizzle), dredge the eggplant slices, one at a time, in the flour, shaking off the excess. Put in the pan, but do not crowd; you will have to cook in batches. Cook for 3 or 4 minutes on each side, until nicely browned, then drain on paper towels. Add some pepper to the slices as they cook, as well as some salt if you did not salt the eggplant. Add more oil to the skillet as needed.

③ Lightly oil a baking dish, then spoon a little of the tomato sauce into it. Top with a layer of eggplant, then a thin layer of each of the cheeses, and finally a few basil leaves. Repeat until all the ingredients are used up, reserving some of the basil for garnish. End with a sprinkling of Parmesan.

④ Bake for 20 to 30 minutes, or until the dish is bubbling hot. Mince the remaining basil and sprinkle over the top. Serve hot or at room temperature.

Eggplant Layered with Vegetables. More in the style of Eastern European dishes: Steps 1 and 2 remain the same. When you remove the eggplant from the oil, sauté 1 diced carrot, 2 diced red bell peppers, 20 peeled cloves garlic, 2 chopped stalks celery, and 1 diced large onion until fairly soft, about 10 minutes. In Step 3, omit the cheese and basil and layer the eggplant and tomato sauce with the cooked vegetables and a liberal amount of chopped parsley. Bake as directed.

Eggplant-Tofu Stir-Fry

MAKES: 4 servings

TIME: 20 minutes with cooked eggplant; 40 from scratch

If, sometime during the day, you have the time to prepare Dry-Pan Eggplant (page 294), you're more than halfway done with this terrific little stir-fry.

Other vegetables you can use: almost anything, especially if it's precooked—broccoli, red peppers, zucchini, winter squash, and so on.

> 2 tablespoons peanut or other oil
>
> 1 pound extra-firm tofu, cubed
>
> 3 or 4 eggplant, cooked according to Dry-Pan Eggplant recipe (page 294) and cut into chunks
>
> About 10 scallions, chopped
>
> 2 tablespoons soy sauce
>
> 2 tablespoons ketchup (to make your own, see page 790)
>
> 1/4 cup chopped fresh cilantro

1 Put the oil in a large skillet or wok over medium-high heat. When hot, add the tofu and cook, undisturbed, until nicely browned on one side, about 5 minutes. Turn the pieces and brown on the other side. Add the eggplant and scallions and toss until hot.

2 Add the soy sauce, ketchup, and 2 tablespoons water, turn the heat to low, and cook until saucy, just a minute or two. Garnish with the cilantro and serve.

Endive, Escarole, Radicchio, and Chicory

This group of bitter plants can be quite confusing. Part of the problem stems from Americans using the term *chicory* to describe all items in this category. Truth is, that's only partly right; they are all members of the composite family (like daisies), but chicory and endive are different species.

Chicory has a solidly green, narrow leaf and grows in a loose head. Related to chicory is the red and white head-shaped radicchio. There are three types of endive: the pale, spear-shaped Belgian endive (aka *witloof*), the open and frilly curly endive (often called *frisée*); and the broad-leafed, lettucelike escarole. Proper botany, size, and shape aside, all endive and chicory are bitter, leafy, and crisp but firm; they add great texture and structure to salads and are also good cooked.

Buying and storing: Look for crisp, unwilted leaves. Belgian endive and all but the very exterior leaves of curly endive should be white to pale yellow in color; green coloring indicates the leaves were exposed to sunlight (a negative for these vegetables) and will be more bitter. Store wrapped loosely in plastic in the refrigerator; chicory and endive keep longer than most salad greens.

Preparing: Trim and wash as you would any lettuce.

Best cooking methods: Sautéing, braising (for Belgian endive and escarole), and grilling (for endive and radicchio).

When are they done? When sautéing or grilling, crisp-tender; when braising, soft but not mushy.

Other vegetables to substitute: Dandelion, turnip, or mustard greens when cooked or any lettuce, arugula, or watercress when raw.

Braised Endive, Escarole, or Radicchio

MAKES: 4 servings

TIME: About 1 hour

Endive makes a nifty little package when braised, and little heads of radicchio, cut into quarters, are also nice. Escarole is not as tidy but tastes just as good. The croutons add a terrific crunch here, though they're not essential.

Other vegetables you can use: just about any bitter green, like romaine lettuce, bok choy, cabbage, or Brussels sprouts, halved or chopped accordingly.

F Fast   **M** Make Ahead   **V** Vegan

3 tablespoons extra virgin olive oil

4 Belgian endives, trimmed at the base and damaged leaves removed; 2 heads radicchio, trimmed and halved; or about 1 pound escarole, washed and roughly chopped

1/2 cup vegetable stock (pages 101–102) or water

Salt and freshly ground black pepper

1 teaspoon freshly squeezed lemon juice or white wine vinegar

1 cup Croutons (page 806), chopped up a bit, or any of the Crumbles (page 805; optional)

1 Put the olive oil in a skillet with a lid over medium heat. When hot, add the endives and cook, turning once or twice, until they begin to brown, 5 to 10 minutes.

2 Add the stock and sprinkle with salt and pepper. Cover and cook over the lowest possible heat, turning occasionally, until very tender, about 45 minutes. Uncover and turn the heat up a bit to evaporate any remaining liquid.

3 Drizzle with lemon juice or vinegar, garnish with Croutons or Crumbles if desired, and serve hot, warm, or at room temperature.

Braised Endive with Orange Juice. The orange juice caramelizes beautifully here, adding a rich sweetness to the bitter flavor of the endive: Substitute butter for the olive oil if you like and orange juice for the stock. Add 2 tablespoons brown sugar and omit the lemon juice or vinegar. Proceed with the recipe, adding the brown sugar with the orange juice.

Grilled or Broiled Radicchio with Balsamic Glaze

MAKES: 4 servings

TIME: About 15 minutes

Ⓕ Ⓜ Ⓥ

With its odd combination of sweet and sour, balsamic vinegar works miraculously to balance the bitterness of radicchio. This makes a fine alternative to a salad and goes especially well with rich, creamy dishes like gratins. It's also nice with some crumbled feta, blue cheese, or grated Parmesan and toasted hazelnuts or almonds on top.

It is also a useful ingredient: Chop it coarsely and stir it into risotto toward the end of cooking or toss together with freshly cooked pasta with some olive oil and Parmesan. Stir it into Crouton Salad (page 87) or combine it with sliced steamed green beans or cooked cannellini beans (page 577).

Other vegetables you can use: endive, chicory, escarole, or romaine lettuce.

4 small or 2 large heads radicchio (about 1 pound)

2 tablespoons extra virgin olive oil

1/4 cup balsamic vinegar

1 tablespoon brown sugar or honey

Salt and freshly ground black pepper

1 Heat a charcoal or gas grill or the broiler to moderately high heat and put the rack about 4 inches from the heat source.

2 Core the radicchio and then halve or quarter them, depending on their size. Rub or brush the radicchio with the olive oil, taking care to keep the wedges intact. Combine the vinegar and sugar in a small bowl until dissolved and keep handy.

3 Put the radicchio wedges on the grill or on a broiler pan, cut sides toward the heat. Grill or broil for a minute or two, then carefully turn and brush (or drizzle) with the vinegar mixture. Cook until just starting to crisp and char around the edges, another couple of minutes. Transfer to a plate or platter and sprinkle with salt and a lot of black pepper. Serve hot or at room temperature.

Mediterranean Slaw. With a sharp flavor and deep color: Just cool down the radicchio and mince the leaves. Then toss with 1/2 cup or so each of chopped parsley and red onion and dress with a little olive oil or mayonnaise (to make your own, see page 771).

Fennel

Anise

Like celery, fennel is used raw and cooked and its flavor and texture are mellowed by cooking. Shaved and used in salads, or sliced and sautéed, it has a pronounced anise flavor. The bulbs range from nearly grapefruit size with celery stalk–size fronds to petite and dainty almost bite-sized bulbs. Fennel can be used interchangeably with celery, as long as you understand that the flavors are not at all alike.

Buying and storing: Fennel bulbs should be clean, white (some green is fine), and tightly packed; avoid those with soft spots or browning. Store wrapped loosely in plastic in the refrigerator; it keeps for about a week.

Preparing: Trim off the fronds and stalks (and reserve them for garnish or seasoning if you like); cut off the hard bottom and slice vertically or into quarters. Or cut the bulb in half lengthwise, cut out the core, and cut into strips.

Best cooking methods: Braising, roasting, and sautéing.

When is it done? When tender enough to pierce easily with a skewer or thin-bladed knife.

Other vegetables to substitute: Celery and fennel are almost always interchangeable.

PREPARING FENNEL

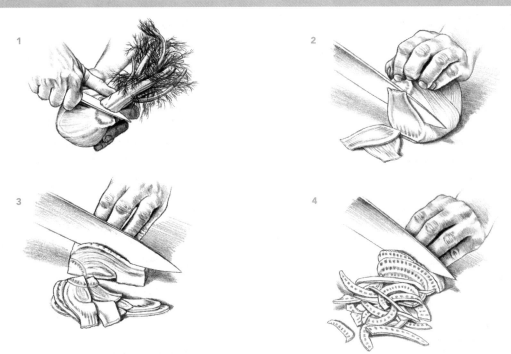

(STEP 1) Trim the hard, hollow stalks from the top of the bulb. Save the feathery fronds for garnish if you like. (STEP 2) Cut a thick slice from one side of the fennel. (STEPS 3–4) Stand the bulb on its side and cut through it vertically. Or cut it horizontally.

Ⓕ Fast   Ⓜ Make Ahead   Ⓥ Vegan

Roast Fennel with Orange

MAKES: 4 servings

TIME: 30 minutes

Fennel is a good candidate for many gratins (see page 382), but because of its unusual anise flavor, it does nicely when combined with the sweet flavor of orange as well.

Other vegetables you can use: celery.

1 large fennel bulb (1 pound or more)

2 navel oranges, peeled

1 medium onion, peeled

3 tablespoons extra virgin olive oil

1 tablespoon fresh rosemary or 1 teaspoon dried

Salt and freshly ground black pepper

1 cup freshly squeezed orange juice

1 Preheat the oven to 500°F. Trim the fennel, reserving some of the dill-like fronds. Cut the fennel, oranges, and onion into $1/8$- to $1/4$-inch-thick slices.

2 Put the oil in a large skillet or flameproof gratin dish. Add the fennel, oranges, onion, and rosemary. Sprinkle with salt and pepper, then pour in the orange juice.

3 Bring to a boil on top of the stove; then transfer to the oven and cook for another 15 minutes or so, or until tender. If much liquid remains, cook a little longer (in the unlikely event that it dries out before the celery becomes tender, add a little more orange juice or some water). Garnish with the reserved fennel fronds and serve hot or warm.

Garlic

Garlic has been around as a culinary and medicinal plant for thousands of years and is probably *the* most important vegetable in recorded history (really), because of its universal value as a seasoning. When raw

it's pungent, hot, and even rank, but while cooking, its aroma is alluring.

Depending on how you handle it, cooked garlic ranges from assertively strong and delicious to sweet and mild. Roasting whole cloves or even the entire head (page 304) is one of the best ways to bring out the rich sweetness of garlic; simply spread it on toast or use it to season just about any dish, sauce, or dressing. Sautéing garlic in oil or butter to season a dish is also magical: chop or slice the cloves and add to the hot oil or butter; sauté it over medium heat just until it softens. Even browned garlic, which is strong and bitter, has a role in certain sauces (see Arrabbiata, page 448).

There are a number of varieties of fresh garlic, but we typically see one or two types at supermarkets, which is a shame since they vary widely in flavor and pungency. The huge elephant garlic has just a few enormous cloves per head and is a bit milder than common garlic. Check out a farmer's market for more variety, including fresh garlic scapes, or flower stalks, which are kind of fun.

Dehydrated garlic, garlic salt, and garlic powder are very poor substitutes for the real thing, as is the chopped garlic in oil found in some markets, though I am a fan of whole peeled garlic in jars, as long as it's fresh.

To remove the garlic scent from your fingers, rinse your fingers in water and rub them on any stainless-steel surface (your sink or faucet will do); this works like a charm.

Buying and storing: Loose heads of garlic are best (avoid the boxed type) because you can select the best; look for hard, unshriveled bulbs that have not sprouted. The color and size of garlic is not especially important, though larger cloves are easier to handle and there's less peeling involved. Store in a dark, cool spot where it's exposed to air; discard it when it becomes soft.

Preparing: When preparing garlic as a vegetable, don't bother to peel it; the cloves will easily slip from their skins when done. For raw garlic, peeling is easiest when the clove is half smashed with the flat side of a knife blade. For larger quantities, simmer the garlic in water to cover for 30 seconds or toast it in a dry pan over medium

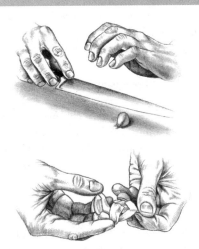

To peel garlic, crush the cloves slightly with the side of a large knife. The peels will come off easily.

heat, shaking the pan frequently, for about 5 minutes. Either of these treatments will loosen the skin and make it easy to slip out the cloves. To chop large quantities, add whole cloves to a food processor with a bit of oil; this will keep well in a sealed container for a few days.

Best cooking methods: Roasting and simmering in oil.

When is it done? When very, very tender, almost mushy. The cloves will easily squeeze out of their skins.

Other vegetables to substitute: Shallots can sometimes fill in, as can onions, but it just isn't the same.

Roasted Garlic

MAKES: 2 heads
TIME: About 1 hour, largely unattended

Ⓜ Ⓥ

Mellow, invaluable, and something you may begin to consider a staple, roasted garlic is a great side, condiment,

or ingredient in sauces and other dishes. And it's pretty much brainless to make. I like to use more olive oil than you need, because the oil itself—as long as it's stored in the fridge and used within a few days—is another great ingredient.

2 whole heads garlic
2 tablespoons extra virgin olive oil, or more as needed
Salt

❶ Preheat the oven to 375°F. Without getting too fussy or breaking the heads apart, remove as much of the papery coating from them as you can. Cut the top pointy part off the head to expose a bit of each clove. Drizzle with olive oil and sprinkle with salt.

❷ Film a small baking dish with a little more oil and add the garlic. Cover with aluminum foil and bake until the garlic is soft (you'll be able to pierce it easily with a thin-bladed knife), 40 minutes or longer.

Faster Roasted Garlic. If you're in a hurry: Break the heads into individual cloves, but do not peel them. Spread them in a pan, sprinkle with salt, and drizzle with oil. Bake, shaking the pan occasionally, until tender, 20 to 30 minutes.

5 Ways to Use Roasted Garlic
You could start and end like this: Spread it on bread and eat. But Roasted Garlic is so useful there's no reason to stop there:

1. Stir into any cooked sauce or soup in which you'd use garlic, usually toward the end of cooking.
2. Spread on any Pizza (pages 721–730) before adding other ingredients.
3. Add to any vegetable purée (pages 387–391) or to Mashed Potatoes (page 341).
4. Add to Vinaigrette (page 762), mayonnaise (to make your own, see page 771), Traditional Pesto (page 768), or almost any other sauce.
5. Add to cooked grain or legume dishes or toss with cooked vegetables.

Garlic Braised in Olive Oil

MAKES: 40 or more cloves
TIME: 45 minutes or less

There are many ways to soften garlic, and some others are on these pages. This is my favorite, though; especially when you begin with pre-peeled garlic, it's incredibly easy. Just keep the heat low and take your time.

You can use this garlic in myriad dishes, including vinaigrette and other sauces; or you can serve it as a vegetable. Use the oil in sauces or for sautéing.

Other vegetables you can use: shallots (use about half as many since they're bigger).

1/2 cup extra virgin olive oil

40 cloves garlic, or more

Salt

1 Put the oil in a small skillet over medium-low heat. When hot, add the garlic. Sprinkle with salt. Adjust the heat so the garlic just sizzles.

2 Cook, turning occasionally so the garlic browns evenly, until it gradually turns golden, then begins to brown. The garlic is done when perfectly tender. Store, refrigerated, in the oil, and peel and use within a few days.

Green Beans

"String" Beans, Wax Beans, Long Beans, and
Haricots Verts

These are all slender beans with edible pods. We're familiar with the common green bean; wax beans are identical except for their yellow color; long beans are originally Chinese (though now grown here too) and are anywhere from a foot to a yard long; and then there are the skinny and tender French haricots verts.

All of these "string" beans—which have had the strings bred out of them for the most part—can be eaten raw (best when they're fresh off the vine), barely cooked so they're still crunchy, or completely cooked and melt-in-your-mouth soft. Summer is the best season for green beans, though most are available year-round.

Buying and storing: Green and wax beans should be crisp, unshriveled, and snap when bent in half. Long beans and haricots verts are more tender and flexible but should still be crisp and unshriveled. Store wrapped loosely in plastic in the refrigerator; use soon— they lose their fresh flavor quickly.

Preparing: Snap or cut off the stem end and leave whole or cut into any length you like. To "French cut" green beans, slice them in half lengthwise. It's a lot of work but results in an appealing look and texture.

Best cooking methods: Steaming, boiling, microwaving, stir-frying, sautéing, roasting, and braising.

When is it done? A matter of personal preference: crisp-tender, just tender, or meltingly soft.

Other vegetables to substitute: Asparagus, peas, or broccoli.

Green Beans Tossed with Walnut-Miso Sauce

MAKES: 4 servings
TIME: 20 minutes

In this traditional Japanese vegan dish, you parboil and blanch green beans, then dress them with a blended sauce of white miso, walnuts, soy sauce, and ginger—all made in less than a minute in a blender. The results are incredible, and the sauce is almost universally useful, on other vegetables as well as for plain rice, noodles, or other cooked grains.

Other vegetables you can use: almost any solid vegetable—peas, snow or snap peas (parboiled and shocked; see page 241); broccoli or cauliflower (parboiled and shocked); potatoes (boiled or baked; see pages 339–341); eggplant (sautéed, not boiled; see pages 295–296); zucchini (steamed or grilled; page 255); and so on.

1 pound green beans, trimmed, parboiled, and shocked

1 tablespoon grated or minced peeled fresh ginger

$^1/_4$ cup light miso

$^1/_2$ cup shelled walnuts

1 teaspoon soy sauce, or to taste

Salt

 Drain the beans and put them in a serving bowl.

② Combine the ginger with the miso, walnuts, 2 tablespoons water, and soy sauce in a blender and blend until smooth, stopping the machine and scraping down its sides if necessary. (You may add a little more water or soy sauce if the mixture is too thick.)

③ Toss the green beans in the sauce and serve warm or at room temperature.

Twice-Fried Green Beans

MAKES: 4 servings
TIME: About 30 minutes
Ⓕ Ⓥ

A Chinese classic, often but hardly necessarily made with pork. I like cashews in this, but Crunchy Crumbled Tempeh (page 674) is also good.

Other vegetables you can use: long beans, cut into 2-inch lengths.

Neutral oil, like grapeseed or corn, for deep frying

$1^1/_2$ pounds green beans, trimmed

Salt

$^1/_2$ cup raw cashews, whole or chopped

1 tablespoon chopped garlic

$^1/_2$ cup chopped scallion

1 teaspoon minced fresh chile (like jalapeño or Thai, page 826), or to taste, or hot red pepper flakes or cayenne to taste

1 tablespoon sugar

2 tablespoons soy sauce

 While you prepare the ingredients, put about 2 inches oil in a countertop deep-fryer or in a deep pan on the stove and turn the heat to medium-high; bring to 350°F (see "Deep Frying," page 26). Make sure the beans are well dried and add them all at once. Cook, stirring occasionally, until they begin to brown, 5 to 10 minutes. Remove them with a slotted spoon and drain; sprinkle with salt.

② Add the cashews to the oil and cook, stirring frequently, until they brown nicely, about 3 minutes. Remove with a slotted spoon and drain on paper towels; sprinkle with salt. Turn off the heat.

③ Put 2 tablespoons of the oil in a heavy skillet over high heat. (You can use the same pan if it's right. Pour off the remaining oil and refrigerate; use it for this dish or other stir-fries another day.) When hot, add the garlic, scallion, and chile and cook for 30 seconds, stirring. Add the beans and cook, stirring, for about 2 minutes. Add the sugar and soy sauce, stir, and turn off the heat. Taste and add salt, chile, or soy sauce if you like. Sprinkle on the fried nuts and serve.

Stir-Fried Green Beans and Tofu Skins

MAKES: 4 servings
TIME: 30 minutes
Ⓕ Ⓥ

Glossy, hot, delicious, this simple combo of tofu skins and green beans is more like a pasta dish than a stir-fry—at a glance, your guests will be sure the skins are noodles—but a super-high-protein one. The pleasantly chewy "skins" go

Ⓕ Fast   Ⓜ Make Ahead   Ⓥ Vegan

great with the crisp-tender beans. Thinly sliced Baked Tofu (page 641) is a good substitute.

Other vegetables you can use: carrots or asparagus.

6 ounces dried tofu skins, or 8 ounces fresh

2 tablespoons peanut or neutral oil, like grapeseed or corn

1 tablespoon dark sesame oil

2 tablespoons minced peeled fresh ginger

Whole dried Thai chiles, to taste (optional)

Salt and freshly ground black pepper

1 pound green or wax beans, trimmed

1 tablespoon soy sauce, plus more to taste

1 Put the tofu skins in a large bowl and cover with warm water. Soak until pliable, about 10 minutes, then drain well and cut into long, wide ribbons. (If using fresh, simply cut them.)

2 Put the oils in a deep skillet or wok and turn the heat to medium-high. Add the ginger and a couple of chiles if you like and sprinkle with salt and pepper. Cook, stirring frequently, until the ginger is soft and starting to turn golden. Add the beans and a spoonful or two of water and cook, stirring frequently, until softened a bit but still crisp, 3 to 5 minutes.

3 Add the tofu skins and another spoonful or two of water. Cook, stirring frequently, until the skins are heated through and the beans are done, a couple of minutes. Drizzle with the soy sauce, taste and adjust the seasoning, and serve.

Stir-Fried Green Beans and Tofu Skins with Peanuts and Cilantro. A full meal with noodles or rice: In Step 3, off the heat, stir in $1/2$ cup each of chopped peanuts and chopped cilantro right before serving.

Horseradish

Though we know it best in a jar, horseradish is quite wonderful fresh and surprisingly mild and delicious when cooked. The fresh root has a narrow branch that ends with a rounded and bulging bulb; it's tan in color and often still covered in dirt. Look for it in the refrigerated produce section near the herbs or next to the garlic.

Buying and storing: Look for firm, crisp, unshriveled specimens. Store it in the refrigerator.

Preparing: It must be peeled before being used; use a sharp knife rather than a vegetable peeler and acknowledge from the outset that you will lose some of the flesh. Grate it for use as a condiment or chop or slice it as needed. Beware: It will make you cry.

Best cooking methods: Boiling, braising, and baking.

When is it done? When it's soft.

Other vegetables to substitute: Radish, parsnips, and celery root all lend a similarly unique flavor to a dish.

Jerusalem Artichokes (*see* Sunchokes, page 369)

Jícama

The taproot of a poisonous tropical vine, jícama is native to Central America and can grow to enormous proportions (up to 5 pounds or more), though we never see any larger than a rutabaga here. Jícama has a turniplike shape and a light tan skin that must be peeled; the flesh is white and crisp, like raw potato or a crunchy pear. Its delicately sweet flavor and crunchy-crisp texture make it excellent for eating raw in salads or simply sliced and eaten as a snack.

Buying and storing: Look for firm, unshriveled specimens that are somewhat heavy for their size. Store in a cool, dry spot (the fridge is fine); it will keep for as long as a month.

Preparing: Use a vegetable peeler or paring knife to remove the skin. Chop, slice, or shred the flesh as you like.

Best cooking methods: It's best raw; quickly sautéing or stir-frying is also nice.

When is it done? When just heated through and still crunchy.

Other vegetables to substitute: Radish, cucumber, or water chestnuts.

Kale and Collard Greens

Kale and collards are mainstays of dark, leafy cooking greens; kale has been cultivated in Europe for thousands of years, and collards are an essential in southern cooking (and are what many southerners mean when they say "greens"). Both have leathery, dark green leaves with thick, sometimes chalky-looking stems. While they are often confused, there are a couple of distinguishing features: collards' leaves are flat and can be quite big (as much as 8 inches across), and kale leaves are ruffled and range in size and color from narrow and very dark green to fat and greenish gray. While they can grow in warmer climates, they're actually at their sweetest and most flavorful when grown in cold areas—even in the snow. Their peak season is midwinter through early spring, but they're available year-round.

Buying and storing: Look for firm, dark green leaves with no yellowing or wilting. Young leaves with stems no thicker than a pencil will be easier to clean, less wasteful, and cook more quickly. They will also have a better texture when cooked. Store wrapped loosely in plastic in the refrigerator for a few days; use before they start to turn yellow.

Preparing: If the stems are thick, strip the leaves, chop the stems, and start cooking them a couple of minutes before the leaves. An easy way to cut the leaves is to roll them up, then cut across the roll.

Best cooking methods: Boiling, steaming, and braising. A great addition to soups and stews as well.

When are they done? When the stems are tender enough to pierce easily with a skewer or thin-bladed knife, unless—and this is sometimes the case—you want the stems on the crunchy side.

Other vegetables to substitute: Cabbage, chard, or beet greens.

(STEP 1) You may remove the stems if they are very thick (or just cook them a little longer than the leaves). Cut on either side of them, at an angle.

(STEP 2) The easiest way to chop large leaves is to roll them up and cut across the log (see chiffonade, pages 21–22).

Rolled Kale with Feta and Olives

MAKES: 4 servings
TIME: 30 minutes

If you've got a nice-looking covered skillet or casserole that can go from stovetop to table, this is the perfect dish for it. With the leaves filled, rolled, and sitting atop the chopped stems, the presentation is dramatic, and everyone will think you worked a lot harder than you did. Be sure to choose kale that has broad, intact leaves or use collards instead. Sliced ricotta salata or fresh mozzarella and dollops of goat cheese are also great filling options here. Serve these with Oven-Roasted Cottage "Fries" (page 345).

F Fast   **M** Make Ahead   **V** Vegan

Other vegetables you can use for this dish: collards, mustard greens, or chard.

About 8 large kale leaves, washed

8 ounces feta cheese

2 tablespoons olive oil, plus oil for drizzling

2 tablespoons minced garlic

Salt and freshly ground black pepper

$1/2$ cup dry white wine, vegetable stock (pages 101–102), or water

1 cup chopped ripe tomato (drained canned is fine)

$1/2$ cup chopped kalamata olives

1 small red onion, minced, for garnish

1 Cut each half of each kale leaf off the stems; reserve the stems. Be careful to keep the leaves intact so you have at least a dozen long, wide kale ribbons. Roughly chop the stems. Cut the feta into sticks about 2 inches long and as thin as you can without crumbling.

2 Put 2 tablespoons of the oil in a deep skillet or casserole with a tight-fitting lid over medium-high heat. Add the garlic and the chopped kale stems and sprinkle with salt and pepper. Cook, stirring occasionally, until the kale is just beginning to soften, about 5 minutes. Remove from the heat.

3 Lay out a ribbon of kale, put a piece of cheese on the end, and roll it up loosely. Put it in the pan on top of the garlic and stems. Repeat until all the ribbons and cheese are used, nestling the rolls in next to each other in a single layer. Pour the wine over all and top with the tomatoes and olives. Return the pan to medium-high heat. When the liquid starts to boil, cover and turn the heat down to medium-low.

4 Cook, undisturbed, for 10 minutes, then check and make sure the kale is tender and the cheese is hot. Garnish with the onion and several grinds of black pepper. To serve, carefully scoop the rolls out and top with some of the bits of vegetables and pan juices. Pass more olive oil at the table for drizzling.

Rolled Kale with Tofu and Fermented Black Beans. A great vegan option to serve with any plain rice:

Instead of the cheese, cut about a pound of tofu (preferably baked, pressed, or prefried) into larger sticks and use them to fill the kale. Use a neutral oil, like grapeseed or corn. Instead of the white wine, use sake or mirin. Instead of the olives, use fermented black beans. Proceed with the recipe, garnishing with sliced scallion if you like and passing soy sauce and dark sesame oil to drizzle at the table.

13 Other Fillings for Rolled Kale or Stuffed Grape Leaves

1. White Beans, Tuscan Style (page 594)
2. Mashed Favas (page 616)
3. Fluffy Cracked Wheat with Mustard and Tarragon (page 559)
4. Kasha with Golden Brown Onions (page 562)
5. Yellow Rice, the Best Way (page 513)
6. Bread and Herb Stuffing (page 395)
7. Pilaf with Currants and Pine Nuts (page 511)
8. Pilaf with Fruit and Nuts (page 511)
9. Simpler Baked Rice with Tomato (page 516)
10. Barley Pilaf (page 539)
11. Whole Wheat Couscous with Cauliflower and Almonds (page 554)
12. Bulgur Pilaf with Vermicelli (page 556)
13. Quinoa with Caramelized Onions (page 559)

Kohlrabi

A somewhat strange-looking vegetable that's actually a member of the cabbage family but is treated like a turnip. The whole plant is edible, but it's the bulbous stem base that's prized for its sweet, slightly piquant flavor and crisp texture. When sold without its stems and leaves, kohlrabi is sphere shaped with several arched ridges (where the stems were attached); its skin is like that of broccoli stems and can be white, light green, or vibrant purple.

Buying and storing: Look for specimens that are firm, crisp, and about the size of a golf ball (larger ones can be woody and tough). Store wrapped loosely in plastic in the refrigerator.

Preparing: Peeling is optional for small kohlrabi and recommended for large ones. Slice or chop as necessary.

Best cooking methods: Steaming, sautéing, and roasting.

When is it done? For steaming or sautéing, when tender but still crisp; for roasting, when soft.

Other vegetables to substitute: Turnips.

Leeks

The leek looks like an enormous scallion and is a member of the allium genus—along with onions, garlic, and scallions. Mild and sweet, silky when cooked, leeks' only downside is that they can be quite expensive. If you're paying by the pound, make sure there is plenty of white on the stalk, since you'll trim off most of the green.

Buying and storing: Generally, the smaller the leek, the more tender it is; but big, plump leeks are wonderful too. Avoid those that are slimy, dried out, browning, or mostly green. Store wrapped loosely in plastic in the refrigerator; they will keep for weeks.

Preparing: Wash well; leeks usually contain sand between layers. Trim the root end and any hard green leaves. Make a long vertical slit through the center of the leek, starting about 1 inch from the root end and cutting all the way to the green end (leaving the root end intact helps keep the leek from falling into pieces when you wash it). Wash well, being sure to get the sand out from between the layers. Or, if you're going to chop them anyway, trim, chop, and wash afterward; this is a much easier and more efficient process, as long as you don't care that the leek is no longer intact.

Best cooking methods: Sautéing, braising, and roasting.

When is it done? When soft—almost melting.

Other vegetables to substitute: Onions, shallots, or scallions.

Leeks Braised in Oil or Butter

MAKES: 4 servings
TIME: 30 minutes

Braised leeks are a great side dish or, when finished with a vinaigrette, as in the first variation, a terrific first course.

Other vegetables you can use: onions or shallots.

½ cup extra virgin olive oil or butter

3 or 4 leeks, about 1½ pounds, trimmed and cleaned

Salt and freshly ground black pepper

½ cup vegetable stock (pages 101–102) or water

Freshly squeezed lemon juice to taste

Chopped parsley leaves for garnish

❶ Put the oil or butter in a skillet or saucepan large enough to fit the leeks in one layer over medium heat. When the oil is hot or the butter is melted, add the leeks; sprinkle them with salt and pepper and cook, turning once or twice, until they're just beginning to brown, about 5 minutes.

❷ Add the stock and bring to a boil. Turn the heat to low, cover, and cook until the leeks are tender, about 20 minutes. Uncover; if the leeks are swimming in liquid, raise the heat a bit and boil some of it away, but allow the dish to remain moist.

❸ Sprinkle about 1 tablespoon of lemon juice over the leeks, then taste and adjust the seasoning. Serve hot, at room temperature, or cold, sprinkled with a little more lemon juice and garnished with parsley.

Leeks Vinaigrette. Good with some thyme added to the braising mix: Use oil instead of butter and cook out almost all of the liquid in Step 2. In Step 3, moisten the leeks with any Vinaigrette you like (pages 762–763), and serve.

Ⓕ Fast   Ⓜ Make Ahead   Ⓥ Vegan

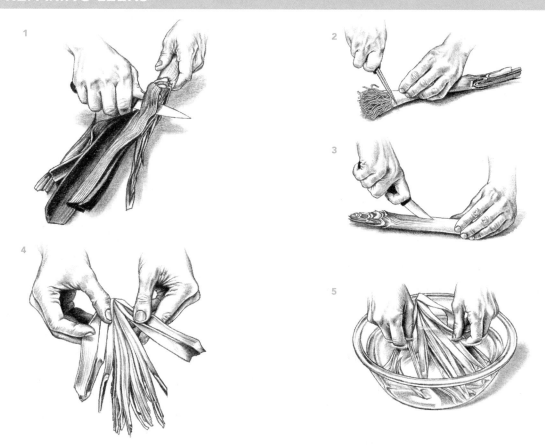

(STEP 1) Always remove the tough green leaves from leeks. (STEP 2) Cut off the root end. (STEP 3) Slice the leek almost in half, just about to the root end. (STEPS 4–5) Fan out the leaves and rinse either under cold running water or in a bowl. (If you're chopping the leeks for cooking, wash after chopping; it will be easier.)

Braised Leeks with Tomato. A little more substantial and much more colorful: Use oil instead of butter, and in Step 2, use 1 cup chopped tomato, preferably fresh, in place of the stock. Proceed with the recipe, finishing with either lemon juice or vinaigrette.

Braised Leeks with Olives. Easy and full of flavor: Use oil instead of butter, and in Step 2, after the liquid comes to a boil, add about 1 cup black olives; best are oil cured (you can leave the pits in), but any will do and all are good. (You'll need less salt.)

Braised Leeks with Mustard. There is a time-honored and wonderful affinity here: In Step 2, before adding the stock, whisk into it 1 tablespoon Dijon mustard, or to taste.

Steamed Leeks

MAKES: 4 servings
TIME: 20 minutes

Ⓕ Ⓜ Ⓥ

A nice alternative to braising, perhaps a little faster and neater, with the leeks finishing somewhat more intact. Dress the leeks as directed here, with any Vinaigrette (pages 762–763), or with a little soy sauce and dark sesame oil. These are also good garnished with toasted slivered almonds or chopped pistachios.

    4 leeks, trimmed and cleaned, cut into 1-inch
        sections

    Salt and freshly ground black pepper

    2 or 3 tablespoons extra virgin olive oil

    1 or 2 tablespoons freshly squeezed lemon juice

❶ Put the leeks in a steamer over about 1 inch of boiling water; steam until the leeks are tender, 10 minutes or more, then transfer to a platter.

❷ Sprinkle with salt and pepper, then drizzle with a couple of tablespoons of olive oil and a tablespoon of lemon juice. Stir gently, then taste and adjust the seasoning, adding more salt, pepper, olive oil, or lemon juice if you like. Serve hot, warm, or at room temperature.

Stir-Fried Leeks or Shallots

MAKES: 4 servings
TIME: 20 minutes

Ⓕ Ⓥ

You can stir-fry leeks in two ways. The first essentially creates a garnish for other dishes; you cook them until they're crisp, then sprinkle them on anything you like. The second is to treat them as a "real" vegetable and stir-fry them—usually with a couple of other vegetables—to serve as a main course. This recipe and the variation cover both.

    2 tablespoons peanut or neutral oil, like grapeseed
        or corn

    1 cup finely chopped or shredded celery, carrot, or
        a mixture

    2 or 3 large leeks or shallots (about 1½ pounds),
        trimmed, sliced, cleaned, and dried well

    1 tablespoon minced garlic

    Salt

    1 or 2 tablespoons soy sauce, to taste

❶ Put the oil in a large skillet or wok over medium-high heat. A minute later, add the carrot and/or celery and raise the heat to high. Cook, stirring occasionally, for about 2 minutes. Add the leeks or shallots and ¼ cup water and continue to cook, stirring, until the vegetables are crisp-tender, about 5 minutes more.

❷ Stir in the garlic and a pinch of salt and cook for 30 seconds. Add the soy sauce and turn off the heat; taste and adjust the seasoning and serve.

Crisp Leeks, Garlic, or Shallots. These can be made in advance and eaten as a snack or used as a garnish: Omit the celery, carrot, garlic, and soy. If using garlic, peel the cloves from 2 to 3 whole heads and coarsely chop or pulse in the food processor a couple of times. Increase the oil to about ½ cup. Cook the leeks, garlic, or shallots, stirring frequently and adjusting the heat so the leeks cook evenly and brown without burning, until nicely browned all over, about 10 minutes. (Be careful: once they start to brown, they brown quickly.) Drain on paper towels and season with salt. Use within a day.

Grilled Leeks

MAKES: 4 servings
TIME: 30 minutes

Ⓕ Ⓜ Ⓥ

If the leeks are very thin, skewer them or sandwich them in a grilling basket so they don't fall through the

 Ⓕ Fast   Ⓜ Make Ahead   Ⓥ Vegan

grill and you can turn them all at once. You can serve these with any Vinaigrette (pages 762–763) or Flavored Oil (pages 758).

Other vegetables you can use: scallions, shallots, onions, garlic.

4 leeks (about 1¹/₂ pounds), trimmed and cleaned

Extra virgin olive oil as needed

Salt and freshly ground black pepper

① Heat a gas or charcoal grill until quite hot and put the rack about 4 inches from the heat source. Brush the leeks lightly with olive oil and sprinkle with salt and pepper.

② Grill, turning occasionally, until nicely browned all over and very tender, 5 to 15 minutes, depending on their thickness.

Grilled Leeks, Asian Style: Substitute dark sesame oil for the olive oil. When the leeks are done, brush them with soy sauce.

Maize (*see* Corn, page 287)

Mushrooms

With countless varieties grown and hunted worldwide, the mushroom is a fungus, whether large or small, white or black, bland or mind-blowingly delicious. Not many of the varieties of these odd plants can be cultivated; this results in steep prices for any truly wild mushroom and especially for its even more luxurious cousin, the truffle, which almost never makes its way into home kitchens in the United States. Fortunately, mushrooms are highly interchangeable (except for the fragile enoki, which is essentially a garnish), and mixing domestic mushrooms with wild is a smart way to add flavor to a dish and stretch your dollar.

Here is a brief primer on the mushrooms—both domestic and wild—you're most likely to encounter in the supermarket:

Button or white: The most common and most bland cultivated variety; white to tan in color; thick caps and stems with gray to dark brown gills; tender and brown when cooked.

Chanterelle: Wild; delicious, and usually expensive. Light to golden yellow in color, shaped like fat trumpets with ruffle-edged caps. The flavor is earthy and nutty.

Cremino (Baby Bella or Portabella): Immature (cultivated) portobello mushrooms. Tan, with dark brown gills; shaped like white mushrooms and more robust in flavor.

Enoki: A delicate Asian mushroom often used as garnish; white with toothpick-sized stems and tiny round caps; very mild in flavor and best used raw or barely cooked.

Morel: Unusually shaped and one of the treasures of cooking, this wild-only mushroom is available fresh in the spring and fall. White or brown, cone shaped with a honeycomb-textured cap and hollow center; wonderful, earthy flavor, both fresh and dried (you should have dried morels in your pantry). Be sure to clean thoroughly as they're usually sandy.

Oyster: Available wild and cultivated in some supermarkets. White to dark gray in color, they grow in clusters with thick stems and a round or oval leaflike "cap"; mild mushroom flavor and slightly chewy texture.

Porcino: The must-have wild mushroom—dried (quite common and should be in your pantry) or fresh (not so common, at least in the States, and usually pretty pricey). It has the most robust and earthy flavor and the meatiest texture of all mushrooms; very plump, tan to dark brown caps and fat, off-white stems when fresh. Buy dried porcini from a reputable dealer (see Sources, page 929) in quantities of at least 1 ounce at a time (the ⅛-ounce packages often sold are rip-offs). Once you get into using them, you'll buy 4-ounce quantities or more.

Portobello: A relatively new supermarket staple, these are mature cremini or brown mushrooms; tan to brown, with giant, flat caps, thick stems, and dense, dark brown gills that darken whatever dish they're cooked with unless they're scraped out first. The flavor is earthy, and they're excellent grilled.

Shiitake: The most flavorful cultivated mushroom. Available fresh and dried; the latter is excellent for stock but has a rubbery though not unpleasant texture when reconstituted and cooked. Tan, flat caps with off-white gills and tough stems when fresh; brown with fatter-looking caps when dried (usually whole); texture is meaty with a hearty, earthy flavor. Always remove stems before eating (they're good in stock).

Buying and storing: Fresh mushrooms should be unbroken, plump, spongy yet firm, and fresh smelling; avoid any that are slimy, bruised, or foul smelling (especially if wrapped in plastic). True fresh wild mushrooms are in season briefly in the fall and spring. White mushrooms should have closed caps that cover the gills. Store wrapped loosely in wax paper or in a brown paper bag with a moist paper towel in the refrigerator; use wild mushrooms almost *immediately*, within 24 hours (they're too expensive to let rot).

Preparing: Rinse fresh mushrooms as lightly as you can (they absorb water like a sponge if they sit in it), but be sure to get dirt out of hidden crevices; with some mushrooms, it's easier to trim them first (morels are easiest to clean if you cut them in half lengthwise, but they don't look as nice afterward). Cut off any hard or dried-out spots—usually just the end of the stem. The stems of most mushrooms are perfectly edible, but those of shiitake should be cut off and discarded or reserved for stock. Clean the stems well, cut them in half if they're

large (as are those of portobellos), and cook them with the caps.

To reconstitute dried mushrooms: See page 317.

Best cooking methods: Sautéing or stir-frying, roasting, and grilling.

When are they done? When tender, though you can cook them until they're crisp too.

Other vegetables to substitute: Mushrooms are largely interchangeable, including reconstituted dried mushrooms. Otherwise there is no substitute.

Sautéed Mushrooms

MAKES: 4 servings
TIME: About 20 minutes

You can make almost any mushroom dish better by taking one of two steps. First, if you can find mushrooms other than button mushrooms, you're off to a good start. But the second technique is easier, as long as you're prepared: Include a portion of reconstituted dried mushrooms—preferably porcini—in the dish. The affinity between fresh and dried mushrooms is such that the exotic dried mushrooms make the tame cultivated ones ten times better.

Then, once you get the hang of it, you'll be in a position to create a world of great mushroom dishes, like these. Start with the basic recipe, then try the additions.

¼ cup extra virgin olive oil or a mixture of oil and butter

About 1 pound mushrooms, preferably an assortment, trimmed and sliced

A handful of dried porcini (optional), reconstituted (see page 317)

Salt and freshly ground black pepper

¼ cup dry white wine or water

1 teaspoon minced garlic

Chopped parsley leaves for garnish (optional)

① Put the oil in a large skillet over medium heat. When hot, add the mushrooms, then sprinkle with salt and pepper. Cook, stirring occasionally, until tender, 10 to 15 minutes.

② Add the wine and let it bubble away for a minute, then turn the heat down to medium-low. Add the garlic, stir, and cook for 1 minute. Taste and adjust the seasoning, then garnish and serve hot, warm, or at room temperature.

Sautéed Mushrooms with Asian Flavors. A world apart with no more work. In Step 1, use peanut oil, start with shiitake mushrooms if possible, add a dried chile or two to the mix, and use lots of black pepper. In Step 2, use water; add 1 tablespoon soy sauce, or to taste, along with the garlic. Finish with cilantro instead of parsley.

6 Additions to Sautéed Mushrooms

1. Use any fresh herb you like, but especially chives (a handful), chervil (a handful), tarragon (a few leaves fresh or a pinch dried), or thyme (a teaspoon or so fresh), along with the garlic.

2. Finish with a teaspoon or more of lemon juice or vinegar.

3. Substitute chopped shallot ($1/4$ cup or so), scallion ($1/2$ cup or so), or onion ($1/2$ cup or so) for the garlic, cooking for 2 or 3 minutes longer.

4. Finish the dish with $1/2$ cup to 1 cup cream or sour cream, simmering gently. This is best if you cook the mushrooms in butter from the start and use scallion in place of the garlic.

5. In the Asian Flavors variation, stir in 1 tablespoon Chile Paste (page 828) or curry paste (to make your own, see page 830), or to taste, along with the garlic.

6. In the Asian Flavors variation, stir in 1 tablespoon toasted sesame seeds (see page 321) with the garlic and finish with a teaspoon or more of dark sesame oil.

Pan-Cooked Mushrooms, Dry Style

MAKES: 4 servings
TIME: 20 minutes

Ⓕ Ⓜ Ⓥ

The technique for what I call "dry-style" mushrooms is a little bit different from a traditional sauté. The idea is to release as much water as possible, then cook it all off. This method requires a little less fat, and the results have a concentrated mushroom flavor, a pleasant chewy texture, and lightly browned, crisp edges; no liquid will remain. Like Sautéed Mushrooms (page 314), this is much better if you use a combination of fresh and dried mushrooms.

Dry-style mushrooms are great whenever you want to add fresh mushroom flavor and meaty texture without any liquid; so use them for topping salads and pizzas, filling sandwiches, tacos, and burritos, or as a garnish or ingredient.

> 2 tablespoons extra virgin olive oil or a mixture of oil and butter
>
> About 1 pound mushrooms, preferably an assortment, cleaned, trimmed, and sliced
>
> A handful of dried porcini (optional), reconstituted (see page 317)
>
> Salt and freshly ground black pepper

① Put the oil in a large skillet with a tight-fitting lid over medium-high heat. Add the mushrooms, sprinkle with plenty of salt and pepper, and give them a quick stir. Cover, turn the heat down to medium-low, and cook, undisturbed, for 5 minutes before checking. You should see a fair amount of liquid in the pan. If not, stir, cover again, and cook until you do, another couple minutes or so.

② Remove the lid and turn up the heat until the liquid bubbles steadily. Cook, undisturbed, until the liquid boils off, 3 to 5 minutes. After that, keep an eye on the mushrooms and stir them just enough to keep them from burning; cook until they're dry, shrunken, and as crisp as you like them, about another 5 minutes more. Remove from the heat, taste and adjust the seasoning, and serve hot or at room temperature.

Mushroom Pâté

MAKES: 6 to 8 servings

TIME: 40 minutes, plus time to chill

Smooth and full of mushroom flavor, this is perfect spread on crackers or toast, in canapés, or in a sandwich. Serve it in a terrine or ramekin or mold it in a dish and turn it out.

3 tablespoons neutral oil, like grapeseed or corn

1 medium onion, chopped

1 carrot, chopped

1 stalk celery, chopped

About 2 pounds cremini or white mushrooms, cleaned, trimmed, and roughly chopped

$1/4$ cup dried porcini (optional), reconstituted (see page 317)

Salt and freshly ground black pepper

2 tablespoons tomato paste

$3/4$ cup dry white wine (optional)

2 tablespoons freshly squeezed lemon juice

1 cup Fresh Bread Crumbs (page 804) or crumbled crackers, plus more as needed

Finely chopped chives or parsley leaves for garnish

1 Put the oil in a large skillet over high heat. When it is hot, add the onion, carrot, and celery and cook until the onion is translucent, about 5 minutes. Add the mushrooms, sprinkle with salt and pepper, and cook for another few minutes, then add the tomato paste and the white wine if you're using it. Stir and cook until the liq-

uid is mostly evaporated, about 10 minutes. Turn the heat off and let the vegetables cool.

2 Transfer the mushroom mixture to a food processor, add the lemon juice and bread crumbs, and purée until smooth. Taste and season with more salt, pepper, or lemon juice as needed. The consistency should be fairly thick but still easily spreadable; add more bread crumbs if it's too thin; add vegetable stock or water if it's too thick.

3 Spoon the pâté mixture into a terrine or ramekin(s) and refrigerate until chilled. Serve at room temperature, garnished with chives or parsley. It will keep in the refrigerator for up to 4 days.

Lentil Pâté. Green, brown, or red lentils work fine: Substitute 2 cups cooked and drained lentils, reserving some of the cooking liquid, for the mushrooms, including the porcini. Add a couple teaspoons minced garlic and a curry powder or garam masala (to make your own, see page 815) if you like, especially with the red lentils.

Walnut Pâté. Not as smooth as mushroom pâté, but quite rich and deliciously nutty in flavor: Substitute 2 cups shelled walnuts for the mushrooms, including the porcini. Omit the tomato paste and add 2 teaspoons minced fresh thyme leaves. No need to cook the walnuts in Step 1. Proceed with the recipe.

Grilled Mushrooms

MAKES: 4 servings

TIME: About 20 minutes

There's a big difference in how mushrooms take to the grill: Ordinary button mushrooms are okay but, well, ordinary. Many wild mushrooms are simply too delicate (though the absolute best grilled mushroom is a fresh

Ⓕ Fast   Ⓜ Make Ahead   Ⓥ Vegan

All you need is a bowl and some hot water to reconstitute dried mushrooms. Soak the mushrooms in the hot water until they are soft, anywhere from 5 to 30 minutes. Occasionally you'll need to change the water for very tough or thick mushrooms. Drain and save the soaking liquid (strained if sand or dirt has settled at the bottom of the bowl) and use it as a stock in soups, stews, and sauces; it has great mushroom flavor. Trim away any hard spots on the mushrooms and use just as you would fresh.

Chinese dried shiitakes are a slightly different story; they must be soaked in boiling-hot water (you might even have to change the water once to get them soft), and they need to be trimmed assiduously. One way to deal with all of this is to cook them in stock (or Kombu Dashi, page 103), then cool, trim, and use them; the process will enhance both stock and mushrooms.

porcino, which is found only in the wild and often sold in markets for $20 a pound and more). The three best of the widely available mushrooms for grilling are shiitake, cremino, and portobello (which are large cremini). Portobellos are the most striking, but big shiitakes can look pretty good too, and they taste great.

Other vegetables you can use: see the chart on page 251.

1/3 cup extra virgin olive oil

1 tablespoon minced shallot, scallion, onion, or garlic

1 teaspoon fresh thyme leaves, if available

Salt and freshly ground black pepper

4 large portobello mushrooms, trimmed and cut in half right down the middle; or 12 to 16 cremini, trimmed and cut in half or left whole; or 12 to 16 shiitakes, stems removed (reserve for stock), caps left whole or cut in half

Chopped parsley leaves for garnish

1 Heat a charcoal or gas grill until quite hot and put the rack about 4 inches from the heat source. Mix together the olive oil, shallot, thyme if you have it, salt, and pepper. Brush the mushrooms all over with about half of this mixture.

2 Grill or broil the mushrooms with the tops of their caps away from the heat until they begin to brown, 5 to 8 minutes. Brush with the remaining oil and turn. Grill until tender and nicely browned all over, 5 to 10 minutes more. Garnish and serve hot, warm, or at room temperature.

Mustard and Turnip Greens

The spicy greens of the mustard and turnip plants, these are tender, peppery, and really delicious when young, but—especially the turnip greens—can become quite bitter and even tough when mature. Which, unfortunately, is how you usually find them in supermarkets. But even then they're not too bad.

Buying and storing: Look for tender, dark green leaves; avoid those with tough, fibrous stems and any yellowing. Store wrapped loosely in plastic in the refrigerator.

Preparing: Wash them very well as they are often full of sand. Remove the stems if they are tough. Tear or chop the leaves.

Best cooking methods: Steaming, braising, and sautéing.

When is it done? When wilted and tender.

Other vegetables to substitute: Mustard and turnip greens are almost always interchangeable; or substitute dandelion, beet greens, broccoli raab, kale, collards, or spinach.

Nuts and Seeds

It would be a mistake to think of nuts and seeds as just salty snacks, though they are great ones, as well as super ways to add texture, flavor, and nutrients to a huge variety of dishes. You can sprinkle them into anything from salads to grains to oatmeal and pancake or waffle batters; grind them up into flours to use in batters and doughs; make nut butters to spread on toast or add to sauces or dips; the possibilities are endless. And they can also play a more prominent role, like in Fast Nut Burgers (page 667) or Traditional Pesto (page 768).

Nuts and seeds cross over many families of plants and are among the most ancient of human food sources: There's evidence that humans were already cultivating nuts around 10,000 B.C.E., and certainly we were foraging for them before that. For a wild food that grows on trees, they can hardly be beat: Almost all nuts and seeds are packed with protein, fat, fiber, minerals, and vitamins (the exception is chestnuts, which have little protein or fat). They're good sources of B vitamins, potassium, and iron; walnuts and flaxseeds have omega-3s; and almonds, Brazil nuts, and hazelnuts are great sources of calcium. Most nuts and seeds contain 5 to 11 grams of protein per serving, with peanuts, sunflower seeds, and soy nuts at the top. And while it's true that up to a whopping 97 percent calories in nuts and seeds can be from fat, in general the majority of that fat is unsaturated.

Nuts and seeds aren't the bulk of anyone's diet these days, but they can play a fantastic role, especially if you take advantage of the techniques and tips outlined here. Roasting, toasting, and blanching your own nuts and making your own nut flours and butters takes only a bit more effort, but is worth it for the money you'll save and the control you'll have over what you eat.

Buying and Storing: If stored properly, unshelled nuts can last up to a year and taste almost as good as on the day you bought them. Look for unshelled nuts that have hard and sound shells; the nuts shouldn't rattle when shaken and should feel heavy for their size.

Shelled nuts have a shorter shelf life—as little as three to four months—so you definitely want to purchase them where there's a high turnover. Look for plump—not shriveled—nuts that are crisp and certainly ones that don't smell rancid. Also check the package or sell by dates on the containers.

All nuts, shelled or unshelled, and seeds need to be stored in an airtight container in a cool, dark, dry place for up to three to four months or in the refrigerator or freezer for up to a year. Hazelnuts and Brazil nuts are the most notorious for going bad quickly; pine nuts and sesame seeds also turn rancid quickly, though the freezer retards this process. These more fragile nuts will keep for only a few weeks.

Shelling Nuts: There's no real mystery to shelling nuts; a nutcracker certainly makes things easier, but a hammer or mallet works too. (To minimize the noise and mess of hammering nuts open, cover them, a few at a time, with a towel.) Pistachios and peanuts can be shelled with your hands; sunflower or pumpkin seeds between your teeth; and chestnuts must be heated before being peeled. Brazil nut shells are notoriously hard to crack, though somewhat easier after roasting.

Roasting and Toasting Nuts and Seeds: Roasting and toasting nuts and seeds enhances flavor and takes no more than patience (and a stove!). The most common mistake people make when roasting or toasting nuts and seeds is trying to do it too quickly with too high heat.

There are generally two ways to roast nuts and seeds: dry or with oil. Naturally, oil roasting adds fat and calories, but it also adds great flavor, especially if you use peanut or sesame oil or butter; extra virgin olive oil isn't bad either. Dry roasting is done with nothing added.

Whether or not you roast with oil, you can control the doneness and the amount and type of seasoning (and also the type of oil if you're using it). See Caramelized Spiced Nuts (page 322) for specific recipes.

F Fast   M Make Ahead   V Vegan

THE NUT AND SEED LEXICON

For simplicity and practicality, I'm defining nuts and seeds by their culinary and common uses, not by botanical properties. Just to be clear, you'll see some items called nuts that are technically seeds or legumes; for instance, peanuts and soy nuts are really legumes. The exceptions are few and insignificant for the purposes of this book.

With their crunchy texture and mild flavor, nuts are widely interchangeable (with the exception of chestnuts). Often choosing what nut to use in a dish is a matter of flavor or simply what you have on hand. Seeds are also fairly exchangeable, though size may also be a factor. I usually always have a good supply of almonds, peanuts, pine nuts, pumpkin seeds (pepitas), sesame seeds, and walnuts or pecans in my freezer, which more than covers the basics; I buy other nuts and seeds in small quantities as I need them for specific uses. Chestnuts appear in their own section on page 286.

NUT	DESCRIPTION	FORMS
Almonds *Sweet Almonds*	A valuable nut of Middle Eastern origin, with sweet and delicate flavor (young fresh almonds, which you see occasionally in spring, are incredible). Most often used in desserts and sweets, but they're also great for adding texture, richness, and a light flavor to savory dishes. The shells are the shape of the nuts, with small indentations. So-called Chinese almonds aren't nuts but apricot seeds that resemble almonds in look and taste; they're always roasted or blanched, because they're slightly toxic when raw.	Shelled and unshelled, blanched, sliced, slivered, roasted and sometimes salted, made into a paste (almond paste or marzipan), ground into flour or meal or butter, pressed into oil, made into "milk," and sometimes sold "green" in their fuzzy, light green shells, which can be eaten whole if young and tender enough or cracked open for just the tender nut.
Brazil Nuts *Para Nuts, Cream Nuts*	Large, oblong, odd-shaped nut in a very hard dark brown shell, with meat that is more tender than crunchy. The majority is harvested from Amazon rain forests. High in unsaturated fat (the "good" fat) and loaded with vitamins and minerals.	Shelled and unshelled, roasted and sometimes salted
Cashews	Originally South American, now primarily grown in India. Shaped like fat commas; the shells are toxic (they are related to poison ivy, if you can believe that!) so they're almost always sold shelled. Cashews are rich and slightly sweet; when cooked, they soften a bit and acquire a somewhat meaty texture. They have a lower fat content than most nuts and are full of iron and folic acid.	Shelled, roasted and sometimes salted, ground into butter
Flax seeds *Linseeds*	Recently "discovered" in the United States for their incredible nutritional properties; packed with protein, fiber, and omega-3 fatty acids. Small, shiny, flat, and nutty-flavored seeds that range in color from tan to dark brown. Get the most nutrients by buying meal or grinding whole seeds.	Whole, ground into meal or flour, and pressed into oil

NUT	DESCRIPTION	FORMS
Hazelnuts *Filberts*	Often used in European pastries, small round nuts that are most often found shelled; in their shells they resemble chestnuts but are smaller and lighter brown. Crunchy, with a mild nutty flavor (perfect with chocolate), and lower in fat than most nuts; the skins are slightly bitter and can be removed by rubbing the nuts between towels or your bare hands while still warm after roasting.	Shelled or unshelled, blanched, roasted and sometimes salted, ground into flour or meal or butter, pressed into oil, and made into milk
Macadamia *Queensland Nuts,* *Maroochi Nuts*	A rich, calorie-laden, high-fat nut native of Australia but also grown in Hawaii. Medium size, round, and creamy white in color; they are always sold shelled because the shells are so hard. A decadent snack or addition to dessert dishes.	Shelled, roasted and sometimes salted, and pressed into oil
Peanuts *Goobers, Groundnuts,* *Ground Peas*	A native South American legume widely considered and eaten like a nut; it really bridges the gap. The peanut is our most popular "nut"; rich in protein, high in fat, and a good source of fiber. Virginia and Spanish are the two most common varieties; Spanish are smaller with a reddish brown papery skin.	Whole and shelled, typically dry-roasted and often salted, boiled, ground into butter, and pressed into oil; occasionally raw (at natural food stores) and fresh (at farmer's markets, Chinese groceries, and on-line)
Pecans	Native to North America and used extensively in southern cooking, like pecan pie; similar to walnuts but flatter, with dark brown skins, and a milder and sweeter, buttery flavor. High fat and low protein content.	Sometimes unshelled, more commonly shelled, in pieces, roasted and sometimes salted
Pine Nuts	The seeds of various types of pine trees. These days China does the largest amount of trade globally, though Native Americans have used pine nuts from native trees since ancient times. They're a slightly golden color, long and slender in shape, with a delicate flavor. Commonly used in cooking both sweet and savory dishes, like Traditional Pesto (page 768).	Shelled, raw or roasted
Pistachios	A pretty green nut often sold in their split tan-colored shells, which crack naturally as the nuts ripen; unopened nuts should be discarded. Originated in the Middle East and grown across the Mediterranean, in California (the largest producer), and in Australia; Middle Eastern (usually Iranian) pistachios are markedly superior in taste. Their flavor is delicious and lends itself to both sweet and savory dishes.	Shelled and unshelled, roasted and sometimes salted, and pressed into an expensive oil with a gorgeous deep green color

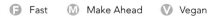 Fast   Make Ahead   Vegan

NUT	DESCRIPTION	FORMS
Pumpkin and Squash Seeds	The seeds of pumpkins or nearly any hard winter squash; medium size, oval with a point, flat, ranging in color from tan to white. The flavor is like a cross between peanuts and sesame seeds; rich and delicious and loaded with protein, fiber, iron, and other minerals. Pepitas are a grayish green color and slightly smaller than whole pumpkin seeds; sometimes ground and used as a thickening and flavoring agent or as a coating (like bread crumbs), tossed into salads, breads, muffins, or eaten out of hand.	Fresh (get them right out of a pumpkin or squash), dried, roasted and sometimes salted, and hulled (often called *pepitas*—Spanish for "little seed"), or roasted and pressed into oil (quite expensive and dark green)
Soy Nuts	Dried and roasted soybeans; they are small, tan, oval-shaped "nuts" that are quite crunchy and loaded with protein but fairly high in fat. Often eaten as a snack or tossed into salads, granola, or trail mix. (For more on soybeans, See "The Legume Lexicon," page 576.)	Raw or roasted and sometimes salted
Sunflower Seeds	A common seed with a black and gray striped shell that's been a staple in vegetarian pantries for decades. From the gigantic sunflower plant, native to North America, and used in everything from breads and muffins to salads and as a crunchy and flavorful garnish for just about anything. Packed with protein, vitamin E, and folic acid and high in fat.	Shelled and unshelled, roasted and often salted, or pressed into oil
Walnuts	One of the most common and oldest known nuts; used in numerous cuisines from the United States to Europe, North Africa, the Middle East, and India. Shells are round with a point, tan colored, and have ridges; nuts are fairly large and unusually shaped (sort of like a brain). Their rich flavor and crisp texture is a nice addition to desserts and savory dishes alike; high in omega-3s, fiber, and minerals. Black walnuts are less common, have harder shells, and are more flavorful.	Shelled and unshelled, in pieces, ground into meal or flour, and pressed into oil

To roast, preheat the oven to 350°F and put the nuts or seeds in an even layer on a baking sheet. Roast them until they are just starting to turn golden brown, 12 to 15 minutes, stirring every so often.

Toasting in a pan on the range is better suited to seeds; heat a pan over medium heat and add the seeds. Toast the seeds, shaking the pan and stirring often, until they are just starting to turn golden brown (pumpkin seeds will puff up slightly, and may pop a bit), 5 to 10 minutes.

Immediately remove the nuts or seeds from the heat and let cool; they will continue to cook a bit and will crisp up as they cool. Be sure to remove them from the heat before they look perfectly golden brown so the carry-over cooking doesn't overdo it; burned nuts are bitter.

Blanching Nuts: Blanched nuts are just nuts with the (sometimes bitter) skins removed. Typically this is done by soaking or boiling them (that's why they're called *blanched*), but you can also do it by roasting or toasting, though it's generally not as effective. Either way, it can be time-consuming; sometimes the skins just slip off, but usually it takes a bit of extra effort. Almonds and hazelnuts are the nuts you're most likely to blanch; walnuts, with their uneven surface, are simply not worth it.

To blanch, bring a pot of water to a boil, add the nuts, and turn off the heat; let soak until you see the skins start to loosen, typically a couple minutes. Drain and pick out the skins. If the skins are stubborn, try rubbing them in a kitchen or paper towel until the skins loosen.

Grinding Nuts into Meal, Flour, or Butter: Almond, hazelnut, or just about any nut meal or flour (it's the same thing) may sound like something really special—and the price you pay for it reinforces that notion—but the truth is that this is an easy process. All you need are nuts and a food processor (or a spice or coffee grinder for smaller quantities). The only exception are chestnuts, which must be dried before being milled into flour; you'll have to fork over the money for that, if you can find it (try Italian markets). Store-bought nut butters—with the exception of peanut butter—can be quite pricey too but are even easier to make than meal or flour.

Don't overdo it when grinding nuts into meal or flour; it's surprising how quickly nut meal turns into nut butter. Pulse the nuts in a food processor until they are finely ground and look like moist flour; if there are still larger bits of nut, either leave them in for texture or sift them out. If you see any bit of the meal clumping, stop processing; it's about to turn into nut butter.

Making nut butter on the other hand is simply a matter of pushing the "on" button and stopping it at the consistency you like; less puréeing for chunky butter, more for smooth butter. Most nut butters are made from roasted or toasted nuts for a richer flavor, but raw nuts make a great butter too. You can also add salt, sweetener,

or spices to enhance or punch up the flavor (see "7 Ways to Season Nut Butters," right). Your average supermarket peanut butter is loaded with salt, sugar, and even added fat.

7 Ways to Season Nut Butters

Nut butters are delicious plain, sweet, and savory. Here are some ideas to add a lot or a little kick to your nut butter.

Keep in mind that adding liquids, like maple syrup or coconut milk, will thin the nut butter; also, adding fresh ingredients like garlic or chiles will make the nut butter more perishable—keep it in the fridge. The following quantities are guidelines for about a cup of butter; I give rough quantities, but really these are to taste.

1. Salt: $1/4$ teaspoon
2. Sweetener: sugar, brown sugar, honey, molasses, or maple syrup; 2 tablespoons
3. Spices: cinnamon, nutmeg, cloves, allspice, cardamom, coriander, cumin, or asafetida to name a few, or any of the spice mixtures (pages 810–819); start with $1/4$ teaspoon
4. Chile: cayenne, hot red pepper flakes, or any dried or fresh chile (see pages 825 and 828 for how to prepare), including chipotle chiles in adobo sauce; start with $1/4$ teaspoon
5. Garlic: raw or roasted (page 304); 1 clove raw or 1 head roasted
6. Ginger: raw or crystallized; about 1 tablespoon
7. Coconut: milk or shredded; a couple tablespoons

Caramelized Spiced Nuts

MAKES: 4 to 6 servings
TIME: 15 minutes

A crisp sugar shell and bit of spice make these not too sweet and not too spicy. Serve a bowl of them with cocktails or other appetizers; they will go quickly, so have

 Fast   Make Ahead   Ⓥ Vegan

backup ready. (For an easier version, see the first two variations.)

Add seeds to the mix as well; sunflower, pumpkin, and sesame seeds all add great flavor and texture along with the nuts.

    2 tablespoons peanut or neutral oil, like grapeseed
        or corn

    2 cups sugar

    2 teaspoons garam masala (to make your own, see
        page 815)

    $1/_2$ teaspoon cayenne

    1 teaspoon salt

    2 cups (about 1 pound) unsalted mixed shelled nuts

1 Preheat the oven to 450°F. Grease a baking sheet with the oil. Put a wide pot or deep skillet over high heat, add 2 cups water and the sugar, and bring to a boil. Stir in the spices, salt, and nuts. Reduce the heat to medium and cook, stirring frequently, until the liquid is reduced to a syrup, 5 to 10 minutes.

2 Turn the heat to low under the nuts and remove with a slotted spoon, letting the excess syrup drain off a bit and then spreading them on the baking sheet. (Be sure to turn off the burner when you've finished).

3 Roast the nuts for 10 minutes, tossing once or twice with a spatula. Remove from the oven and let cool (the sugar coating will be very hot, so resist sampling for a few minutes!); the sugar coating will harden as the nuts cool. Serve or store in an airtight container at room temperature for 2 or 3 days.

Roasted Nuts. No sugar coating, just butter or oil and basic seasoning: Omit the sugar and garam masala; use a tablespoon of butter or peanut oil. Skip Steps 1 and 2; toss the nuts with the butter and seasoning and roast.

Roasted Herbed Nuts. Cook woody herbs, like thyme and rosemary, with the nuts; add more fragile herbs, like parsley, chives, or tarragon, after the nuts have roasted: Omit the garam masala and all but 1 tea-

spoon of the sugar; add 2 tablespoons mixed chopped herbs. Skip Steps 1 and 2.

Fiery Caramelized Nuts. Salty, sweet, and hot: Substitute a tablespoon or more finely minced chipotle chile with the adobo sauce for the garam masala.

Gingered Nuts. The ginger adds a kick: Substitute ground ginger for the garam masala and add a couple tablespoons chopped crystallized ginger if you like. Sprinkle the crystallized ginger on the nuts when they are spread on the baking sheet (Step 2) so it will stick.

Okra

Well loved in the South but largely underappreciated elsewhere, okra is a green (or sometimes purple) oblong, tapered pod covered with a fine fuzz. It can range in size from 1 to well over 6 inches in length, but 3 inches or less is the most tender and flavorful (any larger and it becomes too seedy and even tough). It oozes a slimy liquid when cut and when cooked for a long time; this makes it useful for thickening stews, like gumbo, but it's exactly this feature that those who didn't grow up with okra may find unappealing. Converts are made, however, when okra is fried, especially when coated in cornmeal first.

Buying and Storing: Okra is available year-round in the South and in the summer in the North. Look for unblemished, plump, and firm green pods under 3 inches in length. Large okra, though it may look just as nice, is too often tough and fibrous and not worth eating. Store wrapped loosely in plastic in the refrigerator for up to a few days.

Preparing: Rinse and cut off the stems; you can chop or sliver before cooking if you like. Larger pods must be cut into $1/_2$-inch rounds or smaller.

Best cooking methods: Frying and gently stewing (see pages 324–325).

When is it done? When tender; overcooking makes okra slimy.

Other vegetables to substitute: Green or wax beans or asparagus.

Fried Okra

MAKES: 4 servings
TIME: 30 minutes

A quick soak in buttermilk works wonders on okra. It streamlines the breading process to two steps, while the slime—and let's not pretend it doesn't exist — disappears into a relatively thick coating that won't fall off. The result is super-crunchy okra with silky insides.

If you don't work in batches, the slices will tend to clump up, but even that can work in your favor (see the variation). This fried okra needs nothing but a final dusting with salt, though ketchup (to make your own, see page 790) or Real Ranch Dressing (page 772) turns it into party food.

Other vegetables you can use: any winter or summer squash.

Peanut or neutral oil, like grapeseed or corn,
    for deep frying

1 cup cornmeal

1 cup all-purpose flour

Salt and freshly ground black pepper

Cayenne to taste (optional)

2 cups buttermilk

1½ pounds okra, trimmed

❶ Put at least 2 inches oil in a countertop deep-fryer or in a deep pan on the stove and turn the heat to medium-high; bring to 350°F (see "Deep Frying," page 26). Combine the cornmeal and flour in a shallow bowl or pie plate; sprinkle with a little salt and pepper, and a pinch of cayenne if you like, and stir well. Pour the buttermilk into a large bowl, sprinkle with a little salt, and stir.

❷ If the okra is small, cut it in half lengthwise; cut larger okra into thick slices, slightly on the diagonal to reveal more of the interior. Working in batches, put a handful of okra into the buttermilk, then fish out the slices one by one, roll them around in the cornmeal mixture, and drop them into the hot oil, taking care not to overcrowd the pan.

❸ Cook the okra, stirring gently to cook them evenly, until they are browned all over, 3 to 5 minutes, depending on size. Remove with a slotted spoon to drain on paper towels. Repeat until all the okra are done. Sprinkle with salt and pepper if you like and serve immediately.

Okra Hush Puppies. Even easier: Cut the okra crosswise into ½-inch slices. In Step 2, put the okra into the buttermilk all at once and stir to coat well and release some slime. Use 2 soupspoons to scoop up some of a clump of buttermilk-coated okra slices (trust me; they will be both clumpy and coated) and roll it around in the cornmeal mixture to coat evenly. Drop the clumps—now called *hush puppies* —in the hot oil and fry as described in Step 3 (they might take a minute or two longer to cook).

Okra Stew with Tomatoes

MAKES: 4 servings
TIME: About 1 hour, largely unattended

If you think okra has no potential, try cooking it slowly with tomatoes. For the best texture, you've got to sear the okra first. But after that, there's little to do but let the pot bubble away. To serve this New Orleans style, pour a ladleful into a shallow soup bowl and nestle a scoop of plain white rice in the center.

Other vegetables you can use: any green beans.

3 tablespoons extra virgin olive oil

1 large onion, halved and cut into thick slices

Salt and freshly ground black pepper

1 pound okra, trimmed

2 tablespoons chopped garlic

4 cups chopped tomato (canned, with the juice, is fine)

1 tablespoon minced fresh oregano (optional)

Chopped parsley leaves for garnish

① Put 2 tablespoons of the oil in a deep skillet or large pot over medium-high heat. When hot, add the onion, sprinkle with salt and pepper, and cook, stirring frequently, until soft and turning golden, 2 to 3 minutes. Remove with a slotted spoon.

② Add the remaining oil to the pot and stir in the okra. Cook, stirring occasionally, until it begins to brown a little, then add the garlic and cook for another minute or so, stirring once or twice. Return the onion to the pot and add the tomato, along with a cup of water. Sprinkle with salt and pepper.

③ Bring the mixture to a boil, then lower the heat so it bubbles gently. Cook, stirring every once in a while, until the okra is very tender and the sauce has thickened, about 45 minutes. Stir in the oregano if you like, then taste and adjust the seasoning and serve, garnished with parsley.

Okra Stew with Roux. A simple vegetable gumbo: Increase the oil to 6 tablespoons. Have $1/4$ cup of flour ready. In Step 2, add all the remaining oil ($1/4$ cup) and turn the heat to medium-low. Add the flour and cook, stirring almost constantly, until the mixture— called the *roux*—darkens to the color of tea and becomes quite fragrant. This can take up to 10 minutes; lower the heat if it's sticking or cooking too fast. Add the okra and continue cooking and stirring until the okra starts to soften, another 3 to 5 minutes. Proceed with the recipe.

Olives

Cultivated for thousands of years—its image decorates the walls of Ancient Egyptian tombs— the olive (includ-

ing the fruit, its oil, and the tree itself) has been enormously important to the development of cuisine and even civilization. Originally from the Mediterranean, which is still the world's major producer, olives are now grown in California, Arizona, New Mexico, and much of the rest of the world.

There are dozens of varieties of olives; multiply that by the number of different curing processes (a half dozen or so), and you've got a vast assortment to choose from. Of course, what we see in the United States is just a small fraction of what's available in all of the different countries and regions that produce and cure olives (which is a lot). Go to any Mediterranean market (that's Greek, Italian, Spanish, North African, or Middle Eastern, just to name a few) for a far more comprehensive and regional collection.

Olives are green when unripe and darken (eventually turning black) as they ripen. Most olives are picked green for curing; those intended for olive oil are allowed to ripen further; and some are left on the tree until quite dark. The black olives we see in markets either have been turned black by the curing process or are fully ripe olives.

Curing olives is essential to making them edible; they contain an extremely bitter-tasting chemical called *oleuropin*, which is minimized or eliminated by the curing process. Olives are most often cured in oil, saltwater, lye, or salt; the method will determine the fruit's ultimate flavor, texture, and color. Often herbs or spices are added to further enhance flavor.

These are the olives most commonly found in markets:

Black or Mission: Most often pitted and canned and tasteless; picked when unripe or green; cured in lye and then oxygenated (turning them black).

Kalamata: Widely available, usually pretty salty and sometimes mushy, though not unpleasantly so; dark brown, purple, or black. Picked when ripe or almost ripe, then cured in saltwater or red wine vinegar.

Manzanilla or Spanish: Big, green, rather crisp, and often stuffed with pimientos or garlic cloves. Usually picked young; cured in lye, then brined for six months to a year.

Niçoise: From Nice, France; dark red or brown, small but plump, with a slightly sour flavor. Picked ripe, then cured in saltwater.

Moroccan: Also called *oil-* or *dry-cured*; shriveled, shiny, and jet black. Picked ripe, then cured in oil or salt, sometimes with herbs.

Picholine: From France; green, almond-shaped, and crisp. Picked green, then cured in saltwater or lime and wood ashes, then brined, sometimes with citric acid, giving them a tart flavor.

Buying and storing: There's no guesswork in canned or jarred olives. Loose olives should be firm and not dried out (unless oil- or dry-cured, in which case they are shriveled and not stored in any liquid). Taste one before buying. When ladling out the olives, keep in mind that you're most likely paying by the pound, so any liquid that you include is adding weight; however, olives keep longer in liquid. Best policy: Buy as much as you'll use in a few days. Store in the refrigerator; those in liquid will last weeks if not months.

Preparing: Remove the pit by slicing the flesh lengthwise and digging it out with your fingers, by crushing with the side of a knife and picking out the pit, or by using a pitter. If you like, you can reduce the saltiness by rinsing or soaking in water for 20 minutes or so or boiling for 30 seconds beforehand.

Other vegetables to substitute: Caper berries or capers.

but sautéing them with garlic and herbs adds layers of flavor that make them memorable.

3 tablespoons extra virgin olive oil

2 cloves garlic, smashed

1 pound olives, preferably a combination of black and green, rinsed and pitted

2 sprigs fresh rosemary or marjoram or 4 sprigs fresh thyme

1 tablespoon red wine vinegar

Salt and freshly ground black pepper

Put the oil in a deep skillet over medium heat. When hot, add the garlic and cook for a minute, then add the olives and herbs; cook, stirring occasionally, 4 or 5 minutes. Sprinkle with the vinegar and pepper; taste and add salt if necessary.

Braised Olives with Tomatoes. A fantastic topping for pasta or baked or grilled tofu (page 641 or 642): Just after adding the garlic, add 3 cups chopped tomato (canned—drained—is fine). Cook, stirring occasionally, until the tomato breaks up and the mixture comes together and thickens, about 10 minutes. Add the remaining ingredients and cook for another few minutes.

Sautéed Olives with Croutons. Use on poached eggs, pasta, tofu, Grilled Fresh Cheese (page 216), or Baked Goat Cheese (page 217): Use $1/4$ cup olive oil and add 2 cups diced day-old bread along with the garlic. Cook, stirring often, until the bread browns and crisps, about 5 minutes. Proceed with the recipe.

Sautéed Olives

MAKES: 4 servings
TIME: 10 minutes

A quick and straightforward sauce, topping, or side dish with loads of flavor. Olives don't need cooking, of course,

Tapenade

MAKES: At least 8 servings; about $1^1/_2$ cups
TIME: 20 minutes

A native of southern France, tapenade was made for spreading on toast, but it's also great as a sandwich

 Fast   Make Ahead   Ⓥ Vegan

spread, a dip, or—if used sparingly and thinned with olive oil or even water—a sauce.

Good oil-cured olives are best for tapenade as they make a dark, rich paste, but any other kind of flavorful olive will also work well.

About 1 pound flavorful black olives

$^1/_4$ cup capers, rinsed and drained

2 cloves garlic, peeled and lightly crushed, or more to taste

About $^1/_2$ cup extra virgin olive oil

Freshly ground black pepper

Chopped parsley leaves for garnish (optional)

❶ Pit the olives. If you're using oil-cured olives, you can simply squeeze out the pit; with brined olives you might have to flatten the olive with the side of a knife, which will split it and allow you to remove the pit.

❷ Put the olives, capers, and garlic in a food processor or blender, along with half of the olive oil. Pulse the machine once or twice, then, a bit at a time, add enough of the remaining olive oil (you may not need it all) to make a spreadable and pasty consistency, pulsing between additions. Don't keep the machine running; you want a coarse, chunky, uneven blend as if you had made it with a mortar and pestle (the traditional way).

❸ Stir in the pepper, then garnish and serve or cover and refrigerate for up to a month.

Green Olive Tapenade. Just replace the black olives with green or add a North African twist: Substitute green olives for the black and Preserved Lemons (page 427) for the capers. Add 1 teaspoon toasted cumin seeds (see page 321). Proceed with the recipe.

Dried-Tomato Tapenade. Mild enough to use as a sauce for grilled vegetables or tofu: Replace half if not all of the olives with roughly chopped Oven-Dried (page 377) or store-bought sun-dried tomatoes. Add 2 teaspoons chopped fresh thyme leaves (or 1 teaspoon dried). Proceed with the recipe.

Onions

Yellow (Spanish), White, and Red Onions, Pearl Onions, Scallions (Green Onions), and Cipolline

We usually see dried onions, but they are sold fresh (like "spring" onions) as well, with long green stems. Scallions (often called *green onions*), obviously, are fresh.

But most onions are dried before sale and may be white, yellow, or red; pungent, mild, or sweet—the variety is quite astonishing. The onion itself is the bulb of the plant, which is related to the lily, so the fact that it and other alliums (even garlic) are quite attractive in bloom is not surprising.

Dry onions are essentially interchangeable, though red and white onions are slightly milder than yellow. Red onions' color makes them more attractive for use raw onion, but their color dissipates when cooked. In recent years I've come to think white onions are the best for all-purpose use, but it's not a position I could readily defend.

Sweet onions, including Maui, Vidalia, and Walla Walla, have a less pungent flavor, are juicy and sweet, and usually have a flatter spherical shape than other dry onions. They are best eaten raw, because they become quite insipid when cooked.

On the smaller side are pearl (or boiling) onions and cipolline. Pearl onions are about the diameter of a quarter and are great for boiling, braising, and stewing; their small size allows them to cook through whole. Cipolline can be used the same way as pearl onions, and their completely flattened shape adds an interesting look to any dish.

Scallions and bulb onions with green stems attached are "fresh" onions; they are generally milder in flavor and softer in texture. Scallions in particular are fantastic to use raw as a flavorful oniony garnish on salads and in soups, dips, and other dishes. Their small size makes them extremely valuable as a garnish.

Buying and storing: Fresh onions should have vibrant green, fresh-looking, crisp stems and unblemished white bulbs. Dry onions should be firm and tightly covered in at least one layer of shiny tan to yellow or deep red skins (the outer skin of white onions is more papery). A strong onion aroma is an indication of damaged or rotting

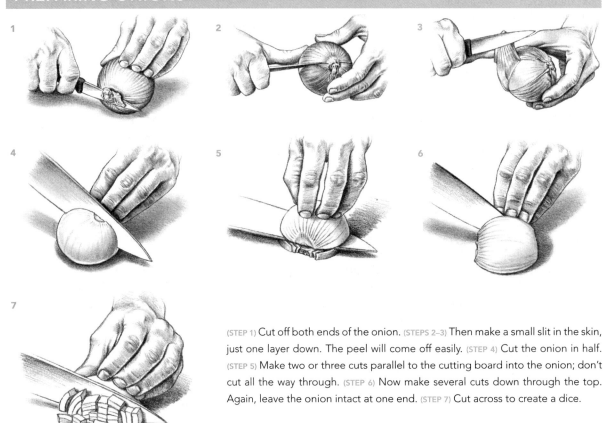

(STEP 1) Cut off both ends of the onion. (STEPS 2–3) Then make a small slit in the skin, just one layer down. The peel will come off easily. (STEP 4) Cut the onion in half. (STEP 5) Make two or three cuts parallel to the cutting board into the onion; don't cut all the way through. (STEP 6) Now make several cuts down through the top. Again, leave the onion intact at one end. (STEP 7) Cut across to create a dice.

onions and should be avoided, as should sprouting onions. Store fresh onions in the refrigerator, and dry onions in a cool, dark, airy spot or in the refrigerator, for weeks.

Preparing: If you have a lot of onions to peel, drop them into boiling water for 30 to 60 seconds, then rinse in cold water. Slice off the stem end and the skins will slip off easily. For just a couple of onions, cut a thin slice off the stem end, then make a shallow cut from one end to the other, just through the skin and top layer of flesh; peel off both together. Then slice or chop as needed.

If you're peeling and chopping a lot of onions, you might consider wearing goggles; but a properly sharpened knife also mitigates the amount of tear-inducing chemical released into the air. (This substance, called *lachrimator,* combines with the moisture in your eyes to form a weak solution of sulfuric acid. No wonder it burns!)

Ⓕ Fast   Ⓜ Make Ahead   Ⓥ Vegan

Leave the root end on onions you will cook whole; they'll stay together better.

Best cooking methods: Caramelizing (below), roasting, and grilling.

When is it done? When very tender but not quite falling apart.

Other vegetables to substitute: Shallots or leeks.

Caramelized Onions

MAKES: 4 servings

TIME: 25 to 60 minutes

If there ever was a dish that you "cook until it's done" this is it, since the possibilities range from barely colored, soft onions, to a deeply colored "jam" that doesn't look—or taste—anything like the raw vegetable. Let the time you have available and the desired result help you decide. (See the chart on below for some guidelines.)

Because onions are made primarily of water, the longer they cook, the more they shrink. (You may as well make as much as your pan will hold; cooked onions keep for days in the fridge.) But their flavor changes as it concentrates, from sharp and pungent to complex and sweet. This process is called *caramelization*.

Other vegetables you can use: Peel all, but keep them whole—whole small onions (like pearl or cipollini), shallots, or garlic.

1½ to 2 pounds onions (6 to 8 medium), halved and thinly sliced or chopped (5 to 6 cups)

2 tablespoons extra virgin olive oil or butter, plus more as needed

Salt and freshly ground black pepper

1 Put the onions in a large skillet over medium heat. Cover and cook, stirring infrequently, until the onions are dry and almost sticking to the pan, about 20 minutes.

2 Stir in the oil and a large pinch of salt and turn the heat down to medium-low. Cook, stirring occasionally, until the onions are done as you like them, adding just enough more oil or butter to keep them from sticking without getting greasy. The onions will be ready immediately or after up to another 40 minutes or so, depending on how you want them. Taste and add pepper, and more salt if necessary, then serve hot or at room temperature.

Sweeter Caramelized Onions. Good with hot, sour, or well-seasoned dishes: In Step 2, add 1 or 2 tablespoons of brown sugar along with the oil and salt. Proceed with the recipe, lowering the heat as necessary to prevent sticking or burning.

PAN-COOKING ONIONS

TIME	WHAT TO EXPECT
20 minutes	Ivory, softened, and still oniony tasting
25 to 30 minutes	Golden, wilted, and sweet, with a slight onion sharpness
40 to 45 minutes	Browned and starting to melt; onion flavor replaced with sweetness
60 minutes	The color of maple syrup, with a jamlike texture and flavor

10 Uses for Caramelized Onions

1. Thicken soups and sauces
2. Garnish cooked or raw foods
3. Fill omelets, sandwiches, and burritos
4. Stir into dips and spreads (or use as a spread by itself!)
5. Top pizza before baking
6. Toss with pasta or noodles—alone or in addition to sauce
7. Stir into quiche mixture before baking
8. Fold into bread doughs and batters
9. Top breads and rolls before baking
10. Eat as a side dish

Creamed Onions

MAKES: 4 servings
TIME: 30 minutes

You can use these as a gravy or sauce for mashed potatoes or pool a big spoonful on a plate and serve The Simplest Bean Burgers (page 660) or Nut Burgers (page 667) on top. They're also classic at Thanksgiving.

Other vegetables you can use: whole shallots or garlic (you'll need lots, or cut the recipe in half).

Salt

6 medium onions (about 1¹/₂ pounds), peeled and trimmed

1 cup light or heavy cream

2 tablespoons butter

Pinch freshly grated nutmeg (optional)

Freshly ground black pepper

1 Put a large pot of water on to boil and salt it. Cut the onions crosswise into thick slices; there's no need to separate them into rings. Plunge the onions into the boiling water and cook for about a minute; drain well.

2 Put the cream and butter in a deep skillet or broad saucepan over medium heat. Add the onion rings and bring to a boil; cook, stirring occasionally, until the onions have absorbed a lot of the cream and the cream is thick, about 15 minutes. Add a tiny bit of nutmeg and sprinkle with pepper; taste and adjust the seasoning and serve hot.

Creamed Spinach. The classic, made by the same technique: Instead of the onions, use 1¹/₂ pounds of trimmed spinach. In Step 1, after draining the spinach, cool it a bit or shock (see page 241), then chop it roughly. Proceed with the recipe.

Vegan Creamed Onions or Spinach. Garnish this with chopped hazelnuts or almonds if you like, depending on the type of milk you use: Instead of the cream, use hazelnut or almond milk and increase the quantity to 1¹/₂ cups. Instead of the butter, use a neutral oil, like grapeseed or corn. Prepare the onions or spinach according to the directions in Step 1. In Step 2, put the oil in the pan alone first and turn the heat to medium-low. Add 2 tablespoons all-purpose flour and cook, stirring constantly, until it turns golden; stir in the nut milk. Then add the onions or spinach and proceed with the recipe.

Roasted Onion Halves

MAKES: 4 servings, plus extra for later
TIME: About 1 hour, largely unattended

Roasted onions are delicious and easy to make in the oven; to keep them intact, try not to fuss with them as they roast. You can use any kind of onion you like here, even sweet ones like Walla Walla or Vidalia, though these sweet varieties will be much softer when done. Serve the onions hot, warm, or at room temperature, garnished, if you like, with chopped herbs or nuts. And, as a bonus, you can use the leftovers as an alternative to raw onions in virtually any dish.

Other vegetables you can use: large shallots, simply peeled and left whole.

2 tablespoons extra virgin olive oil, plus oil for the pan

4 onions, peeled, trimmed, and halved around the equator

Salt and freshly ground black pepper

2 or 3 fresh thyme sprigs (optional)

1 Preheat the oven to 400°F. Grease a small baking or roasting pan with a little olive oil or line it with parchment paper. Rub the onions with the 2 tablespoons olive oil and sprinkle them all over with salt and pepper.

2 Put the onions cut side down in the prepared pan. Roast, undisturbed, until they start to brown, about 20 minutes. Use a spatula to turn them over. Top with the

F Fast   **M** Make Ahead   **V** Vegan

thyme if you like, then return them to the oven for another 15 to 25 minutes, depending on how tender you want them. Check for doneness by sticking a sharp-tipped knife or skewer into the side of one. Serve hot or at room temperature.

Cream-Roasted Onion Halves. Preheat the oven to 350°F. Instead of the olive oil, put ¼ cup cream in a large shallow bowl and roll the onions around in it to coat them all over. Let sit for 30 minutes or so, turning every so often. Proceed with the recipe.

Balsamic-Roasted Onion Halves. With a complex flavor that's tart and sweet: Follow the preceding variation, but use balsamic vinegar instead of cream.

Grilled Scallions (Green Onions)

MAKES: 4 servings

TIME: 15 minutes

A staple in Tex-Mex restaurants across the Southwest, these make a remarkably mild side dish, garnish, or ingredient anywhere you'd use their raw or cooked counterparts. Cook them fast over a relatively hot fire or slowly after you've taken other foods off the grill. Just be careful not to overchar them.

Other vegetables you can use: shallots (on skewers), red or other onions (halved around their equator).

2 bunches scallions or spring onions, trimmed, with a lot of the greens remaining

2 tablespoons extra virgin olive oil

Salt and freshly ground black pepper

2 limes, 1 halved and 1 quartered

Chopped fresh cilantro leaves for garnish

1 Heat a charcoal or gas grill until moderately hot and put the rack about 4 inches from the heat source.

2 Brush or rub the scallions with the oil until well coated. Grill, turning once or twice, until deeply colored and tender, about 5 minutes. Transfer to a plate or platter, sprinkle with salt and pepper, and squeeze the juice of the halved lime over all. Garnish with cilantro leaves and serve hot or at room temperature with the lime wedges.

Roasted Scallions. A good all-purpose treatment that's great with Mediterranean dishes: Preheat the oven to 400°F instead of using a grill. Use lemons instead of limes and parsley instead of cilantro. After rubbing the scallions with oil in Step 2, spread them out on a rimmed baking sheet and put them in the oven. Roast, turning once or twice, until lightly browned and tender, about 20 minutes. Season and garnish as directed.

Roasted Scallions, Asian Style. Excellent as a garnish for all sorts of noodle and rice dishes: Preheat the oven to 400°F instead of using a grill. Instead of the olive oil, use a combination of 1 tablespoon peanut oil and 1 tablespoon dark sesame oil; use 2 tablespoons rice vinegar instead of the limes. After rubbing the scallions with oil in Step 2, spread them out on a rimmed baking sheet and put them in the oven. Roast, turning once or twice, until lightly browned and tender, about 20 minutes. Season and garnish as directed, drizzling with a little soy sauce before serving if you like.

Parsnips

A longtime favorite in Europe (it was once as ubiquitous as the potato is now), this root vegetable looks just like a carrot in all ways but its off-white color. It's a shame that it's not more popular, because it's incredibly delicious—sweeter than carrots, with a nice earthy flavor. Parsnips are available year-round, can be cooked in any number of ways, and keep for weeks.

Buying and storing: Smaller specimens (four to six per pound) are best; larger ones can be woody and tough.

They should be firm and crisp when you buy them. Loosely wrapped plastic in the refrigerator, they'll keep for weeks.

Preparing: Treat as you would a carrot. If the parsnip is large (more than 1 inch thick at its broad end), it's probably best—though not absolutely essential—to remove its woody core: Cut the thinner portion off and set it aside, then cut the thick portion in half lengthwise and dig out the core with the end of a vegetable peeler, a paring knife, or a sharp spoon—neither difficult nor time-consuming.

Best cooking methods: Steaming, braising, "braising and glazing," and roasting. Cooked parsnips make an incredible purée.

When is it done? When tender enough to pierce easily with a thin-bladed knife or skewer but not mushy.

Other vegetables to substitute: Carrots.

Pea Shoots

The tender tendrils or shoots of the green pea plant, pea shoots are a sure sign of spring, especially in Chinese markets. They're the new growth of the pea vine plus a few leaves, vibrant green in color, and delicate; the flavor is a cross between fresh peas and spinach. Pea shoots cook in no time and are delightful quickly stir-fried, stirred into risotto at the last minute, or added raw to green salads. You can find them at farmer's or Asian markets in the spring and summer.

Buying and storing: You want tender, fresh-looking, bright green shoots. Store wrapped loosely in plastic in the refrigerator; use as quickly as possible as they lose their sweetness fast.

Preparing: Wash well; trim away any dried-out stems or yellowing leaves.

Best cooking methods: Quickly stir-fried or sautéed.

When is it done? When just wilted—no more—usually just a couple of minutes.

Other vegetables to substitute: Spinach or snow, sugar, or green peas.

Peas

Shell Peas, Snow Peas (Mange-Tout), Sugar Snap Peas

Peas, which are legumes, come in a variety of forms: Shell peas (aka green or English peas) that must be removed from their inedible shells or pods; pod peas that are entirely edible (pods and all); and field peas, which are nearly always shelled and dried (think black-eyed peas and chickpeas).

Nothing compares to the flavor of shelled fresh peas, but we rarely make time for shucking these days. Snow peas and sugar snap peas, with their edible pods, have made the desire to shell your own green peas even less appealing, since these offer wonderful pea flavor with a lot less work. (Though their strings should—not must, but should—be removed before the pods are eaten; see the illustration for specifics.)

Buying and storing: Fresh shell peas arrive in spring and should be fresh looking and full of medium-size peas. Very large peas are likely to be tough and starchy. To be sure, open one up and taste a couple peas; if you want to keep eating, buy them. Tough peas need to be cooked before being eaten. Snow and snap peas should be crisp, green, and unshriveled. Again, taste one, and if it's sweet and crisp, buy some. Store peas wrapped loosely in plastic in the refrigerator; use as soon as possible as their sweetness is fleeting.

For snow and snap peas, pinch the flower end of the pea pod and pull the string down toward the other end to remove it.

Ⓕ Fast   Ⓜ Make Ahead   Ⓥ Vegan

Preparing: Open the pods of shell peas at the seam and run your finger down the inside to release the peas. Always remove the little string from the peas before cooking.

Best cooking methods: Steaming (and shocking if you like; see page 241), quick-braising in butter, and stir-frying. Peas are almost always a welcome addition to risotto and stir-fries.

When is it done? As soon as they are hot and bright green, usually less than 5 minutes.

Other vegetables to substitute: Green or wax beans, asparagus, or edamame.

Anything-Scented Peas

MAKES: 4 servings
TIME: 20 minutes

Peas have a delicate flavor that can be enhanced in a variety of ways with just a touch of another ingredient, subtlety being the key. (If you've never tasted peas sprinkled with a pinch of sugar during cooking, give it a try.) Use oil and this is vegan.

Other vegetables you can use: about $1^1/_2$ pounds of snow or sugar snap peas.

2 tablespoons butter or extra virgin olive oil

1 tablespoon of any ingredient from the list at right

2 cups peas (thawed and well-drained frozen are fine)

Salt or sugar to taste

❶ Put the butter or oil in a large skillet over medium heat. When the butter is melted or the oil is hot, stir in your ingredient of choice and cook, stirring constantly, until fragrant, just a minute or so.

❷ Add the peas and cook for a couple minutes more, swirling the pan a bit to coat the peas in the pan juices

and soften them a bit. Taste, add a sprinkle of salt or sugar as you like, and serve hot or at room temperature.

11 Possibilities for Anything-Scented Peas

1. Grated lemon, orange, or tangerine zest
2. Minced light herbs, like mint, tarragon, parsley, basil, or chervil
3. Grated peeled fresh ginger or minced crystallized ginger
4. Sesame seeds (white or black)
5. Minced garlic
6. Fermented black beans
7. Grated coconut
8. Minced shallot
9. White wine or sake
10. Any miso paste
11. Minced flowers, like lavender, rose petals, or anise hyssop

Peppers and Chiles

You'll find everything you need to know about both sweet and hot peppers and chiles used for seasoning and garnishing on pages 822–831.

Roasted Red Peppers

MAKES: 4 to 8 servings
TIME: 20 to 60 minutes

Any pepper can be roasted, though red (and yellow) are sweeter than green (which are unripe). This can be done in the oven (where they require almost no attention), over a grill, or in the broiler (some people do it over an open stovetop flame, but I think this is a real nuisance). You can roast as many peppers at once as you like, and the only extra work will be peeling (which isn't, unfortunately, insignificant). But they'll keep for quite a while in the fridge.

8 red, yellow, or green bell peppers, washed

Salt

Extra virgin olive oil as needed

1 The two methods:

To roast or broil: Preheat the oven to 450°F or the broiler and put the rack about 4 inches from the heat source. Put the peppers in a foil-lined roasting pan. Roast or broil, turning the peppers as each side browns, until they have darkened and collapsed, 15 or 20 minutes in the broiler, up to an hour in the oven.

To grill: Heat a charcoal or gas grill until hot and put the rack about 4 inches from the heat source. When the fire is hot, put the peppers directly over the heat. Grill, turning as each side blackens, until they collapse, about 15 minutes.

2 Wrap the cooked peppers in foil (if you roasted the peppers, you can use the same foil that lined the pan) and cool until you can handle them, then remove the skin, seeds, and stems (it's a little easier under running water). Don't worry if the peppers fall apart.

3 The peppers can be served immediately or stored in the refrigerator for up to a few days; bring back to room temperature before serving. When you're ready to serve, sprinkle with a bit of salt and drizzle with olive oil.

7 Things to Do with Roasted Red Peppers

1. Toss with minced fresh or roasted garlic.
2. Splash with balsamic vinegar.
3. Sprinkle with lots of minced fresh herbs like parsley, mint, basil, or chervil; or a little bit of oregano, thyme, or rosemary.
4. Sprinkle with grated Parmesan, Asiago, Romano, or manchego cheese.
5. Use to fill sandwiches or top bruschetta, pizza, and salads.

6. Scramble with eggs.
7. Purée to make a sauce or spread or to mix with other sauces and spreads.

My Mom's Pan-Cooked Peppers and Onions

MAKES: 4 servings

TIME: 40 minutes

When I was growing up, once a week my mother would make us a sandwich of sautéed green peppers and onions, loads of each. It's a great combination and even better if you add some mushrooms and herbs. With oil instead of butter this is vegan.

$1/4$ cup extra virgin olive oil, 4 tablespoons ($1/2$ stick) butter, or a combination

2 bell peppers, preferably red or yellow, roasted and peeled if desired, cored, seeded, and cut into strips

2 medium to large onions, halved and thinly sliced

1 cup trimmed and sliced shiitake or button mushrooms

Salt and freshly ground black pepper

1 teaspoon fresh thyme or marjoram leaves or any fresh herb to taste (optional)

1 Put the oil or butter in a large, deep skillet over medium heat. When the oil is hot or the butter is melted, add the peppers, onions, and mushrooms. Sprinkle with salt and pepper, stir in the thyme, and cook, stirring occasionally and adjusting the heat so the mixture cooks without browning (at least not much), until very tender, at least 20 minutes.

2 Taste and adjust the seasoning, garnish with a bit more herb if you like, and serve as a side dish or piled into rolls or baguettes.

Pan-Cooked Peppers and Onions, Asian Style. A stir-fry where the vegetables are tender, not crunchy: Instead

F Fast   **M** Make Ahead   **V** Vegan

of the olive oil or butter, use peanut or a neutral oil, like grapeseed or corn. Go easy on the salt. Instead of the thyme or marjoram, use 1 tablespoon minced peeled fresh ginger. In Step 2, use a dash of soy sauce and plenty of black pepper for the final seasoning and stir in the cilantro. Serve over Steamed Sticky Rice (page 507) or another plain-cooked rice dish or toss with Chinese-style egg noodles. Garnish with chopped fresh cilantro.

Pan-Cooked Peppers and Onions with Mustard and Cumin Seeds. Use as a warm "chutney" to smear on Essential Flatbread (page 727) or alongside pilafs. In Step 1, put 1 teaspoon of mustard seeds and $^1/_2$ teaspoon of cumin seeds into the pan along with the oil or butter. Omit the thyme, marjoram, or other herbs.

Paprika Peppers

Leczo

MAKES: 4 servings
TIME: 30 minutes

You can vary the flavor and look of this classic Hungarian dish simply by changing the color of the bell peppers you use. All green will result in a piquant, almost bitter taste, while red or yellow will be sweet and brightly colored. If possible, use a mixture, or all red, which is most traditional. Leczo makes a great pasta sauce or topping for baked potatoes, but I like it most scrambled with eggs or included in frittatas. Leftovers are great in cheese sandwiches.

Other vegetables you can use: green beans.

$^1/_4$ cup extra virgin olive oil or 4 tablespoons ($^1/_2$ stick) butter

1 large onion, chopped

2 tablespoons minced garlic

2 tablespoons sweet paprika

Salt and freshly ground black pepper

4 medium bell peppers, cored, seeded, and cut into strips

4 roma tomatoes (drained canned are fine), cored and chopped

Squeeze of lemon juice (optional)

1 Put the olive oil or butter in a deep skillet with a tight-fitting lid over medium heat. When the oil is hot or the butter is melted, add the onion and garlic and cook, stirring once or twice, until soft, about 2 minutes. Stir in the paprika and sprinkle with salt and pepper; cover and turn the heat to low. Cook, undisturbed, for 5 minutes.

2 Turn the heat back up a bit so the pan starts to sizzle, then stir in the peppers. When they start to soften a bit, in a minute or two, again cover, turn the heat to low and let them cook for another 5 minutes.

3 Turn the heat back up a bit and repeat the process with the tomatoes. Remove the lid for the last time, squeeze the lemon juice over all if you like, and give the mixture a good stir. Taste and adjust the seasoning, then serve hot or at room temperature.

Smoked Paprika Peppers. A whole different animal with a deep "barbecue" flavor: Substitute smoked paprika for the sweet variety.

Paprika Peppers with Sour Cream. Rich and creamy but tangy: Follow the main recipe or the variation. In Step 3, after the tomatoes have cooked, stir in 1 cup sour cream. Heat the mixture through, stirring occasionally, taking care not to let it come to a boil. Omit the lemon juice; taste and adjust the seasoning and serve.

Plantains

The plantain is a type of banana, large with thick, leathery skin. It can be used much like a potato when starchy and green or sautéed for a sweet side dish when fully ripe. It's always cooked (and is often called the *cooking banana*)—sautéed, fried, or used in stews and soups.

Like all bananas, plantains ripen nicely off the plant. Leave at room temperature for anywhere from a day to a couple of weeks; the longer they ripen, the softer and sweeter they become. When fully ripe, plantains are deliciously sweet and completely black—the uninitiated would almost certainly toss them in the trash—but hold together well when cooked.

Buying and storing: Plantains are sold at various stages of ripeness; they may take as long as two weeks to ripen fully. They have different uses for different stages of ripeness: used to thicken stews when hard and green; flattened and fried into thick chips (called *tostones*) when just starting to turn yellow and spot; and sautéed or fried when yellow to black. Plantains can be stored in the refrigerator to retard further ripening (the skins may turn black, but the flesh remains the same) for weeks.

Preparing: Plantains require a special peeling technique; begin by cutting off both tips of the plantain; then cut the plantain into three sections. Make three vertical slits in the skin of each section, then peel each piece of the skin off. Trim any remaining skin from the plantain with a paring knife.

Best cooking methods: Sautéing and frying are the best for green plantains; ripe plantains are best for braising and stewing. But you can really cook either any way.

When are they done? Green plantains are done when they're golden brown and slightly tender; ripe are done when they are caramelized, very soft, and starting to fall apart.

Other fruits or vegetables to substitute: When starchy and green, replace with potato, yuca, boniato, or taro root; when sweeter and riper, with sweet potato or yam. Green to green-yellow bananas can often fill in for plantains in recipes; they cook up quite similarly as long as they're not too ripe.

Sautéed Ripe Plantains

Plátanos Maduros

MAKES: 4 servings
TIME: 20 minutes

Sweet, but somehow appropriately so, these are the perfect side dish for any rice and beans dish. Often, fully ripe plantains can be peeled like bananas, but if you have any trouble, peel them as you would unripe plantains; see left.

Other vegetables you can use: just-ripe (yellow but with only a few black spots) bananas.

3 or 4 yellow-black or black plantains, peeled (see left)

Neutral oil, like grapeseed or corn, as needed

Salt and freshly ground black pepper

Lime wedges

1 Cut the plantains into about 1-inch pieces. Put about $1/8$-inch oil in a large skillet over medium heat. When hot, add the plantains and cook, turning as necessary and adjusting the heat so the plantains brown slowly without burning. Be especially careful as they near doneness; there is so much sugar in the plantains that they burn easily. The process will take 10 to 15 minutes.

2 Sprinkle with salt, pepper, and lime juice and serve hot.

Fried Plantain Chips

Tostones

MAKES: 4 servings
TIME: 30 minutes

The wonderful plantain-based side dish, easy to make, as good warm (or at room temperature, as long as

F Fast   **M** Make Ahead   **V** Vegan

they're made not *too* far in advance) as hot. To me, they need nothing more than salt and maybe a little lime, but some people like this with hot sauce, Chile Paste (page 828), Fresh Tomato Salsa (page 750), or another salsa (pages 750–753 and 787–789).

2 green-yellow plantains or green bananas, peeled (see page 336)

Neutral oil, like grapeseed or corn, as needed

Salt

Lime wedges

1 Cut the plantains into $1/2$-inch rounds. Put about $1/8$-inch oil in a large skillet over medium heat. When hot, add the rounds (you'll probably be able to do this in one batch) and sprinkle with salt. Brown lightly, about 5 minutes, then turn and brown the other side, another 5 minutes, transferring to a plate as they brown. (The plantains can be browned an hour or two in advance of eating.)

2 When the plantain rounds have cooled a bit, put each between 2 sheets of wax paper and pound with the side of your fist or the palm of your hand until they spread out and just about double in diameter; they will look squashed and might split a little around the edges, which is right. (This step, also, can be done an hour or two in advance.)

3 Put the remaining oil in the skillet, turn the heat to medium, and again brown the rounds on each side (this time you'll probably have to cook in batches), 5 to 10 minutes total. Serve hot or warm, sprinkled with salt and lime juice.

Potatoes

One of the most abundant and ubiquitous of all vegetables, the humble potato was cultivated in Peru at least seven thousand years ago. But it didn't take root, pardon the pun, in Europe and North America until the eighteenth and nineteenth centuries. Now over 320 million metric tons are produced each year, with China, Russia, and India being the top producers.

There are all sorts of varieties of potatoes, but when it comes to cooking they fall into three basic categories: starchy, waxy, and all-purpose.

Starchy potatoes are, just as the name implies, loaded with starch. They cook to a dry, fluffy, and mealy texture that is great for baking, frying, and mashing. These potatoes crumble and break easily when cooked, which is why they are not a great boiling potato (though there are times when this crumbly quality is a good thing, like in stews and soups, where the starch thickens and adds body). Russet potatoes, which include Idaho, are the archetypal starchy potato and are often called "baking potatoes." They are large and oval with a sandy-feeling, light brown "russeted" skin and off-white flesh.

Waxy potatoes, sometimes called "new" or "boiling" potatoes, have a low starch content; their texture is moister, creamier, and firmer. They are typified by their smooth, thin skin, which is most often a rosy red or yellowish white color, depending on variety. They hold their shape well during cooking and are excellent for boiling, steaming, and roasting.

All-purpose potatoes are in between starchy and waxy potatoes in terms of texture; they're great mashed, fried, and baked but still contain too much starch (thus crumbling easily) to make them ideal for boiling. In my book, Yukon Gold potatoes are the model all-purpose potato with their smooth, golden to brown skins, smooth texture, and yellow flesh.

Buying and storing: All potatoes should be firm, unshriveled, and without soft spots, sprouts, or greening (green coloring—an alkaloid called solanine—is due to sun exposure and is toxic; just cut off that part and the rest of the potato will be perfectly edible). Store in a dark, cool, dry spot (not in the fridge) for weeks.

Preparing: Wash and peel if you like; remove any eyes, dark spots, or greening. If the potato is largely green or has rot, discard it.

People love these, and almost all the work is up front, making them perfect for entertaining. They're also great for single dining and for using up all sorts of leftovers, literally from soup to nuts.

The half-baked, half-mashed concept is simple:

Bake the potatoes, cool them a bit, and scoop their flesh into a large bowl, leaving their skins intact, like a shell. Mash the innards, adding some other ingredients to jazz them up, then pile the works back into the waiting potato skins. Wrap them up in foil (or not, as I generally prefer, so you get a nice crust on top), refrigerate them for up to a few hours if you like, and pop them back into the oven shortly before ready to eat. At 400°F, most will take only 20 to 30 minutes to reheat.

The filling possibilities are endless:

The traditional cheddar, sour cream, bacon, and chives combo is a big bore and hardly vegetarian. So here's a list to get you started in another direction, starting with the subtle approach, adding flavor with relatively few ingredients, then building to more substantial dishes.

Figure a total of about 1/2 cup for each large potato; they won't hold much more. Mash the potato flesh with any additions until as smooth or lumpy as you like. And feel free to thin the mixture a bit with milk, butter, or olive oil as needed.

- Chopped olives, hot red pepper flakes, chopped parsley, and olive oil
- Goat cheese or cream cheese and chopped fresh herbs
- Miso paste, sliced scallion, and dark sesame oil or butter
- Peanut or other nut butter
- Coconut milk and curry powder, garam masala, or chaat masala (to make your own, see page 814, 815, or 816)

- Puréed or finely chopped cooked vegetables, like eggplant, carrots, broccoli, or spinach, with lots of butter or extra virgin olive oil
- Any pesto or herb paste (pages 768–770)
- Cold Mustard Sauce (page 771)
- Seaweed "Mayo" (page 773)
- Ginger-Scallion Sauce (page 779)
- Any chutney (pages 783–787)
- Miso Carrot Sauce with Ginger (page 781)
- Nutty Miso Sauce (page 782)
- Fast Tomato Sauce (page 445)
- Salsa Roja (page 787)
- Mushroom Ketchup (page 791)
- Smooth Green Chile Sauce, Indian Style (page 792)
- Spicy Indian Tomato Sauce (page 793)
- Any nut sauce (pages 794–798)
- Creamy Bistro Dressing or Sauce (page 799)
- Any compound butter (page 801)
- Hollandaise Sauce (page 802)
- Any spice blend (to make your own, see pages 810–819) or chile paste (see pages 828–830) except Pickling Spice; best with a little butter, flavorful oil, or dairy or nondairy milk
- Beans and Greens (page 595)
- Braised Lentils, Spanish Style (page 598)
- Stewed Fava Beans with Tahini (page 604)
- White Beans, Tuscan Style (page 594)
- Any dal (pages 600–604)
- Autumn Millet Bake (page 566)
- Pozole with Mole (page 545)
- Crunchy Crumbled Tempeh (page 674)
- Scrambled Tofu (page 655)
- Any braised tofu (pages 648–652)
- Spicy Ketchup-Braised Tofu (page 651)
- Cheese Fondue (page 221)

 F Fast   **M** Make Ahead   **V** Vegan

Best cooking methods: Any, depending on type (see chart on page 340).

When is it done? When a skewer or sharp knife inserted into one meets almost no resistance.

Other vegetables to substitute: Sweet potato, taro, cassava, boniato, or malanga.

Baked Potatoes

MAKES: 4 servings
TIME: About 1 hour

Dry, fluffy, slightly mealy baked potatoes are easy, though not necessarily fast. First, forget wrapping them in foil or using the microwave, because both techniques will basically steam the potatoes. Second, keep the oven at 425°F, which is the optimum temperature. You can crank it up to 450°F to gain a little speed, though you'll sacrifice some texture.

Other vegetables you can use: Any whole, thick-skinned root vegetable, like rutabaga, turnip, or beet, though none will be as starchy and fluffy as the potato.

4 large starchy potatoes, like Idaho or other russets
Salt and freshly ground black pepper

1 Preheat the oven to 425°F. Scrub the potatoes well, especially if you plan to eat the skins. Use a skewer or a thin-bladed knife to poke a hole or two in each potato.

2 Put the potatoes in the oven, right on the rack or on a rimmed baking sheet. Bake until a skewer or sharp knife inserted into one meets almost no resistance, about an hour, more or less. (You can turn them once during baking, though it's not necessary.)

3 The potatoes will stay hot for a few minutes. To serve, cut a slit lengthwise into each about halfway into the flesh and pinch the ends toward the middle to fluff, sprinkle with salt and pepper, then top if desired (see the list at right for some ideas).

Salted Baked Potato. Not as involved as burying the potatoes in a couple inches of salt—a nice technique itself—but the skins still get a nice crust: After scrubbing, rub each potato with about a teaspoon of extra virgin olive oil or butter. Then rub each all over with a fair amount of salt and bake as directed.

Bay- or Rosemary-Scented Baked Potato. A simple idea with dramatic results: After scrubbing the potatoes, cut a deep slit lengthwise into each and sprinkle with salt and pepper. Put a couple of bay leaves or a sprig of rosemary in each slit and drizzle with extra virgin olive oil, then close them up and set them on a baking sheet. Smear some olive oil around their skins and sprinkle with more salt and pepper. Proceed with the recipe and remove the bay or rosemary before serving.

15 Toppings for Baked Potatoes

1. The Classic: butter, sour cream, and/or minced chives
2. Extra virgin olive oil or any Flavored Oil (page 758)
3. Any cooked or raw salsa
4. Garlic (aïoli) or other flavored mayonnaise (page 771)
5. Soy sauce or any Asian-style dipping sauce (pages 777–780)
6. Any nut sauce (pages 794–798)
7. Cottage cheese
8. A few dashes of hot sauce
9. Worcestershire Sauce, Hold the Anchovies (page 799)
10. Barbecue sauce (to make your own, see page 789)
11. Any Vinaigrette (pages 762–763), especially Mustard Vinaigrette
12. Grated cheese, like cheddar, Parmesan, Asiago, or Jack

13. Goat or cream cheese
14. Ketchup (to make your own, see page 790)
15. Whipped cream (unsweetened)

Boiled Potatoes

MAKES: 4 servings

TIME: About 30 minutes

Many potato dishes start with partially or even fully cooked potatoes; boiling and steaming are the simplest ways to get the job done. You can use these techniques for starchy, waxy, and all-purpose potatoes, though the results will vary; consult the chart below to match the right potato with the dish you plan to make.

In general, it's fine to cut potatoes before boiling or steaming, and obviously that speeds things up; but the results will also be a bit waterlogged (less so if you steam), so if time is not an issue, cook your spuds whole.

If boiled potatoes are your ultimate goal, use any red- or thin-skinned waxy variety.

2 pounds potatoes

Salt

1 Peel the potatoes before cooking if you like. If you're in a hurry, halve or quarter the larger ones. Cut or whole, the idea is to have all the pieces about the same size. Put them in a large, deep pot and cover with cold water. Add a large pinch of salt and bring to a boil.

2 Keep the water rolling until the potatoes are done, anywhere from 15 to 30 minutes, depending on the size of the pieces and how tender you want them. The potatoes are done when a skewer or sharp knife inserted into one meets almost no resistance.

USING POTATOES IN RECIPES

Here is a quick rundown of what type of potato is best in various recipes. Keep in mind that sometimes it comes down to personal preference. If you like the mealy and crumbly texture of starchy potatoes in your potato salad, or the moist and creamy texture of mashed potatoes made from waxy potatoes, then by all means use them. But it's useful to know that, for example, waxy potatoes hold their shape well in cooking and starchy potatoes make wonderful fluffy mashed potatoes.

STARCHY POTATOES	WAXY POTATOES	ALL-PURPOSE POTATOES
Boiled and Steamed Potatoes (above)	Boiled and Steamed Potatoes (above)	Boiled and Steamed Potatoes (above)
Mashed Potatoes (page 341)	Potato Salad (page 68)	Potato Salad (page 68)
Potato Croquettes (page 353)	Potato Salad with Cream Cheese Dressing (page 70)	Potato Salad with Cream Cheese Dressing (page 70)
Baked Potatoes (page 339)	Braised Potatoes, Ten Ways (page 346)	Curried Stir-Fried Potatoes (page 348)
Potato and Leek Soup (page 106)	Potato and Leek Soup (page 106)	Braised Potatoes, Ten Ways (page 346)
Crisp Panfried Potatoes (page 343)	Oven-Roasted Potatoes (page 344)	Potato and Leek Soup (page 106)
Potato "Nik" (page 349)	Grilled or Broiled Potatoes (page 346)	Potatoes Provençal (page 348)
French Fries (page 352)		

③ Drain the potatoes well and let them dry out a bit. If peeling, give them an extra few minutes to cool enough to handle. See the list on page 340 for serving ideas or use in another recipe. To store for later, cool, cover tightly, and refrigerate for up to 3 days. Reheat in the microwave or use in any recipe that calls for cooked potatoes.

Steamed Potatoes. These don't get waterlogged and retain more nutrients: Set up some kind of steaming apparatus (see page 25). Put salted water in the bottom and the potatoes above them. Bring the water to a boil and steam for 15 to 30 minutes.

5 Simple Finishes for Boiled or Steamed Potatoes

Toss hot potatoes with any of the following ingredients—or a combination—and serve immediately.

1. Butter or olive oil with salt and freshly ground black pepper
2. Dark sesame oil, a splash of soy sauce, and a sprinkle of sliced scallion or cilantro
3. Miso, a couple tablespoons
4. Chopped fresh herbs, like chives, tarragon, parsley, rosemary, mint, or chervil
5. Chopped toasted nuts, like hazelnuts, almonds, walnuts, or pecans

Mashed Potatoes

MAKES: 4 servings
TIME: About 40 minutes
Ⓜ

Starchy potatoes make the fluffiest mash, but Yukon Gold or other all-purpose potatoes also yield a creamy texture.

If you like mashed potatoes with bits of the peel included, just scrub them well before cooking. If you like your mashed potatoes lumpy, mash them with a fork or potato masher; if you like them smooth and light, use a food mill or ricer. But whatever you do, keep them away from mixers, food processors, or blenders, because they will become gummy, and almost no one likes them that way.

Once the potatoes are mashed and combined with the milk and butter, they will keep for a little while in a double boiler. But if you want to have better control over them for timing a full meal, it's easier to just boil the potatoes a little ahead of time and let them sit for an hour or so.

Some keys to keeping mashed potatoes fluffy: Cook them whole if possible; cook them with the peel on if possible (the peels will slip off easily after cooking, or you can eat them of course); and refrain from poking them. All of these steps reduce the tendency of the spuds to absorb water, which makes them heavier.

Other vegetables you can use: Any vegetable can be mashed; see "The Basics of Puréed Vegetables" (page 387).

2 pounds starchy or all-purpose potatoes

1 cup milk, plus more if needed

4 tablespoons (½ stick) butter

Salt and freshly ground black pepper

① Boil the potatoes according to the recipe on page 340. (The potatoes can be prepared to this point up to an hour in advance; just leave them in a colander to drain and dry out a bit.)

② While the potatoes are draining, wipe the pot dry and put it back on the stove over medium-low heat. Add the milk and the butter and sprinkle with salt and pepper.

③ When the butter is almost melted, remove the pot from the heat. Rice the potatoes or run them through a food mill set over the pot or add them directly to the milk mixture and mash with a fork or potato masher. Return the pot to the heat and stir constantly with a wooden spoon to reach the desired consistency, adding more milk if necessary. Taste, adjust the seasoning, and serve.

Mashed Baked Potatoes. The drier texture means they'll soak up more milk and butter: Bake potatoes accord-

Beyond milk and butter, there are infinite ways to customize mashed potatoes. Some involve simply adding ingredients to the finished mash, while others require incorporating seasonings earlier. You can mix and match as you like of course, but be careful not to fuse too many strong flavors.

Things to add to the butter as it melts in Step 2:

- Up to $1/2$ cup minced onion, $1/4$ cup minced shallot, or 2 teaspoons to 2 tablespoons minced garlic
- 1 or more heads Roasted Garlic (page 304), peeled
- 1 or 2 tablespoons minced or grated peeled fresh ginger or minced fresh chile (like jalapeño or Thai), hot red pepper flakes, or cayenne to taste
- 1 tablespoon or more curry powder or practically any other spice blend (to make your own, see pages 810–819)
- 2 tablespoons or more horseradish, grated fresh or prepared
- Chile Paste (page 828) to taste

Things to stir into the mashed potatoes as they heat in Step 3 (reduce the milk to $1/2$ cup; you can always add more later):

- Up to 1 cup chopped fresh light herbs, like parsley, mint, chives, basil, or cilantro

- Up to 1 cup grated melting cheese, like Parmesan, Gruyère, cheddar, Jack, or Gouda
- Up to 1 cup fresh goat cheese, cream cheese, or sour cream
- Up to 1 cup Traditional Pesto or any herb paste (pages 768–770):
- Up to $1/2$ cup miso
- Up to $1/2$ cup chopped nuts or olives
- Up to $1/4$ cup soy sauce
- $1/2$ cup or so ketchup (sounds crazy, but it's delicious) or barbecue sauce (to make your own, see pages 789 or 790):
- Up to $1/4$ cup mustard

Ways to garnish mashed potatoes after serving:

- Drizzle with Flavored Oil (page 758)
- Sprinkle with minced chives or other fresh herbs (see above)
- Drizzle with Balsamic Syrup (page 798)
- Drizzle with Traditional Pesto or any herb paste or sauce (pages 768–770)
- Toasted sesame, sunflower, or pumpkin seeds
- Nori "Shake" (page 817)

ing to the recipe on page 339. Peel or not and cut into cubes. Proceed with the recipe from Step 2, adding more milk and butter if you like.

Garlicky Mashed Potatoes. But not overpowering (if you want stronger garlic mash, add a teaspoon or a tablespoon of minced garlic along with the milk and butter): Peel 1 or 2 heads of garlic (or even 3 if you're a fanatic) and boil them along with the potatoes. Proceed with the recipe.

"Smashed" Potatoes. A trendy name for lumpy potatoes without much thinning: Omit the milk. In Step 3, add the potatoes directly to the melted butter in the pan and mash roughly with a fork or masher, leaving lots of lumps. Stir a few times, adding more butter if you like, and proceed with the recipe.

Vegan Mashed Potatoes. Works with either the main recipe or the preceding variations: Instead of the milk, reserve 1 cup or so of the water from boiling the pota-

 Fast   Make Ahead   Ⓥ Vegan

toes; or use vegetable stock (pages 101–102), silken tofu, a dairy-free milk, white wine, beer, or a combination of these liquids. Replace the butter with extra virgin olive oil.

Buttermilk Mashed Potatoes. Tangy and fresh tasting: Instead of milk, use buttermilk.

Joël Robuchon Mashed Potatoes. Only a famous French chef could get away with suggesting so much butter: If you really want to go overboard, replace some or all of the milk with cream. In Step 2, after you drain the potatoes, put 1 cup (2 sticks) of butter in the pot and set it over medium-low heat to melt, taking care not to let it brown. Whisk in the milk or cream. Then proceed with the recipe from Step 3.

Crisp Panfried Potatoes (Home Fries)

MAKES: 4 servings

TIME: About 45 minutes

This technique produces better results than conventional Home Fries (which are the first variation), but you need two things: waxy potatoes, because starchy ones will fall apart before they get crisp; and patience. If you're short on time, make the first variation.

Other vegetables you can use: beets, rutabagas, parsnips, or carrots, though they won't get quite as crisp.

About 2 pounds waxy potatoes

$1/4$ cup peanut, extra virgin olive, or neutral oil, like grapeseed or corn, or more as needed

Salt and freshly ground black pepper

1 Peel the potatoes if you like (it isn't at all necessary since waxy potatoes have thin, delicious skins) and cut them into 1-inch chunks. Put the oil in a large skillet,

preferably nonstick or cast-iron, over medium heat. When hot, add the potatoes and cook, undisturbed, until they begin to brown around the edges and release from the pan, about 10 minutes.

2 Continue cooking, turning to brown all the sides without stirring too often. (This is the part that takes the most patience.) Add more oil if needed to prevent the potatoes from sticking. And if they are browning too fast, turn the heat down just a tad. They'll take up to 20 minutes longer to cook.

3 When the potatoes are tender and golden, turn the heat up a bit to crisp them up. Sprinkle with salt and pepper and toss to coat. Taste, adjust the seasoning, and serve hot or at room temperature.

Last-Minute Crisp Panfried Potatoes. These also take less oil to cook: After cutting the potatoes, boil them in salted water to cover until tender, 10 to 15 minutes. Drain. In Step 2, turn the heat to medium-high instead of medium and start with 2 tablespoons of oil instead of $^1/_4$ cup. Proceed with the recipe, watching the potatoes more closely. They will crisp and turn brown in about half the time.

Crisp and Buttery Panfried Potatoes. Decadent any time of the day, and especially nice if you add an extra tablespoon or two of butter just at the end of cooking: Use 2 tablespoons butter and 2 tablespoons of any oil instead of all oil. If you need to use more, use butter. Proceed with the recipe and stir in about a tablespoon more of butter during the last minute or so of cooking.

Crisp Panfried Potatoes with Onions. The classic home-fry combo: In Step 3, when the potatoes are tender and fairly well browned, add 1 cup chopped onion (any kind, including scallion) to the pan. Cook, stirring occasionally, until the onion softens and turns golden, 3 to 5 minutes more.

Crisp Panfried Potatoes and Eggs. Verging on a skillet breakfast: In Step 3, add 3 or 4 hard-cooked eggs, cut into eighths, and 2 cored, seeded, and chopped tomatoes. Cook for another 2 minutes or so, then taste, adjust the seasoning, and serve.

10 Ways to Season Crisp Panfried or Oven-Roasted Potatoes

Add a spoonful or two of the following ingredients in Step 3, when you add the salt and pepper, and stir for a minute or two, until toasted and fragrant:

1. Minced fresh chile (like jalapeño or Thai), or to taste, or hot red pepper flakes or cayenne to taste
2. Grated Parmesan cheese
3. Finely ground nuts, like hazelnuts, walnuts, almonds, pecans, cashews, or peanuts
4. Minced herbs, like chives, parsley, mint, cilantro, or dill
5. Smoked paprika
6. Curry powder (to make your own, see pages 815–816)
7. Mustard seeds (best added at the beginning, with the oil, and allowed to cook for a moment before adding the potatoes) and a pinch of ground turmeric
8. Poppy seeds and grated lemon zest
9. Grated coconut
10. Chaat masala (to make your own, see page 814)

Oven-Roasted Potatoes

MAKES: 4 servings
TIME: About 1 hour

You can oven-roast any kind of potato, with slightly different but always desirable results. Waxy potatoes will form a brown, crisp crust and, as long as you cook them long enough, a creamy interior, while starchy varieties will tend to darken more easily, become not quite so crisp, and turn very, very soft. Either way, they're great hot from the oven or cooled a bit to room temperature.

Other vegetables you can use: any root vegetable, winter squash, or tropical tuber.

2 tablespoons extra virgin olive oil, plus more as needed

2 pounds potatoes

Salt and freshly ground black pepper

1 Preheat the oven to 400°F. Smear a large roasting pan or rimmed baking sheet with a little of the oil. It should be large enough to hold all the potatoes in a single layer without overcrowding.

2 Scrub the potatoes and peel them if you like. Make sure they're fairly dry and cut them into chunks of equal size, anywhere from 1 to 2 inches wide. Put them in the pan, drizzle with the 2 tablespoons oil, and toss gently to coat. Sprinkle with salt and pepper.

3 Roast, undisturbed, for 20 minutes before checking the first time. If the potatoes release easily from the pan, stir them up a bit or turn the pieces over with tongs.

If they look too dry and are sticking, drizzle with a little more oil and toss. Continue roasting, turning every 10 minutes or so, until crisp on the outside and tender inside, another 20 to 30 minutes, depending on the type of potato and how large the chunks are. The potatoes are done when a skewer or sharp knife inserted into one meets almost no resistance.

④ Remove from the oven, taste, and adjust the seasoning or toss with one of the toppings from "10 Ways to Season Crisp Panfried or Oven-Roasted Potatoes" (page 344).

Oven-Roasted "Fries." Not as crisp as French Fries (page 352), but close, and so much easier and lighter: Cut the potatoes, peeled or not, into French fry–style batons. Grease or line 2 baking sheets with parchment paper. Brush the potatoes with the oil and spread out on the baking sheets without crowding. Proceed with the recipe.

Oven-Roasted Cottage "Fries." So substantial you can eat them like meat: Cut the potatoes, peeled or not, lengthwise into paddles about $1/4$ inch thick or even a little thicker. Grease or line 2 baking sheets with parchment paper. Brush the potatoes with the oil and spread out on the baking sheets without crowding. Proceed with the recipe, turning the potatoes once or twice with tongs until browned evenly.

Crisp Oven-Roasted Cottage "Fries" with Garlic. A simplified version of the French *pommes Anna*: Follow the preceding variation. Use a combination of butter and olive oil, at least 2 tablespoons of each. While the potatoes are roasting, finely mince or press several cloves of garlic and mix them with a tablespoon or so of olive oil. When the fries are nearly done, add the garlic and toss, then return to the oven for a final crisping, which will soften the garlic and turn it golden.

Oven-Roasted Hash Browns. Breakfast potatoes without much fuss: Increase the oil to 3 tablespoons. Peel the potatoes, then grate them on the largest holes of a box grater or with the grating disk of a food processor. Proceed with the recipe, resisting the urge to mess with the potatoes frequently. When they're crisp on the bottom, use a spatula to turn large portions over and press them down a bit like diner hash browns. Serve immediately.

Buttery Oven-Roasted Potatoes. Great color and flavor: Instead of the olive oil, use melted butter. Reduce the oven temperature to 375°F and increase the cooking time by 20 minutes or so. Proceed with the recipe.

5 Dishes Based on Crisp Panfried or Oven-Roasted Potatoes

Patatas Bravas. A Spanish-style dish that's addictive: Drizzle potatoes with Garlic Mayonnaise (page 771) and several dashes of any hot sauce.

Potatoes Benedict. For breakfast, lunch, or dinner: Top each serving of potatoes with a poached egg (or two) and a generous spoonful of Hollandaise Sauce (page 802). Garnish with chopped parsley or fresh chervil and a sprinkle of paprika.

Crisp Potato Salad. Use panfried or oven-roasted potatoes to make Potato Salad (page 68) or simply toss with about $1/2$ cup or so of Vinaigrette (pages 762–763).

Potatoes with Dashi Dipping Sauce. Cut the potatoes into large pieces and instead of olive oil or butter, use peanut oil or a neutral oil, like grapeseed or corn, to cook them. Prepare Dashi Dipping Sauce (page 780) to serve on the side.

Potato Soup with Mexican-Style Garnishes. Use these potatoes instead of tortillas in Tortilla Soup (page 126).

Grilled or Broiled Potatoes

MAKES: 4 servings
TIME: About 40 minutes

The key to grilling or broiling potatoes is to use moderate heat at first; so start them off 6 to 8 inches from the broiler or over a moderate fire; otherwise the insides will be raw and the outsides charred. Once they're situated, you can walk away for 10 minutes at a time and let them do their thing. To get more control over the process, try the variation; they won't be quite as crisp, though the interior will be creamier, so it's sort of a trade-off.

Other vegetables you can use: any tropical tuber or root vegetable; cooking times will vary a bit depending on size and density.

    2 pounds waxy potatoes

    2 tablespoons extra virgin olive oil, plus more
        as needed

    Salt and freshly ground black pepper

① Heat a charcoal or gas grill or a broiler to medium heat and put the rack about 4 inches from heat source in a grill or 6 to 8 inches from the heat source in a broiler.

② Scrub the potatoes and peel if you like. Cut them in half or in thirds lengthwise so the pieces are about $1/2$ inch thick. Toss them in 2 tablespoons of olive oil, adding more as needed to coat; sprinkle with salt and pepper and toss again.

③ Put the potatoes on the grill rack or broiler pan. Grill or broil, undisturbed, for about 10 minutes, then check; they should look blistery but not yet browned. Keep cooking until they start to turn golden, then flip and repeat on the other side, brushing with more oil if needed to keep them from sticking. The potatoes are done when a skewer or sharp knife inserted into one meets almost no resistance; if they aren't yet crisp to your liking, raise the grill heat or move the rack closer to the broiler. Taste and adjust the seasoning, then serve immediately or at room temperature.

Last-Minute Grilled or Broiled Potatoes. Great for skewering with vegetables, tofu, or other ingredients that cook fast because everything will be ready at the same time: After preparing the potatoes in Step 2, boil them (see page 340) until they begin to get tender (about 5 minutes at a steady boil). (The potatoes can be prepared to this point and left on the counter for an hour or so or refrigerated for up to 2 days.) When you're ready to cook, heat the grill or broiler as directed, putting the rack about 4 inches from either heat source. The potatoes will take about half the time to crisp up as they do in the main recipe.

6 Ways to Season Grilled or Broiled Potatoes
When the potatoes are done, toss or smear them with one of the following and return them to the heat for a few minutes to warm the seasonings.

1. Traditional Pesto or herb paste (pages 768–770), about $1/2$ cup
2. Chile Paste (page 828), about $1/4$ cup
3. Tapenade (page 326), about $1/4$ cup
4. Peanut Sauce (page 794)
5. Mashed Roasted Garlic (page 304)
6. Any spice or herb mix, sprinkled judiciously (to make your own, see pages 810–819)

Braised Potatoes, Ten Ways

MAKES: 4 servings
TIME: About 40 minutes

Just like foods rich in protein, potatoes can be seared and then simmered in liquid with aromatic vegetables. The result is a simple stew with a texture that's tough to beat. Try this recipe with small heirloom potatoes like fingerlings and be sure to explore other flavor options using the variations.

Other vegetables or fruits you can use: any root vegetable or winter squash or even apples.

Ⓕ Fast   Ⓜ Make Ahead   Ⓥ Vegan

2 pounds all-purpose or waxy potatoes, like Yukon Gold, "new," or red

3 tablespoons extra virgin olive oil

Salt and freshly ground black pepper

1 small onion, minced

2 cups vegetable stock (pages 101–102) or water

$1/4$ cup chopped parsley for garnish

1 Peel the potatoes and cut them into large chunks, in half if they're mid-sized, and leave them whole if they're small.

2 Put the oil in a large pot over medium-high heat. When hot, add the potatoes and sprinkle with salt and pepper. Cook, stirring occasionally, until coated in oil and beginning to turn golden, about 10 minutes. Add the onion and stir a few times until it softens, a minute or two.

3 Add the stock with enough extra water to barely cover the potatoes with liquid. Bring to a boil, stirring once in a while to make sure the potatoes aren't sticking, then turn the heat down to medium-low so that the mixture bubbles gently. Cook, stirring occasionally, until the potatoes get tender, 20 to 25 minutes. Add more liquid if they start to stick. The potatoes are done when a skewer or sharp knife inserted into one meets almost no resistance. Taste and adjust the seasoning, garnish, and serve hot or at room temperature.

Braised Potatoes with Mustard. Gorgeous color: When you add the stock in Step 3, stir in $1/4$ cup of any mustard, coarse (like Grainy Mustard, Many Ways, page 776) or Dijon.

Braised Potatoes and Garlic. Garnish with grated Parmesan if you like: Omit the onion. Peel 1 or 2 heads of garlic and add them along with the potatoes in Step 2.

Soy-Braised Potatoes. Great with Edamame with Tomatoes and Cilantro (page 583): Instead of the olive oil, use 1 tablespoon dark sesame oil and 2 tablespoons neutral oil, like grapeseed or corn. Instead of the stock, use a mixture of $1/4$ cup soy sauce and $1^3/4$ cups water.

Slice a bunch of scallions and use that instead of the onion. Proceed with the recipe (don't add salt until the potatoes are just about done and taste first, adding salt or more soy). Garnish with cilantro instead of parsley and sprinkle with sesame seeds and minced fresh chile.

Braised Potatoes with Miso. A natural combination with a deep but mellow flavor. Use neutral oil, like grapeseed or corn, instead of olive oil. Omit the onion and, instead of the parsley, use sliced scallion for garnish. Proceed with the recipe through Step 3, taking care not to oversalt. When the potatoes are done, remove them from the heat. Whisk together $1/2$ cup warm stock or water and stir in $1/4$ cup any miso; add this mixture to the potatoes and stir well to combine and warm through. Taste and adjust the seasoning if necessary, garnish, and serve.

Cream-Braised Potatoes. Decadent: Use butter instead of the olive oil. Instead of the stock, use cream and use milk to finish covering the potatoes in Step 3. When the potatoes are done, stir in 1 tablespoon minced fresh tarragon or chervil if you like, instead of the parsley garnish, and serve hot.

Braised Potatoes with Almonds. Rich with almond flavor but not sweet: Instead of the stock, use almond milk or cow's milk, and when you add it in Step 3, add a pinch of saffron if you like. Proceed with the recipe. When the potatoes are done, stir in $1/2$ cup chopped toasted almonds (see page 321). Garnish and serve hot.

Potatoes Braised with Sea Greens. Briny tasting with a silky texture: Instead of the olive oil, use a neutral oil, like grapeseed or corn. When you add the onion in Step 2, stir in $1/4$ cup crumbled sea green, like dulse, arame, or wakame. Proceed with the recipe; you'll probably need to add more liquid as the sea greens absorb it. Garnish with minced red onion or scallion instead of the parsley.

Beer-Braised Potatoes with Horseradish and Cheddar. A nice wintertime dish: Toss 1 cup grated cheddar with 1 tablespoon cornstarch. Instead of the stock, use beer or milk. When the potatoes are almost done, stir in the cheese mixture and a tablespoon or more of freshly grated or prepared horseradish. Add more beer or milk if the potatoes look too dry; they should be a little saucy. Stir until the cheese melts. Garnish and serve hot.

Braised Potatoes with Pineapple in Coconut Milk. Sounds wacky, but it's great, especially with Steamed Sticky Rice (page 507): Replace the olive oil with a neutral oil, like grapeseed or corn. Instead of the onion, finely chop $^1/_2$ small pineapple (or use 1 cup canned crushed pineapple in water, well drained). Instead of the stock, use coconut milk (1 can, slightly less than 2 cups, with a little water, or made from scratch as on page 423). Garnish with chopped fresh cilantro instead of the parsley and minced fresh Thai chile if you like.

Potatoes Provençal

MAKES: 4 to 6 servings

TIME: About 1 hour, largely unattended

This super-easy dish looks great and can be reheated or served at room temperature, which makes it terrific for potluck dinners.

Other vegetables you can use: artichoke hearts (thinly sliced) or sunchokes.

3 tablespoons extra virgin olive oil, plus more for the baking dish

2 pounds all-purpose potatoes, like Yukon Gold

2 large ripe tomatoes

$^1/_2$ cup good-quality pitted black or green olives

3 or 4 sprigs fresh thyme

Salt and freshly ground black pepper

❶ Preheat the oven to 400°F. Grease a large gratin or baking dish with a little olive oil. Scrub the potatoes, but don't bother to peel them. Cut each lengthwise into slices

about $^1/_4$ inch thick. Core the tomatoes and slice them crosswise into $^1/_2$-inch-thick slices.

❷ Put the potatoes and tomatoes into the dish in a single layer, alternating and overlapping them as needed. Distribute the olives among the potatoes and tomatoes and press them in a bit. Top with the thyme and drizzle with the 3 tablespoons olive oil. Sprinkle generously with salt and pepper.

❸ Bake, undisturbed, until the tomato juices evaporate and the whole thing looks golden and toasty. The potatoes are done when a skewer or sharp knife inserted into one meets almost no resistance. Serve immediately or at room temperature.

Potatoes Provençal with Gruyère. Ideal for lunch with nothing more than a green salad: About halfway through cooking, remove the thyme sprigs and sprinkle the top of the potatoes and tomatoes with $1^1/_2$ cups grated Gruyère. Put the sprigs back on top of the cheese if you like and proceed with the recipe, baking until the potatoes are tender and the cheese is bubbly.

Curried Stir-Fried Potatoes

MAKES: 4 servings

TIME: 20 minutes

If you cut potatoes small enough, they'll become tender quickly, but in this dish—inspired by similar creations popular in the Sichuan province of China and throughout India—the potatoes can remain slightly crunchy. Best with homemade curry powder or garam masala; the cumin seeds add a nice bit of crunch, and the cilantro adds a fresh note at the end, but neither is essential.

Other vegetables you can use: cauliflower, broccoli, carrots, turnips, radishes.

3 tablespoons neutral oil, like grapeseed or corn

1 tablespoon cumin seeds (optional)

1 small red onion, finely chopped

Ⓕ Fast   Ⓜ Make Ahead   Ⓥ Vegan

1 1/2 pounds all-purpose potatoes, like Yukon Gold, peeled and shredded or minced

1 tablespoon garam masala or curry powder (to make your own, see pages 815–816), or to taste

Salt and freshly ground black pepper

Pinch cayenne

1/4 cup fresh cilantro leaves, chopped

1 Put the oil in a large nonstick or well-seasoned cast-iron skillet over medium-high heat. When hot, add the cumin seeds if you're using them, fry for 30 seconds, then add half the onion and the potatoes. Add the spice blend along with the salt, pepper, and cayenne. Cook, stirring or tossing, until the onion has caramelized and the potatoes are lightly browned, about 10 minutes; the potatoes need not be fully tender.

2 Add the cilantro to the pan, toss once, and transfer to a serving platter. Garnish with the raw onion and serve immediately.

Stir-Fried Potatoes, Korean Style. As you might expect, heavy on the sesame; great stuff: Omit the cumin, onion, spice mix, and cilantro; use scallion instead of red onion. In Step 1, add 1 teaspoon chopped garlic to the oil (you're going to need 2 teaspoons in all), then half the scallion and the potatoes about 30 seconds later, along with about a tablespoon minced fresh chile (like jalapeño or Thai), or to taste, or hot red pepper flakes or cayenne to taste. In Step 2, add the remaining garlic, along with 1 teaspoon minced peeled fresh ginger, and cook for 30 seconds or so. Garnish with a tablespoon or two toasted sesame seeds (see page 321) and serve.

Potato "Nik"

MAKES: 4 to 6 servings

TIME: About 40 minutes

Like just about everyone, I love the crisp, crunchy potato pancakes also known as *latkes*. But let's face it: they are

(STEP 1) To turn this or any other large pancake, slide the half-cooked cake onto a plate. (STEP 2) Cover with another plate, invert, and slide back into the pan.

not everyday food, especially not for a crowd. The hang-up isn't preparing the batter; it's cooking them one by one in a hot skillet or griddle.

Fortunately there's Potato "Nik," my grandmother's clever solution with the mysterious, unexplained name. I figure one nik equals twenty latkes, and you can actually walk away from it for a few minutes while it cooks. Better still, it stays hot for a long time and is delicious warm or at room temperature. For those occasions when you absolutely crave individual latkes, see the first variation.

One word about sticking: If you don't use a nonstick pan, coat the bottom of your skillet with about 1/8 inch of oil. And turn the thing carefully.

Other vegetables you can use: sweet potatoes (cooked over slightly lower heat for about 5 minutes less per side); a combination of potatoes and sweet potatoes, carrots, or turnips is also good.

About 2 pounds starchy potatoes, like Idaho or russet, peeled

1 medium onion, peeled

2 eggs, beaten

2 tablespoons Fresh Bread Crumbs (page 804) or matzo meal

Salt and freshly ground black pepper

Neutral oil, like grapeseed or corn, as needed

1 Grate the potatoes and onion by hand or with the grating disk of a food processor; drain well in a colander or strainer. Combine the potatoes and onion in a large bowl with the eggs and bread crumbs; sprinkle with salt and pepper.

2 Put about $\frac{1}{8}$ inch of oil in a large, deep skillet, preferably nonstick or cast-iron, over medium-high heat. When the oil is hot (it will shimmer), put the batter into the pan and smooth the top. Cook, shaking the pan occasionally, until the bottom is nicely browned, at least 15 minutes, adjusting the heat so the mixture sizzles but doesn't burn.

3 To turn, slide the cake out onto a large plate, cover with another large plate, and invert the 2 plates together. Add a little more oil to the pan if necessary and slide the pancake back in, cooked side up. Cook for another 15 minutes or so, until nicely browned, then serve hot or warm.

Latkes (Potato Pancakes). The original: Prepare the potato batter in Step 1 and heat the pan as described in Step 2. When the oil is hot, put large spoonfuls of batter into the pan to form individual pancakes. Cook until browned on both sides, about 10 minutes total per pancake. Drain on paper towels and keep warm in a low oven until all of the latkes are finished.

Cheesy Potato Pancakes. Not traditional, but irresistible: Add 1 cup of grated cheddar, Parmesan, Jack, or Asiago cheese to the batter, along with the eggs and crumbs. Proceed with either the main recipe or the first variation.

Potato Pancakes for Purists. Omit everything except for the potatoes, salt, and pepper. Instead of the oil, use 4 to 6 tablespoons of butter, as needed. Grate and drain the potatoes as described and toss with a little salt and pepper. Heat the pan dry for a few minutes before adding a tablespoon or so of the butter. When it melts and bubbles, use a fork to put portions of the potatoes in the pan, pressing down to form small pancakes. Don't crowd them too much; just work in batches. Flip only once, when the bottoms are well browned and crisp, after about 10 minutes, adding more butter as needed. Cook for another 7 to 10 minutes on the other side. Drain on paper towels and keep warm in a low oven until all of the pancakes are finished.

Potato Dumplings. Serve in a bowl of vegetable stock (pages 101–102) for a great soup: Bring a large pot of water to boil and salt it. Stir about $\frac{1}{2}$ cup of all-purpose flour into the potato batter in Step 1. It should stick to your spoon like cookie dough. If not, add a little more. Adjust the water so it bubbles steadily. Make the dumplings with a spoon or your hand, each about the size of a walnut or small egg, and add to the water. Cook for about 3 minutes after they float to the surface; taste one and make sure the potato is done. Drain and serve in stock, alongside any vegetable stew, or simply with a dollop of sour cream.

7 Garnishes for Potato "Nik," Pancakes, or Dumplings

1. Sour cream
2. Applesauce
3. Minced chives or other fresh herbs, like parsley, mint, dill, or chervil
4. Real Ranch Dressing (page 772; outrageous, but great)

Ⓕ Fast   Ⓜ Make Ahead   Ⓥ Vegan

5. Traditional Pesto or other herb paste (pages 768–770)
6. Mayonnaise (to make your own, see page 771, including any of the variations)
7. Tomato Chutney (page 785) or Caramelized Onion Chutney (page 786)

Garlicky Mashed Potato Pie

MAKES: 4 servings

TIME: About 1 hour, partly unattended

This is a big potato cake like Potato "Nik" (page 349), but instead of raw shredded potatoes cooked entirely on the stove, this is made of mashed potatoes and is finished in the oven. The result is a creamy interior and crisp crust. You'll go nuts, especially if you're a garlic lover.

Other vegetables you can use: any winter squash or root vegetable.

2 starchy or all-purpose potatoes, like Idaho, russet, or Yukon Gold, peeled and cut into chunks

$1/_2$ cup cream or milk

2 heads garlic, cloves peeled

6 tablespoons ($3/_4$ stick) butter, melted, or extra virgin olive oil

2 eggs, beaten

Salt and freshly ground black pepper

① Start boiling the potatoes according to the recipe on page 340. Preheat the oven to 425°F.

② Meanwhile, put the cream and garlic cloves in a small pot over medium heat. Cook, stirring occasionally, until the garlic softens, about 15 minutes. Check the potatoes; they're done when a skewer or sharp knife inserted into one meets almost no resistance. Drain well.

③ Mash or rice the potatoes or run them through a food mill. When smooth, stir in 4 tablespoons ($1/_2$ stick)

of the melted butter or oil along with the garlic mixture. Mash and stir with a wooden spoon to smooth out all the lumps. Stir in the eggs. Sprinkle with a fair amount of salt and some pepper.

④ Put the remaining 2 tablespoons melted butter or oil in a large ovenproof skillet, preferably nonstick or cast iron, over medium heat. When the butter is melted or the oil is hot, put the mashed potatoes in the pan and press down a bit to spread them around evenly. Cook, undisturbed, until they brown around the edges, 10 to 12 minutes. Put the pan in the oven and bake until the pie is golden brown on top, about 30 minutes. Cool in the pan for a bit, then run a knife around the edge of the pan to make sure nothing is stuck. Put a plate over the pan and turn the pie out. Serve immediately or at room temperature.

Garlicky Mashed Potato Pie with Cheese. Great for lunch with soup or salad: Follow the recipe through Step 4. While the pie is baking, grate 1 cup cheddar or Gruyère cheese. When the pie is ready, sprinkle the cheese on top and turn on the broiler. Put the pie under the broiler, about 4 to 6 inches from the heat source. Watch carefully and remove the pan as soon as the cheese begins to melt and bubble, only a couple of minutes. Serve immediately.

Garlicky Mashed Potato Hotcakes. Nice topped with sour cream and chives or served like bread with a hearty vegetable stew: Follow the recipe through Step 3. Heat an electric griddle to 375°F or put a large nonstick or cast-iron skillet on the stove over medium-high heat. The surface is ready when a few drops of water dance around enthusiastically. Film the griddle or pan with a little of the remaining melted butter or oil (you might need more than 2 tablespoons), and when it's good and hot, spoon out the mashed potato mixture to form medium-size hotcakes. Cook, undisturbed, until the edges begin to crisp, about 5 minutes or so, then turn and cook the other side, another 3 to 5 minutes. Serve immediately.

French Fries

MAKES: 4 servings

TIME: 30 minutes

It only *seems* like a hassle to double-fry French fries, which is the classic and, shall we say, correct technique; in reality it's a double blessing. Your fries will not only stay crisp longer, but the first step can be done well in advance, leaving you only a quick final frying right before serving. Starchy potatoes are the only option here; waxy potatoes never crisp up quite right.

Purists like to salt the fries and leave it at that, but you can dust them with virtually any spice blend (pages 810–819). Or you can serve a dip, from vinaigrette, ranch dressing, or any mayo-type sauce to Balsamic Syrup, Cooked Tomatillo Salsa, Ponzu Sauce, Tahini Soy Sauce, or any peanut sauce—all in the sauces chapter.

Other vegetables you can use: See the sidebar on at right.

Peanut oil or neutral oil, like grapeseed or corn, for deep frying

2 pounds starchy potatoes, like Idaho or other russet

Salt and freshly ground black pepper

1 Put at least 3 inches oil in a countertop deep-fryer or in a deep pan on the stove and turn the heat to medium-high; bring to 300–325°F (see "Deep Frying," page 26).

2 Scrub the potatoes and peel them if you like. Cut them any way you like—from shoestrings to big batons or chunks—and make sure they're fairly dry. Drop them, a handful at a time, into the oil, adjusting the heat as needed to maintain a constant temperature. Fry the potatoes in one batch, stirring occasionally, for 5 to 10 minutes, depending on the cut. The goal of this first frying is to cook them until just tender and beginning to color slightly. Drain batches on paper towels or a wire rack. (The potatoes may be cooked to this point and set aside

Other Vegetable Fries

Any starchy vegetable can be French-fried, and it will develop a nice crust without needing to be breaded. The cooking times might vary a bit, so watch it the first try and test for doneness. The only trick is to identify what's starchy and what's not. Here's a short list of vegetables that will work:

- Beets (use slightly lower heat to avoid burning)
- Carrots (use slightly lower heat to avoid burning)
- Cassava
- Parsnips (use slightly lower heat to avoid burning)
- Rutabaga
- Sweet Potatoes (or Yams) (use slightly lower heat to avoid burning)
- Taro
- Turnip
- Yuca
- Plantain (use slightly lower heat to avoid burning)

on the counter for an hour or so before proceeding. Be sure to take the oil off the heat.)

3 Heat the oil again, this time to around 350°F. Fry and drain the potatoes a second time—the same way as before—until crisp and deeply colored, just a couple of minutes. Sprinkle with salt and pepper while still hot and serve immediately.

Potato Chips. No prefrying is necessary: You'll need a deeper, larger pot or deep-fryer and be prepared for the potatoes to absorb more oil. Use a mandoline or a sharp knife to cut the potatoes lengthwise. You want them pretty thin, but not too wispy. Heat the oil to about 350°F. Work in batches, using a slotted spoon or strainer to fish them out of the hot oil as they turn golden. Drain on paper towels or brown bags. Season while hot and serve.

 Fast   Make Ahead   Vegan

Potato Croquettes

MAKES: 4 servings

TIME: About 1 hour

The combination of the fluffy mashed potatoes and the crunchy outer coating is irresistible and worth the not-insignificant effort (though you can use left-over mashed potatoes). I prefer panfrying croquettes, though you can certainly deep-fry them if you like.

Ideas for making these main-dish worthy are in the list at right.

Other vegetables you can use: sunchokes or any tropical tuber.

> 4 cups mashed potatoes made with minimal milk and no butter (page 341)
>
> Salt and freshly ground black pepper
>
> 3 tablespoons extra virgin olive oil
>
> 1 medium onion, chopped
>
> 2 tablespoons butter or more oil
>
> All-purpose flour for dredging
>
> 2 eggs, lightly beaten in a shallow bowl
>
> Fresh Bread Crumbs (page 804) for dredging
>
> Lemon wedges

1 Taste the potatoes and sprinkle them with salt and pepper if necessary, taking care not to oversalt. Put 1 tablespoon of the oil in a large skillet over medium-high heat. When hot, add the onion and cook, stirring frequently, just until it softens, 5 minutes or so. Cool a bit, then stir the onion into the potatoes and wipe the pan clean. Form the potato mixture into 4 large or 8 small patties.

2 Add the remaining oil to the pan, along with the butter or additional oil, and turn the heat to medium-high. When the butter melts, dredge each patty in the flour, then run through the egg, then dredge in the bread crumbs, pressing to help the crumbs adhere.

3 Cook the patties as you would hamburgers, turning—carefully, so as not to dislodge the coating—as each side browns, about 5 minutes per side. Since all the ingredients are already cooked, the crust is your main concern; the interior will get hot as long as the exterior browns. Drain briefly and sprinkle with more salt and pepper if you like. Serve immediately with lemon wedges on the side.

Potato Croquettes, Indian Style. Vegan and delicious: Use peanut oil or a neutral oil, like grapeseed or corn. Use cornstarch instead of flour and omit the eggs and bread crumbs. As the onion finishes softening in Step 1, sprinkle it with 2 tablespoons curry powder, chaat masala, or garam masala (to make your own, see page 815) and mix with the potatoes. In Step 2, after forming the patties, simply dredge them in the cornstarch and fry as directed in Step 3. Serve with any chutney, especially Cilantro-Mint Chutney or Crunchy Nut Chutney (pages 783 and 784).

Potato Croquettes, Japanese Style. Super-crunchy: Use peanut oil or a neutral oil, like grapeseed or corn. Use scallion instead of onion and substitute panko for the bread crumbs. To make a simple dipping sauce, combine the juice of 2 lemons with 2 tablespoons soy sauce, or serve with Dashi Dipping Sauce or Ponzu Sauce (page 780).

Potato Croquettes with Roasted Garlic and Parmesan. Terrific with Fast Tomato Sauce (page 445): Omit the onion and 1 tablespoon of the oil. Instead, roast and mash 2 heads of garlic (page 304) and stir this into the potatoes in Step 1, along with 1 cup grated Parmesan.

5 Ways to Make Potato Croquettes More Substantial

Turn any of the potato croquettes into a main dish by stirring about 2 cups of any of the following into the potato mixture along with the onions. Because you'll have more batter, increase the number of eggs to 3 and make sure you have plenty of bread crumbs.

1. Sautéed Mushrooms (page 314)
2. Crunchy Crumbled Tempeh (page 674)

3. Basic Scrambled Tofu (page 655)
4. Any cooked plain beans or bean dish
5. Any cooked greens or cooked greens dish (make sure they're chopped fairly small)

Pumpkins (*see* Squash—Winter, page 363)

Radicchio (*see* Endive, Escarole, and Radicchio, page 300)

Radishes

Red, White, and Black and Daikon

The more common round or oblong radishes come in an array of colors—bright pink to crimson red, purple, and white. We mostly eat them raw, but they are also quite delicious cooked with some butter; try it, especially braised and glazed, below.

Another type of radish is the daikon; it can be huge (as big as your arm) and is often sold cut into pieces. Daikon are ivory white in color, with a mild but distinctively radishy flavor. They are common in Asian cuisines, especially Japanese and Korean, and are often pickled (sometimes colored a bright yellow).

Black radish is a spicy-hot type of radish with a black skin and white flesh; shred and use it as a garnish or eat with buttered bread.

Buying and storing: Radishes with their greens are best (the tender leaves are a spicy addition to salads); the leaves should be green and fresh looking. The radish should be firm, crisp, and smooth. Large specimens (of naturally small radishes) can be woody, so watch out for that. Store wrapped loosely in plastic in the refrigerator.

Preparing: Trim and peel if you like (black radishes should always be peeled); slice or chop as necessary.

Best cooking method: Sautéing (in butter) or braising and glazing.

When is it done? When crisp-tender to fully tender but not mushy.

Other vegetables to substitute: Jícama or water chestnuts if raw; turnips if cooked.

Braised and Glazed Radishes, Turnips, or Other Root Vegetable

MAKES: 4 servings
TIME: 30 minutes

A basic and wonderful way to prepare all kinds of root vegetables. Feel free to jazz this up with a few sprigs of fresh thyme, or a teaspoon of curry powder or other spice mix (to make your own, see pages 810–819) or simply a couple of cloves of garlic. Vegan if you use oil instead of butter.

Other vegetables you can use: anything hard and fibrous, really—carrots, jícama, parsnips, celeriac, carrots, waxy potatoes (but not vegetables that easily become mushy, like starchy potatoes or sweet potatoes).

2 tablespoons butter or extra virgin olive oil

1 pound radishes, trimmed, or daikon radish, turnips, or rutabaga, peeled and cut into chunks

1/2 cup or more vegetable stock (pages 101–102), white wine, or water

Salt and freshly ground black pepper

Freshly squeezed lemon juice (optional)

Chopped parsley leaves for garnish

① Combine the butter, radishes, and stock in a saucepan, sprinkle with salt and pepper, and bring to a boil. Cover and adjust the heat so the mixture simmers; cook until the radishes are tender, 15 to 20 minutes, checking once or twice and adding additional liquid as needed.

② Uncover and raise the heat to boil off almost all the liquid, so that the vegetable becomes glazed in the combination of butter and pan juices; this will take 5 to 10 minutes. Taste and adjust the seasoning, add a little lemon juice if you like, garnish, and serve.

Braised and Glazed Radishes or Other Root Vegetable with Miso Sauce. Great with daikon: In Step 1, add a tablespoon of soy sauce to the mix. In Step 2, as the mixture become glazed, whisk together 2 tablespoons any miso (white is mildest) and an equal amount of stock or water; turn the heat under the radishes to a minimum, add the miso mixture and stir, and heat very gently for a minute or so before serving. (Omit the lemon juice and parsley.)

Rutabagas (*see* Turnips, page 378)

Salsify
Oyster Plant

A root that is better appreciated in Europe than in the United States, salsify has a dark gray or black skin and a pearly white interior that discolors when exposed to air (drop it into acidulated water immediately after peeling or cutting as you would artichokes; see page 257). Salsify can be up to 12 inches long and looks rather like a stick; its flavor is mild and somewhat sweet (some say like an oyster, but I don't get it).

Buying and storing: Look for firm, uniformly shaped roots that aren't too knobby. Store wrapped loosely in plastic in the refrigerator.

Preparing: Peel and chop or slice and rub with lemon juice or put in acidulated water (a tablespoon or two of lemon juice or vinegar mixed into the water will do) until it's ready to be cooked.

Best cooking methods: Boiling, braising, braising and glazing, and roasting.

When is it done? When tender enough to pierce easily with a thin-bladed knife or skewer but not mushy.

Other vegetables to substitute: Parsnips, carrots, or potato.

Scallions (*see* Onions, page 327)

Sea Greens
Sea Vegetables, Seaweed

Sea greens are flavorful, nicely textured, diverse, and incredibly nutritious; they're almost always sold dry, which makes them ultra-convenient as well. For the most part, they're wild, which makes them organic. With the exception of sea beans (which is sold as branches of a whole plant), we eat primarily the leaves. The supply is huge, and they're not expensive. So—although it's been said before—they're destined to become increasingly popular.

Famous last words, I guess, but you should try them if you haven't already.

Most sea greens are very high in protein (nori is at the top of the chart with over 30 percent); an outstanding source of calcium (hijiki and wakame contain as much as fourteen times the amount in milk); and a rich source of vitamins (especially A, B, C, E, and B_{12}, of which there are few nonmeat sources) and minerals (potassium, magnesium, phosphorus, iron, and iodine, which is difficult to obtain from natural sources).

Impressive enough? When you cook with them, you'll be even more impressed.

Buying and storing: There is no guesswork in selecting dried seaweed. The best selection will be in Asian markets, natural food stores, and on-line (see Sources, page 929). Store in a cool, dry spot, where it will keep indefinitely. (Fresh sea beans should be crisp, bright green, and smell like the ocean and should be stored in the refrigerator; use as quickly as possible.)

Preparing: Nori requires no soaking; cut it with scissors as needed. It's often toasted to make it sturdier and tastier before use (see page 357).

For dulse: Use straight out of the package or just give it a rinse in cold water.

For arame, hijiki, kombu, wakame, and alaria: Use a damp paper towel to wipe kombu, but don't rinse. For all of these, soak in warm water until tender, about 5 to 10 minutes. (Save the water for another use.) Chop or slice as you like.

For sea beans: Rinse and chop only if necessary.

Best cooking methods: For arame, hijiki, alaria, and wakame: Boiling and sautéing or stir-frying with other ingredients.

For kombu: Boiling and braising.

For dulse: Quickly sautéing or stir-frying.

For sea beans: 30 seconds in boiling water or a quick stir-fry; but they're just as good raw.

When is it done? When tender.

Other vegetables to substitute: Most sea greens, with the exception of sea beans and kombu, are interchangeable. Substitute French-cut green beans for sea beans.

The Sea Green Lexicon

Following is a primer of the various types of sea greens you're likely to find in some supermarkets, natural food stores, and, of course, Asian markets. (See the "Sea Green (Seaweed) Salads, page 53.)

Arame and Hijiki (Hiziki): Different varieties but similar in look and use; both are slender, almost hairy strands. Arame is finer, milder, and lighter in color; hijiki is black, briny, and expands massively when rehydrated. Either use in salads, soups, and stews or add to sautés or stir-fries.

Dulse: Eaten regularly in New England until the 1920s, dulse is dark red, crumpled looking, and relatively soft. It can be eaten straight out of the package or added to salads, sandwiches, or soups.

Kombu (Kelp): A main ingredient in Kombu Dashi (page 103), kelp contains a substance similar to MSG that enhances flavors. It's great cooked with slow-simmered foods like beans, grains, soups, and stews. Sold in large, thick, hard pieces that are dark green, usually coated with a white powder. Occasionally sold fresh on the West Coast.

Nori (Laver): The familiar thin, shiny sheets that are used to wrap sushi. Deep greenish purple, almost black, brittle when dry and chewy when moistened. Nori dissolves in liquid and has a mild, nutty flavor; it's excellent toasted (see Nori Chips, page 357).

Sea Beans (Samphire, Glasswort): These small, delicate, thin, green "branches" with nubby ends are lovely in salads and used as a garnish; they can also be poached for about 30 seconds, which enhances their flavor slightly. That flavor is as fresh and "sealike" as you can imagine, and the texture is crisp and delightful. If you see it fresh, buy it; when sold pickled, in jars, it's less exciting.

Wakame and Alaria: Used interchangeably; the former is harvested in Japan, the latter in North America. Both are dark green when dried and nearly transparent; they turn emerald green when rehydrated. Their flavor is mild, and they're nice in soups and stews, with grains, or added to salads.

F Fast   M Make Ahead   V Vegan

Sea Green and Celery Stir-Fry

MAKES: 4 servings

TIME: 25 minutes

Among the most nutrient-rich stir-fries you can make; serve it over a whole grain, like brown rice, wheat berries, or quinoa, and you've got yourself a powerhouse of a meal.

Use any combination of arame, hijiki, dulse, kombu, wakame, and alaria. But note that kombu should either be simmered in water for about 15 first or soaked and sliced very finely, and dulse should be added at the last minute.

> 2 tablespoons neutral oil, like grapeseed or corn
>
> 1 tablespoon minced garlic
>
> 1 tablespoon minced and peeled ginger
>
> 1/2 cup trimmed and chopped scallions or onion
>
> 1/2 cup thinly sliced kombu, soaked and simmered in water for 15 minutes
>
> 2 stalks celery, thinly sliced lengthwise or julienned
>
> 2 cups soaked and thinly sliced (if necessary) sea greens, like arame, hijiki, dulse, wakame, and alaria
>
> 1/4 cup any stock or water, or a little more
>
> 2 tablespoons soy sauce
>
> 1 teaspoon dark sesame oil

① Heat a wok or a large, deep skillet over medium-high heat for 3 or 4 minutes. Add the oil and, almost immediately, the garlic, ginger, and scallions. Cook, stirring, for about 15 seconds, then add the kombu, celery, sea greens, and the stock or water and turn the heat to high.

② Cook, stirring constantly, until the vegetables are tender, about 7 minutes. If the mixture is completely dry, add a couple tablespoons more liquid, then the soy sauce

and sesame oil; stir and turn off the heat. Serve or store, covered, in the refrigerator for up to a day.

Sea Green and Mushroom Stir-Fry. Shiitake are best, adding another layer of flavor: Add 1 cup or so sliced mushrooms with the kombu.

Sea Green and Noodle Stir-Fry. Lo mein essentially: Add about 8 ounces fresh Chinese egg noodles or dried Chinese wheat noodles or spaghetti. Bring a large pot of water to a boil and salt it. Cook the noodles until they are tender but not mushy, about 4 minutes for fresh noodles, longer for dried, then drain and rinse; toss with a tablespoon or so of oil to prevent sticking and set aside. Proceed with the recipe; add the noodles and cook, stirring often, until the noodles are hot.

Nori Chips

MAKES: 2 to 4 servings

TIME: 5 minutes

These delicate and crisp "chips," sometimes made as an after-school snack for kids in Japan—are completely addicting. Eat them as a snack—they're great mixed with potato chips, popcorn (cooled, not hot), and Japanese rice crackers—or simply with a bowl of steamed rice and Kimchi (page 96).

> 6 sheets nori
>
> 2 tablespoons dark sesame oil
>
> Salt

① Put a skillet over medium-high heat. Brush the nori with the sesame oil and sprinkle with salt. Put a single nori sheet in the pan and toast it until it shrinks up, about 15 seconds; turn it over and toast the other side for another 15 seconds.

② Use scissors to cut the sheets into rectangular "chips." Serve within a few hours.

Shallots

A member of the allium genus (which contains not only onions and garlic but also lilies), shallots have a mild but complex flavor, making them the Rolls-Royce of the category. They come in individual cloves, not unlike garlic, but bigger and with the flesh and flavor of a mild onion. They have a tan, papery dried outer skin that tightly covers each clove and flesh that is semitranslucent white with a tinge of purple or green. Use them as you would onions, but really good onions.

Buying and storing: Shallots should be firm and have a pretty, shiny tan outer skin. Their shape is distinctive; usually two cloves are held together at the root end to make an oval shape with tapered ends. Don't be fooled by small, round, tan-skinned onions often labeled as shallots. Store in a cool, dry place or in the refrigerator for weeks.

Preparing: Break the cloves apart and remove the dry skins; trim the stem end and slice or chop as you would an onion.

Best cooking methods: Sautéing and roasting.

When is it done? When tender and translucent.

Other vegetables to substitute: Scallions are closest; onion (especially red or white onion) and leek are also good.

Sorrel

These oblong and arrow-shaped green leaves can be anywhere from a couple of inches to a foot long and are a

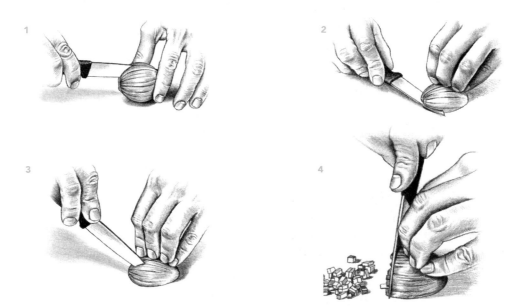

(STEP 1) First peel the shallot, then cut it in half from top to bottom. (STEP 2) Place one half, cut side down, on your cutting board. Make two or three cuts parallel to the cutting board into the vegetable; don't cut all the way through. (STEP 3) Now make as many cuts as are practical down through the top. Again, leave the shallot intact at one end. (STEP 4) Cut across to mince.

    F Fast   **M** Make Ahead   **V** Vegan

cross between an herb and a delicate cooking green. The flavor of sorrel is acidic and lemony (it's sometimes called *sourgrass*), which can be mild or intense, depending on the variety and maturity of the plant (beware: mature leaves can be mouth-puckeringly acidic and sour). Traditionally sorrel is used to make a cream soup and to flavor cream sauces, but young, tender leaves can be tossed into salads or omelets or cooked with spinach and other greens and vegetables for a snappy flavor.

Buying and storing: Look in the herb section of supermarkets, but you're more likely to find it in the spring at farmer's markets. Look for fresh-looking leaves and crisp stems. Store wrapped loosely in plastic in the refrigerator for up to three days.

Preparing: Wash well and trim any tough stems; no need to chop it unless you're using it raw.

Best cooking methods: Cooked into soups, stews, and braises or sautéed for omelets (see pages 171–174). Puréed and stirred with butter, cream, yogurt, or milk, it makes a nice sauce.

When is it done? When the leaves are melted and grayish green in color.

Other vegetables to substitute: Spinach, arugula, or watercress (with a squeeze of lemon juice just before serving).

Spinach

Spinach is among the most convenient vegetables to prepare, with its prepicked, prewashed, prepackaged getup. (Be aware that you're paying as much as $4 per pound for this spinach, when you can get an unwashed, unpicked bunch for half the price. And I strongly suggest you wash bagged spinach or greens anyway.) Bagged or bunched, spinach is finally getting its due as a lovely-tasting vegetable that is equally wonderful slow cooked, flashed in a pan, or tossed as a green salad. The tender flat-leaf variety is slightly better than the more common large, crinkly-leaf type, but more important is where it's grown: Local is better. It's in season in the early spring, but supermarkets carry it year-round.

Buying and storing: Buy vibrantly colored green, crisp leaves; those with the pink-hued stem bases are even better (rinse them well and cook them with the leaves). Store wrapped loosely in plastic in the refrigerator; use it before it turns slimy or wilts.

Preparing: If it's in a bunch, either chop off all the stems (if you're in a hurry) or untie the bunch and pick off only the tough stems, leaving the tender ones on. Wash very thoroughly in several changes of water, especially if it was bunched, as there may be clumps of mud or sand in between the leaves. Chop or slice it after cooking.

Best cooking methods: Steaming and sautéing.

When is it done? As soon as it wilts, though you can cook it longer if you like for extra tenderness (long-and-slow-cooked spinach in butter is dreamy).

Other vegetables to substitute: Arugula, beet greens, or chard.

Spinach with Chiles

MAKES: 4 servings
TIME: 20 minutes

Ⓕ Ⓜ Ⓥ

A simple, flavorful preparation that can be cooked slowly or quickly, with or without liquid (see the variations).

Other vegetables you can use: almost any greens, chopped, though most will take a little longer to cook.

2 tablespoons peanut or neutral oil, like grapeseed or corn

2 dried red chiles, or to taste

5 cloves garlic, peeled, or to taste

1 pound spinach, well washed, large stems removed

Salt and freshly ground black pepper

❶ Put the oil in a large skillet or casserole over medium heat. When hot, add the chiles and garlic and cook until they sizzle, just 30 seconds or so.

❷ Raise the heat to medium-high, then stir in the spinach and about $1/4$ cup water (or stock). Cook, stirring occasionally, until the spinach wilts and is tender, about

10 minutes. Sprinkle with salt and pepper and serve hot or warm.

Spinach with Chiles and Coconut Milk. Like spicy, vegan creamed spinach, nice with a teaspoon of curry powder (to make your own, see page 815), added with the chiles and garlic: Step 1 remains the same. In Step 2, use 1 cup coconut milk in place of the water. Cook slowly for about 30 minutes, stirring occasionally, until the spinach is very soft and tender and the liquid almost evaporated.

Spinach with Currants and Nuts

MAKES: 4 servings
TIME: 20 minutes

Ⓕ Ⓜ Ⓥ

A Mediterranean classic, astringent from the spinach, sweet from the currants (or raisins), crunchy with nuts, and just as good at room temperature as it is hot.

Other vegetables you can use: almost any greens, chopped, though most will take a little longer to cook; broccoli, cooked until quite tender, is also good this way.

1/4 cup dried currants or raisins

1 pound spinach, well washed and trimmed of large stems

1/4 cup extra virgin olive oil

1 teaspoon minced garlic (optional)

1/4 cup broken walnuts or pine nuts, briefly toasted (see page 321)

Salt and freshly ground black pepper

❶ Soak the currants or raisins in warm water for about 10 minutes while you clean and cook the spinach. Steam or parboil the spinach (see page 239) until tender, less than 5 minutes.

❷ When the spinach is cool enough to handle, squeeze all the excess moisture from it; chop it roughly.

Put the olive oil in a large skillet over medium heat. When hot, add the garlic if you're using it and cook, stirring occasionally, until golden, about 3 minutes. Add the spinach and raise the heat to medium-high. Cook, stirring occasionally, for about 2 minutes. Drain the currants and add them, along with the nuts.

❸ Reduce the heat to medium and cook, stirring occasionally, for another 3 or 4 minutes, until everything glistens. Sprinkle with salt and pepper and serve hot or at room temperature.

Spinach with Fresh Cheese and Yogurt

Saag Paneer

MAKES: 4 servings
TIME: 30 minutes with premade cheese

Ⓕ

Great made according to the recipe, this can also made without any special ingredients if you like. The chickpea flour "roux" thickens and flavors the yogurt sauce and keeps it from separating, but regular flour does the trick just as well. And if you don't have any fresh cheese handy or don't have time to make a batch, use cubes of mozzarella or feta. Serve this with the basic version of Rice Pilaf (page 511) or Biryani (page 512), with some Raw Onion or Tomato Chutney on the side (page 783 or 785).

Other vegetables you can use: beet greens, chard, or kale.

1 recipe Fresh Cheese, the Easy Way (page 230; you'll have leftovers), or 6 ounces mozzarella or feta cheese

1 pound spinach, well washed and trimmed

1/4 cup extra virgin olive oil

1/4 cup chickpea or wheat flour

Salt and freshly ground black pepper

2 tablespoons garam masala or curry powder (to make your own, see page 815)

2 cups yogurt, preferably whole milk

Ⓕ Fast   Ⓜ Make Ahead   Ⓥ Vegan

❶ Cut the cheese into $1/2$-inch cubes. You should have about $1^1/_2$ cups. Boil and shock the spinach (see page 241); drain well and roughly chop.

❷ Put the oil and flour in a large pot, sprinkle with salt and pepper, and turn the heat to medium-low. Cook, stirring frequently, until the flour darkens a bit and becomes fragrant, about 5 minutes, lowering the heat if necessary to keep the mixture from scorching.

❸ Stir in the spice mix, then whisk in the yogurt and raise the heat a bit. Cook, stirring frequently, until the yogurt has heated through and thickened a bit, a couple minutes; then fold in the spinach and cheese and cook and stir until hot, another couple of minutes. Taste, adjust the seasoning, and serve.

Baked Spinach with Fresh Cheese and Yogurt. Less stirring, with a little crust on top: Heat the oven to 400°F. Grease a shallow baking or gratin dish. Follow the recipe. In Step 3, stir together the seasoning blend and yogurt, then turn off the heat and fold in the spinach and cheese without waiting for everything to get hot. Taste and adjust the seasoning if necessary. Put the mixture in the prepared dish and pop it into the oven. Bake until hot and bubbly, 15 to 20 minutes, and serve.

Squash—Summer

Yellow Squash, Zucchini, Pattypan (Scalloped), and Chayote (Mirliton)

A quintessential summer vegetable (technically a fruit), summer squash are tender and deliciously mild; great steamed, boiled, sautéed, stir-fried, braised, breaded and fried, roasted, and grilled—often all they need is a pat of butter or a drizzle of olive oil and some salt. In fact, it's rare to feature them alone any other way beyond these simplest preparations. In more complicated vegetable dishes, they're often used as a component.

Beyond the commonplace yellow squash and zucchini, there is the flying saucer–shaped pattypan with its cute scalloped edge, bright colors (yellow and light or dark green), and diminutive size. You want young and tender pattypans under 3 inches in diameter; the older ones, usually white, have less flavorful flesh and tough skin.

And there's also the chayote, or mirliton as it's called in the South. This funny-looking pear-shaped gourd has a bright green, wrinkled exterior skin (sometimes covered with spines) and a pale yellow to white semitranslucent flesh. Its texture is somewhat like that of a melon; the flavor is so mild it picks up that of whatever you cook it with. Use it raw in salads or cooked like any summer squash.

Buying and storing: Look for plump, firm, and unblemished specimens. Store wrapped loosely in plastic in the refrigerator; use as quickly as possible, especially if they are fresh from the garden or farm.

For yellow squash and zucchini: Usually the smaller and more uniformly shaped ones have better flavor and smaller seeds.

For pattypans: Go for small and tender specimens; larger than 3 or 4 inches across and the exterior skin becomes tough.

For chayote: Heavy wrinkles are a sign of being left on the vine too long, so it's best to go with less wrinkled ones.

Preparing: For yellow squash and zucchini: Trim the ends and slice or chop as you like. If the squash is flabby, salt it as you would cucumber (see page 46).

For pattypans: Leave whole if tender enough or halve them.

For chayote: Peeling is optional, but I always do it. Cut in half through the stem end and remove the seed. Leave as halves or chop or slice as you like.

Best cooking methods: Steaming, sautéing, braising (for chayote), roasting, frying, and grilling.

When is it done? When tender but not falling apart; pierce with a skewer or thin-bladed knife to check.

Other vegetables to substitute: Summer squashes are fairly interchangeable.

Sautéed Zucchini or Chayote

MAKES: 4 servings
TIME: 20 minutes

This is the most basic way to cook zucchini, and an excellent introduction to something new. Chayote (also called *mirliton*) looks like a pale avocado but cooks like a summer squash. You can treat it pretty much the same way as any summer squash, but you should peel and pit it first. You can also use pattypan squash (no need to peel).

3 tablespoons extra virgin olive oil

1 tablespoon minced garlic

2 medium zucchini or chayotes (which should be peeled and pitted), sliced

Salt and freshly ground black pepper

2 teaspoons freshly squeezed lemon juice, or to taste

Chopped parsley leaves for garnish

1 Put the oil in a skillet over medium heat. When hot, add the garlic and cook until it sizzles, about a minute. Add the zucchini, sprinkle with salt and pepper, and cook, turning occasionally, until the pieces are tender, 10 to 15 minutes.

2 Just before serving, sprinkle with the lemon juice, then taste and adjust the seasoning; garnish and serve.

FOLDING SUMMER SQUASH IN PARCHMENT

Whether you use parchment paper or foil, crimp the edges of the package tightly to keep as much moisture inside as possible.

Summer Squash and Herbs in Parchment

MAKES: 4 servings
TIME: 30 minutes

Using parchment packages is a great way to reduce fat without losing flavor. The parchment seals in the moisture so the vegetables both steam and simmer in their juices. You can use foil too, though it's not nearly as pretty. If you don't feel like cooking in parchment or foil, just use a covered casserole for very similar results.

Add slices of squeezed tofu (see page 640) to bulk up the dish and add protein; squeezing the tofu first allows it to absorb some of the vegetable juices. This is a vegan dish if you use oil instead of butter.

Other vegetables you can use: chayote, mushrooms, broccoli, cauliflower, asparagus, snap and snow peas, spinach, arugula, or watercress.

$1/_2$ small onion, thinly sliced

2 sprigs fresh tarragon or basil

$3/_4$ pound summer squash, trimmed and sliced $1/_4$ inch thick

$3/_4$ pound zucchini, trimmed and sliced $1/_4$ inch thick

1 tablespoon extra virgin olive oil or butter (optional)

Salt and freshly ground black pepper

Lemon wedges

1 Preheat the oven to 375°F. Cut 4 parchment paper rectangles about 6 × 10 inches, fold in half to crease, then open again. On one half of each rectangle, layer portions of the onion, herbs, and squash, keeping the vegetables close to the center; then drizzle with the olive oil or dot with the butter and sprinkle with salt and pepper.

2 Seal the packages by rolling together the open edges and put them on a baking sheet; bake until the squash is tender, about 20 minutes. Immediately serve the squash in the packages with lemon wedges; be careful of the steam when opening them.

F Fast   **M** Make Ahead   **V** Vegan

Lemon-Scented Pea Shoots in Parchment. Use spinach or watercress if you don't have pea shoots: Omit the onion and herbs; add 1 teaspoon grated lemon zest and 1 clove garlic, thinly sliced. Substitute pea shoots for the squash. Cook for only 5 minutes or until the pea shoots have just wilted.

Shiitakes in Parchment. Any fresh mushroom will work here: Substitute 5 or 6 shiso leaves for the tarragon if you like, stemmed and sliced shiitakes for the squash, and 2 teaspoons dark sesame oil for the olive oil. Add 1 teaspoon minced peeled fresh ginger or garlic if you like too.

Squash—Winter

A member of the gourd family (and technically speaking a fruit) and in season in fall through spring, these squash are marked by their tough skins, unwieldy shapes and sizes, hard and vibrantly colored flesh, edible seeds, and creamy texture when cooked. There are many varieties in this class of vegetables, but the most noteworthy and accessible are the butternut, acorn, pumpkin, spaghetti, delicata, kabocha, Hubbard, crookneck, and calabaza.

The butternut is by far the most convenient as it's easily peeled and cut (no cleavers required), and its flavor and texture are wonderful. Other squash can be daunting to prepare, but don't be afraid to waste some of the flesh to make peeling easier. Winter squash are cheap, so if you have to hack off huge chunks and toss them to get usable flesh, that's not so horrible (and far better than cutting yourself trying to peel all the ridges, bumps, and curves). Or don't peel them; you can roast or steam whole squash and simply scoop out the soft flesh (see the recipes that follow).

Buying and storing: Winter squash should be firm and heavy; avoid any with soft spots, cracks, or punctures. Store in a cool, dry place (not in the fridge) and use when you can, though often they'll keep for months.

Preparing: If you choose to peel winter squash (you don't have to), use a sturdy vegetable peeler or a paring

5 MORE IDEAS FOR VEGETABLES IN PARCHMENT

See the recipe on the previous page. Keep the flavors simple and don't overload the packages with the aromatics.

VEGETABLES	AROMATICS	SEASONINGS
1½ pounds fennel, shaved	1 small onion, thinly sliced	2 teaspoons Citrus Sprinkle (page 818) or minced orange zest
1½ pounds tomatoes, thickly sliced	1 leek, sliced	2 teaspoons chopped fresh marjoram leaves; 3 tablespoons roughly chopped pitted olives
1½ pounds sliced mixed bell peppers (red, orange, yellow, and green)	1 small onion, thinly sliced; 2 teaspoons minced garlic	3 sprigs fresh cilantro; 1 teaspoon chili powder (to make your own, see page 814)
1½ pounds artichoke hearts, sliced	1 teaspoon minced garlic (optional)	2 or 3 sprigs fresh basil or mint
1½ pounds butternut squash, peeled and sliced	2 tablespoons minced peeled fresh ginger	1 tablespoon curry powder or garam masala (to make your own, see page 815 or 816); or ground cumin or a pinch of saffron

knife for butternut; and for tougher, ridged squashes, set the squash on its flat end or cut off an end to create a flat, stable bottom. Use a sharp knife (the larger the squash, the larger the knife should be) and cut off slices of the skin starting from the top where the vegetable starts to curve and slice down to the cutting board; cut off strips around the entire vegetable and then chop off the unpeeled ends.

Use a cleaver or very large, heavy knife to split the squash in half. Scoop out the seeds and stringy fiber and discard or roast the seeds (see page 321).

Best cooking methods: Steaming, braising, braising and glazing, and roasting.

When is it done? When very tender and nicely browned (if panfrying or roasting) but not waterlogged (if boiling).

Other vegetables to substitute: Sweet potato, yam, carrot, or waxy potato.

With winter squash, a little waste is inevitable, so just hack away at the skin with a knife; most squash are simply too tough (and oddly shaped) for a vegetable peeler.

Butternut Squash, Braised and Glazed

MAKES: 4 servings
TIME: 30 minutes

  Ⓥ

This is your go-to recipe for everyday winter squash; it will work with any variety, but I usually turn to butternut because it's so much easier to deal with than all the others. Once you peel and cut the squash, you braise it in a small amount of liquid, then boil off the remaining moisture to glaze it. The main recipe, variations, and list will get you started, but you'll come up with your own ideas in no time.

Other vegetables you can use: any winter squash (except spaghetti), though they will all be more difficult to cut and peel than butternut.

2 tablespoons extra virgin olive oil

1 tablespoon minced garlic

1½ pounds butternut or other winter squash, peeled and cut into ½- to 1-inch cubes

¼ cup vegetable stock (pages 101–102) or water

Salt and freshly ground black pepper

Chopped parsley leaves for garnish

① Put the oil and garlic in a large, deep skillet with a tight-fitting lid over medium heat. When the garlic begins to color, add the squash and stock and sprinkle with salt and pepper. Bring to a boil, cover, and turn the heat down to low. Cook, stirring once or twice, until the squash is tender, about 15 minutes.

② Uncover the pan and raise the heat to medium-high. Cook, shaking the pan occasionally and stirring somewhat less often, until all the liquid is evaporated and the squash has begun to brown, 5 to 10 minutes. Turn the heat back down to low and cook until the squash is as browned and crisp as you like. Taste and adjust the seasoning, garnish, and serve.

Butternut Squash with Soy. Rich tasting and deeply colored: Instead of the vegetable stock, use 2 tablespoons soy sauce and 2 tablespoons water. Use ginger instead of garlic or along with it. Garnish with sliced scallion and sesame seeds instead of the parsley if you like.

Butternut Squash with Pesto. The squash stays coated in the sauce, making a terrific dish to toss with pasta: Increase the stock to ½ cup and omit the garlic if you like. In Step 2, when you uncover the pan, stir in ½ cup Traditional Pesto (page 768).

Ⓕ Fast   Ⓜ Make Ahead   Ⓥ Vegan

Butternut Squash with Coconut Milk and Curry. A saucy dish, perfect with basmati rice: Use peanut or a neutral oil, like grapeseed or corn, instead of the olive oil and increase the quantity to 3 tablespoons. Replace the stock with 1 cup coconut milk, either made from scratch (page 423), or canned. In Step 1, when you put the garlic in the oil, add 1 tablespoon minced peeled fresh ginger and 2 tablespoons curry powder (to make your own, see pages 815–816). Garnish with cilantro instead of parsley if you like.

Butternut Squash, Thai Style. Also saucy; serve with Steamed Sticky Rice (page 507) or toss with wide rice noodles: Use peanut or neutral oil, like grapeseed or corn, instead of the olive oil and increase the quantity to 3 tablespoons. Replace the stock with 1 cup coconut milk, either made from scratch (page 423), or canned. In Step 1, when you put the garlic in the oil, add 1 minced fresh chile (like jalapeño or Thai), or to taste, or hot red pepper flakes or cayenne to taste, and 1 tablespoon minced peeled fresh ginger. Add 2 tablespoons peanut butter along with the coconut milk. Garnish with cilantro instead of parsley if you like.

Butternut Squash with Cream and Walnuts. Luxurious; perfect with whole grains like barley or wheat berries for a hearty meal: Instead of stock, use $^1/_2$ cup heavy cream. In Step 2, when you uncover the pan, stir in $^1/_4$ cup chopped walnuts.

Butternut Squash with Saffron and Almonds. Great tossed with any cooked medium- or short-grain rice and served at room temperature, as a salad: In Step 1, add a pinch of saffron to the pan along with the stock and squash. In Step 2, when you uncover the pan, stir in $^1/_2$ cup chopped almonds. Proceed with the recipe.

7 Simple Ways to Flavor Butternut Squash

Just increase the oil in the basic recipe to 3 tablespoons and stir in any of the following when you uncover the pan in Step 2:

1. $^1/_2$ cup chopped black olives
2. 1 minced fresh chile (like jalapeño or Thai), or to taste, or hot red pepper flakes or cayenne to taste
3. 2 tablespoons curry powder or similar spice blend (to make your own, see pages 815–816)
4. $^1/_2$ cup minced fresh light herbs, like mint, chervil, or basil
5. 1 tablespoon minced fresh pungent herbs, like rosemary, oregano, sage, tarragon, or thyme
6. $^1/_2$ cup chopped nuts (any kind, including coconut)
7. $^1/_4$ cup miso

Whole Winter Squash, Cooked Three Ways

MAKES: 4 to 10 servings, depending on the size of the squash

TIME: 1 to 2 hours, again depending size, completely unattended

Here are the easiest ways to cook and extract the flesh from any winter squash, even the large, thick-skinned varieties, like Hubbard and pumpkin. Oven roasting and steaming whole squash spare you the daunting task of cutting up a raw squash. The second variation describes the more traditional "cut, seed, and roast" method.

With all three methods, the resulting squash will be soft and silky, perfect for purées, soups, or desserts. You can use any quantity or weight of squash here, though of course you're limited by the size of your oven or pot. Expect each pound to yield about a cup of mashed squash.

Other vegetables you can use: eggplant, but it will take a lot less time.

1 or more whole winter squash, 1 to 8 pounds

① Preheat the oven to 375°F. Rinse the squash. Use a sharp narrow knife, ice pick, or long-tined fork to poke several holes in the top of the squash around the stem.

2 Put on a rimmed baking sheet or shallow roasting pan. Roast the squash, undisturbed, for at least 30 minutes. When the sides start to soften and collapse, move it around or turn it over to promote even cooking. Continue roasting until deeply colored and quite soft. Small squash will take 45 minutes or so, large ones up to 1 1/2 hours.

3 Remove the squash from the oven and set it aside to cool almost completely before handling. Cut in half and scoop out the seeds and stringy fiber. Then scoop out the flesh. Use immediately or store, tightly covered, in the refrigerator for several days or in the freezer for several months.

Whole Winter Squash, Steamed. Best for soups or other dishes where the added moisture can be beneficial: Prepare the squash as described in Step 1. Set up a steamer (see page 25). Pour in enough water to cover the bottom of the pot, but leave the container for the food dry and put the squash on top, stem side up. Cover the pot and bring to a boil, then lower the heat so the water bubbles vigorously. Check the pot every so often to make sure there's still water in the bottom; after a half hour or so, turn the squash over (unless it's too big to do so, in which case don't bother). Cooking time will be about the same as for roasting. When the squash is done, put the squash on a plate to cook and proceed with the recipe from Step 3.

Roasted Squash Pieces in the Shell. Slightly faster, with most of your time spent preparing the squash: Preheat the oven to 400°F. Cover a rimmed baking sheet or shallow roasting pan with foil. Cut and seed the squash(es) as directed on page 363. You should be left with squash halves or large pieces. Put the squash in the pan, cut side down, and roast until it's starting to get tender, 20 to 30 minutes, depending on the variety. Turn the pieces over and roast until done, another 20 minutes or so. Cool a bit, then scoop out the flesh.

Winter Squash Slices, Roasted

MAKES: 4 servings
TIME: 30 to 40 minutes

This is prepared most easily and attractively with the top half of butternut squash, the nice seedless cylinder. But as long as you can cut 1/4-inch slices, this will work with any winter squash or root vegetable. It's easy, it looks nice, and it's delicious. It's also vegan if you use oil instead of butter.

Other vegetables you can use: sweet potatoes or any root vegetable.

1 1/2 pounds winter squash, peeled and cut into 1/4-inch-thick slices

4 to 6 tablespoons extra virgin olive oil or melted butter

Salt and freshly ground black pepper

1 Preheat the oven to 400°F. Put half the oil or butter on the bottom of a roasting pan and arrange the squash slices in one layer on top. Sprinkle with salt and pepper and drizzle on the remaining oil or butter.

2 Roast without turning for 20 to 30 minutes, or until the squash is tender. Serve hot or warm.

Panfried Pumpkin with Tomato Sauce

MAKES: 4 to 6 servings
TIME: 45 minutes

This is a straightforward braise: You sear the pumpkin first, then remove it, make a sauce in the same pan, and finally return the pumpkin to finish cooking. The basic dish is simple, but you can garnish and season as you like for a more elaborate presentation; the variations are quite terrific. Serve this over rice or other plain cooked grain or simply with a baked potato or thick slice of bread.

F Fast   **M** Make Ahead   **V** Vegan

Other vegetables you can use: any sturdy winter squash, like kabocha, delicata, calabaza, banana, crookneck, or Hubbard.

$1/4$ cup neutral oil, like grapeseed or corn, plus more if needed

2 pounds pumpkin, peeled, seeded, and cut into large chunks

Salt and freshly ground black pepper

1 large onion, chopped

2 tablespoons minced garlic

2 tablespoons minced fresh chile, or to taste, or hot red pepper flakes or cayenne to taste

$1/2$ cup red wine, any vegetable stock (pages 101–102), or water

3 cups chopped ripe tomato (canned is fine; don't bother to drain), more or less

Chopped parsley leaves for garnish

1 Put the $1/4$ cup oil in a deep Dutch oven or other pot with a tight-fitting lid over medium-high heat. Add some of the pumpkin, taking care not to overcrowd; you'll need to work in batches. Sprinkle with salt and pepper. Cook until the pumpkin is well browned and releases from the pan easily, 5 minutes or so. Then turn and cook the other side the same way. As the chunks cook, transfer them to a plate and add more pumpkin to the pan. Add more oil if necessary to keep the pumpkin from sticking.

2 When all the pumpkin is cooked, pour off all but 2 or 3 tablespoons of the oil and add the onion, garlic, and chile. Cook, stirring frequently, until softened, about 3 minutes.

3 Pour in the wine, scraping up any browned bits from the bottom of the pan. Let the liquid boil off for a few minutes and thicken, then stir in the tomato and its juice. Bring the sauce to a boil, then lower the heat a bit so it bubbles along nicely. Cook, stirring occasionally, until it thickens, about 10 minutes.

4 Return the pumpkin to the pot and let the mixture come back to a boil. Cover and turn the heat to low. Cook, stirring once or twice, until the sauce has thick-

ened even more and the pumpkin is tender but not mushy, about 10 minutes. Taste and adjust the seasoning, garnish, and serve.

Panfried Pumpkin with Tomato Sauce, Yogurt, and Mint. Terrific with Stuck-Pot Rice and Lentils with Pita Crust or Stuck-Pot Rice with Potato Crust (page 525 or 526): Omit the parsley garnish. Follow the recipe all the way through Step 3. While the pumpkin is cooking, whisk 1 cup yogurt (preferably whole milk) with $1/2$ cup chopped fresh mint leaves and season with salt and pepper. When the pumpkin is ready, drizzle with a little of the yogurt mixture, but don't stir it in. Pass the remaining yogurt at the table.

Panfried Pumpkin with Tomato Sauce, Parmesan, and Basil. Great over pasta or for sandwiches, with a little melted mozzarella: Omit the parsley garnish. Follow the recipe all the way through Step 3. While the pumpkin is cooking, grate about $1 1/2$ cups of Parmesan cheese and chop a small bunch of basil. When the pumpkin is ready, sprinkle with a little of the Parmesan and all of the basil, but don't stir them in. Pass the remaining cheese at the table.

Panfried Pumpkin with Tomato Sauce, Cocoa, and Pumpkin Seeds. Sort of like a quick mole: Omit the parsley garnish. Follow the recipe all the way through Step 3. While the pumpkin is cooking, toast 1 cup pumpkin seeds (see page 321), tossing until golden. Chop a small bunch of cilantro. When the pumpkin is ready, stir in the pumpkin seeds along with $1/4$ cup unsweetened cocoa powder and 1 teaspoon ground cinnamon. Garnish with cilantro and serve.

Panfried Pumpkin with Cranberries and Pistachios. Festive all through the fall: Instead of the tomatoes, combine 3 cups cranberries with 2 cups freshly squeezed orange juice. Omit the parsley garnish. Follow the recipe through Step 3, adding the cranberries and juice in place of the tomato. Proceed with the recipe and garnish with $1/2$ cup chopped pistachios instead of the parsley.

Braised Winter Squash in Caramel Sauce

MAKES: 4 servings

TIME: 30 minutes

Like Braised Tofu in Caramel Sauce (page 650), this dish employs a Vietnamese technique that uses sugar to create a unique sauce that perfectly balances sweet and bitter flavors. Here the seasonings are a little different, adding a bit of heat and acidity to the mix. Serve this with simply cooked whole grains, like millet, barley, or wheat or rye berries (see page 537).

Other vegetables you can use: sweet potatoes or yams or any waxy potatoes.

1 cup sugar

$^1/_4$ cup sherry vinegar

2 tablespoons minced garlic

$^1/_2$ cup chopped red onion

1$^1/_2$ to 2 pounds any winter squash, cleaned and cut into 1-inch cubes (about 4 cups)

Salt and freshly ground black pepper

1 tablespoon minced fresh chile (like jalapeño or Thai), or to taste, or hot red pepper flakes or cayenne to taste

① Put a large, deep skillet with a tight-fitting lid (preferably nonstick or cast-iron) over medium heat and add the sugar and a tablespoon or two of water. Cook, gently shaking the pan occasionally, until the sugar liquefies and begins to bubble, about 10 minutes. Cook for another minute or so, until the melted sugar darkens; turn off the heat. Mix the vinegar with $^3/_4$ cup water; carefully, and at arm's length, add the liquid and turn the heat to medium-high. Cook, stirring constantly, until the caramel melts into the liquid, about 2 minutes.

② Add the garlic and onion and cook, stirring occasionally, until they soften, about 5 minutes. Add the squash, sprinkle with salt and pepper, and stir to coat.

③ Turn the heat down to medium-low, cover, and cook, undisturbed, for about 3 minutes. Uncover the pan, stir, and cook, uncovered, stirring occasionally, until the sauce thickens and the squash can be pierced easily with a fork, about 10 minutes. Stir in the chile. Taste, adjust the seasoning, and serve.

Braised Winter Squash in Caramel Sauce with Balsamic Vinegar and Rosemary. Great on top of Simple Risotto (page 517): Instead of the sherry vinegar, use $^1/_2$ cup balsamic vinegar and decrease the water in Step 1 to $^1/_2$ cup. In Step 3, instead of the chile, stir in 1 tablespoon minced fresh rosemary leaves.

Spicy Winter Squash Galette

MAKES: 6 to 8 servings

TIME: 1$^1/_2$ hours, largely unattended

Here's a simple savory free-form pie that tastes even better than it looks. And since you can make it ahead, it's great for entertaining. Serve it with a dollop of sour cream and pass a bowl of salsa at the table. Add a pot of Beer-Glazed Black Beans (page 585) or something similar and you've got a meal.

Other vegetables you can use for this recipe: sweet potatoes.

2 tablespoons extra virgin olive oil

1 medium red onion, chopped

2 tablespoons minced garlic

Salt and freshly ground black pepper

1 tablespoon chili powder (to make your own, see page 814)

$^1/_4$ cup tomato paste

$^1/_2$ cup wine, vegetable stock (pages 101–102), or water

2 pounds any firm winter squash, like kabocha, pumpkin, or Hubbard, peeled, seeded, and cut into 1-inch cubes (about 4 cups)

F Fast   **M** Make Ahead   **V** Vegan

Dough for 1 Savory Piecrust (page 867), chilled but not rolled

① Preheat the oven to 350°F. Grease a large rimless baking sheet or line it with a piece of parchment.

② Put the oil in a deep skillet over medium-high heat. Add the onion and cook, stirring occasionally, until softened, 2 or 3 minutes; add the garlic, stirring constantly, and cook for another minute. Sprinkle with salt and pepper and stir in the chili powder and tomato paste. Cook and stir until fragrant, less than a minute, then stir in the wine and the squash. Bring the mixture just to a boil, give it a few good stirs, then cover and remove the pan from the heat.

③ Roll the piecrust into a circle at least 12 inches in diameter. It's okay if it's not perfectly round. Use the rolling pin to transfer it to the baking sheet (see page 864). Stir the squash mixture again; taste and adjust the seasoning if necessary and carefully spread it on top of the crust, leaving about 3 inches free all the way around the edge. Fold the sides up over the filling. You should have a big circle open in the top. (See the illustrations for "Free-Form Crusts," page 868.)

④ Bake the galette until the crust is nicely browned and the insides are bubbly, 50 to 60 minutes. Cool a bit before slicing or serve at room temperature.

Sunchokes

Jerusalem Artichokes

Not artichokes and not from Jerusalem, these are actually tubers from a type of sunflower native to North America. *Sunchoke* and *sunroot* are arguably more accurate names and are becoming the preferred terms.

Sunchokes look like nubby little fingerling or new potatoes, with a thin, tan-colored skin and firm, off-white, crisp flesh like a raw potato. The flavor is mild and reminiscent of artichoke hearts, and they can be eaten raw and—even better—cooked. Unfortunately, sunchokes contain a type of sugar, inulin, that can cause quite severe flatulence in people with sensitivity to this (you'll know soon enough whether you're among them).

Buying and storing: Look for firm, unshriveled specimens; the smoother, the easier to peel or wash. Store wrapped tightly in plastic in the refrigerator; they'll keep for weeks.

Preparing: Peeling is optional; I prefer to just wash them well. Chop or slice as needed.

Best cooking methods: Sautéing (preferably after a brief simmering) and braising and glazing.

When is it done? When quite tender; taste one.

Other vegetables to substitute: Radishes or jícama when raw or cooked; parsnips, turnips, or potatoes when cooked.

Crisp-Cooked Sunchokes

MAKES: 4 servings
TIME: About 30 minutes

Like pan-cooked potatoes, only with more flavor. Some people peel sunchokes, but I never bother; not only is it a total hassle, but you lose about half the flesh in the process. Just scrub them well before cooking.

Other vegetables you can use: waxy potatoes.

About 1½ pounds sunchokes

3 or 4 tablespoons extra virgin olive oil

Salt and freshly ground black pepper

1 tablespoon minced garlic or shallot or ¼ cup chopped onion

Chopped parsley leaves for garnish

Lemon wedges

① Scrub the sunchokes well, then trim them of any hard or discolored spots. Slice about ⅛ inch thick.

② Put the oil in a large, deep skillet over medium heat. When hot, add the sunchokes, a few slices at a time, spreading them out around the pan; sprinkle with salt and pepper. Cook, stirring and turning occasionally and adjusting the heat so they sizzle without burning, until tender and just about brown, about 20 minutes. Add the garlic and continue cooking until nicely browned and tender, about 5 minutes more. Taste and adjust the seasoning, then garnish with parsley and serve with lemon wedges.

Broiled Sunchokes with Garlic or Parmesan

MAKES: 4 servings

TIME: About 40 minutes

Ⓜ

Parboiling the sunchokes before broiling makes this a two-step process, but each is a snap and you can let the partially cooked vegetable sit in the fridge for a day or two before finishing, which makes the dish more convenient. I'd use either the garlic or the Parmesan here, but not both, so as not to mask all the flavor of the vegetable. The garlic option, obviously, will make this vegan.

Other vegetables you can use: waxy potatoes.

Salt

About 1 ½ pounds sunchokes, well scrubbed

3 tablespoons extra virgin olive oil or butter

1 tablespoon minced garlic (optional)

Freshly ground black pepper

½ cup freshly grated Parmesan (optional)

Chopped parsley leaves for garnish

❶ Bring a large pot of water to a boil; salt it. Add the sunchokes in descending order of size: largest first, followed by somewhat smaller ones a minute or so later, and so on. Cook just until they lose their crispness; poke them with a skewer or thin-bladed knife and you'll be able to tell. Don't overcook or they will become mushy. Remove them as they finish (they will take between 2 and 10 minutes to become tender, depending on their size,

and almost never all become tender at once) and plunge them into ice water. Slice in half lengthwise. Preheat the broiler.

❷ Use half the olive oil or butter to grease a baking dish, then lay the sunchokes in it, tossing with the garlic if you're using it; drizzle with more olive oil or dot with butter. Sprinkle with salt and pepper and the Parmesan if you're using it, then run under the broiler until nicely browned. Garnish and serve hot or warm.

Sweet Potatoes and Yams

First things first: A yam is not a sweet potato. Though they are both tubers and can look very similar, sweet potatoes and yams are two different species of plants. Not that it matters much. The names *yams* and *sweet potatoes* are used interchangeably in the South, and canned "yams" are really sweet potatoes; simply put, take any use of the word *yam* with a grain of salt—it's most likely a sweet potato.

Sweet potatoes are common and sold year-round in every supermarket. There are two basic varieties: one has light tan skin, yellow flesh, and a drier, less sweet texture and flavor; the other type has a reddish brown skin, bright orange flesh, and is soft and sweet when cooked. Other specialty varieties of sweet potato range in color from purple to rose to white flesh.

Real yams, on the other hand, are seldom grown in the United States, nor are they widely available here. When small they are hard to distinguish from sweet potatoes, but they can grow to enormous proportions (like over a hundred pounds) and are often sold cut into chunks and wrapped in plastic (look in Latino markets, where they might be called *ñame*). When cooked their texture ranges from sweet and moist to dry and mealy, depending on type.

Buying and storing: Sweet potatoes should be plump and unshriveled. Avoid any with sprouts. Do not refrigerate; they are best in a cool, dark, dry place. They're fairly perishable for a tuber; use within a couple of weeks, sooner if you can.

Preparing: Peel if necessary; slice and chop as you like.

Best cooking methods: Baking, braising, and roasting.

When is it done? When very tender.

Other vegetables to substitute: Potatoes, carrots, parsnips, or any tropical tuber (see page 377).

Sweet Potatoes, Simply Cooked

MAKES: 4 servings

TIME: 1 hour or less

For basic use, sweet potatoes can be baked, boiled (or steamed), or microwaved. Baked is the best way if you're just going to eat them plain or with butter, but for mashing or use in other recipes, boiling and microwaving are easier.

2 large or 4 medium sweet potatoes, about 1¹/₂ to
    2 pounds total

Salt and freshly ground black pepper

For baking: Preheat the oven to 425°F. Wash the sweet potatoes and poke each with a thin-bladed knife in a few places. Put them in a foil-lined baking pan and bake, turning once, until very tender, about an hour. Serve immediately, with salt and pepper and, if you like, butter.

For boiling or steaming: Peel the potatoes, cut into large chunks, and cook according to Boiled or Steamed Root Vegetables or Tubers (page 240). They'll probably take 20 minutes or less; don't overcook or they'll fall apart.

For microwaving: Peel the potatoes. Cut into large chunks and put on a plate or in a glass baking dish with a couple of tablespoons of water (and a little butter if you like). Cover and microwave on high for at least 10 minutes, or until soft.

Swiss Chard (*see* Chard, page 285)

Tomatillos
Mexican Green Tomatoes

A member of the nightshade family, which makes tomatillo a relative of tomatoes, this green, Ping-Pong ball–sized, tomato-looking fruit has a papery, light brown husk. It's widely used in Mexican cooking, and almost always when firm, green, tangy, and herbaceous (they're yellow and softer when ripe, and there's also a rarely seen purple variety). Their zingy flavor makes excellent raw and cooked green salsas (see Fresh and Cooked Tomatillo Salsa, pages 751 and 788). Although available year-round, they aren't always carried in supermarkets but are always in Latin markets. Canned tomatillos are a decent substitute for fresh.

Buying and storing: Best in summer, but available throughout the year. Look for tightly wrapped husks covering firm, unshriveled, and green fruit. Store in a paper bag in the refrigerator; they'll keep for a couple of weeks.

Preparing: Tear off the husks and rinse off the sticky resin. No need to core. Slice, chop, purée, or leave whole.

Other vegetables to substitute: Green tomatoes and, in a pinch, ripe tomatoes.

Tomatoes

Getting a perfectly ripe and delicious fresh tomato isn't easy: You must wait for the fleeting tomato season, and you must buy locally grown. At peak season, farmer's markets are goldmines of all sorts of tomatoes, and you can often sample the product before buying.

Usually when we think of tomatoes, we picture big, fat red specimens, but tomatoes come in a large array of colors, shapes, and sizes. Red is the most common

They're the darlings of restaurants and farmer's markets across America: brightly colored, often misshapen, usually great-tasting fruits and vegetables known collectively as "heirlooms."

As the name implies, heirloom varieties of fruits and vegetables—and other plants for that matter—were passed down from generation to generation by home gardeners who saved seeds or clippings. When supermarkets became the "normal" way to purchase fresh and processed produce, these varieties lost favor to hybrids that were easier to pick, ship, store, and sell in the mass marketplace. Over time the name has evolved to mean virtually any fruit or vegetable variety that is unusual—often rare—and great tasting. And usually ugly, to boot, because, like most homegrown vegetables, heirlooms are raised for flavor, not appearance.

Even though heirlooms are back in style, they can be tough to find and damned expensive to buy. Generally, though, they do taste better—often much, much better—than their mass-market cousins. Some supermarkets and specialty grocers now sell alternative varieties of tomatoes, but for heirloom potatoes, melons, corn, cucumbers, peppers, and other produce, you'll have to shop at farmer's markets, grow them yourself, or cozy up to someone with a green thumb.

color, but orange and yellow varieties are gaining in popularity for their looks and lower acidity. Heirloom tomatoes can be anything from burgundy to white to striped green. Then there's the unripe green tomato, with its tangy flavor and firm flesh, wonderful fried or broiled.

But the most common tomatoes fall into three basic categories: cherry, plum, and slicing. Cherry tomatoes are small, sweet, and tender, great for snacking, tossing whole into salads, and quickly sautéing or roasting with a sprinkle of fresh herbs. Plum (or roma) tomatoes are medium-size, oval, and meaty. They are available year-round (that doesn't mean they taste good year-round, though in off-season they're usually your best choice) and are great for making a sauce, braising, oven-drying, or stewing. Slicing tomatoes are a broad category of tomatoes that are typically large and spherical (some flattened, some round). Beefsteaks are one of the most common and typical; they're juicy, flavorful, and delicious raw and cooked.

Being a rather delicate fruit that's sensitive to heat and cold, ripe tomatoes do not travel well. The vast majority of supermarket varieties these days—in season or not—are either picked green and ripened off the vine or grown in hothouses; either way, the end result is the same: they don't taste real good. So outside of tomato season, I usually reach for canned tomatoes.

Buying and storing: Tomato season in the United States ranges almost throughout the year if you count the Florida winter plantings, though people in most of the country find really good tomatoes only in summer and early fall. The best fresh tomatoes are undamaged, soft—yielding to light pressure but not mushy—and deeply colored. Store all tomatoes at room temperature (do not refrigerate).

Preparing: To core tomatoes, cut a cone right around the core and remove it. To peel, cut a small X in the flower (smooth, nonstem) end of the tomato and drop into boiling water for ten to thirty seconds, until the skin loosens. Plunge into ice water and peel off the skin. To seed, cut the tomato in half through its equator and squeeze and shake out the seeds (you may want to do this over a strainer to save the liquid).

Best cooking methods: Roasting, grilling or broiling, and pan frying. And, of course, making tomato sauce (see pages 445–446).

When are they done? Whenever you want them to be: they're good from raw to cooked to a mushy sauce.

Other vegetables and fruits to substitute: Tomatillos (beware: they're tangy!), pineapple, peaches, nectarines, or watermelon (for raw tomatoes).

Ⓕ Fast   Ⓜ Make Ahead   Ⓥ Vegan

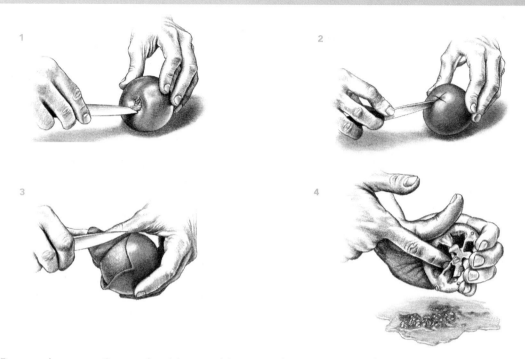

(STEP 1) First core the tomato. Cut a wedge right around the core and remove it. (STEP 2) Then peel the tomato. Cut a small X in the flower (nonstem) end. Drop it into boiling water until the skin begins to loosen, usually less than thirty seconds; then plunge into a bowl of ice water. (STEP 3) Remove the skin with a paring knife. (STEP 4) Finish by seeding the tomato. The easiest way to remove seeds is simply to cut the tomato in half through its equator, then squeeze and shake out the seeds or pop them out with your finger. Do this over a bowl if you want to strain and reserve the juice.

Grilled Tomatoes with Basil

MAKES: 4 servings

TIME: 30 minutes

Ⓜ

When you grill a ripe or even semiripe tomato, the high heat caramelizes some of the fruit's sugars while driving out a bit of its liquid. It also softens the flesh, removing traces of rawness. The whole process takes just 5 or 10 minutes. Heating the grill, of course, takes somewhat longer, though the identical technique can be performed in the broiler or in a heavy skillet over high heat. (And all of this can be done hours before you intend to use the tomatoes.)

From that point on, the possibilities are numerous. You can integrate the cooked tomatoes into a salad or a risotto or simply toss them with pasta. Or you can also serve them as is, drizzled with olive oil and sprinkled with basil.

Without the cheese, these are vegan.

Other vegetables you can use: eggplant (it will take about twice as long to cook on the grill).

3 or 4 ripe tomatoes

Extra virgin olive oil as needed

Salt and freshly ground black pepper

1/3 cup torn or chopped basil, or more to taste

Freshly grated Parmesan cheese to taste (optional)

1 Heat a charcoal or gas grill until moderately hot and put the rack about 4 inches from the heat source. Core the tomatoes and cut each into 3 or 4 thick slices. Brush them with olive oil and sprinkle with salt and pepper.

2 Grill the tomatoes, turning once, until they are soft but not mushy, about 5 minutes; you should be able to lift them from the grill with a spatula without their falling apart, but only barely. As they cook, use tongs to remove and discard the skins. Transfer them to a platter or plates and sprinkle with basil, plus a grating of the cheese if you like.

Grilled Tomatoes and Scrambled Eggs, Chinese Style

MAKES: 2 to 4 servings

TIME: 30 minutes

Grilled tomatoes don't have to have Italian flavors. Here's a quick way to turn them into an appetizer or main dish with Asian flavors.

Other vegetables you can use in this recipe: eggplant (it will take about twice as long to cook on the grill).

3 or 4 ripe tomatoes

2 tablespoons dark sesame oil

Salt and freshly ground black pepper

3 tablespoons neutral oil, like grapeseed or corn

1 teaspoon minced garlic

1 tablespoon minced peeled fresh ginger

6 eggs

2 teaspoons soy sauce, or to taste

1/4 cup minced scallion (optional)

1 Heat a charcoal or gas grill until moderately hot and put the rack about 4 inches from the heat source. Core the tomatoes and cut each into 3 or 4 thick slices. Brush them with half of the sesame oil and sprinkle with salt and pepper. Grill the tomatoes, turning once, until they are soft but not mushy, about 5 minutes; you should be able to lift them from the grill with a spatula without their falling apart, but only barely. As they cook, use tongs to remove and discard the skins.

2 While the tomatoes are cooling, put the neutral oil in a large skillet, preferably nonstick or cast iron, over medium-high heat. Add the garlic and ginger and cook just until they sizzle, about a minute.

3 Beat together the tomatoes and eggs. Add the tomato-egg mixture to the pan and cook, stirring almost constantly, until the mixture forms soft curds, 5 to 10 minutes. Stir in the remaining sesame oil and the soy sauce. Garnish with the scallion if you like and serve.

Broiled Cherry Tomatoes with Herbs

MAKES: 4 servings

TIME: About 5 minutes

Totally simple, amazingly quick, and completely delicious. These tomatoes are good enough to eat alone, one after the other, or spread on Crostini (page 737). Drizzle with cream or good extra virgin olive oil and/or sprinkle with chopped herbs or toasted bread crumbs for even more flavor and texture.

1 pound cherry tomatoes

2 or 3 sprigs fresh oregano, thyme, rosemary, tarragon, or basil

2 tablespoons extra virgin olive oil

Salt and freshly ground black pepper

F Fast   **M** Make Ahead   **V** Vegan

Preheat the broiler and put the rack about 4 inches from the heat source. Toss the tomatoes with the herbs, oil, and salt and pepper and put on a rimmed baking sheet or in a gratin dish. Broil until the skins brown, blister, and crack, 3 to 5 minutes; check the tomatoes often and shake the pan every so often to roll them around a bit; they can burn quickly. Serve straight from the broiler or warm.

Broiled Cherry Tomatoes with Parmesan. Equally delicious with sliced tomatoes: Add $1/2$ cup freshly grated Parmesan; sprinkle it on the tomatoes in the last minute of broiling.

Caramelized Tomato Slices. Use tomatoes at their peak of ripeness; serve them on toast—it's like marmalade: Omit the herbs. Substitute medium or large tomatoes for the cherry and 3 tablespoons brown sugar for the olive oil. Slice the tomatoes about $1/2$ inch thick and sprinkle with the sugar before broiling.

Oven-Roasted Fresh Plum Tomatoes

MAKES: 4 servings
TIME: About 1 hour, largely unattended

It's tough to find good plum tomatoes in the supermarket, even in season. No matter what the time of year, roasting is a great way to make the most of them, because the process concentrates the flavor and eliminates any hint of mealiness. The results are gorgeous.

Once the tomatoes are done, you can use them immediately in sauces, as a garnish, in pilafs or soups, or in other vegetable dishes. Or store them, tightly covered, in the fridge for up to several days.

Other fruits or vegetables you can use: peaches and nectarines.

2 pounds plum tomatoes (about a dozen), cored and cut in half lengthwise

2 tablespoons extra virgin olive oil, plus a little for the pan

Salt and freshly ground black pepper

1 Preheat the oven to 375°F. Grease a large baking sheet or roasting pan with a little of the olive oil.

2 Scoop the seeds out of the tomatoes if you like and put them in the pan, cut side down. Drizzle or brush with the 2 tablespoons olive oil and sprinkle with salt and pepper. Roast until they start to char a bit and shrivel (there's no need to turn), 40 to 50 minutes. (Tomatoes with seeds take a little longer.) Let cool on the pan a bit, then slip the skins off.

Oven-Roasted Canned Plum Tomatoes. A great way to turn a convenience food into something special and far more useful: Instead of the fresh tomatoes, drain two 28- or 35- ounce cans of plum tomatoes, reserving the juice for another use. Omit the salt. Proceed with the recipe.

Oven-Roasted Everyday Tomatoes. Works for heirloom, beefsteak, or hothouse tomatoes, especially when you want to improve imperfect ones: Core the tomatoes and halve them around the equator instead of lengthwise. Squeeze out the seeds (see page 373). Cut the largest pieces in half again and proceed with the recipe.

Tomato Cobbler

MAKES: 6 to 8 servings
TIME: About 1 hour

Everyone is intrigued by the idea of a savory version of one of their favorite desserts, and this one is a beauty. In fact, there's nothing quite like a summertime tomato cobbler, though you can make one with canned tomatoes all year long. (It's just different; see the variation.) The biscuit topping is quickly assembled in a food processor, making this an ideal potluck dish: Not only is the preparation easy, but you serve it at room temperature.

Other vegetables you can use: tomatillos.

Oil or butter for the baking dish

3 pounds ripe tomatoes (8 to 10 medium), cored and cut into wedges

1 tablespoon cornstarch

Salt and freshly ground black pepper

1 cup all-purpose flour, plus more if needed

1 cup cornmeal

$1^1/_2$ teaspoons baking powder

$^1/_4$ teaspoon baking soda

4 tablespoons ($^1/_2$ stick) butter, cut into large pieces and refrigerated until very cold

1 egg, beaten

$^3/_4$ cup buttermilk, plus more if needed

1 Grease a square baking dish or a deep pie plate with the butter or oil. Preheat the oven to 375°F.

2 Put the tomato wedges in a large bowl and sprinkle with the cornstarch and some salt and pepper. Toss gently to combine.

3 Put the flour, cornmeal, baking powder, and baking soda in a food processor along with a teaspoon of salt. Add the butter and pulse a few times until the mixture looks like coarse bread crumbs. Add the egg and buttermilk and pulse a few times more, until the mixture comes together in a ball. If the mixture doesn't come together, add a spoonful or two of flour. If the mixture is too dry, add a few drops of buttermilk.

4 Gently toss the tomato mixture again and spread it in the bottom of the prepared baking dish. Drop spoonfuls of the batter on top and smooth a bit with a knife. (Try to leave some gaps so that the steam from the tomato mixture will have a place to escape as the cobbler bakes.) Bake for 45 to 50 minutes, until golden on top and bubbly underneath. Cool to just barely warm or room temperature. To serve, scoop servings out with a large spoon.

Tomato Cobbler with Cheesy Topping. Great for lunch or a light supper: In Step 3, add 1 cup grated cheddar, Parmesan, Gruyère, or Asiago cheese to the food processor along with the egg and buttermilk.

Tomato Cobbler with Herb Topping. The way to go if you have fresh herbs: In Step 3, when you add the egg and buttermilk, add $^1/_4$ cup chopped fresh herbs, like mint, parsley, basil, or cilantro. Or add 1 tablespoon chopped fresh thyme, oregano, or rosemary.

Tomato Cobbler with Extra Corny Topping. The flavor of summer: In Step 4, before topping the tomatoes, fold 1 cup of fresh corn kernels into the biscuit batter.

Two-Tomato Cobbler. Made hearty with the addition of sun-dried or Oven-Dried Tomatoes (page 377) and good with the main recipe or any of the preceding topping variations: Omit the cornstarch. (The dried tomatoes will soak up the extra juices during baking.) In Step 2, add $^1/_2$ cup coarsely chopped dried tomatoes to the fresh tomato mixture.

Tomato Cobbler with Piecrust Topping. Fancier, richer, and a little more work: Prepare the dough for Savory Piecrust (page 867). In Step 3, instead of preparing the biscuit batter, roll out the pie dough so that it's big enough to cover the top of the baking dish. Proceed with the recipe from Step 4, topping the tomatoes with the prepared pie dough. Tuck in the sides a bit and cut a couple slits in the dough to vent the steam. Bake as directed.

Leek Cobbler. This will work for the main recipe or any of the variations: Omit the cornstarch. Instead of the tomatoes, use 3 pounds leeks. Trim them down to mostly the white part with just a little green, wash them carefully, and cut into 1-inch slices. Proceed with the recipe.

Canned Tomato Cobbler. With a flavor more like tomato sauce than fruit, but still delicious: Instead of fresh tomatoes, use two 28-ounce cans of whole tomatoes and drain them for a bit. (Save the liquid for another

F Fast   **M** Make Ahead   **V** Vegan

use.) If you like, in Step 2, when you add the cornstarch, salt, and pepper, season the tomatoes with a tablespoon of chopped oregano and a pinch of cayenne or hot red pepper flakes.

Oven-Dried Tomatoes

MAKES: 48 pieces

TIME: Several hours, largely unattended

Since tomatoes are really a fruit and not a vegetable, it makes sense they'd dry up in the oven just like apples or grapes (page 412). These are the homemade version of commercially dried tomatoes, but since you control the degree of doneness, you determine the final texture. Just keep in mind that the fully dried and more brittle tomatoes will keep longer than moist and chewy ones.

Other fruits you can use for this recipe: peaches and nectarines.

24 ripe plum tomatoes, cored, cut in half lengthwise, and seeded (see page 373)

1 Preheat the oven to 225°F. Set 2 wire racks on top of 2 baking sheets (preferably rimmed baking sheets). Put the tomatoes on the racks, cut side down. Put in the oven and forget about them for 2 hours.

2 Turn the sheet around and check on the tomatoes. You have several choices: If you just want to intensify the tomato flavor and use them immediately, they're done when still soft but somewhat shriveled, 2 to 3 hours total. If you want to keep them for a few days, they're done when they're shriveled and mostly dry, at least 4 hours total (wrap and refrigerate, or freeze). If you want to keep them for weeks, they're done when they're dark, shriveled, and dry, 6 or more hours total (wrap and refrigerate or store in a jar in the pantry).

Oven-Dried Cherry or Grape Tomatoes. Like big raisins: Instead of plum tomatoes, use 2 pints of cherry or grape tomatoes, halved lengthwise.

Tropical Tubers

Taro (Yuca), Cassava (Manioc), Boniato (Batata), Malanga (Yautía)

A group of tubers that's popular predominantly in Caribbean, South American, Polynesian, and West African cuisines, these are quite starchy—some more than others—and are generally handled the way you do potatoes.

Taro, the main ingredient in the equally loved and loathed Hawaiian dish *poi,* has a brownish gray fiber-covered striped skin and a gray-white flesh with purple stippling. It's more flavorful than potatoes and is great boiled or fried but becomes very dry when overcooked.

Cassava has an elongated, tapered oval shape with a dark brown, woody, and often waxed and shiny skin; the flesh is white, crisp, and loaded with starch (it's what tapioca is made from, which gives you an indication of just how much starch it contains). You can bake it, roast it, fry it, or stew it, but it must be served with some kind of sauce to balance the starchiness.

Boniato looks similar to sweet potato, with smooth, thin skin, but ranges in color from brownish orange to garnet to purple; it's oval with tapered ends and can be short and squat or skinny and lean. Its flavor is like a cross between white and sweet potatoes but with a fluffier texture, and it's lovely baked or boiled.

Malanga (yautía) looks like a cross between a sweet potato and taro; the shape is similar to a sweet potato, but the skin is brown, coarse, striated, and has a rough coat of fibers. The flesh is off-white and has the texture of jícama when raw. It is best boiled, fried, or included in stews—in short, treated exactly like a potato. It's sold at all Latin markets and some supermarkets, sometimes under the name *tannia* or *cocoyam* as well as *malanga* or *yautía.*

Buying and storing: All of these tubers should be firm and unshriveled; avoid any with sprouts or soft spots. Store taro and cassava in the refrigerator and boniato and malanga in a cool, dry, dark spot. Note that unlike other tubers, taro, boniato, and malanga do not keep well; use them within a few days.

Preparing: Peel with a vegetable peeler or, for the tougher cassava, a paring knife; note that some may be waxed, so they *must* be peeled, but otherwise peeling isn't necessary when you're baking one of these. You can chop, slice, or grate the flesh as you like. Raw boniato flesh discolors very quickly when peeled or cut and darkens quite a bit when cooked; immediately immerse in cold water after cutting and be sure to keep it covered with liquid while cooking to minimize darkening.

Best cooking methods:

For taro and malanga: Boiling (see Boiled or Steamed Root Vegetables or Tubers, page 240) and frying (see pages 244–245).

For cassava: Baking (see Whole Winter Squash, Cooked Three Ways, page 365) frying (see French Fries, page 352), and braising (see Braised Potatoes, page 346).

For boniato: Oiling (see Boiled or Steamed Root Vegetables or Tubers, page 240) and baking (see Sweet Potatoes, Simply Cooked, page 371).

When is it done? When a skewer or sharp knife inserted into one meets almost no resistance.

Turnips

White Turnips, Rutabagas, Swedes, Yellow Turnips

Closely related (in fact the rutabaga is thought to be a cross between a turnip and cabbage) and members of the brassicas (cabbages). Most turnips are white and purple on the exterior and solid white inside. Their flavor is mildly cabbagelike, sweet, and lovely braised. Rutabagas look similar to turnips but have a dark yellow and purple exterior and bright to pale yellow flesh; they can be as large as a cantaloupe and have a more assertive (sometimes said to be coarser) flavor.

Buying and storing: Look for small, firm specimens that are heavy for their size. If greens are attached to the turnips (see pages 317–318), they should be fresh looking with no yellowing. Rutabagas are often coated with a thick wax to keep them from drying out. Large turnips and rutabagas are often woody and have a stronger flavor than small ones. Store wrapped loosely in plastic in the refrigerator; they will keep for weeks.

Preparing: Peel and leave whole (if small enough) or slice or chop as you like; rutabagas must be peeled with a paring knife because of their wax coating.

Best cooking methods: Boiling and braising and glazing.

When is it done? When tender or very soft.

Other vegetables to substitute: Turnips and rutabagas are interchangeable; otherwise, parsnips, carrots, or kohlrabi.

Water Chestnuts

Not a chestnut at all—it only resembles one in its shape and dark brown skin—the water chestnut is the tuber of a water plant indigenous to Asia. It's mildly sweet and crunchy and adds great texture to any dish; you've probably eaten them plenty of times in stir-fries and fried rice dishes. When fresh, they have a dark brown skin that covers the off-white, crisp flesh (it's like a raw potato).

Buying and storing: If you can find fresh water chestnuts (which you will if you look in Asian markets), they should be plump, crisp, and heavy for their size. Store wrapped tightly in plastic in the refrigerator. Otherwise, buy canned, which are a decent and readily available substitute, if nearly tasteless.

Preparing: Peel (if fresh) and slice or chop as necessary.

Best cooking method: Stir-frying, added at the last minute.

When are they done? When just heated through and still crunchy.

Ⓕ Fast   Ⓜ Make Ahead   Ⓥ Vegan

Zucchini (*see* Squash—Summer, page 361)

The Basics of Mixed Vegetable Dishes

These are among the most flexible dishes in the entire chapter, because there are really very few rules and most vegetables complement others nicely. Pay attention to size, remembering that similar-size pieces cook at similar rates, and to texture; harder vegetables take longer to cook than softer ones of course. To compensate, either precook the hard ones a bit (see page 240) or just hold out the soft ones until near the end of cooking time.

One further rule: Too many vegetables will muddy the flavor. More is not necessarily better; usually three or four vegetables per dish is sufficient. You can break this "rule" any time you want, of course, but after a while the individuality of each will be lost.

Stir-Fried Vegetables, Vietnamese Style

MAKES: 4 servings

TIME: 30 minutes

For a simple stir-fry, this packs a lot of punch. And the keys are no more than lots of garlic and lots and lots of black pepper, which is really the primary spice used in Vietnam.

Other vegetables you can use: really, any assortment you like, provided you cook each vegetable alone to make sure they are all cooked perfectly.

$1/4$ cup neutral oil, like grapeseed or corn

1 cup broccoli or cauliflower florets in about 1-inch pieces

2 medium carrots, thinly sliced

$1/2$ cup snow or snap peas, trimmed

1 medium to large onion, thinly sliced

2 dried chiles

1 tablespoon minced garlic

2 tablespoons Fishless Fish Sauce (page 778) or soy sauce, or to taste

1 teaspoon ground black pepper, or to taste

Salt

1 Put 1 tablespoon of the oil in a nonstick skillet or wok over high heat. When hot, add the broccoli or cauliflower. Cook, stirring occasionally, for about a minute, then add 2 tablespoons water. Continue to cook and stir until the vegetable is crisp-tender, about 5 minutes. Remove from the pan and repeat the process with the carrots and then the snow peas.

2 Put a little more oil in the pan and add the onion. Cook over high heat, stirring once in a while, until it softens and begins to char, 3 to 5 minutes. Add the chiles and garlic and cook for another 30 seconds.

3 Add $1/4$ cup water, the sauce, and the pepper; return the cooked vegetables to the pan. Cook, stirring, until the mixture is combined and lightly sauced, then taste and adjust the seasoning, adding salt if necessary, and serve.

Quick-Braised Vegetables, Thai Style

MAKES: 4 servings

TIME: 30 minutes

Half stir-fry, half braise, this quick, thick stew can be varied in a number of ways, all delicious. If you like Thai-style curries, this is for you.

3 tablespoons peanut or neutral oil, like grapeseed or corn

1 large white onion, sliced

2 tablespoons chopped garlic

2 dried chiles, 1 fresh chile, minced, or 1 teaspoon Chile Paste (page 828) or red or green curry paste (to make your own, see page 830), or to taste

3 lime leaves, chopped, preferably fresh (dried are okay), or the grated zest of 1 lime

1$^1/_2$ pounds eggplant, zucchini, summer squash, or a combination, peeled as necessary and cut into chunks

1$^1/_2$ cups coconut milk (to make your own, see page 423, or use 1 can, slightly less than 2 cups, with a little water)

3 tablespoons soy sauce or Fishless Fish Sauce (page 778)

Salt and freshly ground pepper

Lime wedges for serving

1 Put the oil in a 10- or 12-inch skillet over medium-high heat. When hot, add the onion and cook, stirring occasionally, until it softens a bit, just 5 minutes or so. Stir in the garlic, chiles, and lime leaves or zest, then add the eggplant. Cook, stirring occasionally and adjusting the heat as necessary so the vegetable cooks quickly without burning, until it softens (zucchini will cook faster than eggplant), 10 to 20 minutes.

2 Add the coconut milk and simmer until thickened, about 5 minutes. Add the soy sauce, then taste and add salt and pepper if necessary. Serve hot, with lime wedges.

13 Easy Additions to Quick-Braised Vegetables, Thai Style

With or without eggplant, this can become a bigger, more interesting dish, made with almost any vegetable you have on hand. For example, add:

1. 1 to 2 cups tomatoes, after the eggplant begins to soften
2. 1 cup corn kernels, just before the coconut milk
3. 1 to 2 cups peeled and cubed winter squash, like butternut, in place of or in addition to the eggplant, at the same time

4. 1 to 2 cups peeled and cubed potato, preferably a waxy variety, in place of or in addition to the eggplant, at the same time
5. 1 cup parboiled and shocked (see page 241) broccoli or cauliflower, just before the coconut milk
6. 2 to 3 cups shredded spinach or other greens, just before the coconut milk
7. 1 to 2 cups peas, snow peas, or snap peas, when the eggplant is about half cooked
8. $^1/_2$ cup toasted nuts (see page 321), any kind, along with the soy sauce
9. $^1/_2$ to 1 cup chopped carrot or celery, along with the onion
10. 1 tablespoon minced peeled fresh ginger, along with the garlic and chile
11. 1 tablespoon curry powder, garam masala, or chili powder (to make your own, see page 814, 815, or 816), or to taste, along with the garlic
12. $^1/_2$ cup or more shredded basil leaves, preferably Thai, at the last second; or use cilantro, mint, or a combination
13. 1 to 2 cups firm to extra-firm tofu (prepared by any of the methods on pages 641–643 or simply blotted dry, cut into $^3/_4$-inch cubes), just before the coconut milk

Baked Mixed Vegetables with Olive Oil

Tian or Ratatouille

MAKES: 4 to 6 servings

TIME: About 1$^1/_2$ hours, largely unattended

The original "What do we have on hand?" recipe: You combine vegetables, herbs, and olive oil in various proportions and cook them on the stove or in the oven until very soft. Since it's widely considered a dish from Provence, zucchini (and/or eggplant) and tomatoes are frequently present, but there are really very few rules here, except longish, slow cooking and lots of good olive oil; herbs help too.

If I had my choice, herbwise, I'd use a teaspoon of thyme or marjoram for the cooking and garnish with a handful of basil or parsley.

Other vegetables you can use: Obviously, you can stew whatever you want, but potatoes and mushrooms are the most common additions that I haven't included here.

$1^1/_2$ to 2 pounds eggplant, preferably small, sliced $^1/_2$ inch thick and salted (see page 46) if time allows

$^1/_2$ cup extra virgin olive oil, plus a little more for garnish

2 large onions, sliced

1 pound zucchini, trimmed and cut into large chunks

2 red or yellow bell peppers, cored, seeded, and sliced

4 plum or 2 round tomatoes, cored and chopped (or use drained canned)

Fresh herbs, according to availability, to taste—thyme, marjoram, rosemary, savory, basil, parsley, or chervil—plus more for garnish

Salt and freshly ground black pepper

10 cloves garlic, peeled and halved

① Preheat the oven to 350°F. If you salted the eggplant, squeeze out excess liquid, then rinse and dry.

② Film a casserole or heavy ovenproof skillet with a couple tablespoons of the olive oil, then make a layer of onion, followed by one of eggplant, zucchini, peppers, tomatoes, herbs, salt, pepper, and garlic cloves (in fact the order doesn't matter at all). Repeat. Drizzle with the remaining olive oil and put in the oven.

③ Bake for about an hour, pressing down on the vegetables occasionally with a spatula, until they are all completely tender. Garnish with more herbs, drizzle with a little more olive oil, and serve hot, warm, or at room temperature.

Stovetop Mixed Vegetables with Olive Oil. This requires a little more attention: Combine all the ingredients in the largest skillet you have (a broad saucepan will also work) and cook, stirring occasionally, over medium heat, adjusting the heat so the mixture simmers in its own juices without browning. Cooking time will be just a little shorter, perhaps 45 minutes or so.

Very Simple Mixed Vegetables. Use either the stovetop or the oven method: Omit the onion and peppers, using only eggplant, zucchini, tomatoes, herbs, garlic, and olive oil.

Roasted Vegetables, Thai Style

MAKES: 4 servings
TIME: About $1^1/_2$ hours, largely unattended

There are other options beyond the preceding recipe's plain, simple, wonderful vegetables baked with olive oil; this is the Southeast Asian version. Like the more common Italian-style roasted vegetables, it's almost easier to list the vegetables that can't be included than the ones that can. What I like are a couple of roots—potatoes, carrots, turnips, and the like—combined with a pea or bean (frozen peas or snap peas and fresh green beans are all good), some eggplant or zucchini, and an assortment of onions, shallots, and garlic. Tomato adds a little moisture, color, and acidity. Some mushrooms—even tofu—are also good here.

Other vegetables you can use: You're more limited by the patience you have to peel and chop than anything else.

$^1/_4$ cup peanut or vegetable oil

1 medium to large potato, peeled and diced

1 medium to large eggplant, diced

1 red bell pepper, cored, seeded, and cut into strips

1 cup peas (frozen are fine; don't bother to defrost)

$^1/_2$ pound green beans, trimmed

4 shallots, peeled, or 1 onion, peeled and quartered

8 to 12 cloves garlic, peeled, to taste

Salt and freshly ground black pepper

2 tomatoes, cut into eighths

$\frac{1}{4}$ cup green, yellow, or red curry paste (to make your own green or red, see page 830) or 1 tablespoon Chile Paste (page 828), or to taste, or cayenne to taste

1 cup coconut milk, (to make your own, see page 423)

$\frac{1}{2}$ cup crunchy "natural" peanut butter

1 tablespoon soy sauce

Chopped fresh cilantro, mint, and/or Thai basil leaves for garnish

1 Preheat the oven to 450°F while you prepare the vegetables. Put a deep ovenproof skillet or casserole on top of the stove over medium heat and add all but a tablespoon of the oil. When hot, add all the vegetables except the tomatoes; sprinkle with salt and pepper and stir. Put the pan in the oven and roast, stirring once or twice, for 30 minutes. Add the tomato, stir, and continue to roast until the vegetables are tender and beginning to brown, about 1 hour total.

2 Put the remaining tablespoon of oil in a small saucepan over medium heat. When hot, add the curry paste and stir; whisk in the coconut milk, peanut butter, and soy sauce and bring to a simmer. Keep warm.

3 When the vegetables are done, stir in the coconut milk mixture. Taste and adjust the seasoning, adding more soy sauce or curry paste if necessary. Garnish with the herbs and serve hot or warm.

The Basics of Gratins

Don't let the fancy words fool you. *Gratin, au gratin,* and *gratinée* are just French terms applied loosely to dishes that are browned on top, usually with cheese or bread crumbs. In essence, they're a family of quick and impressive baked dishes with mind-boggling possibilities for variation: You can enrich them with cheese, cream, eggs, or Béchamel Sauce (page 803); run them under a broiler for extra crisping; or simply finish cooked vegetables with a little sauce and a few minutes in the oven. Almost anything can be made into a gratin in no time, from eggs to vegetables to fruit. (The chart on page 386 demonstrates just how flexible gratins are.) You can even prepare gratins all the way up to the final step a day or two ahead of time, which makes them great for parties or holiday dinners.

The Baking Dish

The recipes here are designed for dishes that hold at least 6 cups of food, so you'll need a dish that will accommodate that much or a little more (use a measuring cup to see how much water it holds if you're not sure of the capacity). Shallow, broad ceramic or stoneware baking dishes—not surprisingly called *gratin dishes*—are best, because they provide a lot of surface area for browning. But you can use baking pans, deep ovenproof platters, pie plates, soufflé dishes, or even skillets.

The Baking Method

For the simple gratins with cheese and/or bread crumbs on cooked vegetables, just use a broiler to brown the topping. The dish should be at least 4 inches from the heat source; keep a close eye on it as the topping can go from barely toasted to charred in a flash. Gratins with raw vegetables, raw eggs, cream, or layers of cheese must be baked until the ingredients are thoroughly cooked or the cheese melted (think Baked Macaroni and Cheese, page 460). During this process, the gratin should brown too. If it doesn't, stick it under the broiler for a couple minutes.

What to Serve with Gratins

By their nature, gratins become the centerpiece of most meals. All you need is some bread or plainly cooked grains or beans and a salad, which should have an acidic vinaigrette-type dressing rather than a rich and creamy one. Pickles are also a good accompaniment for gratins. For more protein, serve them with scrambled or poached eggs.

F Fast   M Make Ahead   V Vegan

6 Other Toppings for Gratins

Ways to add flavor and texture beyond bread crumbs:

1. Cooked grains, like wheat berries, barley, rice, or couscous
2. Crunchy Crumbled Tempeh (page 674)
3. Tofu Croutons (page 656)
4. Nuts (or a combination of nuts and bread crumbs)
5. Coarsely chopped cooked pasta or noodles
6. Crumbled biscuits

Simplest Asparagus Gratin

MAKES: 4 servings

TIME: 10 minutes, with cooked vegetables

Use nearly any cooked vegetable here; simply cover it with cheese and stick it under the broiler until the top is golden brown. Using béchamel (see the variation) makes a more substantial and saucy dish; it works beautifully on an ovenproof platter, where the cheese and/or béchamel bubble and crisp around the edges.

Other cooked vegetables you can use: green or wax beans, broccoli, cauliflower, artichoke hearts, potatoes, fennel, eggplant, leeks, spinach, mushrooms, onions, celery root, parsnips, Jerusalem artichokes, zucchini, winter squash, or sweet potatoes.

1 tablespoon butter or extra virgin olive oil

1$^1/_2$ to 2 pounds cooked asparagus (see page 261)

Salt and freshly ground black pepper

1 cup grated Gruyère or Swiss cheese

$^1/_4$ cup Fresh Bread Crumbs (page 804)

$^1/_4$ cup chopped parsley leaves for garnish

Sprinkle of paprika (optional)

1 Preheat the broiler and put the rack about 4 inches from the heat source. Use the butter or oil to grease a shallow medium baking pan or gratin dish.

2 Put the asparagus in the dish, sprinkle with some salt and pepper, cover with the cheese, and sprinkle on the bread crumbs. Broil for 3 to 5 minutes, until the cheese is melted and golden. Sprinkle with a few more grinds of pepper, the parsley, and the paprika if you like and serve.

Asparagus and Béchamel Gratin. Rich, saucy, and also fabulous with Mornay Sauce: Add Béchamel (page 803) or Mornay (Cheese) Sauce (page 804). Proceed as directed, with or without the cheese on top.

Mushroom and Roquefort Gratin. Any mushrooms and any blue cheese will work nicely: Substitute about 5 cups cooked mushrooms (see page 314) for the asparagus and crumbled Roquefort for all or part of the Gruyère or Swiss.

Potatoes and Manchego Gratin. Lovely with chopped almonds mixed into the bread crumbs: Substitute about 5 cups cooked (roasted, baked, or boiled) potatoes (see pages 339–340) for the asparagus and manchego cheese for the Gruyère or Swiss. Proceed with the recipe. For garnish, sprinkle with smoked paprika.

Roasted Beets and Goat Cheese Gratin. The tang of the goat cheese is perfect with the earthiness of the beets: Substitute about 5 cups sliced roasted beets (see page 267) for the asparagus, crumbled goat cheese for the Gruyère or Swiss, and thyme leaves for the parsley. Sprinkle the beets with the thyme leaves, then the goat cheese, and proceed with the recipe.

Broccoli or Cauliflower and Pesto Gratin. Pesto beyond pasta: Substitute about 5 cups chopped cooked broccoli or cauliflower (see page 270) for the asparagus and Parmesan for the Gruyère or Swiss. Add a cup or so Traditional Pesto (page 768) and omit the parsley. In Step 2, toss the broccoli or cauliflower with the pesto, sprinkle with Parmesan, and proceed with the recipe.

Simplest Onion Gratin. Sweet and satisfying: Instead of the asparagus, use about 5 cups lightly sautéed onions (see page 329).

Potato and Sunchoke Gratin

MAKES: 4 servings

TIME: About 1 hour

This gratin starts with raw vegetables, cream, and cheese that can be assembled up to 2 days in advance of baking—or even baked 2 days ahead and then reheated before serving. A mandoline gives you slices of consistent thickness, which is the key to even cooking, with little work.

Other vegetables you can use: any combination of sweet potatoes, parsnips, celery root, parsnips, rutabagas, winter squash, burdock, celery, carrots, or horseradish (which will mellow while cooking; see page 307).

2 to 3 cups heavy cream, half-and-half, or milk

1 pound potatoes, peeled and thinly sliced

1 pound sunchokes (Jerusalem artichokes), peeled and thinly sliced

1 1/2 cups grated Gruyère or Swiss cheese

Salt and freshly ground black pepper

1 tablespoon thyme leaves

1 Preheat the oven to 375°F. Put the cream in a pot and heat until it's hot.

2 Layer the potatoes, sunchokes, and cheese (be sure to end with cheese) in a gratin or similar ovenproof dish; sprinkle every potato layer with a bit of salt, pepper, and thyme. Pour in enough hot cream to come about three-quarters of the way up the potato layers.

3 Put in the oven and cook, undisturbed, until the potatoes and sunchokes are tender (a thin-bladed knife will pierce them with little or no resistance) and the top is nicely browned, 45 to 50 minutes. Serve immediately or keep warm in the oven for up to 30 minutes.

Potato Gratin. The classic: Use all potatoes (about 2 pounds total).

Potato and Chestnut Gratin. A luxurious winter dish: Substitute prepared chestnuts (see page 287) for the sunchokes, sage for the thyme, and Parmesan for the Gruyère or Swiss.

Cabbage Gratin. Not the usual way we think of cooking cabbage, but a delicious one: Substitute cabbage, thinly shredded, for the potatoes and sunchokes and chopped tarragon leaves for the thyme.

Potato and Cauliflower Gratin with Crème Fraîche or Sour Cream. Nice, with a bit of tang: Substitute cauliflower for the sunchokes and crème fraîche or sour cream for the cheese. (Spread it between the layers with a dull knife.)

Sweet Potato and Cream Cheese Gratin. An excellent brunch gratin: Substitute sweet potatoes for the potatoes and sunchokes and cream cheese for the cheese. Whip the cream cheese with just enough cream to make it spreadable and layer as in Step 1. Top the gratin with grated Parmesan, bread crumbs, or chopped pecans. Sprinkle with freshly grated nutmeg just before serving.

Fennel Gratin. Really fantastic, whether you're vegan or not: Use fennel instead of potatoes and sunchokes and substitute a mixture of chopped hazelnuts or almonds and bread crumbs (about 3/4 cup each) for the cheese. Instead of sprinkling in between the layers, use this mixture as the final topping. Omit the thyme. In Step 1, use vegetable stock (pages 101–102) or almond or hazelnut milk instead of cream and add 2 tablespoons extra virgin olive oil to the pot. Proceed with the recipe.

Savory Peach or Apple Gratin with Coriander: Instead of the potatoes and Jerusalem artichokes, use peaches or apples. (Just quarter them; peel if you like, but you don't need to.) Instead of the cheese, use a mixture of bread crumbs and chopped nuts (about 3/4 cup each). In Step 1, add 1 tablespoon ground coriander to the cream in the pot. Proceed with the recipe.

F Fast   **M** Make Ahead   **V** Vegan

Rich Spinach Gratin

MAKES: 4 servings
TIME: 45 minutes

Practically a custard and totally decadent. Serve this dish in a single large gratin dish or in smaller individual gratin dishes or ramekins. It's a wonderful side dish for an elegant dinner or a fancy luncheon or brunch.

Salt

2 pounds spinach, trimmed of thick stems

1 medium onion, roughly chopped

1 teaspoon minced garlic

3 eggs, lightly beaten

$1/_2$ cup heavy cream, half-and-half, or milk

1 cup freshly grated Parmesan cheese

Freshly ground black pepper

2 tablespoons butter or extra virgin olive oil

$1/_2$ cup Fresh Bread Crumbs (page 804)

① Preheat the oven to 375°F. Put a large pot of water on to boil and salt it. When it boils, add the spinach and onion and cook for just about a minute, until the spinach wilts. Drain thoroughly and cool a bit, then squeeze out as much of the water as you can and chop it.

② Put the spinach and onion in a bowl, along with the garlic, eggs, cream, and about half the Parmesan. Mix well, then add salt and pepper to taste.

③ Use a little of the butter to grease a gratin dish or similar baking dish that will hold the spinach mixture at a depth of about 1 inch. Pour the spinach mixture into the dish, then top with more Parmesan, the bread crumbs, and bits of the remaining butter. Bake until the mixture is hot and set and the top brown, about 20 minutes (if the top threatens to scorch before the mixture is set, lower the heat a bit). Serve hot, warm, or at room temperature.

Smoky Onion Gratin. Pearl onions or cipolline work nicely here; parboil and peel them beforehand (see page 328; you should have about 3 cups): Substitute the prepared onions for the spinach and smoked Gouda (or another smoked cheese) for the Parmesan. Omit the garlic and add 1 tablespoon thyme or rosemary leaves. Proceed with the recipe.

Celery and Leek Gratin. Perhaps the most extravagant way to eat celery: Substitute 1 pound each trimmed celery and leeks for the spinach. Omit the onion and garlic. Julienne the celery and leeks and parboil them in Step 1, but don't chop them afterward.

Butternut Squash and Pecorino Romano Gratin. The tang of the pecorino (use any hard sheep cheese) complements the sweetness of the squash: Substitute butternut squash, peeled and cut into $1/_4$-inch-thick slices, for the spinach and pecorino for the Parmesan. Omit the onion and add 2 tablespoons chopped fresh sage leaves. Skip the parboiling in Step 1. Proceed with the recipe, adding pine nuts along with the bread crumbs if you like.

Mashed Potato Gratin. A great way to gussy up leftover baked or boiled potatoes—or start with raw: If using raw potatoes, substitute an all-purpose or waxy variety for the spinach. Boil them in their skin according to the directions on page 340. Peel and roughly mash. Proceed with the recipe from Step 2. To use cooked potatoes, substitute 3 to 4 cups mashed potatoes for the spinach and proceed with the recipe from Step 2.

Chile Gratin, Mexican Style

MAKES: 4 to 6 servings
TIME: 30 minutes

The basic technique is the same as in the preceding Spinach Gratin, but the cheese plays the starring role here, and the tortilla chips make the topping. If you use queso fresco (page 210), it won't melt entirely but will

MORE VEGETABLE GRATINS

Each of the following gratins makes 4 servings. Just layer the vegetable(s), sauce, and flavorings, sprinkle with the topping, add bits of butter or some extra virgin olive oil over all, and bake at 375°F as for the Potato and Sunchoke Gratin (page 384).

GRATIN	VEGETABLES	LIQUID AND/OR SAUCE	FLAVORINGS	TOPPING
Creamy Green Bean Gratin	2 pounds green or wax beans, trimmed	1¹/₂ cups Creamy Nut Sauce (page 797)	1 tablespoon fresh thyme leaves	Chopped nuts and/or bread crumbs
Mushroom and Pumpernickel Gratin	2 pounds mushrooms, trimmed and sliced	2 to 3 cups heavy cream, half-and-half, or milk	1 tablespoon each minced garlic and chopped fresh thyme leaves	Pumpernickel (or rye) bread crumbs
Tomato Gratin	2 pounds fresh ripe tomatoes, sliced (preferably peeled and seeded)	1¹/₂ to 2 cups vegetable stock (pages 101–102) or cream	Any fresh herb	Any good melting cheese and/or bread crumbs
Eggplant Gratin, Greek Style	2 pounds eggplant, peeled and cut into ¹/₂-inch-thick slices	3 cups Greek-Style Tomato Sauce (page 449)	1 cup crumbled feta cheese and ¹/₄ cup chopped parsley	Bread crumbs
Creamy Parsnip Gratin with Vanilla	2 pounds parsnips, peeled and cut into ¹/₄-inch-thick slices	2 to 3 cups heavy cream, half-and-half, or milk	1 vanilla bean, slit so the seeds can be scraped (page 859) and stirred into the cream or milk	Chopped toasted hazelnuts
Vegan Curry Gratin	1¹/₂ pounds potatoes, peeled and thinly sliced, and 1 cup green peas	3 cups Spicy Indian Tomato Sauce with coconut milk (page 793) or 2 cups chopped tomatoes with 1 cup coconut milk	¹/₄ cup chopped fresh cilantro	Shredded coconut and/or chopped cashews or pistachios

have a great soft and crumbly texture. Serve with Mexican Rice with Vegetables (page 512).

Other vegetables you can use: chayote, zucchini, summer squash, corn kernels (especially Grilled Corn, page 290), or green beans.

- 1 tablespoon neutral oil, like grapeseed or corn
- 12 medium poblano or other mild fresh chiles (see page 826) or bell peppers, roasted and cleaned (page 333)
- 2 cups peeled, seeded, and chopped tomatoes (see page 373), with their juice (canned are fine)
- 3 cups grated cheddar, Monterey Jack, or cotija cheese or crumbled queso fresco
- Salt and freshly ground black pepper
- ¹/₄ cup chopped fresh cilantro leaves
- ¹/₂ cup crushed tortilla chips
- Sour cream for garnish (optional)

1 Preheat the oven to 375°F. Grease a gratin or similar ovenproof dish with the oil.

2 Cut the chiles in half (large pieces are fine). Layer the chiles, tomatoes, and cheese (be sure to end with cheese), sprinkling every now and then with a bit of salt, pepper, and cilantro. Top with the tortilla chips.

③ Put in the oven and bake until the cheese is melted, bubbling, and browned, about 25 minutes. Serve immediately with a dollop of sour cream or keep warm in the oven for up to 30 minutes.

Hot and Smoky Corn Gratin. Chipotles add heat and smokiness: Substitute 4 cups corn kernels (grilled, roasted, or steamed; see pages 288–290) for the chiles. Add 2 to 4 tablespoons chopped canned chipotle chile, with its adobo, to taste, along with the tomatoes.

Summer Squash and Salsa Gratin. Great with any salsa; grilled squash (page 255) is excellent: For the chiles, substitute 3 or 4 medium zucchini or yellow squash, cut into lengthwise slices (about $1/4$-inch thick) and cooked any way you like: Grilled, roasted, steamed, or parboiled and shocked (see page 241). Use Fresh Tomatillo Salsa (page 751) instead of the tomatoes. Add $1/2$ cup of so chopped or whole pumpkin seeds (pepitas) with the tortillas.

The Basics of Puréed Vegetables

Well-made puréed vegetables are a true comfort, super-luxurious and far more sophisticated than baby food: Think of the best mashed potatoes you've ever had, and you've got the idea. The unexpected texture provides the perfect backdrop for a wide range of flavors, and they always add contrast and interest. Puréeing also happens to be a great way to breathe life into leftovers. (See the sidebars on pages 391 and 392.)

How to Prepare and Cook Vegetables for Puréeing

Perhaps the best thing about puréed vegetables is that you don't have to be quite so careful about overcooking them.

You don't want them to be waterlogged or insipid, of course, but they do need to be cooked well beyond the crisp-tender stage, and if you overcook them a bit it doesn't matter much.

Boiling and steaming are the easiest and most obvious ways to cook vegetables before puréeing, but sautéing, roasting, and grilling, which impart deep flavor and color and tend to evaporate excess water, are also good. Whichever method you choose, be sure the vegetables are very tender, well drained, and cooled a bit before puréeing.

As a general rule, peel all vegetables before puréeing. You can peel and cut into manageable chunks before or after cooking, whichever is easier.

The Best Way to Purée

You can often make a crude purée with nothing more than a fork or a potato masher, especially with super-soft, non-fibrous vegetables like eggplant, rutabagas, turnips, sweet potatoes, and winter squashes. Just put the cooked and drained vegetables in a deep, broad bowl and go to work, adding ingredients as needed.

Running vegetables through a food mill (if you have one) gives them a luxurious, almost fluffy texture, but a blender is the easiest way to go for ultra-smooth purées. (A food processor usually delivers a more rustic, slightly chunky grind, and sometimes that's nice, too.) An immersion blender, while excellent for soups, requires too much liquid for these purposes. (See pages 14 to 16 for details about using all of these tools.)

If you're using a blender or food processor, put a small amount of the binder and fat in the container first; then add the seasoned vegetables. (Work in batches if necessary.) Cover and pulse the machine a few times first to get things rolling, then let it run until you achieve the desired consistency. Add liquid as needed—the broth in which you simmered the vegetables is a good choice—but just a little at a time, enough to allow the machine to do its work; you don't want a watery purée that will run all over the plate.

Whatever method you use, transfer the purée to a pot and reheat over medium-low heat, stirring frequently. (A microwave works well here, too.) Taste and adjust the seasoning if necessary. Remove to plates, or a serving vessel; garnish, and serve.

Seasoning Vegetable Purées

In almost every case, I season the vegetables as I'm cooking them. This way aromatics — like ginger, garlic, or onion — are softened and mellowed, and the spices no longer taste raw. (On the other hand, there are times you want them to be raw and assertive; I'll note that when appropriate.) This poses a bit of a problem for steamed vegetables, though you can always cook the seasonings in the oil for a few minutes and then add them to the vegetables.

"Binding" Vegetable Purées

Because vegetables are mostly water, you often need a little fat, and perhaps something starchy or absorbent to keep vegetable purées from separating into solids and liquids on the plate; in many cases, these additions add flavor, too. The standards include rich liquids like cream, half-and-half, or milk, but consider unexpected ingredients, too, like moist fruit, bread, or tofu.

Making Vegan Purées

Any of the combinations in the following chart can be made vegan by replacing the dairy liquid listed with any vegetable stock (pages 101 to 102), non-dairy milk, silken tofu, or some of the alternative binders above. Instead of butter, use extra virgin olive oil, or a neutral oil, like grapeseed or corn. Or just use the vegetable cooking liquid.

Make-Ahead Purées

You can cook the vegetables up to 2 days in advance of puréeing, provided you keep them well-covered to prevent discoloration and loss of flavor. Almost all finished purées can be made in advance, covered tightly, and kept

Which Vegetables to Purée?

You want rich, creamy, flavorful, and (if possible) colorful flesh. Avoid anything watery, stringy, or strangely colored.

Excellent:

- Broccoli
- Carrots
- Cauliflower
- Chestnuts
- Corn
- Eggplant
- Peppers and Chiles
- Root vegetables, virtually all, but especially parsnips, turnips, and beets
- Shell peas
- Spinach and sorrel
- Starchy potatoes (good in combination with other vegetables; to mash or purée them alone, see page 341)
- Winter squash

Not so good:

- Artichokes
- Cabbage and Brussels sprouts
- Celery (but celeriac is good)
- Fibrous greens like chard, kale, bok choy, and so on
- Mushrooms
- Snow and snap peas (but shell peas are great; see the chart on page 390)
- Tomatoes (unless you're making soup)
- Waxy potatoes (they get gummy)
- Zucchini and other summer squash

in the refrigerator for a day or two before serving. Reheat over low heat on the stove, stirring occasionally, or zap in the microwave until hot. To make an impromptu gratin, put the purée in a greased shallow baking or gratin dish, sprinkle with bread crumbs, dot with butter or drizzle

EVERYDAY VEGETABLE PURÉES

These are suggestions for pairing vegetables with seasonings and flavorings. You can mix and match, as long as you choose just one ingredient from each column.

VEGETABLE	BINDER	FAT	SEASONING	GARNISH
2 pounds raw will give you 3 to 4 cups cooked and chopped	Use as much as you like or as needed to reach desired consistency; usually about 1/2 cup or so	2 to 3 tablespoons	1 to 2 tablespoons, in addition to salt and freshly ground black pepper to taste	As much or as little as you like
Beans (see Puréed or Mashed Beans, pages 612 to 617)				
Broccoli	Ricotta cheese	Extra virgin olive oil	A pinch of nutmeg	Grated Parmesan cheese
Butternut squash	Coconut milk	Neutral oil, like grapeseed or corn	Curry powder (to make your own, see pages 815–816)	Toasted shredded coconut
Carrots	Orange juice	Extra virgin olive oil	Minced fresh ginger	Grated orange zest
Cassava	Some of the boiling liquid	Extra virgin olive oil	Lots of garlic, either fried or roasted	Paprika or lots of freshly ground black pepper and a squeeze of lime juice
Cauliflower	Soaked and squeezed Croutons (page 806)	Extra virgin olive oil	Garlic	A drizzle of any herb paste like Traditional Pesto (pages 768–770)
Chestnuts	Cream or crème fraîche	Butter	Honey or maple syrup	Chopped toasted chestnuts
Corn	Sour cream	Butter or extra virgin olive oil	Chili powder (to make your own, see page 814)	Queso fresco, chopped fresh tomato, and minced cilantro
Daikon	A bit of the liquid from boiling the daikon	A few drops of dark sesame oil	None needed	Toasted sesame seeds (page 321) or Nori "Shake" (page 817)
Eggplant	Silken tofu	A few drops of dark sesame oil	Any miso	Sliced scallion (and pass soy sauce at the table)
Eggplant	None needed; it's soft enough, but add a few roasted garlic cloves if you like.	Extra virgin olive oil	Any Middle Eastern spice blend (pages 814–819) or a large pinch of saffron	Chopped fresh parsley or mint leaves
Parsnips	Milk or cream	Melted butter	Seeds scraped from 1 inch of vanilla bean or 1 teaspoon vanilla extract	Finely chopped hazelnuts
Red bell pepper or mild green or red chiles	Usually none needed	Extra virgin olive oil	None needed	Minced fresh cilantro or red onion

VEGETABLE	BINDER	FAT	SEASONING	GARNISH
Rutabagas	Almonds or hazelnuts (ground in the blender or processor with the rutabaga)	Melted butter or extra virgin olive oil	Chopped fresh thyme leaves	Coarse salt and lemon wedges
Shell peas	Cream or half-and-half	Melted butter	Minced tarragon leaves	Stir in a spoonful of Dijon mustard
Turnips	A dab of sour cream	Melted butter or extra virgin olive oil	Minced red onions	Minced parsley

with extra virgin olive oil, and bake in a 375°F oven until hot and bubbly.

How to Serve Purées

Purées make a great "bed" for burgers, cutlets, meatballs, or slices of cooked tofu, tempeh, or seitan. Or use purées underneath whole-vegetable presentations like asparagus, broccoli spears, sliced or cubed eggplant, or roasted chunks of potato. Puréed vegetables can be used as a "sauce" for pasta, rice or risotto, cooked whole grains, baked potatoes, or thick slices of hearty toast. Well-seasoned, warm or room temperature purées are lovely dips for anything from crudités to dumplings to grilled tofu skewers; thin them, if necessary, with a little stock or other liquid. They also make good spreads for sandwiches and fillings for burritos or tacos.

Essential Vegetable Purée

MAKES: 4 servings
TIME: 40 minutes

A straightforward, basic, and model recipe for puréeing almost any vegetable. See the variations below or the chart on page 389 for more ideas.

About 1½ pounds vegetables, one kind or a combination

Salt

2 tablespoons extra virgin olive oil

Freshly ground black pepper

Minced parsley leaves for garnish (optional)

① Peel and trim the vegetables as necessary; cut them into roughly equal-size pieces, 1 or 2 inches in diameter. Put everything in a pot with water to cover and add a large pinch of salt; or put in a steamer above water. Bring to a boil and cook until the vegetable is tender, usually 5 to 15 minutes.

② Drain the vegetables well, reserving some of the cooking liquid. (You may prepare the recipe in advance up to this point; refrigerate, well wrapped or in a covered container, for up to 2 days before proceeding.) Put the vegetables through a food mill placed over the pot or cool slightly and put them in a blender or food processor with as much of the cooking liquid as you need to get the machine going. (You can also mash the vegetables with a large fork or potato masher, adding the cooking liquid as needed.)

③ Add the olive oil and stir, then taste, season with more salt if necessary, and sprinkle with pepper. Serve, keep warm, or allow to cool for reheating later. Garnish before serving.

Rich Vegetable Purée: Replace the olive oil with butter; add up to ½ cup cream, sour cream, half-and-half, or milk.

13. White Beans, Tuscan Style (page 594)
14. Braised Lentils, Spanish Style (page 598)
15. Flageolets, French Style (page 604)
16. Chickpeas in Their Own Broth, with Sun-Dried Tomatoes (page 605)
17. Black Beans with Orange Juice (page 606)

Some of the best purées start out as something else. As long as you keep in mind color—for example, that green and red make brown—any prepared vegetable dish, from garlicky sautéed broccoli to creamy gratins, can produce a lovely purée. Roasted root vegetables make extra-nice purées, as do grilled eggplant slices (even with the skin on) and creamed vegetables like spinach.

Put the vegetables in a blender or food processor along with a little liquid. Have some milk, cream, or olive oil handy to use as needed. You might not need any extra seasoning, but a little lemon juice or vinegar will help brighten the flavor. Purée and heat gently as directed on page 388.

17 Dishes That Make Great Purées

Strain some of the liquid from the soups (and reserve it in case you need to thin the purée) before puréeing. The other recipes should have adequate liquid for the purée, but if not, add a bit of vegetable stock (pages 101–102), water, or one of the liquids used in the recipe.

1. Glazed Carrot Soup (page 105)
2. Cauliflower Soup, Italian Style (page 105)
3. Potato and Leek Soup (page 106)
4. Roasted Beet Borscht (page 109)
5. Chickpea Soup with Saffron and Almonds (page 117)
6. Simplest Split Pea Soup (page 118)
7. Creamy Carrot Soup (page 129)
8. Pumpkin (or Winter Squash) Soup (page 133)
9. Beer-Glazed Black Beans (page 585)
10. Kidney Beans with Apples and Sherry (page 586)
11. Mixed Whole-Bean Dal with Walnuts (page 602)
12. Spicy Red Beans, Indian Style (page 593)

The Basics of Vegetable Pancakes and Fritters

There are a couple ways to approach vegetable-based pancakes—or griddlecakes as some folks call them—and fritters. You can start with cooked and puréed vegetables (see pages 387–388), use chunks of already cooked vegetables, or grate raw vegetables. The recipes in this section cover all these methods, though the concept remains the same: vegetables bound with a little batter.

In the case of pancakes, the somewhat lumpy batter is spread onto a hot greased griddle or pan and cooked until crisp on both sides. (For more tips about cooking pancakes in general, see page 200.) The mixture for fritters is generally thicker and is dropped by the spoonful into hot oil; a little leavening helps keep them light and fluffy.

Pancakes and fritters are easy to improvise. As long as the batter has some flour for structure, some egg and/or cheese for binding, and some liquid for smoothing, you shouldn't have any problems. The recipes provide lots of ideas and starting proportions, but you may need to make minor adjustments, depending on the vegetables you're using and how they were prepared. Too thin: Add a little flour, or some more vegetables. Too thick: Stir in some liquid, a spoonful at a time. The batter should be spoonable but not pourable, essentially vegetables just moist enough to hold together.

Water is the only potential pancake problem. If you're using raw vegetables high in moisture—like zucchini or onions—after grating, wrap them in a towel (or gather up in fistfuls) and give them a good squeeze. If you can, for dipping, drizzle with a syrup, pass a salsa at the table, or pool a sauce on a plate and set the cakes or fritters on top. As long as you avoid cross-cultural clashes, it'll be fine. In other words, a soy dipping sauce isn't a good idea for Parmesan-laced zucchini cakes but would work perfectly if the griddlecakes were seasoned with scallions, ginger, and sesame oil. Here are some possibilities, from the simplest to the most elaborate:

1. Minced fresh herbs or a spice blend (to make your own, see pages 810–819)
2. A pat of butter or Compound Butter (page 801) or a drizzle of olive oil or Flavored Oil (page 758)
3. Sour cream, yogurt, or crème fraîche, either on top or alongside
4. Ketchup (to make your own, see page 790)
5. Any kind of cooked salsa (to make your own, see page 787–789)
6. Any fresh tomato, tomatillo, or fruit salsa (pages 750–752)
7. Fast Tomato Sauce (page 445)
8. Balsamic Syrup (page 798)
9. Traditional Pesto (page 768) or any herb purée (pages 768–770)
10. Any mayonnaise (page 771)
11. Real Ranch Dressing (page 772)
12. Any yogurt sauce (pages 773–775)
13. Any of the Asian-style sauces on pages 777–780
14. A chutney (pages 783–787), as long as it doesn't overpower the pancake or fritter
15. Any peanut sauce (pages 794–796)
16. Hollandaise Sauce (page 802)
17. Béchamel Sauce or any of its variations (page 803)

let them rest on towels for a bit. When using cooked vegetables, make sure they too are well drained or squeezed dried. Then proceed with the recipes.

How to Serve Vegetable Pancakes and Fritters

There are many ways to pair savory pancakes and fritters with accompaniments. You can offer a little something

Vegetable Pancakes

Makes 4 servings

TIME: At least 30 minutes

Vegetables are the main feature here; the batter just serves to hold things together. I love these made with a combi-

  F Fast   **M** Make Ahead   **V** Vegan

nation of turnips and carrots, but they're also great with any of the vegetables listed below.

You cook these a little more slowly than regular pancakes, so give the vegetables a chance to soften and the sides to brown. If you're looking for a more doughy vegetable pancake, use the Everyday Pancakes recipe (page 200) without the sugar and simply stir in up to a cup of grated raw or finely chopped cooked vegetables.

Other vegetables you can use: yellow squash, carrots, parsnips, beets, celery root, or scallions; or cooked, squeezed, and chopped spinach or other greens.

> About 1 pound turnips, zucchini, winter squash, or sweet potatoes, peeled if necessary (about 2 cups packed)
>
> $^1/_2$ onion, grated
>
> 1 egg, lightly beaten
>
> 1 cup flour, more or less
>
> Salt and freshly ground black pepper
>
> Milk, half-and-half, or cream as needed
>
> 2 tablespoons melted butter or extra virgin olive oil, plus more for the pan

① Preheat the oven to 275°F. Grate the vegetable(s) by hand or with the grating disk of a food processor. Mix the vegetables, onion, egg, and flour together. Sprinkle with salt and pepper. Then add just enough milk so that the mixture drops easily from a large spoon. Stir in 2 tablespoons melted butter or olive oil.

② Put a pat of butter or a spoonful of oil in a large skillet or griddle over medium heat. When the butter is melted or the oil is hot, drop in spoonfuls of the batter; use a fork to spread the vegetables into an even layer. (You'll probably have to work in batches; keep pancakes in the oven until all are finished.) Cook, turning once, until nicely browned on both sides, about 15 minutes. Serve hot or at room temperature.

Cheesy Vegetable Pancakes. Add up to 1 cup grated cheese, like cheddar, Parmesan, ricotta salata, or manchego, to the batter, along with the vegetables in Step 1.

Zucchini-Pesto Pancakes. Use zucchini and substitute Traditional Pesto (page 768) for the Parmesan.

Beet Pancakes. Use beets and, if you like, substitute sour cream or goat cheese for the Parmesan; add 1 tablespoon chopped fresh thyme leaves.

Butternut Squash and Hazelnut Pancakes. Use butternut squash and add $^1/_2$ cup finely chopped hazelnuts to the batter.

Crisp Vegetable Pancakes, Korean Style

Pajon

> Makes 6 to 8 servings
> **TIME:** 45 minutes
>

These nearly addictive savory cakes are almost crêpelike in their crisp and chewy texture. That texture is at its best—crisp on the outside, tender and chewy on the inside—if you use rice flour, which is worth the trip to an Asian market if you don't have it on hand. Serve the pancakes hot or room temperature with Soy and Sesame Dipping Sauce and Marinade, Korean Style (page 778), or a mixture of soy sauce and vinegar.

Other vegetables you can use: corn kernels, shredded cabbage or radish (especially daikon).

> 2 cups flour, preferably half all-purpose, half rice flour
>
> 2 eggs, lightly beaten
>
> 1 tablespoon neutral oil, like grapeseed or corn, plus more for the pan
>
> 5 scallions, green parts only, cut into 3-inch lengths and sliced lengthwise
>
> 20 chives, preferably Chinese ("garlic") chives, or parsley or cilantro
>
> 2 medium carrots, grated
>
> 1 small yellow squash or zucchini, grated

1 Mix the flour, eggs, and 1 tablespoon oil with $1^1/_2$ cups water until a smooth batter is formed. Let it rest while you prepare the vegetables. When you're ready to cook, stir the scallions, chives, carrot, and squash into the batter.

2 Heat a large nonstick skillet over medium-high heat and coat the bottom with oil. When hot, ladle in a quarter of the batter and spread it out evenly into a circle. Turn the heat down to medium and cook until the bottom is browned, about 5 minutes, then flip and cook for another 5 minutes. Repeat with the remaining batter.

3 As the pancakes finish, remove them and, if necessary, drain on paper towels. Cut into small triangles and serve with a soy sauce dipping sauce.

Crispy Kimchi Pancake. Spicy: Add about 1 cup chopped Kimchi (page 96) to the batter.

Mushroom Fritters

Makes 4 servings
TIME: 30 minutes

Mushrooms play the starring role in this crunchy fritter, but almost any finely chopped, shredded, or even mashed vegetable can be used in its place. The batter is intended simply to hold the vegetable together. Use a mixture of whole wheat flour or cornmeal to add a subtle nutty or corn flavor.

Fritters are lovely on their own, sprinkled with a bit of lemon juice, or served with a dipping sauce. Salsas (pages 750–753 and 787–789), yogurt sauces (pages 773–775), chutneys (pages 783–787), and mayonnaise—especially Garlic Mayonnaise (aïoli) (page 771)—are good places to look for ideas.

Other vegetables you can use: coconut, eggplant, zucchini, yellow squash, peas, artichoke hearts, asparagus, plantain or banana, sweet potato, cassava, taro, or malanga.

Neutral oil for deep frying, like grapeseed or corn

$1^1/_4$ cups all-purpose flour

2 teaspoons baking powder

Salt and freshly ground black pepper

$^3/_4$ cup milk, plus more if needed

1 egg

2 cups finely chopped mushrooms

1 Put at least 2 inches oil in a countertop deep-fryer or in a deep pan on the stove and turn the heat to medium-high; bring to 350°F (see "Deep Frying," page 26).

2 Combine the dry ingredients in a large bowl. Beat the milk and egg together, then pour them into the dry ingredients, adding a few tablespoons more milk if necessary to make a thick but smooth batter. Stir in the mushrooms.

3 Drop the fritters by the $^1/_4$ cup or large spoonful into the hot oil. Raise the heat to maintain a fairly consistent temperature. Cook the fritters in batches, turning once, until nicely browned on all sides, a total of 4 or 5 minutes per batch. Drain the fritters on paper towels, then eat them as they are done or keep them warm in a 200°F oven until they are all done.

Coconut Fritters. Delicious both savory and sweet: Substitute shredded (sweetened or not) coconut for the mushrooms, and use coconut milk if you like. Proceed with the recipe. Sprinkle with confectioners' sugar if you're serving them sweet.

Cassava Fritters. Any tropical tuber (see page 377) works well here: Substitute 2 cups peeled and diced cassava for the mushrooms; reduce the flour to about $^1/_2$ cup. Put the cassava in a pot, cover with water, and bring to a boil; lower the heat and cook at a slow bubble until tender, about 20 minutes. Mash the cassava with about $^1/_4$ cup of their cooking liquid, let it cool, stir in the liquid ingredients, then the dry ingredients. Proceed with the recipe. Serve with classic Salsa Roja (page 787) or Salsa Borracha (page 788).

Eggplant and Sesame Fritters. Wonderful with a yogurt dip (pages 773–775): Substitute $1^1/_2$ cups chopped, steamed eggplant (page 297) for the mushrooms. Add $^1/_4$ cup each tahini, sesame seeds, and chopped fresh mint leaves; combine with the batter.

The Basics of Stuffed Vegetables

Forget the soggy stuffed cabbage or peppers you remember from the high school cafeteria: These back-to-the-basics recipes will reveal why people invented stuffed vegetables in the first place. The vegetables haven't changed (you'll see the favorites: peppers, tomatoes, cabbage, and eggplant), but the stuffings have gone way beyond the reliably good rice or bread crumbs to a variety of grains and legumes, tofu, cheese, and more that can be as simple or as elaborate as you like. There are dozens of dishes in this book that can be used as stuffing (see "Recipes to Use for Stuffing Vegetables," page 407).

As for what to stuff, you need a vegetable or fruit that has a natural cavity, like peppers or winter squash; or that can be hollowed out, like tomatoes, eggplant, and onions; or that has a leaf that can be rolled or folded (cabbage and other leafy greens). The vegetable or fruit must be able to hold up to cooking as well.

A couple points to keep in mind about the stuffing: While moist stuffings work in any vegetable, dry ones are best reserved for moist vegetables. Secondly, for vegetables with a good deal of their own flavor, like artichokes, tomatoes, or eggplant, it's best to keep the stuffing simpler; bland vegetables, like potatoes, chayote, or cabbage, take well to stuffing with loads of flavor.

Most vegetables require a bit of cooking before stuffing to ensure that the vegetable will be tender and fully cooked, to decrease the final cooking time, and to keep the stuffing from getting too dry. Precooking isn't *always* necessary; vegetables like mushrooms, ripe toma-toes, and small eggplant are naturally tender and cook quickly. I do recommended precooking, though, for most vegetables that take more than 20 minutes to cook, must be hollowed out or peeled, or will be prepared in advance. Boiling, steaming, and roasting are good techniques here, since they allow the vegetable or fruit to keep its shape. You want the precooked vegetable to be just tender—not quite fully cooked—or, for something like peppers or chiles, charred on the outside to make peeling easier.

Most stuffed vegetables finish cooking in a fairly hot oven since the baking or roasting adds a bit of depth and richness to the dish. But steaming, braising, frying, grilling, and broiling also work well. Whatever cooking technique you use, be sure to cook the dish until the vegetable or fruit is tender and the stuffing is hot.

Stuffed vegetables and fruits can be a meal centerpiece, a side dish, or an appetizer (mushrooms are ideal for this). Serve them hot straight out of the oven, steamer, or grill or at room temperature; on their own simply drizzled with extra virgin olive oil, with a sauce, or on a bed of rice, grains, or legumes.

Bread and Herb Stuffing

MAKES: Enough to fill 4 to 6 large tomatoes, peppers, or cabbage leaves

TIME: 15 minutes

Ⓕ Ⓜ

Don't let the word *stuffing* trick you into thinking that's the only use for this; it's an equally great topping for gratins, Baked Macaroni and Cheese (page 460), or simple sautéed vegetables, and if you double the recipe, this makes a nice filling, especially for ravioli or other stuffed pasta.

The amount and type of cheese you use in this recipe can vary depending on how moist you want the stuffing (or topping) to be. For example, since Parmesan is a hard, low-moisture cheese, the stuffing will be drier and will crisp nicely; using blue cheese or a soft, high-moisture cheese will yield a richer, more gooey stuffing.

    3 tablespoons butter or extra virgin olive oil

    1 tablespoon minced garlic

    1$^{1}/_{2}$ cups Fresh Bread Crumbs or Croutons (page 804
    or 806)

    $^{1}/_{4}$ cup chopped fresh herbs: parsley, chervil, cilantro,
    chives, dill, or sage, or smaller amounts of tarragon,
    rosemary, or thyme, or a combination

    $^{1}/_{2}$ cup freshly grated Parmesan or other grated or
    crumbled cheese

    Salt and freshly ground black pepper

❶ Put the butter or oil in a skillet over medium-high heat. When the butter is melted or the oil is hot, add the garlic and bread crumbs and cook, stirring often, until golden brown, about 5 minutes.

❷ Remove from the heat, add the herbs and cheese, and sprinkle with salt and pepper. Stuff into any vegetable you like.

7 Delicious Additions to Bread and Herb Stuffing

Stir any of these into the bread crumb mixture along with the herbs.

1. Nuts: Substitute chopped nuts (almonds, walnuts, pine nuts, pecans, peanuts, etc.) for half the bread crumbs.
2. Olives or capers: Add $^{1}/_{4}$ cup chopped olives or capers.
3. Hard-cooked eggs: Substitute chopped hard-cooked eggs for half of the bread crumbs.
4. Tofu: Substitute chopped firm tofu for half of the bread crumbs or for the cheese.
5. Spinach: Substitute cooked, squeezed, and chopped spinach for half of the bread crumbs.
6. Mushrooms: Substitute cooked and chopped mushrooms for half of the bread crumbs.
7. Dried fruit: Substitute chopped dried fruit for half of the bread crumbs.

Stuffed Onions

MAKES: 4 servings

TIME: About 1 hour, largely unattended

Golden, crunchy, and sweet, stuffed onions always make a dramatic, unusual, and unexpectedly delicious presentation. This two-step process works for many other vegetables that require a little hollowing out before filling, like tomatoes and zucchini. I like to save the insides for another use and stuff the cavity with something interesting, like this spinach and bread crumb combo.

Other vegetables you can use: zucchini or other summer squash, or any small winter squash.

    4 large yellow onions

    1 pound spinach

    $^{1}/_{2}$ recipe Bread and Herb Stuffing (page 395)

    Salt and freshly ground pepper

    $^{1}/_{4}$ cup extra virgin olive oil

❶ Preheat the oven to 375°F. Trim just enough off the ends of the onions so that they stand up; don't peel. Wrap each onion in foil and bake until tender, about 30 minutes.

❷ Boil, shock, drain, squeeze, and chop the spinach according to the directions on page 239. Combine it with the bread crumb stuffing. Taste and adjust the seasoning. Remove the onions from the oven and let them sit until cool enough to handle. (The recipe can be prepared to this point and the stuffing and onions covered tightly and refrigerated for up to a day or so.)

❸ Turn the oven up to 425°F and use some of the oil to grease a small baking dish. Carefully remove the foil and the center onion layers, leaving 2 to 3 outer layers intact, and remove the skins. (Save the insides for another use.) Stuff the onions halfway with the spinach–bread crumb mixture and put them upright in the prepared dish. (If there's any stuffing left over, scatter it around between the onions.) Drizzle the rest of the oil over all and bake until the onions are deeply colored and the stuffing is hot and crisp on top, about 20 minutes. Serve hot or at room temperature.

Stuffed Onions with Béchamel. The béchamel adds a nice richness: Prepare 1 recipe Béchamel Sauce (page 803). Proceed with the recipe; serve with additional sauce if you like.

Stuffed Artichokes

MAKES: 4 to 6 servings

TIME: 30 minutes, with parcooked artichokes

Artichokes must be cooked before being stuffed since they take a while to become tender. Steaming is preferable to boiling for the parcooking so the artichokes don't become waterlogged. But the final cooking is in the oven—as opposed to the steamer—so that the bread stuffing crisps on the top and the artichokes get a bit of that rich roasted flavor.

The olive and hard-cooked egg variations of the Bread and Herb Stuffing are also nice with artichokes.

Other vegetables you can use: onions, winter squash, eggplant, or peppers; mushrooms and tomatoes don't require parcooking.

4 to 6 large artichokes, steamed (see page 258)

$1/4$ cup extra virgin olive oil

Salt and freshly ground pepper

1 recipe Bread and Herb Stuffing (page 395)

① Preheat the oven to 375°F. Pry open the central petals of the steamed artichokes and pull and then scrape out the choke with a spoon (see the illustration on page 258). Drizzle olive oil inside and on the leaves of the artichokes and sprinkle with some salt and pepper.

② Stuff with the bread crumb stuffing, put on a baking sheet or in a pan, and bake until the artichokes are tender and the stuffing is hot throughout, about 20 min-

utes. Test by inserting a metal skewer into the center, removing it, and putting the skewer on your wrist or lip; if it's warm, the stuffing is hot. Serve hot or room temperature.

Stuffed Mushrooms. A great appetizer: Substitute 2 pounds large white mushrooms or cremini for the artichokes—you want mushrooms with good-size caps to hold the stuffing. Remove the stems and scrape out any of the gills to increase the cavity space. No need to parcook the mushrooms. Proceed with the recipe.

Stuffed Eggplant

Imam Bayildi

MAKES: 4 or more servings

TIME: 1 hour, plus time to rest

This meatless variation of a traditional Turkish dish is first pan-roasted to soften the eggplant and give it a good browning. The second roasting adds more depth of flavor and allows the flavors to meld.

You can also use this technique but vary the stuffing. Simply skip Step 2 and prepare another filling. Then use it to stuff the eggplant in Step 3. See the lists of recipes on page 407 for alternate stuffings.

STUFFED EGGPLANT

When stuffing an eggplant—or any other vegetable—don't put so much stuffing in that it spills out.

1/2 cup extra virgin olive oil

4 small eggplant, about 1 pound or a little more, unpeeled

2 medium onions, sliced

4 garlic cloves, sliced

2 ripe tomatoes, cored and diced (drained canned are fine)

1/2 cup chopped parsley leaves

1 tablespoon sugar

Salt and freshly ground black pepper

1 lemon, cut into wedges

① Preheat the oven to 375°F. Heat half the oil in a large skillet over medium-high heat. When hot, add the eggplant and brown on all sides, about 10 minutes, adjusting the heat and turning as necessary. Drain on paper towels. Cut a slit lengthwise in each eggplant, taking care to not cut all the way through, then assemble them in a baking dish that will hold them snugly.

② Add the remaining oil to the skillet and turn the heat to medium-low; cook the onions and garlic, stirring occasionally, until very soft and fragrant, about 10 minutes. Add the tomatoes and cook until softened, about 5 minutes more, then stir in the parsley and sugar and sprinkle with salt and pepper. Remove from the heat.

③ Stuff the onion-tomato mixture into the slits in the eggplant. Pour any remaining pan juices and 3 tablespoons water over the eggplant, cover loosely with foil, and bake for 30 minutes. Remove from the oven, cool to room temperature, squeeze the lemon juice on top, and serve.

Tomatoes Stuffed with Rice

MAKES: 4 or more servings

Time: 50 minutes with cooked rice

Ⓜ

A simple and delicious dish in which tomatoes are stuffed raw and roasted in a really hot oven to maximize caramelization. This single cooking technique works best for vegetables with a good amount of water in the flesh, which you clean of seeds, chop, and mix into the rice and cheese stuffing

The tomatoes can be prepared for stuffing in two ways: by slicing off a "lid" and creating a container out of the whole tomato or by halving the tomato, scraping out the insides, and stuffing each half (best for large tomatoes or for making stuffed-tomato appetizers).

Other vegetables you can use: bell peppers (the insides will be hollow), mushrooms, small eggplant, and summer squash can be stuffed raw; chayote, onions, winter squash, cabbage, or any sturdy cooking green must be parcooked before being stuffed.

4 to 6 firm ripe tomatoes, about 6 ounces each

1 cup cooked white, basmati, brown, or wild rice (see page 505), or any cooked grain

1 cup grated Gruyère, Asiago, manchego, Monterey Jack, or mozzarella cheese

1 tablespoon minced garlic

Salt and freshly ground black pepper

1/2 cup extra virgin olive oil

Chopped parsley or fresh basil leaves for garnish

① Preheat the oven to 450°F. Cut a 1/4-inch slice from the smooth end of each tomato (the stem end is typically flatter and makes for a more stable base). Reserve these slices. Use a spoon to scoop out all of the insides of the tomatoes, leaving a wall about 1/4 inch thick. Discard the woody core and seeds and chop the pulp; mix it with the rice, cheese, garlic, and some salt and pepper.

② Sprinkle the inside of the tomatoes with salt and pepper, stuff them with the rice mixture, and replace the top slices. Spread half the olive oil in a shallow roasting pan that will allow for a little room between the tomatoes and put them in the pan. Sprinkle all with salt and pepper and put the roasting pan in the oven.

③ Roast the tomatoes for 30 to 40 minutes, until they are shriveled and the stuffing is hot. Test by inserting a metal skewer into the center, removing it, and

Note the nice little cap made from the top of the tomato. Do not overstuff!

putting the skewer on your wrist or lip; if it's warm, the stuffing is hot. Serve hot, warm, or at room temperature, drizzled with the remaining olive oil and garnished with the herb.

Red Peppers Stuffed with Quinoa and Goat Cheese. Raw peppers hold their shape and retain a crispness throughout cooking, while preroasted peppers will be very soft; both ways are delicious: Substitute red bell peppers for the tomatoes. Use cooked quinoa and goat cheese; mix the herbs in with the stuffing if you like.

Zucchini Stuffed with Couscous. The seedy center is scooped out to make room for the couscous stuffing: Substitute fat and straight zucchini or yellow squash for the tomatoes and couscous for the rice. Omit the cheese. Add ¼ cup chopped tomatoes and 1 table-spoon each chopped olives and harissa (page 830). In Step 1, halve the zucchini lengthwise and use a spoon to scrape out the seeds. Mix the couscous, tomatoes, olives, and harissa with some salt and pepper. Stuff the zucchini, mounding the couscous about an inch or so high. Proceed with the recipe; garnish with parsley.

Acorn Squash Stuffed with Wild Rice. A wonderful fall or Thanksgiving dish: Substitute 2 or 3 acorn squash for the tomatoes; use wild rice and omit the cheese. Add about 1 cup freshly squeezed orange juice, 2 table-spoons grated orange zest, ½ cup dried cranberries, and chopped pecans to garnish. Halve the squash, scrape out the seeds, and rub the inside flesh with some of the olive oil; roast, cut side down, in a 375°F oven for 25 minutes. Meanwhile, mix the remaining ingredients together. Flip the squash over and fill with the stuffing; continue roasting until the flesh is tender, another 20 minutes or so. Sprinkle with the pecans.

Chiles Rellenos

MAKES: 4 servings
TIME: 1 hour

The classic Mexican stuffed chile dish: the crisp coating is light and ethereal, the chiles soft and yielding, and the cheese oozing. You'll never regret the hour it takes to make these—they are that good. If time is an issue, make the chiles through Step 1, cover, and refrigerate until ready to batter and cook, up to a day in advance.

4 large or 8 small poblano or other mild green fresh chiles (see page 826)

3 cups grated or shredded Chihuahua cheese or Monterey Jack

Neutral oil, like grapeseed or corn, for frying

2 egg whites

½ cup all-purpose flour

½ teaspoon salt

1 cup beer or water

Green Enchilada Sauce or Salsa Borracha (page 788)

Crumbled queso fresco for garnish

1 Roast the chiles as directed on page 333; peel the skins, but leave the stems on. Cut a slit in one side and remove the seeds. Stuff the chiles with cheese and use

toothpicks or a long bamboo skewer to sew them shut; set aside.

② Put at least 3 inches (more is better) of oil in a large, deep saucepan. The narrower the saucepan, the less oil you'll need, but the more oil you use, the more chiles you can cook at the same time. Turn the heat to medium-high and heat the oil to about 365°F (a pinch of the batter will sizzle immediately).

③ Whip the egg whites until they hold soft peaks. Whisk the flour, salt, and beer together in a medium bowl. It should be the consistency of thin pancake batter; add flour or beer if necessary. Gently fold the egg whites into the batter; some white streaks remaining are okay.

④ Dip the stuffed chiles into the batter to coat and immediately fry until crisp and golden brown, about 5 minutes. Use the long skewers to help rotate and remove the chiles or use a spatula; drain on paper towels. Remove the picks or skewers and serve immediately with the sauce, sprinkled with the queso fresco.

Grilled Chiles Rellenos. A quicker, no-peeling, no-frying variation; just stuff and grill. The papery skin blisters a bit and can either be eaten or removed by the diners: Skip the roasting and batter and grill the chiles, turning once or twice, over moderately high heat until the skins are blistered and the flesh is tender. Serve immediately.

Chiles Rellenos with Corn and Pumpkin Seeds. The corn and seeds provide great crunchy texture: Substitute equal parts corn kernels and pumpkin seeds (pepitas) for half of the cheese. Proceed with the recipe.

CHILES RELLENOS

It helps to skewer chiles closed after stuffing; break a wooden skewer in half if necessary.

Chiles Rellenos with Goat Cheese and Walnuts. Tangy from the goat cheese and almost meaty from the walnuts: Substitute 1½ cups each goat cheese and chopped walnuts for the Chihuahua or Jack cheese. Combine the goat cheese and walnuts; use a piping bag (or sturdy plastic bag with the corner cut off) to fill the chiles. Proceed with the recipe.

Cabbage Stuffed with Lentils and Rice

MAKES: 8 to 12 rolls, at least 4 servings
TIME: About 1 hour

Here the cabbage leaves and packages are steamed; this "wet" cooking method makes for a moist and tender dish. You can also braise the cabbage packages in a sauce—see the variation below—or just use vegetable stock. Without the cheese, these rolls are vegan.

Other vegetables you can use: onions, summer squash, chayote, mushrooms, or any sturdy cooking green.

2 tablespoons extra virgin olive oil, plus a little for garnish if you like

½ onion, chopped

2 teaspoons minced garlic

2 cups vegetable stock (pages 101–102), or water

½ cup white, brown, or basmati rice

½ cup dried lentils

Salt and freshly ground black pepper

1 medium head white or Savoy cabbage

Gruyère, fontina, Gouda, or mozzarella cheese slices or butter (optional)

Chopped parsley leaves or chives for garnish

① Put the oil in a medium pot over medium-high heat. When hot, add the onion and cook, stirring occasionally, until it's soft, about 5 minutes. Add the garlic

Ⓕ Fast   Ⓜ Make Ahead   Ⓥ Vegan

and cook for another minute, then add the stock and bring to a boil.

② If you're using brown rice, add it to the pot along with the lentils. If you're using white or basmati rice, add the lentils and cook them for 5 minutes, then add the rice. Turn the heat to medium-low so that the mixture bubbles gently, cover, and cook until the lentils and rice are tender and the liquid is mostly absorbed (you don't want it completely dry), 25 to 30 minutes. If there is excess liquid, take the cover off, turn the heat to high, and boil it off, being careful not to burn the bottom. Sprinkle with salt and pepper and set aside.

③ Meanwhile, use a thin-bladed sharp knife to cut a cone-shaped wedge out of the bottom of the cabbage, removing its core. Pull off 8 to 12 large, untorn leaves and put in a steamer above a couple inches of salted water. Cover and cook until the leaves are just flexible enough to bend. Make a V-cut in each leaf to remove the tough central stem.

④ To stuff the cabbage leaves, put a leaf, curved side up, on a counter or cutting board. Put $1/4$ cup or so of filling in the center of the leaf, near where you cut off the stem. Fold over the sides, then roll up from the stem end, making a little package; you'll quickly get the hang of it. Don't roll too tightly—the mixture will expand as it cooks. Skewer the rolls with a toothpick or two to hold them together or just put them seam side down. (You can make the stuffed cabbage to this point up to a day or two in advance; just cover and refrigerate. Bring the rolls to room temperature before proceeding.)

⑤ Put the cabbage packages in the steamer (check that there is enough water) and cook until the cabbage is tender, 10 to 15 minutes. Top with a slice of cheese and run under the broiler until bubbly if you like or drizzle with olive oil or melt a pat of butter on top. Sprinkle with herbs and serve.

Cabbage Stuffed with Lentils and Rice in Red Wine Sauce. Make a sauce for braising before making the stuffing: Put a tablespoon of olive oil in a deep skillet large enough to hold all the cabbage packages in a single layer over medium-high heat. When hot, add $1/2$ onion, minced, and cook until soft, about 5 minutes; stir in 2 tablespoons tomato paste and cook until rusty brown in color. Add 1 cup red wine, let it cook for a couple minutes, then add 2 cups stock and a couple sprigs fresh thyme; reduce the heat so the sauce bubbles gently. Proceed with the recipe from Step 1. For Step 5, instead of steaming, put the packages in the simmering sauce, cover, and cook until the cabbage is tender (add more stock if the sauce reduces too much).

Cabbage Stuffed with Whole-Grain Bread Salad. A fabulous stuffing—studded with dried figs and dates:

CABBAGE STUFFED WITH LENTILS AND RICE

Stuffing a cabbage or other leaf is much like making a burrito: (STEP 1) Put a not-too-large amount of filling on the third closest to you and fold over that end. (STEP 2) Fold in the sides, then (STEP 3) roll it up.

Substitute the Whole-Grain Bread Salad (page 89) for the lentil and rice stuffing (skip Steps 1 and 2). Proceed with the recipe.

Blue Cheese Apples

MAKES: 6 to 8 servings
TIME: About 1 hour

Nothing says autumn quite like the baked apples that we usually think of as dessert. These, however, are savory, made with blue cheese and sage. They're perfect for a festive buffet table, but because you can make them ahead, they're great everyday food too. Use them to garnish any green salad or as a side dish with any "Meat" loaf (see sidebar on page 664) and Mashed Potatoes (page 341). Drizzle them with honey and they make a great dessert.

Other fruits you can use: peaches or nectarines (reduce each part of the baking time by half).

3 tablespoons butter, melted

6 medium red or green apples, like Pippin, Gala, or Jonathan

$1/4$ cup apple juice or water

1 cup port, red wine, or more apple juice

$1^1/2$ cups crumbled blue cheese (about 6 ounces)

1 tablespoon minced fresh sage leaves or 1 teaspoon dried

Salt and freshly ground black pepper

1 Preheat the oven to 375°F. Grease a 9 × 13-inch baking pan or large gratin dish with 1 tablespoon of the butter.

2 Cut the apples in half lengthwise and remove the seeds and core, creating a little "cup" in each half. Put them in the prepared pan or dish, cut sides down so that the skins face up. Drizzle with the remaining butter and pour the apple juice over all. Bake until they just begin to get tender, 15 to 20 minutes. (You can make the apples to this point up to a day in advance; just cover and refrigerate. Bring them to room temperature before proceeding.)

3 Carefully turn the apples over and pour the port over all. Use a spoon to baste them again with some of the juices in the pan. Fill the cup in each apple half with crumbled blue cheese. Sprinkle with sage, salt, and pepper. Return the apples to the oven and bake until the cheese is hot and bubbly and the apples are tender, about 20 minutes more. Serve the apples hot or at room temperature and pass the pan juices at the table. (If you have the energy, boil some of the liquid out of the pan juices first, to make them syrupy and more saucelike.)

Mascarpone Apples with Almonds. Creamier and milder, with crunch from the nuts: Use 1 cup (4 ounces) mascarpone cheese instead of the blue cheese and thyme instead of the sage. When the apples come out of the oven, sprinkle with $1/2$ cup chopped almonds.

Cheddar Apples with Hazelnuts. The sharper the cheese, the better: Use grated cheddar instead of the blue cheese and thyme instead of the sage. When the

BLUE CHEESE APPLES

Use a melon baller or small spoon to scoop out the seeds and core in each apple half.

F Fast   M Make Ahead   V Vegan

apples come out of the oven, sprinkle with $^1/_2$ cup chopped hazelnuts.

The Basics of Vegetable Pies

Turning a vegetable into a savory pie is an easy way to make something special, an impressive dish to serve for a brunch, potluck, or everyday dinner. Being able to slice it into wedges makes it ideal for feeding a crew, and if you really want to wow your guests you can create individual pies or tartlets in 3- or 4-inch tins.

In this collection of vegetable pie recipes you'll find three recipes, each with a completely different take on the concept. The first is simple and rustic with a crumbly, cakey top and bottom crust; the second is a striking layered and pressed vegetable torte without any crust; and the third has a light and flaky phyllo crust.

If a pie isn't a pie to you unless it has a butter and flour crust, use the Savory Piecrust (page 767) or Savory Tart Crust (page 768).

Kale or Chard Pie

MAKES: 4 to 6 servings

TIME: $1^1/_4$ hours

Ⓜ

A simple and beautiful pie with a tangy, almost biscuit-like (and no-roll!) top and bottom crust. Bake it ahead and serve it room temperature or serve it warm. It's a nice main course but also a fine appetizer when cut into smaller pieces.

Other vegetables you can use: collards, spinach (squeezed and chopped), broccoli, cauliflower, cabbage, and mushrooms.

2 tablespoons butter, plus more as needed

About 8 large kale or chard leaves, thinly sliced

1 medium onion, sliced

Salt and freshly ground black pepper

$^1/_4$ cup chopped mixed herbs, like parsley, thyme, chervil, and chives

6 eggs

1 cup whole-milk yogurt or sour cream

3 tablespoons mayonnaise

$^1/_2$ teaspoon baking powder

$1^1/_4$ cups all-purpose flour

❶ Preheat the oven to 375°F. Put the butter in a large skillet, preferably nonstick, over medium heat. A minute later, add the kale and onion. Sprinkle with salt and pepper and cook, stirring occasionally, until the leaves are quite tender, about 10 minutes; do not brown. Remove from the heat, add the herbs, then taste and adjust the seasoning.

❷ Meanwhile, hard-cook 3 of the eggs (see page 166), then shell and coarsely chop. Add to the cooked kale mixture and let cool while you make the batter.

❸ Combine the yogurt, mayonnaise, and remaining eggs. Add the baking powder and flour and mix until smooth. Lightly butter a 9 × 12-inch ceramic or glass baking dish. Spread half the batter over the bottom, then top with the kale filling; smear the remaining batter over the kale, using your fingers or a rubber spatula to make sure there are no gaps in what will form the pie's top crust.

❹ Bake for 45 minutes; it will be shiny and golden brown. Let the pie cool for at least 15 minutes before slicing it into as many squares or rectangles as you like. Eat warm or at room temperature.

Cabbage Pie. An Eastern European classic: Replace the kale with 1 medium head of Savoy or white cabbage and the mixed herbs with $^2/_3$ cup snipped fresh dill.

Mushroom and Kasha Pie. Meaty in flavor and texture and can be made with almost any cooked grain, including wheat and rye berries: Substitute 3 cups chopped or sliced mushrooms for the kale and add 1 cup cooked kasha (see page 537). Add the kasha to the mushroom mixture along with the herbs.

EVERYDAY STUFFED VEGETABLES

Same techniques—all baked at 375°F—as in the recipes; different vegetable and stuffing combos.

VEGETABLE	PREPARATION	STUFFING	HOW TO COOK AND SERVE
Butternut Squash	Peeling is optional; halve, scrape out seeds, drizzle with olive oil, and roast, cut side down, in a 350°F oven until just tender. You can scoop out some of the flesh in the "neck" to make a larger cavity for stuffing; mix the flesh with the filling.	Mix 1 head Roasted Garlic (page 304) cloves, peeled, bread crumbs, chopped almonds, and dried apricots; season with salt and pepper; fill cavities of squash halves and sprinkle with more bread crumbs.	Bake until the squash is tender; serve with any cooked grain.
Chayote	Don't bother to peel; halve, remove the pit, drizzle with extra virgin olive oil or dot with butter, and bake, covered, in a 350°F oven until tender, about 20 minutes. Scoop out a spoonful of the flesh to make a larger cavity for stuffing; mix the flesh with the filling.	Mix cooked millet, chopped tomato, and any salsa (to make your own, see pages 750–753 and 787–789) with some crumbled queso fresco or grated Monterey Jack; season with salt and pepper; fill cavities of chayote halves.	Bake until the chayote is tender; sprinkle with chopped fresh cilantro leaves.
Eggplant	Peeling is optional; halve lengthwise or—for large, thick eggplant—cut crosswise into 3-inch-thick cylinders; drizzle with olive oil and roast in a 350°F oven until tender. Scoop out the insides or use a spoon to mold a cavity.	Cook chopped onion, celery or fennel, and minced garlic in olive oil until tender; add pine nuts and raisins; sprinkle with a bit of balsamic vinegar and salt and pepper; fill cavities and sprinkle with grated Parmesan or bread crumbs.	Bake until the eggplant is very tender; sprinkle with chopped parsley or basil leaves.
Boston or Butter Lettuce	Pull off the largest whole leaves; rinse.	Mash cooked green peas with ricotta, chopped mint, and some grated Parmesan; sprinkle with salt and pepper; spoon a couple tablespoons of the filling into the "bowl" of the lettuce; fold the sides over and roll; use a toothpick to hold it if necessary.	Steam until the lettuce is wilted and the filling is hot; melt a pat of butter on top and serve.
Napa Cabbage	Pull off the largest whole leaves; steam until just flexible enough to bend; make a V-cut in each leaf to remove the tough central stem.	Mix crumbled or finely diced tofu with chopped scallion, minced peeled fresh ginger, minced garlic, and soy sauce; spoon the filling into the bowl of the cabbage; fold the sides over and roll; use a toothpick to hold it, if necessary.	Steam until the cabbage is tender and the filling is hot; serve with rice.

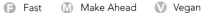 Fast   Make Ahead   Vegan

VEGETABLE	PREPARATION	STUFFING	HOW TO COOK AND SERVE
Pears	Use pears that are still crisp; peeling is optional; halve, core, and set aside.	Mix cooked wheat berries, chopped thyme, parsley, and chervil, and extra virgin olive oil; sprinkle with salt and pepper; pile onto the pears.	Bake until the pears are tender and the filling is hot; serve on a bed of arugula or spinach with a sherry or mustard vinaigrette.
Peaches or nectarines	Halve, remove pit, and drizzle with extra virgin olive oil.	Mix crumbled fresh cheese, chopped nuts, and a pinch or two garam masala (to make your own, see page 815); sprinkle with salt and pepper; pile onto the peaches or nectarine halves.	Bake until the fruit is tender and the filling is hot; serve on a bed of Biryani (page 512).

Layered Vegetable Torte

MAKES: 4 to 6 servings

TIME: At least 2 hours, or a day largely unattended

A really awesome-looking dish, in which the sliced vegetables (you can grill them instead of roasting for even more flavor or if it's more convenient) are layered and pressed to form the torte—you could call it a pie—so that when it's cut you can see the bands of vegetables. This dish makes a really spectacular meal centerpiece or party dish. And it can be assembled and refrigerated up to 2 days ahead; in fact, the longer it's pressed, the better it keeps its shaped when sliced. Omit the garnish and it's vegan too.

Other vegetables you can use: thinly sliced and parcooked butternut squash, summer squash, potato, sweet potato, leeks, onions, turnips, beets, peppers, and chiles.

2 medium eggplant

4 medium zucchini

Salt

4 red bell peppers, roasted and cleaned (see page 333)

$1/_2$ cup or more extra virgin olive oil

Freshly ground black pepper

20 or so fresh basil leaves, some chopped or torn for garnish

Freshly grated Parmesan cheese for garnish (optional)

1 Peel the eggplant if the skin is thick or the eggplant is less than perfectly firm. Cut it and the zucchini into $1/_4$-inch-thick slices; salt the eggplant (see page 46) if time allows. Cut each roasted pepper into thirds or fourths and set aside.

2 Preheat the oven to 400°F. Smear 2 (or more) baking sheets with 2 tablespoons oil each. Lay the eggplant slices on one sheet and the zucchini on the other in a single layer. (You may need to work in batches; cooking the eggplant on the 2 baking sheets, then cooking the zucchini.) Sprinkle with some salt and pepper (if you did not salt the eggplant) and drizzle or brush another couple tablespoons oil over each sheet of vegetables. Roast until the eggplant and zucchini are soft, about 15 minutes for the zucchini, 20 or so for the eggplant.

3 Coat a deep pie dish with some oil. Layer a third of the eggplant slices into the bottom of the pan, covering the bottom (trim the eggplant pieces if necessary), then layer half the zucchini, peppers, and basil, sprinkling each layer with a bit of salt and pepper; repeat the layers, ending with eggplant.

4 Put a plate or other flat object (you want it to distribute weight evenly across the top of the pie) over the

top of the pie and weight it with a large tomato can or something similar. Let it rest at room temperature for at least an hour or in the fridge for a day, then remove the weight; it can be stored in the refrigerator for 2 to 3 days before serving. (Put it on a large plate or platter as juices might be squeezed out.)

⑤ Serve it room temperature or heat it in a 325°F oven until warm, about 30 minutes. Garnish with the basil and Parmesan and cut into wedges.

Cheesy Vegetable Torte. Mozzarella works nicely with the vegetables in the main recipe, but really almost any cheese (except very soft cheeses like ricotta) will work, depending on the vegetables you use in the pie: Grate or slice the cheese and add 1 or 2 layers between the vegetables. After Step 3, bake the pie in a 325°F oven until hot (you want the cheese to melt into the vegetable layers), about 40 minutes. Proceed with the recipe.

Autumn Vegetable Torte. Almost dessert; it's wonderful sprinkled with brown sugar or drizzled with maple syrup and served for brunch too: Substitute peeled butternut squash, peeled sweet potato, and cored apples for the eggplant, zucchini, and red peppers. Instead of the basil, use sage leaves or a couple table-spoons chopped fresh rosemary.

Mushroom and Asparagus Pie with Phyllo Crust

MAKES: 4 to 6 servings
TIME: About 1 hour

Phyllo is magical stuff, and it makes a wonderful base for vegetable pie. Brushing each sheet of phyllo with butter or oil is essential to getting the best crust, and you have to work fast because this paper-thin dough dries out very quickly. But there's not that much effort, or any skill, involved. (See the illustrations for Banana Strudel on page 879.)

The filling can be made and refrigerated up to 2 days ahead, but the phyllo must be done just before baking.

8 tablespoons (1 stick) butter, melted, $1/2$ cup extra virgin olive oil, or a mixture

8 ounces mushrooms, preferably an assortment, trimmed and sliced

A handful of dried porcini, reconstituted (optional)

1 tablespoon minced garlic

Salt and freshly ground black pepper

$1/2$ bunch asparagus, parcooked and chopped, or 1 cup green peas

1 cup grated provolone

12 or so fresh basil leaves, thinly sliced

8 to 12 sheets phyllo dough, thawed

① Preheat the oven to 350°F. Put 3 tablespoons of the butter or oil in a large skillet over medium heat. When hot, add the mushrooms, then the garlic, and sprinkle with some salt and pepper. Cook, stirring occasionally, until tender, 10 to 15 minutes. Turn the mixture out into a bowl and let it cool, then stir in the asparagus, provolone, and basil. Taste and adjust the seasoning.

② Brush a pie or baking dish with some of the butter or olive oil. Keep the phyllo sheets covered with a piece of plastic and a damp towel over the top to keep them from drying out. Remove one sheet at a time and quickly brush it with the butter (see page 879) and lay it in the dish. Continue brushing and layering another 4 or 5 phyllo sheets, turning each one slightly; the edges of the sheets should hang over the rim of the dish.

③ Spoon the mixture over the phyllo, then layer the remaining sheets on top, brushing each one with butter or oil and slightly turning it. Fold in the edges to enclose the pie, sealing with melted butter.

④ Score the top of the pie into squares or diamond shapes and bake for 30 to 40 minutes, until golden brown. Serve warm or at room temperature.

Ⓕ Fast   Ⓜ Make Ahead   Ⓥ Vegan

Dozens of recipes in this book—including any cooked rice or grain and all sorts of legume dishes—can double as stuffings. Seriously, you can pull almost anything out of those chapters and use them here. These are especially appropriate:

Rice and grain recipes:

- Fluffy Cracked Wheat with Mustard and Tarragon (page 559)
- Pearl Couscous Pilaf with Sun-Dried Tomatoes (page 551)
- Kasha with Golden Brown Onions (page 562)
- Yellow Rice, the Best Way (page 513)
- Coconut Rice and Beans (page 507)
- Spiced Rice with Chickpeas and Almonds (page 509)
- Pilaf with Fruit and Nuts (page 511)
- Kimchi Rice (page 512)
- Risotto with Herbs (page 517)
- Japanese Rice with Tomato and Fermented Black Beans (page 532)
- Barley "Succotash" (page 541)
- Bulgur Pilaf with Vermicelli (page 555)
- Quinoa with Caramelized Onions (page 559)
- Millet Miso Mash (page 566)
- Wild Rice with Chestnuts (page 567)

Legume recipes:

- White Beans, Tuscan Style (page 594)
- Mashed Favas (page 616)
- Piquant Kidney Beans with Prunes (page 586)
- Gigantes with Shiitakes (page 588)
- Fresh Favas with Tofu or Feta and Croutons (page 592)
- Twice-Cooked (Refried) Beans (page 592)
- Spicy Red Beans, Indian Style (page 593)
- White Beans with Shiitakes (page 597)
- Braised Lentils, Spanish Style (page 598)
- Flageolets, French Style (page 604)
- Black-Eyed Peas with Smoked Tofu (page 610)
- Mung Beans and Rice with Dried Apricots (page 611)
- Cheesy Puréed Beans (page 613)
- Brazilian Black Beans and Rice (page 620)

Salad, pasta, and other recipes:

- Whole Grain Bread Salad (page 89)
- Tabbouleh (page 43)
- Eggplant Salad with Miso (page 63)
- Ratatouille Salad (page 64)
- Corn Salad with Tomatoes, Feta, and Mint (page 61)
- Broiled Three-Bean Salad (page 74)
- Lemony Lentil Salad (page 75)
- Nearly any rice salad (pages 79–82)
- Bulgur and Tomato Salad (page 83)
- Wheat Berry or Other Whole Grain Salad with Cabbage and Coarse Mustard (page 85)
- Wheat Berry or Other Whole Grain Salad with Peanuts and Fresh and Dried Fruit (page 85)
- Crouton Salad (page 87)
- Orzo Salad, Greek Style (page 93)
- Tofu, Provençal Style (page 649)
- Pasta with Garlic and Oil or any of its variations (page 443)
- Pasta with Butter and Parmesan or any of its variations (page 447)
- Orzo, Risotto Style (page 451)
- Any pasta tossed with any Fast Tomato Sauce (pages 445 and 448–449)
- Pasta with any Nut Sauce (pages 455–458)

Most of these recipes can be made ahead of time and in an hour or less—both crucial elements when you're throwing a party or cooking for the holidays. But the handful of recipes that do take hours to make aren't labor-intensive, so you'll have time to prepare other dishes (or take a break!).

1. Roasted Cauliflower with Raisins and Vinaigrette (page 282)
2. Chard with Oranges and Shallots (page 286)
3. Braised and Glazed Brussels Sprouts (page 272)
4. Lentil Pâté (page 316)
5. Creamed Corn (pages 290–291)
6. Dried Fruit and Lima Stew (page 594)
7. Broiled Eggplant with Peppers, Onions, and Yogurt (page 298)
8. Eggplant Parmesan (page 299)
9. Braised Endive, Escarole, or Radicchio (page 300)
10. Grilled or Broiled Radicchio with Balsamic Glaze (page 301)
11. Roast Fennel with Orange (page 303)
12. Rolled Kale with Feta and Olives (page 308)
13. Leeks Braised in Oil or Butter (page 310)
14. Grilled Watermelon Steak (page 430)
15. Okra Stew with Tomatoes (page 324)
16. Creamed Onions (page 330)
17. Roasted Onion Halves (page 330)
18. Poached Pears (page 433)
19. Joël Robuchon Mashed Potatoes (page 343)
20. Braised Potatoes with Almonds (page 347)
21. Potatoes Provençal (page 348)
22. Potatoes "Nik" (pages 349–350)
23. Potato Croquettes (page 353)
24. Braised and Glazed Radishes, Turnips, or Other Root Vegetable (page 354)
25. Oven-Roasted Fresh Plum Tomatoes (page 375)
26. Tomato Cobbler (page 375)
27. Braised Winter Squash in Caramel Sauce (page 368)
28. Spicy Winter Squash Galette (page 368)
29. Roasted Vegetables, Thai Style (page 381)
30. Asparagus and Béchamel Gratin (page 383)
31. Potato and Sunchoke Gratin (page 384)
32. Rich Spinach Gratin (page 385)
33. Creamy Parsnip Gratin with Vanilla (page 386)
34. Stuffed Onions (page 396)
35. Tomatoes Stuffed with Rice (page 399)
36. Cabbage Stuffed with Lentils and Rice (page 400)
37. Chiles Rellenos (page 399)
38. Blue Cheese Apples (page 402)
39. Layered Vegetable Torte (page 405)

Parsnips and Wheat Berry Pie with Phyllo Crust. Just about any grated root vegetable and any cooked grain will work well here: Substitute 8 ounces peeled parsnips for the mushrooms, $1^1/_2$ cups cooked wheat berries for the asparagus, and thyme for the basil. Grate the parsnips and cook as directed in Step 1.

Dried Fruit and Nut Pie with Phyllo Crust. Loaded with savory flavors: Substitute $1^1/_2$ cups chopped mixed dried fruit, $1^1/_2$ cups chopped walnuts and/or almonds, and cilantro for the mushrooms, asparagus, and basil.

Omit the provolone and add $^1/_4$ cup chopped scallion and 3 tablespoons freshly squeezed lemon juice. Skip the cooking in Step 1 and mix together the dried fruit, nuts, garlic, cilantro, scallion, lemon juice, 3 tablespoons of the butter or oil, and a sprinkle of salt and pepper (cayenne is a great addition too). Toss the mixture into a food processor and pulse until finely chopped (but not puréed) for a less chunky filling.

Spinach and Feta Pie with Phyllo Crust. *Spanikopita*, the classic Greek pie: Instead of the mushrooms and

F Fast   M Make Ahead   V Vegan

asparagus, trim and wash 2 pounds of spinach (page 359). Use crumbled feta cheese instead of the provolone and chop $1/2$ cup parsley or mint or a combination. In Step 1 cook the spinach the way you'd cook the mushrooms. Off the heat, add the feta and herbs, taste and adjust the seasoning, then proceed with the recipe.

22 Dishes That Make Great Filling for Pie with Phyllo Crust

A huge variety of dishes can be used as this pie filling; the only thing you want to avoid is a soupy filling that will make the phyllo crust soggy. With that in mind, make any kind of filling you like—all vegetables, vegetables with cheese, and/or cooked grains or legume:

1. Rice with Cheese (page 508)
2. Rice with Chickpeas (page 509)
3. Brown Rice Pilaf with Two Mushrooms (page 514)
4. Whole Wheat Couscous with Cauliflower and Almonds (page 554)
5. Fluffy Cracked Wheat with Mustard and Tarragon (page 559)
6. Quinoa with Caramelized Onions (page 559)
7. Kidney Beans with Apples and Sherry (page 586)
8. Mung Beans and Rice with Dried Apricots (page 611)
9. Mashed Favas (page 616)
10. Braised Artichoke Hearts or any of its variations (page 259)
11. Beets with Pistachio Butter or any of its variations (page 268)
12. Sautéed Brussels Sprouts or any of its variations (page 273)
13. Red Cabbage with Apples (page 277)
14. Carrots with Dates and Raisins (page 279)
15. Sautéed Eggplant with Hazelnuts or any of its variations (page 295)
16. Braised Endive, Escarole, or Radicchio (page 300)
17. Caramelized Onions (page 329)
18. Paprika Peppers (page 335)
19. Braised Potatoes, Ten Ways (page 346)
20. Spinach with Currants and Nuts (page 360)
21. Oven-Roasted Fresh Plum Tomatoes (page 375)
22. Winter Squash Slices, Roasted (page 366)

The Basics of Cooking Fruit

Everyone enjoys eating naturally sweet and juicy fruit out of hand, but once you get used to the idea of cooking fruit—and seasoning it in ways both sweet and savory—you significantly increase the size of your recipe repertoire. To top it off, cooking makes excellent use of overripe, underripe, or slightly damaged fruit.

Still not sold? Consider this botanical fact: Some of your favorite "vegetables" (tomatoes, eggplant, and olives, just to name a few) are actually fruits, because of an arcane definition of how a plant grows its seeds. So technically you may be already eating cooked fruit without realizing it. Instead of sorting fruits and vegetables into two categories, try thinking of them as a single family of ingredients, with all sorts of different and desirable characteristics, including—but not limited to—sweetness.

Fruit is slightly more forgiving than vegetables when it comes to overcooking, but though the window from just tender to perfect may be slightly longer, the flesh goes from there to mush much faster. That makes slow cooking like poaching, stewing, or roasting most appealing for times you want to walk away from the stove. High-heat methods (grilling and sautéing) require more attention. And because fruit is naturally high in fructose, it will burn more easily if overheated. But this is easy enough to accommodate if you cook fruit at a slightly lower temperature than you would vegetables and keep an eye on it, stirring and turning as necessary.

Firmness is the best way to predict how long a fruit will take to cook: the least fibrous fruits will cook fastest (bananas, strawberries, papaya, and raspberries), while firmer fruits (pineapple, apple, and even citrus) are far more durable.

Like vegetables, fruit will continue to cook as it cools

down. So when in doubt, stick to the tried and true: Use a fork or a knife tip to judge tenderness and remove fruit from the heat before it's completely tender. But really, the worst that can happen—provided you don't burn it—is that you'll wind up with a delicious fruit sauce.

Cooked fruit can be incorporated into all sorts of dishes, not just desserts: Think of halved fruit on the grill and compotes and chutneys; none of these, even the most complex of them, take more than a few minutes to put together. For some ideas about how to season fruit before, during, and after cooking, see page 416. You'll find many more fruit recipes in the Dessert chapter, as well as instructions for making fruit purées on page 862.

To Peel or Not to Peel?

It's a real decision: Peeled fruit will cook through and lose its shape faster than unpeeled fruit, which might make you tend to cook fruit with its peel on. But if the flesh gets even slightly overdone, it tends to separate from the skin, especially during moist cooking methods like poaching and sautéing. Then you're left with the worst of both textures: soft fruit and tough peels. And of course it's simply impractical to remove the skins from fruits like grapes and cherries.

For every rule there's at least one exception, so try to use common sense: If the skin isn't edible—as in melons, mangoes, or papayas—you can usually peel the fruit before cooking. (There are exceptions, like bananas, where the skin is needed to protect the flesh and keep it intact.) However, by the opposite logic, leaving the edible peels on peaches, apples, plums, and pears during high-heat, fast-cook methods like grilling, broiling, or roasting helps hold the flesh together and improves color and flavor. Virtually everything else should be peeled if at all practical (to keep the skins from slipping off small fruits, just be careful not to overcook them).

Fruit-Cooking Techniques

Here's a rundown of the major options for cooking fruit, which are sometimes different from those for vegetables.

For example, you don't steam, boil, or shock fruit. And in some cases you use lower heat.

Poaching

Good candidates for poaching are pears, apples, pineapple, and quince, though cherries, grapes, peaches and nectarines, and plums can all be poached successfully with a little TLC. (Dried fruit is also great poached; see "Poaching Dried Fruit" below.) It's best to poach fruit in a liquid like seasoned juice, vinegar, or wine; water leaches out too much of the flavor.

The idea is to put the prepared fruit in just enough seasoned liquid to cover it. Keep the mixture just barely

Poaching Dried Fruit

Dried fruit slowly absorbs the liquid it's soaked in, becoming plump and tender and taking on the liquid's flavors at the same time (see "Macerating and Seasoning Fruit," page 417). You can speed this process up and intensify the flavors by poaching dried fruit in seasoned liquid. The process is the same as for poaching fresh fruit (see Poached Pears, page 433), and the key is to stop before the fruit falls apart. Timing will vary quite a bit, depending on the type of fruit and how dry it was to begin with (usually it'll be in the range of 10 to 30 minutes). So keep an eye on it and be ready to pull the fruit from the pot—use a slotted spoon—as soon as its wrinkles begin to disappear. Then turn up the heat under the pot and reduce the poaching liquid until it's as syrupy as you like. Cool it a bit and use it as a sauce for the poached fruit (or simply return the poached dried fruit to the syrup).

Refrigerated, poached dried fruit will keep for at least a week. You can use it on top of cooked grains, in sauces or chutneys, or spooned on top of cakes or ice cream. Or serve it plain or topped with a spoonful of yogurt or sour cream—or, if you're feeling indulgent, some heavy cream.

F Fast   M Make Ahead   V Vegan

bubbling and cook, turning it once or twice, until a toothpick or skewer barely pierces to the center. A pear might take 20 minutes or so, while cherries will be done in less than 10. Let the fruit cool in the liquid so it absorbs as much flavor as possible, then remove. Serve with the poaching liquid as is (like a soup) or boil the mixture until it reduces a bit and thickens into a syrupy sauce. Poached fruit keeps in the fridge for a couple of days.

Stewing Fruit

Fruit compote is a fancy name for stewed fruit, and it's the easiest thing in the world to make: Put cut fruit— either one kind or an assortment—into a pan with a tight-fitting lid. Sprinkle with a little sugar or other sweetener (or try salt and freshly ground black pepper). Season as you like. Cover the pan and turn the heat to medium-low. Cook, stirring occasionally until some of the juice is released and the fruit begins to soften, 5 to 20 minutes, depending on the fruit.

You can also "stew" fruit without any cooking at all. See "Macerating and Seasoning Fruit" (page 417).

Microwaving Fruit

In a pinch you can microwave fruit as you would vegetables (see page 237), though it's really just as easy—and only slightly less fast—to stew it on the stove.

Sautéing Fruit

As with vegetables, start with a deep, broad skillet over medium to medium-high heat. Swirl around a little oil or melt a pat of butter in the bottom—just enough to coat the pan and the fruit; figure 1 to 2 tablespoons per pound. When the oil gets hot—but not quite smoking— stir or toss the fruit around in the pan until it's cooked, using sweet or savory seasonings as you like.

Roasting or Baking Fruit

Roasting is one of my favorite ways to cook fruit, because—as with vegetables—it helps develop deep color and flavor. The only trick is to make sure the sugars in

the fruit caramelize, not burn. Start by setting the oven between 325°F and 350°F, a little lower than you would for vegetables. Grease a rimmed baking sheet or shallow roasting pan, or line it with a piece of parchment and add fruit, taking care not to overcrowd. Drizzle or brush with a little oil or melted butter and season if you like. Roast, checking occasionally and turning as necessary, until tender and golden, 15 to 45 minutes, depending on the fruit.

Oven-Drying Fruit

This make-ahead technique leaves fruit chewy, moist, and slightly crisp, and you control the ultimate texture by deciding how long the fruit stays in the oven. See the dried fruit sidebar on page 415 and Oven-Dried Tomatoes (page 377).

Grilling or Broiling Fruit

The heat shouldn't be as intense as with vegetables because the higher sugar content makes them quick to char. For details about preparation, cooking times, and serving ideas, see the chart on pages 413–414.

Frying Fruit

With few exceptions, fruit should be breaded or battered before being deep-fried; coating the fruit not only protects it from overcooking but helps control splattering. Flour, cornmeal, or a mixture of the two is easy enough, though a batter creates wonderful fruit fritters (see Fruit Fritters, page 697). You can either panfry in shallow oil ($^1/_2$ inch deep or so) or deep-fry in enough oil to submerge them (2 or 3 inches of oil in a deep pot).

To panfry: Set a deep skillet over medium to medium-high heat and pour in the oil. It should be very hot but not smoking before you add the fruit (test a small piece first; it should sizzle immediately and energetically).

To deep-fry: The oil should reach a temperature between 350°F and 375°F. (See "Deep Frying," page 26.) Be careful to allow enough room at the top of the pot for the fruit to displace the oil and cause it to rise. And be careful not to overload the pot.

How to Grill Fruit

Grilling is among the best ways to cook fruit, but sadly we don't think to do it very often. Once you get into it, though, you suddenly have a slew of new items to toss on the grill, perhaps changing the way you think about the backyard barbecue. And grilled fruit is more flexible than grilled vegetables because you can often choose between sweet and savory.

Grilled fruit teams beautifully with a green salad, any cooked grain, and a variety of cheeses from fresh cheese to soft (like Brie) to hard (like Parmesan). And check out the grilled fruit salsas on pages 791–792.

Sweet grilled fruit can be served with ice cream, sorbet, granita, rice pudding, or custard or next to cake or other drier desserts. Use it to make a grilled fruit pizza (really great with cream cheese or mascarpone).

The chart on page 413 has tips and suggestions for flavoring, seasoning, saucing, and serving any fruit you can grill, but the basic guidelines are simple, so you can use this as a jumping-off point. In most cases you want to use fruit that is ripe but still somewhat firm, so it will hold together on the grill. It's important to start with a clean grill and keep the heat lower than you would for vegetables but high enough to sear the fruit, bearing in mind that because most fruit are sugar laden they will char fairly quickly, in just a couple of minutes in most cases. And don't neglect to give the fruit a good brushing of oil or melted butter before you put it on the grill or you'll be scraping it off.

---

14 Killer Dishes with Grilled Fruit

Grill the fruit in these recipes for a fabulous twist.

1. Quick Wheat Berry Stew with Citrus, Dried Fruit, and Nuts (page 565)
2. Piquant Kidney Beans with Prunes (add grilled plums at last minute) (page 586)
3. Greens with Fruit, Cheese, and Nuts (page 40)
4. Balsamic Strawberries with Arugula (page 42)
5. Jícama Salad with Pineapple and Mint (page 50)
6. Jícama and Orange Salad (page 50)
7. Six-Layer Avocado Salad with Mangoes (page 53)
8. Avocado Salad with Ginger and Peanuts (page 51)
9. Wheat Berry or Other Whole Grain Salad with Peanuts and Fresh and Dried Fruit (page 85)
10. Jean-Georges's Rice Noodle Salad with Grapefruit and Peanuts (page 93)
11. Papaya and Other Fruit Salsas (page 751)
12. Carmeleized Melon Chutney (page 787)
13. Pineapple Chutney (page 785)
14. Pilaf with Fruit and Nuts (page 511)

The Basics of Other Fruit Preparations

Dried Fruit

Fruit was originally dried to preserve it; drying also intensifies the flavor of many fruits beautifully, sometimes making the dried version superior to most fresh specimens (think of dried apricots and prunes, for example). So dried fruit, available year-round in good quality at reasonable cost, can be anything from a sweet and easy snack or dessert to a lovely flavoring ingredient in baked goods, grains, stews, and more.

Several methods are used to dry fruit, starting with the most basic, primitive, and best (as long as you live near a desert): sun-drying. Here the fruit is often halved or cut into pieces and just left out in the sun for several days. It's as natural a process as you can get, but the long exposure to the sunlight and heat does degrade some of the fruit's vitamins, while leaving it subject to weather variations and insects. Other drying methods include air-

F Fast   M Make Ahead   V Vegan

FRUIT	PREPARATION	FLAVORING IDEAS	HOW TO GRILL	HOW TO SAUCE OR SEASON	SERVING SUGGESTIONS
Apple	Core and slice or cut into wedges; brush with lemon or lime juice and oil or melted butter.	Use Spice-Flavored Oil (page 758); coat with maple syrup or marinate in any vinaigrette for a few minutes—pat dry before grilling; sprinkle with five-spice powder (to make your own, see page 816).	Cook over direct heat, turning occasionally, until browned, 3 to 5 minutes.	Top with Brewhouse Mustard (page 776), Blue Cheese Dressing (page 212), or Arugula "Pesto"; sprinkle with curry powder or garam masala (to make your own, see page 815).	Serve simply with a little grated cheddar or Asiago cheese melted on top; or with Pilaf with Fruit and Nuts (page 511), Simpler-than-Pilaf Baked Rice (page 515), or Nutty Blue Cornmeal Pizza (page 547).
Bananas	Use bananas that are slightly underripe or yellow plantains. Cut off each end; slice in half lengthwise or peel and cut into $1\frac{1}{2}$-inch chunks and skewer; brush with oil or melted butter.	Use Spice-Flavored Oil (page 758); sprinkle with jerk seasoning or hot curry powder (to make your own, see page 815), or sugar, ground cinnamon, or ground ginger.	Cook over direct heat, turning occasionally, until browned, 2 to 5 minutes.	Top with Coconut Chutney (page 784), Crunchy Nut Chutney (page 784), or Simpler Peanut Sauce (page 796).	Serve with Naked Tamales with Chile Cheese Filling (page 547), Baked Curried Black Beans (page 620), or tortilla chips and salsa.
Citrus (any)	Cut in half along their equator or into 1-inch-thick slices; brush with oil or melted butter.	Sprinkle with chili powder or five-spice powder (to make your own, see page 814 or 816), or ground cinnamon or ground cardamom.	Cook over direct heat, turning occasionally, until browned, 3 to 5 minutes.	Top with Chile Paste (page 828) or sprinkle with Citrus Sprinkle (page 818) or minced ginger.	Serve with Whole Wheat Couscous with Cauliflower and Almonds (page 554), Black Beans with Orange Juice (page 606), or Shaved Artichoke Salad (page 50).
Figs	Cut in half through the stem or grill whole; brush with oil or melted butter.	Use Herb- or Aromatic-Flavored Oil (page 758); sprinkle with ground pickling spice or garam masala (to make your own, see page 819 or 815).	Cook, cut side down, over direct heat until browned, 2 to 3 minutes.	Top with Pesto with Butter (page 768), Port Wine Mustard (page 776), Balsamic Syrup (page 798), or Brown Butter (page 801).	Serve with Crêpes (page 196), a spoonful of mascarpone cheese, or simply with buttered bread (it's that good).
Mango	Peel and cut large slices or wedges off the pit; brush with oil.	Use Aromatic-Flavored Oil (page 758); sprinkle with chili powder, hot curry powder, or chaat masala (to make your own, see pages 814 or 815)	Cook over direct heat, turning occasionally, until browned, 3 to 5 minutes.	Top with Fresh Tomatillo Salsa (page 751), Chimichurri (page 769), Cilantro "Pesto" with Ginger and Chile (page 770), Cilantro-Mint Chutney (page 783), or Chile and Coconut Sauce (page 792).	Serve with Coconut Rice (page 507), Stuck-Pot Rice with Yogurt and Spices (page 524), or Braised Tofu in Caramel Sauce (page 650).

FRUIT	PREPARATION	FLAVORING IDEAS	HOW TO GRILL	HOW TO SAUCE OR SEASON	SERVING SUGGESTIONS
Melon	Cut into wedges, peeled or not , or 1½-inch cubes; skewer cubes; oil is optional.	Use Herb-Flavored Oil (page 758); coat with Lemongrass Ponzu (page 780); sprinkle with five-spice powder (to make your own, see page 816).	Cook over direct heat, turning occasionally, until browned, 3 to 5 minutes.	Top with Fresh Tomato Salsa (page 750), Citrus Salsa (page 752), or Mint "Pesto" (page 768); or sprinkle with Citrus Sprinkle (page 818) or lemon or lime juice.	Serve with Beer-Glazed Black Beans with Tamarind (page 586), Spinach Salad with Feta and Nutmeg (page 41), or feta or goat cheese.
Papaya	Peel and cut into wedges or 1½-inch cubes; skewer cubes; brush with oil.	Sprinkle with jerk seasoning (to make your own, see page 818) or Citrus Sprinkle (page 818).	Cook over direct heat, turning occasionally, until browned, 3 to 5 minutes.	Top with Chimichurri (page 769), Mint Dipping Sauce (page 778), or Thai-Style Chile Paste (page 829).	Serve with Huevos Rancheros (page 174) or Espresso Black Bean Chili (page 608).
Peaches and Nectarines	Halve or quarter; brush with oil or melted butter.	Use any Flavored Oil (page 758); coat with Sweet Miso Glaze (page 782); sprinkle with Citrus Sprinkle (page 818) or garam masala (to make your own, see page 815).	Cook, cut side down, over direct heat until browned, 2 to 3 minutes. Flip and cook the other side for a minute or two if you like.	Top with Basil Purée (page 769), Ginger Yogurt Sauce (page 774), Compound Butter (page 801), or Chipotle Paste (page 829). Off the grill, crumble blue or feta cheese on top.	Serve with Basic Wild Rice (page 567) or Green Salad with Caramelized Onion–Thyme Dressing (page 43).
Pineapple	Peel and cut into slices, wedges, or 1½-inch cubes; skewer cubes; brush with oil.	Use Herb- or Aromatic-Flavored Oil (page 758); coat with Tamarind-Date Chutney (page 785); sprinkle with chili powder (to make your own, see page 814).	Cook over direct heat, turning occasionally, until browned, 3 to 5 minutes.	Serve Lime Leaf Dipping Sauce (page 778) for dipping or top with Tropical Teriyaki Sauce (page 779), Ponzu Sauce (page 780), or Jamaican Jerk Ketchup (page 790).	Serve with White Rice and Black Beans (page 510), Basic Fried Rice, with or Without Egg (page 520), or Hot and Sour Edamame with Tofu (page 591).
Plums	Halve or quarter (skewer if you like); brush with oil or melted butter.	Use Spice- or Aromatic-Flavored Oil (page 758); sprinkle with five-spice powder (to make your own, see page 816).	Cook, cut side down, over direct heat until browned, 2 to 3 minutes.	Top with Sweet Yogurt Sauce (page 774), Honey Mustard (page 777), or Nutty Miso Sauce (page 782).	Serve with Balsamic Strawberries with Arugula (page 42), or Couscous Salad with Fennel and Raisins (page 92).

 Ⓕ Fast Ⓜ Make Ahead Ⓥ Vegan

drying (which is a combination of air circulation and low heat), which requires a dehydrator or an oven; sugar-drying (soaking or simmering the fruit in a sugar syrup followed by air-drying—think crystallized ginger); and frying (best for high-starch, low-moisture fruits like bananas). Regardless of the method, many dried fruits are treated with sulfur dioxide, a preservative that helps the fruit hold its color, flavor, and shape, before being processed. If you're sensitive to sulfites—or can taste them—nontreated dried fruits are increasingly available.

If you're interested in drying your own fruit, choose the technique based on the fruit and the results you want. Most fruits, especially those that are naturally sweet or sweet-tart and fleshy (like apricots, peaches, pears, figs, plums, grapes, and tomatoes, to name a few) are best suited for air-drying or dehydrating. Sugar-drying, obviously, loads the fruit with sugar and is good for very tart and/or astringent and less fleshy fruit like cranberries, sour cherries, and ginger (store-bought dried pineapple, cantaloupe, and papaya are often dried using this method, too). Frying is probably the least common and certainly the most fattening drying technique for fruit and is for the most part reserved for bananas and plantains.

Oven-Drying Fruit

Unless you have a dehydrator, oven-drying is your best option; it adds no extra sugar or fat, takes only a few hours, and gives you plenty of control over the dryness of the final product. Your dried fruit can be plump and chewy or shriveled and completely dry, depending on the size of the fruit or pieces and how long you dry it.

There is nothing complicated here: All you need is the fruit and a baking pan fitted with a rack. Small items like grapes, berries, and cherry tomatoes can be left whole. Medium-size fruits should be halved or sliced. Large and/or very hard fruit, like papaya, pineapple, and coconut, need to be sliced. Put the prepared fruit on the rack over the baking sheet—cut side down, if applicable—and put in a 225°F oven for anywhere from 2 to 8 to 12 hours. Rotate the baking sheet every couple of hours and check; they're done when they're as shriveled

29 Recipes That Feature Dried Fruit

From sweet to savory, stewed to "raw," dried fruit is a diverse ingredient.

1. Pilaf with Fruit and Nuts (page 511)
2. Simple Paella with Prunes (page 523)
3. Pearl Couscous Tagine (page 553)
4. Coconut Rice with Coconut Bits (page 508)
5. Simpler Baked Rice with Coconut (page 516)
6. Bulgur Pilaf with Apricots and Pistachios (page 557)
7. Quick Wheat Berry Stew with Citrus, Dried Fruit, and Nuts (page 565)
8. Wild Rice with Dried Fruit (page 568)
9. Mung Beans and Rice with Dried Apricots (page 611)
10. Piquant Kidney Beans with Prunes (page 586)
11. Hot and Smoky Kidney Beans with Chipotle and Dried Cherries (page 586)
12. Hearty Winter Vegetable Burger (page 663)
13. Wheat Berry or Other Whole Grain Salad with Peanuts and Fresh and Dried Fruit (page 85)
14. Whole Grain Bread Salad (page 89)
15. Baked Sweet Omelet with Dried Fruit (page 179)
16. Crunchy Granola (page 573)
17. Goat Cheese and Dried Apricot Soufflé (page 186)
18. Dried Fruit and Nut Chutney (page 784)
19. Pineapple Chutney (page 785)
20. Dried Fruit and Nut Bread (page 692)
21. Saffron Fruit and Nut Bread (page 715)
22. Oatmeal Apple Cookies (page 839)
23. Chewy Almond-Cherry Cookies (page 843)
24. Semolina Apricot Bars (page 845)
25. Dried Fruit Bars (page 847)
26. Raisin or Date Cake (page 854)
27. No-Bake Fruit and Nut Crust (page 869)
28. Nut and Dried Fruit Phyllo "Cigars" (page 880)
29. Coconut–Dried Pineapple Macaroons (page 902)

FRUIT	SEASONING	MACERATING LIQUID
Apples or pears	Ground fennel seeds	White wine and a drizzle of honey
Apricots (fresh or dried)	Ground cardamom and a splash of rose or orange blossom water	Sugar Syrup (page 857) or water
Cherries (fresh or dried)		Port
Citrus segments	Thinly sliced shallot and a pinch of salt	Vodka or water and citrus juice
Dates	Garam masala (to make your own, see page 815)	Water with a splash of sherry or cider vinegar
Figs (fresh or dried)	Chopped fresh thyme leaves	Honey with a bit of water or brandy
Kumquats, halved or sliced	Chopped fresh cilantro or mint leaves or minced lemongrass	Sugar Syrup (page 857)
Lychees	Minced peeled fresh ginger	Kombu Dashi (page 103)
Cantaloupe	Chopped fresh rosemary	Honey with a bit of water
Peaches or nectarines	Ground coriander	Lemon juice
Persimmons	Five-spice powder (to make your own, see page 816) and a sprinkling of salt	Rice vinegar
Pineapple	Chopped fresh tarragon leaves and a sprinkling of salt	Lemon juice and water
Plums		Mustard vinaigrette
Prunes or raisins	Minced capers and garlic	Water with a splash of red wine vinegar and drizzle of extra virgin olive oil
Strawberries	Freshly ground black pepper	Balsamic vinegar
Tomatoes	Chopped fresh basil, salt, and freshly ground black pepper	Extra virgin olive oil

and dried as you like. Completely dried and brittle fruit can be stored almost indefinitely in an airtight container in your pantry; fruit that's still moist should be wrapped in plastic or put in a container and refrigerated; it will keep for at least a few days, probably much longer.

In a dehydrator, the water is evaporated from fruit very slowly, with only a little heat. Most machines have a small electrical element in the base, with a tower of racks and a vent on top. Depending on the fruit and how packed the dehydrator is, it could take up to 24 hours to dry fully,

though as with oven-drying, you can stop the process at any point. Dehydrators are handy (especially if you intend to dry a lot of fruit or vegetables) but not essential.

Preparing fruits for drying is the same whether you use the oven or a dehydrator. Apples, pineapples, coconut, and thin-skinned lemons, oranges, and limes can be thinly sliced and dried until crisp, like chips (use a mandoline for even slices and squeeze lemon juice over the apple slices to prevent discoloring). Put the fruit slices on a lightly oiled baking sheet, set your oven to the low-

           Fast   Ⓜ Make Ahead   Ⓥ Vegan

est setting (turning it on and off if the slices begin to brown), and dry the fruit until completely crisp, 2 to 3 hours. Brush the slices with some sugar syrup (page 857) before drying for a sweeter result. Use fruit chips as a garnish on desserts or salads or just as a crunchy snack.

Macerating and Seasoning Fruit

Macerating fruit—both fresh and dried—is similar to marinating; you soak it in liquid. Juicy fresh fruits, like berries, citrus, and peaches, often need only a sprinkle of sugar or salt to draw out their juices and create the macerating liquid, while other fruits benefit from added liquid like simple syrup, fruit juice, wine or brandy, or even water. The end result is always softened fruit (and plumped if you're using dried) flavored with the soaking liquid. It's a versatile way to add a kick to less-than-perfect fruit (though perfectly ripe fruits are lovely too), because you can make it go either sweet or savory.

Seasoning fruit can be as simple as a sprinkle of spice or layering flavors in maceration. But whatever it is, don't limit your fruit seasoning to cinnamon and sugar; salt, herbs, and all sorts of spices work wonderfully with fruits' sweet, tart, and acidic flavors. See the chart on page 416 for macerating and seasoning ideas; any of the seasonings can be used with or without the macerating liquid.

How to Macerate and Season Fruit

Chop or slice large or medium fruit (small fruit can be left whole) and peel it if the skin is tough or if you prefer it peeled. Mix together the fruit, the macerating liquid, and whatever seasonings you're using. Fresh fruit needs an inch or so of the liquid, but dried fruit absorbs a good amount of liquid and should be covered by an inch or two. Cover and put aside at room temperature or in the refrigerator if your kitchen is warm, stirring every few hours.

Soft and juicy fresh fruit can take as little as 15 to 20 minutes to macerate; denser items, like apple or pineapple, can take 3 or 4 hours; dried fruit requires 12 to 24 hours to soften fully. You want the fruit to be tender but not mushy.

Use macerated and seasoned fruit as a topping for pan-cakes, waffles, yogurt, or ice cream; as a filler for crêpes or blintzes; added to sauces and dressings; and as a garnish for grains, beans, tofu, seitan dishes, and beverages.

The Fruit Lexicon

Following the model of the "Vegetable Lexicon," which begins on page 256, here is an alphabetical listing of fruits—that are commonly eaten as fruits.

Apples

With over 10 billion pounds of apples produced every year, the apple is the primary fruit of the United States. There are thousands of varieties of apples in every shade of yellow, gold, red, and green, ranging from sweet to tart and mealy to crisp. Unfortunately, as is often the case, growers have concentrated on just a few types, and these are among the least interesting; probably the best of the widely grown varieties are McIntosh (even that's become increasingly hard to find) and Golden Delicious. Of course, you'll find the most variety and most interesting apples at local orchards in the fall, especially if you live in the Northeast. And the good news is many apples will keep for weeks in a cool, dry spot, like a garage or basement.

In general, apples are divided into three categories: eating, cooking, and all-purpose. The chart lists some of the most common and some not-so-common—but worth seeking—apples with notes on flavor, texture, and category.

Buying and storing: All apples should be firm and heavy for their size; avoid any with soft spots. Those that are less than perfectly firm are best suited for cooking. Store in a cool, dry place or in the refrigerator for weeks, though some keep better than others. Almost all apples in this country are harvested in the late summer and fall, but wholesalers keep the fruit in reduced-oxygen storage, where they remain in reasonably decent shape for months. But they deteriorate quickly when removed

APPLE VARIETY	DESCRIPTION	FLAVOR AND TEXTURE	CATEGORY
Braeburn	Red with lighter flecks and a green tinge around the stem; yellow flesh	Sweet, slightly tangy, juicy, and crisp	All-purpose
Cortland	Red with bright green patches; white flesh that doesn't turn brown quickly	Sweet, juicy, and tender	All-purpose
Empire	Red with lighter flecks and yellowish green patches; cream-colored flesh	Sweet-tart, juicy, and very crisp but can also be mushy	All-purpose
Fuji	Red with yellow and green mottling; cream-colored flesh	Sweet, juicy, and fairly crisp	Eating
Gala	Red with gold mottling; light yellow flesh	Mild, sweet, and crisp	Eating
Golden Delicious	Greenish gold skin sometimes with a blush of pink; light yellow flesh	Full-flavored, sweet-tart, juicy, and crisp	All-purpose
Granny Smith	Green with light flecks; white flesh	Tart to sweet-tart, juicy, and very crisp; holds shape well when cooked	All-purpose
Ida Red	Large and brilliant red; light green flesh with a touch of pink	Sweet, juicy, and firm; holds shape well when cooked	Cooking
Jonagold	Red with golden yellow flecks and streaks of green; light yellow flesh	Very sweet, juicy, and crisp; better than Golden Delicious but harder to find	All-purpose
Jonathan	Red with some bright yellow streaks; off-white flesh	Sweet-tart with a bit of spice, juicy, and crisp; does not bake whole well	All-purpose
Macoun	A New England favorite; red with green patches and mottling; white flesh; available late fall only	Very sweet, juicy, and tender	Eating
McIntosh	Bright red with green patches; off-white flesh	Sweet and crisp when very fresh; becomes mushy quickly	All-purpose
Pink Lady	Rosy pink and golden yellow; white flesh that doesn't turn brown quickly	Sweet-tart, juicy, and very crisp; lots of flavor	All-purpose
Red Delicious	The most common, but most often mealy; dark red; off-white flesh	Sweet but not complex, often mealy	Eating
Rome	Bright red and round; greenish-hued flesh	Mildly tart and tender	Cooking

from these special storage conditions, so use apples quickly in winter and spring.

Preparing: Rinse and take a bite or peel and cut. For peeling, start at the stem or flower end and work in latitudinal strips or around the circumference; a U-shaped peeler is best.

For coring, you have several options. You can remove the core and leave the apple whole by digging into the stem end with a sturdy melon baller and removing it; this leaves the blossom end intact, a nice presentation for baked apples. Or you can buy a slicer-corer, which will cut the apple into six or eight slices around the core in one swift motion. Finally, you can quarter the apple and dig out each piece of the core with a paring knife.

 Fast   Make Ahead   Ⓥ Vegan

Apples brown quickly once peeled or cut; to prevent browning, drop them into acidulated water (one part lemon juice to about ten parts water) or white wine or toss with lemon or lime juice.

Other fruit to substitute: Pears.

CORING APPLES

You can core an apple either of two ways. For baked apples, use a melon baller and dig into the flower (nonstem) end, taking out a little at a time until the core has been removed.

For other uses, just cut the apple into quarters and remove the core with a melon baller, paring knife, or spoon.

Applesauce

MAKES: About 2 quarts
TIME: About 1 hour, largely unattended

Most people think of applesauce as a sweet, almost dessertlike condiment. And it can be. But I prefer a neutral approach that allows for savory seasonings. See the list that follows for some ideas.

A food mill is the easiest way to go and produces the best applesauce, because the peels lend both their flavor and color and there's no need to do the up-front work. If you don't have one, you must core and peel the apples before cooking. Make as much as your time and the size of your pot allows by doubling or tripling the quantity. Applesauce freezes well and is handy when packed in small containers.

Other fruits that work: pears or cantaloupe.

5 pounds apples, preferably a mixture of varieties
Salt

1 Cut the apples in half or, if they're very large, in quarters. If you don't have a food mill, peel and core. Put about ¹/₂ inch of water and a pinch of salt in the bottom of a large pot and add the apples. Cover and turn the heat to medium.

2 When the water begins to boil, uncover the pot. Cook, stirring occasionally and lowering the heat if the mixture threatens to burn on the bottom, until the apples break down and become mushy, at least 30 minutes. Let sit until cool enough to handle.

3 If you have a food mill, pass the mixture through it, discarding the solids that stay behind. If not, mash if you like with a fork or potato masher. Freeze or refrigerate.

11 Great Seasonings for Applesauce

Just put any of the following ingredients into the pot along with the apples. Start with a teaspoon or so, then taste and add a teaspoon at a time as needed.

1. Freshly ground black pepper
2. Ground cumin, coriander, or caraway seeds
3. Minced fresh chile (like jalapeño or Thai) or hot red pepper flakes or cayenne
4. Chipotle chiles, dried or canned with a little of the adobo sauce
5. Chopped peeled fresh ginger (good with savory or sweet)
6. Roasted Garlic (page 304)
7. Any spice blend (to make your own, see pages 810–819)

8. Granulated or brown sugar
9. A little grating of nutmeg
10. Pinch ground cloves
11. Pinch ground allspice

Apricots

An ancient stone fruit lauded by the ancient Greeks and cultivated in China, its likely birthplace, for thousands of years; the vast majority are now grown in California and the eastern Mediterranean. Good apricots are luxuriously sweet and tart with a silky skin and a fleshy and succulent interior.

But a perfectly ripe, juicy, and flavorful apricot is hard to find, even if you live where they're grown. Ripe apricots are delicate and extremely perishable, so like so much stone fruit, they're picked well before they're ripe. Although they will ripen some after picking, they'll rarely develop into the unbelievably delicious fruit that they should be. You can find them that way in some summer farmer's markets, though again not easily.

Dried apricots are perhaps the best dried fruit; those without sulfur dioxide taste best; those with it have the best color and keep their tender texture longer.

Buying and storing: Fresh summer apricots should be deeply colored (some even with a speckling of dark orange, almost brown), heavy and fragrant and should yield to gentle pressure. Once you've tasted a good one, you'll never want anything less. Leave unripe specimens at room temperature (and in a paper bag to hasten ripening). Store ripe fruit in the refrigerator for a day or two, but eat as soon as possible.

Dried apricots should not be too leathery. When you find ones you like (look in Middle Eastern and Asian markets), buy them in bulk, as they'll keep for a year or more in a cool, dry place, though they do dry out eventually. (Soak them if they become too tough.)

Preparing: Not much to it—tear or cut it in half and remove the pit or just bite into it. The kernels (inside the pit; crack it like a nut) are similar to almonds and can be eaten, but must be roasted beforehand as they're poisonous raw. Peel apricots by plunging in boiling water for about 10 seconds and then slipping off the skin. Dried apricots can be soaked in liquid to soften or cooked.

Other fruits to substitute: Peaches or nectarines.

Bananas

The familiar and favorite banana is a tropical plant with hundreds of varieties (including plantain; see page 385). The most familiar is the yellow—sometimes called *sweet* or *dessert*—banana, but there are also tiny finger bananas and red and even blue varieties, all with varying flavors and sweetness, and some that are superior to those we've grown up with, which is not to take anything away from the staple and quite fine supermarket banana. Yellow and even green bananas are also wonderful cooked, as long as they're not too ripe; they become luxuriously sweet and soft.

Buying and storing: Bananas ripen nicely off the plant, and they are often sold green. Leave at room temperature for anywhere from a day to a week; the longer they ripen, the softer and sweeter they become.

How ripe you want a dessert banana is really a matter of personal preference, and you undoubtedly know yours already. Any banana can be stored in the refrigerator to retard further ripening (the skins may turn black, but the flesh remains the same) for weeks.

Preparing: Peel and eat or chop or slice as needed. Squeeze some lemon or lime juice over the freshly cut banana to prevent discoloring.

Other fruits to substitute: Really, there is no substitute for raw bananas. Substitute plantains (see page 335) for bananas when cooking.

Berries

There are hundreds of types of berries, from all over the world. They all grow on vines or bushes and range in

 Fast   Make Ahead   Ⓥ Vegan

color from white to blue to red, orange, yellow, or black. They can be sweet or tart and everything in between.

In general, berries are expensive and, with the exception of the blueberry, cranberry, and a couple of less common varieties, very perishable. Almost all are now cultivated. Most are picked well before their prime, which is a big problem for us: Because they don't ripen once picked, they sometimes wind up tasting like cardboard (sweetened cardboard if we're lucky). For the best or even good berries, you've got to go local (a farmstand, your garden, or even wild) and in season.

Strawberries are perhaps the most denigrated of all the berries. Anyone who thinks they're getting a good strawberry from the supermarket either doesn't know or has forgotten what a real strawberry tastes like. Most strawberries these days are grown more for their hardiness and disease resistance than for their flavor, and that's a real shame, because a truly ripe strawberry is heavenly. But as good as they are raw—even better with cream—or used in shortcake or jam, that's about the extent of their talent; they just aren't that useful a berry.

Blueberries can be considered the all-purpose berry: hardy (for a berry), fairly inexpensive in season, beautifully colored, delicious, and excellent for eating out of hand and cooking. Occasionally you can even find fresh wild blueberries at farmer's markets. The blueberry's closest relatives, huckleberry and juneberry, are too fragile ever to make it even to a farmer's market.

Blackberries and raspberries, along with all their cousins (boysenberries, loganberries, and dewberries to name a few), are varying degrees of sweet and tart and equally lovely for out-of-hand eating or cooking.

See Cranberries (page 423).

Buying and storing: All berries should be fragrant (especially strawberries), deeply colored, and soft but not mushy. Eat them immediately; they are too perishable and expensive to store.

Strawberries: Taste one. If it's crunchy and flavorless, move on. If it's sweet and flavorful, buy only as many

To prepare strawberries, first remove the leaves, then cut a cone-shaped wedge with a paring knife to remove the top of the core. A small melon baller also does the job nicely.

as you'll use in the next twenty-four hours. Don't refrigerate. Peak season is typically May to June.

Blueberries: Look for plump and unshriveled berries without any green. Inspect prepackaged cartons carefully for mushy and/or moldy berries. Size is irrelevant. Taste one or two to be sure. Peak season is July to August.

Blackberries and raspberries: If you live in the northern half of the United States, you should know that these berries grow wild and in abundance; keep your eyes peeled for low-lying bushes on your next walk through the woods. When buying in plastic containers, inspect the pad of paper underneath the berries; if it's heavily stained with juices, keep looking. Peak season is July to August.

Preparing: Strawberries: See the illustration above. Wash and dry. Pull or cut off the leaves and use a paring knife to dig out the stem and core.

Blueberries: Pick over, remove the stems, and wash.

Blackberries and raspberries: Wash and dry very gently. I do not wash wild berries as long as I'm sure of the source.

Other fruits to substitute: Berries are fairly interchangeable when used raw, or use grapes; blueberries, blackberries, and raspberries can substitute for one another in cooked dishes.

Carambola

Star Fruit

The now-familiar yellow, semitranslucent tropical fruit with five pointed ridges that—when sliced crosswise—creates a pretty star shape. Star fruit are fragrant, juicy, and sweet-tart when perfectly ripe, but often the ones we get here fall short of that. The skin is edible, and they are best eaten raw, lovely sliced into salads or used as garnish.

Buying and storing: Look for fragrant, yellow, and plump fruit that's unblemished and unshriveled. They will ripen some if left at room temperature. When ripe, store wrapped loosely in plastic in the refrigerator.

Preparing: Rinse, dry, and slice crosswise.

Other fruits to substitute: Kiwi (another pretty fruit), orange segments, or table grapes.

Cherimoyas

Custard Apples

A medium-size tropical fruit with green, leathery, scaled-looking skin and—at its best—a white, creamy, dreamy, custardlike interior with a pineapple-banana flavor. Although some are grown in California and Florida, they are not common, and good ones even less so. The best usually come from Central America and Mexico.

Buying and storing: Look for plump, firm fruit, heavy for its size, with no brown patches; they will ripen if left at room temperature and are ready when they yield slightly to gentle pressure; at that point, store wrapped loosely in plastic in the refrigerator.

Preparing: Cut in half, remove the large seeds, and scoop out the flesh with a spoon. Eat raw.

Cherries

I wrote this ten years ago, and it holds true: "Sadly, I think most of us have missed out on the really good cherries; this is the fruit of romance, of fairs, of paradise. Yet none of the cherries we are able to buy come close. Yes, there's an occasional one or two in the batch that makes us pause and think *Oh. Now I remember why I love these.* But these days the fact is that a bowl of cherries is a lot like life—fairly mundane, with some high spots."

Oh, well. It hasn't gotten any better, but we still try. Each bunch of cherries contains a few that remind us of why we love them. When cherries are good, they are succulent, juicy, and fleshy with a sweet, bright, completely lovable flavor.

There are two types of cherries: sweet and sour (or tart). The former is best for eating out of hand, the latter for pie making and cooking. Most of the cherries we find in supermarkets are the sweet, deep red, heart-shaped Bing cherries. Sour cherries are more often sold at farmer's markets and farmstands; they are typically smaller, brighter red, and rounder in shape than the sweet varieties and are too tart to eat raw.

Buying and storing: If you're going to pick them one by one (taste one), look for shiny, plump, and firm specimens with fresh-looking green stems. Otherwise, if the majority look sound, grab by the handful. Store wrapped loosely in plastic in the refrigerator; use as soon as possible; they won't last long.

Preparing: Wash and dry for eating out of hand; additionally stem and pit for cooking. A cherry pitter (which also works for olives) is handy.

Other fruits to substitute: Fresh currants or dried cherries; for cooking, cranberries or blueberries.

Coconuts

The fruit of a tall palm, coconuts grow in tropical regions around the world, from Malaysia (their likely birthplace) to South America. A whole fresh coconut is a large oval-shaped pod with pointed ends and a hard, leathery green or brown exterior, depending on ripeness; this outer husk is usually removed before export to reveal the brown furry fruit we know as a coconut. Beyond this layer is a thin

 Ⓕ Fast   Ⓜ Make Ahead   Ⓥ Vegan

brown skin, then the white coconut meat and the translucent coconut juice (not to be confused with coconut milk; see below). Although fresh whole coconut is wonderful, store-bought shredded fresh and dried coconut is convenient and tastes good too; always buy unsweetened.

Buying and storing: Whole coconuts should be uniformly very hard—check the three eyes especially—and you should be able to hear the juice inside when you shake it. Store in a cool, dry spot for months, depending on ripeness. Sometimes you can find shelled fresh coconut in Asian markets; make sure it looks fresh and moist, then keep in the fridge and use within a few days. Store shredded coconut in a similar spot or in the freezer for up to six months.

Preparing: Use an ice pick, scissors blade, or corkscrew to find the soft eye, then drive the point into the eye and drain out the juice. Put the coconut inside a double layer of plastic grocery or trash bags. Go outside or wherever there is a concrete step or floor; slam the coconut into the concrete as many times as it takes to break it open. Remove the brown skin and chop, slice, or shred the white meat as you like.

Best cooking method: Toasted.
When are they done? When lightly golden brown.
Other vegetables to substitute: None.

Coconut Milk

MAKES: About 2 cups
TIME: 20 minutes

  Ⓥ

Many recipes include coconut milk in this book (see the index for a complete list), and it's an especially important substitute for people who don't drink or use cow's milk. And while it's fine to use canned, homemade coconut milk is super-easy and much more pure in both flavor and ingredients. All you need is dried unsweetened coconut, which is available at natural food stores and Indian, Latin, and Caribbean groceries, as well as many supermarkets.

This recipe gives you a fairly thick milk, akin to canned. Either thin it with water or repeat the process on the coconut again; the second pressing will be thinner.

1 cup unsweetened dried coconut meat

❶ Combine the coconut with 2 cups very hot water in a blender. Pulse on and off quickly, then turn on the blender and let it work for 15 seconds or so (take care that the top of the blender stays in place). Let sit for a few minutes.

❷ Put through a strainer, pressing to extract as much of the liquid as possible. Discard the solids and use the milk immediately or store, covered, in the refrigerator for up to a few days.

Cranberries

Sturdy and long-lasting, cranberries are the ultimate tart berry (they're extremely high in citric acid—vitamin C—which explains their sourness). They are bright red, round, and too hard and astringent to be eaten out of hand, so they are always cooked or combined with other ingredients. There are many species of cranberry (like the Scandinavian lingonberry), but we rarely see any other than Early Black (small and dark red) and Howes (lighter red and more oblong than the Early Black).

Buying and storing: Most are sold in plastic bags in the fall and winter. Toss those that are off-color or shriveled. Store in the refrigerator for weeks or in the freezer indefinitely.

Preparing: Nothing to it: Pick over, wash, and, if necessary, dry.

Other fruits to substitute: Dried cranberries, sour or sweet cherries, fresh currants, or blueberries.

Currants

A small berry that grows in clusters, currants can be brilliant red, purplish black, or white. They're good in pies, jams, jellies, and other desserts. The black variety is made into cassis (the French word for "currant") liqueur. Another fruit—the small seedless Greek grape called *zante* from Corinth—is also called a currant (a bastardization of *Corinth*) when dried, though it is not a true currant. Fresh currants are known by their Latin name, *ribes,* in other parts of the world; it's just the English name that causes confusion about the two fruits. Fresh currants are delicious with other fruits or simply with some cream and sugar.

Buying and storing: Look for firm, plump, intact berries. They are not highly perishable but are best used within a few days. Store, loosely wrapped in plastic i, n the refrigerator.

Preparing: Remove the stems, pick over, wash, and—if necessary—dry.

Other fruits to substitute: Cherries, raspberries, or blueberries.

Dates

Available most often dried, dates are occasionally available fresh—and what a delight! Fresh dates are in season from late summer to the middle of fall, and they're sticky-sweet, tender, and juicy; look for them in Middle Eastern or farmer's markets. Dried dates are even sweeter and chewy, with a papery outer skin; they're available year-round, with or without the narrow pits. The best varieties are medjool; deglet noor and bread dates (khadrawy) are more common but less sweet. The fruit grows in large clusters at the top of hundred-foot-tall palm trees that grow in arid, desert climates like the Middle East (where they originated), California, and Arizona. They are often picked green and allowed to ripen off the tree to a yellow, brown, black, or mahogany color, depending on the variety. Because of their intense sweetness, they are often chopped and added to baked goods, granola, pilafs, and braises.

Buying and storing: Fresh dates should be unblemished and quite moist; they are often sold on the stem. Store on the counter or, for longer storage, loosely

wrapped in plastic, in the refrigerator. Dried dates should be moist and tender; some varieties have a dull and dried-out-looking exterior and others a shiny and succulent appearance, but avoid any that have sugar crystals or are shriveled and hard. As with most dried fruit, it's worth looking for organic specimens in a natural food store. Newly dried dates are much better—they're moister—than stale dried dates. Store on the counter if you're going to eat them right away or for up to six months in a sealed container in the refrigerator.

Preparing: Remove the pits by slicing the fruit lengthwise and pulling the seed out by the tip. Or just squeeze.

Other fruits to substitute: Raisins, prunes, or dried apricots or figs.

Figs

A venerable Mediterranean staple. In the United States, most are grown in California and the Southwest, where they are abundant and relatively cheap in mid- to late summer. (In some Mediterranean lands they are almost too plentiful to sell for several months a year; you can pick them almost anywhere.) When fresh and ripe, figs are supple, sweet, and wonderful. The delicate skin is soft and delicious (and easily damaged), and the interior flesh is succulent, gorgeously white and pink, and loaded with tiny edible seeds. Dried, they are even sweeter, meaty, and lovely as they are, macerated or added to braises or stews.

There are many varieties of figs, but we see only a few in fresh form; the black Mission fig and the green Calimyrna are the most common. They range in color from deep purple to brown, reddish orange to green and yellow, and the shapes can be round to pearlike. Dried are most often black and sometimes brown.

Buying and storing: Ripe fresh figs are usually available toward the end of summer. Since they're extremely delicate and don't travel well at all, in colder areas of the country they are usually not ripe or are very expensive—or, worse, both unripe and expensive. Look for soft, undamaged fruit that's heavy for its size; oozing a bit of

 Ⓕ Fast Ⓜ Make Ahead Ⓥ Vegan

sugary syrup is almost a sure sign of perfect ripeness. Hard or dried-out figs will not ripen and are best macerated or poached. Fresh figs are very perishable and should be eaten as quickly as possible; store wrapped loosely in plastic or covered with a paper towel in the refrigerator for a day or two at most. Dried figs are less guesswork; they should be moist and tender and are a better deal when purchased in bulk than prepackaged. Store in a cool, dark, dry place.

Preparing: Wash and eat fresh ones. Dried figs may be eaten, soaked, or cooked as any dried fruit.

Other fruits to substitute: There is no substitute for fresh figs; dried can be replaced by nearly any dried fruit, like raisins, prunes, or dried apricots.

Grapes

The grape, you may be surprised to learn, is actually a smooth-skinned berry that grows (as you do know) in large clusters. Grapes come in a huge variety of colors, flavors, shapes, and sizes, though we usually see just a few varieties in supermarkets. But there are literally thousands of varieties of grapes that can be used for eating or making wine, raisins, juice, jams, or jellies. They are typically divided into two types: white (also called *green*) and black (often referred to as *red*). White grapes are green to greenish yellow in color, and black grapes range in color from reddish to the deepest of purple.

Generally, table grapes are sweet with a bit of acid and thin-skinned; Americans eat mostly seedless grapes, but, in fact, breeding out the seeds breeds for less flavor. Raisin-, juice-, and preserves-making grapes are typically sticky sweet with a pronounced grape flavor and large seeds (they are also delicious for eating out of hand but aren't commonly available). Wine grapes are usually quite acidic, tannic, and sometimes sweet—when fully ripe, some can be lovely eaten raw, but they're almost never sold for eating.

A wider variety of grapes are usually offered in the late summer to early fall at farmer's markets (especially in California, as you might imagine). Muscat (round and golden green) and Concord (round and bluish purple) are worth seeking out, but so are many of the less common varieties.

Buying and storing: Ideally you want fresh-looking green stems with only some brown; the grapes should be plump, sweet, and flavorful—taste one.

Preparing: Pesticides are used heavily on grapes so rinse them very well.

Other fruit to substitute: Blueberries or cherries.

Grapefruit

West Indian in origin, now widely grown in Florida (which produces the best), California, and elsewhere. Each year, it seems, breeding techniques make grapefruit sweeter and sweeter; and seeds have become a thing of the past. Pomelo (or shaddock) and ugli (aptly if cruelly named) are similar and may be treated as grapefruit.

There are two types of grapefruit, white and red, differentiated more by the color of their flesh than their skin. Red grapefruit were once sweeter than white, but that's no longer really true.

Buying and storing: Look for specimens that are heavy for their size—the heavier, the juicier. Store in the refrigerator after a day or two at room temperature.

Preparing: Cut the grapefruit in half through its equator, around the sides, cutting the flesh from the skin, and then along each of the sides of the segments; eat with a spoon. Or peel and separate the segments as you would an orange; this is especially useful with smaller specimens.

Other fruit to substitute: Orange or pomelo.

Kiwis
Chinese Gooseberries

A native Chinese fruit named in English after New Zealand's national bird (oddly the fruit and the flightless bird do look somewhat similar), the kiwi has become commonplace in our supermarkets. Its oval shape and fuzzy brown exterior belie its brilliant green and white flesh, which is stippled with tiny black and completely edible seeds.

Kiwis are soft, juicy, and sweet-tart when ripe, more on the tart side (though not entirely bad) when not quite ripe enough. There is also a yellow-fleshed variety that is sweeter and has less fuzz. Both green and yellow kiwis make nice additions to fruit salads or a pretty garnish, especially for desserts.

Buying and storing: Most will be fairly hard at supermarkets. Look for unshriveled and unblemished specimens without soft spots. They will ripen if left at room temperature. When ripe, store in the refrigerator.

Preparing: Peel and slice or cut in half and scoop out the flesh with a spoon.

Other fruits to substitute: Carambola (another pretty fruit), grapes, or honeydew.

Kumquats

Kumquats look like tiny oranges. Though the entire fruit is edible, it's the skin that's the best part, believe it or not: It's thin and sweet, while the flesh is heavily seeded and very tart. You can peel them (which is easy) and just eat the skin or slice them thinly, chop them, or poach them whole in sugar syrup. Kumquats are most often available in the winter, frequently still attached to the branch; look for them in specialty or Asian markets.

Buying and storing: Buy firm, unblemished fruits; store in the refrigerator.

Preparing: Wash, dry, and slice, chop, or quarter, removing the seeds, or use whole.

Other fruit to substitute: Orange or tangerine for its flavor, but a lemon or lime for the acidity.

Lemons and Limes

Perhaps the most useful kitchen fruits; a squirt of their juice or a sprinkle of zest can add just the right amount of acid and flavor to perfectly balance a dish, sauce, or beverage. The lemon is the essential fruit in European cooking, while the lime takes center stage in Asian and tropical cooking; I try to keep at least one of each in my kitchen at all times. Be sure not to neglect the zest as it brings the wonderful flavor of the fruit but without the acid (the zest is only the yellow or green outer portion of the peel; the white pith underneath is bitter).

There is a common lemon and common lime variety that you will see everywhere; there are also two less common but prized varieties of both the lemon and the lime: Meyer lemons and key limes. Meyer lemons have a unique floral and piney fragrance; they are a bit less acidic than regular lemons and are not easy to find outside of California. Key limes (mostly from Florida) are tiny and round and, like the Meyer, have a more floral and less acidic flavor than regular limes. Both Meyer lemons and key limes work nicely in desserts.

Buying and storing: Buy plump specimens that are heavy for their size and yield to gentle pressure; very hard or lightweight fruit will be dry. Store in the refrigerator.

Preparing: Cut into halves, quarters, wedges, or slices and remove the pits with the point of a knife. Or cut into halves (or thirds through the axis for limes) and squeeze or press to release juice.

There are a few ways to zest citrus; how you choose to do it should depend partly on how you'll use it. A zester is a nifty tool with small sharp-edged holes that cuts off long, thin strips of zest, which can then be minced; they are great for garnishing when whole. Another method is to use a vegetable peeler or paring knife to remove the peel in long ribbons. Unless you're really skilled with the knife or peeler, this technique inevitably brings part of the bitter white pith with it; to do a perfect job you should then lay the strips down on a cutting board and scrape the white part off with a paring knife, then slice or mince as you like. The third method is using a sharp rasp-type grater (like a Microplane, which results in tiny flecks of zest that are nearly undetectable in dishes except for their flavor.

Other fruit to substitute: Lemons and limes are more or less interchangeable, though they are of course different from one another.

Preserved Lemons

MAKES: 1 quart
TIME: 20 minutes plus 2 weeks to cure

A couple of recipes in this book call specifically for preserved lemons, a staple ingredient in North African cooking. But don't let me or geography come between you and this versatile quick "pickle." Chopped up, it can be added to all sorts of pilafs and braised vegetable dishes. Or make a refreshing drink by muddling a couple in the bottom of a glass, then topping it off with ice and sparkling water. I'm sure you'll find even more ways to use them before your first batch runs out; they keep in the fridge for months.

About 3 pounds lemons, preferably unwaxed, quartered lengthwise

About $^3/_4$ cup kosher salt

Half 3-inch cinnamon stick

2 or 3 cloves

1 star anise

2 or 3 black peppercorns

2 cardamom pods

1 bay leaf

① Fill a 1-quart canning jar with boiling water and soak its lid in boiling water too. Let the water sit while you cut the lemons, then dump the water out.

② Sprinkle a $^1/_4$-inch-deep layer of salt across the bottom of the jar. Nestle a layer of quartered lemons into the bottom of the jar, sprinkle liberally with salt, then repeat, adding the spices as you go. Stop when the jar is about three-quarters full and squeeze the remaining lemons into the jar—seeds and all—so that the fruit is completely submerged in the lemon juice–and–salt brine. (If you don't have enough lemons on hand, top the lemons off with freshly squeezed juice no later than the following day.)

③ Set the jar out on a counter and vigorously shake it once a day for 7 to 10 days—during this time it will start to bubble a little, and the dried spices will swell back to their original size. (You'll be surprised at the size of the cloves!)

④ Put the jar in the refrigerator and let the lemons continue to cure for another week before using. (The lemons will keep for at least 2 months in the refrigerator, though you'll probably want to get into them sooner.) When they have cured, unscrew the lid—after a moment, they should smell sweet and citrusy—an ammonia smell means they've gone wrong somewhere along the line.

⑤ To use in stews, blanch the quarter lemons in unsalted boiling water for 10 seconds, just long enough to leach out a little of the salt. For salads or quick-cooked dishes, scrape the flesh away from the peel, discard the flesh, and blanch the peel in unsalted boiling water.

Lychees
Litchis

Natives of southern China, lychees are $1^1/_2$-inch oval fruits with brilliant red to pinkish tan scaly—sometimes prickly—inedible skin that protects the juicy white flesh, which in turn surrounds a shiny brown inedible seed. The texture of lychees is like that of a fleshy grape, and the flavor is sweet and one of a kind, though akin to that of cherries. (Canned lychees in syrup are mostly just sugary sweet and not worth eating.) They are also dried and sometimes called *lychee nuts,* though they aren't nuts and the seeds are no more edible than when fresh.

Buying and storing: Summer is peak lychee season, where you'll find them in Asian and farmer's markets. Look for fragrant, brightly colored fruit with flexible—not dried out or brittle—skins; they should be heavy for their size. Store wrapped loosely in plastic in the refrigerator; use as soon as possible.

Preparing: Use the stem to break open the skin and gently peel it off; eat the fruit and spit out the seed.

Other fruits to substitute: Grapes, or kiwi or carambola for a tropical flavor.

SKINNING AND PITTING MANGO, VERSION I

(STEP 1) There are two ways to get the meat out of a mango. The first way begins with peeling, using a normal vegetable peeler. (STEP 2) Then cut the mango in half, doing the best you can to cut around the pit. (STEP 3) Finally, chop the mango with a knife.

SKINNING AND PITTING MANGO, VERSION II

(STEP 1) Begin by cutting the mango in half, doing the best you can to cut around the pit. (STEP 2) Score the flesh with a paring knife. (STEP 3) Turn the mango half "inside out" and the flesh is easily removed.

Mangoes

There are dozens of shapes, sizes, and colors of mango, from orange size to melon size; green to yellow, orange, or red; exceedingly tart to syrupy sweet. Both ripe and unripe mangoes are useful: unripe for chutney, pickling, and making amchoor (see page 820) and ripe for eating straight, making salsas, fruit salads, and cooking.

Supermarkets carry the most common yellow and red mango year-round, but you'll find a wider selection in Latin, Asian, and Indian markets. In the United States mangoes are grown in California, Florida, and Hawaii, but the majority are imported from Mexico and farther south.

Buying and storing: Color isn't as important as texture; the softer it is, the riper. Some varieties of mango

🅕 Fast   🅜 Make Ahead   🅥 Vegan

will start to wrinkle a bit at the stem when perfectly ripe. Bought at any stage, however, the mango will ripen if left at room temperature. Once ripe, store in the refrigerator or it will rot.

Preparing: There are a few different ways to go about preparing a mango; how you do it will depend on your knife skills and your patience. (See the illustrations on page 428.) The quick and messy way is to just peel off the skin—a small knife makes quick work of it—and attack. For a neater presentation, trim a piece off the bottom end. Stand the fruit on a cutting board, trim off the skin with a sharp paring knife, then slice the fruit from around the pit.

Other fruits to substitute: Papaya, cantaloupe or other fleshy orange melon, or orange.

Melons

Melons are members of the gourd or cucurbit family—along with squash, pumpkin, and cucumber—and have been cultivated for thousands of years. They are divided into two types: muskmelon and watermelon. Muskmelons have either a netted skin (like the cantaloupe) or a smooth skin (like the honeydew) and a hollow cavity with seeds; their flesh ranges in color from pinkish orange to lime green to nearly white. Watermelons are pretty much what you think they are: they have a smooth skin in varying shades of green, solid or striated, and a watery, sugary sweet flesh with seeds embedded throughout (though, of course, seedless watermelons are increasingly common); the flesh can be the familiar pink or red or, less commonly, yellow, orange, or white.

Melons are summer fruit, and you'll find the widest variety and most flavorful at farmstands and farmer's markets. Selecting the right melon is part skill and part luck. If you're at a farmstand or farmer's market, ask for help. Otherwise, start by smelling it; if it smells sweet and like a melon, that's a good start. Then try shaking it; loose seeds are a sign of ripeness for muskmelons. Last, for muskmelons, gently squeeze the end opposite the

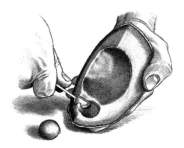

Using a melon baller is intuitive, easy, and fun—just scoop out balls from any cut and seeded melon.

stem—it should yield slightly; for watermelons, slap the side and listen for a hollow sound.

Buying and storing: Eat a ripe melon right away or store it in the refrigerator. Underripe melons can be left out at room temperature for a couple days to sweeten, but they won't ripen to perfection.

Preparing: Cut the melon in half and scrape out the seeds of muskmelons with a spoon; continue cutting it into quarters or slices. Use a paring knife to slice off the rinds if you like. Watermelons can be served casually in wedges with seeds. But if you want to seed them, cut into wedges and slice off the top or "heart" to reveal the row of seeds. Remove them with the tines of a fork. Then cut to desired size.

A melon baller easily lets you scoop out circles of melon. Or you can simply cut the flesh into pieces. Grated melon is great for yogurt sauces and raw salsas; just be sure to do it over a bowl to save the juices.

Allow a chilled melon to come to room temperature before serving; when it's chilled, the flavors are muted. Try a squeeze of lemon or lime juice on the melon—it adds flavor to an underripe melon and complements a ripe one. A sprinkle of salt is an interesting change of pace (as is a dash of ground chile, or some freshly ground pepper and lime juice).

Other fruit to substitute: Melons are interchangeable with each other and with papaya, mango, and (sometimes) cucumber.

Grilled Watermelon Steak

MAKES: 4 to 6 servings

TIME: 30 minutes

I know it sounds gimmicky, but grilled watermelon treated like a vegetable with savory seasoning is delicious. Most of the water cooks out of it, leaving behind a tasty little "steak" with great texture. Plus, it looks terrific. You can broil it, too; just make sure the juices can drain free so it doesn't steam.

Serve this with a baked potato if you like and something with a little protein, like Grilled Tofu (page 642) or Beer-Glazed Black Beans (page 585).

Other fruits or vegetables you can use: any melon, but you'll get smaller slices; and any winter squash.

1 small watermelon

1/4 cup extra virgin olive oil

1 tablespoon minced fresh rosemary leaves

Salt and freshly ground black pepper

Lemon wedges

❶ Heat a charcoal or gas grill or a broiler until moderately hot and put the rack about 4 inches from the heat source. Cut the watermelon in halves or quarters lengthwise, depending on the size of the melon. From each length, cut 2-inch-thick slices, with the rind intact. Use a fork to remove as many seeds from the heart as you can without beating the flesh up too much.

❷ Mix the olive oil with the rosemary and sprinkle with salt and pepper. Brush or rub the mixture all over the watermelon slices. Grill or broil for about 5 minutes on each side. The flesh should be lightly caramelized and dried out a bit. Serve with lemon wedges.

Chile-Rubbed Grilled Watermelon Steak. Great as part of any Mexican-style meal: Instead of the rosemary, use

2 tablespoons chili powder (to make your own, see page 814). Proceed with the recipe, serving with lime wedges instead of the lemon if you like.

Nectarines (*see* Peaches and Nectarines, page 432)

Oranges and Tangerines

The orange tree is a bushy type of evergreen that simultaneously produces leaves, flowers, and fruit; it's grown in warm areas across the globe. (It may surprise you to learn that oranges are native to Southeast Asia—especially considering that the current top three producers are Brazil, the United States, and Mexico.)

There are three types of orange: sweet (like the Valencia, navel, or temple), loose-skinned (any mandarin or tangerine), and bitter (Seville). Sweet and loose-skinned oranges are used for eating and juicing, while bitter ones are used only for making marmalades and other cooked products (we don't see them fresh too often in this country). The outer, orange-colored skin (i.e., zest) and interior flesh are edible, while the white pith on the skin is bitter.

Mandarin oranges are simply a smaller and looser-skinned type of orange. Clementines, Satsuma, and tangerines are all varieties of Mandarins; they are sweet-tart in flavor and are perfect for eating out of hand but great juiced too.

Buying and storing: Oranges are available all year long, though tangerines enjoy a brief season in late fall and winter. Sweet and bitter oranges should be heavy for their size and yield to gentle pressure but have no soft spots. The color of the skin varies by type, but some "russeting" (brown flecks) or "regreening" (green patches) is perfectly fine, if not a sign of ripeness. Mandarin oranges

Ⓕ Fast   Ⓜ Make Ahead   Ⓥ Vegan

(STEP 1) Before beginning to peel and segment citrus, cut a slice off both ends of the fruit so that it stands straight. (STEP 2) Cut as close to the pulp as possible, removing the skin in long strips. You can also remove zest with a zester, which you just pull across the skin as you would a vegetable peeler.

(STEP 3) Cut across any peeled citrus fruit to make "wheels." Or cut between the membranes to separate segments

should be heavy for their size and without any unusually soft spots, though in general they feel softer than sweet oranges.

Preparing: See the illustrations above. Oranges are easiest to eat when cut into eighths rather than quarters. To peel, cut four longitudinal slits from pole to pole, through the skin but not into the flesh. Peel each of these off. Mandarin oranges can be peeled using your fingers without any difficulty.

Other fruit to substitute: Sweet and Mandarin oranges are interchangeable; lemon or lime juice can replace the acidic flavor of bitter oranges.

Papayas

Native to tropical regions of the Americas—the exact place of origin is debated—this tree fruit grows as large as twenty pounds, though most of what we see here are in the one- to two-pound range. It's eaten both green and ripe, ideally with a sprinkle of lime. When ripe, papaya skin is golden yellow with patches of orange; the flesh is soft, melonlike, and a deep orange, and the edible seeds are a shiny greenish gray.

Buying and storing: Often available—and good—year-round, especially in Asian and Latin markets. Green, tart, unripe papayas are hard and solid green. Ripe ones have yellow and orange skin, yield to gentle pressure, and are aromatic; harder specimens will ripen at room temperature. Once ripe, they should be stored in the refrigerator.

Preparing: Wash, peel, cut in half, and scoop out the seeds. Then slice or chop.

Other fruits to substitute: Mango, cantaloupe, or other fleshy orange melon.

Passion Fruit

Egg shaped with purplish brown skin, this tropical fruit has a brightly colored yellow-orange pulp filled with dozens of edible seeds. The flavor is quite tart—almost too tart to eat straight—but sensational, and the fragrance is wonderful. I like to strain the pulp and blend it into juices, smoothies, and ice cream and sorbet bases.

Buying and storing: Look for deeply colored fruit that's firm and heavy for its size. Ripe passion fruit will have a dimpled or slightly shriveled exterior. When ripe, store in the refrigerator.

Preparing: Cut in half and scoop out the flesh with a spoon. For just the juice, use a strainer to separate the seeds; press the flesh to extract as much of the juice as possible.

Other fruits to substitute: The juice can be replaced with orange, guava, or mango juice.

Peaches and Nectarines

Among the best summer eating fruit, peaches and nectarines are closely related stone fruits that originated in China and came to Europe (then the Americas) via the Persian empire. They are nearly identical in shape and color, but peach skin has a soft fuzz and nectarine skin is smooth. (And no, nectarines are *not* a hybrid of peaches and plums, as is so often said.) The flesh is succulent, juicy, and sweet-tart.

Variations in color don't matter much, but there are two broad categories of peaches and nectarines based on how much the flesh clings to the pit: freestone and clingstone. Both are good; freestones are certainly easier to cut up.

Buying and storing: Tree-ripened fruit are best, but these do ripen at room temperature (and quickly, so keep your eye on them). Put hard fruit in a paper bag to hasten ripening or just ripen on the counter. Look for plump, gently yielding, and fragrant specimens without any bruises. Don't buy too many at once, unless you're planning to cook with them; they usually all ripen at the same time.

Preparing: Wash, peel if you like, and eat. To pit, cut in half from pole to pole; twist the halves, which will either come completely free of the pit (freestone) or leave a fair amount of flesh on the pit (clingstone). To peel, drop into boiling water for 10 to 30 seconds, just until the skin loosens; plunge into a bowl of ice water; remove the peel with your fingers and/or a paring knife.

Other fruit to substitute: Peaches and nectarines are interchangeable; otherwise, substitute apricots, plums, or mangoes.

Pears

Pears are one of the few fruits that actually improve after being picked; their flesh softens and sweetens to an almost buttery texture. In fact, they are known as "butter fruit" in several European languages. But actually eating a perfectly ripe pear can be tricky: their peak is fleeting, so we often end up with either a crunchy fruit with little flavor or a mushy one with no texture.

Related to apples—they are both technically members of the rose family—pears are grown throughout the

F Fast   M Make Ahead   V Vegan

world in moderate climates. There are over five thousand varieties, many produced regionally. You're likely to find dozens of varieties beyond the usual Anjou and Bartlett at local farmer's markets and orchards; different varieties of pears have different seasons, though they are most abundant in the fall.

Here are short descriptions of the most common pears:

Anjou: One of the most common varieties; green and red types with a broad oval shape; the flesh is firm (good for poaching), sweet, but not spectacular.

Asian: Round, apple shaped with a yellow to russet-gold color; the flesh is crisp (and is best that way, which is unusual for a pear) and juicy, with a delicate apple-pear flavor.

Bartlett: The most common variety and the only one used for commercial canning and drying. Bell shaped and green when unripe, yellow with a red blush when ripe, with soft, sweet, and juicy flesh; rarely impressive.

Bosc: Somewhat tear shaped with an elongated neck; golden-brown russet color with a juicy, crisp flesh similar to Anjou but more aromatic. At its best, spectacular.

Comice: Squat pear shape with a stubby neck and stem; green with a bronze blush and very sweet, juicy, soft flesh. Wonderful fragrance and probably the best widely available pear.

Packham: Imported in winter from the southern hemisphere; fat, round, and a bit irregular in shape; green to greenish yellow in color, fairly sweet flesh; rarely great.

Seckel: Miniature and precious looking (lovely for poaching whole); green with a deep red blush and a great, spicy flavor. The skin can be tough, but these are worth trying.

Buying and storing: Pears ripen best off the tree, so don't be discouraged if all you can find are hard, green fruit. Leave them at room temperature until the flesh yields gently when squeezed and you can smell a nice pear aroma; some varieties will also change color, from green to yellow. Asian pears are meant to be firm and crunchy. Store ripe fruit in the refrigerator.

Preparing: Peeling is not necessary, but it's easy with a vegetable peeler. Core it by slicing the pear into quarters and then cutting out the core; or halve it and dig out the core with a melon baller; or to keep the fruit whole, dig out the core from the blossom (large) end with a small melon baller.

Other fruits to substitute: Apples.

Poached Pears

MAKES: 4 servings

TIME: About 20 minutes, plus time to cool

You can poach pears at any stage of ripeness, compensating for any lack of fully developed natural sugars simply by adding sugar to the cooking water. So even with an unripe pear, this becomes an impressive, lovely, light dessert. The liquid makes a nice sauce, especially if you have the time and energy to remove the pears and then reduce the cooking liquid to a cup or so, spooning it over the pears at the table.

2¹/₂ cups sugar

¹/₂ vanilla bean, or a whole 3-inch cinnamon stick

4 pears

❶ Combine the sugar and vanilla with 5 cups water in a saucepan large enough to hold the pears over high heat. Peel the pears, leaving their stems on. Core them by digging into the blossom end with a melon baller, spoon, or paring knife.

❷ Lower the pears into the water and adjust the heat so that it simmers gently. Cook, turning the pears every 5 minutes or so, until they meet little resistance when prodded with a thin-bladed knife, usually 10 to 20 minutes. Turn off the heat and allow to cool in the liquid.

③ Transfer the pears to serving plates. (You can cover and refrigerate them for up to a day at this point; bring to room temperature before serving.) Reduce the poaching liquid to about a cup (this can also be stored for a day), then spoon a little over each pear before serving.

Poached Pears with Asian Spices. Add 3 star anise, 5 slices ginger, and 2 cloves to the poaching mix.

Persimmons

A vibrant orange-colored fruit that has a juicy jellylike interior or a crisp applelike quality, depending on the variety. The heart-shaped and traditional Hachiya persimmon—that's the mushy one—is by far the most common, but the squat Fuyu variety is gaining ground.

Hachiya are oblong with a pointed end and are extraordinarily tart—mouth-puckeringly so—when unripe but gradually ripen, becoming soft, mushy, and almost translucent, like a way overripe tomato; the flesh at this point is somewhat gelatinous and deliciously sweet.

The Fuyu, on the other hand, is smaller, tomato shaped, and firm. Unlike the Hachiya, it's deliciously crunchy and sweet with a subtle cinnamon flavor when hard.

Buying and storing: Look for deeply colored fruit; generally the softer the better for Hachiya, and hard like an apple for the Fuyu, if that's how you like it. Bought at any stage, however, the persimmon will ripen at room temperature, which can take up to a month (hasten ripening by putting the fruit in a paper bag). Once it's ripe, store it in the refrigerator.

Preparing: Eat ripe Hachiyas out of hand (over the sink—it's messy) or cut off the top and scoop out the flesh with a spoon. Remove the stem from a hard Fuyu (peeling is optional) and bite in or slice like an apple.

Other fruits to substitute: There is no replacement for a raw, ripe Hachiya; apple or pear can replace a firm Fuyu, but only in terms of texture.

Pineapples

One of the glories of nature, the pineapple is native to Central and South America, and its prickly, diamond-patterned scaly skin ranges from yellow to green to brownish red when ripe. The flesh is juicy, sweet-tart, and acidic. At its best, it's among the best-tasting fruits there is, and this has been known forever; the pineapple is admired and revered, almost worshiped, throughout the world.

And it's changed in the last ten years. Before then, pineapples were picked green and, since they didn't sweeten much after they were picked, were often disappointing. (If they were picked ripe and shipped by air, they were expensive.) But the new "gold" hybrids, which now represent nearly 100 percent of many Hawaiian producers' crops, are almost always sweet and juicy, with lovely golden flesh. Which makes the pineapple among the most reliable fruit you can buy.

Buying and storing: Look for fruit that has a good pineapple aroma, deep yellow or golden color, and yields only slightly to gentle pressure. Underripe pineapples will decrease in acidity if left at room temperature but will not ripen or sweeten. Once it's ripe, eat it immediately or store in the refrigerator and use as quickly as possible.

Preparing: There are a few ways to dismember a pineapple: For either one, first cut off the spiky top. Then, with a chef's knife, peel around the perimeter and remove all of the spiny skin; use a paring knife to dig out any eyes. At that point, cut the pineapple crosswise into round slices or top to bottom into halves or quarters and cut out the woody core. Alternatively, cut straight down from top to bottom with a chef's knife to cut the pineapple in half; then cut each half in half again to make quarters. Use a smaller knife to cut off the woody core portion from each quarter (at the peak of your triangles) and then use a grapefruit or paring knife to separate the flesh from the skin by cutting between the two; cut the quarter into slices and serve.

Other fruits to substitute: Oranges, grapefruit, kiwi, or carambola.

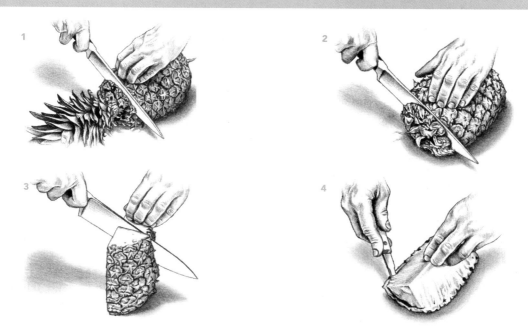

(STEP 1) Cut off the top of the pineapple about an inch below the flower. (STEP 2) Slice off the stem end as well. (STEP 3) Cut the pineapple into quarters. (STEP 4) Use a grapefruit knife to separate the fruit from the rind and a paring knife to dig out any eyes. Remove the core (the hard edge where the fruit comes to a point), slice, and serve.

Plums

Purple, black, red, orange, or green, there are hundreds of varieties of plums, ranging in size, shape, and flavor in addition to color. They can be syrupy sweet, sweet-tart, or mouth-puckeringly tart. My favorite are the dark-red-fleshed, sweet ones, though I recommend trying as many different varieties as you can.

Plums are divided into two general categories, Japanese and European. Japanese types are typically larger, sweet, and juicy, making them great for eating out of hand. European plums are smaller, often used for drying (prunes are dried plums) and cooking but can be equally good eaten fresh.

Buying and storing: Although plums are often available in supermarkets year-round, the best are the local varieties you buy in season, between May and October.

Ripe fruit should be quite soft, even oozing a sugary syrup—eat these right away—but avoid those that are mushy, split, or smell fermented. Underripe fruit will be hard and sour; leave out at room temperature to ripen. You can also refrigerate plums; it will slow down but not stop the ripening process. Prunes, like other dried fruit, are best bought in bulk at a natural food store.

Preparing: Rinse and eat. You can peel them before cooking: Drop into boiling water for about 10 seconds, or until the skins loosen, then peel with a paring knife.

Other fruit to substitute: Apricots, peaches, or nectarines.

Pomegranates
Chinese Apples

An odd fruit and a real pain in the neck to handle, but the rewards in nutrition, flavor, and texture make it worth it. The pomegranate is round and ranges in size from orange to grapefruit size; its exterior skin is speckled dark red and leathery, and the edible (and potassium-rich) seeds are covered with a crisp and snappy ruby-red flesh, which are contained in an inedible white pith. The seeds can be eaten whole or the juicy flesh sucked off and the seeds discarded; it's a matter of personal taste.

When the fresh fruit isn't available, pomegranate molasses and pure juice (which is now readily available) are perfect for bringing the flavor to cooking.

Buying and storing: Pomegranate season is very short—October to November—but the fruit keeps fairly well. Look for unblemished specimens that are heavy for their size and with no soft spots. The will keep in a cool dark spot for a couple weeks at least or in the fridge for several weeks.

Preparing: Either cut in half or cut an inch or so into the top and pry open into segments. You can break the segments apart underwater; the bad seeds and inedible pieces float to the top, the good seeds rest at the bottom, and the staining juice doesn't squirt all over. Or you can seed pomegranates in a plastic bag to contain the mess.

Other fruits to substitute: Cherries, currants, or raspberries.

Quince

Quince, which is related to the apple, has been cultivated and cherished for its fragrance and fruity flavor since the time of Ancient Rome. But it's almost always cooked, because it's incredibly astringent when raw. Its high pectin content makes it a natural for making preserves (in fact, the word *marmalade* is derived from the Portuguese word for quince, *marmelo*).

The fruit is somewhat pear shaped with smooth, golden skin, and a lovely floral fragrance; the flesh is firm, light yellow, and similar to that of a pear. When cooked, it turns a dark orange color. The quince season is short, from October to December, and it's tough to find them at other times.

Buying and storing: Look for firm, unshriveled specimens that are golden yellow in color and fragrant. Store wrapped loosely in plastic in the refrigerator; they will keep for weeks.

Preparing: Peel and remove the core (the seeds are mildly poisonous, not enough to worry about, but don't eat them); chop or slice as needed.

Best cooking methods: Simmering and braising.

When is it done? When very tender or falling apart soft.

Other fruit to substitute: Apples or pears.

Raspberries (*see* Berries, page 420)

Rhubarb

Rhubarb looks like red celery, but don't let that fool you; beyond that and the strings that run its length, they have little in common. Usually used as a fruit in sweet preparations (though not always; see Red Lentils and Rhubarb with Indian Spices, page 600), rhubarb alone is actually extremely tart, and the roots and the leaves are poisonous (the leaves contain toxic levels of oxalic acid). You can take advantages of its tartness or cook it with sugar or

Ⓕ Fast   Ⓜ Make Ahead   Ⓥ Vegan

other sweet fruits, which is why we see it most often made into pies, preserves, and compotes, often paired with strawberries.

Buying and storing: Look for firm and crisp stalks. Store in the refrigerator and use it as quickly as possible.

Preparing: See the illustrations on page 284. Although it's not entirely necessary, rhubarb is best if you string it; grab one end between a paring knife and your thumb and pull straight down to remove the celerylike strings that run lengthwise through each stalk. Remember that rhubarb leaves are poisonous, though only mildly so.

Best cooking methods: Braised or stewed.

When is it done? When very tender and easily pierced with a skewer or thin-bladed knife.

Other fruits to substitute: Cranberries, tart cherries, or fresh currants.

Star Fruit (*see* Carambola, page 422)

Strawberries (*see* Berries, page 420)

Pasta, Noodles, and Dumplings

The only generalization I can make about pasta, noodles, and dumplings—beyond the fact that almost all contain flour and water—is that people love them. There's not even a single term that embraces them all.

Everything else is up for grabs. Most noodles are made from flour and water—and salt of course—and sometimes egg and/or oil. But some contain other grains or vegetables. Most are boiled, but some are baked or pan-fried. Many are noodle shaped—whatever that word means to you, the same basic shape probably comes to mind—but some are simply squares of dough, some are stuffed, and some are eccentric, delightful shapes.

Dried pasta—the kind you buy in a box—is a staple, a reliable and beloved one. It's cheap, convenient, and can be prepared in thousands of different ways. But fresh pasta, which is not that difficult to make (though in truth it's usually not a weekday dish), is really quite special. It's richer, more flavorful, and far more nutritious than dried

as the water is usually replaced by egg. Special, too, are dumplings, ravioli, and other stuffed doughs, which can be time consuming but also can be made in advance.

Finally, there are quasi-noodle things, like gnocchi, spaetzle, and passatelli, which require no rolling or cutting and are most certainly fair game for weeknights, since for the most part they take very little time and effort.

You can make your own pasta (pages 474–480), but unless you have a life transformation it's unlikely you will do so more than occasionally; even the most devoted and skilled home cooks I know make pasta just a few times a year. (There are exceptions; you might make spaetzle, page 490, more often, because it's just so easy.)

So for the most part you're going to buy pasta. You can buy fresh, but know that *fresh* is a relative term: At good Italian or Asian markets, fresh noodles are made regularly and are usually very good. Supermarkets also sell "fresh" pasta that's somewhere between fresh and dried; it varies in quality but is usually too expensive and not all that great.

The Basics of Dried Pasta

Usually you'll buy dried pasta. For most occasions, you want to buy pasta that is 100 percent durum wheat. Ironically, though the flour comes from the States or Canada, the best pasta is made in Italy; it's either the water or the machines used—I don't really know—but it *is* better. Good pasta is easier to keep from overcooking and has a deeper, more appealing color and a texture that grabs the sauce better. For information about pastas made from other flours, see pages 464–465 and 478.

Cooking

With a few exceptions, you must cook pasta in abundant water; figure a gallon or so per pound (even a little more is better). You should salt the water well too—a fistful is about right, but if your hands are small you need more than that (a couple of tablespoons). And it doesn't matter much when you add the salt. While the pasta cooks, adjust the heat to keep the water boiling and stir frequently.

If you have problems with pasta sticking, the problem is either too little water, too little salt, or too little stirring. (And without enough salt, your pasta will be not only sticky but also bland.) No matter what you learned in college, adding oil to the water will not cure the problem. In fact it's counterproductive, because it keeps the sauce from grabbing properly.

If your pot is not deep enough for spaghetti or other long pasta, either break the pasta in half or hold the noodles by one end and dunk the other. As the bunch softens, swirl the strands around until they bend

enough for you to submerge the whole thing. Or get a bigger pot.

Don't undercook or overcook. Easy enough to say, and easy enough to do: when the pasta starts to soften, taste it; it's done when it retains a little bite but is no longer chalky. If you cut a piece in half, you'd still see a little hard white bit in the center. At that point, get ready to drain; it will cook a little more on the way to the table and be *al dente*—literally "to the teeth" or what I call "tender but not mushy"—when you eat it. It doesn't take much practice to get this right.

Don't trust anyone's recommended pasta cooking times. The appropriate time varies from box to box and even day to day. (I've never found one to be right; you could almost take the time on the box and know, at least, *not* to use that as a guide.) Cook by taste and you'll never go wrong. This holds true for every noodle you make, from fresh egg pasta made in your own kitchen to dried rice noodles from Thailand.

Draining, Saucing, and Tossing

Have a heated bowl ready; pasta cools quickly, and you want to eat it hot. A bowl from your cool cupboard is going to rob your pasta of heat immediately. It's best to warm a heatproof bowl with hot water (often you can put it under the colander so that the draining cooking water heats it) or put it in a warm oven while you're cooking. Then drain, quickly but not thoroughly; in most cases the pasta should remain quite moist. (Before draining, dip out

F Fast   M Make Ahead   V Vegan

a cup or so of pasta cooking water and reserve in case you need to thin out your sauce. See below for more on this.)

It was once true—in fact, ten years ago, it was true—that Americans ate more sauce on their pasta than Italians. But as scarcity has decreased in Italy and all but the most traditional Italians have become "modernized," you see what was once considered oversauced pasta all over the place. So, sauce as you like, but for crying out loud don't drown the pasta.

The real problem is that if a sauce is too thick we overcompensate by drowning the pasta with it, in an attempt to make the dish moist enough. If you have a thick sauce, one that is clumping up on the pasta instead of coating it nicely, thin it out with a little pasta cooking water. If the pasta sauce seems too thick (or you don't have enough), just add some of this hot water, a tablespoon or so at a time, until you achieve the desired consistency. This technique is used by most home cooks in Italy and can also be done with water you used for cooking vegetables, stock, or even tomato juice.

Toss quickly; pasta is best very, very hot. Don't worry about solids at the bottom of the bowl; you can scoop them out and over the pasta after it's served. Garnish at the last minute. Serve and eat immediately.

The Pasta Lexicon

Here is a very abbreviated list of pasta shapes; these are the ones you're likely to find without much trouble.

Long Pasta

Capelli d'angelo (angel hair) and capellini: very fine strands

Spaghetti: thin round strands

Bucatini: fat round strands with a hole through the center

Linguine: narrow flat strands

Fettuccine: wide flat strands

Tagliatelle: wide ribbons, between fettuccine and pappardelle

Pappardelle: very wide ribbons

Lasagne: sheets or extra-wide ribbons—sometimes curled at the edges

Cut Pasta

Ditalini: short pencil-width tubes

Chifferi (gomiti): the classic bent elbows

Penne and ziti: smallish tubes cut at an angle

Rigatoni: large (often ribbed) tubes, cut straight

Conchigliette and conchiglie: seashells, small and large (which are good for stuffing)

Cannelloni (manicotti): very large tubes for stuffing; sometimes ribbed

Fancy Pasta

Orecchiette: literally "little ears," small saucer-shaped disks

Cavatelli: small folded disks that look like tiny taco shells

Gemelli: cut pieces of two thick strands of pasta twisted together

Trenne: small three-sided tube

Do Pasta Shapes Matter?

There are countless dried pasta shapes, and new ones are invented all the time. Sometimes the shape you use matters, at least a little bit; when you have a sauce with small solid bits or even larger chunks, it's nice to use a shape that will catch them, like shells. For soup, you want small pasta that will fit on a spoon.

But as you're probably already thinking, this is not exactly critical; using an "inappropriate" shape is not quite the same as using salt instead of sugar. So I (as a confessed non-Italian) would argue, as I always have, that you should rarely change the type of sauce you're making because you don't have the "correct" pasta shape.

Farfalle: what we call butterflies or bowties

Fusilli, rotini, and spiralini: curlicues, corkscrews, and spirals with subtle differences

Radiatore: short tube shapes with lots of deep grooves for collecting sauce

Tortellini: squares, stuffed and folded into ringlike knots

Ravioli: stuffed squares, small to medium in size

Miscellaneous

Couscous: teeny granules of pasta that are cooked like grains (see page 537)

Orzo: shaped like grains of rice, only bigger

What to Expect from Whole Wheat Pasta

I wouldn't call myself a convert exactly, but there is *something* to be said for whole wheat pasta, whether you eat it every once in a while or all the time. Some of the benefit is nutrition-based: It's got more fiber than semolina pasta, for one thing, and a little more protein. But the flavor and texture are different in not-unpleasing ways; it's hearty and satisfying.

And with the growing interest in whole grains, whole wheat pasta has become a supermarket staple. Ideally whole wheat pasta should be flecked with bits of bran, have a pleasantly nutty flavor, and cook from brittle to tender without instantly turning to mush. As with traditional dried pasta, I generally prefer the Italian brands.

You cook and sauce whole wheat pasta the same way you do semolina pasta. It may take a minute or two longer to cook, and you'll never get quite the same creaminess after saucing, because the starch doesn't release the same way. But what you will get is a great vehicle for assertive sauces (especially nut sauces) or sauces that include big chunks of vegetables.

8 Ideal Recipes for Whole Wheat Pastas

Sauce and toss just as you would traditional pasta (page 440); remember to save some cooking water while draining in case the sauce is too thick.

1. Traditional Pesto (page 768)
2. Pasta with Garlic and Oil or its variations (page 443)
3. Fast Tomato Sauce or its variations (page 445)
4. Linguine with Raw Tomato Sauce (page 446)
5. Pasta with Chestnut Cream (page 457)
6. Any of the pastas with vegetables or legumes (pages 451–455)
7. Creamy Baked Noodles with Eggplant and Cheese (page 462)
8. Rustic Pine Nut Sauce or any of its variations (page 796)

Alternative Pastas

From angel hair to fettuccine, penne to lasagne, a staggering array of pastas is made from grains other than durum wheat. Some are available at the supermarket; the rest you can find in natural and specialty food stores or on-line.

The good news about these is that they offer the emphatic, distinctive flavors of their constituent grains—and often more fiber, vitamins, and minerals than noodles made from refined wheat. And they make it possible for diabetics or anyone with wheat allergies or celiac disease to enjoy a bowl of pasta. (If you have dietary restrictions, it's a good idea to check the labels of these, because some contain wheat or wheat gluten to help them behave more like their traditional counterparts.)

But pasta with little or no wheat (and therefore little or no gluten) will never cook to the tender-yet-firm texture of 100 percent durum pasta. Nor will it become quite as creamy when you toss it with sauce, since low-gluten pasta does not have the same binding effect. Instead, these novelty noodles tend to be more fragile, going from firm to mushy in a blink. So it's important to check alternative pasta often for doneness and remove from the heat just before it turns fully tender.

F Fast   M Make Ahead   V Vegan

The roundup that follows includes the handful that are most common, but there is an almost infinite number for you to explore on your own. For more other-than-wheat pastas, see "The Asian Noodle Lexicon" (page 463).

Brown rice pasta: Perhaps the best of the bunch, this is made from flour derived from rice that has had only the hull removed. It is light to medium brown, with the natural sweetness, nuttiness, and nutrition of brown rice; it also tends to retain a nice bite.

Buckwheat pasta: Traditional in both Europe and Asia, this is made from buckwheat flour, often combined with unbleached white or finely ground whole wheat flour to lighten the dough. The buckwheat imparts a nutty flavor and brown color to the noodle, whose texture is pleasantly mealy. Korean buckwheat and soba noodles (see "The Asian Noodle Lexicon, page 463) are examples.

Chestnut pasta: A traditional pasta of the Mediterranean, these days usually made with a mixture of white flour and chestnut flour. (You can make your own; see page 322.) Its subtle, sweet, nutty flavor is best paired with a simple butter sauce or Traditional Pesto (page 768).

Corn flour and cornmeal pastas: Wheat- and gluten-free pasta made from different textures of finely ground cornmeal. They're generally bright yellow, taste of corn, and are grainier in texture than wheat pasta. Nice flavor, but they turn mushy quickly, so watch them carefully.

Jerusalem artichoke (sunchoke) pasta: An old hippie standby, this was one of the first pasta alternatives to hit the shelves. It's made with a combination of semolina and Jerusalem artichoke flour, for a slightly yellow-green color, nutty flavor, and texture similar to egg noodles. But with wheat as the main ingredient, only slightly more protein and slightly fewer carbohydrates than regular pasta, and less fiber than most whole grain noodles, you really have to ask yourself "Why bother?"

Quinoa pasta: The dough of this wheat-free, gluten-free pasta usually combines quinoa and corn. The result is a pasta that is more assertive in flavor and lighter than traditional durum wheat pastas. But the texture is strangely soft yet gritty.

Soy pasta: The kind you find at the supermarkets typically is made with a blend of soy flour and wheat flour, though you may find it made completely from golden, black, or green soybeans at natural food stores. Soy pasta has a relatively high protein content, especially those that are all soy, but the flavor is quite beany and the texture distinctly rubbery. In short: I don't like 'em.

Pasta with Garlic and Oil

Pasta Aglio e Olio

MAKES: 4 servings
TIME: 30 minutes

One of my all-time favorites, the quintessential late-night Roman dish, great as a snack or even a centerpiece when you want something simple. Needless to say, good extra virgin olive oil is key. So is not overcooking the garlic.

Salt

2 tablespoons minced garlic

1 or 2 dried chiles, or to taste (optional)

1/3 cup extra virgin olive oil, or more as needed

1 pound long, thin pasta, like linguine or spaghetti, or any other pasta

1/2 cup chopped parsley leaves (optional)

❶ Bring a large pot of water to a boil and salt it. Put the garlic, chiles, oil, and a pinch of salt in a small skillet or saucepan and turn the heat to medium-low. Let the garlic sizzle a bit, shaking the pan occasionally, just until it puffs and turns golden, then turn off the heat if the pasta isn't ready.

❷ Cook the pasta until tender but not mushy. Drain it, reserving a bit of the cooking water. Reheat the garlic and oil mixture briefly if necessary. Dress the pasta with the sauce, adding a little more oil or some of the cooking water if it seems dry; toss with the parsley if you're using it.

Pasta with Fresh Herbs. A must-learn recipe if you have an herb garden; you'll use it all summer: When the garlic is done, toss in a mixture of 1 cup or more fresh herbs, whatever you have on hand; try, for example, $1/4$ cup minced parsley leaves, $1/4$ cup minced basil or chervil leaves, 1 sprig tarragon, minced, several sprigs of dill, minced, a sprig or two of thyme, leaves stripped from the stem and minced, and 1 tablespoon or more of minced chives (this is merely a suggestion; substitute freely). The mixture will absorb all the oil, so, in Step 2, when you toss it with the pasta, be sure to add more oil or some of the pasta cooking water. Garnish with more chopped herbs.

Pasta with Bread Crumbs. Crunchy and satisfying: Put the oil in a large skillet over medium heat. When it's hot, add $1/2$ cup fresh or dried bread crumbs (page 804) and cook, stirring frequently, until golden and fragrant, 2 to 3 minutes; remove with a slotted spoon. Turn the heat down to medium-low and stir in the chiles, garlic, and a large pinch of salt. Proceed with the recipe from Step 1, using the crunchy bread crumbs as a garnish and stirring in at the last moment.

Pasta with Chickpeas. Good with cut pasta, like ziti, penne, or shells: While you're cooking the pasta, toss about 1 cup cooked chickpeas (canned are fine), with the garlic oil mixture and warm gently.

Pasta with Ground Nuts. Use walnuts, almonds, hazelnuts, or pecans: Chop about $1/2$ cup of nuts in a food processor or by hand. Put the oil in a large skillet over medium heat. When it's hot, add the nuts and cook, stirring frequently, until they start to toast and become fragrant, just a minute or two. Then turn the heat down to medium-low and stir in the chiles, garlic, and a large pinch of salt. Proceed with the recipe from Step 1.

Pasta with Toasted Seeds. Try sunflower, sesame, poppy, or pumpkin: Put the oil in a large skillet over medium

15 Alternative Toppings for Pasta

The most common garnishes for pasta, especially in Italy, are grated cheese (most notably Parmesan and pecorino Romano) and chopped parsley. But fried bread crumbs, for example, are a venerable substitute (cheap, readily available, and crunchy); nuts are used, especially in the South; a variety of herbs will work; and so on. Here's a brief roundup of "alternative" pasta garnishes.

1. Roughly chopped olives
2. Sour cream, crème fraîche, or mascarpone
3. Roughly ground sun-dried tomatoes or dried porcini mushrooms (or both)
4. Fried garlic slivers (slow-cook a couple of cloves of garlic, slivered, in a couple of tablespoons of olive oil until lightly browned)
5. Fried shallots (see page 358)
6. Fried capers (flash-cook a tablespoon or two of capers in a tablespoon of olive oil for 30 to 60 seconds)
7. Chopped or grated hard-cooked egg
8. Toasted nuts or seeds (see page 321) flavored with woody herbs, like walnuts with rosemary or thyme
9. Flash-cooked fresh chile slices, like jalapeño, Thai, or serrano
10. A sprinkling of a spice blend, like garam masala, chili powder, or za'atar (to make your own, see pages 814–818)
11. Bread crumbs, preferably fresh, lightly fried, and seasoned (see page 805)
12. Fried cooked wheat or rye berries or hulled barley (see page 564)
13. Crunchy Crumbled Tempeh (page 674)
14. Any of the crumbles on page 805
15. Crumbled fresh cheese

Ⓕ Fast   Ⓜ Make Ahead   Ⓥ Vegan

heat. When it's hot, add about $1/4$ cup of seeds and cook, stirring frequently, until they start to toast and become fragrant, just a minute or two. Then turn the heat down to medium-low and stir in the chiles, garlic, and a large pinch of salt. Proceed with the recipe from Step 1.

The Basics of Tomato-Based Sauces

Pasta and tomatoes seem to have been made for each other, and the combinations are close to infinite, which makes tomato-based sauces the most popular for pasta. Combined with spices, cheese, butter, or more vegetables, they gain complexity, depth, and flavor.

The first choice is in your tomato. Canned are by far most convenient, and they're reliable as well. But in the summer, fresh tomato sauce should be a staple; peeling the tomatoes—which is optional—is undeniably a bit of work (seeding takes only a second), but the flavor of the sauce is much better than canned, the texture is rich and silky, and the color much prettier. If you want to make fresh tomato sauce regularly (or if you want to make large batches and freeze or can the sauce, as many people do), invest in a food mill (see page 446), which streamlines the process. Or make Raw Tomato Sauce (page 446); it's super-easy and really great.

Since Fast Tomato Sauce is so easy—and a definite kitchen staple—I suggest making double or triple batches and freezing some. Just let the sauce cool; then pack away in freezer bags or tightly sealed containers (small quantities are most useful) and use within six months or so. You can defrost slowly in the fridge or in the microwave or heat gently in a covered pan, stirring occasionally to prevent sticking.

Though straight tomato sauce is great, if you're going to eat pasta regularly, you'll want to experiment with the variations or simple twists that follow the main recipe or the ideas on pages 448–449. Some might add a little bit

13 Sauces, Salsas, or Condiments That Make Terrific Fast Pasta Sauces

1. Avocado–Red Pepper Salsa (page 751)
2. Herb-Flavored Oil (page 758)
3. Spice-Flavored Oil (page 758)
4. Aromatic-Flavored Oil (page 758)
5. Dill Purée, Basil Purée, or Mint Purée (page 769)
6. Caramelized Fennel Chutney (page 787)
7. Roasted Red Pepper Chutney (page 787)
8. Salsa Sofrito (page 788)
10. Mushroom Ketchup (page 791)
11. Rustic Pine Nut Sauce (page 796)
12. Creamy Nut Sauce (page 797)
13. Creamy Bistro Dressing or Sauce (page 799)

of cooking time, though none will take you longer than 45 minutes total. You'll know when tomato sauce is ready because it suddenly goes from looking rather watery to having that familiar saucy look.

Fast Tomato Sauce

MAKES: 4 servings; enough for 1 pound of pasta
TIME: 20 minutes

F M

This is among the most basic and useful pasta sauces and one of those staples, like vinaigrette, that is too easy *not* to make yourself. The main recipe uses basic pantry ingredients and is familiar to just about everyone, but the variations can get pretty wild (try the Peanut Tomato Sauce, for example). This sauce works tossed with any pasta or noodle (pages 441–442), for pizza (page 721), or as an accent to other cooked foods like grain, tofu, eggs, or vegetables. Skip the Parmesan to make this vegan.

Tomatoes Through a Food Mill

A food mill gently purées the tomatoes and extracts nearly all the pulp, leaving the skins and seeds in the mill. But the process for making sauce this way is just slightly different: Halve or quarter whole fresh tomatoes, put them in a pot, and turn the temperature to medium. Once they start to bubble, turn the heat down a bit so they don't scorch and cook, stirring occasionally, until the tomatoes soften, release their water, and then get quite mushy, 45 minutes to an hour. Put the tomatoes and juice in a food mill set over a large bowl and crank them through. Be sure to scrape any purée stuck to the bottom of the food mill into the bowl with a rubber spatula; it's the best part. Use this purée in Fast Tomato Sauce or anywhere you need strong tomato flavor.

3 tablespoons extra virgin olive oil or butter

1 medium onion, chopped

One 24- to 32-ounce can tomatoes, drained and chopped

Salt and freshly ground black pepper

Freshly grated Parmesan or other cheese (optional)

Chopped parsley or fresh basil leaves for garnish (optional)

1 Put the olive oil in a 10- or 12-inch skillet over medium-high heat. When hot, add the onion and cook, stirring occasionally, until soft, 2 or 3 minutes. Add the tomatoes, along with a sprinkling of salt and pepper.

2 Cook, stirring occasionally, until the tomatoes break up and the mixture comes together and thickens, 10 to 15 minutes. Taste, adjust the seasoning, and immediately toss with pasta (garnish with cheese or an herb if you like) or use in other dishes. Or cover and refrigerate for up to several days (reheat gently before serving).

Linguine with Raw Tomato Sauce

Linguine con Salsa Cruda

MAKES: About 4 servings
TIME: About 30 minutes

Sadly, I can't remember the saint who taught me how to make this; but if you have good fresh tomatoes and good basil, there is no higher use for them than this dish. And it's a very fast and easy 30 minutes. Without the Parmesan, it's vegan.

A couple of guidelines: You can use good-quality canned plum tomatoes, as long as you drain them thoroughly first; it won't be the same, but it won't be bad (do not, however, use dried basil, here or anywhere else). And don't smash the garlic too roughly or you'll have trouble removing it before serving.

You can also use this unbeatable sauce for fried foods (or chips, for that matter), on top of soft polenta, or anywhere you'd use raw salsa or relish.

Salt

2 cups cored and roughly chopped ripe tomato

2 tablespoons extra virgin olive oil

2 cloves garlic, lightly smashed

$1/4$ to $1/2$ cup roughly minced fresh basil leaves

Freshly ground black pepper

1 pound linguine or other long pasta

Freshly grated Parmesan cheese (optional)

1 Bring a large pot of water to a boil and salt it.

2 Put the tomato, oil, garlic, and half the basil in a broad-bottomed bowl. Sprinkle with salt and pepper. Mash together well, using a fork or potato masher, but do not purée. (You can make the sauce an hour or two before you're ready to eat and let it rest at room temperature.)

3 Cook the pasta in the boiling water until tender but not mushy. Ladle some of the cooking water into the

F Fast   **M** Make Ahead   **V** Vegan

sauce to thin it out a bit and warm it up. Remove the garlic. Toss the pasta with the sauce and top with the remaining basil; pass the grated Parmesan at the table.

Pasta with Dairy

Pasta exudes starch while it's cooking, which makes it creamy to begin with, but when you combine it with cheese, butter, cream, or other dairy products, it becomes more substantial and rather luxurious. There are times you can substitute extra virgin olive oil for butter, but please don't use margarine. And although other cheeses can fill in for Parmesan, if you're going to use Parmesan, make sure it's real Parmigiano-Reggiano (see page 209).

Pasta with Butter and Parmesan

MAKES: About 4 servings

TIME: 30 minutes

One of the recipes that demonstrates the value of water in pasta sauces: You can use as little as $1/2$ stick of butter here and still make a credible sauce, as long as you thin it slightly with the pasta-cooking liquid. Of course, within limits, more butter is better. See the (many and good) variations.

You can also get great results using cheese other than Parmesan: Pecorino Romano, crumbled Gorgonzola, mascarpone, and finely grated ricotta salata or fontina are all good. Try them alone, in combination, or with Parmesan.

Salt

4 to 6 tablespoons ($1/2$ to $3/4$ stick) butter

1 pound long pasta, like linguine or spaghetti, or any other pasta

1 cup freshly grated Parmesan cheese, plus cheese for serving

Freshly ground black pepper

❶ Bring a large pot of water to a boil and salt it. Bring the butter to room temperature (you can soften it in a microwave, but don't melt it). Put it in a warm bowl.

❷ Cook the pasta until tender but not mushy; drain it, reserving some of the cooking liquid. Toss the pasta with the butter, adding a little of the water if necessary to thin the sauce. Toss with the Parmesan, sprinkle with salt and pepper, and serve immediately, passing additional Parmesan at the table.

Pasta with Butter, Sage, and Parmesan. A classic with browned butter, almost as good with olive oil: Heat 4 or more tablespoons butter with 20 or 30 fresh sage leaves; the butter should brown and the sage sizzle. Cook the pasta and toss the butter, sage, and Parmesan, thinning the sauce with pasta cooking liquid if necessary.

Pasta with Butter, Cream, and Parmesan. Only enough to lightly coat the pasta: Use 4 tablespoons ($1/2$ stick) of butter. In Step 1, when you bring the butter to room temperature, whisk in $1/2$ cup heavy cream.

Fettuccine Alfredo. Maybe overkill, but good nevertheless: Reduce the butter to 2 tablespoons and melt it gently. While the pasta cooks, combine 2 eggs, $1/2$ cup heavy cream, and 1 cup grated Parmesan in a warmed bowl; beat briefly. Sprinkle with pepper. When the pasta is cooked, toss it with the cheese mixture, adding a little of the cooking water if necessary to keep the mixture moist. Drizzle with the butter, toss well, and serve immediately.

Pasta with Butter, Pepper, and Pecorino. A stronger, southern version, good with an egg tossed with the pasta as well: In Step 2, add a lot of coarsely ground black pepper and use pecorino Romano cheese in place of the Parmesan.

Pasta with Fried Eggs. While the pasta cooks, use some of the butter to cook 2 to 4 eggs, sunny side up; keep them very runny. When the pasta is done, finish as in Step 2. Top with the fried eggs, cut them up, and toss with the pasta.

Generally, if you're adding ingredients that need to cook—like vegetables—toss them in the oil, before the tomatoes, and sauté for a bit. If not, just add them along with the tomatoes or after the tomatoes begin to break down. Garnish as in the main recipe unless otherwise directed.

1. Fresh Tomato Sauce. A great option, useful for all the variations here, but only for a couple of months a year; I like this very much with butter: Substitute chopped ripe fresh tomatoes (preferably peeled and seeded; about 2 cups) for the canned. Cooking time will be about the same. Garnish with lots of Parmesan or chopped parsley or basil.

2. Garlicky Tomato Sauce. Lightly crush and peel 2 to 10 (or even more) cloves garlic and cook in place of the onion in the oil or butter over medium-low heat, turning occasionally, until golden brown. Then raise the heat, add the tomatoes, and cook as directed.

3. Spicy Tomato Sauce. Known as *arrabbiata*, a rare dish in which garlic is browned intentionally: Replace the onion with about 1 tablespoon chopped garlic and 3 to 5 (to 10, for that matter) dried red chiles. Cook, stirring, until the garlic is brown, then turn off the heat for a minute, add the tomatoes, and resume cooking. Remove the chiles before serving if you like.

4. Tomato Sauce with Aromatic Vegetables. With the onion, add $1/2$ cup each minced carrot and peeled and minced celery; cook until tender, about 10 minutes, before adding the tomatoes. Especially good puréed (see last variation). Garnish with cheese or the herb.

5. Tomato Sauce with Wine. Add $1/4$ cup dry white or red wine just before the tomatoes; let it bubble away for a moment before proceeding.

6. Tomato Sauce with Bay Leaves. A lot of bang for the buck: Add 5 to 10 bay leaves and about $1/8$ teaspoon ground cinnamon before adding the tomatoes. Remove and discard the bay leaves before serving.

7. Mushroom Sauce. See also Meatless "Meat" Sauce, right: Cook 1 cup trimmed and sliced mushrooms (or, even better, start with Pan-Cooked Mushrooms, Dry Style, page 315, adding onion along with the mushrooms and the tomatoes after the mushrooms are cooked).

8. Fried Olive Sauce. Briny taste and chewy texture: Pit and chop 1 cup olives (any kind or a mixture). Fry in the oil along with the onion until slightly shriveled.

9. Meatless "Meat" Sauce. It's easy to add heft and protein: Prepare 1 recipe The Simplest Bean Burgers (page 660), Fast Nut Burgers (page 667) or Tofu Burgers, Asian Style (page 666); or crumble 8 ounces (about 2 cups) of any tempeh. Increase the oil to $1/4$ cup and omit the onion. In Step 1, add the burger mixture or tempeh to the hot oil and cook, stirring frequently, until crumbly and well browned. Proceed with the recipe, adding any of the "spins" you like from this list. (Or if you have any leftover cooked meatless burgers, simply crumble them up and add them to the sauce toward the end of cooking.)

10. Tomato Sauce with Fresh Herbs. Delightful in summer: At the last minute, add $1/4$ to $1/2$ cup chopped herbs: basil, parsley, dill, and/or mint. Or add smaller amounts of stronger herbs (fresh at the last minute, dried along with the tomatoes): sage (maybe 10 leaves); rosemary (a teaspoon dried or a tablespoon fresh); thyme ($1/2$ teaspoon dried or 1 teaspoon fresh); oregano or, even better, marjoram (1 teaspoon dried or 1 tablespoon fresh); or tarragon ($1/2$ teaspoon fresh or $1/4$ teaspoon dried). Garnish with cheese or a little more herb.

11. Cheesy Tomato Sauce. Changing the cheese completely changes the dish; Parmesan, of course, is standard but hardly essential, and cheeses can be combined: In a warmed bowl, just before adding pasta and sauce, put in $1/2$ cup or more ricotta, goat cheese, or mascarpone for a creamy sauce; a couple tablespoons of grated Parmesan, Grana Padano, manchego, or other hard cheese for a stronger-tasting

one; or up to a cup of grated mozzarella for a gooey pizzalike pasta dish. Garnish with more cheese or some parsley or basil.

12. Vegetable Tomato Sauce. The vegetables must be tender before you add the tomatoes; this is nice puréed (see Puréed Tomato Sauce, below): After the tomatoes are cooked, add a cup of almost any cooked vegetable, chopped or sliced (like eggplant, zucchini, squash, fennel, celery, carrots, peppers, artichoke hearts, mushrooms, cauliflower; grilled vegetables are ideal). Heat through. Garnish with cheese and chopped parsley or basil.

13. Sun-Dried Tomato Sauce. Add $1/4$ cup chopped reconstituted sun-dried tomatoes to the oil before adding the tomatoes. Garnish with cheese or chopped parsley or basil.

14. Tomato Pesto Sauce. Use as much or as little pesto as you like: After the sauce has finished cooking, stir in some Traditional Pesto or one of its variations (page 768). Or, after tossing the pasta, top each serving with a spoonful of pesto; the fragrance at the table is awesome.

15. Red Pepper and Tomato Sauce. With homemade Roasted Red Peppers (page 333), just amazing: Add one or more chopped roasted red peppers along with the tomatoes.

16. Puttanesca Sauce. A Roman classic: Add 2 tablespoons drained capers, some hot red pepper flakes if you like, and $1/2$ cup pitted black olives (preferably oil-cured, like Moroccan).

17. Greek-Style Tomato Sauce. Wonderful over grains; serve with some crumbled feta cheese if you like: Add a smashed large clove garlic with the onion and $1/2$ cup red wine, 1 teaspoon each minced fresh oregano and parsley, a 3-inch cinnamon stick, and a pinch of ground allspice along with the tomatoes. Remove the cinnamon before serving. Garnish with chopped parsley.

18. Creamy Vodka Sauce. Spicy, in a different way: About 2 minutes before the sauce is done, stir in $1/4$ cup or so of vodka and $1/4$ cup heavy or light cream, or to taste.

19. Peanut Tomato Sauce. Best with Asian noodles, even at room temperature (see Cold Sesame or Peanut Noodles, page 466): Add $1/4$ cup peanut butter or tahini along with a teaspoon or two of rice vinegar just during the last minute or so of cooking.

20. Spiced Tomato Sauce. As a dipping sauce for Essential Flatbread (page 727), Paratha, or Chapatti (pages 698–700), unsurpassed: Add a couple teaspoons of garam masala or curry powder (to make your own, see page 815 or 816) during the last minute or two of cooking. Garnish with cilantro and/or wedges of lime.

21. Miso Tomato Sauce. Great with udon noodles: When the sauce is done, remove from the heat and stir in $1/4$ cup red or dark miso. Toss with and garnish with chopped walnuts if you like.

22. Thicker, More Intense Tomato Sauce. Blend in about $1/4$ cup tomato paste just before adding the tomatoes. Garnish with cheese or the herbs.

23. Oven-Roasted Tomato Sauce. Also great thinned with a little vegetable stock (pages 101–102), wine, or water: Use Oven-Roasted Fresh Plum Tomatoes (page 375).

24. Grilled Tomato Sauce. Especially if you've already got a grill going: Cut the tomatoes into thick slices and grill quickly on both sides until browned, about 5 minutes total. Grill a red bell pepper and a jalapeño or two (see page 252), then peel, seed, and chop. Proceed with the recipe, adding a teaspoon minced oregano leaves and a tablespoon or so red wine vinegar after Step 1. Garnish with parsley.

25. Puréed Tomato Sauce. Smooth and creamy: You can finish any sauce by passing it through a food mill or whizzing it in a blender or food processor (for safety's sake, cool it slightly first); add a little cream or ricotta cheese if you like. Reheat it briefly before saucing the pasta. Garnish with cheese or the herbs.

10 Additions to Pasta with Butter and Parmesan

Use alone or in combination, with the basic recipe or any of the variations:

1. About $^1/_2$ chopped herb (or herbs); mint is especially nice
2. About 1 cup cooked peas
3. Up to 2 cups minced drained cooked spinach (plus a little ricotta if you have it)
4. Up to 2 cups cooked and drained broccoli florets
5. 2 or 3 large artichoke hearts, cooked and sliced
6. A tablespoon or so of grated lemon or orange zest
7. 1 tablespoon or so capers
8. Ground dried chiles, like ancho, chipotle, or guajillo, to taste
9. 2 hard-cooked eggs, finely chopped
10. 10 to 20 mashed roasted garlic cloves (see page 304)

Pasta in Broth

There are three ways to prepare pasta in broth, all deeply satisfying. The simplest is akin to noodle soup, where you cook the pasta to near doneness, drain it, and at the last minute drop it into a pot of simmering stock—sometimes along with other simple ingredients. (See 8 Noodle-Loving Soups," page 142.)

The other two ways begin by sautéing the pasta in olive oil or butter, with or without aromatic vegetables or seasonings. In one, the flavored cooking liquid almost entirely bubbles away, leaving a rich pasta "stew," as in the next recipe for vermicelli. The other is cooked and stirred, until the pasta is creamy and the liquid is completely absorbed, as in the orzo recipe that follows.

Garlicky Vermicelli or Fideo

MAKES: 4 to 6 servings
TIME: 25 minutes

The best way to break up the brittle vermicelli or fideo is to put it in a bag and beat it gently; or crush it between your hands, right over the pan. Like Orzo, Risotto Style (page 451), the pasta is toasted in oil before the stock is added; the difference is that the dish is eaten like a stew, with some of the flavorful cooking liquid. So you get the best of both soup and pasta.

$^1/_4$ cup peanut or olive oil

$^1/_2$ pound vermicelli or fideo, broken up

2 tablespoons minced garlic, or more if you like

Salt and freshly ground black pepper

4 to 6 cups vegetable stock (pages 101–102)

1 cup freshly grated Parmesan cheese

$^1/_2$ cup parsley leaves, chopped

1 Put the oil into a deep skillet or large pot over medium-high heat. When hot, add the pasta and garlic, sprinkle with salt and pepper, and cook, stirring frequently, until both are toasted, golden brown, and fragrant, 5 to 10 minutes.

2 Stir in 5 cups of the stock and bring to a boil. Reduce the heat and simmer, stirring occasionally, until most of the liquid is absorbed, about 10 minutes, adding more stock if the mixture starts to get too dry. Test the pasta and cook for another few minutes if it's still too tough. Taste, adjust the seasoning, sprinkle with cheese and parsley, and serve.

Vermicelli or Fideo with Olives. With a striking, almost black, color: Prepare $^1/_2$ cup of Tapenade (page 326). In Step 1, refrain from sprinkling the garlic and pasta with salt; when they're toasted, stir in the olive mixture and cook, stirring frequently, until it darkens a bit, a minute or so. Proceed with the recipe from Step 2. Instead of the cheese, top with Fried Bread Crumbs (page 805) if you like.

 F Fast   **M** Make Ahead   **V** Vegan

Vermicelli or Fideo with Tomatoes and Chile. Garlicky, hot, and tangy: Peel and coarsely chop 3 medium tomatoes (canned are fine; drain most of their juice). Mince a canned chipotle chile and stir it into the tomatoes, with a little of the chile's adobo sauce if you like. In Step 1, when the garlic and pasta are toasted, stir in $1/2$ teaspoon dried or 2 teaspoons fresh oregano and the tomato mixture. Cook, stirring occasionally, until the tomatoes dry out a bit, about 3 minutes. In Step 2, stir in just 4 cups of the stock and proceed with the recipe. Top with grated manchego cheese instead of the Parmesan if you like.

Orzo, Risotto Style

MAKES: 4 servings
TIME: 25 minutes

Even though orzo is rice shaped, this is quite different from true risotto (page 516). But as with risotto, it's important not to skimp on the fat, or the dish runs the risk of seizing up and becoming gummy. You can use any dried small pasta here (like orecchiette or shells) or break long strands into 1-inch pieces. The cooking time and absorption rate might vary a bit, so be sure to add the stock a little at a time and check frequently for doneness.

> 4 to 5 cups vegetable stock (pages 101–102) or water
>
> 2 tablespoons extra virgin olive oil
>
> 1 large shallot, minced
>
> 2 cups orzo
>
> Salt and freshly ground black pepper
>
> $1/2$ cup dry white wine or water
>
> 2 tablespoons butter, softened
>
> $1/2$ cup freshly grated Parmesan cheese, plus more for serving

1 Put the stock in a medium saucepan over low heat. Put the olive oil in a large, deep nonstick skillet over medium heat. When hot, add the shallot and cook, stirring occasionally, until it softens, 2 to 3 minutes.

2 Add the orzo and cook, stirring occasionally, until it is glossy and coated with oil, 2 to 3 minutes. Add a little salt and pepper, then the wine. Stir and let the liquid bubble away.

3 Use a ladle to begin to add the warmed stock, $1/2$ cup or so at a time, stirring after each addition and every minute or so. When the stock is just about evaporated, add more. The mixture should be neither soupy nor dry. Keep the heat medium to medium-high and stir frequently.

4 Begin tasting the orzo 10 minutes after you add it; you want it to be tender but with still a tiny bit of crunch; it could take as long as 20 minutes to reach this stage. When it does, stir in the softened butter and at least $1/2$ cup of Parmesan. Taste, adjust the seasoning, and serve immediately, passing additional Parmesan at the table.

Lemon Orzo, Risotto Style. Tart and creamy: Grate the zest from 2 lemons and squeeze their juice. In Step 2, when you add the orzo, add the zest. Add the lemon juice along with the wine.

Creamy Orzo with Almond Butter. Vegan, but still creamy: Use a combination of almond milk and vegetable stock; instead of the butter, use almond butter. Omit the cheese. Proceed with the recipe, sprinkling with toasted almond slivers for garnish if you like.

Pasta with Vegetables and Legumes

You can turn just about any vegetable into a pasta sauce. Or, to look at it another way, you can toss pasta with many different vegetable dishes. When you think about it, most sauces are nothing more than vegetable combinations that have been reduced until thickened or cooked until soft, so the boundaries are quite vague. But there are some rules worth following to extract and preserve as much flavor as possible.

Think of basic tomato sauce, the model for all

vegetable-based pasta sauces: aromatics are cooked in oil or butter, the tomatoes are added, and they're simmered until they're soft. The process can stop there, or you can add cheese or other vegetables; you can purée the sauce; you can add garnishes. Those are pretty much the options for all vegetables.

There is an alternative: Cook the vegetable in water until it's very soft, then purée or mash, and use that, combined with a little of the water, as a sauce. Generally speaking, this is the less flavorful option, but it's not a bad one. If, for example, you cook spinach until it's done, then chop it and combine it with a little garlic and ricotta, or just oil and salt, you have made a credible sauce without sautéing.

To take a couple of not-so-obvious vegetables as examples: Sauté parcooked broccoli or cauliflower with garlic and oil, adding a little more water so you can cook it until it becomes really soft. Mash it slightly, then toss it with pasta and a bit more oil. Add cheese or toasted bread crumbs if you like; maybe a pinch of hot red pepper flakes. Voilà.

Or grate a sweet potato or butternut squash and put it in a pan with some water, plus some oil or butter if you like. Cook it until it's soft, then toss it with pasta and maybe a little sage or nutmeg, butter, and Parmesan. Very traditional, quite delicious. Again, the alternative is to purée the soft vegetables with flavorings, which almost always makes a fine sauce.

The possibilities are endless; take a look at "39 Vegetable or Legume Dishes That Can Be Tossed with Pasta" (page 456) for more ideas.

Pasta with Broccoli, Cauliflower, or Broccoli Raab

MAKES: About 4 servings
TIME: About 40 minutes

Ⓕ Ⓥ

This is the real shortcut version: You use the same water for the broccoli as you do for the pasta. It's hard to say how much oil you'll wind up adding to this dish: The answer is "enough." I cook the garlic in the $1/4$ cup listed here, but I usually add a teaspoon or two more per serving at the table, more for flavor than for moisture.

Salt

About 1 pound broccoli, cauliflower, or broccoli raab, trimmed and cut into pieces

$1/4$ cup extra virgin olive oil, or more as needed

1 tablespoon chopped garlic, or more to taste

1 pound penne, ziti, or other cut pasta

Freshly ground black pepper

❶ Bring a large pot of water to a boil and salt it. Boil the vegetable until it's fairly tender, 5 to 10 minutes, depending on the type (broccoli raab is fastest, cauliflower slowest) and the size of your chunks. Meanwhile, put the oil in a large skillet over medium-low heat. When hot, add the garlic and cook until it begins to sizzle, about a minute; keep warm. Scoop out the broccoli with a slotted spoon or strainer.

❷ Put the broccoli in the skillet and turn the heat up to medium-high; cook, stirring and mashing the broccoli, until it is hot and quite soft.

❸ Meanwhile, cook the pasta. When the pasta is not quite done, drain it, reserving about a cup of the cooking liquid. Add the pasta to the skillet with the broccoli and a couple of tablespoons of the reserved cooking water; toss with a large spoon until well combined. Sprinkle with salt and pepper, along with some of the pasta water to keep the mixture from drying out. Serve immediately.

Pasta with Greens. Here, if your judgment is good, you can cook the greens at the same time as the pasta; usually you add them to the boiling water during the last minutes of cooking, but the thick stems of kale or collards may take just about as long as the pasta to become tender. Until you're confident, follow the basic recipe, using 1 to $1^1/2$ pounds spinach, kale, collard, chard, mustard, or other greens instead of the broccoli. If the stems are thick, separate them from the leaves; chop the stems no more than 1 inch long and roughly chop the leaves. Cook the stems or whole greens until tender and proceed with the recipe.

10 Ways to Boost Pasta with Broccoli, Cauliflower, or Broccoli Raab

Just a few of the ideas to make this dish more flavorful; many can be combined.

1. Cook 3 or 4 dried chiles along with the garlic or stir in hot red pepper flakes when you toss the pasta.
2. Add a teaspoon or so of minced garlic to the mixture about 30 seconds before you turn off the heat.
3. Cook several threads saffron in the oil along with the garlic.
4. Add $1/2$ cup of so of Traditional Pesto (page 768) when you toss the pasta.
5. Stir in a small can of tomato paste—or a cup of chopped cherry or regular tomatoes—when you combine the pasta and vegetable.
6. Add a couple of tablespoons of Tapenade (page 326) just when you toss the pasta.
7. Add 1 cup sliced mushrooms to the oil once the garlic sizzles and continue to cook, stirring occasionally, until you add the vegetable, then proceed.
8. Toss in a cup or so of quick-cooking, fragile vegetables during the last 30 to 60 seconds of cooking: think pea shoots, shelled fresh peas, chopped spinach, or arugula.
9. Stir in $1/2$ cup of so of Roasted Red Pepper (page 333) purée when you toss the pasta.
10. Serve with a generous sprinkling of freshly grated Parmesan cheese.

Pasta with Caramelized Onions

MAKES: About 4 servings
TIME: About 1 hour

I found this recipe miraculous when I was introduced to it around 20 years ago, and I still love it. The onions are cooked slowly and carefully (see Caramelized Onions, page 329), until they become sweet and incredibly tender.

Many of the ideas found in "10 Ways to Boost Pasta with Broccoli, Cauliflower, or Broccoli Raab" (left) can be used here as well.

5 or 6 medium to large onions (about 2 pounds)
$1/3$ cup plus 2 tablespoons extra virgin olive oil
Salt and freshly ground black pepper
1 pound linguine, spaghetti, capellini, fettuccine, or other long pasta
Freshly grated Parmesan cheese

❶ Thinly slice the onions; this is a good job for a mandoline or (my preference, because this is a lot of onions) the food processor's slicing disk. Put them in a large dry skillet over medium-low heat and cover. Check and stir every 5 minutes. The onions will first give up lots of liquid, then dry out; after 20 to 30 minutes, when they begin to brown and stick to the pan, remove the cover. Add the $1/3$ cup of olive oil, along with a generous sprinkling of salt and pepper. Turn the heat up to medium.

❷ Bring a large pot of water to a boil and salt it. Continue to cook the onions until they are uniformly brown and soft, almost pasty, 10 to 20 minutes more. Cook the pasta until it is tender but not mushy.

❸ Taste the onions and adjust the seasoning; drain the pasta, reserving about a cup of the cooking water. In a warm bowl, toss together the pasta and onions, along with the remaining oil and a little of the cooking water if necessary to allow the mixture to coat the pasta evenly. Toss with some Parmesan and serve, passing more Parmesan at the table.

Pasta with Savory Caramelized Onions. The addition of stronger flavors nicely counters the onions' sweetness. In Step 2, add 2 tablespoons capers or chopped pitted black olives (or both) to the onions as they cook. In Step 3, add 1 teaspoon balsamic or other mild vinegar, or to taste—but be careful not to overdo it.

Pasta with Mushrooms

MAKES: 4 servings

TIME: 30 minutes

In many parts of the world, from Italy to the Pacific Northwest to Chile, you would think to make these, at least seasonally, with fresh porcini. Almost needless to say, it is an amazing dish when made this way, but it's still a very good one when made with shiitakes or even ordinary button mushrooms.

Salt

1 pound shiitake or other fresh mushrooms

$^1/_3$ cup plus 1 tablespoon olive oil

Freshly ground black pepper

2 tablespoons minced shallot or 1 tablespoon minced garlic

1 pound any long or cut pasta

$^1/_2$ cup vegetable stock (pages 101–102)

About $^1/_2$ cup chopped parsley leaves, plus more for garnish

① Bring a large pot of water to a boil and salt it. Remove the stems from shiitakes (discard them or use them for stock). If you're using wild mushrooms, wipe them clean or rinse them quickly if they are very dirty. Trim of any hard, tough spots. Cut the mushrooms into small chunks or slices.

② Put $^1/_3$ cup of the oil in a medium to large skillet over medium heat. When hot, add the mushrooms and sprinkle with salt and pepper. Raise the heat to medium-high and cook, stirring occasionally, until the mushrooms begin to brown, at least 10 minutes. Add the shallot, stir, and cook for another minute or two, until the mushrooms are tender. Turn off the heat.

③ Cook the pasta until tender but not mushy. When it's almost done, add the stock (or pasta cooking water) to the mushrooms, turn the heat to low, and reheat gently. Drain the pasta, reserving a little of the cooking water. Toss the pasta and mushrooms together along with the remaining tablespoon of olive oil; add a little more pasta-cooking water if the dish seems dry. Stir in about $^1/_2$ cup of parsley and serve garnished with more parsley.

Linguine with Fresh and Dried Mushrooms. As in any mushroom recipe, you can enhance the taste of ordinary button mushrooms by using a portion of dried porcini: In Step 1, use ordinary button mushrooms (or shiitakes). At the same time, soak $^1/_4$ to $^1/_2$ cup of dried porcini in hot water to cover for about 10 minutes, or until softened. Drain the porcini and squeeze out excess moisture, reserving the soaking liquid. Cut the porcini into bits and cook them with the fresh mushrooms and shallot. In Step 3, use the mushroom-soaking liquid to augment or replace stock or pasta-cooking water.

Pasta with Lentils or Other Legumes

MAKES: 6 to 8 servings

TIME: About 1 hour

Lentils are ideal for this dish, because they cook so quickly they won't slow you down much. But you can make pasta with almost any legume, as long as it's soft enough; for last-minute cooking, of course, you'll want to start with precooked, canned, or frozen beans. (If you do that, simply cook them with the vegetables until the vegetables are tender.)

The intention here is to have the beans, vegetables, and oil create a kind of sauce that's almost meaty, with the beans playing a substantial role while the pasta provides the bulk. You can also turn this into a more-beans-than-pasta-type dish, like Cannellini Beans with Cabbage and Pasta (page 586), or even a soup, like Pasta e Fagiole (Pasta and Bean Soup, page 123), simply by adjusting the ingredients and the liquid.

$^3/_4$ cup dried lentils, washed and picked over, or $1^1/_2$ to 2 cups cooked small beans

2 carrots, chopped

1 large or 2 medium onions, chopped

2 cups cored and chopped tomato (drained canned are fine)

Salt and freshly ground black pepper

1 tablespoon minced fresh marjoram or oregano or 1 teaspoon dried

3 tablespoons extra virgin olive oil

1 pound elbows, shells, or other cut pasta

1 teaspoon minced garlic

① Combine the lentils, carrots, half the onion, and water to cover in a large pot over medium heat. Simmer until the lentils are tender but not mushy, 20 to 30 minutes (some lentils may take even longer, but check frequently to avoid overcooking). Add the tomato, sprinkle with some salt and pepper and half the marjoram, stir, and cook for another 10 minutes or so; keep warm over low heat. (This sauce may be made ahead up to this point, tightly covered and refrigerated for a day or two, or frozen for several weeks.)

② Bring a large pot of water to a boil and salt it. Put 2 tablespoons of the olive oil in a medium skillet over medium-high heat. When hot, add the remaining onion and cook, stirring, until it begins to brown and become crisp, about 10 minutes.

③ Cook the pasta until it is still quite firm, even a bit chalky in the center. Drain it, reserving a cup or so of the cooking liquid. Stir the pasta into the lentils along with the garlic, the cooked onion, and the remaining marjoram and olive oil. Add enough of the pasta water to moisten the mixture. Cook for 2 or 3 minutes, or until the pasta is tender. Taste, adjust the seasoning, and serve in a warm bowl.

Pasta with Nut Sauces

If you think of pasta as peasant food—a simple base for a sauce of whatever's available—and remember that it orig-

inated in the Mediterranean, it's a short step to seeing the logic of sauces made from nuts, which, after all, grow on trees.

Because nuts are powerful—strong tasting, rich, and textured—one key is keeping it simple; you don't want your pasta swimming in a robust nut sauce, especially if you're using fresh pasta. So it's easy: A dollop of any nut butter thinned with some pasta water instantly adds deep flavor, texture (creamy, crunchy, or both), and makes a great sauce. Add even more flavor—and decadence—by using cream or nut milk to make the sauce. (Pasta with Walnut Sauce, page 458, offers a dairy-free variation that will be a hit with vegans and nonvegans alike.)

Other sauces that feature nuts and are delicious with pasta are—of course—Traditional Pesto (page 768), as well as Rustic Pine Nut Sauce (page 796–797) and Creamy Nut Sauce (page 798). Be sure to see the chart on page 457.

Pasta with Almond Butter

MAKES: About 4 servings

TIME: 30 minutes

Ⓕ **Ⓜ**

Any dried or fresh pasta will work with any nut butter, but Fresh Herb Pasta (page 479) is particularly nice here; for everyday meals, try whole wheat spaghetti or linguine. Omit the Parmesan and the dish becomes vegan.

This fresh nut butter keeps in the refrigerator for a couple weeks, so you can double or triple the recipe and keep it on hand for dressing pasta or vegetables, spreading on toast or sandwiches, and more.

Salt

1/4 cup neutral oil, like grapeseed or corn, or almond oil, or as needed

2 cloves garlic, smashed and peeled

And this is just the beginning . . . if, after saucing, you think the dish needs more moisture, just add a little of the pasta-cooking water or extra oil or butter—or both.

1. Braised Artichoke Hearts (page 259)
2. Roasted or Grilled Asparagus (page 261)
3. Beets with Pistachio Butter (page 268)
4. Sautéed Brussels Sprouts with Hazelnuts (page 273)
5. Buttered Cabbage (page 275)
6. Carrots with Dates and Raisins and its variation (page 279)
7. Breaded Sautéed Cauliflower and its variations (page 281)
8. Chard with Oranges and Shallots (page 286)
9. Pan-Grilled Corn with Tomatoes (page 290)
10. Sautéed Eggplant and its variations (page 295)
11. Eggplant Slices with Garlic and Parsley (page 297); just coarsely chop first
12. Braised Endive, Escarole, or Radicchio (page 300)
13. Roast Fennel with Orange (page 303)
14. Garlic Braised in Olive Oil (page 305)
15. Leeks Braised in Oil or Butter and its variations (page 310)
16. Sautéed Mushrooms (page 314)
17. Anything-Scented Peas (page 333)
18. Roasted Red Peppers (page 333)
19. My Mom's Pan-Cooked Peppers and Onions (page 334)
20. Crisp Panfried Potatoes (Home Fries) and its variations (page 343)
21. Oven-Roasted Potatoes (page 344)
22. Spinach with Currants and Nuts (page 360)
23. Sautéed Chayote (page 362)
24. Crisp-Cooked Sunchokes (page 369)
25. Grilled Tomatoes with Basil (page 373)
26. Oven-Roasted Fresh Plum Tomatoes and its variations (page 375)
27. Oven-Dried Tomatoes (page 377)
28. Butternut Squash, Braised and Glazed, and most of its variations (page 364)
29. Winter Squash Slices, Roasted (page 366)
30. Panfried Pumpkin with Tomato Sauce (page 366)
31. Baked Mixed Vegetables with Olive Oil and its variations (page 380)
32. Gigantes with Brussels Sprouts and its variations (page 587)
33. White Beans, Tuscan Style, and its variations (page 594)
34. Beans and Mushrooms and most of its variations (page 596)
35. Braised Lentils, Spanish Style, and its variations (page 598)
36. Flageolets, French Style, and its variations (page 604)
37. Chickpea Fondue and its variations (page 615)
38. White Bean Purée and its variations (page 612)
39. Tapenade (page 326)

$^{1}/_{2}$ cup blanched almonds

Freshly ground black pepper

1 pound dried or fresh pasta

Chopped mixed fresh herbs for garnish

Freshly grated Parmesan for garnish

1 Bring a large pot of water to a boil and salt it. Put half the oil in a skillet over medium heat. When hot,

add the garlic and cook for about a minute, then add the almonds and cook, stirring often, for about 3 minutes.

2 Remove from the heat, let cool a bit, and transfer to a food processor. Purée until smooth, adding more oil as necessary; the consistency should be thinner than that of peanut butter, just pourable. Taste and add salt and pepper as needed. (The sauce can be made to this point, covered, and refrigerated for up to 2 weeks.)

F Fast   **M** Make Ahead   **V** Vegan

MORE PASTA AND NUT BUTTER COMBINATIONS

You can mix and match here, of course, but the recipes as assembled work very nicely following the basic pattern set out in Pasta with Almond Butter. See, too, "Grinding Nuts into Meal, Flour, or Butter" (page 322) for specifics on making your own nut butter.

PASTA	NUT BUTTER	LIQUID	SEASONING AND GARNISH
Linguine	Pistachio	Pasta water	Cherry tomatoes and chopped basil leaves
Whole Wheat Pasta (fresh, page 478, dried)	Cashew	Stock or pasta water	Chopped capers or olives and parsley leaves
Pappardelle	Hazelnut	Cream or hazelnut or oat milk	Sautéed Mushrooms (page 314) and chopped chives
Corkscrews	Pecan	Cream	Peas and chopped tarragon leaves
Orecchiette	Walnut	Stock or pasta water	Grated or minced lemon zest and chopped rosemary or thyme
Sweet Potato Gnocchi (page 488)	Pumpkin Seed	Stock or pasta water	Roasted Garlic (page 304)

❸ Cook the pasta until tender but not mushy. Drain it, reserving at least $^1/_2$ cup of the cooking water. Mix a tablespoon or so of the pasta water with 3 to 4 tablespoons of the almond butter, then toss with the pasta. If the sauce is too thick, thin with a little more pasta water; add more nut butter if you like. Taste and adjust the seasoning, then serve sprinkled with the herbs and Parmesan.

Pasta with Chestnut Cream

MAKES: About 4 servings
TIME: 30 minutes

Ⓕ Ⓜ

This rich, traditional Mediterranean dish is a perfect first course for a fancy dinner, especially with fresh pasta (page 474). And you can make it vegan just by using nondairy cream and skipping the Parmesan.

Salt

$^1/_2$ cup cream or half-and-half

8 ounces fresh chestnuts, cooked (page 287), or thawed frozen or canned

1 sprig fresh thyme

Freshly ground black pepper

1 pound dried or fresh pasta

Freshly grated Parmesan for garnish

❶ Bring a large pot of water to a boil and salt it. Put the cream, chestnuts, and thyme in a pot over medium heat. Bring it to a boil, then immediately turn off the heat and let the mixture sit for about 10 minutes.

❷ Transfer the chestnut mixture to a food processor or blender and sprinkle with some salt and pepper. Purée until smooth. (You can make the sauce to this point, cover, and refrigerate for up to 4 days.)

❸ Cook the pasta until tender but not mushy. Drain it, reserving some of the cooking water. Toss the pasta with the chestnut cream sauce. If the sauce is too thick, thin with a little of the pasta water. Taste and adjust the seasoning, then serve sprinkled with the Parmesan.

Pasta with Walnut Sauce

MAKES: About 4 servings

TIME: 30 minutes

A rich bread-thickened nut sauce that's unbelievable with stuffed pasta. To make a nondairy version of this sauce, use about $1/2$ cup bread crumbs with nondairy milk and omit the Parmesan.

Salt

1 thick slice Italian bread

$1/2$ cup milk

1 cup walnut or pecan halves

2 cloves garlic

$1/2$ cup freshly grated Parmesan cheese, plus more for serving

2 teaspoons fresh marjoram leaves or $1/2$ teaspoon dried

$1/2$ cup extra virgin olive oil

Freshly ground black pepper

1 pound dried, fresh, or stuffed pasta

1 Bring a large pot of water to a boil and salt it. Soak the bread in the milk. Combine the nuts, garlic, cheese, and marjoram in a food processor and turn the machine on. With the machine running, add the oil gradually, using just enough so that the mixture forms a very thick paste. Squeeze out the bread and add it to the mix, which will be very thick. Now add the milk the bread soaked in and enough water to make a saucy mixture. Sprinkle with salt and pepper.

2 Cook the pasta until tender but not mushy. Drain it—reserve some of the cooking water—and toss with the sauce; if the mixture appears too thick, thin with a little of the pasta-cooking water (or more olive oil). Taste and adjust the seasoning, then serve with more Parmesan.

Pasta with Walnut-Tomato Sauce. The acidity in the tomatoes lightens up the sauce a bit: Add 1 medium tomato, peeled, seeded, and roughly chopped, or $1/2$ cup chopped canned tomato; blend with the nuts in Step 1.

Pasta with Rich Walnut Sauce. Use cream cheese or cream if you don't have mascarpone: Add 3 to 4 tablespoons mascarpone; blend with the nuts in Step 1.

Baked Pasta

Here we have a special group of dishes, some of which are best made with fresh pasta (which usually requires no precooking before being baked), others of which start with parcooked dried pasta. From lasagne to macaroni and cheese, they have in common the fact that they are usually quite substantial. The great thing about these dishes is that you can include practically anything you like in them, whether in the layers (as in lasagne) or in the sauce (as in baked ziti).

Baked Ziti

MAKES: 6 servings

TIME: About 1 hour

Old-school baked ziti with red sauce is basically a short-cut for lasagne, with fewer ingredients and none of the layering hassle. A staple of potluck dinners, it serves at least six people with only a pound of pasta. Whatever you do, don't overcook the pasta! It should be too tough to actually eat when you mix it with the sauce, which will make it perfect after baking.

Salt

3 tablespoons extra virgin olive oil or butter, plus more as needed

1 pound any mushrooms, preferably mixed with some reconstituted dried porcini (page 317)

1 large onion, diced

 F Fast   **M** Make Ahead   **V** Vegan

1 tablespoon minced garlic (optional)

Freshly ground black pepper

One 28-ounce can tomatoes, with their liquid, chopped

1 pound ziti or other large cut pasta

1 pound mozzarella, preferably fresh, grated or chopped

About 1/2 cup freshly grated Parmesan (optional)

1 Bring a large pot of water to a boil and salt it. Preheat the oven to 400°F.

2 Put the olive oil or butter in a large skillet over medium-high heat. When the oil is hot or the butter is melted, add the mushrooms and cook, stirring occasionally, until they soften, release their water, and then begin to dry again, about 5 minutes. Add the onion and, if you're using it, the garlic; sprinkle with salt and pepper. Lower the heat to medium and continue to cook, stirring occasionally, until the vegetables are soft, about 2 minutes.

3 Add the tomatoes and bring to a boil. Turn the heat down so that the mixture bubbles gently and cook, stirring occasionally, while you cook the pasta; don't let the sauce get too thick.

4 Meanwhile, cook the pasta until just tender; it should still be too hard to eat. Drain it (don't shake the colander; allow some water to cling to the noodles) and toss it with the sauce and about half the mozzarella. Grease a large baking dish (9 × 13 or the like) and pour or spoon the mixture into it. Top with the remaining mozzarella and the Parmesan if you're using it and bake until the top is browned and the cheese bubbly, 20 to 30 minutes.

Baked Ziti with Ricotta. Two ways to go: Stir up to 1 cup of ricotta cheese into the sauce right before using and proceed with the recipe. Or, as you're putting the ziti into the baking dish, nestle dollops of ricotta in among the pasta and proceed with the recipe.

Baked Ziti with Goat Cheese and Olives. Full flavored and quite meaty: Instead of the mushrooms, use 1 cup pitted olives (try to keep them in large pieces). Use bits of goat cheese instead of the mozzarella.

Nutty Baked Ziti. Really rich but really good: Instead of making a tomato sauce, omit the mushrooms, onion, garlic, and tomatoes and make the sauce for Pasta with Walnut Sauce (page 458). Toss the ziti with the sauce, along with Pan-Cooked Mushrooms, Dry Style (page 315) if you like. Top with Fresh Bread Crumbs (page 804) and proceed with the recipe.

Vegetable Lasagne

MAKES: 6 to 8 servings
TIME: 1 hour, with prepared pasta sheets and sauce

At its simplest lasagne is a baked layered dish of pasta, sauce, and cheese; adding some cooked vegetables, like spinach, zucchini, or mushrooms, is a no-brainer. Make your lasagne with fresh pasta whenever you can; it's traditional and completely delicious. Surprisingly, store-bought egg roll wrappers work well too. You might also try polenta slices (page 544) instead of pasta.

If you feel that a lasagne isn't a lasagne without mozzarella, substitute shredded mozzarella for half of the ricotta.

Salt

1 recipe any fresh pasta (pages 477–480), rolled into sheets, or 12 dried lasagne noodles

2 tablespoons softened butter or extra virgin olive oil

2 recipes Fast Tomato, Meatless "Meat," or Mushroom Sauce (pages 448–449)

3 cups cooked spinach, squeezed dry and chopped, or any other chopped vegetable

3 cups ricotta, plus more as needed

2 cups freshly grated Parmesan, plus more as needed

Freshly ground black pepper

1. Bring a large pot of water to a boil and salt it. Cut the fresh pasta sheets into long, wide noodles approximately 3 × 13 inches or a size that will fit into your lasagne dish. Cook the noodles (6 at a time for dried noodles) until they are tender but still underdone (they will finish cooking as the lasagne bakes); fresh pasta will take only a minute or less. Drain and then lay the noodles flat on a towel so they don't stick.

2. Preheat the oven to 400°F. Grease a rectangular baking dish with the butter or olive oil, add a large dollop of tomato sauce, and spread it around. Put a layer of noodles (use 4) in the dish, trimming any overhanging edges; top with a layer of tomato sauce, one-third of the spinach, and one-fourth of the ricotta (use your fingers to "crumble" it evenly over top) and Parmesan. Sprinkle some salt and pepper between the layers of tomato sauce and spinach if needed.

3. Repeat the layers twice and top with the remaining noodles, tomato sauce, ricotta, and Parmesan; the top should be covered with cheese; add more ricotta and Parmesan as needed. (The lasagne may be made ahead to this point, wrapped tightly, and refrigerated for up to a day or frozen; bring to room temperature before proceeding.)

4. Bake until the lasagne is bubbling and the cheese is melted and lightly browned on top, about 30 minutes. Remove from the oven and let rest for a few minutes before serving; cool completely, cover well, and refrigerate for up to 3 days; or freeze.

White Lasagne. Seriously rich and delicious: Omit the ricotta and substitute 1 recipe Béchamel Sauce (page 803) for the tomato sauce.

Pesto Lasagne. Alternate layers of pesto and tomato sauce or use all pesto: Substitute Traditional Pesto (page 768) for all or half of the tomato sauce.

Vegan Lasagne. Use puréed tofu: Use Eggless Pasta (page 478) or dried lasagne noodles; substitute puréed silken or soft tofu for the ricotta and bread crumbs for the Parmesan. Add basil leaves between the layers if

you like. Be sure the tomato sauce and spinach are well seasoned. Proceed with the recipe, finishing with a layer of seasoned bread crumbs.

11 Vegetable Dishes for Layering in Lasagne

Layer any of these dishes between your lasagne noodles, with tomato sauce, Béchamel (page 803), cheese, or nothing.

1. Boiled or Steamed Greens (page 239)
2. Roasted Artichoke Hearts (page 259)
3. Grilled or Broiled Eggplant (page 295)
4. Eggplant Slices with Garlic and Parsley (page 297)
5. Sautéed Mushrooms (page 314)
6. Caramelized Onions (page 329)
7. Roasted Red Peppers (page 333)
8. Oven-Roasted Fresh Plum Tomatoes (page 375)
9. Butternut Squash, Braised and Glazed (page 364)
10. Panfried Pumpkin with Tomato Sauce (page 366)
11. Baked Mixed Vegetables with Olive Oil (page 380)

Baked Macaroni and Cheese

MAKES: 4 to 6 servings
TIME: About 45 minutes
Ⓜ

It's a shame to think that some people only know mac and cheese out of a box. The real thing is rich, filling, and delicious. Use nearly any pasta—tube, corkscrew, or cup-shaped ones work best because they grab the sauce—just be sure to slightly undercook whatever pasta you use since it will continue to cook in the oven. Vary the type of cheese you use too: try blue cheese, goat cheese, smoked Gouda, or even mascarpone for a decadent version; see the variations.

Salt

2$\frac{1}{2}$ cups milk (low-fat is fine)

Ⓕ Fast   Ⓜ Make Ahead   Ⓥ Vegan

2 bay leaves

1 pound elbow, shell, ziti, or other cut pasta

4 tablespoons ($1/2$ stick) butter

3 tablespoons all-purpose flour

$1^1/_2$ cups grated cheese, like sharp cheddar or Emmental

$1/2$ cup freshly grated Parmesan cheese

Freshly ground black pepper

$1/2$ cup or more bread crumbs, preferably fresh (page 804)

1 Preheat the oven to 400°F. Bring a large pot of water to a boil and salt it.

2 Cook the milk with the bay leaves in a small saucepan over medium-low heat. When small bubbles appear along the sides, about 5 minutes later, turn off the heat and let stand.

3 Cook the pasta to the point where it is almost done but you would still think it needed another minute or two to become tender. Drain it, rinse it quickly to stop the cooking, and put it in a large bowl.

4 In a small saucepan over medium-low heat, melt 3 tablespoons of the butter; when it is foamy, add the flour and cook, stirring, until the mixture browns, about 5 minutes. Remove the bay leaves from the milk and add about $1/4$ cup of the milk to the hot flour mixture, stirring with a wire whisk all the while. As soon as the mixture becomes smooth, add a little more milk and continue to do so until all the milk is used up and the mixture is thick and smooth. Add the cheddar and stir.

5 Pour the sauce over the noodles, toss in the Parmesan, and sprinkle with salt and pepper. Use the remaining 1 tablespoon butter to grease a 9 × 13-inch or similar-size baking pan and turn the pasta mixture into it. Top liberally with bread crumbs and bake until bubbling and the crumbs turn brown, about 15 minutes. Serve piping hot.

Simpler Macaroni and Cheese. Here the ingredients are just layered and cooked together: Proceed with Steps 1–3 as directed. Butter the baking pan with an extra 1 or 2 tablespoons butter. Layer one-third of the pasta, sprinkle with half of the flour, fleck with half of the butter, cover with about $1/2$ cup of the cheddar, pour half of the heated milk over the top, and sprinkle with salt and pepper. Repeat the layers, using the remaining flour, butter, and milk, and top with the remaining pasta, cheese, and bread crumbs. Bake until bubbling and browned on top, about 30 minutes.

Rich Macaroni and Cheese. Super-creamy and decadent; make this even more special with some sautéed wild mushrooms: Reduce the milk to $3/4$ cup. Omit the bay leaves, the first 3 tablespoons butter, and all of the flour. Substitute mascarpone cheese for the grated cheese. Add about a cup or so sautéed wild mushrooms, if you like, and 1 tablespoon chopped fresh sage leaves (or $1^1/_2$ teaspoons dried sage). Cook the pasta as directed. Mix together the milk, mascarpone, and Parmesan in a large bowl. Add the cooked pasta and the sage, sprinkle with salt and pepper, and combine. Proceed with Step 5.

Nutty Macaroni and Blue Cheese. Substitute 1 cup blue cheese for the Parmesan and reduce the cheddar by $1/2$ cup; use a mild or medium cheddar. Add $3/4$ cup roughly chopped walnuts. Fold the blue cheese and walnuts into the pasta mixture in Step 5 (melting the blue cheese in the sauce will make it gray and not so attractive).

Macaroni and Goat Cheese with Roasted Red Peppers. Nice and tangy from the goat cheese, while rich and sweet from the roasted peppers: Add 2 roasted red peppers, peeled and chopped (page 333), and $1/2$ cup each chopped fresh basil leaves and toasted pine nuts. Substitute 1 cup soft goat cheese for the Parmesan, and reduce the grated cheese by $1/2$ cup. Omit the bay leaves. Proceed with the recipe, stirring in the peppers, basil, and pine nuts with the pasta in Step 5.

Macaroni and Chile Cheese. For a spicy dish, use a hotter chile or add a tablespoon chopped chipotle chile with adobo sauce: Use grated Jack or cheddar for all 2 cups of the cheese. Add 2 medium poblano or other mild green fresh chiles, roasted, cleaned, and chopped (page 333), $^1/_4$ cup or so chopped fresh cilantro leaves, and 1 medium tomato, sliced. Proceed with the recipe, stirring in the chiles and cilantro with the pasta in Step 5, then top with the tomato slices and bread crumbs.

Great Mac and Cheese Combos

Here are some other pastas and cheeses to use in mac and cheese. Of course, any pasta will work with any of the cheeses, so mix up the combinations as you like. Some drier hard cheeses, like Parmesan, Asiago, manchego, and some pecorinos, are better when mixed with softer cheeses; similarly, very strong-flavored cheeses are best mixed with mild-flavored cheeses. Try:

1. Pasta shells with $^1/_2$ cup cream cheese and $1^1/_2$ cups pecorino
2. Fusilli or corkscrew with $1^1/_2$ cups smoked Gouda or mozzarella and $^1/_2$ cup Parmesan
3. Wagon wheels with $1^1/_2$ cups goat cheese and $^1/_2$ cup Romano or Parmesan
4. Rotini or spirals with 1 cup Gorgonzola and 1 cup Bel Paese or fontina
5. Tube pastas, like penne, rigatoni, and ziti, with 1 cup manchego and 1 cup Jack
6. Orecchiette with 1 cup ricotta and 1 cup Parmesan or pecorino

Creamy Baked Noodles with Eggplant and Cheese

MAKES: 4 servings

TIME: About $1^1/_2$ hours, largely unattended

Ⓜ

Inspired by the classic Greek casserole pastitsio, this recipe combines the concept of lasagne with macaroni and cheese, by baking a layer of vegetables between two layers of rich noodles. It's impressive enough to take to a party but simple enough for a weeknight supper when you have a little extra time.

Any (one or all) of the components—the eggplant stuffing, the béchamel, or cooking the noodles—can be done up to several hours in advance. Just cover well and refrigerate until needed, then assemble the dish cold; you'll need to add 10 minutes or so to the baking time. If you double the recipe, the mixture fits perfectly in a large rectangular baking pan, deep gratin dish, or tube pan.

2 tablespoons extra virgin olive oil, plus more as needed

1 pound eggplant, peeled if you like and cut into 1-inch cubes

Salt and freshly ground black pepper

1 small red onion, chopped

1 tablespoon minced garlic

$^1/_4$ teaspoon each ground cinnamon and cloves

Cayenne or hot red pepper flakes to taste

2 cups chopped tomato (canned are fine; use a little of their juice)

4 tablespoons ($^1/_2$ stick) butter

8 ounces ziti, penne, elbows, or other cut pasta

2 tablespoons bread crumbs, preferably fresh (page 804)

$1^1/_2$ cups milk

2 tablespoons all-purpose flour

Pinch of freshly grated nutmeg

2 eggs, beaten

1 cup freshly grated Parmesan or Greek kefalotyri if you can find it

❶ Put the olive oil in a large, deep skillet over medium-high heat. When hot, add the eggplant, sprinkle with salt and pepper, and cook, stirring occasionally and adding a little more oil if necessary, until the eggplant is softened and browned all over, about 5 minutes. Remove with a slotted spoon.

❷ Add more oil to the pan if needed to coat the bottom and return it to the heat. Add the onion and garlic

Ⓕ Fast   Ⓜ Make Ahead   Ⓥ Vegan

and cook, stirring occasionally, until soft, about 2 minutes. Stir in the spice and cayenne, then the tomato. Turn the heat down to medium-low and cook, stirring occasionally, until the sauce thickens, about 10 minutes. Return the eggplant to the pan, taste and adjust the seasoning, then set aside.

③ Bring a large pot of water to a boil and salt it. Preheat the oven to 350°F.

④ Melt the butter in a medium saucepan over low heat. Cook the pasta until barely tender, not quite done enough to eat. Drain well; put the pasta in a large bowl and toss with 1 tablespoon of the melted butter and 1 tablespoon of the bread crumbs. Set aside. Use 1 tablespoon of the melted butter to grease a large square baking pan or small casserole.

⑤ In a small saucepan or microwave, heat the milk until small bubbles appear. Reheat the remaining butter over medium-low heat in its saucepan. Add the flour to the melted butter and stir almost constantly with a wire whisk until the mixture turns golden, about 5 minutes. Slowly add the milk, whisking constantly; cook, whisking, until the mixture thickens, 3 to 5 minutes. Add the nutmeg and sprinkle with salt and pepper.

⑥ Stir a couple of tablespoons of the hot sauce mixture into the beaten eggs, then a little more. Pour this mixture back into the sauce and stir. Add most of the Parmesan or (reserve some for sprinkling later) and stir again.

⑦ Put half the pasta in the baking dish; cover with half the eggplant mixture. Cover with the remaining pasta, then the remaining eggplant and all the cheese sauce. Sprinkle with the remaining Parmesan and the remaining bread crumbs (another little grating of nutmeg here won't hurt either). Bake for about 45 minutes, or until the top turns golden brown. Let rest for a few minutes before cutting and serving.

Creamy Noodles with Mushrooms. For a meatier texture: Replace the eggplant with any fresh mushrooms.

Creamy Noodles with Sliced Eggplant and Tomatoes. A little easier and especially great in the summer, when tomatoes and eggplant are in season: Preheat the broiler and put the rack 4 inches from the heat source. Omit the onion and garlic. Use 1 pound of fresh tomatoes, and instead of chopping the eggplant and tomatoes, cut them into thin slices. Brush the eggplant on both sides with some of the olive oil, sprinkle with salt and pepper, and arrange it on a large baking sheet. Broil until browned (just a few minutes), then turn and sprinkle with salt, pepper, and the spices; broil the other side until browned. Proceed with the recipe, using the eggplant and tomato slices instead of the eggplant-tomato sauce.

Creamy Potatoes with Eggplant and Cheese. Even creamier: Instead of the pasta, use 1 pound all-purpose potatoes. Follow the recipe through Step 2. Instead of Step 3, scrub the potatoes well, put in a large pot, fill with cold water, and salt it. Boil the potatoes according to the directions on page 340. When cool enough to handle, peel the potatoes and cut them into large cubes. Proceed with the recipe, skipping Step 3 and substituting the cooked potatoes for the pasta in Step 4.

The Basics of Asian Noodles

Some Asian noodles—like fresh Chinese egg noodles—are almost identical to their European counterparts. Others, even very common ones like rice noodles (which require only soaking), are radically different in handling, taste, and texture. Once they're cooked, in a pinch you can substitute one for another (what's the worst that can happen?), but a familiarity with Asian noodles will expand your culinary repertoire significantly and probably lead to your keeping your pantry stocked with them.

The Asian Noodle Lexicon

Until recently, if you visited a supermarket the only decision you had to make about Asian noodles was which flavor of instant ramen to buy. Now, however, the assortment of Asian noodles widely available is nothing short of thrilling. To the novice, it can be overwhelming, so here's a rundown of the varieties you're likely to encounter, along with preparation tips and cooking times.

Chinese Egg Noodles

Long, thin, golden egg noodles made with wheat flour; round or flat, fresh or dried. The fresh noodles cook quickly, in 3 minutes or so, or you can add them directly to hot soup. Dried take a little longer, 5 minutes or so; leave them slightly undercooked if you are adding them to soup. Cooking time depends on the thickness of the noodle, of course.

Chinese Wheat Noodles

Like Chinese egg noodles, these are long and thin and can be either round or flat, fresh or dried. They are typically white or light yellow and are made of wheat, water, and salt. Boil the dried noodles for about 5 minutes and the fresh for half that time, roughly. Again, cooking time depends on the thickness of the noodle.

Bean Threads

Mung Bean Threads, Cellophane Noodles, Glass Noodles, or Spring Rain Noodles

These are long, slender, translucent noodles made from mung bean starch. They're usually sold in 2-ounce bundles. To prepare, soak the noodles in hot or boiling water until tender, 5 to 15 minutes; use kitchen scissors to cut them into manageable pieces if necessary. If you're adding them to soup or are deep-frying them, don't bother to soak. You can also cook the noodles by boiling them for a couple of minutes.

Rice Sticks

Mostly from Southeast Asia, these are white, translucent rice noodles that range in width from spaghetti thickness to greater than $1/4$ inch. Soak in hot water for 5 to 30 minutes, until softened. For a stir-fry, soak the noodles for 15 to 20 minutes, then drain and cook them in the skillet or wok for an additional minute or two. For soups,

add the rice sticks directly to the broth or soak them for 5 to 10 minutes and then drop them into the soup.

Rice Vermicelli

Similar to rice sticks, but long and slender; like angel hair pasta. To prepare, soak the noodles in hot water for about 5 minutes or in cold water for 25 to 30. Rinse, drain, and boil for 1 to 2 minutes or stir-fry. If you are adding rice vermicelli to soup, boil for only an additional minute after soaking.

Udon

Round, square, or flat wheat noodles from Japan that are available in a range of thicknesses and lengths and may be fresh or dried. They have a slippery texture and most typically appear in soups and stews, though you can also use them in braised dishes or serve them cold. Boil fresh noodles for a couple of minutes, until tender. Dried noodles require a more complicated cooking method: To begin, add them to boiling water, allow the water to return to the boil, and then add a cup of cold water. When the water returns to the boil, add another cup of cold water and repeat this process until the noodles are *al dente*.

Soba

Long, thin, flat Japanese noodles made from a combination of buckwheat and wheat flour. The buckwheat makes these distinctively nutty and light beige to brownish gray, but they are sometimes green because of the addition of green tea. Generally dried, but you may see fresh. Boil the dried noodles for 5 to 7 minutes, the fresh for 2 to 4.

Somen

White, round, ultra-thin all-wheat noodles that cook in just a couple of minutes.

Ramen and Saimin

Long, slender, off-white Japanese wheat noodles that appear either crinkled in brick form or as rods; fresh, dried, frozen, or instant. The instant variety is typically deep-fried before being dried and packaged to remove

 Fast   Make Ahead Vegan

moisture. (Saimin is similar but made with egg.) When fresh, boil ramen for just a couple of minutes; dried takes around 5. Prepare instant ramen according to the package instructions or see the recipe for Vastly Improved Store-Bought Ramen (page 466).

Fried Chow Mein Noodles

Short, deep-fried egg noodles commonly used to add crunch to salads and stir-fries.

Rice Paper

Rice Paper Wrappers

Translucent sheets made from rice flour and water, almost always sold dried. Soak in hot tap water for about 10 seconds to make pliable before use.

Wonton Noodles

Fine egg noodles often used in soup, available fresh and dried. Cook fresh noodles for 30 seconds or so, dried for about 5 minutes.

Korean Sweet Potato Vermicelli

Dang Myun

Long, slender, translucent noodles, made with sweet potato starch; distinctively chewy. Soak in hot water for 10 to 15 minutes, then finish cooking in a soup or stir-fry. If you are using in a preparation that does not cook them further, boil for about 5 minutes after soaking.

Korean Buckwheat Noodles

Naeng Myun

Made from a combination of potato flour and buckwheat starch, these translucent brown noodles are usually eaten cold but can also be added to soups. Boil the dried version for just a couple of minutes; if the noodles are fresh or frozen, they will take even less time.

Tofu Noodles

These are narrow, flat beige noodles, made from pressed tofu and commonly used in salads and stir-fries. They are available fresh, frozen, and dried. To use the fresh noodles, simply rinse and pat dry; defrost frozen noodles in the fridge, then treat as fresh. Soak dried noodles in warm water for about 15 minutes, then rinse and drain.

Chinese Egg Noodles in Soy Broth

MAKES: 2 main-course or 4 side-dish servings
TIME: 20 minutes

This is a simple, basic noodle soup; check out the chart on page 468 for other ideas.

Salt

$1/2$ pound fresh or dried Chinese egg noodles

$1/4$ cup soy sauce, or to taste

2 tablespoons ketchup (to make your own, see page 790)

Freshly ground black pepper

8 ounces firm tofu, pressed (see page 640) if you have time, cut into small cubes

$1/2$ cup sliced scallion

2 tablespoons chopped peanuts (optional)

1 tablespoon minced fresh chile (like jalapeño or Thai), or to taste, or hot red pepper flakes or cayenne to taste (optional)

① Bring a large pot of water to boil and salt it. Cook the noodles until tender but not mushy. Fresh noodles will take just a few minutes; dried a little longer. Drain, rinse, and put in a bowl of cold water while you prepare the other ingredients.

② Rinse the pot and bring 6 cups of water to a boil; stir in the soy sauce and ketchup. Taste and add a little salt if it needs it, plus lots of black pepper. Keep the broth bubbling.

③ To serve, drain the noodles well and divide them among bowls. Ladle the broth over the noodles and swirl them a bit to make sure they're submerged. Top with tofu and scallion, and peanuts and chiles if you like.

Bean Threads with Coconut Milk and Mint. A splash of Fishless Fish Sauce (page 778) makes the broth even more flavorful: Instead of egg noodles, soak two 2-ounce bundles of glass (mung bean) noodles in hot water. When soft, cut the strands a few times with kitchen scissors to make manageable lengths. Drain, rinse, and return to cold water as described in Step 1. In Step 2, bring 1 quart water to a boil and add 2 cups coconut milk (see page 423 to make your own or use 1 can, slightly less than 2 cups, with a little water). Add both the soy sauce and the ketchup. If you like, use Crunchy Crumbled Tempeh (page 674) instead of the tofu. Use $^1/_4$ cup chopped fresh mint and $^1/_4$ sliced scallion. Proceed with the recipe, adding both peanuts and chiles, unless you can't stand them.

Vastly Improved Store-Bought Ramen. For fifteen cents, you buy a package of ramen, which is really a serving of noodles with a package of nearly poisonous "broth" mixture included. Try this: Use the noodles and cook them as in Step 1, then proceed, using as many or as few of the above ingredients as you like. Or cook the noodles as in Step 1, gently dropping an egg into them when they're about half cooked and reducing the heat to a simmer. When the egg is poached (page 169), gently stir in 1 tablespoon soy sauce, 1 teaspoon dark sesame oil, and a dash of Tabasco or other hot sauce. Garnish if you like, with peanuts, tofu, and/or scallion and serve.

Cold Sesame or Peanut Noodles

MAKES: 2 main-course or 4 side-dish servings
TIME: 30 minutes

This is an easy dish to assemble at the last minute, especially if you do all the gathering, rinsing, trimming, and slicing of ingredients in advance. Serve as part of a larger Chinese meal or in larger portions as lunch or a light supper. To make it more substantial, add $^1/_2$ cup or so of small tofu cubes, cooked soybeans, or few spoonfuls of Crunchy Crumbled Tempeh (page 674).

Salt

1 pound cucumbers

12 ounces fresh Chinese egg noodles or long pasta, like linguine

2 tablespoons dark sesame oil

$^1/_2$ cup tahini, peanut butter, or a combination

2 tablespoons sugar

3 tablespoons soy sauce, or to taste

1 teaspoon minced peeled fresh ginger (optional)

1 tablespoon rice or white wine or other vinegar

Hot sesame oil or Tabasco sauce to taste

$^1/_2$ teaspoon freshly ground black pepper, or more to taste

At least $^1/_2$ cup minced scallion for garnish

1 Bring a large pot of water to boil and salt it. Peel the cucumbers, cut them in half, and, using a spoon, scoop out the seeds. Cut the cucumber into shreds (you can use a grater for this) and set aside.

2 When the water comes to a boil, cook the noodles or pasta until tender but not mushy. While the pasta is cooking, whisk together the sesame oil and paste, sugar, soy, ginger, vinegar, hot oil, and pepper in a large bowl. Thin the sauce with hot water so that it's about the consistency of heavy cream; you will need $^1/_4$ to $^1/_2$ cup. Stir in the cucumbers. When the pasta is done, drain it and run the pasta under cold water. Drain.

3 Toss the noodles with the sauce and cucumbers. Taste, add salt if necessary, then garnish and serve.

Cold Fiery Noodles. Like a salad, really, with lots of crisp vegetables and a light, hot-sweet dressing: Rinse (and trim if you like) $^1/_2$ cup bean sprouts and slice a handful of radishes (any kind). Chop up some cilantro leaves and some peanuts for garnish. When you make the dressing, omit the sesame or peanut paste; increase the vinegar to 2 tablespoons and add $^1/_4$ cup peanut or neu-

tral oil, like grapeseed or corn. When you stir in the cucumbers in Step 2, add the sprouts and radishes and at least a teaspoon of chile paste or minced fresh chile (like jalapeño or Thai). Thin with just a tablespoon or so of water. Proceed with the recipe, garnishing each serving with a sprinkle of scallions, cilantro, and peanuts.

Soba Noodles with Dipping Sauce

MAKES: 4 to 6 servings
TIME: 20 minutes

Lightning-fast, cool, and refreshing, this is a standard summertime soup in Japan, where summers are plenty hot. Soba noodles (page 464), with their marked and pleasant buckwheat flavor, are available at most Asian and many health food markets, but if you can't find them, substitute all-wheat somen noodles or angel hair pasta, both of which will take a few minutes less to become tender.

2 cups Kombu Dashi (page 103), chilled

$^1/_2$ cup soy sauce

2 tablespoons mirin

2 tablespoons light brown sugar

Salt

8 ounces soba (about three 60-gram bundles)

2 scallions, trimmed and minced

Wasabi for serving (optional)

1 Combine the dashi, soy sauce, mirin, and sugar in small mixing bowl. Stir until the sugar dissolves.

2 Bring a large pot of water to a boil and salt it. Drop in the noodles and cook until tender, 2 to 4 minutes, then rinse in a colander under cold running water. (You can prepare this recipe a few hours in advance up to this point; separately cover and refrigerate the noodles and the dipping sauce.)

IMPROVISING ASIAN-STYLE NOODLE BOWLS

This is a mix-and-match chart; you can follow the rows straight across the columns, but you can also use the old "one from column A and one from column B" technique; noodle bowls are like stir-fries in that pretty much anything goes. See pages 463–465 for directions for cooking or soaking the noodles.

NOODLES	BROTH	MAIN INGREDIENTS	GARNISHES (ALONE OR IN COMBINATION)
Udon	Kombu Dashi (page 103)	Spoonfuls of silken tofu	Sliced scallions; Nori "Shake" (page 817)
Soba	Kombu Dashi (page 103)	Folded Omelet (page 173), Japanese Egg Crêpes (page 175), or poached or hard-cooked egg	Pickled Ginger (page 821); Japanese Seven-Spice Mix (page 817)
Somen	Miso	Winter squash cubes, cooked simply (pages 365–366); chopped cooked collards or kale	Chopped toasted walnuts
Rice Sticks (thin)	Any	Tofu Burgers, made into balls (page 666)	Chopped fresh cilantro and minced fresh chile (like jalapeño or Thai), or to taste, or hot red pepper flakes or cayenne to taste
Rice Sticks (medium or wide)	Any vegetable stock (pages 101–102) except mushroom	Kimchi (page 96); cooked soybeans	Chopped fresh cilantro and shredded carrots
Rice Sticks (any kind)	Vegetable stock (pages 101–102) or water	Roasted Vegetables, Thai Style (page 381)	Tofu Croutons (page 656)
Chinese Egg Noodles	Mushroom Stock (page 102)	Stir-Fried Asparagus (page 262) with Mushroom Fritters (page 394) or Pan-Cooked Mushrooms, Dry Style (page 315)	Sesame seeds, cashews, or chopped peanuts
Chinese Egg Noodles	Vegetable stock (pages 101–102) or soy broth	Scrambled Tofu (page 655) or Scrambled Eggs (page 166)	Bean sprouts, sliced scallion, and Five-Spice Powder (page 816)

3 Serve each guest a small bowl of noodles twisted into a little nest on top of a couple of ice cubes and a small bowl with about ¹/₂ cup of the dipping sauce scattered with the sliced scallion on the side. Pass a little dish of wasabi, if desired, to stir into the dipping sauce.

10 Quick Garnishes for Soba Noodles with Dipping Sauce

1. Matchsticks of daikon or other radish
2. Julienne cucumber (seeded)
3. Chopped pickles
4. Grated peeled fresh ginger
5. Tiny cubes of fresh or smoked tofu
6. Minced Hard-Cooked Egg (page 166)
7. Nori "Shake" (page 817) or Nori Chips (page 357)
8. Sesame seeds (black look stunning)
9. Finely shredded Napa or other cabbage
10. Chopped walnuts or other nuts

 Fast   Make Ahead   Ⓥ Vegan

Korean-Style Noodles in Cool Bean Broth

MAKES: 2 main-course or 4 side-dish servings

TIME: 20 minutes, with precooked beans

This version of a classic Korean lunch dish is high in protein and very satisfying, but it's also light and refreshing: the perfect easy summertime meal or snack. Slivers of cucumber and a sprinkle of sesame seeds are the typical garnish, but minced fresh chiles and scallions add nice sharpness and heat.

Salt

8 ounces udon noodles

1 cup cooked soybeans (drained canned are fine)

$\frac{1}{4}$ cup walnuts, pecans, almonds, pine nuts, or a mixture

2 tablespoons sesame seeds, plus more for garnish

2 tablespoons soy sauce

Freshly ground black pepper

1 small cucumber, peeled, seeded, and thinly sliced

Dark sesame oil, for drizzling

Minced fresh chile (like jalapeño or Thai), or hot red pepper flakes or cayenne to taste (optional)

$\frac{1}{2}$ cup sliced scallion

① Bring a large pot of water to a boil and salt it. Add the noodles and cook, stirring occasionally, until tender but not mushy, 5 to 7 minutes. Drain and rinse them under cold water then put them in a bowl or pot of cold water.

② Put the beans, nuts, sesame seeds, soy sauce, and a few grinds of black pepper in a blender with 3 cups of ice water. Purée until smooth, thinning with a little more water if the broth looks to thick. Taste and adjust the seasoning. (You can make the broth up to a day ahead; cover tightly and refrigerate.)

③ Drain the udon noodles well and pile them up in the center of bowls. Ladle the cool broth all around.

Garnish with cucumber and a few sesame seeds, a drizzle of sesame oil, and if you like, some chile and scallion; serve.

Panfried Asian Noodle Dishes

The saucing-and-tossing technique doesn't really apply the same way to Asian-style noodle dishes as it does to pasta. Instead, the noodles are often fried in a little oil, either alone or with other ingredients—more like a stir-fry.

Crisp-Fried Noodle Cake

MAKES: 4 servings

TIME: 20 minutes

Think of this as a crunchy, somewhat impressive alternative to steamed rice. To include it as part of a larger meal, you can cut the cake into wedges or pull it apart with chopsticks as people pass it around the table. Or you can top it with stir-fries or any other saucy braised or roasted vegetable dish. Either way, see the list that follows for some possible accompaniments.

To make these for a crowd, multiply the recipe as needed, fry the cakes in batches, and put them in a warm oven, uncovered, until you're ready to serve (but no longer than you must); or serve at room temperature.

12 ounces fresh Chinese egg noodles or about 8 ounces any dried long noodles or pasta

1 tablespoon soy sauce, plus more for drizzling

1 teaspoon dark sesame oil, plus more for drizzling

$\frac{1}{2}$ cup chopped scallion or chives

$\frac{1}{4}$ cup peanut or neutral oil, like grapeseed or corn

① Bring a large pot of water to a boil and salt it. Add the noodles and cook, stirring occasionally, until tender—this will take only a few minutes. Drain and rinse with cold water. (The noodles can be prepared to this point and left in a bowl of tap water to rest until you're ready to fry; drain well.) Toss the noodles with the soy sauce, sesame oil, and most of the scallion or chives, reserving some for garnish.

② Put 3 tablespoons of the oil in a large nonstick or cast-iron skillet over medium-high heat. When hot, add the noodles. Cook, undisturbed, until brown and crisp on the bottom (adjust the heat so the noodles brown but do not burn). Use a large spatula (or a plate; see page 349) to flip the noodles. Add the remaining oil and brown on the other side, then slide onto a platter. Sprinkle with sesame oil and soy sauce, garnish with the remaining scallion or chives, cut into pieces, and serve.

Crisp-Fried Noodle Soup. The combination of textures is a winner: Boil, drain, and rinse the noodles as described in Step 1. In the same pot, heat 2 quarts vegetable stock (pages 101–102). Taste, adjust the seasoning, and keep hot. Fry the noodles as in Step 3. When done, divide among serving bowls and ladle the hot broth over all. Garnish with chopped scallion, or sesame seeds if you like, or add other ingredients to make a full meal; see "Improvising Asian-Style Noodle Bowls" (page 468).

12 Stir-Fries or Other Dishes to Serve on Crisp-Fried Noodle Cake

Prepare the dish first, then the noodles. Use your judgment on stirring the soy sauce and sesame oil into the noodle mixture before cooking, because some of these dishes are quite heavily seasoned already, and the noodle cake will be serving as a more-or-less neutral base.

1. Stir-Fried Asparagus (page 262)
2. Spiced Stir-Fried Bean Sprouts (page 265)
3. Bok Choy with Black Beans (page 270)
4. Stir-Fried Broccoli (page 270)
5. Steamed Eggplant, pouring the dipping sauce over all (page 297)

6. Stir-Fried Green Beans and Tofu Skins (page 306)
7. Sautéed Mushrooms with Asian Flavors (page 315)
8. Sea Green and Celery Stir-Fry (page 357)
9. Edamame with Tomatoes and Cilantro (page 583)
10. Soybeans with Shiitakes and Sea Greens (page 590)
11. Hot and Sour Edamame with Tofu (page 591)
12. Spicy Soybeans with Kimchi (page 609)

Pad Thai

MAKES: 4 servings
TIME: 30 minutes

Though you probably first fell in love with pad Thai in a Thai restaurant, it's easy to make at home, with a fast-paced stir-frying process that's perfect for either weeknights or entertaining, as long as you have all the ingredients ready to go before you start cooking. Cucumber Salad with Soy and Ginger (page 48), Asian-Style Steamed Mushroom Salad (page 63), and Edamame Salad with Seaweed "Mayo" (page 76) all make great accompaniments.

12 ounces dried flat rice noodles, ¼ inch thick

5 tablespoons peanut or neutral oil, like grapeseed or corn

3 eggs, lightly beaten

4 cloves garlic, minced

8 ounces pressed tofu (page 639) or extra-firm tofu, prepared by any of the methods on pages 640–642 or simply blotted dry, then sliced

2 scallions, trimmed and cut into 1-inch lengths

1 cup bean sprouts

2 tablespoons Fishless Fish Sauce (page 778) or soy sauce

2 teaspoons tamarind paste or ketchup (to make your own, see page 790)

2 teaspoons sugar

Cook udon, soba, somen, or any rice noodles until tender but not mushy. Then add them to the pan with the cooked vegetables and toss until heated through. For more moisture, add a little of the noodle-cooking water or vegetable stock; a splash of soy sauce; or a drizzle of peanut, neutral, or sesame oil.

1. Stir-Fried Vegetables (page 242)
2. Stir-Fried Asparagus (page 262)
3. Spiced Stir-Fried Bean Sprouts (page 265)
4. Quick-Cooked Bok Choy or Bok Choy with Black Beans (page 269)
5. Stir-Fried Broccoli (with or without dried shiitakes) (page 270)
6. Brussels Sprouts in Coconut Milk (page 274)
7. Quick-Braised Burdock and Carrots (page 274)
8. Sautéed Eggplant or any of its variations (page 295)
9. Steamed Eggplant with one of its sauces (page 297)
10. Eggplant-Tofu Stir-Fry (page 300)
11. Green Beans Tossed with Walnut-Miso Sauce (page 305)
12. Stir-Fried Leeks (page 312)
13. Sautéed Mushrooms with Asian Flavors (page 315)
14. Anything-Scented Peas (page 333)
15. Pan-Cooked Peppers and Onions, Asian Style (page 334)
16. Sea Green and Celery Stir-Fry or any of its variations (page 357)
17. Grilled Tomatoes and Scrambled Eggs, Chinese Style (page 374)
18. Butternut Squash with Soy, with Coconut Milk and Curry, or Thai Style (page 364)
19. Stir-Fried Vegetables, Vietnamese Style (page 379)
20. Quick-Braised Vegetables, Thai Style (page 379)
21. Roasted Vegetables, Thai Style (page 381)
22. Grilled or Broiled Tofu (page 642)
23. Agedashi Tofu (page 644)
24. Stir-Fried Tofu with Scallions or any of its variations (page 645)
25. Stir-Fried Tofu with Bell Peppers or Other Vegetables or any of its variations (page 647)
26. Braised Tofu and Peas in Curried Coconut Milk or its variations (page 648)
27. Braised Tofu with Eggplant and Shiitakes (page 650)
28. Fast-Braised Tofu with Tempeh (page 651)
29. Braised Tempeh, Three Ways (page 675)
30. Tempeh Chile with Black Beans (page 677)
31. Edamame with Tomatoes and Cilantro (page 583)
32. Quick-Cooked Edamame with Kombu Dashi or Soy Sauce or any of its variations (page 583)
33. Fried Mung Beans with Sesame or its variations (page 589)
34. Soybeans with Shiitakes and Sea Greens or its variations (page 590)
35. Hot and Sour Edamame with Tofu or its variations (page 591)
36. Black Beans with Dried Shiitakes (page 597)
37. Black Soybeans with Soy Sauce (page 608)
38. Spicy Soybeans with Kimchi or its variations (page 609)
39. Hot, Sweet, and Sour Chickpeas with Eggplant or its variations (page 609)

$1/4$ cup chopped peanuts

$1/4$ cup chopped fresh cilantro

2 chiles, preferably Thai, stemmed, seeded, and sliced (optional)

1 lime, cut into wedges

1 Put the noodles in a bowl and pour boiling water over them to cover. Soak until softened, at least 15 minutes; if you want to hold them a little longer, drain them, fill the bowl with cold water, and return the noodles to the bowl.

❷ Put 2 tablespoons of the oil in a wok or large skillet, preferably nonstick, over medium heat. When hot, add the eggs and scramble quickly for the first minute or so with a fork almost flat against the bottom of the pan; you're aiming for a thin egg crêpe of sorts, one with the smallest curd you can achieve. Cook just until set and transfer the crêpe to a cutting board. Cut into $1/4$-inch strips and set aside.

❸ Raise the heat to high and add the remaining oil. When the oil is hot, add the garlic, tofu, scallions, and half the bean sprouts and cook, stirring occasionally, for 3 minutes. Transfer with a slotted spoon to a plate.

❹ Put the drained noodles, eggs, fishless fish sauce, tamarind, and sugar in the pan and cook, stirring occasionally, until the noodles are heated through, then add the stir-fried tofu mixture. Toss once or twice and transfer the contents of the pan to a serving platter. Top with the peanuts, cilantro, chiles, and remaining bean sprouts. Serve with the lime wedges on the side.

Stir-Fried Wide Rice Noodles with Pickled Vegetables

MAKES: 4 servings
TIME: 30 minutes

Pickled or fermented cabbage is often combined with Asian noodles but requires some forethought. So here I mimic the flavor by "pickling" the vegetables with a little vinegar in the pan. Use the fattest rice noodles you can find for this recipe and feel free to vary the vegetables; asparagus, snow peas, green beans, or even cubes of butternut squash all work well instead of the cabbage. Substitute button mushrooms for the shiitake or skip them altogether. The trick is to work with a relatively hot skillet, quickly sear one vegetable at a time, then remove it. Then you toss everything with the noodles—like a warm salad.

Salt

12 ounces wide rice noodles

$1/4$ cup peanut or neutral oil, like grapeseed or corn

1 large onion, halved and cut into thin slivers

8 ounces shiitake mushrooms, trimmed and sliced

8 ounces Napa or Savoy cabbage or mustard greens

2 tablespoons peeled and minced fresh ginger

1 tablespoon minced fresh chile (like jalapeño or Thai), or to taste, or hot red pepper flakes or cayenne to taste

3 tablespoons rice wine vinegar

2 tablespoons sugar

Freshly ground black pepper

Soy sauce for drizzling

❶ Bring a large pot of water to a boil and salt it. Add the noodles and cook, stirring frequently, until tender but not mushy, about 5 minutes; test occasionally since the cooking times can vary depending on the noodles. Drain, rinse in cold water, and put in a large bowl of cold water.

❷ Put 2 tablespoons of the oil in a large skillet over medium-high heat. When hot, add the onion and cook, stirring occasionally, until it begins to crisp and brown, about 3 minutes; transfer to a large bowl with a slotted spoon. Add the mushrooms and cook and stir until they release their water and begin to brown, about 5 minutes; transfer to the bowl with the onion. Repeat the process with the cabbage, adding enough oil to keep a thin layer on the bottom of the pan; transfer to the bowl with the mushrooms and the onion.

❸ Put the remaining oil in the pan along with the ginger and lower the heat to medium. Cook and stir until it softens, just a minute or so. Stir in the chile, then the vinegar, sugar, and 2 tablespoons of water, scraping up any browned bits from the bottom of the pan. Sprinkle with salt and pepper and pour the dressing over the veg-

Ⓕ Fast   Ⓜ Make Ahead   Ⓥ Vegan

etables. (The recipe can be made to this point up to an hour or so ahead of time; gently warm the vegetable mixture again before proceeding.)

④ Drain the noodles and add them to the bowl of vegetables. Toss gently but thoroughly. Taste, adjust the seasoning, and serve, passing soy sauce at the table for drizzling.

Stir-Fried Brown Rice Noodles with Pickled Vegetables.
A little heartier, with a slight nutty flavor: Substitute brown rice noodles for the wide rice noodles. (They will take a few minutes longer to cook.)

Rice Cakes

Though you may not know rice cakes, few noodle products come in such a dizzying range of flavors, colors, and shapes: savory or sweet; stuffed or plain; pink, green, yellow, or white; round, oblong, crescent, flat as sticks, or thick as ropes. And they can be boiled, stir-fried, braised, steamed, or panfried, all with great success.

Rice cakes are made by pounding glutinous rice until it forms a smooth, elastic dough, which is then either hand-rolled (the traditional method) or extruded or molded by a machine. The texture ranges from soft to dense, but good rice cakes are always pleasantly chewy. There are two kinds of rice cakes that work great in the recipe that follows: noodlelike Korean duk (aka dduk or deok) and Chinese New Year cake, which is formed into long, $1/2$-inch-thick white noodles and either sold whole (usually fresh), cut into sticks, or sliced and frozen. The Japanese mochi, available in various shapes, also work well.

Most Asian markets sell some form of rice cake, often frozen in plastic packages and sometimes available fresh. In areas with large Asian populations there are bakerylike markets that specialize in rice cakes in all forms, flavors, and colors; if you have one of these markets in your area, this is the way to go.

Rice Cakes with Sweet Soy Sauce

MAKES: 4 servings
TIME: 30 minutes

These sautéed or stir-fried rice cakes are sweet, salty, spicy, and addicting. I love them spicy with lots of Chile-Sesame Paste, Korean Style, or any other hot sauce.

1 pound rice cakes, sliced

3 tablespoons soy sauce

1 tablespoon dark sesame oil

1 tablespoon sugar

3 tablespoons Thai-Style Chile Paste (page 829), or to taste

2 tablespoons neutral oil, like grapeseed or corn

Freshly ground black pepper

Chopped scallion for garnish

Toasted sesame seeds (see page 321) for garnish

① If the rice cakes are frozen, soak them in a large bowl of cold water for a few minutes until they're thawed a bit, then cook them in a pot of boiling water until soft, about 5 minutes; drain and reserve some of the cooking liquid.

② Mix together the soy sauce, sesame oil, sugar, and chile-sesame paste and set aside.

③ Put the neutral oil in a large nonstick or cast-iron skillet over medium-high heat. When hot, add the rice cakes, soy sauce mixture, and a sprinkle of the black pepper; cook until the rice cakes are coated in the sauce, 2 to 3 minutes. If the pan dries out, add a couple tablespoons of the reserved cooking liquid. Sprinkle with the scallion and sesame seeds and serve immediately.

Rice Cakes with Sweet Soy Sauce and Vegetables. A quick one-pan dinner: Prepare about $1^1/2$ cups of any combination of thinly sliced shiitakes, onions, carrots, or bell peppers. Add to the hot pan in Step 2; cook until softened, about 3 minutes. Proceed with the recipe, adding more neutral oil as needed.

Rice Cakes with Kimchi. Spicy, of course: Omit the sesame oil, sugar, and chile-sesame paste. In Step 3, add 1 cup or more Kimchi (page 96) a minute or so after the rice cakes.

Rice Cakes with Shaoxing Wine. Shaoxing is similar to dry sherry, which is a good substitute: Reduce the soy sauce to 1 tablespoon and omit the sesame oil, sugar, and chile-sesame paste. In Step 2, add 1 tablespoon minced garlic, $1/2$ cup bamboo shoots, and 2 tablespoons Shaoxing wine.

Braised Rice Cakes. The rice cakes thicken the liquid as they cook, creating a stick-to-your-ribs dish: Add 3 cups stock, dashi, or water and up to 2 cups whatever thinly sliced vegetables you like and/or cubes of tofu. Omit the sugar and neutral oil. Put the stock in a pot and bring to a boil; add the remaining ingredients and cook, at a steady bubble, until the rice cakes are soft (and the vegetables are cooked, if you're using any). Garnish with the scallions and sesame seeds.

Rice or Cellophane Noodles with Sweet Soy Sauce. If you like, add vegetables as in the first variation: Substitute 8 to 12 ounces rice vermicelli, rice sticks, or cellophane noodles for the rice cakes. Drain the noodles and immediately add them to the pan; you may need additional oil. Proceed with the recipe.

Fresh Pasta, Noodles, and Dumplings

Two core doughs—one basically flour and water (sometimes enriched with olive oil), the other enriched with egg yolks—form the backbone of a family of dishes shared by cultures around the world. I count cut pasta, ravioli, and gnocchi and barely formed pastalike dumplings like spaetzle in this category, even though the recipes and techniques are slightly different and the results often more refined than hand-rolled noodles.

However, when you take away the pasta machine, the differences boil down to the same two things: the choice of stuffing ingredients and skill in handling the dough. Luckily, there are plenty of options in this section that require neither experience nor elbow grease.

Unlike store-bought products, you control all the variables here, from the type of flour you choose and the thickness of the dough to the cooking method and sauce. When you make stuffed pasta or dumplings, you add yet another dimension of flavor and texture.

The Basics of Fresh Pasta

The origins of pasta are debatable; it's likely that noodles were first developed in either China or Italy, and each has claims to historical documents and archaeological artifacts that date back thousands of years. But at the end of the day it doesn't really matter on which continent the first noodles were made; in fact they were probably developed more or less simultaneously, because a paste (that's English for pasta, by the way) made of flour, water, and perhaps eggs was a simple enough step in the development of cuisine, and cutting the paste into strands—well, we all know how much fun making clay ropes is. It's a bit of work, but not more than making bread or, really, a pie, and—at least the first time you do it—you will be stunned by what a lovely thing you've produced. You will feel a sense of accomplishment, as if you invented something great. And you did.

This section focuses on Italian-style pastas, and the recipes range from rich and eggy to eggless to bright and herby; they're all pretty much classic. The "holy trinity"—or foundation—for fresh Italian pasta is flour, eggs, and salt (you may occasionally need a few drops of water); it's as simple as that. There are parts of Italy where

Ⓕ Fast   Ⓜ Make Ahead   Ⓥ Vegan

eggs were not used, but more out of scarcity than preference. The gluten in the flour gives the dough its structure and elasticity, the egg adds flavor, moisture, and richness, and salt enhances the subtle flavors of the other two ingredients.

All-purpose flour is the most convenient and conventional flour to use for fresh pasta, and semolina also makes a lovely pasta. But as long as you make some adjustments, you can use any flour for pasta, whether your reason is to change flavor, add nutrients, or avoid wheat gluten; see the sidebar on page 478.

Basic Pasta-Making Techniques

The most traditional way to make fresh pasta is by hand, kneading it to a firm, smooth dough. But it's far easier to start the dough in a food processor, which is easier and much faster, and then roll it thin with a pasta-rolling machine.

For literally handmade pasta, pile your flour on a smooth, clean work surface (for Fresh Egg Pasta) or in a large bowl (for Eggless Pasta) and create a well in the middle of the flour. Put your eggs or liquids into the well and then use a fork or wooden spoon to incorporate the flour. Once a dough begins to form, use your hands to fully incorporate the rest of the flour. It'll be messy at first but should start to come together within a couple minutes. It's at this point when the dough is still shaggy that you want to add more liquid (water or olive oil) or flour in small amounts. You'll know which to add by the look and feel of the dough; if it's mushy and sticking to your hands, you need more flour, or if it's not coming together and separated into dried-out-looking pieces, you need more liquid.

From this point it's a matter of kneading, and although it takes some energy it's not hard and takes only a few minutes (it's much faster than kneading bread dough). Use a hip-height work surface. Form the dough into a ball and sprinkle it and your work surface with some flour. Use the heel of your hand to push into the middle of the dough, fold the dough over, rotate it 90

To make pasta by hand, first make a well in the mound of flour and break the eggs into it.

degrees, and push into it again. Continue kneading until the dough is completely smooth, somewhat skinlike, with some elasticity to it (if you pull off a piece, it should stretch a bit before breaking; if it breaks off immediately, keep kneading). If the dough is sticking to your hands or the work surface, sprinkle it with flour; it doesn't need to be drowning in flour—just enough to keep it from sticking.

The food processor is not for purists, but I like it, and the end result is the same—or nearly the same—as handmade. Put the flour and salt in the processor's container and pulse it a couple times; add the egg and a bit of the liquid you're using and turn the machine on. Gradually add the rest of the liquid(s) until the dough forms a ball. Remove the dough and knead it by hand (see below) or sprinkle it with a good amount of flour and use the pasta rolling machine to knead it. To

To knead the dough, use the heel of your hand to push into the middle of the dough, fold the dough over, rotate it 90 degrees, and push into it again.

use the pasta roller, set the rollers at the thickest setting and work the dough through several times, folding it over after each roll. Slowly work your way down to about the middle roller setting and then let the dough rest.

Using a Manual Pasta-Rolling Machine

If fresh pasta is something you make or intend to make regularly, a good pasta-rolling machine is essential. (You can roll pasta without one; just use a rolling pin, roll from the center out, and keep flouring and turning the dough.) It will cut down your rolling time by at least half, and most come with a cutter attachment, which will also save you time and give you beautifully cut pasta. These machines are simple to use, easy to maintain, and worth the investment, which is only about $40.

For starters, secure the machine on a sturdy counter or tabletop, making sure the crank handle has clearance and that there is surface area on both sides of the machine. Sprinkle the machine and surrounding surfaces with some flour and set the rollers at their thickest setting (most machines use sequential numbers to indicate settings, but some use letters or just tick marks). Dust the portion of dough with some flour and then pass it through the machine. Add more flour if the dough sticks.

Decrease the width of the rollers by one notch and pass the dough through; continue decreasing the width one notch at a time and rolling the dough. If the dough tears or sticks, ball up the dough and start over. When you get to the thinnest setting, cut the sheet of pasta in half so it's a more manageable length. Roll the sheet through twice more; it's now ready for cutting, stuffing, or freezing.

To clean your pasta-rolling machine, just use a clean, dry brush (a pastry or paint brush) and brush off the flour. Use a dinner knife to scrape off any bits of dough stuck to the rollers and wipe off the exterior with a damp cloth or paper towel. Do not wash; the flour in it will gum up and the gears may rust.

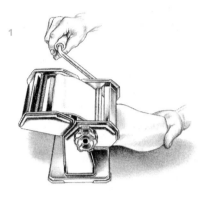

(STEP 1) Begin by putting a piece of dough through the widest setting, usually #1. (STEP 2) Decrease the distance between the two rollers, making the strip of dough progressively thinner. Note that as the dough becomes longer, it will become more fragile. Dust with flour between rollings if necessary.

Cutting Pasta

The fun comes when you cut the pasta into shapes, which can be just about anything (even maltagliati, "badly cut," is traditional; cook the scraps as you would any fresh pasta or add them to a soup or broth). Use your machine cutting attachment for the long, flat fettuccine or tagliatelle or your knife or pasta or pizza cutter (basically the same thing; one is just bigger than the other) for other shapes and sizes (see "Free-Form Pasta," page 490).

Ⓕ Fast   Ⓜ Make Ahead   Ⓥ Vegan

To hand-cut fettuccine, pappardelle, lasagne, or similar ribbonlike pasta, dust the sheet of pasta with some flour, loosely roll it lengthwise, and cut it crosswise as thick or thin as you like. Toss the cut pasta so it doesn't stick together, adding in a bit more flour (or fine cornmeal) if necessary. Pull the noodles apart if they do stick together.

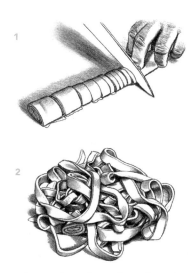

(STEP 1) To make any broad noodle, roll up the pasta sheet, sprinkle it with cornmeal or flour, and cut across the roll at the desired width. (STEP 2) Sprinkle with more cornmeal and leave the noodles in a tangle (short term) or hang individually to dry if not using right away.

What to Do with Fresh Pasta

Keep it simple and toss it with a sauce or pesto or—even simpler—just butter and Parmesan (see "Saucing and Tossing Fresh Pasta," page 480). More time consuming (but rewarding) is making ravioli or other stuffed pastas (see page 481). Baked pasta, like lasagne, is another good option; see page 459. Fresh pasta is a good addition to soups as well, especially for the odd pasta scraps left over after cutting.

Fresh Egg Pasta

MAKES: 4 servings
TIME: At least 1 hour, somewhat unattended

Egg pasta at its best; this Emiglia-Romagna-style pasta is rich and golden in color from the egg yolks. Because this recipe has a good amount of egg in it, the dough is moist and forgiving—a benefit if you're a beginner.

About 2 cups all-purpose flour, plus more as needed

1 teaspoon salt

2 eggs

3 egg yolks

1 With a food processor: Combine the flour and salt in the container and pulse once or twice. Add the eggs and yolks all at once and turn the machine on. Process just until a ball begins to form, about 30 seconds. Add a few drops of water if the dough is dry and grainy; add a tablespoon of flour if the dough sticks to the side of the bowl.

By hand: Combine 1 1/2 cups of flour and the salt on a counter or large board. Make a well in the middle. Into this well, break the eggs and yolks. Beat the eggs with a fork, slowly and gradually incorporating a little of the flour at a time. When it becomes too hard to stir with the fork, use your hands. When all the flour has been mixed in, knead the dough, pushing it against the board and folding it repeatedly until it is not at all sticky and quite stiff.

Sprinkle the dough with a little of the reserved flour and cover with plastic or a cloth; let it rest for about 30 minutes. (You can store the dough in the refrigerator, wrapped in plastic, until you're ready to roll it out, for up to 24 hours.)

2 Clamp a pasta machine to the counter; sprinkle your work surface lightly with flour. Cut off about one-third of the dough; wrap the rest in plastic or cloth while you work. Roll the dough lightly in the flour and use your

USING NONWHEAT FLOURS IN FRESH PASTA

Whole wheat, whole durum wheat, and buckwheat flours are the most common alternatives to all-purpose flour in fresh pasta (and can be used in any of the fresh pasta recipes in this chapter), but spelt, kamut, quinoa, and amaranth are gaining ground. Some you can substitute wholly; others must be blended with white flour because they contain no gluten (essential to forming an elastic, easy-to-handle dough) or because their flavor is too strong when used alone.

FLOUR	QUANTITY TO USE IN RECIPES
Semolina	2 cups semolina
Whole wheat	1 cup whole wheat and 1 cup all-purpose flour
Whole durum wheat	2 cups whole durum wheat
Buckwheat (finely ground)	$1^1/_2$ cups buckwheat and $^1/_2$ cup all-purpose flour
Spelt	2 cups spelt or mixed with all-purpose flour
Kamut	2 cups kamut or mixed with all-purpose flour
Quinoa	1 cup quinoa and 1 cup all-purpose flour
Amaranth	2 cups amaranth or mixed with all-purpose flour
Rye	1 cup rye and 1 cup all-purpose flour

hands to flatten it into a rectangle about the width of the machine. Set the machine to its highest (that is, thickest) setting and crank the dough through. If it sticks, dust it with a little more flour. Repeat. Set the machine to its next-thinnest setting and repeat. Each time, if the pasta sticks, sprinkle it with a little more flour and, each time, put the dough through the machine twice.

3 Continue to work your way down (or up, as the case may be—each machine is numbered differently) through the numbers. If at any point the dough tears badly, bunch it together and start again (you will quickly get the hang of it). Use as much flour as you need to, but in small amounts each time.

4 Pass the dough through the machine's thinnest setting, only once. (If this fails, pass it through the next-thinnest once.) Flour the dough lightly, cover it, and set it aside. Repeat the process with the remaining dough.

5 Cut each sheet into rectangles roughly 16 inches long and as wide as the machine; trim the ends to make it neat. Put it through the machine once more, this time using the broadest (tagliatelle) cutter. Or cut by hand into broad strips (pappardelle). Cook right away or hang the strands to dry for up to a couple of hours.

6 To cook the noodles, drop them into boiling salted water; they'll be done when tender, in less than 3 (and probably less than 2) minutes. Sauce them immediately and serve.

Pizzocheri. A more robust, buckwheat pasta: Use $1^1/_2$ cups fine buckwheat flour and $^1/_2$ cup all-purpose flour.

Eggless Pasta Dough

MAKES: 4 servings

TIME: At least 1 hour, somewhat unattended

Ⓜ

Just as simple and easy to work with as the egg pasta; here the hot water replaces the eggs. The pasta will be less rich

Ⓕ Fast   Ⓜ Make Ahead   Ⓥ Vegan

but still wonderful. Use olive oil instead of butter and it's vegan pasta.

2 cups all-purpose flour, plus more as needed

1 teaspoon salt

2 tablespoons butter or extra virgin olive oil

With a food processor: Combine the flour and salt in the container and pulse once or twice. Turn the machine on and add $^1/_2$ cup hot water and the butter or olive oil through the feed tube. Process just until a ball begins to form, about 30 seconds. Add a few drops of water if the dough is dry and grainy; add a tablespoon of flour if the dough sticks to the side of the bowl.

By hand: Combine the flour and salt in a large bowl. Make a well in the middle. Into this well, add the butter or olive oil and about $^1/_2$ cup hot water. Beat the water with a fork, slowly and gradually incorporating a little of the flour at a time. When it becomes too hard to stir with the fork, use your hands. When all the flour has been mixed in, knead the dough, pushing it against the board and folding it repeatedly until it is not at all sticky and quite stiff. Add water $^1/_2$ teaspoon at a time if the mixture is dry and not coming together; add flour if it is sticky.

Sprinkle the dough with a little of the reserved flour and cover with plastic or a cloth; let it rest for about 30 minutes. (You can store the dough in the refrigerator, wrapped in plastic, until you're ready to roll it out, for up to 24 hours.)

Follow Steps 2 through 6 in the Fresh Egg Pasta recipe (page 477) for rolling, cutting, and cooking instructions.

Pinci. Hand-rolled spaghetti from Tuscany, usually made with semolina flour: Add several grinds of black pepper to the flour and add an egg to the flour well with the butter or olive oil. Add a couple tablespoons water, adding more $^1/_2$ teaspoon at a time if the dough doesn't come together. Transfer the dough to a lightly floured work surface and knead it until it is not at all sticky but still soft and pliable. Roll the dough to $^1/_4$-inch thickness, cut it into 2-inch-wide strips, dust the work surface with cornmeal, and roll the strips into logs. Cut the logs into 3-inch lengths and hand-roll each piece, stretching as you roll, to $^1/_8$-inch-thick noodles. Keep them separate with cornmeal. Cook the pinci as you would the fresh pasta (Step 6).

Herbed Fresh Pasta

MAKES: 4 servings

TIME: At least 1 hour, largely unattended

Fresh herbs are a must in this recipe; they create a pretty, green-tinged pasta that's full of bright flavor.

1 tablespoon minced fresh sage leaves, 1 teaspoon minced fresh rosemary or thyme leaves, or $^1/_4$ cup minced fresh basil, chervil, or parsley leaves

2 cups all-purpose flour, plus more as needed

1 teaspoon salt

3 eggs

With a food processor: Combine the herb with the flour and salt in the container and pulse once or twice. Add the eggs all at once and turn the machine on. Process just until a ball begins to form, about 30 seconds. Add a few drops of water if the dough is dry and grainy; add a tablespoon of flour if the dough sticks to the side of the bowl. The amount of flour you need depends on the amount of herb you use and its moisture content; $^1/_4$ cup of parsley, for example, will take considerably more flour than 1 teaspoon of rosemary.

By hand: Combine $1^1/_2$ cups of flour and the salt with the herbs on a counter or large board. Make a well in the middle. Into this well, break the eggs and yolks. Beat the eggs with a fork, slowly and gradually incorporating a little of the flour at a time. When it becomes too hard to stir with the fork, use your hands. When all the flour has been mixed in, knead the dough, pushing it against the board and folding it repeatedly until it is not at all sticky and quite stiff.

Sprinkle the dough with a little of the reserved flour and cover with plastic or a cloth; let it rest for about 30 minutes. (You can store the dough in the refrigerator, wrapped in plastic, until you're ready to roll it out, for up to 24 hours.)

Follow Steps 2 through 6 in the Fresh Egg Pasta recipe (page 477) for rolling, cutting, and cooking instructions.

Spinach Pasta. Lots of color in this pasta; the spinach flavor is subtle: Add 8 ounces fresh spinach or 4 ounces frozen and about $1/2$ cup flour. Stem and wash the fresh spinach; steam it, then drain, squeeze (get as much water out as possible), and chop it very finely. Add the spinach with the eggs, making sure to break up any clumps of spinach.

Red Pasta. Again, the color is more pronounced than the flavor. Use puréed red bell pepper or beets; the beets will color the pasta more vibrantly than the peppers: Add $1/2$ cup well-drained puréed cooked beets or puréed cooked red bell pepper (page 390), and about $1/2$ cup flour. Add the purée with the eggs.

6 Ways to Flavor Pasta Dough

A few quick add-ins for a touch of extra flavor (and color). Serve the black pepper pasta with Spicy Tomato Sauce (page 448); the saffron, herb, and mushroom are lovely with a rich, creamy sauce; the tomato and roasted garlic simply with extra virgin olive oil and lots of Parmesan or pecorino.

1. Black pepper: Freshly grind about a tablespoon into the flour.

2. Saffron: Steep a large pinch of crumbled threads in a couple tablespoons hot water; add along with the eggs or with the hot water. You may need to add more flour to compensate for the extra liquid.

3. Mushroom powder: Grind dried mushrooms in a clean coffee or spice grinder to a fine powder and add to the flour; you want a tablespoon or two of powder. Porcini are excellent.

4. Dried tomato powder: Use completely dried tomatoes (see Oven-Dried Tomatoes, page 377). Grind

them in a clean coffee or spice grinder to a fine powder and add to the flour; you want a tablespoon or two of powder.

5. Roasted garlic: Mash several cloves roasted garlic (page 304) to a smooth paste; add along with the eggs or hot water, making sure to mix the garlic in very well. You may need to add more flour to compensate for the extra liquid.

6. Whole or very roughly chopped herb leaves: This takes a bit more effort but looks spectacular. Roll out the dough to the thinnest setting, place whole stemmed herb leaves (parsley, chervil, tarragon, or small basil or sage leaves work best) randomly on one sheet of pasta, sprinkle with a tiny bit of water, and put another sheet of pasta on top; roll the sheets together (essentially pressing the leaves between the layers of dough).

Simplest Sauces for Fresh Pasta

Here are a few simple sauces that are lovely with any fresh pasta and can be made in 30 minutes or less.

Saucing and Tossing Fresh Pasta

Fresh pasta is a versatile dish, and it can always be substituted for dried pasta. But you always need to keep in mind three things: Fresh pasta cooks in less than 5 minutes; its simple and delicious flavor is easily overwhelmed by sauce and garnishes; and oversaucing and tossing will quickly turn it to mush.

It's best to add just enough sauce to coat the pasta; if your sauce is too thick and clumping, thin it with some of the pasta-cooking water rather than adding more sauce to compensate (see "Draining, Saucing, and Tossing" in "The Basics of Dried Pasta," page 440). Adding some pasta-cooking water also helps to keep the pasta loose to make tossing quick and easy; if it's too dry, you'll wind up breaking the pasta when you toss it.

 Fast   Make Ahead   Ⓥ Vegan

1. Butter and Parmesan (page 447)
2. Garlic and Oil (page 443)
3. Fresh or Fast Tomato Sauce (page 445)
4. Pistachio Butter (page 268)
5. Chestnut Cream Sauce (page 457)
6. Traditional Pesto (page 768)

The Basics of Stuffed Pasta

Stuffed pasta is a dumpling, really, and ravioli or tortellini differ from many Asian dumplings only in the nature and flavor of the stuffings and the names. But even considering regional distinctions in Italy, there are literally dozens of different types of stuffed pasta from simple rolls to complex folds. I'm focusing on a few basics: ravioli (squares), tortellini (folded loops), and cannelloni (large open-ended tubes).

Stuffing

What you stuff your pasta with is a matter of personal taste. If you like a moist, gooey stuffing, stuff it with a soft cheese; ricotta or another soft and mild cheese is most common, but adding a sharper-tasting cheese, like goat or sheep's milk cheese, gives more character. For contrasting texture, mix in chopped herbs, vegetables, or chopped nuts.

Bread crumbs make a simple stuffing; use the Bread and Herb Stuffing recipe (page 395), with some added Parmesan for extra flavor. Serve the stuffed pasta in a flavorful broth so the stuffing absorbs some of the broth and becomes moist and delicious.

Pumpkin or butternut squash stuffing, popular in northern Italy, makes a sweet and succulent pasta that's a perfect match for a sage and brown butter sauce. Lots of other vegetables work as stuffing; mix with some cheese if the vegetable alone seems dry. See "25 Dishes for Stuffing Pasta" (page 485) for more ideas.

Serving Stuffed Pasta

All stuffed pastas must be boiled (or baked with sauce), but after that they can be sauced immediately, sautéed and sauced, or baked with sauce (if not already done). Consider what kind of sauce you're using: a brown butter sauce with herbs is ideal for sautéing, where a tomato or cream sauce is good for baking. But you also have to take into account what kind of stuffed pasta you're using: cannelloni must be baked, while tortellini are best sauced or added to broth or soup.

As with any pasta, there are lots of sauce options for stuffed pasta, from tomato sauce to pesto to cream sauce. Cheese-stuffed pasta is good with just about any sauce. Bread crumb stuffing, which can be dry, is ideal with a very wet or creamy sauce, especially served in a broth. And when matching vegetable-stuffed pasta you must consider the flavor of the vegetable stuffing and how that will pair with the flavor of the sauce; since the pasta will have a good amount of flavor on its own, keep the sauce on the simple side.

Spinach-Ricotta Ravioli

MAKES: 30 to 60 ravioli

TIME: About 1 hour, with prepared pasta sheets

Ⓜ

A standby stuffed pasta; this stuffing is great in cannelloni too (see the variation). Serve it with Fast Tomato Sauce (page 445), Traditional Pesto (page 768), or the sauce from Fettuccine Alfredo (page 447).

1 egg

$1/2$ cup (about 2 ounces) cooked spinach, squeezed dry and chopped

$1^1/2$ cups ricotta, drained for a few minutes in a strainer

$1/4$ cup chopped parsley leaves

1 teaspoon minced garlic

A small grating of nutmeg

1 cup freshly grated Parmesan

Salt

1 recipe Fresh Egg or Eggless Pasta, rolled into sheets (pages 477 or 478)

① Combine the egg, spinach, ricotta, parsley, garlic, nutmeg, and Parmesan in a bowl and mix well. Cover and refrigerate for up to a day or use immediately.

② Bring a large pot of water to a boil and salt it. Cut each pasta sheet into 2 or more 4-inch-wide strips. Drop heaping teaspoons of the stuffing at about 1½-inch intervals about 1 inch from one long edge of the strip (that is, about 3 inches from the other edge). Fold the dough over onto itself, pressing with your fingers to seal. Trim the dough with a sharp knife or fluted pastry wheel, then cut into individual ravioli. (You can prepare the ravioli up to this point in advance; dust with cornmeal and refrigerate for up to a day or freeze.)

③ Cook the ravioli, 20 or 30 at a time, for just a few minutes, until they rise to the surface. Drain, sauce, and serve immediately.

Spinach-Cheese Cannelloni. Quicker and baked with sauce (tomato or Alfredo is best): Preheat the oven to 375°F. Cut the pasta sheets into rectangles (at least 4 × 6 inches) and boil them for 2 minutes and drain. Use a tablespoon to dollop out a line of the stuffing along the short edge of a piece of pasta, about an inch or so from the edge; roll the pasta into a tube shape. Spread a small spoonful of sauce in the bottom of an ovenproof baking dish and add the cannelloni,

MAKING RAVIOLI

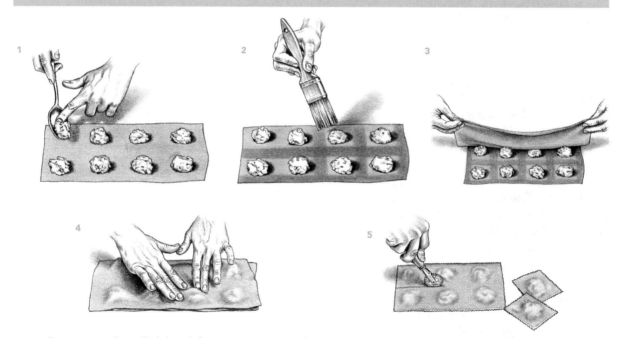

(STEP 1) On a counter dusted lightly with flour, cut any length of fresh pasta dough (pages 477–479) so that it is 4 or 5 inches wide. Place small spoonfuls of filling evenly on the dough, about 1 inch apart. (STEP 2) Brush some water between the filling so the dough will stick together. (STEP 3) Cover with another piece of dough of equal size. (Alternatively, make only one row of filling and fold one half of the dough over onto the other.) (STEP 4) Press down to seal between the ravioli. (STEP 5) Cut with a pastry wheel or sharp paring knife. Keep the ravioli separate until you are ready to cook.

     Ⓕ Fast   Ⓜ Make Ahead   Ⓥ Vegan

putting them side by side and in a single layer; cover with sauce, sprinkle with grated Parmesan, and bake until bubbling, about 20 minutes.

Cheese Ravioli. For stronger flavor, use a sharper cheese, like an aged pecorino, to replace some of the Parmesan; the Herbed Fresh Pasta (page 479) is great here: Substitute bread crumbs for the spinach.

Spinach Ravioli. Or use chard or dandelion greens: Increase the cooked spinach to 2 cups and add $1/4$ cup chopped fresh herbs, like fennel, sage, chervil, basil, or a mixture. Omit the egg and ricotta.

Mushroom-Cheese Ravioli. Use any kind of mushrooms you like: Substitute $3/4$ cup Sautéed Mushrooms (page 314) for the spinach and reduce the ricotta to $1^1/4$ cups. Drain the mushrooms and finely chop.

Butternut Squash Tortellini

MAKES: About 60 tortellini

TIME: $1^1/2$ hours, with prepared pasta sheets

A slightly more complex stuffed pasta; each one requires a bit of work, but you can just make pansotti (see variation) if you don't have the time. Serve the tortellini in a flavorful broth or with Brown Butter (page 801) with sage or rosemary leaves or the "sauce" from Pasta with Garlic and Oil and any of the variations (page 443).

2 cups cooked (preferably baked) butternut squash (page 365)

2 eggs

$1/2$ teaspoon freshly grated nutmeg

Salt and freshly ground black pepper

1 teaspoon sugar, or to taste

$1/2$ cup freshly grated Parmesan cheese

All-purpose flour for dusting

MAKING CANNELLONI

To make cannelloni, put a small amount of filling about an inch up from the end nearest you, spreading it almost but not quite to the sides; then simply roll up.

1 recipe Fresh Egg or Eggless Pasta (pages 477 or 478), rolled into sheets

① Purée the squash, preferably by passing it through a food mill or ricer. Combine it in a bowl with the eggs, nutmeg, salt, and pepper. Taste; if the mixture is not sweet, add a little sugar. Stir in the Parmesan and taste again; add more of any seasoning you like.

② Lightly flour a work surface with some flour. Cut any length of fresh pasta dough so that it is 4 or 5 inches wide. Cut into 2- to 2 $1/2$-inch squares.

③ Brush the dough very lightly with water so it will stick together when you shape the tortellini. Put a small mound (about a rounded teaspoon) of stuffing on each square and fold into a triangle, pressing tightly to seal the edges. Fold the widest point toward the stuffing, then pick up the triangle and press the two bottom points together. Put your finger inside the newly formed ring and fold over the top of the dough inside the circle. Press to seal. Keep the tortellini separate until you are ready to cook. (You can prepare the tortellini up to this point in advance; dust with flour and refrigerate for up to a day or freeze.)

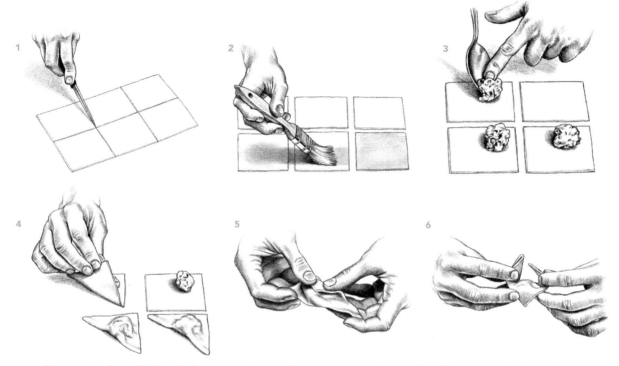

(STEP 1) On a counter dusted lightly with flour, cut any length of fresh pasta dough (pages 477–479) so it is 4 or 5 inches wide. Cut into 2- to 2¹/₂-inch squares. (STEP 2) Brush the dough very lightly with water so it will stick together when you shape the tortellini. (STEP 3) Place a small mound of filling on each square. (STEP 4) Fold into a triangle, pressing tightly to seal the edges. (STEP 5) Fold the widest point toward the filling. (STEP 6) Pick up the triangle and press the two bottom points together. Place your finger inside the newly formed ring and fold over the top of the dough inside the circle. Press to seal. Keep the tortellini separate until you are ready to cook.

④ Bring a pot of salted water to boil. Cook the tortellini, 30 or so at a time, for just a few minutes, until they rise to the surface. Drain, sauce, and serve immediately.

Butternut Squash Triangles. A simpler stuffed pasta—essentially a triangle ravioli (if you really want to cheat, start with store-bought dumpling wrappers): Just fold the pasta into triangles (no further folding necessary). Proceed to Step 4.

Sweet Potato Tortellini. Great boiled and sautéed with extra virgin olive oil and pumpkin seeds (see Pasta with Garlic and Oil, page 443): Substitute cooked sweet potato for the butternut squash and omit the sugar.

Potato Tortellini. Leftover mashed potatoes work great here; serve with Cheesy Tomato Sauce (page 448): Substitute cooked potatoes for the butternut squash, omit the sugar, and add ¹/₄ cup chopped fresh herbs if you like.

 Fast   Make Ahead   Ⓥ Vegan

7 Sauces to Serve with Stuffed Pasta

1. Fast Tomato Sauce (page 445)
2. Traditional Pesto (page 768)
3. Brown Butter (page 801) with sage, rosemary, or thyme leaves
4. The sauce from Fettuccine Alfredo (page 447)
5. The sauce from Pasta with Butter and Parmesan (page 447)
6. The sauce from Pasta with Garlic and Oil (page 443)
7. The sauce from Pasta with Walnut Sauce (page 458)

Ravioli Nudi

MAKES: 4 to 6 servings
TIME: 30 minutes

When you want ravioli but just don't have the energy to make them. With nudi you just turn the stuffing into "naked," uncovered dumplings and serve them with any pasta you like.

1 cup fresh bread crumbs

2 eggs

$^3/_4$ cup freshly grated Parmesan cheese, plus more for garnish

$^1/_2$ cup chopped parsley leaves

$^1/_4$ cup minced onion

Salt and freshly ground black pepper

1 pound fresh or dried pasta, any kind

4 tablespoons ($^1/_2$ stick) butter

20 fresh sage leaves

❶ Combine the bread crumbs in a bowl with the eggs, cheese, parsley, onion, and some salt and pepper. Mix well and let it sit for about 10 minutes. Form into tiny balls, about $^1/_2$ inch in diameter. Refrigerate until you're ready to cook. Bring a large pot of water to a boil and salt it.

25 Dishes for Stuffing Pasta

From caramelized onions to mashed favas. Drain off excess liquids and mash, crumble, or finely chop large pieces.

1. Mashed Cauliflower with Cheese (page 282)
2. Steamed Corn on the Cob (page 288)
3. Dry-Pan Eggplant, Dry Style (page 294)
4. Roasted Garlic (page 304)
5. Steamed Leeks (page 312)
6. Sautéed Mushrooms (page 314)
7. Caramelized Onions (page 329)
8. Anything-Scented Peas (page 333)
9. Roasted Red Peppers (page 333)
10. Mashed Potatoes (page 341)
11. Spinach with Currants and Nuts (page 360)
12. Sweet Potatoes, Simply Cooked (page 371)
13. Broiled Sunchokes with Garlic or Parmesan (page 370)
14. Oven-Roasted Fresh Plum Tomatoes (page 375)
15. Butternut Squash, Braised and Glazed (page 364)
16. Everyday Vegetable Purées (page 389)
17. White Beans, Tuscan Style (page 594)
18. Beans and Mushrooms (page 596)
19. Flageolets, French Style (page 604)
20. Chickpeas in Their Own Broth, with Crisp Bread Crumbs (page 605)
21. Mashed Favas (page 616)
22. Any Vegetable Burger (pages 660–666)
23. Fast Nut Burgers (page 667)
24. Oven-Roasted Seitan with Garlic (page 672)
25. Braised Tempeh, Three Ways (page 675)

❷ Cook the nudi in the water until they come to the surface, about 3 minutes; remove with a slotted spoon and keep warm. Cook the pasta in the same water until it is tender but not mushy. Meanwhile, cook the butter and sage together until the butter is light brown, about 5 minutes.

③ When the pasta is done, drain it, reserving a bit of the cooking water. Dress the pasta with the butter sauce, adding some of the cooking water if it seems dry; top with the reserved nudi and serve, passing grated Parmesan at the table.

The Basics of Gnocchi and Other (Mostly) Italian Dumplings

Gnocchi (pronounced, kind of, nyo-kee) are simple Italian dumplings made from cooked potatoes, flour, and sometimes an egg; they're then boiled and sauced. Starchy potatoes are a must here (waxy ones will not do) as it's the potatoes' starch, in addition to the gluten in the flour, that holds the dough together.

Though these are the standard, not all gnocchi are made from potatoes; other ingredients are substituted and added, from the more common spinach to the anything-but-traditional parsnip (see Parsnip Gnocchi on page 487) to those made from cheese, semolina, or cornmeal. Mostly they're Italian, but the similar Spaetzle (page 490) hail from Alsace, and some of these are modern variations that have no specific European provenance.

Going beyond gnocchi, other dumplings in this section use day-old bread, bread crumbs, flour, and egg to bind their dough. Porcini Dumplings (page 488) have a denser dough with the cooked mushrooms; passatelli is barely held together; and spaetzle is actually a batter rather than a dough. It's the cooking technique that remains essentially the same here, forming a dumpling of dough or batter—whether large or small—and dropping it into a pot of simmering water or stock to cook it.

Gnocchi Technique

Getting the dough just right for gnocchi can be tricky, especially the first time around. It's a delicate balance of potato, flour, and mixing the dough just enough to hold it together. The first time you make it you'll probably use a

Roasting and Baking Gnocchi

Roasting gnocchi or baking them with a sauce adds color, richness, and flavor. Both techniques begin with already-cooked gnocchi.

To roast, put a couple of tablespoons extra virgin olive oil or butter in a skillet and turn the heat to high; when it's hot, add the gnocchi (don't overcrowd the pan; cook in batches if necessary) and cook, stirring as the sides brown, about 5 minutes. Or roast in a 450°F oven: Toss the gnocchi in olive oil or butter and put on a baking sheet; cook, shaking the tray to roll the gnocchi every couple minutes, until the sides are golden brown, 8 to 10 minutes.

To bake, preheat the oven to 425°F. Grease a gratin or any baking dish and add the gnocchi; pour the sauce over top, sprinkle with cheese (or other topping; see "Alternative Toppings for Pasta," page 444), and bake until the sauce is bubbling and hot, about 10 minutes, depending on the size of the dish.

bit too much flour and overmix the dough, but don't be discouraged if your gnocchi aren't delicate and fluffy; you'll improve with each batch, and it will get to the point where it's easy enough to make a batch of gnocchi for lunch.

Potato Gnocchi

MAKES: 4 servings
TIME: 1½ hours

Gnocchi should be ethereal. If all you've ever had are hard and chewy, try these. With just a bit of practice you'll be making the lightest, fluffiest gnocchi you've ever eaten.

1 pound baking (russet or Idaho) potatoes

Salt and freshly ground black pepper

About 1 cup all-purpose flour, plus more as needed

(STEP 1) Start by rolling a piece of the dough into a log. Use flour as needed to prevent sticking, but try to keep it to a minimum. (STEP 2) Cut the dough into approximately 1-inch lengths. (STEP 3) Roll each of the sections off the back of the fork to give it the characteristic ridges.

① Put the potatoes in a pot with water to cover and salt it; adjust the heat so the water simmers and cook until the potatoes are quite tender, about 45 minutes. Drain and peel (use a pot holder or towel to hold the potatoes and peel with a small knife; it will be easy). Rinse the pot and once again fill it with salted water and bring to a boil.

② Use a fork, potato masher, or ricer to mash or rice the potatoes in a bowl, along with some salt and pepper. Add about $1/2$ cup of flour and stir; add more flour until the mixture forms a dough you can handle. Knead for a minute or so on a lightly floured surface. Pinch off a piece of the dough and boil it to make sure it will hold its shape; if it does not, knead in a bit more flour. The idea is to make a dough with as little additional flour and kneading as possible.

③ Roll a piece of the dough into a rope about $1/2$ inch thick, then cut the rope into 1-inch lengths; traditionally, you would spin each of these pieces off the tines of a fork to score it lightly. As each gnocco is ready, put it on a sheet of wax paper; do not allow them to touch.

④ A few at a time, add the gnocchi to the boiling water and stir. A minute after they rise to the surface, the gnocchi are done; remove with a slotted spoon. Put in a bowl and sauce or reheat in butter within a few minutes; these do not keep well.

Spinach Gnocchi. A lovely green color and subtle spinach flavor: Add 10 ounces fresh spinach or 5 ounces frozen spinach and a pinch of nutmeg if you like. Stem and wash the fresh spinach; steam it, then drain, squeeze (get as much water out as possible), and chop it very finely. Add it to the potatoes along with the nutmeg.

Eggplant Gnocchi. Great with Fast Tomato Sauce (page 445): Add 1 pound eggplant, roasted, flesh scooped out and mashed, to the potatoes.

Parsnip Gnocchi

MAKES: 4 servings
TIME: $1^{1}/_{2}$ hours

A twist on the usual potato gnocchi, these are loaded with flavor. The Parmesan and extra flour help hold the dough together and make dense, rich gnocchi. Play up the rich flavor even more by browning them with some butter in a pan (see "Roasting and Baking Gnocchi," page 489). Serve these gnocchi tossed in Oven-Roasted Tomato Sauce (page 449) or with butter, sage, and Parmesan (page 447).

1 pound parsnips, peeled and roughly chopped

Salt and freshly ground black pepper

1 1/2 cups all-purpose flour

1/2 cup freshly grated Parmesan cheese

Pinch freshly grated nutmeg (optional)

1 Roast, steam, or boil the parsnips until very tender (pages 331–332). (If boiling or steaming, be sure to drain well before proceeding.) Bring a large pot of water to a boil and salt it.

2 Purée the parsnips in a food processor until smooth; sprinkle with some salt and pepper. Add about 1 cup of the flour, the Parmesan, and the nutmeg and stir; add more flour until the mixture forms a dough you can handle. Knead for a minute or so on a lightly floured surface. Pinch off a piece of the dough and boil it to make sure it will hold its shape; if it does not, knead in a bit more flour. The idea is to make a dough with as little additional flour and kneading as possible.

3 Roll a piece of the dough into a rope about 1/2 inch thick, then cut the rope into 1-inch lengths; traditionally, you would spin each of these pieces off the tines of a fork to score it lightly. As each gnoccho is ready, put it on a sheet of wax paper; do not allow them to touch.

4 A few at a time, add the gnocchi to the boiling water and stir. A minute after they rise to the surface, the gnocchi are done; remove with a slotted spoon. Put in a bowl and sauce or reheat in butter within a few minutes; these do not keep well.

Sweet Potato Gnocchi. Wonderful with Rustic Pine Nut Sauce (page 796): Substitute sweet potatoes for the parsnips.

Porcini Dumplings

MAKES: 4 servings

TIME: About 1 hour

Ⓜ

These dumplings are full of mushroomy flavor that's almost meaty. Increase the ratio of porcini as you like; fresh shiitakes are a good substitute if you don't have any porcini on hand.

Serve the dumplings in a flavorful broth, add them to Farro Soup (page 141), top with Creamy Nut Sauce (page 797), or toss with spaghetti and Fast Tomato Sauce (page 445) as a twist on spaghetti and meatballs.

2 cups torn or chopped day-old bread or 1 cup Fresh Bread Crumbs (page 804), or use store-bought, or more as needed

1/2 cup milk or cream, or more as needed

3 eggs

1 cup freshly grated Parmesan cheese

2 tablespoons extra virgin olive oil or butter

2 ounces dried porcini, reconstituted (see page 317) and chopped

1 pound any fresh mushrooms, trimmed and chopped

Salt and freshly ground black pepper

2 teaspoons minced garlic

1 teaspoon minced fresh rosemary leaves

① Combine the bread, milk, eggs, and Parmesan in a large bowl, mix well, and set aside.

② Put the oil or butter in a large skillet over medium heat. When the oil is hot or the butter is melted, add the mushrooms, then sprinkle with salt and pepper. Cook for a few minutes, then add the garlic and rosemary. Continue cooking, stirring occasionally, until tender, with some liquid in the pan, another couple minutes or so.

③ Add the mushrooms to the bread mixture, stir well, and let sit for at least 15 minutes or up to a day, covered and refrigerated.

④ Bring a large pot of Mushroom Stock or other vegetable stock (pages 101–102) or salted water to a boil, then reduce the heat so it bubbles steadily. If the batter seems too soft to hold its shape when rolled into balls, add bread crumbs; if it's too stiff, add milk. Form the mixture into balls no more than 1 1/2 inches in diameter and drop the dumplings into the pot as you roll them. When they come to the surface, after about 5 minutes, they are done; remove with a slotted spoon.

Multigrain and Herb Dumplings. Delicious with Garlicky or Spicy Tomato Sauce (page 448): Omit the mushrooms and increase the bread to 4 cups torn or chopped day-old multigrain bread; increase the milk to 2 cups and add 1 cup mixed chopped herbs (parsley, chives, thyme, basil, rosemary, or tarragon). Skip Step 2.

Passatelli in Broth

MAKES: 4 servings

TIME: 45 minutes

Passatelli are delicate dumplings that are served in their cooking liquid. Made from a soft dough that's pressed through a ricer into simmering broth, the end result is somewhere between pasta and dumpling but lighter than either. It's a perfect lunch or first course for dinner on a cold winter day.

2 eggs

2 egg yolks

1 1/2 cups freshly grated Parmesan cheese

1 cup fresh bread crumbs

Pinch freshly grated nutmeg

Salt and freshly ground black pepper

2 quarts vegetable stock (pages 101–102)

① In a bowl, whisk the eggs and yolks until combined. Mix in the Parmesan, bread crumbs, nutmeg, and a sprinkling of salt and pepper to form a very loose dough. Cover and refrigerate for at least 30 minutes or up to a day. The dough should firm up.

② Bring the stock to a boil in a large pot, then reduce the heat so it bubbles gently.

③ Put portions of the dough in a ricer using the large holes and press the dough through, cutting it into 2- or 3-inch segments using scissors or by running a knife along the bottom of the ricer and letting the pieces drop into the bubbling stock. When the passatelli comes to the surface, it's done. Check the seasoning of the stock, adding some salt and pepper as needed. Serve immediately.

Free-Form Pasta

Certainly nicely cut pasta has its place, but if you don't have a cutter or prefer a more rustic-looking pasta, try free-form pasta, which ranges in shape and size from small pinches of dough to fat ribbons or whatever you like. To avoid rolling the dough altogether, check out Passatelli (page 489) and Spaetzle (below), which are very soft or batterlike doughs that are pressed or dropped into simmering water and cooked.

Pasta grattata:

The simplest, usually served in the broth in which it's cooked. Grate (using the large holes on a standard cheese grater) either Fresh Egg Pasta or Eggless Pasta dough (page 477 or 478) right when it comes out of the refrigerator; grate the pasta straight into a pot of simmering stock or over a piece of wax paper, keeping the pasta as separate as possible so it doesn't stick. Or pinch off small pieces of the dough and cook as you would any fresh pasta.

Handkerchiefs:

Roll either Fresh Egg Pasta or Eggless Pasta dough to less than 1/4 inch thick and tear or cut into squares (no larger than 4 inches across); cook as you would any fresh pasta.

Wide ribbons:

Roll either Fresh Egg Pasta or Eggless Pasta dough to less than 1/4 inch thick and cut into ribbons as wide as you like with a knife; cook as you would any fresh pasta.

Spaetzle

MAKES: 4 servings
TIME: 30 minutes

Hailing from Alsace, spaetzle is a cross between a dumpling and pasta; it's made from a pancakelike batter that's dropped into boiling water and cooked. From this point it can be seasoned and served, sautéed, tossed with sauce, or added to a broth or soup. I love it mixed with Mornay Sauce (page 804), put in a gratin dish, topped with grated cheese or bread crumbs, and baked until bubbling—an Alsatian mac and cheese.

The technique for dropping the spaetzle batter into the simmering water is just as varied as the serving possibilities. You can use a spaetzle maker (it looks like a grater without sharp edges, with an attachment that slides across the top), a colander, a squeeze bottle, or simply a spoon. The spoon and squeeze bottle are the most uncomplicated techniques: just load the spoon with about a tablespoon of the batter and let the batter drop into the water. To use a squeeze bottle, just squirt small portions of the batter into the water.

You can also make whole wheat spaetzle by substituting whole wheat flour for about half the all-purpose flour.

Salt

2 cups all-purpose flour

1/2 teaspoon or more freshly ground black pepper

3 eggs

1 cup milk, more or less

2 to 4 tablespoons butter or extra virgin olive oil

Chopped parsley leaves or chives for garnish

1 Bring a large pot of water to a boil and salt it. Combine the flour with the pepper and a large pinch of salt in a bowl. Lightly beat together the eggs and milk in a separate bowl and then stir the egg mixture into the flour. If necessary, add a little more milk to make a batter about the consistency of pancake batter.

2 Scoop up a tablespoon or so of the batter and drop it into the water; small pieces may break off, but the batter should remain largely intact and form an uneven disk. Spoon in about one-third to one-fourth of the batter, depending on the size of your pot. When the spaetzle rise to the top, a couple of minutes later (you may have to loosen them from the bottom, but they'll float right up),

cook for another minute or so, then transfer with a slotted spoon into a bowl of ice water. Repeat until all the batter is used up.

③ Drain the spaetzle (at this point you can toss them with a bit of oil and refrigerate, covered, for up to a day). Put the butter or oil in a large skillet, preferably nonstick, over medium-high heat. When the butter is melted or the oil is hot, add the spaetzle, working in batches, and brown quickly on both sides. Serve hot, garnished with the parsley or chives.

Herb Spaetzle. A mix of parsley, chervil, chives, and tarragon is lovely: Stir about 1 cup chopped fresh herbs into the batter.

Non-Italian Fresh Noodles and Dumplings

The recipes and illustrations in this section will help you explore the world of non-Italian noodles and dumplings. And when you're ready to try some dumplings that break with any and all tradition, see the chart on page 496.

Dumpling Wrappers

MAKES: About 50 wrappers

TIME: 40 minutes

This versatile wrapper can be used to make all sorts of dumplings, pot stickers, wontons, and egg rolls, as well as hand-cut noodles that can be used in Euro-style recipes as well as Asian. The recipe makes enough for two batches of the stuffings that follow; so you can pack away half of the wrappers in the freezer, double the stuffing, or make two different kinds of dumplings.

2 cups all-purpose flour, plus more as needed

1 teaspoon salt

① Put the flour and salt in a large mixing bowl and gradually stir in about $1/2$ cup cold water, until the dough comes together in a ball. The dough should be quite dry. Turn onto a floured surface and knead until smooth and elastic, about 5 minutes, sprinkling with flour as necessary to prevent sticking.

Or use a food processor: Put the flour and salt in the container and add the water gradually while the machine is running; add as much water as necessary to form a dough ball—again, the dough should be dry—then let the machine run for about 15 seconds. Finish the kneading by hand, using as much flour as necessary to keep it from sticking.

② Shape the dough into a ball, dust with flour, and cover with plastic wrap or a damp towel. Let it rest for 20 minutes to 2 hours. (The dough may be made ahead to this point, wrapped tightly, and refrigerated for up to a day; bring to room temperature before proceeding.)

③ Knead the ball for a minute, then cut into 4 pieces. On a lightly floured surface, roll each piece into a 1-inch log, then cut into 1-inch pieces and roll each one out from the center to form a 4-inch round or square, adding a bit more flour if necessary. (You can also roll sheets of dough with a pasta machine, then cut into desired shapes; see page 476.) Use immediately or dust with flour, stack, wrap tightly, and refrigerate (up to a couple of days) or freeze (up to 2 weeks).

Whole Wheat Dumpling Wrappers. Simply use whole wheat flour for all or part of the white flour. You will need to add more water; just do so a little at a time. And the dumplings will need to cook a minute or two longer.

Egg Roll Wrappers or Wonton Skins. You can use these as slightly richer dumpling wrappers or for wontons or egg rolls: Add 1 egg to the flour-salt mix, then reduce the water to a little less than $1/2$ cup. Proceed with the recipe. In step 3, cut the dough ball into 4 pieces and roll out each one. Cut 3-inch squares for dumpling wrappers or wonton skins, 6-inch squares for egg roll wrappers.

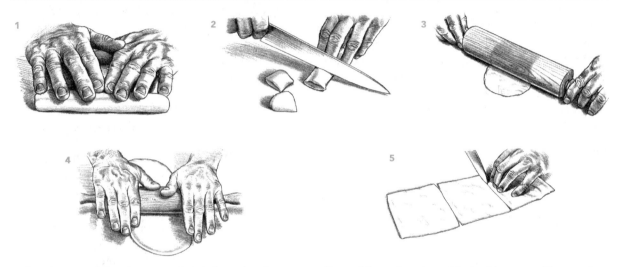

Roll each piece of dough out on a lightly floured surface. (STEP 1) First roll into a log about 1 inch wide. (STEP 2) Then cut into 1-inch pieces. (STEP 3) Roll each one out from the center to form a thin 4-inch circle or square, adding a bit of flour if necessary. (STEP 4) To make larger egg roll wrappers, roll each log into a thin, roughly rectangular shape, then (STEP 5) cut into squares.

Chinese Style Fresh Noodles. Made from either the main recipe or either of the preceding variations: In Step 3, after cutting the dough into 4 pieces, roll out each piece into a rectangle. Try to roll the dough as thinly as possible without ripping it, preferably to $^1/_8$ inch thick. Lightly dust the rectangles, fold into quarters lengthwise, then use a sharp knife to cut each folded rectangle into thin strips. Alternatively, use a pasta machine: Put the dough rectangles through the smallest setting, then roll it through the spaghetti setting. Dust lightly with flour to prevent sticking. Cook in boiling water just until tender, about 3 minutes, then drain, rinse, drain again, and serve immediately.

Steamed Dumplings, Asian Style

MAKES: 24 dumplings; 4 to 6 servings
TIME: 40 minutes

This is a simplified, streamlined stuffing, but you can get as elaborate as you like; there are few limits to the vegetables you can use in dumplings. The only secret is to include something slightly starchy—or bind with an egg—so the stuffing doesn't fall out of the wrapper when you take a bite. If you want to break free of tradition or geography, see the chart on page 496 for many more options.

 Fast   Ⓜ Make Ahead   Ⓥ Vegan

As long as your stuffing isn't too moist, you can refrigerate the stuffed dumplings for an hour or so before cooking or freeze them for up to a few days. Dust them with flour first to prevent sticking. But they really are best if you can stuff and cook in one fell swoop.

8 ounces firm tofu

$1/4$ cup minced scallion

1 cup chopped leek, Napa cabbage, or bok choy

1 teaspoon peeled and minced fresh ginger

1 teaspoon rice wine or dry sherry

1 teaspoon sugar

1 tablespoon soy sauce

1 tablespoon dark sesame oil

1 egg, lightly beaten

Salt and freshly ground black pepper

24 round dumpling wrappers (to make your own, see page 491)

Basil Dipping Sauce (page 777) or Ginger-Scallion Sauce (page 779)

① Put the tofu in a large bowl and mash roughly with a fork to crumble it. Add the scallion, leek, ginger, rice

Store-Bought Wrappers

All sorts of premade dumpling, egg roll, and wonton wrappers are sold in supermarkets. They're undeniably convenient but often contain additives and preservatives, so try to find those with as few ingredients as possible. You can use store-bought wrappers in any of the recipes in this section; sometimes they're a little thick and may need to be rolled a bit thinner. Sometimes they're thinner than ones you might make yourself; adjust the cooking times accordingly and go by visual cues: When the wrapper is slightly puffy and transparent, it's done.

wine, sugar, soy, sesame oil, and egg and sprinkle with a large pinch of salt and lots of pepper. Mix gently but thoroughly.

② Put about 2 teaspoons of the stuffing in the center of a wrapper, then moisten the edge of the wrapper with water and fold over to form a semicircle. Press the seam tightly to seal; it's best if there is no air trapped between the stuffing and wrapper. Set on a lightly floured plate or wax paper. (You can make the dumplings to this point, cover tightly, and refrigerate for up to a day or freeze for a couple of weeks.)

③ Set up a steamer or put a heatproof plate on a rack above 1 to 2 inches of boiling water in a covered pot (page 25). Lightly oil the steamer or plate to prevent sticking. Arrange the dumplings in the steamer so they don't touch and steam, working in batches if you must, for about 10 minutes per batch. Serve immediately with dipping sauce on the side.

Steamed Bean Dumplings. An interesting textural change from tofu: Use $1^1/2$ cups cooked adzuki, soy, or black soybeans instead of the tofu. In Step 1, put the beans into the bowl and roughly mash. Proceed with the recipe.

Steamed Gyoza with Sea Greens and Edamame. The Japanese version of dumplings, made with thinner wrappers; try to find gyoza or wonton wrappers or roll your own as thin as possible. Serve with Ponzu Sauce (page 780), Dashi Dipping Sauce (page 780), or simply with a little soy sauce mixed with a few drops of water: Soak about $1/2$ cup dried wakame or dulse in hot water for 30 minutes. Drain well and chop. Use $1^1/2$ cups edamame instead of the tofu and mash as described in Step 1; use the chopped sea greens instead of the leeks, cabbage, or bok choy. Proceed with the recipe.

Vegan Steamed Dumplings with Bean Threads. Pretty, with a chewy texture: Soak 1 bundle (2 ounces) of bean threads in hot water for 5 minutes (see page

464). Drain and chop into 1-inch pieces. Use the bean thread instead of the egg in the main recipe or any of the variations.

Tofu-Stuffed Wontons

MAKES: 4 to 6 servings
TIME: 30 minutes, with premade wrappers

These are wonderful wontons, with crisp exteriors and soft insides. The best wrappers are super-thin, and some of the store-bought kinds may need a little more rolling. If you're feeling ambitious or have lots of help, make your own following the recipe on page 491.

12 ounces silken tofu

$1/2$ cup chopped fresh chives (if you can find garlic chives, so much the better) or scallion

1 tablespoon peeled minced or grated ginger

1 teaspoon dark sesame oil

Salt and freshly ground black pepper

30 wonton skins (to make your own, see page 491)

Peanut or neutral oil, like grapeseed or corn, as needed

Pot Stickers

Panfried Asian-style dumplings—called *pot stickers*—are actually steamed and fried, which cooks the stuffing and leaves a crisp crust on one side.

Here's how: Put some peanut or neutral oil in a deep skillet with a tight-fitting lid—enough to coat the bottom in a thin layer. When it's hot, put the dumplings into the skillet, seam side up, leaving space between them (you will probably have to cook in two batches). Turn the heat to medium, then cover and cook for about 5 minutes. Add $1/2$ cup water to the skillet, then cover and cook for another 2 minutes. Remove the lid, turn the heat to high, and cook until the water has evaporated, about 3 minutes. Remove the dumplings and serve with the dipping sauce. (Repeat the cooking process as necessary for multiple batches.)

Any Asian-style dipping sauce (pages 777–780) or soy sauce mixed with water

1 Put the tofu in a food processor and let the machine run until it's smooth. By hand, stir in the chives, ginger, and sesame oil in a bowl, sprinkle with salt and pepper, and stir again to combine.

STUFFING AND SEALING HALF MOON–SHAPED DUMPLINGS (OR RAVIOLI)

(STEP 1) To make half-moon pot stickers (or ravioli), put a small amount of filling in the middle of your wrapper. Brush the seam lightly (you can use your fingertip) with water or beaten egg yolk, (STEP 2) then bring one edge of the wrapper over the filling to meet the other. (STEP 3) Secure the dumpling with the thumb of one hand, then press the edges closed.

F Fast   M Make Ahead   V Vegan

2 Put 1 scant tablespoon of the stuffing into the center of each wrapper. Moisten the edges of the wrapper with a few drops of water (use a brush or your finger) and fold into a triangle or semicircle. Press the edges together tightly to seal, making sure no air is trapped between the stuffing and wrapper. If you like, fold the tip of the triangle back and press gently. Set each wonton aside on a floured plate or wax paper.

3 Put at least 2 inches oil in a countertop deep-fryer or in a deep pan on the stove and turn the heat to medium-high; bring to 350°F (see "Deep-Frying," page 26). Working in batches and adjusting the heat as necessary, gently put as many of the wontons into the oil as will fit without crowding and cook, turning once, until golden brown, less than 5 minutes. Drain for a few moments on paper towels, then serve immediately with dipping sauce.

Wonton Soup. To make the soup more substantial, heat the stock with some shredded cabbage or ribbons of bok choy to wilt while the wontons boil: Gently warm about 6 to 8 cups vegetable stock (pages 101–102). In Step 1, bring a large pot of water to a boil. Stuff and seal the wontons as described. Depending on the size of your pot, boil the wontons in 1 or 2 batches for about 5 minutes per batch. Gently stir intermittently to prevent sticking. Immediately transfer to bowls,

SEALING WONTONS

To make wontons, put a small amount of filling on a square dumpling wrapper; brush the seam lightly (you can use your fingertip) with water or beaten egg yolk, then press closed.

ladle the stock over the wontons, and garnish with chopped scallion.

Dumpling Wrappers with Egg

MAKES: About 50 wrappers
TIME: About 60 minutes, partly unattended

Throughout Eastern Europe, the Baltic states, and Central Asia, the dumpling dough is made both with egg and without, but this recipe is used to make rich and creamy vareniki, pelmeni, or pierogi. The dough is very much like fresh pasta dough, only rolled slightly thick—and often uneven—by hand, which makes for a rustic, homey, and utterly irresistible dish.

The recipe makes enough for two batches of the stuffings that follow; so you can pack away half of the wrappers in the freezer, double the stuffing, or make two different kinds of dumplings.

    2 cups all-purpose flour, plus more as needed
    1 teaspoon salt
    2 egg yolks

1 Put the flour and salt in a food processor and pulse to mix. Add the egg yolks and, with the machine running, $^1/_4$ cup water; after that, add water about 1 tablespoon at a time until a dough ball forms; transfer to a lightly floured surface and knead by hand for a couple of minutes.

2 Cut the dough into 2 pieces, form into balls, dust with flour, and cover with plastic wrap, a damp towel, or an upside-down bowl. Let rest for 20 to 60 minutes (you can make the dough to this point, wrap it tightly in plastic, and freeze for up to a couple of weeks; defrost at room temperature before proceeding). Meanwhile, make your stuffing using one of the ideas from the chart on page 496.

3 Knead one of the balls for a minute on a lightly

floured surface. Roll each ball into a thin sheet, about 1/16 inch thick, and cut into 2- to 3-inch squares or use a cookie cutter or glass to form 2- to 3-inch circles. You can form the dumplings immediately or flour the wrappers lightly, stack, and refrigerate (up to a day) or freeze (up to 2 weeks).

Whole Wheat Dumpling Wrappers with Egg. Heartier and great with mushroom stuffing: Replace any or all of the flour with whole wheat flour.

Fresh Egg Noodles. Made with whole wheat or white flour: In Step 3, after cutting the dough into 2 pieces, roll out each piece into a rectangle. Try to roll the dough as thinly as possible without ripping it, $^1/_8$ to $^1/_{16}$ inch thick. Lightly dust the rectangles, fold into quarters lengthwise, then use a sharp knife to cut each folded rectangle into thin strips. Alternatively, use a pasta machine: put the dough rectangles through the smallest setting, then roll it through the fettuccine cutters. Dust lightly with flour to prevent sticking. Cook in boiling water just until tender, about 3 minutes, then drain, rinse, drain again, and serve immediately.

Herbed Fresh Egg Noodles. Pretty and tasty, though they don't freeze well, so use immediately: In Step 1, add $^1/_2$ cup chopped mixed herbs—parsley, mint, and dill is best—to the food processor while mixing the dough. In Step 3, after cutting the dough into 2 pieces, roll out each piece into a rectangle. Try to roll the dough as thinly as possible without ripping it, $^1/_8$ to $^1/_{16}$ inch thick. Lightly dust the rectangles, fold into quarters lengthwise, then use a sharp knife to

DUMPLING COMBOS

Steam, boil, or panfry these dumplings as you like. Because the stuffings are already cooked, you need to cook only long enough to heat the insides and cook the dough until just tender.

WRAPPER DOUGH	STUFFING	DIPPING SAUCE OR OTHER ACCOMPANIMENT
Dumpling Wrapper	Potatoes Braised with Sea Greens (page 347)	Nutty Miso Sauce (page 782)
Dumpling Wrapper	Stir-Fried Leeks (page 312)	Miso Carrot Sauce with Ginger (page 781)
Dumpling Wrapper	Bok Choy with Black Beans (page 270)	Chile-Garlic Paste (page 830)
Dumpling Wrapper	Mixed Whole-Bean Dal with Walnuts (page 602)	Pineapple Chutney or one of its variations (page 785)
Wonton Skin	Spicy Soybeans with Kimchi (page 609)	Ginger-Scallion Sauce (page 779)
Wonton Skin	Basic Scrambled Tofu (page 655)	Seaweed "Mayo" (page 773)
Dumpling Wrapper with Egg	Sauerkraut	Brewhouse Mustard (page 776)
Dumpling Wrapper with Egg	Kasha with Golden Brown Onions or any of the variations except Varnishkes (page 562)	Creamy Cranberry-Nut Sauce (page 798)
Dumpling Wrapper with Egg	Sautéed Mushrooms (page 314)	Creamy Bistro Sauce or Dressing (page 799)
Dumpling Wrapper with Egg	White Beans, Tuscan Style (page 594)	Traditional Pesto (page 768)

 Fast   Make Ahead   Ⓥ Vegan

cut each folded rectangle into thin strips. Alternatively, use a pasta machine: Put the dough rectangles through the smallest setting, then roll it through the fettuccine cutters. Dust lightly with flour to prevent sticking. Cook in boiling water just until tender, about 3 minutes, then drain, rinse, drain again, and serve immediately.

Fresh Egg Noodles with Scallions and Paprika

MAKES: 4 to 6 servings
TIME: About 1 hour; 20 minutes with premade noodles

The noodles are the star here, especially if you make them yourself. But if you can find good-quality Amish-style dried egg noodles, feel free to use them, thereby turning a special-occasion dish into an everyday treat.

Salt

2 bunches scallions, including a couple inches of the green parts

4 tablespoons ($1/2$ stick) butter

Freshly ground black pepper

2 tablespoons sweet paprika

1 recipe Fresh Egg Pasta (page 477) or 1 pound dried Amish-style or other thick-cut egg noodles

① Bring a large pot of water to a boil and salt it. Cut the scallions in half lengthwise, then crosswise into slices about 2 inches long.

② Put the butter and scallions in a deep skillet over medium heat, sprinkle with salt and pepper, and cook, stirring occasionally, until the butter melts and the scallions are soft, about 3 minutes. Stir in the paprika and cook until just fragrant, about a minute, then turn off the heat.

③ Add the fresh or dried noodles to the pot of boiling water. Cook, stirring occasionally, until tender,

about 3 minutes for fresh noodles and about 10 minutes for dried. Rinse and drain well. Turn the heat under the scallion mixture to medium-high and add the noodles to the skillet. Cook, tossing gently to coat the noodles, until everything is hot and the noodles start to sizzle. Taste, adjust the seasoning, and serve immediately.

6 Ways to Jazz Up Fresh Egg Noodles with Butter

If you don't want to go the scallions-and-paprika route, simply heat a tablespoon or two of one of the following ingredients with the butter while it melts in Step 2. Then just proceed with the recipe:

1. Fresh herbs, like tarragon, rosemary, or thyme (a little) or basil, chervil, dill, or parsley (a lot)
2. Minced fresh garlic
3. Curry powder (to make your own, see pages 815–816)
4. Poppy seeds
5. Cider or malt vinegar
6. Golden raisins or dried blueberries

Fried Potato-Stuffed Dumplings

Vareniki or Pierogi

MAKES: 24 dumplings, 4 to 6 servings
TIME: About 1 hour

These dumplings are creamy and savory, made even more rich by frying in butter and serving with cooked onion and some sour cream. Like the dumplings described in the variations, they may be boiled and served with melted butter.

3 tablespoons butter, more or less

1 large onion, diced

Salt and freshly ground black pepper

1 teaspoon minced garlic (optional)

1 cup well-seasoned mashed potatoes (page 341)

24 round or square dumpling wrappers (to make your
    own, with egg, see page 495)

1 egg white, lightly beaten in a bowl

Sour cream for garnish

① Put 1 tablespoon of the butter in a deep skillet over medium heat and add the onion along with a liberal sprinkling of salt and pepper. Cook, stirring occasionally, until the onion wilts, then turns brown. This may take as long as half an hour. It's okay if the onion gets a bit crisp on the edges, but lower the heat as necessary so it doesn't cook too fast; basically you want a kind of onion compote.

② Combine half the onion, and the garlic if you're using it, with the mashed potatoes, then taste and adjust the seasoning. Set the remaining onions aside. There's no need to wipe out the pan. Preheat the oven to 200°F.

③ Lay a wrapper on a work surface, then put 1 to 2 teaspoons of the stuffing in the center of it; brush the edge of the wrapper with egg white. If you have cut circles, form half-moons; if you have cut squares, form triangles. Press the seam tightly to seal; it's best if there is no air trapped between the stuffing and wrapper, so press down slightly. Set on a lightly floured plate or wax paper. (At this point, you may cover tightly and refrigerate for up to a day or freeze for a couple of weeks.)

④ Set a large pot of water to boil and salt it. Working in batches (in combination with the frying technique in Step 5), carefully cook the dumplings in the boiling water until just tender, 3 to 5 minutes. Transfer them with a slotted spoon to the skillet with melted butter.

⑤ Put the remaining 2 tablespoons butter in a large skillet, preferably nonstick or cast-iron, over medium heat. When the butter melts, add as many dumplings as will fit without crowding and brown them quickly, turning once or twice until the dough is tender, about 10 minutes total. When they are done, move them to an ovenproof plate and keep them warm in the oven. Cook the remaining dumplings, adding butter to the skillet as needed. When all are cooked, lower the heat a bit and reheat the remaining onion, then spread it out over the dumplings; serve hot, passing sour cream at the table.

Fried Cheese-Stuffed Dumplings. Decadent in an old-fashioned way: Don't bother with the onion, but mince about $1/4$ cup fresh parsley or dill to use as a garnish. Instead of the potatoes, prepare a cheese stuffing by draining 1 cup cottage cheese in a fine strainer for an hour or so or mashing 1 cup farmer's or pot cheese. Stir in a teaspoon of sugar, a pinch of salt, one egg white, and $1/4$ cup sour cream. Use this to stuff the dumplings. Proceed with the main recipe to fry the dumplings or the following variation to boil them.

Boiled Dumplings. Use this technique for any of the dumplings in this recipe: Melt 2 tablespoons of butter; put a large pot of water on to boil and salt it. Preheat the oven to 200°F. Boil the dumplings, a few at a time, until they rise to the surface; a minute or two later, taste a bit of the dough to see whether it is tender. As they finish, remove them with a slotted spoon and put in an ovenproof bowl; drizzle them with some of the butter and put the plate in the oven. When the dumplings are all done, make sure they are coated evenly with butter; serve with sour cream.

Grains

I learned to cook at a time when a "grain" was either a breakfast cereal or white rice, usually of the instant variety. I had little idea that Wheatena was made from cracked wheat or that the weird stuff my grandmother put in her noodles with onions was kasha, and, like almost everyone else in this country, I'd never heard of quinoa. Later on, I was turned on to brown rice and granola. I tolerated the former to be hip; the latter I actually liked, probably because it contained nuts and sugar and therefore was much like a candy bar.

Years went by. I learned how to cook real rice, and then basmati rice, and then risotto. My grandmother taught me how to make my own kasha varnishkes. I made my own granola, for that matter, equally nutty but less sweet. I experimented with wild rice, learned about bulgur, and finally began to actually enjoy brown rice and wheat berries. Quinoa was a revelation.

But even until three or four years ago, grains other than white rice did not play a major role in my kitchen. Certainly I cooked cracked wheat more often than my friends, but I cooked most unusual food more often than most people.

Researching this chapter, which I began doing way back in 2003, changed all that. The more grains I had in my pantry, the more often I cooked them. The more I cooked them, the more I liked them. And then, of course, it turned out that they are among the few foods of which you can eat your fill and actually feel virtuous. And, in the course of developing this chapter, I made some discoveries that made grain cooking, especially whole grain cooking, easier and more delicious: I learned to parboil brown rice to make it much more convenient, I learned how easy and smart it was to cook grains in advance, I learned how pleasurable it was to eat grains at room temperature and even how to use leftover grains as garnishes.

In short, I'm a convert.

Anyone interested in a vegetarian diet or a vaguely healthy diet or even a more diverse diet should join me. Eating a variety of grains is the most enjoyable way not only to add a ton of fiber to your diet but also to keep your diet from falling into a rice rut.

What You'll Find in This Chapter

As you work your way through this chapter, you'll see that I consider many grains interchangeable much of the time: Most of the recipes contain a line for "other grains you can use," which makes it simpler to use your favorites in more recipes. But I'd still encourage you to try a variety of different grains and stock as many of them as you have room for.

That said, I've put all the rice recipes and relevant info up front, right after the basic information that applies to all grains, because most people still find rice the most enjoyable grain. And with good reason: It's incredibly versatile, it's fast cooking, and there are so many varieties it's a world unto itself. Throw in brown rice—which is now commonly available in short- and long-grain, basmati, sweet, sticky, and a variety of specialty versions—and there's no limit.

After rice, which makes up almost half of this chapter, I go into details about the other grains, and then things get recipe-specific for individual grains. At the end of the chapter are multigrain recipes.

The Basics of Grains

Almost all grains—including rice—are members of the grass family. (The most notable exceptions are buckwheat,

quinoa, and amaranth, which are in another category of plants and distantly related to each other.) All grains have the same basic composition: If you were to look at a single grain and work from the outside in, you would first see the bran, very thin but tough layers that protect the interior. Next comes the germ, which is the "embryo" at the base of the grain, and the endosperm, which makes up the bulk of the grain and provides food for the germ.

We sometimes eat the bran and germ, which contain the most nutrients and fiber, as well as the oil that make grains perishable, but all parts of most grains are edible (we always eat the endosperm). Rice, barley, and oats, however, have an additional protective outer layer, an inedible husk or hull that must be removed before being eaten.

Milling

The process of removing parts of grains to make them edible or (by some standards) more palatable is called *milling*. When the hull is removed from rice, for example, it retains its bran and germ and is called *brown*, as in brown rice, or *whole*, as in whole oats (or, for that matter, whole wheat, which can be eaten with no milling at all). The less grains are milled, the higher they are in both nutrients and flavor, and the longer they take to cook. This is a trade-off and a choice. But keeping precooked grains on hand is a fantastic way to have the best of all worlds—convenience, flavor, and nutrition. (See Cooked Grains, the Easy Way, page 537).

Highly milled grains, like white rice, pearled barley, and rolled oats, contain just the endosperm, the white or light tan interior of the grain, containing little more than starch and protein. These are the grains with which we're most familiar. They're not as nutritious as whole grains, but they're faster cooking, a characteristic it's easy to like. They are also somewhat blander, which generally means more acceptable.

Grains and Health

Ever since spring 2005, when the federal government strongly recommended whole grains in its Dietary

F Fast   M Make Ahead   V Vegan

Guidelines, they're almost everywhere. It's almost all about fiber. Unrefined grains, those that are minimally milled to retain their germ and bran, deliver more fiber than any other food.

This is important, since the general consensus is that adults should eat 25 grams of fiber a day, which is a lot—about eight apples' worth. You're not going to get there very fast if you eat only white rice, with just a couple grams per serving. Though brown rice is somewhat better, a dish that contains wheat berries, cracked wheat, or millet can supply up to 25 to 30 percent of that daily recommendation in a single serving. Eat bulgur or hulled barley and you can get there even faster.

Grains also contain protein, in amounts ranging from modest (rice) to substantial (oats, quinoa, and wild rice), especially when combined with legumes to round out the specific amino acids necessary to form a complete protein. And grains provide, in varying amounts, vitamins, minerals, and phytochemicals—the micronutrients thought to protect us from all sorts of ailments and ills—in quantities that are at least as high as nutrition-packed vegetables like broccoli and tomatoes.

Buying and Storing Grains

Many grains, especially unprocessed whole grains, remain difficult to find in supermarkets. Though that's changing rapidly, your best shopping bets are still specialty supermarkets, natural food stores, and places that sell a lot of foods in bulk (especially for those listed in the "Grains for Enthusiasts" chart on page 536). International markets may be the sources with the best variety and the only sources in your area for grains like farro (Italian), teff (Ethiopian or North African), and hominy (Mexican or Native American). Mail-order and on-line shopping also offer a wide selection; see page 536.

White rice is the least vulnerable of all grains since it has no oils to turn rancid. As with most dry goods, keep it in a cool, dry spot; it will keep indefinitely. Brown rice (including the colored specialty rices) is more sensitive; the natural oils in the bran and germ can turn rancid. Since you never know how long it's already been sitting on the store shelf, brown rice is best stored in the refrigerator, or even your freezer if you have the space. (It need not be defrosted before use.)

Many people keep their grains in closed jars; I try to buy relatively small amounts (a pound or so) of many, many grains and keep them in the freezer, which—especially for whole grains, which contain perishable oils—keeps them fresher. In any case, for best flavor and nutrition (and for the fastest cooking times), use whatever grains you buy within a year or so of purchase.

Rinsing and Draining Grains

Since grains are cleaned in the milling process, there's no need to pick through them as you do legumes, but I like to rinse them briefly before cooking. Rice may have been coated with talc, quinoa may retain a bit of its natural saponin, and any grain may be gritty.

You can either put them in a strainer under cold running water, shaking and tossing them a bit. Or you can put them in the pot you're planning to use for cooking, fill it with water, swish the grains around, then tip the pot to pour off the water; repeat until the water is clear. Don't bother to drain the grains if you're just going to boil them, but if you're making pilaf, it's nice—but not essential—to let them drain a bit if you have time.

The Rice Lexicon

There are thousands of varieties of rice, grown on every continent except Antarctica. Throw in the regional names for each variety and you've got yourself a confusing mass of information. In an effort to clear things up and make this information useful, I'll stick with the varieties that you're most likely to find in the United States, which is still a lot.

Rice is in the same grass family as wheat, oats, barley, rye, and millet. *Oryza sativa* is the cultivated species and is by far the most common, though native wild rice still grows in the northern United States, southern Canada, and parts of Asia. Unlike other grains, rice is best grown in standing water in flooded flats of land or on terraced hillsides. China and India are the top producers (and consumers) of rice, though the United States is a major exporter. But 90 percent of the world's rice supply is grown in the monsoon regions of Asia.

There are two main groups of rices: Indica are long-grain rices, which produce generally fluffy and separated grains when cooked. Indica rices are grown in more tropical regions, like Southeast Asia, India, Pakistan, and the southern United States.

Japonica is the other main group. These are medium- and short-grain rices that are sticky and moist when cooked. They're grown in more northern climates, like northern China, Japan, Korea, Europe, and California.

So, long-grain or short-grain is the basic distinction. But it's not the only one. Here are three other potentially confusing rice terms you'll probably encounter.

Brown Rices

Any rice can be "brown," just as any rice can be milled to be "white" (see "Milling," page 500). Brown rice is rice that has had only its inedible hull removed, leaving on the bran and germ. Brown rice should rightly be called "unmilled" rice, especially since the bran color varies from light tan to red to deep indigo to black. In fact, all the fancy specialty colored rices—red, black, purple, etc.—are just brown rice with a different color bran. But no matter what you call it, more types of whole, unmilled rice are increasingly available, and rightly so: it's more nutritious than white rice and deliciously different to boot.

"Sticky" Rices

Sticky rice is a sticky situation: Knowing what to look for, what to call it, and what you're buying is a challenge. All sorts of sticky rices are used throughout East and Southeast Asia. Some are long-grain, and many are short-grain. Sticky rices go by different names—*glutinous, sweet, waxy, broken,* and even *sushi.* Your best bet is to find a type of sticky rice that works for you and continue to buy the same kind at the same market. I've been using broken jasmine rice, which I buy in a Chinese supermarket, for years, and it works great. But it's not the only option. If you can find "Thai sticky rice," that's another reliable choice; for more details, see page 503.

Converted and Instant Rice

Converted (or parboiled) rice is typically long-grain rice, soaked and steamed before drying and milling. During this process many of the natural vitamins and minerals found in the bran are absorbed by the endosperm, resulting in a slightly more nutrient-rich white rice. Generally, it's more expensive and not worth the cost.

Instant or quick-cooking rice is white or brown rice that's partially or fully cooked and dried. Cooking time is reduced to 5 or 10 minutes, but the flavor and texture (and your wallet!) really suffer. Avoid at all costs; if you're cooking dinner, you have the 15 minutes it takes to cook real rice.

Long-Grain Rices

The Indica family of rice, identified by their slender grains that are at least three times longer than they are wide. When cooked, long-grain rices are fluffy and separated; the flavor is neutral to delicately sweet and nutty. The rice types listed here are organized from most commonly used and easiest to find in the United States to the more specialized.

Southern Long-Grain

Long-Grain

Varieties and Forms: White, brown, converted, instant.

Description: The most common long-grain rice in the world and the most widely grown rice in the United States. If rice is labeled just *long-grain,* it's more than likely this. It has a neutral flavor, and when cooked the grains cling together somewhat.

Availability: Supermarkets.

Ⓕ Fast   Ⓜ Make Ahead   Ⓥ Vegan

Basmati

Varieties and Forms: White, brown.

Description: The best-known and most aromatic rice of South Asia and one of the most expensive rices (which doesn't make it *that* expensive). The premium grade is aged for at least a year; the grains elongate and separate when cooked and have a distinctly nutty aroma and complex flavor. Great stuff, worth keeping on hand all the time.

Availability: Supermarkets; Middle Eastern or Indian markets.

Jasmine

Varieties and Forms: White, brown, broken.

Description: An aromatic rice with a sweet aroma responsible for its name, this Thai specialty is very white and smooth and slightly stickier than basmati, with a milder flavor. Broken jasmine rice makes very good sticky rice.

Availability: Supermarkets, Southeast Asian markets.

American Aromatics

Varieties and Forms: Texmati, Kasmati, Calmati, Jasmati, Della, Wild Pecan, Louisiana Pecan, and Popcorn; white or brown.

Description: Pretty much knockoffs and hybrids of either basmati or jasmine combined with southern long-grain. They usually have *mati* somewhere in the name but don't have the same aroma and flavors as their role models.

Availability: Supermarkets and specialty and natural food stores.

Long-Grain Sticky Rices

Thai, Sticky Jasmine, Glutinous, Sweet, or Kao Niow ("Sticky Rice" in Thai)

Varieties and Forms: White or unmilled (called *Thai black* or *purple, black sticky rice*).

Description: Though it's sometimes called *glutinous rice* or *sweet rice,* that's just to confuse you, or so it seems. To be sure, get broken jasmine or a Thai brand, with long grains that may or may not be broken. Generally, these slender, opaque white kernels turn translucent when cooked. (The black variety is black or dark purple in color.) They're aromatic, with a sweet flavor and very sticky but firm texture (in Thailand and elsewhere, it's formed into small balls and eaten with the hands, kind of like bread). Long-grain sticky rice is best steamed (see page 507). Black sticky rice is traditionally cooked with coconut milk and palm sugar as a dessert.

Availability: Thai, Chinese, and Southeast Asian markets.

Red Rices

Varieties and Forms: California Red, Wehani, Himalayan Red, Thai, Camargue, and Rosematta (a converted rice).

Description: These are really brown rices that, through breeding or accident, have red bran. They're usually more expensive than standard brown rice but not much different in flavor. Like all brown rice, these have a nuttier flavor, chewier texture, and longer cooking times than white rices.

Availability: Specialty stores, mail order (see Sources, page 929).

Kalijira Rice

Baby Basmati

Varieties and Forms: Milled white most commonly.

Description: Grown in Bangladesh and usually reserved for holidays and festivals. Sometimes called *baby basmati* because it looks like miniature basmati and has similar aroma, taste, and texture but cooks in 10 minutes.

Availability: Indian or Central Asian markets, mail order (see Sources, page 929).

Short-Grain Rices

These belong to the Japonica group and are fat, round grains under three times as long as they are wide. They generally have a neutral flavor and are sticky and moist when cooked. The rice types listed here are organized from most commonly used and easiest to find in the United States to the more specialized.

Common Short- and Medium-Grain Rices

Varieties and Forms: The most common variety is Calrose; some is New Variety; others are based on Japanese rices like mochi, Koshihikari, and Akitakomachi. Can be white or brown.

Description: Much of this is from California; the kernels are glossy, sticky but firm, moist, and neutral in flavor. They are good, inexpensive substitutes for Arborio, Valencia, and other short- and medium-grain rices. In general, this is the rice for many dishes associated with Southeast Asia and Japan.

Availability: Supermarkets, Japanese and Asian markets.

Risotto Rices

Varieties and Forms: Most commonly Arborio, but also Carnaroli, Vialone Nano, Baldo, Roma; fino and superfine grades; white and brown (unmilled).

Description: These are traditionally Italian-grown rices that are now also grown in California. They have a white center that remains firm when cooked and starchy outer layers that absorb liquid and create that creamy risotto texture. Superfino is a slightly longer grain than fino risotto rice. Use common short- or medium-grain rice as a substitute if you like; the difference is noticeable but not incredible.

Availability: Supermarkets; specialty stores or mail order for other varieties (see Sources, page 929).

Short-Grain Sticky Rices

Glutinous, Sweet, Waxy

Varieties and Forms: Chinese, Japanese, Korean, mochi; white and brown (unmilled).

Description: Short-grain sticky rices are opaque and plump with a slightly sweet flavor and sticky but firm texture. Usually, but not always, these rices are used in desserts and sweet dishes. Mochi is a Japanese sticky rice that's often made into a dough to make various rice cakes (see page 473).

Availability: Asian markets.

Paella Rices

Spanish

Varieties and Forms: Valencia, Bomba, Bahia, Granza; almost always milled.

Description: A medium-grain rice that produces a creamy texture, similar to risotto. Like risotto, it can absorb a large amount of liquid, but the grains remain more separate. It has a neutral flavor that perfectly absorbs the flavors of the other ingredients in the dish.

Availability: Some supermarkets, specialty stores, mail order (see Sources, page 929).

American Black, Red, and Mahogany Rices

Japonica

Varieties and Forms: Available in various colors and often blended into mixtures.

Description: American-grown specialty aromatic rices that have a nutty and somewhat spicy flavor. The colors are deeply hued and quite beautiful.

Availability: Some supermarkets, specialty stores, mail order (see Sources, page 929).

Bhutanese Rice

Description: A pretty, medium-grain red rice grown in the tiny, high-altitude Himalayan country of Bhutan. It has a nutty and earthy flavor and cooks more quickly than other brown rices.

Availability: Specialty stores, mail order.

F Fast   M Make Ahead   V Vegan

Forbidden Rice

China Black

Description: Said to have been grown originally only for the Chinese emperor, this rice is prized for its black color, soft texture, and earthy taste.

Availability: Specialty stores, mail order.

White Rice

MAKES: 4 servings
TIME: 20 to 30 minutes

There are several ways to cook rice, and all of them get the job done. Unfortunately, the most commonly taught method—in which rice is brought to a boil with one-and-a-half times its volume of water, covered, and cooked for 15 to 17 minutes—is probably the trickiest, the one that takes the most judgment and offers the least flexibility. Far easier and more reliable is the method described here, which will work well for any kind of white rice at all.

You can cook rice ahead, but not that far; 30 minutes is stretching it. Keep it warm over the lowest heat possible, or wrap the pot in a towel.

It's almost as easy to make pilafs (pages 511–516) and other slightly more sophisticated rice dishes as it is to make basic rice, but sometimes this is what you're looking for. Even so, it is, like all grains, vastly better when made with stock or other liquid.

Needless to say, white rice can be served with almost anything, but if you're looking to make it the base for another dish, see the stir-fries on pages 520–522 or "6 Easy Dishes to Serve on Top of Polenta" (page 544).

1¹/₂ cups white rice

Large pinch salt

❶ Put the rice in a small saucepan with water to cover by about 1 inch. Add the salt and bring to a boil over

medium-high heat, then adjust the heat so the mixture boils steadily but not violently. When small craters appear, lower the heat a bit more and, when all visible moisture disappears, turn off the heat entirely—this will be 10 to 15 minutes after you started.

❷ At this point you can serve the rice (it will be moist but fine) or cover it, with the heat off or at an absolute minimum, and let it sit for 15 or even 30 minutes, during which time it will become a bit drier. See "14 Thirty-Second Ways to Jazz Up Plain Rice" (below).

White Rice in the Microwave. Easy enough, especially for two servings: Put 1 cup white rice in a 1-quart measure or bowl and add a large pinch of salt and 1¹/₂ cups water. Cover tightly with plastic wrap and cut a slit in the top of the wrap. Microwave for 12¹/₂ minutes, or until done, then let sit for 5 minutes or so before serving.

14 Thirty-Second Ways to Jazz Up Plain Rice

1. Stir in a tablespoon or more butter.
2. Stir in a tablespoon or more extra virgin olive oil.
3. Drizzle with soy sauce.
4. Add lots of black pepper.

5. Stir in a couple tablespoons minced herbs.

6. Stir in a tablespoon or two minced garlic or chopped onion lightly cooked in olive oil or butter.

7. Top with shredded or minced scallion or shallot.

8. Stir in a teaspoon or more—just a suspicion—vinegar.

9. Add lemon juice to taste (great with butter and black pepper).

10. Mix in $^1/_2$ cup or so grated or crumbled cheese, from mild to strong.

11. Mix in $^1/_2$ to 1 cup cooked beans, with some of their liquid.

12. Top with a bit of Fast Tomato Sauce (page 445).

13. Stir in a *tiny* bit of ground cinnamon, allspice, nutmeg, and/or cloves—exercise restraint and be sure to taste.

14. Season with any spice mixture (to make your own, see pages 810–819).

Brown Rice

MAKES: 4 servings
TIME: About 45 minutes

Brown rice can substitute for white rice in a vast number of recipes, as you'll see in this chapter, so it would be a mistake to think of it as some weird health-food phenomenon. Nutritionally, of course, it's far superior; taste-wise, it's neither better nor worse, only different. Like white rice, indeed like any grain, it's improved by using stock or other liquids instead of water.

Brown rice takes longer to cook than white rice, though the technique is similar. But know this: Brown rice can be cooked very efficiently using the method for Cooking Grains, the Easy Way on page 537). And as long as this is the first thing you tackle when you get in the kitchen, you can still prepare a meal in which brown rice plays a role in just about 45 minutes, certainly under an hour.

1½ cups brown rice

Large pinch salt

1 Put the rice in a small saucepan with water to cover by about 1 inch. Add the salt and bring to a boil over medium-high heat, then adjust the heat so the mixture simmers gently. Cover and cook for 30 to 40 minutes, checking occasionally to make sure the water is not evaporating too quickly (you can add a little more liquid if necessary). When the liquid has been absorbed, taste and see if the rice is tender or nearly so. If not, add about $^1/_2$ cup more liquid and continue to cook, covered.

The Easy Way to Substitute Brown Rice for White

Using brown rice instead of white is as easy as boiling water. All you have to do is precook—"parboil"—the exact same quantity of brown rice first, then substitute that for the raw white rice in any recipe. The techniques after that remain exactly the same—for pilafs, paella, stuck-pot dishes, and, incredibly, even risottos. And the results are terrific. You get the nutty, rich, toasted, satisfying taste of brown rice, but what's most surprising is the texture. Pilafs are still fluffy; risottos are still creamy. In fact, this is one of the most important "discoveries" I made while researching this book.

Start by bringing a large pot of salted water to a boil. Stir in the brown rice and adjust the heat so that the water bubbles along nicely. Don't stir the rice again; just let it cook for 10 to 15 minutes. (Twelve minutes is about perfect, but it's not that precise, so let's not get nuts about this.) Drain the rice, then proceed with whatever recipe you choose. You can even parboil the brown rice up to an hour or so beforehand.

F Fast   M Make Ahead   V Vegan

When the rice is tender, you can serve it or turn the heat off—or keep it at an absolute minimum—and let it sit for 15 or even 30 minutes, during which time it will become a bit drier. See "14 Thirty-Second Ways to Jazz Up Plain Rice" (page 505).

Steamed Sticky Rice

MAKES: 4 servings

TIME: About 2 hours, largely unattended

Among the most incredible one-ingredient preparations in the world, sticky rice is popular throughout East and Southeast Asia. In Thailand, among other places, it's eaten at just about every meal, like bread. It has substance, flavor, and chew, and almost everyone who tries it loves it. Nor is it difficult to make, as long as you plan ahead a bit.

Sticky rice imposes two challenges. One is in buying the right stuff: It may be called sticky rice, sweet rice, or glutinous rice but—unfortunately—not all sweet or glutinous rice is sticky rice. If you buy Thai "sticky rice" or Thai "sweet rice," you'll wind up with the right stuff. Another possibility—and this is also quite reliable—is broken jasmine rice. (There's also black sticky rice, but that's mostly reserved for desserts; see page 503.) Make sure you buy some cheesecloth too; you'll need it for steaming.

The second challenge is simpler: Plan ahead. Sticky rice must be soaked for an hour before steaming, and longer is better.

$1^{1}/_{2}$ cups sticky rice

Salt and freshly ground black pepper or soy sauce

1 Rinse the rice, then soak it in water to cover for at least 1 hour (24 hours is fine also).

2 Drain, then wrap in cheesecloth and put in a steamer above boiling water. Steam for about 30 minutes, until tender. It's almost impossible to overcook

sticky rice, so you can keep it warm over low heat for an hour longer or even more. (You can even cook the rice in advance: Keep it tightly wrapped and refrigerated, and resteam just before serving.) Sprinkle with salt and pepper or soy sauce before serving.

Sticky Rice with Soy Sauce and Coconut Milk. Making a good thing better: Toss the cooked rice with 1 cup coconut milk (to make your own, see page 423) and 1 tablespoon soy sauce. Rewrap and steam (or microwave) for a few minutes to reheat.

Sticky Rice with Shallots and Peanuts or Coconut. This is killer: While it's cooking, toast about $^{1}/_{2}$ cup peanuts or shredded unsweetened coconut in a dry skillet over medium heat until fragrant, about 2 minutes. Chop the peanuts (you don't have to chop the coconut), then toss with $^{1}/_{4}$ cup chopped shallot or scallion, $^{1}/_{4}$ cup chopped fresh cilantro leaves, 1 tablespoon soy sauce, and 2 teaspoons freshly squeezed lime juice. Toss with the cooked rice and rewrap and steam (or microwave) for a few minutes to reheat.

Sticky Rice with Vegetable Filling. Especially nice when wrapped in a lotus or banana leaf, but that step is really unnecessary: When the rice is done, flatten it into a rectangle and spread on about a cup of any filling you like, tossed with a little soy sauce. For example, use Stir-Fried Vegetables with Sautéed Mushrooms (page 242, best with shiitakes). Fold the rice over the filling and rewrap and steam (or microwave) for a few minutes to reheat.

Coconut Rice

MAKES: 4 servings

TIME: 30 minutes

Coconut rice is a near-universal staple, for two reasons: In many rice-growing areas coconuts grow wild, so the combination is a natural. Even the simplest version, which follows, is incredibly delicious. A few other touches make it even better. (And many rice recipes can take on the flavor of coconut simply with coconut milk substituted for all or part of the liquid.)

You can make your own coconut milk (page 423), but canned is easier. And if you don't have quite enough, just top it off with a little water or stock.

3 cups coconut milk or 1$^1/_2$ cups coconut milk plus
    1$^1/_2$ cups water

1$^1/_2$ cups rice, preferably short-grain

Salt

1 Combine the coconut milk and rice in a saucepan; bring to a boil over medium heat, stirring occasionally. Add a pinch of salt, reduce the heat to low, and cover. Cook for 10 minutes, stirring occasionally to make sure the bottom doesn't stick or burn.

2 Uncover and continue to cook, stirring, over low heat until the rice is tender and the mixture is creamy. If liquid evaporates before the rice is done, stir in water, about $^1/_2$ cup at a time, and cook until done.

Sweet Coconut Rice. A real treat: Add $^1/_4$ to $^1/_3$ cup sugar in Step 1.

Spicy Coconut Rice. Bigger: Add 1 tablespoon each peeled and minced fresh ginger, garlic, and fresh chile like jalapeño or Thai; or about 1 tablespoon hot red pepper flakes to the mix. Garnish with chopped fresh cilantro leaves.

Coconut Rice with Coconut Bits. Crunchier: While the rice is cooking, toast $^1/_2$ cup shredded coconut in a dry skillet, shaking occasionally, until lightly browned. Stir into the rice just before serving.

Coconut Rice and Beans. With steamed vegetables, a meal: Step 1 remains the same. Stir 1 cup of moist cooked kidney, pinto, pink, or black beans into the rice about 5 minutes before it finishes cooking.

Coconut Brown Rice. The main recipe or any of the variations can be made with brown rice: Use 1$^1/_2$ cups coconut milk and 2 cups water; increase the covered cooking time to 20 minutes and the uncovered time to about 20 minutes, adding more water if necessary. Alternatively, start with parboiled brown rice (page 506) and treat it exactly as you would the white rice.

Rice with Cheese

MAKES: 4 servings
TIME: 30 minutes

F

This delicious, over-the-top recipe has such a strong dairy component that I wouldn't recommend it to anyone trying to reduce their fat intake or eat vegan style. Everyone else will love it: It's simple, rich, and almost decadent.

Salt

1 cup Arborio or other short-grain rice

3 tablespoons butter

$^1/_2$ cup grated fontina or other good semisoft cheese

Freshly grated Parmesan cheese

Freshly ground black pepper

1 Bring a pot of water to a boil and salt it as you would to cook pasta. Add the rice in a steady steam and stir. When the water returns to a boil, lower the heat and simmer the rice until tender but not mushy, about 15 minutes. Drain.

2 Put the butter in a saucepan large enough to hold the rice and turn the heat to medium. When the butter melts and just begins to turn brown, add the rice and toss together. Stir in the fontina, then a handful of Parmesan, along with a bit of salt and some pepper. Serve, passing more Parmesan at the table.

F Fast   **M** Make Ahead   **V** Vegan

Rice with Peas

MAKES: 4 servings
TIME: 20 minutes

This can be made with leftover rice, but then you're essentially making fried rice, as on page 519. Prepared this way, it's a little more sophisticated.

If you're using frozen peas, defrost them first, either at room temperature or for 15 minutes or so in a bowl of cold water.

Salt

1 cup Arborio or other short-grain rice

4 tablespoons ($^1/_2$ stick) butter or $^1/_4$ cup extra virgin olive oil

1 cup fresh or frozen peas

Freshly ground black pepper

① Bring a pot of water to a boil and salt it as you would to cook pasta. Add the rice in a steady steam and stir. When the water returns to a boil, lower the heat and simmer the rice until tender but not mushy, about 15 minutes. Drain.

② Put half the butter or oil in a saucepan over medium heat. When the butter is melted or the oil is hot, add the peas and cook, shaking the pan occasionally, until hot and tender, about 5 minutes.

③ Toss the rice back in and add the remaining butter or oil; cook, stirring, until hot, just a couple of minutes. Taste and adjust the seasoning, adding plenty of black pepper, and serve.

Rice with Chickpeas

MAKES: 4 servings
TIME: 30 minutes with cooked beans

Chickpeas are a great way to boost the flavor and texture of a rice dish; they add richness to the cooking liquid and

don't turn to mush. (And, with the rice, they provide complete protein.) Add some more vegetables or firm tofu to any of these recipes (especially the curried variation) and you have yourself a lovely little one-pot meal.

Other grains you can use: couscous, bulgur, pearled barley, and quinoa (see "The Basics of Cooking Grains" on page 533 for cooking guidelines).

1 tablespoon olive oil

$^1/_2$ medium onion, finely chopped

2 cloves garlic, minced

$^1/_2$ medium bell pepper, any color you like, cored, seeded, and finely chopped

$1^1/_2$ cups chopped ripe tomato with the juice (about 6 ounces whole or canned; don't bother to drain)

$1^1/_4$ cups vegetable stock (pages 101–102) or water

2 tablespoons dry sherry (optional)

1 bay leaf

Salt and freshly ground black pepper

$1^1/_2$ cups long-grain rice

1 cup cooked (pages 579–580) or drained canned chickpeas

① Put the oil in a medium pot with a lid over medium-high heat. When hot, add the onion, garlic, and bell pepper and cook, stirring occasionally, until the onion softens, about 5 minutes. Add the tomato, stock, sherry if you're using it, bay leaf, some salt, and plenty of pepper; bring to a boil.

② Stir in the rice and chickpeas, cover, and turn the heat down to low so that the mixture bubbles gently. Cook until the liquid is absorbed and the rice is tender, about 20 minutes. Fluff with a fork, taste, and adjust the seasoning if necessary. Serve hot or at room temperature or store, covered, in the refrigerator for up to 2 days (reheat or bring back to room temperature and stir in a little olive oil just before serving).

Spiced Rice with Chickpeas and Almonds. Nicely North African: Omit the bell pepper and sherry. Stir in a tablespoon or so of chili powder, garam masala, or curry powder (to make your own, see pages 814, 815, and 816) with the cooking onions and proceed with recipe. Sprinkle with toasted almond slices before serving.

Curried Rice with Chickpeas. Richer and spicier: Omit the sherry and replace the stock with unsweetened coconut milk if you like. Stir in a tablespoon or so of curry powder (to make your own, see pages 815 and 816) to the cooking onions and proceed with recipe. You can also throw in a handful of peas (fresh or defrosted frozen) during the last 5 minutes of cooking.

Saffron Rice with Chickpeas. Gorgeous color and exotic, lovely flavor: Omit the bell pepper, garlic, and sherry; replace the chopped tomatoes with an additional cup of stock or water. Add $^1/_4$ teaspoon crushed saffron threads and a teaspoon of julienned lemon or orange zest along with the stock in Step 1; proceed with the recipe. Sprinkle with za'atar (to make your own, see page 818) just before serving.

White Rice and Black Beans

MAKES: 4 to 6 servings

TIME: About 2 hours, largely unattended

Seriously delicious and really easy. This technique—semipuréeing the half-cooked beans and adding the rice—makes a great case for cooking all rice and bean dishes this way, because the earthy bean flavor really penetrates the rice. Throw it in the oven and an hour later you have a one-pot meal with an appealingly crisp crust.

2 tablespoons extra virgin olive oil

1 medium onion, finely chopped

1 red or yellow bell pepper, peeled if desired, cored, seeded, and chopped

1 tablespoon minced garlic

$^3/_4$ cup dried black beans, washed, picked over, and soaked if time allows

$1^1/_2$ cups long-grain rice

1 cup chopped tomato (canned are fine; don't bother to drain)

Salt and freshly ground black pepper

$^1/_2$ cup chopped parsley or fresh cilantro leaves

1 Put the oil in a large ovenproof pot over medium heat. A minute later, add the onion, bell pepper, and garlic and cook, stirring occasionally, until the onion is soft, about 5 minutes. Add the beans and cover with water. Bring to a boil, then turn the heat down to low so that the mixture bubbles gently. Cover loosely and cook, stirring occasionally and adding water if necessary, until the beans are about half-done—softening but still tough in the middle—about 40 minutes (an hour or more if you didn't soak the beans at all). Preheat the oven to 350°F.

2 Use an immersion blender or a potato masher to semipurée the beans in the pot (leave at least half unpuréed).

3 Stir in the rice, tomato, and a good amount of salt and pepper. (If you don't want a crust to develop, cover the pot.) Bake in the oven until the rice and beans are tender, anywhere between 30 and 60 minutes, adding a little water if needed. Taste and season with salt and pepper. Sprinkle with parsley and serve or store, covered, in the refrigerator for up to 2 days (reheat and stir in a little water and olive oil just before serving).

Baked Rice and White Beans, Tuscan Style. Omit the onion and tomatoes; the bell pepper is optional: Substitute white beans, like cannellini, navy, or Great Northern, for the black and add 2 to 3 tablespoons chopped fresh sage leaves (or just under 1 tablespoon dried) in Step 1. Proceed with the recipe and drizzle with good extra virgin olive oil just before serving.

Baked Rice and Red Kidney Beans, Jamaican Style. With coconut milk, irresistible: Replace the bell pepper with a fresh hot chile, the black beans with red kidney beans, and a 14-ounce can unsweetened coconut milk for the tomato. In Step 3, add about 2 teaspoons chopped fresh thyme leaves or $^1/_2$ to 1 teaspoon dried thyme, to taste.

Rice Pilaf

What makes a pilaf? Cooking the rice in butter or oil (and often onions or other vegetables) before adding other ingredients, at the very least a flavorful liquid like stock. Yellow rice is a form of pilaf, as is biryani, as, one could argue, is paella. It's a universal technique, and I try to cover many of the bases here. But the key, the aspect they all have in common, is the sautéeing of the rice at the beginning of cooking. That little step makes a world of difference, and pilaf is truly one of the great gems of basic home cooking (risotto, page 517, is more widely praised, and perhaps better known, but it is not better, and it's a little more challenging).

Other than that, much is up for grabs: The rice may be long- or short-grain (personally I think of basmati as the default, but short-grain has its own charm, and in some instances it's better), the liquid may be stock or wine or dairy or nondairy milk (or even yogurt), and the herbs, spices, and solid ingredients can all be varied according to your desires. To make what you might call Golden Pilaf, heat a large pinch of saffron threads (or a teaspoon of ground turmeric, which isn't as good but is a lot cheaper), with the stock.

Even brown rice is fair game, but the technique is slightly different; see page 514.

One other thing that is really great about pilaf: within limits, it can be reheated successfully, either in the microwave or on the stove. Just add a little water first, cover it, and reheat gently.

Rice Pilaf, Nine Ways

MAKES: 4 servings

TIME: About 30 minutes, plus a little time to rest

Only a tiny bit more complicated than plain rice, but with enormous potential, as you'll see. Note that not only may this be made in advance, it *should* be made (slightly) in advance.

2 to 4 tablespoons butter or extra virgin olive oil

1 cup chopped onion

1$^1/_2$ cups rice, preferably basmati

Salt and freshly ground black pepper

2$^1/_2$ cups vegetable stock (pages 101–102), warmed

Minced parsley leaves for garnish

1 Put the butter or oil in a large, deep skillet with a lid over medium-high heat. When the butter is melted or the oil is hot, add the onion. Cook, stirring, until the onion softens, about 5 minutes.

2 Add the rice all at once, turn the heat down to medium, and stir until the rice is glossy, completely coated with oil or butter, and starting to color lightly, about 5 minutes. Season well with salt and pepper, then turn the heat down to low and add the liquid all at once. Stir once or twice, then cover the pan.

3 Cook for about 15 minutes, or until most of the liquid is absorbed. Turn the heat to the absolute minimum (if you have an electric stove, turn the heat off and let the pan sit on the burner) and let rest for another 15 to 30 minutes. Check the seasoning, garnish, and serve.

Red or Green Rice Pilaf. Better known as Arroz Rojo or Verde, these are Mexican versions: Use olive or neutral oil, like grapeseed or corn, and add 1 teaspoon minced garlic just after you stir in the rice. For Arroz Rojo, add about 1 cup chopped tomato (canned is fine; don't bother to drain) just before you add stock; reduce the stock to 1$^3/_4$ cups. For Arroz Verde, add about 1 cup peeled roasted poblano (page 333). Finish with chopped parsley or fresh cilantro leaves and a squeeze of lemon or lime juice.

Pilaf with Currants and Pine Nuts. The Middle Eastern classic: Use butter unless you object. Along with the rice, add $^1/_4$ cup currants or raisins, 2 tablespoons pine nuts, 1 teaspoon ground cumin and $^1/_2$ teaspoon ground cinnamon.

Pilaf with Fruit and Nuts. Similar to the preceding variation, but a little more unusual: Use butter unless you object. Along with the rice, add $^1/_4$ cup slivered blanched almonds. When the rice is ready, stir in 2 tablespoons raisins, 3 or 4 each chopped dried apricots and pitted prunes (or use whatever dried fruit you like), and a tablespoon of honey.

Pilaf with Chickpeas, Peas, Limas, or other Beans: Just before adding the stock, stir in 1 cup cooked chickpeas, raw green peas (frozen are okay, and you need not defrost first), fresh or frozen limas or edamame beans, or drained cooked or canned (or frozen) pigeon peas or black-eyed peas. Season with 1 teaspoon fresh thyme leaves, if available, and a bay leaf.

Vermicelli Pilaf. Related to Bulgur Pilaf with Vermicelli (page 556) and, though not quite as common or classic, really great: Break enough vermicelli or angel hair pasta into 1-inch lengths to make about a cup. Use oil or butter and cook this along with the rice until nicely browned. Proceed with the recipe, increasing the stock to about 3 cups.

Pilaf with Spinach or Other Greens. Add 2 cups trimmed, carefully washed, and chopped spinach, chard, sorrel, or beet greens along with the onion. Add 1 teaspoon minced garlic just after you stir in the rice, then proceed with the recipe, reducing the liquid by about $^1/_4$ cup.

Mexican Rice with Vegetables. Often (and not badly) made with frozen vegetables: In Step 2, just after adding the rice, stir in $^1/_3$ cup each peeled and minced carrot, celery, red or other bell pepper, and trimmed and minced green beans or whole peas. Proceed with the recipe, garnishing with parsley or fresh cilantro.

Kimchi Rice. Use dark sesame oil. Don't salt the rice in Step 1. In Step 2, just after adding the rice, stir in $^1/_2$ cup chopped Kimchi (page 96). Proceed with the recipe, seasoning with soy sauce as needed and garnishing with sliced scallion.

Biryani

MAKES: 4 servings
TIME: About 30 minutes

One of the great pilaf-style dishes of India, almost always made with basmati rice. Indian vegetarians would use paneer (firm, fresh, homemade cheese), but tofu is much more convenient. It can also be made with no protein at all, of course.

A few saffron threads or 1 teaspoon ground turmeric

$1^1/_2$ cups vegetable stock (pages 101–102) or water, warmed

2 tablespoons butter or neutral oil, like grapeseed or corn

6 cardamom pods or 2 teaspoons ground cardamom

Pinch ground cloves

One 3-inch cinnamon stick or $^1/_2$ teaspoon ground cinnamon

2 bay leaves

2 cups chopped onion

1 tablespoon minced garlic

1 tablespoon peeled, minced or grated fresh ginger or 1 teaspoon ground

Salt and freshly ground black pepper

$1^1/_2$ cups long-grain rice, preferably basmati

$1^1/_2$ cups yogurt

1 pound firm tofu or fresh cheese (optional)

Minced fresh cilantro leaves for garnish

1 If you're using saffron, combine it in a pot with the stock. Put the butter or oil in a large, deep skillet with a lid over medium-high heat. When the butter melts or the oil is hot, turn the heat down to medium and add the cardamom, cloves, cinnamon, bay leaf, and turmeric if you're using it. Cook, stirring very frequently, until the spices are fragrant, about 2 minutes.

Add the onion, garlic, and ginger, along with a large pinch of salt and a sprinkling of pepper, and cook, stirring, until the onion softens, about 5 minutes. Add the rice all at once and stir until the rice is glossy and completely coated with oil or butter, 2 or 3 minutes. Lower the heat, then add the yogurt and stock and stir. Stir in the tofu, adjust the heat so the mixture barely bubbles, and cover the pan.

 Cook for 15 to 20 minutes, then check the rice. When the rice is tender and the liquid is absorbed, it's done. If not, cook for 2 or 3 minutes and check again. Remove the cinnamon stick, if you're using it, and the bay leaf (the cardamom pods are good to eat), taste and adjust the seasoning, then garnish and serve.

Rice Cooked in Onions

Soubise

MAKES: 4 to 6 servings
TIME: 1 hour, largely unattended

Ⓜ

This is a great Thanksgiving dish: It'll keep warm for a long time or can be kept hot over a very low flame (and, if it browns on the bottom, so much the better). I've modified it in a few ways since I first made it (with thanks to Julia Child), reducing the fat (or at least making a portion of it optional), adding saffron (for glorious color), increasing the amount of rice (and using basmati), and cooking the onions a bit longer at the beginning.

The most difficult part of the preparation lies in slicing the onions, but the food processor's slicing disk was created for tasks exactly like this one: From the time you set it up to the time the onions are sliced, about 5 minutes should pass, and you will not end up in tears.

Salt and freshly ground black pepper

3 to 6 tablespoons butter

1 cup basmati rice

6 to 8 cups sliced onion (about 4 or 5 large)

Large pinch saffron threads (optional)

1/2 cup heavy cream (optional)

Chopped parsley leaves for garnish

 Bring a saucepan of water to a boil and salt it. Meanwhile, melt 3 tablespoons butter over medium heat in a broad, deep skillet or casserole with a lid.

 When the water boils, cook the rice in it, stirring occasionally, until it loses its translucence, about 5 minutes. Add the onion to the melted butter along with a large pinch of salt and some pepper and cook, stirring occasionally, just until the onion begins to soften, about 5 minutes. Drain the rice (leave it wet) and add it to the onion along with the saffron if you're using it. Stir, turn the heat to minimum, and cover.

 Cook, stirring occasionally, for about 45 minutes, or until the onion is very soft and the rice cooked through; don't stir at all during the last 10 or 15 minutes, so that the bottom browns a bit. Taste and adjust the seasoning, then stir in the heavy cream and/or remaining butter if you like. Heat through once more, turn off the heat, and let sit for 10 minutes or so (or longer; this will retain its heat for at least 30 minutes and can be reheated gently if you like). Garnish with the parsley and serve.

Yellow Rice, the Best Way

MAKES: 4 servings
TIME: 30 minutes

Ⓕ

There is the right way to make this and a number of easy ways; even the easy ways are good, but this right here—with saffron and other spices and a couple of vegetables—is really the ultimate. Vegan with oil instead of butter.

2 1/2 cups vegetable stock (pages 101–102) or water

Large pinch saffron threads

2 to 4 tablespoons butter or extra virgin olive oil

1 cup chopped onion

1 red bell pepper, cored, seeded, and chopped

1 tablespoon minced garlic

1^1/$_2$ cups white rice

Salt and freshly ground black pepper

1 ripe tomato, cored, seeded (pages 372–373), and chopped

^{1}/$_8$ teaspoon ground allspice

2 bay leaves

1 cup fresh or frozen peas

Chopped parsley leaves for garnish

Lemon wedges

❶ Warm the stock with the saffron. Put the butter or oil in a large, deep skillet over medium-high heat. When the butter melts or the oil is hot, add the onion and bell pepper and cook, stirring occasionally, until the onion turns translucent, about 5 minutes.

❷ Stir in the garlic and the rice, sprinkle everything with salt and pepper, turn the heat to medium, and stir until the rice is glossy, completely coated with oil or butter, and starting to color lightly, about 5 minutes. Add the tomato, allspice, bay leaves, peas, and stock; stir, adjust the heat so that the liquid boils steadily but not violently, and cover.

❸ Cook for about 15 minutes, or until most of the liquid is absorbed. Turn the heat to the absolute minimum (if you have an electric stove, turn the heat off and let the pan sit on the burner) and let rest for another 15 to 30 minutes. Check the seasoning, garnish, and serve with lemon wedges.

Yellow Rice, the Fast Way. Omit the red pepper, tomato, allspice, bay leaves, and peas: Bring 3 cups of stock or water to a boil. Put 2 tablespoons olive oil in the skillet over medium-high heat. When hot, add the onion and a sprinkling of salt and pepper. Cook, stirring occasionally, until the onion softens and becomes translucent, about 5 minutes. Add the rice to the onion and cook, stirring occasionally, until glossy. Add the saffron if you're using it (or use 1 teaspoon ground turmeric), then the boiling stock. Adjust the heat and finish cooking as directed.

Brown Rice Pilaf with Two Mushrooms

MAKES: 4 servings
TIME: About 1 hour, largely unattended

You can substitute brown rice for white in any pilaf, simply by using parcooked brown rice as described in the sidebar on page 506. But cooking the raw brown rice in oil first, then adding the onion and other vegetables, gives it incredible flavor and decreases the overall cooking time somewhat without making the onion mushy. By beginning this way, you can incorporate any of the variations or suggestions for the white rice pilafs on pages 511–512, adjusting the amount of liquid and the time accordingly.

I make another change here, though it isn't essential: Cooking the shiitake mushrooms separately makes them crisp and adds a nice textural contrast. But you could just add the shiitakes to the simmering rice during the last 10 or 15 minutes of cooking.

Brown basmati is definitely the way to go here; not that other rices are unusable, but the aroma of brown basmati sautéing in olive oil will just knock you out. If you want to use white basmati, use 1^1/$_2$ cups with the same amount of liquid and decrease the cooking time in Step 2 to 20 minutes.

^{1}/$_2$ cup dried porcini or other mushrooms

2^1/$_2$ cups vegetable stock (pages 101–102), Mushroom Stock (page 102), or water

6 tablespoons extra virgin olive oil (or half oil and half butter)

1^1/$_4$ cups brown basmati rice

1 cup sliced onion

Salt and freshly ground black pepper

1½ cups sliced shiitake mushroom caps (reserve the stems for stock if you like)

1 Combine the dried porcini with the stock in a small saucepan and warm while you begin cooking the rice. Add half the oil to a deep skillet with a lid over medium-high heat. When hot, add the rice and cook, stirring occasionally, until it is extremely aromatic and beginning to brown, about 10 minutes.

2 Toss in the onion and the softened porcini (hold off on the stock) and continue to cook, sprinkling with salt and pepper and stirring occasionally, until the onion begins to soften, about 5 minutes. Add the liquid all at once, adjust the heat so that the mixture bubbles very gently, and cover. Total cooking time from this point will be about 40 minutes; check after 20 and 30 minutes to make sure there's enough liquid and, if there is not, add about ½ cup more.

3 About 15 minutes before the pilaf is done, put the remaining oil in a skillet over medium-high heat. When hot, add the shiitakes, along with a large pinch of salt and some pepper, and cook, stirring occasionally, until the mushrooms brown on the edges, about 10 minutes.

4 When the rice is tender, uncover and cook over medium heat until almost all the liquid is gone. Stir in the browned shiitakes, taste and adjust the seasoning, and serve immediately.

Simpler-Than-Pilaf Baked Rice

MAKES: 4 servings

TIME: 30 minutes

F

This basic, valuable technique is used worldwide; it's a kind of combination of pilaf and paella, but simpler than either, especially if you omit the spices and go with just salt and pepper. Use oil and the pilaf is vegan.

Absolutely use white basmati here if you have it. Nothing else is the same.

2 tablespoons butter or 1 tablespoon neutral oil, like grapeseed or corn

One 3-inch cinnamon stick

2 cloves

5 white cardamom pods

1 cup long-grain rice, preferably basmati

Salt and freshly ground black pepper

1 Preheat the oven to 350°F. Put half the butter or all of the oil in an ovenproof pan with a lid over medium heat. When the butter is melted or the oil is hot, add the spices and cook for about a minute. Add the rice and some salt and pepper and cook, stirring, for about a minute.

2 Add 1½ cups water, bring to a boil, put in the oven, and bake for 10 minutes. Remove the rice from the oven, but do not uncover; let it rest in a warm place for another 10 minutes. Remove the cinnamon and cloves (the cardamom pods are good to eat); taste and adjust the seasoning if necessary, stir in the remaining butter if you're using it, and serve immediately.

Simpler Baked Brown Rice. The main recipe and any of the variations can be made with brown rice: Increase the liquid to 2 cups, the baking time to 30 minutes, and the resting time to 15 minutes. Alternatively, start with parboiled brown rice (see page 506) and treat it exactly as you would the white rice.

Simpler Baked Rice with Herbs. This is good with a tablespoon or so of minced shallot, garlic, or scallion cooked with the herb in Step 1: Omit the cinnamon, cloves, and cardamom. Start with about ¼ cup shredded or roughly chopped fresh basil, shiso, parsley, or dill. Cook half the herb in the butter in Step 1. Stir in the rest at the end of the resting time.

Simpler Baked Rice with Curry. A near-pilaf and a nobrainer: Add, in Step 1, a pinch of saffron threads if you have it, a teaspoon of cumin seeds, and a teaspoon of curry powder or garam masala (to make your own, see page 815 or 816). Garnish, if you like, with minced fresh cilantro.

Simpler Baked Rice with Coconut. Omit the cinnamon, cloves, and cardamom. In Step 1, cook $^1/_2$ cup shredded coconut in the butter or oil until lightly browned; remove half of it and set it aside before adding the rice. Proceed with the recipe, stirring in the coconut at the end of the resting time.

Simpler Baked Rice with Tomato. Omit the cinnamon, cloves, and cardamom: Start with 1 medium to large chopped tomato or about $^3/_4$ cup drained canned tomato, $^1/_4$ teaspoon cayenne (or to taste), and, if you have it, a large pinch of saffron threads. Reduce the water to 1 cup and stir in $^1/_4$ cup roughly chopped parsley or fresh basil at the end of the resting time.

6 Ideas for Simpler-Than-Pilaf Baked Rice

Following the pattern in the recipe, try any of these possibilities, alone or in combination:

1. Legumes: Use $^1/_2$ to 1 cup cooked beans, chickpeas, or lentils or raw (frozen are fine) peas, snap peas (chopped), green beans (chopped), or limas.
2. Nuts and fruit: Use about $^1/_4$ cup each pine nuts (or other nuts) or raisins (or currants or other dried fruit).
3. Aromatics: Start with a couple tablespoons each of finely chopped onion, celery, and carrot (a teaspoon of garlic wouldn't hurt) and a couple of sprigs of thyme. Increase the initial cooking time to 2 minutes before adding the rice.
4. Mushrooms: Use $^1/_2$ to 1 cup fresh mushrooms, like button or shiitake, or reconstituted porcini or shiitake mushrooms, removing about half of them after the initial cooking in butter (increase this time to 2 minutes) and returning them to the rice after it's cooked.
5. Vegetables: Use $^1/_2$ to 1 cup cooked and chopped carrot, potato, turnip, or other root vegetable.
6. Other spices: In the initial toasting, try mustard seeds, cumin seeds, coriander seeds, nigella seeds, or minced fresh or dried chiles.

The Basics of Risotto

Risotto is about three things: short-grain rice, the patience to stir in good-tasting liquid while it cooks, and whatever seasonings and ingredients you choose to integrate. Of all the sophisticated rice dishes in a cook's repertoire, none (save pilaf, page 511 is simpler once learned, and none can be varied with quite the freedom. When you master risotto, the sky's the limit. It just takes a little practice and really not even much of that.

According to the canon, you must use Arborio or one of its relatives (see page 504) to make "real" risotto. (Of course according to the canon, you must use rich chicken stock too. And, according to the canon, you must stir nonstop. So much for the canon.) But I've long had success with most short-grain rice, especially the common short-grain varieties, which cost about a fifth of the ridiculously overpriced Arborio; try them. You may even make risotto with short-grain brown rice (see "The Easy Way to Substitute Brown Rice for White," page 506). You will lose creaminess but may feel that it's made up for in deep, nutty flavor.

Many people have been scared off of making risotto by the claim that it must be stirred constantly. The truth is that the liquid must be added a bit at a time, and the heat must be kept fairly high, and there's a lot of stirring. But though you must pay attention while making risotto, that doesn't mean constant stirring.

Let's just stay once you start the process, you shouldn't leave the stove for more than a minute or so at a time. Because the heat is relatively high and there's a delicate balance between rice and liquid, the danger of scorching is real (nonstick skillets are helpful but not essential). Just be careful not to overcook, but to handle just as you would pasta: remove the rice from heat when there is still a tiny bit of crunch in the center of the rice kernels.

Once you've made risotto a couple of times, you can start to experiment with ingredients. The recipes here will help get you started, but you can add virtually anything to a risotto during the last few minutes of cooking. This makes risotto a terrific way to use leftovers like cooked vegetables.

It is customary to pass additional Parmesan cheese at the table, but that's not the only way to add a final jolt of luxurious flavor. Try drizzling on a spoonful of pesto or one of the other herb pastes in that section (page 766). Or veer away from Italian tradition with a little Chile-Garlic Paste (page 830), Citrus Sprinkle (page 818), or even a dusting of garam masala, curry powder, or za'atar (see page 815, 816, or 818).

For vegans, it's easy enough to use oil and skip the cheese but a little trickier to duplicate the creaminess they lend to the dish. Replacing some of the stock or water with rice, oat, or nut milk (specifically hazelnut or almond) will help a lot, though they're all slightly sweet and none is entirely neutral in flavor (soy milk, in fact, is simply too strong). See page 29 for more about making vegan substitutions.

Simple Risotto

MAKES: 4 to 6 servings
TIME: 45 minutes

Read the preceding text, learn the basic technique here, then use the recipes and suggestions that follow to build on it. If you don't have vegetable stock on hand, I suggest making Simple, Easy, and Fast Vegetable Stock (page 101) or just poaching a carrot, an onion, a celery stalk, and a garlic clove in water for 20 minutes and using that. If you must use straight water, up the other flavorings a bit. If you use oil instead of butter and omit the cheese, you'll have vegan risotto.

4 to 6 cups vegetable stock (pages 101–102)

Large pinch saffron threads (optional)

4 to 6 tablespoons butter or extra virgin olive oil, to taste

1 medium onion, minced

1 1/2 cups Arborio or other short- or medium-grain rice

Salt and freshly ground black pepper

1/2 cup dry white wine or water

Freshly grated Parmesan cheese (optional)

1 Put the stock in a medium saucepan over low heat; add the saffron if you're using it. Put 2 tablespoons of the butter or oil in a large, deep nonstick skillet over medium heat. (Allow the remaining butter to soften while you cook.) When the butter is melted or the oil is hot, add the onion and cook, stirring occasionally, until it softens, 3 to 5 minutes.

2 Add the rice and cook, stirring occasionally, until it is glossy and coated with butter, 2 to 3 minutes. Add a little salt and pepper, then the white wine. Stir and let the liquid bubble away.

3 Use a ladle to begin to add the warmed stock, 1/2 cup or so at a time, stirring after each addition and every minute or so. When the stock is just about evaporated, add more. The mixture should be neither soupy nor dry. Keep the heat medium to medium-high and stir frequently.

4 Begin tasting the rice 20 minutes after you add it; you want it to be tender but with still a tiny bit of crunch; it could take as long as 30 minutes to reach this stage. When it does, stir in 2 to 4 tablespoons softened butter or oil (more is better, at least from the perspective of taste!) and at least 1/2 cup of Parmesan if you're using it. Taste, adjust the seasoning, and serve immediately, passing additional Parmesan at the table if you like.

Risotto with Herbs. Fresh herbs change the character of any risotto: Along with the cheese, stir in 1/4 to 1/2 cup chopped leaves of parsley, basil, dill, mint, chervil, oregano, marjoram, or a combination.

Risotto with Vegetables and Herbs. In Step 1, add 1 stalk celery and 1 medium carrot, chopped, along with the chopped leaves of 1 sprig fresh rosemary or thyme or 1/2 teaspoon dried. Cook until the vegetables are glossy and the onion softens, then proceed with the recipe.

Risotto with Lemon. Follow the preceding variation, but when the rice is almost done (Step 4), stir in the grated zest of a lemon. Stir in the juice of the lemon along with the butter at the very end. Add the Parmesan and serve as directed.

Risotto with Red Wine. Omit the saffron and white wine. Substitute a bottle of decent red wine for the stock (use water or stock to make up the difference). The color will be a lovely reddish brown.

Risotto with Four Cheeses. It's worth noting that good, creamy Gorgonzola can almost always substitute for Parmesan in finishing risotto; but this combo is over the top: When you would ordinarily stir in the Parmesan, add equal amounts (about $^1/_4$ to $^1/_3$ cup each) of grated Parmesan or pecorino Romano, chopped Gorgonzola or other creamy blue cheese, and shredded or chopped fontina or other semisoft but not-too-mild cheese. Other cheeses that will do nicely: cubed or shredded mozzarella; shredded mild cheese, like jack; any hard cheese, like Grana Padano.

Risotto with Nuts. Chop about $^1/_4$ cup toasted hazelnuts or almonds (see page 321) or shelled pistachios and stir them in with the cheese.

Risotto with Dried and Fresh Mushrooms

MAKES: 4 to 6 servings
TIME: 45 minutes

To me, this is an important version of risotto: not only does its intensity come with very little labor, but I always have dried mushrooms on hand (the addition of fresh mushrooms is a bonus). Note that any vegetable—artichoke hearts, green beans, snow peas, and so on—can be cooked on the side and stirred into the risotto at the last minute, as

the shiitakes are here (see the list that follows). Use the oil and skip the cheese, and the risotto becomes vegan.

> $^1/_2$ cup dried porcini mushrooms
>
> 4 to 5 cups vegetable stock (pages 101–102)
>
> Large pinch saffron threads (optional)
>
> 4 to 6 tablespoons butter or extra virgin olive oil, to taste
>
> 1 medium onion, minced
>
> $1^1/_2$ cups Arborio or other short- or medium-grain rice
>
> Salt and freshly ground black pepper
>
> $^1/_2$ cup dry white wine or water
>
> 1 cup slivered shiitake or portobello mushroom caps
>
> Freshly grated Parmesan cheese (optional)

1 Rinse the dried mushrooms once or twice, then soak them in hot water to cover. Put the stock in a medium saucepan over low heat; add the saffron if you're using it. Put 2 tablespoons of the butter or oil in a large, deep nonstick skillet over medium heat. (Allow the remaining butter to soften while you cook.) When the butter is melted or the oil is hot, add the onion and cook, stirring occasionally, until it softens, 3 to 5 minutes.

2 Add the rice and cook, stirring occasionally, until it is glossy and coated with butter, 2 to 3 minutes. Add a little salt and pepper, then the white wine. Stir and let the liquid bubble away. Drain the porcini and chop them, then stir them in, along with about half of their soaking liquid.

3 Use a ladle to begin to add the warmed stock, $^1/_2$ cup or so at a time, stirring after each addition and every minute or so. When the stock is just about evaporated, add more. The mixture should be neither soupy nor dry. Keep the heat medium to medium-high and stir frequently. Meanwhile, put the remaining butter or oil (more will make a creamier risotto) in a small skillet over medium-high heat. When the butter is melted or the oil is hot, add the fresh mushrooms and cook, stirring occasionally, until lightly browned and almost crisp, about 10 minutes.

4 Begin tasting the rice 20 minutes after you add it; you want it to be tender but with still a tiny bit of crunch; it could take as long as 30 minutes to reach this stage. When it does, stir in the cooked mushrooms, with their butter, and at least ¹/₂ cup of Parmesan if you're using it. Taste, adjust the seasoning, and serve immediately, passing additional Parmesan at the table if you like.

3 Simple Substitutions for Risotto with Mushrooms

Use the dried mushrooms or not, as you like. Then substitute one of the following for the fresh mushrooms.

1. Fresh peas, snow peas, snap peas, or green beans (cut up): Cook until bright and just tender; stir in at the last minute.
2. Beets, turnips, potatoes, carrots, or other root vegetables: Cut into small cubes and parboil (page 241) just until tender (or use leftovers); cook quickly in butter until lightly browned, then stir in at the last minute.
3. Other vegetables, like broccoli or cauliflower: Cut (or break) into small florets and parboil very quickly, just until tender; cook in butter for a minute or two, then stir in at the last minute.

The Basics of Fried Rice

This basic dish of China is almost as easily varied as pasta and has one distinct advantage: It can be made with leftover rice. In fact, oddly enough, it *should* be made with leftover rice—or at least rice that's been cooked ahead. Warm, just-made rice inevitably clumps together, which is why so many novice cooks (I remember this vividly) believe that well-made fried rice is somehow impossible to produce at home. But when cooked rice is chilled—even for a few hours, though a day or so is even better—it dries out, separates into individual grains, and can be stir-fried with a minimum of oil.

Ironically, the rice that is delivered with Chinese takeout meals is pretty good for this purpose, but your own-made basmati—brown or white or both—is even better.

The choices of vegetables and other major ingredients is unlimited, but if you follow the proportions in this

prototypical recipe you will never go far wrong. There are some other points to make, however; see the sidebar above.

Simplest Fried Rice with Peppers

MAKES: 4 servings
TIME: 20 minutes with cooked rice

The easiest fried rice dish, mildly flavored, not earth-shattering, but very fast, very good, and a respectful treatment of a revered leftover. Move to the next recipe if you're looking for something more complex or exciting.

- 1/4 cup peanut or neutral oil, like grapeseed or corn
- 2 cups bell pepper strips, preferably a mixture of red and yellow
- Salt and freshly ground black pepper
- 3 to 4 cups cooked white or brown rice (start with about 1 1/2 cups raw), preferably long-grain
- 2 tablespoons soy sauce, or to taste
- 1 tablespoon dark sesame oil

1 Put the oil in a large skillet, preferably nonstick, over medium-high heat. A minute later, add the peppers, sprinkle on some salt and pepper, and raise the heat to high. Cook, stirring occasionally, until they begin to brown, about 10 minutes.

2 Add the rice, separating it with your hands as you do so. Cook, stirring and breaking up the rice lumps, until it is hot and begins to brown, about 10 minutes. Stir in the soy sauce and sesame oil, taste and adjust the seasoning, and serve.

Simplest Fried Rice with Onions. If you like, use half peppers and half onions, but cook the onions on their own for a few minutes first: Substitute 2 cups thinly sliced onion for the peppers.

Fried Rice, with or without Egg

MAKES: 4 to 6 servings
TIME: 20 minutes with cooked rice

A little more complex than the preceding recipe, made just like a standard stir-fry: You choose your other main ingredients in whatever combination you like—here, vegetables and tofu, at least to start—and cook them one or two at a time, each in a little bit of oil (a nonstick or well-seasoned pan is an essential piece of equipment) over high heat, until they are pretty much done. Then set them aside in a bowl.

Add a bit more oil and the basic aromatics, like garlic and ginger, followed by the rice. When that is hot and glossy, you can add an egg or two if you like, return the cooked ingredients to the mix, and add soy sauce and other seasonings.

The quality and freshness of the dish will be a revelation. Vegan without the eggs.

- 1 cup fresh or frozen peas
- 3 tablespoons peanut or neutral oil, like grapeseed or corn
- 1 medium onion, roughly chopped
- 1 bell pepper, cored, seeded, and roughly chopped
- 1 1/2 cups cubed firm tofu
- 1 tablespoon minced garlic, or to taste
- 1 tablespoon peeled and minced fresh ginger, or to taste
- 3 to 4 cups cooked white or brown rice (start with about 1 1/2 cups raw), preferably basmati or jasmine
- 2 eggs, lightly beaten (optional)
- 1/4 cup Shaoxing wine, sherry, white wine, stock, or water
- 2 tablespoons soy sauce
- 1 tablespoon dark sesame oil
- Salt and freshly ground black pepper to taste
- 1/4 cup minced scallion or fresh cilantro

1 If the peas are frozen, soak them in cold water to defrost while you begin cooking. Put 1 tablespoon of the oil in a wok or large skillet over high heat. A minute later, add the onion and bell pepper and cook, stirring occasionally, until they soften and begin to brown, 5 to 10 minutes. Lower the heat if the mixture threatens to scorch. Use a slotted spoon to transfer them to a bowl.

2 Add the tofu and cook, again over high heat, stirring infrequently, until nicely browned, 5 to 10 minutes. Add to the bowl with the vegetables. Drain the peas if necessary and add them to the skillet; cook, shaking the skillet, for about a minute, or until hot. Add them to the bowl.

❸ Put the remaining oil in the skillet, followed by the garlic and ginger. About 15 seconds later, begin to add the rice, a bit at a time, breaking up any clumps with your fingers and tossing it with the oil. When all the rice is added, make a well in its center and break the eggs into it if you're using them; scramble them a bit, then incorporate them into the rice.

❹ Return the tofu and vegetables to the pan and stir to integrate. Add the wine and cook, stirring, for about a minute. Add the soy sauce and sesame oil, then taste and add salt and pepper if necessary. Turn off the heat, stir in the scallion, and serve.

Basic Fried Rice with Frozen Vegetables. No apologies; this is better than you might think: For the peas, substitute mixed peas and carrots or peas, carrots, and corn. You can even use frozen bell pepper strips if you like and probably never notice.

Basic Fried Rice, Thai Style. In Thailand, they call this Chinese food: In Step 4, stir in a teaspoon or two (or to taste) red curry paste (to make your own, see page 830). Garnish with cilantro and scallion.

Basic Fried Rice with Lettuce. Surprised? Try it: In Step 4, stir in 2 cups thinly sliced iceberg or romaine lettuce.

Pineapple Fried Rice. Undeniably popular, for good reason: In Step 4, stir in $1^1/_2$ cups chopped fresh pineapple (or, okay, you can use canned, but unsweetened please, and drained) when adding the rice; adding a diced tomato at the same time, along with a little ketchup, will give you a more complex and fun-looking dish. Proceed with the recipe.

13 Good Additions to Fried Rice

The list of things you can add to fried rice is longer than the list of things you cannot. But they basically fall into three categories: vegetables, protein, and seasonings.

Vegetables:

1. Very tender vegetables, or those that can be eaten raw, can be stirred in at the last minute, like the lettuce in the variation.
2. Those that will cook in about the same amount of time as the onion or pepper (scallion, shredded zucchini, corn kernels, etc.) should be cooked with or instead of the onions.
3. "Harder" vegetables—broccoli, cauliflower, eggplant, potato, winter squash—should either be cut into very tiny bits, so they will cook in just about the same amount of time as the onions, or quickly parboiled (or deep-fried if you prefer) before incorporating as any other vegetable.
4. Tomatoes are a special case: Cut them into small wedges and add just after the rice, or you will have tomato sauce. (Not that there's anything wrong with that, and if that's what you want, add the tomatoes when the onions are about half cooked.)
5. You can also garnish with raw vegetables, like cucumbers made according to the Quick-Pickled Vegetables recipe (page 95), chopped cabbage, or tomato wedges.

Protein:

6. Any tofu—smoked, pressed, flavored, frozen and thawed, you name it—is great here. Add as you would the tofu in the main recipe.
7. Also good are cubed or crumbled tempeh or seitan. I like to fry them in a little oil as if they were a vegetable.
8. Hard-cooked egg is another good option, either chopped or sliced and added right after the rice.

Seasonings:

9. Fresh chiles, minced, at the beginning, or chile paste of any kind at the end, always to taste.
10. Hoisin sauce (or ketchup; they're really not that different), stirred in just after the rice.
11. Basil (preferably Thai) 10 or 15 big leaves, torn up and added at the last moment, instead of or in addition to cilantro.

12. Curry powder or almost any other spice mix (to make your own, see pages 810–819), stirred in just before you add the rice.

13. Nori "Shake" (page 817) is good, as are toasted sesame seeds (see page 321).

The Basics of Paella

In Spain, home-cooked paella is a Sunday ritual designed to expand the week's leftovers into a filling meal. Take a bit of chicken here, some sausage there, top with a bit of seafood, and cook it all together with rice in an open-air pan that concentrates their flavors. Fresh vegetables are usually an afterthought.

The challenge of vegetarian paella, though, is not the technique but simply that it hasn't been popularized. If you choose vegetables that drip savory juices into the rice while it's cooking, and the right combination of seasonings, it's the meat and fish that become the afterthought. And there are plenty of vegetables—and even fruits— that do the job perfectly, as many Spaniards have known for centuries.

My vegetarian paella shares much with the more common type: First you make the sofrito, usually a mixture of aromatic vegetables—onions or garlic—herbs, and sometimes tomato paste, fried in olive oil until it becomes a thick paste in which the rice is cooked. Saffron is the traditional seasoning of choice, but I think smoked paprika is a great addition (or substitution) and adds deep flavors.

Another trick is to season the paella again at the end of cooking or with a condiment like garlic mayonnaise (Aïoli, page 771) or the less-than-orthodox Chimichurri (page 769). The real deal, however, is the pan: It need not be a paellera (a traditional two-handled paella pan), but it should be wide enough to hold the grains of rice in a thin layer. This will help develop the crusty bits of rice that can develop at the bottom of the pan (called *socarat*) that are many people's favorite part.

Since most home cooks (including me) don't own such a big pan, and using two pans is such a hassle, I pre-fer starting paella on the stove in a roasting pan or my largest skillet and moving it to the oven. There, whatever you decide to put on top does its magic on the rice, roasting along merrily while you go do something else. And, to properly develop the socarat, just put the pan back on the stove for a couple minutes before serving.

Paella with Tomatoes

MAKES: 4 to 6 servings
TIME: 30 minutes

Ⓕ Ⓥ

With caramelized tomatoes on top and a dish on the table in half an hour, this is gorgeous and stunningly easy. When tomatoes aren't in season, try one of the variations.

3¹/₂ cups vegetable stock (pages 101–102) or water

1 pound ripe tomatoes, cored and cut into thick wedges

Salt and freshly ground black pepper

¹/₄ cup extra virgin olive oil

1 medium onion, minced

1 tablespoon minced garlic

1 tablespoon tomato paste

Large pinch saffron threads (optional)

2 teaspoons smoked or other paprika

2 cups Spanish or other short-grain white rice or parcooked short-grain brown rice (see page 506)

Minced parsley for garnish

❶ Preheat the oven to 450°F. Warm the stock in a saucepan. Put the tomatoes in a medium bowl, sprinkle with salt and pepper, and drizzle them with 1 tablespoon of the olive oil. Toss gently to coat.

❷ Put the remaining oil in a 10- or 12-inch oven-proof skillet over medium-high heat. Add the onion and garlic, sprinkle with salt and pepper, and cook, stirring occasionally, until the vegetables soften, 3 to 5 minutes. Stir in the tomato paste, saffron if you're using it, and paprika and cook for a minute more. Add the rice and cook, stirring occasionally, until it's shiny, another minute or two. Carefully add the warm stock and stir until just combined.

③ Put the tomato wedges on top of the rice and drizzle with the juices that accumulated in the bottom of the bowl. Put the pan in the oven and roast, undisturbed, for 15 minutes. Check to see if the rice is dry and just tender. If not, return the pan to the oven for another 5 minutes. If the rice looks too dry at this point, but still isn't quite done, add a small amount of stock, wine, or water. When the rice is ready, turn off the oven and let it sit for at least 5 and up to 15 minutes.

④ Remove the pan from the oven and sprinkle with parsley. If you like, put the pan over high heat for a few minutes to develop a bit of a bottom crust before serving.

Simple Paella with Eggplant. Instead of the tomatoes, use 1 pound eggplant—peeled if you like—and cubed. When you put it in the bowl, increase the olive oil you toss it with to 2 tablespoons.

Simple Paella with Mushroom Caps. Instead of the tomatoes, use 1 pound of fresh mushrooms, like cremini, shiitake, or baby bellas. Trim the stems and save them for another use, but leave the caps whole. Proceed with the recipe, putting the caps on top of the rice, smooth side up.

Simple Paella with Spinach and Lemon Zest. You'll have to pile the spinach up on top of the rice, but it will cook down and form a lovely green topping: Instead of the tomatoes, use 1 pound fresh spinach, coarsely chopped. When you put it in the bowl with the olive oil, add 1 tablespoon minced lemon zest.

Simple Paella with Eggs. I love this one: Use the main recipe or the mushroom variation. Or omit the tomatoes and feature only eggs. In Step 3, use a large spoon to make 4 indentations in the rice mixture and carefully crack an egg into each. Proceed with the recipe.

Simple Paella with Oranges, Olives, and Saffron. Warm and complex: Add a pinch of saffron to the stock or water as it warms. Instead of the tomatoes, use 2 medium oranges, preferably Valencia. Zest one of them. Peel and slice them crosswise into wheels. In Step 2, toss them with the olive oil, along with a handful of chopped pitted green olives and a few strands of the orange zest.

Simple Paella with Fava Beans. You could also make this with limas or edamame: Instead of the tomatoes, use 1 cup shelled and peeled fava beans (frozen are fine).

Simple Paella with Prunes. Wacky-sounding and takes about 15 minutes longer, but deeply flavored and delicious and perfect when tomatoes are out of season: Instead of the tomatoes, use 8 or 10 pitted prunes; cut them all in half. When you toss them with the olive oil, add $1/4$ cup warm red wine or port and 2 teaspoons minced fresh rosemary. Cover the bowl and let the prunes steep for 15 minutes. Proceed with the recipe, pressing the fruit down into the rice a bit after you put them on top.

The Basics of Stuck-Pot Rice

If you love the browned crusty bits of rice, potatoes, or anything else that sticks to the bottom of a pan, these three stuck-pot recipes and variations may be your dream come true. Plus, they're among the easiest ways to get an impressive rice dish on the table: You just set up the pan, then walk away for a while. And the upside-down tumble of rice, with the crust sitting on top, is drop-dead gorgeous.

Use brown rice here if you like. Just increase the pre-cooking time to 15 minutes. The kernels will be slightly less starchy than with white basmati rice, but the flavor will be deep and delicious.

And don't worry if the crust at the bottom of the pan comes out in several pieces, which it sometimes does. In central Asia, where this dish originates, that part is often just broken into crisp chunks and served alongside the mound of rice.

A final word: If your lid isn't absolutely tight-fitting (and even if it is), it's worth the extra step to line the pot lid with a cloth. This absorbs water so the condensation from the lid doesn't drip back into the rice. Normally that doesn't matter, but when you're trying to dry out the bottom of the pan to form a crisp crust, you need every drop of water you can get on top to cook the rice through.

Stuck-Pot Rice with Yogurt and Spices

MAKES: 4 servings

TIME: 40 minutes

Here the rice itself forms the crust at the bottom of the pot, making this dish super-simple, super-crunchy, and utterly addictive. You'd think the yogurt might clump up or even curdle, but just the opposite is true; the rice has an unbeatable creamy texture and tangy flavor.

Salt

$1^1/_2$ cups white or brown basmati rice

Freshly ground black pepper

$^1/_4$ cup peanut or neutral oil, like grapeseed or corn

$^1/_4$ cup yogurt, preferably whole milk

1 tablespoon freshly squeezed lime juice

1 tablespoon curry powder (to make your own, see page 816)

❶ Bring a medium pot of water to a boil and salt it. Stir in the rice and return to a boil, then lower the heat so the water bubbles along nicely. Cook undisturbed—white rice for about 5 minutes, brown rice for about 15 minutes. Drain and set aside. Taste (the rice will be only partially done), add salt if necessary, and sprinkle with pepper.

❷ Put 2 tablespoons of the oil in a large bowl and whisk in the yogurt, lime juice, and curry powder. Sprinkle with salt and pepper and keep whisking until smooth. Add the rice and use a fork to toss gently, coating it with the yogurt mixture.

❸ Put the remaining oil in a large, heavy pot with a tight-fitting lid over medium-high heat. Add the rice mixture, pressing it down in the pan with a fork. Wrap a clean kitchen towel around the lid of the pot so that it completely covers the inside of the lid, with the corners gathered on top so they don't fall anywhere near the stove. Then carefully cover the pot to seal the rim. The mixture will sizzle immediately. But when you start to smell the spices and the rice cooking—in 3 to 5 minutes—turn the heat down very low. Cook, completely undisturbed, for about 30 minutes, or until the rice smells toasty—you will know—but not burned. Remove from the heat and let sit for another 5 minutes.

❹ Carefully remove the lid and the cloth and turn the pot upside down over a plate. If the rice crust comes out in a single piece, terrific. If not, use a spatula to scrape the crisp pieces out of the pan and put them on top of the remaining rice. Serve immediately, sprinkled with a bit of salt and pepper if you like.

Stuck-Pot Rice with Yogurt and Mango. Astonishing stuff and very pretty: In Step 2, instead of whisking the yogurt mixture together, put those ingredients in a food processor. Peel and chop a medium mango (page 428; you should have about 1 cup) and about an inch of fresh ginger and add them to the food processor. Purée until smooth. Now toss the rice with $^1/_3$ cup of this mixture, cover the rest, and set it aside in the refrigerator. Proceed with the recipe from Step 3. Serve the finished rice along with a bowl of the mango-yogurt mixture as a sauce to pass at the table.

Stuck-Pot Rice with Sour Cream and Chiles. Hot and cool, spicy and rich: Instead of the yogurt, use sour cream. Replace the curry with chili powder (to make your own, see page 814). Proceed with the recipe, garnishing the finished dish with $^1/_4$ cup chopped fresh cilantro and a few lime wedges if you like.

Ⓕ Fast   Ⓜ Make Ahead   Ⓥ Vegan

Stuck-Pot Rice and Lentils with Pita Crust

MAKES: 4 to 6 servings

TIME: 1½ hours, largely unattended

Pita makes a wonderful crust for this stuck-pot recipe, but you can use tortillas or lavash instead (see the Stuck-Pot Rice and Beans with Tortilla Crust variation). This dish is quite complex in both flavor and texture, and the earthy lentils with lightly caramelized onions and sweet bits of dates or raisins are delicious. Use oil and this becomes vegan.

Salt

1 cup lentils, washed, picked over, and soaked if you like

1½ cups white or brown basmati rice

Freshly ground black pepper

4 tablespoons (½ stick) butter or ¼ cup extra virgin olive oil

Large pinch saffron threads (optional)

1 large onion, thinly sliced

½ cup chopped pitted dates or raisins

1 large or 2 small pita breads with pocket, split and halved

① Bring a medium pot of water to a boil and salt it. Stir in the lentils and return to a boil. Add the rice and return to a boil, then lower the heat so the water bubbles along nicely. (If you're using brown rice, add the rice and lentils to the boiling water at the same time.) Cook undisturbed—white rice for about 5 minutes, brown rice for about 15 minutes. Drain and set aside. Taste (the rice and lentils will be only partially done), add salt if necessary, and sprinkle with pepper.

② Melt the butter in a small bowl or pot (or just put the oil in) and stir in the saffron if you're using it.

③ Put half of the melted butter or oil in a large, heavy pot with a tight-fitting lid over medium-high heat. Add the onion, sprinkle with salt and pepper, and cook, stir-ring occasionally, until lightly browned, about 10 minutes. Stir in the dates, remove, and turn off the heat.

④ Add the remaining butter or oil to the pot. Cover the bottom with the pita pieces. Add half of the rice and lentil mixture, then the onion, and finally the other half of the rice and lentils. Sprinkle it all with ⅓ cup water. Wrap a clean kitchen towel around the lid of the pot so that the corners are on top and don't fall anywhere near the stove and cover the pot. Turn the heat to medium-high. When you hear sizzling—about 5 minutes—turn the heat down to very low. Cook, completely undisturbed, for about 30 minutes, or until the pita starts to smell toasty—you will know—but not burned. Remove from the heat and let sit for another 5 minutes.

⑤ Carefully remove the lid and the cloth and turn the pot upside down over a plate. If the pita comes out in a single crust, terrific. If not, use a spatula to scrape the pieces out of the pan and put them on top of the rice. Serve immediately, sprinkled with a bit of salt and pepper if you like.

Stuck-Pot Orange-Scented Rice and Lentils with Pita Crust. Add the julienned zest from 1 orange to the dates (or eliminate the dates if you like) and add ½ cup mixed nuts (like pistachios, almonds, and pine nuts) in Step 3. Sprinkle the rice with ½ teaspoon or more coarsely ground cardamom seeds.

Stuck-Pot Spicy Rice and Lentils. Here it's the rice that makes the crust: Eliminate the saffron, dates, and pita. Add chopped hot fresh chile to taste and about a tablespoon peeled and minced fresh ginger to the onion in Step 3. Stir in a tablespoon or so of curry powder or garam masala (to make your own, see page 815), then gently stir in the rice and lentils.

Stuck-Pot Rice and Beans with Tortilla Crust. Omit the lentils, saffron, and dates. Add a chopped bell pepper (any color) with the onion in Step 3. In Step 4, line the pot with tortillas instead of pita. Layer the rice with the onion mixture and a cup or so of drained cooked beans (like black, pinto, or kidney beans).

Stuck-Pot Rice with Potato Crust

MAKES: 4 to 6 servings

TIME: 1½ hours, largely unattended

This is the first of these types of dishes I learned how to make (with thanks to the late great food writer Paula Peck). Potatoes provide the crust here, complemented by the bright flavors of fennel and saffron. If fennel isn't available (or isn't your thing), use celery or neither or try one of the variations.

Salt

1½ cups white or brown basmati rice

Freshly ground black pepper

4 tablespoons (½ stick) butter or ¼ cup extra virgin olive oil

Large pinch saffron threads (optional)

1 large or 2 small waxy potatoes, like Yukon Gold or other thin-skinned variety

1 medium fennel bulb, trimmed and thinly sliced

1 Bring a medium pot of water to a boil and salt it. Stir in the rice and return to a boil, then lower the heat so the water bubbles along nicely. Cook undisturbed—white rice for about 5 minutes, brown rice for about 15 minutes. Drain and set aside. Taste (the rice will be only partially done), add salt if necessary, and sprinkle with pepper.

2 Melt 2 tablespoons of the butter in a small bowl or pot (or just put the oil in) and stir in the saffron if you're using it. Peel the potatoes and cut crosswise into thin slices.

3 Put the remaining butter or oil in a large, heavy pot with a tight-fitting lid over medium-high heat. Add the fennel, sprinkle with salt and pepper, and cook, stirring occasionally, until soft, about 2 minutes. Remove and turn off the heat.

4 Add ¼ cup water and the saffron mixture (or the plain melted butter or oil) to the pot. Carefully cover the

bottom of the pan with a layer of potato slices. Add half the rice, then the fennel, and finally the other half of the rice. Wrap a clean kitchen towel around the lid of the pot so that the corners are on top and don't fall anywhere near the stove and cover the pot. Turn the heat to medium-high. When you hear the water spattering—about 5 minutes—turn the heat down to very low. Cook, completely undisturbed, for about 45 minutes, or until the potatoes start to smell toasty—you will know—but not burned. Remove from the heat and let sit for another 5 minutes.

5 Carefully remove the lid and the cloth and turn the pot upside down over a large plate. If the potatoes come out in a single crust, terrific. If not, use a spatula to scrape the pieces out of the pan and put them on top of the rice. Serve immediately, sprinkled with a bit of salt and pepper if you like.

Stuck-Pot Rice with Lima Beans. Replace the saffron with 2 tablespoons chopped fresh dill or 1 tablespoon dried. Instead of the fennel, use 1½ cups lima beans (fresh or frozen). Everything else stays the same.

Stuck-Pot Rice with Lemon and Herbs. Brighter in flavor: Instead of saffron, use ½ cup minced mild fresh herbs—like parsley, mint, or a combination—or 1 teaspoon minced strong herb leaves, like tarragon, thyme, or rosemary, or a couple teaspoons of oregano or marjoram. Use 2 thinly sliced lemons (peels and all) instead of the fennel and proceed with the recipe from Step 3.

Stuck-Pot Red Rice with Aromatic Vegetables. Instead of brown rice, use red rice. Replace the fennel with 2 carrots and 1 stalk celery, all thinly sliced.

Stuck-Pot Rice with Almonds, Sesame Seeds, and Ginger. Omit the saffron. Instead of the fennel, cook a mixture of ½ cup sliced almonds, 2 tablespoons sesame seeds, and 2 tablespoons minced peeled fresh ginger. (It will take 3 or 4 minutes to soften and get fragrant.)

F Fast   M Make Ahead   V Vegan

The Basics of Sushi

The ingredients for making great sushi at home are simple, easy to find, and inexpensive: short-grain rice, rice vinegar, a few sheets of nori, and any filling you want. This can be sliced cucumbers, carrots, or avocado, Japanese pickles (page 98), or more elaborate items like stir-fried vegetables (page 242), Grilled or Broiled Tofu (page 642), or simply cooked edamame.

Sushi comes in many forms. The simplest are sushi bowls (*chirashi*), a mound of seasoned Sushi Rice with tasty hot, cold, or room-temperature ingredients scattered on top.

Then there's rolled sushi (*maki*), where you use a bamboo mat to wrap sheets of nori around the rice and filling. Finger sushi (*nigiri*) is sushi rice formed into a small rectangular brick and topped with whatever you choose. (A ribbon of nori can help hold everything together if you like.) With practice, you can master both of these. (I'm not saying you're going to stand behind a counter and start yelling at people when they walk in the door, but you can make good-looking sushi.)

Part of the sushi mystique is the presentation, but you really can't go wrong here, especially if you pay even the slightest attention to color and texture; the chart on page 529 will help you get started with possible ingredient combinations. In fact, a platter of simply cut sushi rolls and finger pieces is an impressive and fairly easy party dish.

Ultimately, remember that sushi is not really special-occasion food: A sushi bowl is one of the best ways ever to use small bits of leftover vegetables, beans, and sauces.

Sushi Rice

MAKES: 4 servings

TIME: 40 minutes

Ⓥ

Though sushi rice is often served cool (in Japan it's considered best warm), it cannot be made ahead by more than a couple of hours or it loses its great texture.

1 recipe White Rice or Brown Rice (page 505 or 506), made with short-grain rice

¼ cup rice vinegar

2 tablespoons sugar

1 teaspoon salt

❶ While the rice is cooking, combine the vinegar, sugar, and salt in a small saucepan over medium heat and cook, stirring, until the sugar dissolves, less than 5 minutes. Put the saucepan in a bowl filled with ice and stir the vinegar mixture until cool.

❷ When the rice is done, put it in a bowl more than twice the size needed to hold the rice—probably the largest bowl you have. Begin to toss the hot rice with a flat wooden paddle or spoon or a rubber spatula—as if you were folding egg whites into a batter, but much faster and not quite as gently. While you're tossing, sprinkle the rice with the vinegar mixture (if the paddle becomes encrusted with rice, dip it in some water, then shake the water off and proceed). The idea is to cool the rice quickly as it absorbs the vinegar.

❸ Sushi rice will not keep for long, but if you cover it with a damp cloth, you can wait a couple of hours to proceed. Or eat it right away: see Sushi Bowls and Sushi Rolls, following.

Sushi Bowls

Chirashi Sushi

Think of chirashi sushi as unstructured sushi (*chirashi* means "scattered"). There is no real recipe for chirashi sushi other than starting with Sushi Rice (above). Top the rice with anything from Japanese pickles to Kimchi (page 96) to Sea Green Salsa (page 753 can't go wrong.

Sushi bowls are the perfect one-person meal, ideal for using up leftovers. They also make great party food. All you have to do is set up a colorful buffet of several dishes, condiments, and sauces and let guests have at it.

You can combine any of the items from the chart on page 529, but here are a few classic combos:

1. Quick-Braised Burdock and Carrots (page 274) and Japanese Egg Crêpes (page 175); serve with Pickled Ginger (page 821)
2. Stir-fried vegetables and Nori "Shake" (page 817)
3. Cucumbers and carrots marinated in Ponzu Sauce (page 780)
4. Sea Green Salsa (page 753) with toasted sesame seeds.
5. Edamame Salad with Seaweed "Mayo" (page 76) and Cherry Tomato Salad with Soy Sauce (page 57)

Sushi Rolls

MAKES: 6 rolls
TIME: 10 minutes with premade rice and filling

These days you can find almost anything in sushi rolls. And though it's hardly traditional sushi, I don't think there's anything wrong with that. Use the items listed in the "Improvising Sushi Bowls" chart or your own ideas, but keep these points in mind: Sushi roll filling works best when it's cut into thin strips (julienned) so you can set the slices down the length of the roll. And overstuff-

ROLLING AND CUTTING MAKI SUSHI

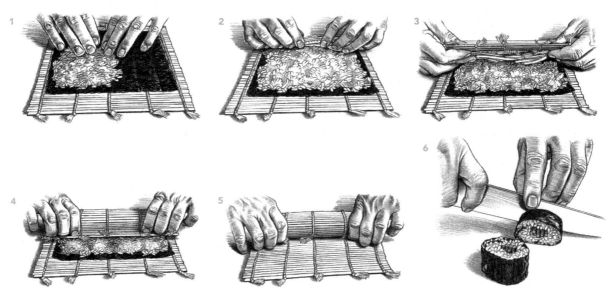

(STEP 1) First put a square of toasted nori onto a bamboo sushi-rolling mat; then press a bed of sushi rice onto it, 1/2 inch thick. (STEP 2) Put any filling you like about 1/2 inch in from the edge nearest you. Do not overfill! (You will at first, but you'll stop soon enough.) (STEP 3) Start rolling, tucking in the edge of the nori as you do so. (STEPS 4–5) Keep rolling, as tightly as you can; you will soon get the hang of it. (STEP 6) Cut the roll into 1-inch lengths.

     Fast   Make Ahead   Ⓥ Vegan

IMPROVISING SUSHI BOWLS

Pick a "Centerpiece," drizzle with a spoonful or two from the "Sauce or Marinade" column, and finish with as much or as little "Garnish" as you like. The only advice I have is to match plain things—like simply cooked dried beans—with more complicated sauces or marinades and vice versa; you don't want too many complicated components competing with one another. Once you get the hang of it, you'll be rifling through the book to make up your own combinations (or just improvising from your refrigerator).

CENTERPIECE	SAUCE OR MARINADE	GARNISH
Sliced avocado	Sake, mirin, or rice wine vinegar	Nori "Shake" (page 817)
Stir-Fried Vegetables (page 242)	Ponzu Sauce (page 780)	Pickled Ginger (page 821)
Marinated cucumbers, carrots, onions, or radish, using any of the sauces or marinades listed to the right	Ponzu Sauce (page 780) Dashi Dipping Sauce (page 780) Strong green tea	Cherry Tomato Salad with Soy Sauce (page 57)
Japanese Egg Crêpes (page 175)	Dashi Dipping Sauce (page 780)	1 cup toasted and crumbled nori (see page 357)
Grilled or Panfried Eggplant (page 295 or 244) or Eggplant Salad with Miso (page 63)	Mushroom Ketchup (page 791) or Sautéed Mushrooms (page 314)	Japanese Seven-Spice Mix (page 817)
Precooked small dried beans, like white or black soybeans, adzuki, edamame, or mung (page 581)	Any miso sauce (pages 781–782)	Edamame Salad (page 76), with or without the Seaweed "Mayo"
Kimchi (page 96) or Sea Slaw (page 55)	Peanut Sauce, Six Ways (page 794)	Wasabi paste
Tofu skin, frozen or dried, or deep-fried pouches, lightly poached (see page 640), or simple cubes of raw, baked, or fried tofu (pages 640–642)	Soy sauce	Chopped shiso leaves
Sea Green Salsa (page 753)	Soy and Sesame Dipping Sauce and Marinade, Korean Style (page 778)	Kimchi, made with daikon (page 96)
Japanese pickles, any kind found in a Japanese market or any Miso-Cured Vegetables (page 98)	Seaweed "Mayo" (page 773)	Thinly sliced scallions
Quick-Braised Burdock and Carrots (*Kinpira Gobo*) (page 274)	Kombu Dashi (page 103)	Toasted sesame seeds (see page 321)

ing will get you in trouble; think of the filling as a seasoning and the rice as the main component.

Sushi rolls can be made a couple of hours ahead: Wrap the rolls in damp paper towels and plastic and store them in a cool place (do not refrigerate, which will harden the rice).

6 sheets nori

2 tablespoons rice or other mild vinegar

1 recipe Sushi Rice (page 527)

Wasabi paste as needed

1 cup filling (see "Centerpiece" and "Garnish" columns from the chart, above)

① Begin by toasting 6 squares of nori: Use tongs to hold them, one at a time, over a medium-high flame for a few seconds, until they change color. If you have an electric stove, run them under the broiler for 15 seconds to a minute on each side. Mix 1 cup water with the vinegar (this is called "hand water").

② Put a square of nori, shiny side down, on the bamboo mat. Spread it evenly with a $^1/_2$-inch layer of sushi rice, leaving a 1-inch border on all sides; rinse your hands in the hand water as needed. (Although rolling is easy, you won't do it perfectly at first, so you might start with a slightly thinner layer of rice.) Smear the rice with a finger full of wasabi (careful; it's hot), then top with some of your filling.

③ Use the mat to tightly roll the nori around the rice, forming it into a log; you can unroll the mat at any time and check to see how things are going. This takes a little bit of practice but is not at all difficult; you'll quickly get the hang of it. To roll, follow the illustrations on page 528. Slice the rolls into 1-inch sections and serve with pickled ginger and soy sauce.

Nigiri Sushi

MAKES: 24 to 36 pieces
TIME: 20 minutes with premade rice and topping

Nigiri is simple hand-shaped sushi, which takes less practice than rolled (maki) sushi; see the accompanying illustrations. To top, you can use any filling from the "Improvising Sushi Bowls" chart. For example, try stacked strips of Japanese Egg Crêpes (page 175), pickled or marinated vegetables, or Kimchi (page 96). Just cut

---

FORMING NIGIRI SUSHI

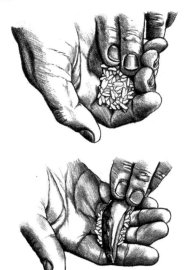
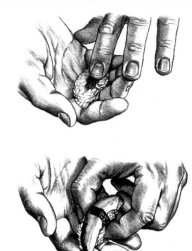

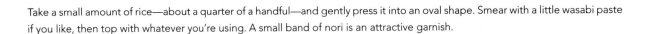

Take a small amount of rice—about a quarter of a handful—and gently press it into an oval shape. Smear with a little wasabi paste if you like, then top with whatever you're using. A small band of nori is an attractive garnish.

Ⓕ Fast   Ⓜ Make Ahead   Ⓥ Vegan

whatever topping you choose into pieces that will fit onto your molded rice.

Nigiri can be made an hour or so ahead: Drape the pieces with damp paper towels, cover with plastic, and store them in a cool place. Do not refrigerate, which will harden the rice.

1 sheet nori, toasted (see page 357; optional)

2 tablespoons rice or other mild vinegar

1 recipe Sushi Rice (page 527)

$1/4$ cup wasabi paste (optional)

36 small pieces of topping (see "Centerpiece" and "Garnish" columns from the chart, page 529)

Soy sauce

Pickled Ginger (page 821) for garnish

1 If you're using the nori, cut it into about $1/2 \times$ 5-inch strips (using scissors is easiest). Mix 1 cup water with the vinegar (this is called "hand water").

2 Put about 2 tablespoons or so of the rice in the palm of your hand; cup your hand and use your other hand to help shape the rice into a small oblong piece, about 1×3 inches; rinse your hands in the hand water as needed. Smear the nigiri with a fingerful of wasabi (careful; it's hot), then add your topping.

3 If you like, wrap a strip of nori over the middle of the nigiri, securing the topping in place, and seal the end by dampening it with the hand water. Serve with pickled ginger and soy sauce.

Mixed Rice, Japanese Style

Kayaku Gohan

MAKES: 4 servings

TIME: 40 minutes

Kayaku gohan ("mixed rice") may be thought of as Japanese paella. It's less sophisticated than sushi and, in the home at least, far more common. Like paella, it may be made with or without seafood. Like paella, it relies on good ingredients, including rice and stock, and, like paella,

it's pretty straightforward to prepare and easy to vary. But unlike paella, it's made entirely on top of the stove.

Kayaku Gohan (along with, it seems, about a million other dishes in Japan) uses dashi for the liquid. Dashi can be made spontaneously and keeps well. If you use mirin instead of the honey, this dish is vegan.

Almost needless to say, nearly any green vegetable can be used in place of the peas; asparagus tips are especially wonderful. Or try edamame or lima beans for a little extra protein and great flavor.

1 quart Kombu Dashi (page 103)

5 shiitake mushroom caps (save the stems for stock if you like), fresh, dried, or a combination

2 tablespoons neutral oil, like grapeseed or corn

1 medium onion, chopped

1 burdock root, peeled and julienned or finely chopped (optional)

1 carrot, julienned or finely chopped

$1^3/4$ cups short-grain white rice

1 cup fresh or thawed frozen peas or about 1 cup snow peas, slivered

2 tablespoons soy sauce

1 tablespoon mirin or honey

Salt

1 sheet nori, lightly toasted (see page 357; optional)

1 Warm the dashi (do not boil); if you're using dried shiitakes, add them to it; remove them when they're tender, about 10 minutes later. Slice whichever mushroom caps you're using.

2 Put the oil in a deep 10-inch skillet or fairly broad saucepan with a lid over medium-high heat. Add the onion, sliced mushroom caps, burdock if you're using it, and carrot and cook, stirring occasionally, until the mushroom edges are brown, about 10 minutes.

3 Turn the heat down to medium, add the rice, and cook, stirring, until combined. Add the peas and the dashi, along with the soy sauce and mirin. Stir, reduce the heat to medium-low, and cover. A minute later, check that the mixture is simmering and adjust the heat if necessary; cook for 15 minutes.

④ When you remove the cover, the mixture should still be a little soupy (add a little dashi or water if it's dried out); raise the heat a bit and cook until the rice is tender and the mixture is still moist but not soupy. Taste and add salt or soy sauce, then serve, with the nori crumbled on top.

Japanese Rice with Edamame and Sea Greens

MAKES: 4 servings
TIME: 30 minutes

If you haven't yet discovered the wonders of sea greens (you might call them seaweed), this is your opportunity. And please try dashi here: It adds a complex flavor that simply can't be replaced and shouldn't be missed.

Though it can be eaten on its own, this rice is great with Stir-Fried Vegetables (page 242), or any straightforward tofu dish. A few pinches of Japanese Seven-Spice Mix (page 817) or Citrus Sprinkle (page 818) on top add great flavor.

   1¹/₂ cups short-grain white rice or parcooked brown (see page 506)

   Kombu Dashi (page 103) or water as needed

   4 dried shiitake mushrooms

   ¹/₂ small onion, finely chopped

   1 teaspoon toasted sesame seeds (see page 321)

   Dash dark sesame oil

   Soy sauce

   1 cup shelled edamame

   ¹/₂ cup soaked and chopped hijiki, wakame, or kombu (page 356)

① Put the rice in a pot with a lid; add enough dashi to cover the rice by about an inch. Bring to a boil, then reduce the heat to low so that it bubbles gently, cover,

and cook for about 10 minutes. Meanwhile, soak the shiitakes in hot water to cover. When they're soft, chop them roughly and toss their water into the rice.

② Add the shiitakes, onion, sesame seeds, sesame oil and soy to taste, edamame, and hijiki to the rice and continue to cook until the rice is tender and most of the liquid is absorbed (you don't want it soupy, but not dry either), about 15 minutes. Taste and add sesame oil and soy sauce as necessary. Serve hot or at room temperature or store, covered, in the refrigerator for up to 2 days (reheat or bring back to room temperature and stir in a little sesame oil just before serving).

Japanese Rice with Tomato and Fermented Black Beans. Totally unorthodox and really delicious: Add 1¹/₂ cups chopped tomato (or about a 12-ounce can, drained) in Step 2 and substitute ¹/₄ cup rinsed fermented black beans for the edamame.

Sushi-Style Rice with Edamame and Shiso. Shiso adds a mysterious flavor: Omit the onion, sesame oil, and soy sauce; add 4 or 5 shiso leaves. In a small pan, combine ¹/₃ cup rice vinegar, ¹/₄ cup sugar, and a tablespoon of salt; heat until the sugar is dissolved and set aside. Proceed with the recipe and then stir in the vinegar mixture and chopped shiso just before serving.

Black Thai Rice with Coconut Milk and Edamame. A savory version of a classic Thai dessert: Use black Thai rice instead of regular white or brown. Substitute unsweetened coconut milk for the dashi or water and omit the shiitakes, sesame oil, and sea greens.

Rice Balls

Onigiri

MAKES: 4 to 8 servings
TIME: 30 minutes

Rice balls are a part of daily life in Japan, a fast snack, something to be grabbed on the run or part of a boxed

Ⓕ Fast   Ⓜ Make Ahead   Ⓥ Vegan

lunch—and clearly somewhat "healthier" than potato chips. There's almost nothing to them: cooked short-grain rice, gently pressed together and shaped with salt-coated hands—they should be quite tender, shaped just firmly enough to hold together—sometimes stuffed with a piece of food, sometimes wrapped with nori, sometimes both and sometimes neither. They can also be grilled after shaping, which is a nice touch.

Serve these as a side dish with Japanese dishes like Edamame Salad with Seaweed "Mayo" (page 773) or as an appetizer with Simple Miso Dipping Sauce (page 781), Dashi Dipping Sauce (page 780).

Salt

4 cups cooked white or brown short-grain rice (pages 505 to 507), still warm

Pickled plums (umeboshi), pickled daikon (takuan), and/or lightly salted cucumber (page 46; optional)

Soy sauce

4 sheets nori, lightly toasted (page 357)

1. Work with wet hands; sprinkle a little salt on your hands, then grab about $1/2$ cup of rice and gently shape it into a ball; the rice should hold together easily. If you want to stuff the rice balls, poke a hole in each and put in a bit of any of the fillings. Reclose the hole.

2. Brush each ball lightly with soy sauce.

3. Brush each of the nori sheets with a little soy sauce, then cut each piece in half (most easily done with scissors). Wrap each ball with a piece of nori, shiny side out. Serve within a few hours.

Rice Balls with Sesame. Sprinkle the balls with toasted sesame seeds (see page 321) before wrapping.

Grilled Rice Balls. Before wrapping in nori, gently grill the rice balls over a medium-low flame, turning and basting with soy sauce as they're grilling, for a total of 5 to 10 minutes. Serve hot or warm, wrapped in nori or not, as you choose.

The Grain Lexicon

As I said at the beginning of this chapter, almost all grains are grasses. Beyond that commonality, though, each grain is distinct in terms of flavor, texture, color, and cooking times. Still, most are interchangeable, to an extent that may surprise you. To help you experiment and make the best use of whatever you have on hand, I've included the line "Other grains you can use" in recipes that work with other options.

You can start to familiarize yourself with grains with the following charts. I hope you'll try as many of these as possible, but I've divided the grains into two charts, one on grains you can find easily and will probably eat most regularly and one for those you might want to seek out.

The Basics of Cooking Grains

If you know *nothing* about cooking grains, just start with Cooking Grains, the Easy Way (page 537), which covers most bases in a general way that will make you feel comfortable pretty quickly. Generally speaking, though, cooking grains is straightforward: You boil them in water or other liquid. They may be toasted (cooked in a dry skillet) or sautéed (cooked in a skillet with a little oil or other fat) before further cooking, but for the most part there's not much more to it than that.

Microwaves, pressure cookers, rice cookers, and slow-cookers might all seem like logical tools to turn to in the quest for faster-cooking whole grains, but straightforward techniques like the basic recipe are really your best choice. A few exceptions worth noting: The microwave oven works well only for white rice and quinoa; see the variation to White Rice (page 505). The pressure cooker isn't much faster than the stovetop and is a hassle to check for doneness; use for beans but not grains. The slow cooker works for long-cooking grains, but you cannot "set it and forget it"; again you must check frequently to capture the moment before the grain kernels burst unexpectedly. The rice cooker works well for white rice because white rice is

EVERYDAY GRAINS

These grains are loosely organized first around cooking times, from shortest to longest, and second around what's most common and versatile (and my personal favorites).

GRAIN	COOKING TIME	DESCRIPTION	FORMS AND VARIETIES
Couscous	5 to 15 minutes, depending on the type	Traditionally tiny, yellow, hand-rolled semolina dough. Now bits of rough-looking pasta, and the national "grain" (it isn't) of Morocco, served with almost every stew. "Israeli" couscous is also made from semolina dough, but extruded through a round mold and toasted, giving it a more uniform and larger, pearllike shape, a nuttier flavor, and a chewier texture; it's also more forgiving during cooking.	Usually made from semolina flour, sometimes in varying colors. Whole wheat couscous is also available and very good. The larger type is called *Israeli couscous, super couscous, maftoul, pearl couscous,* or *Israeli toasted pasta.*
Bulgur *Bulghur, Burghul, Bulger (often confused with cracked wheat, which it is not; see next page.)*	10 to 20 minutes, depending on the grind	Finely ground wheat kernels, first steamed, then hulled, dried, and ground to varying degrees. Fine grind is quick and convenient:, usually edible after soaking. Its nutty, mild flavor and fluffy, dry texture make it perfect for soaking up liquids and turning into salads. A good rice alternative.	Available in fine, medium, coarse, and sometimes very coarse grinds, which are sometimes identified by numbers, from #1 for fine to #3 or even #4 for the coarsest.
Cornmeal *Grits (usually from white corn; sometimes from hominy); Polenta*	20 to 30 minutes	Yellow or white (occasionally blue or red) dried corn kernels, ground to varying degrees. Fine grind is usually used in baking; medium grind is best for polenta; coarse makes a grittier polenta or grits (page 543).	Fine, medium, and coarse grinds; water, stone, or steel ground. Water or stone ground is a more traditional method and arguably superior to steel ground, because the bran and germ remain intact. (This makes cornmeal perishable, however, so be sure to store it in the fridge or freezer).
Rolled Oats *Old-Fashioned Oats*	15 to 20 minutes	Whole oats are toasted, hulled, steamed, and flattened with giant rollers to make these familiar flakes. The quick-cooking variety is cut before being steamed and flattened; instant is cut, precooked, dried, steamed, and then flattened. Stay away from these if you want any flavor at all.	Raw or quick-cooking (steamed) rolled oats, instant oats. Some are more heavily processed than others.
Quinoa (pronounced keen-wa) *Mother Grain, Supergrain*	About 20 minutes	Originally from the Andes, the most common quinoa is light tan, disk shaped and pinhead size ($\frac{1}{16}$ inch). Nutty and grassy in flavor, with a slightly crunchy but soft texture. Even plain, it's as good as grains get.	Three main cultivated varieties, generally differentiated by color: white, red, and black; you can find whole grains of each. Also made into flakes, which can be used like rolled oats.
Pearled Barley *Peeled Barley, Polished Barley*	About 20 minutes	Barley that has been hulled, steamed, and polished (the bran removed). Creased, oval-shaped, dull white and tan grains that cook fairly quickly and have a creamy, chewy texture when cooked. Super rice alternative.	This is the familiar barley, sold everywhere and cooked much like rice, for which it can almost always be substituted. You may occasionally see barley flakes, which can be treated like rolled oats.

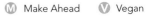 Fast   Make Ahead   Vegan

GRAIN	COOKING TIME	DESCRIPTION	FORMS AND VARIETIES
Kasha *Roasted Buckwheat*	20 to 30 minutes	Hulled and roasted buckwheat kernels, brown, triangular, and distinctively nutty. Usually toasted in a skillet, sometimes with egg, before adding liquid.	Whole grains
Buckwheat Groats *Peeled Buckwheat*	20 to 30 minutes	Essentially raw kasha, buckwheat groats are hulled and crushed; they're greenish tan, triangular, and fresher tasting than kasha—almost grassy in fact.	Whole grains; also rolled into flakes
Cracked Wheat	20 to 30 minutes	Often confused with bulgur (see above), cracked wheat is raw. It offers the same nutty wheat flavor as bulgur and wheat berries, but with a chewier, heartier texture than bulgur and quicker cooking times than wheat berries.	Fine, medium, and coarse grains (see bulgur, above), but most commonly available in medium grind
Millet	20 to 30 minutes	Small, yellow, and beadlike, with a tiny spot at one end. Pleasant tasting, mildly nutty and cornlike; cooks up fluffy. Said to be one of the first grains used by humans, it remains a staple in Africa and South Asia.	Whole grains are most common. Occasionally you may find puffed millet, but it's rare.
Steel-Cut Oats *Oat Groats, Whole Oats, Scotch Oats, Irish Oats, or Porridge Oats*	45 to 60 minutes	Like rolled oats, oat groats (with only the outer hull removed) have a nutty, sweet flavor. But they're slow cooking and quite chewy. Cut grains cook faster and are often used for breakfast cereal.	Whole grains or cut grains
Wild Rice *Indian Rice, Manomin, Water Oats*	45 to 60 minutes	A marsh grass native to the Great Lakes region, once a staple for many Native Americans. Long, narrow, deep brown cylinder-shaped grains that crack open to reveal the white interior when cooked.	Whole grains. There is both farm-raised "wild" rice and truly wild rice, which tends to be less uniform in color, better tasting, and more expensive.
Whole Wheat *Wheat Berries*	60 to 90 minutes	The second-largest grain crop in the world (after corn), whole wheat is unmilled kernels with the bran and germ still intact. Light brown, rounded, oval-shaped grain with a nutty flavor and very chewy texture.	Varieties are named for the seasons they are grown in and the traits of their hulls: hard red winter, hard white winter, soft white spring, etc. Grains come whole, cracked (see above), and "peeled," which is slightly faster cooking. Flakes are also available and cook in about half the time.
Hominy *Pozole, Posole*	Up to 2 hours	A native American ingredient, hominy is corn that has been processed—usually with lime or lye—to remove the germ and bran. In appearance, hominy looks like giant sweet corn kernels only lighter; the flavor is uniquely corny.	Dried whole kernels, partially cooked whole kernels (*nixtamal*), canned, broken, or ground; there are yellow, white, red, and blue varieties (for more details see "The Maize Maze," page 542).

GRAINS FOR ENTHUSIASTS

Because they're generally less well known, these grains are listed from the most common and versatile (and my personal favorites) to the least, and also loosely organized around cooking times, from shortest to longest.

GRAIN	COOKING TIME	DESCRIPTION	FORMS AND VARIETIES
Farro *Often confused with spelt (below)*	20 to 30 minutes	An ancient wheat-related grain, popular in early Rome, recently "rediscovered" in Tuscany. Tan colored and oval shaped, not unlike peeled wheat in appearance, farro has a nutty, wheaty flavor and retains a chewy texture when cooked. With a starch similar to short-grain rice, it's a nice whole grain substitute in risotto.	Whole, and crushed or "cracked" grains
Hulled Barley *Whole Barley, Pot Barley, Scotch Barley*	45 to 60 minutes	The least processed form of barley, with just the outer hull removed. It takes longer to cook than pearled barley and has a chewier texture, but it also has a higher nutritional value. The grains are a light brown color and oval shaped with pointed ends.	Whole grains and the slightly more processed Scotch barley (aka *pot barley*), which has more of the outer layers of the grain removed and is quicker cooking, less chewy, and somewhat less nutritious
Teff *Lovegrass*	45 to 60 minutes	The smallest grain in the world (less than $1/32$ inch). A staple in Ethiopia, with a mild, slightly sweet, nutty flavor. Cooked teff is soft and a little gummy. When ground into flour, teff is used to make injera, the bread of Ethiopia.	Whole grains: ivory, beige, dark brown, or deep purple-brown, depending on variety
Amaranth	10 to 15 minutes	Closely related to quinoa, amaranth is tiny ($1/32$ inch) and round. It can be cooked like porridge, puffed like popcorn, or toasted and used as garnish. Its flavor is mildly nutty and malty. Cooked grains get a bit sticky (and rubbery if cooked too long) but retain a nice crunch.	Whole grains, most common; puffed is rare. Usually beige in color, though other varieties vary in shades of tan and brown.
Spelt *Sometimes mistakenly labeled farro*	60 to 90 minutes	Spelt, cultivated for thousands of years, is in the wheat family and has a pleasant, mild flavor. Its appearance is similar to brown rice, though it's a bit plumper. Its low gluten levels can often be tolerated by gluten-sensitive people.	Whole berries and flakes. (Flakes cook in about half the time.)
Whole Rye *Rye Berries*	60 to 90 minutes	Rye plays an integral role in the cuisines of northern Europe and Russia, but isn't as widely popular in the United States—a shame, since it's delicious. The berries are unmilled kernels with bran and germ still intact. The flavor is nutty, the texture firm.	Whole grains and flakes. (Flakes cook in about half the time.)

 Fast   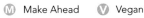 Make Ahead   Vegan

GRAIN	COOKING TIME	DESCRIPTION	FORMS AND VARIETIES
Kamut® (pronounced KAH-moot) QK-77	60 to 90 minutes	A modern breed of an ancient variety of wheat, kamut is tan, with kernels two to three times larger than common wheat. It's also more nutritious, with a sweeter, more buttery flavor.	Whole berries and flakes. (Flakes cook in about half the time).
Triticale	60 to 90 minutes	A hybrid of wheat (*triticum*) and rye (*secale*) in both name and biology, triticale is a relative newcomer, officially made a viable fertile crop in 1937. Grown primarily in Europe, the rye-flavored grains are a tan color and have a somewhat angular oval shape.	Whole grains

a more consistent product than whole grains. But don't bother trying it for other grains.

Grain cooking, like that of many other foods, follows a number of rules. Some of these are so self-evident that they're easy to overlook, so at the risk of stating the obvious, here goes:

Grains and Liquid

Grains are dried plant foods; they are not "fresh" in the way that broccoli is fresh but dried, like most beans. This means they must be rehydrated while they're cooking. (Like beans, some can benefit from presoaking, though this extra step is never essential.)

As grains rehydrate, they swell, gaining volume by absorbing liquid. The amount of time this process and the accompanying cooking takes, and the amount of liquid the grain needs to become fully cooked, depends on five factors:

1. The nature of the grain: Larger takes longer, and some are just tougher than others.
2. How dry the grain is: Older grains are drier than newer ones.
3. How many of its outer layers have been removed: Brown rice has a hull; white rice does not.
4. How much it has been milled: "Rolling" or "cutting" oats exposes more surface area.
5. Whether it has been precooked to some extent: Kasha is toasted buckwheat, bulgur is precooked

cracked wheat, and some rice is sold "converted" or parboiled. (You can also precook grains yourself; see below.)

Cooking Grains, the Easy Way

MAKES: 4 servings

TIME: 10 minutes to more than 1 hour, depending on the grain

This process will allow you to cook almost any grain, perfectly, every time. You really don't even have to measure anything. I'm providing a recipe for the method, but you don't need it: Put the grains in a pot with water and cook them until they're done the way you like them. Period.

The worst thing that can happen is that the inside of the grain will absorb so much liquid its interior bursts from its outer layer (or you'll let the water evaporate and burn the bottom of the pot). Eventually it will turn to mush, but some people actually prefer their grains burst—the starch that is released makes grains creamier.

1 cup pearl couscous, quinoa, barley (any type), oat groats, buckwheat groats, wild rice, cracked wheat, hominy, whole rye, farro, teff, spelt, kamut, or triticale or 1½ cups wheat berries

Salt

Extra virgin olive oil, other oil, or butter

1 Combine the grain with a large pinch of salt and water to cover by at least an inch in a 4- to 6-cup saucepan. (Use 3 cups water for pearled barley, which predictably absorbs a more precise amount of water.) Bring to a boil, then adjust the heat so the mixture bubbles gently.

2 Cook, stirring occasionally, until the grain is tender. This will take as little as 7 or 8 minutes with couscous and as long as 1 hour or more for some brown rice, unpearled or hulled barley, wheat berries, and other unhulled grains. Add boiling water as necessary to keep the grains covered, but—especially as the grain swells and begins to become tender—keep just enough water in the pot to keep the grain from drying out.

3 The grain is done when it tastes done; whole grains will always have some bite to them, but milled or cut grains will become mushy if overcooked, so be careful. Ideally, you'll have cooked out all of the water at about the same time the grain is tender, but if any water remains, strain the grain.

4 Toss the grain with olive or other oil or butter to taste if you're serving right away or see "5 Ways to Enhance Cooked Grains" (below). If you're storing it, toss it with a couple of tablespoons of olive or other oil to keep the grains from sticking together too much, then cover and refrigerate or freeze.

5 Ways to Enhance Cooked Grains

In Step 4, use a large fork to toss any of the following ingredients in with the grains and butter or oil:

1. Just-tender cooked vegetables, like peas, chopped greens, broccoli or cauliflower florets, or chopped root vegetables
2. A couple spoonfuls of a simple sauce, like any Flavored Oil (page 758) or Compound Butter (page 801) (omit the butter or oil); or any Chile Paste (page 828) or Miso Sauce (pages 781–782); or any of the Asian-Style Sauces on pages 777–780
3. $^1/_4$ to $^1/_2$ cup finely grated or crumbled cheese, like Parmesan, feta, any blue cheese, or goat cheese

4. 2 or 3 tablespoons minced fresh herbs, like chives, parsley, rosemary, or mint
5. 1 to 2 cups of any cooked beans

Cooked Grains with Butter or Oil

MAKES: 4 servings
TIME: About 10 minutes

No matter how you cook grains—I'd suggest following the preceding recipe—you can store them in the refrigerator and reheat them, with flavorings, in a snap. *Even if you do nothing more than warm them in olive oil, perhaps with a little garlic, they'll be delicious.* And, as you can see from the variations, you can take this in plenty of different directions. The grains are vegan if you use the oil.

3 tablespoons olive oil, butter, or a combination

1 teaspoon minced garlic (optional)

3 to 4 cups any cooked grain

Salt and freshly ground black pepper

1 Put the oil and/or butter in a large skillet over medium heat. When the oil is hot or the butter is melted, add the garlic if you're using it and cook, stirring, for about 30 seconds.

2 Add the grains and cook, stirring occasionally, until hot, 10 minutes at the most. Sprinkle with salt and pepper; taste, adjust the seasoning, and serve.

Precooked Grains with Onions. You can add 1 tablespoon minced fresh chile (like jalapeño or Thai), or to taste, or hot red pepper flakes or cayenne to taste if you like here too: In Step 1, use the garlic or not, as you like. Add about 1 cup chopped onion and cook, stirring occasionally, until just beginning to brown, about 10 minutes. Proceed to Step 2.

Precooked Grains with Onion and Mushrooms. Reduce the onion in the preceding variation to about $^1/_2$ cup and add $^1/_2$ cup sliced shiitake mushroom caps or other mushrooms. Cook, stirring occasionally, until both onion and mushrooms brown at the edges, about 10 minutes. Proceed to Step 2.

Precooked Grains with Toasted Spice. Here's a place you can really have some fun: To the heating oil or butter, add 1 tablespoon (or to taste) curry powder, chili powder, or virtually any spice mixture (to make your own, see pages 810–819). Proceed (you can use either of the preceding variations if you like), making sure to taste and adjust the seasoning before serving.

Precooked Grains with Vinaigrette, Pesto, or Other Sauce. As long as you don't overdo it, this is among the easiest, simplest ways to make grains really special: Cook the basic recipe or either of the first two variations and then, when the grain is heated, stir in about $^1/_3$ cup Vinaigrette or any variation (pages 762–763), Traditional Pesto or other herb paste (pages 768–770), or Brown Butter (page 801).

Precooked Grains with Nuts or Seeds. This is good combined with the Toasted Spice variation: In Step 1, use the garlic or not, as you like. Add about $^1/_2$ cup whole or roughly chopped nuts (cashews are good, as are pistachios, but any nut or seed is fine here) and cook for 30 seconds (for sesame seeds) to a minute or two (for cashews), or until the nut or seed is fragrant but not browned. Proceed to Step 2.

Barley

Barley Pilaf

MAKES: 4 servings
TIME: 45 minutes

Here you sauté barley before cooking it with stock (preferably, though water is okay). It's a simple recipe and one that can be varied in all the same ways as Rice Pilaf (page 511). It also becomes vegan if you use oil instead of butter.

Other grains you can use: millet, quinoa.

2 tablespoons butter or extra virgin olive oil

$^1/_2$ cup chopped scallion or onion

1 cup pearled barley

1 teaspoon chopped fresh tarragon or $^1/_2$ teaspoon dried or 1 tablespoon chopped fresh chervil, mint, dill, or parsley

3 cups vegetable stock (pages 101–102) or water, warmed

Salt and freshly ground black pepper

Chopped parsley leaves for garnish

❶ Put the butter or oil in a medium to large skillet over medium-high heat. When the butter is melted or the oil is hot, add the scallion and cook, stirring, until softened, about 5 minutes.

❷ Add the barley and cook, stirring, for a minute or so, until glossy; add the herb, liquid, and salt and pepper. Bring to a boil.

❸ Turn the heat down to low, cover, and cook for 30 minutes. Check the barley's progress: It's done when tender and all the liquid is absorbed. Continue to cook if necessary, adding a tablespoon or two more liquid if all the liquid has been absorbed and the barley is not quite done. Or, if the barley is tender but a little liquid remains, simply cover and turn off the heat; the barley will absorb the liquid within 10 minutes. If $^1/_4$ cup or

more of liquid remains (unlikely), uncover and raise the heat a bit; cook, stirring, until the barley is fluffy and the liquid evaporated.

Barley and Mushroom Stew

MAKES: 4 servings
TIME: About 1 hour

Here barley almost plays a supporting role, as a toothsome component of a hearty vegetable stew. Use any root vegetables you like here and serve with crusty bread.

1 cup chopped onion

2 medium carrots, cut into chunks

2 celery stalks, roughly chopped

2 medium potatoes, preferably low-starch (see page 337), peeled and quartered

8 garlic cloves, peeled (optional)

2 cups sliced mushrooms, preferably an assortment, or 1 cup sliced button mushrooms and $^1/_2$ cup dried porcini or other dried mushrooms, reconstituted in hot water to cover

$^1/_3$ cup pearled barley

1 teaspoon fresh thyme leaves or $^1/_2$ teaspoon dried

Salt and freshly ground black pepper

3 cups vegetable stock (pages 101–102) or water

Chopped parsley or celery leaves for garnish

❶ Combine all the ingredients except the parsley in a saucepan. (If you used dried mushrooms, include their strained liquid and reduce the amount of stock or water accordingly.) Bring to a boil over medium-high heat, then turn the heat down so the mixture barely bubbles. Cover and cook for about 30 minutes, stirring once or twice.

❷ The stew is done when everything is tender; taste, adjust the seasoning, garnish, and serve.

Deeper Barley and Mushroom Stew. Slightly more complex (and complicated!): Put 2 tablespoons extra virgin olive oil or butter in the saucepan first and turn the heat to medium-high. When the oil is hot or the butter is melted, add the onion, carrots, celery, potatoes, and garlic and cook, stirring occasionally, until the vegetables brown a bit, 10 to 15 minutes. Stir in the mushrooms and cook for another 5 minutes or so, stirring occasionally. Stir in the barley and cook, stirring, until it glistens, then add the remaining ingredients (except the parsley) and proceed with the recipe.

Barley "Succotash"

MAKES: 4 servings

TIME: 30 minutes for pearled barley; 1 hour for hulled

Ⓜ

Barley stars here, with corn and beans adding flavor, texture, bulk, and nutrition. The result is a fortified version of the summertime classic that manages to be immensely satisfying and fresh tasting at the same time.

You can use either pearled or hulled barley; the first will take less time to cook and give you a creamier, lighter dish. The more nutritious hulled barley will take about twice as long to cook but will produce more contrast and chew. Whichever way you go, serve this hot or at room temperature with some thick slices of ripe red tomato and grilled veggie burgers (pages 660–668). Leftovers reheat well in the microwave for a quick lunch. Vegan with oil instead of butter.

4 tablespoons ($^1/_2$ stick) butter or $^1/_4$ cup extra virgin olive oil

1 cup pearled or hulled barley

Salt and freshly ground black pepper

1 tablespoon minced garlic

$^1/_2$ cup lima beans (frozen are fine) or chopped green or wax beans

1 cup fresh (from 2 large ears) or frozen corn kernels

$^1/_2$ medium red or orange bell pepper, cored, seeded, and chopped

2 scallions, thinly sliced

$^1/_2$ cup chopped parsley

1 tablespoon minced fresh tarragon leaves (optional)

❶ Put 2 tablespoons of the butter or oil in a medium saucepan over medium-high heat. Add the barley and cook, stirring frequently, until lightly toasted and fragrant, 2 to 3 minutes. Sprinkle with salt and pepper. Stir in $2^1/_2$ cups water. Bring to a boil, then cover and reduce the heat to low. Cook, stirring a couple of times to promote creaminess, until the water has nearly been absorbed, about 20 minutes for pearled barley, 30 to 40 for hulled.

❷ Put the remaining 2 tablespoons of butter or oil in a deep skillet over medium-low heat. Add the garlic and cook, stirring occasionally, until plump, a minute or two. Add the beans and sprinkle with salt. Cover and cook, shaking the pan once or twice to prevent them from sticking, until just tender, about 5 minutes.

❸ Stir in the corn, bell pepper, and scallion and cook the mixture for a minute or two. Stir in the barley and whatever cooking water remains in the pot (it should be only a tablespoon or two). Cover and cook, stirring occasionally, until the vegetables have softened slightly and the succotash is creamy, another 5 minutes or so. Stir in the parsley and the tarragon if you're using it, then taste, adjust the seasoning, and serve.

The Maize Maze

Fresh corn is pretty easy to understand, but when it's dried things get downright confusing, which explains why whole books are devoted to this quintessential American grain. Trying to understand pozole, hominy, polenta, grits, and cornmeal is complicated by foreign languages, outdated names, and healthy doses of ignorance and misinformation. To muddle things even further, many dishes are named after the type of corn food that's in them.

To understand dried corn products, first you must know that they are either simply dried or dried and processed along with something alkaline to easily remove the hull and germ. This second category—which gives the kernels that distinctive flavor you immediately associate with warm tortillas—has been around for thousands of years. The earliest American inhabitants discovered that soaking corn along with wood ashes (which contain lime—not the fruit but the agricultural product, more technically calcium hydroxide) made the corn more digestible and therefore more beneficial.

The Corn Lexicon

Here's a lexicon to help you sort through the most common dried corn products and preparations, which all begin with either whole hominy or corn kernels.

Hominy

See the "Everyday Grains" entry on page 535: The traditional wood ashes are no longer used except ceremonially. Instead, whole dried corn kernels are soaked in slaked lye (lime) before removing the hull and germ. (In Mexico, the dried corn is cooked in a lime solution called *cal.*) Usually large field corn is used for hominy, so the kernels

are big, and they can be white, yellow, or even red or blue. (Cooked and canned hominy is also sold simply as "hominy.") Dried kernels cook faster if you soak them for a few hours, as you would beans.

Pozole or Posole

This comes from the Aztec name for hominy. It is also the name of any stew that features hominy.

Nixtamal

Whole hominy, partially cooked in a lime solution. It is usually ground into masa (see below) and used for making tortillas or tamales. It's a pain to make yourself, but fortunately, you can buy nixtamal at some Hispanic markets and most tortilla bakeries. Nixtamal must be refrigerated and keeps for only a couple of days. Rinse it well to wash away all the bitter lime solution before cooking. Because it's partially cooked, it takes much less time to become tender than dried hominy, and it has a fresher taste. All in all, great stuff, so buy it if you see it.

Masa

The "dough" or paste that comes from grinding nixtamal. When coarsely ground, it's used for tamales; when finely ground, it is the base for tortillas. You might be able to get a tortilla bakery to sell you its masa, or you can make your own by simply running some damp nixtamal through the food processor.

Masa Harina

This is masa dried into a convenient mix for making dough for tortillas, tamales, and other Mexican dishes. Its texture is somewhere between flour and fine cornmeal. Most supermarkets now carry masa harina, and some also have a relatively new, coarsely ground variation that is especially for making tamales. Store masa harina for up to six months or so, preferably refrigerated.

Samp

Hominy kernels that are cracked but not ground. Samp is a popular ingredient in some African stews and, like pozole,

 Fast   Make Ahead Ⓥ Vegan

gives its name to a particular dish that combines cracked hominy and beans. (See Pozole with Beans, page 544.)

Dried Corn

Not very common, but available at some health food stores. It can be cooked just like any other whole grain, only because it still has the hull and bran, it is tougher to digest than hominy and not nearly as tasty.

Cornmeal

Cornmeal is ground dried corn without the lime. It can be fine, medium, or coarse. You'll find it both heavily processed (usually under heat, which winds up not tasting like much) and stone ground (a much better choice). When cooked, most Americans call it "cornmeal mush." But raw cornmeal also goes by two other names that are the same as finished dishes:

- **Polenta:** This Italian specialty is best made from medium-ground yellow cornmeal (or a combination of fine and coarse).
- **Grits:** True hominy grits are indeed ground from hominy, though this is not the common grits of the South today, which are simply coarsely ground white cornmeal.

Corn Flour

Finely ground from dried corn (more finely ground than cornmeal) and used for baking, usually in combination with wheat flour since it has no gluten and can be heavy.

Popcorn

There are two explanations for why popcorn pops. One is that it contains spirits, which escape when exposed to heat, leaving their exploded shell behind. I like this story, but it's more believable that the starch and water content in popcorn is relatively high, which makes the hull explode under high heat. When heated in oil (see the recipe on page 292), popcorn is the classic snack. Boiled popcorn is edible, but not as good as either dried corn or hominy.

Polenta

MAKES: 4 servings
TIME: 20 minutes

As with risotto, a big deal was made of the difficulty of preparing polenta when it first became popular in the United States twenty or so years ago. Like risotto, the big deal was exaggerated. The bottom line is that polenta is easy: You can make it for lunch in about the time it takes to clean and pan-cook some spinach or make a quick tomato sauce to put on top of it.

If you want to make grilled polenta (see the variation), you should reduce the amount of water slightly (or cook it a little longer) so the polenta is thick rather than creamy and soft.

You can make polenta with water only, but it's a little richer and creamier with some milk in there. (You can use oat, rice, almond, or hazelnut milk if you prefer; opt for oil and skip the cheese, and you'll have vegan polenta.) Another nice touch: Stir in about a cup of fresh corn kernels when the polenta is just about done.

Other grains you can use: grits and teff (see variation).

1/2 cup milk, preferably whole

Salt

1 cup coarse cornmeal

1 tablespoon butter or extra virgin olive oil, or more (optional)

Freshly grated Parmesan cheese (optional)

Freshly ground black pepper

① Combine the milk with 2 cups of water and a large pinch of salt in a medium saucepan over medium heat. Bring just about to a boil, then add the polenta in a steady stream, whisking all the while to prevent lumps from forming. Turn the heat down to low and simmer, whisking frequently, until thick, 10 or 15 minutes. If the mixture become too thick, simply whisk in a bit more water. For polenta you're serving right away, you want a consistency about as thick as sour cream; for Grilled or

Fried Polenta (see the variation), you want something approaching thick oatmeal.

② Add the butter and/or cheese if you're using them, then taste, add salt if necessary and lots of pepper, and serve (or prepare it for Grilled or Fried Polenta or Polenta Gratin).

Polenta with Herbs. This is also good for Grilled or Fried Polenta, below: Add a teaspoon of fresh sage leaves or $1/2$ teaspoon dried and a teaspoon of fresh rosemary or $1/2$ teaspoon dried, along with the cornmeal. When the mixture is done, stir in $1/2$ teaspoon minced garlic if you like and a tablespoon or two of extra virgin olive oil or butter. Cheese remains optional.

Polenta Gratin. Looks like a big deal, but easy enough: Immediately after cooking, spoon or pour the polenta into a buttered baking dish of a size that will give you a layer about 1 inch thick. Top with about a cup of freshly grated Parmesan cheese and broil until the cheese melts and browns slightly. Cut into squares and serve hot or at room temperature.

Grilled or Fried Polenta. A summertime staple: Make sure the polenta is fairly thick when cooked and omit the butter and cheese. Pour the cooked polenta out onto a board or into a loaf pan. Let cool for at least 10 minutes (it can really sit there all day), then cut into $1/2$-inch-thick slices. When you're ready, brush with olive oil and grill with a little salt and pepper or brown the slices in hot olive oil in a pan.

Microwave Polenta. To me, this is more trouble than it's worth, but it works, and it's a little faster: Combine the milk, water, salt, and cornmeal in a bowl and whisk until smooth. Cover and microwave for about 2 minutes; whisk. Re-cover and repeat the process, microwaving for 1 minute at a time, until the mixture is creamy and smooth. (Total time will be around 5 minutes or a little longer.) Again, if it thickens too fast, whisk in a little more water. Finish as directed.

Angá. Brazilian "Polenta": Start by cooking 1 cup chopped onion and 1 tablespoon minced garlic in a saucepan with 2 tablespoons extra virgin olive oil; cook, stirring occasionally, until the onion begins to brown. Stir in $2^{1}/_{2}$ cups water, bring just about to a boil, and proceed as in Step 1.

Panissa. Basically polenta made with chickpea flour (see page 633), from the Ligurian region of Italy. The results will be less gritty and more prone to lumping, so be sure to stir vigorously: Replace the cornmeal with chickpea flour. In Step 1, put the chickpea flour in a strainer to sift (shake) it into the boiling water and milk mixture while stirring with your other hand. Proceed with the recipe and treat exactly as you would polenta.

Foolproof Teff, Polenta Style. Cocoa-colored and deeply flavored: Instead of cornmeal, use teff. Cook and stir for a total of 20 to 25 minutes. Add butter and cheese if you like and sauce as you would polenta. Or let cool and slice to fry or grill.

6 Easy Dishes to Serve on Top of Polenta

1. Fast Tomato Sauce (page 445)
2. Fried Olive Sauce (page 448)
3. Puttanesca Sauce (page 449)
4. Roasted Butternut Squash (add butter and Parmesan; see page 366)
5. Sautéed Mushrooms (page 314)
6. Sautéed Eggplant with Tomatoes (page 296)

Pozole with Beans

MAKES: 6 to 8 servings
TIME: At least an hour, largely unattended

Pozole is made and used everywhere there's corn and goes by a variety of different and confusing names. (The most common of these names is *hominy*, but as the Mexican population in the United States grows, that is changing.) It's got a terrific, corny flavor, but also that distinctively

Ⓕ Fast   Ⓜ Make Ahead   Ⓥ Vegan

bright, slightly sour taste you probably associate with tortillas (which, ultimately, are made from pozole).

Pozole takes time to cook, though this time can be reduced significantly if you soak the dried kernels first. But it's also sold precooked and canned, as pozole or hominy, depending on where you live. Starting with nixtamal (see page 542) can also speed the process.

> 1 cup dried hominy (preferably soaked as you would beans) or about 3 cups precooked hominy (page 537), nixtamal (page 542), or canned hominy
>
> 1 cup dried pink or red beans or black-eyed peas (preferably soaked; see pages 579–80) or about 3 cups precooked (page 581) or canned beans
>
> Salt and freshly ground black pepper
>
> 1 tablespoon fresh marjoram or oregano or 1 teaspoon dried
>
> 1 teaspoon minced fresh chile (like jalapeño or Thai), or to taste, or hot red pepper flakes or cayenne to taste
>
> 1 tablespoon ground cumin, or to taste
>
> 1 large onion, chopped
>
> 1 tablespoon minced garlic
>
> Chopped fresh cilantro leaves for garnish
>
> Lime wedges

1 If you're starting with dried or soaked hominy and beans, combine them in a pot with water to cover and cook until nearly tender, at least an hour. If using precooked or canned, proceed to Step 2.

2 Combine the hominy, beans, salt, pepper, marjoram, chile, cumin, and onion in a saucepan that will hold them comfortably. Add water or some of the hominy-cooking liquid to cover by about an inch and turn the heat to medium-high. Bring to a boil, then adjust heat so the mixture simmers steadily. Cook, stirring occasionally, until the beans are quite tender, about 30 minutes, adding a little liquid if necessary; the mixture should be a bit soupy.

3 Stir in the garlic and cook for a few minutes more. Taste and adjust the seasoning, then serve in bowls, garnished with the cilantro and the lime wedges.

Samp and Peas. Sometimes the hominy (called samp, or stampmielies, or stamp, or mealies, in some African dialects and by some African-Americans) here is crushed, which you can do before cooking (put it in a sturdy paper bag and go over it with a rolling pin) or afterward (mash it a bit or use an immersion or regular blender). It can be as simple as samp, peas, and salt or a little more complicated, with fresh vegetables—cabbage and potatoes, for example: Use black-eyed peas in place of the beans; omit the marjoram and cumin, and proceed with the recipe.

Pozole with Mole

MAKES: At least 8 servings
TIME: 3 to 4 hours, largely unattended; 1 hour with cooked hominy

This Mexican dish is fabulous at parties, and you can build an entire evening around it: The ingredients are inexpensive, it can feed a crew, and, though the recipe takes some planning, it's really easy. Serve it with a stack of warm tortillas, Red or Green Rice Pilaf (page 511) or Mexican Rice with Vegetables (page 512), a full spread of assorted cooked vegetables (like cubed potatoes, carrots, or chayote; sliced chard or kale; or green beans), and loads of garnishes (see the list on page 546). Everyone will love the variety of colors and flavors.

Mole sauces and bases are available premade, in all sorts of forms. Most are full of preservatives and frankly don't taste very good. So unless you have an excellent source of "homemade" moles nearby (and some Hispanic markets offer them), I say make your own. It takes a little time but freezes well and is always worth the effort. The pozole and mole can be made ahead separately to Step 4; just cool, cover, and store them in the fridge for up to 2 days. Reheat before serving; the flavor will be better than if you served it immediately after making.

2 cups dried hominy, soaked as you would beans, 6 cups precooked hominy (page 537), or 6 cups nixtamal (page 542)

1½ cups freshly toasted pepitas (pumpkin seeds; see page 321)

4 to 6 cups vegetable stock (pages 101–102) or water

1 large onion, chopped

4 cloves garlic, chopped

4 medium poblano or other mild green fresh chiles, roasted and cleaned (page 333)

2 serrano or other hot green fresh chiles, roasted and cleaned (page 333)

1 pound tomatillos (16 to 20, depending on size), husked and rinsed (canned are okay; include their juices)

1 cup chopped fresh cilantro

¼ cup chopped parsley

2 tablespoons chopped epazote or radish greens (optional)

1 tablespoon chopped fresh oregano or marjoram leaves

Salt and freshly ground black pepper

¼ cup neutral oil, like grapeseed or corn

① If you're using precooked hominy, proceed to Step 2. Put the soaked hominy in a large pot with water to cover. Bring to a boil, then turn the heat down to medium-low to produce a steady bubble. Cover and cook, stirring occasionally and adding water as necessary to keep the mixture covered, until the hominy is burst and tender, about 3 to 4 hours. (If you're using nixtamal, rinse it and treat it like soaked hominy; the cooking time will be shorter.)

② Meanwhile, put the pepitas and 1 cup of the stock in a blender or food processor; purée until smooth; transfer to a large bowl. Put the onion, garlic, chiles, tomatillos, herbs, and a large pinch of salt and pepper in the blender or food processor and purée until smooth (add a bit more stock or water if necessary). Mix the tomatillo purée with the pepita purée.

③ Put the oil in a large pot over medium-high heat; add the mixed purée and cook, stirring frequently, until it's dry, 10 to 15 minutes. (Be careful when adding the purée—it will splatter when it hits the hot oil.) Gradually stir in another 3 cups of the remaining stock or water; reduce the heat to a gentle bubble and cook, stirring occasionally, until thickened, another 15 minutes or so.

④ Add the hominy (with some or all of its cooking liquid and more stock or water if you want to thin the mole). Taste and adjust the seasoning. Serve hot with various garnishes or cool and store, covered, in the refrigerator for up to 3 days.

Corn with Mole. Use 6 cups freshly shucked corn kernels instead of the hominy (or pan-roast or grill the corn first if you like; see page 290). Add it in Step 4.

Vegetable Mole. Replace the hominy with any or a variety of vegetables, like cubed potatoes, carrots, or chayote; sliced chard or kale; or green beans. Add the vegetables in Step 4 and cook in the mole until tender, adding more stock if necessary.

Creamier Pozole with Mole. Before adding the hominy in Step 4, put up to half of it in a food processor or blender along with its cooking liquid or water. Purée to the consistency you like. Add it along with the remaining whole-kernel hominy and proceed with the recipe.

10 Garnishes for Pozole with Mole

1. Chopped cilantro leaves
2. Crumbled queso fresco or farmer's cheese or goat cheese
3. Diced avocado
4. Crunchy Crumbled Tempeh (page 674)
5. Sliced scallions, radishes, and cabbage
6. Lime wedges
7. Minced jalapeño or other fresh chile
8. Crumbled guajillo or other dried chile
9. Salsa (pages 750, 753, and 787–789) or hot sauces
10. Mexican crema or sour cream

Polenta "Pizza"

MAKES: 4 servings
TIME: About 40 minutes

This is a fun way to eat polenta, especially if you've got kids eager to get into the kitchen. Pizza toppings beyond sauce and mozzarella will also work here, though you end up with something a lot closer to polenta than pizza, so you'll definitely need a fork. For a handheld—and more involved—corn-flavored pie, start with Crunchier Pizza Dough (page 725).

You can actually prepare this crust in advance. Make a batch of polenta (make extra, so you can eat some warm) and, when it's cool, mix in the oil and spread it on a pan or even a plate. Cover, and refrigerate for up to a day or so.

Other grains you can use: grits.

3 tablespoons extra virgin olive oil, plus oil for the pan

1 recipe Polenta (page 543), made with 2¹/₂ cups water and without butter or cheese

Salt and freshly ground black pepper

1¹/₂ cups Fast Tomato Sauce (page 445)

1¹/₂ to 2 cups grated mozzarella, Parmesan, Gorgonzola, or fontina cheese or a combination

Minced fresh herbs, like basil, parsley, oregano, or marjoram, or a mixture

❶ Preheat the oven to 400°F. Brush a thin layer of olive oil on a pizza pan or cookie sheet. Stir 1 tablespoon of the oil into the cooked polenta and pour and spoon it onto the prepared pan. Work quickly so the polenta doesn't stiffen and spread it evenly.

❷ When the polenta is cool enough to handle, cover it with a sheet of plastic wrap or wax paper. Use your hands to flatten it to a thickness of about ¹/₂ inch all over and sprinkle with salt and pepper. Spread the tomato sauce over the polenta, then sprinkle with the cheese and the herbs. Drizzle with another tablespoon or so of olive oil and place in the oven.

❸ Bake until the cheese is melted and the pizza is hot, 12 to 15 minutes. Cut into slices and serve hot or at room temperature.

Mexican-Style Cornmeal Pizza. Use either grits or polenta. Substitute Salsa Roja (page 787) for the tomato sauce. Instead of the Italian cheeses, use cotija, Chihuahua, or Monterey Jack. Omit the herbs before baking and garnish with minced fresh cilantro and scallion when the pizza comes out of the oven.

Nutty Blue Cornmeal Pizza. Use Rustic Pine Nut Sauce (page 796) instead of the tomato sauce. (You won't have as much, but it's very rich.) Instead of the cheeses listed, choose a blue cheese like Gorgonzola, Maytag blue, or Roquefort and crumble about a cup on top of the nut salsa. Instead of the herbs listed, use 1 tablespoon chopped fresh sage or 1 teaspoon dried.

Breakfast Polenta Pizza. I love this on weekend mornings, especially with leftover polenta: Omit the tomato sauce. Make 4 indents in the polenta crust and crack an egg into each. Top with a grating of cheese (cheddar is fine here) and some snipped herbs (I like sage). Bake until the eggs are set, 10 to 15 minutes.

Naked Tamales with Chile Cheese Filling

MAKES: 8 to 12 individual tamales; 4 to 6 servings
TIME: About 2 hours, largely unattended

These cornhusk-free tamales are for the practical, not the purist, though if you make the husk-wrapped variation you'll come pretty close to the real thing. The advantage of forming them in ramekins is ease, which only means you get to make them more often. (For real ease, see the first variation, which uses a baking pan.)

Nixtamal (partially cooked hominy; see page 542) is available from most tortilla shops and many Hispanic groceries. Or, you can make it yourself by cooking hominy about halfway through: Just follow the directions in Cooking Grains, the Easy Way (page 537) and stop after a half an hour or so, when the grains are tender but still quite chalky. The flavor is deliciously corny, though masa harina (also on page 542) makes a pretty good tamale too, without any of the hassle.

Traditional tamales are made with lard or vegetable shortening, because the creamy texture helps make the dough light and fluffy. The first is made from animal products and the second, which is all trans fat, tastes lousy. The best solution, I think, is solidified olive oil, which whips up very nicely, has good flavor, and makes for much lighter tamales than those made with butter (another option).

Much of this recipe can be done in advance: Put the oil in the freezer, cook the hominy if you need to, prepare the onion and pepper mixture (or any of the other fillings), and even the sauce. With these tasks done, it'll take only a little over an hour to get the tamales on the table, and most of that time is unattended.

$^2/_3$ cup extra virgin olive oil, plus more for greasing the pan

2 medium onions, halved and sliced

1 tablespoon sugar

3 medium red bell peppers, roasted and peeled (page 333) if you like, then sliced

2 poblano or Anaheim chiles, roasted and peeled (page 333) if you like, then sliced

Salt and freshly ground black pepper

4 cups nixtamal (about 1$^1/_2$ pounds) or 2 cups masa harina

1 to 2 cups vegetable stock (pages 101–102) or water at room temperature

1 teaspoon baking powder

4 ounces Chihuahua, Monterey Jack, or mild cheddar cheese, grated (about 1 cup)

2 cups Salsa Roja or Red Enchilada Sauce (pages 787–788) or Fast Tomato Sauce (page 445), warmed

$^1/_4$ cup sliced scallion or minced red onion for garnish

$^1/_4$ cup chopped parsley or fresh cilantro for garnish

1 An hour or more before cooking, put $^1/_2$ cup of the olive oil in the freezer to solidify. Preheat the oven to 400°F. Grease eight to twelve ramekins with a little more olive oil. You will need a roasting pan (or two) that holds them comfortably.

2 Put 2 tablespoons of oil in a large skillet with a lid over medium-high heat. Add the onions and cook, stirring frequently, until they just begin to color, about 5 minutes. Stir in the sugar, reduce the heat to medium, and cook, stirring occasionally, for 5 minutes more. If you're using fresh, not roasted and peeled, peppers and chiles, add them too the pan now, along with some salt and pepper. Cover and reduce the heat to low. Cook, stirring occasionally, until very soft and compact, about 25 minutes. If you're using roasted peppers and chiles, add them to the onions after about 15 minutes of cooking. When done, turn off the heat and set aside. (You can make the filling ahead to this point, then cool and refrigerate it for up to 2 days. Bring it to room temperature when you're ready to proceed.)

3 Bring a kettle of water to boil. If you're using nixtamal, rinse it well and drain. Put it in a food processor and grind for several minutes until a thick paste forms. If you're using masa harina, put it in the food processor, turn on the machine, and add stock, $^1/_4$ cup at a time, until a thick paste forms. (This paste is called a masa, or dough.)

4 Add the frozen olive oil, baking powder, and a large pinch of salt to the masa. Pulse a few times, then, with the machine running, add more stock, $^1/_4$ cup at a time, until the masa is the consistency of thick batter. It should take a little tap to plop off a spoon.

5 Fill each prepared ramekin about a third full with masa. Spoon a heaping tablespoon of the onion/pepper mixture on top of the masa (try to keep it in the middle if you can), followed by a sprinkling of cheese. Fill the ramekins almost to the top with the remaining masa.

F Fast   M Make Ahead   V Vegan

Soak 16 dried corn husks—available in Latin grocery stores and even many supermarkets—in warm water for at least 3 hours or overnight. Drain, then separate and clean the husks. Continue to soak until ready to use. Follow the directions for making both the masa and the filling in Naked Tamales with Chile Cheese Filling (page 547), or the masa and any of the fillings listed on page 550.

1. For each tamale, drain a husk and pat dry with paper towels. Spread 2 tablespoons of the masa dough in the center of the husk, then wet your fingers and pat into a 4 × 3-inch rectangle along the right edge of the husk, leaving at least 2 inches on each side.

2. Spoon 1 tablespoon of filling lengthwise down the center of the dough rectangle. To wrap the tamales, fold the dough rectangle in half, bringing the right side of the dough over the filled center.

3. Continue rolling tightly to the end of the husk.

4. Then secure the open ends with kitchen string. Repeat with the remaining ingredients.

To cook: Prepare a large steamer by setting a steamer rack about 2 inches above gently boiling water. Stack the tamales, seam down, on the rack. Cover and steam until done, about 45 minutes. To test for doneness, remove a tamale and open the husk—the filling should be firm and come away easily from the husk. Serve tamales in their husks, passing the sauce on the side.

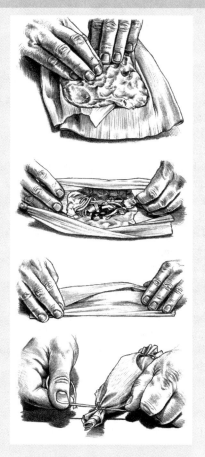

Cover each with a little piece of foil and put them in the roasting pan(s).

⑥ Carefully pour the boiling water into the pan to come halfway up the ramekins. Put the whole thing in the oven and bake for 40 to 45 minutes, until the masa is done and pulling away from the sides of the ramekins. (They'll keep warm for 15 minutes or so in the water bath.) When ready to serve, put the warm sauce on the bottom of individual plates or a platter, turn the tamales upside down onto the sauce, sprinkle with scallion and parsley, and serve.

"Naked" Tamale Loaf, Pie, or Cake. Even easier than individual tamales: Instead of using ramekins, grease a standard bread loaf pan, a 10-inch cake pan, or a deep 9-inch pie plate. Follow the recipe through Step 4. Put half the masa in the prepared pan. Top with the onion/pepper mixture and the cheese. Put the remaining dough on top. Cover the pan with foil and put in the roasting pan. Pick up the recipe again at Step 5, but bake for about an hour, or until the masa is done and pulling away from the sides of the ramekins. Cut the loaf, cake, or pie into slices or wedges, sprinkle with scallion and parsley, and pass the warm sauce at the table.

13 Dishes That Make Great Tamale Fillings

You can use these fillings with or without cheese:

1. Beer-Glazed Black Beans or any of its variations (page 585)
2. Twice-Cooked (Refried) Beans or any of its variations (page 592)
3. Chopped grilled vegetables, like eggplant, zucchini, tomatoes, chiles, or squash (see "Grilling Everyday Vegetables," page 251)
4. Roast Fennel with Orange (page 303)
5. Leeks Braised in Oil or Butter or Braised Leeks with Tomato (page 310)
6. Caramelized Onions (page 329)
7. My Mom's Pan-Cooked Peppers and Onions (page 334)
8. Spinach with Currants and Nuts (page 360)
9. Any oven-roasted tomatoes (page 375)
10. Butternut Squash with Saffron and Almonds (page 365
11. Panfried Pumpkin with Tomato Sauce, Cocoa, and Pumpkin Seeds (page 367)
12. Chile Scrambled Tofu (page 655)
13. Tempeh Chile with Black Beans (page 677)

8 Sauces to Serve with Tamales

1. Fresh Tomatillo Salsa (page 751)
2. Cooked Tomatillo Salsa (page 788)
3. Creamy Nut Sauce (page 797)
4. Smooth Green Chile Sauce, Indian Style (page 792)
5. Grilled Pineapple and Onion Salsa (page 791)
6. Either of the sauces made for Cheese Enchiladas with Red Mole (page 223) or Pozole with Mole (page 545)
7. Fresh Tomato Salsa (page 750)
8. Grilled Tomato Sauce (page 449)

Grits Gratin with Arugula and Garlic

TIME: 45 minutes, with prepared grits
MAKES: 4 to 6 servings

Part warm salad, part comfort food, this one-dish meal shows that grain dishes don't have to be heavy. As the garlicky arugula wilts, the slices of grits form a yummy golden crust akin to croutons.

You can use yellow cornmeal here, but the more pronounced corn flavor of hominy grits stands up better to the other assertive flavors. Either way, make the grits up to a day in advance, pour it into a loaf pan or rimmed baking sheet, and let it set before proceeding.

Other grains you can use: coarse cornmeal.

$1/4$ cup extra virgin olive oil, plus oil for the pan

3 or 4 cloves garlic, crushed

$1/2$ teaspoon sugar

4 cups arugula leaves

Salt and freshly ground black pepper

2 tablespoons balsamic or sherry vinegar

1 recipe Polenta (page 543), made with grits and molded according to Grilled or Fried Polenta

$1/2$ cup freshly grated Parmesan cheese

① Preheat the oven to 400°F. Grease a shallow 2-quart gratin dish or oblong baking pan with a little olive oil.

② Put 2 tablespoons of the oil in a large, deep skillet over medium-low heat. Add the garlic and sugar and cook, stirring occasionally, until the garlic is soft, plump, and starting to color, about 10 minutes. Turn off the heat and add the arugula. Sprinkle with salt and pepper, toss gently once or twice, and spread the leaves into the bottom of the prepared dish. Drizzle with the vinegar.

③ Turn the grits out of the pan and cut into $1/2$-inch-thick slices; sprinkle with salt and pepper to taste. Carefully spread them out on top of the arugula, overlapping

Ⓕ Fast   Ⓜ Make Ahead   Ⓥ Vegan

them a little if necessary. Drizzle with the remaining oil and sprinkle with the cheese. Bake until the topping is golden and bubbling, 20 to 25 minutes. Serve, topped with lots of black pepper.

Grits Gratin with Escarole, Garlic, and Lemon. Instead of the arugula, use torn escarole leaves. Substitute lemon juice for the vinegar.

Grits Gratin with Arugula, White Beans, and Garlic. You can simply add beans to the preceding variation, but I like this better: When you toss the arugula with the garlic and olive oil in Step 2, add 1 cup cooked white beans.

Smothered Grits Gratin with Arugula and Garlic. This is much heartier: You'll need 2 cups of warmed tomato sauce (you can use almost any one you like; see page 448) and 8 ounces fresh mozzarella cheese, cut into thin slices, plus some extra Parmesan cheese. After greasing the baking dish in Step 1, spread a thin layer of the sauce in the bottom. Then add the arugula and vinegar as per Step 2. In Step 3, while putting the sliced grits on top, alternate them with the mozzarella slices, overlapping them as needed. (Don't cover the grits entirely with the cheese or it won't brown.) Finish by sprinkling on the Parmesan and baking for 25 to 30 minutes. Pass the extra sauce and Parmesan at the table.

Couscous

Pearl Couscous Pilaf with Sun-Dried Tomatoes

MAKES: 4 servings
TIME: 20 minutes

Pearl couscous is so forgiving: It won't turn to mush with too much liquid, it can be served hot or at room tempera-ture, it reheats well, and it's delicious in a number of different guises (note all the variations). Highly recommended.

2 tablespoons extra virgin olive oil

$1/2$ onion, minced

1 cup pearl couscous

4 sun-dried tomatoes, reconstituted as you would mushrooms (page 317) and chopped

1 clove garlic, minced

3 tablespoons chopped pitted black olives

$1^1/_4$ cups vegetable stock (pages 101–102) or water

Salt and freshly ground black pepper

Chopped fresh basil, mint, or oregano leaves for garnish

❶ Put the oil in a pot with a lid over medium-high heat. Add the onion and pearl couscous and cook until the couscous is lightly browned and the onion is soft, about 5 minutes. Add the sun-dried tomatoes, garlic, and olives and cook for another 2 minutes.

❷ Stir in the stock, sprinkle with a bit of salt (remember the olives will add salt) and a good amount of pepper, and bring to a boil. Turn the heat to low so that the mixture bubbles gently, cover, and cook until the liquid is absorbed and the couscous is al dente, about 10 minutes. Taste, adjust the seasoning, sprinkle with chopped herbs, and serve hot or room temperature. Or store, covered, in the refrigerator for up to 2 days (reheat or bring back to room temperature and stir in a little olive oil just before serving).

Pearl Couscous Pilaf with Preserved Lemons. A great use for Preserved Lemons (to make your own, see page 427, or buy them at a North African market): Delete the sun-dried tomatoes and add 2 to 3 tablespoons each chopped preserved lemons and toasted almond slivers.

Eggplant Pearl Couscous Pilaf. A bigger, more filling dish: Omit the olives if you like and add about a cup of eggplant in $1/2$-inch or smaller pieces, instead of or in addition to the tomatoes. Cook until the eggplant is nearly done, about 5 minutes.

Spinach Pearl Couscous Pilaf. Quite Sicilian in spirit, if not tradition: Delete the onions, sun-dried tomatoes, and olives. Double the garlic and add about a cup of cooked chopped spinach, squeezed almost dry, and $1/4$ cup each pine nuts and raisins.

Curried Pearl Couscous Pilaf. Omit the sun-dried tomatoes and olives; add a tablespoon each minced ginger and curry powder (to make your own, see page 816).

Spicy Pearl Couscous Pilaf. Replace the sun-dried tomatoes and olives with $1/2$ cup roasted corn kernels (page 290) and 2 roasted poblano chiles (page 333), chopped. Add a teaspoon ground cumin in Step 1 and chopped cilantro leaves to garnish.

Pearl Couscous "Risotto" with Artichoke Hearts

MAKES: 4 servings

TIME: 30 minutes (faster with marinated artichokes)

Ⓕ Ⓜ

Unlike the real thing, this "risotto" doesn't quite have that special, creamy texture. But it's a good, light dish, like the Orzo, Risotto Style on page 451. The couscous releases some starch to thicken the sauce, and its al dente texture resembles that of Arborio rice. The round pearl shape also gives it a distinctive look.

As usual, sunchokes (aka Jerusalem artichokes; see page 369) are an excellent substitute for the artichoke hearts. Use oil instead of butter to make this dish vegan.

Other grains you can use: pearled barley or farro (increase the cooking time and the liquid a bit).

3 tablespoons butter or extra virgin olive oil, plus 1 tablespoon butter, softened (optional)

2 tablespoons minced shallot, scallion, or onion

1 cup chopped fresh mushrooms

1 cup pearl couscous

1 teaspoon minced fresh oregano, marjoram, or thyme leaves or $1/2$ teaspoon dried

4 artichoke hearts, cleaned and cut into bite-sized pieces (drained marinated are fine)

Salt and freshly ground black pepper

$1/2$ cup dry white wine

4 to 6 cups vegetable stock (pages 101–102), warmed

Minced parsley leaves for garnish

❶ Put the butter or oil in a medium to large, deep skillet or casserole over medium heat. When the butter is melted or the oil is hot, add the shallot and mushrooms and cook, stirring, until softened, about 5 minutes.

❷ Add the pearl couscous and cook, stirring, until it is glossy, about 1 minute. Add the herb, artichokes (add marinated hearts in the last couple minutes of cooking), some salt and pepper, and the white wine; turn the heat up to medium-high and let the wine bubble away while you stir.

❸ Return the heat to medium and begin to add the stock, $1/2$ cup or so at a time, stirring after each addition and every minute or so. When the stock is just about evaporated, add more. The mixture should be neither soupy nor dry; stir frequently.

❹ Keep adding liquid until the couscous is tender, about 15 minutes. Stir in the softened butter if you're using it, garnish, and serve.

Creamy Pearl Couscous "Risotto." No work, quite nice: Stir in $1/4$ to $1/2$ cup cream just before serving.

Pearl Couscous "Risotto alla Milanese." Lovely, deep yellow color: Delete the artichokes and herb and add a large pinch of saffron threads to the stock.

Pearl Couscous "Risotto" with Butternut Squash. I like this a lot; if you want to make it really great, roast the squash, as in the recipe on page 366, before adding it: Substitute 1 cup diced butternut squash for the artichokes and use sage. In Step 1, cook the squash in the butter or oil until lightly browned, about 5 minutes, then add the shallot.

Spicy Tomato Pearl Couscous "Risotto." Omit the artichokes and reduce the stock by about a cup. Add 1/4 cup mixed finely chopped celery and carrot and cook with the shallot. In Step 2, add 1 cup cored, peeled, seeded, and chopped tomatoes and a tablespoon or so of Harissa (page 830) or hot red pepper flakes to taste.

Pearl Couscous Tagine

MAKES: 4 to 6 servings
TIME: 40 minutes

Tagine, the name of both the cooking vessel and the national dish of Morocco, is typically a stew with vegetables and spices, served with couscous. The curious pot, with its bowl-shaped bottom and conical lid, makes sense: It's designed to allow just the right amount of steam to escape through the hole in the top and condensation to drip back down into the stew simmering below. But you don't need a tagine to cook a great tagine; any deep skillet or Dutch oven with a snug-fitting lid will do.

2 tablespoons extra virgin olive oil

1 onion, chopped

2 cloves garlic, minced

One 1-inch piece ginger, peeled and minced

1 1/2 teaspoons ground cumin

2 teaspoons ground turmeric

Two 3-inch cinnamon sticks

1/3 cup chopped dried apricots, dates, or raisins

1 1/2 cups chopped ripe tomato (about 1 pound whole, preferably peeled and seeded, or drained canned)

2 cups vegetable stock (pages 101–102)

1 cup cooked or drained canned chickpeas

2 medium carrots, cut into bite-size chunks

1/2 head cauliflower, cut into bite-sized chunks

2 zucchini, cut into bite-sized chunks

Salt and freshly ground black pepper

1 cup pearl couscous

1 Put the oil in a deep skillet with a lid over medium-high heat. Add the onion and cook until it softens, about 5 minutes. Add the garlic, ginger, cumin, turmeric, and cinnamon; cook, stirring often, until fragrant, 2 minutes.

2 Add the dried fruit, tomato, stock, chickpeas, carrots, cauliflower, and zucchini, a large pinch of salt, and a good amount of pepper; bring to a boil. Reduce the heat to a gentle simmer, cover, and cook until the vegetables are just tender. (The dish can be made ahead to this point, cooled, covered, and refrigerated for up to 2 days. Bring it to a simmer before proceeding.)

3 Add the couscous and cook until al dente, about 10 minutes. It should have a stewy consistency. Taste and adjust the seasoning. Serve hot or store, covered, in the refrigerator for up to 2 days and then reheat.

Pearl Couscous Tagine with Caramelized Butternut Squash. Replace the apricots with pitted prune, and the chickpeas with 1/2 cup mixed almonds and chopped Preserved Lemons (page 427). Omit the carrots, cauliflower, and zucchini. Add a medium (about 1 pound) butternut squash, peeled and cut into 1/2-inch slices. In Step 1, cook the butternut squash in the oil until golden brown on both sides, about 10 minutes. Add the onion once you've flipped the squash to cook the other side. Proceed with recipe.

Whole Wheat Couscous with Cauliflower and Almonds

MAKES: 4 servings

TIME: About 20 minutes

Cauliflower has an affinity for whole grains (see Millet Mash, on page 565) and whole wheat pastas (which is what couscous really is anyway). When finely chopped and fried as in this recipe, its crumbly texture mimics cracked grains.

Other grains you can use: regular couscous, bulgur.

1/2 cup whole almonds

3 tablespoons extra virgin olive oil

1 large shallot or small red onion, minced

1 small cauliflower, finely chopped (about 3 cups)

Salt and freshly ground black pepper

1 cup whole wheat couscous

2 teaspoons smoked paprika

1 1/2 cups vegetable stock (pages 101–102), white or rosé wine, water, or a combination

1/2 cup chopped fresh parsley

Freshly grated manchego or other semihard sheep's milk cheese for garnish (optional)

1 Put a dry deep skillet with a lid over medium-high heat. Add the almonds and cook, stirring constantly, until toasted and fragrant, just a couple of minutes. Remove them from the pan with a slotted spoon and set aside to cool. Return the pan to the heat and add the olive oil.

2 Add the shallot and cook, stirring occasionally, until soft and beginning to color, about 2 minutes. Add the cauliflower and sprinkle with salt and pepper. Cook, stirring frequently, until it is coated in the oil and starts to pop and sputter in the pan, 5 to 10 minutes. Stir in the couscous and keep stirring until it too is coated in oil and begins to toast, another 3 to 5 minutes.

3 Sprinkle the mixture with smoked paprika and stir to combine. Stir in the stock and bring to a boil. Cover and turn the heat down very low. Cook, undisturbed, for 15 minutes (5 minutes for regular couscous). Chop the almonds as finely as you can. Add them along with the parsley and fluff gently with a fork. Return the lid and turn off the heat. Let the couscous rest for a minute or two, then taste and adjust the seasoning. Serve immediately, garnished with grated manchego if you like, or let cool and serve at room temperature, up to an hour later.

Whole Wheat Couscous with Broccoli and Walnuts. Toast 1/2 cup walnuts instead of the almonds. Instead of cauliflower, use a few stalks of broccoli. Omit the smoked paprika. Instead of cheese, garnish with Fresh Bread Crumbs (page 804) if you like.

Pearl Couscous Gratin with Pesto and Goat Cheese

MAKES: 4 servings

TIME: 40 minutes, largely unattended, with cooked pearl couscous

Lots of vegetables can be substituted for either the asparagus or the mushrooms in this recipe; green beans, peas, zucchini, and artichoke hearts would all work nicely. For a more dressed-up look, serve individual portions in four 6-ounce (or six 4-ounce) ramekins. The pearl couscous can be cooked up to 2 days ahead, making this dish even more appealing.

2 tablespoons extra virgin olive oil or butter, plus more for the dish

1 shallot, finely chopped

1 cup chopped wild mushrooms, like morels, chanterelles, or porcini (or any variety)

8 ounces asparagus, trimmed and peeled if necessary, cut into 1-inch pieces

Salt and freshly ground black pepper

$^1/_2$ cup cream, milk, vegetable stock (pages 101–102), or water

$^1/_2$ cup Traditional Pesto (page 768) or Parsley or Lighter Cilantro "Pesto" (page 768 or 769)

1 egg

$2^1/_2$ cups cooked pearl couscous

4 ounces goat cheese

① Grease a 2-quart soufflé or gratin dish or an oblong baking pan. Preheat the oven to 350°F.

② Put 2 tablespoons oil or butter in a large skillet over medium-high heat. When the oil is hot or the butter is melted, add the shallot and cook, stirring frequently, until softened, less than a minute. Add the mushrooms and cook for a minute or two, then add the asparagus and a sprinkle of salt and pepper; cook until the asparagus is just tender, another 5 minutes.

③ Whisk the cream, pesto, and egg together in a small bowl until blended. Sprinkle with salt and pepper and set aside. When the asparagus mixture is done, stir in the couscous and heat until warmed through. Turn off the heat, taste, and adjust the seasoning.

④ Spread the asparagus and couscous mixture in the bottom of the prepared dish. Drizzle the cream and pesto mixture over it all. Evenly distribute the goat cheese (small clumps are fine) on top.

⑤ Bake until the edges and top are browned and bubbling, 30 to 40 minutes, depending on how deep your baking dish is. Serve immediately or let rest for up to an hour and serve at room temperature.

Pearl Couscous Gratin with Caramelized Onions and Blue Cheese. Richer and fancier: Omit the asparagus and mushrooms; use Parsley "Pesto"; substitute blue cheese for the goat. Replace the shallots with 2 thinly sliced onions and cook until browned, about 20 minutes. In Step 3, whisk in half of the blue cheese. In Step 4, add $^1/_2$ cup chopped walnuts or pecans and then evenly distribute the remaining blue cheese on top. Proceed with the recipe.

Pearl Couscous Gratin with Roasted Tomatoes. Delete the asparagus and mushrooms and add about 1 cup chopped Oven-Roasted Fresh Plum Tomatoes (page 375). Replace the goat cheese with freshly grated Parmesan if you like.

Bulgur

Basic Bulgur

MAKES: 4 servings
TIME: Less than 30 minutes

Because bulgur is partially cooked, it's easier to prepare than other grains; it's also light and fluffy, with a dry texture that's perfect for soaking up butter or oil, pan juices, dressings, and sauces.

1 cup fine- or medium-grind bulgur

① Bring a kettle of water to a boil. Put the bulgur in a bowl and pour $2^1/_2$ cups boiling water over it. Stir once and let sit.

② Medium bulgur will be tender in 15 to 20 minutes, coarse bulgur in 20 to 25. If any water remains when the bulgur is done, squeeze the bulgur in a cloth or put it in a fine-meshed strainer and press down on it. Season and serve as you like.

Creamed Bulgur with Spinach

MAKES: 4 to 6 servings
TIME: 30 minutes

A rich, thick porridge, far from breakfast cereal but an excellent side dish with any grilled or roasted vegetables. Substitute nondairy milk or cream and you have a vegan dish.

Other grains you can use: quinoa, cracked wheat, farro, millet, or precooked wheat berries, rye berries, kamut, spelt, or hominy.

3 tablespoons butter or extra virgin olive oil

1 onion, thinly sliced

About 1/2 pound (1 pound before trimming) spinach or chard leaves, well washed and chopped

1 cup fine- or medium-grind bulgur

1 cup cream, half-and-half, or whole milk

2 cups vegetable stock (pages 101–102) or water

Salt and freshly ground black pepper

Freshly grated nutmeg to taste

1 Put the butter or oil in a pot over medium heat. When the butter is melted or the oil is hot, add the onion and cook, stirring occasionally, until soft, about 5 minutes.

2 Add the spinach, stir until wilted, about 3 minutes, then add the remaining ingredients. Turn the heat down to low, cover, and cook for 10 minutes. Turn off the heat and let sit until the bulgur is tender, about 15 minutes. Taste, adjust the seasoning, and serve hot or store, covered, in the refrigerator for up to 2 days before reheating.

Creamed Bulgur with Leeks. Milder and a tad more elegant: Replace the spinach with 1 large or 2 medium leeks, with some green parts remaining, cleaned and thinly sliced (about 2 cups).

Creamed Bulgur with Fennel. Substitute a fennel bulb, thinly sliced, for the spinach. Lightly brown the fennel in the butter or oil and proceed with the recipe.

Creamed Bulgur with Saffron. Omit the spinach if you like and add a pinch of saffron threads.

Creamed Bulgur with Sunchokes. More substantial: Replace the spinach with 1 cup peeled and sliced sunchokes (Jerusalem artichokes).

Bulgur Pilaf with Vermicelli

MAKES: 4 servings

TIME: 30 minutes

This pilaf is simple but seriously delicious; at its core is nearly any type of small dried pasta or broken bits of larger pasta. You can change the flavor profile by adding the tomato paste or tossing in some chopped fresh herbs before serving; see the variations and list on page 557. Use oil instead of butter to make this vegan.

Other grains you can use: whole wheat or regular couscous.

4 tablespoons (1/2 stick) butter or 1/4 cup extra virgin olive oil

1 large or 2 medium onions, chopped

1/2 cup vermicelli, broken into 2-inch-long or shorter lengths, or other, smaller pasta

1 cup fine- or medium-grind bulgur

Salt and freshly ground black pepper

1 tablespoon tomato paste (optional)

2 1/4 cups vegetable stock (pages 101–102) or water, heated to the boiling point

1 Put the butter or oil in a medium skillet or saucepan with a lid over medium heat. When the butter is melted or the oil is hot, add the onion and cook, stirring, until soft, about 5 minutes.

2 Add the vermicelli and the bulgur and cook, stirring, until coated with the butter or oil. Sprinkle with salt and pepper, add the tomato paste if you're using it, and add the boiling stock. Turn the heat to low, cover, and cook for 10 minutes, then turn off the heat and let sit until the bulgur is tender, about 15 minutes. Adjust the seasoning and serve.

Tomato Bulgur Pilaf with Cinnamon. More complex and quite delicious: Omit the vermicelli; add a tablespoon of minced garlic, 1 bay leaf, one 3-inch cinnamon stick, and 1/2 teaspoon hot red pepper flakes; replace 1 cup stock with chopped canned or fresh tomato with the juice.

Bulgur Pilaf with Green Beans and Soy Sauce. A nice veggie-grain combo: Omit the vermicelli; replace half the butter or olive oil with dark sesame oil, the onion with 3 chopped scallions, and $^1/_4$ cup stock or water with soy sauce. Add 1 tablespoon each minced garlic and ginger and 1 cup trimmed and halved green beans.

Bulgur Pilaf with Cabbage, Lebanese Style. Delete the vermicelli; add a small leek, chopped, 1 cup shredded cabbage, 2 teaspoons or so ground pickling spice (to make your own, see page 819), a squeeze of lemon juice, and a dash of Worcestershire Sauce, Hold the Anchovies (page 799), if you like.

5 More Bulgur Pilafs

1. Bulgur and Beet Pilaf: Add a cup of diced beets, a minced shallot, 2 sprigs fresh thyme, and a tablespoon or two of dry sherry.
2. Bulgur Pilaf with Apricots and Pistachios: Stir in $^1/_2$ cup each chopped dried apricots and pistachios and $^1/_2$ teaspoon cayenne; garnish with a squeeze of lemon juice and some chopped fresh mint leaves.
3. Bulgur Pilaf with Black-Eyed Peas: Add 1 cup cooked and drained black-eyed peas and $^1/_2$ teaspoon cayenne, or to taste.
4. Mediterranean Bulgur Pilaf: Add $^1/_4$ cup each chopped black olives and Preserved Lemon (page 427) and 2 teaspoons chopped fresh oregano leaves or 1 teaspoon dried; garnish with crumbled feta.
5. Bulgur Pilaf with Lentils: Add the tomato paste, 1 cup cooked and drained lentils, and 1 teaspoon each minced garlic, hot red pepper flakes, and ground cumin.

Bulgur Chili

MAKES: 6 to 8 servings
TIME: 1 hour, largely unattended

In this chili, bulgur takes the place of the usual protein, and beans are not essential, though they can easily be incorporated (see the variation). The bulgur provides body and thickening power, and the preparation and cooking are relatively fast. And, like most stews, this one will actually taste better the next day, which makes it a super make-ahead dish.

All sorts of vegetables can be incorporated here: corn kernels, zucchini, squash, carrots, celery, and more. Toss them in in Step 1.

Other grains you can use: cooked grains like wheat, rye, kamut, spelt, hominy, and millet. Adjust the stock or water to just 2 cups.

2 tablespoons extra virgin olive oil

1 onion, chopped

2 bell peppers, any color, cored, seeded, and chopped

2 tablespoons minced garlic

3 tablespoons tomato paste

2 to 4 cascabel, guajillo, ancho, or other dried hot red peppers, soaked, cleaned, and chopped

3 cups chopped ripe tomato (about $1^1/_2$ pounds whole or canned; don't bother to drain)

1 quart vegetable stock (pages 101–102) or chile-soaking liquid or water

2 tablespoons chili powder (to make your own, see page 814)

Salt and freshly ground black pepper

1 cup fine- or medium-grind bulgur

Sliced scallion, chopped cilantro leaves, grated Monterey Jack or cheddar cheese, and sour cream for garnish

❶ Put the oil in a large pot over medium-high heat. When hot, add the onion, bell peppers, and garlic. Cook, stirring occasionally, until the onion is soft, about 5 minutes. Stir in the tomato paste until it's evenly distributed and begins to color, another minute or two. Add the chiles, tomato, stock, chili powder, and a good sprinkling of salt and pepper.

❷ Bring to a boil and then turn the heat down so the mixture bubbles gently; cook, stirring occasionally, until slightly thickened, about 30 minutes. Stir in the bulgur and cook for 10 minutes, then turn off the heat and let sit until the bulgur is tender, about 15 minutes. Garnish as you like and serve hot or store, covered, in the refrigerator for up to 3 days before reheating.

Bulgur Chili with Beans. Add 2 to 3 cups cooked or drained canned kidney, pinto, black, or other beans.

Smoky and Hot Bulgur Chili. Add 2 to 4 canned chipotle chiles, with their adobo, minced.

Bulgur Croquettes with Walnuts

MAKES: 4 to 6 servings

TIME: 25 minutes with cooked bulgur

A nutty, quick, and delicious side dish or starter. Browse through the sauces chapter for dipping sauces to serve with the croquettes or use the suggestions here.

Other grains you can use: cooked grains like quinoa, millet, kasha, and farro.

1 recipe Basic Bulgur (page 555)

1 cup chopped walnuts

$^1/_4$ cup all-purpose flour, plus flour for dredging

$^1/_2$ onion, finely chopped

1 tablespoon chopped fresh sage, thyme, or rosemary leaves (optional)

3 eggs

Salt and freshly ground black pepper

Neutral oil, like grapeseed or corn, for frying

Bread crumbs for dredging, preferably homemade (page 804), or panko

❶ Put the bulgur, walnuts, flour, onion, chopped herbs, 1 egg, and a good pinch of salt and pepper in a medium bowl; mix well. If the mixture is too loose to form into cakes, add some more flour; if it's too dry, add a little milk.

❷ Put $^1/_4$ inch of oil (or at least $^1/_8$ inch) in a large skillet over medium heat. Whisk the remaining eggs together in a shallow dish and sprinkle with salt and pepper; set aside.

❸ Form the bulgur mixture into small patties or $1^1/_2 \times 3$-inch logs (this amount will make 20 to 24). (The croquettes can be made to this point a day ahead; cover and refrigerate.) Dredge each croquette in the flour, then run through the whisked eggs, then dredge in the bread crumbs, pressing to help the crumbs adhere. Carefully put batches of the croquettes in the hot oil, gently rotating them for even cooking and browning on all sides, 5 to 7 minutes.

❹ Drain the croquettes on paper towels and immediately sprinkle with salt and pepper. Serve hot or at room temperature with Parsley "Pesto" (page 768), plain old ketchup (to make your own, see page 790) or Mushroom Ketchup (page 791), just about any yogurt sauce (pages 773–775), or simply lemon wedges.

Bulgur Croquettes with Plantains. You can also make these with sweet potatoes or yams: Replace the walnuts with chopped green (or yellow, but not black) plantains; add $^1/_2$ teaspoon cayenne or paprika, or to taste, and $^1/_3$ cup chopped peanuts. Proceed with the recipe and serve with Green Olive Mojo (page 769), Basil Dipping Sauce (page 777), or ketchup or lemon wedges.

Bulgur Croquettes with Mashed Potatoes. A great way to use leftover mashed potatoes: Replace the walnuts with $1^1/_2$ cups Mashed Potatoes (page 341); eliminate the flour and the first egg; add $^1/_2$ cup chopped cooked vegetables (like mushrooms, carrots, celery, fennel, any color bell pepper, roasted fresh chile, or peas) and dust the croquettes with Sambar Powder (page 816) before frying, if you like. Proceed with the recipe—serve with Smooth Green Chile Sauce, Indian Style (page 792), Spicy Indian Tomato Sauce (page 793), any chutney (see pages 783–787), or lime wedges.

Cracked Wheat

Fluffy Cracked Wheat with Mustard and Tarragon

MAKES: 4 servings
TIME: About 20 minutes

The difference between savory, fluffy cracked wheat and breakfast porridge is basically a lot less water and a fork. Don't confuse (as I did for years) cracked wheat (which is raw) with bulgur (which is precooked and dried). If you use bulgur here instead of cracked wheat, you will wind up with mush.

Omit the butter and this is vegan.

Other grains you can use: steel-cut oats, Israeli (pearl) couscous.

2 tablespoons extra virgin olive oil

1 cup cracked wheat

Salt and freshly ground black pepper

$^1/_4$ cup white wine (optional)

2 teaspoons Dijon mustard

1 tablespoon minced fresh tarragon leaves

Pat of butter (optional)

1 Put the oil in a medium pan with a lid over medium-high heat. When hot, add the cracked wheat and sprinkle with salt and pepper. Cook, stirring frequently with a fork, until it smells like fresh toast, 3 to 5 minutes. Add the wine if you're using it, stir briefly to combine, and cook until it almost boils off, a minute or two.

2 If you didn't add wine, add a cup of water. If you did add wine, add $^3/_4$ cup of water. Either way, stir again briefly with the fork, bring to a boil, cover, and reduce the heat to low. Cook, undisturbed, for about 15 minutes.

3 Lift the lid and use the fork to stir in the mustard, the tarragon, and the butter if you like. Cover again, turn the heat off, and let sit for at least 5 and up to 15 min-

utes. Taste and adjust the seasoning, then fluff one last time with your fork and serve.

6 Additions to Fluffy Cracked Wheat

Instead of mustard and tarragon, try stirring these combos into the cracked wheat in Step 3 (always with a fork), either with or without the butter:

1. Stir in 3 finely chopped scallions and 2 tablespoons sunflower seeds.
2. Stir in 2 tablespoons of your favorite Chile Paste (page 828).
3. Add 2 tablespoons maple syrup (or less, to taste) and a pinch of cayenne (and honest, it's still not breakfast cereal).
4. Add $^1/_2$ cup fresh or frozen peas and $^1/_4$ cup minced fresh mint leaves. (A dollop of plain yogurt goes great with this.)
5. Throw in a couple dozen halved seedless grapes and $^1/_2$ cup chopped toasted almonds, hazelnuts, or pecans, along with lots of black pepper.
6. Use dark sesame or peanut oil instead of extra virgin olive oil, and finish by stirring in 1 tablespoon or so of soy sauce, $^1/_2$ cup chopped roasted peanuts, and $^1/_2$ cup chopped fresh cilantro.

Quinoa

Quinoa with Caramelized Onions

MAKES: 4 servings
TIME: About 1 hour, largely unattended

This dish makes an unbeatable bed for grilled vegetables or Braised Artichoke Hearts (page 259). The quinoa adds a subtle crunch to the deep and sweet flavor of slow-cooked onions, and, if you make it with red onions, the color is almost lavender. Molasses contributes a slightly smoky flavor.

Other grains you can use: amaranth, cracked wheat, or steel-cut oats.

4 medium yellow or red onions (about 1 pound), halved and thinly sliced

3 tablespoons extra virgin olive oil

2 tablespoons brown sugar or molasses

$^3/_4$ cup quinoa

Salt and freshly ground black pepper

1$^1/_2$ cups vegetable stock (pages 101–102), beer, or water

2 or 3 sprigs fresh thyme (optional)

① Put the onions in a large skillet with a lid over medium heat. Cover and cook, stirring infrequently, until the onions are dry and almost sticking to the pan, about 20 minutes. Add the oil and the brown sugar and cook, stirring occasionally, until the onions brown, another 10 to 15 minutes. (The onions can be cooked ahead to this point, covered, and refrigerated for a day or two. Gently reheat them in the covered skillet and proceed with the recipe.)

② Turn the heat up to medium-high, add the quinoa, and sprinkle with salt and pepper. Stir as the grains start popping and toasting, a couple of minutes, then add the stock and bring to a boil. Stir one last time, add the thyme if you're using it, cover, and reduce the heat to low. Cook, undisturbed, for 15 minutes.

③ Uncover and test the quinoa for doneness. If the kernels are still sort of hard, make sure there's enough liquid to keep the bottom of the pan moist and cover them to cook for another 5 minutes or so. When ready, taste, adjust the seasoning, and remove the thyme if necessary, adding a few extra grinds of pepper. Serve immediately or let cool to room temperature.

Quinoa with Caramelized Leeks. More elegant: Use about 1$^1/_2$ pounds leeks instead of the onions. Trim them until just a little green remains, rinse them carefully, and thinly slice.

Quinoa with Silky Cabbage. The technique and quantities are identical, but everything except the quinoa changes: Instead of the onions, use about a pound of any cabbage (1 small head or $^1/_2$ head of Napa or Savoy). Slice into thin ribbons. Instead of the olive oil, use 2 tablespoons peanut oil and 1 tablespoon dark sesame oil. Cut a few coins of peeled ginger to use instead of the thyme. Season with soy sauce instead of some of the salt and garnish with $^1/_2$ cup sliced scallion.

Quinoa and Parsnip Rösti

MAKES: 4 to 6 servings
TIME: 1 hour, largely unattended
Ⓜ

Switzerland is known for a spectacular but rustic potato pancake known as rösti. Here parsnips—with their sweet, herbaceous flavor and unbeatable creaminess—replace the potatoes, while quinoa adds yet another element of texture and loads of nutrition. So what you have is a crisp meal-in-a-cake, really great with a dollop of sour cream or yogurt or alongside Kidney Beans with Apples and Sherry (page 586).

Other grains you can use: plain or whole wheat couscous, pearled barley, millet.

Salt

1 pound parsnips (4 to 6, depending on size)

1 cup cooked quinoa (page 537), drained well

Freshly ground black pepper

6 tablespoons ($^3/_4$ stick) butter, melted

2 tablespoons minced fresh chives for garnish

① Bring a large pot of water to a boil and salt it. Cut the parsnips in half if necessary to fit the pot. When the water boils, add the parsnips and cook, checking once or twice, until they can be pierced with a tip of a knife but there's still some resistance, 10 to 15 minutes. Drain and set aside to cool.

② Put the quinoa in a large bowl, sprinkle with salt and pepper, and drizzle with 2 tablespoons of the butter. Toss lightly with your hands or a large fork.

③ Peel the parsnips and coarsely grate them over a strainer. Use a large spoon or a potato masher to press down on them and extract as much water as possible. Add them to the bowl with the quinoa and toss just enough to combine. Taste and adjust the seasoning.

④ Put 2 tablespoons of the remaining butter in a deep skillet over medium-high heat. When the butter is melted and hot but not smoking, add the quinoa mixture all at once, firmly pressing it down into the pan to form a solid "cake." Turn the heat down to low and cook, undisturbed, until the rösti starts to smell toasted—you'll know—20 to 25 minutes.

⑤ Remove the lid, carefully put a large dish over the skillet, and flip it to turn out the rösti. Add the remaining 2 tablespoons butter to the pan, swirl it around, and turn the heat up to medium. Carefully slide the rösti off the plate and back into place. Leave the skillet uncovered and cook the second side for 10 minutes or so, peeking once or twice to make sure it's browned nicely. Slide the finished rösti back onto the plate and sprinkle with chives. Serve immediately or at room temperature, cut into wedges.

Spicy Quinoa and Carrot Rosti. Instead of parsnips, use carrots, which will take only 5 minutes or so to boil and become crisp-tender. Add 1 teaspoon ground cumin and a pinch of cayenne to the butter as it melts.

Roasted Quinoa with Potatoes and Cheese

MAKES: 4 to 6 servings

TIME: 1 hour

Ⓜ

When you boil quinoa for a couple of minutes, then roast it in oil, it develops a crispness that's almost like nuts. Here the crisp-roasted quinoa almost coats the potatoes, and you finish the whole thing off with melted cheese.

If you can find purple potatoes, use them here. With a simple green salad—and in summer, sliced ripe tomatoes—this is a perfect lunch or light supper. With scrambled eggs, warm tortillas, and salsa, it's weekend breakfast. Add any good bean dish and you have a satisfying dinner.

Other grains you can use: amaranth, fine bulgur (#1).

1/4 cup extra virgin olive oil

1 pound small waxy potatoes, like fingerling, new red, or Peruvian purple, peeled if you like and cut lengthwise into wedges

3 to 4 cloves garlic, peeled

Salt

3/4 cup quinoa

Freshly ground black pepper

1/2 cup sliced scallion

1 medium red bell pepper, cored, seeded, and chopped

1 or 2 tablespoons minced fresh chile (like jalapeño or Thai), or to taste, or hot red pepper flakes or cayenne to taste

6 ounces cheese, preferably smoked, like cheddar, Gouda, or mozzarella, grated (about 1 1/2 cups)

1/4 cup minced parsley for garnish

① Preheat the oven to 400°F. Grease an 8 × 10-inch roasting pan with a tablespoon or so of the olive oil.

② Put the potato wedges and garlic in a large pot with water to cover, salt it, and turn the heat to high. When the water begins to boil, stir in the quinoa. Adjust the heat so that the water boils assertively and cook, stirring once or twice, for about 5 minutes.

③ Drain the quinoa, garlic, and potatoes in a strainer, but leave them fairly wet. Spread them into the prepared pan, sprinkle with salt and pepper, drizzle with the remaining olive oil, and gently toss with a spatula. Spread them out again. Roast, undisturbed, for

15 minutes. Gently toss again, scraping up any browned bits from the bottom of the pan, and return the pan to the oven for another 10 minutes or so, until the potatoes are tender on the inside and golden on the outside.

④ Add the scallion, bell pepper, and chile and toss everything one last time. Taste and adjust the seasoning, keeping in mind that the cheese will add some saltiness. Spread the cheese over all and return to the oven for another 5 to 8 minutes, until the cheese is melted and bubbling. Sprinkle with parsley and serve.

Kasha

Kasha with Golden Brown Onions

MAKES: 4 servings
TIME: 30 minutes

This is the basic and classic Eastern European kasha dish, and, with its deeply browned onions, it's delicious. Many people toss their kasha with an egg before cooking, because it keeps the grains separate. But toasting it in oil accomplishes the same goal, so take your pick. (Without either, the kasha will become mushier, which is fine too.) Omit the butter to make this vegan.

3 cups chopped onion

3 tablespoons neutral oil, like grapeseed or corn

1 egg or 2 more tablespoons neutral oil, like grapeseed or corn

1 cup kasha

Salt and freshly ground black pepper

2 cups vegetable stock (pages 101–102) or water, warmed

1 to 2 tablespoons butter (optional)

① Put the onion in a large skillet with a lid over medium heat. Cover the skillet and cook for about 15 minutes, until the onion is dry and almost sticking to the pan. Add the oil, raise the heat to medium-high, and cook, stirring, until the onion is nicely browned, another 15 minutes or so.

② Meanwhile, if you're using the egg, beat it, then toss it in a bowl with the kasha. (If not, proceed to Step 3.) Put the mixture along with some salt and pepper in a heavy, large, deep skillet over medium-high heat. Cook, stirring, until the mixture smells toasty, about 3 minutes.

③ If you're using the oil instead of egg, put it in a heavy, deep skillet over medium-high heat. When hot, add the kasha, along with some salt and pepper, and cook, stirring, until the mixture smells toasty, about 3 minutes.

④ Turn the heat to a minimum and carefully add the stock. Cover and cook until the liquid is absorbed, about 15 minutes. Turn off the heat. Stir in the onion, taste, and adjust the seasoning. Serve or let the kasha sit for up to 30 minutes before serving.

⑤ When you're ready to serve, fluff with a fork, adding the butter if you like at the same time.

Kasha Varnishkes. Possibly the best-known and best use of kasha, with pasta: Add 1 pound bowtie, shell, or broad egg noodles. Cook the pasta in boiling salted water until tender but still firm; drain and combine with the kasha and caramelized onions.

Kasha with Parsnips. A nice midwinter dish: Replace the onion with 2 cups or so (about a pound) of peeled and chopped parsnips. In Step 1, put the oil in the pan first, then add the parsnips; cook until the parsnips are golden brown and tender, about 15 minutes. Proceed with the recipe.

Kasha with Carrots. Replace the onion with 2 cups or so (about a pound) peeled and chopped carrots. In Step 1, put the oil in the pan first, then add the parsnips; cook until the carrots are golden brown and tender, about 15 minutes. Proceed with the recipe.

Kasha with Mushrooms. Very flavorful and meaty: Replace the onion with 2 cups or so (about 8 ounces) chopped or sliced mushrooms, like shiitake, cremini, portobello, button, or a mixture. In Step 1, put the oil in the pan first, then add the mushrooms; cook until the mushrooms are golden brown and soft, about 5 minutes. Proceed with the recipe.

Kasha with Radicchio or Escarole. You like bitter? This is it: Replace the onions with 2 cups chopped radicchio or escarole. In Step 1, put the oil in the pan first, then add the green and cook until softened, about 3 minutes. Add 1/4 cup freshly squeezed orange juice and a pinch of sugar and cook until the mixture is dark brown and nearly dry, 5 to 8 minutes. Proceed with the recipe.

Kasha Pilaf with Caramelized Endive. Replace the onion with 3 Belgian endives, chopped; reduce the oil to 3 tablespoons. In Step 1, put the butter or oil in the pan first, then add the endive; cook until softened and golden brown, about 10 minutes. Add 1/4 cup freshly squeezed orange juice and cook until the mixture is golden and nearly dry, 5 to 8 minutes. Proceed with the recipe.

Buckwheat Groats

Buckwheat Stew with Tofu and Kale

MAKES: 4 servings
TIME: 40 minutes

Buckwheat groats, or peeled buckwheat as it's sometimes called, is not the same as kasha, which is pre-roasted (see page 535). What nonkasha buckwheat has is a certain freshness, almost grassiness, that can be quite refreshing when treated properly. It takes some pan-toasting in oil to bring out its charm, but believe me, that charm is evident here. Unlike kasha, this never turns mushy: the nutty texture remains through the cooking.

Other grains you can use: farro, millet, pearled barley.

1/4 cup peanut or neutral oil, like grapeseed or corn

1 onion, chopped

1 potato, peeled and chopped, or 1 cup white or wheat vermicelli, broken into 1-inch pieces

1/2 cup buckwheat groats (not kasha)

8 to 10 cloves garlic, peeled

Salt and freshly ground black pepper

4 cups kale or collards with no stems over 1/4 inch thick, washed and chopped

8 to 10 ounces firm tofu, cut into 1/2-inch cubes

About 2 cups stock or water (1/2 cup of this could be white wine)

1 teaspoon Chile Paste (page 828), or to taste

2 tablespoons soy sauce, or to taste

❶ Put the oil in a deep skillet with a lid over medium heat. Add the onion, potato, buckwheat, and garlic and cook, stirring, until everything is pretty much dry and sticking to the pan; sprinkle with salt and pepper.

❷ Add the greens and cook, stirring, until they wilt a little, about 5 minutes; add the tofu and cook, still stirring, until the tofu browns a little, about 5 more minutes.

❸ Add about 1/2 cup of liquid, wine first if you're using it, and stir with a wooden spoon to release all the browned bits on the bottom of the pan. Add another cup of liquid, then adjust the heat so the mixture simmers and cook, checking and stirring every 5 minutes or so and adding additional liquid as necessary, until the buckwheat is just about tender, about 20 minutes.

❹ Stir in the chile paste and soy sauce and cook until both buckwheat and greens are tender, another 5 minutes or so; enough liquid should remain so the mixture is saucy, not soupy or dry. Taste and adjust the seasoning, then serve.

Wheat Berries

Summer Vegetable Stew with Wheat Berries

MAKES: 4 to 6 servings
TIME: About 20 minutes with cooked grains

A stew of wheat berries may bring to mind anything but summer, but a pot of bright, crisp summer vegetables combined with chewy wheat berries is both refreshing and satisfying.

Other grains you can use: hulled barley, rye berries, and hominy.

3 tablespoons extra virgin olive oil, plus oil
    for drizzling

1 medium leek, including a little green, thinly sliced

Salt and freshly ground black pepper

1/4 pound green or wax beans, sliced into 1-inch
    pieces (1 scant cup)

1 small zucchini, pattypan, or summer squash,
    thinly sliced

1/2 cup white wine, vegetable stock (pages 101–102),
    or water

2 cups cooked wheat berries (page 537)

2 medium ripe tomatoes, cored and cut into wedges

1/2 cup chopped fresh basil or parsley leaves

1 Put the oil in a large saucepan or deep skillet with a lid over medium-high heat. When hot, add the leek and sprinkle with salt and pepper. Cook, stirring occasionally, until soft, about 2 minutes. Add the green beans and zucchini and stir to coat with the oil. Stir in the wine.

2 Reduce the heat to medium-low, cover, and cook, stirring once or twice, until the vegetables are just start-

F Fast   M Make Ahead   V Vegan

ing to get tender, 5 to 7 minutes. Raise the heat a bit and stir in the wheat berries.

③ Cook, stirring frequently, until hot and bubbling, a minute or two. Stir in the tomatoes, season again with salt and pepper, cover, and turn off the heat. After about 5 minutes, add the herb and fluff the stew gently with a fork. Taste and adjust the seasoning. Serve right away or at room temperature (up to an hour or so later), drizzled with a little more olive oil if you like.

Quick Wheat Berry Stew with Fall Vegetables. You can make this right through the winter: Instead of the leeks, green beans, and zucchini, use 1 medium yellow onion, a couple of medium turnips or carrots, chopped, and an acorn squash, peeled, seeded, and chopped. Increase the cooking time in Step 2 to 15 to 20 minutes. Instead of the tomatoes, cut several cabbage or Swiss chard leaves into ribbons (enough to make a heaping cup) and stir them into the pot. Cook for about 5 minutes more, then finish with a tablespoon minced fresh sage leaves (or a teaspoon dried) in place of the basil or parsley.

Quick Wheat Berry Stew with Citrus, Dried Fruit, and Nuts. A nice change of pace: Instead of the leeks, green beans, and zucchini, use 2 tablespoons minced peeled fresh ginger, 3 or 4 small Valencia oranges or tangerines (peeled, thinly sliced crosswise, and seeded), and $1/2$ cup dried cranberries or cherries. Instead of the tomatoes, stir $1/2$ cup chopped dried apricots or dates into the pot. Finish with $1/4$ cup chopped almonds or pistachios in place of the basil or parsley.

Quick Wheat Berry Stew with Spring Vegetables. A celebration: Instead of the leeks, green beans, and zucchini, use 2 or 3 scallions, snap or snow peas, and a handful of asparagus spears (sliced into 1-inch pieces). Instead of the tomatoes, use $1/2$ cup fresh peas. Finish with fresh chopped fresh mint leaves in place of the basil or parsley.

Millet

Millet Mash

MAKES: 4 servings
TIME: 45 minutes, largely unattended

Some version or another of these millet "mashed potatoes" has been making the rounds in vegetarian circles for a long time. The secrets to the texture are cauliflower and the cooking water. With the protein from the millet, these will stick to your ribs longer than Mashed Potatoes (page 341), and virtually all the variations and additions you find there will work with this too, though I've included some millet-specific combinations in the variations here.

2 tablespoons neutral oil, like grapeseed or corn

1 cup millet

Salt and freshly ground black pepper

$1/2$ head cauliflower, coarsely chopped (about $1 1/2$ cups)

3 cups vegetable stock (pages 101–102) or water

1 head Roasted Garlic (page 304), squeezed from the skin (optional)

① Put the oil in a large pot with a lid over medium heat. Add the millet and stir constantly until it toasts and turns golden, about 3 minutes.

② Sprinkle with salt and pepper and add the cauliflower and $2 1/2$ cups of the stock. Bring to a boil, then lower the heat so the mixture bubbles gently, cover, and cook, stirring occasionally, until the millet bursts, about 30 minutes. Add a little stock anytime the mixture gets too dry.

③ Remove from the heat and use an immersion blender to purée the millet and cauliflower in the pan. Or cool the mixture slightly, pour into a food processor or food mill (which will make the mash very fluffy), and carefully purée. Return the mash to the pot, add the roasted garlic if you're using it, and reheat gently, stirring in more stock if needed. Taste, adjust the seasoning, and serve.

Creamy Millet Mash. Richer, but no more difficult: Instead of plain water, cook the millet and cauliflower in $2^1/_2$ cups whole milk (or nondairy milk). It might take a little bit longer, and you will still have to add water if the mixture gets too dry. Proceed with the recipe from Step 3, adding 2 tablespoons of butter at the end if you like.

Cheesy Millet Mash. Richer: Make either the main recipe or the preceding variation. After puréeing, in Step 3, add 1 cup grated cheddar, manchego, or Gruyère cheese to the mash, along with $1/_4$ cup or so of milk and a pat of butter if you like.

Millet Miso Mash. Great flavor: Skip the garlic. After puréeing, in Step 3, add $1/_4$ cup white miso to the mash along with a splash of water or sake if you like. Serve, garnished with sliced scallion.

Millet Tahini Mash. Dense yet lively: Skip the garlic. After puréeing, in Step 3, add $1/_4$ cup tahini and the juice of a lemon to the mash.

Millet Carrot Mash with Ginger, Sesame, and Soy. Skip the garlic and use peanut oil instead of neutral oil, but while you're toasting the millet, add 2 tablespoons peeled and minced fresh ginger to the pot. Instead of the cauliflower, use 8 ounces carrots, chopped. After puréeing, in Step 3, season the mash with a little soy sauce instead of the salt. Drizzle each mound of mash with a little sesame oil and sprinkle with toasted sesame seeds (see page 321).

Autumn Millet Bake

MAKES: 4 to 6 servings

TIME: About $1^1/_2$ hours, largely unattended

Ⓜ Ⓥ

Though this is perfect for Thanksgiving, you'll probably want to eat it more than once a year. The slightly sweet flavor of the squash, which makes the dish creamy without adding dairy, is nicely balanced with tart fresh cranberries and the nutty flavor of millet.

Other grains you can use: quinoa, amaranth, teff, cracked wheat.

$1/_4$ cup extra virgin olive oil, plus oil for the dish

$3/_4$ cup millet

1 medium butternut or other winter squash or 1 small pumpkin, peeled, seeded, and cut into 1-inch cubes

1 cup fresh cranberries (about 4 ounces)

Salt and freshly ground black pepper

1 tablespoon minced fresh sage leaves or 1 teaspoon dried

2 tablespoons maple syrup or honey

1 cup vegetable stock (pages 101–102) or water, warmed

$1/_4$ cup pumpkin seeds or coarsely chopped hazelnuts

❶ Preheat the oven to 375°F and grease a 2-quart casserole, a large gratin dish, or a 9 × 13-inch baking dish with olive oil.

❷ Put 2 tablespoons of the oil in a small skillet over medium–high heat. When hot, add the millet and cook, stirring frequently, until fragrant and golden, about 3 minutes. Spread in the bottom of the prepared baking dish.

❸ Scatter the squash or pumpkin cubes and the cranberries on top of the millet. Sprinkle with salt and pepper and the sage and drizzle with syrup. Carefully pour the warmed stock over all. Cover tightly with foil and bake, without disturbing, for 45 minutes.

❹ Carefully uncover and turn the oven up to 400°F. As discreetly as possible, sneak a taste and adjust the seasoning. If it looks too dry, add a spoonful or two of water or stock. Sprinkle the pumpkin seeds on top (a good way to camouflage your taste) and return the dish to the oven. Bake until the mixture bubbles and the top is browned, another 10 minutes or so. Serve piping hot or at room temperature.

Autumn Millet Bake with Cream. Richer, obviously: Use a mixture of 1 cup heated cream and $^1/_2$ cup stock, instead of all stock.

Wild Rice

Basic Wild Rice

MAKES: 4 servings
TIME: 40 minutes

Wild rice is indigenous to North America and has been harvested since prehistoric times, when it was eaten by Native Americans in the Great Lakes region and a main source of protein and other nutrients. Now there is cultivated wild rice, which usually comes from California, and wild rice, which still comes mostly from Minnesota and neighboring states and provinces. Either can be quite good and either can taste like pine needles, but though wild rice is a nice change, there are other, more interesting grains that don't cost five or six bucks a pound. Whatever you do, don't buy the little boxes you find in the supermarket, which are inferior; mail order is better (see Sources, page 929).

You can cook wild rice with brown, white rice, or pearled barley (I like this combo very much) in equal quantities and integrate its flavor into almost any other rice dish. But beware that it takes almost as long as brown rice to cook, so plan ahead a bit (or parboil it according to the instructions on page 506 before combining it with white rice). The easiest way to cook it by itself is with the recipe for Cooked Grains, the Easy Way (page 537), but this is a little more sophisticated.

Skip the butter to make this vegan.

1 cup wild rice
3 cups vegetable stock (pages 101–102) or water
1 bay leaf
Salt and freshly ground black pepper

1 tablespoon butter or extra virgin olive oil (optional)
Minced parsley leaves for garnish

❶ Combine the wild rice, stock, bay leaf, and some salt and pepper in a medium saucepan over medium-high heat and bring to a boil.

❷ Cover, turn the heat down to low, and cook, undisturbed, for 30 minutes. Check the progress: The rice is done when the grains have puffed up and are quite tender, regardless of whether the liquid has been absorbed. If the rice is not done, continue to cook, adding more liquid if necessary. If it is done, drain if necessary.

❸ Stir in the butter if you like, garnish, and serve.

Wild Rice with Curried Nuts. Instead of using plain butter, while the rice is cooking, melt 2 tablespoons butter or peanut or neutral oil, like grapeseed or corn, in a large skillet. Add 1 tablespoon curry powder or any other spice mix (to make your own, see pages 810–819) and cook, stirring, for 1 minute. Stir in $^1/_2$ to 1 cup broken (not finely chopped) cashews, almonds, pecans, or walnuts. Cook, stirring, until they begin to brown. Turn off the heat until the rice is done, then drain the rice if necessary and add it to the nut-butter mixture. Cook over medium-low heat, stirring, until hot.

Wild Rice with Brussels Sprouts. Why this is such a great combination I don't know, but the two work very well together: While the rice is cooking, prepare 8 ounces Brussels sprouts according to the recipe for Roasted Brussels Sprouts with Garlic, page 273. Stir them into the rice just as it is finishing cooking and serve.

Wild Rice with Roasted Winter Squash. This screams autumn: Roast about 1 cup butternut or other winter squash (page 366) with butter or olive oil; stir into the rice just as it finishes cooking and serve.

Wild Rice with Chestnuts. Also fall-like and good combined with the Brussels sprouts (above) or mushrooms (next page): Roast or deep-fry about 12 chestnuts (see page 287 or 238). Peel, roughly chop, stir into the rice just as it finishes cooking, and serve.

Wild Rice with Mushrooms. While the rice is cooking, cook about 1 cup shiitake mushroom caps, sliced, in 2 tablespoons butter or extra virgin olive oil until crisp, about 10 minutes. Stir into the rice just as it finishes cooking and serve.

Wild Rice with Dried Fruit. When you add the butter or olive oil and parsley, stir in $1/2$ cup chopped dried fruit, like apricots, cherries, cranberries, mango, or apple. Put the lid back on for a minute or two to warm through and plump.

Rye Berries

Rye Berry Gratin with Leeks and Tomatoes

MAKES: 4 servings

TIME: 1 hour, largely unattended, with cooked rye berries

Ⓜ

Whole grain kernels make gorgeous and easy gratins. It helps if your grains are slightly underdone when you start, because they cook a bit more in the oven, while the custard and topping set and crisp around them.

Here the recipe here is topped with ripe fresh tomatoes, but in the off-season you might try a thinly sliced zucchini, a handful of whole asparagus spears, or even a smattering of whole pitted black olives. This gratin is also good without any vegetables at all; just reduce the baking time to 30 minutes or so and finish with an extra dusting of cheese.

Other grains you can use: wheat, kamut, or spelt berries; hulled or pearled barley; kasha, farro, or hominy.

3 tablespoons extra virgin olive oil or butter, melted, plus more for the dish

1 large or 2 medium leeks, including some green, washed and thinly sliced (about 2 cups)

2 tablespoons minced garlic

Salt and freshly ground black pepper

$1/2$ cup milk or cream

1 egg

$1/4$ cup freshly grated Parmesan cheese, plus cheese for garnish

$1/4$ teaspoon freshly grated nutmeg

$2^{1}/2$ cups cooked rye berries (page 537)

3 medium ripe tomatoes, cored and cut crosswise into thin slices

Several sprigs fresh thyme

❶ Grease a 2-quart soufflé or gratin dish or an oblong baking pan. Preheat the oven to 350°F.

❷ Put 2 tablespoons of the oil or butter in a deep skillet with a lid over medium-high heat. When the oil is hot or the butter is melted, add the leeks and garlic and sprinkle with salt and pepper. Cook, stirring frequently, until softened and dry, about 2 minutes. Turn the heat down to low, cover, and cook, stirring occasionally, until melting, about 5 minutes.

❸ Whisk the milk with the egg in a small bowl until blended. Add the cheese and the nutmeg and set aside. When the leeks are done, stir in the rye berries and heat until warmed through. Turn off the heat, taste, and adjust the seasoning. (Remember, you'll be adding Parmesan to the dish.)

❹ Spread the leek and rye mixture into the bottom of the prepared pan. Drizzle the egg and cheese mixture over it all. Top with the tomato slices and thyme sprigs. Drizzle with the remaining tablespoon of oil or butter.

❺ Bake until the edges and top are browned and bubbling, 45 to 55 minutes, depending on how deep your baking dish is. Remove the thyme if you like and sprinkle with additional cheese, salt, and pepper. Serve immediately or let rest for up to an hour and serve at room temperature.

Creamy Rye Gratin with Leeks and Tomatoes. For a creamier, less custardy texture, omit the egg and use heavy cream.

Vegan Rye Gratin with Leeks and Tomatoes. Add $1/2$ cup chopped hazelnuts or almonds to the leek mixture.

Ⓕ Fast   Ⓜ Make Ahead   Ⓥ Vegan

Omit the egg and the cheese and use $^1/_2$ cup hazelnut or almond milk instead of the milk or cream.

Hominy Baked with Chile, Cheese, and Tomatoes. Instead of rye, use cooked hominy (page 537; canned is fine too, provided you drain it well). Replace the leeks with 2 fresh poblano chiles or 1 medium red bell pepper, cored, seeded, and thinly sliced). Instead of the Parmesan, use grated cheddar or Jack cheese and increase the quantity to $^1/_2$ cup.

Rice Baked with Chile, Cheese, and Tomatoes. Follow the preceding variation, substituting 3 cups cooked white or brown rice (preferably a long-grain variety; see page 502) for the hominy.

Grain Griddlecakes

If you don't already love leftover grains, these will do the trick. Don't think of them as pancakes. You start with cooked food, adding a little binder (usually egg, but see page 29 for a substitute), filler (usually flour), and leavening (baking powder) to create a savory main dish or accompaniment. And it doesn't take much leftover grain—a cup or so will suffice—to jump-start a batch of griddlecakes.

To cook, use an electric griddle, stovetop griddle, or heavy skillet (cast-iron is best). Heat it to about 375°F—a drop of water will dance for a moment and quickly evaporate—and spread enough butter or oil across the surface to make sure the batter won't stick. Add a little more butter or oil between batches if necessary.

Resist the temptation to flip griddlecakes prematurely. Though the right time to turn won't be quite as obvious with grain cakes as with pancakes, they will have some bubbles and begin to look dry and firm around the edges. Use your nose, too: they will smell toasty when the bottom is cooked correctly.

Griddlecakes are always best eaten immediately, but you can keep them warm while you continue cooking large batches: Just put a wire rack set on a cookie sheet, a heatproof plate, or a pan in a 200°F oven and set the finished griddlecakes in there for a few minutes.

Parmesan Rice Cakes

MAKES: 4 servings

TIME: About 20 minutes

Cheese ensures these griddlecakes are crisp, well browned, and rich. Feel free to substitute aged cheddar, Gruyère, a semidry or dry pecorino, or even crumbled feta cheese for the Parmesan. Serve these with any tomato sauce (pages 445–449) or Mushroom Ketchup (page 791).

Other grains you can use: pearled or hulled barley, farro, kamut, rye, spelt, or wheat berries.

2 eggs

$^1/_2$ cup milk, half-and-half, or cream, plus more as needed

$1^1/_2$ cups cooked white or brown rice

$^1/_2$ cup freshly grated Parmesan cheese

$^1/_2$ cup all-purpose flour

$^1/_2$ teaspoon baking powder

Salt and cayenne to taste

$^1/_4$ cup neutral oil, like grapeseed or corn, or 4 tablespoons ($^1/_2$ stick) butter

$^1/_4$ cup minced parsley for garnish (optional)

1 Heat a heavy skillet or griddle to a temperature of about 375°F.

2 Whisk the eggs and milk together in a medium bowl until well combined. Whisk in the rice and cheese. Switch to a spoon, add the flour and baking powder, and sprinkle with just a little salt and as much cayenne as you like. Add enough extra milk to make a smooth, medium-thick batter.

3 When a drop of water skips across the skillet or griddle before evaporating, it's ready. Put a little oil or butter in the pan and let it bubble. Using a large spoon, scoop up a bit of the batter and put it in the pan. It should spread about 3 inches. Cook as many griddlecakes at once as will fit comfortably, turning them after a couple of minutes, when they are brown. Total cooking time will run between 5 and 8 minutes. Serve immediately, ideally straight from the pan, sprinkled with parsley if you like.

Griddlecakes Made from Oatmeal (or Other Porridge)

MAKES: 4 servings
TIME: 30 minutes with cooked oatmeal

Porridge—any grain that cooks up soft and creamy—is naturally "wetter" than whole-kernel cooked grains and therefore easier to make into cakes. In fact, when you take a bowl of leftover porridge out of the fridge, it's a solid mass that can be cut up and panfried or grilled like polenta (page 543). These griddlecakes are delicious with herb sauces like Mint Purée and Chimichurri (page 769).

Other "porridges" that are good in this recipe: grits, polenta, sticky rice, cracked wheat, or anything made from grain flakes (see pages 534–537).

About $^1/_4$ cup neutral oil, like grapeseed or corn, or 4 tablespoons ($^1/_2$ stick) butter

$^1/_2$ cup finely minced onion

Salt and freshly ground black pepper

1 egg

$^1/_4$ cup milk, half-and-half, or cream

2 cups cooked oatmeal

$^1/_4$ cup all-purpose flour

$^1/_2$ teaspoon baking powder

1 Put 2 tablespoons of the oil or butter in a small skillet over medium-high heat. When the oil is hot or the butter is melted, add the onion, sprinkle with salt and

pepper, and cook, stirring frequently, until the onion is soft and starting to brown, about 2 minutes. Turn the heat down to medium-low and continue cooking, stirring occasionally, until well caramelized, 5 to 7 minutes more. Remove from the heat and set aside.

2 Heat a heavy skillet or griddle to about 375°F.

3 Whisk the egg and milk together. Add the oatmeal and keep whisking until smooth. Switch to a spoon and add the flour, $^1/_2$ teaspoon salt, and the baking powder. Stir until just combined, then stir in the cooked onion.

4 When a drop of water skips across the skillet or griddle before evaporating, it's ready. Put a little oil or butter in the pan and let it bubble. Using a tablespoon, scoop up a bit of the batter and put it in the pan. Cook as many griddlecakes at once as will fit comfortably, turning them after a couple of minutes, when they are brown. Total cooking time will run between 5 and 8 minutes. Serve immediately, ideally straight from the pan.

Savory Oatcakes with Peas and Carrots. In Step 1, when you turn down the heat, add $^1/_4$ cup peas (frozen are fine) and $^1/_4$ cup chopped carrot to the pan.

Curried Oatcakes. Use scallions. In Step 1, when you turn down the heat, add 1 tablespoon curry powder (to make your own, see pages 815–816). Serve the oatcakes with Raita or Sweet Yogurt Sauce (page 774) or Cilantro-Mint Chutney (page 783).

Crunchy Amaranth Griddlecakes

MAKES: 4 servings
TIME: About 20 minutes with cooked amaranth

Amaranth works best as an ingredient, not a stand-alone grain, because even when fully cooked it retains a super-firm texture. And that's exactly what makes these simple griddlecakes so appealing. Serve these with Dried Fruit and Lima Stew (page 594), any Beans and Greens (page

595) or as part of any grilled vegetable meal (don't forget your favorite yogurt sauce; page 774).

Other grains you can use (but that won't be quite as crunchy as amaranth): bulgur (any grind), regular or whole wheat couscous, cracked wheat, kasha, millet, quinoa, wheat berries, wild rice.

1 egg

1 cup cooked amaranth

Salt and freshly ground black pepper

$1/2$ cup all-purpose flour

$1/4$ teaspoon baking powder

Milk, half-and-half, or cream as needed (no more than $1/4$ cup)

1 tablespoon minced fresh thyme leaves

2 to 3 tablespoons neutral oil, like grapeseed or corn, or butter

1 Heat a heavy skillet or griddle to about 375°F.

2 Whisk the egg in a bowl until well beaten. Whisk in the amaranth and sprinkle with salt and pepper. Whisk in the flour and baking powder. Add enough milk to make a smooth, medium-thick batter. Whisk in the thyme.

3 When a drop of water skips across the skillet or griddle before evaporating, it's ready. Put a little oil or butter in the pan and let it bubble. Using a large spoon, scoop up a bit of the batter and put it in the pan. It should spread about 3 inches. Cook as many griddle-cakes at once as will fit comfortably, turning them after a couple of minutes, when they are brown. Total cooking time will run between 5 and 8 minutes. Serve immediately, ideally straight from the pan.

11 Additions to Crunchy Amaranth Griddlecakes

Whisk these in, either alone or in combination, with the egg before adding the grain.

1. A minced shallot
2. A couple cloves Roasted Garlic (page 304), squeezed from their skins
3. A tablespoon or so of soy sauce (reduce the salt)
4. Horseradish (freshly grated or prepared), to taste
5. A tablespoon of chopped fresh chives
6. $1/4$ cup finely chopped nuts, like almonds, walnuts, hazelnuts, or pecans
7. $1/4$ cup peanut butter
8. $1/4$ cup minced scallion
9. $1/4$ cup chopped dried fruit, like apricots, cherries, cranberries, or apple
10. $1/2$ cup chopped cooked greens, like kale, spinach, or chard, squeezed dry
11. $1/2$ cup corn kernels (thawed frozen are fine)

Risotto "Frittata"

MAKES: 2 servings

TIME: 20 minutes with leftover risotto

Suppose you've just made a batch of risotto and now have leftovers: Here's one thing to do with them. Because it's more rice than eggs, it's more like a griddle-cake than a real frittata, but it is a perfect next-day lunch or supper.

If you want to make a bigger batch (and this is a great dish to take to a party), make a full recipe of risotto a little in advance and double the other ingredients. Instead of cooking the mixture in a skillet, spread it in a greased oblong pan and bake it at 375°F long enough to set the eggs, 20 minutes or so. Then run it under the broiler for a minute or two to brown the top.

2 to $2^1/2$ cups leftover risotto (page 517)

2 eggs

2 tablespoons milk or cream

$1/4$ teaspoon baking powder

Salt and freshly ground black pepper

2 to 3 tablespoons extra virgin olive oil

Freshly grated Parmesan cheese for garnish (optional)

1. Take the risotto out of the fridge for a few minutes to take the chill off before starting.

2. Whisk the eggs, milk, and baking powder together. Sprinkle with salt and pepper and fold in the risotto. Stir until everything is integrated into one semi-thick mass.

3. Put 2 tablespoons of the olive oil in a deep skillet (not too large) with a tight-fitting lid over medium-high heat. When the oil is hot but not smoking, add the risotto mixture all at once, firmly pressing it down into the pan to form a solid cake. Turn the heat down to low and cook, undisturbed, until the frittata starts to smell toasted—you'll know—10 minutes or so.

4. Remove the lid, carefully put a large dish over the skillet, and flip it to turn out the frittata. Add the remaining oil to the pan if it looks dry, swirl it around, and turn the heat up to medium. Carefully slide the frittata off the plate and back into place. Leave the skillet uncovered and cook the second side for 5 minutes or so, peeking once or twice to make sure it's browned nicely. Slide the finished frittata back onto the plate and sprinkle with some cheese if you like. Serve immediately or at room temperature, cut into wedges.

The Basics of Grains for Breakfast Cereal

Oatmeal and Wheatena aren't your only whole grain options at the breakfast table. One basic cooking technique can be applied to whatever grain you want to cook for a hot and hearty breakfast cereal. To add even more variety, you can substitute regular, soy, nut, or grain milk for half the water or stir in a bit of the milk, cream, or half-and-half at the end of cooking.

Fast-cooking grains that are good for hot breakfast cereal: farina, cracked wheat, cornmeal (grits or polenta), amaranth, teff, rolled barley, rolled spelt.

Slow-cooking grains that are good for hot breakfast cereal: wheat berries, rye berries, kamut, spelt, barley.

1. Combine $1/2$ cup any of the grains listed above, rinsed, with a large pinch of salt and water to cover by at least an inch in a saucepan. Bring to a boil, then adjust the heat so the mixture bubbles gently.

2. Cook, stirring occasionally, until the grain is tender. This will take as little as 3 minutes with farina, as long as 20 minutes or more for cracked wheat and teff, as long as an hour for wheat berries. Add additional boiling water as necessary to keep the grains covered and to adjust the consistency. Be sure there's enough water in the pot to keep the grain from drying out.

3. The grain is done when it tastes cooked and is as tender as you like it. Stir in some butter or any milk or cream and add whatever garnishes you like (see "9 Great Things to Stir into Oatmeal and Other Cooked Grains" on page 573 for ideas).

Oatmeal or Other Creamy Breakfast Cereal

MAKES: 2 servings

TIME: 15 minutes

Ⓕ　Ⓜ

You can cook any kind of rolled or flaked grain this way; try wheat, rye, quinoa, millet, kamut, or brown rice flakes. And please don't bother with quick-cooking or instant oats; the old-fashioned style takes barely 5 minutes more, and the flavor and texture are far better. This recipe gives you a fairly creamy oatmeal; if you prefer it thicker, use a bit less water.

Skip the butter and milk to make this vegan.

Dash salt

1 cup rolled oats

Butter (optional)

Salt, sweetener (such as maple syrup, sugar, or honey), and/or milk or cream as desired

① Combine $2^{1}/_{4}$ cups water, the salt, and the oats in a small saucepan over high heat. When the water boils, turn the heat down to low and cook, stirring, until the water is just absorbed, about 5 minutes. Add butter to taste if desired, cover the pan, and turn off the heat.

② Five minutes later, uncover the pan and stir. Add other ingredients as desired and serve.

9 Great Things to Stir into Oatmeal and Other Cooked Grains

When feeding a crew, provide an array of garnishes for your guests to dress their own cereals.

1. Ground spices, like cinnamon, nutmeg, cloves, allspice, cardamom, or anise
2. Chopped dried fruit
3. Chopped nuts and/or seeds
4. Fresh fruit, chopped or sliced if necessary: apples, bananas, strawberries, apricots, peaches, blueberries, cherries, or raspberries
5. Jam, jelly, marmalade, preserves, or fruit compote (page 411)
6. Shredded coconut (great when toasted)
7. Crunchy Granola (below)
8. Grated cheese
9. Chopped Hard-Cooked Egg (page 166)
10. Poached Egg (page 169) (You can also poach eggs directly in cooking grains, simply by cracking an egg into the simmering mixture during the last 3 to 5 minutes of cooking.)

Crunchy Granola

MAKES: About 8 cups
TIME: 30 minutes

The basic technique for making granola is always the same; it's what you put in it that makes it special. Think of this recipe as a guideline for a basic granola and then customize it in any way you like; there are lots of ideas in these pages.

Rolled oats are the most common grain, but you can use lots of other rolled and flaked grains, like wheat, rye, quinoa, millet, kamut, or brown rice flakes. Increase or decrease the other ingredients as you like and toss in other ingredients like nut butters, vanilla, or citrus zest. See the variations and the "Customizing Crunchy Granola" chart for ideas. Use maple syrup instead of honey to make vegan granola.

6 cups rolled oats (not quick cooking or instant)

2 cups mixed nuts and seeds, like sunflower seeds, chopped walnuts, pecans, almonds, cashews, and sesame seeds

1 cup shredded coconut

1 teaspoon ground cinnamon, or to taste

Dash salt

$^{1}/_{2}$ to 1 cup honey or maple syrup, or to taste

1 cup raisins or chopped dried fruit

① Preheat the oven to 300°F.

② Put a 9 × 13-inch roasting pan over medium-low heat (put the pan over 2 burners if it's convenient). Add the oats and cook, stirring occasionally, until they begin to change color and become fragrant, 3 to 5 minutes.

③ Add the nuts and seeds and continue to cook, stirring frequently, for 2 minutes. Add the coconut and cook, stirring, for 2 minutes more. Add the cinnamon, salt, and sweetener, stir, and put in the oven. Bake for 20 minutes, stirring once or twice.

④ Add the dried fruit, stir, and cool on a rack, continuing to stir once in a while until the granola reaches room temperature. Transfer to a sealed container and store in the refrigerator; it will keep indefinitely.

Peanut Butter Granola. Any nut butter or tahini will work nicely here; toss in some chocolate chips if you like very sweet granola: Add $^{1}/_{2}$ cup peanut butter and mix with the $^{1}/_{2}$ cup honey or maple syrup until blended. Proceed with the recipe; stir the granola

CUSTOMIZING CRUNCHY GRANOLA

Swap or mix sweeteners, spices, flavorings, nuts, dried fruit, and so forth to get a completely customized granola. The possibilities are nearly endless.

SWEETENERS	SEASONINGS	FOR CRUNCH AND CHEW
Honey	Spices: cinnamon, nutmeg, cloves, cardamom, anise, coriander, allspice	Nuts: peanuts, almonds, walnuts, pecans, pistachios, cashews, hazelnuts, macadamias
Maple syrup	Vanilla extract or beans	Dried fruits: apricots, dates, cranberries, cherries, blueberries, pears, papaya, mango
Brown sugar	Peanut butter, nut butter, or tahini	Seeds: sesame, sunflower, flax
Molasses	Ginger: fresh, ground, or crystallized	Chocolate or carob chips
Corn or brown rice syrup	Orange, lemon, or grapefruit zest	Dried, roasted soybeans; toasted amaranth (see page 536)

every few minutes while it's baking to prevent the peanut butter from burning.

Tropical Granola. Macadamia nuts are killer here: Substitute coconut milk (to make your own, see page 423) or $1/2$ cup coconut milk with $1/4$ cup or more honey for the honey or maple syrup and chopped dried papaya, mango, pineapple, banana chips, and crystallized ginger for the raisins.

Real Vanilla Granola. Using real vanilla beans is pricey, but the flavor is delicious: Add 1 split vanilla bean or 2 tablespoons vanilla extract to the sweeteners. Omit the coconut if you like. Heat the honey or maple syrup over low heat, scrape the insides of the vanilla bean, and put the seeds in the honey along with the pod; steep for about 10 minutes.

Spiced Granola. Use any spice combination you like: Add another teaspoon ground cinnamon, 1 teaspoon ground ginger, $1/2$ teaspoon each ground anise and cardamom, $1/4$ teaspoon each freshly grated nutmeg and ground cloves, and 2 teaspoons vanilla extract.

Ginger-Molasses Granola. Crumbled gingersnaps are a great addition: Substitute molasses for half of the sweetener and add a 1- to 2-inch piece ginger, peeled and grated into the sweetener. Add $1/4$ cup chopped crystallized ginger along with the dried fruit.

Almond-Orange Granola. The marzipan adds that intense, fabulous, sweet almond flavor, but a teaspoon or two of almond extract instead is also quite delicious: Substitute 1 cup each blanched almonds and pistachios for the nuts and $1/4$ cup or more marzipan or almond paste for some of the sweetener. Omit the coconut. Add the grated zest of 2 to 3 oranges. Blend the marzipan or almond paste along with the orange zest into the sweetener; heat the mixture to help blend it. Proceed with the recipe. Golden raisins, dried apricots, or cherries are a nice addition.

 Ⓕ Fast   Ⓜ Make Ahead   Ⓥ Vegan

Legumes

I adore beans and have cooked them regularly for my entire adult life. As I've traveled, as I've experimented, as I've discovered new varieties and the joys of fresh beans, I've grown to love them more and more.

There was a time when I could barely imagine cooking a pot of beans without "seasoning" it with meat. But beans, as most people (and all vegetarians) know, have tremendous flavor and great texture. And when you play off their natural characteristics, then build in other ingredients and seasonings, the results can be stunning.

Some of my favorite flavorings for beans—after olive oil and garlic, or just butter—are the simplest: soy sauce, roasted garlic, smoked or fresh chiles, mushrooms, cheese, and all kinds of greens. Either together or alone, added just after the beans become tender or at the last minute, these ingredients provide dimension and depth. This chapter features legumes in combina-

tion with all of these ingredients, as well as simple cooking techniques that will launch you on your own explorations.

Since legumes are largely interchangeable—in terms of both cooking and usage—I've arranged the recipes around the cooking methods. If you've got cooked beans (or, in a pinch, canned beans), bean sautés (I call them "skillet beans" in this chapter) are the fastest dishes to make; they're sort of like stir-fries. Stovetop bean stews make up the bulk of this chapter, and these dishes cook virtually unattended, which is nice. Purées and mashes are a more luxurious way to eat beans that deserve attention of their own. The collection of baked bean recipes in this

575

chapter, which includes gratins, are hearty do-ahead dishes that are perfect for entertaining. And remember that some of the most satisfying and interesting ways to eat beans—and to use up leftovers—are in fritters, dumplings, croquettes, and cakes.

The Basics of Legumes

All beans, lentils, peas, peanuts, and certain kinds of grasses belong to the Leguminosae family. These plants produce their seeds in a pod, and it's these seeds we eat. (When both the pods and the seeds are eaten, as in green beans or snow peas, the legumes are commonly categorized as vegetables.) Around the world, anything in this large plant family that humans eat is called a *pulse*. Americans tend to call everything *beans, legumes,* or *shell beans.*

Early farmers learned that legumes were easily dried and preserved for storage and future use. Though you can sometimes (happily) find beans that have not been dried—see "Fresh and Frozen Shell Beans" on page 589—most legumes must be cooked for a relatively long period of time so they rehydrate and become edible.

You probably know that legumes are the most nutritious plant food. When eaten with grains they make complete protein, meaning that the two contain complementary types of amino acids that cannot be produced by our bodies. All beans contain about the same amount and types of protein (except soybeans, which are notably higher). They're high in fiber, too, rich in complex carbohydrates, and relatively low in fat, and the fat they contain is of the more beneficial, unsaturated kind. In short, there's no reason not to eat them frequently.

Buying and Storing Legumes

Since beans are dried, they rarely go bad. But they do get old. In extreme cases they might taste musty, especially if they've been stored in damp conditions, but more often old beans just require more water and longer cooking to soften up. Unfortunately, you have little way of knowing when beans were dried, though there are some visual cues

you can use when you're buying them: Avoid packages with a large percentage of broken beans, imperfect skins, or discoloration. Ideally, you'd buy beans at a place where they're sold and restocked frequently.

Store beans in a cool, dry place, like the pantry, not the fridge. Make sure they are tightly sealed, in either their original packaging or (better) a plastic container or glass jar. Some people freeze their dried beans, but as this dehydrates them further, it's probably not such a great idea.

The Legume Lexicon

From everyday to trendy heirlooms, high-tech hybrids, and the downright obscure, the world of legumes is endless. Fortunately you can find some of the best beans at international groceries and natural food stores, and many specialty and even regional legumes are now within reach on-line, though usually at a premium.

I've divided this lexicon into two categories: legumes you can find in supermarkets or specialty stores and those for enthusiasts, who don't mind hunting them down and/or paying a little (or a lot!) extra. Note that this list is far from complete: There are hundreds of varieties of beans available to gardeners and habitués of farmer's markets, but all of them come close in appearance and/or treatment to something listed here.

Each of these two dozen or so legumes has a particular appearance, along with sometimes subtle differences in flavor and texture. Though tradition almost demands that certain beans be used for certain dishes, I don't think the rules need be so rigid: Many beans are truly interchangeable, though some swaps are better than others. You can generally substitute any white bean for another white bean, pink for pink, and red for red. But color isn't the only determining factor: Flavor, texture, and how well a bean holds together during cooking play important roles too. Sometimes it boils down to a personal choice, and with experience making substitutions will become second nature. To help you along, most recipes in this chapter include the line "Other beans you can use. . . ."

 Fast   Make Ahead   Ⓥ Vegan

LEGUME	DESCRIPTION	FORMS
Black Beans *Turtle Beans,* *Frijoles Negros*	Medium size, oval, and deep black. Rich and earthy, almost mushroomlike. (Don't confuse with Chinese fermented black beans, which are actually soybeans.)	Dried, frozen, and canned
Black-Eyed Peas *Cowpeas*	Small, plump, ivory-colored beans with a black spot. They cook quickly, absorb flavors well, and in the United States are most popular in the South.	Dried, fresh, frozen, and canned
Cannellini Beans *White Kidney* *Beans*	Large, kidney shaped, off-white, with nutty flavor and a creamy consistency	Dried and canned
Chickpeas *Garbanzo Beans,* *Ceci, Channa Dal,* *Kabli Channa*	One of the most useful. Acorn-shaped tan (sometimes red or black) beans with robust and nutty flavor. They take a long time to cook, but the cooking liquid is very flavorful. Popular internationally.	Dried, fresh, frozen, canned, or ground into flour (called *besan;* see page 633)
Fava Beans *Broad, Faba, Haba,* *Fève, Horse,* *Windsor Beans*	Large, flattened, wide oval beans, light brown when dried and green when fresh. Tedious to peel, but nutty and creamy when dried, a bit sweet when fresh.	Dried (get the split favas, which are already peeled), fresh (still in the pod, usually, in spring and fall), and frozen
Great Northern Beans	All-purpose white beans; large, oval, and widely available	Dried, frozen, and canned
Kidney Beans	Shiny, red, light red or pink, reddish brown, or white (see Cannellini Beans), up to an inch long; kidney shaped (duh!), they keep their shape when cooked, and absorb flavors well.	Dried, frozen, and canned
Lentils	Tiny, thin skinned, disk shaped, and quick cooking; hundreds of varieties	Mostly dried, sometimes split and peeled, and less often canned
Lima Beans *Butter Beans,* *Butter Peas*	Generally pale green when fresh and white when dried, both large and small limas are flat, kidney shaped, and have a hearty texture and nice buttery flavor. Several varieties that vary in color and size. The most common are large; Christmas limas have pretty reddish purple markings. When fresh, firm pods are best (bulging beans will be starchy). Baby lima beans cook more quickly.	Fresh, frozen, and canned
Navy Beans *Pea, Boston,* *Yankee Beans*	Small, round, plump, white, common, and very useful. Dense and mild flavored with a creamy consistency that makes great purées and baked beans.	Dried, frozen, and canned
Peanuts *Goober,* *Groundnut,* *Ground Pea*	A legume, eaten like a nut, but really bridges the gap	Whole and shelled in jars, cans, and bags and as peanut butter, usually dry roasted
Peas, Dried *Split peas, Maquis* *Peas, Matar Dal*	Small and round, these peas are grown specifically for drying. When cooked, they're starchy and earthy. Green and yellow are nearly the same in all ways but color.	Most commonly sold split, either dried or canned

LEGUME	DESCRIPTION	FORMS
Pigeon Peas *Gandules, Congo, Goongoo, Gungo Pea, Toovar Dal*	Tan and nearly round, with one side flattened; sweet and a bit mealy. Many different colors: tan, black, brown, red, yellow, and spotted. Popular worldwide.	Usually dried, sometimes split and peeled; also fresh, frozen, and canned
Pink Beans *Chili Beans*	Virtually interchangeable with pintos. Slightly kidney shaped, rounder, and solidly pinkish tan. Common in the Caribbean.	Dried and canned
Pinto Beans	Medium size, oval, with a reddish tan and brown speckled exterior (*pinto* means "painted" in Spanish). Earthy and creamy. Commonly refried.	Dried, frozen, and canned
Soybeans *When young and green: Edamame*	Round, small, yellow or black, and nutty; the most widely grown bean in the world. Edamame are immature soybeans: large, shiny, and usually green, a good substitute for fresh lima or fava beans.	There are hundreds of varieties of soybeans, available dried, canned, and sometimes fresh or frozen. Edamame are available fresh or in their pods or already shucked. Fermented black beans are made from black soybeans. (Soybeans are also the basis of tofu and many other products.)

LEGUMES FOR ENTHUSIASTS

LEGUME	DESCRIPTION	FORMS
Adzuki Beans *Aduki*	Small, oval, and maroon, with a streak of white. Earthy and slightly sweet; dense and creamy. Used most often in sweet dishes in East Asia.	Dried, canned, fresh, and as sweet red bean paste (used in Asian cuisines)
Anasazi Beans *Anastazi, Cave, New Mexico Cave Beans*	Found in the ancient cave dwellings of the Anasazi Indians (New Mexico), these are mottled with white and burgundy and are mild, sweet, and mealy.	Dried and sometimes fresh
Appaloosa Beans	Named after the Appaloosa horse for its distinct markings of color on one end and white to tan on the other. Slender and oval shaped with a creamy texture and rich flavor.	Dried and sometimes fresh and canned
Cranberry Beans *Borlotti, Roman, Romano*	Beautiful dried or fresh; creamy, with bright to deep red dappling; similar in flavor and texture to pinto beans. Delicious fresh.	Dried, fresh, and sometimes frozen
Flageolets	Immature kidney beans, small, kidney shaped, and a pale green. A favorite in France, they are quick cooking with an herbal, fresh taste.	Dried, fresh, and canned
Gigantes *Great White Beans, Gigande, Hija*	Huge, off-white, and sweet, with potatolike texture; popular in Greek, Spanish, and Japanese dishes	Dried and canned (sometimes with tomato sauce)

 Fast   Make Ahead    Vegan

LEGUME	DESCRIPTION	FORMS
Lupini Beans *Tremoços*	Flat, yellow, and somewhat square, with a hole at one end, lupinis can be bitter due to a naturally high level of alkaloids, so they must be soaked and cooked for a long time, then peeled. Because of the labor-intensive preparation, they are often sold cooked. To eat, squeeze or suck the sweet, firm beans from their skins.	Dried, canned, jarred (and sometimes pickled), and fresh
Mung Beans *Mung Dal, Green Grams*	Tiny, pellet shaped, and usually khaki (when whole) or yellow (when peeled) but also green or black; tender and slightly sweet when cooked. Used in dals; ground and used to make bean thread noodles in China; they also make the most familiar sprouts.	Dried or peeled and split. For dal, see page 600–604
Tarbaises	Named after a small town (Tarbes) in the foothills of the Pyrenees. Oval, white in color, sweet and buttery in flavor.	Dried
Urad Dal *Black Gram*	Used primarily in dals	Dried. Sold three ways: Whole, with grayish black skins intact (sabat urad), and split, both with skins (chilke urad dal) and without (the most commonly used form, known simply as *urad dal*).
White Coco Beans *Coco Blanc, Haricots Cocos*	Pretty, almost-egg-shaped, medium-size white bean from France. Creamy texture, mild flavor.	Dried and occasionally fresh

The Basics of Cooking Legumes

Beans are an ideal staple—satisfying, hearty, and, of course, nutritious. Not only are they easy to store, but once they're cooked they keep for days in the fridge or months in the freezer, which makes them a perfect make-ahead food. They're also appealing at different degrees of doneness and in different forms. Cook them al dente and they remain independent, toothsome components for salads, stuffings, sautés, or garnishes; cook them a little more and you have a creamy, comforting stew. Mashed or puréed, beans can be anything from a substantial side dish to a vehicle for sauces or gravies or the base for a whole family of fritters, pancakes, dumplings, and croquettes. (And, though it's not covered in this chapter, processed beans—soybeans in particular—are the basis of some of the tastiest and most nutritious plant foods there are: tofu, tempeh, soy sauce, and miso.

Preparing, Cooking, and Serving Beans

My recipes, and most others, always instruct you to wash and pick over raw beans. You will often find discolored or bug-eaten beans. There might even be pebbles, twigs, leaves, or small dirt clods that slipped into the batch, especially if they're not overly processed. Just take a minute to put the beans in a strainer or colander, run them under cold water, and swish them around with your hands while you give them a visual once-over.

Dried beans require a fair amount of water—and heat—to become edible. How much water they absorb and how long it takes to cook them varies, depending on when the beans were harvested and dried, how they've been stored, and whether you presoak them. That makes exact cooking times literally impossible to pinpoint; but they absorb a lot of water during soaking—especially when the water is heated—which can significantly shorten their cooking time (See "Cooking Beans: the Quick-Soak Way" on page 581).

Cooking: The amount of water beans absorb is finite, so if you soak you'll need less water during cooking. This is important to remember because legumes are best cooked when they bubble gently in water just to cover. You don't want to cook beans "pasta style"—at a vigorous boil—then drain a lot of water off. For one thing, the skins will break and tear too soon. For another, a more concentrated cooking liquid is flavorful, nutritious, and more saucelike.

Over the years I've tried all sorts of formulas for cooking beans in all different styles. Generally, I prefer beans that are creamy, but there are times I want firm beans, for salad or a skillet dish, and you may prefer them that way. There's no big mystery here: Just taste them as they cook and take the pot off the heat when they're done the way you want them. Creamy beans take a little longer, until their skins burst and the insides start to melt into the cooking liquid. (Salt and acidic ingredients like vinegar or lemon juice change how beans cook; see "Tips for Determining the Texture of Cooked Beans," page 584.)

If this all sounds imprecise, it is, and that's a good thing: For many bean dishes, you don't even really need a recipe; few kitchen chores are simpler than cooking beans. You put the cleaned—and probably soaked—beans in a pot, cover them with cold water, and turn the heat on. It takes just a couple of minutes to bring the pot to a boil, at which point you lower the temperature so the beans bubble gently. Then you walk away for a while. The timing varies, but little else changes except for ingredients you might add. For example, you might choose—even routinely—to cook aromatic vegetables like onion, garlic, ginger, celery, or carrots in the pot with the beans and water.

Serving: Some recipes call for you to drain the beans before serving them, but even then you might save the cooking liquid, to cover any leftover beans before storing or to enrich soups or stocks. (Chickpea-cooking liquid is especially good for this.) But in most recipes, ideally you want to end up with about an inch of cooking liquid when the beans are done to your liking. This is easy enough: Check the pot every half hour or so while the beans cook and add about a cup of water if they threaten to dry out.

Plain Talk About Legumes and Gas

You don't hear about this issue as much as you once did, even a decade ago, and I suspect it's because beans have become more prevalent in our diets. I've never been a fan of additives that minimize flatulence, and in fact I often don't bother to drain off the water after quick-soaking legumes, which is supposed to be one of the ways to minimize beans' negative effects. If you eat a lot of high-fiber plant foods, your system is probably efficient at digesting them; it's as simple as that. However, some people are allergic to beans, and constant gastric distress is one signal. If you're uncomfortable after eating legumes, see your doctor.

Storing Home-Cooked Beans in the Fridge or Freezer

If you get in the habit of cooking a pound of dried beans at a time—or even two—you'll find that you almost never rely on canned beans. Your own beans, frozen, keep well, taste better, and cost less.

Let the cooked beans cool in their liquid, then put beans and liquid into either large or serving-size plastic containers with tight-fitting lids. Put a splash of white vinegar or lemon juice in if you want to help keep the beans intact, then cover and refrigerate for up to five days or freeze for up to six months (though, as with all frozen foods, you are better off using them sooner).

To cook from the freezer, either thaw for a day or so in the fridge, thaw in the microwave, or put the block of beans and liquid in a covered pan with a little water in the bottom and turn the heat to medium-low. Check

Ⓕ Fast   Ⓜ Make Ahead   Ⓥ Vegan

Most of the recipes here start with 1 pound of beans, which generally makes between five and six cups cooked (each type of bean has a slight different yield), or six to eight servings, depending on what else you're serving. This is my general practice, so I can refrigerate or freeze what I don't need immediately (usually about half). Though canned beans are fine in a pinch—and getting better, thankfully, all the time—I'd much rather eat home-made beans: The flavor and texture are much better (they're cheaper too). You can, of course, make half of the recipe if you prefer.

Store cooked beans in a plastic container, covered with their cooking liquid and a tight-fitting lid. They'll keep for up to a week in the refrigerator or for months in the freezer (see "Storing Home-Cooked Beans in the Fridge or Freezer," page 580.)

occasionally to make sure they have enough water but don't overstir or try to break up the ice block, or the beans will break into bits. How long they take will depend on the size of the container, but generally beans can go from frozen to hot in less than 30 minutes.

Cooking Beans, the Quick-Soak Way

MAKES: 6 to 8 servings

TIME: 2 hours to soak, plus 30 minutes to 2 hours to cook, largely unattended

The recommended method and the easiest way to cook beans because for most of the time they aren't cooking at all; they're soaking. Incredibly, if you start a pot of dried beans from scratch without soaking and start another pot

following this method, both will be ready at about the same time, with no difference in taste or texture. What changes is that with the presoaking method you don't have to check as much or add water as often.

    1 pound any dried beans, split peas, or peeled and
        split beans, washed and picked over
    Salt and freshly ground black pepper

1 Put the beans in a large pot with a tight-fitting lid and cover with cold water by 2 to 3 inches. Bring to a boil and boil the beans, uncovered, for about 2 minutes. Cover the pot and turn off the heat. Let the beans soak for about 2 hours.

2 Taste a bean. If it's tender (it won't be done), add a large pinch of salt and several grinds of black pepper and make sure the beans are covered with about an inch of the soaking water. (If not, add a little water.) If the beans are still raw, don't add salt yet and cover with about 2 inches of water.

3 Bring the pot to a boil, then reduce the heat so that the beans bubble gently. Partially cover and cook, stirring occasionally, checking the beans for doneness every 10 or 15 minutes, and adding a little more water if necessary. If you haven't added salt yet, add it when the beans are just turning tender. Stop cooking when the beans are done the way you like them, taste and adjust the seasoning, and use immediately or store.

Cooking Beans, the No-Soak Way

MAKES: 6 to 8 servings

TIME: 30 minutes to 4 hours, largely unattended

This is the only method you need for lentils and split peas, which cook pretty fast and don't absorb a lot of water.

The main advantage of cooking other beans this way is that they go from raw to mushy very slowly. So compared to soaked beans, you have more control and less chance of missing the moment when the beans are perfectly tender with their skins intact. The downside is that you will also need to watch the water level more closely than you do with either of the soaked methods.

1 pound any dried beans, split peas, or peeled and split beans, washed and picked over

Salt and freshly ground black pepper

1 Put the beans in a large pot with a tight-fitting lid and cover with cold water by 2 or 3 inches. Bring the pot to a boil, then reduce the heat so that the beans bubble gently. Partially cover and cook, stirring occasionally, checking the beans for doneness every 10 or 15 minutes, and adding a little more water if necessary.

2 When the beans start to get tender, add a large pinch of salt and several grinds of black pepper. As the beans get closer to being finished, they need to be covered with only an inch or two of water. Stop cooking when the beans are done the way you like them, taste and adjust the seasoning, and either use immediately or store.

Cooking Beans, the Long-Soak Way

MAKES: 6 to 8 servings

TIME: Up to 12 hours to soak, plus 30 minutes to 2 hours to cook, almost completely unattended

Many recipes instruct you to soak beans "overnight" before cooking. But that means they could be soaking for up to 24 hours before you start making dinner, which often leaves you with a mushy, bland pot of beans. To me, a long soak is 8 to 12 hours. Conveniently, this is about the length of the average workday: You set them up in the morning and cook them when you get home. Easy, assuming you have enough time to let them simmer. There is a downside, however: The beans absorb so much liquid during soaking that once you start cooking them, they turn

from tender to mushy rather fast. Bottom line: Very convenient and fast, but you gotta watch 'em on the stove.

1 pound any dried beans, split peas, or peeled and split beans, washed and picked over

Salt and freshly ground black pepper

1 Put the beans in a large pot with a tight-fitting lid and cover with cold water by several inches. Let them soak for 8 to 12 hours.

2 Drain the beans and return them to the pot. Check a bean for doneness. If it's tender but not yet done, add a large pinch of salt and several grinds of black pepper and make sure the beans are covered with about an inch of water. If the beans are still raw, don't add salt yet and cover with about 2 inches of water.

3 Bring to a boil, then reduce the heat so that the beans bubble gently. Partially cover and cook, stirring

occasionally, checking the beans for doneness every 10 minutes or so, and adding a little more water if necessary. If you haven't added salt yet, add it when the beans are just turning tender. Stop cooking when the beans are done the way you like them, taste and adjust the seasoning, and either use immediately or store.

Skillet Beans

No rule says you have to cook beans in a pot, and in fact precooked legumes make great one-pan dishes—sautés, or skillet beans—especially when combined with crunchy vegetables, rich oils and condiments, or full-flavored ingredients like mushrooms, garlic, ginger, or onions. And they couldn't be simpler: Start with a little fat, then layer on ingredients until everything is lightly cooked and hot.

Edamame with Tomatoes and Cilantro

MAKES: 4 servings
TIME: 25 minutes

This simple but high-powered recipe can take two completely different forms depending on technique: Cook the tomatoes with their juices for a saucy dish or add them at the last minute for a fresher, more saladlike dish. Other cooked vegetables can be tossed in as well: Try corn kernels, cubed eggplant, summer squash, chopped cauliflower, or broccoli.

Other fresh beans you can use: any fresh bean—like lima, fava, or cranberry—will work nicely.

2 tablespoons extra virgin olive oil

1 small onion or 3 scallions, chopped

1 tablespoon minced garlic

1 teaspoon ground cumin

$1^1/_2$ cups chopped ripe tomato (canned are fine, drained or not)

2 cups edamame, fresh or thawed frozen

Salt and freshly ground black pepper

$^1/_4$ cup chopped fresh cilantro leaves

① Put the oil in a skillet over medium-high heat. When hot, add the onion and garlic and cook, stirring occasionally, until the onion is soft, about 3 minutes.

② Add the cumin and tomato and cook at a gentle bubble until the tomatoes begin to break apart, about 10 minutes.

③ Stir in the edamame and sprinkle with salt and pepper. Cook until the edamame are tender, 5 to 7 minutes. Taste and adjust the seasoning, sprinkle with cilantro, and serve.

Edamame with Tomatoes and Olives. A Mediterranean take: Substitute 8 pitted and sliced black olives for the cumin and basil leaves for the cilantro.

Edamame with Tomatoes and Roasted Chiles. Use any chile in the quantities you like here (see "The Basics of Chiles and Peppers" on page 822): Delete the cumin and add 1 or 2 roasted, cleaned, and chopped fresh chiles (see page 333).

Edamame with Dijon and Wax Beans. So it's not classical French—or Japanese!—it's still good: Omit the garlic, cumin, tomato, and cilantro. Add a couple tablespoons water along with the edamame, cook for a couple minutes, then add 2 teaspoons chopped fresh tarragon or thyme leaves, 3 tablespoons Dijon mustard, and a cup of trimmed and cooked wax beans.

Quick-Cooked Edamame with Kombu Dashi or Soy Sauce

MAKES: 4 servings
TIME: 15 minutes

This super-easy and delicious little dish cooks up in no time and makes a terrific lunch—hot or cold—on top of

You can control the texture of any beans you cook by using a few simple techniques:

To keep beans from breaking apart and becoming gritty: Don't salt beans during soaking or the early stages of cooking. Salt breaks down their skins so they burst before the insides are done and you end up with tough bits and pieces. (You should, however, add salt when the beans begin to get tender; salted beans cook slightly faster and develop better flavor.)

For beans that are firm but tender, with intact skins: This is what you want for salads, garnishes, or sautés: Add up to 2 tablespoons white (distilled) vinegar or freshly squeezed lemon juice to the cooking water when you add the salt. This fortifies the skins against breaking, which in turn keeps the insides from overabsorbing water. The beans will taste a little more acidic, but that's not necessarily a bad thing, especially if you plan to use them in salads or add other strong-flavored ingredients.

For richer, creamier beans: Add a cup or two of any milk—dairy or nondairy—to the pot toward the end of cooking. Cow's or goat's milk and coconut, oat, soy, nut, and rice milks are all fair game. And, of course, butter or flavorful oil, like extra virgin olive or nut oil, will also make beans rich and creamy; add them anytime during cooking.

For thicker, creamier bean dishes: Before adding cooked beans to any recipe, put $1/2$ cup or so on a small plate and mash them with a fork. Then just add them with the rest of the beans as directed. This works for soupy bean stews as well as sautés, whenever you want a little more body. (You can also simply put an immersion blender in the pot and whiz briefly.)

soba noodles or rice. If you don't have dashi or stock, use soy sauce as directed; even quicker and easier and nearly as good.

Other fresh beans you can use: any fresh bean—like lima, fava, or cranberry—will work.

1 tablespoon neutral oil, like grapeseed or corn

1 tablespoon minced peeled fresh ginger

$1/4$ cup chopped scallion

1 cup Kombu Dashi (page 103), vegetable stock (pages 101–102), bean-cooking liquid, or $1/4$ cup good-quality soy sauce mixed with $3/4$ cup water

1 small carrot, julienned or finely chopped

$1/2$ cup snow peas, trimmed and julienned or finely chopped

2 cups edamame, fresh or thawed frozen

Salt and freshly ground black pepper

1 Put the oil in a skillet over medium heat. When hot, add the ginger and scallion and cook, stirring occasionally, until the scallion is soft, about 3 minutes.

2 Add the dashi and bring to a steady bubble. Add the carrot, snow peas, and edamame and sprinkle with salt and pepper.

3 Cook until the vegetables are tender, about 5 to 7 minutes. Taste, adjust the seasoning, and serve.

Quick-Braised Edamame with Sea Greens. This is good with almost any sea green, though I like hijiki: Replace the carrot and snow peas with about $1/2$ ounce ($1/3$ cup) hijiki; soak it in cold water for 10 minutes and drain.

Quick-Braised Edamame with Green Tea. Replace the scallion with 5 or 6 chopped shiso leaves and substitute freshly brewed, not-too-strong green tea for the dashi.

Quick-Braised Edamame with Ponzu. The zing of the yuzu juice is fantastic: Add roughly the same amount of julienned daikon as carrot and delete the snow peas. Substitute $3/4$ cup Ponzu Sauce (page 780) for the dashi.

Quick-Braised Edamame with Fishless Fish Sauce. Replace the ginger with 1 or 2 hot fresh chiles (preferably Thai), minced, or to taste, or hot red pepper flakes to taste. Substitute $3/4$ cup Fishless Fish Sauce (page 776) for the dashi. Proceed with the recipe and add 4 or so chopped fresh Thai basil leaves and chopped roasted peanuts before serving.

F Fast   **M** Make Ahead   **V** Vegan

Not long ago, you saw edamame—green soybeans—only in Japanese restaurants. Now these quick-cooking beans are everywhere, including the freezer case of most supermarkets. Colorful, plump, and sweet, with a buttery texture and super-high protein content, they can substitute for fresh or frozen limas or favas virtually anywhere.

Buying and storing: Edamame are immature soybeans, harvested after about 80 percent of their growth. They're available both in the pod and shelled, usually frozen. Fresh beans are also showing up in supermarkets. Store fresh edamame in plastic bags in the fridge for up to a week or so. Frozen and well wrapped, the beans will keep for months.

Preparing: Wash both shelled and in-the-pod edamame under cold running water. Use a brush to scrub some of the fuzz off of the pods if you like, though it's not necessary.

Cooking: Because they are immature and not dried, edamame cook fast, like any other vegetable, and a lot faster than mature fresh or frozen shell beans.

In their shells, edamame make terrific finger food for appetizers. Just boil a pound or so at a time in lots of salted water for a few minutes and drain. Or steam them, partially covered, in the microwave. Serve them hot, warm, or chilled, sprinkled with a little more salt. To eat edamame from the pod the traditional way, hold the pod between your teeth and use them to squeeze the beans into your mouth. It's also easy to shell them like peanuts or peas and pluck them from the pods.

Beer-Glazed Black Beans

MAKES: 4 servings

TIME: 20 minutes with cooked beans

It's amazing how much flavor you get from adding a cup (or a bottle) of beer to black beans, and nearly any type of beer will work: Lagers and wheat beers will generally make a lighter and fruitier dish; porters will be rich, and stouts richer still, with deep, caramelized flavors. For a meal that emphasizes the beer's origins, try eating this with a dish like Grain Griddlecakes (page 569).

You can make this dish vegan by using molasses in place of honey.

Other beans you can use: pinto, pink, pigeon peas, black-eyed peas, or appaloosa.

2 tablespoons extra virgin olive oil

1 onion, chopped

1 tablespoon minced garlic

1 cup beer

3 cups cooked or canned black beans, drained but still moist, liquid reserved

1 tablespoon chili powder (to make your own, see page 814)

1 tablespoon honey

Salt and freshly ground black pepper

1 Put the oil in a skillet over medium-high heat. When hot, add the onion and cook, stirring occasionally, until soft, about 5 minutes. Add the garlic, cook for about a minute, then add the beer, beans, chili powder, honey, and a good sprinkling of salt and pepper.

2 Bring to a steady bubble and cook until the liquid is slightly reduced and thickened, about 15 minutes. Taste and adjust the seasoning. Serve hot or store, covered, in the refrigerator for up to 3 days.

Beer-Glazed Black Beans and Tomatoes. Any form of tomato—fresh, canned, or paste—is good here: Add 1 cup chopped ripe tomato or 1 to 2 tablespoons tomato paste in Step 1. Proceed with the recipe.

Beer-Glazed Black Beans and Chiles. Use your favorite chile, dried or fresh (see "The Basics of Chiles and Peppers," page 822): Add 1 or 2 fresh chiles, cored, seeded, and chopped, along with the onion in Step 1. Or add 1 or 2 dried chiles, soaked and cleaned (see page 825) with the beans in Step 1. Proceed with the recipe.

Beer-Glazed Black Beans with Tamarind. For a bit of tang and quite mysterious: Stir in a couple teaspoons tamarind paste and a pinch of brown sugar if you like, in Step 1. Proceed with the recipe.

Beer-Glazed Black Beans, Asian Style. Add a tablespoon peeled and minced fresh ginger and 2 tablespoons or so fermented black beans with the garlic in Step 1. Stir in some soy sauce before salting.

Beer-Glazed Black Beans with Thai-Style Chile Paste. The heat of this paste melts right into the beans: Stir in a dollop of Thai-Style Chile Paste (page 829), in Step 1 with the beans.

Kidney Beans with Apples and Sherry

MAKES: 4 servings

TIME: 20 minutes with cooked beans

Sautéing produces a texture completely different from that of stewed bean dishes, with distinct, separate ingredients. The apples make this dish especially nice with simple boiled cabbage or other greens and a thick slice of hearty whole grain bread. Vegan with oil instead of butter.

Other beans you can use: any firm and nutty or rich-flavored beans, like appaloosa, cranberry, pinto, or edamame.

  2 tablespoons extra virgin olive oil or butter, plus a little more for garnish (optional)

  2 shallots, sliced, or 1 small onion, chopped

  1 1/2 cups chopped or sliced Golden Delicious or Granny Smith apples

  2 teaspoons chopped fresh thyme leaves

  1/4 cup dry (fino) sherry

  3 cups cooked or canned kidney beans, drained but still moist

  Salt and freshly ground black pepper

1 Put the 2 tablespoons oil or butter in a large skillet over medium heat. When the oil is hot or the butter is melted, add the shallots and the apples and cook, stirring occasionally, until softened and golden, 5 to 7 minutes.

2 Add the thyme and sherry; bring to a boil and cook until nearly dry, about 2 minutes. Add the beans and a good sprinkling of salt and pepper; cook for 5 minutes or so. Taste and adjust the seasoning. Serve hot, with a pat of butter or a drizzle of olive oil over the top if you like.

Kidney Beans with Pears and Wine. Replace the apples with chopped or sliced firm pears and substitute rosemary for the thyme and dry white wine for the sherry.

Kidney Beans with Apples and Red Wine. For a richly colored and flavored dish: Use kidney beans and a simple dry red wine instead of the sherry.

Piquant Kidney Beans with Prunes. A sweet-and-sour variation: Replace the apples with 1 cup halved pitted prunes, the thyme with cilantro, and the sherry with 2 teaspoons tamarind paste (or brown sugar) and 1 tablespoon balsamic vinegar.

Hot and Smoky Kidney Beans with Chipotle and Dried Cherries. Replace the apples with 1/2 cup dried cherries and 1 or 2 canned chipotle chiles (with their adobo to taste), the thyme with cilantro, and the sherry with tequila or beer if you like.

Cannellini Beans with Cabbage and Pasta

MAKES: 4 servings

TIME: 30 minutes

Serve this wonderfully rustic dish piping hot on a cold day or at room temperature when it's warm outside. Fla-

Ⓕ Fast   Ⓜ Make Ahead   Ⓥ Vegan

vorful stock is key here. The cavatelli is my first choice, but any small pasta is fine. Use oil and omit the cheese to make this a vegan dish.

Other beans you can use: It's important to use firm beans that won't break apart when tossed with the pasta, like cranberry, appaloosa, pinto, or chickpeas.

Salt

$^1\!/_2$ head cabbage, preferably Savoy, cored and chopped

$^1\!/_2$ pound cavatelli, conchiglie, or orecchiette

2 tablespoons extra virgin olive oil or butter

1 large or 2 medium leeks, including some green parts, washed and thinly sliced (about 2 cups)

1 stalk celery, chopped

2 sprigs fresh thyme

$^1\!/_4$ cup dry white wine (optional)

1 cup vegetable stock, preferably One-Hour Vegetable Stock (page 101) or Roasted Vegetable Stock (page 102)

3 cups cooked or canned cannellini beans, drained but still moist

Freshly ground black pepper

Freshly grated Parmesan or pecorino Romano cheese for garnish

❶ Bring a large pot of salted water to a boil over high heat. Add the cabbage and cook for about 3 minutes, until just tender; use a slotted spoon or a small strainer to fish it out; drain and set aside. When the water returns to a boil, add the pasta and cook until tender but firm, 7 minutes or so, then drain it.

❷ Meanwhile, put the oil or butter in a large skillet over medium heat. When the oil is hot or the butter is melted, add the leeks and celery and cook until softened, about 5 minutes. Add the thyme, and the wine if you're using it, and cook for another minute, until almost dry. Add the stock, beans, and reserved cabbage. Sprinkle with salt and pepper and cook until the flavors blend and everything is well heated, about 5 minutes more.

❸ Combine the bean mixture and the pasta in the large pot and stir gently. Taste and adjust the seasoning, sprinkle with Parmesan, and serve.

Cannellini Beans with Spinach and Cavatelli. Replace the cabbage with a pound or so of cleaned and trimmed spinach; but instead of blanching it, just add it to the large skillet in Step 2 after the leeks and celery have softened. Add a handful of raisins or currants if you like in Step 3.

Cranberry Beans with Artichokes and Cavatelli. Use artichoke hearts or whole baby artichokes: Substitute 2 or 3 cups quartered artichoke hearts or 10 or so trimmed and quartered baby artichokes for the cabbage. Add a squeeze of lemon juice to the artichoke's boiling water in Step 1. Cook the pasta separately and proceed with the recipe.

Chickpeas with Cabbage and Pearl Couscous. Add a tablespoon or so of Harissa (page 830) for a North African twist: Replace the cavatelli with 1 cup pearl couscous and the cannellini with chickpeas. Increase the vegetable stock to 2 cups. In Step 2, after cooking the thyme and wine, add the 2 cups stock; bring to a boil and add the pearl couscous. Cover and cook until just tender, about 5 minutes. Proceed with the recipe.

Gigantes with Brussels Sprouts

MAKES: 4 servings
TIME: 20 minutes with cooked beans

The varied textures and rustic flavors of this dish make it a real winner. It's incredibly versatile as well: Substitute just about any vegetable for the Brussels sprouts and use any roasted nuts and fresh herb you have on hand.

You can also use all sorts of beans instead of the somewhat hard-to-find gigantes, but these huge beans are worth seeking out. Their potatolike flavor and texture is amazing, making them a great standby bean to have in the pantry. And how many beans can you eat with a knife and fork?

If you use oil instead of butter, this dish is vegan.

Other beans you can use: Many hearty beans, like lima (especially the large ones), cranberry, pinto, or kidney beans, will work nicely.

2 tablespoons extra virgin olive oil or butter

12 ounces Brussels sprouts, trimmed and halved

1 tablespoon minced garlic

1/2 cup vegetable stock (pages 101–102) or water

3 cups cooked or canned gigantes, drained but still moist

Salt and freshly ground black pepper

1/2 cup roasted and chopped hazelnuts or almonds (see page 321)

Chopped fresh sage leaves for garnish

1 Put the oil or butter in a skillet over medium-high. When the oil is hot or the butter is melted, add the Brussels sprouts and cook, stirring occasionally, until golden brown, about 10 minutes. Add the garlic and cook for another minute.

2 Add the stock and bring to a boil. Add the beans and a good sprinkling of salt and pepper; reduce the heat to a steady simmer and cook until heated through, about 5 minutes. Taste and adjust the seasoning, sprinkle with the hazelnuts and sage, and serve.

Gigantes with Shiitakes. Use any sturdy mushroom: Replace the Brussels sprouts with about 2 cups quartered shiitake mushroom caps.

Gigantes with Cherry Tomatoes. Brighter in color and flavor: Substitute about 2 cups cherry tomatoes for the Brussels sprouts and pine nuts for the hazelnuts. Proceed with the recipe and sprinkle with chopped fresh basil or oregano leaves for garnish.

Gigantes with Preserved Lemon. A bit of Morocco: Delete the Brussels sprouts. Add 2 or 3 tablespoons chopped Preserved Lemon (page 427) and 1/4 cup pit-

ted green olives with the beans in Step 2. Use almonds instead of hazelnuts.

Briny Black-Eyed Peas

MAKES: 4 servings

TIME: 20 minutes with cooked beans

Throughout the Lone Star State, marinated black-eyed peas are a popular dish known as "Texas Caviar"; elsewhere, lentils are referred to as "poor-man's caviar." This vegetarian "caviar" is more like the real deal, with a briny flavor derived from a glaze seasoned with sea greens. I like it chilled or at room temperature, served with typical caviar accompaniments: minced red onion, crumbled hard-cooked eggs, crème fraîche (or sour cream or yogurt), and chopped cornichons or sweet pickles.

For a little kick, include some minced fresh chile or hot red pepper flakes or cayenne in the mix. You can also eat these unadorned, with Sushi Rice (page 527) or tossed with plain soba or udon noodles.

Other beans you can use: Any small beans with skins intact and a slightly firm bite after cooking—Le Puy lentils are great (as are black lentils if you can find them); so are adzuki beans or black soybeans.

1/4 cup dried dulse, arame, or other mild sea green

2 tablespoons neutral oil, like grapeseed or corn

1 shallot, minced

1 cup Kombu Dashi (page 103), sake, or water

2 tablespoons mirin or honey

Salt and freshly ground black pepper

3 cups cooked or canned black-eyed peas, drained until as dry as possible

1 Put the sea greens in a clean spice or coffee grinder and pulse until the threads are almost ground to a powder.

❷ Put the oil in a deep skillet over medium-high heat. When hot, add the shallot and cook, stirring constantly, until soft, about a minute. Stir in the sea greens, dashi, and mirin. Sprinkle with a little salt and pepper and let the mixture bubble away until it reduces and thickens into a thin syrup, 5 to 7 minutes.

❸ Stir in the peas and keep stirring until heated through and coated with the glaze, just a couple more minutes. Taste and adjust the seasoning, then serve immediately or cool, cover tightly, and refrigerate for up to a week.

Fried Mung Beans with Sesame

MAKES: 4 servings

TIME: 15 minutes with cooked beans

  Ⓥ

Super-simple, especially if you have cooked beans on hand. And because the beans are not at all soupy, you can use this as an ingredient to fortify other recipes like Fried Rice (page 520), Mashed Potatoes (page 341) or the dough for Essential Flatbread (page 727); just fold in the cooked beans at the last minute. Be sure to cook the beans in a pan big enough to hold them without crowding so the skins crisp up a little and the beans don't get mashed.

Other beans you can use: dried soybeans (white or black), kidney beans, and chickpeas.

2 tablespoons dark sesame oil, plus more as needed

3 cups cooked mung beans, tender but still intact and drained until dry

2 tablespoons sesame seeds (black are striking if you can find them)

2 tablespoons minced fresh chives

Salt and freshly ground black pepper

❶ Put the sesame oil in a large skillet over medium heat. When hot, add the beans and stir gently to coat with the oil. Cook without stirring until they begin to

spatter and pop, a couple of minutes or more, depending on how wet they were to begin with. Shake the pan a bit to keep the beans moving and frying until the skins begin to color a bit and crisp, another 2 or 3 minutes.

❷ Add the sesame seeds to the pan and use a spatula to toss them gently so that the beans are coated in the seeds. Add a couple more drops of oil if needed. Remove from the heat and carefully stir in the chives, a little salt, and lots of pepper. Taste, adjust the seasoning, and serve.

Fried Mung Beans with Mung Bean Sprouts. Sort of a warm salad: In Step 1, heat an extra tablespoon of oil in the skillet (be sure to use a pan with a lid). In Step 2, before you take the pan off the heat, stir in 2 cups mung bean sprouts, then cover the pan and take it off the heat. Let the mixture rest for 5 minutes or so, then add the chives, salt, and pepper. Add a few drops of rice wine vinegar if you like or a squeeze of lime juice. Toss with a fork, taste and adjust the seasoning, and serve.

Fried Mung Beans with Chile Paste. Hot as you like it: In Step 2, instead of adding the sesame seeds, try using a spoonful or two of Thai-Style Chile Paste (page 829) or one of the other variations on that page. (You probably won't need the salt and pepper.)

Fried Mung and Fermented Black Beans. In Step 1, heat an extra teaspoon of sesame oil in the skillet. When you add the sesame seeds in Step 2, add $^1/_4$ cup fermented black beans. You won't need much salt here.

Soybeans with Shiitakes and Sea Greens

MAKES: 4 servings
TIME: 30 minutes

Ⓕ

This combination of soybeans, shiitakes, and sea greens is brilliant, with the soybeans providing a hearty backdrop for the rich earthiness of the shiitakes and the sea greens keeping it light and adding a nice crunch. Vegan with mirin instead of honey. Serve on top of rice or with soba or udon noodles.

Other beans you can use: black beans or uncooked edamame.

About 1 ounce (about $^3/_4$ cup) hijiki

5 dried shiitake mushrooms

2 tablespoons extra virgin olive oil

2 medium or 1 large carrot, shredded

2 cups cooked or canned soybeans, drained but still moist

1 cup Kombu Dashi (page 103) or vegetable stock (pages 101–102)

2 tablespoons mirin or 1 tablespoon honey

$^1/_4$ cup soy sauce, or to taste

Salt

❶ Soak the hijiki in cold water to cover for about 10 minutes; soak the shiitakes in very hot water to cover for 10 minutes, or until tender enough to trim (change the water once or twice if they're stubborn). Meanwhile, prepare the remaining ingredients. Slice the shiitakes, discarding the tough stems but reserving the soaking liquid.

❷ Put the oil in a 12-inch skillet over medium-high heat. When the oil is hot, drain the hijiki and put it in the skillet; stir once, then add the carrot and the shiitakes. Stir in the beans, shiitake-soaking liquid, dashi, mirin, and soy sauce. Stir, turn the heat to medium-low, and cook, stirring occasionally, until the carrot is tender, about 10 minutes. Reduce the liquid further if necessary—the mixture should be stewy but not soupy—then taste, add more soy sauce or salt if necessary, and serve.

Soybeans with Morels and Asparagus. Luxurious and wonderful and even better with $^1/_2$ cup or so of cream added along with the wine: Replace the hijiki with about a cup of chopped asparagus, the shiitakes with 12 or so dried morels, and the soy sauce with dry white wine. Delete the mirin and substitute a squeeze of lemon juice.

Soybeans with Shiitakes and Miso. Nice, deep flavor, with no extra work: Omit the hijiki, mirin, and soy sauce. Add a tablespoon each of chopped garlic and peeled chopped ginger and cook it in the olive oil in Step 2. Stir in a dollop of miso at the end of Step 2.

Hot and Sour Edamame with Tofu

MAKES: 4 servings
TIME: 30 minutes

Here the fermented black beans provide a briny backbone for the tang of the vinegar and wine and the fresh blandness of the edamame; It's a complex, mouthwateringly delicious dish—and vegan as long as you use the sugar and not the honey. Serve with white or brown rice.

$^1/_4$ cup peanut or neutral oil, like corn or canola

8 ounces firm tofu, cut into 1/2- to 1-inch cubes and drained on paper towels

1 onion, chopped

2 teaspoons minced garlic

1 tablespoon peeled and minced fresh ginger

2 hot dried red chiles, stemmed, seeded, and minced, or hot red pepper flakes to taste

1 tablespoon fermented black beans

$^1/_3$ cup Shaoxing wine or dry (fino) sherry

2 tablespoons soy sauce

$^1/_4$ cup rice vinegar or white wine vinegar

2 teaspoons sugar or honey

$^1/_2$ cup vegetable stock (pages 101–102), or water, mixed with 2 teaspoons cornstarch

2 cups edamame, fresh or thawed frozen

① Put half the oil in a nonstick skillet over high heat. When hot, add the tofu and cook, stirring occasionally, until lightly golden brown, about 8 minutes. Remove from the pan.

② Put the other half of the oil in the hot pan and add the onion; cook until soft, 3 to 5 minutes. Add the garlic, ginger, chiles, and black beans; cook for another minute, stirring.

③ Stir in the wine, soy sauce, vinegar, sugar, and stock mixture and bring to a boil. Turn the heat down to low and add the edamame and browned tofu; cook at a gentle simmer until the edamame is tender, 5 to 7 minutes. Taste and adjust the seasoning, adding more soy sauce if necessary, and serve.

Sweet and Sour Edamame with Vegetables. Replace the tofu with about 2 cups any chopped vegetable, like bok choy, carrots, celery, daikon, mushrooms, bell pepper, snow peas, green beans, asparagus, broccoli, or cabbage.

Ma Po Edamame with Tofu. Traditionally a simmered ground pork and tofu dish: Omit the fermented black beans, wine, and vinegar; reduce the oil by half; replace the firm tofu with soft or silken and the onion with $^1/_2$ cup chopped scallion. Skip Step 1 and proceed with the recipe.

Fresh Favas with Eggs and Croutons

MAKES: 4 servings
TIME: 30 minutes

Fresh fava beans are a delicious springtime treat, with fresh, verdant flavors that make the shucking and peeling worth the effort. Substituting frozen favas or lima beans is perfectly fine out of season or when time is an issue, but it won't be the same.

Other beans you can use: Just about any fresh or frozen bean you can find will be delicious—lima, edamame, black-eyed peas, or cranberry.

$^1/_4$ cup extra virgin olive oil

8 ounces bread, preferably day-old, cubed

3 cups fresh fava beans (about 3 pounds in pods), blanched and peeled, or thawed frozen

Salt and freshly ground black pepper

2 tablespoons freshly squeezed lemon juice

2 Hard-Cooked Eggs (page 166), peeled and chopped

Chopped parsley for garnish

1 Put half the oil in a skillet over medium heat. Add the bread cubes and cook, stirring frequently, until golden brown, about 5 minutes.

2 Add the remaining oil and the favas and sprinkle with salt and pepper; cook for about 2 minutes. Stir in the lemon juice and eggs, stir, then taste and adjust the seasoning. Garnish with parsley and serve immediately.

Fresh Favas with Tofu and Croutons. An eggless, vegan version: Substitute about $1/2$ cup chopped tofu for the eggs and add with the favas.

Herbed Fresh Favas with Egg and Croutons. Use whatever fresh herb you have on hand: Add 2 to 3 tablespoons chopped fresh herbs, like dill, basil, mint, chives, or chervil; or add a dollop of any of the pestos or herb pastes on pages 668–670.

Fresh Favas with Feta and Croutons. Perfect over hot or even room-temperature orzo: Replace the eggs with $1/2$ cup or more crumbled feta cheese and sprinkle with chopped fresh marjoram or oregano leaves.

Twice-Cooked (Refried) Beans

MAKES: 4 servings
TIME: 20 minutes with cooked beans

F **V**

This is an instance in which you want to avoid canned beans: Since there are so few ingredients—and vegetarians obviously can't use the traditional lard—the predominant flavor and texture comes from the beans themselves. For more assertive seasoning, try adding a couple sprigs of epazote (fresh or dried), a bay leaf or two, and some garlic to the pot as the beans simmer.

Twice-Cooked Beans can be more than just a side dish. Try them as a bed for Fried Eggs (page 168) or thinned with a little Salsa Roja (page 787) for a hearty enchilada or tamale sauce. Puréed, they make an excellent base for all sorts of Bean Dips (page 612).

Other beans you can use: black beans.

$1/4$ cup neutral oil, like grapeseed or corn

1 cup chopped onion

1 tablespoon ground cumin, plus more if desired

3 cups cooked pinto or other red beans

Salt and freshly ground black pepper

$1/4$ teaspoon cayenne, plus more if desired

1 Put the oil in a large skillet over medium heat. When the oil is hot, add the onion and cook, stirring, until golden brown, about 10 minutes.

2 Add the cumin and cook, stirring, for 1 minute more. Add the beans and mash with a large fork or potato masher. Continue to cook and mash, stirring, until the beans are more or less broken up (some remaining chunks are fine).

3 Sprinkle with salt and pepper and add the cayenne and more cumin if you like. Taste, adjust the seasoning, and serve.

Creamier Refried Beans. This is in no way traditional but will give you a more velvety texture: Instead of the neutral oil, use $1/3$ cup coconut oil.

Buttery Refried Beans. Also nontraditional (and nonvegan) but delicious: Instead of the neutral oil, use up to $1/2$ cup butter.

10 Flavorings for Twice-Cooked (Refried) Beans

1. Minced fresh chile (like jalapeño or Thai), or to taste
2. Minced pickled chile
3. Chopped scallion or white onion
4. Minced peeled fresh ginger or garlic
5. Chopped Quick-Pickled Vegetables (page 95)
6. Chopped seeded tomato
7. Cilantro
8. Chopped black olives
9. Grated cheddar, Monterey Jack, or Chihuahua cheese or crumbled queso fresco
10. Cooked brown or white rice

Spicy Red Beans, Indian Style

MAKES: 8 servings

TIME: About 2 hours

The spicy combination of beans and tomato sauce will remind you of chili, only with a twist. This freezes well, but if you don't want the leftovers or aren't feeding a crowd, it's easy enough to cut the recipe in half.

If you have cooked beans in the fridge or freezer, use them and cut the total time to about 20 minutes. (Just skip down to Step 2.) This doesn't require much of the cooking liquid anyway, since most of the flavor is in the tomato sauce.

Other beans you can use: chickpeas, black beans.

1 pound dried red beans, washed, picked over, and soaked if you like (see "The Basics of Cooking Legumes," page 579)

$^1/_2$ teaspoon cayenne, or to taste

2 tablespoons neutral oil, like grapeseed or corn

1 tablespoon peeled and minced fresh ginger

1 tablespoon minced garlic

1 teaspoon fennel seeds

1 teaspoon ground cinnamon

Pinch ground cloves

1 tablespoon ground cardamom

1 bay leaf

1 teaspoon ground turmeric

2 cups chopped tomato (canned are fine; don't bother to drain)

Salt

1 tablespoon garam masala or curry powder (to make your own, see page 815 or 816), or to taste

❶ Cook the beans in water to cover with the cayenne until they are just about tender; this will take 1 to 2 hours, depending on their freshness and whether you soaked them.

❷ Meanwhile, put the oil in deep skillet or large pot over medium heat. When hot, add the ginger, garlic, fennel, cinnamon, cloves, cardamom, bay leaf, and turmeric and cook, stirring, for about a minute. Add the tomato and cook, stirring occasionally, until it breaks up a bit, 5 minutes or so.

❸ Drain the beans, reserving a little of their cooking liquid, and add them to the tomato sauce along with a large pinch of salt. Continue to cook until the beans are fully tender, adding a little of the bean cooking liquid if necessary. When the beans are done, add the garam masala, taste and adjust the seasoning, and serve.

Bean Stews

The long cooking times here are deceptive, because these recipes are actually ultra-simple to prepare. With few exceptions, everything goes into one pot and cooks unattended. It's also true that almost all of these dishes taste better rewarmed the next day. And remember that lentils cook in less than 45 minutes.

White Beans, Tuscan Style

MAKES: 6 to 8 servings

TIME: 1 to 2 hours, largely unattended

A rustic and almost indispensable bean dish—one of my kids used to love it as an after-school snack—that can be served hot, cold, or at room temperature. Serve it with a salad and some crusty bread or toss it with a bit of cooked small pasta (like orecchiette) or greens (like cabbage), and you have a fantastic lunch or dinner. It reheats perfectly too; just add a bit of water if the beans are too dry.

Other beans you can use: gigantes, lima, fava, pinto, kidney, appaloosa, anastazi, black-eyed peas, green or brown lentils, or soybeans.

> 1 pound dried white beans—cannellini, navy, Great Northern, or lima—washed, picked over, and soaked if you like (see "The Basics of Cooking Legumes," page 579)
>
> 20 fresh sage leaves or 1 tablespoon dried
>
> Salt and freshly ground black pepper
>
> 2 teaspoons minced garlic, or more to taste
>
> 1 tablespoon extra virgin olive oil, or more to taste

1 Put the beans in a large pot with water to cover. Turn the heat to high and bring to a boil. Add the sage and turn the heat down so the beans bubble steadily but not violently. Cover loosely.

2 Cook, stirring occasionally, until the beans begin to soften; add a good sprinkling of salt and pepper. Continue to cook until the beans are very tender; add water if the beans dry out.

3 Drain the cooking liquid if necessary, then add the garlic. Taste and adjust the seasoning, stir in the olive oil, and serve.

Favas with Scallions. Replace the white beans with fava beans and delete the sage. Use $^1/_4$ cup chopped scallion instead of or in addition to the garlic.

Chickpeas with Jalapeños. Substitute chickpeas for the white beans and a chopped onion for the sage. Add 2 tablespoons minced jalapeño with the garlic.

Pinto Beans with Red Bell Pepper. Cilantro stems, loaded with flavor, can withstand longer cooking than the more fragile leaves: Use pinto beans instead of white beans and 2 tablespoons chopped cilantro stems instead of the sage. Add 1 cup sliced red bell pepper; cook it in 1 tablespoon olive oil over medium-high heat until soft, then add it with the garlic in Step 3. Proceed with the recipe and garnish with chopped cilantro leaves.

Dried Fruit and Lima Stew

MAKES: 4 servings

TIME: 1 hour with cooked, fresh, or frozen limas

With its chewy texture and bold flavor, dried fruit makes an excellent base for a stew as long as it's not overcooked (when it is, it falls apart, which isn't the worst thing in the world). Use oil instead of butter and skip the optional cream and you have a vegan stew.

Other dried fruit you can use: dried peaches or apples.

> 8 ounces dried lima beans or 1 pound fresh or frozen
>
> 2 tablespoons butter or neutral oil, like grapeseed or corn
>
> 2 large onions, sliced
>
> 1 tablespoon peeled and minced fresh ginger
>
> 1 tablespoon minced garlic
>
> 1 cup port, not-too-dry red wine, or water
>
> 1 cup chopped tomato (canned are fine; don't bother to drain)
>
> 12 dried plums (prunes)
>
> 12 dried apricots

F Fast   **M** Make Ahead   **V** Vegan

Salt and freshly ground black pepper

1 tablespoon sugar

$^1/_2$ teaspoon cayenne, or to taste

$^1/_2$ cup cream (optional)

❶ If you're using dried limas, cook them (see Cooking Beans, the Quick-Soak Way, page 581), a day or two in advance if you like. If they're fresh or frozen, proceed to Step 2.

❷ Put the butter or oil in a casserole, Dutch oven, or similar pan over medium heat. When the butter is melted or the oil is hot, add the onions and cook, stirring occasionally, until very soft, at least 15 minutes. Add the ginger and garlic and cook for 30 seconds. Add the port, raise the heat a bit, and cook for a minute, until some of the liquid bubbles away. Add the tomato, dried fruit, salt, pepper, sugar, cayenne, and drained limas.

❸ Bring to a boil, lower the heat, cover, and simmer, stirring occasionally, until the fruit is tender, the tomato "saucy," and all the flavors combined, about 15 minutes. Raise the heat and boil off any excess liquid (you want stew, not soup); taste and adjust the seasoning. (You can make the stew in advance to this point, then cool, cover, and refrigerate until you're ready to eat; reheat and proceed.) Stir in the cream if you're using it. Cook for another 30 seconds and serve.

Beans and Greens

MAKES: 4 servings

TIME: 1 to 2$^1/_2$ hours

Ⓜ Ⓥ

I never tire of this classic combination, especially since there are so many possible variations. Regardless of the flavors, it's a texture thing; the beans should be somewhat creamy and the greens should be silky without disinte-

grating. The secret is to add the greens—and lots of garlic and oil—after the beans are almost there.

8 ounces dried chickpeas, washed, picked over, and soaked if you like (see "The Basics of Cooking Legumes," page 579)

1 medium onion, unpeeled

1 bay leaf

1 clove

Salt and freshly ground black pepper

1 bunch (about 1$^1/_2$ pounds) broccoli raab, roughly chopped

1 tablespoon minced garlic, or more to taste

1 tablespoon plus 1 teaspoon extra virgin olive oil, or more to taste

$^1/_2$ cup Fried Bread Crumbs (page 805) for garnish

❶ Put the beans in a large pot with water to cover. Turn the heat to high and bring to a boil.

❷ Cut a slit in the onion and insert the bay leaf; insert the clove into the onion as well and put the onion in the pot. Turn the heat down to medium-low so the mixture bubbles gently, cover partially, and cook, stirring occasionally.

❸ When the beans begin to soften (anywhere from 30 to 60 minutes, depending on the bean), sprinkle with salt and pepper. Continue to cook, stirring occasionally, until the beans are tender but still intact (which will be about as much more time as it took for them to get tender). Add water if necessary.

❹ Add the broccoli raab to the pot and continue to cook until tender, 10 to 30 minutes, depending on the thickness of the stems. If you want a soupy mixture, add more water.

❺ Remove the onion. Taste and adjust the seasoning. About 3 minutes before serving, add the garlic and olive oil and stir. Spoon the beans and greens into individual bowls and garnish with bread crumbs. Serve immediately.

OTHER BEANS AND GREENS

These are some of my favorite combinations, though you can mix and match as you like. The quantities remain the same as in the recipe, except where noted.

BEAN	GREEN	FAT	GARNISH
Adzuki beans	Bok choy	Dark sesame oil	Soy sauce and minced fresh chile (like jalapeño or Thai), hot red pepper flakes, or cayenne to taste
Black beans	Kale	Extra virgin olive oil	Chopped toasted Brazil nuts
Cannellini	Escarole	Extra virgin olive oil or melted butter	Grated or shaved Parmesan cheese
Cannellini	1 large or 2 small heads radicchio	Extra virgin olive oil or melted butter	Balsamic Syrup (page 798)
Chickpeas	Chard	Extra virgin olive oil	Chopped toasted almonds
Gigante or other large dry white beans	Romaine lettuce (cooked like a green)	Extra virgin olive oil	Crumbled feta cheese
Lentils, brown	Cabbage	Extra virgin olive oil or melted butter	A spoonful of coarse mustard
Lentils, green (preferably Le Puy)	1 bunch sorrel	Melted butter	Crème fraîche
Lentils, green (preferably Le Puy)	1 large fennel bulb	Extra virgin olive oil or melted butter	Golden raisins, stirred in with the garlic and oil or butter
Navy beans	Broccoli	Extra virgin olive oil or butter	1 cup grated cheddar cheese
Pinto beans	Spinach	Extra virgin olive oil	Fresh Tomato or Tomatillo Salsa (page 750 or 751)
Soybeans, black or white	Mustard greens	Dark sesame oil	A tablespoon or so of soy sauce and a sprinkle of sesame seeds

Beans and Mushrooms

MAKES: 4 servings

TIME: 1 to 2^1/$_2$ hours, depending on the bean

The earthy flavors of beans and mushrooms complement each other perfectly; use dried or fresh mushrooms, in virtually any combination—see the variations.

To emphasize the mushroom flavor, cook the beans in Mushroom Stock (page 102) instead of water or double the amount of mushrooms. You might also garnish the dish with Sautéed Mushrooms (page 314), using shiitakes if you can and getting 'em nice and crisp. Use the oil instead of the butter to make this vegan.

Other beans you can use: cannellini, navy, gigantes,

F Fast   M Make Ahead   V Vegan

lima, pinto, kidney, appaloosa, anastazi, green or brown lentils, or soybeans.

8 ounces dried cranberry beans, washed, picked over, and soaked if you like (see "The Basics of Cooking Legumes," page 579)

2 ounces dried porcini

1 medium onion, unpeeled

1 bay leaf

Salt and freshly ground black pepper

1 tablespoon minced garlic, or more to taste

1 tablespoon chopped fresh sage leaves,
    or 1 teaspoon dried

$^{1}/_{4}$ cup extra virgin olive oil or 4 tablespoons ($^{1}/_{2}$ stick) melted butter

1 Put the beans in a large pot with water to cover. Turn the heat to high and bring to a boil. Meanwhile, soak the mushrooms in hot water to cover.

2 Cut a slit in the onion, insert the bay leaf, and put the onion in the pot. Turn the heat down to medium-low so that the mixture bubbles gently, cover partially, and cook, stirring occasionally.

3 When the mushrooms are soft, drain them, reserving the soaking liquid. Squeeze them dry, trim away any hard spots, and chop them.

4 When the beans begin to soften (anywhere from 30 to 60 minutes, depending on the bean), sprinkle with lots of salt and pepper and stir in the reserved mushroom-soaking liquid. Continue to cook, stirring occasionally, until the beans are tender but still intact (which will be about as much time as it took them to get tender). Add the mushrooms to the pot and continue to cook for 10 to 15 minutes.

5 Remove the onion. Taste and adjust the seasoning. About 3 minutes before serving, add the garlic, herbs, and olive oil and stir. Spoon the beans and mushrooms into individual bowls and serve immediately.

Black Beans with Dried Shiitakes. Asian flavors work well with the black beans' earthy flavor: Replace the cran-berry with black beans and the porcini with dried shi-itakes. Substitute 2 tablespoons chopped fermented black beans for the sage and dark sesame oil for the olive oil. Season with soy sauce instead of salt and pro-ceed with the recipe.

Chickpeas with Cremini or Shiitakes. Add a sprinkling of just about any spice or spice mixture (to make your own, see pages 810–819) if you like: Substitute chick-peas for the cranberry beans and use about 1 pound fresh cremini or shiitake mushrooms, chopped or quartered, instead of the porcini. Skip Step 2 and use Mushroom Stock (page 102) to replace the mushroom-soaking liquid in Step 5. Replace the sage with cilantro or parsley.

White Beans with Shiitakes. The shiitakes add complex-ity: Replace the cranberry beans with any white bean and the dried porcini with about 8 ounces fresh shi-itakes, stems removed and reserved. In Step 2, soak the stems in the hot water or in hot Mushroom Stock (page 102) for more mushroom flavor. Substitute rosemary or thyme for the sage.

Flageolets with Morels. Dried or fresh morels are good here, as is a touch of cream added at the end: Use flageolets and morels instead of the cranberry beans and porcini. If you're using fresh morels, use about 8 ounces, cleaned and halved, skip Step 2, and use Mushroom Stock (page 102) to replace the mushroom-soaking liquid in Step 5. Replace the sage with tarragon or chervil and use the melted butter instead of the olive oil.

Fava Beans with Chanterelles. Use any dried wild mush-room if chanterelles are not available, or shiitakes if that's all you can find: Use fava or lima beans instead of cranberry beans and chanterelles instead of porcini. If you're using fresh mushrooms, skip Step 2 and use Mushroom Stock (page 102) to replace the mushroom-soaking liquid in Step 5. Replace the sage with chives or parsley and use the melted butter instead of the olive oil.

Braised Lentils, Spanish Style

MAKES: 4 servings

TIME: 45 minutes

Earthy and slightly smoky (use Spanish pimentón, the wonderful smoky paprika). Make it saucy but not soupy—you want enough liquid to sop up with crusty bread. Add a salad and you have a good, simple meal.

Double the recipe if you like, because the leftovers will keep in the fridge for a couple of days and reheat perfectly for lunch or a super-quick dinner.

Other beans you can use: Earthy-flavored legumes work best, Le Puy or black Beluga lentils if you can find them.

2 tablespoons extra virgin olive oil

$^{1}/_{2}$ onion, chopped

1 stalk celery, chopped

1 carrot, chopped

2 teaspoons minced garlic

$^{1}/_{2}$ teaspoon crumbled saffron threads (optional)

1 tablespoon smoked Spanish paprika (pimentón)

1 bay leaf

$^{1}/_{2}$ cup dry red wine

2 cups vegetable stock (pages 101–102) or water, or more as needed

1 cup dried brown lentils, washed and picked over

Salt and freshly ground black pepper

Chopped parsley for garnish

1 Put the oil in a medium pot over medium-high heat. When hot, add the onion, celery, and carrot; cook, stirring occasionally, until the onion is soft, 5 to 7 minutes. Add the garlic, saffron, and paprika and cook for another minute.

2 Add the bay leaf, wine, stock, and lentils. Sprinkle with salt and pepper and bring to a boil. Turn the heat down to medium-low so that the mixture bubbles gently, cover partially, and cook, stirring occasionally and adding stock or water if necessary to keep the lentils from sticking and burning, until the lentils are tender, 25 to 30 minutes. The lentils should be saucy but not soupy. Taste and adjust the seasoning, sprinkle with parsley, and serve or store, covered, in the refrigerator for up to 3 days.

Braised Lentils, Moroccan Style. A more heavily spiced dish: Double the onion and omit the celery, carrot, paprika, and wine. Add 1 teaspoon each ground turmeric, cinnamon, and ground cumin. Replace 1 cup of the stock with $1^{1}/_{2}$ cups chopped ripe tomato with their juices. Proceed with the recipe and garnish with chopped cilantro leaves.

Braised Lentils, Ethiopian Style. Loads of spices and a bit of heat: Omit the celery, carrot, saffron, and bay leaf. Add 1 tablespoon peeled and minced fresh ginger and $^{1}/_{2}$ teaspoon each ground allspice, fenugreek, coriander, cardamom, and cayenne. Replace the Spanish paprika with 2 tablespoons sweet paprika.

Braised Lentils with Roasted Winter Squash. The caramelized roasted squash adds depth: Add any medium winter squash, like acorn, butternut, kabocha, or turban, peeled, seeded, and cut into 1- to 2-inch cubes (about 2 cups); toss it in olive oil to coat and roast it in a 375°F oven on a baking sheet until tender and caramelized (see page 366 for more details on roasting squash). Eliminate the saffron and paprika and use white wine instead of red. Proceed with the recipe; add the squash to the lentils in the last 10 minutes or so of cooking.

Braised Lentils with Celery. The clean flavor of the celery pairs nicely with the earthiness of the lentils. Or use $^{1}/_{2}$ cup chopped lovage stems and leaves: Double or triple the amount of celery and eliminate the carrot, garlic, saffron, and paprika. Use white wine instead of red and add a teaspoon of grated orange zest.

Braised Lentils with Parsnips. A great fall or winter dish; add a bit of cream for extra richness: Replace the carrot with about a cup of peeled and chopped parsnip and eliminate the garlic, saffron, and paprika. Use $^{1}/_{4}$ cup dry (fino) sherry instead of the red wine. Proceed with the recipe, sprinkling with nutmeg just before serving.

Lentils, along with barley and wheat, were among the first cultivated foods, probably about ten thousand years ago in what is now Iraq. Now few foods are as widely eaten around the world. Lentils are staples in the Middle East and especially India, where they are a vital protein source for the large vegetarian populations. On the other end of the spectrum is the United States, which is among the largest producers of lentils but exports more than 75 percent of the crop. Simply put, Americans aren't lentil lovers, which is a shame—they're delicious, cheap, and easy to cook. They're also incredibly nutritious, loaded with protein (second only to soybeans), fiber, minerals, and vitamins and low in fat.

Lentils are classified into three groups, each of which contains a number of varieties; I'm describing only the most popular and widely available here:

BROWN LENTILS are the most commonly available lentil (look in any supermarket), have darker seed coats—ranging from brown to black—and generally hold their shape during cooking.

Spanish Brown. Spanish Pardina, Continental, Indian Brown, Egyptian, German: Your basic lentil, found in every supermarket. Dull, light brownish green in color, flat, with an earthy, slightly peppery flavor. These hold their shape during cooking but can start to split if overcooked.

Black Beluga. Beluga, Petite Beluga: Small, rounded, and jet black—they look a little like caviar—they take on a shiny green-black color when cooked. They hold their shape well, have a rich earthy flavor, and a soft texture. Not unlike lentilles du Puy, right.

Marrone. A tan-colored flat lentil with an earthy and nutty flavor.

Ivory White. Urad dal.

GREEN LENTILS (mostly French Green and Lentilles du Puy) have glossy dark green to green-brown seed coats and hold up well to cooking but generally take the longest to cook. You're more likely to find these lentils at specialty markets.

Lentilles du Puy. Le Puy Lentils, French Green du Puy: Nicknamed the "poor man's caviar," the most revered lentil for its robust earthy flavor and ability to hold its shape in cooking. Lentilles du Puy are grown only in Puy, France.

French Green. A (usually) American-grown version of the famed lentilles du Puy, at about half the price. They vary in color from slate to dark green, are rounded, and have an earthy and peppery flavor.

RED LENTILS—usually orange—are most often peeled and split and found by their Indian names: masoor (or masar) or just plain dal. Some uneducated people (like me) call them "orange lentils," because they're really orange. These are super-quick-cooking (like 15 minutes) and tend to fall apart when tender. Despite their being the world's most popular lentils, you may have to go to an Indian or Middle Eastern market to find red lentils. And you sometimes see them whole, with skins (sabat masoor), or split, with skins (chilke wali masoor). They are used in many Indian-style dals, like Simplest Dal on page 600.

Red Chief. Peeled and varying from red to salmon-colored. Quick cooking, with a mild, earthy flavor.

Crimson, Petite Crimson. Small, extremely quick cooking. They fall apart completely, making them great for thickening soups and stews.

Petite Golden. Small, peeled, and golden-yellow in color; they're rounder in shape and don't fall apart as easily as other red lentils.

Canary, Sutter's Gold. A hard-to-find peachy-yellow peeled lentil; quick cooking, and if not overcooked can hold their shape.

Simplest Dal

MAKES: 4 servings

TIME: 40 minutes, largely unattended

The most basic dal—the classic lentil staple of India—flavorful and creamy (if you add butter or oil, the dish becomes more luxurious). In addition to the usual ways of eating dal hot, you can also serve this at room temperature or even cold, to spread on toasted wedges of pita or Flaky Indian-Style Flatbread (page 698). Leftovers make a terrific sandwich spread. Use oil instead of butter to make this vegan.

Other beans you can use: yellow split peas, split mung beans without skins (moong dal).

1 cup dried red lentils, washed and picked over

2 tablespoons minced peeled fresh ginger

1 tablespoon minced garlic

4 cardamom pods

1 tablespoon mustard seeds

2 cloves

1 teaspoon cracked black pepper

1 ancho or other mild dried chile (optional)

Salt

2 tablespoons cold butter or peanut oil (optional)

Chopped fresh cilantro leaves for garnish

1 Combine the lentils, ginger, garlic, cardamom, mustard seeds, cloves, pepper, and chile in a saucepan and add water to cover by about 1 inch. Cook at a steady simmer until the lentils are quite soft, 20 to 30 minutes, salting as the lentils soften.

2 Remove the cloves and, if you like, the cardamom pods (they're kind of fun to eat, though). Stir in the butter or oil if you're using it. Taste and adjust the seasoning, then garnish with cilantro and serve.

Red Lentils and Rhubarb with Indian Spices. The rhubarb almost dissolves into this, leaving behind its trademark flavor: To the pot along with the other ingredients, add 3 or 4 stalks rhubarb, strings removed (see illustrations, page 284) and fruit chopped.

Red Lentils with Radish. Crunch and flavor: Peel and cut 1 large daikon radish into large chunks (about 2 cups). You can also use smaller white or red radishes.

Red Lentils with Celery Root. Peel, chop, and add 1 medium celery root (or $^2/_3$ of a large one).

Red Lentils with Fresh Tomatoes. Really nice color and a little acidity: Core 4 ripe medium tomatoes and cut them into wedges; stir them in during the last 5 minutes or so of cooking.

Red Lentils with Chaat Masala. In the main recipe or any of the variations, omit the ginger, garlic, cardamom, mustard seeds, chile, and cloves (essentially all the other seasonings besides salt and pepper) and use a teaspoon or more of chaat masala (to make your own, see page 814).

Lentils and Potatoes with Curry

MAKES: 4 servings

TIME: About 1 hour

You may want to double this recipe so you have some handy in the fridge or freezer, because it reheats beautifully. Don't worry if the potatoes crumble a bit on the second go-round; they will only add body to the dish.

Other beans you can use: yellow or green split peas or split mung beans without skins (moong dal), the cooking time reduced by 15 minutes or so.

1 cup dried brown lentils, washed and picked over

$3^1/_2$ cups water, coconut milk, either made from scratch (page 423) or canned (use 1 can, slightly less than 2 cups, with a little water), or vegetable stock (pages 101–102), plus more if needed

Dal is the Indian word used to describe both beans and the family of dishes made from them, and anyone who has ever eaten in an Indian restaurant—or any hip vegetarian joint for that matter—has eaten a dal of some kind, a soupy stew of beans, usually spooned over basmati rice or served with bread. But with all due respect to the cuisines of India, I suggest that you think of dal as an approach to eating beans in the Indian style rather than a rigid kitchen doctrine. Interchanging one bean for another in recipes may not be strictly authentic, but it will result in delicious dishes even if all you ever use are supermarket brown lentils.

Butter, and often lots of it, is the key to the richest dals. (The first time I was in India, I was stunned by the amount of butter people used. Delighted too.) Ghee—a super-clarified butter that keeps really well and can withstand high cooking temperatures—is traditional, and relatively easy to make, but plain butter works just fine. (You can also buy ghee in Indian groceries, but I think butter is better.) Peanut oil and more neutral oils like grapeseed and corn are fine alternatives for vegans.

Dal can be eaten with a spoon, like soup, but I prefer slightly thicker but still-soupy dishes that you pour over something else—usually rice—and "dry" dal, where the beans remain intact. And some of my favorite ways to eat dal (remember, the word is used for all beans) don't involve boiling water at all. In Sambar Powder (page 816), raw yellow or red lentils are ground with other spices and used as a seasoning. And there's a whole family of fritters, "doughnuts," pancakes, and breads—from India and elsewhere—made with batters based on soaked and puréd beans and lentils, like Falafel (page 625), Mung Bean Pancakes (page 631), and Dosa and Uttapam (pages 744).

You can always serve dals with plain-cooked basmati or jasmine rice (page 503) or hot or at room temperature with The Simplest Indian-Style Flatbread (page 698), Essential Flatbread (page 727), or homemade (page 719) or store-bought pita for dipping. But soupy dals also make an effective and creamy sauce for simply cooked vegetables, like potatoes, eggplant, summer or winter squashes, carrots, and greens. Add more water or stock, or cream or coconut milk, and they become soup. At room temperature or chilled, they're a fine dip for Crudités (page 88). Dals even make surprisingly good sandwich fillings, especially with lettuce or sprouts and tomatoes.

1 tablespoon curry powder (to make your own, see page 816)

2 medium russet potatoes, peeled and cut into large chunks

Salt and freshly ground black pepper

Yogurt for garnish

Minced fresh cilantro leaves for garnish

❶ Combine the lentils, liquid, and curry powder in a medium saucepan and bring to a boil over medium-high heat. Turn the heat down to medium-low so that the mixture bubbles gently, cover partially, and cook, stirring occasionally, until the lentils start to absorb the water a bit, about 15 minutes.

❷ Add the potatoes and cover the pan completely. Cook, undisturbed, for 10 minutes or so, then stir gently and check to make sure the lentils aren't too dry. If so, add a little more liquid. Add salt as the lentils become tender.

❸ Cover and continue cooking until the lentils are soft and beginning to turn to mush and the potatoes are tender at the center, another 5 to 10 minutes; add liquid if necessary. The mixture should be moist but not soupy. Add lots of black pepper, stir, then taste and adjust the seasoning and serve, garnished with yogurt and cilantro.

Buttery Lentils and Potatoes with Curry. A little smoother and more flavorful: When you stir and check the mixture in Step 2, stir in 2 tablespoons cold butter. (Use peanut oil if you want to keep the dal vegan.)

Mung Bean Dal with Apples, Coconut, and Mint

MAKES: 4 to 6 servings
TIME: About 1 hour, largely unattended

Many dals rely on deep flavors, but here's an example of how fresh, bright ingredients can set off the natural heaviness of beans. The result is a hearty dish that manages to be refreshing, even in summer.

Other beans you can use: pigeon or black-eyed peas or chickpeas, cooked for up to an hour longer.

- 1$^{1}/_{2}$ cups dried mung beans, washed, picked over, and soaked if you like (see "The Basics of Cooking Legumes," page 579)
- $^{1}/_{2}$ cup shredded coconut
- 2 medium green apples, cored, peeled, and chopped
- 2 tablespoons peeled and minced fresh ginger
- 2 tablespoons minced garlic
- Pinch ground turmeric (optional)
- 2 cups coconut milk, either made from scratch (page 423), or canned (use 1 can, slightly less than 2 cups, with a little water)
- $^{1}/_{4}$ cup brown sugar, or to taste
- Salt and freshly ground black pepper
- $^{1}/_{2}$ cup chopped fresh mint leaves
- $^{1}/_{2}$ cup sliced scallion
- Juice of 1 lime

1 Combine the beans, coconut, apples, ginger, garlic, turmeric if you're using it, coconut milk, and brown sugar in a large pot. Add enough water to cover. Bring to a boil over high heat, then turn the heat down to medium-low so the mixture bubbles steadily but not violently. Cook, stirring occasionally and adding some salt as the beans become tender, until the beans are quite soft, 45 to 60 minutes, adding water or coconut milk as needed to keep everything moist.

2 When the beans are tender and the liquid is thickened, sprinkle with pepper and stir in the mint, scallion, and lime juice. Cook for a minute or two more, then taste, adjust the seasoning, and serve.

Mung Bean Dal with Carrots, Cashews, and Thai Basil. A nice twist: Instead of the apples, use 3 or 4 medium carrots. Use whole cashews instead of the coconut. Add a couple dried Thai chiles to the pot if you like and replace the mint leaves with Thai (or other) basil.

Mixed Whole-Bean Dal with Walnuts

MAKES: 4 to 6 servings
TIME: About 1 hour, largely unattended

Here I cook the onion and seasonings in a little oil, then add the tomato paste, nuts, and finally beans. It's a little more work than other dals, but it lends a toastiness that helps make this a true main dish, and adzuki beans add both natural sweetness and creaminess.

Other beans you can use: You can make this a single-bean dal using all small navy beans or black-eyed peas. Black, dried lima, or kidney beans are also good, alone or in combination.

- 2 tablespoons butter or peanut oil
- 1 large yellow onion, chopped
- 1 tablespoon fragrant curry powder or garam masala (to make your own, see page 815 or 816)
- $^{1}/_{4}$ cup tomato paste

1 cup chopped walnuts

$^1/_2$ cup each dried small navy beans, black-eyed peas, and adzuki beans, washed, picked over, and soaked if you like (see "The Basics of Cooking Legumes," page 879)

Salt and freshly ground black pepper

$^1/_2$ cup yogurt for garnish

$^1/_4$ cup chopped parsley for garnish

1 Put the butter or oil in a large pot over medium heat. When the butter is melted or the oil is hot, add the onion and cook, stirring occasionally, until soft and golden, about 5 minutes. Stir in the spice blend and keep stirring for a few seconds, until it becomes fragrant. Add the tomato paste and cook, stirring frequently, until it darkens, another couple of minutes.

2 Add the walnuts and stir to coat them in the onion mixture. Cook and stir just long enough for them to warm a bit. Add the beans and enough water to cover by an inch or so.

3 Bring to a boil, then turn the heat down to medium-low so the mixture bubbles steadily but not violently. Cook, stirring occasionally and adding some salt as the beans become tender, until the beans are soft, about 30 to 45 minutes, adding more water as needed to keep everything moist.

4 When the beans are tender and creamy, sprinkle with pepper, then stir well, taste, and adjust the seasoning. Serve, garnished with a dollop of yogurt and a little parsley.

Mixed Whole-Bean Dal with Cabbage and Walnuts. A little more substantial: Instead of the tomato paste, add 2 cups finely chopped cabbage. Cook long enough for the cabbage to wilt and color, 5 to 8 minutes, before adding the walnuts and proceeding with the recipe.

Mixed Whole-Bean Dal with Cauliflower and Almonds. Finely chop a small head of cauliflower and add it to the pot instead of the tomato paste. Cook long enough for it to soften a bit, about 5 minutes. Use almonds instead of walnuts and proceed with the recipe.

Urad Dal with Poppy Seeds and Cilantro

MAKES: 4 servings

TIME: About 30 minutes, largely unattended

Ⓕ Ⓜ Ⓥ

The best translation for *urad dal* is "peeled and split black lentils," but that's not quite right either. Never mind; you'll find them in Indian and Asian markets and sometimes good natural food stores. This fast recipe uses a *tarka*—spices, quickly toasted in butter or oil—to season the beans after they have cooked. If you don't happen to have poppy seeds handy, omit them or substitute sesame or sunflower seeds.

The color of this dish is unusual, with the ivory urad dal providing the backdrop for the specks of poppy seeds and fresh herbs. The consistency depends on how much water you add during cooking. I love it as a thick sauce, to pour over basmati rice and Grilled or Broiled Eggplant (page 295). It's vegan with oil instead of butter.

Other beans you can use: any kind of lentil or split pea.

$1^1/_2$ cups dried urad dal, washed, picked over, and soaked if you like (see "The Basics of Cooking Legumes," page 579)

2 or 3 dried Thai chiles (optional)

4 tablespoons ($^1/_2$ stick) butter or $^1/_4$ cup peanut oil

2 tablespoons peeled and minced fresh ginger

Salt and freshly ground black pepper

2 tablespoons poppy seeds

1 cup minced fresh cilantro or a mixture of parsley and cilantro

1 Put the dal in a medium pot with the chiles if you're using them and add enough water to cover by about $^1/_2$ inch. Bring to a boil, then turn the heat down to medium-low so the mixture bubbles steadily but not violently. Cook, stirring occasionally, until the beans are soft, about 20 minutes or so, adding more water as needed to keep everything moist and reach the consistency you like.

2 While the beans are cooking, put the butter or oil in a small skillet over medium heat. When the butter is melted or the oil is hot, add the ginger and cook, stirring constantly, until soft and golden, about 3 minutes. Sprinkle with lots of salt and pepper, then add the poppy seeds, stirring to coat with the oil and toast for just a minute or so. Add the herbs and cook until just wilted and brightly colored. Turn off the heat.

3 When the beans are tender, stir in the poppy seed mixture. Taste, adjust the seasoning, and serve.

Stewed Fava Beans with Tahini

MAKES: 4 servings
TIME: About 1½ hours, largely unattended

Cooked beans and tahini always make a great combo, with real depth, richness, and incredible flavor. This mix can also be puréd and served as a dip with toasted pita chips, like Hummus (page 614). Or add a little more liquid and serve this as a stew. Be sure to use a good, fruity olive oil. Vegan without the optional egg.

Other beans you can use: lima, gigantes, navy, or Great Northern.

    8 ounces dried peeled and split fava beans, washed,
        picked over, and soaked if you like (see "The Basics
        of Cooking Legumes," page 579)

    1 onion, chopped

    2 tablespoons tahini

    Salt and freshly ground black pepper

    3 tablespoons extra virgin olive oil

    2 tablespoons freshly squeezed lemon juice

    Chopped parsley for garnish

    Chopped Hard-Cooked Egg (page 166) for garnish
        (optional)

1 Put the beans in a large pot with water to cover. Turn the heat to high and bring to a boil.

2 Turn the heat down so the beans bubble gently. Cover loosely. When the beans begin to soften, after about 30 minutes, add the onion, tahini, and a good pinch of salt and pepper. Continue to cook, stirring occasionally, until the beans are very soft, about 1 hour; add water if necessary. Taste and adjust the seasoning, then drizzle with the olive oil and lemon juice, garnish with the parsley and egg, and serve.

Stewed Favas with Za'atar. The sesame flavor remains but with a bit of thyme and the zing of sumac: Substitute za'atar (to make your own, see page 818) for the tahini.

Stewed Favas with Potatoes and Spiced Onions. A bulkier, heartier, and quite delicious dish: Add 1 or 2 cups cubed potatoes after the first 30 minutes, then proceed with the recipe. Meanwhile, cook a chopped onion and 2 cloves chopped garlic in olive oil until soft. Add a teaspoon each ground coriander and cumin and sprinkle with salt and cayenne to taste, stir well and cook for another minute. Top the stewed favas with the spiced onion and garnish with chopped cilantro.

Tomatoey Stewed Favas. Delete the tahini. Add a cup or so chopped fresh or canned tomato with the juices and 2 teaspoons chopped fresh marjoram leaves or 1 teaspoon dried.

Flageolets, French Style

MAKES: 4 servings
TIME: 1 to 2 hours, largely unattended

Ⓜ

Flageolets, the small pale green beans that are actually immature kidney beans, are adored in Western Europe and are known for their delicate flavor. The addition of cream simply enhances it (they've been doing this in

France for centuries). To vary the flavor, replace the thyme sprigs with tarragon or garnish with chopped tarragon, chives, or chervil.

Other beans you can use: cranberry, navy, or lima.

8 ounces dried flageolets, washed, picked over, and soaked if you like (see "The Basics of Cooking Legumes," page 579)

1 medium onion, unpeeled

1 bay leaf

1 clove

1 carrot, cut into chunks

4 sprigs fresh thyme or $1/2$ teaspoon dried

Salt and freshly ground black pepper

2 tablespoons butter

1 tablespoon minced shallot

1 cup cream, preferably not ultra-pasteurized

Chopped parsley leaves for garnish

① Put the beans in a large pot with water to cover. Turn the heat to high and bring to a boil.

② Cut a slit in the onion and insert the bay leaf; insert the clove into the onion as well and put the onion in the pot. Add the carrot and thyme. Turn the heat down so the beans bubble gently and cover loosely.

③ When the beans begin to soften, after about 30 minutes, season with salt and pepper. Continue to cook, stirring occasionally, until the beans are tender but still intact, about 45 minutes; add water if necessary.

④ Drain the beans and discard the onion and carrot. Put the butter and shallot in a deep skillet large enough to hold the beans. Turn the heat to medium and cook, stirring occasionally, until the shallot softens, about 5 minutes. Add the cream and the beans and continue to cook, stirring, until the beans are hot and have absorbed some of the cream, about 10 minutes. Taste and adjust the seasoning, garnish, and serve.

Flageolets with Fennel. Adding a delicate anise flavor: Replace the onion and carrot with about 1 cup chopped fennel; discard the bay leave and clove but not the fennel in Step 4. Garnish with a couple teaspoons grated lemon zest or Citrus Sprinkle (page 818).

Flageolets with Tomatoes. Great color, different flavor: Add 1 cup or more chopped fresh or canned tomato in Step 2.

Flageolets with Lettuce. The fresh flavor of the lettuce enhances that of the flageolets: Stir in 1 to 2 cups shredded lettuce or radicchio in Step 4.

Chickpeas in Their Own Broth, with Crisp Bread Crumbs

MAKES: 4 servings

TIME: 30 minutes with cooked chickpeas

Ⓕ Ⓜ Ⓥ

Chickpeas and their broth are so flavorful they hardly need anything else to be completely delicious, but a bit of garlic and a good olive oil make this dish spectacular. Cooking your own chickpeas is really essential here, because canned chickpeas just don't have the flavor.

One roughly 6-inch piece French or Italian bread, a day or two old

$1/2$ cup extra virgin olive oil

Salt and freshly ground black pepper

3 cups cooked chickpeas, with about 2 cups of their cooking liquid (5 cups total; see "The Basics of Cooking Legumes," page 579)

1 tablespoon minced garlic

Chopped parsley leaves for garnish

① Roughly chop the bread and put it in a food processor; pulse until it is shredded, with no chunks larger than a pea but most not much smaller either. Put all but 2 tablespoons of the olive oil in a skillet over medium heat. Add the bread and a sprinkling of salt and cook, shaking the pan occasionally, until the crumbs are nicely browned, 5 to 10 minutes. Use a slotted spoon to remove the bread crumbs from the skillet (drain them on paper towels).

2 Warm the chickpeas in their broth with the garlic and add a good sprinkling of salt and pepper. Top with the bread crumbs, garnish with parsley, and serve or store, covered, in the refrigerator for up to 3 days. Gently reheat and garnish right before serving.

Chickpeas in Their Own Broth, Catalan Style. A bit of wine and tomato for a slightly more sophisticated dish: After Step 1, cook a chopped onion and the garlic in 3 or 4 tablespoons extra virgin olive oil until soft. Add a splash of white wine and a tablespoon of tomato paste, then cook for a minute or two. Add a bay leaf and continue with Step 2.

Chickpeas in Their Own Broth, Cuban Style. Loads of garlic and tangy lime juice: After Step 1, cook a chopped bell pepper along with 2 or 3 tablespoons of minced garlic, in 3 or 4 tablespoons extra virgin olive oil until soft. Add a teaspoon ground cumin and continue with Step 2. Sprinkle with lots of lime juice just before serving.

Nutty Chickpeas in Their Own Broth. Even more toastiness and crunch: After Step 1, pan-roast about a cup of almonds, pine nuts, hazelnuts, or chestnuts in olive oil or butter until aromatic and continue with Step 2.

Chickpeas in Their Own Broth, with Sun-Dried Tomatoes. The tomatoes finish reconstituting themselves in the chickpea broth, absorbing loads of flavor in the process: Add about $1/2$ cup chopped soaked sun-dried tomatoes in Step 2 and cook until they are soft, about 10 minutes.

Chickpeas in Their Own Broth, with Tahini. A classic combination, just a different form: Add a tablespoon or two of tahini in Step 2. Garnish with a squeeze of lemon juice before serving.

Black Beans with Orange Juice

MAKES: 4 servings
TIME: 30 minutes with cooked beans

An odd-sounding combination, but trust me, a delicious one. The sweet acidity of the orange juice works nicely with the earthy flavor of the black beans. Using a fruity red wine complements the orange flavor and also adds to the complexity of the dish.

Other beans you can use: Rich, earthy beans, like kidney and pinto, work best.

3 cups cooked or canned black beans, with about 1 cup of their cooking liquid (4 cups total; see "The Basics of Cooking Legumes," page 579)

$1^1/2$ teaspoons ground cumin

Salt and freshly ground black pepper

1 orange, well washed

2 tablespoons extra virgin olive oil

1 onion, chopped

1 bell pepper, preferably red or yellow, peeled if desired (see page 237), cored, seeded, and chopped

1 tablespoon minced garlic

$1/2$ cup dry red wine

Chopped fresh cilantro or parsley leaves for garnish

1 Put the beans in a pot over medium heat; add the cumin and a good pinch of salt and pepper.

2 Halve the orange. Peel one half and add the skin to the beans, then divide the sections and set aside. Squeeze the juice out of the other half and set aside.

3 Put the olive oil in a skillet over medium heat. Add the onion and bell pepper and cook, stirring occasionally, until the pepper softens, 8 to 10 minutes. Add the garlic and cook, stirring, for 1 minute more. Add to the beans.

4 Turn the heat to high and add the red wine to the skillet. Cook until the wine is reduced by about half, about 5 minutes. Add to the beans along with the reserved orange juice. Taste and adjust the seasoning. Serve with rice, garnished with the reserved orange sections and some cilantro, or store, covered, in the refrigerator for up to 2 days.

Black Beans and Beets with Orange Juice. Quite sweet, but acidic as well and unmistakably *not* dessert: Add 1 cup peeled and chopped beets in Step 1; cook until the beets are tender.

Black Beans and Chiles with Orange Juice. Terrific contrast; use any fruity or smoky chile (see "The Basics of Chiles and Peppers," page 822) or chili powder (to make your own, see page 814): Add 1 or 2 fresh chiles (like New Mexico or habanero), cleaned and chopped, or 1 or 2 dried chiles (like chile de árbol or piquín), soaked, cleaned, and chopped, in Step 1.

White Beans with Lemon. A lighter version: Replace the black beans with any white beans, the cumin with 1 tablespoon chopped rosemary, and the red wine with white. Eliminate the bell peppers. In Step 2, substitute about 1 tablespoon julienned or chopped lemon zest for the orange peel; set aside the juice of half the lemon.

Chili non Carne

MAKES: 6 to 8 servings
TIME: About 2 hours, largely unattended

A straightforward and delicious chili that can be completely customized to your taste. Increase or decrease just about anything or add pressed tofu, tempeh, or even nuts to bulk up the texture and flavor. Serve it with lots of garnishes—always great when feeding a crew—like minced onion or scallion, hot sauce, sour cream, and grated cheddar, Monterey Jack, or queso fresco, as well as rice, crackers, or tortilla chips.

Other beans you can use: kidney, dried soybeans, or any pink or red beans.

> 1 pound dried pinto beans, washed, picked over, and soaked if you like (see "The Basics of Cooking Legumes," page 579)
>
> 1 onion, unpeeled, plus 1 small onion, minced

Salt and freshly ground black pepper

1 cup bean-cooking liquid, vegetable stock (pages 101–102), or water

1 fresh or dried hot chile, seeded and minced, or to taste (optional)

1 teaspoon ground cumin, or to taste (optional)

1 teaspoon minced fresh oregano leaves or 1/2 teaspoon dried (optional)

1 tablespoon minced garlic

Chopped fresh cilantro for garnish

① Put the beans in a large pot with water to cover. Bring to a boil over high heat, add the whole onion, turn the heat down so the beans bubble steadily but not violently, and cover loosely.

② When the beans begin to soften, after 30 minutes to an hour, season with salt and pepper. Continue to cook, stirring occasionally, until the beans are quite tender but still intact, 1 to 2 hours; add water if necessary.

③ Drain the beans, reserving the cooking liquid if you choose to use it. Discard the whole onion and add the minced onion, the liquid, the chile, cumin, and/or oregano if you're using them, and the garlic. Turn the heat to medium and bring to a boil. Cover and turn the heat down to low.

④ Cook, stirring occasionally and adding more liquid if necessary, until the beans are very tender and the flavors have mellowed, about 15 minutes. Taste, adjust the seasoning, and garnish with cilantro.

Chili con Tofu. A great way to add heft: Put 3 tablespoons neutral oil, like grapeseed or corn, in a large skillet over high heat. Add 1/2 to 1 pound cubed firm, pressed, or smoked firm tofu and cook, stirring frequently, until browned. Add the tofu to the chili in Step 4.

Chili con Tempeh. Adds bit of earthy flavor and more texture: Put 3 tablespoons neutral oil, like grapeseed or corn, in a large skillet over high heat. Add 1/2 to 1 pound firm crumbled tempeh and cook, stirring frequently, until browned. Add to the chili in Step 4.

Chili con Nuts. Add about 8 ounces or so chopped walnuts or other nuts in Step 4.

Espresso Black Bean Chili

MAKES: 6 to 8 servings

TIME: 1¹/₂ to 2 hours, largely unattended

This deep, richly flavored chili has enough caffeine to keep you awake—literally. (Bear this in mind when you're serving it; use decaffeinated espresso if you or your guests are caffeine sensitive or reserve it for lunch or early dinner.) Serve this with rice, a stack of warm tortillas, or tortilla chips, some crumbled queso fresco or sour cream, and parsley or cilantro.

Other beans you can use: Earthy-flavored beans that can stand up to the other flavors—pinto, kidney, or dried soybeans—work best.

    3 tablespoons neutral oil, like grapeseed or corn

    2 onions, chopped

    2 tablespoons minced garlic

    3 cups chopped ripe tomato (about 1¹/₂ pounds whole; canned is fine; don't bother to drain)

    ¹/₂ to 1 cup freshly brewed espresso, 1 to 2 cups brewed coffee, or 2 tablespoons espresso powder

    2 tablespoons chili powder (to make your own, see page 814)

    ¹/₄ cup dark brown sugar or 3 tablespoons molasses

    One 3-inch cinnamon stick

    1 pound dried black beans, washed, picked over, and soaked if you like (see "The Basics of Cooking Legumes," page 579)

    Salt and freshly ground black pepper

❶ Put the oil in a large pot with a tight-fitting lid over medium-high heat. When hot, add the onions and cook, stirring occasionally, until soft, about 5 minutes. Add the garlic and cook for another minute.

❷ Stir in the tomato, espresso, brown sugar, cinnamon, and beans and add water to cover. Bring to a boil, then lower the heat so the liquid bubbles steadily but not violently. Cover and cook, stirring occasionally, until the beans are beginning to soften, 30 to 40 minutes. Add a good pinch of salt and pepper.

❸ Continue cooking until the beans are tender, anywhere from another 45 minutes to 1¹/₂ hours. Taste and adjust the seasoning, adding more sugar, salt, or pepper. Serve or store, covered, in the refrigerator for up to 3 days.

Smoked-Tea Chili. The rich and smoky flavor of Lapsang Souchong—a Chinese smoked black tea—is fantastic in this chili with other Chinese flavors: Add 1 tablespoon minced peeled fresh ginger; omit the tomato; replace the espresso with 5 to 6 cups freshly brewed Lapsang Souchong tea or any smoked black tea, and the chili powder with hot red pepper flakes to taste. Substitute 1 teaspoon Sichuan peppercorns for the cinnamon and dried soybeans for the black beans. Add water to cover the beans if necessary and proceed with the recipe.

Chocolate Chili. Closer to a deeply flavored Oaxacan mole: Replace the espresso with ¹/₂ cup chopped Mexican chocolate or ¹/₄ cup chopped bittersweet chocolate. Decrease the sugar by half if you're using the Mexican chocolate.

Black Soybeans with Soy Sauce

MAKES: At least 4 servings

TIME: About 2 hours

A popular side dish in Korea and Japan, these are intensely flavored and delicious, with an unusual and wonderfully firm texture.

Other beans you can use: regular soybeans or black beans.

    ¹/₂ pound dried black soybeans, soybeans, or black beans, washed, picked over, and soaked if you like (see "The Basics of Cooking Legumes," page 579)

1/4 cup sugar, or more to taste

2 tablespoons mirin or a little more sugar

1/4 cup soy sauce

2 tablespoons dark sesame oil

1 tablespoon sesame seeds

① Put the beans in a pot with water to cover and bring to a boil over medium-high heat. Partially cover and adjust the heat so the mixture simmers steadily. Cook, stirring occasionally, until the beans are nearly tender and most of the water is evaporated, at least an hour and probably more. (Add water as necessary to keep the beans covered, but bear in mind that eventually you will want no water at all, so don't drown them.)

② Add the sugar, mirin, and soy and raise the heat a bit. Continue to cook, stirring frequently, until the beans are glazed and still firm, not quite as tender as you're used to; leave them quite moist (the soy sauce will burn if the mixture dries out). Stir in the sesame oil.

③ You can serve the beans immediately, at room temperature, or chilled. Just before serving, toast the sesame seeds in a small dry skillet over medium heat, shaking the pan frequently until the seeds color slightly. Sprinkle the beans with the seeds and serve.

Spicy Soybeans with Kimchi

MAKES: 4 servings

TIME: 1 1/2 hours

Ⓜ   Ⓥ

A wonderful way to incorporate kimchi into a main dish. The kimchi's pungency and spice are absorbed by the soybeans, creating a deeply flavored and warming one-pot meal.

Other beans you can use: pinto, kidney, adzuki, or black-eyed peas.

8 ounces dried yellow soybeans, washed, picked over, and soaked if you like (see "The Basics of Cooking Legumes," page 579)

2 tablespoons rice wine

2 teaspoons dark sesame oil

1 1/2 cups chopped Kimchi (page 96)

2 cloves garlic, chopped

1/4 cup soy sauce, or to taste

1/2 teaspoon cayenne, or to taste (if your kimchi is strong, you may not need any)

Chopped scallion for garnish

① Put the beans in a medium pot with water to cover and bring to a boil over medium-high heat, stirring frequently. Immediately turn the heat down to low so that the mixture bubbles gently; cook until the beans are nearly done, about 45 minutes, stirring often and adding water to cover as necessary.

② Add the wine, sesame oil, kimchi, garlic, soy, and cayenne and cook until the beans are soft, about 30 minutes more. Taste and adjust the seasoning, adding more soy sauce and cayenne if necessary. Serve hot, garnished with scallion, or store, covered, in the refrigerator for up to 3 days.

Spicy Soybeans with Kimchi and Stir-Fried Tempeh. Just before serving the beans and kimchi, stir in 1 recipe (more or less) Crunchy Crumbled Tempeh (page 674).

Puréd Spicy Soybeans with Kimchi. Once the beans are soft, use an immersion blender to puré the soybeans in the pot. Or cool the mixture slightly, pour into a blender or food processor, and purée carefully. Proceed with the recipe.

Hot, Sweet, and Sour Chickpeas with Eggplant

MAKES: 4 servings

TIME: 25 minutes

Ⓕ Ⓜ Ⓥ

Fresh curry leaves make a real difference, so try to get your hands on some. And, if you can find them, black chickpeas will make this South Asian classic even more stunning. Look for both in Indian markets.

Other beans you can use: Although none of these produce as flavorful a liquid as the chickpeas, kidney beans, split peas, or pink beans all make for a mean dish.

2 tablespoons neutral oil, like grapeseed or corn

1 medium eggplant, cut into bite-sized pieces

1 tablespoon minced peeled fresh ginger

2 hot fresh chiles, seeded and minced, or hot red pepper flakes to taste

1 sprig fresh curry leaves or several dried leaves (optional)

3 cups cooked black or regular chickpeas, with about 2 cups of their cooking liquid

1 tablespoon Sambar Powder (page 816) or curry powder (to make your own, see page 815)

1 teaspoon ground turmeric

Pinch of asafetida (optional)

2 tablespoons brown sugar

1 tablespoon tamarind paste or freshly squeezed lime juice to taste

Salt and freshly ground black pepper

Chopped fresh cilantro leaves for garnish

Chopped roasted peanuts for garnish

1 Put the oil in a skillet over medium-high heat. When hot, add the eggplant and cook, stirring occasionally, until golden brown, 5 to 10 minutes. Add the ginger, chiles, and curry leaves, stir, and cook until fragrant, about a minute.

2 Add the chickpeas, sambar, turmeric, asafetida if you're using it, brown sugar, tamarind, and a good sprinkling of salt and pepper. Bring to a boil, reduce the heat so the mixture bubbles gently, and cook, stirring occasionally, until the eggplant is very tender and the sauce has thickened, about 15 minutes.

3 Taste and adjust the seasoning, adding more sugar or tamarind paste as needed. Garnish and serve hot or reserve the cilantro and peanuts for later and store, covered, in the refrigerator for up to 2 days. Reheat gently and garnish right before serving.

Sweet and Sour Chickpeas with Tomatoes. Tomatoes create another layer of flavor: Replace the eggplant with 2 cups chopped fresh tomato; add them in Step 2 with the chickpeas.

More Sweet than Sour Chickpeas with Eggplant. The natural sweetness of the coconut is a lovely addition: Replace a cup of the chickpea liquid with unsweetened coconut milk.

Black-Eyed Peas with Smoked Tofu

MAKES: 6 to 8 servings
TIME: About 2½ hours, largely unattended

In all good conscience I can't call this hoppin' John, the classic southern bean and rice dish, because it doesn't have a ham hock. And since I'm not a fan of faux meats, I'm not going to recommend them for this—or any—vegetarian dish.

On the other hand, smoked tofu doesn't pretend to be meat. Its slightly dense, chewy texture and strong smoky flavor is unique and enjoyable, especially cooked whole, as it is here, which keeps it moist.

Because hoppin' John is traditionally served with stewed greens for good luck on New Year's Day, I suggest eating this with Boiled or Steamed Greens (page 239) or even Sea Slaw (page 55). A wedge of Corn Bread (page 687) and you're set. Even with all that, this is an easy meal to get on the table.

Other beans you can use: cowpeas or pigeon peas.

1½ cups dried black-eyed peas, washed, picked over, and soaked if you like (see "The Basics of Cooking Legumes," page 579)

2 quarts vegetable stock (pages 101–102) or water

1 brick (about 14 ounces) smoked tofu

2 medium onions, finely chopped

2 tablespoons minced garlic

1½ cups long-grain white rice

Salt and freshly ground black pepper

Tabasco sauce to taste (optional)

1 Put the peas, stock, tofu, onions, and garlic in a large pot with a tight-fitting lid. Bring to a boil, then lower the heat so it bubbles steadily but not violently. Cook, stirring occasionally, until the beans are tender but not mushy, 1 to 2 hours. (The beans may be made ahead to this point, cooled, and refrigerated for up to 2 days. Reheat gently before proceeding.)

2 When the beans are ready, make sure you have about 3 cups of liquid; if not, add more or spoon some out to make 3 cups. Stir in the rice, sprinkle with salt and pepper, and cover. Reduce the heat to low and cook, undisturbed, for 20 minutes or so.

3 Remove the lid; if any water remains, turn the heat to high for a minute or two to boil it off. Remove the tofu, cut it into cubes, and return it to the pot. Use a fork to gently fluff the rice, beans, and tofu. Add a dash or two of Tabasco if you like, taste, and adjust the seasoning. Put the lid back on and let the dish rest for at least 5 minutes and up to 15 before serving.

One-Pot Bean Gumbo. More like a casserole than a soup, with the rice and beans all together: When you add the rice in Step 2, add 1½ cups chopped tomato (canned is fine; don't bother to drain) and 1 cup chopped fresh or frozen okra. When you fluff the rice and beans in Step 3, stir in ½ cup minced red bell pepper with the Tabasco if you like.

Black-Eyed Peas with Smoked Tofu and Mushrooms. Extra earthiness and chew: While the beans are cooking, make 1 recipe Sautéed Mushrooms (page 314). When you fluff the rice and beans in Step 3, stir in the mushrooms, along with ½ cup chopped parsley if you like.

Black-Eyed Peas with Sliced Smoked Tofu. Here the tofu shares the plate with the beans and rice (you can use more of it if you like): In Step 3, instead of cubing the tofu and adding it back to the pot when you fluff the rice, remove it, fluff the rice and peas without it, and

keep the tofu bricks warm. When you're ready to serve, thinly slice the tofu and serve it alongside the peas and rice.

Mung Beans and Rice with Dried Apricots

MAKES: 4 to 6 servings

TIME: 1½ hours, largely unattended

A Central Asian take on beans and rice. The cooking technique of boiling and then steaming the beans and rice is a wonderful way to cook basmati; the grains elongate and become fluffy and separate.

If you want a crispy crust on the bottom of the pan, just drizzle in a tablespoon or more of olive oil or melted butter. (For more recipes like this, see pages 523–526.) Stick to olive oil in the recipe and it becomes vegan.

Other beans you can use: any lentil or split pea.

Salt

1 cup dried mung beans, washed, picked over, and soaked if you like (see "The Basics of Cooking Legumes," page 579)

1½ cups white or brown basmati rice, soaked if you like (see page 501)

Freshly ground black pepper

4 tablespoons (½ stick) butter or ¼ cup extra virgin olive oil

Large pinch saffron threads (optional)

1 large onion, thinly sliced

¾ cup chopped dried apricots

1 teaspoon ground cardamom

1 teaspoon ground cumin

2 teaspoons ground cinnamon

½ teaspoon cayenne

1 Bring a medium pot of water to a boil and salt it. Stir in the mung beans and return to a boil. Add the rice and return to a boil, then lower the heat so the water bubbles along nicely. (If you're using brown rice, add the rice and mung beans to the boiling water at the same time.) Cook, undisturbed—white rice for about 5 minutes, brown rice for about 15 minutes. Drain and set aside. Taste (the rice and mung beans will be only partially done), add salt if necessary, and sprinkle with pepper.

2 Melt the butter in a small bowl (or just put the oil in) and stir in the saffron if you're using it.

3 Put the melted butter or oil in a large, heavy pot with a tight-fitting lid over medium-high heat. When the butter is melted or the oil is hot, add the onion, sprinkle with salt and pepper, and cook, stirring occasionally, until lightly browned, about 10 minutes. Stir in the dried apricots and spices and cook for a minute.

4 Add the rice and mung bean mixture and fold everything together, sprinkling with salt and pepper. Sprinkle it all with $1/3$ cup water. Wrap a clean kitchen towel around the lid of the pot so that the corners are on top and don't fall anywhere near the stove and cover the pot. Turn the heat to medium-high. When you hear sizzling—after about 5 minutes—turn the heat down very low. Cook, completely undisturbed, for about 30 minutes, until the mung beans and rice are tender. Remove from the heat and let sit for another 5 minutes.

5 Carefully remove the lid and the cloth, taste and adjust the seasoning, and serve immediately.

Split Yellow Peas and Rice with Prunes. Replace the mung beans with split yellow peas and the apricots with prunes; omit the cinnamon. Add 1 cup chopped tomato with its juice in Step 3, along with the prunes and spices.

Spiced Mung Beans and Rice with Carrots. Omit the apricots and spices. In Step 3, add 1 cup chopped tomato with its juice, $3/4$ cup shredded carrot, and $1^1/2$ tablespoons garam masala (to make your own, see page 815).

Puréed or Mashed Beans

These dishes present legumes at their most luxurious—creamy, rich, and satisfying. And puréeing or mashing is a smart way to rejuvenate leftover cooked beans, though in almost all of the recipes that follow you can use canned beans in a pinch.

White Bean Purée

MAKES: 4 servings
TIME: 10 minutes with cooked beans

One of the most useful bean preparations there is, this purée can serve as a side dish, sauce, spread, or dip (and is great as an appetizer served with bread or pita chips and carrot and celery sticks or other sliced vegetables). Furthermore, it can be whipped up in no time. Serve it as a spread for Crostini (page 737) or as a side dish with Seitan and Mushroom Loaf (page 670) or Fast Nut Burgers (page 667); or pool it under Grilled Mushrooms (page 316). For a smoother, richer, more luxurious purée, add $1/4$ cup or so cream to the main recipe or to any of the first three variations.

Make the purée vegan by using oil instead of butter.

Other beans you can use: nearly any—cannellini, Great Northern, dried favas and limas, chickpeas, pinto, kidney, appaloosa, anastazi, soybeans, or black beans, and lightly cooked fresh beans like fava, edamame, or lima.

3 cups cooked or canned navy or other white beans, drained but still moist, liquid reserved

About 1 cup bean-cooking liquid, vegetable stock (pages 101–102), or water

3 tablespoons butter or extra virgin olive oil

Salt and freshly ground black pepper

Chopped parsley leaves for garnish

1 Purée the beans by putting them through a food mill or using a blender; add as much liquid as you need to make a smooth but not watery purée.

2 Put in a microwave-safe dish or medium nonstick saucepan along with the butter or olive oil. Heat gently

until the butter melts, or the oil is hot, and the beans are hot; season with salt and pepper.

③ Garnish and serve hot as a side dish or warm or at room temperature as a dip or spread.

Bean Purée with Roasted Garlic. Many kinds of beans work beautifully with roasted garlic; any white bean, favas, chickpeas, pinto, black-eyed peas, and soybeans are all great: Add 15 to 20 cloves of Roasted Garlic (page 304) and 1 teaspoon fresh thyme leaves in Step 1.

Garlicky Puréed Beans. A little lemon zest is good here too: Add 1 teaspoon or more minced garlic and a few fresh rosemary leaves or ¹/₂ teaspoon dried in Step 1.

Cheesy Puréed Beans. Stir in ¹/₄ cup finely grated Parmesan, pecorino, fontina, or Gouda in Step 2. Heat until the cheese is melted, stirring frequently, then proceed with the recipe.

White Bean and Celery Root or Parsnip Purée. Even more substantial and a great substitute for mashed potatoes: Add 1 cup cooked chopped celery root (page 285) or parsnips (page 332) in Step 1.

Chickpea and Eggplant Purée. A dollop of tahini adds a rich, nutty flavor: Grill, or roast in a 500°F oven, 1 medium eggplant, pierced with a skewer or small knife several times, until soft and blackened, 20 to 30 minutes. Let it cool, then split the skin, scoop out the flesh, and add it to the food mill or blender with the beans in Step 1. Add about 3 tablespoons freshly squeezed lemon juice, or to taste.

Lima Bean Purée with Fennel and Orange Juice. A terrific spread for Bruschetta (page 735) or Crostini (page 737): Add 1 medium bulb fennel, trimmed and sliced, and ¹/₂ cup freshly squeezed orange juice. Cook the fennel in 2 tablespoons olive oil over medium heat until very soft; add the orange juice, and cook until the liquid is nearly evaporated. Add the fennel mixture to the blender with the beans in Step 1.

Black Bean Purée with Chipotles. Spicy and smoky; perfect with Naked Tamales (page 547) or Chiles Rel-lenos (page 399): Add 1 or 2 tablespoons chopped canned chipotle chiles in adobo sauce in Step 1. Proceed with the recipe and garnish with cilantro.

Refried Bean Dip

MAKES: At least 8 servings
TIME: 10 minutes with cooked beans

A basic bean dip that's great with tortilla chips, though you could serve it with almost anything: raw sliced vegetables; grilled, broiled, or fried tofu cubes; pita, toast, or crackers—you name it.

Use 3 cups cooked pinto or other beans if you don't have Twice-Cooked (Refried) Beans on hand, but be sure to increase the seasoning.

1 recipe Twice-Cooked (Refried) Beans (page 592)

About 1 cup bean-cooking liquid or vegetable stock (pages 101–102), or as needed

¹/₂ cup minced red bell pepper

¹/₂ cup minced onion

¹/₂ cup drained diced peeled tomato (optional)

1 tablespoon minced fresh chile (like jalapeño or Thai), or to taste, or cayenne or hot sauce to taste

1 teaspoon red wine or other vinegar

Salt and freshly ground black pepper

① Put all but 1 cup of the beans in a food processor or blender. Add enough bean-cooking liquid to start the purée.

② Lightly mash the remaining beans by hand, using a fork or potato masher; combine with the puréed beans. Stir in the bell pepper, onion, tomato if you're using it, chile, and vinegar. Sprinkle with salt and pepper. Taste and adjust the seasoning; thin with more liquid if necessary. Serve immediately or cover and refrigerate for up to 2 days; bring to room temperature or reheat gently before serving.

6 MORE BEAN DIP VARIATIONS

The technique remains the same as in the Refried Bean Dip recipe. Use the bean-cooking liquid, stock, or water to thin the purée when a liquid isn't listed. The flavorings, like the roasted red peppers or caramelized onions, can be puréed with the beans if you like.

BEANS (3 CUPS COOKED AND DRAINED)	FLAVORINGS	SEASONINGS
Black beans	1¹/₂ cups chopped roasted red peppers (pages 333) or sun-dried tomatoes; 2 teaspoons minced garlic	1 tablespoon ground coriander
Pink beans	1 cup chopped Caramelized Onions (page 328); ¹/₂ cup diced tomato	2 teaspoons smoked paprika (pimentón)
Red lentils or yellow split peas (no need to drain)	1 tablespoon each minced peeled fresh ginger and garlic; 1 cup yogurt	1 or 2 tablespoons chaat masala (to make your own, see page 814); ¹/₄ cup chopped fresh cilantro
Lima beans	¹/₂ cup toasted pine nuts; ¹/₂ cup grated Parmesan cheese; 2 teaspoons minced garlic	1 cup chopped fresh basil leaves
Soybeans	¹/₂ cup white or yellow miso; ¹/₂ cup chopped scallion; 1 tablespoon minced peeled fresh ginger	2 tablespoons rice vinegar
Fava beans	1 tablespoon minced garlic; ¹/₂ cup fruity extra virgin olive oil	2 teaspoons grated lemon zest; 2 tablespoons freshly squeezed lemon juice; lots of freshly ground black pepper

Fast Bean Dip. Save a few minutes and some chopping by using prepared salsa: Substitute 1¹/₂ cups Fresh Tomato Salsa (page 750) or Fresh Tomatillo Salsa (page 751) for the bell pepper, onion, tomato, chile, and vinegar.

Creamy Bean Dip. Use sour cream for a richer dip; yogurt for a tangy and lower-fat dip: Substitute sour cream or yogurt for the bean-cooking liquid or stock.

Cheesy Bean Dip. Easy-melting cheeses work best here; harder cheeses must be grated more finely: Add about ³/₄ cup grated cheese, like cotija, cheddar, or Monterey Jack. After Step 1, gently heat the beans over low heat; stir in the cheese until melted. Proceed with the recipe and serve hot or warm.

Hummus

MAKES: 4 to 6 servings

TIME: 15 minutes with cooked chickpeas

Ⓕ Ⓜ Ⓥ

A Middle Eastern classic that's become a standby dip or spread in many homes in the United States, hummus has that distinctive chickpea flavor mixed with the nuttiness of tahini. Make it as nutty, garlicky, lemony, or spiced as you like; I love it with lots of lemon juice. It's also great with a good sprinkling of za'atar (to make your own, see page 818).

If you're serving this as a dip, you may need to add more of the bean-cooking liquid (or water) to thin it adequately so that items can be dipped in.

 Fast   Make Ahead   Ⓥ Vegan

2 cups drained well-cooked or canned chickpeas, bean-cooking liquid reserved if possible

$\frac{1}{2}$ cup tahini with some of its oil if you like, or more to taste

$\frac{1}{4}$ cup extra virgin olive oil, plus more for garnish

2 cloves garlic, peeled, or to taste

Juice of 1 lemon, plus more as needed

Salt and freshly ground black pepper

1 tablespoon ground cumin or paprika, or to taste, plus a sprinkling for garnish

Chopped parsley leaves for garnish

1 Put the chickpeas, tahini, plus oil if you're using it, olive oil, garlic, and lemon juice in a food processor, sprinkle with salt and pepper, and begin to process; add chickpea-cooking liquid or water as needed to allow the machine to produce a smooth purée.

2 Taste and adjust the seasoning, adding more salt, pepper, tahini, garlic, or lemon juice as desired. Serve, drizzled with some olive oil and sprinkled with a bit of cumin and some parsley.

Edamame Hummus. Beautiful green and full of flavor: Substitute cooked edamame for the chickpeas and cilantro for the parsley if you like. Omit the cumin or paprika.

Lima Hummus. Use fresh lima beans if you have them, but frozen are good too: Substitute cooked lima beans for the chickpeas; lime juice for the lemon; and cilantro for the parsley.

Chickpea Fondue

MAKES: 6 to 8 servings

TIME: 20 minutes with cooked chickpeas

Throughout the Mediterranean, chickpeas are often puréed to make rich sauces, and that's the idea behind this wonderful spin on fondue. When you cook chick-

peas yourself (which is what I recommend; canned is definitely a distant second here) it's loaded with distinctive chickpea flavor, rich with roasted garlic, and silky smooth—sort of like a warm, smooth hummus, perfect for dipping as described here or as a sauce for everything from pasta or rice to grilled or roasted vegetables.

Serve this traditional fondue style (see Cheese Fondue, page 221), surrounded with things for dipping: cherry tomatoes; cauliflower florets; slices of cucumber and bell pepper; cubes of feta, kasseri, havarti, or fried tofu (page 642); boiled or roasted potato; cubes or slices of roasted or grilled eggplant; bits of pita or crusty bread; Mushroom Fritters (page 394) or Bulgur Croquettes with Walnuts (page 558). (It's okay if you don't have the equipment to keep this fondue warm on the table, because it won't harden like cheese fondues. Just make sure it's pretty hot to start out.)

Other beans you can use: cannellini, Great Northern, navy, or cranberry.

3 cups cooked chickpeas with 3 to 4 cups of their cooking liquid

20 or so cloves Roasted Garlic (page 304) or 2 raw cloves

3 tablespoons extra virgin olive oil

Salt and freshly ground black pepper

3 tablespoons freshly squeezed lemon juice

Chopped parsley for garnish

1 Put the chickpeas with 3 cups of their cooking liquid in a blender and add the garlic and oil; sprinkle with some salt and pepper. Purée and let the machine run for a minute or two, until the mixture is very smooth—almost light and fluffy. Add more cooking liquid (or use vegetable stock or water) until the consistency is like a smooth dip or thick soup.

2 Transfer the purée to a pot over medium heat; heat through while stirring constantly. Add the lemon juice, taste, and adjust the seasoning, adding more salt, pepper, or lemon juice as needed. Serve warm, garnished with the parsley.

Hummus Fondue. The same delicious sesame flavor: Use the raw garlic instead of the roasted, and in Step 2 add about 2 teaspoons ground cumin and 2 to 3 tablespoons tahini, or to taste.

Cheesy Chickpea Fondue. Here you need a nutty-flavored cheese that melts easily: In Step 2, add ¹/₂ cup or more grated cheese, like Parmesan, Gruyère, raclette, Comté, Emmental, or fontina. Or try a blue cheese, like Maytag, Roquefort, or Gorgonzola. Proceed with the recipe, heating the mixture until the cheese is fully melted.

6 Additions to Chickpea Fondue

Stir in any of these just before serving, either alone or in combination.

1. Up to ¹/₄ cup of any herb pesto, herb paste, or sauce, like Traditional Pesto (page 768), Parsley "Pesto" (page 768), or Lighter Cilantro "Pesto" (page 769); omit the roasted garlic if you like)
2. A tablespoon or so any Chile Paste (page 828)
3. A large pinch of crumbled saffron threads, steeped first in a couple tablespoons hot water
4. A dollop or two of Mushroom Ketchup (page 791)
5. Up to ¹/₄ cup of finely chopped nuts, like walnuts, almonds, or pistachios
6. A tablespoon or so of any curry powder or similar spice blend (to make your own, see pages 810–819)

Mashed Favas

MAKES: 4 servings
TIME: About 1 hour
Ⓜ Ⓥ

A true Mediterranean classic, a perfect use for favas, and a great mashed potato substitute, with lots of possibilities; see the list at right.

Other beans you can use: limas, gigantes, or cranberry beans.

> 8 ounces dried peeled and split fava beans, washed, picked over, and soaked if you like (see "The Basics of Cooking Legumes," page 579)
>
> 1 onion, chopped
>
> 1 carrot, chopped
>
> 1 stalk celery, chopped
>
> Salt and freshly ground black pepper
>
> ¹/₃ cup extra virgin olive oil for garnish
>
> 2 tablespoons freshly squeezed lemon juice for garnish

❶ Put the beans in a large pot with water to cover. Bring to a boil over high heat, then turn the heat down so the beans simmer steadily but not violently; cover loosely. When the beans begin to soften, after about 30 minutes, add the onion, carrot, celery, and a good pinch of salt and pepper. Continue to cook, stirring occasionally, until the beans are very soft, about 1 hour; add water if necessary.

❷ When the favas are done, drain them. Mash them with a potato masher or wooden spoon or put them through a ricer or food mill. Taste and adjust the seasoning, then drizzle with the olive oil and lemon juice and serve.

10 Additions to Mashed Favas

Many of these can be used in combination; lemon zest, shallots, and lemon juice, drizzled with olive oil and sprinkled with parsley, for example, are super.

1. Chopped fresh herbs, like parsley, basil, cilantro, chives, tarragon, chervil, dill, or mint
2. Grated lemon zest
3. Sautéed or Roasted Garlic (page 304)
4. Chopped fresh tomato
5. Feta cheese
6. Roasted or boiled potato
7. Chopped steamed broccoli

8. Chopped steamed or roasted cauliflower
9. Cooked and chopped greens, like dandelion, escarole, collards, kale, spinach, mustard, or broccoli raab
10. Chopped shallot or mild onion

Smashed Edamame and Potatoes with Miso

MAKES: 4 servings
TIME: 30 minutes

Any miso can be used in this recipe. White will add a bit of sweetness, the darker ones more earthiness. Be sure to salt to taste, as some miso is much saltier than others. Bear in mind, too, that edamame don't "smash" as easily as most other cooked beans, so you'll need to give them a whirl in a food processor or blender.

Other beans you can use: Any fresh bean will work nicely; try lima, fava, or cranberry.

2 medium potatoes, peeled and cubed

2 cups edamame, fresh or thawed frozen

2 to 3 tablespoons miso mixed with $^1/_4$ cup water

Salt and freshly ground black pepper

Chopped scallion for garnish

1 Boil the potatoes in water to cover until soft, about 20 minutes.

2 Meanwhile, in another pot, bring about 1 quart water to a boil; add the edamame and cook for 5 to 7 minutes. Drain the edamame, transfer to a blender or food processor, and pulse until roughly chopped (do not purée).

3 Drain the potatoes when done (reserve a bit of their cooking water), add the edamame and the miso, and smash the potatoes with a masher or wooden spoon (it should be fairly chunky). Add a little of the reserved potato water if the mixture is too dry. Taste and adjust the seasoning, adding salt and pepper or more miso as needed. Garnish with scallion and serve.

Smashed Edamame and Potatoes with Sesame and Soy. Replace the miso with soy sauce mixed with 2 tablespoons water and add 2 teaspoons each dark sesame oil and toasted sesame seeds (see page 321).

Smashed Edamame and Potatoes with Thai-Style Chile Paste. A bit of heat and lemongrass: Replace the miso with Thai-Style Chile Paste, (page 829).

Smashed Edamame and Potatoes with Red Curry Paste. Add more or less curry paste and coconut milk to your taste: Substitute 2 tablespoons or so red curry paste (to make your own, see page 830) mixed with coconut milk instead of water.

Smashed Edamame and Potatoes with Curry Powder. Potatoes and Indian spice blends are a natural; edamame is an unlikely but delicious addition: Substitute 1 to 2 tablespoons curry powder (to make your own, see page 816) for the miso. In a small pot, heat $^1/_4$ cup coconut milk and add the curry powder; boil for a minute and then add in Step 3. Proceed with the recipe.

Baked and Roasted Beans

The dry heat of an oven works magic on both cooked and uncooked beans. When covered, as with Baked Beans (page 618), you get plump, creamy, individual beans coated in a rich sauce. Bake uncovered, as in Boulangerie Beans and Potatoes (page 620), and wind up with a wonderful combination of a crunchy crust surrounding tender beans and vegetables; add cheese and you get yet another layer of flavor and texture.

Many of these recipes can be prepared and assembled in baking dishes in advance; just cover well with plastic or foil and refrigerate until you're ready, then let them come to room temperature or so before baking.

Roasted Chickpeas

MAKES: 4 servings

TIME: 25 minutes, with cooked chickpeas

Roasting cooked chickpeas in a little oil—first briefly on the stove and later in the oven—leaves their insides tender while adding crunch to their exterior; they make both a great side dish and a perfect snack. After you take them out of the oven, try dusting with a little chili powder, curry powder, or other spice mixture (to make your own, see pages 810–819) or drizzle with a little extra virgin olive oil, some lemon juice, and a lot of black pepper.

3 tablespoons extra virgin olive or neutral oil, like grapeseed or corn

2 cups cooked or canned chickpeas, drained until as dry as possible

1 tablespoon minced garlic

Salt and freshly ground black pepper

1 Preheat the oven to 400°F. Put the oil in a large ovenproof skillet or a roasting pan large enough to hold the chickpeas in one layer and put on the stove over medium heat. When hot, add the chickpeas and garlic and sprinkle with salt and pepper. Shake the pan so that all the chickpeas are well coated with oil and are sitting in one layer.

2 Transfer the skillet or pan to the oven and roast, shaking the pan occasionally, until the chickpeas begin to brown, about 15 or 20 minutes. Remove from the oven and cool slightly. If desired, sprinkle with additional seasonings or salt and pepper (see headnote). Serve hot or at room temperature.

Roasted Chickpeas and Pistachios. Great party food: Replace 1 cup of the chickpeas with 1 cup of shelled pistachios.

Baked Beans

MAKES: 6 to 8 servings

TIME: About 3 hours, largely unattended

It's tough to find a vegetarian version of baked beans with bacon, with that creamy texture and delicate balance of sweet and smoky flavors. Enter kelp, also known as *kombu*, the sea green used to make dashi (page 103). Kelp contains a natural acid that tenderizes the beans as the seaweed itself melts away, leaving behind a luxurious sauce with complex flavor. If you're looking for extra texture and flavor, try the hearty variation with dulse stirred in at the last minute.

Once you cook the onions and put everything in the pot, which takes about 10 minutes—tops—you can literally walk away for two hours. If you don't have time (or forgot) to soak the beans first, the beans will probably take another hour in the oven. Serve bowls of baked beans with Boston Brown Bread (page 690) or Biscuits (page 694) and Marinated Garden Vegetables (page 67) on the side.

Other beans you can use: pinto or pink, Great Northern, black, and kidney beans, though they might take slightly longer to cook.

$^1/_4$ cup neutral oil, like grapeseed or corn

2 medium onions, chopped

$^1/_4$ cup tomato paste

One 5-inch piece kombu

1 pound dried navy, pea, or other white beans, washed, picked over, and soaked if you like (see "The Basics of Cooking Legumes," page 579)

$^1/_2$ cup molasses, or more to taste

2 teaspoons dry mustard or 2 tablespoons prepared, or more to taste

Salt and freshly ground black pepper

1 Preheat the oven to 300°F. Put the oil in a large ovenproof pot or casserole with a lid over medium-high heat. When hot, add the onions and cook, stirring frequently, until soft and golden, 7 to 8 minutes. Add the tomato paste and stir until deeply colored, another minute or so. Stir in 6 cups water, scraping up any browned bits from the bottom of the pot.

❷ Add the kombu, beans, molasses, and mustard. Cover and bake for 2 hours, ignoring it. Stir, then add water if needed to keep the beans covered, then cover again and cook until the beans are completely cooked, another 30 minutes or more.

❸ Sprinkle with salt and pepper, stir well to help break up the kombu, then taste and add more molasses or mustard if you like. Turn the oven up to 400°F. Return the pot to the oven, uncovered, and bake until the beans are creamy and the liquid has thickened, another 30 minutes or so. Taste, adjust the seasoning, and serve. (Or cool the beans down a bit, cover, and refrigerate for up to 3 days; reheat gently.)

Buttery Baked Beans. Not vegan or even traditional, but rich and luxurious: Instead of using neutral oil in Step 1, cook the onions in 4 tablespoons ($^1/_2$ stick) butter.

Maple-Baked Apple Butter Beans. Lighter in color and flavor: Instead of the tomato paste, use $^1/_2$ cup apple butter. Instead of the molasses, use maple syrup.

Heartier Baked Beans. Closer to bacon-baked beans: Add $^1/_2$ cup shredded dried dulse (page 356) to the pot after uncovering the pot in Step 3. Make sure there is still enough water to cover.

Baked Beans with Cracker Crumb Crust. After uncovering the beans and raising the oven temperature at the end of Step 3, sprinkle the top of the beans with about $1^1/_2$ cups of crumbled soda or saltine crackers. Return the pot to the oven and cook until the crust is golden (20 to 30 minutes), then serve.

Curried Baked Beans. The coconut milk adds incredible creaminess: Omit the tomato paste and the molasses.

After you cook the onions in Step 1, stir in 2 tablespoons curry powder (to make your own, see page 816). Reduce the amount of water to 1 quart; in Step 2, stir in 2 cups coconut milk, either made from scratch (page 423) or canned (use 1 can, slightly less than 2 cups, with a little water).

Baked Brazilian Black Beans

MAKES: 4 servings

TIME: About 1 hour with cooked beans, largely unattended

A tropical party dish, one you can make in large quantities and ahead of time (it will taste even better the next day). Serve with lots of rice, some warm tortillas or Rich Golden Bread (page 714), and Spicy No-Mayo Coleslaw (page 49), Grilled Pineapple and Onion Salsa (page 791), Fresh Tomato Salsa (page 750), or Radish Salsa (page 752).

Other beans you can use: black-eyed peas, pinto, or kidney beans or any medium-size heirloom beans you might find, like appaloosa or anastazi.

2 tablespoons extra virgin olive oil

1 onion, chopped

2 tablespoons minced fresh chile (like jalapeño or Thai), or to taste, or hot red pepper flakes or cayenne to taste

1 tablespoon peeled and minced fresh ginger

$1^1/_2$ cups chopped ripe tomato (about 12 ounces; canned are fine; don't bother to drain)

1 large yellow-black plantain or ripe banana, peeled and cut into chunks

3 cups cooked or canned black beans with about 1 cup of their cooking liquid

1 tablespoon fresh thyme leaves

Salt and freshly ground black pepper

① Preheat the oven to 350°F. Put the oil in a skillet over medium-high heat. When hot, add the onion and cook, stirring occasionally, until softened, about 3 minutes. Add the chile and ginger and cook for another minute, stirring.

② Transfer the onion mixture, along with the tomato and plantain, to a food processor or blender and purée.

③ Combine the tomato mixture with the beans and thyme in an ovenproof dish. Taste and add salt and pepper, then cover and bake until bubbling, about 40 minutes. Serve hot or store, covered, in the refrigerator for up to 3 days.

Baked Curried Black Beans. More Caribbean: Replace the thyme with a couple of fresh or dried curry leaves and add them with the chile in Step 1. Add a tablespoon curry powder (to make your own, see page 816) in Step 3.

Smoky Baked Black Beans. Subtly smoky and delicious: Substitute garlic for the ginger, plus more if you like. Add 1 or 2 tablespoons smoked Spanish paprika (pimentón) and $1/2$ cup cubed smoked tofu in Step 3.

Brazilian Black Beans and Rice. Simple and more substantial: Stir in $1^1/2$ cups long-grain rice and 1 cup vegetable stock (pages 101–102) or water in Step 3; bake until the rice is tender.

Boulangerie Beans and Potatoes

MAKES: 4 servings

TIME: $1^1/2$ hours with cooked beans, largely unattended

Boulangerie potatoes, a classic French dish, was traditionally baked in the local baker's ovens for hours until supper time; the potatoes became meltingly soft, and the stock reduced to a rich glaze over top. The beans in this version add bulk and delicious flavor; it could easily be a main course or a side dish. I strongly recommend cooking your own beans for this dish; canned beans just won't be the same.

Other beans you can use: pink or red beans.

2 tablespoons fresh thyme leaves, or 1 teaspoon dried thyme

3 cups cooked white beans, drained but still moist

Salt and freshly ground black pepper

3 medium russet or other high-starch (baking) potatoes or all-purpose potatoes, peeled

1 cup vegetable stock (pages 101–102) or water

3 tablespoons butter

① Preheat the oven to 325°F. Stir a tablespoon of the thyme into the beans, taste, and sprinkle with salt and pepper. Spread the beans in a baking dish and set aside.

② Halve the potatoes lengthwise and thinly slice into half-circles. Lay the potatoes in overlapping rows to cover the beans. Pour the stock over the top, dot with pieces of butter, and sprinkle with salt, pepper, and the remaining thyme.

③ Cover with foil and bake for 45 minutes. Remove the foil and continue baking until the top is browned and glazed, another 45 minutes or so. Serve immediately or let rest for up to an hour and serve at room temperature.

Creamy Boulangerie Beans and Potatoes. A little luxury, with no work: Add $1/2$ cup cream to the beans.

Tomatoey Boulangerie Beans and Potatoes. Prettier, with a little acidity and more flavor: Add 1 cup chopped ripe tomato (canned is fine; drain them first) or about $1/2$ cup chopped sun-dried or Oven-Dried Tomatoes (pages 377) to the beans.

Boulangerie Beans and Potatoes with Leeks. Approaching elegance: Cook 2 cups chopped leeks in butter until very soft—almost melting—about 20 minutes. Top the beans with the leeks and then the potato slices.

Ⓕ Fast   Ⓜ Make Ahead   Ⓥ Vegan

Boulangerie Beans and Potatoes with Spanish Paprika. The smokiness of the paprika is so good with thyme: Add about a tablespoon of smoked Spanish paprika (pimentón) to the beans and sprinkle some over the potatoes before baking if you like.

Boulangerie Beans and Sweet Potatoes. Use pinto beans and sweet potatoes. Stir into the beans a tablespoon or two of Worcestershire Sauce, Hold the Anchovies (page 799), and add a pinch of ground allspice or cinnamon if you like. Proceed with the recipe; sprinkle the top with brown sugar before baking.

Baked Lima Beans Parmigiana

MAKES: 6 servings
TIME: 40 to 60 minutes

The slightly grainy texture of limas works perfectly with cheese, but you can use virtually any fresh or cooked dried bean. In any case, the trick is to make sure the beans' skins have not yet burst so they remain intact during cooking.

This dish makes the case for cooking extra of staples like tomato sauce and beans and keeping them handy in the fridge, because it's a snap when you've prepared these two main components up to three days ahead.

You need little more than crusty bread and a salad to make this a meal, but you can also serve it with plain rice or over pasta.

Other beans you can use: fresh fava beans or edamame, cooked cannellini or gigante beans, or cooked chickpeas.

1/4 cup extra virgin olive oil

1 recipe Fast Tomato Sauce (page 445), well seasoned and warmed

4 cups fresh, thawed frozen, or cooked dried lima beans

Salt and freshly ground black pepper

1 cup cubed mozzarella, preferably fresh

1 cup Fresh Bread Crumbs (page 804), or plain store-bought crumbs

1/2 cup freshly grated Parmesan cheese

1/2 cup chopped parsley for garnish

1   Preheat the oven to 400°F. Use a tablespoon or so of the oil to grease a 2-quart soufflé or gratin dish or a 9 × 13-inch baking dish.

2   Spread the tomato sauce in the dish and spoon the beans on top. Sprinkle lightly with salt and pepper. Spread the mozzarella cubes around evenly, pressing them into the sauce and beans a bit. Sprinkle with the bread crumbs, then the Parmesan, and drizzle with the remaining olive oil.

3   Bake until the cheese has melted, the sauce is bubbly, and the bread crumbs are browned, 20 to 30 minutes, depending on the size of your dish. Remove from the oven, sprinkle with parsley and a few more grinds of black pepper if you like, and serve.

Baked Lima or Fava Beans with Ricotta and Parmesan. Basically a noodleless lasagne: Use either lima or fresh fava beans and 1 cup ricotta cheese instead of the mozzarella. In Step 2, spoon small dollops of ricotta around the beans, then proceed with the recipe. If you like, garnish with chopped fresh basil leaves instead of the parsley.

Baked Pinto Beans, Enchilada Style

MAKES: 6 servings
TIME: 40 to 60 minutes

Like Baked Lima Beans Parmigiana (page 621), this dish is dead easy (especially if beans and salsa have been made ahead) and versatile. Serve with hot tortillas, shredded

cabbage, hot sauce, sour cream, and lime wedges—the works, in other words.

Other beans you can use: black or kidney beans or any red or pink heirloom bean like appaloosa, cranberry, or anastazi.

- 1/4 cup extra virgin olive oil
- 1 recipe Salsa Roja or Cooked Tomatillo Salsa (page 787 or 788, either chunky or puréed as in the variations), warmed
- 4 cups cooked or drained canned pinto or pink beans
- Salt and freshly ground black pepper
- 1 cup cubed Monterey Jack or Chihuahua cheese
- 1 cup crushed tortilla chips
- 1/2 cup crumbled queso fresco
- 1/2 cup chopped fresh cilantro for garnish

❶ Preheat the oven to 400°F. Use a tablespoon or so of the olive oil to grease a 2-quart soufflé or gratin dish or a 9 × 13-inch baking dish.

❷ Spread the salsa in the dish and spoon the beans on top. Sprinkle lightly with salt and pepper. Spread the cheese cubes around evenly, pressing them into the sauce and beans a bit. Sprinkle with the tortilla crumbs, then the queso fresco, and drizzle with the remaining olive oil.

❸ Bake until the cheese has melted, the sauce is bubbly, and the tortilla chips are browned, 20 to 30 minutes, depending on the size of your dish. Remove from the oven, sprinkle with the cilantro and a few more grinds of black pepper if you like, and serve.

Baked Pinto Beans and Sweet Potatoes, Enchilada Style. Heartier and, well, sweeter: Peel 2 large sweet potatoes and cut them into 1-inch cubes. In Step 2, spread them out in the salsa, cover the baking dish with foil, and bake (without the beans and other ingredients) for 15 minutes. Remove the foil, add the beans and other ingredients, and proceed with the recipe.

Baked Black Beans and Corn, Enchilada Style. Use black beans instead of the pinto or pink beans. Add 1 cup corn kernels (frozen are fine; don't bother to thaw them) to the beans and salsa.

Baked Chickpeas with Fresh Cheese

MAKES: 6 servings
TIME: 40 to 60 minutes

Fresh cheese—called *paneer* in India and sold in many Asian and natural food stores—is easy to make and is great combined with beans, especially with the tasty Spicy Indian Tomato Sauce. Paneer is not unlike firm tofu in texture, but with a taste like ricotta; in its place, use tofu, feta cheese, farmer cheese, or even queso fresco. Serve this with Biryani (page 512) or The Simplest Indian-Style Flatbread (page 698) or even over baked potatoes.

Other beans you can use: kidney or mung beans.

- 4 tablespoons (1/2 stick) butter, melted
- 1 recipe Spicy Indian Tomato Sauce (page 793), warmed
- 4 cups cooked or drained canned chickpeas
- Salt and freshly ground black pepper
- 1 1/2 cups cubed fresh cheese
- 1/2 cup chopped fresh cilantro or parsley for garnish

❶ Preheat the oven to 400°F. Use a tablespoon or so of the butter to grease a 2-quart soufflé or gratin dish or a 9 × 13-inch baking dish. Make sure the tomato sauce is warm and seasoned.

❷ Spread the tomato sauce in the dish and spoon the beans on top. Sprinkle lightly with salt and pepper. Spread the cheese cubes around evenly, pressing them into the sauce and beans a bit. Drizzle with the remaining butter.

❸ Bake until the sauce is bubbly and the tops of the cheese and beans have browned a bit, 20 to 30 minutes, depending on the size of your dish. Remove from the

Ⓕ Fast   Ⓜ Make Ahead   Ⓥ Vegan

oven, sprinkle with cilantro and a few more grinds of black pepper if you like, and serve.

Baked Chickpeas with Paneer and Spinach. A kind of glorified version of *saag paneer*, the common Indian-restaurant dish: Blanch, squeeze dry, and chop a pound of fresh spinach according to the directions on page 239. In Step 2, after you pour the sauce into the baking dish, spread the spinach evenly around. Then add the chickpeas and proceed with the recipe.

Baked Chickpeas with Paneer and Cauliflower. Core and trim a small head of cauliflower into medium florets (see the illustrations on page 280). In Step 2, after pouring the sauce into the baking dish, spread the florets evenly around, then add the chickpeas and proceed with the recipe.

White Bean and Celery Root Gratin

MAKES: 4 servings

TIME: 1 hour with cooked beans, largely unattended

A good cold-weather dish, one that can be made with all sorts of vegetables. Add more Parmesan for a cheesier gratin or eliminate the Parmesan altogether (and use oil instead of butter) for a dairy-free variation; just add more liquid if the beans are too dry.

Other beans you can use: navy, Great Northern, cannellini, flagolet, or cranberry.

Other vegetables you can use: potatoes, eggplant, cauliflower, broccoli, fennel, carrots, parsnips, summer squash, green beans, asparagus, or cabbage.

$^{1}/_{4}$ cup extra virgin olive oil or 4 tablespoons ($^{1}/_{2}$ stick) butter, plus more for greasing the baking dish

$1^{1}/_{2}$ pounds celery root, peeled, and cut into 1-inch cubes (about 2 cups)

1 onion, chopped

Salt and freshly ground black pepper

2 cloves garlic, chopped

3 cups cooked or canned white beans, drained but still moist, liquid reserved

1 teaspoon sweet or Spanish smoked paprika (pimentón; optional)

2 teaspoons chopped fresh marjoram leaves or 1 teaspoon dried or fresh oregano

$^{1}/_{2}$ cup freshly grated Parmesan cheese, plus more for garnish (optional)

$^{1}/_{2}$ cup bread crumbs, fresh (page 804) or store-bought

1 Grease a 2-quart soufflé or gratin dish or a 9 × 13-inch baking pan with some of the butter. Preheat the oven to 400°F. Put 3 tablespoons of the oil or butter in a deep skillet over medium heat. When hot, add the celery root and cook until it starts to brown, about 8 minutes. Add the onion and sprinkle with salt and pepper; cook until the celery root and onion are soft and golden, another 3 minutes or so.

2 Turn off the heat and stir in the garlic, beans, paprika, and marjoram; add the reserved bean liquid if the mixture is too dry (it should be like a thick stew). Taste and adjust the seasoning.

3 Spread the bean and vegetable mixture in the prepared pan. Top with Parmesan and bread crumbs and drizzle with the remaining tablespoon of oil or butter. Bake until the edges and top are browned and bubbling, 45 to 55 minutes, depending on how deep your baking dish is. Serve immediately or let rest for up to an hour and serve at room temperature.

White Bean and Celery Root Gratin, Tuscan Style. Just a little simpler: Omit the red bell pepper and paprika and replace the marjoram with rosemary or sage.

White Bean and Tomato Gratin. Juicier: Replace the celery root with 4 or 5 ripe plum tomatoes, quartered and seeded. Cook the tomatoes as you would the celery root in Step 2. Proceed with the recipe, using several of the tomato pieces to decorate the top of the gratin.

White Bean and Vegetable Gratin with Bulgur Crust. Put $^1/_2$ cup fine-grind bulgur in a heatproof bowl, pour 1 cup boiling water over the top, stir, cover with plastic wrap, and let sit for 15 to 20 minutes. Fluff the bulgur with a fork, drizzle with extra virgin olive oil or melted butter, sprinkle with salt and pepper, and set aside. Add 2 cups any chopped vegetables (see the list in the headnote) and use any fresh or dried herb you like. Proceed with the recipe, then top the gratin with the bulgur and bake.

Pinto Bean Tart with Millet Crust

MAKES: 6 to 12 servings
TIME: 1 hour with cooked beans, largely unattended

Nearly any bean will produce delicious results in this creamy tart, one that features a cooked-grain crust, but lighter-colored beans are definitely more attractive. (Black beans can look a bit scary, but topping the tart with cheese is a simple and tasty solution.) If you start with cooked beans and you have a food processor, the whole process is very quick. A few roasted chiles (even canned are good) mixed into the filling with the bell pepper are nice.

You can use any cooked grain you like for the crust, as long as it will hold together. Short- or medium-grain rice, quinoa, cornmeal, or bulgur all work nicely.

Other beans you can use: any red, pink, or white beans.

1 tablespoon neutral oil, like grapeseed or corn, plus more for greasing the pan

$^1/_2$ cup millet

Salt

2 cups cooked or drained canned pinto beans

$^1/_2$ small onion, chopped

1 small red bell pepper, cored, seeded, and chopped

2 cloves garlic, chopped

$1^1/_2$ teaspoons chopped fresh rosemary or thyme, or about 1/2 teaspoon dried

$^3/_4$ cup cream, vegetable stock (pages 101–102), bean-cooking liquid, or water

Freshly ground black pepper

$^1/_2$ cup corn kernels (frozen are fine; don't bother to thaw)

3 egg yolks

① Preheat the oven to 350°F. Put the oil in a small pot over medium heat. When hot, add the millet and cook, stirring frequently, until fragrant and golden, about 3 minutes. Add 1 cup water and a good pinch of salt; bring to a boil. Immediately turn the heat down to low so that the mixture bubbles gently. Cover and cook until the liquid is absorbed and the millet is tender, 20 to 30 minutes. Set aside.

② Put the beans, onion, bell pepper, garlic, rosemary, cream, a pinch of salt, and a good amount of pepper in a blender or food processor; purée until smooth (add a tablespoon or so more liquid if necessary). Taste and adjust the seasoning, transfer to a bowl, and mix in the corn and egg yolks.

③ Grease a pie or tart pan and press the millet into it to form a crust, then pour the bean mixture into the pan. Put in a larger baking dish and put in the oven; add water to the baking dish to come as far up the sides of the pan as is practical, then bake until set but still slightly jiggly in the middle, about 30 minutes. Remove from the oven and cool it on a rack for a few minutes. Slice and serve warm or at room temperature.

Cheesy Pinto Bean Tart with Millet Crust. Even more body: In Step 2, add about $^1/_2$ cup grated or fresh cheese, like Chihuahua, Monterey Jack, mozzarella, farmer, queso fresco, ricotta, or cottage cheese, plus more for garnish.

Souffléed Pinto Bean Tart with Millet Crust. For a lighter tart: Beat 3 egg whites with a pinch of salt until they

F Fast   **M** Make Ahead   **V** Vegan

hold soft peaks. Gently fold the egg whites into the bean purée and put in the prepared dish. Bake the tart until it has risen and browned. Check the interior with a thin skewer; it's done when the skewer is barely moist. Serve immediately.

White Bean and Sage Tart with Quinoa Crust. A little more sophisticated: Use olive oil to grease the pan, cooked quinoa for the crust, and white beans; add 4 or 5 chopped fresh sage leaves. Decorate the top with a few whole sage leaves if you like.

Black Bean Tart with Millet Crust, Mexican Style. Top with cheese for a prettier dish: Use black beans and add $1/4$ cup chopped fresh cilantro leaves and a chopped roasted poblano chile (see page 333). Proceed with the recipe and top with crumbled queso fresco or other fresh cheese, like farmer's or ricotta, just before serving.

Bean Fritters, Dumplings, Croquettes, and Cakes

If you eat a lot of beans, variety becomes increasingly important. The recipes in this section turn ordinary legumes into beloved snacks, accompaniments, and main dishes. The transformation is so complete that you might not even recognize the beans anymore. But the results are usually crisp, always tasty, and super-easy, because you almost always start with cooked (or canned) beans.

Falafel

MAKES: 6 servings

TIME: 1 hour plus 24 hours to soak the beans

Ⓜ

One of the things that makes falafel different from other bean fritters is that it's made from uncooked beans. It's best when the beans are soaked for a full day in plenty of water; the result is a wonderfully textured and moist interior and a crispy, browned exterior. The spices and aromatics only add to the fabulous bean flavors, and it wouldn't be unheard of to double or even triple the amount of garlic. Serve the falafel in pita with lettuce, tomatoes, cucumbers, and other raw vegetables; with a green salad; or on their own, but always with Tahini Sauce (page 796) or any yogurt sauce (page 774); some Harissa (page 830) or other Chile Paste (page 828) is great also.

Other beans you can use: dried lima beans (also see the variations).

$1^3/4$ cups dried chickpeas or 1 cup dried chickpeas and $3/4$ cup dried split fava beans

2 cloves garlic, peeled and lightly crushed

1 small onion, quartered

1 teaspoon ground coriander

1 tablespoon ground cumin

1 scant teaspoon cayenne, or to taste, or mild chile powder, to taste

1 cup chopped parsley or fresh cilantro leaves

1 teaspoon salt

$1/2$ teaspoon freshly ground black pepper, or to taste

$1/2$ teaspoon baking soda

1 tablespoon freshly squeezed lemon juice

Neutral oil, like grapeseed or corn, for frying

① Put the beans in a large bowl and cover with water by 3 or 4 inches—they will triple in volume as they soak. Soak for 24 hours, checking once or twice to see if you need to add more water to keep the beans submerged.

② Drain the beans well and transfer them to a food processor with all the remaining ingredients except the oil; pulse until almost smooth, scraping down the sides of the bowl as necessary; add one or two tablespoons of water if necessary to allow the machine to do its work, but keep the mixture as dry as possible. Taste and adjust the seasoning, adding more salt, pepper, cayenne, or lemon juice as needed.

③ Put neutral oil to a depth of at least 2 inches in a large, deep saucepan (more is better); the narrower the saucepan, the less oil you need, but the more oil you use, the more patties you can cook at the same time. Turn the heat to medium-high and heat the oil to about 350°F (a pinch of the batter will sizzle immediately).

④ Scoop out heaping tablespoons of the mixture and shape them into balls or small patties. Fry in batches, without crowding, until nicely browned, turning as necessary; total cooking time will be less than 5 minutes. Serve hot or at room temperature.

Sesame Falafel. I love this flavor combination: In Step 2, add ¼ cup sesame seeds and 3 tablespoons tahini to the food processor.

Falafel with Za'atar. Tang from the sumac, nuttiness from the sesame seeds: Use parsley and add ¼ cup za'atar (to make your own, see page 818), or 2 tablespoons sesame seeds, 1 tablespoon sumac (page 821), and a teaspoon of dried thyme to the food processor in Step 2.

Nutty Falafel. Lots of good texture from the chopped nuts: Replace ½ cup of the beans with walnuts, almonds, peanuts, or hazelnuts (don't soak the nuts). Omit the garlic, cumin, and cayenne and use the parsley or a tablespoon or so fresh thyme leaves instead of the cilantro.

Mung Bean Fritters, Asian Style. Serve with equal parts soy sauce and vinegar or with Soy and Sesame Dipping Sauce and Marinade, Korean Style (page 778): Replace the chickpeas or favas with split mung beans without skins (moong dal; see page 631); soak for 2 to 3 hours. Replace the onion with ¼ cup chopped scallion, the coriander with cracked Sichuan peppercorns, and the cumin with minced peeled fresh ginger. Omit the cayenne and use rice vinegar instead of the lemon juice.

Black-Eyed Pea Fritters. Street food in West Africa and totally addictive: Replace the chickpeas or favas with black-eyed peas, the onion with ½ cup chopped scallion, the coriander with hot red pepper flakes, and the cumin with minced peeled fresh ginger.

Chickpea-Ricotta Gnocchi

MAKES: 4 servings
TIME: About 1 hour

Like standard gnocchi (page 486), these are small boiled dumplings. Since they're based on chickpeas, not potatoes, they're heartier and more nutritious. Another benefit: The dough is a little easier to handle. In any case, you can treat exactly as you would gnocchi: sauced like pasta, sauced and baked, or simply tossed in butter or oil. See the list on page 627 for some ideas specific to this recipe.

A food mill here will produce a finer texture than a food processor, but either gives great results. The trick is to keep the chickpeas as dry as possible, so resist the temptation to add any extra water. Just keep scraping the sides of the work bowl or food mill until you get a smooth and fluffy consistency.

Other beans you can use: cannellini or gigante.

Salt

3 cups cooked or canned chickpeas (page 606), drained until as dry as possible

Freshly ground black pepper

½ cup ricotta cheese

½ teaspoon freshly grated nutmeg

About ½ cup all-purpose flour

① Bring a large pot of water to a boil and salt it Put the chickpeas and a little salt and pepper in a food mill set over a large bowl and run them through. (Or use a food processor to mash them as smooth as possible, then put them in a large bowl.) You should have about 2 cups.

② Use a fork to stir in the cheese and nutmeg. Add ¼ cup of the flour and stir; add more flour until the mixture forms a dough you can handle, but just barely. Knead for a minute or so on a lightly floured surface. Pinch off a piece of the dough and boil it to make sure it will hold its shape; if it does not, knead in a bit more flour.

③ Roll a piece of the dough into a rope about ½ inch thick, then cut the rope into 1-inch lengths; traditionally,

Ⓕ Fast   Ⓜ Make Ahead   Ⓥ Vegan

you would spin each of these pieces off the tines of a fork to score it lightly, but you don't need to. What you do need to do is be gentle and handle them as little as possible. As each gnoccho is ready, put it on a sheet of wax paper; do not allow them to touch.

④ A few at a time, add about half of the gnocchi to the boiling water and stir gently. After they rise to the surface, count to 20 (or so) and remove with a slotted spoon. (Taste one or two to make sure your timing is right.) Put in a bowl with a little warm sauce or keep warm in a pan with melted butter within a few minutes first, then finish. These do not keep at all.

4 Great Ways to Finish Chickpea-Ricotta Gnocchi

1. Toss gently with warm Tahini Sauce (page 796) and sprinkle with grated Parmesan or crumbled feta cheese. Garnish with chopped black olives and parsley if you like.
2. Add a spoonful or two of Harissa (page 830) to Fast Tomato Sauce (page 445) and sauce them with that.
3. Serve with Spicy Indian Tomato Sauce (page 793).
4. Float a few in bowls of Smooth Chickpea Soup (page 118).

Bean Croquettes

MAKES: 4 servings

TIME: 20 minutes with cooked beans

These are fast, straightforward, and dead easy. Mix in some finely chopped vegetables, spices, or fresh herbs or change the kind of beans you use—there are tons of variations.

Though this basic recipe needs no coating, it's easy enough to add if you want more crunch: roll the shaped croquettes in cornmeal, bread crumbs, panko, ground rice or lentils, or even crushed tortilla chips. For extra crispness, coat the croquettes in beaten egg, then roll them in the coating.

Other beans you can use: any cooked beans you have on hand, including many leftover bean dishes (see the chart on page 628).

> 2 cups cooked or canned white or other beans, drained but with a few tablespoons bean-cooking liquid reserved
>
> 1/2 cup minced onion
>
> 1/4 cup minced parsley leaves
>
> 1 egg, lightly beaten
>
> Salt and freshly ground black pepper
>
> About 1/2 cup coarse cornmeal or Fresh Bread Crumbs (page 804)
>
> Peanut or other oil for frying

① If you want to serve the croquettes hot, preheat the oven to 200°F. Mash the beans by putting them through a food mill or into a blender or food processor. Use a little bean-cooking liquid (or other liquid, such as water or stock) if the beans are too dry to mash. Do not purée; you want a few bean chunks in this mixture.

② Combine the beans with the onion, parsley, and egg and sprinkle with salt, and pepper. Add cornmeal or bread crumbs by the tablespoon until you've made a batter that is barely stiff enough to handle. You should be able to shape it with your hands without its sticking, but it should be quite fragile or the cakes will be dry.

③ Cover the bottom of a large, deep skillet with about 1/8 inch of oil; turn the heat to medium. Shape the bean mixture into patties 2 to 3 inches across or into 1 1/2 × 3-inch logs and when the oil is hot, put them in the skillet. Don't crowd them; you may have to work in batches.

④ Cook the croquettes until nicely browned on all sides, adjusting the heat so that they brown evenly without burning before turning, 7 or 8 minutes total. Keep warm in the oven until ready to serve—for up to 30 minutes—or serve at room temperature.

Spicy Black Bean Croquettes. Serve with salsa: Use black beans and replace the parsley with cilantro. Add 2 teaspoons ground cumin and 2 tablespoons minced jalapeño or other fresh chile or hot sauce to taste. Use

TURNING LEFTOVER BEAN DISHES INTO CROQUETTES

You can make bean croquettes from a variety of leftover dishes. Some ideas to get you started:

COMBINE LEFTOVERS FROM . . .	WITH . . .	AND USE AS A COATING . . .
Chili non Carne (page 607)	Corn kernels	Crushed tortilla chips
Spicy Soybeans with Kimchi (page 609)	Chopped scallion (optional)	Ground rice or panko
Stewed Favas Beans with Tahini (page 604)	Chopped Preserved Lemon (page 427) or olives	Bread crumbs
Mung Bean Dal with Apples, Coconut, and Mint (page 602)	Diced apple (optional)	Shredded coconut
Buttery Lentils and Potatoes with Curry (page 602)	Peas	Ground lentils or shredded coconut

cornmeal instead of the bread crumbs and proceed with the recipe.

Adzuki Croquettes. An Asian twist: Use adzuki beans; replace the onion with 2 tablespoons minced scallion and 1 tablespoon each minced garlic and peeled fresh ginger. Omit the parsley and use Sichuan peppercorns instead of black pepper for seasoning. Dip the croquettes in beaten egg, then roll in panko instead of cornmeal or bread crumbs.

Hot and Smoky Red Bean Croquettes. Use red beans and Chipotle Barbecue Sauce (page 789) or any barbecue sauce with a chopped chipotle chile and some of its adobo sauce mixed in, instead of the bean-cooking liquid. Coat the croquettes in crushed tortilla chips or cornmeal and proceed with the recipe.

A Choice of Sauces for Bean Croquettes

With basic Bean Croquettes (page 627)

1. Traditional Pesto or Parsley "Pesto" (page 768)
2. Garlic Mayonnaise (page 771)
4. "Bleu" Ranch Dressing (page 772)
5. Port Wine or Brewhouse Mustard (page 776)
6. Homemade or Mushroom Ketchup (page 790)

With Spicy Black Bean Croquettes (page 627) or Chili non Carne Croquettes (above)

1. Puréed Salsa Fresca (page 750)
2. Chimichurri (page 769)
3. Real Ranch Dressing (page 772)
4. Salsa Borracha (page 788)
5. Cooked Tomatillo Salsa (page 788)

With Adzuki Croquettes (page 628) or Spicy Soybeans with Kimchi Croquettes (above)

1. Seaweed "Mayo" (page 773)
2. Basil Dipping Sauce (page 777)
3. Soy and Sesame Dipping Sauce and Marinade, Korean Style (page 778)
4. Ginger-Scallion Sauce (page 779)
5. Simple Miso Herb Dipping Sauce (page 781)

With Hot and Smoky Red Bean Croquettes (left)

1. Papaya and other fruit salsas (page 751)
2. Lighter Cilantro (or Other Herb) "Pesto" (page 769)
3. Avocado Yogurt Sauce (page 774)
4. Fresh Tomatillo Salsa (page 751)

Ⓕ Fast   Ⓜ Make Ahead   Ⓥ Vegan

With Stewed Fava Beans with Tahini Croquettes (page 628)

1. The Simplest Yogurt Sauce (page 774)
2. Tahini Sauce (page 796)
3. Roasted Garlic Tahini Sauce (page 796)
4. Puréed Pine Nut Sauce (page 797)
5. Harissa (page 830)

With Mung Bean Dal with Apples, Coconut, and Mint (page 628) or Buttery Lentils and Potatoes with Curry Croquettes (page 628)

1. Raita or Ginger Yogurt Sauce (page 774)
2. Pineapple Chutney (page 785)
3. Tomato Chutney (page 785)
4. Chile-Yogurt Sauce (page 793)
5. Indian-Style Chile Paste (page 829)

Baked White Bean Cakes

MAKES: 4 servings
TIME: 20 minutes with cooked beans

If you've got leftover White Beans, Tuscan Style, you're in luck: Just drain them of any liquid and use them here. The sage and the extra garlic will add a great layer of flavor. But if not, use any cooked white beans here, even canned. I eat these hot from the oven, with a sprinkling of cheese and a salad on the side. For a fancier presentation, try warming a little Fast Tomato Sauce (page 445) to serve with them.

Other beans you can use: any white bean, like navy or Great Northern. See the variations for some other ideas for other beans.

3 cups cooked white beans

2 eggs

1/4 cup freshly grated Parmesan cheese

1/4 cup extra virgin olive oil or 4 tablespoons (1/2 stick) melted butter

1/4 cup minced red onion

2 tablespoons minced garlic

2 teaspoons minced fresh rosemary leaves or 1 teaspoon dried

1/4 cup all-purpose flour, plus more if needed

1/2 teaspoon baking powder

Salt and freshly ground black pepper

1 Preheat the oven to 375°F. Put the beans in a large bowl and mash lightly with a fork. Add the eggs and cheese and whisk with the fork until combined.

2 Put 2 tablespoons of the oil or butter in a small skillet over medium-high heat. When the oil is hot or the butter is melted, stir in the onion and garlic and cook, stirring frequently, until they are soft and golden, 2 to 3 minutes. Stir in the rosemary and remove from the heat.

3 Put the flour, baking powder, and a sprinkling of salt and pepper (taking into account how well seasoned your beans were to start with) into the bowl with the beans. Add the onion mixture and stir with the fork until just combined. The consistency should be like thick cookie dough. If not, add a little more flour.

4 Use the remaining oil or butter to grease a baking sheet. Use a large spoon or your hands to form the bean mixture into 8 bean cakes and put them on the prepared pan. Bake until golden and crisp, about 30 minutes, and serve hot or at room temperature.

Cheesy Baked Red Bean Cakes. Terrific with salsa: Use red beans instead of white, grated Monterey Jack or cheddar instead of the Parmesan, and epazote or oregano instead of the rosemary.

Black Bean Cakes with Queso Fresco. Great texture, with the cheese staying semifirm. Serve with plain white rice and Chimichurri (page 769): Use black beans instead of white, crumbled queso fresco instead of the Parmesan, and sage or parsley instead of the rosemary.

Baked Lentil Cakes with Gruyère. Best with Le Puy or other small black or green lentils, but brown lentils are good too: Use lentils instead of the white beans, grated Gruyère or Swiss cheese, and thyme or tarragon instead of the rosemary. Proceed with the recipe, drizzle with Mustard Vinaigrette and serve with Braised Potatoes with Mustard (page 347).

Bean Griddlecakes

MAKES: 4 servings

TIME: About 30 minutes

A little more work than Baked White Bean Cakes (preceding recipe), but also more elegant. Use virtually any cooked beans here and see the lists that follow for some ideas about seasoning them and pairing specific beans with side sauces and accompaniments. All you really need, though, is a sprinkle of cheese, a dollop of sour cream or any pesto, a drizzle of vinaigrette, or a small bowl of salsa for dipping.

> 2 cups cooked or canned beans (any type), drained until as dry as possible
>
> 1 cup half-and-half or whole milk, plus more if needed
>
> 1 egg
>
> 2 tablespoons melted butter, extra virgin olive oil, or neutral oil, like grapeseed or corn, plus more for cooking the griddlecakes
>
> 1 cup all-purpose flour
>
> Salt and freshly ground black pepper

① Set a skillet over medium-high heat or heat an electric griddle to 375°F. Put the beans in a large bowl and mash them roughly with a fork. Use the fork to stir in the half-and-half, the egg, and 2 tablespoons of the melted butter or oil. Stir until the mixture is thoroughly combined.

② Add the flour and sprinkle with salt and pepper (keeping in mind how well seasoned the beans were to begin with). Stir with the fork just enough to fold in the flour, adding more half-and-half if necessary to reach the consistency of thick pancake batter.

③ Start cooking when a drop of water dances on the surface of the skillet or griddle. Working in batches, use a little more butter or oil to grease the cooking surface. Spoon on the batter to form 3- or 4-inch pancakes. Cook until bubbles form on the surface, then turn and cook the other side until golden, about 4 minutes per side. Keep the finished griddlecakes in a warm oven if you like while you finish the others. Serve hot or at room temperature.

Bean Sprout Griddlecakes. Serve with soy sauce or one of the Asian-Style Sauces on pages 777–780: Instead of whole cooked beans, use 3 cups washed and drained mung or soy bean sprouts. Use 2 tablespoons dark sesame oil instead of the butter or other oil in the batter, then use a neutral oil, like grapeseed or corn, to grease the pan. Add ½ cup sliced scallion to the batter if you like.

8 Great Additions to Bean Griddlecakes

1. 2 tablespoons minced mild fresh herbs, like parsley, mint, basil, chives, chervil, or cilantro
2. 2 teaspoons minced potent fresh herbs, like rosemary, thyme, tarragon, oregano, or epazote
3. 2 teaspoons peeled and minced fresh or crystallized ginger
4. 1 teaspoon minced fresh garlic
5. Up to ¼ cup chopped or sliced scallion or minced red onion
6. Minced fresh chile (like jalapeño or Thai), hot red pepper flakes, or cayenne to taste
7. 1 tablespoon any spice blend, like curry powder, chaat masala, za'atar (to make your own, see pages 814–818), or Japanese Seven-Spice Mix (page 817)

Ⓕ Fast   Ⓜ Make Ahead   Ⓥ Vegan

8. Up to $^1/_4$ cup chopped nuts, like almonds, walnuts, pecans, peanuts, or hazelnuts

7 Terrific Accompaniments for Bean Griddlecakes

1. Adzuki griddlecakes with Basil Dipping Sauce (page 777)
2. Chickpea griddlecakes with Grilled or Broiled Eggplant (page 295) and Harissa (page 830)
3. Edamame griddlecakes with Teriyaki Sauce (page 779) or Simple Miso Dipping Sauce (page 781)
4. Cannellini griddlecakes with Fast Fresh Tomato Sauce (page 445) or Braised Endive, Escarole, or Radicchio (page 300)
5. Black bean griddlecakes with Fresh Tomatillo Salsa (page 751)
6. Pinto bean griddlecakes, tostada style, topped with shredded lettuce, chopped scallion and tomato, minced fresh cilantro, and crumbled queso fresco
7. Mung bean griddlecakes, served with Curried Stir-Fried Potatoes (page 348)

Mung Bean Pancakes

MAKES: 4 to 6 servings

TIME: 40 minutes with soaked beans

Delicious, highly spiced, and nutritious pancakes (called *bindae duk* in Korea, where they're from) that are easy to love. Make them as large or small as you like and serve them with Soy and Sesame Dipping Sauce and Marinade, Korean Style (page 778), or soy sauce mixed with an equal amount of vinegar.

Mung beans come whole, split, or peeled. For best texture in this recipe, use split and peeled mung beans, called *moong dal* in Indian markets. It's also important to soak the beans for 2 to 3 hours ahead of time, or they won't purée to the right consistency for the batter.

Other beans you can use: split peas, red or brown lentils, channa dal, or urad dal.

1 cup split mung beans without skins (moong dal), washed and picked over (see "The Basics of Legumes and Preparing Beans," page 576), soaked overnight if you have time and drained

2 eggs

1 tablespoon minced garlic, or to taste

1 tablespoon minced fresh chile (like jalapeño or Thai), or to taste, or hot red pepper flakes or cayenne to taste

$^1/_2$ cup chopped scallion

1 large carrot, finely julienned or grated

Salt and freshly ground black pepper

$^1/_4$ cup or so dark sesame oil, peanut oil, or neutral oil, like grapeseed or corn

1 Put the mung beans in a blender or food processor and add about $^3/_4$ cup water. Purée until a smooth and somewhat thick batter is formed; add more water if necessary.

2 Transfer to a bowl and stir in the eggs, garlic, chile, scallion, carrot, and a large pinch of salt and pepper. The batter should be the consistency of pancake batter.

3 Heat a large skillet over medium-high heat and coat the bottom with oil. Ladle in the batter to form several pancakes or one large pancake. Turn the heat down to medium and cook until the bottom is browned, about 5 minutes, then flip and cook for another 5 minutes. Repeat with the remaining batter.

4 As the pancakes finish, remove them, and, if necessary, drain on paper towels. Cut into small triangles or serve whole with a dipping sauce.

Mung Bean Pancakes with Kimchi. Approaching fiery: Replace the chile and carrot with 1 cup chopped or sliced Kimchi (page 96).

Mung Bean Pancake, Southeast Asian Style. Serve this with Fishless Fish Sauce (page 778) or Basil Dipping Sauce (page 777) or any of their variations: Add

1 tablespoon minced peeled fresh ginger and $^1/_4$ cup chopped fresh cilantro or Thai basil leaves. Cook with the neutral oil.

Brown Lentil Pancakes. A basic lentil pancake that is a fabulous foundation for a delicious yogurt sauce (page 774): Replace the mung beans with brown (regular) lentils and add 1 to 2 teaspoons any ground spice you like (cumin, coriander, caraway, or fennel works nicely). You can delete the chile or scallion, as you prefer.

Spiced Red Lentil Pancakes. Accompanied with just about any chutney (pages 783–787), these are utterly fantastic: Substitute red lentils for the mung beans; add 1 tablespoon minced peeled fresh ginger and $1^1/_2$ tablespoons or so curry powder, chaat masala, or garam masala (to make your own, see pages 814–816).

Crisp-Fried Bean Sprouts

MAKES: 4 to 6 servings
TIME: 30 minutes

Unlike Bean Sprout Griddlecakes (page 630), where the ingredients are bound together in a batter before frying, here the bean sprouts are lightly coated and gently stirred in the hot oil. If some stick together, fine; if not, that's good too. What you get is something akin to shoestring French fries. This is good without the garnishes, terrific with them. At the same time, make some Fried Tofu (page 642) and cool Jícama Salad with Pineapple and Mint (page 50). Serve it all with Steamed Sticky Rice (page 507) and you've got a feast.

Other bean sprouts (or cooked beans) you can use: soybean sprouts or adzuki bean sprouts, which you'll probably have to make yourself (see page 77); or cooked chickpeas, gigantes, or edamame.

Peanut or neutral oil, like grapeseed or corn, for deep frying

1 pound bean sprouts (about 4 cups), washed and drained well

$^1/_4$ cup soy sauce

2 cups all-purpose flour, rice flour, or cornstarch

Salt and freshly ground black pepper

1 cup chopped roasted peanuts for garnish (optional)

1 cup chopped fresh cilantro for garnish (optional)

Minced fresh chile (like jalapeño or Thai), or hot red pepper flakes or cayenne to taste for garnish (optional)

Lime wedges for garnish (optional)

❶ Put at least 2 inches of oil in a saucepan or other deep vessel over medium-high heat; bring to about 350°F on a deep-frying thermometer.

❷ Put the bean sprouts in a large bowl, drizzle the soy sauce over all, and toss gently to moisten. Add the flour to the mixture, a few spoonfuls at a time, and toss until the sprouts are evenly coated.

❸ When the oil is hot, add about a cup or so of the bean sprouts to the pan. Turn and stir them occasionally with a slotted spoon, until crisp and golden on all sides, 3 to 5 minutes. Transfer to paper or cloth towels or brown paper to drain. Sprinkle with salt and lots of black pepper while hot. Repeat until all the sprouts are done. Serve immediately, garnished with peanuts, cilantro, chile, and lime wedges as you like.

Crisp-Fried Bean Sprouts in Lettuce Wraps. Fun to eat as an appetizer or part of the main course: Wash and dry a dozen or so large (clean) outer leaves of a head of Bibb, iceberg, or green leaf lettuce. To eat, put a couple spoonfuls of fried sprouts in the center of each, garnish as desired, and roll gently to enclose. Serve with Ginger-Scallion Sauce (page 779) for dipping if you like.

F Fast   **M** Make Ahead   **V** Vegan

The Basics of Chickpea Flour

Chickpea flour—also called *besan* or *gram flour*—can be found in Indian, Middle Eastern, some Asian and health food markets, and often in Italian markets as well. It's used around the world, from Europe to the Middle East and throughout Asia—and it'll become a regular in your kitchen too once you've tried it. Like chickpeas themselves, it has a great nutty and robust flavor and is instantly likable. (It can used to make a version of Polenta, page 544.)

The Chickpea Pancake is a classic throughout Provence and Liguria, where it's called *socca* and *farinata,* respectively, and has been made for hundreds of years. Traditionally cooked in wood- or coal-burning ovens—in France on disk-shaped copper plates called *plaques*—they are simple, rustic, everyday dishes that are sold piping hot, wrapped in paper and sold as snacks in shops and by vendors on the streets. (I'm salivating just writing about it.)

Both the Chickpea Pancake (below) and the Chickpea Fries (page 634)—as well as their easy variations—are wonderful as they are or dressed up with herbs, spices, or cheeses. One of my favorite combinations is Chickpea Fries sprinkled with chili powder.

Chickpea Pancake

Socca or Farinata

MAKES: 4 to 6 appetizer servings
TIME: 1 hour plus time for the batter to rest

Ⓜ Ⓥ

This is one of those dishes you can toss together in the morning and forget about until dinner. The flavors are simple but wonderful, and the pancake is easy enough to dress up. The dominant flavor: black pepper. The onions and rosemary are strictly optional; many chickpea pancakes contain no more than flour, water, oil, salt, and pepper.

1 cup chickpea flour

1 teaspoon salt

1 teaspoon ground black pepper, or more to taste

5 to 6 tablespoons extra virgin olive oil

$1/_2$ small yellow onion, thinly sliced ($1/_4$ to $1/_2$ cup, loosely packed, to taste; optional)

1 tablespoon fresh rosemary leaves (optional)

Freshly ground black pepper

❶ Pour $1^1/_2$ cups lukewarm water into a mixing bowl and sift the chickpea flour into it. (You can do this with a sifter or just by shaking the chickpea flour through a fine-meshed strainer; the goal is to eliminate any lumps of chickpea flour, which are ubiquitous.) Whisk the chickpea flour, water, salt, pepper, and 2 tablespoons of the olive oil together, cover the bowl with a towel, and let the batter sit on the kitchen counter for at least a few minutes and as long as 12 hours.

❷ Preheat the oven to 450°F. Put 2 tablespoons olive oil in a well-seasoned or nonstick 12-inch pizza pan or skillet. Stir the sliced onion and rosemary leaves into the batter—it will be a little thicker than it was originally—then pour the batter into the greased pan. Bake for about 15 minutes, or until the pancake is firm and the edges are set. Preheat the broiler and brush the top of the socca with another tablespoon or two of oil.

❸ Set the pancake a few inches away from the broiler for a minute or two, just long enough to brown it spottily, but not long enough to color it evenly or burn it. Cut it into wedges and serve hot or at least warm.

Socca Pizza. A fabulous thin-crust pizza, but be careful not to overload it: Sprinkle your toppings onto the socca in the last 10 minutes or so of cooking and continue to bake (do not broil).

Chickpea Flapjacks. Great for serving with vegetable stews and dead easy: Make the batter using either the main recipe or the preceding variation. Instead of heating the oven, heat a griddle or a large skillet to medium-high and grease it well with olive oil. Spoon the batter onto the hot surface to make individual 3- or 4-inch pancakes. Cook until crisp, 3 to 4 minutes on each side.

Chickpea Fries

Panelle

MAKES: 4 to 6 appetizer servings
TIME: 45 minutes

Ⓜ

Among the best appetizers ever, these fries are crisp, tasty, and satisfying. They can be made in a relatively short time or ahead (up to cooking them), flavored in at least a dozen different ways, and cut into all kinds of shapes. Serve them over and over with slight variations in form and flavor, and no one will ever suspect it's all the same basic recipe. Skip the cheese and the fries are vegan.

> Neutral oil, like corn or grapeseed, for greasing and frying
>
> 1 cup chickpea flour, sifted
>
> Salt and freshly ground black pepper
>
> 2 tablespoons extra virgin olive oil
>
> Finely grated Parmesan cheese for garnish (optional)

❶ Grease a baking sheet or pizza pan with a rim and set aside. Bring 2 cups of water to a boil in a medium pot. Gradually add the chickpea flour, with a large pinch of salt and pepper, whisking constantly to prevent lumps from forming. Reduce to a gentle bubble, stir in the olive oil, and cook for just a minute.

❷ Scoop the chickpea mixture onto the prepared pan and spread into an even layer. Let cool for a few minutes and then cover loosely with parchment or plastic. Refrigerate until chilled through, about 30 minutes (but up to a day, covered tightly after it's completely cool).

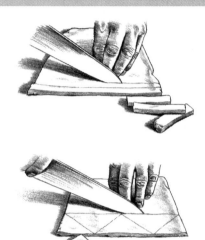

Spread the chickpea mixture on a rectangular sheet and let it firm up. Then you can cut it into triangles or fries before deep-frying.

❸ Put enough oil to come to a depth of at least $\frac{1}{8}$ inch ($\frac{1}{4}$ inch is better) in a large skillet over medium heat. Meanwhile, cut the chickpea mixture into $3 \times \frac{1}{2}$-inch fries (or into triangles, or rounds using a cookie cutter). Gently put batches of the fries in the hot oil, gently rotating them for even cooking and browning on all sides, about 3 to 4 minutes.

❹ Drain the fries on paper towels and immediately sprinkle with salt, lots of pepper, and a good dusting of Parmesan if you like. Serve hot or at room temperature with lemon wedges or sauce (see the list on page 635).

Peanut and Chickpea Fries. The peanut flour adds a great nutty flavor—serve savory or sweet, sprinkled with confectioners' sugar: Replace half of the chickpea

Turning bean dishes into the main feature of a meal is simple: Serve them over rice or just about any grain and you have a complete protein. To bulk up the dish, add some vegetables, Grilled or Broiled Tofu (page 642), Baked Tofu (page 641), Seitan (page 669), or Crunchy Crumbled Tempeh (page 674). You might even sprinkle a handful of Tofu Croutons (page 656) over the top.

Some dishes make great bean tacos, tostadas, or enchilada stuffing, like the Beer-Glazed Black Beans (page 585), any of the chilis (pages 607–608), or Twice-Cooked (Refried) Beans (page 592). Serve with flour or corn tortillas and a spread of toppings—grated cheese, shredded lettuce or cabbage, chopped radishes and scallions, any salsa (pages 750–753 and 787–789), hot sauce, Guacamole (page 263), or sour cream.

1. Baked Beans (page 618)
2. Baked Brazilian Black Beans (page 619)
3. Baked Chickpeas with Fresh Cheese (page 622)
4. Baked Lima Beans Parmigiana (page 621)
5. Baked Pinto Beans, Enchilada Style (page 621)
6. Baked White Bean Cakes (page 629)
7. Bean Croquettes (page 627)
8. Black-Eyed Peas with Smoked Tofu (page 610)
9. Boulangerie Beans and Potatoes (page 620)
10. Cannellini Beans with Cabbage and Pasta (page 586)
11. Chickpea-Ricotta Gnocchi (page 626)
12. Chickpea Pancake (page 633)
13. Chickpeas in Their Own Broth, with Crisp Bread Crumbs (page 605)
14. Chili non Carne (page 607)
15. Espresso Black Bean Chili (page 608)
16. Falafel (page 625)
17. Fresh Favas with Egg and Croutons (page 591)
18. Hot and Sour Edamame with Tofu (page 591)
19. Hot, Sweet and Sour Chickpeas with Eggplant (page 609)
20. Mung Beans with Rice and Dried Apricots (page 611)
21. Pinto Bean Tart with Millet Crust (page 624)
22. Spicy Red Beans, Indian Style (page 593)
23. Spicy Soybeans with Kimchi (page 609)
24. Stewed Fava Beans with Tahini (page 604)

flour with peanut flour (see page 322). Proceed with the recipe.

8 Sauces to Serve with Chickpea Fries

1. Fast Tomato Sauce (page 445)
2. Spicy Indian Tomato Sauce (page 793)
3. Chimichurri (page 769)
4. Garlic Mayonnaise (page 771)
5. Ketchup (to make your own, see page 790)
6. Just about any yogurt sauce or raita (page 774)
7. Nearly any chutney (page 783)
8. Tahini Sauce (page 796)

12 Fabulous Additions to Chickpea Pancakes and Fries

Most of these are best stirred into the batter just before cooking; cheese is best sprinkled over the top of the cooked pancakes. Try combinations like chopped parsley with lemon zest and capers; cilantro, green olives, and preserved lemon; or sage, sunflower seeds, and pecorino.

1. Chopped fresh herbs, like parsley, basil, cilantro, chives, tarragon, dill, sage, thyme, or rosemary
2. Minced raw garlic or several cloves Roasted Garlic (page 304)

3. Chopped scallion or shallot
4. Grated lemon zest
5. Chopped or sliced black or green olives
6. Chopped or sliced fresh chiles
7. Chopped sun-dried tomatoes
8. Chopped Preserved Lemon (page 427)
9. Chopped or whole capers
10. Pine nuts, pumpkin seeds, or sunflower seeds

11. Spice mixtures like curry powder, chaat masala, or chile powder (to make your own, see pages 814–816)
12. Finely grated cheeses: Hard cheeses, like Parmesan, pecorino, Asiago, manchego, or Comté, added to the batter; semihard or soft cheeses, like Roquefort or Gorgonzola, goat cheese, or mozzarella, as toppings for the pancakes or for pizza

 Fast   Make Ahead   Vegan

Tofu, Vegetable Burgers, and Other High-Protein Foods

Calling tofu and its cousins "meat substitutes" would be a bit of an insult; it reminds me that there are parts of the world where these assumptions are flipped. In India, for example, you're either a "normal" eater or a "nonvegetarian." The point is that one could just as easily call pork a "seitan substitute."

Whatever you call them, the focus of this chapter is food that is more center-of-the-plate than many other vegetarian options. Generally, these are hearty dishes that offer big flavors and lots of "chew," the role traditionally played by meat, poultry, and fish in most of North America.

I'm betting that you'll be adding to your own center-of-the-plate list when you try some of the recipes here. No doubt you're familiar with tofu, but when you experiment with some of these marinating and precooking techniques you may discover flavors and textures you didn't expect from bean curd. You might even try making tofu yourself, a process that yields more delicious results than you can imagine and isn't as difficult as you might think.

A big focus here is what's most easily referred to as "burgers" but embraces the whole world of things that can take the place of ground meat in all its forms. I use a variety of vegetables, legumes, tofu, nuts, tempeh, and grains to create not only the kind of patties that go great in a bun but also "meat"balls, "meat" loaf, cutlets, and more. These all taste great, but one of the many surprises is how quickly and easily they can be put together. If a traditional burger takes 10 or 15 minutes, start to finish,

The Umami Factor

Just as people have sweet teeth, or people adore salty food, there are those of us who simply cannot get enough of *umami*, a word used to describe the flavor what we might otherwise call "savory-ness." Animal protein is a common vehicle for this flavor, but when I think of vegetarian sources of umami I think of some of my favorite ingredients: soy sauce, for example, and Parmesan—two of the greatest culinary inventions of the human race, and perfect examples of umami-packed foods. If you take these, or any of a hundred other ingredients—from reduced stock to dried mushrooms to ripe tomato—and add them to other foods (like the ones found in this chapter) you boost their umami, which means, in short, you make them taste better, and often more "meaty." On the other hand, if you eat "stinky" cheese, or miso soup, or you drink good red wine, you're experiencing umami in a fairly pure form.

these take 15 or 20. (Even if you eat meat, this is not a huge sacrifice to make to get out of the ground meat rut.)

I take tremendous delight in the seitan section in this chapter. While assembling these pages, I began to sample seitan—pronounced SAY-tan and sometimes called "wheatmeat"—from a variety of sources and realized how much I liked it. Its meatiness and flavor are incomparable, as everyone I cooked it for agreed. It's even better (and considerably cheaper) if you prepare it yourself, from scratch and about as difficult as making pancakes.

A word about portion sizes: This is the one chapter in the book where the dishes might be considered main-dish size. If you want smaller portions—as part of a larger vegetarian meal or as appetizers or party food—you'll get more servings out of the recipe than the quantity listed. With the veggie burgers, simply make small patties (and make more of them) or form them into bite-sized balls (see page 660).

The Basics of Tofu

Whether you're vegetarian or not, tofu is among the most valuable foods on the planet, a nutritional powerhouse and as versatile as the egg. It comes in myriad forms and shapes and can be used in just about any way imaginable—fried, stir-fried, baked, grilled, poached, braised, broiled, whipped, blended, even served cold right out of the package, included in smoothies, or used in sauces.

Though tofu is a recent discovery for Americans, it's been around in China for a couple thousand years (it's thought to have been produced as early as the second century B.C.E., but the exact date is debatable). The word *tofu*, used by most Americans and much of the Western world, is Japanese; it's also called *bean curd* or *dofu* (Chinese).

Whatever the name, tofu is nothing but coagulated soy milk, closely related to fresh cheese and made in much the same way. A salt- or acid-based coagulant is stirred into the soy milk, which forms curds from the protein. For the most common tofu, the curds are drained from the whey and then pressed into a mold. It's a simple process, really, and one you can follow at home without too much effort or cost (see Homemade Tofu, page 656).

The Tofu Lexicon

Your local Asian market may stock tofu in so many forms that you'll be astonished; I'll stick with the basics, which are still pretty formidable. You can find brick-formed regular and silken tofu at your supermarket; other types may require a trip to a health food store or, better yet, an Asian market.

"Regular" Tofu

Brick, Momen, or Chinese Tofu

The most familiar tofu, brick shaped and sold sealed in plastic tubs with water or—in Asian and some health food markets—in an open bucket or tub of water. To make it, the water is pressed out of the curds to form a dense, crumbly tofu. There are levels of firmness: soft, medium, firm, and extra-firm, determined by their water content. In general, regular tofu absorbs flavors very well and is good marinated. The firm and extra-firm varieties hold their shape and are suitable for just about any cooking technique: stir-frying, baking, braising, grilling, or frying. Since soft and medium tofu hold their shape when cut but not necessarily when cooked, they're best served raw or used as thickeners or blended to replace eggs or dairy.

Silken Tofu

Kinugosh or Japanese Tofu

Also brick shaped and usually sold in aseptic boxes, silken tofu has the texture of custard—soft and delicate. And making it is different: Curds are not formed before molding (the coagulant—often GDL or nigari; see the chart on page 657 for more on coagulants—is stirred into the soy milk in the mold) and excess liquid is not drained off, so it has a very high moisture content (consequently, it's slightly less nutritious). Sold in soft, firm, and extra-firm varieties, it's a great thickener or replacement for eggs or dairy, and firm and extra-firm versions can be diced and added to broths and soups, crumbled, deep-fried, or even stir-fried gently.

Pressed or Extra-Firm Tofu

Not to be confused with tofu you press yourself (page 656), this is subjected to high pressure to form a *very* firm tofu that has the density of Swiss cheese. It's ideal for marinating or grilling or whenever you want a meaty texture. In Asian groceries, pressed tofu might be called any number of things, so you've got to go by looks: it's compact and generally thinner than blocks of firm tofu. Elsewhere it's often called *extra-firm tofu*.

You might also see a seasoned pressed tofu, usually spiked with soy and five-spice powder. This is labeled a number of ways but is always brown and dense, sold whole or cut into thin strips and used like noodles It's delicious and is a great addition to soups, stir-fries, or marinated and used in a salad, like Pressed Tofu Salad (page 652). Not bad for snacking, either.

Smoked Tofu

Firm or extra-firm tofu that is completely delicious and could become a staple in your fridge (it is in mine); I use it in stir-fries, with beans and lentils, in salads, and other places. It makes a good sandwich too.

You can also smoke tofu yourself by squeezing any firm or extra-firm tofu (see page 640) and then putting it in a low-heat wood-burning grill over indirect heat for 20 minutes or longer, depending on how smoky you like it. (You can also use a stovetop smoker if you prefer.)

Fried Tofu

There are all sorts of various Chinese and Japanese styles of fried tofu, sold in different packaging. They may be firm or pressed tofu and are sometimes seasoned in a sweet and salty liquid. One specific type (*aburage or inari-age*) has a pocket and can be filled with sushi rice for Nigiri Sushi (see page 530). It's simple enough to fry your own; see Deep-Fried Tofu (page 643).

Baked Tofu

Sold with all sorts of added flavors. I recommend baking your own; see Baked Tofu (page 641).

Fermented or Pickled Tofu

A type of jarred condiment that has taken a strange path from China through Vietnam to early-twentieth-century America and can now be found in all kinds of Asian cooking here. Traditionally, the tofu is first cut into cubes, air-dried, and allowed to ferment from naturally occurring spores and bacteria; unfortunately, it's hard to find; the commercially made variety is injected with fungus. The cubes are then soaked in water seasoned with salt, vinegar, rice wine, and chiles or a soybean and rice paste; the red variety is soaked in a jujube (Chinese red date) or fermented red rice paste. The texture is smooth and quite creamy, and the taste and smell are akin to strong cheese. Good stuff if you can find it, and wonderful in stir-fries.

Dried Bean Stick, Yuba, Bean Curd Sheets or Skins

A skin forms on top of warm soy milk as it's coagulating; if you skim that off and dry it, you get "tofu skin," usually used as a wrapper or added to stir-fries and soups. Available dried and frozen; you can find it fresh if you live near a good Chinatown. Reconstitute in water (and fry if you like), unless you're adding it to a soup or broth.

Buying and Storing Tofu

Like all perishable products, tofu is best when fresh: It has a more defined texture, whether creamy or crumbly, and the flavor is brighter and usually not at all sour. If you can find locally made tofu, try some soon after it's made; it's a rare treat, and you may decide one that's worth it. And I urge you to try making tofu at home (page 656). Your efforts will be rewarded not only with a sense of accomplishment but with *very* delicious tofu.

Refrigerated tofu (typically the kind sold in plastic tubs) has an expiration date; once opened it can be stored (refrigerated) in fresh water, which should be changed daily, for up to four days. Once opened, aseptic-boxed tofu can be stored, refrigerated, for up to two days. Tofu has spoiled when it smells and/or tastes sour and the storing water is cloudy (though cloudy water alone does not mean the tofu is off). For longer storage, tofu can be frozen; see right.

Because tofu is a main source of vegetarian protein in meals, I think of it the same way as I do animal proteins. So the recipes here for main-dish tofu call for $1^1/_2$ to 2 pounds for 4 people, or 6 to 8 ounces each. So for many of these recipes, you'll need two bricks.

Preparing Tofu

Though it's perfectly fine to drain tofu, pat it dry, and use it right away, you can easily vary the texture of tofu before cooking, a practice you'll take up if you eat a lot of it. Here is a rundown of the techniques called for in the recipes whenever I mention "prepared tofu":

Freezing: Not only the only way to store tofu for long periods, but even in the short term it creates a darker, firmer, chewier, and meatier brick. Freezing makes the water in tofu expand; when thawed, this water is released, resulting in tofu with a dry and spongy texture that's perfect for grilling, stir-fries, or braised dishes.

To freeze, drain the tofu and pat it dry; wrap it in plastic (or put in a container) and freeze for several hours, or until you need it, up to three months. For extra chew, cut the tofu into cubes, dry them well, and freeze them in a freezer bag. Allow enough time to defrost tofu before slicing and cooking.

Squeezing: Here you just press some of the liquid from a brick to give it a drier and firmer texture that makes it denser and easier to handle and cook. Cut the tofu in half through its equator and put the halves on four sheets of paper towels, then cover with another four sheets. Cover with a can of food, a heavy cutting board, or a similar weight so the tofu bulges at the sides slightly but doesn't crack. Wait 20 to 30 minutes, or as time allows (even the few minutes it takes you to prepare other ingredients will help); change the towels if they become saturated. Of course, the longer you squeeze the tofu, the more liquid it will release and the drier it will become. (Drier tofu absorbs more flavors, which is especially important for marinating.)

Puréeing: Pretty self-explanatory, though the uses of puréed tofu may not be as obvious. Running silken tofu in a food processor or blender creates a yogurtlike consistency, while puréeing regular tofu makes a much

Put cut tofu between four layers of paper towels, weight evenly (about a pound, no more than two, is right), and let sit for a few minutes, up to a half hour or so.

thicker consistency— like buttercream frosting. The results vary slightly depending on what firmness you use. This technique is used to create the gentle curds in Scrambled Tofu with Mushrooms (page 655). And because puréed tofu acts as a binder, it can replace dairy, eggs, or thickeners in smoothies, shakes, sauces, dips, or dressings.

Poached Tofu

MAKES: 4 or more servings
TIME: 20 minutes

The easiest precooking method and one that gives the tofu a swollen but firm texture that is entirely pleasant. And—more than baking, grilling, or frying—it does not mess with the tofu's subtleties. (In Kyoto, where this technique is popular, the tofu is served almost unadorned.)

Use as you would fried or baked tofu—in stir-fries or other dishes—or serve drizzled with soy sauce, Ponzu Sauce (page 780), or any of the suggestions listed in "10 Ideas for Precooked Tofu" (page 644).

Salt
1 or 2 pounds tofu

1 Choose a pot large enough to hold the tofu comfortably; fill it with water, salt it, and bring to a boil.

2 Gently add the tofu in one piece to the boiling water. Adjust the heat so the mixture bubbles gently and cook until the tofu floats, 5 to 10 minutes, and no longer. Remove with a slotted spoon and drain on paper towels. Use immediately or cool, wrap, and refrigerate for up to 3 days.

Dashi- or Kombu-Boiled Tofu. Each of these is lovely drizzled with plain soy or, even better, some Ponzu: If you already have Kombu Dashi (page 103), bring a couple of cups to a slow simmer. Cook the tofu as directed; serve the tofu, if you like, with some of the dashi, mixed with a little soy sauce and, if you have it, sake. If you have no dashi, heat a 4-inch piece of kombu (kelp) in the salted water, but do not boil. When the water steams, poach the tofu as directed.

Baked Tofu

MAKES: 4 or more servings
TIME: About 1 hour

Treated this way, tofu acquires a terrific, firm crust, while its interior gains the texture of a pleasant custard, almost egglike. It's basic, essential, and—for some reason—relatively unknown. It's also distinctively easier, neater, and leaner than the more common deep frying. Cooled and sliced or cubed, baked tofu is ready for anything: sandwiches, salads, stir-fries—you name it—virtually anywhere you'd use Deep-Fried Tofu. (See "10 Ideas for Pre-Cooked Tofu," page 644.)

1 to 2 pounds firm tofu
Salt

1 Preheat the oven to 350°F. Dry the tofu with paper towels—you don't have to be too compulsive about this; just blot off excess water—and sprinkle it with salt. Put in a nonstick skillet or baking pan.

2 Bake for about 1 hour, undisturbed. The tofu is done when the crust is lightly browned and firm. Remove and use immediately or cool, wrap, and refrigerate for up to 3 days.

Soy-Baked Tofu. About 10 seconds more work and—for many uses—a significant improvement. After blotting off water, brush liberally with good soy sauce. You may still want to sprinkle with salt, but very lightly. Bake as directed.

Miso-Baked Tofu. Now you're adding serious flavor, but still quite easily: Thin a couple of tablespoons of any miso with sake, white wine, vegetable stock, or water, just to brushable consistency. After blotting off water, brush the tofu liberally with this mixture and bake as directed.

Barbecue-, Teriyaki-, or Ponzu-Baked Tofu. Perhaps better suited to Grilled or Broiled Tofu (right), but easier, more leisurely, and not at all bad: After blotting off water, brush the tofu liberally with any barbecue sauce (to make your own, see page 789), Teriyaki Sauce (page 779), or Ponzu Sauce (page 780).

Crispy Panfried Tofu

MAKES: 4 or more servings
TIME: 20 minutes

Panfrying tofu gives you crisp, almost baconlike slices without a lot of extra oil. For super-crunchy, chiplike wafers, slice the tofu as thinly as you can. If you want a crisp-tender texture, cut thicker pieces. In addition to being added to hot dishes, tofu prepared like this is great for sandwiches, salads, and simple saucing. (See "10 Ideas for Precooked Tofu," page 644.)

2 to 3 tablespoons neutral oil, like grapeseed or corn

1 to 2 pounds tofu, sliced crosswise 1/4 to 1 inch thick (see headnote) and patted dry

Salt

❶ Put the oil in a deep skillet over medium heat. When hot, slide in the tofu, taking care not to overcrowd the slices (you'll have to work in batches).

❷ Cook until the bottoms are crisp and golden, 3 to 4 minutes, then carefully flip and cook the other side. As they finish, transfer them to paper towels and sprinkle with salt if you like. Use immediately or cool, wrap, and refrigerate for up to 3 days.

Grilled or Broiled Tofu

MAKES: 4 to 6 servings
TIME: 30 minutes

Not quite as simple as other basic preparations, because it's almost essential to freeze or press the tofu (see page 640) before grilling or broiling. But once that's done, the process is easy enough, especially if you use the broiler. (Of course if you already have a grill going, so much the better.)

Like baking, frying, and poaching, this method can be used to prepare tofu for other dishes, including stir-fries, but it is also great on its own, especially when prepared with miso as in the variation. In fact, for most people, this method produces an appealing tofu "steak," one you're likely to eat as a center-of-the-plate meat substitute.

1 1/2 to 2 pounds tofu, frozen (see page 640) or squeezed (see page 640), cut in half horizontally

Salt

Soy sauce

Mirin or corn syrup (optional)

❶ Heat a charcoal or gas grill or a broiler to moderately high heat and put the rack about 4 inches from the heat source. Pat the tofu dry if necessary and sprinkle lightly with salt.

❷ Cut the tofu into large cubes and skewer if you like or simply put the whole pieces on the grill or under the broiler. Carefully cook until lightly browned, then brush with soy sauce or soy sauce mixed with mirin or corn syrup. Continue to grill or broil until nicely browned; total cooking time will be less than 10 minutes.

❸ Serve immediately (whole or sliced), with a little more soy sauce drizzled on top or with any of the sauces listed in "10 Ideas for Precooked Tofu" (page 644) or cool, wrap, and refrigerate for another use.

 Fast   Make Ahead   Ⓥ Vegan

Miso Grilled or Broiled Tofu. Use any miso you like here, but any dark (red or brown) miso is best, I think: Warm together $1/2$ cup red miso with 2 tablespoons sake or white wine and 2 tablespoons mirin or corn syrup; taste and add a little sugar if you like. In Step 2, brush the tofu liberally with this mixture and continue to cook, turning and basting, until the tofu is dark brown. Serve immediately.

Barbecue-, Teriyaki-, or Ponzu-Grilled or Broiled Tofu. In Step 2, brush the tofu liberally with any barbecue sauce (to make your own, see page 789), Teriyaki Sauce (page 779), or Ponzu Sauce (page 780) and continue to cook, turning and basting, until nicely browned. Serve immediately.

Rubs and Sauces for Grilled Tofu

Grilled tofu is great with almost any rub or sauce you'd use on other grilled foods; its flavor is neutral enough to both complement and absorb almost anything you put on it.

In general, rubs are typically dry spice blends or pastes that are spread on the tofu before cooking. Whatever you choose, let it marinate for about 10 (and up to 30) minutes if you have the time. The sauces are best put on the tofu after it's grilled or in the last couple of minutes of cooking so they don't burn.

Rubs

1. Chili powder (to make your own, see page 814)
2. Jerk seasoning (to make your own, see page 818)
3. Za'atar (to make your own, see page 818)
4. Japanese Seven-Spice Mix (page 817)
5. Any curry powder (to make your own, see pages 815–816)
6. Garam masala (to make your own, see page 815)
7. Chaat masala (to make your own, see page 814)
8. Sambar Powder (page 816)
9. Five-spice powder (to make your own, page 816)
10. Any miso paste (page 152)
11. Red curry paste (to make your own, see page 830)

Sauces

1. Barbecue sauce (to make your own, see page 789)
2. Teriyaki Sauce (page 779)
3. Any raw or cooked salsa (pages 750–752 and 787–788)
4. Raw Onion Chutney (page 783)
5. Tomato Chutney (page 785)
6. Caramelized Onion Chutney (page 786)
7. Fishless Fish Sauce (page 778)
8. Ponzu Sauce (page 780)
9. Soy and Sesame Dipping Sauce and Marinade, Korean Style (page 778)
10. Simple Miso Dipping Sauce (page 781)
11. Nutty Miso Sauce (page 782)
12. Sweet Miso Glaze (page 782)
13. Fast Tomato Sauce (page 445)
14. Peanut Sauce, Six Ways (page 794)
15. Tahini Sauce (page 796)
16. Creamy Bistro Dressing or Sauce (page 779)
17. Chile-Garlic Paste (page 830)

Deep-Fried Tofu

MAKES: 4 or more servings
TIME: 20 minutes

Deep frying is a standard precooking preparation for tofu, used throughout Asia to produce a nice crust and tender interior. It's faster than baked tofu, but—needless to say—a little bit messier. Fried tofu can be simply sauced and served, as in the variations or used later in stir-fries, sandwiches, salads, whatever you like. (See "10 Ideas for Precooked Tofu," page 644.)

There are two ways to prepare the tofu for frying. One is to cut it in half horizontally; this is easy and fast, but it exposes less of the surface area to frying, so you have fewer crisp edges. The other is to cube, slice, or cut it into rectangles, triangles (traditional), or circles for that matter; this takes a little more effort initially, but it reduces cooking time and gives slightly better results. Either way, pat the tofu dry before frying to reduce spattering.

Neutral oil, like grapeseed or corn

1 to 2 pounds tofu, cut in half horizontally, cubed, or sliced (see headnote), and patted dry

Salt

1 Heat oil to a depth of 2 inches or more in a deep, heavy skillet or saucepan (see " Deep-Frying," page 26) over medium heat to 350°F.

2 When the oil is hot, slide in the tofu—in batches if necessary—and fry, turning occasionally, until golden brown and puffy, just a few minutes; do not overcook or the tofu will toughen. Remove with a slotted spoon, drain on paper towels, and sprinkle with salt if you like. Use immediately or cool, wrap, and refrigerate for up to 3 days.

Slightly More Refined Deep-Fried Tofu. Many Japanese prefer to rinse the tofu after frying, to remove traces of oil; this practice does yield a cleaner (and obviously less oily) taste, and it's not much more work. There are two ways you can proceed: Bring a pot of water to a boil; after the tofu has drained for a minute, poach it in the water for 30 seconds or so; you can repeat if you like. Alternatively, simply put the fried tofu in a colander and rinse it for a minute or so with hot water (as hot as you can make it), straight from the tap. Drain, pat dry, and use immediately or cool, wrap, and store.

Agedashi Tofu. A staple appetizer of Japanese restaurants, best with firm or extra-firm silken tofu: Before frying the tofu, combine 1 cup Kombu Dashi (page 103), 2 tablespoons good soy sauce, and 2 tablespoons mirin (or 1 tablespoon honey or corn syrup) in a small saucepan. Heat until steam arises, then keep warm. Cube the tofu before frying, then fry as directed. Put the fried tofu in a bowl and pour the sauce over it (or use the sauce for dipping). Garnish with minced or shredded scallion, grated daikon, toasted sesame seeds, crumbled toasted nori (page 357), and/or peeled and grated fresh ginger.

10 Ideas for Precooked Tofu

Starting with bottled ketchup (or, if you're feeling more ambitious, one of your own; see page 790) and ending with . . . I don't know what—there must be scores of ways to top precooked tofu. Some of my favorites:

1. Plain soy sauce
2. Soy sauce mixed with garlic, chile, ginger, and sugar; with sesame seeds or sesame oil; or both if you like
3. Peanut Sauce (page 794)
4. Ponzu Sauce (page 780)
5. Any of the miso sauces (pages 781–782)
6. Soy and Sesame Dipping Sauce and Marinade, Korean Style (page 778)
7. Ginger-Scallion Sauce (page 779)
8. Seaweed "Mayo," (page 773), especially with Deep-Fried Tofu (page 643)
9. Black Bean Ketchup (page 791)
10. Peanut or Miso Tomato Sauce (page 449)

The Basics of Stir-Fried Tofu

You can stir-fry every type of tofu, though some varieties require pretreatment. For the absolute easiest stir-fries, start with store-bought pressed tofu, the brown-skinned stuff (see page 639) that is so dry, firm, and meaty that it will not fall apart (or even, unless you really abuse it, stick) no matter how roughly you treat it. Given its long shelf life and incredible convenience, there's no reason not to have a package or two in your refrigerator at all times.

Most other types of tofu should really be firmed up and dried out a bit before being stir-fried. You can use firm and extra-firm tofu almost straight from the package, but even those benefit from drying (at least blot dry with towels before cooking, as described in the recipes).

 Fast   Make Ahead   Ⓥ Vegan

All of the methods outlined on pages 640–644—pressing, freezing, poaching, baking, and deep-frying—are appropriate in readying tofu for stir-frying. Of these, freezing is probably the easiest (though it takes forethought); pressing the simplest; and poaching or deep-frying the fastest. But they're all easy enough.

Once the tofu is prepared for stir-frying, you can wrap it and refrigerate it, for anywhere from an hour to a day or longer (or, for that matter, you can freeze it). When you're ready to go, use it in any of the following recipes.

In general it's best to stir-fry most ingredients separately, combining them only at the last minute. And, with tofu, which has a tendency not only to stick but also to fall apart, it's important to stir-fry in a nonstick or well-seasoned cast-iron pan; in most instances you want the tofu to hold together, as it will have a different, meatier consistency than anything else you're including in the dish. Allowing it to crumble and fall apart would defeat one of its main purposes, which is to add a nice, chunky consistency to dishes that are otherwise dominated by the textures of vegetables.

Stir-Fried Tofu with Scallions

MAKES: 4 servings
TIME: 20 minutes

The most basic stir-fry you can make and one you can build on indefinitely. Master this and you master the world, at least the world of stir-frying tofu, which is not insignificant.

- 1$\frac{1}{2}$ to 2 pounds firm to extra-firm tofu, prepared by any of the methods on pages 640–644 or simply blotted dry
- 3 tablespoons peanut oil or neutral oil, like grapeseed or corn
- 1 tablespoon garlic, chopped
- 1 tablespoon chopped peeled fresh ginger (optional)
- 2 dried chiles (optional)
- 1 or 2 bunches scallions, trimmed and cut into 2-inch lengths, white and green parts separated (about 2 cups total)
- $\frac{1}{3}$ cup vegetable stock (pages 101–102) or water
- 2 tablespoons soy sauce, or to taste
- 1 tablespoon toasted sesame seeds (see page 321; optional)

1 Cut the tofu into $\frac{1}{2}$-inch or slightly larger cubes. Put the oil in a large skillet or wok, preferably nonstick, over high heat. When hot, add the garlic and the ginger and chiles if you're using them and cook, stirring, for about 10 seconds. Add the tofu and the white parts of

the scallions; cook, stirring occasionally, until the tofu begins to brown, a couple of minutes. Add the stock and cook, stirring, until about half of it evaporates; add the green parts of the scallions and stir for about 30 seconds.

2 Add the soy sauce, stir, taste and adjust the seasoning, garnish if you like, and serve.

Stir-Fried Tofu with Scallions and Walnuts. You can use cashews, peanuts, or other nuts here if you like: In Step 1, before cooking the tofu, use an additional tablespoon of oil to stir-fry 1 cup of shelled nuts (they may be whole or broken) until glossy and just beginning to brown, about a minute. Remove with a slotted spoon and set aside, then proceed with the recipe.

Stir-Fried Tofu with Scallions and Black Beans. Black beans are a simple but huge flavor-booster for any stir-fry: Before cooking, soak 2 tablespoons fer-

mented black beans in $^1/_4$ cup Shaoxing wine, sherry, or water for about 10 minutes. In Step 1, reduce the stock to $^1/_4$ cup and add the black bean mixture along with the green parts of the scallions. Proceed with the recipe.

Stir-Fried Tofu with Scallions, Orange Zest, and Chiles. An old favorite, not often made at home; use an exhaust fan or the chile smoke may get to you: In Step 1, before cooking the tofu, use an additional tablespoon of oil to stir-fry the peeled zest of a navel orange (you want the zest in large pieces, not shreds) and 3 to 50 dried red chiles (traditionally a handful, but you can use less), until glossy and just beginning to brown, about a minute. Remove with a slotted spoon and set aside, then proceed with the recipe. Do not eat the chiles; they'll just lend a pleasant heat and smokiness to the dish.

7 Additions to Stir-Fried Tofu with Scallions

You can build on this recipe by moving on to Stir-Fried Tofu with Bell Peppers or Other Vegetables, which follows, but here are some other, slightly quicker ideas:

1. $^1/_2$ cup (or to taste) Crunchy Crumbled Tempeh (page 674), along with the tofu
2. 2 teaspoons five-spice powder, or to taste (to make your own, see page 816) and/or a few star anise, added with the tofu (this is good with hoisin sauce, see number 6 below)
3. 1 medium to large tomato, cored, halved, and seeded, then chopped, added with the white parts of the scallions
4. 1 cup bean sprouts, along with (or instead of) the scallion greens
5. 1 tablespoon sugar (or to taste), honey, or other sweetener, along with the green parts of the scallions
6. 1 tablespoon (or to taste) Chile Paste (page 828) or hoisin sauce, along with the soy sauce
7. 1 tablespoon (or to taste) dark sesame oil, along with the garnish

 Fast Make Ahead Vegan

Stir-Fried Tofu with Bell Peppers or Other Vegetables

MAKES: 4 servings

TIME: 30 minutes

As with any stir-fry, this one is infinitely variable: You pull what you have out of the refrigerator, and not long afterward you're ready to eat. If you make the main recipe, then the variations, you'll soon be combining at will, without much more than a glance at these pages. (See "The Basics of Stir-Frying Vegetables," page 242, for more on how to treat different types of vegetables.)

Shaoxing wine is named for a specific region in China where it originated, though it's made throughout the country now. It's fermented from rice, sometimes with other grains added; the better ones are said to be aged for a hundred years. The cooking types aren't of this quality, of course, and aren't much good for drinking anyway since they're often salted. But the sherrylike flavor benefits almost any stir-fry.

> 1¹/₂ to 2 pounds firm to extra-firm tofu, prepared by any of the methods on pages 640–644 or simply blotted dry
>
> 3 tablespoons peanut oil or neutral oil, like grapeseed or corn
>
> 1 large onion, halved and sliced
>
> 1 each green, yellow, and red bell pepper, or any combination, cored, seeded, and sliced
>
> 1 tablespoon chopped garlic
>
> 1 tablespoon chopped peeled fresh ginger
>
> ¹/₄ cup Shaoxing wine, sherry, sake, white wine, or water
>
> ¹/₃ cup vegetable stock (pages 101–102) or water
>
> 2 tablespoons soy sauce
>
> ¹/₂ cup roughly chopped scallion

1 Cut the tofu into ¹/₂-inch or slightly larger cubes. Put 2 tablespoons of the oil in a large skillet or wok, preferably nonstick, over high heat. When hot, add the onion and cook, stirring occasionally, until it begins to soften, a couple of minutes. Add the peppers and continue to cook, stirring occasionally, until both onions and peppers are crisp-tender and a little charred at the edges, about 5 minutes. Remove with a slotted spoon and set aside for a moment.

2 Add the remaining oil, then the garlic and ginger, and cook, stirring, for about 10 seconds. Add the tofu and cook, stirring occasionally, until it begins to brown, a couple of minutes. Add the wine and stock and cook, stirring, until about half of it evaporates; return the pepper-onion mix to the pan and cook, stirring, for a minute or so to reheat.

3 Add the soy sauce and scallion and cook, stirring, until the scallion becomes glossy, about 30 seconds. Serve immediately.

Stir-Fried Tofu with Peas, Snow Peas, or Snap Peas. Use these singly or in combination: In Step 1, the onion is optional. In place of the peppers, add 2 cups peas (frozen are fine, but they should be defrosted first if at all possible) and cook until bright green and just beginning to brown; snow peas and snap peas should not soften too much. Remove and proceed with the recipe.

Stir-Fried Tofu with Shiitake Mushrooms. You can use any mushrooms, of course, but shiitakes (including dried ones) seem to have been made for this: In Step 1, use the onion; you can also use 1 bell pepper if you like. After scooping both out of the pan, cook 2 cups sliced shiitake mushroom caps (stems are good for stock only) in a tablespoon of oil over high heat, stirring, until browned and almost crisp. Remove them with a slotted spoon, then add a tablespoon of oil and proceed with the recipe.

Stir-Fried Tofu with Broccoli or Cauliflower. Parboiling isn't absolutely necessary but actually saves time and effort: In Step 1, in place of the peppers, use 2 cups bite-sized pieces of broccoli and/or cauliflower that have been parboiled for just a minute or two. Cook, stirring occasionally, until tender but not soft. Remove and proceed with the recipe.

Stir-Fried Tofu with Cabbage, Kale, Collards, or Other Greens. If you use no stems thicker than $1/8$ inch or so, no parboiling is necessary: In Step 1, the onion is optional. Add 3 cups shredded or chopped cabbage, kale, collard, or other greens (mustard, turnip, cress—whatever you like); cook, stirring occasionally, until wilted and tender, about 5 minutes. Remove and proceed with the recipe.

The Basics of Braising Tofu

Braising—you might think of it as stewing—is most frequently used to tenderize tough proteins, especially meats. But it's a useful technique even for tofu, which of course needs no tenderizing at all, because it's one of the best ways to meld flavors and impart the characteristics of stronger-tasting foods to milder ones.

Whereas meat-braised dishes take hours, those featuring tofu take minutes, because tofu quickly absorbs the flavors of the braising liquid. And the results are rewarding, especially given the small amount of work. If possible, use prepared tofu—fried, pressed, frozen, or whatever method you prefer (see pages 640–644)—because it will absorb more flavor than when braised straight from the package.

You can choose almost any flavor profile you like for braising tofu. Here I focus on a few from Asia and one from Europe.

Braised Tofu and Peas in Curried Coconut Milk

MAKES: 4 servings
TIME: 40 minutes

Ⓥ

This recipe features a classic Indian technique for making a deep-flavored "gravy." Preparing the tofu in advance by frying, pressing, or freezing (pages 640–641) makes for a subtle improvement, but you can skip it because the tofu essentially "boils" in this broth anyway and becomes plump and firm.

I like peas in this recipe, because they're easy (for the most part, I rely on frozen peas), and I like the way their bright green color stands out. But—as you'll see from the variations—you can use almost any vegetable.

Serve this over rice or with The Simplest or Flaky Indian-Style Flatbread (page 698 or 699).

3 large onions, quartered

One 28- or 35-ounce can tomatoes with their liquid

2 tablespoons neutral oil, like grapeseed or corn

Salt and freshly ground black pepper

2 tablespoons garam masala or curry powder (to make your own, see page 814 or 816), or to taste

$1^{1}/_{2}$ to 2 pounds firm to extra-firm tofu, prepared by any of the methods on pages 640–644 or simply blotted dry, cut into $3/4$-inch cubes

$1^{1}/_{2}$ cups peas (frozen are fine; defrost in cold water and drain)

$1^{1}/_{2}$ cups coconut milk, either made from scratch (page 423) or canned (about 1 can plus a little water)

Chopped fresh cilantro leaves for garnish

1 Combine the onions and tomatoes in a food processor and purée; depending on the size of your machine, you may have to do this in 2 batches. Put the oil in a deep skillet or broad saucepan over medium heat. When hot, add the onion-tomato mixture, along with some salt and pepper and the spice mixture, and cook, stirring occasionally, until it thins and becomes saucelike, about 10 minutes.

2 Add the tofu and peas and cook for about 5 minutes, until the tofu swells slightly and the peas are tender; stir in the coconut milk and bring just about to a boil, stirring occasionally. Taste and adjust the seasoning, garnish with the cilantro, and serve as described above.

Ⓕ Fast   Ⓜ Make Ahead   Ⓥ Vegan

Faster Tofu and Peas in Coconut Milk. You can live without both the tomatoes and the onions if you're in a hurry: Put the oil (or use butter) in a skillet and toast the spice mixture in it, stirring, for about 30 seconds. Add the tofu and continue to cook, stirring, for about a minute. Stir in the coconut milk and peas and cook, stirring, until the peas are cooked through. Garnish and serve.

Really Spicy Tofu and Peas in Coconut Milk. Add 5 or more cloves peeled garlic and 1 or more dried chiles (1 will give you some heat, 2 will make it fairly hot, and 3 or more will really elevate the heat quotient) to the food processor with the onions and tomatoes. When you add the tofu to the mix, throw in another 10 or 20 dried chiles, which are primarily for appearance (you do not want to eat these). Add a tablespoon or more lime juice just before serving.

Creamy Tofu, Peas, and Rice in Coconut Milk. Think of an Indian risotto: Be sure to use a pan that can be covered. In Step 1, before you add the onion-tomato mixture to the hot oil, stir in 1 cup of any short-grain white rice. Cook and stir until toasted and fragrant, then add the onion-tomato mixture, the tofu, and the coconut milk. Bring to a boil, cover the pot, and reduce the heat to low. Let cook for 15 minutes instead of 10. In Step 2, put the peas into the pan on top of the rice mixture, return the lid, and remove from the heat. After 5 minutes, stir the peas into the rice along with the cilantro. Taste, adjust the seasoning, and serve.

4 More Ideas for Braised Tofu and Vegetables in Curried Coconut Milk

Using the main recipe or any of the variations, you can easily turn this into a one-pot stew that will feed a small crowd:

1. Add to the pan, along with the onion-tomato mixture, 2 cups diced (about $1/2$-inch pieces) potatoes, carrots, parsnips, or turnips, alone or in combination. These will cook to tenderness in about 15 minutes.

2. Along with the tofu, add about 2 cups bite-sized broccoli or cauliflower florets that have been par-cooked by boiling for a minute or two.

3. Use fresh or frozen snow or snap peas instead of shell peas.

4. Along with the coconut milk, add about 3 cups shredded spinach, Napa cabbage, bok choy, or other greens (some, like kale, will take a little longer to cook).

Tofu, Provençal Style

MAKES: 4 servings
TIME: 40 minutes

Hardly anyone in Provence eats tofu (yet), but combining it with the traditional, straightforward, and super-savory ingredients of that area makes for an excellent dish. It's best to start with one of the fried tofus (page 642 *or* 643) here, but frozen and pressed tofu (page 640) are also good, as is plain firm tofu. Do not use store-bought pressed (or smoked) tofu, as its Asian flavors will clash with those of the sauce.

If you like, add some cubed zucchini or eggplant along with the onions and peppers.

2 tablespoons extra virgin olive oil

1 tablespoon minced garlic

1 large or 2 medium onions, chopped

1 red bell pepper, cored, seeded, and chopped

Large pinch saffron threads (optional)

1 teaspoon fresh marjoram, oregano, or thyme
or $1/4$ teaspoon dried

2 tablespoons drained capers

2 cups chopped tomato (canned is fine), with juices

1 cup good-quality black or green olives
or a mixture, pitted

$1^{1}/_{2}$ to 2 pounds firm to extra-firm tofu, prepared by any of the methods on pages 640–644 or simply blotted dry, cut into $3/_{4}$-inch cubes

Salt and freshly ground black pepper to taste

Chopped fresh parsley leaves for garnish

1 Put the oil in a large, deep skillet, preferably nonstick, over medium heat. When hot, add the garlic and cook, stirring occasionally, until it begins to take on some color, just a minute or so. Add the onions and the bell pepper and cook, stirring occasionally, until softened, about 10 minutes. Add the saffron, herb, and capers and stir, then add the tomato and olives. Stir, bring to a boil, and cook until the sauce thickens a bit, about 10 minutes.

2 Add the tofu and cook, stirring once or twice, until it's swollen slightly and heated through, about 5 minutes. Taste and add salt if necessary and plenty of black pepper. Garnish and serve.

Braised Tofu with Eggplant and Shiitakes

MAKES: 4 servings
TIME: 30 minutes

A more-or-less traditional Sichuan preparation, creamy and delicious with soft-cooked eggplant, made crisp by the addition of sautéed shiitakes. Substitute green beans for the eggplant if you like.

$^1/_4$ cup peanut oil or neutral oil, like grapeseed or corn

1 cup sliced shiitake caps (reserve stems for stock or discard)

Salt and freshly ground black pepper

1 tablespoon chopped garlic

1 tablespoon peeled and minced fresh ginger (optional)

$1^1/_2$ pounds eggplant, trimmed, cut into $1^1/_2$-inch chunks, and salted, rinsed, and dried if you like (page 46)

1 tablespoon Chile Paste (page 828), or to taste (optional)

$^1/_2$ cup vegetable stock (pages 101–102) or water

2 tablespoons soy sauce

1 pound tofu, prepared by any of the methods on pages 640–644 or simply blotted dry, cut into $^3/_4$-inch cubes

1 tablespoon dark sesame oil for garnish (optional)

Chopped fresh cilantro leaves for garnish (optional)

1 tablespoon toasted sesame seeds (see page 321) for garnish (optional)

2 tablespoons minced scallion for garnish (optional)

1 Put half the oil in a deep skillet or shallow saucepan over medium-high heat. When hot, add the shiitakes and some salt and pepper and cook, stirring occasionally, until the mushrooms are crisp, 5 to 10 minutes. Remove with a slotted spoon and set aside.

2 Add the remaining oil and, a few seconds later, the garlic and the ginger if you're using it. As soon as it sizzles, add the eggplant. Cook, stirring every minute or so, until the eggplant browns, 5 to 10 minutes. Add the chile paste if you're using it, along with the stock. Stir, scraping the bottom of the pan if necessary to release any stuck bits of eggplant. Cook until the eggplant is really tender, 10 to 15 minutes more, adding a little more liquid if necessary (unlikely, but not impossible).

3 Stir in the soy sauce and tofu and cook, stirring occasionally, until the tofu is heated through, about 5 minutes; stir in the reserved shiitakes and turn off the heat. Taste and adjust the seasoning, then garnish as you like and serve.

Braised Tofu in Caramel Sauce

MAKES: 4 servings
TIME: 30 minutes

There were two things I couldn't get enough of in Vietnam: crunchy lemongrass dishes and caramel sauce dishes. Here's one of the latter, in which the caramel sauce—essentially melted sugar, which becomes oddly bitter while retaining its sticky sweetness as it browns—is used to poach the tofu. Make sure you use lots of black pepper, which is one of the characteristic seasonings of Vietnam, and serve this unusual, delicious dish with rice.

 Fast   Make Ahead   ⓥ Vegan

1 cup sugar

1/2 cup Fishless Fish Sauce (page 778) or soy sauce

1/2 cup peeled and sliced shallot

1 teaspoon freshly ground black pepper, or more to taste

Freshly squeezed lime juice to taste (from at least 2 limes)

1 1/2 to 2 pounds tofu, prepared by any of the methods on pages 640–644 or simply blotted dry, cut into 3/4-inch cubes

Chopped fresh cilantro leaves for garnish

1. Put a large, deep skillet, preferably nonstick or cast iron, over medium heat and add the sugar and a tablespoon or two of water. Cook, occasionally shaking the pan gently, until the sugar liquefies and begins to bubble, about 10 minutes. When the sugar has liquefied, cook for another minute or so, until it darkens; turn off the heat. Mix the Fishless Fish Sauce with 1/2 cup water; carefully, and at arm's length, add the liquid and turn the heat to medium-high. Cook, stirring constantly, until the caramel melts into the liquid, about 2 minutes. Add the shallot and cook, stirring occasionally, until they soften, about 5 minutes.

2. Add the black pepper and some lime juice, then put the tofu in the sauce. Simmer, stirring occasionally, until the tofu is slightly swollen and heated through, about 5 minutes. Taste and add more lime juice or pepper if necessary, then garnish and serve.

Fast-Braised Tofu with Tempeh

MAKES: 4 servings
TIME: 20 minutes

A take on the classic ma po tofu, this substitutes crisp crumbled tempeh for the more common pork, and a wonderful substitution it is: The texture is just as crunchy and the flavor if anything more complex. Be sure to start a pot of rice before you do anything else

since you don't have to prepare the tofu in any way and the whole recipe takes just 20 minutes or so.

1/4 cup peanut oil or neutral oil, like grapeseed or corn

4 ounces (about 1 cup) tempeh

2 tablespoons minced garlic

2 tablespoons minced peeled fresh ginger

1/4 teaspoon hot red pepper flakes, or to taste

1 cup chopped scallion, green part only

3/4 cup vegetable stock (pages 101–102) or water

1 pound soft or silken tofu, cut into 1/2-inch cubes

1/4 cup soy sauce

Salt

Minced fresh cilantro for garnish (optional)

1. Put half the oil in a large skillet over medium-high heat. When hot, use 2 forks or your fingers to crumble the tempeh into the oil. Cook, stirring frequently and scraping up any browned bits, until the tempeh is deeply colored and crisp on all sides, 10 to 15 minutes. Remove the tempeh with a slotted spoon and drain on paper towels.

2. Add the remaining oil to the skillet. When hot, add the garlic, ginger, and red pepper flakes and cook just until they begin to sizzle, less than a minute. Add the scallion and stir; add the stock, then the tofu. Cook, stirring once or twice, until the tofu is heated through, just a few minutes.

3. Stir in the reserved tempeh and the soy sauce; stir gently once or twice. Taste and add salt and pepper flakes as necessary. Garnish with the cilantro if you like and serve.

Spicy Ketchup-Braised Tofu

MAKES: 4 servings
TIME: 20 minutes

Vaguely Chinese, more honestly American, this is delicious stuff. It can be served on bread or on top of rice or noodles. Given the ease of preparation, it's amazing.

1/2 cup peanut oil or neutral oil, like grapeseed or corn

1 1/2 to 2 pounds firm or extra-firm tofu, cut into 8 slices and squeezed lightly (see page 640)

All-purpose flour for dredging

Salt and freshly ground black pepper

1 tablespoon minced garlic

1 1/2 cups ketchup (to make your own, see page 790)

Cayenne to taste

Freshly squeezed lemon juice to taste

① Put about 1/3 cup of the oil in a large skillet over medium-high heat. When hot, dredge the tofu slices lightly in the flour and add them, one at a time, to the skillet. Do not crowd: you may have to cook in batches. Sprinkle the tofu with salt and pepper as it cooks. As the pieces brown, turn them and brown the other side; total cooking time per piece will be 4 to 6 minutes. When the pieces are done, transfer them to a plate. Wipe out the skillet.

② Add the remaining oil to the skillet over medium heat; immediately add the minced garlic. Cook for a minute or two, until fragrant but not colored, then add the ketchup and some cayenne (start with about 1/4 teaspoon). Cook, stirring, for about 5 minutes, until the sauce bubbles, thickens, and starts to caramelize around the edges of the pan. Taste and add salt, pepper, or cayenne as necessary.

③ Return the tofu to the sauce and turn until evenly coated; add lemon juice to taste, stir, and serve.

Other Great Tofu Dishes

This is a grab bag of tofu dishes, ranging from a simple salad to croutons you can use in a salad to dumplings, "pancakes," and a couple of others. They demonstrate, quite convincingly I think, the broad range of forms that tofu can take and the many roles it can fill.

Pressed Tofu Salad

MAKES: 4 to 6 appetizer servings
TIME: 20 minutes, plus 2 hours to marinate

There are two keys to this salad. The first is to buy dry, pressed tofu, which is sold in most Asian food markets and some natural food stores. It's much firmer than regular tofu and has a dense, chewy texture and deep ivory skin—or, if seasoned or precooked—a brown skin.

The second is to allow the salad to marinate long enough for the tofu to absorb the flavors of the dressing. That part's easy, but it does require some planning.

1 pound dry pressed or extra-firm tofu or firm tofu, squeezed (see page 640)

2 medium to large carrots, peeled

2 large celery stalks, trimmed

2 tablespoons soy sauce

2 teaspoons Chile Paste page 828), or store-bought chile paste

1/4 cup dark sesame oil

① Cut the tofu into 2-inch matchsticks; grate the carrots and celery. Whisk together the liquids.

② Toss everything together and marinate for at least 2 hours in the refrigerator. Toss again immediately before serving.

Marinated Tofu

MAKES: 4 servings
TIME: 30 minutes, plus time to marinate

You can grill, broil, or pan-cook marinated tofu, and you can use pretty much any marinade you can think of as a base, from Japanese style to Italian style to barbecue sauce.

1/4 cup extra virgin olive oil

3 tablespoons freshly squeezed lemon juice

2 tablespoons minced or grated onion or shallot

1 teaspoon minced garlic

Salt and freshly ground black pepper

1½ to 2 pounds firm to extra-firm tofu, prepared by any of the methods on pages 640–644 or simply blotted dry, cut into 12 to 16 slices and squeezed lightly (see page 640)

Chopped fresh parsley leaves for garnish (optional)

Lemon wedges

① Combine the oil, lemon juice, onion, garlic, and some salt and pepper in a shallow bowl broad enough to hold the tofu in one layer. Add the tofu and marinate, turning occasionally, for 30 minutes or longer (24 hours is okay; refrigerate if it will be longer than an hour or two).

② To broil: Put the tofu on a rack set about 4 inches from the heat source. Broil until lightly browned, then turn and broil the other side. Total time will be 10 minutes or less.

To grill: Grill over medium to low heat, about 4 inches from the heat source. Grill until lightly browned, then turn and grill the other side. Total time will be 10 minutes or less.

To panfry: Add a couple more tablespoons of olive oil to a nonstick or well-seasoned cast-iron skillet over medium-high heat. When hot, sear on both sides, for a total of about 5 minutes.

③ Garnish with parsley if you like and serve with lemon wedges.

Marinated Tofu with Japanese Flavors. Marinate in 3 tablespoons soy sauce, 2 tablespoons dark sesame oil, 1 tablespoon mirin or corn syrup, 1 teaspoon minced peeled fresh ginger, and 1 tablespoon rice vinegar. Grill or broil, or panfry in neutral oil, like grapeseed or corn, or in dark sesame oil. Garnish with parsley or shiso and serve with lemon wedges.

Marinated Tofu with Spanish Flavors. Add about 1 teaspoon ground cumin and 1 teaspoon smoked paprika (pimentón) to the mix.

Marinated Tofu with Barbecue Sauce. Marinate in barbecue sauce (to make your own, see page 789). Best to broil or grill rather than panfry.

Crisp Marinated Tofu. For ultra-crisp and crunchy slices. This technique works for the main recipe or any of the variations: Slice the tofu even more thinly, say into 18 to 24 slices, broiling, grilling, or panfrying until the slices are very crisp and dry. (You may have to work in 2 batches.)

Tofu Escabeche

MAKES: 4 servings

TIME: 45 minutes, plus time to cool

Escabeche (ESS-ka-beh-chay) is a kind of backward marinating. Originally a method used for preserving, it is essentially a mild pickle applied to protein (probably fish originally) after it has been cooked. The technique is not at all difficult; here the tofu is floured and pan-cooked, then layered in a dish or shallow bowl. A highly seasoned marinade—it can be almost anything spicy, acidic, or even sweet—is then cooked in the same pan and poured over the tofu. The whole thing is refrigerated—for a couple of hours or a couple of days—then served cold or at room temperature.

You can add almost any vegetables or seasonings that you might like slightly pickled to the mixture in Step 2, along with the garlic: Bell or chile peppers, mushrooms, fennel, onion, olives, capers, and so on, are all good.

½ cup extra virgin olive oil

1½ to 2 pounds firm or extra-firm tofu, cut into 8 slices and squeezed lightly (see page 640)

All-purpose flour for dredging

Salt and freshly ground black pepper

10 cloves garlic, peeled and lightly crushed

2 bay leaves

5 sprigs fresh thyme or 1 teaspoon dried

1/2 teaspoon cayenne, or to taste

1 cup red wine vinegar or other vinegar

1 cup red wine

1 cup vegetable stock (pages 101–102) or water

Chopped parsley leaves for garnish

1 Put about 1/3 cup of the oil in a large skillet over medium-high heat. When hot, dredge the tofu slices lightly in the flour and add them, one at a time, to the skillet. Do not crowd: you may have to cook in batches. Sprinkle the tofu with salt and pepper as it cooks. As the pieces brown, turn them and brown the other side; total cooking time per piece will be 4 to 6 minutes. When the pieces are done, transfer them to a platter or gratin dish; they may overlap slightly.

2 Cool the pan and wipe it out. Add the remaining oil and turn the heat to medium. A minute later, add the garlic and cook, stirring occasionally, until it begins to turn color. Add the bay leaves, thyme, and cayenne and stir; add the vinegar, bring to a boil, and simmer for a minute. Add the wine, bring back to a boil, and simmer for about 5 minutes. Add the stock, bring back to a boil, and cook quickly to reduce the mixture to about half its volume.

3 Pour the liquid over the tofu and refrigerate. The escabeche will remain good for at least a couple of days. You can serve it cold or bring it back to room temperature before garnishing and serving.

Tofu Pancakes, Six Ways

MAKES: 4 servings
TIME: 30 minutes

Ⓕ Ⓜ Ⓥ

Simple and delicious as this recipe is, it has chameleon-like qualities: Add garlic, ginger, and scallions for an Asian twist; garlic, ginger, cilantro, and Sambar Powder (page 816) for an Indian flavor; or capers, olives, and basil—or a spoonful of Traditional Pesto (page 768)—for a Mediterranean flair. See the variations.

1 1/2 pounds firm tofu, patted dry

3 tablespoons tahini or any nut butter

1/3 cup soy milk or water

1/2 cup all-purpose, rice, or whole wheat flour

Salt or soy sauce

1/4 cup chopped fresh herbs, like parsley, basil, cilantro, dill, or chives (optional)

2 to 3 tablespoons peanut, dark sesame, or neutral oil, like grapeseed or corn

1 Put the tofu, tahini, and soy milk in a food processor and purée until the tofu is smooth.

2 Transfer to a large mixing bowl and sprinkle with the flour, some salt or soy sauce, and the fresh herbs if you're using them; stir well to combine. It should be the consistency of a thick batter; add more liquid or flour to adjust the consistency if necessary. (The batter can be made ahead to this point, covered with plastic, and refrigerated for up to a day.)

3 Put the oil in large nonstick or well-seasoned cast-iron skillet over medium heat. Spoon the batter into the pan in whatever size cakes you like but leaving enough room to flip. Cook, undisturbed, until they turn golden and release easily from the pan, about 4 minutes. Flip carefully and cook until done, another 3 minutes, then serve.

Tofu Pancakes, Asian Style. Lovely with any of the Asian-style sauces on pages 777–781: Add 1 tablespoon each minced garlic and peeled fresh ginger and 2 tablespoons minced scallion. Use the rice flour, season with soy sauce, and cook in dark sesame oil.

Tofu Pancakes with Kimchi. Great with Soy and Sesame Dipping Sauce and Marinade, Korean Style (page 778): Substitute Chile-Garlic Paste (page 830) for the tahini or omit the tahini altogether. Add 1/2 cup or more chopped Kimchi (page 96). Cook the pancakes in dark sesame oil.

Tofu Pancakes, Thai Style. My favorite is with Peanut Sauce, Six Ways (page 794), but Basil Dipping Sauce (page 777) and Fishless Fish Sauce (page 778) are delicious too: Substitute peanut butter for the tahini. Add a tablespoon each minced garlic, ginger, and lemongrass and 1 or 2 Thai chiles, seeded and thinly sliced (page 826). Use cilantro for the fresh herbs and cook the pancakes in the peanut oil.

Tofu Pancakes, Indian Style. Perfect with an assortment of chutneys (pages 783–787): Substitute 2 tablespoons Sambar Powder (page 816) for the tahini and add a tablespoon each minced garlic and peeled fresh ginger. Use cilantro for the fresh herb.

Tofu Pancakes, Mediterranean Style. Substitute $^1/_4$ cup chopped sun-dried tomatoes or Roasted Red Peppers (page 333) for the tahini and add $^1/_4$ cup each pitted black olives and pine nuts; pulse in the food processor until finely chopped before adding the tofu. Use basil for the fresh herb.

Scrambled Tofu with Mushrooms

MAKES: 4 servings
TIME: 20 minutes

Scrambled tofu is surprisingly similar to the texture of eggs scrambled until they are dry, and if you use turmeric they'll even be a familiar golden color. The trick is to smooth the tofu out in a food processor before cooking, though the quicker crumbled tofu variation is good too. I like to scramble tofu with cooked vegetables; vary the vegetables and seasonings as you like depending on the time of day, the accompaniments, or your mood.

1 pound firm tofu, drained, patted dry, and cut into chunks

Salt and freshly ground black pepper

$^1/_2$ teaspoon ground turmeric (optional)

2 tablespoons neutral oil, like grapeseed or corn

8 ounces button or shiitake mushrooms, trimmed and sliced

$^1/_4$ cup chopped parsley for garnish (optional)

1 Put the tofu into a food processor and purée until smooth. (This will take a couple minutes; just let the machine run.) Sprinkle with salt and pepper and add the turmeric if you like. Pulse a few more times to mix well.

2 Put the oil in a deep skillet over medium heat. When hot, add the mushrooms, sprinkle with salt and pepper, and cook, stirring occasionally, until they are dry and starting to brown.

3 Stir in the tofu and continue cooking and stirring until the tofu is heated through and as dry as you like it, anywhere from 4 to 6 minutes. Taste, adjust the seasoning, and garnish with the parsley if you like.

Basic Scrambled Tofu. Perfect as an ingredient to combine with stir-fries, sautés, and noodle or rice dishes. Increase the amount of tofu to $1^1/_2$ to 2 pounds and sprinkle in just a little more turmeric. Omit the mushrooms.

Scrambled Tofu with Bean Sprouts. Perfect on top of rice or noodles: Replace the mushrooms with 2 cups bean sprouts. Proceed with the recipe, garnishing with sliced scallion instead of the parsley if you like.

Smoky Scrambled Tofu with Onions. Barbecue sauce (to make your own, see page 789) is perfect with this: Use smoked tofu instead of regular tofu. Replace the mushrooms with a large onion and chop it roughly. Proceed with the recipe.

Chile Scrambled Tofu. Spicy and sweet: Instead of the mushrooms, core, seed, and chop 1 medium red bell pepper and 1 or 2 minced fresh chiles (like jalapeño or Thai), or to taste, or hot red pepper flakes or cayenne to taste.

Miso Scrambled Tofu. Follow the directions for the main recipe or the Basic Scrambled Tofu variation: In Step 3, when the tofu is cooked nearly how you like it, add a tablespoon or two of any miso paste and scramble until well combined.

The Simplest Scrambled Tofu. Without the food processor, with a more rustic texture: Skip Step 1 and simply crumble the tofu with your hands or 2 forks in a small bowl. Season as you like and use this in the main recipe or any of the variations.

5 Ways to Eat Scrambled Tofu

1. As a filling for burritos, tacos, or enchiladas
2. In any vegetable stock (pages 101–103), preferably with cooked noodles, rice, or other grain
3. On top of toasted bread for Crostini (page 737)
4. Stuffed into Baked Potatoes (page 339)
5. In a Sushi Bowl (page 527) or simply tossed with cooked rice noodles, dark sesame oil, and a little soy sauce

Tofu Croutons

MAKES: 4 to 6 servings
TIME: About 1 hour

Super-crisp, slightly chewy, and tangy with the flavor of tofu, these little nuggets can be used on a lot more than soups and salads. Try them in sauces, with Asian-style noodle dishes, or in stir-fries. You can season them the same way you would croutons made with bread; see the list on page 806 for ideas.

1¹/₂ to 2 pounds firm tofu, patted dry and cut into
    ¹/₂-inch cubes

1 to 2 tablespoons neutral oil, like grapeseed or corn

1 Preheat the oven to 350°F. Line a baking sheet with parchment if you like. Put the tofu cubes on the baking sheet and drizzle with the oil. Toss gently to coat.

2 Bake, undisturbed, for about an hour. The croutons will have shrunk quite a bit and be nicely golden. Cool slightly before using (they'll release more easily from the pan) and use immediately or cover tightly and

refrigerate for up to 3 days. Bring the croutons to room temperature before using.

Homemade Tofu

MAKES: 4 to 6 servings
TIME: About 2 hours, largely unattended

Tofu kits typically come with good equipment for making tofu at home: coagulant, liner, press, and often a soy milk maker. But the old way is simple enough: You make a tofu press out of any kind of container you're able to punch a few holes into, like a plastic tub from store-bought tofu, a reusable plastic storage container, or a loaf pan; even a strainer will work fine. See "Types of Tofu Coagulants" (page 657) for specific information on where to find coagulants.

1 gallon soy milk

PRESSING HOMEMADE TOFU

(STEP 1) Put the tofu in a purchased or homemade draining container lined with cheesecloth or a not-too-fine towel.

(STEP 2) Fold the cloth over the top and weight.

F Fast   **M** Make Ahead   **V** Vegan

TYPES OF TOFU COAGULANTS

Different types of coagulants give tofu different textures and flavors. The three common coagulants used in mass manufacturing are calcium sulfate or calcium chloride, magnesium chloride, and glucono delta-lactone; they are often used in combination to balance the texture (you can find out what's been used by reading the label). But for homemade tofu, alternatives or equivalents are available (see Sources, page 929); here I list them in order of the ease with which you'll find them; all work well.

COAGULANT	AKA	DESCRIPTION
Distilled vinegar		Available everywhere, but makes a slightly rubbery tofu (which some people prefer) and may impart a slightly sour flavor. You might start here, or with lemon juice, because if you like the results you're essentially home free in the ingredient department.
Lemon or lime juice		Like vinegar, this produces springy tofu with a mildly tangy flavor.
Epsom salt	Magnesium sulfate	Epsom salt is easy to come by in just about any drugstore or from a pharmacist. Must be dissolved first in a little boiling water.
Nigari		Derived from evaporated seawater, nigari, like magnesium chloride (below), makes a smooth tofu, typical of Japanese-style tofu. Look for it in health food stores and Japanese markets or see Sources.
Calcium sulfate or chloride	Gypsum (the common name for calcium sulfate)	This makes a more crumbly tofu and adds loads of calcium. You need food grade, which can be found on-line (see Sources) if not elsewhere.
Magnesium chloride (see Nigari, above)		Produces a smooth tofu. See Sources or look for it in drugstores or ask a pharmacist. Do *not* use the magnesium chloride used for deicing sidewalks!
Glucono delta-lactone	GDL	This acid is often used to make silken and very soft—almost jellylike—tofu; it's not easy to find.

2 tablespoons distilled vinegar; 1/4 cup freshly squeezed lemon or lime juice; or 2 teaspoons nigari, calcium sulfate or chloride, or epsom salt, dissolved in 1/4 cup warm water

1. Put the soy milk in a large pot over medium-low heat and bring to 140°F. Stir half of the coagulant into the warm soy milk; continue stirring for 5 minutes.

2. Add the remaining coagulant and reduce the heat to low; cook until the mixture begins to form curds, about 15 minutes, then turn off the heat.

3. Ladle or spoon the curds into a tofu mold or fine-meshed strainer lined with a tea towel or cheesecloth; fold the ends of the towel over the top of the curds and set a 3- to 5-pound weight (a large can or jar of water on a plate or something similar is okay) on top. Drain for about 20 minutes or more for firmer tofu, then remove the tofu from the mold.

4. Put the tofu in a bowl or dish of cold water in the refrigerator for about an hour to let it set. Use it or store it in the water, covered and refrigerated, for up to 5 days, changing the water daily.

The Basics of Veggie Burgers

If you read the labels of premade veggie burgers, you'll think you need two dozen ingredients to make a good one at home (and, unfortunately, many recipes lead you down this same path). But that is far from the case. Like traditional burgers, those made without meat don't need a lot of ingredients (or money) or an elaborate process to be delicious. Whether based on legumes, vegetables, nuts, tofu, or whatever, these can be flavored in a wide variety of ways and take a number of forms. The same mixtures used for burgers can produce cutlets, "meat" loaf, or "meat"balls.

My favorite, most common, and simplest veggie burger starts with cooked or canned beans; but no matter what you use, a food processor is essential for most of these recipes, because you almost always want to pulse the primary ingredient into small bits. (Occasionally you'll want to purée part of the mix, and the food processor does this well too.) You can use a combination of hand chopping, mashing, and a blender, but it's going to be more time consuming.

Some ingredients—like mushrooms, greens, and other watery vegetables—must be cooked first to concentrate their flavor and evaporate excess water. This makes vegetable burgers an excellent way to use leftovers, especially grains, beans, and potatoes, where even a small amount will give the burger shape and body.

There are three keys to cooking these burgers so they develop a crisp outer crust and a tender inside. First, be sure you have enough fat in the pan and that it's hot before adding the burgers. Then let them cook—undisturbed—until the first side is nicely browned. (If you're not using a nonstick pan, you'll know they're brown enough to turn when they release from the pan easily.) And finally, don't overcook your veggie burgers. You want them hot but not dry. Of course you can also broil or bake a veggie burger and even grill some of them; see page 660.

Flavoring

As long as you follow the basic principles of good cooking—fresh ingredients combined with a balanced approach to seasonings—your vegetable burgers are going to taste great. The best foundation for deep, rich flavors comes from common ingredients like beans, mushrooms, caramelized onions, smoked chiles, soy sauce, and toasted nuts.

There are also a few recipes here based on seasonal vegetable combinations. The fall and winter burgers are rich and substantial, while the bright flavors of their spring and summer counterparts make nice alternatives to heavier patties, especially in warm weather, when you crave something lighter. They're still filling but don't have much protein, so you might want to serve them with a side of beans, tofu, or eggs or top them with a slice of cheese.

Whether you start with bright or deep flavors, though, you simply add other seasonings, being careful only not to add too much liquid or overdo it. I almost always cook aromatics like onions, garlic, and ginger in a little oil first; it helps to take the rawness off, since burgers don't cook that long. Spices and fresh herbs are usually warmed gently to activate their flavor before they are added to the mixture.

Binding and Shaping

Vegetables, legumes, and nuts don't have the components of ground meat that help hold patties together, so they need a little binder to create a cohesive mass that can be shaped and handled. The idea is to use ingredients that bridge the gap between liquids and solids by capturing the moisture and transforming it into a sort of culinary glue. The starch found in potatoes, beans, grains, or bread crumbs does the trick nicely, as does a little flour, egg, or even butter. In other cases (like the Tofu Burger on page 666), simply puréeing some of the tofu, which has both protein and fat, holds everything together without adding much else.

Vegetable burgers hold together best and are most manageable when they're not too big; $3/4$ to 1 cup each is ideal. They can be on the thick side, but remember that they don't cook too long; make them too fat and the interior won't get hot enough. I'd say no thicker than an inch is a good rule of thumb. The recipes here all make 4 to 6

F Fast   M Make Ahead   V Vegan

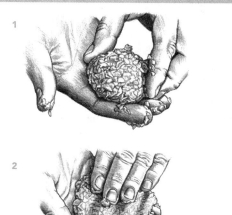

(STEP 1) Gently form the mixture into a ball (it helps if your hands are wet), then (STEP 2) press—again, gently—into a patty.

burgers, depending on how big a diameter you want. (Cook and refrigerate or freeze any leftovers; they reheat very well—see right.)

To shape, handle them as little as possible. Cup a little of the mixture in your hands, form it into a ball, then flatten to a patty; that's it. If you press down on a hard surface, the patties are likely to crack around the sides, so try to smooth the edges as you apply pressure on top. To assure the finished patties don't stick to anything before you cook them, you can set them on wax paper, though it's certainly not necessary (see the next section). A spatula may help you move them around without any damage.

You can use these recipes to make loaves, balls, and cutlets too. Check out the sidebars on pages 664, 666, and 661.

Making Burgers in Advance

Every burger recipe in this section takes about 30 minutes from the time you start assembling ingredients to your first bite. If that's not fast enough, consider making them in advance.

There are two ways to go. The first is to cook the burgers, wrap them well, then store them for a few days in the fridge or up to three months or so in the freezer. Thaw and heat the burgers in the microwave or wrap in foil and heat in a 350°F oven for 20 to 30 minutes. (If you want a crunchy crust, you'll have to sauté them again, which kind of defeats the whole purpose and probably will result in a dried-out interior.)

You can also make the mixture ahead to shape and cook later. I like to prepare the burgers (and even shape them) a few hours in advance, which is perfect for entertaining or getting a quick supper on the table. Any longer than that and you must wrap everything well (ideally in a zipper bag) and either refrigerate or freeze the mixture until needed. Once frozen, it will take 24 to 36 hours for everything to thaw in the fridge. (Don't let the package sit out on the counter; some of the recipes contain eggs.)

Serving Burgers

As with any burger, you can just slide these onto a bun and dress with the usual fixings, like ketchup, mustard, onion, lettuce, or tomato. You can make cheeseburgers, sauce with virtually any dressing or salsa, or splash with a little soy or hot sauce.

Or you can skip the bun and serve the patties as you would any center-of-the-plate item, with mashed potatoes, rice, pasta, or noodles and more vegetables or a salad. Or bread the patties and turn them into "cutlets" (see the sidebar on page XXX). Either way, whip up a complementary sauce, chutney, or salsa and you're set.

5 Ways to Serve Cooked Meatless Meatballs

1. Add to vegetable stock (pages 101–102), and stir in cooked grains, noodles, pasta, or vegetables if you like.
2. Simmer in any cooked sauce until warm, being careful not to stir too much and break them apart. Then serve over rice or grains.

3. With a toothpick and dipping sauce.
4. In Sushi Bowls (page 527).
5. With eggs and toast for a hearty brunch.

The Simplest Bean Burgers

MAKES: 4 to 6 servings

TIME: 20 minutes with cooked beans

F

This is the way to go when you want a burger and have neither the time nor the inclination to fuss. When made with chickpeas, they're golden brown and lovely; with black beans, much darker; with red, somewhere in between. Lentils give you a slightly grainy texture.

There are, of course, an infinite number of ways to jazz these up (see the variations, as well as "13 Ways to Build Delicious Burgers," page 662), but this has good flavor and texture and is excellent served on a bun with the usual fixings.

If you start with beans you've cooked yourself—especially well-seasoned ones—the results will be even better, and you can put the bean-cooking liquid to good use (I usually don't use the liquid from canned beans, which often has a tinnier taste than the beans themselves). Like almost all veggie burger mixtures, these will hold together a little better if you refrigerate them first (ideally you'd refrigerate both before and after shaping, but that's only if you have the time).

> 2 cups well-cooked white, black, or red beans or chickpeas or lentils, or one 14-ounce can, drained
>
> 1 medium onion, quartered
>
> 1/2 cup rolled oats (preferably not instant)
>
> 1 tablespoon chili powder or spice mix of your choice (to make your own, see pages 810–819)
>
> Salt and freshly ground black pepper
>
> 1 egg
>
> Bean-cooking liquid, stock, or other liquid (wine, cream, milk, water, ketchup, etc.) if necessary

SHAPING VEGGIE "MEAT"BALLS

"Meat"balls are easier if they're made small and if your hands are slightly wet. Simply shape gently into balls.

F Fast   **M** Make Ahead   **V** Vegan

Extra virgin olive oil or neutral oil, like grapeseed or corn, as needed

1 Combine the beans, onion, oats, chili powder, salt, pepper, and egg in a food processor and pulse until

Making Vegetarian Cutlets

When you shape the burgers a little more thinly and bread them before frying, they instantly become vegetable cutlets—a gussied-up cousin of the casual burger that's classic and terrific.

To make cutlets, take any burger mixture and shape the patties so they are fairly thin—$1/2$ inch thick or so. If you like, use less mixture for each to keep the size more manageable. Chill them for at least 15 minutes (an hour or two is fine) to give them time to set. Meanwhile, prepare three shallow, wide bowls: Beat a couple eggs together in one; put a cup of flour in another; and put a cup of bread crumbs (fresh, dried, or panko) in the other. Have another cup of crumbs handy, just in case you need more. Put at least $1/8$ inch neutral oil, like grapeseed or corn, in a deep skillet over medium heat.

After the patties have chilled, carefully dip the patties first in the eggs, then in the flour, and finally in the bread crumbs. Try to coat both sides evenly with all three. When the oil is hot, cook the patties, undisturbed, until deeply golden, 5 to 7 minutes. Carefully flip and cook the other side. Drain on paper towels. Sprinkle with salt and freshly ground black pepper if you like and serve immediately.

3 Ways to Serve Vegetarian Cutlets

1. With lemon wedges
2. Parmesan style (like Eggplant Parmesan, page 299) with Fast Fresh Tomato Sauce (page 445) and grated mozzarella and Parmesan cheese
3. With large lettuce leaves and cilantro stalks for wrapping, and Fishless Fish Sauce (page 778) or Basil Dipping Sauce (page 777)

chunky but not puréed, adding a little liquid if necessary (this is unlikely but not impossible) to produce a moist but not wet mixture. Let the mixture rest for a few minutes if time allows.

2 With wet hands, shape into whatever size patties you want and again let rest for a few minutes if time allows. (You can make the burger mixture or even shape the burgers up to a day or so in advance. Just cover tightly and refrigerate, then bring everything back to room temperature before cooking.) Film the bottom of a large nonstick or well-seasoned cast-iron skillet with oil and turn the heat to medium. A minute later, add the patties. Cook until nicely browned on one side, about 5 minutes; turn carefully and cook on the other side until firm and browned.

3 Serve on plates with any of the accompaniments listed in "Serving Burgers" (page 659), or on buns with the usual burger fixings. Or cool and refrigerate or freeze for later use.

Simplest Vegan Bean Burger. Many options: Omit the egg, obviously. Add $1/2$ cup Mashed Potatoes (page 341); or $1/2$ cup cooked oatmeal or short-grain rice (white or brown); or $1/4$ cup Vegannaise (page 772); or $1/4$ cup miso or $1/2$ cup tofu.

Bean-and-Cheese Burger. As a flavor-adder, cheese can't be beat, plus there are two bonuses: You don't have to

SHAPING VEGETARIAN CUTLETS

Using your hand as a shaper, form a cutletlike patty out of the mixture.

mess with melting cheese on top of the burger, and—for the most part—it acts as a binder. Add $^1/_2$ to 1 cup grated Parmesan, cheddar, Swiss, Jack, mozzarella, or other cheese to the mix (you can omit the egg if you like).

Bean-and-Spinach Burger. Of all the veggies you can add to a burger, I like spinach. You can leave it uncooked and just shred it if you prefer (figure about 2 cups), but this gives better results; it's great with a little garlic added: Squeeze dry and chop about 1 cup cooked spinach (you'll need about 8 ounces of raw spinach to start, or you can use frozen spinach); add it to the mix and proceed with the recipe.

Bean-and-Veggie Burger. Many options, but don't overdo it or the burger will fall apart (for more veggie-laden burgers, see page 658): Add up to $^1/_2$ cup carrots, bell peppers, shallots, leeks, celery, potato, sweet potato, winter squash, zucchini, or a combination. Cut into chunks as you do the onion and grind with the beans or shred or mince and add afterward.

High-Protein Bean Burger. The soy gives it just a little boost: Instead of rolled oats, use rolled soy (soy flakes).

13 Ways to Build Delicious Veggie Burgers

There are more ways to vary the burgers in this section than I can imagine, but here are a few ideas. The basic rules are to make sure the mixture is neither too dry nor too wet (if you find yourself in the first situation, add a liquid ingredient; in the second, add some oats, ground rice powder or flour, cornmeal, flour, bread crumbs, or the like). But as for flavors, the sky's the limit.

1. Fresh herbs. You can almost not go wrong with fresh herbs, as long as you don't use overwhelming amounts. Add up to $^1/_2$ cup parsley, basil, or dill leaves; somewhat less of mint, cilantro, or chervil; a tablespoon of oregano or marjoram; or only a teaspoon or so of fresh thyme, tarragon, or rosemary.

2. Dried herbs. Use by the pinch; to really get the seasoning right, taste and adjust it (you can cook a little bit first if you don't want to taste it raw).

3. Spices. The spice mix—chili or curry powder, for example (to make your own, see page 814–816)—is an easy way to go, but you can combine fairly small amounts (usually $^1/_4$ to $^1/_2$ teaspoon) of various spices as you like. Try, for example, smoked paprika, cumin, and ground chiles; coriander, cumin, ginger, and cardamom; or anything else that appeals to you.

4. Garlic. Can't go wrong, really. Add 1 teaspoon or more minced garlic to the mix, or a tablespoon or more Roasted Garlic (page 304), with a little of its oil.

5. Chiles. For heat, you can simply add cayenne, hot red pepper flakes, or the like. But if you want some texture, you might include $^1/_4$ cup or more roasted (or canned) green or red chiles.

6. Soy sauce or miso. Just a tablespoon or so of soy sauce, but up to $^1/_4$ cup of any miso; you can omit the egg if you like.

7. Ketchup, salsa, or mustard. Up to $^1/_3$ cup of ketchup or salsa (both of which are pretty good); 1 tablespoon or so of Dijon or other mustard.

Burger Mix as Ground "Meat"

All of the recipes in this section can be cooked without being shaped to make a loose, slightly crunchy mixture that's perfect anywhere you'd use ground meat or meat substitute. Just prepare the burger mix—don't form patties—and heat a little oil or butter in a large deep skillet. When it's hot, add the burger mixture. Resist the urge to stir until it's crisp and brown; then stir and break the pieces apart a bit, continuing to cook until it's as done as you like. Use the delicious results to fill tacos, burritos, omelets, savory pastries, and sandwiches. Or stir into Fast Tomato Sauce (page 445) for a topping for pizza or pasta.

F Fast   M Make Ahead   V Vegan

8. Nuts or seeds. The nice thing about nuts is the crunch; see Fast Nut Burgers on page 667 for more details. Add $1/4$ cup or so of sesame or sunflower seeds and up to $1/2$ cup nuts or pumpkin seeds toward the end of the processing so they don't become too powdery.

9. Lemon, lime, or orange zest. The slight acidity brightens the taste.

10. Tomato paste. A tablespoon or two will give the burgers nice color and a more complex flavor.

11. Mushrooms. Add a tablespoon or so of dried mushrooms, soaked and cooked, as you would any other vegetable (see number 12). Or use up to about $1/2$ cup raw, trimmed and added along with the oats and beans.

12. Cooked veggies. Milder flavor, softer texture than raw veggies (see Bean-and-Veggie Burger, page 662): Add up to a cup of cooked vegetables— onions, greens, broccoli, potatoes, sweet potatoes, winter squash, zucchini—whatever you like. If you use potatoes and add them to the food processor along with the beans, you can omit the egg and oats.

13. Cooked grains. All-grain burgers tend to be mushy and uninteresting, but adding a bit of grains to other burgers results in a terrific light texture. Feel free to add up to a cup of cooked grains, along with the beans. Omit the oats and, if you like, the egg.

Hearty Winter Vegetable Burger

MAKES: 4 to 6 servings
TIME: 45 minutes

Ⓜ

Dried fruit is the secret ingredient in these rich and gorgeous burgers. Because the flavor is sweet and slightly earthy, these are delicious on a whole grain bun with lots of mustard. Or you can serve them on a bed of Braised and Glazed Brussels Sprouts (page 272) or any winter green for a more elegant meal.

> 1 pound beets, trimmed, peeled, and grated
> $1/2$ cup packed pitted dates or dried plums (prunes)
> $1/2$ cup almonds
> 1 inch peeled ginger, cut into coins
> $1/2$ cup bulgur
> Salt and freshly ground black pepper
> $3/4$ cup boiling red wine or water
> 1 tablespoon Dijon or other mustard
> Cayenne or hot red pepper flakes to taste (optional)
> A little all-purpose flour, if needed, for binding
> 2 tablespoons extra virgin olive oil or butter

❶ Combine the beets, dates, almonds, and ginger in a food processor and pulse several times until everything is well chopped but not quite a paste.

❷ Put the mixture in a large bowl with the bulgur and a sprinkle of salt and pepper. Stir in the boiling wine, mustard, and cayenne if you're using it and cover the bowl with a plate. Let steep for 20 minutes. Taste and adjust the seasoning if necessary. Let the mixture rest for a few minutes if you can before shaping it into patties; if it seems too wet, stir in a little flour to help bind it. (You can make the burger mixture or even shape the burgers up to several hours in advance. Just cover tightly and refrigerate, then bring everything back to room temperature before cooking.)

❸ Shape the mixture into 4 to 6 patties. Put the oil or butter in a skillet with a lid over medium heat. When the oil is hot or the butter is melted, carefully slip the burgers into the pan. Cook, undisturbed for 5 minutes or so, until nicely browned on the bottom; carefully flip the burger, cover, and cook the other side for 5 minutes.

❹ Serve on plates with any of the accompaniments listed in "Serving Burgers" (page 659) or on buns with the usual burger fixings. Or cool and refrigerate or freeze for later use.

Fresh Spring Vegetable Burger

MAKES: 4 to 6 servings

TIME: 45 minutes

When spring's first vegetables and herbs appear, here's a way to bind them lightly with mashed potatoes and eat them on a bun. The mixture also makes great bite-sized party food. These burgers are fine with ketchup, of course, but even better with some crumbled blue cheese or Blue Cheese Dressing (page 212), Creamy Bistro Dressing or Sauce (page 799), or Real Ranch Dressing (page 772). Of course you'll want to omit the dairy toppings and use the oil instead of butter if you're looking for a vegan burger.

1 pound small waxy potatoes, like "new" or fingerling, quartered

Salt

3 to 4 tablespoons butter or extra virgin olive oil

4 ounces asparagus, green beans, or snow peas, finely chopped (about 1 cup)

1 cup peas (frozen are fine, just thaw them in cold water)

$\frac{1}{2}$ cup mixed fresh herbs, like parsley, mint, chives, and chervil

Freshly ground black pepper

A little all-purpose flour, if needed, for binding

Turning Burgers into Loaves

For meatless meat loaves, simply double any of the burger recipes and preheat the oven to 350°F. Pat the mixture into a greased standard (6-cup) loaf pan and cover with foil. Bake for 30 minutes or so, then uncover and bake until crisp and golden, another 20 to 30 minutes. Cool a bit, then slice and serve with ketchup (to make your own, see page 790) or any of the accompaniments suggested in the recipe.

① Put the potatoes in a large pot with water to cover; salt it. Bring to a boil and lower the heat so that the water bubbles vigorously. Cook until the potatoes are very tender, about 20 minutes. Drain well.

② Meanwhile, put a tablespoon of the butter or oil in a deep skillet over medium heat. When the butter is melted or the oil is hot, add the asparagus and cook, stirring frequently, until crisp-tender, just a couple of minutes. Add the peas and the herbs, sprinkle with salt and pepper, and cook until just hot, another couple minutes. Remove from the heat and put the mixture into a large mixing bowl.

③ Add the potatoes and mash roughly, leaving some larger pieces but making sure it's combined well. Taste and adjust the seasoning. Let the mixture rest for a few minutes if you can before shaping it into patties; if it seems too wet, stir in a little flour to help bind it. (You can make the burger mixture up to several hours in advance. Just cover tightly and refrigerate, then bring everything back to room temperature before cooking.) Wipe out the skillet.

④ Shape the mixture into 4 to 6 patties. Put 2 tablespoons of the remaining butter or oil in the skillet and turn the heat to medium. When the butter is melted or the oil is hot, carefully slip the burgers into the pan. Cook until nicely browned on one side, about 5 minutes; turn carefully and cook on the other side until firm and browned, adding the remaining butter or oil if necessary.

⑤ Serve on plates with any of the accompaniments listed in "Serving Burgers" (page 659) or on buns with the usual burger fixings. Or cool and refrigerate or freeze for later use.

Midsummer Vegetable Burger

MAKES: 4 to 6 servings

TIME: 45 minutes

This light, colorful burger, which gets its crunch from corn, is terrific on a bun, especially with a little Salsa

Roja (page 787), Chile Mayonnaise (page 771), or Roasted Pepper Mayonnaise (page 771) or with sliced ripe tomatoes and drizzled with Traditional Pesto (page 768).

Serve it with substantial side dishes like Ratatouille Salad (page 64), Warm Chickpea Salad with Arugula (page 73), Sweet Potato and Quinoa Salad (page 84).

$1/4$ cup extra virgin olive oil

1 small red onion, halved

2 cloves garlic

1 minced fresh chile (like jalapeño or Thai), or to taste, or hot red pepper flakes or cayenne to taste

Salt and freshly ground black pepper

1 medium zucchini, grated (about 1 cup)

2 cups corn kernels, fresh if possible

$3/4$ cup cornmeal

A little all-purpose flour, if needed, for binding

1 Put 2 tablespoons of the olive oil in a deep non-stick or cast-iron skillet with a lid over medium heat. Put the onion, garlic, and chile in a food processor and pulse a few times to grind almost smooth. Add the mixture to the pan with a sprinkle of salt and pepper and cook and stir.

2 Stir the zucchini into the onion mixture along with $1/2$ cup of the corn and another sprinkle of salt and pepper. Put the remaining corn into a food processor and let the machine run until it becomes a thick paste. Continue to cook and stir the zucchini mixture until the vegetables release all their water and it starts to evaporate, about 5 minutes. Stir in the corn paste and the cornmeal. Remove from the heat, cover, and let rest for 10 minutes. If the mixture seems too wet, stir in a little flour to help bind it. Taste and adjust the seasoning.

3 Form 4 to 6 patties and let sit for a few minutes if you have time. (You can make the burger mixture or even shape the burgers up to several hours in advance. Just cover tightly and refrigerate, then bring everything back to room temperature before cooking.) Wipe out the pan,

put in the remaining 2 tablespoons of oil, and turn the heat to medium. A minute later, add the patties. Cook until nicely browned on one side, about 5 minutes; turn carefully and cook on the other side until firm and browned.

4 Serve on plates with any of the accompaniments listed in "Serving Burgers" (page 659) or on buns with the usual burger fixings. Or cool and refrigerate or freeze for later use.

Fresh Summer Vegetable Burger with Cheese. A little richer and creamier: In Step 2, when you stir in the corn paste and cornmeal, add $1/2$ cup grated cheddar, mozzarella, Jack, or Parmesan cheese.

Spicy Autumn Vegetable Burger

MAKES: 4 to 6 servings

TIME: 30 minutes with cooked beans and kale

F **M**

Here's a burger flecked with bits of green and orange vegetables, with both creamy and chewy textures. It's also a handy way to use leftover greens like kale, chard, cabbage, or spinach. If you don't have any handy, just cook and shock them according to the directions on page 241. It will add only a few minutes to the recipe.

Serve these on a crusty roll with barbecue sauce (to make your own, see page 789) or put them on a plate naked, next to a big spoonful of Millet Mash (page 565) with Caramelized Onion Chutney (page 786) on the side.

Vegan if you use the oil.

2 cups cooked kale or other winter green, like collards, turnip or mustard greens, or broccoli raab (about 8 ounces raw)

2 cups cooked or canned cannellini or other beans, drained well

4 or 5 tablespoons extra virgin olive oil or butter

1 medium sweet potato (about 12 ounces), peeled and grated (about 1 cup)

Salt and freshly ground black pepper

$1/2$ cup Fresh Bread Crumbs (page 804) or panko

$1/2$ teaspoon ground cinnamon

$1/4$ teaspoon freshly grated nutmeg

Pinch cayenne, or to taste

A little all-purpose flour, if needed, for binding

1 Squeeze all the water out of the kale and finely chop it. Put the cannellini beans in a large bowl and mash them roughly. Stir in the greens with a fork.

2 Put 2 tablespoons of the oil or butter in a deep skillet over medium heat. When the oil is hot or the butter is melted, add the sweet potato and sprinkle with salt and pepper. Cook, stirring frequently, until it begins to soften and color, about 5 minutes. Stir in the bread crumbs and remaining spices and cook and stir for another minute or so.

3 Stir the sweet potato mixture into the bean mixture with a fork, mixing until well blended. Let the mixture rest for a few minutes if you can before shaping it into patties. If it seems too wet, stir in a little flour to help bind it. Taste and adjust the seasoning. (You can make the burger mixture up to several hours in advance. Just cover tightly and refrigerate, then bring everything back to room temperature before cooking.) Wipe out the skillet.

4 Shape the mixture into 4 to 6 patties. Put 2 tablespoons of the remaining butter or oil in the skillet and turn the heat to medium. When the butter is melted or the oil is hot, carefully slide the burgers into the pan. Cook until nicely browned on one side, about 5 minutes; turn carefully and cook on the other side until firm and browned, adding the remaining butter or oil if necessary.

5 Serve on plates with any of the accompaniments listed in "Serving Burgers" (page 659) or on buns with the usual burger fixings. Or cool and refrigerate or freeze for later use.

Tofu Burgers, Asian Style

MAKES: 4 to 6 servings
TIME: 30 minutes

Sea greens add both taste and texture to tofu, which makes a perfect backdrop for a burger with Asian seasonings. Serve these with Steamed Sticky Rice (page 507) and Sea Slaw (page 55). Or for cocktail food, make miniburgers (or "meat"balls; see below) to spear with toothpicks and dip in Miso Carrot Sauce with Ginger (page 781) or Fishless Fish Sauce (page 778).

$1/4$ cup arame or other dark sea green, like kombu or wakame

1 bunch scallions

$1^1/2$ pounds firm tofu, patted dry

$1/2$ cup panko or Fresh Bread Crumbs (page 804)

Making Meatless Meatballs

Whether baked (page 660) or fried, for dinner or for appetizers, vegetarian meatballs are almost as easy to make as burgers. I suggest you roll them relatively small, at least until you get the hang of it; they cook up fast and crisp without falling apart. Start with a heaping tablespoon or so and gently squeeze them in your hands, rolling lightly to smooth and even the outside. Set them on wax paper until all are done. (See the illustration on page 660.)

They'll take between 15 and 20 minutes to bake (you probably won't have to turn them at all), depending on the burger recipe. To fry, film a nonstick or cast-iron skillet with oil or butter and turn the heat to medium. Add some meatless balls—they need a little space between them, but you can fit quite a few in a pan—and cook, undisturbed, until crisp and golden, 3 to 5 minutes. Roll them around a bit to cook the other sides until they're cooked all over.

1/4 cup sesame seeds

1 tablespoon soy sauce

2 teaspoons dark sesame oil

Salt and freshly ground black pepper

2 to 3 tablespoons peanut oil or neutral oil, like grapeseed or corn

1 Pour boiling water over the arame and soak for 1 or 2 minutes. Drain well.

2 Trim the scallions, put in a food processor, and pulse a few times, until minced. Transfer to a large mixing bowl. Put about half of the tofu and the arame in the processor (no need to wash it out) and pulse a couple of times, until just crumbled. Add to the mixing bowl.

3 Put the remaining tofu into the processor and let it run until the tofu is smooth. Add it to the mixing bowl, along with the crumbs, sesame seeds, soy sauce, and sesame oil. Sprinkle with a little salt and lots of pepper and stir well to combine. Form into 4 to 6 patties. Let rest if you have some extra time. (You can make the burger mixture or even shape the burgers up to a day or so in advance. Just cover tightly and refrigerate, then bring everything back to room temperature before cooking.)

4 Put the oil in a large nonstick or well-seasoned cast-iron skillet over medium heat. When hot, use a spatula to slip the burgers into the pan. Cook, undisturbed, until they turn golden and release easily from the pan, about 5 minutes. Flip carefully and cook until done, another 3 to 4 minutes.

5 Serve on plates with any of the accompaniments listed in "Serving Burgers" (page 659) or on buns with the usual burger fixings. Or cool and refrigerate or freeze for later use.

Tofu-Walnut Burger. Rich and silky: Reduce the tofu to 1 pound and omit the sesame seeds. In Step 2, with the first half of the tofu, add 1/2 cup chopped walnuts (or cashews, almonds, or hazelnuts) and pulse until the mixture is crumbly. In Step 3, with the second half of the tofu, add 1/4 cup chopped walnuts and process until smooth. Proceed with the recipe.

Tofu Sesame Burger with Adzuki Beans. Nice reddish brown color and meaty texture: Reduce the amount of tofu to 1 pound. In Step 1, add 1 cup well-drained adzuki beans to the processor with the arame and tofu and pulse a few times until crumbled. Proceed with the recipe.

Tofu-Tempeh Burger. Deeply flavored: Replace 8 ounces of the tofu (about a third) with 8 ounces of tempeh. In Step 2, pulse it in the food processor along with the sea greens and a little bit of the remaining tofu until crumbly. Proceed with the recipe.

Fast Nut Burgers

MAKES: 4 to 6 servings
TIME: 20 minutes

If you have a food processor, these take almost no time, making them perfect for lunch or a fast dinner. And you can make a batch of twelve, then shape and freeze them (see page 659), almost as easily as a batch of four. (You can even precook them, freeze them, and defrost in a microwave, albeit with some sacrifice in flavor.)

1 medium onion

1 cup walnuts, pecans, almonds, cashews, or other nuts, preferably raw

1 cup (raw) rolled oats or cooked short-grain white or brown rice

2 tablespoons ketchup, miso, tomato paste, nut butter, or tahini

1 teaspoon chili powder or any spice mix you like (to make your own, see pages 810–819), or to taste

Salt and freshly ground black pepper

1 egg

2 tablespoons peanut oil, extra virgin olive oil, or neutral oil, like grapeseed or corn

1 Grind the onion in a food processor. Add the nuts and oats and pulse to chop, but not too finely. Add the ketchup, spice mix, salt, pepper, and egg. Process briefly; don't grind the mixture too finely (the results will not be terrible, but a little tougher, if you do so). Add a little liquid—water, stock, soy sauce, wine, whatever is handy—if necessary; you want a mixture that is moist but not loose.

2 Let the mixture rest for a few minutes if you have the time, then shape it into 4 to 6 patties. (You can make the burger mixture or even shape the burgers up to a day or so in advance. Just cover tightly and refrigerate, then bring everything back to room temperature before cooking.) Put the oil in a large nonstick or well-seasoned cast-iron skillet over medium heat. When the oil is hot, add the burgers to the skillet. Cook for about 5 minutes, more or less undisturbed (you may want to rotate the patties for even browning), then turn. Lower the heat a bit and cook on the other side 3 or 4 minutes more, or until firm.

3 Serve on plates with any of the accompaniments listed in "Serving Burgers" (page 659), or on buns with the usual burger fixings. Or cool and refrigerate or freeze for later use.

Nuttier Nut Burger. Handled carefully, these are fine. They're a bit more delicate, but they taste great: Use $1^1/_2$ cups nuts and reduce the oats or cooked rice to $^1/_2$ cup.

Nut-and-Seed Burger: Substitute up to $^1/_2$ cup sesame, sunflower, or pumpkin seeds for half of the nuts or oats.

Vegan Nut Burger. With a little ground nori, these are so good: Omit the egg. Use miso or nut butter, not ketchup, and use soy sauce for the liquid. Add $^1/_2$ sheet crumbled Nori Chips (page 357) to the food processor.

The Basics of Seitan

If you've ever eaten "mock duck" or "mock chicken" in a Chinese restaurant, you've had seitan, the chewy, tasty wheat product that has long been used in Asia as a meat or tofu substitute. Seitan is versatile, keeps for a long time, and is foolproof to make. It goes by a variety of other names, including wheatmeat, and with good reason: Among nonanimal products, it has a uniquely chewy texture, absorbs flavorings extremely well, and can be roasted, panfried, breaded, or even grilled or broiled—just as if it were meat.

You can buy seitan, usually in the refrigerated section of natural food stores, and most is of acceptable quality. But it is relatively expensive and is tough to find whole, since it's usually cut into small chunks and packaged in its simmering liquid.

Making seitan yourself is far cheaper and allows you to control the seasonings and size of the pieces. Happily, it's relatively easy, and all you need is a single ingredient.

That ingredient is called *vital gluten flour*, a concentrated, high-protein flour that's available in the same stores where you find seitan (which could be your supermarket, a natural food store, or an Asian grocery), or see the Sources at the back of the book for on-line and mail-order suppliers. (It's possible to rinse and knead plain flour into seitan dough, but it's absurdly labor-intensive.)

Making and Using Seitan

Vital gluten flour is slightly yellow and very fine, almost powdery. Made after the starch, ash, and other components of wheat flour have been separated and washed away, it boasts a whopping 12 percent of its weight—or as much as 24 grams per 6-ounce serving—in protein. When mixed with water it becomes instantly elastic and rubbery, which is exactly why seitan has such meaty texture. Once you've mixed this dough, seitan must cook for a while before you proceed; you just roll it into free-form loaves, flavor a little water or stock, and let the seitan gently bubble away in a pot of liquid for an hour or so. As it cooks, the gluten absorbs water and flavor while the loaves triple in size. Simmering makes the proteins tighten, which gives seitan its chewy texture.

You can control the texture of your seitan simply by adjusting the cooking time. If you prefer a dense interior, turn off the heat after around an hour. Let it go a little longer if you like a lighter, spongier texture. (Just cut into the loaf during cooking and take a peek; you'll be a pro by the second or third time you make it.) Once the loaves are done, let them cool in the cooking liquid. At that point, you've got a couple options. You can slice and use it immediately, refrigerate it in the cooking liquid for up to several days, or freeze it for several months.

The recipe for seitan and the simmering liquids here will give you ready-to-eat wheat protein, seasoned two different ways. All you have to do is slice; the sauce and serving ideas are here too. But I like to put a little crust on seitan by either pan-searing, roasting, or broiling or grilling it. (See the recipes that follow for each technique.)

One of the easiest ways to become familiar with seitan is to substitute it for tofu in stir-fries and braised dishes. For the tofu recipes on pages 645–652, simply use equal quantities of seitan and follow the directions the same way.

Seitan

MAKES: 4 to 6 servings (1 to 1^1/$_2$ pounds)

TIME: About 1^1/$_2$ hours, largely unattended

The first time you make seitan is shocking: The dough comes together almost instantly, is astonishingly elastic, and is very easy—even fun—to work. It's important to knead it thoroughly, either by hand or by machine, and to let the dough rest before forming the loaves. To finish the seitan, prepare either the Dark or the Golden Simmering Liquid on page 671 and follow the directions here.

1 cup vital gluten flour

1 recipe Dark or Golden Simmering Liquid for Seitan (page 671)

1 Put the vital gluten flour in a large bowl. Or, if you're mixing and kneading by machine, put it in a food processor fitted with the short plastic blade or in the bowl of an upright mixer fitted with a dough hook.

2 Add ^{3}/$_4$ cup water and mix until it is all absorbed. Knead (by hand or machine) for a minute or two. If loose flour remains, add a couple more drops of water, but be careful not to add too much. The dough should be one big, slightly rubbery mass. Continue kneading right in the bowl by hand for 5 minutes or so, by mixer for a couple of minutes, or by food processor for just 30 seconds or so. Cover the dough with a cloth and let it rest for at least 20 minutes but no more than 30. Meanwhile, mix up either the Dark or the Golden Simmering Liquid in a large pot with a lid.

3 Pull or cut the dough into 2 equal portions. Stretch, pull, and roll the dough into 2 logs. (Don't worry; they'll plump considerably.) Set them in the simmering liquid and bring to a boil. (It's okay if they aren't submerged.)

4 Lower the heat so that the mixture bubbles gently and cover. Cook, using tongs to turn the seitan once or twice, for about an hour. Test by cutting a slice off the end with a knife, and if you want it a little less dense, cook another 15 to 30 minutes. Cool in the liquid before storing or using.

5 Seasonings for Seitan Dough

Combine any of these ingredients with the vital gluten flour and salt called for in the recipe before adding water. You can use them alone or in combination, but don't use more than ^{1}/$_4$ cup total.

1. Toasted wheat germ
2. Whole wheat flour
3. Seasoning blends, like any curry or chili powder (to make your own, see pages 814–816)

(STEP 1) Pull or cut the dough into two equal portions. (STEP 2) Stretch and pull each ball to lengthen it. (STEP 3) Pat and roll the stretched dough pieces into logs. The dough will be ragged and elastic, so it's okay if they are not perfectly shaped. Each will plump to even out and triple in size during cooking.

4. Chopped or pulverized nuts
5. Chopped or pulverized dried sea greens, such as kombu, arame, or wakame

Seitan and Lentil Loaf

MAKES: 4 to 6 servings (1 to 1^1/$_2$ pounds)

TIME: About 2 hours, largely unattended

Think of a vegetarian meat loaf, only with a chewier, less crumbly texture. This is among the most versatile recipes in this chapter—indeed, in the entire book—and just may become a permanent ingredient in your fridge or freezer. For appetizers, cool it down and slice it thinly to eat it like pâté, with mustard and crackers. Chopped, it becomes a tasty and protein-rich addition to Fast Fresh Tomato Sauce (page 445). Or cut the loaf into cubes and use it in stir-fries.

^{3}/$_4$ cup vital gluten flour

^{1}/$_3$ cup dried lentils

1 recipe Dark or Golden Simmering Liquid for Seitan (page 671)

1 Put the vital gluten flour and lentils in a large bowl. Or, if you're mixing and kneading by machine, put it in a food processor fitted with the short plastic blade or in the bowl of an upright mixer fitted with a dough hook.

2 Add ^{3}/$_4$ cup water and mix until it is all absorbed. Knead (by hand or machine) for a minute or two. If loose flour remains, add a couple more drops of water, but be careful not to add too much. The dough should be one big, slightly rubbery mass. Continue kneading right in the bowl by hand for 5 minutes or so, by mixer for a couple of minutes, or by food processor for 30 seconds or so. Cover the dough with a cloth and let it rest for at least 20 minutes but no more than 30. Meanwhile, mix up either the Dark or the Golden Simmering Liquid in a large pot with a lid.

3 Shape the dough into an oval loaf, rolling it around the bowl to capture any stray lentils. (Don't worry; it will plump considerably.) Set the loaf in the simmering liquid and bring to a boil. (It's okay if it isn't submerged.)

4 Lower the heat so that the mixture bubbles gently and cover. Cook, using tongs to turn the seitan once or twice, for about an hour. Test by cutting a slice off the end with a knife, and if you want it a little less dense, cook for another 15 to 30 minutes. Cool in the liquid before storing or using.

Seitan and Mushroom Loaf. Use a food processor fitted with a metal blade to pulverize about ^{1}/$_4$ ounce of dried shiitake or porcini mushrooms. You should have about $^1/_3$ cup, and it's okay if there are still some small chunks. Use the mushrooms instead of the lentils and proceed with the recipe.

Dark Simmering Liquid for Seitan

Use this simmering liquid if you plan to use the seitan in Asian-style dishes or with deeply flavored foods like mushrooms, caramelized onions, or root or winter vegetables. The soy sauce colors the seitan a light brown.

If you use oil to further cook or season dark-simmered seitan, use a neutral oil like grapeseed or corn or peanut or dark sesame oil.

6 cups vegetable stock (pages 101–102) or water

$^1/_3$ cup soy sauce

Combine the stock or water and the soy sauce in a large pot that can be covered. Follow the simmering directions in the main recipe.

Golden Simmering Liquid for Seitan

Cook the seitan in this lighter seasoning liquid if you want a more neutral color and flavor or plan to use seitan with spring or summer vegetables. It's best with non-Asian dishes and seasonings. The color will be, well, golden.

If you use oil to further cook or season golden-simmered seitan, use a neutral oil like grapeseed or corn or extra virgin olive oil.

6 cups vegetable stock (pages 101–102) or water

1 cup white wine, apple juice, or cider

1 tablespoon salt (if using water)

Combine the ingredients in a large pot with a lid and follow the simmering directions in the main recipe.

7 Other Seasonings for Seitan-Simmering Liquid

Use alone or in combination, with either the dark or golden base liquid.

1. 1 or 2 bay leaves
2. About 1 tablespoon peppercorns, black or Sichuan
3. 6 or 8 garlic cloves, lightly crushed
4. Fresh herb sprigs like rosemary, thyme, sage, oregano, parsley, cilantro, or mint
5. Up to 1 tablespoon tea leaves
6. Warm spices like cinnamon (1 stick), cloves (2 or 3), star anise (1 or 2), or cardamom (4 or 6 pods)
7. A pinch of asafetida

Pan-Seared Seitan

MAKES: 4 to 6 servings

TIME: 10 minutes with prepared seitan

F **V**

The simplest way to cook seitan is to cut it in slices and fry it in a little oil. For more elaborate dishes, substitute seitan for tofu in any of the stir-fry recipes on pages 645–648. Seared pieces of seitan are also great on salads or in soups.

Any cooking oil is fine here, but pick one that goes with the other seasonings you plan to use: peanut with Asian flavors; extra virgin olive oil with Mediterranean. Or use a neutral oil like grapeseed or corn.

2 to 3 tablespoons oil

1 to 1$^1/_2$ pounds seitan, cooled, thinly sliced, and patted dry

Salt and freshly ground black pepper

Put 2 tablespoons of the oil in a large nonstick or well-seasoned cast-iron skillet over medium-high heat. When the oil is hot, add the seitan, taking care not to overcrowd (you will have to work in batches). Cook until the pieces are well browned and release from the pan, 3 to 5 minutes, then flip and cook the other side. Drain on paper towels, taste, and sprinkle with salt and pepper if you like.

Grilled or Broiled Seitan

MAKES: 4 to 6 servings

TIME: 30 minutes with prepared seitan

The smoky flavor from a live fire is especially good with seitan, though broiling inside can also give you a nice light char. Generally I prefer to sauce the seitan toward the end of cooking so that everything gets crisp, but you can certainly baste with sauce if you like. See "25 Sauces and Accompaniments for Seitan" (right) for some ideas.

1 to 1$^1/_2$ pounds seitan, cooled and patted dry

Neutral oil, like grapeseed or corn, as needed

Salt and freshly ground black pepper

1 Start a charcoal or gas grill or preheat a broiler to medium-high heat and place the rack 3 or 4 inches from the heat source. Pat the seitan dry again if necessary and brush with oil.

2 Cut the seitan into large cubes and skewer if you like or simply put the whole pieces on the grill or under the broiler. Cook carefully until lightly browned, brushing with more oil as needed. Continue to grill or broil until nicely browned; total cooking time will be less than 10 minutes. Taste and sprinkle with salt and pepper if you like. Serve whole or sliced or cool, wrap, and refrigerate for another use.

Oven-Roasted Seitan

MAKES: 4 to 6 servings

TIME: About 1 hour with prepared seitan, largely unattended

With a crunchy crust and a tender interior, this is one of my favorite ways to cook seitan. When it's done, you just slice it thinly and eat, either as you would meat with vegetable and starch side dishes or stirred into rice, noodle, or bean dishes.

1 to 1$^1/_2$ pounds seitan, cooled and patted dry

2 tablespoons neutral oil, like grapeseed or corn, plus more as needed

Salt and freshly ground black pepper

1 Preheat the oven to 350°F. Put the seitan loaf or loaves on a roasting rack in a large pan and brush with 2 tablespoons of the oil. Roast, undisturbed, until they start to turn golden, about 30 minutes.

2 Use tongs to turn the loaves over and brush with more oil if you like. Continue roasting until the seitan is deeply colored, another 15 to 20 minutes. Cool slightly before slicing. Taste and sprinkle with salt and pepper if you like.

Oven-Roasted Seitan with Garlic. Crush 2 cloves of garlic. In Step 2, when you turn the loaves, use a fork to smear the crushed garlic over the top. Proceed with the recipe, roasting until the garlic is lightly browned.

Oven-Roasted Seitan with Ginger. Use dark sesame oil. Follow the preceding variation, replacing some or all of garlic with ginger.

Oven-Roasted Seitan with Chile. A spicy filling for tacos or in a pot of beans: In Step 2, when you turn the loaves, sprinkle them with a tablespoon of chili powder (to make your own, see page 814).

Oven-Roasted Seitan with Curry. In Step 2, when you turn the loaves, sprinkle them with a tablespoon of any curry powder (to make your own, see pages 815–816).

23 Sauces and Accompaniments for Seitan

1. Fresh Tomato Salsa (page 750)
2. Fresh Tomatillo Salsa (page 751)
3. Sea Green Salsa (page 753)
4. Traditional Pesto or any herb purée (pages 768–769)

 Fast   Make Ahead   Vegan

5. Grainy Mustard, Many Ways (page 776)
6. Basil Dipping Sauce (page 777)
7. Fishless Fish Sauce (page 778)
8. Soy and Sesame Dipping Sauce and Marinade, Korean Style (page 778)
9. Teriyaki Sauce (page 779)
10. Ginger-Scallion Sauce (page 779)
11. Dashi Dipping Sauce (page 780)
12. Ponzu Sauce (page 780)
13. Raw Onion Chutney (page 783)
14. Crunchy Nut Chutney (page 784)
15. Tomato Chutney (page 785)
16. Miso Sauce (pages 781–782)
17. Fast Fresh Tomato Sauce (page 445)
18. Mushroom Ketchup (page 791)
19. Ketchup (to make your own, see page 790)
20. Barbecue sauce (to make your own, see page 789)
21. Spicy Indian Tomato Sauce (page 793)
22. Peanut Sauce, Six Ways (page 794)
23. Rustic Pine Nut Sauce (page 796)

The Basics of Tempeh

Tempeh (pronounced tem-pay), which originated in Indonesia several hundred years ago, is relatively new to America. Like soy sauce, miso, and vinegar, tempeh is fermented, with a complex yeasty flavor and a high umami quotient (see page 638, The Umami Factor); think of mushrooms, strong cheese, or hearty bread. Like blue cheese, tempeh is "inoculated" with an edible mold, so it looks pretty wild: an ugly, lumpy, compressed cake of beans (and sometimes grains), usually less than an inch thick. It's more of an acquired taste than many foods, but if you make Crunchy Crumbled Tempeh (page 674), my guess is you'll be fond of it pretty quickly.

Tempeh is very high in protein, up to 19 percent by weight, which means about 15 grams in a $1/2$-cup serving—just about all you really need on many days. Unlike tofu, tempeh is a whole soybean food, so it's also rela-

tively high in fiber and all the nutrients found in whole soybeans, including B vitamins and many amino acids.

You can buy tempeh in natural food stores and some supermarkets—fresh (usually vacuum-sealed for a longer shelf life) or frozen, in many different varieties. All-soybean is the classic and most common, but tempeh can also be made with soybeans and wild rice, brown rice, or other grains. Always check the date on the package to find the freshest available; once opened, tempeh keeps for only a few days.

It's a good idea to cook tempeh before eating it, mostly because it will taste better; it's not really a safety concern. Some people like it steamed or sliced and fried, and you can bake it whole too. But I like it best crumbled and crisped in a little hot oil.

Crunchy Crumbled Tempeh

MAKES: 4 servings

TIME: 10 minutes

Ⓕ Ⓜ Ⓥ

My favorite way to use tempeh is crumbling it into other foods, which distributes delicious bits throughout the dish and makes the most of tempeh's unique flavor. Think of how you might use grated cheese, only it doesn't melt. And the crispness is a treat.

2 tablespoons neutral oil, like grapeseed or corn

8 ounces (about 2 cups) tempeh

Salt and freshly ground black pepper

❶ Put the oil in a large skillet over medium-high. When hot, use 2 forks or your fingers to crumble the tempeh into the hot oil. Cook, stirring frequently and scraping up any browned bits, until the tempeh is deeply colored and crisp on all sides, 5 to 7 minutes.

❷ Remove the tempeh with a slotted spoon and drain on paper towels. Sprinkle lightly with salt and pepper. Use immediately or cool a bit, cover tightly, and refrigerate for up to 3 days.

Seasoned Crumbled Tempeh. Use any spice mixture (to make your own, see pages 810–819) or simply the salt and black pepper: When the tempeh is just about done, sprinkle it with spice to taste—a tablespoon or so—and a little more salt and pepper. Cook and stir for another minute or two to take the rawness out of the seasonings, then proceed with the recipe from Step 2.

Crunchy Crumbled Tempeh with Fresh Herbs. All cilantro or half cilantro and half parsley are naturals here, though you can certainly experiment with basil or mint too: When the tempeh is just about done, stir in 1 cup of chopped mild fresh herb leaves and a little more salt and freshly ground black pepper. Cook and stir for another minute or two to take the rawness out of the seasonings, then proceed with the recipe from Step 2.

Crunchy Crumbled Tempeh with Chile Paste. Deeply flavored with a hot finish: When the tempeh is basically done, stir in up to $^1/_4$ cup of Chile Paste (page 828). Cook and stir for another minute or two, then proceed with the recipe from Step 2.

Crunchy Crumbled Tempeh with Wheat Berries. Use this combination for about 3 cups of a milder-tasting version of the main recipe or any of the variations: Increase the amount of oil to 3 tablespoons. Along with the tempeh, stir in 1 cup of cooked wheat berries. Proceed with the recipe. Taste and adjust the seasoning.

10 Ways to Use Crunchy Crumbled Tempeh

1. Fill burritos, tacos, or enchiladas.
2. Sprinkle on pizzas before baking.
3. Sprinkle on top of green salads.
4. Fluff with any cooked rice or grain pilaf right before serving.
5. Stir into any cooked sauce as it simmers for a "meaty" enrichment
6. Stir-fry into any Fried Rice (page 519–520).
7. Add to soups at the last minute.
8. Stir into a pot of beans or chili during the last few minutes of cooking.
9. Toss with Asian-style noodle dishes (see pages 463–474).
10. Add to Sushi Bowls (page 527).

Braised Tempeh, Three Ways

MAKES: 4 to 6 servings
TIME: 30 minutes

Tempeh gives any cooking liquid—even water—a haunting flavor that provides a great backdrop for other, more assertive flavors like coconut milk, vinegar and chiles, or soy and tomatoes. The result is three very different dishes with one simple technique. If you add cooked vegetables to this dish (virtually any will work; just stir them in with the bean thread), you have a quick one-bowl dinner.

Try replacing the bean thread here with 2 or 3 cups cooked rice vermicelli (page 464) or whole wheat angel hair pasta; both are great.

2 tablespoons peanut oil or neutral oil, like grapeseed or corn

8 ounces (about 2 cups) tempeh

1 tablespoon peeled and minced fresh ginger

1 tablespoon minced garlic

Salt and freshly ground black pepper

1 tablespoon curry powder (to make your own, see page 816)

2 cups vegetable stock (pages 101–102) or water

2 cups coconut milk, either made from scratch (page 423) or canned (use 1 can, slightly less than 2 cups, with a little water)

3 cups chopped cabbage, preferably Napa

4 ounces (2 bundles) bean thread noodles, soaked and cut (see page 464)

$^1/_2$ chopped fresh basil leaves, preferably Thai, or parsley

$^1/_2$ cup sliced scallion

❶ Put the oil in a deep skillet or Dutch oven over medium-high heat. When hot, use 2 forks or your fingers to crumble the tempeh into the hot oil. Cook, stirring frequently and scraping up any browned bits, until the tempeh begins to color and gets crisp on all sides, about 5 minutes. Stir in the ginger and garlic and sprinkle with salt and pepper. Keep cooking and stirring until the vegetables soften and the tempeh is deeply colored, another minute or two. Stir in the curry powder.

❷ Add the stock and coconut milk. Turn the heat to high and bring to a boil, then lower the heat so that the mixture bubbles somewhat assertively. Leave uncovered and cook, stirring occasionally, until the liquid thickens a bit, about 10 minutes.

❸ Stir in the cabbage and give it a minute or two to wilt. Add the noodles, basil, and scallion, and when the mixture just begins to bubble again, taste, adjust the seasoning, and serve.

Hot and Sour Braised Tempeh. Increase the oil to 3 tablespoons. Along with the ginger and garlic, add 1 tablespoon minced fresh chile (like jalapeño or Thai), or to taste, or hot red pepper flakes or cayenne to taste. Use sugar instead of the curry powder. Omit the coconut milk and increase the amount of stock or water to $3^1/_2$ cups. When you add the liquid in Step 2, stir in $^1/_4$ cup each of soy sauce and rice wine vinegar. Proceed with the recipe, using cilantro instead of the basil if you like.

Braised Tempeh with Soy and Tomato Sauce. Try this with pasta instead of the bean thread noodles or omit the noodles entirely and spoon this over polenta (page 543): Omit the curry powder. In Step 2, instead of the stock and coconut milk, use 4 cups chopped tomato (canned is fine; include the juice), plus $^1/_4$ cup soy sauce. You will need to cook the mixture for another 5 minutes or so to thicken it up. Use spinach instead of the cabbage if you like. Proceed with the recipe, finishing with basil or parsley.

Tempeh with Rice and Spinach

MAKES: 4 servings
TIME: About 40 minutes, largely unattended

Lemon zest and juice makes this a brightly flavored one-pot dish. It's also great for picnics and patio parties because you can serve it at room temperature.

2 lemons

3 tablespoons extra virgin olive oil

8 ounces (about 2 cups) crumbled tempeh

2 tablespoons minced garlic

Hot red pepper flakes or cayenne, to taste

Salt and freshly ground black pepper

1 cup any white long-grain rice

1 pound fresh spinach leaves, washed

1 Remove the zest from one of the lemons (see page 426) and mince it. Squeeze the juice from both lemons and reserve it.

2 Put the oil in a deep pot with a lid over medium-high heat. When hot, add the tempeh and cook, stirring frequently and scraping up any browned bits, until it is deeply colored and crisp on all sides, 5 to 7 minutes.

3 Stir in the garlic, red pepper flakes, minced lemon zest, and sprinkle with salt and pepper. Cook and stir for a minute or so, then stir in the rice and toss to coat. Add enough water to the pot to cover the rice by an inch and bring to a boil. Then adjust the heat so the mixture boils steadily but not violently. When small craters appear, lower the heat a bit more and, when all visible moisture disappears—this will be 10 to 15 minutes after you started—put the spinach and the reserved lemon juice on top of the rice, cover the pot, and turn off the heat entirely. Leave undisturbed for at least 10 minutes and up to 20 or so. Fluff with a fork to combine and taste and adjust the seasoning if necessary, adding lots of black pepper. Serve immediately or at room temperature.

Tempeh with Rice and Peas. Terrific texture and great with a splash of soy sauce: Omit the spinach and use 2 cups of peas instead (frozen are fine). Proceed with the recipe.

Tempeh with Rice and Mushrooms. Especially good with lots of parsley stirred in at the end: Omit the spinach and clean and slice 1 pound mushrooms (one kind or a combination). After cooking the tempeh in Step 2, add the mushrooms, and cook, stirring frequently, until they give off their liquid and start to get dry again. Then proceed with the recipe from Step 3, simply adding the lemon juice to the rice when it's ready and covering the pot as directed.

Tempeh with Brown Rice and Spinach. You have two choices here; either one works for the main recipe or either of the variations: Follow the directions for substituting brown rice for white in the sidebar on page 506 or substitute brown rice for white and follow the recipe. In Step 3, when the pot comes to a boil, adjust the heat so the mixture simmers gently, and cover. Cook for 30 to 40 minutes, checking occasionally to make sure the water is not evaporating too quickly (you can add a little more liquid if necessary). When the liquid has been absorbed, taste and see if the rice is tender or nearly so. If it is, proceed. If not, add about $1/2$ cup more liquid and continue to cook, covered, until it is, another 5 minutes or so. Then add the spinach and lemon juice and proceed with the recipe.

Tempeh Hash

MAKES: 4 servings

TIME: About 1 hour

Ⓜ Ⓥ

You'll be amazed at how close this is to "real" hash. The soy and sesame seasoning enhances the richness of the tempeh and adds an interesting twist to an old favorite. Some patience is required here to cook each of the main elements separately, though you can easily prepare the components a couple hours in advance and assemble the hash at the last minute. All you need with this are some sliced ripe tomatoes or simple steamed vegetable like carrots or broccoli. Of course you might want to top this with a poached egg or two.

$1/4$ cup neutral oil, like grapeseed or corn, or peanut oil

2 or 3 large white potatoes, peeled if you like and cut into small dice

Salt and freshly ground black pepper

8 ounces (about 2 cups) crumbled tempeh

1 large yellow onion, chopped

2 tablespoons peeled and minced fresh ginger

1 tablespoon minced garlic

1 tablespoon minced fresh chile (like jalapeño or Thai), or to taste, or hot red pepper flakes or cayenne to taste

1 tablespoon soy sauce, or more to taste

1 tablespoon dark sesame oil

1 teaspoon rice wine vinegar

1 teaspoon sugar

1 medium red bell pepper, cored, seeded, and finely chopped

1 cup chopped fresh cilantro

❶ Put 2 tablespoons of the neutral oil in a large skillet over medium-high heat. When hot, add the potatoes, sprinkle with salt and pepper, and cook undisturbed until the edges brown and they release easily from the pan, about 5 minutes. Toss the potatoes gently, scraping up any bits from the bottom of the pan, and turn the heat down to medium. Cook, stirring occasionally, until they are crisp and golden on all sides and tender inside, about 10 to 15 minutes more. Transfer them to a platter or baking pan.

❷ Put 1 tablespoon of the remaining neutral oil into the skillet and return the heat to medium-high. Add the tempeh and cook, stirring frequently and scraping up any browned bits, until it is deeply colored and crisp on all sides, 5 to 7 minutes. Add the tempeh to the potatoes, but don't stir them up yet.

❸ Put the last tablespoon of the neutral oil in the skillet over medium-high heat. Add the onion, ginger, and garlic and cook, stirring frequently, until they begin to soften, a minute or two. Then reduce the heat to medium-low and cook, stirring occasionally, until caramelized, about 20 minutes. When done, remove from the heat.

❹ Meanwhile, whisk together the chile, soy sauce, sesame oil, vinegar, and sugar. (The hash may be prepared to this point and assembled up to 2 hours later.)

❺ To finish the dish, put the onion mixture over medium heat. Return the tempeh and potatoes to the skillet and stir for a few minutes until hot and sizzling. Add the chile-soy mixture and toss to coat, scraping up any browned bits from the bottom of the pan. Stir in the bell pepper and cilantro. Taste and add a little salt if necessary and lots of black pepper.

Tempeh Hash with Kimchi. Hot and vinegary: Omit the chile. Coarsely chop 1 cup Kimchi (page 96) and add it to the hash along with the bell pepper and cilantro in Step 5.

Tempeh Chili with Black Beans

MAKES: 4 to 6 servings

TIME: About 2 hours, largely unattended

This is the smokiest, most deeply flavored chili in the book, rich with the combination of tempeh, roasted garlic, black beans, and chipotle chiles. For balance, a little honey helps each bite to end on a slightly sweet note (use sugar to make the chili vegan). Serve bowlfuls with a wedge of Corn Bread (page 687) or use to fill burritos. You might also consider making a double batch and freezing some.

Use canned beans here if you must; just add them after the chili thickens up a bit, during the last few minutes of cooking.

2 heads garlic

3 tablespoons extra virgin olive oil, plus more for coating the garlic

12 ounces (about 3 cups) crumbled tempeh

2 onions, chopped

¼ cup honey or 2 tablespoons sugar

3 medium carrots, chopped

2 tablespoons chili powder (to make your own, see page 814)

1 tablespoon chopped fresh sage or 1 teaspoon dry

2 to 5 canned chipotle chiles, chopped with some of their adobo, to taste

3 tablespoons tomato paste

4 cups chopped ripe tomato (about 2 pounds whole; canned are fine; don't bother to drain them)

2 cups vegetable stock (pages 101–102) or water

1 cup dried black beans, preferably quick-soaked (page 581)

Salt and freshly ground black pepper

1 cup chopped fresh cilantro

1 cup chopped radishes

1 Coat the whole heads of garlic with a little of the olive oil and roast according to either of the recipes on page 304.

2 Meanwhile, put 2 tablespoons of the remaining oil in a large pot with a lid over medium-high heat. Add the tempeh and cook, stirring frequently and scraping up any browned bits, until it is deeply colored and crisp on all sides, 5 to 7 minutes. Transfer with a slotted spoon to a shallow bowl. Return the pot to the stove over medium-high heat.

3 Add the last tablespoon of oil to the pot along with the onions and cook, stirring frequently, until soft, 2 or 3 minutes. Stir in the honey and turn the heat down to medium-low. Cook, stirring occasionally, until the onions are caramelized and deeply colored, about 20 minutes.

4 Add the carrots, chili powder, and sage; cook for a minute or two, until fragrant. Stir in the chipotles and adobo, followed by the tomato paste, tomato, stock, beans, and tempeh. Bring to a boil, then lower the heat so the mixture bubbles gently and cook, stirring occasionally, until the liquid thickens and the beans are tender, about an hour. (Add more stock or water if it starts to look dry.) Taste, sprinkle with salt and pepper, and partially cover.

5 By now the garlic should be done and cooled enough to handle. Squeeze the flesh into the pot and stir well. Taste again and adjust the seasoning if necessary, adding more chipotle or honey if you like. Serve, garnished with cilantro and radishes.

Breads, Pizzas, Sandwiches, and Wraps

There is nothing like home-baked bread. The great irony is that it's developed a reputation for being difficult, yet you can become competent in making bread about as easily as in making soup. Thanks to reliable

leavening, like instant yeast (and of course baking powder), consistent ovens, a variety of good flours, and the food processor, bread making has never been more straightforward.

If there's no denying that it still takes a little time, let me also assure you that almost all of that time is pretty much unattended. The batter for quick breads is not much more complicated than that for pancakes, so most of the time is taken up by baking. And with yeast breads, from baguettes to pizza, the mixing—and this includes kneading, takes less than a minute (again, thanks to the food processor), and the rising and shaping, though they occur over a period of hours, need little input from you.

In fact, when I'm too busy to cook, I still find myself making bread; it's easy enough to integrate into the rhythm of life even when the rhythm is upbeat: a few minutes at night, a few in the morning, and then an hour or so to keep an eye on the oven sometime later in the day. The effect that this engagement with so ancient and natural a process has on my mood—and on what I grab to eat when I get hungry—is quite striking. It's not a last-minute thing, bread baking. But it is as rewarding a kitchen process as there is, and I hope you'll give it a shot.

This chapter is divided into several sections. First I outline the basics of flour and leavening agents and then offer quick bread recipes and the details you'll need to make them; with these go muffins (a form of quick bread, really), biscuits, and scones.

Next are a few basic recipes for flatbreads, fritters, crackers, and other smaller categories of breads. Then it's on to an elementary treatment of yeast breads and pizzas, a huge topic that I try to handle succinctly and in a way that will lead you to begin experimenting on your own. Finally: stuffed doughs, sandwiches, and wraps. (You gotta do something with all that bread you'll be baking!)

The Basics of Flour

The backbone of all baking is flour, which is ground ("milled") from wheat or other grains. Though the milling determines the texture of the flour, the way it bakes is ultimately a reflection of the characteristics of the original grain; in other words, nothing will perform exactly like white flour.

"Other" flours include everything but basic, all-purpose white—flours milled from other grains, nuts, and even roots, all of which are readily available. Though they're called "flour," they don't have the same baking qualities (see "The Magic of Gluten?" on page 708), and they don't taste the same.

Many, however, offer distinctive flavor, satisfying texture, and good nutrition. (And those that are entirely gluten or wheat free can be enjoyed by celiacs and the wheat intolerant.) But without gluten—the protein specifically found in wheat—you're never going to get the same texture. That's because protein makes the dough sturdier and more elastic; low-protein flours produce a finer, tender crumb desirable in desserts, not breads.

One way to get around the lack of gluten and lighten whole grain breads is to add some white flour or, a very neat trick, a little vital gluten (see "The Basics of Seitan," page 668). Substitutions vary depending on the type of bread and the kind of flour you're trying to incorporate into the recipe; there's a chart with some basic guidelines on page 684.

The Flour Lexicon

Virtually any grain, bean, or starchy food can be ground into flour, including quinoa, amaranth, barley, triticale—even water chestnuts. Some are hard to find and tricky to use; others may make their way into the regular rotation at your house. Here, then, are the primary flours you'll need for baking the breads in this chapter, plus a few more if you want to experiment further.

White Flours

These are "regular" flours, the finely ground endosperm of the wheat kernel, without the bran or germ. I use only unbleached flour; the bleaching process uses harsh chemicals and serves no purpose other than cosmetic (it's actually illegal in some European countries). Besides, flour that is properly milled and aged lightens naturally as it oxidizes; oxidizing also improves the quality of protein and in turn helps make doughs more elastic. So just buy good-quality unbleached flour and your baked foods will look and taste great.

All-Purpose Flour

This is the workhorse of flours. Milled from hard wheats or a combination of hard and soft, A-P flour, as it's often known, may be enriched with vitamins and nutrients in an attempt to compensate for those that are stripped through the removal of the bran and the germ. It contains 8 to 11 percent protein, which allows it to work well in a range of applications, including cakes, cookies, pastries, noodles, quick breads, and yeast breads. (The protein content of every flour is listed on the label; if not specifically, just check the number of grams of protein in the nutritional information; since that's listed per 100 grams of flour, it's a percentage. So 4 grams of protein means the flour is 4 percent protein.)

Bread Flour

Milled from hard wheats, bread flour has more protein than A-P flour (up to 14 percent), and therefore greater gluten strength, which makes it the flour of choice for

 Fast   Make Ahead   Ⓥ Vegan

elastic, easy-to-handle doughs that produce chewy crumb and sturdy crust. Typically unbleached, bread flour is sometimes conditioned with ascorbic acid, though I prefer those that are not, because I think even moderate quantities can make the finished dough taste slightly sour.

Cake (Pastry) Flour

Milled from soft wheat, this flour has a low protein content (less than 9 percent). This means doughs and batters don't develop much elasticity, so it produces a tender, delicate crumb in cakes and pastries.

Self-Rising Flour

Also called *phosphated flour,* this is essentially A-P flour plus salt and a leavening agent like baking powder. Self-rising flour works for biscuits and quick breads but not yeast breads. In any case, it's a silly concept, since it's more expensive and can't substitute for all-purpose flour; furthermore, it's easy enough to add those two ingredients to regular flour.

Whole Wheat Flour

Produced by grinding all three components of the wheat kernel—the bran, the germ, and the endosperm. This means more fiber and nutrients than white flour (and up to 14 percent protein), as well as a pleasantly assertive flavor, especially in breads. But anything made with 100 percent whole wheat flour will be heavy and dense, so most people—including me—combine it with some white flour for best results.

Whole wheat flour is available in a variety of grinds from ultra-fine to coarse, though the most common supermarket types are relatively coarse. Finer grinds produce a more even texture and behave more like white flour in terms of rising and elasticity. To incorporate whole wheat flour into a recipe without making other adjustments, just replace half of the white flour with whole wheat. But don't expect the results to be the same.

Whole Wheat Pastry Flour

Milled from soft wheat, with about 10 percent protein. Like its white counterpart, it produces a delicate crumb in cakes and pastries, but with the characteristics of whole wheat, including a downside: baked goods made with whole wheat flour are almost always heavier than those made with white pastry flour.

White Whole Wheat Flour

Similar to conventional whole wheat flour in baking performance and nutritional profile, this relatively new variety is milled from white wheat instead of red wheat. It has a relatively mild flavor, so it's great for people who don't like the strong flavor of conventional whole wheat flour but want the nutritional advantage. Again, it has the baking characteristics of whole wheat, which means most baked goods relying on it are on the heavy side.

Rye Flour

Graded dark, medium, or light, depending on how much bran is milled out. The darker the flour, the stronger the flavor and the higher the protein and dietary fiber, which makes this a nice substitute for a small amount of the white flour in bread recipes. Because it has a low gluten content, it is almost always combined with white flour. But even if your ratio is high in wheat flour, baked goods made with rye flour tend to be moist, dense, deeply colored, and slightly (deliciously) sour tasting. Pumpernickel flour is just dark coarsely ground whole-grain rye.

Cornmeal

Ground dried corn, available in fine, medium, or coarse grinds and in yellow, white, or blue, depending on the color of the corn. Stone-ground cornmeal—which is generally what you want—retains the hull and germ, so it's more nutritious and flavorful than common steel-ground cornmeal, though also more perishable (store it in the freezer). In yeast breads, you can generally substitute up to 10 percent cornmeal for wheat flour without adjusting the recipe. But you will see corn bread recipes that are anywhere from 50 to 100 percent meal.

Corn flour is just another name for finely ground cornmeal (but be careful; in recipes written in the UK, it means cornstarch). You can make corn flour by grinding medium or coarse cornmeal in a food processor for a few minutes.

Buckwheat Flour

Milled buckwheat groats (see page 535), gluten free and graded dark, medium, and light, depending on how much hull remains after milling. The dark variety, milled from whole groats, is most common and is sometimes labeled *supreme*. By contrast, the flour milled from hulled groats is sometimes called *fancy*. As with rye flour, the darker the color, the stronger the flavor. Buckwheat flour is slightly sour; it's most commonly used in pancakes, but you can also use it in waffles, blintzes, crêpes, muffins, and noodles. In yeast breads it must be combined with a gluten-rich flour.

Rice Flour

Also called *rice powder, ground rice,* and *cream of rice,* this is ground, sifted raw white rice. In Southeast Asia it's used to make noodles, pastries, and sweets and as a thickening agent and coating. Gluten free, so it must be combined with gluten-rich flours in yeast breads.

Brown Rice Flour

Milled from rice that has had only the outer hull removed. Higher in protein and fiber than white rice flour, brown rice flour adds a nutty flavor and slight color to baked goods. It has a grainy, gritty texture that yields a dry, fine crumb.

Glutinous Rice Flour

Sometimes called *sweet rice flour,* glutinous rice flour is most commonly used to make Asian sweets that have a resilient, chewy texture.

Nut Flours

Made by finely grinding nuts, nut flours, or *meals* as they're also called, are gluten free and high in protein and fat. (Grinding your own, page 322, can be tricky, because a blender or food processor may turn nuts to paste before

they're ground finely.) Nut flours work great in quick breads or for breading vegetables or croquettes, but you must mix them with gluten-rich flours in yeast breads; generally you can substitute up to 25 percent nut flour for wheat flour in baking without making other adjustments.

Almond flour is the most widely available nut flour, with a consistency that resembles cornmeal. It's typically made from blanched almonds; almond meal is made from either blanched or whole almonds. Similarly, hazelnut flour is made from ground, partially skinned hazelnuts; chestnut flour, which has a complex, slightly sweet flavor and is used to make pasta (see page 443), is made from ground chestnuts.

Soy Flour

Made from roasted soybeans. Full-fat soy flour (sometimes called *natural*) retains the oils of the soybean; defatted soy flour has had them removed. Both are high in protein, though the defatted type has a higher concentration—about 47 percent compared to 35 percent in full-fat flour. Soy flour is gluten free and must be blended with a high-gluten flour in yeast bread recipes; it also has a pronounced bean flavor that not everyone likes (I'm not wild about it myself). You can use it to replace about 15 percent of all-purpose flour to make a dense, moist loaf. For baked goods that do not contain yeast, you can substitute as much as one-quarter soy flour for regular flour.

Spelt Flour

A high-protein, low-gluten flour made from ground spelt. Spelt flour has a pleasant nutty flavor and is a good wheat substitute for people with a low tolerance for wheat, though some people with wheat allergies are also allergic to spelt. You can find both white and whole grain spelt flour.

Oat Flour

Milled from oat groats, rolled oats, or oatmeal, oat flour produces baked goods that are moist, crumbly, and nutty

 Fast   Make Ahead   Ⓥ Vegan

tasting; nice. You can grind your own coarse oat flour by giving rolled oats a whirl in the blender or food processor. For yeast breads, use no more than 30 percent oat flour and the rest high-gluten flour. (Because oats contain some of the proteins that form gluten, people who are very sensitive to gluten often can't eat oats.)

Potato Flour

Gluten-free flour made from steamed dried potatoes; most often seen during Passover, when it's used to make baked goods. It also works well, though, to help bind croquettes and fritters or thicken sauces. Its pronounced potato flavor helps improve the taste of gluten-free baked foods. Don't confuse it with potato starch.

Garfava Flour

A blend of chickpea flour (aka *besan,* page 633) and fava bean flour. Substitute it for chickpea flour for an added dimension of flavor.

Arrowroot Flour

Helpful in small quantities when baking with other gluten-free flours because of its good binding properties. See "Thickening Sauces" (page 795*).*

Tapioca Flour

The ground dried starch of the cassava root. Like arrowroot, tapioca flour is mostly as a thickener in puddings, fruit pies, and soups, but its gelatinous qualities can also add some chewiness to baked foods.

Gluten-Free Baking Mixes

These are commercially made blends that generally combine rice flour, potato starch, and tapioca flour or other gluten-free ingredients. You can substitute this directly for wheat flour in many recipes, though with mixed results. Available in some supermarkets and most natural food stores, as well as on-line (see Sources, page 929).

The Leavening Lexicon

Leavening—the word *leaven* means "lighten"—gives baked goods lift. Yeast, baking soda, baking powder, and natural starters like sourdough are all leaveners. And they all work the same way: by producing carbon dioxide bubbles that are trapped by the dough's structure, and in turn, make the dough rise.

The process is as old as baking—that is, thousands of years—but it's been understood only since the mid–nineteenth century, when ol' Louis Pasteur discovered that yeasts are living, single-cell fungi that produce carbon dioxide through fermentation (baking and brewing have a lot in common). Before then, most breads were risen with sourdough starters, which contain wild yeasts, but shortly thereafter commercial yeast production began. Now, of course, you can buy yeast in various forms at the supermarket, including fresh, active dry, and instant, which is the most recent addition to the group and by far the most convenient. Yeast (especially combined with sourdough) adds a distinctive, unmistakable, and delicious flavor to breads.

Baking soda and baking powders are used in quick breads, cookies, cakes, and the like; they don't add the distinctive flavor of yeast (which is not always welcome), though they do have flavor of their own, albeit milder.

Natural starters, like sourdough, are formed when a mixture of flour and water is left at room temperature to catch wild yeast and bacteria, always present in the air. They can take weeks or even months to develop (though you can hasten the process; see page 709) and can be kept active for centuries if maintained properly (I have one that is purported to have been started during the Alaska gold rush). The *Lactobacillus* bacteria are responsible for the distinctive flavor of sourdough breads.

More detail on leavening agents:

Yeast

Instant Yeast

Also called *fast-acting, fast-rising, rapid-rise,* and *bread machine yeast,* this is the yeast I use. It's a type of dry yeast

SUBSTITUTING FLOURS IN BAKING

Use this chart as a quick reference for replacing all-purpose flour in yeast and quick breads. (The results are usually better in quick breads, where you generally don't want a chewy texture.) You can mix and match, but don't go over the maximum percentage for any one flour.

One easy way to measure these substitutions is to put the estimated amount of alternative flour (or flours) in the measuring cup first, then fill the remainder with all-purpose wheat flour and level it off.

FLOUR	QUANTITY TO USE IN RECIPES
Whole Wheat	Up to 50 percent
Rye	
light	Up to 40 percent
medium	Up to 30 percent
dark	Up to 20 percent
Buckwheat	Up to 20 percent
Cornmeal	Up to 10 percent
Soy	Up to 15 percent
Spelt	Up to 100 percent; then either decrease water by 25 percent or increase flour by 25 percent
Nut	Up to 25–30 percent
Oat	Up to 25–30 percent
Rice	Up to 25–30 percent

(see below) and by far the most convenient: It can be added directly to the dough at almost any point, it's fast, and it's reliable.

Instant yeast has ascorbic acid added (and sometimes traces of other ingredients too); this helps the dough stretch easily and increases loaf volumes. In most breads, you won't notice any difference in flavor.

Fresh Yeast

Also known as *cake* or *compressed yeast,* fresh yeast is usually sold in foil-wrapped cakes of about $2/3$ ounce. It should be yellowish, soft, moist, and fresh smelling, with no dark or dried areas. Fresh yeast must be refrigerated

(you can freeze it if you like); it has an expiration date and will die within ten days of being opened.

It must also be "proofed" before being added to a dough. This means you must combine it with liquid; when you do, it will foam and smell yeasty (if it doesn't, it's dead). Many bakers contend that fresh yeast tastes better than dry, but I don't see it. It is kind of fun to work with, but for me instant yeast is the way to go.

Active Dry Yeast

ADY is kind of in between fresh and instant and was used by most home bakers until instant yeast came along. ADY is fresh yeast that has been pressed and dried until

 Fast   Make Ahead Vegan

the moisture level reaches about 8 percent. Unlike instant yeast, ADY must be rehydrated in 110°F water; below 105°F, it will remain inert; above 115°F, it will die. So use a thermometer!

ADY is sold in ¼-ounce foil packets; you don't need to refrigerate them, because they are sealed for a shelf life of up to two years. ADY is also sold loose in bulk quantities (sometimes in jars), which you must store in the refrigerator.

Baking Soda

Baking soda (sodium bicarbonate) produces carbon dioxide only in the presence of liquid and acid, or an acidic liquid like buttermilk, yogurt, or vinegar. Every recipe that uses baking soda must have an acidic component or it won't rise.

Baking soda releases all of its gas at once, so it's best to add it with the flour, at the last minute. Once it hits the acid and liquid it goes to work, and you want those bubbles formed in the oven, not on the counter.

You also must be careful not to add too much baking soda, because it's quite salty. Plus, whenever you add more baking soda you must add more acid, which could make the recipe unpleasantly acidic. (The recipes here take all of this into account.)

Baking Powder

Baking powder is simply baking soda with a dry acid added to it (along with some starch, which keeps the baking powder dry and therefore inert until it's added to a recipe). Single-acting powders generally contain cream of tartar as the acid, which is activated by moisture, so the batter must be baked immediately after being mixed, just like those containing baking soda. Double-acting powder, however, usually contains both cream of tartar and the slower-acting sodium aluminum sulfate, so it releases gas in two phases.

When double-acting baking powder is added to a batter, the cream of tartar combines with the soda and produces the first leavening. The second leavening occurs during baking. So batters using double-acting baking powder (which is the most common kind) can sit at room temperature for a few minutes before being baked; but just a few. (And why bother, really? Just mix the flour/baking powder mixture into the wet ingredients at the last moment.)

Be careful about the amount of baking powder you add: too much can give baked goods a bitter taste and—if the air bubbles grow too big and break—even cause them to collapse.

Sourdough

Also called *levain* or *mother dough,* sourdough is a natural starter that doesn't rely on yeast. (Though, as you'll see from my recipes, and I'm not alone in this, I think a bit of yeast helps sourdough along and improves its flavor.) To make sourdough (page 709), you mix flour, water, and a pinch of yeast and leave them at room temperature where, over a period of days, the mixture will catch wild yeast and *Lactobacillus* bacteria. (Or you get some sourdough starter from a friend, which is the easy way and makes sense; everyone with sourdough is happy to share.) This slow fermentation creates a characteristic tang and deep flavor. The day before you're ready to bake, you feed the sourdough, let it sit for a while, then use some of it as leavening in your bread dough; see page 710. You also put some aside for the next time; a good sourdough will keep for a couple of weeks or longer in the fridge without being fed.

Sponge

Sometimes called by their Italian or French name *biga* or *poolish,* a sponge—essentially a predough mixture—is made with flour, water, and yeast or sourdough. You let the sponge sit for a few hours or overnight and then combine it with more flour and water to make the dough; this technique improves flavor and texture enormously and is my preferred method when not using sourdough (above).

LEAVENING AGENT	AMOUNT	SUBSTITUTION
Baking powder, double-acting	1 teaspoon	1/4 teaspoon baking soda plus 1/2 teaspoon cream of tartar plus 1/4 teaspoon cornstarch OR 1 1/2 teaspoons single-acting baking powder OR 1/4 teaspoon baking soda plus 1/2 cup buttermilk, sour milk, or yogurt to replace 1/2 cup nonacidic liquid
Baking powder, single-acting	1 teaspoon	2/3 teaspoon double-acting baking powder OR 1/4 teaspoon baking soda plus 1/2 teaspoon cream of tartar plus 1/4 teaspoon cornstarch
Baking soda	1/2 teaspoon	2 teaspoons double-acting baking powder (must replace acidic liquid in recipe with nonacidic liquid) OR 1/2 teaspoon potassium bicarbonate
Yeast, active dry	1 packet (1/4 ounce)	1 cake fresh (3/5 ounce) OR 1 scant tablespoon active dry OR 2 teaspoons instant

The Basics of Quick Breads and Muffins

The mixtures used for quick breads and muffins are identical; the only difference is the shape in which you bake them. Quick breads are (usually) rectangular loaves; muffins are, well, baked in muffin cups. The batter—it can't be called a dough, because it's pourable, not kneadable—is rich, usually containing eggs, butter, and milk, often with at least a little bit of sugar or other sweetener. (Vegan quick breads and muffins are a special case and not really related that closely to the originals; see page

687.) Instead of being raised with yeast, the batter is usually leavened with baking powder, though you can sometimes use baking soda, and there are times when a combination is best.

In a very real way, quick breads and muffins are more like cakes than they are like yeasted breads (though I resist and resent the commercial tendency to make cakes in muffin form and call them muffins; muffins and quick breads should be slightly sweet and are great with coffee or tea, but they're not dessert). The batter is relatively light, and the goal is a delicate, cakelike crumb, moist interior, and nicely browned but still tender crust with a

Ⓕ Fast   Ⓜ Make Ahead   Ⓥ Vegan

little chew but no real crunch. To achieve this you need some fat, which contributes to flavor and tenderness, and special handling.

Not that it's difficult handling. Making quick breads is easy: You combine the dry ingredients, then combine the wet ingredients, then combine the two, and then bake. No special techniques or equipment are needed. You don't even really need a bread pan; you can bake quick breads in a square baking tin or even an ovenproof skillet.

The special handling means this: Overmixing the batter will make quick breads tough. While in most yeast breads you want to develop gluten to get a tough crust and chewy crumb, in quick breads you want to retard its development to keep the bread nice and light. (This is why you use only all-purpose flour, not bread flour.) So heed this warning: Combine dry and wet ingredients as quickly as you can and don't beat or even stir any more than is necessary. When you see no more dry bits of flour, the job is done; don't worry about any remaining lumps.

As a general rule, quick breads do not keep as well as yeasted breads, so it's best to eat them the same day they're made. It's fine to bake them a few hours in advance; once they cool, keep them wrapped in wax paper or foil. To freeze them for later (or to keep leftovers), just wrap them tightly in plastic and foil and pop them in the freezer for later. Thaw in the refrigerator if time allows and remove the plastic. Rewrap in the foil if you want to warm quick breads; use a 300°F oven.

Corn Bread

MAKES: About 6 servings
TIME: About 45 minutes

Corn bread is indispensable, especially to a vegetarian diet, where its full flavor and slightly crunchy texture are welcome at any meal. And few dishes deliver so much for

so little work. Be sure to experiment with the variations (the Lighter, Richer Corn Bread is what many people think of as standard, though the admittedly slightly spartan main recipe is the more traditional) and the suggestions in "12 Additions to Virtually Any Quick Bread, Muffin, Biscuit, or Scone" on page 688.

$1\frac{1}{4}$ cups buttermilk, milk, or yogurt (or $1\frac{1}{4}$ cups milk plus 1 tablespoon white vinegar; see Step 2), plus more as needed

2 tablespoons butter or extra virgin olive oil

$1\frac{1}{2}$ cups medium-grind cornmeal

To Make Any Bread Vegan

The classic French or Italian breads (pages 707–711) are essentially vegan by nature, containing only flour, water, yeast, and salt. But richer yeast breads, and most quick breads, often contain dairy milk and eggs.

Replacing the milk is the easy part: You can use any nondairy milk, though I generally recommend oat or rice milk for baking because of their neutral flavors. Almond and hazelnut milk are great when you've got nuts in the recipe or want to add a subtle nutty flavor.

Replacing eggs, though, is a little trickier, because they have both protein and fat, as well as some leavening properties. First choice: For each egg, substitute 3 (level) tablespoons of soft silken tofu and $\frac{1}{4}$ teaspoon of baking powder. If tofu isn't a good choice for you, for each egg, mix together 1 teaspoon cornstarch, 3 tablespoons neutral oil, like grapeseed or corn, and $\frac{1}{4}$ teaspoon baking powder. Stir either substitution mixture together with a fork until smooth and add it when the recipe calls for the egg.

And, of course, whenever a recipe suggests honey, simply use molasses, maple syrup, or granulated sugar.

I'm not going to pretend that the vegan versions of the recipes in this section are the same as the originals, but they're good and no more difficult.

$^{1}/_{2}$ cup all-purpose flour

$1^{1}/_{2}$ teaspoons baking powder

1 teaspoon salt

1 tablespoon sugar, plus more if you like sweet corn bread

1 egg

1 Preheat the oven to 375°F.

2 If you're using buttermilk, milk, or yogurt, ignore this step. If not, make the soured milk: Warm the milk gently—1 minute in the microwave is sufficient, just enough to take the chill off—and add the vinegar. Let it rest while you prepare the other ingredients.

3 Put the butter in a medium ovenproof skillet or an 8-inch square baking pan over medium heat; heat until good and hot, about 2 minutes, then turn off the heat. Combine the dry ingredients in a bowl. Mix the egg into the buttermilk. Stir the liquid into the dry ingredients (just enough to combine); if it seems too dry, add another tablespoon or two of buttermilk. Pour the batter into the prepared skillet or pan, smooth out the top if necessary, and put in the oven.

4 Bake about 30 minutes, until the top is lightly browned and the sides have pulled away from the pan; a toothpick inserted into the center will come out clean. Serve hot or warm.

Lighter, Richer Corn Bread. Use 4 tablespoons ($^{1}/_{2}$ stick) of butter (do not use other fat). Increase the sugar to $^{1}/_{4}$ cup. Use 2 eggs; stir their yolks into the milk and beat the whites until stiff but not dry, then gently stir them into the prepared batter after the yolks and milk have been incorporated.

Corny Corn Bread. You have some options here: Add 1 cup of fresh or frozen corn kernels or about a cup of creamed corn to the liquid ingredients in Step 3.

Corn and Bean Bread. I love this: Use 2 eggs and 1 cup buttermilk or soured milk; omit the white flour. Stir $1^{1}/_{2}$ cups well-cooked white beans (canned are fine), puréed and strained, into the milk-egg mixture before adding to the dry ingredients.

12 Additions to Virtually Any Quick Bread, Muffin, Biscuit, or Scone

You can adjust the recipes in this section simply by adding an ingredient (or two or three) to the liquid ingredients just before combining them with the flour mixture. If you use a little common sense so flavors and textures don't clash, you'll never go wrong.

1. Spice blends, like chili powder or curry powder (to make your own, see pages 814–816) or even single spices like cumin, saffron, cardamom, or caraway seeds; generally 1 tablespoon or so
2. Traditional Pesto (page 768) or any other herb paste (pages 768–770); up to $^{1}/_{4}$ cup (It's great to drizzle it onto the batter once it's in the pan and use a knife to swirl it in like marble cake.)
3. Minced or sliced pickled jalapeños; from a tablespoon to $^{1}/_{4}$ cup or to taste
4. Grated cheese, either soft, melting, or hard types—anywhere from $^{1}/_{2}$ to 1 cup
5. Molasses or honey in place of the sugar (if there is any); about $^{1}/_{4}$ cup
6. Minced herbs—up to $^{1}/_{4}$ cup of mild ones like mint, parsley, or cilantro; up to 2 tablespoons of strongly flavored ones like rosemary, oregano, or thyme
7. Sautéed onions, shallots, or leeks; about $^{1}/_{2}$ cup (With this and other very savory additions, stock in place of half the milk is nice.)
8. Finely chopped nuts or seeds, like almonds, pecans, or pumpkin, poppy, or sesame seeds—up to $^{1}/_{2}$ cup
9. Dried cherries, blueberries, or cranberries or raisins (soak in a little warm water first and drain well); up to 1 cup
10. Cooked wheat or rye berries or hulled barley; up to 1 cup
11. Grated citrus zest; about 1 tablespoon
12. Sprinkle the tops of unbaked quick bread or muffins with some sugar (raw sugar is particularly nice) or a mixture of cinnamon and sugar

F Fast   **M** Make Ahead   **V** Vegan

Quick Whole Wheat and Molasses Bread

MAKES: 1 loaf

TIME: About 1¼ hours, largely unattended

The basic, quintessential, not-too-sweet quick bread—quick, simple, hearty, and rich despite the fact that it contains no eggs or butter. Although you can use it for sandwiches, this is best served warm, as part of a meal.

Oil or butter for greasing the pan

1²/₃ cups buttermilk or yogurt (or 1½ cups milk plus 2 tablespoons white vinegar; see Step 2)

2½ cups (about 12 ounces) whole wheat flour

½ cup cornmeal

1 teaspoon salt

1 teaspoon baking soda

½ cup molasses

❶ Preheat the oven to 325°F. Grease an 8 × 4-inch or 9 × 5-inch loaf pan.

❷ If you're using buttermilk or yogurt, ignore this step. If not, make the soured milk: Warm the milk gently —1 minute in the microwave is sufficient, just enough to take the chill off—and add the vinegar. Let it rest while you prepare the other ingredients.

❸ Mix together the dry ingredients. Stir the molasses into the buttermilk. Stir the liquid into the dry ingredients (just enough to combine), then pour into the loaf pan. Bake until firm and a toothpick inserted into the center comes out clean, about an hour. Cool on a rack for 15 minutes before removing from the pan.

Lighter Whole Wheat Quick Bread. A little cakier: Use 1½ cups whole wheat and 1½ cups all-purpose flour; omit the cornmeal. Substitute honey for the molasses for lighter flavor and color. Beat 1 egg into the wet ingredients in Step 3.

Whole Wheat Quick Bread with Sweet Milk. It's a lot of baking powder, so you might taste it, but if you don't want to use yogurt or sour milk, here you go: Use sweet (regular) milk and substitute 2 tablespoons baking powder for the baking soda. Beat 1 egg into the wet ingredients in Step 3.

Olive Oil Salt Bread

MAKES: 4 to 6 servings

TIME: About 45 minutes, largely unattended

There is no quicker, hassle-free way to get fresh warm bread on the table, especially if you make the griddled variation. Rich and flaky with olive oil, this biscuitlike dough is easy to handle and takes to all sorts of additions, like cheese, chopped olives, or seasonings (see the list on page 688). Just knead them in with your hands after processing. Like most unyeasted breads, it doesn't keep for more than a day and is best eaten still warm from the oven.

⅓ cup olive oil, plus more for greasing the pan

3 cups all-purpose flour

1 tablespoon baking powder

1 teaspoon salt, preferably coarse or sea salt, plus more for sprinkling

❶ Preheat the oven to 375°F. Grease an 8-inch skillet or square baking pan with about a tablespoon of olive oil. Put the flour, baking powder, and salt in a food processor and turn the machine on. Pour through the feed tube first ⅓ cup of the olive oil, then most of 1 cup of warm water. Process for about 30 seconds, then remove the cover. The dough should be in a well-defined, barely sticky, easy-to-handle ball. If it is too dry, add the remaining water 1 tablespoon at a time and process for 5 or 10 seconds after each addition. If it is too wet, which is unlikely, add a tablespoon or two of flour and process briefly.

❷ Put the dough into the prepared pan and press until it fits to the edges. Flip it over and press again. Cover with foil and bake for 20 minutes; then remove the foil, sprinkle the top with a little coarse salt, and bake for another 20 to 25 minutes, until the top is golden and springs back when touched gently. Cool in the pan a bit, then cut into wedges or squares and serve.

Griddled Olive Oil Salt Bread. Even faster to the table: Instead of preheating the oven, heat a griddle or set a heavy pan over medium heat. Have the extra olive oil handy for greasing. In Step 2, divide the dough into 8 to 12 pieces and pat them into patties between your hands until they're about ½ inch thick. When the griddle or pan is hot, use enough olive oil to film the bottom and put in as many breads as will fit comfortably without crowding (you will probably have to work in batches). Cook, undisturbed, until they begin to brown around the edges and the tops bubble a bit, about 5 minutes. Then turn and cook the other side until crisp and golden.

Boston Brown Bread

MAKES: 1 large or 2 small loaves
TIME: About 1½ hours, largely unattended

Ⓜ

This soft-crusted bread, traditionally eaten with Baked Beans (page 618), is best with a mixture of flours. Although it can be baked or steamed, I prefer baking. Stir up to 1 cup of raisins into the prepared batter if you like.

Butter or neutral oil, like grapeseed or corn, for the pans

2 cups buttermilk or yogurt, or 2 cups less 2 tablespoons milk plus 2 tablespoons white vinegar (see Step 2)

3 cups assorted flours, such as 1 cup each rye, cornmeal, and whole wheat or all-purpose

1½ teaspoons salt

1¼ teaspoons baking soda

¾ cup molasses or maple syrup

❶ Preheat the oven to 300°F. Liberally grease two 8 × 4-inch loaf pans or one 9 × 5-inch pan.

❷ If you're using buttermilk or yogurt, ignore this step. If not, make the soured milk: Warm the milk gently—1 minute in the microwave is sufficient, just enough to take the chill off—and add the vinegar. Let it rest while you prepare the other ingredients.

❸ Mix the dry ingredients, then add the sweetener and buttermilk. Stir just until mixed; this is a loose batter, not a dough. Pour or spoon into the loaf pan(s) and bake for 1 hour or a little longer, until a toothpick inserted into the center of the loaf comes out clean. Let cool on a rack for 10 minutes before removing from the pans; eat warm.

Irish Soda Bread

MAKES: 1 round loaf
TIME: About 45 minutes

Of all quick breads, this classic recipe from Ireland is the most like yeasted bread, with a fine crumb and slightly sour flavor. It's particularly good made with half white and half whole wheat flour, and things like raisins and caraway seeds are often added to the dough. Like many yeasted breads, it doesn't keep for much more than a day and is best shortly after baking, but it's quite good the next day when thinly sliced and toasted.

Butter or neutral oil, like grapeseed or corn, for the baking pan

About 1½ cups buttermilk or yogurt, or 1½ cups milk plus 1½ tablespoons white vinegar (see Step 2)

4 cups all-purpose flour or 2 cups all-purpose plus 2 cups whole wheat flour

2 teaspoons salt

¾ teaspoon baking soda

¾ teaspoon baking powder

❶ Preheat the oven to 375°F. Use the butter or oil to grease a baking sheet.

Ⓕ Fast   Ⓜ Make Ahead   Ⓥ Vegan

2 If you're using buttermilk or yogurt, ignore this step. If not, make the soured milk: Warm the milk gently —1 minute in the microwave is sufficient, just enough to take the chill off —and add the vinegar. Let it rest while you prepare the other ingredients.

3 This is an easy enough dough to handle by hand, but it's even easier in a food processor: Combine all the dry ingredients and process (or stir) to combine. Add enough buttermilk to make a soft but not too sticky dough. Process for 30 seconds in the food processor or knead for about 3 minutes by hand; the dough will be smooth and elastic. Let the dough rest for a few minutes.

4 Shape the dough into a round loaf. Slash the top with a razor blade (see the illustrations on page 704). Bake for at least 45 minutes, or until the loaf is golden brown and sounds hollow when you thump the bottom (its internal temperature will be about 210°F). Let cool thoroughly before cutting into slices or wedges.

Banana Bread

MAKES: 1 loaf
TIME: About 1 hour

The best banana bread is a balancing act: It requires a fair amount of fat to keep it moist and lighten the crumb; a little whole wheat flour gives it some substance. And in my opinion, the result should be sweet, but not overly so. Though coconut is my favorite secret ingredient, feel free to omit it or add more nuts, raisins, or other dried fruit instead. This bread keeps better than most quick breads, though it probably won't be around too long.

8 tablespoons (1 stick) butter, plus butter for the pan

1¹/₂ cups all-purpose flour

¹/₂ cup whole wheat flour

1 teaspoon salt

1¹/₂ teaspoons baking powder

³/₄ cup sugar

2 eggs

3 very ripe bananas, mashed with a fork until smooth

1 teaspoon vanilla extract

¹/₂ cup chopped walnuts or pecans

¹/₂ cup shredded dried coconut

1 Preheat the oven to 350°F. Grease a 9 × 5-inch loaf pan.

2 Mix the dry ingredients together. With a hand mixer or a whisk or in the food processor, cream the butter and beat in the eggs and bananas. Stir this mixture into the dry ingredients just enough to combine (it's okay if there are lumps). Gently stir in the vanilla, nuts, and coconut.

3 Pour the batter into the loaf pan and bake for 45 to 60 minutes, until nicely browned. A toothpick inserted into the center of the bread will come out fairly clean, but because of the bananas this bread will remain moister than most. Do not overcook. Cool on a rack for 15 minutes before removing from the pan.

Fruit-and-Nut or Vegetable-and-Nut Bread

MAKES: 1 loaf
TIME: About 1¹/₄ hours

This is the master recipe for making a whole family of breads, like Cranberry-Pecan, Zucchini-Sunflower, or Carrot-Walnut—you name it; more combinations are suggested in the variations and the list on page 692. If the fruit is really juicy (like peaches), put the pieces in a strainer and let them drain for an hour or so before proceeding. Feel free to experiment with the seasonings as well as the fruits and nuts.

To make muffins, prepare the batter as directed, then divide it among greased muffin cups, increase the oven temperature to 400°F, and bake for 20 to 30 minutes. (See Muffins, Infinite Ways, page 692.)

4 tablespoons (¹/₂ stick) cold butter, plus butter for the pan

2 cups all-purpose flour

1 cup sugar

1¹/₂ teaspoons baking powder

¹/₂ teaspoon baking soda

1 teaspoon salt

³/₄ cup fruit juice (like orange or apple) or milk

1 tablespoon minced or grated orange or lemon zest

1 egg

1 cup any raw fruit or vegetable: berries left whole, anything else peeled and grated or chopped

¹/₂ cup chopped walnuts or pecans

1 Preheat the oven to 350°F. Grease a 9 × 5-inch loaf pan.

2 Stir the dry ingredients together. Cut the butter into bits, then use a fork or 2 knives to cut it into the dry ingredients until there are no pieces bigger than a small pea. (Using a food processor makes this step quite easy, but don't use the food processor for the remaining steps or the bread will be tough.)

3 Beat together the juice, zest, and egg. Pour into the dry ingredients, mixing just enough to moisten; do not beat and do not mix until the batter is smooth. Fold in the fruit and nuts, then pour and spoon the batter into the loaf pan. Bake for about an hour, or until the bread is golden brown and a toothpick inserted into the center comes out clean. Cool on a rack for 15 minutes before removing from the pan.

Dried Fruit and Nut Bread. Not as heavy as traditional holiday fruitcake: Instead of fresh fruit, use ³/₄ cup dried fruit, any single kind or a combination, coarsely chopped. Before beginning the recipe, heat the fruit juice gently, then pour it over the dried fruit. Let steep for 30 minutes. When you get to Step 3, add the zest and the egg to the fruit mixture and then proceed with the recipe, folding in only the nuts before baking.

Whole Grain Fruit-and-Nut or Vegetable-and-Nut Bread. Makes a slightly denser loaf: Substitute whole wheat, buckwheat, cornmeal, or other flour —either alone or in combination —for up to ¹/₂ cup of the all-purpose flour.

Pumpkin Ginger Bread with Hazelnuts. Different from the usual version, because the pumpkin isn't cooked and puréed first: Grate enough pumpkin or other winter squash to yield 1 loosely packed cup. Use hazelnuts. Instead of the zest, use minced peeled fresh ginger or 1 teaspoon ground.

Brown Sugar Carrot Bread with Almonds. Gorgeous color: Instead of granulated sugar, use dark or golden brown sugar. Grate enough carrots to yield 1 loosely packed cup. Use sliced almonds.

7 Great Fruit or Vegetable and Nut Combinations

1. Zucchini and cashews
2. Winter squash and hazelnuts
3. Sweet potatoes and pecans
4. Cherries (pitted) and almonds
5. Cranberries and pistachios
6. Grapes (halved) and peanuts
7. Apples and walnuts

Muffins, Infinite Ways

MAKES: 8 large or 12 medium muffins

TIME: About 40 minutes

The only real difference between muffins and the preceding quick breads is the pans you bake them in. But those little cups allow for a lot more potential variation, depending on what you do at the last minute before baking.

Anything goes when it comes to this recipe and the next one (which will give you a more dessertlike muffin), including the suggestions in Fruit-and-Nut or Vegetable-

F Fast   **M** Make Ahead   **V** Vegan

and-Nut Bread on page 691. Also see "12 Additions to Virtually Any Quick Bread, Muffin, Biscuit, or Scone" on page 688 for more ways to spike either recipe.

3 tablespoons melted butter or neutral oil, like grapeseed or corn, plus fat for the pan

2 cups all-purpose flour

$1/4$ cup sugar, or to taste

$1/2$ teaspoon salt

3 teaspoons baking powder

1 egg

1 cup milk, plus more if needed

1 Preheat the oven to 400°F. Grease a standard 12-cup muffin tin or line it with paper or foil muffin cups if you like.

2 Mix the dry ingredients together in a bowl. Beat together the egg, milk, and melted butter or oil. Make a well in the center of the dry ingredients and pour the wet ingredients into it. Using a large spoon or rubber spatula, combine the ingredients swiftly, stirring and folding rather than beating and stopping as soon as all the dry ingredients are moistened. The batter should be lumpy, not smooth, and thick but quite moist; add a little more milk or other liquid if necessary.

3 Spoon the batter into the muffin tins, filling them about two-thirds full and handling the batter as little as possible. (If you prefer bigger muffins, fill the cups almost to the top. Pour $1/4$ cup water into those cups left empty.) Bake for 20 to 30 minutes, or until the muffins are nicely browned and a toothpick inserted into the center of one of them comes out clean. Remove from the oven and let rest for 5 minutes before taking them out of the tin. Serve warm.

Banana-Nut Muffins. These are good with half bran or whole wheat flour: Add $1/2$ cup roughly chopped walnuts, pecans, or cashews to the dry ingredients. Substitute 1 cup mashed very ripe banana for $3/4$ cup of the milk. Use honey or maple syrup in place of sugar if possible.

Bran Muffins. The classic: Substitute 1 cup oat or wheat bran for 1 cup of the all-purpose flour (you can use whole wheat flour for the remainder if you like). Use 2 eggs and honey, molasses, or maple syrup for sweetener. Add $1/2$ cup raisins to the prepared batter if you like.

Blueberry or Cranberry Muffins. Great with cornmeal substituted for up to $1/2$ cup of the flour: Add 1 teaspoon ground cinnamon to the dry ingredients; increase the sugar to $1/2$ cup. Stir 1 cup fresh blueberries or cranberries into the batter at the last minute. You can also use frozen blueberries or cranberries here; do not defrost them first. Blueberry muffins are good with $1/2$ teaspoon grated or minced lemon zest added to the batter along with the wet ingredients. Cranberry muffins are excellent with $1/2$ cup chopped nuts and/or 1 tablespoon grated or minced orange zest added to the prepared batter.

Spice Muffins. Perfect during holiday season: Add 1 teaspoon ground cinnamon, $1/2$ teaspoon each ground allspice and ground ginger, and 1 pinch ground cloves and mace or nutmeg to the dry ingredients; use 1 cup whole wheat flour in place of 1 cup all-purpose flour. Add $1/2$ cup raisins, currants, dates, or dried figs to the prepared batter if you like.

Sour Cream or Yogurt Muffins. Rich and tender, with a hint of sourness: Reduce baking powder to 1 teaspoon, and add $1/2$ teaspoon baking soda to dry ingredients. Substitute 1 $1/4$ cups sour cream or yogurt for the milk and cut the butter or oil back to 1 tablespoon. Proceed with the recipe.

Coffee Cake Muffins. Crunchy and sweet: Mix together $1/2$ cup packed brown sugar; 1 teaspoon ground cinnamon; 1 cup finely chopped walnuts, pecans, or cashews; and 2 extra tablespoons melted butter. Stir half of this mixture into the original batter with the wet ingredients and sprinkle the rest on top before baking.

Lighter Muffins. A little more work, with noticeable results: Use 2 eggs and separate them. Add the yolks as usual; beat the whites until stiff but not dry and fold in very gently at the last moment.

Savory Muffins. Cut the sugar back to 1 tablespoon. Add up to 1 cup minced cooked onion or leek and shredded cheese to the batter just before baking.

Sweet and Rich Muffins

MAKES: 8 large or 12 medium muffins

TIME: About 40 minutes

These muffins have more butter, eggs, and sugar than the classic muffin. Any of the flavor variations for Muffins, Infinite Ways (page 692) or the suggestions listed in "12 Additions to Virtually Any Quick Bread, Muffin, Biscuit, or Scone" (page 688) will work here. The results will be more like mini-cakes.

6 tablespoons (³/₄ stick) butter at room temperature, plus butter the pan

³/₄ cup sugar

¹/₂ teaspoon salt

3 teaspoons baking powder

2 cups all-purpose flour

2 eggs

¹/₂ cup milk, plus more as needed

❶ Preheat the oven to 400°F. Grease a standard 12-cup muffin tin or line it with paper or foil muffin cups if you like.

❷ Use a wooden spoon or an electric mixer to cream the butter and sugar together. Mix the salt, baking powder, and flour together; beat the eggs with the milk.

❸ Add about a third of the dry ingredients to the butter-sugar mixture, then moisten with a little of the milk. Repeat until all the ingredients are used up. The batter should be lumpy, not smooth, and thick but moist; add a little more milk or other liquid if necessary.

❹ Spoon the batter into the muffin tins, filling them about two-thirds full and handling the batter as little as possible. (If you prefer bigger muffins, fill the cups almost to the top. Pour ¹/₄ cup water into those cups left empty.) Bake for 20 to 30 minutes, or until the muffins are nicely browned and a toothpick inserted into the center of one of them comes out clean. Remove from the oven and let rest for 5 minutes before taking them out of the tin. Serve warm.

Yogurt or Buttermilk Biscuits

MAKES: 10 or more biscuits, depending on size

TIME: 20 to 30 minutes

The easiest and best way to make biscuits is with yogurt, because the results are tangy, tender, and flaky. Buttermilk is my second choice, but if you have neither just make the Baking Powder Biscuits variation. For an extra-soft crumb, use cake flour. Vary these biscuits with any of the ideas listed in "12 Additions to Virtually Any Quick Bread, Muffin, Biscuit, or Scone" (page 688).

2 cups all-purpose or cake flour, plus more as needed

1 scant teaspoon salt

1 tablespoon baking powder

1 teaspoon baking soda

2 to 5 tablespoons cold butter (more is better)

⁷/₈ cup yogurt or buttermilk

❶ Preheat the oven to 450°F.

❷ Mix the dry ingredients together in a bowl or food processor. Cut the butter into bits and either pulse it in the food processor (easier) or pick up a bit of the dry ingredients, rub them with the butter between your fingers, and drop them again. Make sure all the butter is thoroughly blended into the flour mixture before proceeding.

 Fast Make Ahead Ⓥ Vegan

③ Use a large spoon to stir in the yogurt just until the mixture forms a ball. Turn the dough out onto a lightly floured surface and knead it 10 times; no more. If it is very sticky, add a little flour, but very little; it should still stick to your hands a little.

④ Press the dough into a $3/4$-inch-thick rectangle and cut into 2-inch rounds with a biscuit cutter or glass. Put the rounds on an ungreased baking sheet. Gently reshape the leftover dough and cut again.

⑤ Bake for 7 to 9 minutes, or until the biscuits are a beautiful golden brown. Serve within 15 minutes for them to be at their best.

Baking Powder Biscuits. Slightly different flavor but good texture: Increase the baking powder by a teaspoon and omit the soda. Use sweet milk in place of yogurt or buttermilk.

Drop ("Emergency") Biscuits. Not quite as good, though you'll save 5 minutes: Increase the yogurt or buttermilk to 1 cup and drop tablespoons of the dough onto a greased baking sheet. Bake as in the main recipe.

Sweet Potato Biscuits. Southern-style goodness; great with Creamy Peanut Soup (page 125): Grease the baking sheets. Stir 1 cup cooked, drained, and puréed sweet potato or winter squash into the butter-flour mixture. Add only enough yogurt or buttermilk to form the dough into a ball, usually between $1/2$ and $3/4$ cup (if your potatoes are very dry, you may need the whole $7/8$ cup. Roll the dough a little thinner— about $1/2$ inch thick. Cut as directed, into about 24 biscuits, and bake at 450°F for 12 to 15 minutes.

Scones

MAKES: 10 or more scones
TIME: 20 minutes

Ⓜ

Real scones are just ultra-rich biscuits, with cream as the primary ingredient. Sure, you can use milk, but then they won't be nearly as flaky and light. Substitute something from "12 Additions to Virtually Any Quick Bread, Muffin, Biscuit, or Scone" (page 688) for the currants or raisins if you like.

2 cups (about 9 ounces) all-purpose or cake flour, plus more as needed

1 scant teaspoon salt

1 tablespoon plus 1 teaspoon baking powder

2 tablespoons sugar

5 tablespoons cold butter

3 eggs

$3/4$ cup cream

$1/3$ cup dried currants or raisins

① Preheat the oven to 450°F.

② Mix the dry ingredients together in a bowl or food processor, reserving 1 tablespoon of the sugar. Cut the butter into bits and either pulse it in the food processor (easier) or pick up a bit of the dry ingredients, rub them with the butter between your fingers, and drop them again. Make sure all the butter is thoroughly blended into the flour mixture before proceeding.

③ Beat 2 of the eggs with the cream; with a few swift strokes, combine with the dry ingredients. Fold in the currants. Turn the dough out onto a lightly floured surface and knead it 10 times; no more. If it is very sticky, add a little flour, but very little; it should still stick to your hands a little.

④ Press the dough into a $3/4$-inch-thick rectangle and cut into 2-inch rounds with a biscuit cutter or glass. Place the rounds on an ungreased baking sheet. Gently reshape the leftover dough and cut again; this recipe will produce 10 to 14 scones. Beat the remaining egg with 1 tablespoon of water and brush the top of each scone; sprinkle each with a little of the remaining sugar.

⑤ Bake for 7 to 9 minutes, or until the scones are a beautiful golden brown. These keep better than biscuits but should still be eaten the same day you make them.

Cheese Shortbread

MAKES: 30 to 40 puffs
TIME: 30 minutes

Ⓕ Ⓜ

After just one of these crisp, melt-in-your-mouth snacks you'll never want another of those bright orange cheese puffs (gougères). The dough can be made ahead of time or the shortbreads baked a day ahead and stored in an airtight container, making them ideal for parties.

8 tablespoons (1 stick) cold butter, cubed

2 cups grated Emmental, Gruyère, cheddar cheese, or other semihard cheese

1 1/2 cups all-purpose flour

1 egg, lightly beaten

1/2 teaspoon salt

1/2 teaspoon cayenne

1 tablespoon paprika (optional)

1 Preheat the oven to 400°F. Put the butter, cheese, flour, egg, salt, and cayenne into a food processor and pulse, just until the mixture resembles coarse meal; do not overprocess. (You can also use a pastry blender or a fork to cut the mixture to the same consistency.) Wrap the dough in plastic and refrigerate until you're ready to bake the puffs or proceed.

2 Form the dough into 1-inch balls. Put the balls 2 inches apart in rows on a nonstick or lightly greased baking sheet. Slightly flatten each ball with your fingers.

3 Bake until the pastries are puffed and golden brown, about 10 minutes. Cool completely on a wire rack, then sprinkle with paprika and serve.

Blue Cheese Shortbread. All blue cheese makes the puffs an unattractive gray color; a half-and-half ratio still gives you that tangy blue cheese flavor and an appealing color: Substitute 1 cup crumbled blue cheese for a cup of the Emmental.

Pecorino Cheese Shortbread. Add Italian sheep cheese for great, tangy flavor: Substitute 1 cup each grated pecorino and Parmesan for the Emmental.

Herbed Cheese Shortbread. A simple addition: Add 1/4 cup chopped mixed fresh herbs like parsley, chives, dill, and/or basil, with a little tarragon.

Spiced Cheese Shortbread. A pinch of spice changes everything. Use 2 to 3 teaspoons garam masala or hot curry powder (to make your own, see page 815) for an Indian flair, caraway for an Eastern European flavor, or toasted cumin seeds for a North African twist.

Doughnut Puffs, Sweet or Savory

MAKES: About 2 dozen
TIME: 30 minutes

Ⓕ

For everyone who craves bread and pastry, fried dough is the ultimate decadence; no wonder virtually every culture has both sweet and savory versions of it. This recipe is basically a pâte à choux, a fancy but simple pastry that begins by cooking butter, water, and flour into a pastelike batter. It's quick, versatile, and can be baked instead of fried, which makes an even easier fresh hot bread. See the variations for some specific ideas, then start experimenting.

Peanut or neutral oil, like grapeseed or corn, for frying

1 tablespoon granulated sugar

8 tablespoons (1 stick) butter

1/4 teaspoon salt

1 cup all-purpose flour

3 eggs

1/4 cup confectioners' sugar for dusting

1 Put at least 2 inches oil in a countertop deep-fryer or in a deep pan on the stove and turn the heat to medium-high; bring to 350°F (see "Deep-Frying," page 26).

Ⓕ Fast   Ⓜ Make Ahead   Ⓥ Vegan

② Combine the sugar, butter, salt, and 1 cup of water in a saucepan over high heat and bring to a boil. Turn the heat down to low and add the flour all at once. Stir constantly until the mixture pulls away from the pan and forms a ball, about 30 seconds. Remove from the heat and beat the eggs one at a time into the mixture, stirring until smooth after each addition.

③ Carefully drop spoonfuls of the dough into the hot oil, only as many as will fit comfortably at once. Cook, turning as they brown, for a total of 5 to 10 minutes.

④ Use a slotted spoon to remove the doughnuts from the oil and drain them on paper towels. Put the confectioners' sugar in a shaker or tea strainer and immediately dust the tops with powdered sugar. Serve hot or at least warm.

Churros. The easy way or the authentic way: Instead of confectioners' sugar, combine $^1/_2$ cup granulated sugar with 1 teaspoon ground cinnamon on a plate. Follow the recipe through Step 2. Then you can either drop the dough into the hot oil (the easy way) or make the signature churro sticks by spooning it into a pastry bag with a large star tip (more authentic). Press strips of dough about 4 inches long into the hot oil. Proceed with the recipe, rolling the hot churros around in the cinnamon-sugar mixture before serving.

Fruit Fritters. Try unexpected fruits like figs, pineapple, or papaya or more common ones like apples, berries, peaches, or plums: Trim, peel, and cut the desired fruit into slices or chunks. You should have about 2 cups. Sprinkle with a little sugar and put in a strainer to drain excess juice. Prepare the dough as directed in Steps 1 and 2. Heat the oil. Now either dip large pieces of fruit in dough or fold several smaller pieces of fruit into a spoonful of dough to form a loose ball. Either way, carefully put the fritters into the hot fat and proceed with the recipe.

Savory Doughnuts. Endless seasoning possibilities: Omit the granulated and confectioners' sugar. Increase the salt to $^1/_2$ teaspoon. Prepare a seasoning for the hot doughnuts: coarse salt, smoked or sweet paprika, any spice blend (see pages 810–819), or grated Parmesan cheese, for example. Proceed with the recipe, dusting the hot doughnuts with seasoning before serving.

Cheese Puffs. Another name for gougères: Omit the granulated and confectioners' sugar. After mixing in the eggs in Step 2, stir in 1 cup grated melting cheese, like Gruyère, Emmental, or cheddar, and 1 cup hard cheese like Parmesan or manchego. Proceed with the main recipe or the following Baked Puffs variation.

Baked Puffs. A lot less mess and fat: Instead of preparing oil for deep frying, preheat the oven to 425°F. Line a couple baking sheets with parchment paper or grease them or use nonstick sheets. Prepare any of the preceding sweet or savory doughs; drop spoonfuls onto the baking sheets. Bake until crisp and golden, 10 to 15 minutes.

Cream Puffs. Also known as *profiteroles* and even better with thinned Chocolate Ganache (see page 860) drizzled on top: Prepare a custard recipe (page 863) or whip and sweeten to taste 2 cups of whipping cream (see page 856). Prepare the main recipe, only instead of preparing oil for deep frying, bake as in Baked Puffs. After the puffs have cooled a bit, carefully cut them in half like a sandwich roll and spoon in some of the prepared custard or cream; replace the top.

The Basics of Unleavened Flatbreads

These easy-to-mix, easy-to-handle doughs are shaped simply by pressing or rolling. I say "simply"—even though some home cooks have an innate fear of rolling pins—because, as with pizza (which is also a flatbread), it's not important if the resulting breads and crackers are perfectly round. Who cares? They're all delicious and appealing looking, whether they come out oval, squarish, or amoeba shaped. Once you free yourself of the stress of creating perfect circles, shaping becomes an utterly simple and fast task. (Though the fact is that if I can make near-circles—and I can—so can you.)

Unleavened breads have neither yeast nor baking powder or soda to make the dough rise. But this doesn't mean they're dense: Each has a unique texture unlike any of their leavened cousins, and some are quite light.

Crackers

MAKES: 4 servings

TIME: About 15 minutes

Homemade crackers are super-easy to make, with lots of room for improvising. You can blend a little cheese, nuts, garlic, or herbs into the dough before rolling or replace some of the white flour with whole wheat, rye, or cornmeal. Or just before baking, dust the tops with coarse salt, sesame seeds, or poppy seeds. It's virtually impossible to overwork the dough since you are essentially looking for all crust, so it can become completely tough. Use oil and these are vegan.

> 1 cup all-purpose flour, plus more for rolling
>
> $^1/_2$ teaspoon salt
>
> 2 tablespoons butter or neutral oil, like grapeseed or corn

1 Preheat the oven to 400°F. Lightly dust 2 baking sheets with flour or put a baking stone in the oven. Put the flour, salt, and butter in a food processor and pulse until combined. Add about $^1/_4$ cup of water and let the machine run for a bit; continue to add water a little at a time until the mixture holds together but is not sticky.

2 Roll out the dough on a lightly floured surface until $^1/_4$ inch thick or even thinner, adding flour as needed. Score lightly with a sharp knife or razor if you want to break the crackers into nice squares or rectangles later on.

3 Use a spatula, pastry blade, or peel to transfer the crackers to the prepared baking sheets or stone. Bake until lightly browned, about 10 minutes. Cool on a rack; serve warm or at room temperature or store in a tin for up to a couple days.

Cream Crackers. Rich and delicious, they really need nothing on top but a little salt: Increase the butter to 4 tablespoons ($^1/_2$ stick). Substitute milk or cream for the water.

Parmesan Crackers. Perfect with salads or grilled vegetables: In Step 1, add $^1/_2$ cup grated Parmesan cheese to the mixture in the food processor.

The Simplest Indian-Style Flatbread

Chapati

MAKES: 4 servings

TIME: At least 1 hour

True chapatis are made with a finely ground whole wheat flour (called *atta* or *chapati flour*) and then quickly twice-cooked—first on a dry griddle and then over an open flame—so that the dough traps steam and puffs up dramatically. If you have a gas stove or can combine the main recipe with the grilled variation, you can duplicate this technique with just a little extra work. But fortunately, the straight recipe here still makes a bread that is unbelievably simple, nutritious, and delicious.

You can mix the dough in advance, but chapatis must be eaten immediately after a batch is cooked. Line a basket or plate with a cloth napkin before starting, and as the chapatis come off the griddle, pile them up and wrap loosely. This will keep them warm while you cook the rest.

Eat chapati with any food, Indian or not. They're best with stews and soups, especially bean dishes and their traditional accompaniment, dals (pages 600–604).

2¼ cups whole wheat flour

1 cup all-purpose flour, plus more for dusting

1 teaspoon salt

1 Set a fine-mesh strainer or a flour sifter over the bowl of a food processor, add the flours, and sift. Discard the coarse bran or save for another use.

2 Add the salt to the flour mixture and, with the machine running, pour in 1 cup of warm water. Process for about 30 seconds, then remove the cover. The dough should be in a well-defined, barely sticky, easy-to-handle ball. If it's too dry, add more water 1 tablespoon at a time and process for 5 or 10 seconds after each addition. If too wet, which is unlikely, add a tablespoon or two of flour and process briefly. Turn the dough out onto a lightly floured surface, cover, and let rest for at least 30 minutes or up to 2 hours. (The dough may be made ahead to this point, wrapped tightly in plastic, and refrigerated for up to a day; bring to room temperature before proceeding.)

3 Pinch off pieces of dough; the recipe will make 8 to 12 chapatis. Using flour as necessary, pat each piece into a 4-inch disk. Dust lightly with flour to keep them from sticking and cover them with plastic or a damp cloth while you pat out the others and set aside until you finish all the pieces. (It's okay to overlap them a bit, but don't stack them.)

4 Put a griddle or cast-iron or stainless-steel skillet over medium heat. When it's hot, roll out a disk until it's fairly thin, about ⅛ inch, dusting as necessary with flour; the shape doesn't matter (as long as it fits on the griddle or pan). Pat off the excess flour and put the chapati on the griddle or pan, count to 15 or so, then use a spatula to flip and cook the other side until it starts to blister, char, and puff up a bit, about a minute. (Use this time to finish rolling out the next disk.) Turn and cook the first side again, until dark and toasty smelling. Transfer to the cloth-lined basket and repeat until all are cooked. Serve immediately.

Grilled Chapati. Rustic, smoky, and puffy. Perfect for when you've already got a fire going and have some room on the grill: Heat a charcoal or gas grill until moderately hot and put the rack about 4 inches from the heat source. Oil the grates well. If you have the space, take the disks outside for the final rolling. If not, roll all the chapatis out, flour them well, and stack between layers of wax or parchment paper. Cook the chapatis, several at a time, as described in Step 4, only directly on the grill grates instead of the griddle.

4 Ways to Vary Chapati Dough

1. Replace up to ½ cup of the whole wheat flour with cornmeal, brown rice flour, or chickpea flour (besan; see page 633).
2. Replace the all-purpose flour with whole wheat; the dough will be slightly more difficult to handle, but the results are delicious.
3. Reduce the water to ½ to ¾ cup and add ½ cup yogurt to the flour at the same time.
4. Brush the chapati with oil, coconut milk, or melted butter during cooking.

Flaky Indian-Style Flatbread

Paratha

MAKES: 8 to 12

TIME: At least 1 hour

Unlike chapati (the preceding recipe), this dough is enriched with butter or oil, which gives it a lovely flaky texture. (Use oil if you want the parathas to be vegan.) Like chapatis, these must be eaten immediately after being cooked: Line a basket or plate with a cloth napkin before starting and, as they finish, pile them up and wrap loosely.

You can also grill these; follow the directions in the variation for grilling chapatis.

1½ cups whole wheat flour, or more as needed

1½ cups all-purpose flour

1 teaspoon salt

About 4 tablespoons (½ stick) melted butter or about ¼ cup neutral oil, like grapeseed or corn

① Combine the flours and salt in a food processor. Turn the machine on and add $3/4$ cup water through the feed tube. Process for about 30 seconds, adding more water, a little at a time, until the mixture forms a ball and is slightly sticky to the touch. If it's dry, add another tablespoon or two of water and process for another 10 seconds. (In the unlikely event that the mixture is too sticky, add flour a tablespoon at a time.) Remove the dough and, using flour as necessary, shape into a ball; wrap in plastic and let rest for at least 20 minutes or up to several hours at room temperature. (Or refrigerate for up to a day or freeze for up to a week.)

② Pinch off pieces of dough; the recipe will make 8 to 12 parathas. Using flour as necessary, roll each piece into a 4-inch disk and brush with melted butter or oil. Roll up like a cigar, then into a coil not unlike a cinnamon bun; set aside until you finish all the pieces.

③ Put a griddle or cast-iron or skillet over medium heat. When it's hot, press one of the coils flat, then roll it out into a thin disk. Put on the griddle or pan and cook until lightly browned on one side, 3 to 5 minutes; brush the top with butter or oil, flip, and brown on the second side, another few minutes. Continue until all the breads are done, then serve.

Spinach Paratha. Almost as easy but with a great twist: Cook 1 pound of fresh spinach and squeeze well to dry (see page 239). In Step 1, add the spinach and a squeeze of lemon juice along with the oil and process as directed, adding more water or flour as needed. Proceed with the recipe.

Flaky Indian-Style Flatbread Stuffed with Potato

Aloo Paratha

MAKES: 8 to 12
TIME: At least 1 hour

I adore this bread and was fortunate enough to learn how to make it from an expert, the great Indian cook and cookbook writer Julie Sahni. This is essentially her recipe, though I've modified it over the years.

You can cook this paratha ahead and keep it at room temperature for up to 24 hours to serve without reheating or warm it briefly in a dry skillet or even a microwave. But there is nothing like one fresh from the skillet.

Ajwain comes from carom seeds, which look like celery but taste like very strong, slightly coarse thyme.

$1^{1}/_{2}$ cups whole wheat flour

$1^{1}/_{2}$ cups all-purpose flour, plus more for rolling

Salt

1 teaspoon ajwain, dried thyme, or ground cumin

2 tablespoons neutral oil, like grapeseed or corn, plus more for brushing the breads

$1^{1}/_{2}$ pounds baking potatoes, peeled and cut in half

1 jalapeño or other hot chile, seeded and minced

2 teaspoons ground coriander

Freshly ground black pepper

Juice of $1/_{2}$ small lemon

Melted butter (optional)

① Combine the flours with 1 teaspoon salt and the ajwain in a food processor. Turn the machine on and add the oil and $3/4$ cup water through the feed tube. Process for about 30 seconds, adding more water, a little at a time, until the mixture forms a ball and is slightly sticky to the touch. If it's dry, add another tablespoon or two of water and process for another 10 seconds. (In the unlikely event that the mixture is too sticky, add all-purpose flour, a tablespoon at a time.) Remove the dough and, using flour as necessary, shape into a ball; wrap in plastic and let rest while you make the potato mixture. (Or refrigerate for up to a day or freeze for up to a week.)

② Put the potatoes in a large saucepan and add water to cover and a large pinch of salt. Bring to a boil over high heat, then turn the heat down so the mixture simmers steadily; cook until the potatoes are tender, 15 to 20 minutes, then drain. Mash with the chile, coriander, a large pinch of salt, some pepper, and the lemon juice;

F Fast   M Make Ahead   V Vegan

taste and adjust the seasoning (you may prefer more chile; sometimes aloo paratha is quite hot).

③ When the dough has rested, set out a bowl of flour and a small bowl of neutral oil, with a spoon or brush, on your work surface. Lightly flour your work surface and your rolling pin. Break off a piece of dough about the size of a golf ball. Toss it in the bowl of flour and then roll it in your hands to make a ball. Flatten it into a 2-inch disk, then use a floured rolling pin to roll it into a thin round, about 5 inches in diameter, dusting with flour as necessary.

④ Mound about 2 tablespoons of the filling into the center of one of the rounds of dough. Bring the edges of the round up over the top of the filling and press them together to make a pouch. Press down on the "neck" of the pouch with the palm of one hand to make a slightly rounded disk. Turn the disk in the bowl of flour and roll it out again into a round, about 6 to 7 inches in diameter. Pat it between your hands to brush off the excess flour. Put the paratha on a plate and cover with a sheet of plastic wrap. Continue to roll all of the remaining dough into parathas and stack them on the plate with a sheet of plastic wrap between them. You can keep the paratha stacked like this for an hour or two in the refrigerator before cooking them if necessary.

⑤ Heat a griddle or cast-iron skillet over medium-high heat for a minute or two, then put a paratha (or two if they'll fit) on and cook until it darkens slightly, usually less than a minute. Flip the paratha with a spatula and cook for another 30 seconds on the second side. Use the back of a spoon or a brush to coat the top of the paratha with oil. Flip and coat the other side with oil. Continue cooking the paratha until the bottom of the bread has browned, flip, and repeat. Do this a few times until both sides of the paratha are golden brown and very crisp, 2 to 3 minutes total for each paratha. As the parathas finish, remove them from the pan and brush with melted butter if you're going to serve hot; otherwise wait until you've reheated them.

Cauliflower Paratha. Traditional and similar, but with that distinctive cauliflower flavor: Instead of the pota-toes, use 1 small head cauliflower. Use mustard seeds instead of the ground coriander.

The Basics of Yeast Bread

You can make very good yeast bread today even if you've never made it before—really. If you have a food processor, you can be pulling it from the oven two or three hours from now. You can make it even faster if you push. And it'll be good, very good, better than what is served to you in most restaurants.

But I don't want to kid you: To make great bread, the kind that makes you think you should be eating bread at every meal, the kind that makes you really proud, is an accomplishment. It takes practice, even skill, good ingredients, much more time (though not much more work once you get the rhythm down), and even a bit of luck. More than most foods, bread is alive; yeast, even today's standardized yeast, is a little unpredictable. And the best breads are risen with a bit of sourdough, or at least a sponge, and not entirely by yeast.

Do not fear. As I said, you can produce very good bread right away and get 90 percent down the road to great bread in a season of bread making. The last 10 percent is the hardest, and, except for a couple of great home bread makers I know, few of us make it there (I, for example, have not).

Equipment

What you don't want is a bread machine. What you absolutely need is a bowl and a wooden spoon and an oven. In between, there are ranges of requirements. Here's what I have, and what I recommend you acquire eventually, if not all at once.

A food processor. If you're going to cook regularly, you want one anyway; after the refrigerator, and maybe the dishwasher, it's the most useful kitchen appliance invented in the twentieth century. What it does for bread making is remarkable; it turns the process of making dough from a laborious chore (which has its upsides, especially if you're a Zen type, but nevertheless discourages many people from even getting started) into a task that takes less than a minute. Literally. The hardest part is washing the workbowl afterward (and that's where the dishwasher comes in!).

A pizza stone. You buy one (see Sources, page 929), shove it in your oven, and forget about it. It can stay there forever, won't hurt anything else you cook in there, and will noticeably improve your breads as well as crank the quality of your pizza up about ten notches.

An instant-read thermometer. You should have one anyway.

A small strainer. A good tool for dusting flour; not essential, but nice.

A 5-pound bag of garden stones. This is getting a little advanced, but steam makes great bread (professional bread ovens have steam injectors). Hold off on buying these until you get frustrated with crusts that are just too hard and want something a little more on the tender-crisp side.

That's it. You don't need bread pans, at least for European-style breads (you will for sandwich loaves, of course). And you can live without all of the above, although if you become a devoted or even a regular bread maker you'll wind up getting them eventually.

Ingredients

Pretty simple, really. All-purpose flour is good, bread flour is better; see page 680 for details. A bit of rye or whole wheat adds flavor, variety, and of course some fiber. You need yeast; I prefer instant (see page 683), because it's the most convenient. Water and salt: The best you have, but from the tap and the table are just fine. A bit of olive oil now and then is a nice addition. And then of course you can add whatever flavorings you want, but I'm talking the basics here.

Making the Dough

Dough making is the key to good bread making; starting with the wrong dough will guarantee an unsatisfactory bread no matter how perfect your baking. Starting with the right dough, however, will usually give you a good bread even if everything else is imperfect.

Many of the best breads begin with a sponge or a sourdough starter; it isn't much more work, but it takes hours longer than the simplest bread, which begins by tossing the ingredients together in the food processor.

Eventually you will learn to mix and knead and judge dough by sight and feel alone (really); for now, just follow the recipes, which are detailed enough. I swear a ten-year-old child can make very good dough on the first try by following these directions. Make dough by hand once or twice if you want to get a sense of history or of how it feels when it all comes together; or don't. (And I must pause here to thank, once again, the guru of food processor dough making, Charlie Van Over, who didn't invent the process but has nearly perfected it and made it accessible and logical.)

Kneading—which can be done entirely in the food processor—allows the flour-and-water mixture to develop gluten (page 708), the protein that gives bread structure, chewiness, and essentially the character you're looking for. The food processor is ideal because it allows you to maximize the water-to-flour ratio, and the best yeast doughs for rustic-style breads are difficult to handle with your hands. This is why food processor dough is not only easier but better than hand-kneaded dough: The food processor doesn't care how sticky the dough is; in fact, it should be rough looking, what bakers call "nearly shaggy," halfway through the processing. It becomes a smooth ball when you continue to process beyond this point—the part of the processing that is the machine kneading.

Rising the Dough

Within limits, slower rising is better; it allows flavor to develop and improves the final product in subtle but noticeable ways. Some bakers rush through the rising

 Fast   Make Ahead   Ⓥ Vegan

period by increasing the amount of yeast (a practice I do not recommend because it's hard to control) or by letting the dough rise in a warm (no more than 110°F) oven, but if you have the time, you might consider a schedule like this: Mix the dough in the morning, let it rise at room temperature until noon or early afternoon, then shape it (or deflate the dough and allow it to rise again) and let it rest for another hour or more before baking. Contrary to older recipe directions, there are no precise rising times; dough is really quite flexible.

Shaping the Dough

I guess this is the hard part, though it's also the most fun. And it's a matter of taste. You can use your dough to make small rolls or baguettes, which are the trickiest route, or you can make a big round, almost free-form loaf, which is probably the easiest. You can use loaf pans (or baguette pans, though I find them more trouble than they're worth because the dough tends to get stuck in the holes in the pan).

You can make any shape you like with basic bread dough, including pizza (see page 721). Just remember to lightly flour all your work surfaces before putting the dough on them (you can use cornmeal if you prefer, which will add a little crunch to the bread). Following are illustrations for making the most popular shapes.

A boule ("ball" in French), or free-form loaf, is the simplest shape. Take the risen dough and turn it in your hands, shaping it into a round ball (you can make a long oval if you prefer) and smoothing it over so that the seams are on the bottom. Pinch the seams closed. For the final rising, line a medium bowl with a clean towel and sift a bit of flour onto it. Put the dough ball, seam side

SHAGGY VS. SMOOTH DOUGH

Dough about halfway through the mixing process—note that it's still quite shaggy.

When the dough is ready, it will be ball shaped and easy to handle.

KNEADING DOUGH

1

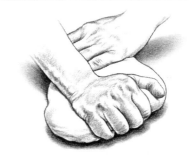

2

(STEP 1) Using as little flour as possible, press the lump of dough down with your hands. (STEP 2) Repeatedly fold and press until the dough becomes far less sticky and quite elastic.

SHAPING BOULES

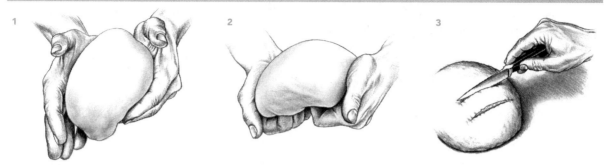

(STEP 1) To make a boule, or round loaf, shape the dough into a ball. (STEP 2) Working around the ball, continually tuck the dough toward the center of the bottom, stretching the top slightly and creating surface tension. Pinch together the seam created at the bottom of the dough. (STEP 3) Just before baking, make a few shallow slashes in the surface of the dough.

SHAPING ROLLS

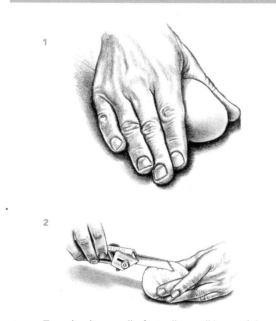

(STEP 1) To make dinner rolls, first roll a small lump of dough on a lightly floured surface until the seam is closed and smooth. (STEP 2) Just before baking, make a few shallow slashes in the surface of the dough.

up, in the towel; sprinkle with little more flour and fold the towel over the top. Let rise for at least an hour and preferably two or three. To bake, turn the dough over onto a lightly floured peel, wooden board, or flexible cutting board, slash it, and slide directly onto a pizza stone or turn it onto a lightly oiled baking sheet, slash it, and put the sheet into the preheated oven.

To make rolls, simply divide the dough into anywhere from six to twelve pieces and shape each as you would a boule. Treat them the same way from that point on, though baking time will obviously be shorter.

Baguettes are a little more complicated, but easy enough with practice. Press the dough into a rectangle; it may be any length that will fit into your oven. Fold each long side of the rectangle up into the middle, then roll into a log and use your fingers to press the resulting seam together tightly. If you'd like, you can then shape the loaf into a ring, just by pinching the ends together. Spread a large piece of heavy canvas or cotton (you can use a large tablecloth, folded into quarters to give it extra stiffness) on a table or countertop and sprinkle it lightly with flour. Or use baguette pans, sifting a little bit of flour into them or oiling them lightly. Cover if necessary and let rise for 1 to 2 hours at room temperature; the loaves will be about one and a half times their original size.

Ⓕ Fast   Ⓜ Make Ahead   Ⓥ Vegan

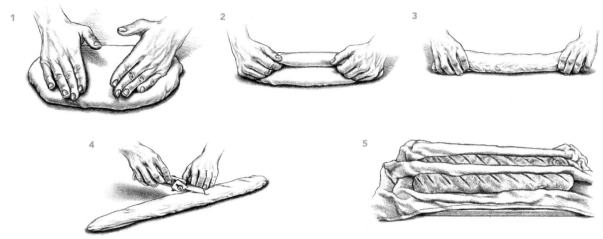

(STEP 1) Press the dough into a rectangle of any length that will fit into your oven. (STEP 2) Fold each long side of the rectangle up into the middle. (STEP 3) Roll into a log and use your fingers to press the resulting seam together tightly. (STEP 4) Just before baking, make a few shallow slashes in the surface of the dough. (STEP 5) You can create a couche for your baguettes to rise with a piece of heavy canvas, a towel, or a tablecloth.

If you'd like, you can start by making a baguette (STEPS 1 THROUGH 3) and shape the loaf into a ring or crown.

Slashing

To allow some of the steam built up in the dough to escape in a controlled fashion, most bakers slash the top of their dough in several places just before baking. It's not essential, but it usually results in a more attractive loaf. Use a sharp knife or razor blade; with baguettes, make three or four crosswise cuts, each about $1/4$ inch deep. With boules, make a crosshatch or similar pattern. With rolls, just make an X.

Baking

Baking technique is important (it's easy, though), especially when you start to fine-tune your baking. This is where the pizza stone and rocks come in. Preheat the oven to 400°F (higher if you want a thick, hard crust). Give it a good half hour, even more, to come to temperature, especially if you have a pizza stone. While it's heating, put in it an ovenproof pot (preferably cast iron) half-filled with rocks. This will absorb heat like mad and hold it there. Boil some water. Just before putting the bread in the oven, carefully pour boiling water to just over the top of the stones. You will get lots and lots of steam. (I always take my glasses off first.) Close the oven door. A minute later, start baking and turn the heat down to 375°F.

There are a zillion variations possible on this technique, but this is how I do it these days, and I'm pleased with the results. I've tried every way of getting steam into the oven, from using a spray bottle to dumping ice cubes on the bottom, but the rock technique (courtesy of the genius Beatrice Ojakangas, thank you!) works best.

At this point you can more or less ignore your bread until it's done, though I turn it after ten or fifteen minutes just to make sure it bakes evenly. I do keep an eye on

The fact is that you can tailor bread's rising schedule to your own. Here are a few possible scenarios:

The simplest is to make dough in the morning and leave it in the fridge while you're gone for six or eight or ten hours. Before you start to prepare dinner, take the dough out and shape it, let it rise, and then bake it.

Or you can mix the dough—or, better still, replenish your sourdough (page 710) or make a sponge—at night and let it rise in a cool place (or the refrigerator) overnight, then turn the sponge into dough and let it rise again throughout the day, again in a cool place or the fridge.

Since dough freezes well, you can whip up a double batch of regular dough, enough to make six dough balls. Let the dough rise all day or overnight, then divide it, wrap the balls in plastic, and toss them in the freezer. When you know you'll want bread for dinner but don't have the time or energy or foresight to make dough, remove a dough ball from the freezer when you wake up (if company is coming, take out two). This sits on the counter if you're going to be around during the day, in the fridge if you're away. Late in the afternoon, shape the dough; while making dinner, bake it. Dough balls keep well in the freezer for a few weeks; after that the yeast begins to lose power. (Dough prepared this way is really great for pizza or pita, where maximum rise is not that important.)

In a pinch, you can even skip rising: Make the dough, shape it, let it rest while you heat the oven, and bake it. This won't be the tastiest bread you've ever had, but it'll still beat most loaves you buy in the supermarket. There are many options, as you will see by the time you've made a few loaves; most of them are outlined in these pages.

Combine half the flour with the salt and yeast and stir to blend. Add all the water and stir with a wooden spoon until smooth. Add the remaining flour a bit at a time; when the mixture becomes too stiff to stir with a spoon, begin kneading (see "Making the Dough," page 702), adding as little flour as possible—just enough to keep the dough from being a sticky mess. Knead until smooth but still quite moist, about ten minutes. Proceed with the recipe.

it, but even that isn't essential as long as the heat isn't too high. Most bread is done when it makes a hollow sound when you thump it or when an instant-read thermometer inserted into the center of the loaf reads 210°F. If you're going to reheat it, which is often the case, underbaking is no big deal, and you can consider anything above 190°F "done." Boules usually take about 40 minutes, baguettes about 20, rolls about 15. But there are a lot of variables, so keep your eyes open.

Storing Bread

As I've already noted, you can store unbaked dough, well wrapped in aluminum foil or plastic, in the freezer for a couple of weeks. You can also store baked bread, wrapped in wax paper—plastic makes the crust soggy—on the counter for up to a few days (especially if you like toast); large loaves containing some whole grain flour keep better than small ones baked with just white flour, because the whole grain contains some fat (and bread baked with added fat, like those on pages 711–721, keep even better).

Baked bread can also be frozen; in this instance aluminum foil or heavy plastic bags are fine, because you'll need to recrisp the bread anyway. Unwrap, then place thawed or unthawed bread in a preheated 350°F oven for five to fifteen minutes, until thawed and crusty again.

 Fast   Make Ahead   Ⓥ Vegan

Making These Recipes with a Standing Mixer

To make yeast bread (including pizza dough) with a standing mixer, the machine must be fairly powerful or it will stall. Combine half the flour with the salt, yeast, and all of the water; blend with the machine's paddle. With the machine on slow speed, add flour a little at a time, until the mixture has become a sticky ball that pulls away from the sides of the bowl (switch to the dough hook if necessary). Knead for 1 minute by hand, adding as little flour as possible, then proceed with the recipe.

If your standing mixer is always on the counter (or you have a portable mixer), using it for quick breads might be marginally faster than making them by hand. Just be careful not to overmix: First stir the dry ingredients together in a bowl. Then, using the paddle in the mixer, cream the fat and the sugar until well blended and add the milk or other liquid in the recipe. With the machine at its lowest setting, add the dry ingredients all at once and stir until just combined; stop the machine, scrape down the sides with a spoon, and stir by hand once or twice. Don't worry about any lumps.

All of this may sound like a lot, but making bread—unlike making cakes, for example, or even brownies—offers loads of latitude. The schedule can be molded to meet your own, and as long as your yeast is alive, the chances are good you'll be far more successful than you imagine.

European-Style Yeast Breads

There was a time, in my overenthusiasm for things European, when I would have said these were the best breads in the world. I've since come to a greater appreciation for Indian breads, American-style quick breads, and even a good old anadama loaf, so I will no longer go that far. But these are great breads and ultra-rewarding to make at home. Containing nothing more than flour, water, yeast, and salt, they are miracles of nature, with great flavor and texture and amazing crust. This dough can be made in any shape, including rolls. They are not fancy; they're just nearly perfect.

Three levels of commitment here: a version that can be made very quickly, with little work; one that takes all day, also with little work; and one that takes twenty-four hours or so, with just a bit more work. Read "The Basics of Yeast Bread" (page 701) for more details.

Fast French Bread or Rolls

MAKES: 3 or 4 baguettes, 1 boule, or 12 to 16 rolls
TIME: About 2 hours, largely unattended

This bread can be made by hand or with an electric mixer (see left), but the food processor, as usual, is the tool of choice and will save you tons of time.

3$\frac{1}{2}$ cups all-purpose or bread flour, plus more as needed

2 teaspoons salt

1$\frac{1}{2}$ teaspoons instant yeast

❶ Put the flour in the food processor, add the salt and yeast, and turn the machine on. With the machine running, pour about a cup of water through the feed tube. Process until the dough forms a ball, adding a little water at a time until it becomes smooth; if the dough begins sticking to the side of the bowl, you've added too much water. No harm done: add $\frac{1}{4}$ cup or so of flour and keep going. You're looking for a moist, well-defined ball. The whole process should take about 30 seconds, and it will once you get good at it. If the dough is too dry, add water 1 tablespoon at a time and process for 5 or 10 seconds after each addition. If it is too wet, add another tablespoon or two of flour and process briefly.

The Magic of Gluten

You can't talk about baking without mentioning gluten, the magical compound that allows yeast dough to rise and gives breads their characteristic "chew." To make gluten, it takes water and two proteins, glutenin and gliadin, both of which are abundant in wheat and present (usually in much lesser quantities) in many other grains. And since these proteins are even more accessible when the grains are ground, wheat flour is extremely high in gluten.

As you mix and knead wheat-based batters or doughs, the gluten develops into a weblike structure that supports the flour's starch and other components, which in turn traps the carbon dioxide bubbles produced by yeast during fermentation (or by other leaveners, like baking powder; see page 685). This structure becomes permanent as the bread, cake, muffin, or cookie bakes and moisture evaporates to create the nooks, crannies, and air pockets we call "the crumb."

Significant gluten development is really desirable only in making crusty, chewy breads, where you can use high-protein bread flour and work the dough vigorously. When you want a tender bread crumb, it's better to start with a relatively low protein flour, like all-purpose or even cake flour, and be careful not to knead the dough too much; if you overwork a delicate yeasted pastry dough, it becomes tough. In fact, to ensure a tender crumb in quick breads, cakes, cookies, and other nonyeasted baked foods, you usually blend the flour in briefly and as lightly as possible at the end of the recipe. That's why you often see the instruction "stir only until the flour is incorporated."

Some people can't digest gluten and may develop celiac disease, a condition that impairs the ability of the small intestine to absorb nutrients. Unfortunately it is impossible to duplicate the effects of gluten exactly, though people with gluten and wheat intolerances do have some options. See "The Basics of Flour" (page 680).

2 Dump the lump of dough into a large bowl or simply remove the blade from the processor bowl and leave the dough in there. Either way, cover with a plastic bag or plastic wrap and let sit for at least an hour at room temperature.

3 Use a small strainer or your fingers to dust a counter or tabletop with a little flour. Shape the dough as you like, into small loaves, one big one, baguettes, or rolls (see the illustrations on pages 704–705), sprinkling with flour as necessary but keeping the flour to a minimum. Preheat the oven (see page 705) to 400°F while you let the loaves or rolls rest, covered with a towel.

4 When you're ready to bake, slash the top of each loaf once or twice with a razor blade or sharp knife (see pages 704–705). If the dough has risen on a cloth, slide or turn it onto floured baking sheets or gently move it onto a lightly floured peel, plank of wood, or flexible cutting board, then slide the bread directly onto a baking stone. Or you can bake on lightly oiled baking sheets. Turn the heat down to 375°F.

5 Bake until the crust is golden brown and the internal temperature of the bread is at least 210°F (it can be lower if you plan to reheat the bread later). Remove, spray with a bit of water if you would like a shinier crust, and cool on a wire rack.

More Leisurely and Flavorful French Bread or Rolls. Basically, all you do here is slow down the process, which improves the quality some: Step 1 remains the same. In Step 2, let the dough rise longer to help it develop flavor—2 or 3 hours at room temperature or up to 12 hours refrigerated (bring it back to room temperature before proceeding). In Step 3, after shaping, let the loaves or rolls rise for 2 to 3 hours (or longer, refrigerated, bringing them back to room temperature before baking). Steps 4 and 5 remain the same.

Whole Grain French Bread or Rolls. You can add color and flavor to this bread by adding whole wheat, rye, or barley flour or cornmeal, alone or in combination; or you can use a 7- or 9-grain preblended flour. Simply substi-

 F Fast   **M** Make Ahead   **V** Vegan

tute the whole grain flour for some of the all-purpose or bread flour. If you keep the addition to $1/2$ cup or less, you will retain the great texture of this bread. You may add much more—up to one-third of the total amount of flour, or just over 1 cup—and still have a very good bread with a crisp crust. Adding more than that produces the soft crust and doughy crumb typical of breads high in whole grain; better, at that point, to make one of the other breads designed specifically for whole grain, like Black Bread (page 716).

Overnight French Bread or Rolls

MAKES: 3 or 4 baguettes, 1 boule, or 12 to 16 rolls

TIME: About 24 hours, largely unattended

This bread requires two mixings, one to make a sponge and one to finish the dough. And you must start at least twelve hours before, and preferably the night before, you plan to eat the bread. Otherwise, nothing changes from the preceding Fast French Bread or Rolls recipe. If you're using a portion of whole grain flour, add up to a cup of it to the sponge for best results.

$3^{1}/_{2}$ cups bread or all-purpose flour, plus more as needed

$1^{1}/_{2}$ teaspoons instant yeast

2 teaspoons salt

❶ Put 2 cups of the flour in a food processor, add the yeast and half the salt, and turn the machine on. With the machine running, pour about a cup of water through the feed tube. Process until a smooth pancakelike batter is formed. Cover and let rest in a cool place overnight or for at least 6 hours.

❷ Add the remaining flour and salt to the mixture, turn the machine on again, and add water, a little at a time, until a moist, well-defined ball forms. If the dough begins sticking to the side of the bowl, you've added too much water; add $1/4$ cup or so of flour and keep going. If the dough is too dry, add water 1 tablespoon at a time and process for 5 or 10 seconds after each addition. If it is too wet, add another tablespoon or two of flour and process briefly.

❸ Dump the lump of dough into a large bowl or simply remove the blade from the processor bowl and leave the dough in there. Either way, cover with a plastic bag or plastic wrap and let sit for at least an hour at room temperature.

❹ Use a small strainer or your fingers to dust a counter or tabletop with a little flour. Shape the dough as you like, into small loaves, one big one, baguettes, or rolls (see the illustrations on pages 704–705), sprinkling with flour as necessary but keeping the flour to a minimum. Preheat the oven (see page 705) to 400°F while you let the breads or rolls rest, covered with a towel.

❺ When you're ready to bake, slash the top of each loaf once or twice with a razor blade or sharp knife (pages 704–705). If the dough has risen on a cloth, slide or turn it onto floured baking sheets or gently move it onto a lightly floured peel, plank of wood, or flexible cutting board, then slide the bread directly onto a baking stone. Or you can bake on lightly oiled baking sheets. Turn the heat down to 375°F.

❻ Bake until the crust is golden brown and the internal temperature of the bread is at least 210°F (it can be lower if you plan to reheat the bread later). Remove, spray with a bit of water if you would like a shinier crust, and cool on a wire rack.

Sourdough Bread

MAKES: 3 or 4 baguettes, 1 boule, or 12 to 16 rolls

TIME: At least 48 hours the first time, roughly 24 hours thereafter, largely unattended

You can make sourdough bread that's *really* sour (see the variation), but I prefer this method, which uses a bit of yeast each time; it's faster, I think it's got more complex flavor, it's easier, and it's not too sour for me. I'm including rye flour in the basic recipe because that's my favorite way to go, but you can use all white flour or mix in whole wheat instead of or in addition to rye. (As usual, you can do pretty much whatever you want with this dough; see "17 Ingredients to Add to Any Yeast Bread," page 718.)

Note that the first time you make this will take longer, because you have to create a sourdough starter (unless someone gives you one). After that it's a pretty straightforward, simple process. The starter must, however, be used every couple of weeks or so or it will die (I've left mine for a month and it ended up okay, but I felt this was risky). You can simply feed the starter some flour and water, but every time you make bread you're replenishing it, so as long as you make bread every now and then it will be fine.

4$^1/_2$ cups bread or all-purpose flour, plus more
   as needed

$^5/_8$ teaspoon instant yeast

2 teaspoons salt

1 cup rye flour

1 At least 2 days before you plan to bake the bread (3 days is better), mix together 1$^1/_2$ cups of the bread flour, $^1/_8$ teaspoon of the yeast, and 1 cup warm water. Stir with a wooden spoon, cover loosely, and place on top of your refrigerator or in some other out-of-the-way place. Stir every 8 to 12 hours; the mixture will become bubbly and eventually develop a slightly sour smell. If your kitchen is very warm, this may happen in 24 hours; usually it takes a couple of days. When it's done, you've made sourdough starter!

2 This is how you'll make the bread; begin at this step every time from now on: The night before you're ready to bake, combine the starter with 2 cups of the remaining bread flour and about 1$^1/_2$ cups of warm water. You can do this in a food processor or a bowl;

process or mix until smooth. Cover and let rest overnight; the mixture will bubble and foam a bit. (You can cut this process to 6 hours or so if you like.)

3 Transfer half the starter to a covered container and refrigerate until the next time you're going to make bread. What's left is the basis for your bread; put it in the food processor with the remaining $^1/_2$ teaspoon yeast, the salt, the rye flour, and the remaining cup of bread flour and turn the machine on. Add water (you may not need much, because the starter should be quite wet) a little at a time until a moist but well-defined ball forms. If the dough begins sticking to the side of the bowl, you've added too much water; add $^1/_4$ cup or so of flour and keep going. If the dough is too dry, add water 1 tablespoon at a time and process for 5 or 10 seconds after each addition. If too wet, add another tablespoon or two of flour and process briefly.

4 From this point on, you're making bread as you would normally: Dump the lump of dough into a large bowl or simply remove the blade from the processor bowl and leave the dough in there. Either way, cover with a plastic bag or plastic wrap and let sit for at least an hour at room temperature.

5 Use a small strainer or your fingers to dust a little flour onto a counter or tabletop. Shape the dough as you like, into small loaves, one big one, baguettes, or rolls (see the illustrations on pages 704–705), sprinkling with flour as necessary but keeping the flour to a minimum. Preheat the oven (see page 705) to 400°F while you let the breads or rolls rest, covered with a towel.

6 When you're ready to bake, slash the top of each loaf once or twice with a razor blade or sharp knife (see pages 704–705). If the dough has risen on a cloth, slide or turn it onto floured baking sheets or gently move it onto a lightly floured peel, plank of wood, or flexible cutting board, then slide the bread directly onto a baking stone. Or you can bake on lightly oiled baking sheets. Turn the heat down to 375°F.

7 Bake until the crust is golden brown and the internal temperature of the bread is at least 210°F (it can be lower if you plan to reheat the bread later). Remove,

    F Fast   **M** Make Ahead   **V** Vegan

spray with a bit of water if you would like a shinier crust, and cool on a wire rack.

Breadsticks

MAKES: 50 to 100

TIME: A day or so, largely unattended

In Piedmont, Italy—where breadsticks are called *grissini*—you wouldn't bother to adorn these with anything. But their slightly sweet flavor is also good with a sprinkling of poppy seeds or sea salt right before baking. To make them rustic looking, roll the strips of dough lightly on the countertop—they'll get skinny and crooked. If you want a more professional appearance, cut them with a pastry wheel or use a pasta machine (see Step 4).

3 cups all-purpose or bread flour

2 teaspoons instant yeast

1 teaspoon sugar

2 teaspoons salt

2 tablespoons extra virgin olive oil, plus more as needed

$1/2$ cup semolina flour or cornmeal

1 Combine the flour, yeast, sugar, and salt in a food processor; pulse once or twice. Add the oil and pulse a couple of times. With the machine running, add 1 cup warm water through the feed tube. Continue to add water, a tablespoon at a time, until the mixture forms a ball. It should be a little shaggy and quite sticky.

2 Put a little oil in a bowl and transfer the dough ball to it, turning to coat well. Cover with plastic wrap and let it rise for 1 hour in a warm place. Reshape the ball, put it back in the bowl, cover again, and let rise in the refrigerator for several hours or, preferably, overnight.

3 Preheat the oven to 400°F. Lightly grease 2 baking sheets with olive oil and sprinkle very lightly with semolina flour or cornmeal.

4 Cut the dough into 3 pieces; keep 2 covered while you work with the other. To roll by hand: On a well-floured surface, roll a piece of dough out as thinly as possible into a large rectangle, about a foot long. Use a sharp knife or pastry wheel to cut the dough into roughly $1/4$-inch-thick strips (slightly smaller is better than slightly bigger).

To roll with a pasta machine: Roll out the dough to $1/4$-inch thickness by hand. Put it through the machine at the largest setting, then cut it using the fettuccine setting and cut the strips into 1-foot lengths.

5 Transfer the strips to the baking sheets, spaced apart, and brush with olive oil. Bake until crisp and golden, 10 to 20 minutes, then cool completely on wire racks. Serve immediately or store in an airtight container for up to 1 week.

Herbed Breadsticks. Add to the dough mixture 2 teaspoons fresh rosemary, thyme, or sage along with the olive oil.

Parmesan Breadsticks. Try dipping in tomato sauce: Add up to $3/4$ cup grated Parmesan cheese to the food processor along with the flour in Step 1.

Olive or Dried Tomato Breadsticks. Darkly colored and full flavored: Before beginning to make the dough in Step 1, use the food processor to purée $1/2$ cup pitted olives (green or black) or dried tomatoes along with the olive oil (instead of adding it after the flour). Then add the dry ingredients to the processor and proceed with the recipe.

Sesame Rice Breadsticks. Fun to serve with Asian dishes: Replace 1 cup of the flour with brown rice flour. Sprinkle the breadsticks with light or black sesame seeds before baking.

Sandwich Breads

The difference between dough for European-style breads and American-style sandwich loaves is not only shape: It's fat. Though you can make any dough any shape you like, sandwich breads tend to have a softer crust, a finer crumb, and a more tender texture, which makes them easier to slice and easier to eat. You achieve these textural changes by adding fat, usually in the form of milk and sometimes butter as well. (Vegan versions of sandwich bread are easy to make; just use oil and nondairy milk, as suggested below.)

Like that for any bread, the dough for sandwich breads can be made in a food processor pretty quickly. Because they don't depend on the interaction between yeast and flour for all of their flavor, sandwich breads generally have quicker rising times and are almost always made directly, without sponges or sourdough; so in some ways they're actually easier than many of the European-style loaves. Beginners may find them a tad tricky to shape, but you'll quickly get the hang of that.

Sandwich Bread, 6 Ways

MAKES: 1 large loaf
TIME: At least 3 hours, largely unattended

The typical white bread is not only richer than the European-style breads on pages 707–711 but also typically baked in a loaf pan, which helps to keep the crust tender. To make this bread by hand or with a standing mixer, follow the guidelines on page 706 or 707. You can make this bread vegan by substituting nondairy milk.

3$^1/_2$ cups all-purpose flour, plus more as needed

2 teaspoons salt

1$^1/_2$ teaspoons instant yeast

1 tablespoon sugar or honey, or more to taste

SHAPING A SANDWICH LOAF

(STEP 1) If the dough has risen in an oiled bowl, you need no flour; otherwise, work on a very lightly floured surface. Use the heel of your hand to form the dough into a rectangle. (STEP 2) Fold the long sides of the rectangle over to the middle. (STEP 3) Pinch the seam closed, pressing tightly with your fingers. (STEP 4) Fold under the ends of the loaf. (STEP 5) Use the back of your hand to press the loaf firmly into the pan.

Ⓕ Fast   Ⓜ Make Ahead   Ⓥ Vegan

2 tablespoons neutral oil, like grapeseed or corn, or butter (at room temperature if you're working by hand), plus more for the bowl and the pan

Scant 1^1/$_3$ cups cool milk, preferably whole or 2 percent (warm the milk to at least 70°F if you're working by hand)

1 Put the flour in a food processor, add the salt and yeast, and process for 5 seconds. With the machine running, add the sweetener, the oil, and most of the milk through the feed tube (you'll need a little less milk if you're using a liquid sweetener). Process for about 30 seconds, then remove the cover. The dough should be in a well-defined, barely sticky, easy-to-handle ball. If it's too dry, add milk 1 tablespoon at a time and process for 5 or 10 seconds after each addition. If too wet, which is unlikely, add a tablespoon or two of flour and process briefly.

2 Use a little more of the oil to grease a large bowl. Shape the dough into a rough ball, place it in the bowl, and cover with plastic wrap or a damp towel. Let rise for at least 2 hours, until nearly doubled in bulk. Deflate the ball and shape it once again into a ball; let rest on a lightly floured surface for about 15 minutes, covered.

3 Using only enough flour to keep the dough from sticking to your hands or the work surface, flatten it into a rectangle, then shape it into a loaf (see page 712 for illustrations). Use the remaining oil or butter to grease a standard (8^1/$_2$ x 4^1/$_2$) loaf pan. Place the loaf in the pan, flattening the top of it with the back of your hand as shown on page 712. Cover and let rest for 1 hour, or until the top of the dough is nearly level with the top of the pan.

4 Preheat the oven to 350°F. Brush the top of the loaf lightly with water, then put in the oven. Bake for about 45 minutes, or until the bottom of the loaf sounds hollow when you tap it (it will fall easily from the loaf pan) or the internal temperature reads about 210°F. Remove the loaf from the pan and cool on a wire rack before slicing.

Half Whole Wheat Sandwich Bread. Standard, something like what you get in the supermarket, though not fluffy: Substitute whole wheat flour for half of the white flour. Use honey for the sweetener, adding 2 tablespoons or more. Proceed as directed, increasing the rising times to at least 2 hours in Step 2 and the resting time to 45 to 60 minutes in Step 3.

Bran and Oat Sandwich Bread. Decrease the flour to 2 cups. Add ^{1}/$_2$ cup wheat or oat bran and ^{3}/$_4$ cup whole wheat flour. Use about ^{1}/$_4$ cup honey or maple syrup for the sweetener and decrease the milk to about 1 cup. Knead in ^{3}/$_4$ cup rolled oats by hand. (If you wet your hands, it will be easier to handle.) Proceed with the recipe.

Anadama Bread. A New England classic: Substitute ^{1}/$_2$ cup cornmeal for ^{1}/$_2$ cup flour. (You may also substitute 1 cup whole wheat flour for 1 cup white flour at the same time.) Replace the sugar or honey with ^{1}/$_2$ cup molasses and use a little less milk.

100 Percent Whole Grain Bread

Turns out vital gluten—the same flourlike ingredient used to make seitan (see page 668)—makes phenomenal whole grain breads that are almost as light as white. The technique doesn't change at all, so the variation is still just as easy to make, and vital gluten is readily available at natural food stores and some large supermarkets.

Here's how: For any of the yeast breads in this section, use all whole grain flour—like whole wheat, rye, or mixed-grain flour—using white flour only for kneading and dusting as necessary. Then add 2 tablespoons vital gluten to the mix. The dough will be stiffer than usual, so when shaping for a loaf pan, pat it into a log that's just a little smaller than the pan, smoothing out any wrinkles or cracks by turning it and patting. Put the log in the pan and use the back of your hand to flatten it (see the illustration on page 712). For panless breads, simply form as usual, letting the dough rest during shaping as needed. Then rise and bake as directed in the recipe.

English Muffins. Much easier than you think, in some ways easier than bread, and really lovely; use the main recipe or either of the variations. In Step 3, cut the dough into 12 roughly equal pieces (if you want perfectly sized muffins, use a scale). Using just enough flour to enable you to handle the dough, shape each into a 3- to 4-inch disk. Dust with flour and let rise for 30 to 45 minutes, or until puffy. Heat a griddle or large skillet over low heat for about 10 minutes; do not oil it. Sprinkle it with cornmeal, then pan-bake the muffins, a few at a time, on both sides, turning occasionally, until lightly browned; a total of about 15 minutes. Cool on a rack and split with a fork before toasting.

Rich Golden Bread, 6 Ways

MAKES: 2 round loaves, 1 huge round loaf, or 1 large sandwich loaf

TIME: At least 3 hours, largely unattended

I love brioche, challah, and all the other tender, melt-in-your mouth breads based on loads of butter and eggs. Who doesn't? Often, though, the recipes are complicated and difficult, which has convinced many people that they're better off heading to the bakery or reserving them for special occasions.

This, however, is a version you can make whenever you like: it's a rich, extremely versatile dough that you can quickly turn into anything from sandwich bread to coffee cake. All will have a golden crumb and shiny crust and be better than most bakery loaves. The variations and illustrations outline a few different examples, but the possibilities are endless. For more ideas for adding flavor and ingredients to any of these shapes, see "17 Ingredients to Add to Any Yeast Bread" (page 718).

3¹/₂ cups all-purpose or bread flour, plus more as needed

2 teaspoons instant yeast

2 teaspoons coarse kosher or sea salt

1 tablespoon sugar

2 tablespoons cold butter

2 eggs

About 1 cup milk, preferably whole

Softened butter as needed

Melted butter as needed

❶ Combine the flour, yeast, salt, sugar, and butter in a food processor. Pulse the machine on and off until the butter is cut throughout the flour. Add the eggs and pulse a few more times. With the machine running, slowly add ³/₄ cup of the milk through the feed tube.

❷ Process for about 30 seconds, adding more milk if necessary, a little at a time, until the mixture forms a ball and is slightly sticky to the touch. If it's dry, add another tablespoon or two of milk and process for another 10 seconds. (In the unlikely event that the mixture is too sticky, add flour, a tablespoon at a time.)

❸ Turn the dough onto a floured work surface and, by hand, knead a bit. (Now's the time to add extra ingredients to the dough if you like.) Form a smooth, round dough ball, put in a bowl, and cover with plastic wrap; let rise until the dough doubles in size, 1 to 2 hours. (You can cut this rising time short if you're in a hurry, or you can let the dough rise more slowly, in the refrigerator, for up to 6 or 8 hours.) Proceed to Step 4 or wrap the dough tightly in plastic wrap and freeze it for up to a month. (Defrost in a covered bowl in the refrigerator or at room temperature.)

❹ When the dough is ready, form it into a ball and divide it into 2 pieces if you like or leave it whole; roll each piece into a round ball. Place each ball on a lightly floured surface, sprinkle with a little flour, and cover with plastic wrap or a towel. Let rest until the dough puffs slightly, about 20 minutes.

❺ Pinch the bottom of the ball(s) to seal the seam as best you can. Butter 1 or 2 shallow baking dishes or cake pans that will comfortably hold the loaves; they should not (yet) quite fill the pans. Cover and let rise for an hour and preferably longer, up to 2 hours. It's okay if the dough rises over the pans a bit.

F Fast   **M** Make Ahead   **V** Vegan

6 Preheat the oven to 350°F and set a rack in the middle. Brush the top of the loaf or loaves with melted butter, then put the loaf or loaves in the oven. Bake for about 40 minutes, until the crust is golden brown and the internal temperature of the bread is at least 210°F when measured on an instant-read thermometer. Immediately turn the breads out of their dishes or pans and cool on a wire rack. Cut with a serrated knife—the bread will be rich and delicate.

Rich Golden Rolls. Slightly crisp on the outside, airy on the inside: In Step 5, instead of shaping the dough into a loaf or loaves, keep dividing it in half until you have 16 medium or 24 small balls. (See the illustrations on page 704.) Grease a couple of baking sheets or line them with parchment. Put the rolls on the sheets, a couple inches apart, cover, and let rise for about an hour. Proceed with the recipe; reduce the baking time to 20 to 30 minutes, depending on the size of the rolls.

Rich Golden Sandwich Bread. In Step 5, instead of greasing the baking dishes or cake pans, grease a large 9 × 5-inch loaf pan. Shape the dough into one large rectangle; fold it under and seal the seam as you would for sandwich bread. (See the illustrations on page 712.) Proceed with the recipe.

Saffron Fruit and Nut Bread. Like a fancy holiday bread, with less work: In Step 1, add a large pinch of saffron to the flour mixture before running the food processor. While the dough is rising for the first time, put 1 cup of dried fruit—like golden raisins, cherries, cranberries, or chopped apricots—in a small bowl; heat $^1/_2$ cup of brandy, rum, or apple juice, pour it over the fruit, and let the fruit soak for about 30 minutes, then drain well. Coarsely chop $^1/_2$ cup of almonds, pecans, or walnuts. In Step 3, knead in the fruit and nuts as directed. Proceed with the recipe.

Streusel Pull-Apart Coffee Cake. Also known as "monkey bread," this is the easiest way to shape all kinds of yeast dough and then slip it into any kind of pan you

Roll the dough into balls and put them, touching each other, into a baking pan.

like: Prepare a recipe of Sweet Crumble Topping (page 870). In Step 5, butter an angel food tube pan or other large loaf or cake pan and sprinkle the bottom lightly with some of the topping. Instead of shaping the dough into loaves or rolls, pinch off small pieces of dough—about a tablespoon's worth—and roll it into a ball on a lightly floured surface. As you finish each ball, put it in the greased pan, forming an even layer in the bottom. (See the illustration above.) Once you have a layer of balls, sprinkle with some of the topping. Repeat until you use up all of the dough and topping. Proceed with the recipe. When the coffee cake comes out of the oven, turn it out onto a serving platter and let the gooey coffee cake cool a bit before slicing.

Cinnamon Buns. In Step 5, butter a 9 × 13-inch baking pan or dish. In a small bowl, combine 2 tablespoons ground cinnamon with $^3/_4$ cup sugar. Press and roll the dough into a large oblong about the size of the baking dish. (If the dough is very elastic, you may need to roll, then let it rest for a few minutes and roll again.) Sprinkle the cinnamon sugar evenly over all. Wet your hands and shake a few drops of water over all (or spray lightly with a water bottle if you have one); use a fork to rub the cinnamon sugar and water into the dough a bit; it should be a light paste. Roll

(STEP 1) Press and roll the dough into a oblong and spread the filling mixture evenly across the top.

(STEP 2) Roll it up the long way.

(STEP 3) Slice it into swirls.

the dough up lengthwise and seal the seam as best you can. You'll have a long log. Slice it crosswise into 15 pieces. Put each, cut side up, into the prepared dish or pan, 3 across and 5 lengthwise. (See the illustrations above.) Proceed with the recipe; reduce the baking time to about 30 minutes. If you like, when the cinnamon rolls cool down a bit, sprinkle them with confectioners' sugar or drizzle with a glaze (pages 857–858). Serve right from the pan.

Braided Rich Golden Bread. Like challah but easier: In Step 3, shape the dough into one large ball. In Step 5, divide the dough into 3 balls; roll each of the balls into a rope about 14 inches long and 1 inch thick. Braid them on a lightly greased baking sheet, as illustrated on page 717. Right before baking, brush with egg wash if you like (see "How do I Get That Shiny Crust?" on page 717) and sprinkle with poppy seeds (also optional). Proceed with the recipe; reduce the rising time to about an hour and the baking time to 30 to 35 minutes.

Black Bread

MAKES: 2 small loaves or 1 large loaf
TIME: 3 hours, largely unattended

This bread features a one-step mixing technique that keeps the process simple, and in return you get a full-flavored, fairly dense, almost-black Russian-style loaf that's perfect with hearty soups and stews or a wedge of sharp cheddar cheese, some pickles, and a smear of Grainy Mustard (page 776). And it tastes like it was a lot more difficult to make than it is. I like to shape the dough into two smaller loaves and keep one in the freezer.

1/2 cup 100 percent bran cereal (not flakes)

2 cups all-purpose or bread flour

1 cup medium rye flour

1 cup whole wheat flour

2 tablespoons cocoa powder

2 tablespoons sugar

1 tablespoon instant yeast

2 teaspoons salt

4 tablespoons (1/2 stick) butter, softened, or 1/4 cup neutral oil, like grapeseed or corn, plus more for the pan

Ⓕ Fast   Ⓜ Make Ahead   Ⓥ Vegan

$^1/_4$ cup molasses

2 tablespoons cider vinegar or freshly squeezed lemon juice

$1^1/_4$ cups strong black coffee

1 Put the cereal in a food processor and let it run for about 10 seconds, until it's finely ground. Add the flours, cocoa, sugar, yeast, and salt and pulse. Add the butter or oil and the molasses and pulse a few more times. With the machine running, pour the vinegar and most of the coffee through the feed tube. Process for about 30 seconds; then remove the cover. The dough should be a well-defined,

How Do I Get That Shiny Crust?

It's easy: Right before the bread or rolls go into the oven, make an egg wash by beating one egg yolk with a table-spoon of water. Lightly brush the top of the loaves or rolls with a little egg wash and pop them into the oven. You can use an egg wash on any type of bread, though sweet doughs like the one for Rich Golden Bread are the most traditional.

MAKING CHALLAH

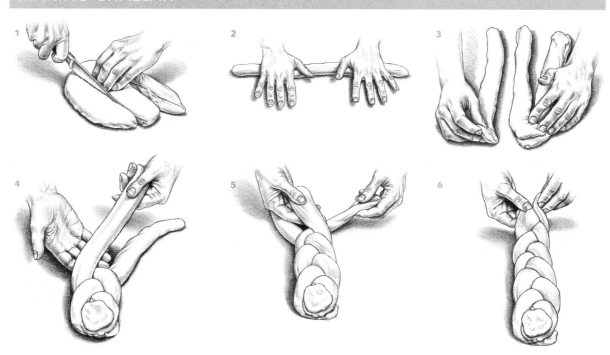

(STEP 1) Cut the dough into 3 equal pieces. (STEP 2) Roll each piece into a rope about 14 inches long. (STEP 3) Lay the ropes next to each other and press their ends together. (STEP 4) Braid, just as you would hair. (STEPS 5–6) Finish braiding and use your fingers to tightly press the ends together.

Here are some ways to add flavor and texture to virtually any yeast bread. See the chart on page 720 for some specific ideas and combinations.

Add any of these ingredients along with the flour and yeast (before the water) if you're making a direct dough recipe or along with the final wheat and salt if making a bread from a sourdough or sponge recipe:

1. Spice blends: 1 to 2 tablespoons, depending on pungency, toasted lightly in a dry pan if you like
2. Spice seeds, like caraway or cumin: up to 1 tablespoon, toasted lightly in a dry pan if you like
3. Cooked whole grains: up to $1/2$ cup
4. Finely ground coffee or tea: up to $1/4$ cup
5. Wheat germ: up to $1/4$ cup, toasted lightly in a dry pan if you like

Knead any of these ingredients into the dough during the final shaping:

1. Chopped nuts or seeds, toasted if you like, up to 1 cup per recipe

2. Chopped dried fruit (including dried tomatoes) or raisins, up to $1/2$ cup
3. Chopped bean or seed sprouts: up to 1 cup
4. Chopped pitted olives: up to $1/2$ cup
5. Lightly mashed drained cooked beans: up to 1 cup
6. Grated hard cheese, like Parmesan, manchego, or ricotta salata: up to 1 cup per recipe
7. Grated medium-hard cheese, like cheddar, Asiago, or pepper Jack: up to $1/2$ cup per recipe
8. Bits of soft cheese, like goat, blue cheese like Gorgonzola, or cream cheese: up to $1/2$ cup per recipe
9. Minced fresh herbs: up to $1/4$ cup of mild ones like parsley, mint, cilantro, dill, or chives; no more than 1 tablespoon of strong ones like rosemary, sage, or oregano
10. Minced fresh chile (like jalapeño or Thai), or hot red pepper flakes or cayenne: to taste
11. Caramelized Onions (page 329): up to $1/2$ cup
12. Roasted Garlic (page 304), lightly mashed or coarsely chopped: up to $1/2$ cup

barely sticky, easy-to-handle ball. If it's too dry, add coffee 1 tablespoon at a time and process for 5 or 10 seconds after each addition. If too wet, which is unlikely, add a tablespoon or two of flour and process briefly.

② Use a little more butter or oil to grease a large bowl. Shape the dough into a rough ball, place it in the bowl, and cover with plastic wrap or a damp towel. Let rise for at least 2 hours, until nearly doubled in bulk. Deflate the ball and shape it once again into a ball; let rest on a lightly floured surface for about 15 minutes, covered. (You can make the dough ahead to this point, cover it well, and refrigerate for several hours or overnight; return it to room temperature before proceeding.)

③ Using only enough flour to keep the dough from sticking to your hands or the work surface, knead the

dough a few times and shape the dough into a large oval loaf (or divide it in half and make 2 smaller round loaves). Use the remaining oil or butter to grease a baking sheet. Put the loaf or loaves on the sheet. Cover again and let rest for 1 hour, or until the dough has plumped up again considerably.

④ Preheat the oven to 325°F. Bake for 55 to 60 minutes for a large loaf or 40 to 45 minutes for smaller ones, or until the bottom sounds hollow when you tap it (it will fall easily from the loaf pan) or the internal temperature reads about 210°F. Carefully slide the loaf from the sheet and cool on a wire rack before slicing.

Pumpernickel-Raisin Bread. You can omit the raisins, of course. Soak 1 cup raisins in enough hot water or cof-

Ⓕ Fast   Ⓜ Make Ahead   Ⓥ Vegan

fee to barely cover them. Drain well. In Step 3, knead the raisins into the dough along with a tablespoon of caraway seeds.

Black Bread with Chocolate. Great with a smear of cream cheese or sour cream: Coarsely chop a 4-ounce piece of bittersweet chocolate into chunks. In Step 3, knead the chocolate into the dough.

Pita

MAKES: 6 to 12 pitas, depending on size

TIME: At least 2 hours, somewhat unattended

Ⓜ

You can buy pita (also called *pide*), of course, though it's tough to find the real thing: the chewy, slightly puffed rounds that are the standard flatbread of the eastern Mediterranean. Luckily baking your own is a simple enough task for bread makers, even novices. As with any bread dough, you can control the time it takes to make this by slowing the rising in the refrigerator. If you've got a pizza stone, use it for these, though a cookie sheet is okay too. If you have the time and patience, dry-bake them on top of the stove in one or two heavy skillets. Skip the butter to make the pita vegan.

3 cups all-purpose or bread flour, plus more as needed

3 tablespoons extra virgin olive oil

2 teaspoons instant yeast

2 teaspoons coarse kosher or sea salt

$\frac{1}{2}$ teaspoon sugar

Melted butter (optional)

❶ Combine the flour, olive oil, yeast, salt, and sugar in a food processor. Turn the machine on and add 1 cup water through the feed tube.

❷ Process for about 30 seconds, adding more water, a little at a time, until the mixture forms a ball and is

5 Things to Do with (Slightly) Stale Bread

You don't want to use rock-hard bread, but dried-out one- to three-day-old bread is perfect for:

1. Fresh Bread Crumbs (page 804)
2. Any of the bread puddings on pages 885–886
3. One of the bread salads on pages 87–90
4. Melba toast: Slice bread as thinly as possible— $\frac{1}{8}$ inch thick if possible. Put on a baking sheet and toast in a 250°F oven for about 30 minutes, turning once, or until thoroughly dry. Cool on a rack and store in a tin.
5. Croutons (page 806)

slightly sticky to the touch. If it's dry, add another tablespoon or two of water and process for another 10 seconds. (In the unlikely event that the mixture is too sticky, add flour, a tablespoon at a time.)

❸ You can simply cover the food processor bowl with plastic wrap (remove the blade first) or turn the dough onto a floured work surface and knead by hand for a few seconds to form a smooth, round dough ball. Put the dough in a bowl and cover with plastic wrap; let it rise until the dough doubles in size, 1 to 2 hours. (You can cut this rising time short if you're in a hurry, or you can let the dough rise more slowly, in the refrigerator, for up to 6 or 8 hours.) Proceed to Step 4, or wrap the dough tightly in plastic wrap and freeze for up to a month. (Defrost in a covered bowl in the refrigerator or at room temperature.)

❹ When the dough is ready, form it into a ball and divide it into 6 or more pieces; roll each piece into a round ball. Place each ball on a lightly floured surface, sprinkle with a little flour, and cover with plastic wrap or

BREAD FLAVORING COMBOS

Here are some specific flavor combinations to get you started; as long as you don't overload the dough with too many ingredients (which will keep it from rising properly), you can mix, match, and experiment freely. See the list on page 718 for the quantities and timing of the stir-ins.

BREAD DOUGH RECIPE	FLAVORINGS
Fast French Bread or Rolls (page 707)	Chopped black or green olives, plus a little olive oil; minced rosemary leaves
Whole Grain French Bread or Rolls (page 708), made with some rye flour	Toasted caraway seeds and minced fresh dill (optional)
Whole Grain French Bread or Rolls (page 708), made with whole wheat or seven-grain flour	Cooked whole grain berries, like wheat or rye and sunflower seeds
Overnight French Bread or Rolls (page 709)	Parmesan cheese and roasted garlic
Sourdough Bread (page 709)	Cheddar cheese and minced parsley
English Muffins (page 714)	Caramelized Onions (page 329) and black pepper
Anadama Bread (page 713)	Golden raisins or dried apricots and chopped pecans
Half Whole Wheat Sandwich Bread (page 713)	Raisins or dates and cinnamon sugar
Sandwich Bread with all white flour (page 712)	Curry powder (to make your own, see pages 815–816) and sesame seeds

a towel. Let rest until they puff slightly, about 20 minutes.

⑤ Roll each ball out to less than ¼-inch thickness, using flour to prevent sticking as necessary. As you work, spread the flat disks out on a floured surface and keep them covered. When all the disks are rolled out, preheat the oven to 350°F (the disks should rest for at least 20 minutes after rolling). If you have a pizza stone, use it, on a rack set low in the oven; if not, lightly oil a baking sheet and put it in the oven on a rack set in the middle. Alternatively, lightly oil and wipe out a heavy skillet.

⑥ To bake on a stone, slide the individual disks—as many as will fit comfortably—directly into the oven, using a peel or a large spatula. Or bake 2 disks at a time on a cookie sheet. Or bake over medium to medium-low heat in the skillet. For whichever method, bake pita until lightly browned on first side, then flip and brown on the

other side. Total baking time will be between 5 and 10 minutes, generally only 5 or 6.

⑦ As the breads finish baking, remove them from the oven. If you're going to eat them fairly soon, brush with melted butter. Otherwise cool, then store in wax paper or plastic bags; reheat gently before using.

Whole Wheat Pita. Substitute whole wheat flour for half of the all-purpose or bread flour.

Stuffed Pita

MAKES: 6 large pitas
TIME: 20 minutes with premade dough

This half-open bread—with the filling partially enclosed and baked right into the dough—is a street treat found

 Fast   Make Ahead   Ⓥ Vegan

throughout the eastern Mediterranean, ideal for lunch or a snack. Or cut the hearty pitas into wedges to serve at parties or picnics; they're also great at room temperature.

1 recipe pita dough (page 719)

2 cups crumbled feta or blue cheese

4 tablespoons ($1/2$ stick) butter at room temperature

4 eggs

1 cup snipped fresh dill

Freshly ground black pepper

Lightly toasted sesame seeds (see page 321; optional)

1 When you reach Step 5 in making pita, put the feta, butter, eggs, and most of the dill in a bowl, along with a good sprinkling of black pepper; stir to combine. Put a portion of this filling on each of the disks and bring the sides up to seal; do not enclose entirely (the traditional filled pita is longer than it is wide, kind of boat shaped; you can make any shape you want).

2 Bake as you would pita, but for a little bit longer, perhaps 10 minutes. Sprinkle with the remaining dill and a few sesame seeds and eat hot or at room temperature.

10 Dishes You Can Fold into Stuffed Pita

You'll need 3 cups of fairly dry filling total, about $1/2$ cup for each pita. If there's too much liquid, drain some off for a bit. It's best to have the dish at room temperature: too hot and it "cooks" the dough before baking and makes it soggy; too cold and it never heats through properly.

1. Lentils and Potatoes with Curry (page 600)
2. Mixed Whole-Bean Dal with Walnuts (page 602)
3. Beans and Greens (page 595)
4. Stewed Fava Beans with Tahini or with Za'atar (page 604)
5. White Bean Purée or any of its variations (page 612)
6. Mashed Favas with any of the additions (page 616)
7. Baked Chickpeas with Fresh Cheese (page 622)
8. Hummus (page 614)
9. Beets with Pistachio Butter or any of its variations (page 268)
10. Mashed Eggplant with Honey and Lemon (page 298)

The Basics of Pizza

Home-baked pizza is a completely different animal, and a different experience, from calling the delivery guy. You have complete control over ingredients, and once you get good at it you'll be in love with the results. But you have to plan ahead.

Pizza is no trickier than making a simple bread, with the crust using essentially the same ingredients and the toppings simple—tomatoes, cheese, mushrooms, olives . . . just what you'd expect—and best kept to a minimum. But at home you have the option of using universally better ingredients than the ones used at a pizzeria, and that makes a huge difference.

The biggest challenge is shaping, which can be intimidating. But if you let go of the idea that the pie has to be perfectly round and uniform, that hurdle is soon cleared too.

Preparing the Dough

Just as with bread, a food processor is the most convenient tool for making pizza dough. You can certainly use a standing mixer (see "Making These Recipes with a Standing Mixer," page 707) or mix and knead the whole thing by hand, first in a big bowl, then on a floured board. In any case, start to finish, you can have pizza dough ready in about an hour, but to develop more flavor—and turn this into a make-ahead dish—you can let it rise and ferment in the refrigerator for 6 to 8 hours, even overnight.

The Shaping

The romantic image of pizza makers spinning, stretching, and tossing the dough into a perfect circle is hard to

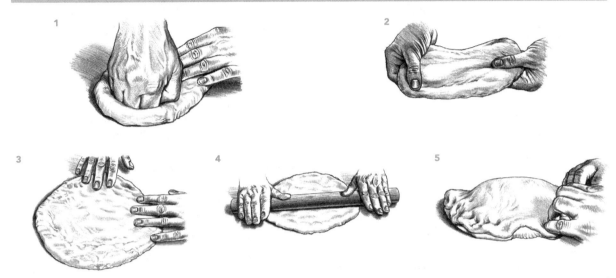

(STEP 1) Punch the dough down and (STEP 2) stretch it with your hands. If at any point the dough becomes very resistant, cover and let rest for a few minutes. (STEPS 3–4) You can press the dough out with your hands or roll it with a pin; either is effective. Use a little flour or olive oil to keep it from sticking. (STEP 5) To make a calzone, add your filling, fold the dough over onto itself, and pinch the seams closed.

shake. No denying that kind of treatment yields a gorgeous crust, though it's a technique that's neither practical nor necessary. Enthusiasts with even modest experience can get equally good results by laying the dough on a work surface and gently pressing it with opened fingertips until it dimples and slowly stretches into shape. (This is how professionals make focaccia, which is just another form of pizza.)

But the easiest way for home cooks to shape pizza is to flatten the dough a bit, then roll it. Like the best bread doughs, pizza dough should be relatively moist, so even if the dough seems sticky and unruly, use only as much flour as you need to keep it from being totally unmanageable while you're kneading and shaping.

Patience is the key to shaping pizza dough. Your goal is to coax the dough into shape by pressing or rolling and stretching. It's easiest if you allow the dough to rest between steps: when you divide it, when you flatten it, and even during stages of rolling. You can plow right through from start to finish, but whenever you handle the dough it becomes more elastic and more difficult to work (that's the gluten doing its thing). The rest periods let it relax, which in turn makes it easier for you.

Thick or Thin?

You can make any size or thickness of pizza—even focaccia, which can be quite thick—with the same recipe and technique. It all depends on how you divide and shape the dough. Large, thin pizzas are the hardest

Ⓕ Fast   Ⓜ Make Ahead   Ⓥ Vegan

to handle because they tend to tear during rolling no matter how experienced you are. I usually divide the dough into at least two pies; three or four if they're going on the grill.

No matter how thin you roll the crust, it will just about double in thickness as it bakes. (The temperature of your kitchen, the toppings, and even how you shaped the dough can affect this formula a bit, but it's generally a good rule of thumb.) You can increase the thickness of the crust somewhat by letting the dough rise for a few extra minutes after you shape it and before topping it. Just be careful not to overproof the dough by letting it puff up too much and lose its elasticity. Otherwise your pizza will have big bubbles and sunken valleys.

The Toppings

Topping pizza is much like saucing pasta; distinct, clean flavors are better than a mishmash of ingredients. You can stick to classic combinations: tomatoes, basil, and Parmesan; tomato sauce and mozzarella; or roasted peppers and olives. You can even experiment with different vegetables and cheeses, like grilled eggplant and feta or caramelized onions and Gorgonzola. After the pizza comes out of the oven, try adding a sprinkle of minced fresh herbs or dust the pie with a spice blend or finely ground nuts. There's nothing wrong with being untraditional; pizza is a great vehicle for enjoying some of your favorite ingredients.

But when you start getting into "house special" territory, you're in trouble. Too many ingredients taste muddled on a pizza, and they do no favors to your crust, which really deserves equal billing with whatever you put on it. So go easy on the sauce and cheese. A smear and a sprinkle will do it. If you smother the dough, it will steam as it bakes, turning a potentially crisp and light crust into a soggy mess. This is a difficult temptation to resist, especially if you're used to pizza parlor pies. (That's why pizza is in the bread chapter: The crust is the most important part.)

Baking

Pizza must be baked in a very hot oven; 500°F and even higher if your oven can handle it. (Professional pizza ovens are around 700°F.) The best way to cook pizza is directly on a pizza stone, which crisps up the bottom of the crust and dries it out perfectly. And be sure the oven is thoroughly preheated—to fully heat the stone, it's best to wait a good half hour after turning the oven on—before popping the pizza inside. That said, pizza's also just fine baked on a flat baking sheet; one with a small lip is perfect for focaccia. (And, of course, there's always pizza on the grill, see page 724.)

The ideal pizza stone is a large rectangle that can hold a whole pie or two small ones. It should be unglazed and relatively thick. Once you've got the stone, you really need a peel—the board with a handle that looks like a large Ping-Pong paddle —to simplify the whole process. Sprinkle flour or cornmeal on it and you can roll the dough directly on the peel, then just slide it right onto the stone. The peel also makes removing and serving the pie a breeze. Wooden peels are more attractive than metal ones but can get a little dingy-looking after a while (I sand mine when it gets too stained); metal peels are much easier to clean.

One more thing to remember about equipment: If you use a baking sheet to bake the pizza, grease it with a little olive oil to keep the dough from sticking, rather than dusting the surface with flour or cornmeal as you would with a peel. Once you do that, just press the dough right onto the pan as you shape it.

Cutting and Serving Pizza

Let pizza rest for a couple minutes to set the toppings before cutting, especially if there's gooey cheese involved. Pizzas with little or no cheese—or other rich ingredients that might congeal when cooled—are also good served at room temperature, like bread. You can cut pizza into

Pizza on the Grill

This is a whole different universe and a fantastic one. Grilled pizza is fun to make and easier than you'd think, especially if your grill has a cover. Wood fires are the trickiest fuel to control but impart a great flavor to the crust; gas grills are naturally the easiest for baking pizzas, and charcoal lies somewhere in between.

Whatever fuel you use, you'll want a grill with a broad surface area so you can handle a few small pizzas at a time. You also want a fire that is hot enough to brown the dough but not hot enough to scorch it before the interior cooks; a good fire is one you can hold your hand a few inches above for three or four seconds. An ideal fire is one where part of the grill is fairly hot and part of it quite cool. On a gas grill, this means setting one side at high and the other at low or using some similar arrangement. With a charcoal grill, simply build your fire on only one side. Use the hot side for the initial browning of the dough, the cool side to heat the toppings. If you're making smaller pizzas, you can turn them with tongs as soon as they firm up a bit; if the pizza is larger, you may need a peel or two spatulas to turn it.

Having said all that, I'll say this too: It's possible to get too fussy. You can grill pizza on whatever grill you have and on just about any fire you build as long as it's not so hot that it scorches the dough.

The process is straightforward: Grill one side of the pizza, just enough to firm it up and brown it a bit, then flip it (again, if the pizzas are small, you can use tongs; otherwise a spatula aided by your fingers does the trick) and add toppings. If you want the toppings to get very hot, cover the grill. If you don't care whether they actually cook, but just warm up a bit, you can leave the grill open.

It's even more important to use flavorful toppings and keep them to a minimum when you're grilling pizza. Fully loaded grilled pizzas won't cook properly and will be impossible to handle. One way around this is to grill pizzas with one or two ingredients, then top them with another when you remove them from the fire.

wedges like pie or small squares if you're feeding a crowd or just want smaller pieces.

Pizza Dough

MAKES: 1 large or 2 or more small pies
TIME: 1 hour or more

You won't believe how simple it is to make pizza at home. And because pizza dough freezes very well for at least a couple of weeks, it's even practical to whip up a batch for one or two people, wrap up half of the dough tightly in plastic wrap or a resealable plastic bag, and tuck it away for another day.

To make pizza dough by hand, use a bowl and a heavy wooden spoon instead of the food processor. When the dough becomes too heavy to stir, use your hands.

3 cups all-purpose or bread flour, plus more as needed

2 teaspoons instant yeast

2 teaspoons coarse kosher or sea salt, plus extra for sprinkling

3 tablespoons extra virgin olive oil

① Combine the flour, yeast, and salt in a food processor. Turn the machine on and add 1 cup water and 2 tablespoons of the oil through the feed tube.

② Process for about 30 seconds, adding more water, a tablespoon or so at a time, until the mixture forms a ball and is slightly sticky to the touch. If it's dry, add another tablespoon or two of water (but no than a total of $1/4$ cup in this step) and process for another 10 seconds. (In the unlikely event that the mixture is too sticky, add flour a tablespoon at a time.)

③ Turn the dough onto a floured work surface and knead by hand for a few seconds to form a smooth, round dough ball. Put the remaining olive oil in a bowl, turn the dough ball in it, and cover the bowl with plastic wrap; let rise until the dough doubles in size, 1 to 2 hours. (You can cut this rising time short if you're in a hurry, or you can let the dough rise more slowly, in the refrigerator, for up to 6 or 8 hours.) Proceed to Step 4 or wrap the dough tightly in plastic wrap or a resealable plastic bag and freeze for up to a month. (Defrost in the bag or a covered bowl in the refrigerator or at room temperature; bring to room temperature before shaping.)

4 When the dough is ready, form it into a ball and divide it into 2 or more pieces if you like; roll each piece into a round ball. Place each ball on a lightly floured surface, sprinkle with a little flour, and cover with plastic wrap or a towel. Let rest until they puff slightly, about 20 minutes. Proceed with any of the pizza recipes that follow.

Whole Wheat Pizza Dough. Still chewy and light but a little heartier, with a nutty taste and a little more fiber: Use half whole wheat and half all-purpose or bread flour. You'll probably need to use closer to $1^1/_2$ cups water or maybe even a little more.

Crunchier Pizza Dough. This dough may be a little more difficult to handle, but it has superior flavor and a pleasant crunch: Substitute $^1/_2$ cup cornmeal for $^1/_2$ cup of the flour.

6 Quick Ideas for More Flavorful Pizza Dough

You can mix and match a bit, as long as you don't overdo it and overpower the natural flavor of the crust or make it soggy. But before adding the water to the dough, try the following, alone or in combination:

1. Add $^1/_2$ to 1 teaspoon freshly cracked black pepper.
2. Add 1 teaspoon to 1 tablespoon chopped fresh herbs.
3. Add $^1/_4$ to $^1/_2$ cup chopped nuts or seeds.
4. Substitute $^1/_2$ to 1 cup rice, semolina, or other alternative flour for the white flour (see "The Basics of Flour," page 680).

5. Add 1 tablespoon puréed cooked garlic (roasted, page 304, is best) or $^1/_2$ teaspoon minced raw garlic, or to taste.
6. Use flavored olive oil, like garlic or rosemary oil, in place of regular olive oil.

White Pizza

MAKES: 1 large or 2 or more small pies
TIME: About 3 hours, largely unattended

In southern Italy, *pizza bianca* (as pizza without tomato sauce is called) is the mother of all pizzas. This may seem spare compared to what we're used to in this country, but I urge you to try it and experiment with some of the possible additions and tweaks that follow the recipe, because it's among the best breads you'll ever eat.

I always use a good coarse salt for white pizza, because salt is almost a primary ingredient. See "The Basics of Salt" on page 806 for a rundown of your options.

1 recipe Pizza Dough (page 724), mixed and risen

Extra virgin olive oil as needed

Coarse kosher or sea salt

1 tablespoon or more roughly chopped fresh rosemary leaves

Several fresh rosemary sprigs (optional)

1 When the dough is ready, knead it lightly, form it into a ball, and divide it into 2 if you like; roll each piece into a round ball and place each ball on a lightly floured surface. Sprinkle with a little more flour, cover with plastic wrap or a towel, and let rest while you heat the oven.

2 Preheat the oven to 500°F or higher. Roll or lightly press each dough ball into a flat round, lightly flouring the work surface and the dough as necessary (do not use more flour than you need to). Let the rounds sit for a few minutes; this will relax the dough and make it easier to roll out. If you have a peel and baking stone,

roll or pat out the dough on the peel, as thinly as you like, turning occasionally and sprinkling it with flour as necessary. If you're using baking sheets, oil them, then press each dough ball into a flat round directly on the oiled sheets.

3 Sprinkle the top with some salt and the chopped rosemary and drizzle with a little more olive oil; if you have some rosemary sprigs, decorate the top with them. Slide the baking sheet into the oven on a rack set in the middle (or the pizza itself onto the stone, which should be set on a lower rack). Bake for 6 to 12 minutes, depending on the oven heat, until nicely browned. Serve immediately or at room temperature (these will keep for a few hours).

Margherita Pizza. The ultimate summertime treat: Top the pies with sliced fresh tomatoes, extra virgin olive oil, a little mozzarella, preferably fresh, and some basil leaves, salt, and Parmesan.

Marinara Pizza. All tomatoes, no cheese: Top the pies with fresh sliced tomatoes, thinly sliced garlic (or Fast Tomato Sauce, page 445), extra virgin olive oil, and, if you like, a few chopped black olives or whole capers.

White Pizza with Mint. Unexpected and refreshing: Instead of the rosemary, scatter about $1/4$ cup chopped fresh mint leaves on top along with the salt and press them down into the dough a bit.

White Pizza with Mushrooms. Earthy and satisfying: Omit the rosemary. Top each pizza with some Sautéed Mushrooms (page 314). Use plenty of minced fresh parsley leaves; sage is also good. If you're grilling, add the toppings after turning, then cover the grill if possible. If you're baking, add the toppings about halfway through the cooking.

White Pizza with Caramelized Onions and Vinegar. This takes some work in advance: Omit the rosemary. Make Caramelized Onions (page 329), cooked fairly dark. Season to taste with salt and pepper, then stir in 1 tablespoon balsamic vinegar, or to taste. Top each pizza with a portion of these onions and some minced fresh basil, thyme, or sage leaves. A sprinkling of plain bread crumbs is also good. If you're grilling, add the toppings after turning, then cover the grill if possible. If you're baking, add the toppings about halfway through the cooking.

White Pizza with Lemon. Use thin slices of Preserved Lemons (page 427) if you have them and eliminate the salt: Omit the rosemary if you like. Remove the zest from 2 lemons in strands as large as possible; or cut away big pieces of zest then slice them into super-thin julienne. When you add the salt and the rosemary in Step 3, spread the lemon zest around on top and gently press it into the dough. Proceed with the recipe and, when the pizza comes out of the oven, top it with some shaved Parmesan cheese if you like and lots of black pepper.

Pizza with Tomato Sauce and Mozzarella

MAKES: 1 large or 2 or more small pies

TIME: About 3 hours if you need to make sauce, largely unattended

Ⓜ

This recipe is more like American-style pizza than White Pizza, with a smear of tomato sauce and a fair amount of mozzarella. It's a little too loaded to grill as is (see the variation), but the good news is that the cheese helps other unwieldy toppings—like broccoli, bell peppers, or olives—stick to the pie. For more variations, see "15 Ideas for Pizza Toppings" (page 728).

1 recipe Pizza Dough (page 724), mixed and risen

About 2 tablespoons extra virgin olive oil

2 cups Fast Tomato Sauce (page 445) or any other tomato sauce

2 cups (about 8 ounces) grated mozzarella

Salt and freshly ground black pepper

1 When the dough is ready, knead it lightly, form it into a ball, and divide it in two if you like; roll each piece into a round ball and place each ball on a lightly floured surface. Sprinkle with a little more flour, cover with plastic wrap or a towel, and let rest while you heat the oven.

② Preheat the oven to 500°F or higher. Roll or lightly press each dough ball into a flat round, lightly flouring the work surface and the dough as necessary (do not use more flour than you need to). Let the rounds sit for a few minutes; this will relax the dough and make it easier to roll out. If you have a peel and baking stone, roll or pat out the dough on the peel, as thinly as you like, turning occasionally and sprinkling it with flour as necessary. If you're using baking sheets, oil them, then press each dough ball into a flat round directly on the oiled sheets.

③ Drizzle the rounds with the olive oil, then top them with the sauce and cheese; sprinkle with salt and pepper. Put the baking sheet in the oven or slide the pizza directly onto the stone and bake until the crust is crisp and the cheese melted, usually 8 to 12 minutes. Let stand for several minutes before slicing to set up the cheese.

Pizza with Tomato Sauce and Fresh Mozzarella. Since the cheese doesn't melt the same way and tends to be fairly moist, use less and slice it; don't grate it. Use less than 8 ounces fresh mozzarella —usually 1 medium ball packed in water. Drain well and cut into thin slices. After you top with the oil and cheese, spread the slices on top of the pizza (you will have gaps in between so the pizza can breathe and crisp up). Proceed with the recipe. When it comes out of the oven, sprinkle with chopped fresh basil or oregano if you like and some grated Parmesan.

Pizza with Tomato Sauce, Mozzarella, and Broccoli. Best with broccoli raab: Sauté about 8 ounces of broccoli florets (or broccoli raab spears), with a little garlic if you like, making sure you stop cooking them as soon as they're just tender. In Step 3, after you put the cheese on the pizza, distribute the broccoli around the top and press gently into the cheese. Bake as directed.

Grilled Pizza with Tomato Sauce and Mozzarella. Great on the grill as long as you pare down the toppings: Reduce the sauce to 1 cup and the grated mozzarella to 1 cup. Follow the directions for cooking, flipping, topping, and finishing grilled pizzas on page 724, drizzling a little extra olive oil onto the pizza before grilling if you like.

4 Tips for Foolproof Pizza Toppings

Whether you grill or bake, the trick is for the toppings and the dough to cook in sync. Just keep in mind the following rules.

1. Vegetables must be cooked—boiled, steamed, grilled, sautéed, or roasted—before being added to pizzas. Pizza just doesn't bake long enough for most raw vegetables to become tender, and raw vegetables will leech too much water into the crust, turning it soggy. It's best to use slices rather than chunks, which will just burn on top. Just about any vegetable is fair game on pizza; the list on page 728 includes some of my favorites.

2. Think before topping oven-baked pizzas; delicate ingredients may overcook if left in the oven for the full baking time. It may be better to add them about halfway through the cooking.

Essential Flatbread

Quite possibly the easiest bread in the world to make. Tear or cut off pieces to eat with everything from Dals (pages 600–604) to stir-fries, dips and spreads like Hummus (page 614), yogurt sauces (see pages 773–775), or chutneys (pages 783–787). If you like, for a neutral flavor, make the Pizza Dough recipe—or any of its variations—with a neutral oil, like grapeseed or corn. Or omit the olive oil, coarse salt, and rosemary from the White Pizza, then shape the dough into one or two large flatbreads or several small ones; irregular shapes have a great rustic appeal.

3. When you add moist ingredients such as cheese or tomatoes to grilled pizzas, cover the grill if possible or they may not cook through.

4. Don't overload grilled pizzas; you risk losing part of the topping. Switch to the oven instead.

15 Ideas for Pizza Toppings

Use the following ingredients alone or in combination on any of the pizzas in this section.

1. Shredded mozzarella

2. Small amounts of Gorgonzola or other blue cheese or fontina or other semisoft cheese; gratings of Parmesan are almost always welcome

3. Soft goat cheese or ricotta

4. Minced raw or mashed Roasted Garlic (page 304)

5. Minced fresh chile (like jalapeño or Thai) or hot red pepper flakes or cayenne to taste

6. Pitted black olives, especially the oil-cured kind (good on White Pizza with Caramelized Onions and Vinegar, page 326), or green olives

7. Reconstituted sun-dried tomatoes (or Oven-Dried Tomatoes, page 377)

8. Thin-sliced tomatoes and basil, with olive oil and/or grated Parmesan. Or peeled, seeded, and chopped tomatoes tossed with basil.

9. Traditional Pesto or other herb paste or sauce (pages 768–770)

10. Sliced boiled waxy or all-purpose potatoes

11. Well-washed and dried tender greens, especially spicy ones such as arugula and watercress, added after baking or grilling, which will wilt from the heat from the crust in about 1 minute

12. Sautéed spinach (page 359), strewn around in a thin layer

13. Marinated Roasted Red Peppers (page 333)

14. Grilled or Broiled Eggplant (page 295) or the pan-cooked eggplant slices from Eggplant Parmesan (page 299)

15. Slices of grilled zucchini (see Grilling Everyday Vegetables, page 255)

5 Alternative Crusts for Pizzas

You can make a pizza without making pizza dough. Try any of these:

1. Flour tortillas

2. Pita bread

3. Polenta (see Polenta "Pizza," page 547)

4. Lightly toasted English muffins

5. Lightly dampened large crackers, like matzo or crisp lavash, dampened lightly by spraying with a water bottle or blotting them with a clean wet cloth

6 Things Vegans (or Anyone Else) Can Use Instead of Cheese

For a nice crunchiness and deep golden color, try tossing the following ingredients in a drizzle of extra virgin olive oil or a neutral oil, like grapeseed or corn, before topping the pizza. Press gently so that the topping sticks to the crust. Or if you're not using tomato sauce, smear the top with a layer of silken tofu.

1. Chopped nuts

2. Crumbled tofu (or tiny cubes)

3. Crumbled tempeh

4. Crumbled firm tofu

5. Cooked beans, lightly mashed

6. Fresh Bread Crumbs (page 804)

Focaccia

MAKES: 1 focaccia

TIME: About 3 hours, largely unattended

Focaccia is like pizza, but the dough is lightly seasoned and baked in a pan like bread. You generally top it a little differently too: minimally, with literally a handful of strong-flavored ingredients, like minced fresh herbs, thinly sliced tomatoes of any kind, Caramelized Onions (page 329), pitted black or green olives or Tapenade (page 326), grated Parmesan or other sharp cheese, or thin slices of peeled

Ⓕ Fast   Ⓜ Make Ahead   Ⓥ Vegan

fruit like peaches, nectarines, apples, or plums, or halved grapes.

To turn focaccia into a thick-crust Chicago-style pizza, bake the dough for about 10 minutes, then top as you like with sauce, cheese, and other ingredients and finish baking; see Pizza with Tomato Sauce and Mozzarella (page 726) and "15 Ideas for Pizza Toppings (page 728).

1 recipe Pizza Dough (page 724), made with an extra tablespoon olive oil, mixed and risen

3 tablespoons extra virgin olive oil

Coarse kosher or sea salt

1 When the dough is ready, knead it lightly, form it into a ball, and place it on a lightly floured surface. Sprinkle with a little more flour and cover with plastic wrap or a towel; let it rest for 20 minutes.

2 Use 1 tablespoon of the oil to grease an 11 × 17-inch jelly-roll pan. Press the dough into a small rectangle and place it in the pan; let it relax there for a few minutes. Press the dough to the edges of the pan. If it resists stretching, stretch it gently, then let it rest for a few minutes. Sometimes this takes a while, because the dough is so elastic. Don't fight it; just stretch, let it rest for 5 minutes, then stretch again. Try not to tear the dough.

3 Cover the dough and let it rise for at least 30 minutes, or until somewhat puffy. Meanwhile, preheat the oven to 425°F. Uncover the dough and dimple the surface all over with your fingertips. Drizzle with the remaining olive oil and sprinkle with plenty of salt.

4 Put the focaccia in the oven, lower the temperature to 375°F, and bake for about 30 minutes, or until the focaccia is golden. Remove and cool on a rack before serving. Cut focaccia into squares and serve with meals or as a snack. Or cut squares in half horizontally and use to make sandwiches. Focaccia, well wrapped (first in plastic, then in foil), freezes fairly well for 2 weeks or so. Reheat, straight from the freezer (unwrap, remove plastic, and then rewrap in foil), in a 350°F oven for 10 to 15 minutes.

Calzone

MAKES: 2 calzones, enough for 4 main-dish servings
TIME: About 3 hours, largely unattended

Here's how I "discovered" calzone: One day I messed up on sliding a pizza into the oven; it folded onto itself in a heap on the stone. I couldn't take it back out, and I couldn't bake it the way it was. So I quickly folded it over (and not too neatly), encasing the filling entirely in the dough. It was what you call making the best of a bad situation.

Intentionally made calzone is better than that. While you can make calzone using any pizza topping as a filling (see "15 Ideas for Pizza Toppings," page 728, for suggestions), it's best with cheese and vegetables rather than all cheese. While the filling should be substantial, it should also be fairly dry; very liquid fillings will leak or make the dough soggy; that's why drained ricotta, which is moist but not wet, is the ideal base.

You can serve calzone with Fresh Tomato Sauce (page 445) or any other tomato sauce, for dipping or topping.

1 recipe Pizza Dough (page 724), mixed and risen

2 cups ricotta cheese

1 cup finely chopped cooked spinach or other greens, such as chard or broccoli raab (see page 239)

1 cup chopped or grated mozzarella cheese

1 cup freshly grated Parmesan cheese

Salt and freshly ground black pepper

1 When the dough is ready, knead it lightly and cut it in two. Form 2 balls and place them on a lightly floured surface. Sprinkle with a little more flour and cover with plastic wrap or a towel; let them rest for 20 minutes. If the ricotta is very moist, drain it in a fine strainer for 10 minutes or so to remove excess moisture.

2 Combine the spinach or other vegetable, ricotta, mozzarella, and Parmesan. Taste and add salt, if necessary, and pepper. Preheat the oven to 350°F.

❸ Roll or lightly press each dough ball into a flat round, lightly flouring the work surface and the dough as necessary (do not use more flour than you need to). Let the rounds sit for a few minutes; this will relax the dough and make it easier to roll out. Roll or pat out the dough into an 8- to 10-inch round, not too thin, on a floured pizza peel or lightly oiled baking sheet.

❹ Put half the filling into the middle of each dough round. Moisten the edges with a little water. Fold one edge over onto the other and press closed with your fingertips.

❺ Bake the calzones on a baking sheet or directly on a baking stone for 30 to 40 minutes, or until nicely browned. Serve hot or warm.

9 Great Dishes for Filling Calzones

Calzones are perfect for using up leftovers. Reduce the ricotta to 1 cup and use 1 cup of the following, drained of any excess liquid, instead of the spinach.

1. Gigantes with Brussels Sprouts (page 587)
2. White Beans, Tuscan Style (page 594)
3. Roasted Chickpeas (page 618)
4. Roasted or Grilled Asparagus (page 261)
5. Eggplant Slices with Garlic and Parsley (page 297)
6. Leeks Braised in Oil or Butter (page 310)
7. Sautéed Mushrooms (page 314)
8. Roasted Red Peppers (page 333)
9. Winter Squash Slices, Roasted (page 366)

The Basics of Sandwiches

You know the concept: two pieces of bread—or a roll or loaf cut in half—with some kind of filling. The sandwich has been around for a few hundred years—supposedly named after its accidental inventor, the Earl of Sandwich, though who really believes that? Whoever "invented" bread probably made the first sandwich—and runs the gamut from simple peanut butter and jelly to something as deluxe as poached eggs with caramelized onions (open-faced, of course).

Sandwiches are a staple at lunch and make regular appearances at the dinner table as well, especially hot sandwiches. Frankly, more elaborate sandwiches (like the Seitan and Mushroom Loaf with Gruyère and Red Cabbage with Apples in the chart on page 733), are excellent main courses when made using a large loaf of ciabatta or thick focaccia and cut into individual pieces. Alternatively, downsize a sandwich to finger food or canapés (small open-face sandwiches served as hors d'oeuvres) by using thin slices of bread (with the crusts cut off if you like) and cutting the sandwich into pieces. Bottom line: There is a sandwich for every occasion.

Bread

Of course, a sandwich couldn't be a sandwich without bread, but the role of the bread goes beyond function. You want to be able to taste the bread, which means store-bought white is not the best choice.

Yeast or flat breads and rolls are usually the best sandwich breads because they have the structure to support the filling and a nice chewy texture. But some yeast breads simply aren't cut out for sandwiches; those with very hard or thick crusts can make sandwiches nearly impossible to eat, and breads with large holes just can't hold the filling. Crumbly quick breads can work but are best as open-face sandwiches with simple and small amounts of topping. (The charts on pages 731–734 give bread pairing suggestions for all sorts of sandwiches.)

Beyond the type of bread you use, cooking—toasting, grilling, and broiling—also alters the flavor and texture of the sandwich. It goes without saying that heating bread dries it out, making it crisp and adding a toasty flavor. It's largely a matter of whether you like your sandwich bread soft or crunchy, but keep in mind that some breads, like crusty, rustic-style ones, can be difficult, even painful, to eat when cooked.

Fillings and Spreads

With the exception of soupy and small, unbound items, like peas or rice, almost anything can be a sandwich filler, which makes for a huge range of possibilities (use pita or

Ⓕ Fast   Ⓜ Make Ahead   Ⓥ Vegan

COLD SANDWICHES

There are the classics, like egg salad and cucumber, and the more modern TLT (that's tofu (smoked), lettuce, and tomato). Although the sandwich itself is served cold, any of the bread can be toasted to add a lovely crunch and touch of toasty flavor. Feel free to mix and match; these are just ideas to get you thinking.

BREAD	SPREAD	FILLINGS	CONDIMENTS
Sandwich Bread: Half Whole Wheat, or Bran and Oat (page 713)	none	Egg Salad (page 179); tomatoes; lettuce or watercress	Mayonnaise with minced sweet pickles (page 771; optional)
Sandwich Bread (page 712) or Pita (page 719)	none	Hard-Cooked Eggs (page 166), sliced; chopped black olives; tomatoes; lettuce	Roasted Pepper Mayonnaise (page 771)
Pita (page 719)	Hummus (page 614)	Falafel (page 625; optional); tomatoes; cucumbers; lettuce	The Simplest Yogurt Sauce (page 774)
Sourdough Bread (page 709), Focaccia (page 728), or any Italian-style bread	Traditional Pesto (page 768) or torn basil leaves and a drizzle of extra virgin olive oil	Fresh mozzarella; tomatoes; sprinkled with salt and freshly ground black pepper	none
Sourdough Bread (page 709) or Fast French Bread (page 707)	none	Smoked tofu; avocado; tomatoes; lettuce	Homemade Mayonnaise (page 771); Brewhouse Mustard (page 776)
Rich Golden Sandwich Bread (page 715) or Sourdough Bread (page 709)	Dried-Tomato Tapenade (page 327)	Marinated Tofu (page 652); tomatoes; arugula	Cold Mustard Sauce (page 771)
Whole Grain Bread (page 713) or Rich Golden Sandwich Bread (page 715)	none	Tofu Escabeche (page 653); manchego cheese; tomatoes; arugula	Garlic Mayonnaise (page 771)
Half Whole Wheat Sandwich Bread (page 713) or Rich Golden Sandwich Bread (page 715)	Blue Cheese Spread (page 212)	Grilled or broiled tomato slices (page 255); watercress	Tomato Mustard (page 777) or Cold Mustard Sauce (page 771)
Fast French Bread (page 707)	walnut pâté	Brie (preferably at room temperature); sliced pear or apple; frisée	Rosemary or Honey Mustard (page 777)
Rich Golden Sandwich Bread (page 715) or English Muffin (page 714)	Any cheese spread (pages 212–213) (optional)	Poached or Fried Egg (page 169 or 168); Caramelized Onions (page 329); frisée or spinach	Grainy Mustard (page 776) or Dijon
Anadama Bread (page 713) or Pita (page 719)	Lighter Cilantro (or other herb) "Pesto" (page 769)	Grilled eggplant, zucchini, or yellow squash; Monterey Jack; tomatoes; lettuce	Chile Mayonnaise (page 771)

BREAD	SPREAD	FILLINGS	CONDIMENTS
Fast French Bread (page 707) or Sourdough Bread (page 709)	goat cheese spread (page 213) or plain goat cheese	Roasted (or grilled) Red Peppers (page 333); tomatoes; arugula or spinach	Green Sauce, French Style (page 771)
Fast French Bread (page 707)	none	Soy- or Miso-Baked Tofu (page 641); tomatoes; alfalfa or other sprouts	Mayonnaise with wasabi (page 771)
Half Whole Wheat or regular Sandwich Bread (page 712)	Cream cheese with chives or scallions	Cucumber slices; radish slices (optional); broccoli or other sprouts	none

HOT SANDWICHES

Grilled, broiled, griddled, or toasted, there's a lot to be said for a sandwich with a steaming filling, some melted cheese, and toasty or completely soft bread. Here the sandwiches are either assembled from separate cooked items or cooked as sandwiches (à la grilled cheese).

Again, mix up these combos as you like, drawing inspiration rather than rules from this chart.

BREAD	SPREAD	FILLING	CONDIMENTS	COOKING
Anadama Bread (page 713) or hamburger buns	none	Marinated Tofu with Barbecue Sauce (page 653); tomatoes; onions; lettuce	Mustard Relish (page 776); Homemade Mayonnaise (page 771)	Grill the tofu, the onions if you like, and the bread until toasted; assemble the sandwich.
Fast French Bread (page 707) or Rich Golden Sandwich Bread (page 715)	none	Grilled or Broiled Tofu (page 642); grilled or broiled onions (page 254); arugula	Peach Melon Tomato Salsa (page 752); Homemade Mayonnaise (page 771)	Grill or broil the tofu and onions; toast the bread if you like; assemble the sandwich.
Whole Grain Bread (page 713) or Bran and Oat Sandwich Bread (page 713)	none	Crispy Panfried Tofu (page 642); tomatoes; Spicy No-Mayo Coleslaw (page 49)	Homemade Mayonnaise (page 771; optional)	Fry the tofu and toast the bread; assemble the sandwich.
Half Whole Wheat Sandwich Bread (page 713), Whole Grain Bread (page 713), or Pita (page 719)	red bell pepper purée (see page 389)	Bean Croquettes (page 627) or any bean cake or fritter; Monterey Jack; red onions; lettuce	Chile Mustard (page 777); Homemade Mayonnaise (page 771)	Fry or warm the croquettes and melt the cheese on top; heat the bread in a 300°F oven with the purée spread on a piece; assemble the sandwich.

BREAD	SPREAD	FILLING	CONDIMENTS	COOKING
Black Bread (page 716) or Whole Grain Bread (page 713)	Mushroom Ketchup (page 791) or Sautéed Mushrooms (page 314)	Grilled or Broiled Seitan (page 672); Swiss or fontina cheese; onions; spinach	Homemade Mayonnaise (page 771) with Worcestershire Sauce, Hold the Anchovies (page 799)	Grill or broil the seitan and melt the cheese on top with the onions; grill or toast the bread; assemble the sandwich.
Black Bread or Poppy Seed Swirl Bread (page 716)	none	Seitan and Mushroom Loaf (page 670), sliced; Gruyère or Emmental; Red Cabbage with Apples (page 277)	Chile Mayonnaise (page 771) or horseradish; Dijon mustard	Toast the bread; spread on the mustard, and add the hot seitan and cheese on one slice; heat in a 300°F oven until the cheese is melted; heat the cabbage and drain off any liquid; assemble the sandwich.
Sourdough Bread (page 709), Focaccia (page 728), or any Italian-style bread	Roasted Garlic (page 304)	Grilled endive or radicchio (page 253); fontina or Gruyère	Rosemary or Grainy Mustard (pages 776–777) or Dijon	Grill the endive or radicchio and bread, melting the cheese on one slice; spread the garlic and mustard on the other slice; assemble the sandwich.
Fast French Bread (page 707) or hamburger buns	Caramelized Onion Chutney (page 786) or Caramelized Onions (page 329)	Grilled Mushrooms (portobellos; page 316); tomatoes; lettuce	Mango or Grainy Mustard (pages 776–777)	Grill the portobellos and the bread if you like; spread the chutney on one slice, the mustard on the other; assemble the sandwich.
Sourdough Bread (page 709) or Sandwich Bread (page 712)	none	Caramelized Onions (page 329); Oven-Roasted Fresh Plum Tomatoes (page 375); manchego cheese (optional); spinach or arugula	Mayonnaise with smoked paprika	Toast the bread; add the onions and tomatoes and top with the cheese; broil until the cheese is melted; assemble the sandwich.
Quick Whole Wheat and Molasses Bread (page 689)	Applesauce (page 419; optional)	Smoked cheddar; sliced apple; frisée	Mayonnaise with chopped pecans or walnuts	Toast the bread; spread the apple purée on one slice of bread and layer the cheese and apple; broil until the cheese is melted; assemble the sandwich.

BREAD	SPREAD	FILLING	CONDIMENTS	COOKING
Focaccia (page 728) or Sourdough Bread (page 709)	Tapenade (page 326; optional)	Mozzarella, Roasted Red Peppers (page 333)	Extra virgin olive oil	Spread the tapenade on both slices of bread; layer the mozzarella and roasted peppers; drizzle with olive oil; assemble the sandwich; put the sandwich in a hot pan or on a grill and cook until the bread is toasted and the cheese is soft.
Rich Golden Sandwich Bread (page 715) or Nut-and-Fruit Bread (page 691)	Goat cheese	Sliced figs (fresh or dried); chopped walnuts and/or almonds; arugula	Port Wine Mustard (page 776)	Toast the bread; spread the cheese thickly on one piece of bread and add the figs; broil the bread with the cheese until the cheese is melted and lightly browned; add the chopped walnuts; assemble the sandwich.
Fast French Bread (page 707) or Sandwich Bread (page 712)	Almond or any nut butter	Banana slices; chocolate chips or marshmallows (optional)	none	Assemble the sandwich; melt a pat of butter in a hot pan, then add the sandwich and cook until both sides are golden brown and toasted.

make a wrap and the filling can be as tiny as you like). Whether it's grilled, roasted, breaded and fried, boiled, or puréed vegetables; salads (egg salad or tabbouleh for pita); poached, fried, scrambled, hard-cooked and sliced eggs; fritters or burger patties; or dozens of cheeses or tofu preparations, you won't run out of sandwich fillers anytime soon.

There are few rules for fillings and even fewer for spreads. Obviously you don't want a filling that's so moist that it sogs up the bread or so dry that you need a gulp of water with every bite (remember the bread is dry too). At the same time, you want the filling thin enough that you can get your mouth around the sandwich, but not in such small pieces that the filling falls out of the bread. (When in doubt, just stuff a pita pocket.)

The spreads should be full of flavor and provide some moisture and/or creaminess to the sandwich. Cheese spreads, soft cheeses, and vegetable and bean purées are ideal for this. Or skip the filling and use just the spread. Most spreads, like hummus, make simple but tasty sandwiches that can easily be transformed into bite-sized hors d'oeuvres.

Top 8 Things to Have on Hand for Filling Sandwiches

1. Tofu (for baking, frying, grilling, broiling, marinating, and more)
2. Hard-Cooked Eggs (page 166, for egg salad or just slicing)

 Fast   Make Ahead   Ⓥ Vegan

3. Hummus (page 617) or any bean spread or purée
4. Cheese spread or slices
5. Tomato slices
6. Onion slices
7. Lettuce, arugula, watercress, or spinach
8. Condiments or dressings: standbys like mustard, mayo, ketchup, and relish, but also Traditional Pesto and other herb sauces, barbecue sauce, chutney, cooked or fresh salsa (pages 750–792)

6 Tips for Preventing a Sandwich from Getting Soggy

Aside from the obvious—eating it immediately—here's how to keep a packed sandwich fresh.

1. Use cold or room-temperature ingredients; heat will create steam and condensation, which the bread will absorb.
2. For picnics and traveling, wrap the components separately and assemble the sandwich just before eating.
3. Omit the tomato; substitute Roasted Red Pepper (page 333) pieces, blotted dry with paper towels.
4. Use a less moist filling or blot a moist filling with paper towels.
5. Use a dry, dense, crusty bread, which will be far more resilient than a very soft, fluffy bread and will soften up after a few hours of being wrapped with the fillings.
6. Make a wrap using a large flour tortilla (see "Wraps," page 736); tortillas don't absorb moisture as readily as bread.

Bruschetta

MAKES: 4 servings
TIME: About 20 minutes

At its simplest, bruschetta is simply crisp, hot bread rubbed gently with a clove of garlic, drizzled with lots of good olive oil, and sprinkled with salt; a snack, or a starter. But depending on how you top it, it can become a side dish or even a light meal. For some more elaborate topping suggestions, see the variations and the list on page 737.

Once you get beyond the smoky grilled flavor, the important thing is the texture: a combination of crunch and body that can be achieved only when you add the olive oil *after* cooking. For classic bruschetta, use the best rustic Italian-style bread you can get your hands on—or use one of the home-baked European-style breads on pages 707–711. Slice it yourself, up to 1 inch thick, so that the outside gets crunchy while the inside stays moist.

8 thick slices rustic bread
Extra virgin olive oil as needed
1 to 4 garlic cloves, halved or peeled and crushed
Salt and freshly ground black pepper

❶ Heat a charcoal or gas grill until moderately hot, or heat the broiler and put the rack about 4 inches from the heat source. Grill or broil the bread until lightly browned on both sides, ideally with some grill marks or light charring.

❷ While the bread is still hot, rub the slices with the garlic on one or both sides. Put it on a plate, then drizzle it with olive oil (a tablespoon or so should do it) and sprinkle it with salt and pepper. Serve warm.

Broiled Bruschetta. When you don't feel like firing up the grill: Preheat the broiler and put the rack about 4 inches from the heat source.

Bruschetta with Tomatoes and Basil. Excellent with an assortment of summer tomatoes: Core about a pound of ripe tomatoes, squeeze most of the seeds out (page 373), and coarsely chop them. If you have time, put them in a strainer for a few minutes to drain the excess water. When the bread is ready to cook, combine the tomatoes and about a cup of torn basil leaves in a bowl, along with a drizzle of olive oil and a sprinkle of salt. Toss to combine. After rubbing the garlic on the bread in Step 2, put the tomato mixture on top of the bread. Sprinkle with pepper and serve.

WRAPS

A wrap is a kind of sandwich/burrito hybrid, where the filling is as varied as any sandwich and then some. Because wraps are folded and rolled like a burrito, they can hold items that would otherwise fall out of two pieces of bread or make a soggy mess of sandwich bread (like beans and rice). On top of any sandwich filling, load up wraps with any dressed salad, grains, legumes, stir-fried vegetables, or chopped vegetables.

Any large, flat and flexible bread will work as a wrapping; tortillas and lavash are the most common, though you can also use Pita (page 719). The wrapping plays a supporting role, providing more structure than flavor; even most flavored tortillas are mildly flavored at best and are for looks more than anything else. Substituting one type of wrap for another is always fine.

Lavash comes in two forms, the soft bread (basically freshly baked) and the hard cracker (where the bread has been allowed to dry). Both can be used for wraps. Soften the hard cracker by running it under water on both sides, place it in a plastic bag, seal it, and let it sit in a cool place or refrigerator until it's completely soft, about 3 hours (the same holds for the large ak-mak, which also has instructions on the side of the package).

WRAP	SPREAD	FILLING	CONDIMENTS
Lavash or ak-mak	Bean dip with red lentils (page 614)	Grilled Tofu (page 742); cucumbers; tomatoes	Creamy Cilantro-Mint Chutney (page 784)
Lavash or ak-mak	Tahini or Spice-Marinated Feta (page 211)	Tabbouleh (page 43); grilled eggplant (page 252; optional)	Onion Yogurt Sauce (page 774; optional)
Plain or flavored tortilla	none	Breaded and fried tomatoes and/or zucchini and yellow squash (page 246); romaine; chopped chives or scallions	Blue Cheese Dressing (page 212) or Real Ranch Dressing (page 772)
Lavash or ak-mak	Spicy Mashed Eggplant with Yogurt and Mint (page 298)	Tomatoes; onion or scallions; crumbled feta (optional)	Za'atar (to make your own, see page 818)
Plain tortilla	Guacamole (page 263)	Chile Scrambled Tofu (page 655); corn kernels; tomatoes; queso fresco, cheddar, or Monterey Jack	Any salsa you like (pages 750–753 and 787–789); sour cream
Lavash or ak-mak	none	Braised Tofu and Peas in Curried Coconut Milk (page 648) or Quick-Braised Vegetables, Thai Style (page 379); basmati or jasmine rice; lettuce; cilantro sprigs	Chile Paste (page 828)
Plain tortilla	Hoisin or vegetarian oyster sauce	Grilled Tomatoes and Scrambled Eggs, Chinese Style (page 374); Spiced Stir-Fried Bean Sprouts (page 265) or steamed Asian greens, like bok choy, gai lan, or tatsoi (page 239)	Ginger-Scallion Sauce (page 779) instead of the hoisin or oyster sauce
Lavash, ak-mak, or plain tortilla	Teriyaki Sauce (page 779) or Ginger-Scallion Sauce (page 779)	Tofu Burger, Asian Style (page 666), crumbled, or Teriyaki- or Ponzu-Grilled or Broiled Tofu (page 643); shredded carrot and daikon; chopped scallions	Chile-Garlic Paste (page 830)
Plain or flavored tortilla	Fast Fresh Tomato Sauce (page 445)	Eggplant Parmesan (page 299); mozzarella; spinach (optional)	none

 Fast   Make Ahead   Ⓥ Vegan

Crostini. Thinly sliced and ultra-crisp, these Italian-style croutonlike toasts until recently were known in America as "toast points": Slice the bread more thinly and into smaller pieces so you have between 16 and 24 pieces. Crisp them on a grill, under a broiler, or in a 400°F oven until golden on all sides. Rub them with garlic if you like and top them in any of the ways described on page 735 or in the list below.

25 Unexpected Toast Toppers

You have a lot of options when it comes to topping bruschetta, beyond the usual open-face sandwich ideas. Some are like serving the croutons underneath a more substantial dish. And don't forget that you can slice virtually any other bread—whole grain, sandwich, or even corn bread or focaccia—and give them the toast-and-top treatment. For each of the following suggestions, put the bread on a plate immediately after cooking (without the garlic and oil) and top.

1. Any vinaigrette, with or without a green salad (page 762)
2. Balsamic Strawberries with Arugula (page 42)
3. Parsley and Herb Salad (page 42)
4. Shaved Artichoke Salad (page 50)
5. Seaweed Romaine Salad (page 56)
6. Heirloom Tomato Salad with Hard-Cooked Eggs (page 59)
7. Ratatouille Salad or its variation (page 64)
8. Roasted Cauliflower with Raisins and Vinaigrette (page 282)
9. Corn Salad with Tomatoes, Feta, and Mint or its variation (page 61)
10. Mushroom Salad, Italian-American Style (page 62)
11. Essential Bean Salad, Italian, French, or Greek Style (page 72)
12. Warm Chickpea Salad with Arugula (page 73)
13. Lemony Lentil Salad or its variation (page 75)
14. Broiled Three-Bean Salad or its variations (page 74)
15. Fresh Cottage Cheese or Ricotta (page 230)
16. Cheese Fondue or any of its variations (page 221)
17. Kidney Beans with Apples and Sherry (page 586)
18. Beans and Greens (page 595)
19. Beans and Mushrooms or any of its variations (page 596)
20. Chickpea Fondue or its variations (page 615)
21. White Bean Purée or its variations (page 612)
22. Mashed Favas (page 616)
23. Sautéed Eggplant with Tomatoes (page 269)
24. Leeks Braised in Oil or Butter or its variations (page 310)
25. Sautéed Mushrooms or its variations (page 314)

6 Great Spreads for Bruschetta or Crostini

After toasting the bread, you might think about smearing the top of each piece with one of these:

1. Blue Cheese Spread or its variations (page 212)
2. Mushroom Pâté or its variations (page 316)
3. Egg Salad or its variations (page 179)
4. Tapenade or its variations (page 326)
5. Hummus and bean dips (page 614)
6. Virtually any puréed vegetable (pages 387–391)

The Basics of Tacos and Burritos

Tacos and burritos have a lot in common: They use tortillas; can be filled with beans, rice, vegetables, salsas, etc.; and, mostly, are eaten with your hands. But they don't share the same origins. In fact, tacos are authentic—if not quintessential—Mexican food, made with corn or flour tortillas, while burritos are a north-of-the-border Tex-Mex invention, and always made with flour tortillas.

Heritage aside, both tacos and burritos are fantastic convenience foods that can be assembled quickly from a huge variety of ingredients and eaten quickly or even on the run. They can also become part of a do-it-yourself buffet loaded with various fillings, toppings, and extras.

Most name-brand tortillas are made with vegetable shortening; vegetarians should beware that some traditionally made tortillas sold in Mexican or Latin markets may contain lard.

Most supermarkets sell a half dozen varieties of tortillas these days, varying in type (corn or flour), size, and flavor. Though they don't compare in terms of flavor and texture to those made fresh daily at a local tortilleria, they will certainly do the job. But if you live near a Mexican or Latin market, it's worth the trip to buy really good tortillas.

Flour tortillas are soft and subtle, almost neutral in flavor; when fresh, they are delicious and almost fluffy, but more often than not they are dull and rubbery. A variety of types are available in most supermarkets, including plain, whole wheat, and others flavored (and colored) with things like spinach or tomato. Flour tortillas range in size from small (2 or 3 inches) to very large (12 inches or so, ideal for burritos), and are almost always served and used soft but are occasionally fried crisp.

Corn tortillas—both white and yellow and sometimes even blue—offer more texture and flavor than flour, and, like flour, the fresh ones are completely different from those that sit on the supermarket shelves for weeks at a time. The best corn tortillas have a fresh corn flavor and a soft and pliable texture when raw; they're rarely more than 6 inches in diameter. Cooked corn tortillas can be either soft or crisp, depending on your taste or how fresh the tortilla is—serve them soft if they're fresh; fry them if they're stale.

Cooking Tortillas

Soft tortillas should be served hot or warm. Heat them over direct heat, like a grill or the flame of a gas stove, turning them every few seconds, or in a dry skillet or wrap them in a damp kitchen towel and heat in the microwave for about 30 seconds. To keep the tortillas hot, put them in a tortilla holder (a shallow round container with a lid) or wrap them in a towel or two.

Corn tortillas are served crisp more commonly than flour, but both fry up nicely. There are two methods: Panfry in a skillet with hot oil until crisp (flip it over as the edges brown; you can mold it into a taco shape when it's still slightly soft and flexible); or stuff tortillas with filling, secure with toothpicks, and panfry them in $1/4$ inch or so of hot oil until both sides are golden, bubbly, and crisped. (Drain the tortillas on paper towels for several seconds before serving.)

ROLLING BURRITOS

(STEP 1) Put the filling on the third of the tortilla closest to you. (STEP 2) Fold in the sides a little bit and (STEP 3) roll up, tucking in the sides and the top edge to form a fairly tight roll.

Ⓕ Fast   Ⓜ Make Ahead   Ⓥ Vegan

10 TACO AND BURRITO IDEAS

Here are some suggestions for filling tacos and burritos; mix and match as you like. Sprinkle on Crunchy Crumbled Tempeh (page 774) or any other crumble (page 805) for extra texture, especially in combination with soft tofu or bean fillings or in soft tortillas.

Also see Breakfast Burritos (pages 174–175) for some delicious ideas using scrambled eggs.

TACO OR BURRITO	FILLINGS	SALSAS, TOPPINGS, AND EXTRAS
Taco (corn or flour tortilla) or burrito (any tortilla)	Any tofu (pages 641–644); Beer-Glazed Black Beans (page 585; optional)	Corn Salsa (page 751) or Super-Spicy Chile-Garlic Salsa (page 789); Crunchy Corn or Minimalist Guacamole (page 263)
Taco (corn tortilla) or burrito (whole wheat flour tortilla)	Chile Scrambled Tofu (page 655)	Garlic-Scallion Sauce (page 779); Bean Salsa (page 751) or Fresh Tomatillo Salsa (page 751); bean or nut crumbles (page 805)
Taco (corn or flour tortilla) or burrito (flour tortilla)	Twice-Cooked (Refried) Beans (page 592); Mexican Rice with Vegetables (page 512; optional)	Radish Salsa (page 752), Jícama Salsa (page 751), or Pepita Pico de Verde (page 751)
Burrito (whole wheat or flavored tortilla)	White Rice and Black Beans (page 510); fried plantains (optional)	Minimalist Guacamole (page 264); Cooked Tomatillo Salsa (page 788) or Chipotle-Cherry Salsa (page 752)
Taco (corn or flour tortilla)	The Simplest Bean Burgers (page 660) or Midsummer Vegetable Burger (page 664), crumbled	Avocado–Red Pepper Salsa (page 751) or Charred Salsa Roja (page 788)
Taco (corn or flour tortilla) or burrito (flour or whole wheat tortilla)	Spicy Black Bean Croquettes (page 627), crumbled	Avocado and Dried Tomato Spread (page 264); Peach Melon Tomato Salsa (page 752) or Radish Salsa (page 752)
Taco (corn or flour tortilla) or burrito (whole wheat or flavored tortilla)	Breaded and fried eggplant, zucchini, yellow squash, tropical tubers, or any vegetable (see chart on page 246)	Fresh Tomato Salsa (page 750) or Mexican Cheese Salsa (page 751)
Taco (corn tortilla)	Grilled or Broiled or Pan-Seared Seitan (pages 672 or 671)	Salsa Borracha (page 788) or Smoky and Hot Salsa Roja (page 788)
Burrito (whole wheat or flavored)	Tempeh Chili with Black Beans (page 677)	Cooked Tomatillo Salsa (page 788) or Green Tomato Pico De Verde (page 751)
Taco (corn or flour tortilla)	Beer-Battered Squash Blossoms (page 247)	Crunchy Corn Guacamole (page 263); Puréed Salsa Fresca (page 750) or Fresh Tomatillo Salsa (page 751)

Filling Tortillas

Beans and rice are a traditional and excellent filling for tacos and burritos; not only are they delicious, but they also provide complete protein. Be sure the beans are well seasoned and not too soupy (especially important for tacos); partially mash whole beans to vary the texture and absorb some excess liquid if there's too much. Add more texture by using firmer grains, like wheat berries, instead of rice.

Vegetables are another option, especially when grilled or breaded and fried, which give tacos and burritos an irresistible crunchy-soft texture. You can use just about any vegetable you like, bearing in mind the various limitations of the cooking method (see "How to Grill Vegetables," page 249, and Battered and Fried Vegetables, page 245).

The least traditional fillings are not Mexican at all: tofu, seitan, and tempeh. But you don't have to let tradition stand in your way. All of these fillings offer an excellent variety of flavors, textures, and cooking methods. Frying, baking, and grilling tofu or tempeh gives it a great meaty texture, and grilled seitan offers that lovely char flavor and a pleasantly chewy texture.

The Right Salsa

Homemade salsa can improve tacos and burritos immeasurably. Check out the raw and cooked salsas on pages 750–753 and 787–789 and don't forget Crunchy Corn Guacamole (page 263), which adds creamy richness, especially valuable when you're using a vegetable filling.

Of course, shredded lettuce, chopped tomatoes, grated cheese, sour cream (or yogurt), and hot sauces are givens; serve them in bowls on the table for everyone to dress his or her own tacos and burritos if you like.

Rolling Burritos

Rolling a solid burrito doesn't take too much skill. The biggest impediment is usually caused by overstuffing. The solution: Fill it with less stuffing or use a larger tortilla. On the other hand, because tortillas are so elastic, you can use more filling than with most other stuffed things. To keep them together after rolling, put the burritos seam side down on a plate or wrap the bottom half in foil or wax paper until you're ready to cook.

10 Other Great Fillings for Tacos and Burritos

With some of these ingredients—like bean cakes and veggie burgers—you'll be crumbling or chopping them up before filling.

1. Winter squash slices, roasted (page 366)
2. My Mom's Pan-Cooked Peppers and Onions (page 334)
3. Sautéed Ripe Plantains (page 336) or Fried Plantain Chips (page 336)
4. Sautéed Chayote (page 362)
5. Cassava Fritters (page 394)
6. Bulgur Chili (page 557) or any chili with rice or grains
7. Any grilled or roasted vegetable (like eggplant, mushrooms, any summer squash, peppers or chiles, and onions) (pages 251–255)
8. Pinto Beans with Red Bell Pepper (page 594)
9. Chili non Carne (page 607) or Espresso Black Bean Chili (page 608)
10. Black Bean Cakes with Queso Fresco (page 629)

Other Filled Breads and Wrappers

Beyond sandwiches, wraps, burritos, and tacos is a world of stuffed breads, doughs, and wrappers. But like their Americanized cousins, these can be served as appetizers, snacks, or the centerpiece of a larger meal. You can make some of them with store-bought breads; others you must make from scratch, though none are particularly difficult.

Ⓕ Fast   Ⓜ Make Ahead   Ⓥ Vegan

Chile-Bean Quesadillas

MAKES: 6 main-dish or 12 appetizer or side-dish servings
TIME: 15 minutes

To me, quesadillas are more like grilled cheese sandwiches than tacos or burritos. The secret is to resist overstuffing them. Too much cheese, for example, and they ooze all over the place; too many extra ingredients, and the cheese never melds the two tortillas together. But these are both advantages, because few hot dishes are easier or make better use of teeny amounts of leftovers. (See the charts and lists in The Basics of Tacos and Burritos on page 737–741 for ideas.)

2 tablespoons neutral oil, like grapeseed or corn, plus more as needed

2 cloves garlic, minced

3 or 4 poblano or other mild fresh chiles, stemmed, seeded, and chopped (page 826)

1 cup cooked or well-drained canned pinto beans

1/4 cup chopped fresh cilantro leaves

Twelve 6-inch corn tortillas or eight 8-inch flour tortillas

1 cup grated Mexican melting cheese, like cotija or queso blanco, or mild cheddar or Monterey Jack, or a combination

1/4 cup salsa (pages 750–751), guacamole (page 263), or sour cream or yogurt (optional)

1 Put the oil in a large skillet, preferably nonstick or well-seasoned cast-iron, over medium heat. When hot, add the garlic and chiles and cook, stirring occasionally, until softened, about 2 minutes. If the mixture begins to brown, add a little water to the skillet. Stir in the beans and cook them just long enough to warm (it's okay if they get a little mashed). Remove from the heat and stir in the cilantro. Transfer to a bowl and wipe out the skillet.

2 Set the skillet over medium-low heat. Add just enough oil to coat the bottom lightly. Build your quesadilla: Put a tortilla on the skillet, spread on an even layer of cheese and the chile-bean mixture, then top with another tortilla. When the cheese begins to melt, after about 2 minutes, use a spatula to flip the quesadilla over. Cook just until the bottom tortilla is warm and lightly toasted, about 2 minutes. Repeat with the remaining ingredients.

3 Cut the quesadillas into wedges and serve immediately with salsa, guacamole, or sour cream. (Or you can keep the quesadillas warm in a 200°F oven for a few minutes if you like before garnishing.)

Quesadilla for One. Great for snacking: Scale the quesadilla ingredients back to a drizzle or two of olive oil, a teaspoon of minced garlic, 1 chile, 2 tablespoons beans, a sprinkle of chopped cilantro if you like, 2 corn or flour tortillas, and about 3 tablespoons of grated cheese.

Grilled Chile-Bean Quesadillas. Heat a charcoal or gas grill until moderately hot and put the rack about 4 inches from the heat source. Brush one side of a tortilla with oil and set on the grill. Build your quesadilla as instructed in Step 2 and brush oil on the top tortilla. Proceed as directed.

All-Cheese Quesadilla. Perfect in its simplicity: Omit the beans and chiles and increase the amount of cheese to 2 cups (a mixture is great).

Egg Rolls

MAKES: 20 egg rolls
TIME: 45 minutes

Homemade egg rolls are a different breed from the mass-produced ones sold in freezer cases and most restaurants, even if you start with store-bought wrappers. They also make a terrific side dish, served with any number of dipping sauces, like a basic soy sauce and vinegar mixture, hoisin, or Chile-Garlic Paste (page 830).

Use rice paper (page 465) instead of egg roll wrappers for an even crisper, Southeast Asian–style egg roll. See the list of other vegetables you can use in this recipe; mix and match as you like. You can even fill egg rolls with other cooked grain or bean dishes and fry them up just like this.

To make egg roll wrappers yourself, and for even more filling and saucing ideas, see Dumpling Wrappers (page 491) and the handful of recipes and lists that follow.

1 teaspoon sugar

2 teaspoons soy sauce

2 teaspoons rice wine or dry sherry

8 ounces pressed tofu (page 639) or squeezed tofu (page 640), julienned

Peanut or neutral oil, like corn or grapeseed, as needed

5 fresh (or reconstituted and drained; see page 317) shiitake mushrooms, stems discarded, sliced

3 scallions, roughly chopped

2 cups bean sprouts or shredded Napa cabbage

1 tablespoon peeled and minced fresh ginger

20 egg roll wrappers (to make your own, see page 492)

1 Whisk together the sugar, soy, and wine and then toss with the tofu. While it sits, put 2 tablespoons of oil in a large skillet over medium-high heat. When hot, add the mushrooms, scallions, and bean sprouts and cook, stirring occasionally, for about 3 minutes. Remove from the pan with a slotted spoon.

2 Add another tablespoon of oil to the skillet and cook the ginger, stirring, until fragrant, about 30 seconds. Add the tofu and its marinade and cook until it's hot, stirring occasionally to separate the pieces, about 3 minutes. Return the vegetables to the pan, mix well, and cook for another minute. Remove the mixture with a slotted spoon. (You can store the filling, covered, in the refrigerator for up to a day.)

3 Put at least 3 inches oil in a countertop deep-fryer or in a deep pan on the stove and turn the heat to medium-high; bring to 350°F (see "Deep-Frying," page 26). Meanwhile, moisten the edges of an egg roll wrapper with water and put 2 tablespoons of the filling in a line down the center; fold in the sides and roll tightly. Seal the seam with a few drops of water.

4 Working in batches, put the egg rolls in the oil and turn occasionally to brown evenly; the cooking will be easy and quick, about 5 minutes per batch (you just have to heat them through and brown the outside; everything inside is already cooked). Adjust the heat as necessary so that the egg rolls brown evenly. As they finish, drain on paper towels. Serve hot, with any of the sauces you like.

Panfried Egg Rolls. This cooking method uses less oil, though it's not necessarily low-fat: Put the oil to a depth of about $1/2$ inch in a deep skillet over medium-high heat. When the oil is hot, after about a minute, add some of the egg rolls, rolling them as they cook to brown all sides.

Smoked Tofu and Turnip Egg Rolls. Slightly smoky, slightly sweet: Substitute smoked tofu for the pressed or squeezed tofu and thinly julienned turnip for the bean sprouts.

11 Other Vegetables to Use in Egg Rolls

Finely julienne, thinly slice, or finely chop as necessary:

1. Carrots
2. Daikon
3. Burdock
4. Snow peas
5. Celery
6. Leeks
7. Spinach (cooked, squeezed dry, and chopped; see page 239)
8. Broccoli

 Fast   Make Ahead   Vegan

9. Water chestnuts
10. Green peas
11. Corn kernels

Summer Rolls

MAKES: 8 rolls (4 to 8 servings)
TIME: 40 minutes

This classic Vietnamese appetizer, with its pliable white rice paper wraps, saladlike filling, and flavorful dipping sauces, takes a little practice, but not much: You'll get good at it pretty quickly. Think of this recipe as an outline for any kind of summer roll you like; the filling can be anything from tofu to shredded vegetables to slices of fruit.

Working with rice paper is not rocket science—it's not even cooking. All they need is a dip in hot water to soften up and become pliable; they'll continue to soften a bit after they've been rolled. The two most common mistakes people make with rice paper is letting them soak too long (they become mushy and tear easily) and making the rolls too far in advance, which results in a dried-out and overly chewy rice paper wrapper. So remember to keep the hot water dip short and to serve the rolls immediately or wrap well and serve within an hour. And as with other stuffed wrappers, be careful not to overfill.

For dipping, try Peanut Sauce, Six Ways (page 794), Fishless Fish Sauce (page 778), Ponzu Sauce (page 780), Basil Dipping Sauce (page 777), Vietnamese- or Thai-Style Chile Paste (page 829), Chile-Garlic Paste (page 830), or just soy sauce with vinegar or water.

8 sheets rice paper, 10 or 12 inches in diameter

8 to 10 tender lettuce leaves, like Boston, washed, dried, and torn

One 4-ounce bundle rice vermicelli, soaked in hot water until softened (about 10 minutes) and drained

2 scallions, cut into 2-inch pieces and sliced lengthwise

2 carrots, finely julienned or grated

1/2 cup fresh mint leaves

1/2 cup fresh cilantro leaves

1/2 cup fresh basil leaves, preferably Thai

Lime wedges for garnish

1 Set up a work station: Lay out a damp kitchen or paper towel on the counter and a large bowl of hot water (110 to 120°F, which is about what hot water measures from most taps). Dip a sheet of the rice paper in the hot water, turning once, until soft, about 10 seconds. Lay it flat on the towel.

2 On the bottom third of the rice paper, spread an eighth of each of the remaining ingredients except lime in a line. Fold in the bottom edge and both sides and then roll tightly into a cylinder (like a burrito; see page 738). The rice paper will adhere to itself. Repeat this process with the remaining ingredients.

3 Serve immediately or wrap in damp paper towels and plastic wrap and serve within an hour or so, with a dipping sauce and the lime wedges.

10 Great Fillings for Summer Rolls
Not all of these are traditional, but they are all good.

1. Pressed, squeezed, or smoked tofu slices (page 610 and 640)
2. Deep-Fried, Crispy Panfried, or Marinated Tofu (pages 643, 642, or 652)
3. Daikon, peeled and finely julienned or grated
4. Spinach leaves
5. Asparagus, steamed (see page 240)
6. Green or wax beans, cooked and shocked (page 241)
7. Hothouse cucumber, peeled and finely julienned or grated
8. Green papaya, peeled and finely julienned or grated

9. Mango or ripe papaya, peeled and thinly sliced
10. Steamed Sticky Rice (page 507) or Coconut Rice (page 507), warm or room temperature

Rice and Lentil Crêpes

Dosas

MAKES: 16 to 20 dosas
TIME: 2 days, largely unattended

When you first see a dosa, usually in an Indian restaurant, you think it's a work of art, as hard to create as to conceive. But then you start dreaming of re-creating them at home.

The good news is that these thin, crisp, oversized pancakes, made from a batter of ground lentils and rice, are not an especially difficult cooking adventure, though the recipe takes some planning. I'm grateful to have two great teachers—Monica Bhide and Suvir Saran, both friends who have written extensively about Indian cooking—streamline the process for us.

You can eat dosas as you would bread, but filled and rolled, they become a meal (see the list on page 745 for filling ideas). Eat them with any dal (pages 600–604) or chutney (pages 783–787); they're also good with yogurt sauce (pages 773–774).

Finally, you might consider doubling this recipe, so a day or two later you can make more with the extra batter. Or just save half of the recipe if you don't want to make 16 to 20 dosas. Leftover dough keeps in the refrigerator for a couple days.

$^1/_2$ cup white urad dal (also sold as dhuli urad; available at all Indian markets)

2 cups basmati rice

2 to 3 tablespoons vegetable oil, as needed

Salt

1 Soak the dal and rice in separate bowls in water to cover for 4 to 6 hours, or overnight if you prefer.

2 Turn your oven to its lowest temperature. Drain the dal and put it a blender with a tablespoon or two of water. Purée it to a smooth consistency, adding as little additional water as necessary, but enough to allow the machine to do its work. Transfer the purée to a large mixing bowl.

3 Drain the rice and add half of it to the blender (there's no need to clean between batches) with about $^1/_4$ cup water. Again, purée (it won't become as smooth as the dal), adding as little additional water as possible.

FORMING DOSA

(STEP 1) To make dosa, spread the batter onto a greased, heated griddle. Use the bottom of a ladle or measuring cup to spread it thin. (STEP 2) when the dosa is ready, put a small amount of filling in the middle and (STEP 3) roll it up.

Ⓕ Fast   Ⓜ Make Ahead   Ⓥ Vegan

Repeat with the remaining rice. Add the puréed rice to the dal and stir the two together; the resulting mixture should have the texture of a thick pancake batter. Cover the bowl with plastic wrap, turn the oven off, and let the batter ferment overnight in the warmed oven.

④ Heat a large rectangular nonstick or cast-iron griddle over medium heat for a full minute before greasing it with a film of oil. Season the dosa batter with a large pinch of salt and stir to incorporate. Use a measuring cup or a ladle to pour $1/4$ cup of batter into the center of the pan, then use the bottom of the measuring cup to spread the dough across the pan into a large oval shape not much more than $1/8$ inch thick; don't worry if the thickness is inconsistent. (It's the same motion a pizza maker would make—concentric circles with the bottom of the ladle—to spread tomato sauce thinly and evenly across pizza dough.)

⑤ Tiny bubbles will form across the surface of the dough, and the bottom will crisp and turn a deep golden brown in 3 to 5 minutes. Use a spatula to loosen the edges of the dosa, then roll it onto itself to make a cylinder and remove it from the griddle. Repeat with the remaining batter, greasing the griddle as necessary. Serve hot.

Brown Rice Dosa. A little more dense, with a pleasant earthy flavor: Simply substitute brown basmati rice for the white.

5 Great Fillings for Dosa

In Step 5, right before you remove the dosa from the griddle, spread a few spoonfuls of filling down one-third of the crêpe before rolling it up. (Drain any excess liquid from the dish first or use a slotted spoon to scoop it into the dosa.)

1. Curried Stir-Fried Potatoes (page 348)
2. Caramelized Onions (page 329)
3. Curried Eggplant with Coconut Milk (page 296)
4. Braised Potatoes with Pineapple in Coconut Milk (page 348)
5. Brussels Sprouts in Coconut Milk (page 274)

Baked Lentil Samosas

MAKES: 20 to 30 filled dumplings
TIME: $1^{1}/_{2}$ hours, partially unattended

This makes a nice big batch for party food—or stash some in the freezer to make later. You can use virtually any thick dal or bean dish instead of the quickly prepared lentils. See the variations and the list on page 747 for even more filling possibilities. As for dipping, I like samosas with yogurt sauce; "The Basics of Yogurt Sauces" (page 773) has lots of ideas.

1 cup dried lentils (any kind), washed, picked over, and soaked if you like

2 tablespoons neutral oil, like grapeseed or corn

1 small onion, finely chopped

Salt and freshly ground black pepper

1 medium carrot, finely chopped

1 stalk celery, finely chopped

2 tablespoons minced garlic

2 tablespoons peeled and minced fresh ginger

2 cups vegetable stock (pages 101–102) or water

2 tablespoons garam masala or curry powder (to make your own, see pages 815–816)

2 cups all-purpose flour, plus more as needed

2 tablespoons cold butter, plus more for greasing the pans

2 tablespoons yogurt

① Drain the lentils if you've soaked them. Put the oil in a deep skillet or medium pot over medium heat. When hot, add the onion, sprinkle with salt and pepper, and cook, stirring occasionally until golden, 2 to 3 minutes. Add the carrot, celery, garlic, and ginger and keep cooking and stirring until all the vegetables start to wilt and are fragrant, another 3 to 5 minutes.

② Add the lentils, stock, and garam masala to the pan with enough water to cover the lentils by about $1/2$ inch. Turn the heat to high. When the mixture begins to boil, lower the heat so it bubbles gently.

Cover and cook, stirring every so often, until the lentils and vegetables are very soft, about 45 minutes or more. Add stock or water during cooking only if needed to keep the lentils from scorching. The lentils should be fairly stiff and dry when they're done; if not, remove the lid, turn up the heat a bit, and let some of the liquid bubble away. Taste, adjust the seasoning, and set aside to cool.

3 While the lentils are cooking, combine the flour with a large pinch of salt, the butter, and the yogurt in a food processor; turn on the machine and, a few seconds later, add about $1/2$ cup water. Let the machine run, adding a little more water if necessary, until a dough ball forms. Knead the dough for a moment by hand, adding a little more flour if necessary, wrap it in plastic, and refrigerate for at least 30 minutes. (You can make both the lentils and the dough to this point up to 1 day in advance. Cover or wrap tightly and refrigerate and bring to room temperature before proceeding.)

4 Preheat the oven to 350°F. Lightly grease a couple of baking sheets or line them with parchment paper. Sprinkle a work surface with flour, then divide the dough into quarters. Cover three of the pieces and divide the fourth into 6 pieces; roll each piece into a round ball. Roll each ball out to a 3-inch diameter. When you have rolled out the first six, put about 1 tablespoon of the filling in the center of each. Brush the rim (you can use your fingertip) with a little water, then fold over and seal. Put the samosas—about 1 inch apart—on the prepared baking sheets. Keep covered with plastic wrap while you repeat with the remaining dough. Bake the samosas until golden brown, turning as needed, about 30 minutes, and serve hot.

Fried Lentil Samosas. Use this technique for the main recipe or any of the variations: Put at least 3 inches peanut or neutral oil, like grapeseed or corn, in a countertop deep-fryer or in a deep pan on the stove and turn the heat to medium-high; bring to 350°F (see "Deep-Frying," page 26). Put as many as will fit without crowding in the hot oil, until lightly

FILLING AND FORMING SAMOSAS

(STEP 1) Put a small amount of filling on one side of the rolled samosa dough. (STEP 2) Fold over and pinch closed.

browned, about 5 minutes, turning once or twice. Drain on paper towels and serve hot. (Or keep them warm in a low oven, or serve at room temperature, but in any case within an hour.)

Potato and Pea Samosas. Made rich with coconut milk: Instead of the lentils, peel 1 pound of potatoes and cut into cubes (you should have between 3 and 4 cups). Thaw about $1/2$ cup of frozen peas (or shell fresh peas). If you like, instead of the masala or curry, combine 1 tablespoon each of mustard and cumin seeds and have them handy. Prepare the recipe through Step 1, substituting the spices. In Step 2, use the potatoes instead of the lentils and coconut milk instead of the stock. Proceed with the recipe, cooking the potatoes until very tender, 20 minutes or so, checking to make sure they're not too dry or too wet. Mash the potatoes roughly; stir in the peas and set aside to cool. Proceed with the recipe from Step 3.

F Fast   M Make Ahead   V Vegan

Spinach and Cheese Samosas. The cheese doesn't melt, for a terrific texture: Crumble about 1 cup fresh cheese, mozzarella, queso fresco, or feta. Boil and shock 1 pound of spinach (see page 241), drain well, and coarsely chop. Combine with the cheese, sprinkle with salt and pepper, taste, and adjust the seasoning. Using this mixture to fill the samosas, proceed with the recipe from Step 3.

5 Other Great Fillings for Samosas

1. Coconut Rice and Beans (page 508)
2. Any vegetable stew with wheat berries (page 564)
3. Dry-Pan Eggplant, mashed and seasoned (page 294)
4. Winter Squash Slices, Roasted; lightly mash and season (page 366)
5. Any Bean Burger, cooked and crumbled (pages 660–662)

Bean and Cheese Empanadas

MAKES: 12

TIME: About 1 hour with cooked beans

There's nothing stopping you from filling these little turnovers from Central America and the Caribbean with anything you like. Beans, cheese, and sturdy vegetables are the traditional vegetarian fillings. Serve empanadas hot or at room temperature, with any cooked or raw salsa.

1^1/$_2$ cups all-purpose flour, plus a little more

^{1}/$_2$ cup masa harina, fine cornmeal flour, or more all-purpose flour

1^1/$_2$ teaspoons baking powder

1 teaspoon salt

^{1}/$_2$ cup plus 2 tablespoons solid vegetable shortening or vegetable oil

2^1/$_2$ cups cooked and well-seasoned beans, like Twice-Cooked (Refried) Beans (page 592)

2 cups grated or crumbled queso fresco, Monterey Jack, or cotija cheese

^{1}/$_2$ cup milk

❶ Mix the flour, masa harina, baking powder, and salt together in a food processor and process for about 5 seconds. With the machine running, add the ^{1}/$_2$ cup shortening and process for 10 seconds. Then, with the machine running, add about ^{1}/$_2$ cup cold water, just enough for the dough to form a ball. Don't add more water than necessary; the dough should be fairly dry. Knead by hand until smooth, just a minute or so.

❷ Divide into 12 pieces, roll into balls, and wrap in plastic or cover with a damp towel and let rest for at least 20 minutes. (You can refrigerate the dough overnight; be sure to let it come to room temperature before proceeding.) On a well-floured surface, roll each piece into a 6-inch circle, adding flour as necessary.

❸ Preheat the oven to 450°F. Place a couple of tablespoons of the beans in the center of each circle of dough, followed by a sprinkling of cheese, then fold each circle over; seal the seam with a few drops of water and press with the tines of a fork to close. Put on an ungreased baking sheet and brush lightly with milk. Bake until the dough is golden brown and hot, about 20 minutes. Serve immediately or at room temperature.

Corn and Cheese Empanadas. Especially good filled with Pan-Grilled Corn with Chile (page 289): Instead of the beans, use 2^1/$_2$ cups lightly cooked corn. (Mash it a little if necessary to help give it some body.)

Roasted Peppers and Cheese Empanadas. Smoky and tender inside: Instead of the beans, use 2^1/$_2$ cups Roasted Red Peppers (large pieces are nice).

Vegan Vegetable Empanadas. Super-quick with leftovers: Use 3 cups of any thick or rich vegetable dish to fill the empanadas.

Sauces, Condiments, Herbs, and Spices

In contemporary cooking, all the news about sauces is good: They have become fresher tasting, healthier, more exciting, more exotic, and easier to make. What could be better?

In the "old days"—say, until the 1980s and for a hundred years before that—almost every sauce was cooked, almost every sauce was thickened, and almost every sauce contained a binder like flour, a big-time fat, and stock or another major ingredient. Now many sauces are modeled on pesto or salsa; the first is essentially an herb ground with flavorings, and the second is basically a vegetable or fruit chopped with seasonings.

I still enjoy some traditional French sauces, but it's the simpler ones like vinaigrettes (pages 762–763) and mayonnaise (page 771), which can be used in a hundred different ways, that I turn to often. You'll find hollandaise, béchamel, and a few other classics in this chapter too.

But many of the old standbys seem tame compared to the chutneys, cooked vegetable and fruit sauces, yogurt sauces, and chile pastes and spice blends found in American home kitchens today.

The building blocks of today's sauces are easy to find and easy to understand. Here are detailed descriptions of oils, chiles, salt and pepper, and literally hundreds of ideas for using fast sauces in everyday cooking. The fact is that you could take the blandest grain recipe (how about basic Brown Rice, page 506?) and put fifty different sauces on it, and have a completely different dish once a week for a year. These sauces, combined with the other recipes from this book, can give you exciting meals for a lifetime.

Some store-bought sauces and spice blends are bound to be staples in your kitchen. Let's face it: though there is a recipe for ketchup here, and it's a great one, I certainly don't expect everyone to rely on homemade ketchup. There are plenty of good store-bought condiments, and there's no reason not to use them, as long as they're of good quality, with few or no additives.

But when it comes to spice blends, like curry and chili powder, for example, you'll discover that your own blends are far superior, last longer, and, because they are customized, are more appealing than anything you can buy.

This chapter is loosely divided into two main parts: sauces and spice blends (or similar seasonings). The sauces begin with the easiest and freshest—including salsas, flavored oils, herb pastes, chutneys, and Asian sauces. Then the recipes get progressively more complex and time consuming as you explore the sections on cooked sauces and condiments. The rest of the chapter is devoted to spice blends—seasonings that you can make in advance and keep on hand for spontaneous flavor and variety.

Fresh Salsas

A classically trained French chef might scoff at calling a bunch of tomatoes, onions, chiles, and seasonings, chopped together and loosely piled on a plate, a "sauce." Yet this is exactly what most Americans consider their favorite condiment, and if salsa isn't a sauce, I don't know what is.

The building blocks are simple and generally low in fat. Of course tomatoes are a staple, but so are fruits, green tomatoes, tomatillos, citrus, even seaweed. All can be combined with herbs, and raw onions and garlic, a bit of oil, citrus juice, and chiles—mild or hot—usually play a role as well. The final product may be left chunky and loose or puréed into something that looks a little more like a classic sauce. In any case the flavors are fresh, bright, and immediate, which also means fresh salsas are generally best within an hour or two.

Fresh Tomato Salsa

Salsa Fresca

MAKES: About 2 cups
TIME: 15 minutes

Salsa fresca (or *pico de gallo*) is easy, fast, really tasty, and extremely useful. The basic ingredients are simple enough: ripe tomatoes, onions, citrus juice or vinegar, fresh chiles, and fresh herbs. Of course, it's great with chips as well as grilled vegetables, simply cooked grains, any kind of eggs, and whatever else you like. And if you double the recipe, you can serve this like a chunky gazpacho and eat it with a spoon.

If you prefer a milder onion flavor, soak the minced onion in cold water for a few minutes, or even just rinse it in cold water, before adding it to the salsa. Or use two or three minced scallions.

- 2 large ripe fresh tomatoes, chopped
- $1/2$ large white onion, minced
- 1 teaspoon minced garlic, or to taste
- 1 habanero or jalapeño chile, seeded and minced, or to taste
- $1/2$ cup chopped fresh cilantro leaves
- 2 tablespoons freshly squeezed lime juice or 1 tablespoon red wine vinegar
- Salt and freshly ground pepper

1 Combine all the ingredients in a bowl, taste, and adjust the seasoning.

2 If possible, let the flavors develop for 15 minutes or so before serving, but by all means serve within a couple of hours.

Puréed Salsa Fresca. For a less chunky version: Toss the salsa into a food processor and blend as you like.

Chilean Salsa. A little more assertive, but less acidic: Increase the minced garlic to a tablespoon; add 1 teaspoon chopped fresh oregano leaves and 1 to 2 tablespoons of olive oil; omit the lime juice.

F Fast   **M** Make Ahead   **V** Vegan

Salsa Cruda. This makes a good pasta sauce: Eliminate the onion and pepper; substitute basil leaves for cilantro and balsamic vinegar for the lime juice. Add a tablespoon or more of good extra virgin olive oil.

Avocado–Red Pepper Salsa. Add a chopped avocado and a Roasted Red Pepper (page 333).

Bean Salsa. Black beans are most traditional, but pintos or even chickpeas work well too: Add a cup of your favorite cooked beans, substitute red onion for the white, and add a teaspoon of ground cumin. Let sit for about 30 minutes for the flavors to develop.

Mexican Cheese Salsa. Add $^1/_2$ cup or more crumbled queso fresco and replace the garlic with $^1/_2$ English cucumber, peeled and chopped.

Fresh Tomatillo Salsa

Pico de Verde

MAKES: About 2 cups
TIME: 10 minutes

Super-fresh and perfect in summer. Tomatillos are more readily available these days than in years before (you may even find them in unusual colors, like purple). They're most often sold with the papery husks still on; look for firm, unshriveled fruit with tight husks (be sure to rinse the sticky residue off before using them). If fresh tomatillos are not available, canned are okay.

Poblanos and some other fresh chiles have tough skins that are best removed. The easiest way is to char the skin, which has the added benefit of giving the salsa a light smoky flavor. You can, however, skip this step if you're rushed.

2 medium poblano or other mild green fresh chiles

2 cups husked and chopped tomatillos

3 scallions, finely chopped

2 teaspoons minced garlic, or to taste

$^1/_4$ cup chopped fresh cilantro leaves

3 tablespoons freshly squeezed lime juice, or to taste

Salt and freshly ground black pepper

① If you like, roast and clean the chiles according to the directions on page 333. Mince the chiles.

② Put the tomatillos, scallions, garlic, cilantro, and lime into a medium bowl with the chiles and sprinkle with salt and pepper. If you're serving immediately, taste and adjust the seasoning; or cover and refrigerate for up to 2 days (bring back to room temperature and taste and adjust again before serving).

Green Tomato Pico de Verde. Good in fall, when green tomatoes are plentiful and cheap: Substitute green tomatoes for the tomatillos.

Chile Pico de Verde. Stronger, but not much: Replace the tomatillos with 2 cups chopped fresh mild green chiles, like more poblano or New Mexican; increase the minced garlic to 2 tablespoons; substitute parsley for the cilantro and lemon for the lime juice.

Pepita Pico de Verde. Easily made from the pantry: Replace half of the tomatillos with toasted pepitas (page 321). Serve immediately.

Corn Salsa. Distinctive and delicious: Substitute 2 cups corn kernels from Corn on the Cob, Grilled or Roasted (page 290), for the tomatillos.

Jícama Salsa. Very crunchy: Replace the tomatillos with peeled and chopped jícama and substitute peeled and minced fresh ginger for the garlic. Add 2 tablespoons chopped fresh mint leaves. Let sit for about 30 minutes before serving.

Papaya and Other Fruit Salsas

MAKES: About 2 cups
TIME: 20 minutes

Citrus juices—not just lime, but many others, as you'll see in the variations—make fruit salsas special. They're sweet and sour, sometimes hot, usually appetizing and exciting. But you must taste while you're assembling them: balancing the sweetness of the fruits (which, of course, varies each time you buy fruit) with the acidity of the citrus juice and the heat of the chiles is essential.

2 cups firm but ripe papaya, cut into $1/2$-inch chunks

$1/2$ cup diced red onion

$1/2$ cup diced red, yellow, or green bell pepper or a combination

2 tablespoons minced fresh chile (like jalapeño or Thai), to taste, or hot red pepper flakes or cayenne to taste

$1/4$ cup or more chopped cilantro fresh leaves

1 tablespoon extra virgin olive oil

3 tablespoons freshly squeezed lime juice, plus more to taste

Salt and freshly ground black pepper

1 Put all the ingredients in a medium bowl and stir to combine. Let sit for about 5 minutes, then taste and adjust the seasoning, adding more chile, lime, or salt as needed.

2 Serve immediately or refrigerate for up to a couple of hours. (Bring back to room temperature before serving.)

Persimmon Salsa. If you have persimmons, this is a good place for them: Replace the papaya with Fuyu persimmons; omit the peppers and add 2 teaspoons minced peeled fresh ginger. Substitute equal parts chopped fresh basil and mint leaves for the cilantro.

Citrus Salsa. Lovely in winter: Make this salsa just before serving it. Substitute a combination of orange, grapefruit, and lemon segments (see page 431) for the papaya. Omit the olive oil.

Peach Melon Tomato Salsa. Perfect in summer: Use 1 medium ripe tomato, 2 medium peaches, and $1/4$ small cantaloupe (you should still have about 2 cups of fruit). Use basil or mint instead of cilantro if you like. Proceed with recipe and serve within 30 minutes.

Chipotle-Cherry Salsa. Unusual and wonderful: Replace the papaya with pitted cherries (fresh or frozen); omit the peppers and chile and instead add 1 tablespoon chopped canned chipotle chiles in adobo sauce. Serve at room temperature or cover and refrigerate for up to 2 days.

10 Fruits for Salsa

You can use almost any juicy, ripe fruit to make a good salsa. You can even use nonjuicy fruits, like apple or avocado, as long as you increase your oil or citrus to get the consistency you want.

1. Mango
2. Pineapple
3. Watermelon, cantaloupe, honeydew, Crenshaw, or other melons
4. Peaches, nectarines, apricots, plums, or other stone fruit
5. Pomegranate seeds and orange segments
6. Avocado and orange segments
7. Seedless grapes, cut in half
8. Grapefruit segments
9. Tart apples, like Granny Smith (serve immediately)
10. Blueberries or blackberries

Radish Salsa

MAKES: About 2 cups
TIME: 30 minutes

F **M** **V**

Radishes are hardly a classic salsa ingredient, but the technique—mixing a vegetable (or fruit) with onion, an acid, chiles, and fresh herbs—is downright traditional, and that's the important part. Serve this colorful salsa with any tamale (page 547) or quesadilla (page 741), Red or simply a big bowl of tortilla chips.

2 cups (about 1 pound) chopped radish, like daikon or red or a combination

1/2 English cucumber, peeled and diced

1/2 small red onion, minced

1 scallion, thinly sliced

1 teaspoon minced garlic

1 tablespoon minced fresh chile (like jalapeño or Thai), or to taste, or hot red pepper flakes or cayenne to taste

2 tablespoons freshly squeezed lemon juice, or more to taste

1/4 cup chopped fresh cilantro leaves

Salt and freshly ground black pepper

1 Put all the ingredients in a medium bowl and mix thoroughly.

2 Taste and adjust the seasoning, adding more chile, lemon, or salt as needed. Serve immediately or cover and refrigerate for up to a day.

Cucumber Salsa, Thai Style. A common and flavorful garnish: Replace the radishes with additional diced cucumber and carrot (about 1 medium each), red onion with shallots, and lemon with lime juice. Add a tablespoon of rice vinegar. Omit the garlic.

Green Papaya Salsa, Thai Style. Sort of a mini papaya salad: Substitute peeled, seeded, and shredded green papaya for the radishes, use lime instead of lemon juice, and replace the scallion and red onion with a thinly sliced shallot. Add a tablespoon or so of rice vinegar.

Sea Green Salsa. Practically work-free: Replace the radishes with 1 cup arame, hijiki, or wakame (see page 356). You'll need to soak the sea greens in warm water to cover for about 10 minutes, then drain well. Add 1 teaspoon minced peeled fresh ginger and about 2 tablespoons rice vinegar.

The Basics of Oil-Based Sauces

When I wrote the original *How to Cook Everything*, America had nearly abandoned butter and was gradually making the move away from trans fats to healthier vegetable oils. At the time, people thought canola oil was miraculous. Though olive oil was making inroads, it had just begun to be found regularly on supermarket shelves.

What a difference a decade makes. Most of us now have a completely different mind-set about oils; we use them not only for cooking and salad dressing like vinaigrettes but also for "drizzling," a concept that barely existed in the States ten years ago. And olive oil is dominant.

I don't believe in pigeonholing oils (or, for that matter, any other kind of real food) as "good" or "bad." But, really, from a health and flavor perspective, the oils I reach for most happen to be the tastiest, healthiest, and easiest to use. Not surprisingly, olive oil—the easiest to make, the most ancient, natural, and traditional, the most useful, and among the best tasting—heads the list.

Oils are the ultimate condiments. When you cook with them, their differences affect the flavor and texture of the food. But when you use them raw, whether in dressings or as a last-minute drizzle, the strongest-tasting ones act as a true seasoning.

Before I run down my favorite oils and how to use them, here's an overview of how oils are made, what they contain, and how to store them, all useful information in choosing which to buy:

The Extracting Process

There are a number of ways to coax oil from fruit (like olive), vegetables (corn), seeds (rapeseed, which produces canola), nuts (peanut), or legumes (soy). Most "oil seeds"—and these are among the most common—are first crushed, washed in a solvent called *hexane*, then heated.

The result is a clear, virtually flavorless oil that withstands high heat and has a long shelf life. These oils don't say anything on the label about how they are extracted, and hexane, a petroleum solvent approved by the U.S. Food and Drug Administration (FDA) for this purpose, isn't listed as an ingredient since it is not supposed to remain in the finished oil. There is some evidence that some does, and for this reason (as well as the fact that chemically extracted oils don't taste that great), I rarely use commercially produced seed oils.

Better oils tend to be "cold pressed," which means that the seeds are put under intense pressure to extract their oil. No hexane is used, and temperatures remain below 180°F. The result is oil that may be cloudier, with deeper color and a distinct flavor that reminds you of its source. These oils are also less stable, less tolerant of heat, and quicker to turn rancid, but these are all factors that can be easily dealt with, and cold-pressed oils are usually your best choice.

The term *extra virgin*—associated only with olive oil—refers to the first cold pressing of the fruit. (This was once done by simply pressing the olives between mats, using a large screw, but is now done by machine. Still, it's a much simpler process than chemical extraction.)

"Expeller-pressed" oils fall somewhere in between chemical extraction and cold pressing. They too are pressed, not chemically extracted, though the process involves high heat. These oils still have some flavor, but they are generally more stable for cooking and storage, and hexane residues are not a concern. They're a good choice also.

After oils are extracted, they may be refined further—by heating or filtering—to remove impurities and improve their shelf life. Refined oils can handle higher heat than their unrefined counterparts, but they don't have as much flavor.

Oils, Fats, and Health

Oils contain saturated, monounsaturated, or polyunsaturated fats, usually in combination. Olive oil, for example, is the best known for being high in monounsaturated fats. Soy, seed, and vegetable oils tend to be high in polyunsaturated fats. Coconut oil is a mostly saturated fat, like animal fats.

There is a lot of debate about striking the right balance between these three types of fats, and some research indicates that you should limit or even avoid some. If you have a history of high cholesterol or heart disease, you should educate yourself more on these distinctions, but for most people it's enough to know that you should limit your intake of saturated fat and even watch your consumption of polyunsaturates. Virtually all plant oils contain no cholesterol.

Much recent research has focused on how antioxidants help thwart cancer and other diseases, or at least keep your body functioning better. These micronutrients seem to neutralize the potential damage caused by free radicals or oxidants, chemical components in your cells that seek and destroy other, beneficial components. Fruits and vegetables are high in antioxidants, and so are olive, sesame, and other oils. Omega-3s are "long-chain" fatty acids that are essential to human health and appear to protect against heart disease and certain cancers. Fish is the most concentrated source of omega-3s, but there are smaller amounts in ground flaxseeds and flaxseed oil (your body can't obtain the oil from whole seeds) and, to a lesser degree, walnuts, soybeans and their oils.

Trans fats are made when liquid vegetable oil, usually from soybeans or cottonseed, is turned into a semisolid form through the process of hydrogenation, or adding hydrogen. Solid shortening is the most common source of trans fatty acids or trans fat in our diets, but there is so much concern about the negative health effects of trans fat that it is now identified on the Nutrition Facts label of every food product. Like just about everyone else these days, I now avoid these foods; in fact, I never use solid shortening or margarine, and I see no reason for anyone else to either.

Storing Oils

Not only does rancid oil taste bad—it might be bad for you. When oil starts to turn rancid, it oxidizes, a process that converts some of its components into free radicals. Since cold-pressed oils—which are the best oils—spoil fastest, you have to watch out for this.

But it's easy: Keep your oil in a dark, cool place, preferably not stored in clear glass containers. If you buy large quantities, put a pint or so in a bottle and keep the rest in a dark place or, even better, in the refrigerator. It's not a terrible idea to keep all your oil, even that you're using daily,

F Fast   M Make Ahead   V Vegan

EVERYDAY OILS

Listed in order of preference and usefulness, though not too strictly, because many oils are interchangeable.

OIL	TYPE OF FATS	DESCRIPTION	USES	SUBSTITUTES
Extra Virgin Olive Oil	Mostly monounsaturated	The best are like wines, balancing the flavor of olives with a little acidity for a nice round finish. They range from pale gold to radiant green, and widely in price. Buy extra virgin olive oil in 1-liter bottles or 3-liter cans; it's a commodity, so it tastes different each time, but it's almost always good. The expensive stuff has the equivalent of "vintages" too—some years are better than others.	Dressings and cold sauces, Flavored Oils (page 758), drizzling, low-heat cooking or warming	Nothing. Nada. Niente. You gotta have it.
Grapeseed Oil	Mostly polyunsaturated	My go-to oil for high-heat cooking or for times I want almost no flavor, grapeseed oil is both neutral and versatile. These can vary a bit; darker, greener ones have a pleasant but mild flavor.	Sautéing, panfrying, grilling, roasting	Corn oil
Peanut Oil	Slightly more polyunsaturated than monounsaturated and a teeny bit of saturated fat	I love peanut oil for deep- and stir-frying because it can withstand high heat and has a distinctive flavor that is perfect for many Asian dishes. As with other oil, cold pressed is best.	Deep frying, panfrying, grilling, roasting, some baking	Grapeseed or corn oil
Corn Oil	Mostly polyunsaturated	A good oil for all-purpose cooking. It's mild, full bodied, and nicely colored. It works especially well in Mexican, Caribbean, and Latin American dishes. Cold pressed is best.	Sautéing, panfrying, grilling, roasting, deep frying	Grapeseed oil
Dark Sesame Oil	Almost 50/50 mono- and polyunsaturated, with a little saturated fat	The quintessential Asian condiment, full flavored, with a distinctive taste and aroma. A little goes a long way. If you're cooking with it—which is sometimes quite nice—watch it well; it has a low smoking point.	Salads, dipping sauces, drizzling, seasoning	There are none, though toasted nut oils (page 757) come close.

in the fridge. (Olive oil will become solid—you can use it as a butter substitute!—but will quickly liquefy at room temperature.) If you do store your oil at room temperature, you ought to smell it after a month or two before using it. You'll know when it's rancid; if it has, toss it.

A Word About Smoke Points

If oil gets hot enough, it will smoke (this is called its *smoke point*) and will eventually catch fire. The smoke point can vary from 200°F to 400°F, depending on how the oil was pressed, filtered, and refined. Minimally processed oils have lower smoke points. Obviously you want to avoid starting a kitchen fire, but beyond that oil that is heated to smoking has off flavors, loses its potential health benefits, and may even be higher in free radicals.

I have never had a problem cooking with any oil—even dark sesame oil, which has a relatively low smoke point—because I always watch the pan carefully and adjust the heat as needed. And a little smoke—as long as it goes no further than that—is not a bad thing.

Knowing an oil's exact smoke point is helpful, but in reality few home cooks ever use a thermometer for anything other than deep frying (see page 26). Let your senses be your guide. Oil becomes more fragrant as it gets hot, and when it's ready for cooking the surface begins to ripple and shimmer. Tilt the pan a bit (carefully of course) and you'll notice that the oil seems thinner than straight from the bottle. Those are the signals that it's about to smoke (and, usually, that it's ready for cooking). Adding food automatically lowers the temperature of the oil, especially if your ingredients come straight from the fridge.

The Oil Lexicon

Instead of stocking just one or two oils, many of us now keep on hand a variety that impart different flavors to foods either during cooking or after. The first two charts that follow will help you decide which you want to have around regularly and which are good for experiments. The last chart gives you some perspective on the oils that many of us used to consider staples but that I think aren't worth using except in a pinch.

The Basics of Flavored Oils

By taking the flavor of an herb, spice, or aromatic and infusing its essence into fat, you create something delicious, akin to compound butter (page 801).

The oil itself is far more of a variable here than it is with butter. It's not only the quality you're looking at but the type: Do you want olive oil, another flavorful oil like peanut or dark sesame oil, or a neutral oil like grapeseed or corn? This is a judgment call you make on a case-by-case basis, but it's mostly common sense. When you know

an herb or spice is going to be used mostly in a certain type of cuisine, you can usually figure out which oil to pair with it. You're likely to pair rosemary with olive oil, for example, because both are most often used in Mediterranean cooking; you're likely to pair star anise with peanut oil, because both are likely to be used in Asian cooking. But whenever you're in doubt, reach for your neutral oil; you can't go wrong here. (In any case, do not use your best olive oil for flavored oils; it will not make the final product any better.)

Flavored oils have three major uses: in vinaigrettes, in cooking, and as a last-minute drizzle. In each of these cases they will save you a step and a few moments, but in many cases you'll have the time to make a flavored oil while you're cooking.

Much has been made of the "threat" of flavored oils, and, in fact, there have been some documented cases of botulism resulting from flavored oils gone bad. You need not worry about this if you follow these directions:

The simplest way to stay safe is to make flavored oils pretty much as you need them. I've included three basic versions in one recipe that makes $1/2$ cup. The idea is to make enough to store comfortably in the refrigerator and use in a week or two. You don't want it sitting around much longer than that.

If, however, you want to make an assortment of flavored oils to give to others—and, indeed, they are fine gifts—simply multiply these recipes as needed. Strain the warmed oil into small, clean (preferably wide-mouthed) containers (if you're compulsive, you'll sterilize them, but it really won't help the shelf life much), refrigerate, and instruct your friends that this is a perishable product, to be refrigerated and used within a month or two. This is pretty much standard in my book, since I believe most oils should be refrigerated anyway.

Refrigerating many oils causes them to solidify, but this is not at all a problem. For one thing, it makes these even more like compound butter: You can spoon some onto your dish and watch it "melt." Or, you can use it as a spread. Not only that, any refrigerated oil will turn

F Fast   M Make Ahead   V Vegan

OILS FOR ENTHUSIASTS

These are not oils, or even a category of oils, you'll need to have around, but they have their appeal or at least some usefulness.

OIL	TYPE OF FATS	DESCRIPTION	USES	SUBSTITUTES
"Pure" Olive Oil	Mostly monounsaturated	Sometimes labeled "pure," sometimes just "olive oil." At one time I used this for high-heat cooking and to save money. But the flavor is not nearly as intense as that of extra virgin, and the price differential has grown so small that I don't bother now. ("Lite" olive oil is further processed and almost tasteless. It's not worth bothering with; use grapeseed oil instead.)	Roasting, sautéing, grilling, pizzas and bread, Italian-style baking	Grapeseed oil, which is not as flavorful
Nut Oils	This varies: Almond and hazelnut contain predominantly monounsaturated fats, while walnut is mostly polyunsaturated.	Nut oils are super-flavorful, which makes them fun to use, especially on salads. Almond, walnut, and hazelnut are the most common; there are also roasted nut oils (check out pistachio oil if you ever see it), but their strong flavors limit their use.	Salads and drizzling; more refined nut oils work well for low-heat cooking and baking.	They are fairly interchangeable within this category but otherwise utterly distinctive.
(Light) Sesame Oil	Almost 50/50 mono- and polyunsaturated, with a little saturated fat	Untoasted, a good neutral oil that withstands cooking well. It's both milder and lighter in color than its roasted cousin.	Salads, stir-frying, and baking	Neutral oils, like grapeseed or corn
Very Exotic Oils: Apricot Kernel, Coconut, and Avocado	Varies, depending on the oil, so read the labels	Coconut oil has the potential to raise metabolism despite the fact that it's nearly all saturated fat. It's solid at room temperature, though, so you can't use it for salads. Nothing beats apricot kernel oil for high-heat roasting and cooking. Avocado oil is tasty on salads.	Varies, depending on the oil	These are one-of a kind, special-occasion oils.
"Health" Oils: Rice Bran, Hemp Seed, Wheat Germ, and Flaxseed Oils	Varies, depending on the oil, so read the labels	Most researchers suggest simply incorporating small amounts of these into your diet, mostly as a replacement for other oils. They're all quite different, and some taste better than others. A couple— like flaxseed oil—are downright bitter. Because of their high antioxidant value, you don't want to heat these anything above "warm."	People eat them by the spoonful, but I use them judiciously—and only very rarely—for drizzling.	These are all individual tastes and are increasingly available, though you might find them refrigerated, along with other supplements, not in the food aisles.

OTHER OILS

I don't use the following oils. All are designed for all-purpose cooking and baking, but you can find all your needs met by the superior oils described on the previous pages. Still, it doesn't hurt to know about them.

OIL	TYPE OF FATS	DESCRIPTION
Soybean Oil	Mostly polyunsaturated, though about 30% monounsaturated and some saturated fat	The predominant mass-produced oil in the world, in both liquid and hydrogenated form. Until recently, it was the supermarket staple (see "Vegetable Oil," below), but now there are many other choices.
Canola Oil	Mostly monounsaturated, but a relatively large proportion of polyunsaturated fats too	Canola is made from rapeseeds, which are not edible. It almost always has a slightly off flavor (sometimes worse than that) and turns rancid quickly. Though it's cheap and popular, it's just not that good.
"Vegetable Oil"	Varies somewhat depending on the oil, but mostly polyunsaturated	This is the neutral-tasting, all-purpose oil, now being replaced by individual oils (soy, canola, and corn, for example) and specialty vegetable oil blends, like canola-olive and so on. If the bottle just says "vegetable oil," there's an excellent chance it's all soybean oil, but check the fine print on the label: it could be cottonseed, sunflower, or safflower oil (or a combination).

back to liquid form in less than an hour at room temperature and in seconds in the pan.

One last word: Don't bother to make flavored oils with ground spices or herbs. These flavor oil (or anything else) so quickly that there is no reason to do so in advance. And they're too easy to burn.

Flavored Oil

MAKES: ¹/₂ cup
TIME: 20 minutes, plus time to cool

It's almost impossible to use too much of the flavoring ingredients in this preparation, but if you do—if your oil becomes too strong—simply dilute it with a little fresh oil. You can certainly mix or match among the "or" options here, but remember combinations—especially the more creative ones!—will limit the range of the oil's usefulness.

¹/₄ cup washed and dried fresh herb leaves: rosemary, thyme, bay leaf (dried will do in this case), tarragon, marjoram, oregano, etc.

OR

1 tablespoon spice: star anise, peppercorn, cloves, allspice, nutmeg, chiles (dried), etc.

OR

Aromatics: 2 garlic cloves, lightly crushed, or 2 tablespoons ginger slices, or roughly chopped shallots or scallions, or celery leaves, or a combination

Pinch salt

¹/₂ cup extra virgin olive oil or neutral oil, like grapeseed or corn

❶ Combine the flavor ingredient (or ingredients) and the oil in a saucepan and turn the heat to low. Warm gently until the mixture sizzles, then continue to cook until the oil is very fragrant, another 5 minutes.

❷ Cool, then strain into a clean bottle or other container. Refrigerate and use within a week.

 Fast   Make Ahead   Vegan

A Tribute to Olive Oil

These days most experienced home cooks, when asked to name their default cooking fat, would name olive oil. And the advantages of olive oil are so marked that it's quickly becoming universal. People cook with it in Japan, and they cook with it in Sweden, and it's about as traditional in those places as butter is in China.

Why? Olive oil is easily made, it's relatively inexpensive (or becoming increasingly so), it's arguably the healthiest common cooking fat (or at least way up on the list), it's ubiquitous, and it tastes terrific. Though some people won't deep-fry in olive oil, there's little reason not to.

In fact, the only sane argument you can make against olive oil is that it tastes too good; or, that is, tastes too much. This is why some people don't like to use it to deep-fry, and the flavor is so distinctive that there are roles for which it seems unsuited, especially in Asian cooking. (Though sometimes I wonder if this isn't just a long-held prejudice that will gradually fade as we increasingly think of olive oil as the default.) At those times, it makes sense to use a neutral oil, like grapeseed or corn, or an oil with a different flavor profile, like peanut, or . . . butter.

But for most European and American cooking, you cannot beat olive oil. When raw, it's smooth textured and complex in flavor. When warmed—as it is, passively, when you drizzle it on hot foods, it blooms beautifully and is, in essence, the simplest "sauce" there is and one of the most delicious. And, of course, when used in cooking, its sensational aroma fills the kitchen like nothing else. Especially when it's cooked with garlic . . .

The Basics of Vinegar

Any vinegar can provide acidity, which by itself is valuable for balance and brightness, but only good vinegar—usually made from wine, or at least fruit—adds flavor, depth, and complexity.

Citrus or Vinegar?

You can use freshly squeezed citrus juice wherever you'd use vinegar, except when you're pickling or preserving. Lemon juice is the most common substitute, though limes, tangerines, oranges, blood oranges, and even grapefruits have their place, especially in salad dressings. Of course the flavor isn't at all like vinegar, and the acidity is considerably lower (usually about 3 percent versus 5 percent or higher). But that makes citrus juice a good choice when you want lower acidity levels or just a different flavor.

Like wine or spirits, vinegar can be fermented from just about any fruit, vegetable, or grain. The process takes two steps: an alcoholic fermentation converts sugars in the base material to alcohol; then an acetic fermentation converts the resulting brew to (acetic) acid. To jump-start the second step an inoculation of bacteria—known as a "mother"—is added to the liquid. This is the cloudy, thick sediment you sometimes see floating around the bottom of your vinegar bottle.

Always keep vinegar in nonreactive glass or ceramic containers, preferably with corks, or glass or lined-metal lids. (This is how it is packaged, though sometimes you see inexpensive vinegars in plastic.) Kept in a cool, dark place and used regularly, it will be gone before it ever goes bad.

The Mother of All Dressings: Vinaigrettes

If vinaigrette—pronounced, by the way, vinn-a-gret, not vinegar-ette—was important twenty years ago (and it was), it's even more so now, arguably one of the true foundations of modern cuisine. Americans have largely lost interest in butter-based sauces and don't have time to

TYPES OF VINEGAR

I think sherry vinegar is the best value in vinegar these days, and it's now sold in most supermarkets. That's why you'll find it at the top of the following chart. The order in which the vinegars are listed in the chart is a combination of personal preference and availability. Near the bottom are vinegars that are interesting and good but have limited uses, are hard to find, or, in the case of ordinary white vinegar, without flavor.

VINEGAR	ACIDITY	DESCRIPTION	USES	SUBSTITUTES
Sherry Vinegar	8%	The best and most flavorful vinegar for the money (the bottle must say *Vinaigre de Jerez* for it to be genuine). Very acidic, so start by using less than of other vinegars, or cut it with a little water.	Wherever you'd reach for balsamic, this will work, from salads to cooked dishes	White wine or champagne vinegar
Rice Vinegar	4.5%	A must-have for Japanese and other East Asian cooking as well as all sorts of good light vinaigrettes. Check the ingredients; you don't want "seasoned" rice vinegar. (Rice wine vinegar is also good.) Note that this is very low in acid, which has its advantages.	Virtually any Asian salad, cooked dish, or sauce; or anytime you want to use less oil (and therefore vinegar) in a salad	No good ones, but in a pinch, white vinegar diluted with water; or lemon juice
Balsamic Vinegar	about 6%	Most is distilled vinegar flavored with caramel syrup, but even that may have a pleasant flavor, is fine in salads, and is perfect for Balsamic Syrup (pages 798–799). *Aceto Balsamico Tradizionale di Modena*—real balsamic vinegar—is hard to make, hard to find, and hard to afford. Look for one made from wine vinegar and aged at least a little while in wood barrels.	Vinaigrette (page 762), though some of the more traditional Italian ways are wonderful.	Sherry vinegar or Chinese black vinegar
Red Wine Vinegar	6–7%	Unless you're going to spend the money ($8–30) for a good one, sherry vinegar is a better bet.	Salads and cooked dishes (though remember it turns brown when cooked)	Sherry vinegar
White Wine Vinegar; Champagne Vinegar	5–7%	Like white wine, white wine vinegar can be dull or delightful. Real Champagne vinegar is among the best, but in general, these are disappointing—buy neither cheapest nor most expensive.	Vinaigrettes and refrigerator (not preserved) pickles	Rice vinegar or fresh citrus juice
Malt Vinegar	4–8%	Made from malted grain, this actually tastes malty, with a slight lemon aroma and flavor. As beer varies in alcohol, this varies in acidity. Get real brewed malt vinegar—not a "nonbrewed condiment," which is nothing more than water, acetic acid, and coloring.	Pickling, splashing on fried or roasted foods	Cider vinegar

 Fast   Make Ahead   Ⓥ Vegan

VINEGAR	ACIDITY	DESCRIPTION	USES	SUBSTITUTES
Chinese Black Vinegar	Usually about 5%, but may vary	Made from glutinous rice, with a delicious, almost haunting flavor. Look for one with a short list of ingredients and the word *Chinkiang* (or something similar) on the label; that's the province in which it's traditionally made.	In stir-fries and cooked dishes like Fried Rice (page 519) and as a dipping sauce or dressing by itself	A mixture of rice vinegar, soy sauce, and brown sugar—but it just won't be the same.
Cider Vinegar	5%	Real cider vinegar can have a distinctively fruity flavor. The quality varies from flavored white vinegar to small-batch, imported, and domestic vinegars worthy of the best salads and vegetables.	The complex ones make rich dressings and sauces; others are good for pickling, chutneys, and glazes.	White or malt vinegar
Plum Vinegar *Umeboshi Vinegar*	4–6%	The rather salty, slightly fruity flavor of this Japanese vinegar can be addictive; it's made from *umeboshi*, which are dried and pickled stone fruit, similar to a plum.	Dipping sauces (delicious with Cold Soba Noodles, page 467, for example), sauces and glazes for tofu	Red wine vinegar with a little soy sauce
Cane Vinegar	4–6%	This ranges in color from golden to deep brown and can come from the Philippines, Louisiana, or most anyplace else. At its best, it's a well-balanced, all-purpose vinegar with a slightly syrupy taste.	Cooking mostly, as well as for sauces and dressings	Sherry vinegar or brown rice vinegar
Raspberry Vinegar	4–6%	Raspberry vinegar peaked in popularity in the nineties, though it still has its fans and its uses. Light, fruity, and very pink, it's got a distinct fruity flavor balanced by acidity.	Dressing cucumbers, radishes, and spinach; fruit salsas, especially those with cantaloupe or watermelon; a few drops on fresh cheese, like cottage or ricotta	Rice vinegar and lightly crushed raspberries
Coconut Vinegar	4–6%	With its cloudy white color and tangy bite, coconut vinegar has specialized appeal. It works best in Southeast Asian–style dishes.	Stir-fries, noodle and rice dishes, dipping sauces, and glazes	White vinegar
Verjuice *(Verjus)*		Literally "green juice" in French, this isn't a vinegar, but rather a sour liquid made from underripe (green) red or white grapes. Its mild, fruity taste is both refreshing and wine-friendly.	Salad dressings; light sauces	Lemon juice, unsweetened grape juice, or white wine

make stock, let alone stock-based sauces, from scratch. What's left are two basic categories of sauce: vinaigrette, which is oil-based, and salsa, which—though mostly vegetable based—could be considered a variation on vinaigrette.

Not that it matters; these are just names. What's important is that vinaigrette is all-purpose, as simple as oil and vinegar, as creative as you care to make it. And even the most complicated vinaigrettes are five-minute affairs, quickly made mixtures that can be combined with a fork, a whisk, a blender, an immersion blender, or in a jar. The keys, the constants, are good oil and vinegar (or citrus juice) and seasonings.

The components—oil, acid, seasonings: Vinaigrette is more than the sum of its parts, and within each of these three essential components you have endless options. What happens if you take good extra virgin olive oil, some kind of good vinegar, salt and pepper, and a piece of garlic or shallot, and maybe an herb or a little good mustard and combine them into one entity? You have something astonishingly delicious, the kind of thing chefs amaze people with, something you can make every day, serve with pride, and vary for the rest of your life. You can drizzle this mixture on everything from salad to grilled vegetables to cold hard-cooked eggs—almost anything, really.

I discuss oils on pages 753–759 and vinegars on the preceding pages, but it's enough to say here that most vinaigrettes start with good extra virgin olive oil and whatever vinegar you have on hand or happen to like. Variations can employ more flavorful oils, like those made from nuts, or less flavorful ones, like those made from corn or grapeseed. Vinegar may be sherry (my favorite), balsamic, rice (which is milder than most), red or white wine. Or you can skip the vinegar entirely and use citrus juice, or even wine or sake. Spices, herbs, solid ingredients like tomatoes or chopped pickles, creamy ones like mustard or egg or roasted garlic—all of these are good but optional. You'll get a better sense of the range of possibilities in the next few pages.

Demystifying emulsifying: Novices may wonder how to turn these components into a creamy, cohesive dressing. The process itself is called *emulsification* (many vinaigrettes are emulsions, as is mayonnaise)—think of it as forcing oil and water to combine—and it takes some energy. Of course this need not be your energy; it can be electrical energy powering a blender, which can produce a vinaigrette so stable that it can be prepared hours before serving time.

Bottled dressing—trust me or read the long list of ingredients yourself—is an emulsion of inferior oil (usually soy or "vegetable") and liquid (often water, with some vinegar), seasonings (often artificial, or at least far from fresh), and preservatives. Try this little experiment: Put vegetable oil and water together in a blender and turn it on. The mixture will turn white and creamy; add salt, pepper, and a few other flavorings, and you have something you can sell for $3 a cup, as long as you're a multinational food company.

I emphasize this because I'm trying to convince you to make your own vinaigrette rather than to buy bottled dressing. Do it in a blender, by shaking the ingredients in a jar, by beating them with a fork or whisk, or with an immersion blender. Hand tools—like forks—won't emulsify much, though there's nothing wrong with that (or with a "broken" vinaigrette, in which the oil and vinegar are barely combined), but for a creamy, rich emulsion, just use a blender, which also has the advantage of puréeing whatever solids you're adding and producing a vinaigrette that will keep nicely.

The right proportion: The standard ratio is three parts oil to one part vinegar, but many people prefer more oil; a ratio of four to one can be quite delicious. If you use mild vinegar and strong-tasting olive oil, you may prefer two parts oil to one part vinegar or something even a little stronger. Somewhere in that range, between four to one and one to one, you're going to find a home for your own taste. But that's the key: Taste your vinaigrette, then taste it some more. Eventually your palate will find a home that it loves.

Vinaigrette

MAKES: About $3/4$ cup
TIME: 5 minutes

From here grow all other vinaigrettes. Use your instincts or any of the suggestions on the following pages to vary the basic recipe. My everyday dressing almost always includes a bit of mustard (see the second variation), which helps emulsify the dressing while adding tang.

$^1/_2$ cup extra virgin olive oil

3 tablespoons good wine vinegar, or more to taste

Salt and freshly ground black pepper

1 large shallot (about 1 ounce), cut into chunks (optional)

① Combine all the ingredients except the shallot in a blender and turn the machine on; a creamy emulsion will form within 30 seconds. Taste and add more vinegar a teaspoon or two at a time until the balance tastes right to you.

② Add the shallot and turn the machine on and off a few times until the shallot is minced within the dressing. Taste, adjust the seasoning, and serve. (This is best made fresh but will keep, refrigerated, for a few days; bring it back to room temperature and whisk briefly before using.)

Lemon Vinaigrette. Light, fresh tasting, and all purpose: Use $^1/_4$ cup or so freshly squeezed lemon juice for the acid and plenty of black pepper. A tablespoon of warm water will help the mixture emulsify.

Mustard Vinaigrette. Simply add 1 heaping teaspoon (or more) of any good mustard to the blender. It doesn't have to be Dijon; whole grain is fine too. You can also use dry mustard; start with about $^1/_2$ teaspoon.

Soy Vinaigrette. One of my favorite quick dressings: Add a tablespoon of soy to the mix, along with dark sesame oil to taste, about a teaspoon. Lemon juice, lime juice, and vinegar are all just fine here.

Ginger Vinaigrette. Add a 1-inch piece of ginger, peeled and roughly chopped, to the blender. Use a mixture of 1 tablespoon sherry vinegar, 1 tablespoon freshly squeezed lime juice, and about 1 tablespoon luke-warm water for the liquid; be sure to taste and adjust the seasoning, using plenty of black pepper.

Honey-Garlic Vinaigrette. Strong, sweet, and delicious: Use balsamic vinegar for the acid. Add about 1 clove garlic and 1 tablespoon honey to the mix.

Coconut Curry Vinaigrette. Use rice wine or coconut vinegar. Instead of the olive oil, use coconut milk, either made from scratch (page 423) or canned (use it straight from the can without any extra water). Blend in a tablespoon of curry powder (to make your own, see page 816).

25 Simple Additions to Vinaigrette

1. Any fresh herb: For tender, milder herbs like parsley, basil, or dill, use as much as a quarter cup; for stronger, tougher herbs like rosemary, tarragon, or thyme, a teaspoon is enough.

2. Any dried herb or spice: Here it's harder to offer general guidelines, but start with as little as a pinch—$^1/_8$ teaspoon or so—and work your way up from there. Be careful not to blow away the vinaigrette; dried herbs and spices can be quite strong.

3. Minced fresh ginger: Start with a teaspoon.

4. Minced fresh garlic: Start with a small clove. For milder garlic flavor, let a crushed clove sit in the vinaigrette for a few minutes, then fish it out. Or wipe your salad bowl with a crushed clove of garlic and discard. Roasted Garlic (page 304) makes a terrific addition and emulsifies like crazy; because it's mild, you can use 5 cloves or more.

5. Minced red onion, scallion, shallot, mild white onion, or leek: Start with a tablespoon or so.

6. Soy sauce or other liquid seasonings: Use as much as a tablespoon.

7. Honey, maple syrup, or other sweeteners, within reason: Don't use more than a tablespoon or so.

8. Freshly grated Parmesan (or other hard cheese; see page 210) or crumbled blue cheese, feta, or goat cheese: Anything from a tablespoon to $^1/_4$ cup will add flavor.

9. Minced crunchy vegetables—red or yellow bell pepper, cucumber, celery, carrot, or fennel, for example: Try a couple tablespoons.

10. Minced pickles, preferably cornichons: Go with a tablespoon to $^1/_4$ cup.

11. An egg or fresh or sour cream, yogurt, or puréed soft tofu: A couple of tablespoons will add incredible creaminess to your vinaigrette.

12. Prepared or freshly grated horseradish: Use at least 1 teaspoon.

13. A tablespoon or two of minced tomato (seeded and, preferably, skinned) or bits of reconstituted sun-dried tomato.

14. Roasted Vegetable Stock (page 102): Add just a tablespoon or two.

15. Minced nuts or seeds, especially peanuts, almonds, walnuts, hazelnuts, pecans, or pumpkin seeds: A small handful will do it.

16. Roasted and peeled bell pepper (see page 333): One is usually enough.

17. Avocado: Blend in the flesh of 1 small or medium.

18. Poppy seeds: 2 tablespoons is a wonderful addition to Lemon Vinaigrette in particular.

19. Canned chipotle: 1 pepper is plenty, with just a tiny bit of its adobo.

20. Soaked and softened sea vegetable, like arame, hijiki, or wakame: $1/2$ cup is about right.

21. Small cooked whole grains, like cracked wheat, amaranth, millet, or quinoa: Stir in up to $1/4$ cup after blending.

22. Peach, pear, or apple: Peel, seed, and cut 1 small one into chunks.

23. Salsa Roja (page 787): Use $1/4$ cup.

24. Dried fruit, like blueberries, cherries, raisins, apricots, pineapple, or mango: Add up to $1/4$ cup.

25. Any pitted black or green olives: $1/4$ cup or even more if you like, but be sure to add these before you salt the vinaigrette.

The Basics of Herbs

Herb pastes and purées, beginning with pesto and going from there, are complex and delicious and an important part of the home cook's sauce repertoire. The herb is always the dominant flavor (just look at the quantities!), even when it's combined with spices or garlic. It's simple: When you start with basil or parsley, the two most commonly used herbs in pastes, as you do in the recipes in this section, you are going to end up with great flavor. But herbs by themselves are also essential to flavorful cooking. Following are charts containing brief descriptions of the herbs you're most likely to use in the kitchen.

The Herb Lexicon

The charts that follow are self-explanatory: The herbs are in alphabetical order. The first lists the herbs used most frequently in today's cooking. There are literally thousands of plants used as herbs, and in the second chart I focus on those that are sometimes found in supermarkets, often used in cooking, and at least mentioned in this book.

Unfortunately, no herb is a direct substitute for any other. There are many situations, however, in which you're not necessarily looking for a distinct flavor but rather a certain freshness that an herb will provide. In these cases, of course, you can substitute parsley for basil, or cilantro for mint, and so on. Just don't expect the end product to be the same.

Fresh herbs keep best when stored in the refrigerator. For most, simply wrap them in damp paper towels and slip them into a plastic bag. For those with fragile leaves—like basil, chervil, dill, mint, or parsley—you can set them stem-side down in a jar of water with a plastic bag over the leaves, and change the water every couple of days. They'll keep a few days or longer if they were very fresh to begin with. Store dried herbs in tightly sealed jars, away from sunlight, for up to a year, but after six months or so taste them before using to make sure they haven't gotten musty.

F Fast   M Make Ahead   V Vegan

EVERYDAY HERBS

HERB	DESCRIPTION	USES
Basil *Basilico*	The most familiar varieties (like Genovese) have flavors of licorice and cloves; the more exotic, like Thai, are peppery and more minty. Sold everywhere, and easy to grow in warm weather.	Best raw or cooked only briefly. Use the leaves whole or tear them; or chop them if you don't mind the leaves turning black. The flowers are edible and great thrown in salads.
Bay Leaves *Sweet Bay, Sweet Laurel, Bay Laurel*	Glossy, green, and leathery when fresh; grayed and brittle when dried. Fresh are much stronger than dried, though both are good; whole dried leaves are far better than ground. Turkish (small, round leaves) are superior to Californian (2- to 3-inch-long narrow leaves). Easy to grow in Mediterranean climates.	In stocks, soups, sauces, poaching liquids, to flavor vinegars; with roasts of all kinds (throw a few leaves in the next time you're roasting vegetables)
Chervil	Looks similar to parsley but smaller, with lacy leaves and an anise-basil flavor. Fresh only; dried is useless. Easy to grow in not-too-hot climates, but so delicate it's not easy to find in supermarkets.	A delicate herb best used raw or tossed in at the end of cooking. Delicious in omelets, sauces, in salads, and with vegetables.
Chives	Bright green, hollow, and grasslike, with a mild onion flavor. Garlic chives have wider and flatter leaves and a more garlicky taste, but aren't as common. Fresh are far preferable, sold everywhere, and easy to grow.	Best raw or cooked only briefly. An assertive addition to soft cheese spreads and compound butter.
Cilantro *Coriander, Chinese Parsley, Mexican Parsley*	Tender and parsley-like in appearance, but distinctive (some might say *soapy*), in aroma and flavor. Only fresh leaves are desirable; dried is useless. (The seeds are considered a spice; see Coriander, page 812.) Sold everywhere, and easy to grow.	Like basil and many other herbs, best added at the last minute. Widely associated with the flavors of Mexican, Thai, and Indian cooking. Use the roots in stews or other long-cooked dishes.
Dill *Dill Weed*	Stalks with blue-green, feathery, tender leaves, with familiar flavor. Fresh is superior to dried, which has less flavor but at least retains the character of the fresh leaves. Sold in most supermarkets and easy to grow in not-too-hot weather. Dill seed is useful too.	Use at the end of cooking, as its flavor is diminished by hot temperatures (though tying stems in a bundle and cooking with stews gives a nice flavor). Super in dishes made with sour cream, yogurt, or mustard, or tossed into a green salad.
Marjoram *Sweet Marjoram, Knotted Marjoram (Wild Marjoram is sometimes Oregano)*	Short, square stems with light green, fuzzy, oval leaves. Often confused and interchangeable with oregano, but superior. Dried marjoram isn't too bad, though it's far more pungent than fresh. Sold in most supermarkets, and an easy-to-grow perennial in most climates.	Add fresh toward the end of cooking; crumble dried leaves between your fingers and use less than if you were using fresh. Wonderful with green salads, vinaigrettes, eggs, beans, all sorts of vegetables, and especially tomato sauces.
Mint	Square stems with bright green, wrinkled leaves (spearmint), or smooth ones (peppermint and other varieties). Best fresh; dried is a decent substitute, at least in savory dishes. Sold in most supermarkets, and easy to grow (invasive, in fact).	Fresh leaves should be chopped or crushed to release their flavor. Traditional with peas or potatoes, goes well with many vegetables and fruits; perfect in yogurt-based sauces, as well as in chutneys and many Southeast Asian dishes. Ideal for herbal teas and cocktails.

HERB	DESCRIPTION	USES
Oregano *Greek Oregano, Wild Marjoram*	Square stems with dark green, fuzzy, spade-shaped leaves. Stronger and spicier than marjoram, especially Mexican oregano. Dried is especially pungent. Fresh is infinitely better, but dried is acceptable. Sold in most supermarkets, and an easy-to-grow perennial in most climates.	Fresh and dried can be cooked or used as a garnish in small amounts. Good with tomatoes, cheeses, pizza, vegetables, beans, and vinaigrettes.
Parsley	Crisp stems with bunches of dark leaves with fresh flavor. Dried is not worth buying. There are two varieties: curly and flat-leaf (Italian) parsley; the latter is somewhat better, but it's not worth making a big deal about. Sold everywhere, and easily grown as an annual.	Impossible to overstate its importance. Inexpensive and versatile, used in just about everything: soups, salads, vinaigrettes, sauces, vegetables, eggs, pasta, and as a garnish. Especially valuable in winter for its freshness.
Rosemary	Grayish-green needles on woody branches, with crisp, piney aroma and flavor. Fresh rosemary is sold increasingly in supermarkets, and is easy to grow as a perennial (warmer climates) or annual, but dried leaves are flavorful.	Wonderful with beans, also with most vegetables, egg dishes, pasta, and breads. The woody branches make perfect skewers for broiling or grilling too.
Sage	Soft, woolly, oval shaped grayish-green or multicolored leaves. Sharply flavored, slightly bitter and very aromatic. Fresh leaves are best; dried are stronger and somewhat mustier, but not bad. Increasingly sold in supermarkets, or can be grown as a perennial almost anywhere.	When using fresh leaves, use them whole or chopped. Crumble dried leaves with your fingers. One of the most important herbs of Italy; wonderful with beans, stuffings, breads, biscuits, and pasta.
Tarragon	Narrow, lance-shaped, bright to dark green leaves, with strong, complex flavor and aroma, faintly licorice-like. Fresh is always best; dried is less flavorful but usable. Often sold in supermarkets, and easily grown as a perennial in most climates. (If you have a choice, grow French tarragon.)	Whole or minced fresh leaves can be cooked; flavor is not at all tamed by heat, so use it sparingly. Crumble dried tarragon between your fingers to release essential oils.
Thyme	A small shrub with tiny green or gray-green leaves. Minty, lemony, and earthy. Fresh is more pungent and aromatic than dried, though dried thyme is useful. Often sold in supermarkets, and easily grown as a perennial in most climates.	The classic French cooking herb, often used in long-simmering or braising recipes. Use fresh leaves and tips as a garnish, but very sparingly—its strong flavor easily overwhelms everything else. Perfect teamed with olive oil and garlic at the beginning of many sautés.

Pesto, Herb Purées, and Herb Sauces

Pesto, which originated in and around Genoa, keeps fairly well. Don't add the Parmesan until you're ready to use it, however, and to help retain its bright green color, drizzle a layer of olive oil over the top once you've put the pesto in a container. Herb pastes made with less oil do not fare as well, so eat them sooner rather than later. If you have a garden filled with basil, by all means make as much pesto as you can and throw it into the freezer. But if you're using store-bought basil, unless it's incredibly cheap you might as well just make it in the quantities given here and enjoy it fresh.

 Fast   Make Ahead   Ⓥ Vegan

SPECIALTY HERBS FOR ENTHUSIASTS

HERB	DESCRIPTION	USES
Epazote *Mexican Tea, Wormseed, Pigweed*	Bright green, jagged, and pointed leaves with green stems, usually sold in bunches when fresh. Its aroma is unusual, and its taste powerful, so use it carefully. But it adds a mysterious, valuable, and unique flavor. Fresh leaves are better, but dried are more common. Sold in Mexican and Latin American markets and easily grown as an annual.	Use chopped or whole fresh or dried leaves in small quantities; 1 tablespoon of fresh or 1 teaspoon dried is sufficient for most recipes serving 4 to 6 people. Traditionally used with beans, and some moles; also good with corn and other summer vegetables in quesadillas, and in scrambled eggs.
Lavender	Narrow gray-green leaves with long purple or pink flower spikes; only the flower buds are commonly available dried. The scent and flavor is minty and floral—you'll recognize it immediately. Can be grown as a perennial in any moderate climate.	Use sparingly; it's strong and can be bitter. Fresh leaves and flowers can be minced and tossed into salads and fruit dishes or cooked in sauces, candies, and pastries.
Lemongrass *Citronella Root, Sereh*	A stiff, narrow stalk that could be mistaken for a scallion. Strong citrus flavor and aroma (think citronella candles), but without acidity. Best fresh; dried is acceptable. The powdered form, called *sereh*, is not as good. Sold in supermarkets and Asian markets (especially Vietnamese and Thai). Easy to grow in warm climates or as an annual in temperate zones.	Cut off woody tops and peel tough outer layers; mince or pound the pieces to release their flavor and aroma. Soak dried lemongrass in hot water for at least 30 minutes before using.
Lime Leaves *Kaffir Lime Leaves*	Tough, shiny green leaves that often look like two conjoined leaves. Very aromatic, with unusually floral and limy flavor. Fresh is best, but dried are good. Sold in most Asian markets, and can be grown wherever citrus will grow.	In Southeast Asian dishes of all types. Mince or toss the whole leaves in during cooking; use double the amount of dried leaves for fresh. Or use a teaspoon of grated or minced lime zest for each leaf.
Shiso *Perilla, Japanese Basil or Mint, Beefsteak Plant*	Flat, bright green or reddish purple leaves with a jagged edge. Combination of basil, mint, and cinnamon flavors. Dried is less flavorful but somewhat useful. Sold in many Asian (especially Japanese) and some Mexican markets; easy to grow inside or out (like mint, it is invasive and will spread like mad).	As you would use basil or mint. Traditionally served with sashimi and sushi, as well as with cucumbers, pickles, tempura; in salads, soups; when dried, sprinkled over rice.

There are five main ingredients in pesto. To take them in turn:

Basil: You can now find decent, aromatic basil, even in winter; it gets expensive, of course, but availability is no longer an issue. Remove large, thick (and bitter) stems, but if you're taking basil from the garden (and you're sure no pesticides were used), including a few flowers won't hurt. Wash well in a salad spinner; it need not be completely dry before you begin, but you don't want too much water clinging to the leaves.

Oil: Again, it's no longer a problem to find—or, for most people, afford—extra virgin olive oil. If you have some really fine oil, don't use it for the bulk of the pesto but consider stirring in a tablespoon or two at the end. You can cut extra virgin olive oil with a little grapeseed or corn oil if you'd like to economize, but don't go overboard or the pesto will suffer mightily.

Nuts: Not optional in true pesto, which is made in some areas with pine nuts (*pignolis*) and in others with walnuts. Both are good.

Cheese: Not optional in Genoa, but I often omit it because basil, simply puréed with oil and nuts, is already so good. Real Parmigiano-Reggiano is usually the cheese of choice, but Grana Padano is almost as good here, and many people in Liguria use hard sheep's milk cheese, like pecorino Romano. (There's more about these cheeses on page 210.)

Garlic: I've had some pesto in which the garlic taste is overwhelming, and I am not a huge fan of raw garlic, so I often start with 1/2 clove. This can and should be adjusted to your own taste. Another idea is to use Roasted Garlic (page 304), which is super-mild; it also has an emulsifying quality, so it will thicken your pesto. Start with a couple of tablespoons and take it from there.

Traditional Pesto

Pesto Genovese

MAKES: About 1 cup
TIME: 10 minutes

The best pesto is made with a mortar and pestle. And in Genoa, where pesto originated—it's properly called *pesto Genovese,* and everyone there will tell you not to even bother to *try* to make it elsewhere, because no one else's basil is as good (a ridiculous notion, by the way)—few people will admit to using a food processor. But when you get into their kitchens, that's just what they do. And so do I.

Although it is not traditional, you can substitute parsley for all of some of the basil, with fine results. Without the cheese, this is vegan.

2 loosely packed cups fresh basil leaves, rinsed and dried

Salt

1/2 clove or more garlic

2 tablespoons pine nuts or walnuts

1/2 cup extra virgin olive oil, or more

1/2 cup freshly grated Parmesan, pecorino Romano, or other hard cheese (optional)

1 Combine the basil with a pinch of salt, the garlic, the nuts, and about half the oil in a food processor or blender. Process, stopping to scrape down the sides of the container if necessary and adding the rest of the oil gradually.

2 Add more oil if you prefer a thinner mixture. Store in the refrigerator for a week or two or in the freezer for several months. Stir in the Parmesan by hand just before serving.

Pesto with Butter. Toss this with pasta or rice or use it as you would a compound butter (page 801); it's really quite special: Blend in 2 tablespoons softened butter along with the last bit of oil (do not store this version).

Mint or Dill "Pesto." Try it on pasta or grilled vegetables: Substitute mint or dill for the basil; the garlic is optional. Use a neutral oil, like grapeseed or corn, instead of olive oil and omit the cheese. Finish, if you like, with a squeeze of lemon juice. Use within a day.

Arugula "Pesto." Terrific with grilled vegetables or plain rice: Substitute arugula—tough stems removed—for the basil. Omit the cheese. Use within a day.

Parsley "Pesto" or Parsley Purée

MAKES: About 1 cup
TIME: 10 minutes

Simpler, purer, less complex than traditional pesto, parsley purée is—to me at least—more of a standby. For one thing, you can find decent parsley year-round. For another, it's a brighter, fresher purée and therefore less

F Fast   **M** Make Ahead   **V** Vegan

There's a fine line between herb paste and herb purée or sauce. The difference? No more than thickness. As much as I love them, pesto and other herb pastes make great-tasting pasta and finishing sauces, but they tend to be a little bit dry. So what can you use to thin herb pastes without watering them down?

Actually, you *can* water them down: Water provides the solution, as long as you add only a little so the oil continues to bind everything. One of the oldest tricks in the world is to use pasta-cooking liquid (which contains at least a little starch and flavor) to thin pesto or other herb pastes down to sauce consistency. Another, more modern technique is to add water to whatever you're puréeing in a food processor—the sauce will become thinner but will still be creamy and emulsified; you might need to run the machine a bit longer, but that's it.

Other liquids work well too. Lime, lemon, or other freshly squeezed citrus juices are delicious and make the foundations of Caribbean mojos like the green olive one at right. Dry or sweet white wine, rice vinegar, even apple cider can contribute to many herb sauces, especially those destined for whole grains or bland vegetables like cabbage. From there it's not too big a leap to using fresh fruits and vegetables to thin herb sauces. Choose the juicy ones like peaches, melons, and plums; they'll give you more body than straight liquid, while still thinning the paste into a sauce. In either case, be sure to taste and add a little sugar or honey if needed, depending on the acidity of the additions.

specific in its uses. And, as you can see from the variations, it is equally useful with different herbs.

2 cups parsley leaves (thin stems are okay), rinsed and dried

Salt

½ clove garlic, or more to taste

½ cup extra virgin olive oil, or more

1 tablespoon sherry vinegar or freshly squeezed lemon juice

1 Combine the parsley with a pinch of salt, the garlic, and about half the oil in a food processor or blender. Process, stopping to scrape down the sides of the container if necessary, and adding the rest of the oil gradually.

2 Add the vinegar, then a little more oil or some water if you prefer a thinner mixture. Taste and adjust the seasoning, then serve or cover and refrigerate for up to a couple of days.

Cilantro Purée, Dill Purée, Basil Purée, or Mint Purée. These are good; cilantro purée is delicious with grilled chicken, mint with lamb, and so on: Substitute any of these herbs (leaves only or very thin stems too) for the parsley.

Chimichurri. Very strong: Use 3 or more cloves garlic, 2 tablespoons vinegar or lemon juice, and at least a teaspoon of hot red pepper flakes. Do not refrigerate.

Green Olive Mojo. Caribbean and intense: Reduce the olive oil to ¼ cup; use ¼ cup freshly squeezed lime juice, or to taste, in place of the vinegar. After puréeing, use the food processor to pulse in 1 cup pitted green olives; or chop the olives by hand and add them. In any case, do not purée them.

Lighter Cilantro (or Other Herb) "Pesto"

MAKES: About 1 cup
TIME: 10 minutes

Here just enough oil is added to thicken the mixture a bit; it doesn't become creamy as does normal pesto, but it retains a vibrant herb flavor. Wonderful drizzled over

vegetables or stirred into soups. You can also make this with parsley, basil, dill, mint, or a combination.

2 cups loosely packed fresh cilantro leaves

Salt

1 clove garlic

3 tablespoons peanut or neutral oil, like grapeseed or corn

1 tablespoon freshly squeezed lime juice

① Combine the cilantro with a pinch of salt, the garlic, and the oil in a food processor or blender. Process, stopping to scrape down the sides of the container if necessary.

② Add the lime juice and blend for a second; add a little water if necessary to thin the mixture, then purée. Taste and adjust the seasoning, then serve or cover and refrigerate for up to a couple of days.

Cilantro "Pesto" with Ginger and Chile. Serious kick here and a must for chile lovers: Double the garlic, add about 1 tablespoon roughly peeled and chopped ginger, and hot chile (like habanero or jalapeño, seeded,) to taste, or hot red pepper flakes to taste.

The Basics of Mayonnaise

Like basic Vinaigrette (page 762), mayonnaise is an emulsion, where one ingredient (oil)—is dispersed into another (eggs) by vigorous stirring. The result is something that doesn't look at all like the original components.

Most beginning cooks find the whole idea of making mayonnaise from scratch downright perilous. If failure is your phobia, there's a cure: practice. While a separated or "broken" mayonnaise may not be very appetizing, it's certainly not the end of the world. Simply try making it again. Your sauce will be a zillion times better than anything you'll ever eat out of a jar. It won't keep as long, but it'll keep for a week or more.

Then there's the fear of getting food poisoning from raw eggs, a fear you either have or don't. If you do, then simply choose from the eggless recipes that follow or buy the best mayo you can find and doctor it up with some of the suggestions in this section.

Demystifying Mayo

Homemade mayos go south because you either added the oil to the egg too fast or (less often) added too much. Temperature fluctuations can cause some instability, so try to make sure your eggs aren't too cold and your oil is at room temperature. (This is really quite a minor point, but I want to give you every chance at success; once you get the hang of mayo, it will never intimidate you again.)

To help you add the oil in a slow, steady stream, try putting it in a squeeze bottle or a liquid measuring cup with a spout. Or use a teaspoon to start with literally drops at a time. (There's more about specific technique in the recipe instructions.)

For general purposes, I like grapeseed oil best because of its stability and neutrality, especially if you're planning on adding extra flavors and ingredients; corn oil delivers slightly more flavor and golden color. Use olive oil if you want a particularly Mediterranean taste, which is often the case. Asian ingredients go better with a mayonnaise made from grapeseed, corn, or, for a more pronounced flavor, peanut oil. All of these decisions should be based on how you plan to use the mayo.

For vinegar, I like sherry or white wine vinegar (page 760) as the default, but try lemon or even lime juice for a brighter flavor.

In addition to classic Homemade Mayonnaise, I've included four somewhat unorthodox emulsions here that are very mayolike. All are rich tasting and creamy. One—I'm calling it Vegannaise—is based on tofu and can be substituted for mayonnaise in any of the recipes in the book; the other is made from sea greens, which contain natural emulsifiers. Weird, maybe, but really good. Then there's *real* ranch dressing here.

Homemade Mayonnaise

MAKES: 1 cup
TIME: 10 minutes

Ⓕ Ⓜ

I have made whole-egg mayonnaise countless times with blender, food processor, and whisk, and though the machines make things marginally easier, all techniques are foolproof if you follow the simple suggestions in "The Basics of Mayonnaise" and the specific instructions here.

1 egg yolk

2 teaspoons Dijon mustard

1 cup neutral oil, like grapeseed or corn, or extra
   virgin olive oil

Salt and freshly ground black pepper

1 tablespoon freshly squeezed lemon juice, sherry
   vinegar, or white wine vinegar

❶ To make by hand: Put the yolk and mustard in a medium bowl. Beat together with a wire whisk. Begin to add the oil as you beat, a little at a time (a squeeze bottle, a measuring cup with a spout, or a tablespoon is perfect for this, but with a little practice you can simply use a measuring cup), adding more as each bit is incorporated. You'll notice when a thick emulsion forms, and then you can add the oil a little faster. Depending on how fast you beat, the whole process will take about 5 minutes.

To make by machine: Put the yolk and mustard in a blender or food processor and turn the machine on. While it's running, add the oil in a slow, steady stream (see Step 1 for tools to do this, or—if you're lucky—your food processor will have a teeny hole you may never have noticed in the insert in the top). When an emulsion forms, you can add it a little faster, until all the oil is combined into the yolks.

❷ Add salt and pepper, then stir in the lemon juice. Taste and adjust the seasoning.

Garlic Mayonnaise (*Aïoli*). A Mediterranean classic, strong but addictive: Peel between 3 and 8 cloves of garlic, to taste. If mixing by hand, mince; if using a machine, roughly chop. Replace at least half of the oil with olive oil and proceed with the recipe, adding the garlic in Step 2.

Chile Mayonnaise. Use mild chiles, like ancho, or hot, like Thai or dried chipotle: Soak 1 or 2 dried chiles in warm water until soft. Drain and pat dry. Or use 1 canned chipotle and a little of its adobo sauce. If mixing by hand, mince the chiles; if using a machine, roughly chop. Proceed with the recipe, adding the chile in Step 2.

Roasted Pepper Mayonnaise. Pretty and more complex: Roast and clean 1 medium red, yellow, or orange bell pepper (see page 333). If mixing by hand, mince; if using a machine, roughly chop. Add the pepper in Step 2.

Green Sauce, French Style. Easier by machine: After the emulsion is made, add to the blender or processor container 1 sprig fresh tarragon, about 10 sprigs watercress (thick stems removed), 10 chives, and the leaves of 5 parsley stems. Process until not quite puréed but definitely green.

Cold Mustard Sauce. Delicious sandwich spread: Add 1 heaping tablespoon Dijon-style or whole grain mustard along with the other ingredients in Step 2. Thin with a tablespoon or two of cream—fresh, fraîche, or sour—to the desired consistency.

Rémoulade Sauce. By machine or hand, make these additions to the finished mayonnaise: $1/4$ cup chopped parsley, $1/4$ cup chopped scallions, 3 tablespoons Dijon or coarsely ground mustard, 1 tablespoon ketchup, and grated horseradish and cayenne to taste.

12 Ideas for Flavoring Mayonnaise

After the mayo is done, stir, blend, or process in any of the following ingredients, alone or in combination. If working by hand, there will always be bits and pieces of the stir-ins for a more rustic sauce. By machine, the mayonnaise will be smooth and evenly colored.

1. A pinch of saffron threads
2. Up to 1 tablespoon minced strong fresh herb leaves, like rosemary, oregano, tarragon, marjoram, epazote, or thyme
3. Up to $1/4$ cup mild fresh herb leaves, like parsley, cilantro, chives, chervil, or basil
4. Up to $1/4$ cup minced sweet pickle
5. 2 tablespoons soy sauce, or to taste
6. 1 teaspoon wasabi powder (see page 776), or to taste
7. 1 teaspoon (or more) grated citrus zest
8. At least a teaspoon of prepared horseradish
9. A few dashes Tabasco, Worcestershire Sauce, Hold the Anchovies (page 799), or other prepared sauce
10. Up to $1/2$ cup toasted chopped almonds, walnuts, or pecans
11. 1 tablespoon peeled and minced fresh ginger
12. Up to 2 tablespoons chili powder (to make your own, see page 814)

Real Ranch Dressing

MAKES: 2 cups
TIME: 10 minutes

The big secret to ranch dressing is buttermilk powder, which is probably in the baking section of your supermarket. Nothing else delivers that characteristic buttermilk twang, and it works as a thickener to boot.

1 cup mayonnaise (to make your own, see page 771)

1 cup buttermilk

$1/4$ cup buttermilk powder

Salt and freshly ground black pepper

$1/4$ cup chopped fresh chives or parsley (optional)

1 Put the mayonnaise, buttermilk, and buttermilk powder in a medium jar with a tight-fitting lid. Sprinkle with a little salt and lots of freshly ground black pepper.

Add the chives or parsley if you like, put on the lid, and shake vigorously for 30 seconds or so.

2 Taste and adjust the seasoning, then use immediately or store in the refrigerator for a few days. (It will keep longer if you don't add the fresh herbs.)

Chile Ranch Dressing. Add 2 teaspoons chili powder (to make your own, see page 814) to the mixture.

Curry Ranch Dressing. Add 1 tablespoon curry powder (to make your own, see page 816) to the mixture.

Parmesan Ranch Dressing. Add 2 tablespoons freshly grated Parmesan cheese to the mixture and cut back on the salt.

"Bleu" Ranch Dressing. Add $1/4$ cup finely crumbled blue cheese to the jar.

Vegannaise

MAKES: Almost 1 cup
TIME: 10 minutes

F **M** **V**

If you crave a vegan sandwich spread, salad dressing, or dip base, something you can use in place of traditional mayonnaise, you can stop buying commercially made substitutes *now*. In fact, you can whip this up in the time it takes to pull the jar from the store shelf and walk to the checkout counter. If you've tried store-bought products and don't like them, you should give homemade Vegannaise a chance. (And if you think these ingredients sound weird, you might start reading the labels on mass-produced products you consider ordinary!)

A few technical details: Cider vinegar lends a more mayonnaiselike flavor; lemon juice is brighter. For a slightly golden tint, add the pinch of turmeric (or, if you have it, saffron). Don't skimp on the blending time; your reward will be a creamy, airy consistency. All the variations to Mayonnaise (page 771) and the add-ins work for this recipe too.

F Fast   **M** Make Ahead   **V** Vegan

6 ounces (about ³/₄ cup) extra-firm silken tofu

¹/₄ cup extra virgin olive oil

2 tablespoons cider vinegar or freshly squeezed lemon juice

2 teaspoons Dijon mustard

¹/₄ teaspoon salt, plus more to taste

Pinch of ground turmeric (optional)

1 Put all the ingredients in a blender. Turn the machine to medium speed and let it run for a minute or two, then turn it off.

2 Scrape the sides of the container with a rubber spatula, turn the blender back on, and let it run for 3 minutes. Stop and scrape again, then run the blender for a minute or so more. Taste and add more salt if necessary. Serve immediately or store in a jar in the refrigerator for up to several days.

Sweeter Vegannaise, Salad Dressing Style. Like really good Miracle Whip, if that makes sense: Add a tablespoon of sugar or honey along with the other ingredients.

Thicker Vegannaise. The consistency will be more like store-bought: Reduce the oil to 2 tablespoons and the vinegar to 1 tablespoon. You will have to stop and scrape the sides more frequently.

Vegetarian Caesar Dressing. It's no longer vegan, but it doesn't contain eggs: Add ¹/₄ cup finely grated Parmesan cheese, 1 tablespoon Worcestershire Sauce, Hold the Anchovies (page 799), and several grinds of black pepper.

Seaweed "Mayo"

MAKES: About ³/₄ cup

TIME: About 40 minutes, largely unattended

Like eggs, seaweed has the ability to thicken liquids naturally, which is why it makes such a stable vegan "mayonnaise"; it also makes one with a distinctive and very good flavor.

Use this as a dip for crudités (page 88) or as a sandwich spread. It's terrific with Grilled Tofu (page 642) and grilled vegetables or tossed with hot or cold rice, udon, or soba noodles.

The color will vary depending on which type of seaweed you use. For a vibrant green, try the instant wakame. Hijiki "mayo" will be mocha colored with little dark brown flecks, while arame is greenish brown.

1 cup arame, hijiki, or ¹/₄ cup instant wakame (page 356)

2 tablespoons dark sesame, peanut, or grapeseed oil, or a combination

1 tablespoon sake or rice wine vinegar

Salt

1 Put the arame in a medium bowl and cover with warm water. Let soak until very soft, about 30 minutes. Drain, reserving the soaking liquid.

2 Combine all the ingredients in a blender with a sprinkle of salt and 2 tablespoons of the soaking water (save the rest for another use if you like). Turn the machine on; a creamy emulsion will form in 30 about seconds. Stop and push down any stray seaweed that didn't make it into the dressing and blend again. Taste and add more salt if needed. Use immediately or keep in a jar for up to 3 days. (If any water separates, just stir it back in.)

The Basics of Yogurt Sauces

Yogurt-based sauces have played a huge role in the cooking of nearly every place with a tradition of using dairy, especially the Middle East and India, but also of Eastern Europe and Russia. Where the French made butter and cheese as ways of preserving milk, much of the rest of the world simply made yogurt.

Good yogurt (you can make your own; see page 207) is sour and rich and is practically a sauce on its own; add a little salt and you're set. The group of recipes here builds on that fact, taking yogurt and adding various sea-

Without much work, you can turn this simple sauce into a number of different sauces or condiments. Here are a few ideas that can be used alone or in combination.

Herbed Yogurt Sauce. Add ¼ cup chopped fresh mint leaves, or to taste. Or use parsley, dill, cilantro, or any other tender herb. Dried mint or dill, about a teaspoon, is also acceptable (other dried herbs are not as good).

Onion Yogurt Sauce. Add a tablespoon or more minced onion, shallot, or scallion; you can omit the garlic or not, as you like.

Richer Yogurt Sauce. Top with a tablespoon or so of good extra virgin olive oil, along with a sprinkling of paprika or cumin if you like.

Avocado Yogurt Sauce. Stir in (or purée in a food processor) half (or more) of a ripe avocado, along with a little extra lemon juice.

Raita. The classic Indian yogurt sauce: Add about 1 cup chopped cucumber (peeled if you like, seeded, and salted if necessary; see page 46) or peeled, seeded, and diced tomato or any mixture of vegetables, like those you'd use in Chopped Salad (page 38).

Ginger Yogurt Sauce. Stir in a tablespoon or so of minced peeled ginger.

Fiery Yogurt Sauce. Add hot red pepper flakes, chili powder (to make your own, see page 815), or minced fresh chile, to taste.

Spicy Yogurt Sauce. Cumin, paprika, cayenne, dry mustard, saffron (let stand for a while before using; or use turmeric, which will give the same color, though not as much good flavor), and ground ginger are all useful.

Yogurt Sauce with Beans. Add a cup of drained cooked (or canned) beans, especially chickpeas.

Sweet Yogurt Sauce. A spoonful of honey—either alone or in combination with any of the above—goes great with heavily seasoned food, and the sweetness helps round out yogurt's natural acidity.

Blue Cheese Dressing. Good with sour cream too: Add about ½ cup crumbled blue cheese (Roquefort, for example) along with a bit of freshly squeezed lemon juice. Omit the garlic.

---

sonings or chopped vegetables to it, in the traditions of (mostly) the Middle East and India, where yogurt sauces are called *raitas*.

There is so much good yogurt around these days, including some made from goat milk, that you should really avoid the brands that contain gelatin or pectin and those that don't contain live cultures. The best yogurt may be thick or thin, it may have a hard, almost cream cheese layer on top, or it may not, but what it does have is a fresh, sweet-sour smell and delicious flavor. Good yogurt is not only something you eat to be "healthy" (though it seems to be undeniably good for you) but also something you crave, even when it isn't laden with sugar.

The Simplest Yogurt Sauce

MAKES: 1 cup
TIME: 3 minutes

Ⓕ   Ⓜ

You might not even think of this as sauce, but I swear, if you use it on grilled or roasted vegetables or as a dip, people will think you're a genius. Add a few drops of lemon juice if your yogurt isn't quite sour enough, which is sometimes the case.

1 cup yogurt, preferably whole milk

1 teaspoon minced garlic

Ⓕ Fast   Ⓜ Make Ahead   Ⓥ Vegan

Salt and freshly ground black pepper

Freshly squeezed lemon juice if necessary

① Combine the yogurt with the garlic, a pinch of salt, and a grind or two of pepper. Taste and adjust the seasoning, adding the lemon juice if necessary.

② Serve immediately or refrigerate for up to a few hours; bring back to near room temperature before serving.

6 Uses for Yogurt Sauce

Any of the yogurt sauces can be used in myriad different ways. Some ideas:

1. Thin with a little lemon juice and olive oil and use as a salad dressing.
2. Top grilled or steamed vegetables or baked potatoes.
3. Use as a dip for raw veggies or chips.
4. Stir into cooked rice or other grains for extra creaminess, body, flavor, and protein.
5. Cook on top of roasted vegetables as you might cheese (don't overcook, but add during the last 5 or 10 minutes of cooking).
6. For a more complex fruit salad, stir into chopped raw fruit.

The Basics of Mustard

The pungent mustard plant belongs to the same family—the brassicas—as broccoli, cabbage, and turnips. We eat the leaves, the flowers, and the seeds, which are either used whole or cracked as a seasoning or ground into the paste we call *mustard*. Like all spices, mustard seeds contain volatile oils that can get rancid and turn bitter when old, so store them as you would other spices (page 809).

Here are some of the common forms of mustard:

Yellow and white mustard seeds: The largest of the mustard seeds, these are also the mildest. Their tart flavor makes them good for everyday ground and prepared mustards, though when used without blending with other mustards, their flavor is one-dimensional.

Brown mustard seeds: The most pungent mustard, these seeds range in color from reddish to brown. The sharpest Chinese-, German-, and English-style mustards are all based on these.

Black mustard seeds: Indian cooking often features these slightly oblong seeds, which are sharp. In ground mustards they help add another dimension and deepen the color.

Dry mustard: When seeds are ground very finely, the result is a powder or "flour." The mustard you can make from powder—like Coleman's—is acceptable in a pinch. All you have to do is mix about $1/4$ cup with a sprinkle of salt and a spoonful or two of sugar. Then stir in water, wine, or beer a little at a time until you get the desired consistency. The paste will be very strong, though the sugar rounds it out a bit. For a more appealing use of dry mustard, see Chinese Mustard Dipping Sauce, below.

Dijon-style mustard: This is the name given to the smooth, pleasantly hot, wine-based mustards modeled after those from Dijon, France. Since getting such a smooth grind with everyday kitchen equipment is impossible, you've simply got to buy it. American-made Grey Poupon is the most familiar brand; Maille (from France) is another good choice, and there are more. Use Dijon mustard for salad dressings, sauces, and all-purpose smearing.

Coarse-ground, whole-grain, or stone-ground mustard: If bits of the seeds remain intact, the mustard has a slight crunch with an almost nutty flavor. (See the recipe on page 776.) Perfect for hearty dishes (for example, the Wheat Berry or Other Whole Grain Salad with Cabbage and Coarse Mustard on page 85) or whenever you want a more assertive flavor combined with texture.

Chinese mustard: This saucelike mustard from American Chinese restaurants is also found in Asian markets and well-stocked grocery stores. It tends to be on the thin side and quite sharp. To make your own, just make a thinner version of the dry mustard recipe above. But it's easy enough to make delicious Chinese Mustard Dipping Sauce by adding a little sesame oil and a splash of soy sauce. Serve this with any dumpling (page 491) or Egg Rolls (page 741) or deep-fried vegetables, like those on page 245.

Flavored mustards: So-called gourmet mustards, mostly made by small companies, are spiked with all sorts of things, from tarragon to beer to roasted shallots to fruit. Some are better than others and even worth the steep prices, though you're generally better off making your own.

Prepared yellow mustard: Unless you're eating hot dogs in a ballpark (which you probably aren't), there's no reason to bother with old-fashioned neon-yellow mustards. About the only thing they have going for them is their mildness, which isn't really a plus, and most have extra ingredients you don't want anyway.

Wasabi: Natural, fresh wasabi is a rhizome (a stem that grows underground like ginger). It's bright green, with a heat that will clear your sinuses. But mustard is the main ingredient of the prepared wasabi we most often use.

Grainy Mustard, Many Ways

MAKES: 1 1/2 cups

TIME: 15 minutes, plus a day or two to soak the seeds

If you're a mustard enthusiast, you'll be amazed by how easy and cheap it is to make your own—and how good it is. You can customize the flavor in many ways with minor adjustments; see the list at right. The only rule you must follow is to mix yellow mustard seeds with brown or black; otherwise the results will be too harsh. And if you use red wine instead of water, expect the color to be a deep reddish brown.

> 1/4 cup (about 1 1/2 ounces) yellow mustard seeds
>
> 1/4 cup (about 1 1/2 ounces) brown or black mustard seeds
>
> 1/2 cup red wine or water
>
> 1/2 cup sherry or malt vinegar (or any vinegar with at least 5 percent acidity; see page 760)
>
> Pinch of salt

1 Put all the ingredients in a jar with a tight-fitting lid or another sealed glass or ceramic container. (Don't use metal; it will corrode.) Shake or stir, then set aside to soak for a day or two.

2 Put the mixture in a blender and purée for several minutes to grind, adding a little extra water as needed to keep the machine running. Stop and scrape the sides down once or twice and repeat. You'll never get the mustard as smooth as Dijon, but you can vary the coarseness by how long you let the blender run.

3 Return the mustard to the container and cover tightly. Store in a cool, dark place (or the refrigerator) for up to several months. The mustard will be quite sharp at first but will thicken and mellow with time.

Port Wine Mustard. Instead of the red wine or water, use 1/2 cup ruby or tawny port.

Brewhouse Mustard. Instead of the red wine or water, use 1/2 cup strong-flavored beer, like stout, porter, bock, or dark or amber ale.

14 Great Additions to Grainy Mustard

Stir any of the following into 1/2 cup mustard, keeping in mind that you'll be able to keep the flavored mustard for only a week if you add fresh herbs, fruit, or vegetables.

1. Mustard Relish: 1/2 cup minced sweet pickle and 1/4 cup each minced red onion and red bell pepper

2. Tarragon Mustard: 1 tablespoon minced fresh tarragon leaves

3. Rosemary Mustard: 1 teaspoon minced fresh rosemary leaves

4. Tomato Mustard: 1 tablespoon tomato paste

5. Honey Mustard: 2 tablespoons honey

6. Horseradish Mustard: 1 teaspoon freshly grated or prepared horseradish, or more to taste

7. Molasses Mustard: 1 tablespoon molasses

8. Balsamic Mustard: 1 to 2 tablespoons balsamic vinegar, to taste

9. Creole Mustard: $1/4$ teaspoon cayenne, or more to taste

10. Roasted Garlic Mustard: 2 to 3 cloves Roasted Garlic (page 304), smashed with a fork

11. Chile Mustard: 1 teaspoon minced fresh chile (like jalapeño or Thai), or to taste, or hot red pepper flakes or cayenne to taste

12. Peach Mustard: $1/4$ cup fresh peach purée (1 medium peach, peeled, pitted, sliced, and mashed with a fork)

13. Mango Mustard: $1/4$ cup fresh mango purée ($1/2$ medium mango, peeled, pitted, cubed, and mashed with a fork)

14. Nori Soy Mustard: 1 sheet toasted and crumbled nori (page 357), plus 1 tablespoon soy sauce

Asian-Style Sauces

This section serves as a good introduction to the sauces of Asia. Many feature soy sauce or one of its relatives, but chiles, ginger, sesame seeds, and fresh herbs like basil and cilantro are also important building blocks. Most are also balanced with sweetness and acidity, often in the form of lime juice or rice vinegar. In many of these, a simple ingredient addition or replacement—like using fresh cilantro instead of basil or tahini instead of sesame seeds—can create a whole new sauce in flavor, texture, or both.

And though we call them sauces, many make fine marinades. Try the Soy and Sesame Dipping Sauce and Marinade, Korean Style and condiments like Teriyaki Sauce. Others, like the Ginger-Scallion Sauce and Chile Pastes (not all of which are Asian, but I've kept them together anyway), can be integrated into stir-fries, soups, and other recipes. No recipe here takes more than 15 minutes to make, and they all keep in the refrigerator for days if not weeks, so they're ideal for busy schedules.

Basil Dipping Sauce

MAKES: About $1/2$ cup
TIME: 15 minutes

This dead-easy sauce is even better than it might seem, because you can completely change the way it tastes just by replacing the basil with cilantro, mint, lemongrass, lime leaves, or even a different type of basil. If you want to make the flavors much more complex, add the optional ingredients, but it's delicious and well balanced as is.

Any of the variations would make a fantastic dipping sauce for Vietnamese Summer Rolls (page 743).

1 clove garlic, minced

2 tablespoons soy sauce, plus more to taste

2 tablespoons rice wine vinegar

1 tablespoon sugar

1 or 2 fresh Thai chiles, seeded and thinly sliced (page 828)

$1/4$ cup thinly sliced fresh basil leaves, preferably Thai

Whisk all the ingredients with 2 tablespoons water until the sugar is dissolved. Let sit for 5 minutes for the flavors to meld.

Cilantro Dipping Sauce. Substitute fresh cilantro for the basil.

Mint Dipping Sauce. Substitute fresh mint leaves for the basil.

Lemongrass Dipping Sauce. Replace the basil with 1 stalk lemongrass, peeled, trimmed, and minced.

Lime Leaf Dipping Sauce. Replace the basil with 1 lime leaf, minced, or the grated zest of a lime.

Fishless Fish Sauce

Makes: About ¹/₂ cup

Time: 15 minutes

Based on the classic fish sauces of Southeast Asia—Thai *nam pla* is the best known—but without the fish. The sea green (dulse) helps maintains the salty pungency of the real thing, but if you don't have any handy, you won't go far wrong by combining the remaining ingredients.

1 tablespoon crumbled or ground dulse (see page 356; optional)

1 clove garlic, minced

2 tablespoons light soy sauce

4 limes

1 tablespoon palm sugar (see page 836) or brown sugar

❶ Whisk the dulse, garlic, and soy with 2 tablespoons water in a small bowl.

❷ Grate the zest of 2 limes into the same bowl, then juice all 4 limes and add the juice. Add the palm sugar and stir well. Let sit for 5 minutes for the flavors to meld.

Thai-Style Dipping Sauce. Usually called *nam prik* and ideal for spring rolls, grilled tofu, or drizzled over steamed vegetables: Add anywhere from 1 to 10 hot fresh chiles (preferably Thai), minced, or to taste, or hot red pepper flakes to taste and a tablespoon or so of finely shredded carrot.

Vietnamese-Style Dipping Sauce. Aka *nuoc cham gung:* Add 1 or 2 hot fresh chiles (preferably Thai), minced, or to taste, or hot red pepper flakes to taste, and a tablespoon of peeled and minced ginger. Squeeze in the juice of another lime, too.

Soy and Sesame Dipping Sauce and Marinade, Korean Style

MAKES: About 1¹/₂ cups

TIME: 15 minutes

This finger-licking-good sauce is quintessentially Korean, with its soy, sesame, sugar, and garlic. It just might be the perfect marinade for grilled tofu and is also wonderful for saucing Sushi Bowls (page 527) or dipping Crudités (page 88).

¹/₂ cup soy sauce

2 tablespoons sake or rice vinegar

2 tablespoons dark sesame oil

¹/₄ cup toasted sesame seeds (see page 321)

1 tablespoon sugar

2 large cloves garlic, minced

1 tablespoon finely peeled and minced or grated fresh ginger

¹/₄ cup minced scallion

Combine all the ingredients and stir until sugar is dissolved. Use immediately or refrigerate for up to 2 days.

Tahini Soy Sauce. Thicker and richer, super with Steamed Eggplant (page 297): Substitute ¹/₄ cup mirin or honey for the sake and tahini for the toasted sesame seeds. Omit the ginger and scallions. Add a pinch of hot red pepper flakes if you like.

F Fast   **M** Make Ahead   **V** Vegan

Teriyaki Sauce

MAKES: About 1 cup
TIME: 15 minutes

Familiar and widely loved, teriyaki sauce is also fast and simple. You can slather it on broiled or deep-fried tofu, add it to stir-fried vegetables—which in turn can be served over rice or noodles—or use it as a ketchup replacement on any of the veggie burgers on pages 661–668, or anywhere else for that matter.

$1/2$ cup soy sauce

$1/2$ cup mirin or honey

1 tablespoon finely peeled and minced or grated fresh ginger

1 clove garlic, minced

$1/4$ cup minced scallion

Combine the soy sauce and mirin in a small saucepan. Cook over medium-low heat until bubbling, about 2 minutes. Turn off the heat, stir in the remaining ingredients, and use immediately or cool, then refrigerate for up to a day.

Tropical Teriyaki Sauce. Think of this as Polynesian: Substitute $1/4$ cup passion fruit or pineapple juice for half of the mirin.

Mushroom Teriyaki Sauce. A little deeper: Substitute 2 tablespoons mushroom soy sauce for 2 tablespoons of the regular soy sauce and add $1/2$ cup finely chopped mushrooms—shiitake, cremini, or button are all fine—before cooking.

Caramelized Onion Teriyaki Sauce. Put about $1/2$ onion, thinly sliced, in a small saucepan over medium heat. Cover and cook, stirring infrequently, until the onion is dry and almost sticking to the pan, 10 to 15 minutes. Add 1 tablespoon corn other neutral oil and cook, stirring occasionally, until the onion browns, another 10 minutes or so. Proceed with the recipe in the same pan used for the onion.

Roasted Garlic Teriyaki Sauce. Rich, delicious, and only a little more work: Increase the garlic (don't bother to peel) to 2 whole cloves, wrap in foil, and roast in a 375 F oven for 20 minutes, or until soft. Remove the skin from the garlic, mash the pulp into a paste, and add it to the soy sauce and mirin.

Ginger-Scallion Sauce

MAKES: About 1 cup
TIME: 15 minutes

The fresh, bright combination of ginger and scallions is the traditional and perfect accompaniment to Steamed Dumplings, Asian Style (page 492). It's also a fabulous addition to soups and, with a bit more oil, a convenient way to start a stir-fry. Finally (well, probably not finally—you'll think of other uses), it's terrific on top of plain, thin, Chinese-style egg noodles (page 496).

If chopping and mincing isn't your thing, just throw a big chunk of peeled ginger and three or four scallions into the food processor, along with the garlic, and pulse until finely chopped—but do not purée.

$1/4$ cup peeled and minced fresh ginger

$1/2$ cup chopped scallion

1 clove garlic, minced

1 teaspoon salt, or more to taste

$1/2$ cup peanut or neutral oil, like grapeseed or corn

❶ Mix the ginger, scallion, garlic, and salt together thoroughly in a heatproof bowl.

❷ Put the oil in a small saucepan or skillet over high heat until smoking. Carefully pour the oil over the ginger-scallion mixture, mix well, and serve or store, refrigerated, for up to 3 days (bring back to room temperature before serving).

Garlic-Scallion Sauce. Less complex but more powerful: Increase the garlic to $1/4$ cup and omit the ginger.

Chile-Scallion Sauce. A little heat: Add 3 tablespoons (or to taste) of your favorite finely chopped fresh chile (see the chart on page 826). Increase the garlic to 2 large cloves and reduce the ginger to 1 tablespoon or omit it entirely.

Dashi Dipping Sauce

MAKES: About 1 cup

TIME: 5 minutes, plus time to cool

A complex, delicious sauce that couldn't be any easier to prepare, especially if you already have dashi on hand. It's wonderful with Tempura (page 248), Steamed Gyoza with Sea Greens and Edamame (page 493), and Asian-Style Noodle Bowls (pages 465–469).

1 cup Kombu Dashi (page 103)

$^1/_4$ cup mirin or 2 tablespoons honey or sugar

2 tablespoons soy sauce

Combine all the ingredients in a small pot and bring to a boil. Turn off the heat and let cool. Use or cover and refrigerate for up to 3 days.

7 Quick Additions to Dashi Dipping Sauce

This stuff is so easy to spice you won't believe it—once it's cooked, you can stir in almost anything. Use the amounts here as guidelines; really, you can just add to taste.

1. Ginger, about 1 tablespoon grated or 1 teaspoon ground
2. Daikon, about $^1/_4$ cup grated
3. Wasabi, about 1 tablespoon wasabi paste
4. Sesame, about 1 tablespoon toasted seeds (page 321) or tahini
5. Garlic, about 1 teaspoon raw or 1 tablespoon roasted (page 304)
6. Scallion or shallot, about $^1/_4$ cup minced
7. Chile (pages 826–828), about 1 teaspoon minced fresh or dried

Ponzu Sauce

MAKES: About 2 cups

TIME: 10 minutes, plus time to rest

The famous Japanese dipping sauce usually contains shavings of dried bonito, a relative of tuna. In this version seaweed replaces the fish more than adequately. If yuzu (a Japanese citrus) isn't available—and it probably won't be—use a combination of lemon and lime or check out the other citrus options.

One 3- to 5-inch piece kombu or about 1 tablespoon dulse

1 cup soy sauce

$^1/_3$ cup mirin or honey

1 cup fresh yuzu juice or $^1/_2$ cup each freshly squeezed lemon and lime juice

1. In a small pot, combine the kombu, soy sauce, and mirin. Heat gently over medium-low heat—do not boil—then turn off the heat and let cool to room temperature.

2. Remove the kombu and stir in the yuzu juice. Cover and refrigerate indefinitely; serve at room temperature if at all possible.

Citrus Ponzu. Use any citrus juice—grapefruit, pomelo, orange, blood orange—instead or in addition to the yuzu (or lemon and lime) juice.

Lemongrass Ponzu. Another twist: Increase the mirin to $^3/_4$ cup, reduce the soy sauce to $^1/_4$ cup, and add $^1/_2$ cup water (or Kombu Dashi, page 103) and a stalk of lemongrass, peeled, trimmed, and crushed, to the pot with the kombu. Simmer for 15 minutes, strain, and serve warm or at room temperature. Omit the yuzu juice.

 Fast   Make Ahead   Vegan

Miso Sauces and Dressings

This is the most exotic and perhaps misunderstood group of Asian sauces, yet among the easiest and most useful. You probably know miso mostly through soup, but it makes an incredibly convenient and delicious sauce base. Few vegetable-based ingredients deliver such complex and subtle flavors in a single spoonful, and its uses are legion. There are many kinds of misos, categorized by both color and the base grain or legume (this is all explained on pages 151–152).

I've given serving suggestions for each of the following recipes, but you don't have to take them too seriously: A "dressing," for example, need not go on a salad but can be used as a dipping sauce or sandwich spread instead. And virtually all of these sauces work well either cold, at room temperature, or warmed gently. So use them anywhere and everywhere.

Simple Miso Dipping Sauce

MAKES: about 1 cup (4 servings)
TIME: 15 minutes

Richer and more subtle than Ponzu Sauce (page 780) or other soy-based dipping sauces, this is perfect for dunking or dressing heartier foods like boiled or grilled potatoes (page 340 or 346), whole wheat pastas, and Meatless "Meat"balls (page 660). Serve it in small bowls for dipping sauce or as a dressing or standard sauce.

The type of miso you choose (see page 151) will make this sauce lighter or heavier, but it's good all ways. Warm it gently on the stove if you like; just don't let it come to a boil or you will weaken the flavor.

6 tablespoons miso paste

$^3/_4$ cup warm water or sake

1 teaspoon sugar

1 tablespoon mirin or honey

1 tablespoon rice vinegar, or more to taste

Salt

① Put everything except the salt in a small bowl and whisk together. Taste and add more vinegar and salt if needed.

② Serve immediately, heat gently, or chill in the refrigerator. Covered tightly, the sauce will keep for about a week.

Simple Miso Herb Dipping Sauce. Lots of bang for your buck: Add $^1/_2$ cup minced fresh cilantro, basil, Thai basil, or mint or a combination. For a smooth green sauce, combine everything in the blender.

Simple Miso Citrus Dipping Sauce. Brighter and fresher: Instead of the rice vinegar, add a tablespoon or two of freshly squeezed lemon, lime, orange or tangerine juice. If you like, finely grate some zest and float a sprinkle on top of each little bowl.

Simple Miso Soy Dipping Sauce. A no-brainer: Add a tablespoon or two of soy sauce to the main recipe or either of the preceding variations.

Miso Carrot Sauce with Ginger

MAKES: About 1$^1/_4$ cups
TIME: 15 minutes

This colorful dressing is the high-quality version of the goopy stuff they put on salads in many Japanese restaurants. I make it in the food processor, but if you prefer something smoother, just throw everything in a blender.

Use this as a salad dressing but also on warm or chilled chickpeas or edamame. Or just toss a few spoonfuls into any plain cooked whole grain.

$^1/_4$ cup peanut oil

$^1/_4$ cup rice vinegar

3 tablespoons mild or sweet miso, like yellow or white

1 tablespoon dark sesame oil

2 medium carrots, cut into big pieces

1 inch fresh ginger, peeled and cut into coins

Salt and freshly ground black pepper

 Put all the ingredients except the salt and pepper in a food processor and pulse a few times to mince the carrots. Then let the machine run for a minute or so until the mixture is chunky-smooth.

 Taste and adjust the seasoning if necessary and serve immediately or cover tightly and refrigerate for up to several days.

Nutty Miso Sauce

MAKES: About 1 cup (4 servings)
TIME: About 15 minutes

Ⓕ Ⓜ Ⓥ

When the Japanese chef Yumiko Kano showed me this sauce, she used it to dress blanched and shocked green beans (page 241). But now I toss it on all sorts of vegetables, from grilled eggplant or mushrooms to steamed kale or broccoli. Try a dollop on thickly sliced tomatoes, use a bowlful as a dip for raw celery, or just spoon it onto boiled rice or soba, somen, or udon noodles.

Virtually any unsalted roasted nut and most seeds will work here. For starters, try almonds, cashews, hazelnuts, peanuts, or pumpkin or sunflower seeds.

One 1-inch-long piece ginger

1/4 cup light (white or sweet) miso (page 152)

1 cup shelled walnuts

1 teaspoon soy sauce, or to taste (optional)

Grate the ginger over a bowl, then place in a small fine-meshed strainer and press out the juice, about a teaspoon. Combine the ginger juice with the remaining ingredients in a blender and blend until smooth, stop-

ping the machine and scraping down the sides if necessary. Add a little water or soy sauce until the mixture is the desired thickness. Serve immediately or cover tightly and refrigerate for up to 3 days.

Tahini Miso Sauce. Faster and easier; just use a whisk: Instead of the walnuts, use 1/2 cup tahini and 1/2 cup water.

Sweet Miso Glaze

MAKES: About 1/2 cup
TIME: 10 minutes

Ⓕ Ⓜ Ⓥ

Miso works well as a basting sauce for grilling, broiling, or roasting vegetables or tofu. (I especially like this sauce made with red miso on mushrooms.) You can use any miso (page 151) for the base, but it's best to pair stronger-tasting red miso with full-flavored vegetables so as not to overpower them; the converse is also true, as strong-tasting miso can drown out subtler tastes.

The sugar in the mirin helps promote browning and gives a deep sheen to whatever you're preparing. But if you don't have mirin (or if you can find only mirin that is essentially corn syrup, use honey, a sweet and fruity after-dinner-style wine, or—for that matter—sugar.

1/2 cup miso

1/4 cup mirin

Salt

 Whisk together the miso and mirin in a small bowl until smooth. Taste and add salt if needed.

 Use immediately or cover tightly and refrigerate for a day or two.

Sweet and Hot Miso Glaze. Mince 1 clove garlic and 1 small hot or medium fresh chile, like Thai or serrano; add them to the glaze mixture.

Chutneys

Although chutneys rely on many of the same (tropical) ingredients as salsas—lime, cilantro, chile, mango, and so on—and are used the same way, as dips, condiments, dressings, and relishes, there are differences. Chutney is a bit denser, often crunchier or nuttier, and more of a condiment than a sauce. And instead of tasting bright with acidity and chile, it's usually a more complex combination of sweet, sour, and salty that is best described as piquant.

Raw Onion Chutney

MAKES: About ³/₄ cup
TIME: 1 hour, largely unattended

I love chutneys bursting with chiles and ginger and herbs, but when you're pairing a chutney with richly flavored legumes like the dals on pages 600–604, sometimes a simpler, more directly assaultive accompaniment is in order. This onion-based chutney—a standard in India—certainly fits that bill: It's fresh, bright, pungent, and mind-bogglingly easy. White onions, shallots, or chopped scallions work equally well here, and since whatever you use will essentially be pickled in the vinegar, it will keep in the refrigerator, covered, for up to a month.

2 small to medium or 1 large red or Vidalia onion, quartered and thinly sliced or chopped

1 teaspoon salt, or more to taste

¹/₂ teaspoon coarsely cracked black peppercorns

¹/₄ cup red wine vinegar

1 teaspoon or more paprika

Pinch cayenne, or to taste (optional)

Pinch chaat masala (to make your own, see page 814), or to taste (optional)

❶ Separate the layers of the onion and combine with the salt, peppercorns, vinegar, and paprika in a small bowl; let sit for an hour.

❷ Stir in the cayenne and/or chaat masala if you're using them and serve.

Hot Pepper Chutney. Not necessarily fiery: Replace the onion with 4 to 5 hot fresh red chiles (or use a red bell pepper or a combination for a milder version). Substitute 2 cloves peeled garlic for the black peppercorns. Pulse in a food processor until coarsely chopped (do not purée). This will keep well in the refrigerator, covered, for at least 2 weeks; bring back to room temperature before serving.

Cilantro-Mint Chutney

MAKES: 1¹/₂ cups
TIME: 15 minutes

This recipe plays up the wonderful affinity of cilantro and mint for one another. Made with either herb alone, the chutney will still be worthwhile, but with both it's almost magical, as it would be with Thai or regular basil substituted for the mint.

Depending on your tolerance for heat, you may adjust the number of chiles in the recipe; but remember that raw garlic and ginger pack a punch too.

1¹/₂ cups firmly packed chopped fresh cilantro leaves

¹/₂ cup firmly packed fresh mint leaves

1 to 2 Thai or other hot fresh green chiles, or to taste, or hot red pepper flakes to taste

2 inches ginger, peeled and cut into chunks

¹/₂ large or 1 small-to-medium red onion, quartered

2 cloves garlic, peeled

¹/₄ cup freshly squeezed lime juice

¹/₂ teaspoon salt, or more to taste

❶ Combine the herbs, chiles, ginger, onion, and garlic in a food processor and pulse until finely ground.

❷ Add the lime juice and salt and process until nearly

smooth (you may need to add up to $1/4$ cup water to help the food processor get going); taste and adjust the seasoning. Serve at room temperature or cover and refrigerate for up to a day.

Creamy Cilantro-Mint Chutney. This cools the whole thing down a bit and makes it closer to a Raita (page 774): Add $1/2$ cup or more good-quality yogurt, then taste, adjust the seasoning, and serve.

Long-Lasting Cilantro-Mint Chutney. Increase the garlic to 5 cloves and use $1/2$ cup white wine vinegar instead of the lime juice. Covered and refrigerated, this will last up to several weeks.

Coconut Chutney

MAKES: About 1 cup
TIME: 10 minutes

This fresh, chewy chutney goes well with just about any Indian-inspired rice dish and is not only exotic but could barely be any easier. In a pinch, you can make it with ingredients from the pantry, and if you don't have coconut, it's equally interesting and delicious (and more colorful) with chopped carrots or beets.

$1/2$ cup shredded coconut

1 inch ginger, peeled and chopped, or
   1 teaspoon ground

1 hot fresh green or red chile or hot red pepper flakes
   to taste

$1/2$ bunch cilantro, leaves only

$1/4$ teaspoon ground cumin

2 tablespoons freshly squeezed lime juice

Salt

① Put the coconut, ginger, chile, cilantro, and cumin in a food processor or blender and pulse until finely ground.
② Add the lime juice and a pinch of salt and pulse again, until nearly but not quite smooth; taste, adjust the seasoning, and serve at room temperature.

Crunchy Nut Chutney

MAKES: About 1 cup
TIME: 15 minutes

This is a beauty, easy to make and very unusual. Serve it with Whole Winter Squash, Cooked Three Ways (page 365). It's most often made with peanuts and cashews, but you can also try macadamia nuts, almonds, walnuts, pumpkin seeds, or watermelon seeds; really, any nut or seed will work here. The key to success is to taste and adjust, because nuts vary widely in freshness, bitterness, and sweetness depending on how old they are, so be prepared to add more salt or garlic. Add a little brown sugar or oil if the mixture seems too bitter or dry.

1 teaspoon cumin seeds

1 teaspoon coriander seeds

1 dried Thai or other red chile, or to taste

1 cup roasted unsalted peanuts or cashews

1 teaspoon each salt and freshly ground black pepper,
   or more to taste

1 clove garlic, peeled

① Toast the seeds and chile in a small dry skillet over medium heat, shaking the pan frequently, until the seeds color slightly, 3 to 5 minutes. (If the nuts are raw, you can toast them the same way.)
② Grind all the ingredients together in a blender or food processor, stopping the machine to scrape down the sides if necessary; you're looking for a coarse grind, short of peanut butter. Serve immediately or refrigerate for up to a week (bring back to room temperature before serving).

Dried Fruit and Nut Chutney. Built-in sweetness: In Step 2, add $3/4$ cup dried fruit, like dates, apricots, raisins, cranberries, or cherries. Again, go for a coarse grind, not a purée.

Coconut and Nut Chutney. The special flavor of coconut comes through nicely here: In Step 2, add $3/4$ cup unsweetened shredded coconut and a tablespoon or so of freshly squeezed lime juice.

Ⓕ Fast   Ⓜ Make Ahead   Ⓥ Vegan

Real Garlicky Nut Chutney. If you want a chunky chutney, roughly chop the nuts, garlic, and coconut by hand: In Step 2, add 2 to 3 cloves garlic with or without $1/2$ cup unsweetened shredded coconut and a tablespoon or so of freshly squeezed lime juice.

Walnut and Yogurt Chutney. In Step 2, use walnuts and a fresh green chile, like jalapeño or Thai, if you like. Proceed with the recipe and then stir in $1/2$ cup yogurt, or more to taste.

Pineapple Chutney

MAKES: About 2 cups
TIME: 30 minutes

This jammy, sweet-and-spicy chutney has its roots in both traditional Indian chutneys and spicy fruit preserves from Renaissance Europe. The secret is mixing fresh fruit with dried. It's perfect as a sweet-hot foil to bland foods—try it with Coconut Rice (page 507) or Deep-Fried Tofu (page 643)—but, like good old jam, it's pretty good on buttered toast too.

2 cups minced pineapple (canned is okay; drain excess juices)

$1/2$ cup chopped dates or dried apricots

$1 1/2$ tablespoons peeled and minced fresh ginger

$1/2$ teaspoon dry mustard or mustard seeds

$1/2$ teaspoon cumin seeds

$1/4$ cup freshly squeezed lime juice

2 tablespoons brown sugar

1 tablespoon minced fresh chile (like jalapeño or Thai), or to taste, or hot red pepper flakes or cayenne to taste

Salt

1 Put all the ingredients in a saucepan, mix well, and cover. Bring to a boil over high heat and uncover.

2 Turn the heat to medium or medium-low and simmer for 15 minutes, stirring occasionally.

3 Remove the chutney from the heat and cool to room temperature; taste and adjust the seasoning if necessary. This keeps well, covered and refrigerated, for at least a week; bring back to room temperature before serving.

Cranberry Chutney. A joy in the winter: Substitute cranberries for the pineapple, $1/4$ teaspoon ground cloves for the cumin, and orange juice for the lime juice. Use only 1 fresh red chile or none at all. If you like, cool the chutney slightly, then partially purée with an immersion blender or in a food processor.

Tamarind-Date Chutney. As exotic as it gets: Replace the pineapple with $1/2$ cup tamarind pulp dissolved in $1 1/2$ cups hot water (or $3/4$ cup tamarind paste, dissolved in 2 cups hot water and strained; increase the dates to $3/4$ cup. Omit the mustard and lime juice. Add more brown sugar if you like.

6 Fruit Combinations for Chutney

1. Peaches or apricots with dried apricots
2. Sour cherries (fresh or frozen, pitted) with dried cherries or cranberries
3. Plums or seedless red grapes with dried figs or prunes
4. Seedless red grapes with dried pineapple or pears
5. Rhubarb with raisins
6. Blueberries or blackberries with dried cherries or blueberries

Tomato Chutney

MAKES: About $2 1/2$ cups
TIME: 20 minutes

I like almost any tomato-based condiment; the truth is that I'm an unapologetic ketchup lover. This one, from my friend the New York–based chef Suvir Saran, is spicy, sweet, aromatic, chunky, and more interesting than most. Serve it with eggs.

1/4 cup unsalted peanuts

3 tablespoons butter or peanut oil

2 teaspoons black mustard seeds

6 whole cloves

3 dried Thai or other hot red chiles

1 teaspoon cumin seeds

1 large red onion, cut into 1/2-inch pieces

Salt

2 large tomatoes or 2 cups canned tomatoes, chopped

3 tablespoons tomato paste

1/2 teaspoon curry powder (to make your own, see page 816)

1 Put the peanuts, butter, mustard seeds, cloves, and dried chiles in a large cast-iron or nonstick skillet or wok over medium heat. Cook, stirring, for 1 to 2 minutes, until the spices are fragrant, then add the cumin and cook, stirring, until the peanuts take on a light golden color, another 2 minutes.

2 Add the onion and a large pinch of salt and cook, stirring, until the onion begins to soften, then add the tomatoes, tomato paste, and curry powder and cook, stirring often, until the sauce is slightly thickened, about 5 minutes. Taste and adjust the seasoning. Cool to room temperature and serve or cover and refrigerate for up to 3 days. Bring to room temperature before serving (you can remove the cloves too if you like).

Grilled Tomato Chutney. Especially easy if you already have a grill going: Heat a charcoal or gas grill to moderately hot and put the grate 3 inches from the heat. Cut the tomatoes into thick slices and grill quickly on both sides until browned, about 5 minutes total. Proceed with the recipe.

Green Tomato Chutney. A terrific way to use up those green tomatoes: Replace the cloves with a teaspoon of coriander seeds. Substitute green tomatoes for the ripe ones and eliminate the tomato paste and curry powder. Stir in 1/4 cup chopped fresh cilantro leaves before serving.

Green Tomato–Apple Chutney. Omit the peanuts if you like and replace the black mustard and cumin seeds with 1 teaspoon yellow mustard seeds and 1 teaspoon garam masala (to make your own, see page 815). Replace the tomatoes with a cored green apple and a green tomato; omit the tomato paste and curry powder.

Sweet Tomato Chutney. Substitute 1 stick of cinnamon for the black mustard and cumin seeds. Add 3 tablespoons brown sugar along with the tomato paste.

Caramelized Onion Chutney

MAKES: About 1 1/2 cups
TIME: 45 minutes

This recipe harnesses the richness of onions cooked until they're dark and sweet to create a strongly flavored, almost smoky condiment. In fact, if you plan in advance or if you're going to be serving this chutney with a meal off the grill, grill the onions (see the variation).

1 large or 2 medium yellow onions, sliced

Salt

1 tablespoon neutral oil, like grapeseed or corn

1 jalapeño or other fresh green chile (optional)

1 fresh hot red chile, stemmed

1 teaspoon mustard seeds

1 teaspoon ground cumin

1 teaspoon coriander seeds

1 teaspoon brown sugar

1 Put the onions in a large skillet over medium heat. Cover and cook, stirring occasionally, until the onions are dry and almost sticking to the pan, about 20 minutes. Add a large pinch of salt and all the remaining ingredients except the sugar and cook, uncovered, stirring occasionally, until the onions brown, at least 15 minutes more.

2 Stir the sugar into the onion mixture, then transfer the contents of the pan to a food processor and process until nearly smooth; taste and adjust the seasoning if necessary.

Grilled Onion Chutney. Definitely a step up if you have the time: Cut the onions into thick slices and brush with the oil; impale each disk of onion on a wooden skewer so they won't fall through the grate. Cook over low or indirect heat until very soft and nearly charred, about 20 minutes, while toasting the spices in a dry skillet on the stove (page 321). Proceed with the recipe.

Caramelized Fennel Chutney. Sweet and rich: Replace the onions with 1 or 2 bulbs fennel, trimmed and thinly sliced. Heat a large skillet over medium heat and add 2 tablespoons oil and the fennel; cook until the fennel begins to brown, about 10 minutes. Substitute fennel seeds for cumin.

Roasted Red Pepper Chutney. If you have roasted red peppers on hand or can grill them with the onions as in the first variation, this is a nice route: Substitute 1 or 2 seeded and peeled Roasted Red Peppers (page 333) for the onions. Eliminate the chiles if you like. Proceed with the recipe, adding the juice of $^1/_2$ lemon or lime.

Caramelized Carrot Chutney. The cooking time will be longer, but this is unusual and impressive: Replace the onions with 1 pound carrots, chopped (about 3 cups).

Caramelized Melon Chutney. A summer delight: Use 1 medium honeydew, cassava, or cantaloupe (about 2 pounds), cleaned and cut into small cubes or slices (about 3 cups total). These will cook *much* faster than the onions.

Cooked Sauces and Condiments

This is the more traditional, largely more familiar world of cooked sauces, starting with cooked salsas and moving on to a zillion variations on the tomato theme—which include not only barbecue sauces but also ketchup—and then to some more obscure cooked sauces. Cooked sauces are, of course, a little more time consuming than raw ones, but then they're more substantial, complex, and polished as well.

Salsa Roja

MAKES: About 2 cups
TIME: 45 to 50 minutes

This classic cooked tomato and chile sauce can be served as is or puréed and used for enchiladas or tacos. The guajillo chiles lend a complex, smoky flavor, as well as moderate heat. If you want a milder salsa, substitute ancho or another mild chile (see the chart on page 827).

Save the chile soaking water to thin the salsa if it gets too thick or use it in Tortilla Soup (page 126).

> 2 large guajillo or other medium-hot dried chiles, toasted, soaked, and cleaned (see pages 822–825)
>
> $^1/_4$ cup neutral oil, like grapeseed or corn
>
> 2 large onions, chopped
>
> 4 cloves garlic, minced
>
> 2 pounds tomatoes, cored, peeled, seeded, and chopped, with their liquid (about 3 cups; canned are fine)
>
> 1 tablespoon sugar
>
> Salt and freshly ground black pepper
>
> $^1/_4$ cup chopped fresh cilantro
>
> 3 tablespoons freshly squeezed lime juice

1 Mince the chiles. Put the oil in a medium saucepan or deep skillet with a lid over medium-high heat. When hot, add the chiles, onions, and garlic and cook, stirring occasionally, until the onions soften, about 5 minutes. Add the tomatoes, sugar, some salt, and plenty of pepper.

2 Adjust the heat so the mixture bubbles gently and

cook, stirring occasionally, until the mixture has thickened and come together, about 20 minutes.

③ Stir in the cilantro and lime juice. Taste and adjust the seasoning. Serve hot or at room temperature. Store, covered, in the refrigerator for up to 2 days.

Red Enchilada Sauce. Essential on enchiladas (page 223): Use an immersion blender to purée the sauce in the pan. Or cool the mixture slightly, pour it into a blender or food processor, and purée carefully.

Salsa Borracha. Translates as "drunk salsa" because it's cooked with beer and finished with tequila: In Step 1, add a bottle of beer with the tomatoes. (It might take a little longer to thicken.) In Step 3, use an immersion blender to purée the sauce in the pan. Or cool the mixture slightly, pour it into a blender or food processor, and purée carefully, scraping down the sides as necessary. Finish with 2 tablespoons (about a shot) of tequila if you like.

Charred Salsa Roja. If you have the grill going already, why not? Cut the tomatoes and onions into thick slices and grill on both sides until charred, about 10 minutes total. Proceed with the recipe; add 2 tablespoons or so of chopped fresh mint if you like, in Step 3.

Smoky and Hot Salsa Roja. Toast, soak, and clean a dried chipotle chile along with the others. Or add a canned chipotle chile with its adobo along with the tomatoes.

Salsa Sofrito. Substitute roasted red or yellow bell peppers (page 333) for the guajillos; replace the cilantro with a tablespoon or so of chopped fresh oregano leaves and use red wine vinegar instead of the lime juice.

Cooked Tomatillo Salsa

Salsa Verde

MAKES: About 2 cups
TIME: 30 minutes

Ⓕ Ⓜ Ⓥ

Salsa Verde is a good all-purpose salsa that keeps in the fridge for at least a week. Spoon it onto scrambled eggs

and roll in a flour tortilla with a little cheese or serve a bowlful with Naked Tamales or any of the variations (page 547).

To keep this on the mild side, substitute another poblano for the hot chile. But if in-your-face heat is what you're looking for, add even more hot chiles or some of their seeds.

10 to 12 tomatillos, husked and rinsed

3 tablespoons neutral oil, like grapeseed or corn

2 large onions, diced

5 cloves garlic, minced

2 medium poblano or other mild fresh green chiles, roasted and cleaned (page 333)

1 or 2 serrano or other hot fresh green chiles, roasted and cleaned (page 333; optional)

1 teaspoon dried oregano, preferably Mexican

1 cup vegetable stock (pages 101–102) or water

Salt and freshly ground black pepper

$1/2$ cup chopped fresh cilantro

$1/4$ cup freshly squeezed lime juice

① Preheat the oven to 400°F. Put the tomatillos on a baking sheet and roast until the skins are lightly browned and blistered, about 20 minutes. Remove the tomatillos; when they're cool enough to handle, chop them finely, along with the chiles, saving their juices.

② While the tomatillos are roasting, put the olive oil in a large deep skillet over medium heat. When hot, add the onions and garlic and cook, stirring occasionally, until very soft and lightly browned, about 10 minutes. Add the tomatillos, chiles, oregano, stock, and a large pinch of salt and pepper; stir and bring to a low simmer. Cook, stirring occasionally, until the mixture is slightly thickened, 10 to 15 minutes.

③ Stir in the cilantro and lime juice and taste and adjust the seasoning. Serve at room temperature or cover and refrigerate for up to 2 days (bring back to room temperature before serving).

Green Enchilada Sauce. For Squash Enchiladas (page 224): Use an immersion blender to purée the finished sauce in the pan. Or cool the mixture slightly, pour into a blender or food processor, and purée carefully.

Green Chile Salsa. Milder and simpler: Increase the chiles to 5 poblanos; omit the tomatillos and serranos. Decrease the stock to $1/4$ cup, more or less, as needed. Proceed with Steps 1 and 2; then use an immersion blender to purée the salsa. Or cool the mixture slightly, pour into a blender, and purée carefully. Proceed with Step 3. This salsa will keep in the refrigerator, covered, for a couple of days.

Super-Spicy Chile-Garlic Salsa. Blistering—really: Substitute 3 to 5 habaneros for the poblanos and serranos; omit the tomatillos, onion, oregano, and stock. Put the habaneros and garlic in a small skillet over medium heat. Cook, shaking the skillet occasionally, until the garlic and chiles are brown (or partially wrap the garlic and chiles in foil and roast in a 400°F oven for about 30 minutes). Stem and seed the chiles (wear gloves, if you have them, or wash your hands thoroughly). Put the chiles, garlic, cilantro, and lime juice in a food processor or blender and purée until pasty. Serve immediately or refrigerate, covered, for up to several days.

Pumpkin Seed Sauce. Thick and with a toasted nut flavor like green mole, only much easier: Toast or roast 1 cup green pumpkin seeds (pepitas; see page 321) and pulse them several times in a food processor until finely chopped. Add them to the onion-garlic mixture in Step 2 along with 1 tablespoon minced fresh epazote if you like.

Fast, Down-Home Barbecue Sauce

MAKES: About 2 cups
TIME: 20 minutes

I'm a ketchup fan, so one of my standard barbecue sauces simply builds on its well-balanced, tomatoey sweetness. If you want to use this sauce for basting during grilling or roasting, make sure you add it toward the end of the cooking time to prevent burning.

You can also use this as a rub, dip, or spread: Try it on Bean-and-Veggie Burger (page 662), grilled or broiled seitan (page 672), or simple Grilled Tofu (page 642) or vegetables. If you want to add some heat, use some chili powder, cayenne, or your favorite bottled hot sauce, like Tabasco.

> 2 cups ketchup (to make your own, see page 790)
>
> $1/2$ cup dry red wine or water
>
> $1/4$ cup wine vinegar or rice vinegar
>
> 1 tablespoon Worcestershire Sauce, Hold the Anchovies (page 799) or soy sauce
>
> 1 tablespoon chili powder (to make your own, see page 814), or to taste
>
> 1 tablespoon minced onion
>
> 1 clove garlic, minced or crushed
>
> Salt and freshly ground black pepper

1 Combine all the ingredients except the salt and pepper in a small saucepan over medium-low heat. Cook, stirring occasionally, until the flavors have a chance to blend, about 10 minutes.

2 Taste and add salt and pepper if necessary. Use immediately or cool, cover, and refrigerate for up to a week.

Curry Barbecue Sauce. More fragrant: Add a teaspoon or more of curry powder (to make your own, see page 816) along with the other ingredients.

Horseradish Barbecue Sauce. The later you add this in the recipe, the more kick it will have: To taste, add up to $1/4$ cup freshly grated horseradish or up to 2 tablespoons prepared horseradish, along with the other ingredients.

Mustardy Barbecue Sauce. Reduce the vinegar to 2 tablespoons. Add $1/4$ cup Dijon or stone-ground mustard.

Chipotle Barbecue Sauce. Serious heat: In a small bowl, use a fork to mash 1 or 2 canned and minced chipotle chiles along with some of their adobo sauce into a paste. Add to the sauce with the rest of the ingredients.

Bourbon Barbecue Sauce. There's some woody complexity in this one: Instead of wine, use $1/2$ cup bourbon.

Beer Barbecue Sauce. More down-home: Instead of wine, use $1/2$ cup beer (the darker the better—use stout or porter if you can).

Light Barbecue Sauce. A tad more elegant: Replace 1 cup of the ketchup with 1 cup vegetable stock (pages 101–102).

Asian Barbecue Sauce. Even better with Black Bean Ketchup (page 791) in place of the hoisin: Replace 1 cup of the ketchup with 1 cup hoisin sauce. Use plum wine instead of the red wine if you like, use the rice vinegar, and substitute soy sauce for the Worcestershire. Add 1 tablespoon minced peeled fresh ginger and 1 tablespoon Chinese mustard (page 775) if you like.

Homemade Ketchup

MAKES: About 1 quart
TIME: About 2 hours

Ⓜ Ⓥ

Need a reason to make your own ketchup? How about this: It tastes incredible, it can be adjusted to your taste, and it's not loaded with high-fructose corn syrup like most bottled ketchup (in fact, it has just a bit of sugar).

Finally, if you're a gardener, you must try the Green Ketchup variation.

$3/4$ cup cider vinegar

2 tablespoons pickling spice (to make your own, see page 819)

2 tablespoons neutral oil, like grapeseed or corn

1 red or yellow bell pepper, cored and roughly chopped

1 large onion, roughly chopped

1 stalk celery, roughly chopped

2 cloves garlic, peeled and crushed

2 tablespoons tomato paste

6 cups chopped ripe tomato, about 3 pounds whole (canned are fine; don't bother to drain)

$1/4$ cup brown sugar

Salt

Cayenne

❶ Heat the vinegar and pickling spice in a small pot; turn off heat and let the spices steep until ready to use, at least 45 minutes.

❷ Meanwhile, put the oil in a large pot over medium-high heat. When hot, add the bell pepper, onion, celery, and garlic. Cook, stirring occasionally, until the onion is soft. Stir in the tomato paste until it is distributed evenly and begins to color, another minute or two. Add the tomato and stir well, scraping the bottom of the pot. Turn the heat down so that the mixture bubbles gently and cook, stirring occasionally, until slightly thickened, about 45 minutes, taking care not to let the tomatoes stick to the bottom and burn.

❸ Strain the spiced vinegar and stir it into the tomato mixture along with the remaining ingredients; cook for 45 minutes longer, until just a little thinner than bottled ketchup. Taste and adjust the seasonings. Use an immersion blender to purée the ketchup in the pot or pass it through a food mill. Or cool the mixture slightly, pour it into a blender, and purée carefully. Cool and serve or cover tightly and store in the refrigerator for up to 2 weeks.

Green Ketchup. Very useful for gardeners: Replace the red or yellow pepper with a green one and use 2 pounds green tomatoes and 1 pound peeled and cored tart apples instead of red tomatoes (you should have about 6 cups total). Substitute a seeded jalapeño for the garlic if you like. Omit the tomato paste and increase the brown sugar to $1/2$ cup. Add a cup or so of water when you add the green tomatoes in Step 2.

Jamaican Jerk Ketchup. Could become your standard: Substitute jerk seasoning (to make your own, see page 818) for the pickling spice. Replace 1 cup of the chopped tomato with 1 cup mashed banana (about 2 medium bananas).

Black Bean Ketchup. Better than bottled hoisin, by far: Replace the cider vinegar and pickling spice with Chinese black vinegar and five-spice powder (to make your own, see page 816). Add $1/4$ cup rinsed fermented black beans along with the tomato in Step 2.

Tomatoless Ketchup. Here the lines between ketchup and chutney begin to blur: Replace the tomatoes with 3 pounds peeled and chopped carrots and 2 pounds peeled and chopped beets. Add 2 cups water and $1/2$ cup freshly squeezed lemon juice along with the carrots and beets in Step 2. Omit the tomato paste if you like.

Mushroom Ketchup

MAKES: About 1 quart
TIME: 26 hours, largely unattended

Mushroom ketchup has been made in England for at least four hundred years, and with good reason: It has a rich, earthy flavor and velvety texture, and it's terrifically versatile. Spread it on toast (spectacular served with a fried egg), on a sandwich, over rice or pasta, or added to a soup or sauce for a boost in flavor. It keeps well too, though it won't last that long. And don't let a mere 26 hours stand between you and this sauce; 24 of those hours are for mindless marinating.

$1^1/2$ pounds white mushrooms, halved

1 tablespoon salt

1 ounce dried porcini or shiitake mushrooms

$1/4$ cup sherry vinegar or white wine vinegar

$1/2$ cup roughly chopped shallot or onion

1 clove garlic, peeled

Freshly ground black pepper

$1/4$ cup dry sherry (optional)

① Put the fresh mushrooms in a food processor and pulse until roughly chopped. Transfer to a large bowl; sprinkle with the salt and mix until the salt is distributed evenly. Cover with a cloth and let sit at room temperature for about 24 hours, stirring 3 or 4 times (the mushrooms will turn dark).

② An hour before you're ready to make the sauce, put the dried mushrooms in a medium bowl and cover with about 2 cups boiling water. Use a plate if necessary to keep them submerged and soak until soft, about an hour.

③ Transfer the fresh mushrooms to a food processor. Use a slotted spoon to move the dried mushrooms to the processor. Then ladle or pour in $1/2$ cup of their soaking liquid, trying not to disturb the grit settled at the bottom of the bowl. Add the vinegar, shallot, garlic, and lots of pepper; purée until smooth.

④ Put the mushroom mixture in a pot over medium-high heat and bring to a boil, stirring occasionally. Lower the heat so it bubbles gently and cook, stirring occasionally, until the mixture appears homogenous and thick, an hour or so. (To test the consistency, dab a small spoonful onto a plate and let sit for a few minutes; if liquid is released, it needs to cook longer.)

⑤ Cool until safe to handle, then put the ketchup in a blender and purée until smooth, almost velvety in texture. Add the sherry if you're using it and adjust the seasoning. Let cool to room temperature, then serve or store, refrigerated, in a covered container for up to 2 weeks.

Grilled Pineapple and Onion Salsa

MAKES: About $2^1/2$ cups
TIME: 20 minutes

Grilled fruit makes a fabulous base for salsa; its caramelized sweetness is offset perfectly by the tang of the lime juice and the crisp heat from the chiles. Use this sauce to dress a green salad, as a dip for tacos, or alongside Cheesy Baked Red Bean Cakes (page 629) or Huevos Rancheros (page 174).

> 1 pineapple, peeled, cored, and cut into thick rings (see page 435; canned rings are okay; drain excess juices)
>
> 1 large red onion, cut into thick slices
>
> 3 tablespoons extra virgin olive oil
>
> 1 tablespoon minced fresh chile (like jalapeño or Thai), or to taste, or hot red pepper flakes or cayenne to taste
>
> 1 stalk lemongrass, peeled, trimmed, and minced (see page 767)
>
> 2 tablespoons chopped fresh Thai basil or mint leaves
>
> 2 tablespoons freshly squeezed lime juice
>
> Salt and freshly ground black pepper

1 Heat a charcoal or gas grill to fairly low heat and put the rack about 4 inches from the heat source. Brush the pineapple and onion slices with the olive oil; if you're worried about the slices falling through the grate, thread them on soaked wooden skewers. Cook, turning once or twice, until soft and slightly charred, about 8 minutes total. Remove the slices as they finish cooking and, when cool enough to handle, discard the skewers and chop into bite-sized chunks, saving as much of the juice as possible.

2 Put the pineapple and onion into a medium bowl with the chile, lemongrass, basil, and lime juice. Sprinkle with salt and pepper and stir to combine. Let sit for about 5 minutes, then taste and adjust the seasoning, adding more chile, lime, or salt as needed.

Grilled Apricot and Onion Salsa. *If* you can get good apricots—and it's a big *if*—this is terrific; but it's not bad with good dried apricots, soaked in water or wine to cover until soft: Substitute about 8 halved apricots for the pineapple, a tablespoon of peeled and minced fresh ginger for the lemongrass, and lemon for the lime juice.

Grilled Peach and Corn Salsa. A nice midsummer salsa: Replace the pineapple with 3 or 4 ripe peaches, halved, and use a tablespoon of peeled and minced fresh ginger instead of the lemongrass; add a cob or two of Corn on the Cob, Grilled or Roasted (page 290) and 2 chopped scallions. Use lemon or lime juice.

Smooth Green Chile Sauce, Indian Style

MAKES: 4 to 6 servings
TIME: 20 minutes

Nothing about this chile sauce is subtle; the color is deep green, the aroma is mouth-watering, and the flavors are intense. It's delicious with Dosa (page 644) and Dry-Pan Eggplant (page 294). Add some yogurt (see the first variation), to mellow the sauce a bit.

If the relatively mild poblanos aren't strong enough for you, you can increase the heat by adding some serrano or other hot chiles; see "The Basics of Chiles and Peppers" (page 822). And for a quicker, somewhat milder sauce, you can use a can or two of green chiles instead.

> 6 medium poblano or other mild fresh green chiles, roasted and cleaned (page 333)
>
> 1 tablespoon peeled and minced fresh ginger
>
> 2 teaspoons cumin seeds
>
> ¼ cup chopped fresh cilantro
>
> Pinch asafetida (optional)
>
> ¼ cup neutral oil, like grapeseed or corn
>
> Salt and freshly ground black pepper
>
> 3 tablespoons freshly squeezed lime juice

1 Put chiles, ginger, cumin, cilantro, and asafetida if you're using it in a blender or food processor; purée until smooth, adding a tablespoon or so of water if necessary.

② Put the oil in a medium saucepan over medium-high heat. Add the chile purée and cook, stirring frequently, for about 2 minutes. (Be careful when adding the chile purée—it will splatter when it hits the hot oil.) Reduce the heat and cook, stirring occasionally, until thickened, another 2 to 3 minutes.

③ Season with salt and pepper to taste and stir in the lime juice. Serve hot or store, covered and refrigerated, for up to 3 days.

Chile-Yogurt Sauce. A wonderful combo of cool and hot, ideal with Samosas (page 745) or as a dip: Let the chile sauce cool and then add a $^1/_2$ cup or more of yogurt. Serve at room temperature.

Chile and Coconut Sauce. Rich, spicy, creamy, and delicious: In Step 2, stir a 14-ounce can of coconut milk (or about 2 cups homemade coconut milk, page 423) into the simmering chile purée.

Red Chile Sauce, Indian Style. Lovely color, deep flavor: Replace the poblanos with 6 New Mexico or other mild red fresh chile, roasted and cleaned (page 333).

Red Chile Sauce, North African Style. Replace the poblanos with 6 New Mexico or other mild red fresh chiles. Substitute 2 cloves peeled garlic for the ginger; add $^1/_2$ teaspoon each caraway, coriander, and fennel seeds; omit the asafetida.

Spicy Indian Tomato Sauce

Makhani

MAKES: 2 cups
TIME: 30 minutes

Ⓕ **Ⓜ**

A tomato-based sauce from India, quite rich, almost sweet, a little hot, and spicy. The butter roasting of the cumin and mustard seeds—used essentially as a garnish—is an Indian technique called *tarka,* sometimes translated as "tempering." You can also add some minced garlic or ginger to the mix.

I love using this sauce with Hard-Cooked Eggs (page 166), cubes of fried tofu (page 642) or fresh cheese and green peas or another vegetable. I also like it as a dipping sauce for Flaky Indian-Style Flatbread Stuffed with Potato (page 700), or Dosa (page 644). The sauce is vegan if you use oil and coconut milk.

4 tablespoons ($^1/_2$ stick) butter or $^1/_4$ cup neutral oil, like grapeseed or corn

1 medium onion, chopped

2 cloves garlic, minced

One 1-inch piece ginger, peeled and minced

1 tablespoon minced fresh chile (like jalapeño or Thai), or to taste, or hot red pepper flakes or cayenne to taste

2 teaspoons garam masala or curry powder (to make your own, see pages 815–816)

$^1/_2$ teaspoon chili powder (to make your own, see page 814)

Large pinch sugar

Salt and freshly ground black pepper

2 cups chopped ripe tomato (about 1 pound whole), preferably peeled and seeded (see pages 372–373), or drained canned tomatoes

$^1/_2$ cup cream or coconut milk (to make your own, see page 423)

$^1/_2$ cup chopped fresh cilantro leaves

1 teaspoon cumin seeds

1 teaspoon mustard seeds

① Put 3 tablespoons of the butter or oil in a deep skillet over medium-high heat. When the butter is melted or the oil is hot, add the onion, garlic, ginger, and chile. Cook, stirring occasionally, until the onion is soft, about 5 minutes. Stir in the garam masala, chili powder, and sugar and sprinkle with salt and pepper;

cook and stir until the spices become fragrant, a minute or two more.

② Add the tomato and cook, stirring frequently, until it starts to release its liquid, about 3 minutes. Add the cream and the cilantro and keep cooking and stirring until the mixture comes to a boil.

③ Turn the heat down so that the sauce bubbles gently and cook, stirring occasionally, until the tomato breaks up and the mixture comes together and thickens, about 30 minutes. Taste and adjust the seasoning. (The sauce may be made ahead to this point, cooled, covered, and refrigerated for up to 3 days. Reheat gently before proceeding.)

④ Put the remaining butter or oil in a small pan over medium-high heat. When the butter is melted or the oil is hot, add the cumin and mustard seeds and toast them until they begin to pop. Spoon over the sauce just before serving.

Nut and Seed Sauces

If you don't like nut sauces, my guess is you're either allergic or have never tried one. High in complex carbohydrates and protein, nuts add spectacular flavor and texture to whatever they touch. The recipes in this section feature them whole, chopped, and finely ground for a variety of different uses. Mostly, they're so delicious you can eat them with a spoon, and some will probably surprise you with their complexity.

Specific nuts are often associated with different cuisines: almonds with Spanish cooking, peanuts with Southeast Asian, pumpkin seeds with Mexican, walnuts with the Middle East, and so on. But nuts are often interchangeable (and when I say "nuts," I'm including even sunflower and pumpkin seeds), and in today's world we're not limited by what's local. So see that as an opportunity to break some of those rules; let your taste guide you here. (For general information about nuts, see page 318.)

Peanut Sauce, Six Ways

MAKES: 2 cups
TIME: 35 minutes

Though you may be tempted to eat this sauce for dessert, you'll more likely toss this Thai-style sauce with Chinese egg noodles (page 496) or pool a couple spoonfuls on the bottom of a plate and top with slices of grilled or fried vegetables or tofu. It also makes a fine dip for celery, red bell pepper, cherry tomatoes, and rice crackers. If you want a smooth sauce, use peanut butter instead of chopped peanuts.

3 hot fresh red chiles, seeded, or cayenne or hot red pepper flakes to taste

3 garlic cloves, peeled

2 shallots, peeled

1 stalk lemongrass, white part only, thinly sliced (optional)

2 teaspoons ground turmeric

1 tablespoon peanut or neutral oil, like grapeseed or corn

1 cup coconut milk (to make your own, see page 423)

1 tablespoon brown sugar

2 tablespoons soy sauce

2 tablespoons freshly squeezed lime juice

1/2 cup chopped roasted peanuts or crunchy peanut butter

Salt

① Combine the chiles, garlic, shallots, lemongrass, and turmeric in a food processor and grind until fairly smooth; scrape down the sides of the machine once or twice if necessary.

② Put the oil in a medium saucepan or skillet over medium heat. When hot, cook the chili-garlic mixture until fragrant, about 1 minute. Add the remaining ingredients and whisk until smooth. Simmer, stirring occa-

I've got the same general attitude about thickening sauces as I do about thickening soups: If you want them thicker—and sometimes you will—use less liquid or cook a little longer (essentially "reducing"). Here are the ways you can add body and sheen to many of the cooked sauces in this chapter.

Reducing

This is the most common, reliable, and natural method of thickening a sauce: Simply let a lot of the liquid bubble away. The result is a thicker sauce with concentrated flavor. (Juice-based sauces are especially good reduced.) Just be sure to watch the pot to make sure nothing is burning or sticking and go easy on the salting, since boiling off the water also concentrates the seasonings.

Puréeing

Chunky sauces turn smooth and luxurious when puréed. An upright blender will give you the best results (always cool food to a safe temperature before putting it in a blender); an immersion blender is easier, but not as powerful. A food processor or food mill will give you a slightly rougher texture.

Enriching

Adding cream, sour cream, yogurt, egg yolks, or small bits of very cold butter will give body to cooked sauces. But beware of excess heat: cream and butter are relatively stable even if the sauce bubbles a bit, but boiling will curdle sauces made with yogurt or eggs. (Eggs are best tempered before being added to sauces; stir a bit of the hot sauce into beaten egg to warm it, then stir that mixture back into the sauce.)

Starting with a Roux

Cooking butter or oil and flour—together in equal proportion, stirring constantly over medium heat—is a classic way to thicken sauces. (There's also a technique for this purpose that combines butter and flour without cooking—*beurre manié* or "kneaded butter"—but I'm not a fan of that raw flour taste.) You can cook the roux first and then whisk a liquid like stock or milk into it (this is the technique used in Béchamel, page 803) or add the cooked roux to a simmering sauce. The darker you cook the roux, the deeper and nuttier the flavor; just be careful not to let it burn.

Adding a Slurry

When you dissolve a little starch in water or a bit of the sauce you want to thicken, the result is a cloudy mixture known as a *slurry*. You want the slurry to be the consistency of cream before adding it to the sauce. A general formula to get you started: Dissolve 1 tablespoon starch in $1/2$ cup of liquid to thicken 2 to 4 cups of sauce. Whisk it smooth with a small fork or spoon, then reincorporate the slurry into the sauce, which quickly thickens, clarifies, and gets shiny as it is heated gently.

A variety of starches are available, and all work virtually the same way. See "Vegetarian Thickeners at a Glance" on page 882 for specifics on using them. Cornstarch is probably the most common; potato and rice starches and flours are a little less so. You can even make a slurry with whole wheat flour, though I find this way too pasty.

---

sionally, until the sauce thickens, about 15 minutes. Taste and add a sprinkle of salt or a little more soy sauce if necessary. Serve immediately or store, covered and refrigerated, for up to a week; gently rewarm over very low heat or in a microwave before using.

Curry Peanut Sauce. Another layer of flavor: Omit the chiles, lemongrass, and turmeric. Instead, put one 2-inch piece peeled fresh ginger and 2 tablespoons curry powder or paste (to make your own, see page 816) in the food processor along with the shallots.

Sweet Peanut Sauce. Indonesian in spirit: Add ¹/₄ cup ketchup (to make your own, see page 790) along with the coconut milk.

Lighter Peanut Sauce. Substitute any vegetable stock (pages 101–102) for the coconut milk.

Simpler Peanut Sauce. More peanutty (and makes less): Omit everything except for the chiles, sugar, soy sauce, and peanuts. Use the food processor to blend, adding a little water or more soy sauce to get the consistency you like. Then gently heat the sauce in a small saucepan over low heat or in the microwave. Finish with ¹/₄ cup each sliced scallion and minced fresh cilantro.

Southern-Style Peanut Sauce. Peanut sauce, down-home style: Omit the chiles, lemongrass, turmeric, and soy sauce. You can hand-mince the shallots and garlic if you like, instead of using the food processor. Proceed with the recipe, but use cream instead of coconut milk and lemon juice instead of lime juice.

Tahini Sauce

MAKES: About 1 cup

TIME: 10 minutes

Ground sesame paste (tahini) serves as the base for one of the fastest, easiest, richest sauces on the planet. You don't even really need a food processor, though it makes the sauce much smoother and the variations super-simple. (If you're just whisking the sauce together, mince the garlic first.)

The most common way to eat tahini sauce is on Falafel (page 625) or on a little salad of cucumbers, tomatoes, and onions. But you can use it to dress all sorts of salads or drizzle on virtually any grilled vegetable. It's even good on spaghetti, along with a handful of chopped tomatoes and some feta cheese. Or add a cup or so of cooked or canned chickpeas to the processor and you have automatic hummus.

¹/₂ cup tahini, with a tablespoon or two of its oil

Juice of 1 lemon, or more to taste

1 clove garlic, or more to taste

¹/₂ teaspoon ground cumin (optional)

Salt and freshly ground black pepper

1 Put the tahini, ¹/₂ cup water, the lemon juice, the garlic, and the cumin if you're using it in a food processor and sprinkle with salt and pepper. Process until smooth.

2 Taste and adjust the seasoning if necessary, adding more lemon juice, oil, water, or garlic as you like. Serve immediately or cover tightly and use within a day or so.

Yogurt Tahini Sauce. Richer: Instead of water, use yogurt (whole milk, low-fat, or nonfat).

Coconut Tahini Sauce. Dynamite: Instead of water, use ¹/₂ cup coconut milk (to make your own, see page 423).

Roasted Pepper Tahini Sauce. Quite pretty: Use either the main recipe or the preceding variations and add a Roasted Red Pepper (page 333) to the food processor.

Roasted Garlic Tahini Sauce. Deep and delicious: Instead of the raw garlic, use the soft flesh from 1 head Roasted Garlic (page 304).

Minty Tahini Sauce. Add a cup of fresh mint leaves to the food processor.

Curry Tahini Sauce. Omit the cumin and add up to 2 tablespoons curry powder (to make your own, see pages 815–816).

Rustic Pine Nut Sauce

MAKES: About 2 cups

TIME: 30 minutes

The mild creaminess of pine nuts provides a terrific foundation for this Italian-style sauce, one that is both versatile and complete. Almost anything you decide to put it on, from plain pasta or rice to grilled mushrooms or steamed spinach, instantly becomes a meal.

    1/4 cup extra virgin olive oil

    1 small red onion, halved and thinly sliced

    2 tablespoons minced garlic

    Salt and freshly ground black pepper

    1 cup coarsely chopped pine nuts

    1/2 cup coarse Fresh Bread Crumbs (page 804)

    1 to 2 tablespoons drained capers or chopped pitted green olives (optional)

    1/4 cup red or white wine (depending on what you plan to use this on), vegetable stock (pages 101–102), or water

    1/2 cup chopped fresh basil or parsley leaves

❶ Put the olive oil in a deep skillet over medium-high heat. When hot, add the onion and garlic and sprinkle with a little salt and lots of pepper. Cook, stirring occasionally, until soft, about 2 minutes. Turn the heat down to medium and continue cooking, stirring occasionally, until the onion is golden and very soft, about 10 minutes more.

❷ Stir in the pine nuts and bread crumbs and cook, stirring frequently, until the crumbs start to toast and brown, 7 to 10 minutes. Add the capers, if you're using them, along with the wine. Raise the heat a bit and bring to a boil, then cook for just a minute or two more. Turn off the heat and stir in the basil. Taste, adjust the seasoning, and serve.

Lemony Pine Nut Sauce. Nice sparkle: Substitute lemon juice for the wine. Add a tablespoon of grated lemon zest instead of the capers in Step 2.

Ancho–Pine Nut Sauce. A little heat: Rehydrate 1 or 2 dried ancho chiles according to the directions on page 825. (This will take an extra 30 minutes or so.) Remove their stems and seeds and chop. Add them to the olive oil along with the onion and garlic in Step 1. Omit the capers.

Pine Nut Sauce with Tomatoes. Super on pasta: After the pine nuts and bread crumbs have turned golden in Step 2, add 1 cup chopped tomato (canned is fine). Cook for an additional 5 minutes or so, until wilted, then proceed with the recipe.

Rustic Pine Nut Sauce with Cheese. When you add the herbs, also add 1 cup crumbled feta cheese or grated Parmesan, manchego, or ricotta salata.

Puréed Pine Nut Sauce. Not so rustic: When the sauce is done, use an immersion blender to purée it in the pan. Or cool the mixture slightly, pour into a blender, and purée carefully.

Creamy Nut Sauce

MAKES: About 2 cups
TIME: 30 minutes

This is rich, almost over the top, but delicious: Pulverizing the nuts until they're almost the consistency of cornmeal and cooking them in some butter or oil forms a nutty "roux" (page 322), which in turn thickens the cream-based sauce.

Any nut or seed works here, so choose your favorite. The most obvious use for this is as a pasta sauce (there's a traditional one just like this made in northern Italy), though it also works as an easy base for gratins (page 382) or for "creaming" vegetables.

    1 cup unsalted nuts, preferably cashews, walnuts, almonds, or hazelnuts

    1/4 cup extra virgin olive oil or 4 tablespoons (1/2 stick) butter

    1/4 teaspoon freshly grated nutmeg (optional)

    Salt and freshly ground black pepper

    1 cup cream, plus more for thinning if desired

    Milk or vegetable stock (pages 101–102) for thinning if desired

❶ Use a food processor or blender to grind the nuts to the consistency of coarse meal.

2 Put the oil or butter in a deep skillet over medium heat. When the oil is hot or the butter is melted, add the ground nuts. Cook, stirring constantly, until the mixture becomes fragrant, about a minute. Turn the heat down to medium-low and continue cooking and stirring until the mixture darkens and forms a sort of paste. (This is the roux.) Sprinkle with nutmeg if you like, salt, and pepper.

3 Pour in the cream and stir or whisk to blend with the roux. Gently cook the sauce without boiling, stirring frequently, until it thickens, 5 to 7 minutes. Taste, adjust the seasoning, thin with milk if you like, and serve.

Creamy Nut Sauce with Arugula or Sorrel. Thinned, this makes a lovely soup: After the roux is cooked and seasoned, stir in $^1/_2$ cup finely chopped arugula or sorrel and cook for a minute or two before adding the milk. Proceed with the recipe. Serve as is, or use an immersion blender to purée the sauce in the pan or cool the mixture slightly, pour into a blender, and purée carefully.

Boozy Nut Sauce. A little kick: After the roux is cooked and seasoned, carefully stir in $^1/_4$ cup bourbon, brandy, or dark rum; keep stirring until the roux dissolves and the liquid almost evaporates, a couple of minutes. Add the cream and proceed with the recipe.

Creamy Cranberry-Nut Sauce. Pistachios are gorgeous here: After the roux is cooked and seasoned, stir in $^1/_2$ cup finely chopped cranberries and 2 tablespoons sugar. Cook, stirring frequently, until the fruit is soft, about 5 minutes. Then add the cream and proceed with the recipe.

4 Additions to Creamy Nut Sauce

When the sauce is done, stir in any of these for an extra flavor boost. You may need to thin the sauce a little bit.

1. $^1/_2$ cup grated cheese, like Parmesan, Gruyère, or sharp cheddar
2. $^1/_4$ cup chopped mild fresh herb leaves, like mint, parsley, or basil
3. 1 tablespoon minced potent fresh herb leaves, like rosemary, oregano, or thyme
4. 2 chopped Hard-Cooked Eggs (page 166)

Vinegar-Based Sauces

The most famous use of vinegar in sauces is certainly Vinaigrette (pages 762). Vinegar plays an essential supporting role in dozens of other recipes in this chapter, but here it stars again—and each of the following three select sauces showcases a different vinegar.

Balsamic Syrup

MAKES: $^1/_4$ cup
TIME: About 15 minutes

Inexpensive balsamic vinegar is both sweet (it usually contains sugar) and sour, so it naturally goes well with both savory and sweet foods. And this simple reduction, which begins with inexpensive balsamic vinegar, is a nice substitute for the high-priced stuff. Just be sure to start with a clean-testing balsamic vinegar, because reducing it will concentrate both good and bad aspects.

1 cup balsamic vinegar

1 Put the balsamic vinegar in a small nonreactive pan over medium-low heat. Bring to a boil, then immediately lower the heat so it bubbles gently.

2 Reduce at a low simmer to $^1/_4$ cup, about 20 minutes; it should be thickened and syrupy. (It will thicken a little more as it cools.) Serve warm or store in a covered container indefinitely.

8 Great Additions to Balsamic Syrup

For more flavor, slip any of the following ingredients into the pan while the vinegar is reducing. When you're done, strain the syrup or fish the solids out with a slotted spoon.

 Fast   Make Ahead   Ⓥ Vegan

1. Raw or Roasted Garlic (page 304), to taste
2. $^1/_2$ cup Caramelized Onions or shallots (page 329)
3. Herbs: a sprig of the stronger ones like rosemary, tarragon, or thyme; a few sprigs of the milder ones like parsley, mint, or basil
4. $^1/_4$ cup fresh, fruity red wine
5. $^1/_2$ cup chopped fruit or berries, like raspberries, apples, figs, strawberries, blackberries, pears, grapes, or cherries
6. $^1/_3$ cup chopped dried fruits, like dates, apricots, pears, cherries, strawberries, or figs
7. 2 tablespoons molasses, maple syrup, or honey
8. $^1/_2$ cup freshly squeezed orange juice

Where to Drizzle Balsamic Syrup

1. Simple Green Salad, page 38
2. Roasted or grilled veggies (especially roasted red peppers with toasted pine nuts)
3. Broiled Tomato and Blue Cheese Salad and its almond-Brie variation (page 58)
4. A slice of aged goat cheese, blue, Parmesan, or manchego or a dollop of mascarpone
5. Fresh strawberries
6. Cubes of watermelon
7. Grilled or roasted fruit (especially figs, peaches, or nectarines, page 411)
8. Vanilla ice cream or fruit sorbets (especially raspberry or strawberry)

Creamy Bistro Dressing or Sauce

MAKES: About 1 cup
TIME: 20 minutes, plus time to chill

Ⓕ Ⓜ

It's not often you fire up the stove for salad dressing, but this French-inspired double-duty drizzle is well worth it. Still warm, it's delicious on Baked Potatoes (page 339) or teamed with Asparagus Done Simply (page 261). Cool it

down and you can use it on salads. Well covered, a batch will keep in the fridge for a couple of days.

2 tablespoons extra virgin olive oil

2 shallots, thinly sliced

Sugar

$^1/_4$ cup red wine vinegar or sherry vinegar

1 cup cream

Salt and freshly ground black pepper

❶ Put the olive oil in a small nonreactive skillet over medium-high heat. Add the shallots and a pinch of sugar and cook, stirring constantly, until softened and just turning color, 3 to 4 minutes.

❷ Stir in the vinegar and let it bubble away for a minute or two. When the mixture becomes thick and syrupy, reduce the heat a bit and carefully stir in the cream, then sprinkle with salt and pepper. Keep stirring until it starts to bubble a bit, then lower the heat and cook without boiling for a couple of minutes, until thickened. Cool, then cover and chill in the refrigerator for at least an hour. (The dressing will keep, well covered, in the refrigerator for up to 3 days. Thin as needed by stirring in a little more cream or some milk before serving.) Before serving, whisk briefly and taste and adjust the seasoning.

Creamy Tarragon Bistro Dressing. Use white wine vinegar. After the cream has thickened, add 2 tablespoons minced fresh tarragon leaves.

Creamy Mustard Bistro Dressing. After the cream has thickened, add 1 tablespoon Dijon mustard.

Worcestershire Sauce, Hold the Anchovies

MAKES: About $1^1/_2$ cups
TIME: 30 minutes

Ⓕ Ⓜ Ⓥ

Having a completely vegetarian Worcestershire sauce in the pantry opens up all kinds of seasoning possibilities, from Vegetarian Caesar Dressing (page 773) to meatless "meat" balls (page 660) to seitan (page 668). The combination of ingredients may seem wacky, but if you've ever read the label on the real stuff, you'll see where I'm coming from. Tamarind paste is important to get the precise Lea & Perrins flavor and color, but apricot preserves make a fine alternative.

- 1½ cups Chinese black vinegar
- 2 tablespoons dulse or kombu
- 2 tablespoons brown sugar
- 2 teaspoons tamarind paste or apricot preserves
- 1 teaspoon black peppercorns
- 1 teaspoon whole cloves
- ½ teaspoon hot red pepper flakes, or more to taste
- 1 tablespoon soy sauce
- 1 tablespoon molasses
- One 1-inch piece real black licorice (optional)

1 Put the vinegar, dulse, brown sugar, tamarind paste, peppercorns, cloves, and hot pepper in a small saucepan over medium-high heat. Bring the mixture to a boil, stirring once or twice.

2 Once the mixture starts boiling, immediately take it off the heat and add the soy sauce, the molasses, and the licorice if you're using it. Set aside to steep until completely cool, 20 to 25 minutes. Strain into a glass jar or bottle with a tight-fitting lid and store in the pantry or refrigerator for 6 months.

Butter-Based Sauces

For many people, butter has ceased to be a staple; they just cannot justify eating straight gobs of fat the way our physically harder-working ancestors could. But when viewed as a luxury, butter takes on a new dimension. (You don't have to think much further than a slab of nicely toasted good bread slathered with butter to get the juices flowing, do you?)

Here, then, are a few simple butter-based sauces: compound butters, which are simply butter flavored with herbs or other ingredients; brown (and black) butter, quickly made sauces based on butter and little else; and the classic hollandaise and béchamel sauces. None is likely to be daily fare for you, as flavored oils (page 756) might, but all are good to have in your repertoire, especially when you want to treat yourself or your guests to something special.

The Basics of Compound Butters

Compound butter is nothing more than butter mixed with a flavorful ingredient: an herb, like parsley; a spice, like cumin; an aromatic, like garlic; a bit of fruit, like lemon; or a prepared ingredient, like mustard or soy sauce. The possibilities are endless, though traditionally it's been used as a finishing ingredient in sauces and also on grilled or broiled items. But those limits need not concern you; since it can be made in advance, compound butter is a handy way to add quick flavor and a luxurious texture to pasta, grains, beans, veggies—whatever.

And making it is literally as simple as softening butter to near room temperature and mixing in your flavoring ingredient or putting it in a small food processor and whizzing the two together. There is no exact ratio you need remember and no reason to limit yourself to the options here; you can blend almost anything you want into butter. But use good-quality unsalted butter and certainly avoid margarine. (If you want to avoid butter, see Flavored Oil, page 758.)

Compound butter can be refrigerated for days or frozen for a month or so. Make it, then roll it into a log; wrap in two or three layers of plastic before freezing. When you need some, cut a piece off and keep the rest in the freezer.

F Fast   **M** Make Ahead   **V** Vegan

Compound Butter

MAKES: about 5 tablespoons
TIME: 10 minutes

Ⓕ Ⓜ

Herb butters are the basic, most essential compound butters; variations follow. But bear in mind that some herbs are stronger than others—and spices stronger still—so adjust the amount based on common sense and taste.

> 2 tablespoons fresh herbs like parsley, chervil, cilantro, chives, dill, or sage, or smaller amounts of tarragon, rosemary, or thyme, or a combination
>
> 4 tablespoons (1/2 stick) butter, at near room temperature
>
> Salt and freshly ground black pepper
>
> Juice of 1/2 lemon (optional)

❶ Mince the herbs and use a fork to cream them with the butter; add salt as needed, and pepper and lemon juice if you like.

❷ Use or wrap and refrigerate or freeze until needed.

11 Uncooked Add-Ins for Compound Butter

These can be used in conjunction with an herb or not, as you prefer (same with the lemon juice) or combined with one another. Amounts are approximate and should be adjusted to suit your taste:

1. 2 tablespoons minced scallion
2. 1 tablespoon minced peeled fresh ginger; for a sweet compound butter, add a tablespoon or two of honey or minced crystallized ginger
3. 1 teaspoon grated lemon or lime zest, along with 1 tablespoon freshly squeezed lemon or lime juice
4. 1 tablespoon capers, rinsed and mashed, with 1 teaspoon minced lemon zest
5. 1 tablespoon balsamic vinegar, with 1 tablespoon minced shallot if you like
6. 1 tablespoon Dijon mustard or 1 teaspoon wasabi powder
7. 2 teaspoons Spanish paprika
8. 2 tablespoons minced pitted green or black olives
9. 1 teaspoon minced garlic
10. Mashed flesh of 1/2 peach, plum, or pear
11. 1 or 2 teaspoons soy sauce

5 Cooked Ingredients to Add to Compound Butter

Almost as easy and perfect when you want to take the edge off raw-tasting aromatics or vegetables. Let cooked aromatics cool a bit before mixing with the butter.

1. Add 2 or more cloves Roasted Garlic (page 304).
2. Mix in 1 teaspoon minced garlic cooked in 1 tablespoon butter for 2 to 3 minutes, or until soft. You can also add 1 teaspoon minced peeled fresh ginger just before the garlic is done. A little soy sauce mixed into the butter with this is even better.
3. Roast 2 finely chopped scallions or shallots with a tablespoon or two of butter in a pan over medium-low heat and then add.
4. Roast about 3 tablespoons chopped cashews or other nuts with a tablespoon or two of butter in a pan over medium-low heat until light golden, then add.
5. Try about 2 tablespoons minced carrot, cooked over medium-low heat in a tablespoon or two of butter until very soft. Very nice with parsley.

Brown Butter

MAKES: 1/4 cup
TIME: 15 minutes

As butter browns when cooked it develops both color and a range of complex flavors. Try this anywhere you might use a pat of butter. It takes only a few minutes to make, even with the additions, which add even more flavor.

> 4 tablespoons (1/2 stick) unsalted butter

1 Put 3 tablespoons of the butter in a small saucepan over medium heat. Stir, scraping down the sides with a rubber spatula, until the butter foam subsides and the butter turns nut brown.

2 Turn off the heat and keep warm until you're ready to use, but use as quickly as you can, certainly within 15 minutes.

Black Butter Sauce. One step further and more dramatic: Cook the brown butter until black flecks start to form, another 2 or 3 minutes. Immediately drizzle the butter over whatever food you're serving and "rinse" the pan with 2 tablespoons sherry vinegar or white wine vinegar, shaking and letting about half the vinegar evaporate. Add 1 tablespoon drained capers if you like and $1/4$ cup minced parsley. Sprinkle with salt and pepper and drizzle this mixture over the food. Toss if necessary and serve.

4 Great Additions to Brown Butter

Stir in any of these during the last minute of cooking, when the butter is just about where you want it to be (this is easily recognized once you've made brown butter a couple of times). If you want to use them in combination, increase the quantity of butter by 2 tablespoons for each additional ingredient.

1. $1/4$ to $1/2$ cup finely ground nuts (page 322): The usual ones like hazelnuts, cashews, pistachios, walnuts, or almonds, but also macadamia nuts, or sunflower or pumpkin seeds. Whole pine nuts are another good choice.

2. Minced fresh herbs: Use a tablespoon or so of oregano, rosemary, sage, thyme, or tarragon or up to $1/4$ cup of milder herbs like parsley, cilantro, mint, dill, or basil.

3. Mustard: Up to a tablespoon of either Dijon or whole-grain, to taste; whisk it in a bit.

4. Vinegar: Sherry or balsamic works best. Add about a tablespoon. It won't emulsify into the butter but instead makes a so-called broken sauce.

Hollandaise and Béchamel

For most home cooks—and even for many of the world's best restaurants—the world of traditional (and mostly French) cooked sauces has been left behind. This is especially true for vegetarians, since many of those sauces are based on chicken or veal stock, but it's becoming a universal truth as cooks and eaters increasingly prefer the lighter, fresher sauces of the Third World to the old-fashioned and often belabored concoctions of nineteenth-century Western Europe.

Nevertheless, a spoonful of hollandaise might make you think differently; it always makes me think differently. Akin to mayonnaise, but with butter instead of oil and a higher proportion of egg yolks, hollandaise is a guilty luxury, but oh what a guilty luxury. The amount in the recipe here—about a cup—will grace a plate of asparagus, broccoli, or other lightly steamed green vegetable for four or even eight people and will turn any meal into a feast. Really. As a once- or twice-a-year thing, it's simply amazing and not at all difficult to make.

The other traditional but less indulgent sauce that deserves our continuing attention is béchamel, a flour-based sauce (no eggs) that is most useful as the basis for top-grade lasagne and macaroni and cheese. Béchamel can be varied in many ways and is almost always a terrific way to turn ordinary grain and vegetable dishes into something special.

Hollandaise Sauce

MAKES: About 1 cup
TIME: 10 minutes
F

You can make hollandaise in a blender (see the variation), but the stovetop version is perhaps a little finer, pretty much foolproof, and a bit more fun. Depending on how

F Fast   **M** Make Ahead   **V** Vegan

you're using it, you can stir a bit of minced fresh tarragon (a teaspoon), dill (a tablespoon), chervil (a tablespoon), or other herb into the finished sauce.

3 egg yolks

Salt

6 tablespoons (³/₄ stick) butter, softened

1 teaspoon freshly squeezed lemon juice

Pinch cayenne (optional)

1 Put the yolks in a small saucepan with 2 tablespoons water and a pinch of salt; turn the heat to very low and cook, whisking constantly, until light, foamy, and slightly thickened. (If at any point during this process the yolks begin to curdle, immediately remove from the heat and continue to whisk for a minute before returning them to the stove.)

2 Remove from the heat and stir in the butter, a tablespoon or two at a time. Return to the heat and continue to whisk until the mixture is thick and bright yellow. Add the lemon juice, then taste and adjust the seasoning (add the cayenne now if you're using it) and serve. (If you like, you can keep the finished sauce warm over extremely low heat or—better—over very hot water, for 15 or even 30 minutes, whisking occasionally.)

Blender Hollandaise. Melt the butter in a small saucepan over low heat or in the microwave; do not let it brown. Combine all the other ingredients in the blender and turn on the machine. Slowly drizzle in the butter; the mixture will thicken. Taste and add more lemon juice or other seasonings if necessary.

4 Dishes That Hollandaise Will Turn into Luxurious Affairs

1. Steamed broccoli or asparagus
2. Boiled potatoes
3. Barley Pilaf (pages 539–540) or any plain grain dish
4. Poached Eggs (page 169)

Béchamel Sauce, 11 Ways

MAKES: About 1 cup
TIME: 10 to 20 minutes

These creamy sauces all begin with flour and butter (you can use oil), cooked together to make a thickening paste (roux). To guarantee success, cook the fat-and-flour mixture long enough to rid the flour of its raw taste; this takes just a couple of minutes but requires nearly constant stirring. And add the milk or other liquid slowly enough, whisking all the while, so that no lumps form. (If they do form, you can beat or blend them out, but that's more work.)

2 tablespoons butter or extra virgin olive oil

2 tablespoons all-purpose flour

1 to 1¹/₂ cups milk

Salt and freshly ground black pepper

1 Put the butter or oil in a small saucepan over medium-low heat. When the butter melts or the oil is hot, use a wire whisk to incorporate the flour. Turn the heat to low and cook, whisking almost constantly, until the flour-butter mixture turns tan, about 3 minutes.

2 Stir in the milk, a little bit at a time, whisking all the while. When about a cup of the liquid has been stirred in, the mixture will be fairly thick. Add more milk, a little at a time, until the consistency is just a little thinner than you like, then cook, still over low heat, until the mixture thickens up again.

3 Sprinkle with salt and pepper and serve immediately or keep warm over gently simmering water for up to an hour, stirring occasionally.

Brown Sauce. A pinch of thyme is good here: In Step 1, cook the flour-fat mixture until brown. Use Roasted Vegetable Stock (page 102) in place of the milk.

Shallot Sauce. Cook ¹/₄ cup minced shallot, onion, or scallion (or 1 tablespoon minced garlic) in the butter until softened before adding the flour.

Nut Sauce. Cook 1 or 2 tablespoons pine nuts or other chopped nuts in the butter until lightly browned before adding the flour.

Mustard and/or Caper Sauce. Whisk in 1 tablespoon or more prepared mustard, capers, or both during the last minute of cooking.

Lemon Sauce. Season to taste with lemon (at least a tablespoon) or vinegar during the last minute of cooking.

Beurre Noisette Sauce. Cook the butter until it's brown before adding the flour. This adds a distinctively nutty flavor (but your béchamel will not be white, in case you care.)

Mushroom Sauce. Use mushroom-soaking liquid for part of the stock and add 1 or 2 tablespoons minced reconstituted dried mushrooms during the last minute of cooking.

Herb Sauce. Stir in any minced fresh or dried herbs you like during the last minute of cooking.

Light Tomato Sauce. Add about a tablespoon tomato paste about a minute before removing the sauce from the heat.

Mornay (Cheese) Sauce. Add ¹/₂ to 1 cup grated Emmental, Gruyère, or other good cheese to the mixture after it has thickened.

Curry Sauce. Add 1 tablespoon curry powder (to make your own, see page 816), or to taste, along with the flour.

Crisp Toppings and Garnishes

Before grated cheese and fresh herbs were so widely available, people frequently used stale bread—always on hand—as garnishes. We don't need this type of garnish anymore, but it remains popular because the crunch is so appealing. When you make your own bread crumbs

you're not only linking to an ancient tradition, you're not only reusing something you'd otherwise toss, but you're improving vastly on any bread crumbs you've ever purchased. Check it out, as well as the other crunchies here.

Fresh Bread Crumbs

MAKES: About 2 cups
TIME: 10 minutes

Bread crumbs have a special place in a vegetarian diet, where they instantly add texture and substance to almost anything. Sometimes they work like a seasoning or garnish. Other times, as in stuffings, they become the main attraction. Try to make your own whenever possible—the coarse texture is always preferable to finely ground store-bought—starting with homemade bread or a good bakery loaf.

That said, it's always a good idea to stock the pantry with a pack of panko crumbs, the Japanese-style bread crumbs that are now available everywhere and work in all types of cuisines. They're good in a pinch.

About ¹/₂ large loaf of French or Italian bread, preferably a day or two old

❶ Tear the bread into pieces and put about half in a food processor. Pulse a few times, then let the machine run for a few seconds, until coarsely chopped.

❷ Remove and repeat with the remaining bread. Use immediately or store in an airtight container for up to a month.

Toasted Bread Crumbs. They're less likely to become too fine if you toast the crumbs *after* grinding: After grinding, put the bread crumbs on a baking sheet and bake in a 350°F oven, shaking the pan occasionally, until lightly browned, about 15 minutes; these may be stored as fresh (though it makes more sense to

Think of crumbles as crisp bread crumbs or small croutons, only not made from bread. The idea is to turn common foods—cooked beans or noodles or nuts, to name a few—into toppings for anything from soups and salads to mashed potatoes and grilled vegetables. (There's a tradition of this technique in Japan, where fried bits of tempura batter—*agedama*—are used as a final garnish.) In fact, whenever you fear that your dish lacks spark, these crunchy, tasty tidbits are a good solution.

You can handle them all the same way: Start with a large, deep skillet and enough grapeseed or corn oil to cover the pan to a depth of $1/8$ to $1/4$ inch. Turn the heat to medium-high while you prepare your ingredient (see the list below). When the oil is hot but not smoking, cook the crumbles, turning gently, stirring, and breaking the pieces up so that they brown and crisp all sides. Use a slotted spoon to remove them as they brown and crisp and set them on towels to drain. While they're still hot, sprinkle them with salt and freshly ground black pepper.

They're even better sprinkled with a bit of your favorite spice blend (pages 810–819). Choose one that goes with the food you plan to put the crumbles on and use 1 to 2 teaspoons, depending on the strength of the seasonings. Try, for example, za'atar with falafel batter, chaat masala with chickpeas, or Japanese seven-spice mix with cut-up soba noodles.

Great Ideas for Crumbles

Each of these is enough for 4 or so servings:

- Falafel Crumbles. Next time you make Falafel (page 625), save $1/2$ cup of the batter to make crumbles. (It'll keep in the fridge for a day or two.) Use a small fork to distribute the batter in the hot oil, and when it starts to set, stir carefully to form small bits.
- Bean Crumbles. Start with 1 cup cooked (or canned) chickpeas, beans, or lentils. Make sure they're well drained. Use a fork to mash them a bit, then put them in the hot oil. As they cook, carefully break them up even more.
- Nut Crumbles. Pulse $1/2$ cup of your favorite nuts in a food processor a couple of times (or chop by hand) until they're about the size of split peas. Put them in the hot oil and fry until deeply golden, stirring constantly to keep them from burning. (They'll be ready in just a minute or so.)
- Noodle Crumbles. Start with 1 cup cooked long noodles, like spaghetti, angel hair, or Asian noodles. Whole grain kinds give you the most flavor and texture. Chop the strands into $1/2$-inch pieces. Add them to the hot oil and cook, stirring occasionally, until crisp, browned, and wavy.
- Crumbled Grains. Take $1/2$ cup of large cooked whole grains, like wheat or rye berries, hominy, or farro (page 537). Just cook them in the hot oil, stirring occasionally, until golden.
- Potato Skin Crumbles. Coarsely chop the peels from 2 potatoes (assuming they were well scrubbed). Add them to the oil when it's hot and stir gently to keep them separate while they cook.

store untoasted bread crumbs and toast just before using).

Fried Bread Crumbs. These are delicious, and seasoning sticks to them better than uncoated bread crumbs; but they don't keep as well, so use them immediately after frying: Heat $1/4$ cup extra virgin olive oil in a large skillet and add the bread crumbs; cook, stirring occasionally, until lightly browned, about 5 minutes. Season with salt or any spice blend (to make your own, see pages 810–819) and drain on paper towels; use immediately.

Croutons

MAKES: 4 servings

TIME: 15 minutes

The difference between homemade croutons and the packaged variety cannot be overstated; the former are delicious, reasonably healthful, and entirely addictive. (There are times when I make soup or a nice big salad just as an excuse to make and eat croutons. I'm not kidding, and I'm not apologizing.) Start with good bread and good olive oil, try some of the variations, and you'll be a convert.

Remember that you can make croutons from any good bread. Corn bread, olive bread, whole grain and whole wheat breads, even raisin or other specialty breads are all excellent candidates.

> $^1/_4$ cup or more extra virgin olive oil
>
> 1 clove garlic, peeled and smashed (optional)
>
> Four to twelve $^1/_2$-inch-thick slices good bread
>
> Salt
>
> Freshly ground black pepper (optional)

1 Put the oil and the garlic if you're using it in a skillet large enough to hold the bread in one layer and turn the heat to medium. When the oil shimmers or the garlic sizzles, add the bread. Sprinkle it with salt and, if you like, pepper.

2 When the bread browns lightly, after about 5 minutes, turn and brown the other side. If the pan dries out (which it likely will), add more olive oil if you like. When the second side is browned, after another 5 minutes or so, remove the croutons. Use immediately or store in a tin or wax paper for up to a day.

Cubed Croutons. Before beginning, cut the bread into $^1/_2$- to 1-inch cubes. Cook them in the oil, tossing occasionally, until lightly browned all over.

Herbed Croutons. Best with cubes: As the bread browns, stir in about $^1/_4$ cup finely minced parsley, dill, or chervil or a combination.

Highly Seasoned Croutons. Use plenty of black pepper, along with about 1 teaspoon chili or curry powder (to make your own, see pages 814–816).

Dry-Baked Croutons. Perfect for large batches; when kept in an airtight container, these will stay crunchy for at least a week. Plus, there's no fat: Preheat the oven to 400 F. Omit the oil and garlic. Slice or cube the bread, spread on a rimmed baking sheet, and bake, undisturbed, until the croutons begin to turn golden, about 15 minutes. Then turn the slices or shake the pan to roll the cubes around a bit. Continue baking until they're the desired color, anywhere from 5 to 15 minutes more. Sprinkle with salt and pepper or other seasoning if you like.

The Basics of Salt

Though all salts are created naturally—in the rock and seas of the earth—they are *not* created equal. Common table salt is mined, milled, refined, and "enhanced" with iodine and other ingredients into small, free-flowing grains. But consistency has a downside: the flavor of table salt is harsh, with iodine the predominant mineral taste.

At the other end of the spectrum is an array of specialty salts, pulled from both oceans and clay, with nuances of flavor and color you may or may not think are worth the expense. In between are a handful of everyday salts—either coarsely milled from deposits in rock or made by evaporating ocean water. These are the ones I use both in the kitchen and on the table.

Salt gets its name and primary flavor from sodium chloride, the major compound present in all types in varying degrees. The subtle flavors of sea salts (which may be described as "briny," "metallic," or "earthy") come from their most common trace minerals—magnesium, calcium, and potassium. The more trace minerals, the less sodium chloride, which is why many sea salts taste less "salty" than table and kosher salts.

Once you banish iodized salt and start cooking with

kosher, flake, or any kind of sea salt, you automatically stop treating salt as an ingredient and begin to think of it as a condiment. You might even use less. (And if you doubt this is true, just try a quick side-by-side taste test.)

Availability

Kosher and sea salts are now common in supermarkets—sometimes even in several types. The specialty salts, like Maldon (from England) and fleur de sel (Brittany), and smoked sea salts from various places are usually available in gourmet shops and definitely by mail order (see Sources, page 929).

Storing Salt

Even the wettest sea salts are extremely long-lived and stable. But because salts can have a corrosive effect, you should keep them in glass, ceramic, crockery, or wood containers—definitely not metal. Plastic is okay for short periods of time.

A Word About Grinding Salt

Some very coarse salts require additional grinding. Use a special salt mill designed for this purpose or crush small amounts in a mortar and pestle. Again, the idea is to avoid metal parts, which will only corrode and rust.

Seasoning Salt

It's easy enough to season your own salt with herbs and spices. For example, try putting a sprig of fresh rosemary, lavender, oregano, or thyme into a small shaker bottle of salt for a few days (then remove). Or toast a spoonful of coriander, cardamom, or cumin seeds or even a dried chile and stir into the salt, either whole or ground. Use these during cooking or as a last-minute finish.

Using Salt

Put small quantities of salt in tiny bowls—sometimes called *saltcellars*—on your countertop and table. Stick a wee spoon in them if you want, though it is perfectly acceptable just to grab a pinch. For many people—me included—the act of touching and sprinkling salt is part of the enjoyment of food.

Salt in My Recipes

Because I believe salting food is a matter of personal taste, my recipes almost always call for simply "salt" (usually with "freshly ground pepper") in the ingredient list. This frees you to use whichever salt you like best, in whichever quantity you enjoy. But I won't totally leave you in the dark. The instructions will suggest when to season with salt—usually more than once during the process and definitely at the end—and give you an idea how much to add with words like "pinch" or "sprinkle."

I do specify exact measurements in rare dishes where a precise amount of salt really makes a difference and of course in baking recipes—where quantity is more about science than about taste. For baking, I almost always use kosher salt; sea salt is less uniform and might have overpowering mineral flavors.

The Salt Lexicon

Kosher Salt

This usually comes in big boxes, either flaked or coarsely ground. I like the flaked best, but both are fine. It's as white as table salt, but the flavor is clean and slightly mineral, with no lingering aftertaste.

Uses: This is my all-purpose salt for baking, salting cooking water, and last-minute seasoning.

Generic Sea Salt

There are many different kinds of what I call generic sea salts, made by either heating saltwater in pipes and tubs or open-air evaporation. The processes are akin to true sun-dried tomatoes and heat-dried tomatoes, where the method matters less than the tomato you start with. In other words, the most complex sea salts generally start with the most complex saltwaters. That said, connoisseurs will argue that heating the water destroys some flavor. Try a few different ones and see what you think; your palate may be more sensitive than mine.

Uses: Because these tend to be more expensive than other kinds of salt, I generally reserve them for cooking and final seasoning rather than add sea salt to pasta water and the like. And I never use them in sweet baking recipes.

Fleur de Sel

Literally "flower of the sea," this prized sea salt from the coast of France (Brittany) is fine, grayish white, and slightly damp.

Uses: After cooking, as the final seasoning. It's so good you can use it to "dress" fresh salad greens, either alone or with a light squeeze of lemon.

Maldon Sea Salt

Made by a special process in England, this salt is rolled flat and flaky. The result melts on your tongue and on hot food unlike any other salt, leaving behind a pleasant flavor that builds slowly. It can be tough to find (though easy by mail), but when you do it's usually relatively inexpensive.

Uses: Absolutely the best on piping-hot fried foods, roasted potatoes, and scrambled eggs.

Table Salt

As mentioned above, this is the common salt of shakers and paper packets across America. Iodine was added several decades ago and remains in the mix today, frequently along with other noncaking ingredients. The fine grains dissolve faster than most coarse salts, though I like the crunch of undissolved salt.

Uses: Anywhere, but table salt is quite "salty," so you may want to use less.

Rock Salt

This less-pure salt is commonly used in roasting and ice cream making to conduct heat or cold. A small bit probably wouldn't kill you, but you definitely don't want to eat it.

Salts for Enthusiasts

A rainbow of colors and flavors to try: Look for the ivory Ravidà from Sicily, bright red Alae salt from Hawaii, black salts from India, and Celtic gray sea salt from France. Some may be tough to find, but each is renowned for conveying the distinct flavors of the earth and sea from which they came.

The Basics of Pepper

If you were to buy only one whole spice for your pantry, it should be black pepper. Native to India, and now cultivated throughout the hot and humid regions of the world, this vine-growing fruit has been fought over and fought for throughout history, and with good reason. The flavor is deep, sharp, smoky, slightly acidic, and pleasantly hot, a balance that cannot be duplicated with anything else. It's become ubiquitous, and its value can't be overstated. But it's easy to lose sight of this if you use packaged preground pepper.

Don't confuse peppers with chiles (see page 822). Peppercorns are technically fruit—not seeds—that grow in clusters on long "spikes." They are harvested ripe as they begin to mature from green to red or yellow-green fruit. After curing in the sun, they shrivel and turn black.

White peppercorns are skinned before drying, while the just-ripe green peppercorns are freeze dried, preserved in brine or, by those lucky to be in growing areas, eaten fresh. True red, or fully mature, peppercorns are not widely available. What you see instead are pink "peppercorns" from a completely different plant related to roses.

A Word About Grinding Pepper

Until recently, I didn't push the "freshly ground black pepper" issue in my cookbooks. But now I feel differently. What you grind at the moment doesn't taste at all like the same spice you shake out of a can or jar and barely resembles its home-ground kin that's a few hours

Ⓕ Fast   Ⓜ Make Ahead   Ⓥ Vegan

old. That said, if you really can't bear to grind as you go, do it every few weeks in small batches and keep the ground pepper in a tightly sealed container.

There are many types of peppermills for table and kitchen grinding. Ideally you want a sturdy metal or wooden mill with a screw at the top or bottom to adjust the grind. Of course you can also grind pepper in a spice or coffee grinder (see "Buying, Toasting, Grinding, and Storing Spices" below). You may also simply crack pepper into large chunks with the flat side of a big knife. Or put them in a plastic bag and take a hammer to them.

The Peppercorn Lexicon

Black Peppercorns

There are many varieties, known mostly by the region in which they were raised, but what you will usually find is a blend simply labeled *black pepper*. Take a whiff if possible to make sure the aroma is complex and sharp without being acrid. Store these and other dried peppercorns whole, in tightly sealed containers in a cool, dark place.

White Peppercorns

Because the skins have been removed, white pepper is milder than black. It's perfect for everything from cream sauces to fruit desserts, anytime you're looking for the range of pepper flavors with a little less punch and a lack of black specks. But if you're going to use it, commit to buying another pepper mill and grind your own.

Green Peppercorns

These are best—but rare—fresh, where their mild fruity and grassy flavor is at its peak. After that, I like them packed in brine. You may as well not even bother with dried green peppercorns unless they are very high quality and you plan on reconstituting them in hot water like dried chiles or mushrooms. Ground, I don't think you'll notice much difference from black pepper. Brined green peppercorns should be refrigerated after opening.

Pink Peppercorns

Once the darling of nouvelle cooking in the 1980s, these have fallen out of favor but are still available—at a price. Remember that they are not from the same plant as pepper, though the flavor is very similar to black pepper, only slightly sweet.

Sichuan Peppercorns

Chinese Peppercorns, Anise Pepper, Fagara, Flower Pepper, Sansho

Like pink peppercorns, Sichuan pepper isn't from the pepper vine at all, though in this case it's the flower of a small tree. Its flavor is unique and essential to Sichuan cooking—a flowery, slightly smoky aroma combines with a somewhat lemony-medicinal flavor and a tongue-numbing, unhot "spiciness" that feels almost like local anesthesia. (This is how Sichuan food can contain so many chiles without being overwhelmingly hot.)

You can also buy oil seasoned with them or try infusing some yourself in a little peanut or dark sesame oil (see page 758).

The Basics of Spices

The average American currently eats more than 3 pounds of spices a year, which is twice as much as twenty years ago. And there's no end in sight. When I wrote *How to Cook Everything*, right in the middle of that boom a few of the seasonings I used seemed a bit obscure. Now most of them are downright mainstream.

Buying, Toasting, Grinding, and Storing Spices

I suggest you buy spices from somewhere that either specializes in them or at least sells them in bulk, where they'll be cheaper and fresher. That generally means Asian or Indian markets, gourmet shops, on-line, or by mail order (see Sources, page 929). Most whole spices keep so well, for so long, you'll need to stock up only once or twice a year.

Whole spices have huge advantages over preground: They tend to be of higher quality to begin with. They keep much better. You can toast them at the last minute, which help brings out their flavor. And the last-minute grinding means you get all that flavor; it doesn't dry out over the course of months (or, if you're like most of us, years) of storage.

Having said all of that, everyone uses preground spices; they're just too convenient. Still, I'd say toast and grind whole spices when you can. Even if "when you can" means every fifth time, even if it means every tenth time, it's worth it.

Spices get their flavor from the essential ("volatile") oils that are captured and concentrated during drying. It doesn't matter whether the spice is a seed, a flower, a piece of bark, or a dehydrated version of something fresh (like amchoor and ginger). Gentle warming activates and releases these oils and makes the spices aromatic. But too much direct heat burns them, resulting in a bitter taste; so if they happen to burn, toss them.

When I can, I toast whole spices just before grinding or when spices are used as a finishing seasoning. If your spices are big, like cinnamon sticks or nutmeg, break them up or crush into pieces in whatever way you need to—with your fingers, the back of a knife, a hammer, the bottom of a pan, whatever. If they're encased in pods, like cardamom, lightly crush the pods and remove the seeds (discard the husks).

Then set a dry skillet over medium-high heat. Add the spices and cook, swirling the pan or stirring constantly with a wooden spoon, for just a minute or two; you'll know when they're ready because they'll smell alluring. Remove them from the pan immediately, because the spices will easily burn.

Whiz the spice or spices in your coffee or spice grinder. (You can use a cheap one, which costs ten bucks; purists use a mortar and pestle.) Unplug it, then wipe it out as best you can. (If you're feeling really energetic,

grind a little rice to a powder after removing the spices; the rice powder will remove the seasonings when you dump it out.)

Store the ground spices in a tightly covered container, preferably an opaque one (or at least away from light). They'll stay potent as long as any other ground spices, which is to say a few weeks.

Whole spices stay potent for months, up to a year, sometimes even longer. Sunlight, moisture, and heat are their only potential enemies. So just keep them in a tightly covered opaque container or in a jar in a dark place. The cooler, the better, though the refrigerator is not ideal because it's too humid. Some people recommend storing spices in the freezer, though I've never had the need to.

The Spice Lexicon

In the first chart that follows are the basic spices most people use to cook and bake. It's not a comprehensive list—"Spices for Enthusiasts" contains many others—but you can certainly get by, and cook well, with the everyday spices alone.

These are, however, judgment calls; if you were going to cook a lot of North African or Middle Eastern dishes, you'd put sumac in the first list instead of the second; similarly, if you weren't interested in Chinese cooking, you'd forget about star anise (and Sichuan peppercorns, which are described along with other peppercorns on page 809). For real Indian cooking, you must have asafetida.

A note about garlic powder, which is probably conspicuous by its absence: I simply see no reason to use anything but fresh garlic, which is cheap, easy to use, keeps for a long time, and is one of the most important flavors in cooking.

For mustard seeds, see "The Basics of Mustard" (page 775); chiles are described in two charts on pages 826–828.

Ⓕ Fast   Ⓜ Make Ahead   Ⓥ Vegan

EVERYDAY SPICES

SPICE	DESCRIPTION	USES
Allspice *Jamaica Pepper, Myrtle Pepper, Newspice, Pimento*	Berries that come from the aromatic evergreen pimento trees, which are not to be confused with pimientos, the peppers (see "The Basics of Chiles and Peppers," page 822). Small and shriveled, they look like large reddish brown peppercorns, smell a bit like a combination of cloves and nutmeg, and taste slightly peppery. Jamaican allspice is the best. Available as whole berries and ground.	By the pinch; a little goes a long way. Particularly delicious with grains like bulgur, couscous, rice, and polenta and vegetables like beets, carrots, parsnips, winter squashes, and sweet potatoes. Extremely useful in pies, puddings, gingerbread, and some chocolate desserts. Good in mulled wines or sprinkled in tomato or cranberry juice.
Cardamom	Whole pods are shaped like teeny walnuts and may be green, brown-black, or whitish. Each contains about 10 brown-black seeds, which are slightly sticky. Cardamom has a rich spicy scent, a bit like ginger mixed with pine and lemon. Cardamom is available in several forms of three main varieties: green, black, and white. You may find whole pods, or "hulled," meaning just the seeds. Unfortunately, ground cardamom is the most commonly sold form, but it is also the least potent. I buy whole pods (mostly white, which after all is not *that* rare).	Cardamom is a staple in Indian and some Middle Eastern cooking. Sometimes pods are cooked whole, especially in braised dishes where they soften (I like to eat them this way). Otherwise, gently crush the pods with the flat side of a knife or a heavy pan, remove the seeds, and grind or crush as required. Cardamom is usually combined with other spices, as in curry powder, garam masala, and kebsa. It is also used throughout the world (especially in Scandinavia) in cakes, pastries, and sweets.
Celery Seeds	Tiny tan-colored whole seeds, usually from lovage, a relative of celery that has an intense celery flavor.	A little goes a long way. Often used in pickling brines, cheese spreads, and salad dressings or baked into breads and biscuits.
Cinnamon *Canela, Ceylon or Sri Lanka Cinnamon*	Cinnamon is the aromatic bark of a tropical laurel tree. Cassia—cinnamon's less expensive cousin—is often sold as cinnamon; it's the bark from a laurel tree native to China (also called poor man's cinnamon, Chinese cinnamon, or false cinnamon). The bark dries into long, slender, curled sticks that are a reddish light brown color. Ground cinnamon is useful, though it's easy enough to grind sticks if necessary. Cassia is redder and usually comes in chip form; its flavor is more biting and bitter, making it better suited to savory dishes than sweet ones.	Use whole cinnamon sticks or pieces of cassia in soups, stews, chilis, and curries or add to rice or other grains. True cinnamon is excellent in pastries, as well as in rice puddings and other concoctions that feature sweet cream. It's delicious paired with apples, or in mulled cider or cold fruit soups.
Cloves	Cloves are the unripe flower buds of a tall evergreen tree native to the islands of Southeast Asia. Pink when picked, they are dried to a reddish brown color, separated from their husks, and dried again. Whole cloves should be dark brown, oily, and fat, not shriveled. They have a sweet and warm aroma and a piercing flavor. Both whole and ground forms are common, and both are useful.	Use cloves sparingly—their flavor can be overwhelming—and try to remove whole pods before serving (or at least warn people to look out for them!). To make this easier, you can stud an onion with cloves and then remove the onion; or wrap them in cheesecloth. Ground cloves—just a pinch, usually—are good in spice blends, batters and doughs, fruit pie fillings, and stewed fruit.

SPICE	DESCRIPTION	USES
Coriander	Seeds of the cilantro plant, they are small, round, and vary in color from pale green when fresh to light or dark brown when dried. The lemony flavor is somewhat like cilantro leaves, but the overall taste is much more complex, with hints of cumin, fennel, and even cloves. Both whole seeds and ground are common.	Coriander seeds can be cooked whole into dishes (and are quite pleasant to eat) or ground first; if you're grinding, you might consider toasting first (page 321), for a bit more flavor. Coriander is more often used in conjunction with other spices, especially cumin and cardamom, and is an important part of many spice mixtures or alone in both Asian- and Latin American–style stews, soups, and some breads and pastries.
Cumin *Comino*	Cumin seeds are the highly aromatic dried fruit of the cumin plant, a relative of parsley. Because they look similar, brown cumin and caraway are often confused, though they don't taste alike at all. If you find cumin bitter; seek out the black seeds, which are more peppery and sweet. Whole seeds and ground are available in brown (the most common), black, and white varieties. (Black and white cumin can usually be found in Indian markets.)	Lightly toasting the seeds before using enhances their flavor. Like coriander, it's frequently included in spice mixtures, like garam masala, kebsa, and chili powder. But it's also used solo a great deal, especially in Latin American and Middle Eastern cooking.
Dill	The seeds are light brown, oval, and flat. They have a stronger taste than the fresh or dried herb and a good one. Seeds and leaves are both common, though the leaves are considered an herb (see page 765).	Often used whole, though occasionally ground. Excellent with cucumbers, radishes, potatoes, and sauces made with sour cream, yogurt, or mustard. They are also featured in pickling spice.
Fennel *Sweet Cumin*	From bulbless fennel, these seeds are small, pale greenish- brown ovals with tiny ridges and an aromatic, warm, sweet taste reminiscent of licorice. Not as strong as anise and a bit more useful. Whole seeds are most common.	Delicious in salad dressings, yogurt sauces; used in Indian dishes, as well as many pilafs; one of the five ingredients in five-spice powder and some curry powders. A popular flavor in Italy and southern France. When ground, fennel seed makes an interesting addition to spice cookies, short bread, and quick breads.
Ginger	Yellowish tan and powdery, with the distinctive aroma of ginger. Available almost always ground (or, obviously, fresh). Dried ginger is inferior to fresh but useful nevertheless. Crystallized (candied) ginger is delicious out of hand and can be used in cooking, too.	Ground ginger is often used in sweets, like cakes, cookies, quick breads, but is so convenient in spice mixtures that it is among the most useful spices.
Nutmeg	Nutmeg is the egg-shaped kernel inside the seed of the fruit of a tropical evergreen tree; it's dark brown and about 1 inch long. (Its covering is called mace; see page 821.) It is sometimes a whitish color, the result of being dusted with lime to discourage insects (wash this off before grating or grinding). Available whole or ground; since the whole keeps nearly forever and is easily grated, there's no reason to buy ground.	Nutmeg is very strong and slightly bitter, so use sparingly, by grating it directly (just put the unused portion back in the jar or bag) or by breaking into pieces first (use a hammer). A sweet and warm spice, it's lovely with fruit dishes, custards, cakes and other sweets, as well as vegetables, especially spinach. It also works well with cream and cheese sauces for pasta. Nutmeg is used in many spice mixtures, including jerk seasoning and some curry powders.

 Fast   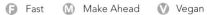 Make Ahead   Vegan

SPICE	DESCRIPTION	USES
Paprika *Pimentón*	A light red-orange powder with a spicy-sweet aroma; anything turning brown is too old. Varying in heat from mild (sweet) to hot, peppery to smoky (usually Spanish). Varieties include sweet, Hungarian, and Spanish. The best paprika comes from Spain (pimentón, which may be smoked, and is really good) or Hungary (*Szegedi* is a good word to look for). California paprika is usually quite mild and not as good. (See "The Basics of Chiles and Peppers," page 822.)	As you would any ground dried chile (that's what it is). Delicious with grains, eggs, cheese, and many vegetables and in soups, stews, sauces, rice, and potato dishes. You can substitute ground mild chile (like ancho) for paprika with no problem.
Saffron *Zafran, asafran*	Very expensive, but at $30 or so an ounce, worth having around; really. (It's a mistake to buy smaller quantities, which instead of being $480 a pound wind up being more like $4,000 a pound. And if it's much cheaper than that, it's probably not saffron at all, but marigold.) The threads should be strong, long, and a brilliant orange-red color. It's highly aromatic, warm, and spicy, with a slightly bitter taste, and gives food a distinctive and lovely yellow color and an exotic, wonderful flavor. If you want to approximate its color, you can use annatto or turmeric, but nothing tastes like saffron or has the same glow. Buy only threads; ground is useless.	Use saffron sparingly (a good pinch is about right); too much can give food a medicinal taste. Add threads directly to the dish or steep them in some of the cooking liquid or oil for a few minutes first. Used in many traditional breads and cakes; as well as in rice (like Yellow Rice, The Best Way, page 513), pasta, and cheese dishes.
Sesame Seeds *Benné seeds*	Small, oval with a pointed tip, flat seeds; a light tan (white), rusty red, or black color. A nice nutty, somewhat sweet, flavor, especially when toasted. Available in whole seeds, paste (tahini), or roasted and pressed into oil. White (most common), red, and black varieties; also unhulled white seeds, which are slightly bitter and harder to digest. (You can also buy pretoasted sesame seeds, but they sometimes have an off flavor.)	With their rich natural oils and nutty flavor, sesame seeds are an important flavoring in the cooking of China, Korea, Japan, India, and the Middle East; they are also used in Europe and are often lightly toasted before use. They are delicious as a coating for fried foods or as a garnish, sprinkled into sauces, dressings, and salads. Store in the refrigerator or freezer to prevent rancidity.
Star Anise *Chinese Anise*	The fruit of an evergreen tree native to China; pods are a dark brown, eight-pointed star, about 1 inch in diameter, with seeds in each point—perhaps the strangest-looking spice you'll ever buy, and quite lovely. Although it has a licorice like flavor, it is botanically unrelated to anise. Available whole.	Both pod and seeds are used. Whole stars make an attractive garnish. If less than a whole star is required, break the star into individual points. You may want to wrap the points in cheesecloth and remove them before serving. Use in soups, marinades, and spice mixtures; part of five-spice powder.

SPICE	DESCRIPTION	USES
Vanilla Beans	From the seed pod of a climbing orchid, native to the humid tropical forests of Central and South America. Good pods are about 4 to 5 inches long, dark chocolate brown, tough but pliant, and sometimes covered with white crystals, called *givre* ("frost") in French. Inside, they have hundreds of tiny black seeds, which are what we see in top-quality vanilla ice cream. Good vanilla is expensive, so be suspicious of cheap beans. Wrap tightly in foil or seal them in a glass jar and store them in a cool place or the refrigerator. Available in whole pods (superior) and extract (convenient).	You can steep pods whole in sauces or syrups, but it's usually best to split the pod lengthwise and scrape the seeds into the liquid. Make vanilla sugar by burying a couple of whole beans in a jar of sugar, which will absorb their aroma after a few days. Replenish the sugar in the jar as you use it. Exceptional with chocolate and coffee, used to flavor all kinds of desserts. Other traditional uses include flan (page 887) and crème anglaise. Good with fruits: try poaching pears, apples, figs, or pineapple in a syrup flavored with vanilla.

Spice Mixtures

With a few spice mixtures in your pantry, suddenly the whole world is literally at your fingertips; if you have any doubt, sprinkle one piece of boiled potato with chili powder and another with curry and see what happens.

This versatility makes spice mixtures the ultimate convenience food. Blend one or two at a time and keep them at the ready for weeks or months in advance. It's a sure way to keep your cooking vibrant and interesting, whether you're entertaining or just warming up leftovers.

$^1/_2$ teaspoon black peppercorns

2 teaspoons cumin seeds

2 teaspoons coriander seeds

1 tablespoon dried Mexican oregano

❶ Put all the ingredients in a small skillet over medium heat. Toast, shaking the pan occasionally, until the mixture is fragrant, 3 to 5 minutes.

❷ Grind until powdery in a spice or coffee grinder. Store in a tightly covered container for up to several weeks.

Chili Powder

MAKES: About $^1/_4$ cup
TIME: 5 minutes

Do yourself and everyone you cook for a favor and toss out any taco seasoning or packaged chili powder tucked away. Not only will this version blow anything you can buy out of the water, but it's easy to make.

2 tablespoons ground ancho, New Mexico, or other mild chile

$^1/_2$ teaspoon cayenne, or to taste

Chaat Masala

MAKES: About $^1/_2$ cup
TIME: 5 minutes

Chaat masala is among my favorite spice blends, with an unusual and instantly appealing flavor. The secret is the sourness of the amchoor (see page 820), a powder made from dried mangoes that's available in Indian and some Asian markets (where you'll find the other unusual ingredient, hing).

Sprinkle a pinch or two of chaat masala on everything—plain rice, salads, beans (especially one of the

  Fast   Ⓜ Make Ahead   Ⓥ Vegan

dals, pages 600–604), and fresh cheese (page 228) to The Simplest Indian-Style Flatbread (page 698), right out of the oven.

  ¹/₄ cup amchoor (dried mango powder)

  2 teaspoons ground cumin

  2 teaspoons freshly ground black pepper

  2 teaspoons ground coriander

  2 teaspoons ground ginger

  ¹/₄ teaspoon asafetida (hing)

  ¹/₄ teaspoon cayenne

  Pinch of salt

Put all the ingredients in a tightly covered opaque container and shake or stir to combine. Use immediately or store for up to several months.

Garam Masala

MAKES: About ¹/₄ cup
TIME: 15 minutes

Literally "warm mixture," this North Indian spice blend should be made in small quantities and used quickly so it's as fresh as possible. Like the curries in this section, it can be customized to your taste and used wherever a recipe calls for curry powder.

  10 cardamom pods, seeds only (discard the hulls; see page 811)

  One 3-inch cinnamon stick

  1 teaspoon whole cloves

  ¹/₂ teaspoon nutmeg pieces

  1 tablespoon cumin seeds

  1 tablespoon fennel seeds

❶ Put all the ingredients in a medium skillet over medium heat. Cook, shaking the pan occasionally, until lightly browned and fragrant, just a few minutes.

❷ Cool, then grind to a fine powder in a spice or coffee grinder. Store in a tightly covered opaque container for up to several months.

Hot Curry Powder

MAKES: About ¹/₄ cup
TIME: 10 minutes

The word *curry* is a fairly generic reference to what we think of as an Indian-style blend of spices, though it can also describe a cooking technique or a particular type of spicy dish. Curries are generally quite personalized—no two ever taste quite the same—so definitely adjust this recipe to your taste. If this one sounds too hot for you (the black peppercorns alone pack quite a punch), try the one that follows or just reduce the amount of chiles.

  2 small dried Thai or other hot chiles

  1 tablespoon black peppercorns

  1 tablespoon coriander seeds

  1 teaspoon cumin seeds

  1 teaspoon fennel seeds

  1 teaspoon ground fenugreek

  1 tablespoon ground turmeric

  1 tablespoon ground ginger

  Cayenne (optional)

❶ Put the chiles, peppercorns, and seeds in a medium skillet over medium heat. Cook, shaking the pan occasionally, until lightly browned and fragrant, just a few minutes; for the last minute of cooking, add the ground spices.

❷ Cool, then grind to a fine powder in a spice or coffee grinder; add the cayenne at this stage if you're using it. Store in a tightly covered opaque container for up to several months.

Fragrant Curry Powder

MAKES: About $\frac{1}{4}$ cup
TIME: 10 minutes

A mild and complex spice mix, perfect when you're looking for loads of flavor without heat.

$\frac{1}{4}$ teaspoon nutmeg pieces

5 white cardamom pods, seeds only (discard the hulls; page 811)

3 whole cloves

One 3-inch cinnamon stick

1 teaspoon black peppercorns

2 tablespoons cumin seeds

$\frac{1}{4}$ cup coriander seeds

2 bay leaves

2 dried curry leaves (optional)

1 teaspoon ground fenugreek

1 Put all the ingredients except the fenugreek in a medium skillet over medium heat. Cook, shaking the pan occasionally, until lightly browned and fragrant, just a few minutes; for the last minute of cooking, add the fenugreek.

2 Cool, then grind in a spice or coffee grinder to a fine powder. Store in a tightly covered opaque container for up to several months.

Sambar Powder

MAKES: About $\frac{1}{2}$ cup
TIME: 15 minutes

This spicy mix is traditionally used in a well-loved South Indian lentil soup called *sambar*. The mix itself is made with lentils or peas, which lend a nutty flavor and act as a thickener when added to soups, stews, and sauces.

Asafetida (also called *hing*) is a particularly pungent spice; the odor from even a small container can overwhelm a large pantry with a funky garlic and onion aroma, and a small pinch goes a long, long way. But the flavor is wonderful.

4 to 5 small dried Thai, Chinese, or other hot dried chiles or 1 tablespoon hot red pepper flakes, or to taste

$\frac{1}{4}$ cup coriander seeds

1 tablespoon brown mustard seeds

1 tablespoon fenugreek seeds

1 teaspoon black peppercorns

1 tablespoon dried pigeon peas

1 tablespoon yellow split peas

Pinch of asafetida (hing; optional but good)

1 Put all the ingredients except the asafetida in a medium skillet over medium heat. Cook, shaking the pan occasionally, until fragrant, just a few minutes.

2 Cool, then grind to a fine powder in a spice or coffee grinder. Mix in the asafetida and use immediately or store in a tightly covered opaque container for up to several months.

Five-Spice Powder

MAKES: About $\frac{1}{4}$ cup
TIME: 5 minutes

Sichuan peppercorns make this spice blend unusual and unforgettable. Once banned from import due to a contagious disease they can carry, these are now happily returned to the shelves of Asian markets thanks to a flash-heat treatment that kills the nasty little bacteria. This tiny fruit pod (it's not really a peppercorn; see page 809) has an unusual smoky, citrusy flavor.

Use this classic Chinese spice blend in stir fries, for

F Fast   **M** Make Ahead   **V** Vegan

spiced nuts, and even sprinkled on desserts, like ice cream or poached pears.

    1 tablespoon Sichuan peppercorns or black
      peppercorns
    6 star anise
    1¹/₂ teaspoons whole cloves
    One 3-inch stick cinnamon
    2 tablespoons fennel seeds

Put all the ingredients in a spice or coffee grinder and grind to a fine powder. Store in a tightly covered opaque container for up to several months.

Japanese Seven-Spice Mix

Shichimi Togarashi

MAKES: About ¹/₄ cup
TIME: 5 minutes

This Japanese spice mix is a perfect last-minute addition to soba or udon noodles, soups, salads, vegetables, and anything grilled.

You can make your own dried tangerine peels (or those of any citrus) by removing the outer skin with a zester or vegetable peeler (avoid getting too much of the bitter white pith) and dehydrating in a very low oven for an hour or two or leaving the pieces on a paper towel overnight, or until dry.

    1 tablespoon Sichuan peppercorns or black
      peppercorns
    2 teaspoons white sesame seeds
    1 tablespoon crumbled dried nori sheets
    1 tablespoon dried tangerine or orange peel
    1 tablespoon chili powder
    1 teaspoon black sesame seeds
    1 teaspoon poppy seeds

① Put the Sichuan peppercorns and white sesame seeds in a spice or coffee grinder and grind to a coarse powder. Add the nori and tangerine peel; grind quickly, about 5 seconds.

② Mix in the remaining ingredients. Store in a tightly covered opaque container and refrigerate for up to 3 months.

Nori "Shake"

MAKES: About ¹/₄ cup
TIME: 20 minutes

This seaweed "shake" is not a green smoothie, but an American translation for the ubiquitous family of Japanese seasonings that you sprinkle on food as a last-minute condiment, either with your fingers, with a spoon, or out of some kind of big-holed shaker (thus the name). Sushi Rice (page 527) is a good place to use Nori Shake; so are bowls of broth with soba or udon noodles, and Eggless Vegetable Tempura (page 249).

I like to make shakes in small batches because they stay fresh for only a little while. This recipe makes enough for four 1-tablespoon servings. But if you're going to use it all within a week or so, go ahead and double or triple the recipe.

    2 sheets nori
    1 tablespoon sesame seeds
    1 teaspoon salt, preferably sea salt
    Cayenne pepper (optional)

① Set a large skillet (preferably cast-iron) over medium heat. When it's hot, put a nori sheet in the pan and toast until it turns slightly green, which will take only a few seconds. Turn and quickly toast on the other side. Set aside to cool and repeat with the other nori sheet.

② While the pan is still hot, toast the sesame seeds, stirring or swirling the pan constantly to keep them from burning. When they are fragrant and beginning to turn golden, put them in a small bowl, sprinkle with salt, and stir.

3 Crumble the nori into the bowl with the sesame seeds and salt. Or if you want a finer shake, whir the nori in a spice grinder for a few pulses and then add. Stir in the cayenne if you're using it. Store, tightly covered, in a dark place for up to a week.

Dulse "Shake": Instead of the nori, toast 3 tablespoons of crumbled dulse.

Jerk Seasoning

MAKES: About ¼ cup

TIME: 5 minutes

In Jamaica, jerk seasoning is typically used as a rub or marinade for grilled chicken or pork, but there's really no reason you can't use this on your grilled vegetables or tofu. It's also an easy way to spice up Quesadillas (page 741) or Grilled Fresh Cheese (page 216).

1 tablespoon allspice berries

¼ teaspoon nutmeg pieces

1 teaspoon black peppercorns

2 teaspoons dried thyme

1 teaspoon cayenne, or to taste

1 tablespoon paprika

1 tablespoon sugar

2 tablespoons salt

2 teaspoons minced garlic

2 teaspoons peeled and minced fresh ginger or
    2 teaspoons ground

1 Put the allspice, nutmeg, peppercorns, and thyme in a spice or coffee grinder and grind to a fine powder.

2 Mix in the remaining ingredients and use immediately or store in a tightly covered container for up to several weeks and add the garlic and ginger as you use the seasoning.

Za'atar

MAKES: About ½ cup

TIME: 10 minutes

A tangy, nutty seasoning used throughout the Arab world, this herb and seed blend is a good addition to Hummus (page 614) and can be used sprinkled on olives, over vegetables, rice, slices of feta cheese, or toasted pita bread drizzled with olive oil. For a fast dip, mix it with some plain yogurt and extra virgin olive oil (see Simplest Yogurt Sauce, page 774).

Sesame seeds turn rancid quickly, so keep this in the fridge for longer storage.

2 tablespoons dried thyme

2 tablespoons ground sumac

¼ cup toasted sesame seeds (page 321)

Salt and freshly ground black pepper

1 Use your fingers to crumble the thyme into a small jar or bowl or put it in a spice or coffee grinder and coarsely grind.

2 Stir in the sumac and the seeds and season with a little salt and pepper. Store in a tightly covered opaque container in the refrigerator for up to a month.

Citrus Sprinkle

MAKES: About ¼ cup

TIME: 2 hours, largely unattended

Sun-dried citrus peels or leaves from citrus trees are popular seasonings throughout the Middle East, Southeast Asia, and the Mediterranean, where they're often blended with other so-called warm seasonings, like cardamom, cinnamon, and coriander seeds. Unfortunately, these citrus ingredients are often tough to find in the United States, and their quality is often suspect.

Here, then, is an easy and versatile substitute, a tangy blend that works on everything from egg dishes to fresh fruit to rice pudding. And because it's mostly citrus, you can also use it to add character to other spice blends, like Za'atar (page 818) or Japanese Seven-Spice Mix (page 817).

4 limes

3 lemons

2 oranges (not navel; blood, Valencia, or bitter oranges are best)

1 tablespoon freshly ground black peppercorns (optional)

1 tablespoon coriander seeds

❶ Preheat oven to 200°F. Use a vegetable peeler or zester to remove the peels from all the citrus; take care to remove as much of the bitter white pith as you can from the peels. Spread the peels into a small pan or on a small piece of foil and toast in the oven until dry, curled, and slightly golden, about 1 hour. Shake them occasionally to promote even drying.

❷ When cool, put the peels, the pepper if using, and the coriander in a spice or coffee grinder and grind into a coarse powder. Store in a tightly covered opaque container for up to a month.

Pickling Spice

MAKES: About 1 cup

TIME: 10 minutes

A traditional spice blend that gives a pickled flavor to virtually anything; see the pickle recipes in the salad chapter. You can also use this spice mix to season Mashed Potatoes (page 341).

Two 3-inch cinnamon sticks

10 bay leaves

2 small hot dried red chiles or 1 tablespoon hot red pepper flakes, or to taste

$^1/_4$ cup mustard seeds

2 tablespoons allspice berries

2 teaspoons whole cloves

2 tablespoons black peppercorns

2 tablespoons coriander seeds

2 teaspoons cardamom seeds

2 tablespoons dill seeds

❶ Break the cinnamon sticks, bay leaves, and chiles into pieces.

❷ Roughly chop (or crush by pressing on the spices with a heavy skillet) all the other ingredients, leaving most of the seeds whole.

❸ Stir to combine the spices and store in a tightly sealed container for several months.

The Basics of Ginger

Spicy, aromatic, and in many cuisines essential, this unusual-looking tropical plant is often called a root but is actually a rhizome—an underground stem. Ginger is important in cuisines from North Africa to India to China and many more and is used fresh, dried, ground, candied, and preserved. It's tan colored with a papery skin that must be peeled; the flesh is off-yellow, pungent in flavor and fragrance, and has fibers running the length of it. Typically, the younger the ginger, the less pungent and spicy (and more translucent the skin); more mature ginger can be downright hot—after all, the active chemical in it is related to capsaicin, the substance that makes chiles hot.

Buying and storing: Look for an unwithered, plump piece that is heavy for its size and not too fibrous. Don't be afraid to break off a piece from a large branch, and if it doesn't make a clean break there are too many fibers; move on to a fresher piece if that's an option. Store loosely wrapped in plastic in the refrigerator for as long as two weeks; use it before it shrivels.

SPICE	DESCRIPTION	USES
Amchoor *Amchur, Green Mango Powder*	Made from unripe green mangoes, which are peeled, sliced, dried, and ground, amchoor has a tangy sour taste. Used much like lemon juice, primarily in Indian cooking. Available powdered or in dried slices.	Sift if necessary to remove lumps before using. Best with curries, chutneys, and pickles, and especially in the blend chaat masala.
Anise Seeds *Aniseed, Sweet Cumin*	Tiny, crescent-shaped, greenish brown seeds from the anise plant, with a sweet licorice flavor. Star anise or fennel can usually fill in for these and vice versa. Available whole or ground.	Although most common in desserts, anise works well in both sweet and savory dishes that include apples, cucumbers, carrots, turnips, or cabbages; or in fruit salads, salad dressings, pickles, stuffings, and sauerkraut.
Annatto *Achiote*	The triangular, brick-colored seeds of the annatto tree smell earthy or musky and taste slightly peppery, but their flavor is subtle. Traditionally used in Latin American dishes. Available whole, ground, or less frequently as a prepared paste.	The seeds are too hard to crush easily and must be soaked for 10 minutes in boiling water first. Once cool and drained, grind them with a mortar and pestle or in a clean spice mill. More often, whole seeds are used to color and flavor oil as a first step in cooking dishes; just be sure to fish them out before adding the other ingredients.
Asafetida *Hing, Devil's Dung, Stinking Gum*	A fascinating spice made from the dried sap exuded from the stem of giant fennel. The lumps are a waxy brownish black, and the powder is a beige color. Its unfortunate high-sulfur odor— like rotten garlic—can overcome your kitchen. But with a bit of cooking, it is transformed into a haunting flavor that smells a bit like onion. Available in big lumps (preferred) or ground. The powder is undeniably easier to use, but it's generally less pure, so go for the lump form if you can find it. Your reward is that asafetida doesn't have its characteristic (and generally considered unpleasant) odor until it is ground.	Indian cuisine primarily, especially vegetables, beans, potatoes, and in chutney, pickles, and sauces, usually in spice mixtures, like sambar powder. It is very potent, so use only by the pinch. Try adding a tiny amount to plain boiled rice. To minimize the smell, double-pack powdered asafetida in a jar inside another jar, or it will stink up your pantry. A lump will keep indefinitely and should be pulverized just before use.
Caraway	Slender, ridged, whole brown seeds from a parsley-related plant; with an anise and cumin flavor	Traditionally used in rye bread, caraway is delicious with a variety of cabbage and potato dishes and other hearty soups and stews.
Fenugreek *Methi*	The distinctive rectangular seeds are small, brownish yellow, and very hard. They have a pungent, almost acrid aroma and an earthy, somewhat bitter taste that is found in many Indian dishes. Available whole and ground.	Fenugreek is used mainly in the cuisines of India and northern Africa: in chutneys, dals (lentils), and curries. It goes especially well with eggplant and potatoes. An essential ingredient in many curry powders, giving them their distinctive aroma, and sambar powder.
Juniper Berries	The berrylike cones from the evergreen juniper tree; they are the size of dried peas, blue-black in color. They taste like a mix of pine, fruit, and lemon peel in taste and are the dominant flavor in gin. Delicious, but limited in use.	Juniper berries are very pungent, so use them in moderation. Toasting them briefly in a dry skillet before use will bring out their aroma, and crushing them releases their flavor. You can also use them whole, in a cheesecloth bag or tea ball, and then remove them before serving. Classic in stuffings, sauerkraut, sauces, and pickling.

F Fast   **M** Make Ahead   **V** Vegan

SPICE	DESCRIPTION	USES
Mace	Mace is the hard, lacy coating—or aril—that covers the pod that contains the nutmeg kernel. When the fruit first opens, mace is bright red. After drying and pressing, it becomes a dried yellow-brown color. Its flavor is very similar to that of nutmeg, though more bitter. Usually available ground; called "blades" when whole.	Add ground mace directly to savory dishes toward the end of cooking. Whole blades can be used as is in soups or stews and then removed before eating. Commonly used in cakes and other sweets, traditional in doughnuts and pumpkin pie. Nutmeg is almost always an adequate substitute.
Poppy Seeds	Poppy seeds come from the same plant as opium but contain no traces of the drug. The teeny seeds, which are about the size of a pinhead, come from inside the flower's pods. Most of the seeds we use in the United States are slate blue, but those used in India are usually smaller and a yellow-white color. Poppy seeds add a nutty flavor and a subtle crunch to foods. Available whole or crushed into a paste; black is the most common variety, though there are also white poppy seeds.	They're more like a seasoning than a nut or seed. For a nuttier flavor, lightly toast them—carefully so they don't burn. Used in Europe and the Middle East in or on sweets and baked goods. Good in salad dressings, fruit salads, and with Eastern European–style noodle dishes. In India, poppy seeds are toasted, ground, and used to flavor and thicken curries. The paste is used as a filling for strudel-type pastries and in other baked foods. Very finely ground almonds or almond paste is a good substitute. The results will be very different, but quite good.
Sumac *Summaq*	The dried fruits of a type of sumac; used as a souring agent, much like lemon, in the Middle East. The brick-red (though sometimes deep purple) berries also lend a bit of color. Available in whole dried berries or ground, which is more common.	To use whole, crack them and soak in water for 15 to 20 minutes, then wrap in cheesecloth and squeeze to extract the juice, which can be used much like lemon juice. Powder is usually added during the last few minutes of cooking, or as a last-minute sprinkle. Used with grilled items; on salads or in dips like hummus or baba ghanoush. Mixed with thyme and toasted sesame seeds in the spice mix za'atar.
Turmeric *Indian Saffron*	Darker skinned than ginger (like ginger, it's a rhizome), with thin fingers; its flesh is bright orange-red and difficult to grind. Available ground (most common) or in dried pieces.	Turmeric is most frequently used dried in spice blends, but if you see some fresh, try mincing some in pickles (page 94). But use it sparingly, because too much turmeric tastes bitter. Typical in Indian vegetarian cooking, where its deep flavor is welcome in dal and curries; also good with rice and other grain dishes, like couscous.

Preparing: Scrape off the papery skin with the blunt side of your knife blade, the edge of a spoon, or a vegetable peeler. Grate the ginger or julienne and mince it.

Other vegetables to substitute: Really, there is no substitute for fresh ginger—except perhaps galangal if you can find it. Dried ground ginger is useful in many sweet and savory dishes, including gingerbread and curries.

Pickled Ginger

MAKES: 4 servings

TIME: At least a day, largely unattended

This is more delicious than the pink-tinted pickled ginger you know from Japanese restaurants. Try to find young, thin-skinned ginger, because the results will be a little more delicate. But any type will make an easy pickle that keeps in the fridge for two weeks. Use as a condiment with Sushi Bowls (page 527), Sushi Rolls (page 528), and sandwiches of all kinds. Or mince and try in recipes that call for fresh ginger, especially dressings and sauces.

About 1/4 pound fresh ginger

1 tablespoon salt

Rice vinegar as needed

2 tablespoons sugar, or more to taste

1 Peel and thinly slice the ginger, using a mandoline if you have one. Toss it with the salt and let stand for an hour. Rinse thoroughly, drain, and put in a 1-pint glass or ceramic container with a tight-fitting lid.

2 Combine about 1/4 cup rice vinegar with an equal amount of water and the sugar; heat, stirring to dissolve the sugar. Taste and add more sugar if you like. Cool slightly and combine with the ginger. If the liquid does not cover the ginger, add more vinegar and water, again, in equal parts. Cover and refrigerate.

3 You can begin eating the ginger within a day, though it will improve for several days and keep for a few longer, up to a couple of weeks.

Citrus-Pickled Ginger. Brightens up anything you put it on: In Step 2, to the rice vinegar and sugar mixture add the zest from 1 orange, lemon, or tangerine; 2 limes; or 1/2 a grapefruit. Proceed with the recipe and use or eat the zest along with the ginger.

The Basics of Chiles and Peppers

One of the most frequently used ingredients in this chapter is the chile: dried, fresh, chopped, whole, seeded, not, processed, pasted—it's everywhere. This isn't surprising, since we have become a nation of hot heads, gobbling down more chiles than ever before. What that means for you is more choices in more places; these days, even average supermarkets stock a couple of kinds of chiles.

Though the world of chiles is complicated, I've tried to simplify things here (and included sweet peppers as well; it's all the same family) to make it as easy as possible to choose and use these huge flavor boosters.

Types of Chiles

All chiles and peppers are in the same botanical genus, *Capsicum*. There are literally thousands of varieties, ranging from fingernail size to foot-long, from sunset orange to purplish green. Their flavors vary in terms of heat (some, like bell peppers, are not hot at all) and complexity, sometimes as much from pepper to pepper as from variety to variety, which can make things a bit unpredictable. Where you live has a lot to do with the kinds you will find, as does your proximity to Hispanic or Asian communities, which tend to offer larger selections.

But really, if you go to the store and find only one type of chile, you might as well just buy it. Even if it's the super-hot habanero (unlikely), you'll take a few home, slice a teeny-tiny piece out of one when you're preparing a dish, and taste. Then you'll decide how much to use. This is still the way I cook with chiles and, really, it's the only foolproof method. Habaneros are hot, poblanos are mild, but "hot" and "mild" vary wildly. You gotta taste.

The Heat Factor

Chiles should enhance the enjoyment of food. Sometimes their heat is meant to dominate, but both mild and hot chiles offer complex flavors too; you might taste citrus, grass, smoke, wood, or simply a vague, haunting flavor. Sometimes, as the heat subsides, other tastes take over your palate, sort of in waves, and in different places. That's because your lips, tongue, mouth, and nasal pas-

USING SPICE MIXTURES

Once you have made up a spice mixture, it makes sense to get some mileage out of it. Though I don't always call for these blends in specific recipes, here are some suggestions for when and where to improvise.

SPICE MIXTURE	HOW TO USE	WHAT TO USE ON OR IN
Hot Curry Powder Fragrant Curry Powder Garam Masala	Stir/mix into	Soups, stews, braises, or sauces; dough or batter before or while cooking; beans, lentils, vegetables, tofu, etc.
	Sprinkle over	Vegetables or tofu while roasting, sautéing or stir-frying; rice or other grains; roasted nuts
Sambar Powder	Stir/mix into	Soups, stews, braises, or sauces before or during cooking; rice dishes, like pilafs and Stuck-Pot Rice, during the last few seconds of sautéing the rice
Za'atar	Stir/mix into	Dough or batter; plain yogurt with olive oil; or just olive oil, as a dip
	Sprinkle over	Hummus and other bean purées; raw or cooked vegetables; rice or other grains; salads, bread (drizzled with olive oil and toasted), sliced cheese
	Marinate (with added oil)	Vegetables, olives
Citrus Sprinkle	Stir/mix into	Bread doughs, cake batters (eliminate the salt), -inaigrette (page 762)
	Sprinkle over	Rice and grains, fresh cut melon, feta cheese
	Marinate (with added oil)	Vegetables, olives
Five-Spice Powder	Stir/mix into	Soups, stews, braises, sauces; batter and cookie dough
	Sprinkle over	Sautéing or stir-frying vegetables, tofu; desserts like cobblers, vanilla ice cream, baked apples, poached pears
Japanese Seven-Spice Mix	Sprinkle over	Soba or udon noodles; soups, salads, vegetables, or anything grilled; rice or other grains
Red Curry Paste Green Curry Paste	Stir/mix into	Used as a sauté base. Curries, soups, stews, braises, sauces, or stir-fries before or while cooking
	Marinate (with added liquid/oil)	Vegetables, tofu, or tempeh
Chili Powder	Sprinkle over	Cornbread batter, right before baking
	Stir/mix into	Bean, rice, or vegetable dishes while cooking

SPICE MIXTURE	HOW TO USE	WHAT TO USE ON OR IN
Chili Powder	Stir/mix into	Soups, stews, braises, sauces; dough or batter before or while cooking
	Sprinkle over	Roasting, sautéing or stir-frying vegetables or tofu; roasted nuts
Pickling Spice	Stir/mix into	Pickling liquid; soups, stews, braises, or sauces in small quantities before or while cooking; stirred into mashed potatoes
Jerk Seasoning	Stir/mix into	Soups, stews, braises, sauces; dough or batter before or while cooking
	Sprinkle over	Roasting, sautéing or stir-frying vegetables (especially potatoes); tofu; rice or other grains; roasted nuts
	Marinate (with added liquid/oil)	Vegetables or tofu

sages awaken to the irritants in the chile and become mildly inflamed, which in turn heightens the way you experience the other pungent flavors on your fork, like sourness and saltiness. To me, this is the ideal chile experience. (If you don't like your food even a tiny bit spicy, though, just leave the chiles out of the recipe.)

There are ways to measure a particular chile's heat—or at least give a range for the heat you can expect from a specific variety. Scoville units are the most common, but there are others. I don't find these scales useful at all, since each chile is different; indeed, each part of a chile can be different. Yes, most habaneros are hotter than most jalapeños, but each can work in a dish, and each can kill a dish.

In the following chart I've identified particular peppers as hot to very hot, medium, or mild; it's all relative, but jalapeños, generally speaking, are hot. A few generalizations: Small peppers tend to be hotter than large ones (with a few notable exceptions), while mature (red or orange) peppers pack a bigger wallop than green ones. And the seeds and veins (the pith) are the hottest parts of the chile. Any chile can be tamed (again, at least relatively), by removing the seeds and pith. Simply include some seeds if you want to pump up the heat.

Remember this: Chiles can burn. If you've got rubber gloves, think about using them. If not, every time you touch a chile, wash your hands with warm soapy water—twice is better than once—and be careful not to touch your eyes or any other tender areas for a while. If your hands are chapped or cut, chiles will irritate them. Some people's skin is sensitive no matter what they do.

And if your mouth is on fire, don't reach for that margarita. Well, you can, but it won't give you the relief that a glass of milk will, strange as that may sound. Plain bread or crackers are good options.

Buying, Storing, and Using

Look for firm, smooth fresh chiles, with shiny skins and fresh-looking stems. Keep them in the fridge, wrapped loosely in a plastic bag, for a week to two, maybe even longer.

Dried chiles that are still somewhat pliable are ideal—there's no need for "dried" chiles to be bone-dry—but they should never be dusty, musty, dank, or moldy. When you get them home, put them in an airtight container and tuck them away in a dark corner of your pantry or spice shelf. Soak, grind, or crumble them as needed.

 Fast   Make Ahead   Ⓥ Vegan

Most often I call for either fresh or dried chile, in a generic sort of way, with a couple of suggested types. If you don't have fresh handy, use dried chiles, or—as a last resort—hot red pepper flakes (when I'm looking for just a little heat, hot red pepper flakes will definitely do). When it really matters to the flavor of a dish, I call for a specific variety, though this is rare (and usually limited to milder chiles, or to chipotle, which has a distinctively smoky taste; most hot chiles are roughly equivalent in taste). You can always substitute dried chile (which obviously stores better, so you can always have some around) for fresh, and vice versa. There's more about how to prepare dried chiles below.

The bottom line, though, is this: Use what you like, what you can find, and as much as you think tastes good.

For the sake of measurements, here are two general rules. Every square inch of chile flesh—not including seeds, pith, or the core—will yield about 1 tablespoon when minced. One medium bell pepper—cored, seeded, and chopped—will yield about a cup.

Preparing Chiles

Unless they're stuffed (page 399), fresh chiles are almost always cut before using; the hotter ones finely minced, the medium and mild ones (like poblanos or bell peppers) chopped. They may be cooked along with aromatic vegetables like onions, garlic, and ginger, before adding other ingredients, or they may be used as a last-minute garnish, or they may be thrown in there anywhere in between.

There are many ways to use dried chiles. Toasting dried chiles for a few minutes in a dry skillet (over medium heat) is the best way to bring out their smoky flavor before using them; though it's a step I take only when the chile will be featured prominently. The simplest approach is to use them whole and remove them before serving. The only problem with this is that you have no idea what level of heat they will contribute to the dish.

Next easiest is to remove the stem—and the seeds and veins too if you want less heat—then toss them into a spice grinder and pulse until you get the desired texture. (Be careful when you open the lid; the aroma could be powerful.) Stored tightly covered in a dark place, this ground chile—it's pure chile powder, not the "chili" powder that contains other spices and seasonings—will remain potent for months. And you can taste it before adding it to anything you're cooking.

Soaking is a way to return dried chiles to something more like their original fresh texture. Cover the chiles in hot water and soak until they're soft and pliable. Then remove the seeds and veins. Some of the larger chiles will separate from their tough skins, so remove those too. Strain and save the soaking water (which can be very potent) if you want. Now you can chop and use the chiles, or purée them, either in a soup or stew or with a little of the soaking water and served as a straight chile sauce.

Because chiles and peppers are actually fruits and not vegetables, the mildest ones can be really quite sweet. Minced, chopped, or sliced, they are versatile both cooked and raw. The only thing you don't want to do is simmer them in liquid for too long; they'll turn bitter.

The Chile Lexicon

The chiles in this lexicon are divided into three charts: everyday fresh, everyday dried, and mild ones. Then they're organized by heat, in the order that I use them most frequently. Each entry identifies substitutes in case you can't find a specific chile. There are specialty peppers for enthusiasts you may run across by accident or want to seek out. If you can't find them in stores near you, check the mail-order sources on page 929.

One more thing that might move you to try a variety of chiles: Chiles have a little extra going for them. They're high in vitamin C and contain some antioxidants (especially the red ones, which contain beta-carotene). Then they have capsaicin, the thing that gives peppers their heat and releases "feel good" endorphins in the brain. Recent studies indicate chiles might even help lower cholesterol and increase metabolism.

EVERYDAY FRESH CHILES

CHILE	DESCRIPTION	HEAT	OTHER FORMS	SUBSTITUTIONS
Habanero *Scotch Bonnet (not technically the same, but virtually interchangeable)*	Round and fairly small, like teeny bell peppers, ranging in color from neon green to yellow, gold, and orange, depending on maturity and variety. The flavor is slightly fruity and bright if you can get past the fire.	Very hot	Dried	Nothing has the same complex flavor (or packs quite the same wallop)
Cayenne *Finger Chile*	Long, slightly gnarled, and slender; green to red when mature	Very hot	Also available dried whole and ground into powder	Thai bird, or use dried powder
Thai *Thai Bird*	Pinky size or smaller; green to red when mature	Very hot	Dried (see page 827) and sometimes pickled	Cayenne
Giant Thai	Basically a bigger Thai pepper (see above)	Hot	Usually fresh only	Thai or jalapeño (use more)
Chile de Arbol *Red Chile*	Finger length and slender; green to red when mature	Hot	Dried (more common)	Jalapeño
Serrano	Finger size or smaller, thin skinned; sold either red (mature) or green	Hot	Dried	Cayenne or Thai (use less); jalapeño (use more)
Jalapeño	Sold green mostly, though sometimes red; the flavor is slightly herbaceous and grassy	Hot to medium	Smoked and dried (see Chipotle page 827)	Serrano or chile de arbol
Fresno	Like jalapeños, only with thinner flesh; usually red (mature), but sometimes available green	Hot to medium	Usually only fresh	Serrano or jalapeño
Poblano	Like a smaller, flatter bell pepper; usually very dark green or purple or sometimes red (mature). Great for stuffing (you should peel first), grilling, and roasting.	Medium to mild	Dried (called *ancho*, see page 828)	Anaheim or New Mexico
Anaheim *Chile Colorado (when red)*	Long and wide, somewhat flat; available both green and red (mature). Used for stuffing, grilling, roasting; egg dishes, mild salsas, sauces, and dressings.	Medium to mild	Dried (see California, page 828)	Poblano or New Mexico
New Mexico *Green Chiles or Red Chiles, depending on maturity*	Similar to Anaheim, only pointed on both ends, available both green and red (mature). Used for stuffing, grilling, roasting, puréeing into sauces and chilis.	Medium to mild	Both available dried	Anaheim

F Fast   M Make Ahead   V Vegan

EVERYDAY DRIED CHILES

CHILE	DESCRIPTION	HEAT	OTHER FORMS	SUBSTITUTIONS
Dried Habanero	Small, roundish, reddish brown, very wrinkled. Use judiciously in chiles, soups, broths.	Very hot	Fresh (see page 826) and sometimes smoked and dried	Dried chipotle
Chipotle *Chile Seco; Smoked Jalapeño*	Dried, shades of brown from light to reddish; canned, quite dark, almost purple. Because they're smoked, the flavor is incomparable—smoky, hot, deep, and complex. These give a rich smokiness to chilis, stews, cooked salsas. If using dried, grind to a powder and use judiciously as a seasoning like cayenne. Minced or puréed, canned chipotle—with a little of their adobo—add body along with the heat.	Very hot to hot	(Fresh, they're jalapeños, page 826)	Nothing, really
Piquin *Pequin or Piquín*	Fingernail size and shape, bright red; somewhat shiny skins; very complex flavors	Very hot to hot	Fresh (rare)	Dried Thai chiles
Chile de Arbol *Red Chile (see Thai, below)*	Unlike many dried chiles, these retain a bright reddish brown to almost orange color; narrow and a couple inches long; nice heat and depth of flavor.	Very hot to hot	Fresh (less common; see page 826)	Guajillo (which is milder too)
Thai *Same as other small Asian or American varieties, but virtually interchangeable*	Small, narrow, brownish red	Hot	Fresh (see page 826)	Chile de Arbol, Chinese Chile
Hot Red Pepper Flakes *Crushed Red Pepper; Dried Red Pepper; Ground Red Pepper*	The ubiquitous combination of seeds and bits of pepper, sometimes suspended in oil, always red. With supermarket kinds, assume that a variety of peppers are used to achieve a level of heat specified by the manufacturer. Use whenever you want to add plain old heat.	Hot to medium		Crumble or grind any whole, dried red pepper like Thai or serrano; or for a milder flavor, use California
Cascabel *Chile Bola or Rattle Chile (because the seeds shake around inside)*	Smooth skinned and puffy—kind of like brown Ping-Pong balls, only smaller, with deep, smoky flavor.	Hot to medium	Fresh (rare)	Chile de arbol
Guajillo	Dark reddish brown with shiny, thick skin; flat and about an inch wide and a couple inches long	Medium	Fresh guajillo (rare)	New Mexico or ancho
New Mexico—Red and Green	Long, somewhat wide and flat; red or green	Medium	Fresh (see page 826)	California or ancho

CHILE	DESCRIPTION	HEAT	OTHER FORMS	SUBSTITUTIONS
Ancho	Almost purple or black; compact, squarish; medium size. The classic in mild chili powder and an excellent mild dried chile.	Medium to mild	Fresh (and called *poblano*; see page 826)	Pasilla or California
Pasilla *Chile Negro*	Almost black, very wrinkled, long and narrow	Hot to mild, depending on the variety	Fresh (less common)	New Mexico
California	Longish and narrow, slightly flat, with rusty red color	Medium to mild	Fresh (see Anaheim, page 826)	Ancho
Paprika *Hungarian Paprika or Spanish Paprika*	Usually found ground in cans or jars in sweet or smoked varieties (especially Spanish)	Mild	Rarely found fresh	none

Chile Paste, 8 Ways

MAKES: About ¹/₂ cup

TIME: 45 minutes, largely unattended

Like spice blends and rubs, chile pastes are not exactly sauces but cooking ingredients that are useful in dressings, sauces, and marinades and for smearing on foods before grilling or roasting.

The base ingredient here: pure dried chiles. Use relatively mild ones like ancho, Anaheim, or poblano (which will make the paste green). Guajillo or chipotle will be much hotter. The best, though, is a combination that includes both heat and complexity (my favorite is mostly ancho with a hit of chipotle). The variations simply build additional flavors into the all-chile paste. Whichever kind you make, if fresh herbs or aromatics are involved, refrigerate and use within a day or so for maximum freshness and oomph. Otherwise, chile paste made with dried seasonings will last a couple of weeks.

PREPARING PEPPERS

To core a pepper, first cut around the stem. Then pull the core out; rinse to remove the remaining seeds. Alternatively, cut the pepper in half, break out the core, and scrape out the seeds.

Ⓕ Fast   Ⓜ Make Ahead   Ⓥ Vegan

PEPPER	DESCRIPTION	FORMS
Bell Peppers *Sweet Peppers; Holland Peppers; also called by their color, red, yellow, orange, or green*	The familiar large bell pepper, thick walled and moister than hot peppers; crisp, with a grassy or sweet flavor, depending on maturity. They range in color from shades of green (usually bitter, because immature) to yellow, orange, or red (or even purple).	Fresh
Shishito *Guernika*	Of Japanese or Spanish origin; finger sized, slightly gnarled, pale green. Serve grilled or fried, with salt.	Only fresh
Pimiento	Narrower and slightly smaller than a bell pepper, with a pointed end; more intense, sweet flavor, and red only.	More commonly found in jars, but sometimes you see fresh.
Banana Peppers	Slightly larger than a jalapeño, yellowish green; don't confuse them with the hot Hungarian wax peppers)	Fresh

2 ounces dried whole chiles (see page 827 for some ideas), 6 to 12 total, depending on size

Salt

2 tablespoons neutral oil, like grapeseed or corn

 ➊ Toast and clean the chiles (see page 825). For a hotter paste, set aside some of the seeds. Put the chiles in a bowl and cover with boiling water and a small plate to keep them submerged. Soak for about 30 minutes, until soft.

 ➋ Drain the chiles, saving the soaking liquid. Put the chiles, any seeds you might be using, and a pinch of salt in a blender or food processor. Purée until smooth, adding a spoonful of soaking water at a time, until you reach the desired consistency.

 ➌ Put the oil in a small skillet and turn the heat to medium-high. Cook the paste, stirring constantly, until deeply colored and fragrant, about 2 minutes. Use immediately or cool, cover tightly, and refrigerate for up to 2 days. Just before serving, taste and adjust the seasoning.

Mexican-Style Chile Paste. Use all guajillo or other dark chile (page 827): To the blender or processor, add 2 cloves garlic, 1 teaspoon ground cumin, and 2 tablespoons epazote, Mexican oregano, or regular oregano.

Chipotle Paste. Hot. Hot. Hot: Use some or all dried chipotle pods. Or skip Step 1 and use 1 small can of chipotles with their adobo sauce (about $1/3$ cup).

Thai-Style Chile Paste. Quite complex: Use 2 or 3 Thai chiles along with the mild chiles. To the blender or processor, add 1 inch lemongrass, cleaned and chopped (see page 767) and $1/4$ cup fresh cilantro or Thai basil leaves. Use peanut oil if you like instead of grapeseed.

Vietnamese-Style Chile Paste. Use 2 or 3 Thai chiles along with the mild chiles. To the blender or processor, add 3 or 4 cloves garlic and 2 tablespoons Fishless Fish Sauce (page 778) and $1/4$ cup fresh mint leaves. Use peanut oil if you like instead of grapeseed. After cooking, squeeze in the juice of 1 lime.

Indian-Style Chile Paste. Very useful to add some heat to Indian-style dishes: To the blender or processor, add 1 tablespoon garam masala (to make your own, see page 815), or more to taste. Use peanut oil if you like instead of grapeseed.

Harissa. Quite complex: To the blender or processor, add 1 tablespoon ground coriander seeds, 2 teaspoons ground cumin, and 1 to 3 cloves garlic. Use extra virgin olive oil instead of grapeseed.

Chile and Black Bean Paste. To the blender or processor, add 2 tablespoons fermented black beans and eliminate the salt until you taste for seasoning. Use peanut oil if you like instead of grapeseed.

6 Ways to Use Chile Pastes

Some uses of chile pastes are obvious. Others take a bit of thought. Some of each:

1. Toss a spoonful or two of any chile paste with cooked vegetables, pasta, grains, or more complex dishes.
2. To turn chile paste into a "real" sauce, heat a batch with $^1/_4$ cup or so of oil, butter, cream, stock, tomato sauce, or even water, then use.
3. Stir chile paste directly into yogurt, sour cream, or mayonnaise for a quick chilled sauce.
4. Mix with a little extra virgin olive or neutral oil, like grapeseed or corn, and brush on vegetables as they come off the grill.
5. Stir a little into nut pastes for a spicy spread for toasted bread.
6. Smear a little on sandwiches (especially grilled cheese!).

Chile-Garlic Paste

MAKES: About 2 cups
TIME: 10 minutes

Chile-garlic paste is among the most ubiquitous and versatile Asian sauces, used in hundreds of dishes and other sauces. As with the preceding, simpler recipe, you can learn to make this instinctually, and you can customize the heat level by using milder chiles (like New Mexico) or hotter ones (Thai, chile de arbol, pequin, or habanero); see the chart on page 827. You can also reduce the heat

level some by removing the seeds from the chiles before crushing them.

  1 cup hot dried red chiles, like red Thai, chile de arbol, pequin, or red New Mexico

  $^1/_4$ cup chopped garlic

  $^1/_4$ cup white wine vinegar or distilled vinegar

  2 teaspoons sugar

  1 teaspoon salt, or to taste

Combine all the ingredients in a blender or food processor with $^1/_4$ cup hot water and purée to a smooth paste. Add additional hot water by the tablespoon if the paste is too thick. Use immediately or refrigerate for up to 3 months.

Red Curry Paste

MAKES: About $^3/_4$ cup
TIME: 25 minutes

Cilantro roots—the roots of the cilantro plant, often attached to the bunch of cilantro you buy in the supermarket—lend that bright cilantro flavor without using the entire bunch. Just be sure to rinse them very well to get all the sand and dirt off before using. Use the remaining cilantro for garnish, the Cilantro-Mint Chutney (page 783), or Lighter Cilantro "Pesto" (page 769).

  10 Thai or other medium to hot dried red chiles, seeded, or to taste

  4 dried lime leaves, fresh lime leaves, finely chopped, or 1 tablespoon minced lime zest

  One $^1/_2$-inch piece fresh galangal or 4 dried quarter-sized pieces or one 1-inch piece fresh ginger, peeled and roughly chopped

  1 teaspoon coriander seeds

  1 teaspoon cumin seeds

  2 stalks lemongrass, peeled, trimmed and roughly chopped (see page 767)

F Fast   **M** Make Ahead   **V** Vegan

2 shallots, peeled and roughly chopped

4 cloves garlic, peeled and smashed

2 tablespoons cilantro roots (see headnote), rinsed well, or 3 tablespoons chopped fresh cilantro stems

3 tablespoons peanut oil

1 Soak the chiles, along with the lime leaves and galangal if you're using dried, in warm water for about 15 minutes.

2 Put the coriander and cumin seeds in a small skillet over medium heat. Cook, shaking the pan occasionally, until lightly browned and fragrant, about 3 minutes. Cool, then grind to a powder in a spice or coffee grinder.

3 Drain the chiles and lime leaves and, along with all the remaining ingredients except the oil, transfer to a blender or food processor; grind to a paste, stopping the machine to scrape down the sides as necessary. Gradually add the oil while blending; you're looking for a fairly smooth, thick paste. Store in a tightly covered container and refrigerate for up to 2 weeks.

Green Curry Paste. Substitute fresh green chiles for the red chiles and add 1 tablespoon ground turmeric in Step 3.

Desserts

While every chapter in this book approaches cooking with what might be called a vegetarian sensibility, this one is perhaps the most creative. It's also among the most exciting; although most vegetarians eat the same

desserts as most omnivores (obviously, it's the rare dessert that contains meat, poultry, or fish), I took a different approach here, developing, discovering, testing, and providing a new collection of great-tasting recipes that acknowledges the basics but also presents a host of desserts that are healthful, made with the least fuss possible, and quite terrific. These will be appealing not only because they're sweet (good enough reason for many of us) but because—like the rest of the recipes in this book—they contain more whole grains, natural sweeteners, unexpected ingredients like vegetables and herbs, and more international and unexpected flavors. All without getting weird.

These recipes are ideal endings for vegetarian meals or any other meal, and they're a welcome change from the routine desserts found in almost every other large cookbook. Try for example, Brown Sugar Cookies with Sea Salt, Coconut-Lime Bars, Olive Oil Cake, or Poached Pear Tart with Dark Chocolate Ganache. All have a perfectly contemporary sensibility—delicious, creative, and a little unusual.

The Basics of Sweeteners

Desserts, by their nature, are sweet. The question is how to make them so. For people who don't avoid refined sweeteners, white sugar is the staple. It's cheap, convenient, eminently useful, and effective. Even if sugar is the default, however, sweeteners are important ingredients in desserts and should be chosen for their flavor and cooking performance—just like you'd choose a type of fat or flour.

Different chemical compounds—sucrose, fructose, glucose, dextrose, and maltose—make different sweeteners. All are carbohydrates, with varying degrees of complexity. And each has a different level of sweetness and solubility, which dictates how it will behave during cooking. Here's a rundown of common and less common sweeteners and some ideas for what to do with them.

Granulated Sweeteners

White sugar may be the choice that makes the most sense, but there are certainly other possibilities among granulated sweeteners.

White Sugar

White sugar is the most common granulated sweetener. Whether from sugar cane or sugar beets, all white sugars are highly refined, and all are sucrose. Sugar comes in various granule sizes and types, each with its optimal uses: Granulated sugar is the equivalent of all-purpose flour; you can use it almost everywhere when recipes call for sugar. The grains are medium size and dissolve well when heated or combined with a relatively large proportion of liquid (or with liquid that's been warmed). All of the following are forms of white sugar.

- Powdered sugar (also called *confectioners', icing, 10X, 6X,* or *4X sugar*), is just regular sugar ground to a fine powder, with cornstarch added to prevent caking and crystallization. It's used mostly in icings (it dissolves very easily) or for sifting over desserts. The kind in supermarkets is 10X, which in theory refers is to the number of times the sugar has been processed; you may see 4X or 6X as well.
- Superfine sugar (aka *castor, caster,* or *baking sugar*) is somewhere between white sugar and powdered sugar. It's great to use in light cakes or anything that won't be cooked but has some liquid—like meringues—because the fine crystals dissolve

quickly. You can make your own by grinding granulated sugar in a food processor for a few seconds.
- Coarse (*decorator's* or *pearl sugar*) is processed to small, roughly shaped round grains, larger than those of granulated sugar and therefore much slower to dissolve. Use it as a garnish on cookies, cakes, or sweet breads. Crystal sugar is similar, though the crystals are pellet shaped, not round.

Brown Sugar

Brown sugar is just refined white sugar with molasses added; this gives it a deeper, more complex taste. It is gritty and moist and comes in light or dark, depending on how much molasses has been added. Generally the darker the brown sugar, the more intense the flavor, but the difference is subtle (I use light and dark interchangeably). In most dessert recipes, you can substitute brown sugar for white, as long as you remember the color and flavor will be different; just be sure to pack the cups down before leveling them off as you measure.

Raw Sugar

Made exclusively from sugar cane in a couple of different ways, these coarse-grained brown or golden sugars contain the molasses naturally present in the plant. You can use raw sugar in place of white sugar in many recipes, provided the grind is fine or the cooking time long enough to dissolve it completely. I like it best sprinkled on top of baked goods like scones and cookies to add a mildly sweet crunch. Here are the common raw sugars:

- Turbinado: This is light brown and coarse grained, with a mild molasses flavor.
- Demerara: Originally from Guyana, this dry, coarse sugar is amber in color and toffeelike in flavor.
- Muscovado: From Barbados, finer grained than Demerara; moist, with an assertive molasses flavor and color that ranges from light to dark brown.

Maple Sugar

Produced by boiling the water out of maple syrup, which crystallizes its sucrose into a sugar. Sticky, with almost

 Fast   Make Ahead   Ⓥ Vegan

twice the sweetening power of granulated cane sugar. (See "Real Maple Syrup—Making the Grade," page 205). Best used in recipes that feature sugar (since it's a little pricey). The results will be sweeter but with a more complex flavor.

Other Granulated Sweeteners

Fructose, a simple sugar found in honey, fruit, berries, and some root vegetables, is often recommended to diabetics because it is metabolized differently from cane sugar. But it's super-concentrated and loses power when heated or mixed into liquids, so it's tricky to use; I don't mess with it.

Date sugar is made from dehydrated, finely ground dates; it's tasty and nutritious, but it's hard to find and hard to use since it doesn't dissolve easily and varies in sweetness from one batch to the next.

Stevia is a natural sweetener from the plant by the same name, a shrub indigenous to South America. It contains no calories and is up to three hundred times sweeter than cane sugar, but the FDA has limited it to being sold as a supplement in the United States; this hardly matters, since most people find the flavor is a taste you either acquire or avoid. It falls into the realm of artificial sweeteners, like saccharin, Splenda (the current darling and as of early 2007 not shown to be harmful), and aspartame, which at best taste funny and at worst might be hazardous to your health.

Liquid Sweeteners

Honey

Made, as you know, by bees. Because the source of the nectar determines the flavor of the honey, there are more than 300 varieties of honey in the United States alone, including orange blossom, clover, and eucalyptus. Many commercially produced honeys are a blend from different plant sources. All are about 25 percent sweeter than conventional sugar, so you use less of it to achieve the same sweetness. Start by replacing just some of the sugar in your favorite recipe (remember that the color of honey will darken foods slightly) and see what happens; cookies, for example, are tricky, because honey causes them to spread more than cookies baked with sugar.

Some guidelines for baking with honey:

1. Reduce the liquid by $1/4$ cup for each cup of honey used.
2. For every cup of honey, add $1/2$ teaspoon baking soda to balance the honey's acidity.
3. When you substitute honey for sugar in quick breads, cookies, and cakes, reduce the oven temperature by 25°F to prevent overbrowning.

Molasses

A brown, heavy syrup produced during the sugar-making process. The first boiling produces light molasses, which can be used like honey; the second produces dark molasses (a thick, full-flavored, not-so-sweet syrup for cooking); and the third produces blackstrap molasses, the darkest, thickest, most nutritious, and least useful of the bunch. You can cook and bake with blackstrap, though it's best to blend it with light molasses or honey.

Corn Syrup

A thick, sticky sweetener processed from cornstarch. Light corn syrup is clarified, while the dark is flavored with caramel, which makes it sweeter and (duh) darker. It's very useful in making Caramels (page 907) and some other candies and sauces (like hot fudge), but otherwise you can live without it. Generally, if you want sugar in a syrup form, try Sugar Syrup, page 857.

Rice Syrup (Rice Honey)

When the starches in whole grain rice are processed, they become the complex sugars maltose and glucose, which metabolize more slowly than sucrose. Rice syrup is about half as sweet as cane sugar, has a mildly sweet butterscotch taste, and generally produces baked goods that are crisper than those made with cane sugar. You cannot substitute it directly for sugar in most recipes, but you can use it instead of maple, corn, or sugar syrup.

Other liquid sweeteners: Malt syrup, made from

sprouted barley, is most often used in the production of beer; it has a mild, sweet flavor. (Made into a powder, it's used to make malted milk shakes.) Treacle, which is popular in Europe, is similar to molasses; the light variety is called "golden syrup," and the dark type is called "black treacle." Sorghum is another molasseslike sweetener made from a European grain; use it as you would honey or molasses. Palm syrup is made by boiling the sap of the date palm tree (palm sugar has the same source); it's sweet and dark and is often added to desserts in Asia.

The Basics of Chocolate

Like cheese, coffee, and wine, chocolate has become the food of serious connoisseurs, complete with highbrow terminology and potential snobbery. But for those of us who eat chocolate for sheer enjoyment, the important things remain simple.

I approach chocolate the same way I do cheese or wine: no matter how many variables there are, you basically want to start with a delicious ingredient, the best quality that you can afford and find without hassle. Cooking won't hide off flavors or strange textures, but if the chocolate tastes great when you bite into it, it's certainly good enough for cooking. This is why I avoid chocolate chips and premade sauces; they're usually not delicious when eaten straight, and it's simple enough to chunk, chop, or melt a good eating chocolate. Your desserts will be much better for that small bit of extra work.

And it's easy to find good chocolate; in general, even supermarkets carry better brands than they did just a few years ago. One thing many people don't know is that you can use good "candy-bar" chocolate for cooking—you're not limited to whatever happens to be on the shelf next to the flour. Go by quality first, then the type of chocolate. For most desserts—and for eating, actually—I turn to bittersweet or semisweet chocolate. To help you make the best decisions, here are the basics, from bean to bar.

Anatomy of a Cacao Bean

Chocolate is made from cacao beans, which are seeds of the tropical cacao tree. Twenty to fifty of them grow in an oblong pod; it takes about four hundred seeds to make a pound of chocolate. The most common type of tree is the Forastero, and the chocolate that comes from it tastes generally earthy and moderately acidic. A more fruity chocolate comes from the Criollo tree; Trinitario is a hybrid of the other two. But these variety names alone mean virtually nothing, since other things—like where the trees are grown and how the chocolate is processed and blended—also affect the quality and flavor of the final product.

Once the seeds and the pulp are collected, they're fermented, a process that changes their chemistry and develops chocolate's unique flavor; from here out they're called *cocoa beans*. The beans are dried (by machine or, preferably, in the sun; you can begin to see how it's possible to become as obsessive about chocolate as it is about wine). They're then sorted, roasted, and shelled. All this produces the nib, which is ground and refined into chocolate liquor (which contains no alcohol but can be thought of as a straight shot of chocolate). Separating the solids from the fat in chocolate liquor results in two products: unsweetened cocoa powder and cocoa butter.

To get to edible chocolate, the liquor is mixed with other ingredients—sugar, vanilla, additional cocoa butter, and sometimes milk, vegetable oils (yuck), or other additives, then gently stirred or "conched." Before chocolate can be molded and sold, it is tempered, a heating and cooling process that keeps it from crystallizing and makes the chocolate hard, smooth, and glossy. It's a complicated procedure, and here's the bottom line: High-quality ingredients, few additives, and attention during the production process are what distinguishes good chocolate from bad.

The Chocolate Lexicon

The types of chocolate are determined by the percentage of cocoa solids (essentially the chocolate liquor content)

Ⓕ Fast   Ⓜ Make Ahead   Ⓥ Vegan

and how they are processed. Some names are used interchangeably, so it's best to read the label to know exactly what you're getting. A general rule of thumb: The higher the percentage of solids, the less sweet the chocolate, because there's less sugar in the formula. (Generally, higher percentages of chocolate solids mean not much else to muck up the flavor.)

Here's a quick rundown of the lingo:

Unsweetened Chocolate

Baking Chocolate, Chocolate Liquor

A combination of cocoa solids and cocoa butter and nothing else; 100 percent cocoa. Unsweetened chocolate is too bitter to eat but useful for home chocolate making, cooking, and baking.

Bittersweet Chocolate

Semisweet, Dark, Extra Dark, Extra Bittersweet

This is the type of chocolate I use for cooking and baking. The solid cocoa content ranges from 35 to 99 percent, with less than 12 percent milk solids. That's a big range, so look for an exact number, and if none is mentioned, check out the ingredient lists to see what else is included. Just having a high percentage of solids doesn't automatically guarantee good quality, but it does mean there isn't a lot of room for fillers. Try a few brands before settling on your favorites for cooking. First listen to the snap when you break a piece in two; it should sound crisp. Many good-quality bittersweet chocolates taste almost chalky if you're not used to them, but they coat your mouth evenly without any waxiness or grittiness (that's the cocoa butter at work). As the chocolate melts on your tongue, you should register all sorts of flavors, from coffeelike roasted notes to fruit and acidic tones. (This is why excellent chocolate is universally appealing.)

Dark Chocolate

Sweet

Contains 15 to 34 percent cocoa solids and no more than 12 percent milk solids. *Sweet chocolate* is the "official"

name, though it's commonly called *dark chocolate*. The good stuff is fine for eating, though not really for cooking. I prefer to control the sweetness of my chocolate desserts.

Milk Chocolate

Must contain a minimum of 10 percent cocoa solids, 12 percent milk solids, and 3.39 percent milk fat. If you like sweet, melt-in-your mouth chocolate, this is it. But don't skimp. Make sure it includes real ingredients and tastes rich and almost buttery. Milk chocolate should be as complex as bittersweet or dark chocolate, with the flavors muted against a backdrop of creaminess.

German Sweet Chocolate

This is not from Germany; the name comes from its inventor, Samuel German, who in 1852 invented a sweetened baking bar for the Baker's Chocolate Company. It is sweeter than bittersweet chocolate. (And yes, the famous cake comes from this brand of chocolate, not the country.) Not super-high-quality.

Cocoa Powder

After cocoa butter is pressed out of the nibs—or separated from the chocolate liquor—the solids are finely ground into a powder. Be sure to use unsweetened cocoa powder. "Dutched," "Dutch process" or "alkalized" cocoa is the most common; it's been treated with an alkaline ingredient to reduce acidity and darken the color. "Natural" cocoa powder is harder to find but worth the hunt (and worth the extra expense). It's light brown and more acidic but usually has more true chocolate flavor. Basically, they're interchangeable in the recipes here. (The only potential problem is leavening cakes and quick breads; if you use natural cocoa and there's no baking soda in the recipe, add a pinch to balance the acidity and improve leavening.)

White Chocolate

White chocolate is technically not chocolate, but a confection made from cocoa butter. It must contain at least

20 percent cocoa butter, 14 percent milk solids, and 3.39 percent milk fat. To me, it's a completely different ingredient rather than a substitute for chocolate, though you can substitute white chocolate in any of the recipes here. But there's a huge difference between good white chocolate and the cheap stuff. First, scan the label for strange-sounding ingredients; cocoa butter should be the first ingredient. Always taste it before you cook with it. Good white chocolate has a subtle flavor and should never be waxy, gritty, or bland. At its best, white chocolate melts very slowly in your mouth and is something like what you might imagine eating straight vanilla would be like. It doesn't keep nearly as long as dark chocolate; only a few weeks.

Carob

Not chocolate at all, but made from a legume; commonly used as a cocoa substitute for people who are allergic to chocolate. It tastes more grassy and vegetative, and without the fat of cocoa butter, it has a more grainy texture.

Storing Chocolate

There's no need to refrigerate chocolate, but you should keep it in a cool, dry place (I think the fridge is as good a place as any). Stored properly, chocolate can last for at least a year; bittersweet chocolate can even improve as it ages.

Sometimes chocolate develops a white or gray sheen or thin coating. If this happens, don't panic. The chocolate hasn't gone bad; it's "bloomed," a condition caused by too much moisture or humidity or fluctuating temperatures that cause the fat or sugar to come to the surface of the chocolate and crystallize. In either case the chocolate is still perfectly fine for cooking, as long as you're not making coated candy. It's also okay to eat bloomed chocolate out of hand, though the texture will be grainy.

Cooking with Chocolate

Good-quality chocolate bars are fine for melting or finely chopping, but if you want big chunks or decorative shav-ings, buy a piece from a larger brick; specialty and many natural food stores sell chocolate like this.

Chop chocolate with a chef's knife on a cutting board, pressing down firmly but carefully to cut it into first big pieces, then smaller, until you get the size you want. To make chocolate shavings, put the chocolate on a clean cloth and carefully pull the knife toward you, or use a vegetable peeler. It might take a couple passes to get the hang of it, but they're surprisingly easy to make.

Be careful when you melt chocolate, because it scorches easily. First, chop the chocolate (pieces melt faster than big chunks). Then either boil a pot of water, take it off the heat, set a small glass bowl with your chocolate in it, and stir until melted (or use a double boiler). Or melt the chocolate directly over the lowest possible heat, keeping a close eye on it. Or microwave the chocolate for a minute or two at the lowest setting; watch it like a hawk and interrupt to stir once or twice. Melting chocolate with liquids is trickier, so I always melt the chocolate alone, then work with it.

The Basics of Cookies

You don't need to be told about cookies; everyone eats 'em. They're a simple and wonderful dessert that can be whipped up at a moment's notice or made days or even weeks ahead, because with very few exceptions cookie dough can be frozen for months.

It's likely that you already have the traditional and basic ingredients for cookies in your kitchen: butter, flour, sugar, and eggs. In general, butter makes cookies tender, flour makes them cakey, sugar adds crispness (and, of course, sweetness), and eggs give richness, structure, and chew. But olive oil can fill in for butter; honey, brown sugar, or other sweeteners for some or all of the sugar; and all sorts of flours for the usual all-purpose flour. The flavorings run from just about any ground spice to rolled grains, dried fruit, nuts, candy, even spices and chiles.

All-purpose flour is the flour of choice for cookies, but it's by no means the only flour you can use. Whole

 Fast   Make Ahead   Ⓥ Vegan

wheat lends a good nutty flavor while also adding nutrients; rice flour and cornmeal are great alternatives when you want a very tender cookie (or if you're allergic to wheat); and other flours can add flavor and/or texture. See Substituting Flours in Baking (page 684) for more information and ratios.

A couple of other things affect the character of cookies: In general, "drop" cookies—those that are dropped by the spoonful onto baking sheets—are sturdier than those that are refrigerated, rolled, and sliced (generally called *refrigerator cookies*), which are finer and more delicate. Drop cookies easily take stir-in ingredients (like chocolate pieces or chips), while their tender-crumbed counterparts require finely ground or chopped additions (see "Tips for Improvising Cookies," right). Baking times also have an important effect on texture; shorter cooking times produce softer, chewier cookies, while longer ones make them crispier. You can play with this, even with the same recipe, and see which you prefer.

Cookie making moves much more quickly if you have two or even three cookie sheets so you can avoid baking in small batches. Many cookies can be baked on ungreased pans (especially if the pans are nonstick), but batter-based cookies, like Tuiles (page 843), require greasing and flouring or lining the pan with a silicone mat or a piece of parchment paper. You can use a mat or parchment for any cookie, especially if you don't want to promote browned bottoms.

Oatmeal Apple Cookies

MAKES: About 3 dozen
TIME: About 1 hour

Dried apples make a nice updated version of this American classic, but whole grain fans won't want to stop there. Anything rolled is up for grabs (they're all made like rolled oats); quinoa is especially good. And just about any dried fruit can be used instead of apples; raisins (nat-

urally), dried cranberries, cherries, blueberries, strawberries, dates, mango or papaya bits, chopped apricots or prunes, and shredded coconut are all delicious. If you like your cookies fully loaded, this recipe can handle up to another $1/2$ cup—maybe even a little more—of chopped nuts, chocolate, or both. And whether you have dietary restrictions or not, the vegan variation is one terrific cookie.

Other rolled grains you can use: quinoa, whole wheat, spelt, triticale, or barley.

8 tablespoons (1 stick) unsalted butter, softened

$1/2$ cup granulated sugar

$1/2$ cup packed brown sugar

2 eggs

$1^1/2$ cups all-purpose flour

2 cups rolled oats (not instant)

$1^1/2$ cups (about 5 ounces) chopped dried apples

$1/2$ teaspoon ground cinnamon

Pinch salt

2 teaspoons baking powder

$1/2$ cup milk

$1/2$ teaspoon vanilla or almond extract

1 Preheat the oven to 375°F. Use an electric mixer to cream the butter and sugars together; add the eggs one at a time and beat until well blended.

2 Combine the flour, oats, apples, cinnamon, salt, and baking powder in a bowl. Alternating with the milk, add the dry ingredients to the batter by hand, a little a time, stirring to blend. Stir in the vanilla.

3 Put tablespoon-size mounds of dough about 3 inches apart on ungreased baking sheets. Bake until lightly browned, 12 to 15 minutes. Cool for about 2 minutes on the sheets before using a spatula to transfer the cookies to a rack to finish cooling. Store in a tightly covered container at room temperature for no more than a day or two.

Vegan Oatmeal-Apple Cookies. Substitute $1/2$ cup neutral oil, like grapeseed or corn, for the butter, $1/4$ cup applesauce for the eggs, and any nondairy milk for the cow's milk.

Oatmeal Carrot (or Parsnip) Cookies. These are especially great with rolled quinoa: Substitute peeled and grated carrots (or parsnips) for the raisins. Add a pinch of freshly grated nutmeg and/or cloves if you like.

Peanut Oatmeal Cookies. Peanut butter (or any nut butter) replaces some of the butter for a rich flavor: Substitute $1/4$ cup peanut butter for half of the butter.

Whole Grain Apple Spice Cookies. Straight-out cooked whole grain (like bulgur, barley, wheat or rye berries, buckwheat, or even short-grain brown rice) replaces rolled oats with tender but chewy results: Substitute cooked whole grain (see page 537) for the rolled oats and fluff it with a fork to separate the kernels before combining with the other ingredients. Omit the milk. In Step 2, increase the cinnamon to a teaspoon and add $1/2$ teaspoon ground ginger and $1/4$ teaspoon each ground allspice and nutmeg. Proceed with the recipe, combining the dry ingredients with the egg mixture in Step 3 all at once, without adding any milk.

Brown Sugar Cookies with Sea Salt

MAKES: 3 to 4 dozen

TIME: About $1^1/2$ hours, largely unattended

Ⓜ

With their slightly salty finish and subtle sweetness, these cookies offer the best of both worlds. Semolina makes the texture tender and crumbly, almost shortbreadlike with buttery richness. It's best to roll the dough into a relatively small narrow log so the cookies are less fragile. Use finely ground cornmeal if you don't have semolina; all all-purpose flour is fine too. But it's important to use sea salt for the final sprinkling.

$1/2$ pound (2 sticks) unsalted butter, softened

$1/2$ cup dark packed brown sugar

1 egg yolk

1 cup semolina flour

$1/2$ cup all-purpose flour

Ⓕ Fast   Ⓜ Make Ahead   Ⓥ Vegan

$^1/_4$ teaspoon salt

About 1 teaspoon coarse sea salt for sprinkling

① Use an electric mixer on low speed to mix the butter and sugar together just until combined, 30 seconds or so. Still on low speed, beat in the egg yolk, then the flours and salt, until the mixture barely holds together; this will take a few minutes.

② Turn the dough out onto a clean work surface and shape it into a round, triangular, or rectangular log about 1 inch in diameter; wrap it in plastic wrap and refrigerate or freeze until firm, about 30 minutes. (Or freeze the log, well wrapped, for up to 3 months.)

③ Preheat the oven to 325°F. Unwrap the dough and slice it $^1/_4$-inch thick, put the slices on an ungreased baking sheet, sprinkle each with a little sea salt, and bake right away until the cookies are firm but not browning, 15 to 20 minutes. Remove from the oven, let them cool in the pan for a minute or two, and then transfer the cookies to a rack to cool. Store in an airtight container for up to 2 days.

Pine Nut Cookies. All sweet, not salty. Drizzle the tops with Orange Glaze or Berry Jam Glaze (page 858) for even more sweetness and flavor: Substitute granulated sugar for the brown and 1 whole egg for the yolk. Omit the sea salt for sprinkling. In Step 1, add 1 cup toasted pine nuts (see page 321) along with the flour.

Ginger Spice Cookies. A more tender and mild gingersnap: Substitute all-purpose flour for the semolina and in Step 1 add 2 teaspoons grated or finely minced peeled fresh ginger and $^1/_2$ teaspoon each ground cinnamon, allspice, and cloves along with the egg and flour.

Black Pepper Cookies. With a kick of black pepper and a fine grainy texture: Substitute granulated sugar for the brown. Add $^1/_2$ teaspoon coarsely ground black pepper. Proceed with the recipe, but instead of the sea salt, sprinkle an additional grind of black pepper on top of each cookie just before baking.

Sichuan Peppercorn Cookies. Substitute granulated sugar for the brown. In Step 1, add $^1/_2$ teaspoon ground Sichuan peppercorns along with the eggs and flour.

Maple Snaps

MAKES: 3 to 4 dozen
TIME: About 1$^1/_2$ hours, largely unattended

These are not quite your grandma's maple cookies, especially if you try any of the variations. Rice flour makes the dough tender and snappy, but if you don't have any handy, cornmeal, semolina, or simply all all-purpose flour still make crisp cookies. Just be sure to give them space on the cookie sheet since they spread.

There's some room for variation here, provided the additions are finely chopped or ground: Add up to $^3/_4$ cup finely ground pecans or minced dried fruit (or a combination) if you like. Smear on Not-Too-Sweet Maple Buttercream Frosting (page 860). Or contrast the flavors of the glaze; see Orange Glaze or Apricot Jam Glaze and their variations on pages 857–858 for other ideas.

12 tablespoons (1$^1/_2$ sticks) unsalted butter, softened

$^1/_2$ cup maple syrup

$^3/_4$ cup dark packed brown sugar

2 eggs

$^1/_2$ cup rice flour

1$^1/_2$ cups all-purpose flour

1 teaspoon baking powder

Pinch salt

① Preheat the oven to 350°F. Use an electric mixer set on medium to cream the butter, maple syrup, and brown sugar together; add the eggs one at a time and beat until well blended (it's okay if the mixture doesn't look smooth).

② Combine the flours, baking powder, and salt in a bowl. Add the dry ingredients to the batter by hand, a little a time, stirring to blend. (If you're adding any nuts or dried fruit, now is the time.)

❸ Drop tablespoon-size mounds of dough about 3 inches apart on ungreased baking sheets. Bake until lightly browned, 12 to 15 minutes. Cool for about 2 minutes on the sheets before using a spatula to transfer the cookies to a rack to finish cooling. (If icing or glazing, wait until they are cool, then decorate them right on the rack for a cleaner look and let set for about 10 more minutes.) Store in a tightly covered container at room temperature for no more than a day or two.

Coconut Snaps. Substitute $1^1/_2$ cups granulated sugar for the syrup and brown sugar. Add 2 cups finely chopped or ground shredded coconut and make a batch of Coconut Glaze (page 858). Proceed with the recipe, adding 1 cup of the coconut to the dough at the end of Step 2. After the cookies have cooled, put the remaining coconut on a plate; glaze each cookie and quickly dip it into the coconut, which will stick to the top.

Chile Snaps. Substitute $1^1/_2$ cups granulated sugar for the syrup and brown sugar and cornmeal for the rice flour. If you like, make a batch of Lime Glaze (page 858). Add 2 teaspoons hot red pepper flakes or 1 teaspoon ground dried chile, like chipotle, guajillo, ancho, or New Mexico, at the end of Step 2. Proceed with the recipe, glazing the cookies after they have baked and cooled.

Coriander Snaps. Substitute 1 cup granulated sugar for the syrup and brown sugar and add 1 tablespoon freshly ground coriander seeds at the end of Step 2.

Saffron Olive Oil Cookies

MAKES: About 3 dozen cookies
TIME: 40 minutes

Ⓜ

Another not-too-sweet cookie (perfect for glazing), only this time a hint of saffron gives the cookies a gorgeous gold color, and their cakey texture will remind you of an elegant vanilla wafer. The olive oil is a fresh-tasting alternative to butter, even if you're not looking to cut down on saturated fat.

> Small pinch (about $1/_8$ teaspoon) crumbled saffron threads
>
> 2 cups all-purpose flour
>
> $1/_4$ teaspoon baking powder
>
> Pinch salt
>
> $3/_4$ cup sugar
>
> $1/_2$ cup extra virgin olive oil
>
> 2 eggs
>
> 2 teaspoons grated or finely minced orange zest
>
> 2 tablespoons Grand Marnier, other orange liqueur, or orange juice

❶ Preheat the oven to 350°F. Combine 1 tablespoon boiling water with the saffron in a medium bowl, stir, and steep for a few minutes. Combine the flour, baking powder, and salt in a large bowl.

❷ Add the sugar and olive oil to the saffron mixture and beat until light, a minute or two. Add the eggs and continue beating until creamy and fluffy, another couple of minutes. Beat in the orange zest and liqueur. Gently stir the liquid mixture into the dry one, just until well combined.

❸ Use 2 teaspoons to drop mounds of dough about 3 inches apart on ungreased baking sheets. Bake until lightly browned on the bottom, 12 to 15 minutes. Immediately transfer the cookies to a rack to finish cooling. Store in a tightly covered container at room temperature for no more than a day or two.

Cardamom-Pistachio Cookies. Almost any nut oil, nut, and spice will work in place of the cardamom-pistachio combo (or just stick with the olive oil): Substitute 1 tablespoon ground cardamom for the saffron and add $1/_2$ cup ground pistachios. Skip the boiling water/steeping in Step 1. Proceed with the recipe. Sprinkle the pistachios on the cookies and gently press them into the dough before baking.

Ⓕ Fast   Ⓜ Make Ahead   Ⓥ Vegan

Date–Olive Oil Cookies. Omit the saffron. Substitute $^1/_2$ cup whole wheat flour for $^1/_2$ cup of the all-purpose flour if you like. Add $^3/_4$ cup chopped dates. In Step 1, steep the dates in water instead of the saffron and substitute the whole wheat flour in the dry ingredients if you're using it. Proceed with the recipe.

Chile–Olive Oil Cookies. Omit the saffron. Add 1 to 2 tablespoons cored, seeded, and minced jalapeño or other hot fresh chile or cayenne to taste. Skip the boiling water/steeping in Step 1.

Cinnamon Chocolate Cookies. Use cinnamon instead of the saffron; coarsely chop $^1/_2$ cup dark (semisweet) chocolate (about 3 ounces) and melt it. In Step 1, omit the water and combine the cinnamon and chocolate in a small bowl and stir well. Use this mixture in place of the saffron water in Step 1. Proceed with the recipe.

Chewy Almond-Cherry Cookies

MAKES: 3 to 4 dozen
TIME: About 2$^1/_2$ hours, largely unattended

Finely chopped nuts, sugar, and egg whites are the base of this cookie; the nuts add flavor and texture, while the sugar and egg whites make them crisp and chewy, sort of like a flat macaroon. Don't let the time deter you; two hours of it is just for chilling, which can be done overnight too, making this a great make-ahead recipe.

3 cups almonds

1$^1/_2$ cups granulated sugar

5 egg whites

1 teaspoon vanilla extract

1$^1/_2$ cups chopped dried cherries

Confectioners' sugar for dusting (optional)

❶ Put the almonds and granulated sugar in a food processor and pulse until the almonds are finely chopped.

❷ Put the egg whites in a large bowl and beat until foamy; add the vanilla and beat a bit more. Gradually add the almond mixture and cherries, stirring until a loose, sticky dough forms. Cover and chill in the refrigerator for at least 2 hours or overnight.

❸ When you're ready to bake the cookies, preheat the oven to 350°F. Put teaspoon-size or larger mounds of dough about 3 inches apart on nonstick baking sheets or sheets lined with parchment or wax paper. Bake until lightly browned and hardened on the outside, 20 to 25 minutes. (Keep the remaining dough in the refrigerator while the first batch bakes.) Cool the cookies completely on the sheets, then remove with a spatula. Dust with confectioners' sugar before serving if you like. These keep well in an airtight container for up to 3 days.

Chewy Mocha Cookies. Always a good combination; hazelnuts are excellent here: Substitute 3 tablespoons cocoa powder and 1$^1/_2$ tablespoons instant espresso or coffee for the cherries. Proceed with the recipe.

Chewy Chestnut Cookies. Fresh roasted chestnuts are *the* best: Substitute 3 cups roasted, peeled, and mashed chestnuts (see page 287) for the almonds and omit the cherries.

Chocolate Tuiles

MAKES: 3 to 4 dozen
TIME: About 30 minutes

Thin, light, crisp, *and* chocolaty, these cookies are spread onto the baking sheets instead of being mounded and dropped. They're showstoppers, but this version is super-easy to make. When the cookies are still warm, they are removed and molded into various shapes—like cones—or just twisted or curled by being draped over ramekins, glasses, rolling pins, or wire racks or shaped by hand while still warm. As the cookies cool, they become crisp (and harder to manipulate, so work quickly).

4 egg whites

1 cup confectioners' sugar

$^{1}/_{4}$ cup cocoa powder

$^{3}/_{4}$ cup all-purpose flour

8 tablespoons (1 stick) unsalted butter, melted, plus a little more if needed, as well as some soft butter for greasing the baking sheets

① Preheat the oven to 375°F. Grease 2 baking sheets or cover them with parchment or a silicone mat.

② Whisk the egg whites until foamy. Mix in the sugar, cocoa, and flour, scraping down the sides of the bowl as necessary. Add the melted butter and stir until just incorporated. The dough will be more like a very thick batter than a cookie dough. If it's not spreadable, add more melted butter, a teaspoonful at a time.

③ Spoon the batter onto the prepared sheets and use the back of the spoon to spread the batter into thin (less than $^{1}/_{4}$ inch thick) 2- to 3-inch circles. Bake until firm and slightly darkened around the edges, 8 to 10 minutes. While still hot, use a metal spatula or butter knife to transfer the cookies to a rack to cool flat or drape over a dowel or rolling pin to form the traditional curved tuile shape.

Chocolate Rice Cookies. Super-crisp and light, but also a little more fragile: Substitute rice flour for the all-purpose flour.

Chocolate Dessert Cups. Great for holding berries, pudding, ice cream, or flavored whipped cream. Prepare the recipe as directed. When the cookies come out of the oven, drape them over inverted small ramekins or coffee cups to cool, pressing gently to form a cup on the inside. Fill as you like, just before serving so they don't get soggy.

8 Things to Sprinkle on Chocolate Cookies

Sprinkle the cookies with any of these just before baking:

1. Black and white sesame seeds or poppy seeds
2. Crumbled lavender buds
3. Crushed pink peppercorns
4. Anise or fennel seeds
5. Finely chopped nuts
6. Chopped pumpkin seeds or sunflower seeds
7. Ground spices, like cinnamon, nutmeg, cloves, allspice, star anise, cardamom
8. Citrus Sprinkle (page 818)

MOLDING TUILES

To obtain the classic tuile shape, lay the baked but still soft cookies over a rolling pin, dowel, or similar object.

Brownies and Bars

Here is a variety of cookielike recipes that you bake whole, in a pan, and then cut into squares or rectangles—bars, that is. Brownies are the classic example, but the world of bars is larger than that, the junction of cookies, cakes, and tarts. And a good world it is. The best bars have a bit of chew to them; generally, you want to take them out of the oven when the edges are starting to firm up and the middle is still a bit soft, because they will continue to cook as they cool.

Blondies

MAKES: About a dozen squares

TIME: 40 minutes

These are essentially brownies *sans* chocolate. If you don't want to use whole wheat flour, that's okay: all all-purpose flour is fine too.

 Fast   Make Ahead   Ⓥ Vegan

If you like, toss in chocolate chunks, bits of butter-scotch candy or peanut butter, or chips of either; nuts or seeds; or whole or chopped dried fruit.

8 tablespoons (1 stick) unsalted butter, plus a little for greasing the pan

1 cup packed brown sugar

1 egg

1 teaspoon vanilla extract or $^1/_2$ teaspoon almond extract

Pinch salt

$^3/_4$ cup all-purpose flour

$^1/_4$ cup whole wheat flour

1 Preheat the oven to 350°F. Grease an 8- or 9-inch square baking pan or line it with aluminum foil and grease the foil.

2 Melt the butter over low heat. Transfer it to a bowl and use an electric mixer to beat in the sugar until very smooth, then beat in the egg and vanilla, scraping down the sides of the bowl every now and then if necessary.

3 Add the salt, then gently stir in the flours. Pour into the prepared pan and bake for 20 to 25 minutes, or until just barely set in the middle (if it looks like they're baking unevenly, rotate the pan about halfway through cooking). It's better to underbake blondies than to overbake them. Cool on a rack before cutting. Store, covered and at room temperature, for no more than 1 day.

Peanut-Caramel Bars. The saltiness of the peanuts contrasts with the sweetness of the caramel and batter; use any nuts, salted or unsalted: Add $^1/_2$ cup salted peanuts and $^1/_2$ cup chopped Caramels (page 907). Stir in the peanuts and caramels after the flour in Step 3.

Semolina-Apricot Bars. Chopped pecans or walnuts are lovely but not essential here: Substitute semolina flour for all-purpose; add $^3/_4$ cup chopped dried apricots and $^1/_2$ cup chopped nuts if you like.

Almond Bars. Richly almond-flavored and wonderful; great with tea or coffee: Substitute almond flour for the whole wheat; add $^3/_4$ cup chopped toasted almonds and $^1/_4$ cup almond paste (or stick with almond extract). Mix the almond paste in with the butter in Step 2.

Coconut-Lime Bars

Makes: About a dozen squares

TIME: About 1 hour

Tangy and sweet, with a tropical twist from the coconut, this variation on gooey lemon bars is incredibly easy to prepare. Be sure not to overbake them; they're done when the edges are firming up and the middle is still a bit soft and jiggly. Rotate the pan as they bake if they are cooking unevenly. To make a bigger batch, double the recipe and use a 9 × 13-inch pan.

8 tablespoons (1 stick) unsalted butter, softened, plus a little for greasing the pan

$1^3/_4$ cups sugar

Pinch salt

1 cup plus 3 tablespoons all-purpose flour

2 teaspoons grated or finely minced lime zest

3 eggs

$^1/_4$ cup freshly squeezed lime juice

$^1/_2$ teaspoon baking soda

$^3/_4$ cup shredded coconut

1 Preheat the oven to 350°F. Grease an 8- or 9-inch square baking pan.

2 Use an electric mixer to cream the butter with $^1/_4$ cup of the sugar and the salt. Stir in 1 cup of the flour and the zest. This mixture will be quite dry; press it into the greased pan and bake for 20 minutes, no longer; it should just be turning golden Remove from the oven and cool slightly.

❸ Beat together the eggs, lime juice, and remaining 1¹/₂ cups sugar until lightened and thick. Mix in the remaining 3 tablespoons flour and the baking soda. Pour over the crust, sprinkle with the coconut, and bake until firm on the edges but still a little soft and jiggly in the middle, 25 to 30 minutes. Cool completely before cutting into squares. Serve immediately or store, covered and refrigerated, for up to 2 days.

Lemon-Rosemary Bars. A sophisticated flavor that's great after a rich meal: Substitute lemon juice and zest for the lime and add 1 teaspoon chopped fresh rosemary leaves (or lavender if you can find it). Omit the coconut. Proceed with the recipe and sprinkle with confectioners' sugar before serving.

Mango Bars. Tropical and tangy; use ripe, juicy mango here: Add ¹/₄ cup mango purée (see page 862) and reduce the lime juice to 2 teaspoons. Omit or keep the shredded coconut as you prefer.

Buttermilk Bars. Creamy, mildly sour, and really simple: Substitute ¹/₄ cup buttermilk for the lime juice and zest. Omit the coconut.

Caramel Walnut Bars

MAKES: About a dozen squares
TIME: About 1 hour

Ⓜ

A baked crust topped with walnuts coated in a rich and buttery caramel; it's simultaneously crunchy, chewy, and soft—not to mention completely delicious. Any nuts will work here.

¹/₂ pound (2 sticks) unsalted butter, softened, plus a little for greasing the pan

1¹/₄ cups sugar

1 cup all-purpose flour

¹/₂ cup cream

Pinch salt

¹/₄ cup honey

1 cups roughly chopped walnuts

❶ Preheat the oven to 350°F. Grease an 8- or 9-inch square baking pan.

❷ Use an electric mixer to cream 1 stick of the butter with ¹/₄ cup of the sugar. Stir in the flour. This mixture will be quite dry; press it into the greased pan and bake for 15 minutes, no longer. Remove from the oven and cool slightly.

❸ Put the remaining cup of sugar and a tablespoon of water in a saucepan over medium-high heat and cook until it melts and turns a light brown color, 5 to 8 minutes.

❹ Carefully stir in the remaining stick of butter, the cream, and the salt; stir until the mixture is combined, then add the honey and walnuts. Immediately pour the walnut mixture over the baked crust and refrigerate until set. Cut into squares or rectangles and serve. Store, covered, for up to 5 days.

No-Bake Granola Bars

MAKES: About a dozen squares
TIME: 15 minutes

Ⓕ   Ⓥ

A better-tasting, good-for-you version of store-bought snack squares. These are a lot of fun to fool around with; see the variations.

³/₄ cup honey

¹/₂ cup packed brown sugar

¹/₄ cup neutral oil, like grapeseed or corn

3 cups Crunchy Granola (page 573)

❶ Put the honey, brown sugar, and oil in a small pot and bring to a boil. Put the granola in a large bowl and pour the sugar mixture over the top while mixing; stir until the granola is well coated.

Ⓕ Fast   Ⓜ Make Ahead   Ⓥ Vegan

2 Press into an 8- or 9-inch square pan and let cool in the fridge. Cut into squares or rectangles and serve. Store in an airtight container for up to 4 days.

Dried Fruit Bars. Use just about any dried fruit here; dates or dried figs are great, as are dried apricots, raisins, plums, pears, and more: Substitute $1^{1}/_{2}$ cups dried fruit for the honey and brown sugar. Put the dried fruit and oil in a food processor and purée until smooth, stopping the machine to scrape down the sides if necessary. (Add small amounts of water if the fruit is dried out and not processing.) Proceed with the recipe.

Orange-Spice Granola Bars. Great with some chocolate chips in the mix: Add 1 tablespoon chopped orange zest, 2 teaspoons ground cinnamon, 1 teaspoon each ground cardamom and ginger, and $^{1}/_{2}$ teaspoon ground cloves.

Nutty Granola Bars. Loaded with nuts and seeds: Substitute 1 cup mixed or single toasted roughly chopped nuts and whole seeds for 1 cup of the granola.

Peanut (or Any Nut) Butter Granola Bars. Practically a power bar: Substitute peanut or any nut butter for the brown sugar.

Dried Cherry–Chocolate Granola Bars. A great picnic or brown-bag lunch dessert: Add 1 cup dried cherries and $^{1}/_{2}$ cup or more melted semisweet chocolate. Add the cherries to the granola. Proceed with the recipe; after the granola is pressed into the pan, drizzle the top with the melted chocolate, then cool in the fridge.

Double Chocolate Bars

MAKES: About a dozen squares
TIME: 40 minutes

Ⓜ

Somewhere between a brownie, a cookie, and fudge.

8 tablespoons (1 stick) unsalted butter, softened, plus
    a little for the greasing pan

3 ounces unsweetened chocolate, chopped

$^{3}/_{4}$ cup sugar

1 egg

Pinch salt

$^{3}/_{4}$ cup all-purpose flour

1 cup chopped white, milk, or semisweet chocolate

$^{3}/_{4}$ cup chopped walnuts or pecans (optional)

1 Preheat the oven to 350°F. Grease an 8- or 9-inch square baking pan or line it with aluminum foil and grease the foil.

2 Melt the butter and unsweetened chocolate over low heat. Transfer to a bowl and use an electric mixer to beat in the sugar until very smooth, then beat in the egg, scraping down the sides of the bowl every now and then if necessary.

3 Add the salt, then gently stir in the flour, chocolate chunks, and nuts if you're using them. Pour into the prepared pan and bake for 20 to 25 minutes, or until just barely set in the middle (if it looks like they're baking unevenly, rotate the pan about halfway through the baking). It's better to underbake the bars than to overbake them. Cool on a rack before cutting. Store, covered and at room temperature, for no more than 1 day.

Chocolate Peppermint Bars. Great for the holidays: Add $^{1}/_{2}$ teaspoon peppermint extract and/or $^{3}/_{4}$ cup crushed peppermint candies or candy canes; stir into the batter along with the salt in Step 3. Proceed with the recipe.

Chocolate Cranberry or Cherry Bars. Bits of sweet-tart dried fruit contrast with the rich chocolate: Substitute dried cranberries or cherries for the nuts.

Chocolate Swirl Bars. Cream cheese is swirled into the batter: Add 8 ounces softened cream cheese, $^{1}/_{4}$ cup additional sugar, and another egg; beat them together until soft and well combined. Proceed with the recipe, putting the chocolate batter in the pan, then adding the cream cheese mixture in dollops; use a knife tip to swirl it into the batter. Bake as directed.

The Basics of Cakes

Cakes come in a huge variety of flavors, shapes, textures, and flavors: vanilla, chocolate, almond, spice, or plum; loaves, sheets, layers, or tubes; simple and complicated. Some whip up in an hour or less, while others take hours from start to finish. But in sum—believe it or not—most cakes are pretty straightforward to make. You stir together a few basic ingredients, maybe whip some egg whites to a puffy foam, fold it all together, pour it into a pan, and bake it. There's little technique or even much skill involved; do it just a couple of times and you're practically a pro. Frosting, it should be said, is a little more complicated, and decorating I leave to the hobbyists.

Like many desserts, cakes are made from flour, butter or oil, eggs, some leavening, and sugar. Different styles of cake call for different ratios of one ingredient to the other, so, unlike for a custard or ice cream, there isn't one fairly standard ratio to follow. And you can't throw just any quantity of flour, butter, eggs, baking powder, and sugar into a bowl and get a cake, unless you get lucky. Unlike with many savory dishes, there's only so much fiddling you can do to a cake recipe before it affects the outcome, usually negatively. Baking is chemistry, not improvisation; you're always better off following a recipe here.

Given that, you don't really need to understand what's going on to bake; you just need to follow the steps. But knowing what roles ingredients play will help you figure out what went wrong if something does. And it will also, eventually, let you tinker with your cakes so that you can make them lighter, denser, sweeter, richer, and so on, according to your taste. In cakes, five basic kinds of ingredients all make different contributions:

- Flour provides structure; it's the basic building block.
- Eggs provide moisture, binding (if the flour is brick, the eggs are mortar), richness, flavor, and leavening (especially when the whites are beaten).
- Sugar provides moisture, sweetness, and good color.
- Baking powder and soda provide leavening (and nothing else).

- Butter or oil provides moisture, tenderness, and flavor.

A Little More About Flour

All-purpose flour, as you'd expect, is a reliable option for just about any cake. But if you want a tender cake with a fine crumb, you're better off using cake or pastry flour. These flours have less protein than all-purpose flour, so less gluten is produced, making the cake more tender. The same is true for nut flour or meals and alternative flours, like rice, barley, and cornmeal, which contain little to no gluten. Except for cake flour, you'd typically use these as a substitute for some of the all-purpose flour; if you used them exclusively, the cake would fall apart.

If you want to use whole wheat flour, whole wheat pastry flour is the best choice; second is white whole wheat flour. If you can't find either, use whole wheat all-purpose, but always mixed with regular A-P flour (see "Substituting Flours in Baking," page 684). Whole wheat flours don't absorb as much liquid as their white derivatives, so they will usually produce a drier and denser cake. (See "The Basics of Flour" on page 680 for more details.)

Cake Pans

You have several pan options for baking these cakes; the most common are mentioned in each recipe. But most cooks often find they have exactly the "wrong" pans. So here's how to wing it when you find yourself in that situation: If the recommended pan is an 8- or 9-inch square pan or a loaf pan, you can double the recipe and bake the cake in a 9 × 13-inch rectangular pan or a tube or bundt pan. Any cake that goes in a rectangular pan or 2 round pans for layers can also be baked in a tube or bundt pan. Just be sure to keep an eye on the cake; chances are it will take a little longer to bake.

As for greasing and flouring pans: I generally skip flouring, in part to save the hassle and mess, but also to avoid the gummy crust that forms on cakes baked in floured pans. The new nonstick pans make this a safe bet,

 Fast   Make Ahead   Vegan

but if your pans are old or you want to ensure a clean release and less browning, line the bottom of the greased pan with a piece of parchment and grease that. In almost every case you can skip flouring.

Baking and Doneness

Baking times in these and all cake recipes are approximate and will vary a little or a lot depending on the accuracy of your oven, the size of pan or pans you use, even the temperature of your batter. I strongly suggest you get an oven thermometer if you're going to bake a lot. You don't want to open the oven too frequently, but about three-quarters of the way through, take a peek and see what's going on; rotate the pan if the cake is cooking unevenly.

You can stick a toothpick into a cake, and if it comes out clean it's done. But I prefer to use my nose: When you start to smell it is usually the first time to take a look. And for the final test, press gently in the center of the cake with one finger. It should immediately spring back. If it leaves a mark, let the cake go a bit longer.

Cornmeal Pound Cake

MAKES: 1 loaf (at least 8 servings)

TIME: About 1¹/₂ hours, largely unattended, plus time to cool

I love regular pound cake, but I love the sweet and mild corn flavor of this even more. Thanks to whipped egg whites, it's light and tender, not leaden as you might expect, provided you use finely ground cornmeal. And it's flavorful enough to eat on its own or with any number of toppings, from powdered sugar to Berry Jam Glaze.

Sauces, glazes, and frostings you can use with this cake: Drizzle with Lemon-Clove Glaze (page 858) or Berry Jam Glaze (page 858) or spoon on any fruit purée (see page 862).

¹/₂ pound (2 sticks) unsalted butter, softened, plus butter for the pan

1 cup all-purpose flour

1 cup cornmeal

1¹/₂ teaspoons baking powder

Pinch salt

1 cup sugar

5 eggs, separated

1 teaspoon vanilla extract

① Preheat the oven to 325°F. Grease a 9 × 5-inch loaf pan. Combine the flour, cornmeal, baking powder, and salt in a bowl and set aside.

② Use an electric mixer to cream the 2 sticks of butter until it's smooth. Add ³/₄ cup of the sugar and beat until it's well blended. Beat until the mixture is light in color and fluffy, scraping down the sides of the mixing bowl as necessary. Beat in the egg yolks one at a time. Add the vanilla and stir until blended.

③ Mix in the dry ingredients by hand just until smooth; do not overmix and do not beat. In a separate bowl, beat the egg whites until they foam, then sprinkle in the remaining ¹/₄ cup sugar while beating to soft peaks. Fold them gently but thoroughly into the batter (the base batter is very thick).

④ Turn into the prepared pan and bake until a toothpick inserted in the center comes out clean, about 1 hour and 15 minutes. Let the cake rest in the pan for 5 minutes before inverting it onto a rack. Remove the pan, then turn the cake right side up. Cool before slicing. Store at room temperature, covered with wax paper, for a day or two; you can gain a couple more days by wrapping in plastic, but at some loss of texture.

Ginger Pound Cake. Use fresh ginger for its flavor alone; crystallized ginger for its flavor and chewy bits: Substitute grated or very finely minced peeled fresh ginger and/or 2 to 4 tablespoons chopped crystallized ginger for the vanilla extract.

Vanilla-Lime Pound Cake. Using real vanilla beans makes a lot of difference here: Substitute 1 vanilla bean for

Creaming: One Technique That Matters

Creaming butter (or oil) and sugar together is not just a mixing technique; it plays a role in leavening the cake as well. The quick beating (most easily done in a standing mixer, but there are other techniques; see Boozy Apple Cake, page 851) breaks up the fat with the sugar crystals and forces air bubbles into the mixture, which helps "lift" the cake as it bakes. (The eggs or egg yolks usually added at the last stage of creaming enrich and lighten the batter even further.)

the vanilla extract and add 2 teaspoons grated or very finely minced lime zest. Split the vanilla bean in half lengthwise and use a small sharp knife to scrape the seeds into the butter mixture; add the zest.

Yogurt Pound Cake. Yogurt replaces some of the butter for a lighter, even moister cake: Substitute $3/4$ cup yogurt for half of the butter.

Almond Cake

MAKES: 1 single-layer cake (about 8 servings)
TIME: About 1 hour, plus time to cool

Ⓜ

A rich cake for any almond lover. Almost all the almond flavor comes straight from the nuts, which are ground into a flour, with almond milk and extract playing supporting (and optional) roles to boost the flavor. Check out the Flourless Chocolate Nut Torte variation for an even more intense taste and texture. And feel free to use any nut or combination of nuts here.

Sauces, glazes, and frostings you can use with this cake: Spread on Not-Too-Sweet Buttercream Frosting (page 860), cover with Chocolate Glaze (page 861) or

Anise-Plum or Cherry Sauce (page 863), or simply dust with powdered sugar.

> 8 tablespoons (1 stick) butter, softened, plus butter for the pan
>
> 1 cup almonds
>
> 1 cup all-purpose flour
>
> 1 $1/2$ teaspoons baking powder
>
> $1/2$ teaspoon salt
>
> 1 cup sugar
>
> 2 eggs
>
> 1 teaspoon vanilla or almond extract
>
> 1 teaspoon grated or finely minced lemon zest
>
> $1/4$ cup almond milk or cow's milk

❶ Preheat the oven to 350°F. Grease one 9-inch layer or springform cake pan with some of the butter.

❷ Put the almonds in a food processor and pulse until finely ground. Mix the almond flour with the dry ingredients.

❸ Use an electric mixer to beat the stick of butter and the sugar together until creamy, then add the eggs one at a time and beat until thick and fluffy, scraping down the sides of the mixing bowl as necessary (this will take 5 to 7 minutes); add the extract and zest and beat to combine. Add the dry mixture, mixing until smooth. Add the milk and mix on low speed until well blended.

❹ Turn the batter into the prepared pan and bake until a toothpick inserted in the center comes out clean, 30 to 40 minutes. Let the cake cool in the pan for 15 minutes before inverting it onto a rack. Cool completely before glazing or frosting and slicing. Store at room temperature, covered with wax paper, for up to a day or two; use plastic wrap and it will keep for an extra day or so.

Amaretto Cake. Crumble amaretti cookies over the top of the batter just before baking if you like: Substitute $1/4$ cup amaretto for the almond milk.

Flourless Chocolate Nut Torte. Omit the stick of butter and just use enough to grease the pan. Add another

Ⓕ Fast   Ⓜ Make Ahead   Ⓥ Vegan

whole egg and 2 egg whites, plus $^1/_2$ cup cocoa powder and another cup of almonds. Omit the flour, baking powder, and almond milk. Grind all the nuts as directed in Step 2. In Step 3, beat the eggs and sugar together until thick and frothy, then just fold in the ground nuts, cocoa, and salt. Pour into the pan, bake, and cool as directed.

Boozy Apple Cake

MAKES: 1 rectangular cake (12 to 16 servings)
TIME: About 1 hour

Ⓜ

This toffee-style soaked cake is gooey, fruity, and relatively familiar, whether you finish it with the bourbon or vanilla cake soak. (If you'd prefer a more traditional approach, simply substitute Not-Too-Sweet Buttercream Frosting on page 860.) The recipe makes a large cake, perfect for entertaining. And as we know from carrot cake, you can get excellent results using vegetables in cakes, so be sure to check out the nontraditional variations.

12 tablespoons (1$^1/_2$ sticks) butter, softened, plus some for greasing the pan

2 medium apples (about 8 ounces), peeled, cored, and quartered

1$^1/_2$ cups sugar

2$^1/_2$ cups all-purpose flour

2 teaspoons baking powder

$^1/_2$ teaspoon salt

4 eggs

$^1/_2$ cup milk

Double recipe Boozy Cake Soak (page 859) or Vanilla Cake Soak (page 858)

❶ Preheat the oven to 350°F. Grease a 9 × 13-inch rectangular pan with a little butter. Put the apples in a blender or food processor with $^1/_2$ cup of the sugar and

Dressing Your Cake

You can top a cake as simply as this: Put some confectioners' sugar in a strainer and tap it over the top (use a stencil if you want to get fancy). Whipped cream (or lightly sweetened sour cream or crème fraîche) is great and almost as simple (it's best to put these over individual pieces, or you'll have to refrigerate the leftovers, which won't hold up very well).

But glazing, frosting, and ganache are fancier and—brushed, dabbed, or smeared onto the exterior—add their special flavors as well as moisture. Sauces are another good option, from simple puréed fruit to something more complicated. All of these can be used to decorate the cake or be served beneath or on top of individual slices.

The ultimate flavor and moisture enhancer is a cake soak. Most cakes are like sponges, soaking up any liquid that's poured onto them; when allowed to sit for an hour or more, every bit of the cake will become saturated. I like this technique a lot, as you can see on page 858.

With any cake dressing, you don't want to overwhelm the flavor and texture of the cake but to add just enough to enhance the cake's flavor and moisten it as necessary. When pairing a dressing with your cake, try to match or contrast flavors; for example, orange is a wonderful flavor contrast for the sweetness of Beet Cake (page 852), and Coconut-Pineapple Cake Soak (page 860) complements Coconut Cake (page 853) perfectly.

pulse a few times to purée. You should have about 1 cup. (Save any extra for another use, like to flavor yogurt.)

❷ Combine the flour, baking powder, and salt in a large bowl. In a separate bowl, use an electric mixer to beat the 1$^1/_2$ sticks of butter and the remaining 1 cup sugar until creamy. Add the eggs one at a time and beat until light and smooth. Beat in the apple purée. Mix in about a third of the flour mixture, followed by about half of the milk; add another third of the flour, followed by the rest of the milk, then finally the last of the flour. Stir gently until the batter just evens out.

③ Turn the batter into the prepared pan and bake until the middle is set (your fingers should leave only a small indentation when gently press the cake), 45 to 50 minutes. Meanwhile, prepare the cake soak. Leave the cake in the pan. Cool for about 10 minutes, then pour the cake soak all over the top; let it sit for at least an hour before serving. Store at room temperature, covered with wax paper, for up to 2 days; use plastic wrap and it will keep for an extra day or so.

Beet Cake with Orange Glaze. Substitute 2 medium raw beets for the apples (peel and quarter them before puréeing). Instead of the cake soak, prepare 1 recipe Orange Glaze (page 857). Proceed with the recipe, except instead of finishing with the soak, let the cake cool completely, then glaze.

Parsnip or Carrot Cake with Not-Too-Sweet Buttercream Frosting. Another sweet vegetable that should get more play in desserts: Substitute parsnips (or carrots) for the apples and add $^1/_4$ teaspoon freshly grated nutmeg to the dry ingredients if you like. Prepare 1 recipe Not-Too-Sweet Buttercream Frosting (page 860). Proceed with the recipe, except instead of finishing with the soak, let the cake cool completely, then glaze.

Fennel Cake with Grapefruit Glaze. With a subtle anise flavor: Substitute finely chopped fennel for the apples, grapefruit zest for the lemon zest, and prepare 1 recipe Grapefruit Glaze (page 857) instead of the cake soak. Proceed with the Beet Cake variation above.

Olive Oil Cake

MAKES: 1 rectangular cake or 2 layers (12 to 16 servings)

TIME: About 1 hour, plus time to cool

This is by no means for die-hard health fanatics; truly, it's an entirely delicious cake that uses olive oil for flavor and not just to replace the butter, which it does with excellent results. This cake is fluffy, moist, and extremely versatile.

Sauces, glazes, and frostings you can use with this cake: Serve with Basil–Apple, Pear, or Pineapple Sauce (page 862) or any fruit purée (see page 862), or warm the cake and top with a dollop of Cassis–Orange Marmalade Glaze (page 858).

Butter, for greasing the pan

2 cups all-purpose flour

$1^1/_2$ teaspoons baking powder

$^1/_4$ teaspoon salt

$^1/_2$ cup extra virgin olive oil

1 cup sugar

4 eggs, separated

$^1/_3$ cup freshly squeezed orange juice

2 teaspoons grated or finely minced orange or lemon zest

① Preheat the oven to 350°F. Grease two 8- or 9-inch layer cake pans or one 9 × 13-inch pan with a little butter. Combine the flour, baking powder, and salt in a bowl and set aside.

② Use an electric mixer to beat the $^1/_2$ cup oil with $^3/_4$ cup of the sugar until creamy, then add the egg yolks and beat until thick and fluffy, scraping down the sides of the mixing bowl as necessary (this will take 5 to 7 minutes).

③ Mix in the dry ingredients until smooth. Add the orange juice and zest and stir until blended. In a separate bowl, beat the egg whites until they foam, then sprinkle in the remaining $^1/_4$ cup sugar while beating to soft peaks. Stir them thoroughly but as gently as possible into the batter (the base batter is very thick).

④ Turn into the prepared pan and bake until a toothpick inserted in the center comes out clean, about 35 minutes. Let the cake cool in the pan for 15 minutes before removing it from the pan if you're using the layer cake pans; leave the cake in the 9 × 13-inch pan.

⑤ Frost or glaze if you like (see the headnote for suggestions). Store at room temperature, covered with wax paper, for up to a day or two; use plastic wrap and it will keep for an extra day or so.

F Fast   M Make Ahead   V Vegan

For a fancy presentation without having to deal with elaborate frostings or even slicing the cake, babycakes—individually sized cakes, sort of like cupcakes—are a great option. Just grease a few 6- or 8-ounce ramekins, pour the batter in, and bake.

Because the cakes are smaller, they will cook more quickly, sometimes in only half the original recipe's baking time; so check them frequently. Allow the cakes to cool in their ramekins and serve as is or turn them out as directed. Glaze, soak, coat, or frost and garnish as you would a large cake.

Cupcakes are another great option, one that never goes out of style. The difference, of course, between cupcakes and babycakes is those little accordion cups, which you set into muffin tins and fill. (This also makes them a little smaller.) You can be as plain or as fancy as you like with the decorating. The important thing is that cupcakes turn cake into a hand-held, portable food, perfect for picnics, road trips, and snacking.

Coconut Cake. Dense, rich, and very flavorful: Substitute coconut oil for the olive oil and coconut milk (to make your own, see page 423) for the orange juice. Add 1 cup shredded coconut and omit the orange zest. Proceed with the recipe, folding the shredded coconut in with the coconut milk.

Blueberry–Olive Oil Torte. Also a denser cake, studded with blueberries: Reduce the eggs to 4 yolks and 2 whites. Substitute $^3/_4$ cup milk for the orange juice. Add 4 tablespoons ($^1/_2$ stick) melted butter and 2 cups blueberries (frozen are fine). Grease and flour a 10-inch springform pan. Mix all the ingredients in a bowl like a pancake batter, adding the blueberries last. Proceed to Step 4. Remove from the pan to serve.

Plum-Rosemary Upside-Down Cake

MAKES: One 9-inch cake (at least 8 servings)
TIME: About 1 hour

Juicy, ripe plums caramelize beautifully to create a rich, caramelized topping when the cake is inverted. Use a skillet if you want to maximize this browning effect. The touch of rosemary gives the cake a pleasant floral flavor, which complements the fruit.

Other fruit you can use: apples, blackberries, pitted cherries, cranberries, or apples.

8 tablespoons (1 stick) unsalted butter, melted

$^1/_2$ cup packed dark brown sugar

1 teaspoon finely chopped fresh rosemary leaves

4 or 5 ripe sweet plums, halved, pitted, and cut into chunks

1 cup buttermilk

2 eggs

$^1/_2$ cup sugar

2 cups all-purpose flour

1 teaspoon baking soda

$^1/_4$ teaspoon salt

❶ Preheat the oven to 350°F. Liberally grease a 9-inch round cake pan or cast-iron skillet with half of the butter. Sprinkle the brown sugar and rosemary evenly over the bottom of the pan and spread the plums in the pan in a single layer; set aside.

❷ Whisk the remaining melted butter, buttermilk, eggs, and sugar together until foamy. In a separate bowl, combine the flour, baking soda, and salt. Gradually add the egg mixture to the flour mixture and stir until well incorporated.

❸ Carefully spread the batter over the plums, using a spatula to make sure it's evenly distributed. Bake until the top of the cake is golden brown and a toothpick inserted in the center comes out clean, 50 to 60 minutes. Let the cake cool in the pan for just 5 minutes.

④ Run a knife around the edge of the pan. Put the serving plate on the top of the cake pan and flip the pan so that the serving plate is now on the bottom and the cake pan upside down and on top. The cake should fall out onto the serving plate. If the cake sticks, turn it right side up and run the knife along the edge again, then use a spatula to lift gently around the edge. Invert the cake again and tap on the bottom of the pan. If any of the fruit sticks to the pan, don't worry; simply use a knife to remove the pieces and fill in any gaps on the top of the cake. Serve warm with ice cream.

Fresh Pineapple Upside-Down Cake. Use the sweetest pineapple you can find: Omit the rosemary. Substitute six ¹/₂-inch-thick slices peeled fresh pineapple (see page 435), or as many as will fit in the pan, for the plums and ¹/₂ cup cornmeal for half the all-purpose flour.

Sweet Green Tomato Upside-Down Cake. Use 'em if you have 'em: Omit the rosemary. Substitute 6 or more thick slices green tomatoes for the plums and ¹/₂ cup cornmeal for half the flour if you like.

Pear and Almond Upside-Down Cake. Small Seckel pears look elegant, but full-size pears work too: Substitute ¹/₄ cup chopped almonds for the rosemary; 3 to 4 small ripe pears, peeled, cored, and halved, for the plums; and ¹/₂ cup ground almonds for half the flour. Mix 3 tablespoons almond paste in with the butter.

Honey-Spice Cake

MAKES: 1 loaf (8 or more servings)
TIME: About 1 hour, plus time to cool

Ⓜ

An Eastern European cake with deep, rich gingerbread-like taste and dark color. It's loaded with flavor from the rye flour, spices, honey, and coffee. Add up to a cup of chopped dried fruit and/or nuts if you like.

Sauces, glazes, and frostings you can use with this cake: Drizzle with Mocha Glaze (page 858), soak in Spiced Coffee Cake Soak (page 859), or spread on Not-Too-Sweet Honey Buttercream Frosting (page 860).

2 tablespoons butter, plus butter for the pan

1 tablespoon grated or finely minced orange zest

1¹/₂ cups all-purpose flour

¹/₂ cup rye or whole wheat flour

1 teaspoon baking soda

¹/₂ teaspoon ground cinnamon

Pinch salt

Pinch each ground allspice, nutmeg, cloves, and ginger

2 eggs

¹/₂ cup sugar

¹/₂ cup honey

¹/₂ cup freshly brewed coffee

① Preheat the oven to 350°F. Grease a 9 × 5-inch loaf pan (if you double the recipe, you can use a tube pan). Combine the 2 tablespoons butter and the zest in a small saucepan over medium heat; cook until the butter sizzles, then turn off the heat. Combine the dry ingredients in a large bowl.

② Beat the eggs and sugar together until the mixture is light and thick; beat in the honey and coffee, followed by the butter/zest mixture. Add the dry ingredients by hand, stirring just to combine; do not beat. Pour into the prepared loaf pan and bake for 40 to 50 minutes, or until a toothpick inserted in the center of the loaf comes out clean. Let the cake rest in the pan for 5 minutes before inverting it onto a rack. Remove the pan, then turn the cake right side up. Let cool before slicing.

Raisin or Date Cake. The dried fruit is soaked and puréed, which adds even more deep color and flavor: Add 1 cup raisins or chopped dates. Soak the raisins or dates in the coffee and honey until they soften a bit, then puree until smooth. Proceed with the recipe.

Ⓕ Fast   Ⓜ Make Ahead   Ⓥ Vegan

Molasses-Spice Cake. Really rich in color and flavor: Substitute molasses for the honey. Increase the spices to one large pinch each. Proceed with the recipe.

Chocolate Vanilla Layer Cake

MAKES: One 2-layer cake (about 12 servings)

TIME: About 1 hour, plus time to cool

Though usually viewed as opposite flavors, chocolate and vanilla combine beautifully. Vanilla's perfumy and musky aroma and flavor provide a wonderful backdrop for the earthiness of the chocolate. To get every bit of flavor from the vanilla bean, the whole thing—pod and all—is minced and incorporated into the batter. They sort of melt away into soft bits. If you don't think you can finely mince the whole pod, then scrape out the seeds (see page 859) or use another teaspoon of vanilla extract.

Sauces, glazes, and frostings you can use with this cake: Not-Too-Sweet Buttercream Frosting, Not-Too-Sweet Chocolate Buttercream Frosting (page 860), or Chocolate Ganache (page 860). Fill the inside with raspberry jam if you like.

1 vanilla bean, ends trimmed and finely minced

$^{1}/_{2}$ cup boiling water

1 cup cake or all-purpose flour

$^{3}/_{4}$ cup cocoa powder

$1^{1}/_{2}$ teaspoon baking powder

$^{1}/_{2}$ teaspoon salt

4 large eggs, separated

$1^{1}/_{4}$ cups sugar

$^{1}/_{4}$ cup neutral oil, like grapeseed or corn, or nut oil

1 teaspoon vanilla extract

① Preheat the oven to 350°F. Grease two 8- or 9-inch cake pans. Put the vanilla bean in a large bowl and cover with the boiling water. Let steep for a few minutes while you prepare the other ingredients.

② Combine the flour, cocoa, baking powder, and salt. In a separate bowl, use an electric mixer to beat the egg whites to stiff peaks.

③ Add the yolks, sugar, oil, and extract to the vanilla water and beat until creamy and bubbly. Mix in the dry ingredients until smooth. By hand, fold the egg whites into the batter gently but thoroughly.

④ Spoon the batter into the prepared pans and let it settle for a few seconds. Bake until a toothpick inserted in the center comes out clean, 20 to 25 minutes. Cool for at least 10 minutes before carefully inverting onto racks. Cool completely before frosting first between the layers, then the sides and on top.

Chocolate Nib Layer Cake. These little bits of cocoa beans are now available wherever you can find excellent chocolate: Instead of the minced vanilla bean, use $^{1}/_{4}$ cup finely chopped or ground chocolate nibs.

Chocolate Ginger Layer Cake. Rich chocolate with a kick of ginger: Substitute 2 teaspoons grated or very finely minced peeled fresh ginger or $^{1}/_{4}$ cup finely chopped crystallized ginger for the vanilla bean. Proceed with the recipe. Add crystallized ginger to the buttercream if you like.

Chocolate Cinnamon Layer Cake. Substitute 2 teaspoons ground cinnamon for the vanilla bean.

Glazes, Sauces, Soaks, and Frostings

This section is for those times when you can't resist serving a cake, tart, pie, cobbler, cookie—whatever—with a little something extra. The addition doesn't need to be that sugary; in general, richness and flavor are preferable to added sweetness. Nor are you limited to the traditional concept of "topping." The recipes here provide a range of possibilities, from a dollop of perfectly whipped cream to an ultra-chocolaty (but incredibly easy) ganache, from tasty liquids for soaking to simple fruit-based glazes and sauces.

No special skills are required to master these recipes, but you may need to slightly alter your thinking about finishing, garnishing, and serving desserts. Approach it like you put together any other part of the meal—with components that complement, contrast, or enhance both flavor and texture—and you'll be fine.

Feel free to mix and match any of these recipes with others in the chapter. It's all fair game. The headnotes, variations, and lists have lots of ideas to get you going.

The Basics of Whipped Cream

Whipping cream is so easy there's absolutely no need to buy the canned stuff (which doesn't taste nearly as good and contains ingredients you don't want). You can easily whip smaller amounts of cream with a whisk, though of course a mixer—whether hand-held or upright—is faster.

There are various stages to whipped cream that are good to know for any kind of cooking (they also apply to whipped egg whites; see page 899). Before you start whipping, be sure you have well-chilled cream with as few additives as possible, a clean metal or glass bowl (oil residues will effect the cream's ability to whip up), and a balloon whisk or a mixer fitted with the whisk attachment. One cup of cream will double in volume when whipped and generally serve four to six people. Add the sweetener or flavorings when the cream is just starting to hold a shape.

Then, to know when to stop beating, dip the whisk or beater into the cream and pull up: Once the process is going, you will see these, in order of time:

- Soft peaks: The cream will just make a low peak with a tip that readily folds onto itself.
- Medium peaks: A solid peak but still soft with a tip that folds over but not onto itself.
- Firm peaks: A fairly stiff peak with a tip that hardly bends; dragging your finger through the cream will

leave a distinct mark. It should *not* be clumpy, though (see below).
- Overwhipped: The cream will be clumpy and rough looking. Add a couple tablespoons more cream and stir it in to smooth it out. (Or keep whipping; you'll get butter.)

You can vary the stiffness of the peaks according to the dessert: If you want the cream to melt into the dish, use soft peaks or cream whipped only enough to thicken a bit and drizzle over the top; stiff peaks are good for using as a frosting or filling for cakes or cookies.

Another way to vary your whipped cream is by adding various flavors, like vanilla, ginger, or rose water (see the list below). Alternatively, you can also add a tablespoon or two of sour cream; or whip crème fraîche or mascarpone, which will be tangier or thicker, respectively.

8 Ways to Flavor Whipped Cream

Start with 1 cup of cream and beat until it holds shape before adding any of the following:

1. Vanilla Whipped Cream: Scrape the seeds from $1/2$ pod into the cream or use 1 teaspoon good-quality vanilla extract.
2. Honey Whipped Cream: Use honey instead of sugar.
3. Maple Whipped Cream: Use some maple syrup in place of sugar (add just enough to flavor the whipped cream; if you want it sweeter, add sugar so you don't liquefy the whipped cream).
4. Cinnamon or Nutmeg Whipped Cream: Sprinkle in ground cinnamon, nutmeg, cardamom, or any finely ground sweet spice.
5. Boozy Whipped Cream: Add 1 to 2 tablespoons bourbon, brandy, Kahlúa, Grand Marnier, framboise, amaretto, etc.
6. Citrus Whipped Cream: Add $1/2$ teaspoon or so of grated citrus zest.
7. Ginger Whipped Cream: Add $1/2$ teaspoon finely grated or very finely minced peeled fresh ginger.

8. Rose or Orange Blossom Whipped Cream: Add 1 to 2 teaspoons rose water or orange blossom water.

Sugar Syrup

MAKES: 2 cups
TIME: 10 minutes

Also called *simple syrup,* this is perfect for adding sweetness to something without worrying about the sugar dissolving. It comes in handy when making sorbets, granitas, and iced drinks, including tea, coffee, and cocktails.

Make this syrup in any quantity you need; the ratio—equal parts water and sugar—is always the same.

2 cups sugar

❶ Combine the sugar with 2 cups water in a small pot; bring to a boil and cook until the sugar is dissolved, stirring occasionally. Set aside and cool to room temperature. Use immediately or store in a clean container or jar, covered, in the fridge for up to 6 months.

7 Ways to Flavor Sugar Syrup

Steep the flavoring in the hot syrup for 5 to 10 minutes, then strain out or leave in (for larger items, like vanilla pods).

1. Vanilla bean (page 859), with the scraped pod if you like
2. Cinnamon sticks, whole cloves, allspice, or crushed cardamom pods
3. Citrus zest, any kind, grated, minced, or strips
4. Coffee beans, whole
5. Ginger, peeled and grated or minced
6. Lavender buds (just a bit or it'll taste soapy)
7. Fresh herbs, whole stems, especially mint, peppermint, verbena, and basil

6 Uses for Sugar Syrup

Obviously it sweetens; here's where to use it:

1. Sorbet and granita bases (pages 892–895)
2. Cake soaks (pages 858–860)
3. Dessert soups (pages 903–905)
4. Iced tea, coffee, and cocktails
5. Fruit purées (page 862)
6. Macerating fruit (page 417)

Orange Glaze

MAKES: Enough for any cake
TIME: 10 minutes

This glaze has just the right amount of orange flavor, so it won't overwhelm even the most delicate desserts. Drizzle it on cakes, tarts, or quick breads or decrease the orange juice (or other liquids in the variations) slightly to make a thicker glaze that can be spread on cookies.

Use nearly any citrus in place of the orange; tangerine, grapefruit, and blood orange are all delicious.

1/2 cup freshly squeezed orange juice

1 tablespoon grated orange zest

1/2 teaspoon vanilla extract (optional)

3 cups confectioners' sugar, plus more as needed

Combine all the ingredients and beat until combined and smooth; it should be about the consistency of thick maple syrup—just pourable. Adjust the consistency by adding a little more liquid or a little more sugar. Use immediately or store, covered, in the refrigerator for up to 2 weeks.

Creamy Orange Glaze. Richer with a touch of cream and butter; perfect for cookies: Substitute 1/4 cup cream for half of the orange juice and add 3 tablespoons very soft butter. Whisk until smooth and glossy.

Lemon or Lime Glaze. A bit more zing: Substitute $^1/_4$ cup freshly squeezed lemon or lime juice and $^1/_4$ cup water for the orange juice. Omit the vanilla.

Mocha Glaze. Great for a breakfast or brunch Coffee Cake Muffins (page 693) or Honey-Spice Cake (page 854): Substitute freshly brewed coffee for the orange juice and add 1 ounce melted semisweet or bittersweet chocolate or 3 tablespoons cocoa powder. Omit the zest.

Rose Water Glaze. Omit the orange juice and zest and the vanilla. Use $^1/_2$ cup water, milk, or cream instead of the orange juice and stir in 2 teaspoons (more or less to taste) rose water for the vanilla extract.

Lemon-Clove Glaze. Lovely drizzled on Pine Nut Cookies (page 841): Substitute $^1/_4$ cup freshly squeezed lemon juice and $^1/_4$ cup water for the orange juice, lemon zest for the orange zest, and $^1/_4$ teaspoon ground cloves for the vanilla.

Coconut Glaze. A wonderful glaze for Coconut Snaps (page 842): Substitute coconut milk (to make your own, see page 423) for the orange juice and $^1/_4$ cup shredded coconut for the zest. Omit the vanilla.

Apricot Jam Glaze

MAKES: Enough for any cake
TIME: 15 minutes

Ⓕ Ⓜ Ⓥ

There is no glaze easier than this one, which is jam thinned with water; add the cardamom and it instantly becomes exotic. This glaze can be whipped up in minutes and kept in the fridge for a couple of weeks. Since it's pretty sticky, it must be drizzled or brushed onto cakes; use it to smear on cookies as a glaze or filling for cookie "sandwiches" (see page 839) or on sweet quick breads or muffins (see pages 691–695), including Scones (page 695), Doughnut Puffs (page 696), and Fruit Fritters (page 697).

This glaze is great on Coriander Snaps (page 842), Olive Oil Cake (page 852), or Yogurt Pound Cake (page 850).

1 cup apricot jam or preserves
1 teaspoon ground cardamom (optional)

Put the jam and cardamom with 1 cup water in a small pot over medium heat. Bring to a low bubble and cook to a syrupy consistency, about 10 minutes. Set aside to cool; use immediately or store, covered, in the refrigerator for up to 2 weeks.

Berry Jam Glaze. Strawberry, raspberry, blackberry, and blueberry are all delicious; use it on Ginger Pound Cake (page 849): Substitute any berry jam for the apricot and add 2 teaspoons finely minced peeled fresh ginger if you like.

Cassis–Orange Marmalade Glaze. A great combination of flavors; use it on Almond Cake (page 850): Substitute orange marmalade for the apricot jam and add $^1/_4$ cup cassis liqueur.

Port–Cherry Jam Glaze. More serious, deeper flavors; use it on Chocolate Vanilla Layer Cake (page 855): Substitute cherry jam or preserves for the apricot and add $^1/_2$ cup port wine.

Vanilla Cake Soak

MAKES: Enough for any single-layer square or round cake
TIME: 10 minutes

Ⓕ Ⓜ

If you've never soaked a cake before, you're missing a real treat. The process turns it into something else entirely, almost like a pudding, only with more structure. And depending on the soak you choose, the flavor can run from subtle to pronounced. Using real vanilla beans in this cake soak is key; the rich flavor can't be replicated by vanilla extract. That doesn't mean you *can't* use vanilla extract, but don't expect the same results.

 Fast   Make Ahead   Ⓥ Vegan

For oblong or other large cakes baked in bundt or tube pans, double this recipe.

$^1/_2$ cup sugar

2 tablespoons butter

1 vanilla bean or 1 tablespoon vanilla extract

1 Put $^1/_2$ cup water, the sugar, and the butter in a small pot. Split the vanilla bean in half lengthwise and use a small sharp knife to scrape the seeds into the butter mixture; add the pod. Cook at a slow bubble, whisking frequently, until the sugar is dissolved and the liquid is slightly thickened, about 10 minutes. Let it cool to room temperature, then remove and discard the pod.

2 Leave the cake in the pan (or return it if it was out cooling); pour the soak over the cake and let it sit for at least an hour. (Or put the soak in a jar and refrigerate for a day or two; bring to room temperature before using.)

Vanilla–Brown Sugar Cake Soak. For a caramelized flavor: Simply substitute brown sugar for white sugar.

Boozy Cake Soak. For adults only; use it on Boozy Apple Cake (page 851): Substitute bourbon or Calvados, whiskey, brandy, cognac, limoncello, or any compatible liquor for the water: For Step 1, either proceed as directed or combine the sugar, butter, and vanilla; cook and let sit, then add the alcohol. Proceed with the recipe.

Spiced Coffee Cake Soak. Excellent with Honey-Spice Cake (page 854); substitute freshly brewed strong coffee for the water and $^1/_4$ teaspoon each ground cinnamon, allspice, and cardamom for the vanilla. In Step 1, combine the sugar, butter, and spices; cook and let sit, then add the coffee. Proceed with the recipe.

Using a Vanilla Bean

(STEP 1) To use a vanilla bean, split it in half the long way.

(STEP 2) Scrape out the seeds. Reserve the pod for vanilla sugar (see "Everyday Spices," pages 811–814).

Real vanilla beans can make a tremendous difference in many desserts, though they are becoming *very* expensive—as much as $8 for a single bean. You want to get as much flavor out of such an expensive item as possible—down to the last tiny seed.

Use a small sharp knife to split the bean lengthwise; use the tip of the blade to scrape the seeds out of each half. Put the seeds in the other ingredient(s) and give the pods another scraping.

If you're adding the seeds to a liquid, you can add the emptied pods to the liquid to extract more flavor from the pods. Otherwise, bury the pods in a container with some sugar; cut into pieces and add to your vanilla extract; or steep with your next pot of tea or coffee. Whatever you do, don't let the pods' remnant vanilla flavor go to waste.

See the Vanilla Beans entry in "Everyday Spices," page 814, for more information.

Jasmine Tea Cake Soak. Good-quality, fragrant jasmine tea is key here; use it with a plain vanilla or angel food cake: Substitute strong jasmine tea for the water and omit the vanilla.

Vanilla Milk Cake Soak. The milk cuts the sweetness and adds richness; good with the Almond Cake (page 850): Substitute dairy or any nondairy milk or cream for the water.

Coconut-Pineapple Cake Soak. Tropical and "creamy" from the coconut milk; add a splash of rum if you like; pairs great with Coconut Cake (page 853): Substitute coconut milk (to make your own, see page 423) for the water and 1 cup pineapple juice for the water. Omit the vanilla.

Not-Too-Sweet Buttercream Frosting

MAKES: Enough for any cake
TIME: 10 minutes

A close relative of true buttercream frosting, but a little more buttery and a little less sweet. It's rich and flavorful, though, so you'll probably find yourself using less than you would traditional buttercream, just a smear instead of piling it on. For a real treat, you can also use this frosting instead of butter on pancakes, waffles, and French toast or on sweet quick breads, muffins, or scones.

12 tablespoons (1¹/₂ sticks) butter, softened

2¹/₂ cups confectioners' sugar

Pinch salt

¹/₄ cup plus 2 tablespoons cream or milk, plus a little more if needed

2 teaspoons vanilla extract

① Use a fork or an electric mixer to cream the butter. Gradually work in the sugar and salt, alternating with the cream and beating well after each addition.

② Stir in the vanilla. If the buttercream is too thin, refrigerate; it will thicken as the butter hardens.

Not-Too-Sweet Chocolate Buttercream Frosting. Not too sweet, not too chocolaty; wonderful with Chocolate Vanilla Layer Cake or any of its variations (page 855): Add 2 ounces melted and cooled unsweetened chocolate to the mixture after adding about half the sugar. Start with 2 tablespoons cream and add more if needed.

Not-Too-Sweet Maple Buttercream Frosting. Great for cakes as well as pancakes, waffles, and French toast: Substitute ¹/₂ cup maple syrup for 1 cup of the confectioners' sugar. Omit the vanilla extract. Start with 2 tablespoons cream and add more if needed.

Not-Too-Sweet Honey Buttercream Frosting. Wonderful on Honey-Spice Cake (page 854): Substitute ¹/₂ cup honey for 1 cup of the confectioners' sugar. Omit the vanilla. Start with 2 tablespoons cream and add more if needed. Proceed with the recipe.

Chocolate Ganache

MAKES: About 1¹/₂ cups
TIME: 15 minutes

Ganache, one of the most useful of all dessert sauces, sounds far more difficult than it is, thanks to its French name. But it's a snap to make and can take on a number of different guises (see "4 Uses for Chocolate Ganache," page 861).

You can use milk or white chocolate in place of bittersweet chocolate; just decrease the cream to ³/₄ cup.

1 cup cream

8 ounces bittersweet chocolate, chopped

① Put the cream in a pot and heat it until it's steaming. Put the chocolate in a bowl, pour on the hot cream,

Few dessert sauces have as many uses as ganache; here are my favorites.

Cake Coating: Put your cake on a wire rack over a baking sheet with sides. Warm the ganache; it should be slightly thicker than heavy cream so it can spread over the cake. Pour or ladle the ganache onto the cake from the middle outward, letting it flow down the sides of the cake as well. Do not spread the ganache as it will pick up cake crumbs and ruin the smooth coating. Transfer the cake—rack, pan, and all—to the fridge until the ganache sets, about 30 minutes. Transfer the cake to the serving plate and scrape up the leftover ganache in the pan; use it for filling or truffles (it will have crumbs in it, so it's not suitable as a coating or sauce). Lovely with Almond Cake (page 850) or Chocolate Vanilla Layer Cake (page 855).

Cake Filling: Starting with a sturdy cake that doesn't crumb much, warm the ganache so it's spreadable; use a warm spatula to spread a layer of ganache $1/4$ inch thick or so over the surface of the cake. (For a fragile cake that crumbles easily, follow the directions in "Cake Coating" above.)

Sauce: Thin the ganache with additional cream; it should be easily pourable and not harden too much when cooled to room temperature. To test the consistency, spread a small spoonful on a plate; it should thicken but remain very soft if not saucy. Pair it with Banana Strudel (page 880), Spiced Walnut Bread Pudding (page 886), or Cream Puffs (page 697).

Quick Truffles: Chill the ganache in the fridge until it's solid all the way through, 1 to 2 hours, depending on quantity. Scoop out a tablespoonful, quickly roll it into a 1-inch ball (wearing latex gloves helps to prevent melting); repeat, lining the truffles on a plate or baking sheet. If the truffles become too soft to handle, stick them in the fridge or freezer for a few minutes. Roll them in cocoa powder, confectioners' sugar, or a sugar and ground cinnamon mixture. Serve immediately or store, wrapped with plastic, in the fridge for a day or so.

and whisk until the chocolate is melted and incorporated into the cream.

2 Use immediately as a sauce or coating or let cool to room temperature and whip to a smooth frosting.

Chocolate Glaze or Frosting. Use ganache as it is, or beat in confectioners' sugar $1/4$ cup at a time until the mixture is the desired sweetness and consistency.

5 Ways to Flavor Ganache

Here are a few simple ways to make the flavor of ganache more complex.

1. Orange zest, grated or finely minced
2. Crystallized ginger, minced, or peeled and very finely minced fresh ginger
3. Ground spices, like cinnamon, cardamom, allspice, nutmeg, and star anise
4. Earl Grey tea (steep in the hot cream for about 10 minutes or so, then strain)
5. Freshly brewed espresso or instant espresso powder

Vanilla-Berry Sauce

MAKES: About 2 cups (6 to 8 servings)
TIME: 15 minutes

A model for any fruit sauce, this is straightforward and equally wonderful on cake, cheesecake, ice cream, custard, pancakes, waffles, and crêpes. Leave it chunky with the pieces of fruit providing some texture (especially nice with whole berries) or put it in the blender and purée it for a smooth sauce. And of course you can always skip the vanilla.

2 cups any berries, whole or chopped as necessary

$^1/_4$ cup sugar, or as needed

$^1/_2$ vanilla bean

1 Put the berries, sugar, and $^1/_2$ cup water in a saucepan. Split the vanilla bean in half lengthwise and use a small sharp knife to scrape the seeds into the berry mixture; add the pod.

2 Cook at a slow bubble, stirring occasionally, until the sugar is dissolved and the berries are softened but not mushy, about 5 minutes, depending on ripeness and berry type; discard the vanilla pod. Serve warm, room temperature, or chilled or store, covered, in the fridge for up to 4 days.

Basil-Apple, Pear, or Pineapple Sauce. Serve with Basil Ice Cream (page 890): Substitute 2 cups sliced apple, pear, or pineapple (peel and core as necessary) for the berries and 2 stems basil for the vanilla. Remove the basil leaves and finely chiffonade (see page 21). Proceed with the recipe, stirring in the basil leaves just before serving.

Citrus-Mango Sauce. Almost sweet-tart; if the mangoes are ripe, you'll hardly need any sugar; serve it with Coconut Ice Cream (page 890) or Frozen Yogurt (page 892): Substitute diced mango for the berries and 2 tablespoons mixed grated or finely minced lemon, lime, and orange zests for the vanilla. Add 2 tablespoons any citrus juice. Proceed with the recipe, stirring in the citrus juice just before serving.

Creamy Apricot Sauce. A creamy sauce with a sweet richness, especially good puréed; lovely drizzled over Cornmeal Pound Cake (page 849) or Leftover Pound Cake Strudel (page 881): Substitute ripe diced apricot for the berries and cream for the water. Keep or omit the vanilla. Proceed with the recipe; purée in a blender if you like.

Fruit Purées

Puréed fruit makes a light and delicious sauce and is also a common ingredient in dessert recipes. Both raw and cooked fruit make great purées, and both are easy to prepare since nearly any fruit can be puréed, from berries to peaches, melons to apples. Obviously, you want to remove large pits, seeds, thick or tough skin, stems, and other inedible bits.

There are three good ways to purée fruit. The best method is using a blender; it's quick and makes a smooth if not velvety purée. The food processor is equally quick; it won't make a super-smooth purée with hard fruit like raw apples, but soft or cooked fruit becomes perfectly smooth. The third option is the hand method; use a fork or potato masher or press the fruit through a fine-meshed strainer set over a bowl—this works well only for cooked or very soft fruit, and it's more time consuming.

Occasionally you'll want to add liquid to the purée—for flavoring, sweetness, or simply if the fruit is hard and needs some liquid to get the purée going. Fruit juice, water, cream, or lemon or lime juice are good options, depending on the fruit and your intention. If you're adding the liquid for the purpose of getting the purée going, add the liquid by the tablespoonful so you don't add more than you need and dilute the fruit flavor.

For fruits that brown, like raw apples, pears, and bananas, always add a good squeeze or two of lemon or lime juice to minimize browning. Additionally, before puréeing, coat the fruit and cutting board in the juice before chopping it; add a few drops after each cut. This also prevents browning, though there will be some.

Strawberries, raspberries, blackberries, seeded grapes, and other fruit with tiny seeds that you can't easily remove beforehand should be strained after puréeing. So should fibrous fruit, like mangoes. Otherwise, strain as you think it's necessary to remove unwanted bits of flesh or skin. You will probably need to use a wooden spoon or the back of a ladle to push the pulp through a strainer; be sure to scrape the underside of the strainer to remove every last drop of puréed fruit.

 Fast   Make Ahead   Ⓥ Vegan

Anise-Plum or Cherry Sauce. Serve with Cornmeal Pound Cake (page 849) or Almond Cake (page 850): Substitute chopped plums or pitted cherries (frozen is fine) for the berries and 1 teaspoon anise seed for the vanilla.

Almond Custard Sauce

MAKES: About 2 cups (6 to 8 servings)
TIME: 15 minutes

Ⓕ Ⓜ Ⓥ

A spin on crème Anglaise, the English-style custard sauce, only this one-step, one-pot method is super-easy and lends itself to many more variations. See "Infusing Liquids with Flavor" (page 894) for some ideas; since you strain the sauce anyway, just add ingredients right into the pot as the custard cooks. If you prefer a richer sauce, use cream in place of some or all of the milk. Feel free to use hazelnuts, cashews, peanuts, or pistachios here. I love this with Almond Cake (page 850), but it's also delicious drizzled over Cream Puffs (page 697) or for dipping Churros (page 697).

$3/4$ cup chopped almonds

2 cups milk

$1/2$ cup sugar

4 egg yolks

❶ Put the almonds in a medium saucepan over medium heat. Cook, shaking the pan occasionally, until fragrant and beginning to toast, about 3 minutes.

❷ Add the remaining ingredients and whisk well to combine. Cook, whisking almost constantly, until the mixture thickens and reaches 175–180°F. Do not let it boil. (There will be a thick coating on the back of a spoon; see the illustration on page 884.)

❸ While still hot, strain the sauce through a sieve and let cool a bit. You can serve warm or chilled. The sauce keeps, tightly covered, in the refrigerator for up to 3 days.

Vanilla Custard Sauce. The classic: Omit the almonds and skip to Step 2, adding 1 split vanilla bean to the pot.

Chocolate Custard Sauce. Omit the almonds (or not). In Step 2, add $1/2$ cup (about 3 ounces) chopped semisweet or bittersweet chocolate to the pot and let it melt as the mixture heats.

Pies, Tarts, Cobblers, and Crisps

Once a fundamental part of American home cooking, these desserts are considered a big deal by many people today. But pies, tarts, cobblers, and crisps are far from difficult, and they're not even that time consuming. Most pies and tarts can be started and finished in an hour or so (and much of that time is barely attended baking), and cobblers and crisps are even faster.

What they all have in common is some form of crust, a universally loved treat that almost always depends on a fair amount of fat—usually butter—to make it light, flaky, and delicious. What distinguishes pies and tarts from cobblers and crisps is the composition of the crust, how it is formed, and whether it's on top or on bottom.

The Basics of Crusts

A crust can just about make or break a pie or tart; that's why people who make "perfect" crusts—your aunt Ida, perhaps?—are legendary. And dedicated pie makers do get better and better at producing flaky, flavorful, nicely shaped, and beautifully colored crusts. But it need not take years of trial and error to get the technique just so; in fact, you can make really good crusts for pies, tarts, cheesecakes, crisps, and more your first time out, and you'll improve quickly and steadily if you use the right ingredients and techniques.

First, ingredients: There are so few ingredients in a

basic crust—many are nothing but butter, flour, water, and maybe a little salt and sugar—that it's absolutely vital that each one be of good quality and flavor. The best crusts start with butter, and although there are people who use a percentage (sometimes a very high percentage) of shortening, I use all butter: It gives the crust a rich, delicious flavor and good color (shortening does help with texture, but it has a neutral or even negative impact on flavor, not to mention the concerns over partially hydrogenated fats).

Technique turns that butter and other basic ingredients into something magical. But it isn't difficult; I routinely use my food processor to mix the dough for crusts, and I recommend you do too—it's quick, easy, efficient, and nearly foolproof. You can mix the dough by hand, of course, pinching the butter with flour between your fingers, or using various utensils like a pastry blender or two forks. However you do it, the idea is to get small bits of butter coated in flour, which will make for a flaky and light crust. When the dough is formed, you will be able to see bits of butter in it; this is a good thing—don't think it needs to be mixed more. In fact, the dough for pies and tarts should be handled minimally, because you don't want the gluten to develop as it does in bread dough; in these crusts you want tenderness, not chew.

Once you make a dough, it's best to let it rest in order to relax the gluten further. This is done in the refrigerator or freezer so the bits of butter in the dough harden, which makes rolling easier. Equally important, it helps the crust hold its shape in baking and become flaky. Once the dough is frozen, it can be stored in the freezer for weeks or even months (be sure to wrap it well to prevent freezer burn).

Rolling the Dough

Transforming dough from a ball or disk to a fairly uniform $1/4$-inch-thick round crust results from a combina-

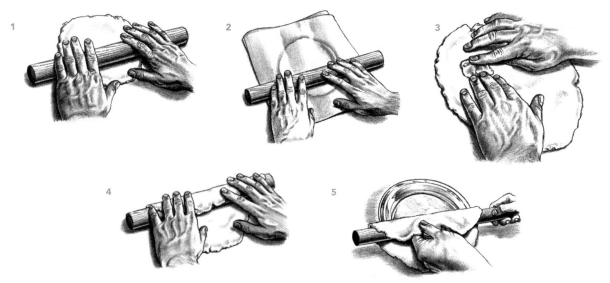

(STEP 1) Roll with firm, steady, but not overly hard pressure, from the inside out, sprinkling with tiny amounts of flour if necessary. (STEP 2) You can also roll between 2 sheets of plastic wrap, which is sometimes easy. If at any point during rolling the dough becomes sticky, refrigerate it for 15 minutes or so. (STEP 3) You can patch any holes with pieces of dough from the edges. (STEP 4) When the dough is ready, pick it up using the rolling pin (flour the dough and pin very lightly first and then (STEP 5) drape it over your pie plate.

Ⓕ Fast   Ⓜ Make Ahead   Ⓥ Vegan

tion of patience and practice. Ideally, you'll roll the dough out only once, because rerolling will make it tougher. At first, though, you may need more than one try. Although rolling tart dough makes a more even and flat crust, it can just be pressed into the pan.

Here are some tips that will make rolling dough easier:

- Start with dough that is firm but not cold or frozen. It should yield a bit to pressure, but your fingers shouldn't sink in (if they do, refrigerate or freeze for a while longer).
- Flour the work surface and the top of the dough to prevent sticking to the counter and the rolling pin. Beginners should use flour liberally; as you get the hang of it, you'll use less and less flour. Alternatively, put the dough between two pieces of plastic wrap and roll it in there; as long as the dough is not too sticky, this will work just fine.
- Roll from the middle of the disk outward, rotating the rolling pin and the dough to make sure it's rolled evenly. Apply even and firm but gentle pressure to the rolling pin.
- Fix any holes with pieces that break off at the edges; add a dab of water to help seal your patches in place. Don't try to pinch the hole closed.
- If the dough becomes sticky, slide it onto a baking sheet and stick it in the freezer for a few minutes.
- When the dough is rolled out, move it to the pie plate or tart pan by draping it over the rolling pin and moving it into the plate or by picking up your plastic wrap, removing one side, laying it in place, then removing the other side.
- Press the dough firmly into the plate all over. Refrigerate for about an hour before filling (if you're in a hurry, freeze for a half hour or so).

Once the dough is in the pan, you can trim it and make the edge more attractive.

Tarts typically have a simple edge: Just use a knife to cut away the excess dough. Fluted tart pans make a pretty, ruffled-looking edge without any extra work on your part.

You can flute the edges of a piecrust in a variety of different ways. Three of the easiest are:

Pinch the dough between the side of your forefinger and your thumb.

Press a knuckle from one side into the space made by your thumb and forefinger on the other.

Simply press down with the tines of a fork along the edges of the dough.

Piecrusts, on the other hand, have more elaborate edges. Different pie makers prefer different techniques, some more complicated than others. Here are three that you can master quickly:

- **Pinching method:** Pinch the edges of the dough between the side of your forefinger and your thumb.
- **Knuckle method:** Use the thumb and forefinger of one hand (usually your left) to hold the dough in place from the inside. Then press a knuckle from your other hand against the crust, pushing it into the space made by your thumb and forefinger.
- **Fork method:** Simply press down with the tines of a fork along the edges of the dough.

Baking the Crust

There's not much mystery behind baking crust. There are a couple ways to go about it: either baking the whole pie, filling and all, or prebaking ("blind baking") the crust alone first. Though it adds a step, in many if not most cases prebaking the crust gives better results; see "Prebaking Pie and Tart Crusts," page 872, for more information.

When you're baking a filled pie, always put it on a cookie sheet; it encourages bottom browning and prevents spillovers from cooking onto your oven floor. If your crust edges start to get too dark, loosely wrap a ring of foil around them.

Sweet Piecrust

MAKES: Enough for an 8- to 10-inch single-crust pie

TIME: 20 minutes, plus time to rest

Ⓕ Ⓜ

I've used this recipe and technique for years and always been pleased with the results. The crust is flaky and flavorful, and it holds its own no matter what the filling. This may be basic, but piecrusts don't get any better.

See "Prebaking Pie and Tart Crusts" (page 872) when using a very moist filling, like a custard or juicy fruit filling or when using a precooked or raw filling.

1 cup plus 2 tablespoons (about 5 ounces) all-purpose flour, plus more for rolling

$1/2$ teaspoon salt

1 teaspoon sugar

8 tablespoons (1 stick) cold unsalted butter, cut into about 8 pieces

3 tablespoons ice water, plus more if necessary

❶ Combine the flour, salt, and sugar in a food processor and pulse once or twice. Add the butter and turn on the machine; process until the butter and flour are blended and the mixture looks like cornmeal, about 10 seconds.

❷ Put the mixture in a bowl and add 3 tablespoons ice water; mix with your hands until you can form the dough into a ball, adding another tablespoon or two of ice water if necessary (if you overdo it and the mixture becomes sodden, add a little more flour). Form into a ball, wrap in plastic, and freeze for 10 minutes or refrigerate for at least 30 minutes. (You can refrigerate for up to a couple of days or freeze for up to a couple of weeks.)

❸ Sprinkle a clean countertop with flour, put the dough on it, and sprinkle the top with flour. Use a rolling pin to roll with light pressure, from the center out. If the dough is hard, let it rest for a few minutes. If the dough is sticky, add a little flour (if it continues to become sticky, and it's taking you more than a few minutes to roll it out, refrigerate or freeze again). Roll, adding flour and rotating and turning the dough as needed; use ragged edges of dough to repair any tears, adding a drop of water while you press the patch into place. (See the illustrations on page 864.)

❹ When you've rolled the dough to a diameter 2 inches larger than that of your pie plate, move it into the pie plate by draping it over the rolling pin and moving it into the plate. Press the dough firmly into the plate all over. Refrig-

 Ⓕ Fast   Ⓜ Make Ahead   Ⓥ Vegan

erate for about an hour before filling (if you're in a hurry, freeze for a half hour or so).

⑤ Trim the excess dough to about $^1/_2$ inch all around, then tuck it under itself around the edge of the plate. Decorate the edges with a fork or your fingers, using any of the methods illustrated on page 865. Freeze the dough for 10 minutes or refrigerate it for 30 minutes.

⑥ When you're ready to bake, either fill it or prick it all over with a fork for prebaking (see page 872).

Savory Piecrust. What you want for savory quiches, tarts, and so forth: Omit the sugar. Any of the other variations can be made savory by omitting the sugar as well.

Wheat Piecrust. Adding whole wheat flour gives the crust a more intricate, slightly nutty flavor and a deeper, golden brown color; there's some sacrifice in texture, but it's a worthwhile trade-off: Substitute $^1/_2$ cup whole wheat for $^1/_2$ cup of the all-purpose flour. A bit more ice water may be necessary.

Oat Piecrust. Oats give this crust great texture: Substitute just over $^1/_2$ cup rolled oats (not instant) for $^1/_4$ cup of the all-purpose flour. Pulse the oats in a food processor for a few seconds until they are partially ground (mostly flour, but with some roughly chopped pieces).

Nut Piecrust. Rich and delicious, especially with macadamias: Substitute $^1/_4$ cup finely chopped or ground nuts for $^1/_4$ cup of the all-purpose flour. Pulse a few extra times in the food processor before adding the butter in Step 1.

Sweet Tart Crust

MAKES: Enough for an 8- to 10-inch tart
TIME: 20 minutes, plus time to rest

Ⓕ Ⓜ

This contains more butter than the preceding piecrust, and an egg makes it extra-rich and perfect for tarts. You might think of this as a large cookie, and, like a cookie, it has many possible variations.

1$^1/_4$ cups all-purpose flour, plus more for rolling

$^1/_2$ teaspoon salt

2 tablespoons sugar

10 tablespoons frozen or cold butter, cut into chunks

1 egg yolk

3 tablespoons ice water, plus more if necessary

① Combine the flour, salt, and sugar in a food processor and pulse once or twice. Add the butter all at once; process until the mixture is uniform, about 10 seconds (do not overprocess). Add the egg and process for another few seconds.

② Put the mixture in a bowl and add the ice water; mix with your hands until you can form the dough into a ball, adding another tablespoon or two of ice water if necessary (if you overdo it and the mixture becomes sodden, add a little more flour). Form into a ball, wrap in plastic, and freeze for 10 minutes or refrigerate for at least 30 minutes. (You can refrigerate for up to a couple of days, freeze for up to a couple of weeks.)

③ Sprinkle a countertop with flour and put the dough on it; sprinkle the top with a little flour. Use a rolling pin to roll with light pressure from the center out. If the dough is sticky, add a little flour (if it continues to become sticky, and it's taking you more than a few minutes to roll it out, refrigerate or freeze again). Roll, adding flour and rotating and turning the dough as needed; use ragged edges of dough to repair any tears, adding a drop of water while you press the patch into place.

④ When you've rolled the dough to a diameter about 2 inches larger than that of your tart pan, move the dough into the tart pan by draping it over the rolling pin and moving it into the pan. Press the dough into all the nooks and crannies in the pan, being careful not to overwork it, and use a knife to cut the edges

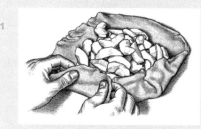

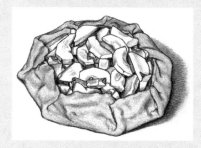

(STEP 1) To make a free-form galette, roll out the dough, then spread it with the topping, to just an inch or two within the edge. Fold the edges over, crimping them so they remain in place, (STEP 2) until you've gone around the entire circumference of the dough.

The simplest—and most rustic—tarts are baked free-form, without a tart pan. Called *galettes* in France, these can be made with both sweet or savory dough and fillings and virtually any relatively pliable tart crust. See Spicy Winter Squash Galette (page 368).

Here's how to make one using regular dough. Gather the ingredients for Sweet Tart Crust (page 867), only set aside 2 tablespoons of the butter. Prepare and rest the dough as directed.

When you're ready to bake, preheat the oven to 425°F. Either roll the crust out on a board sprinkled with flour or sprinkle it lightly with flour and roll it between two sheets of plastic or parchment. It doesn't have to be perfectly round. Put the crust directly on a baking sheet. Melt the remaining butter.

Cover the round with filling, leaving about a 1$\frac{1}{2}$-inch border all around. You'll need 2 to 3 cups; make sure it's not too wet. Fold up the edges of the crust around the fruit, pinching them together. Don't try to cover all of the fruit, just the outer rim of it. Brush the exposed dough with most of the butter and brush a little onto the fruit as well. Bake until the crust is golden brown and the fruit bubbly, 20 to 30 minutes. Remove from the oven and cool on a rack; serve warm or at room temperature.

at the rim of the pan. Refrigerate for about an hour before filling (if you're in a hurry, freeze for a half hour or so).

Savory Tart Crust. What you want for savory tarts or for any type of sugarless tart crust: Omit the sugar. Most of the other variations can be made savory by omitting the sugar as well.

Nut Tart Crust. A bit of nuts adds great flavor and texture: Substitute $\frac{1}{2}$ cup ground nuts, like almonds, hazelnuts, walnuts, pecans, macadamias, or peanuts, for $\frac{1}{2}$ cup of the all-purpose flour.

Chocolate Tart Crust. An even richer-flavored crust; be sure it doesn't overwhelm the filling: Add $\frac{1}{4}$ cup cocoa powder along with the flour.

Baked Crumb Crust

MAKES: Enough for an 8- to 10-inch tart or pie
TIME: 20 minutes

Ⓕ Ⓜ

A simple crust that is great when you want to whip something together without having to chill, rest, or roll a more

Ⓕ Fast   Ⓜ Make Ahead   Ⓥ Vegan

traditional crust. It has a slightly crumbly texture that is lovely with more structured fillings—like cheesecake—that don't rely on the crust to hold them together.

This is a little different from the traditional graham cracker crust, where you use melted butter to moisten the crumb-and-sugar mixture before you press it into the pan. This technique makes a more cohesive, finer crust. It's worth the extra few minutes. If you use dried crumbs from a plain loaf of bread, you might want to increase the sugar by a tablespoon or so, depending on the filling. Taste it after mixing and see. If you use the oil instead of butter, the crust will become vegan.

1½ cups dried bread or graham cracker crumbs

3 tablespoons brown sugar

Pinch salt

4 tablespoons melted butter or neutral oil, like grapeseed or corn, or extra virgin olive oil

1 Preheat the oven to 350°F. Put the crumbs, sugar, and salt in a food processor or a bowl. Slowly add the butter, processing or stirring until well blended.

2 Press the crumb mixture into the bottom and sides of a pie or tart pan. Bake the crust until it just begins to brown, 10 to 15 minutes. Cool on a rack before filling; it will crisp up as it cools.

Baked Savory Crumb Crust. This is really great with quiche: Instead of the graham cracker crumbs, use bread crumbs (either alone or in combination with cooked grains) and omit the sugar. If you like, add about 2 tablespoons minced shallot or onion; ¼ cup chopped mild fresh herbs, like parsley, cilantro, chives, chervil, or basil or 2 tablespoons stronger herbs, like rosemary, oregano, marjoram, or thyme; and freshly ground black pepper.

Baked Gingersnap Crumb Crust. Any crisp cookie—from vanilla wafers to chocolate cookies—works here; if the cookie is very buttery, reduce the butter or oil by 1 or 2 tablespoons: Substitute gingersnap cookie crumbs for the bread or graham cracker crumbs.

No-Bake Fruit and Nut Crust

MAKES: Enough for an 8- to 10-inch tart or pie
TIME: 10 minutes

There's no messing up this sweet, chewy, and crunchy crust; it's so straightforward. Use any nuts and any dried fruit you want; the nuts provide great flavor and texture, while the dried fruit provides sweetness and a pliable and chewy texture to form a pasty "dough" that is pressed into the pan.

1 cup almonds or any nuts

¾ cup pitted and packed dried fruit, like dates, raisins, dried cherries, figs, or apricots

1 Put the nuts in a food processor and pulse until ground (but not puréed into nut butter); transfer it to a bowl. Put the dried fruit in the food processor, add a teaspoon or so of water, and pulse until finely chopped and a bit pasty (some fruit will need a bit more water than others); add to the bowl. Mix the nuts and dried fruit until well combined. (At this point, you can form the mixture into a disk, wrap it in plastic, and refrigerate or freeze until about 30 minutes before you're ready to use it; defrost if necessary and proceed with the recipe.)

2 Press the mixture into the bottom and sides of a pie or tart pan or individual pans or ramekins and add the filling. To make free-form individual pies, simply divide the dough into 8 pieces and press to shape on a piece of wax paper or parchment.

No-Bake Fruit and Coconut Crust. Sweet and coconutty: Substitute 1½ cups shredded coconut for the nuts. You can skip the pulsing of the coconut if you like, though doing so will create a more finely textured crust.

7 No-Bake Ways to Fill Any No-Bake Tart Crust

Form the crust and fill it with any of the following for a quick and lovely tart.

1. Whole or sliced berries, macerated in some sugar and a splash of orange-flavored liqueur if you like
2. Chocolate Ganache (page 860), topped with toasted nuts
3. Any cooked pudding (page 895), including Rice Pudding (page 895), garnished with fruit if you like
4. Mascarpone or softened cream cheese topped with fig, strawberry, apricot, or peach or nectarine slices
5. Any mousse (page 897) spread or piped in (page 902), frozen if you like
6. Nutella or any chocolate-hazelnut spread with sliced banana or pitted cherries
7. Sliced apples sautéed in butter and sugar or poached pears (page 433)

Sweet Crumble Topping

MAKES: About 2 cups
TIME: 10 minutes

Ⓕ Ⓜ

Essentially a streusel, this topping is like a delicate—and crumbled—nut cookie. It's lovely on any crisp (page 878), as well as sprinkled on quick breads, muffins, or tarts and pies before baking. Use the whole wheat flour for a more robust flavor; change the nuts and spices to vary the flavor or complement a particular flavor in the dish in which it's being used; add about 3 tablespoons cocoa powder for a chocolate crumble topping.

8 tablespoons (1 stick) butter

1 cup packed brown sugar

$1/2$ cup chopped walnuts or pecans

1 tablespoon freshly squeezed lemon juice

$1/2$ teaspoon ground cinnamon, or to taste

1 cup all-purpose or whole wheat flour, plus more as needed

Pinch salt

❶ Cream the butter and brown sugar together using an electric mixer, food processor, or fork. Stir or pulse in the remaining ingredients until combined and crumbly; it won't hold together like a dough. (You can make this in advance if you like; pile onto a piece of plastic and wrap, then refrigerate or freeze until about 30 minutes before you're ready to use it. Defrost if necessary, then use.)

❷ Crumble the mixture over a crisp, quick bread, or muffins. Or bake in a 350°F oven until golden brown and use as a filling for crêpes (page 196).

Citrus-Spice Crumble Topping. Perfect with Cherry Crisp (page 878): Add 1 tablespoon mixed grated or finely minced citrus zest, like lemon, lime, orange, or grapefruit. Substitute $1/2$ teaspoon each ground coriander and freshly ground black pepper for the cinnamon. Proceed with the recipe.

Oat Crumble Topping. The classic for crisps: If you like, substitute maple syrup or corn syrup for the brown sugar, and $1/2$ cup rolled oats (or other rolled grain) for half of the flour. Proceed with the recipe.

Rice Flour Crumble Topping. Rice flour makes this very delicate: Substitute rice flour for the all-purpose flour. Proceed with the recipe.

Cracked Wheat Crumble Topping. Bulgur, wheat berries, or brown rice will work just as well: Substitute cooked cracked wheat (page 537) for the nuts. Proceed with the recipe.

Coconut Crumble Topping. Use this with Banana-Date Cobbler (page 878): Substitute shredded coconut for the walnuts. Omit the cinnamon, if you like. Proceed with the recipe.

Hazelnut or Almond Crumble Topping. A delicious sweet, nutty flavor; it's particularly good baked and used as a crêpe filling (page 196): Substitute hazelnuts or almonds, preferably blanched, for the walnuts or pecans, and 3 tablespoons hazelnut or almond paste

Ⓕ Fast   Ⓜ Make Ahead   Ⓥ Vegan

for the flour. Reduce the brown sugar to $^{1}/_{2}$ cup if the paste is very sweet. Proceed with the recipe.

11 Great Additions to Any Pie or Tart Crust

1. Nut flour or nut butter (page 322)
2. Chopped or whole seeds, like sesame, poppy, sunflower, or pumpkin seeds
3. Shredded coconut
4. Crumbled or ground cookies, like gingersnaps, vanilla wafers, graham crackers, amaretti cookies, and more
5. Almond or hazelnut paste
6. Finely chopped dried fruit
7. Ground spices, such as cinnamon, nutmeg, allspice, star anise, anise, cardamom, or coriander
8. Grated or finely minced fresh ginger, minced crystallized ginger, or ground ginger
9. Grated or finely minced citrus zest
10. Crunchy Granola (page 573)
11. Cooked grains, like sticky or short-grain rice, couscous, or bulgur, used in small amounts (less than $^{1}/_{2}$ cup) and sweetened with honey or brown sugar

The Basics of Making Pies, Tarts, Cobblers, and Crisps

All of these have two essential building blocks: the filling and the crust or topping. The role of each is obvious. The filling provides loads of flavor and (usually) a soft jammy or creamy texture. Fillings may be cooked or raw fruit, pudding or custard, chocolate ganache, citrus curd, and more. All should have good, intense flavor (underripe or insipid-tasting fruit will not do) or sublime richness. And it may go without saying, but you should be able to eat the filling with a fork; if a filling spills out of the crust so it must be eaten with a spoon, or is impossible to cut without a knife, it doesn't make the grade.

Getting that perfect, flaky, flavorful, and golden brown crust for your pie or tart is always the goal; the details are discussed separately in "The Basics of Crusts" (page 863). Although it takes only a jiffy to mix up a pie or tart crust, and you can just have a batch frozen for whenever you need it, undeniably there are still times when a store-bought crust is a convenient option. It will never be as flaky and flavorful as a homemade crust (and they can be loaded with preservatives, so look at the ingredients), but it will do in a pinch.

You'll notice that all the pies in this section are single-crust (bottom crust only). It's a matter of personal taste, but I think one well-made crust is perfectly fine for just about every pie I like; two crusts are overkill.

The toppings for cobblers and crisps may be even more important, to the point where they share the spotlight with the filling. Those for cobblers should be somewhere between a biscuit and a cookie: fluffy, a bit flaky, buttery, and at least slightly sweet. The key is not overmixing the dough; get it so that it's just combined, barely holding together, then drop it onto the filling in mounds, leaving space for steam to escape from the cooking fruit.

Crisps, as their name indicates, are all about having a topping with a bit of crunchy texture, which can be like a crumbly buttery cookie or more robust like a granola. Again, keep the mixing to a minimum and crumble the dough into $^{1}/_{2}$- to 1-inch pieces; anything smaller may dissolve into the filling.

Buttermilk-Blueberry Pie

MAKES: 8 to 12 servings
TIME: 45 minutes with a prepared crust, plus time to chill

A lovely custard pie that is at once rich, tangy, and sweet. I love the whole berries that float to the top and become almost jammy. The recipe makes enough to fill a deep-dish pie plate, and that's my favorite way to bake it. But

Why Prebake?

Generally, you want to prebake—or "blind" bake—pie and tart crusts, for a number of reasons. Prebaking minimizes shrinking and helps produce a nicely shaped crust. It also ensures that the crust cooks through, giving it ideal flavor and color (browned crusts look and taste better than pale ones). And a prebaked crust is less likely to become soggy when the filling is particularly moist (as in, for example, Buttermilk-Blueberry Pie, page 871). Finally, when the filling is precooked or served raw (as in Pineapple Tart (page 874), for example), you have no other choice than to prebake. Both Sweet Piecrust and Sweet Tart Crust recipes and all their variations can be prebaked; Baked Crumb Crust is always prebaked, as it's a moist and crumbly crust that turns mushy when the filling is added without prebaking.

How to Prebake

To prebake, you need butter, foil, and a cup or two of raw rice or dried beans (or pie weights if you prefer). The weight helps prevent the crust from shrinking and bubbling with air pockets while it's baking. They aren't absolutely essential (you can prick the bubbles with a fork as they appear throughout the baking), but they make things easier, and your crust will look better.

Preheat the oven to 425°F. Be sure the crust is pressed firmly into the pan, adequately pricked with a fork, and well chilled before baking; hard butter and the fork pricks will help the crust keep its shape.

Butter one side of a piece of foil large enough to cover the crust; press the foil onto the crust, butter side down. Weight the foil with a pile of dried beans or rice (they can be reused for the same purpose) or pie weights. Bake for 12 minutes; remove from the oven and remove the weights and foil. Reduce the oven temperature to 350°F and continue baking the crust until it has a golden brown color, another 10 minutes or so. Continue baking until the crust is completely golden brown if the pie's filling requires no additional baking (cool the pan on a wire rack before filling) or cool, fill, and finish baking according to the individual recipe.

it works in a regular pie dish too. You'll have some filling left over, and the pie will be ready on the early end of the baking range given. Like cheesecake, this might crack a bit on the top, but to me that only adds to its old-fashioned appeal.

Other crusts that are good in this recipe: Wheat Piecrust (page 867) or Oat Piecrust (page 867).

1 recipe Sweet Piecrust (page 866) in a 9- or 10-inch
  pie plate

1 cup buttermilk

1 cup cream or half-and-half

4 eggs plus 2 egg yolks

1/2 cup sugar

Pinch salt

1 teaspoon vanilla extract (optional)

1 cup blueberries

❶ Bake the crust (see "Prebaking Pie and Tart Crusts," above). Start the filling while the crust is in the oven. When the crust is done, set the oven temperature at 350°F and cool the crust slightly on a rack.

❷ Put the buttermilk and cream in a small pot and heat until steaming. Whisk together the eggs, yolks, sugar, salt, and vanilla if you're using it; gradually pour in the buttermilk and cream while whisking. Pour the buttermilk mixture into the cooled crust, evenly distribute the blueberries in the mixture, and return to the oven.

❸ Bake until the mixture is not quite set—it should jiggle a bit in the middle—35 to 45 minutes. Use your

Ⓕ Fast   Ⓜ Make Ahead   Ⓥ Vegan

judgment; it will set and thicken more with cooling. Remove and let cool to room temperature on a wire rack, then cover and chill in the refrigerator for at least 2 hours. Serve or store in the refrigerator for up to 4 days.

Dark Chocolate–Buttermilk Pie. Deeply flavored and decadent; excellent with Nut Tart Crust (page 868): Substitute 12 ounces chopped bittersweet chocolate for the blueberries. Put the chocolate in a bowl, pour the hot buttermilk mixture over the top, stir until the chocolate is melted and incorporated, then stir into the egg mixture. Proceed with the recipe. Serve with whipped crème fraîche.

Ginger–Sweet Potato Pie. Use Baked Gingersnap Crumb Crust (page 869): Increase the cream to $1^1/_2$ cups. Substitute $1^1/_2$ cups sweet potato purée (page 390) for the buttermilk and 2 tablespoons minced crystallized ginger or 2 teaspoons minced peeled fresh ginger for the blueberries. Proceed with the recipe, stirring the ginger in with the purée in Step 2. Serve with a dollop of Ginger Whipped Cream (page 856).

Banana-Butterscotch Pie. Sweet and creamy: Substitute packed dark brown sugar for the white sugar, milk for the buttermilk, and 2 medium bananas for the blueberries. Peel and cut the bananas into $^1/_4$-inch-thick slices; arrange the slices overlapping each other in the baked pie crust in a single layer (you may not need all the banana slices). Gently pour the butterscotch mixture over the bananas so as not to dislodge any. Proceed with the recipe and serve with a good dollop of Vanilla Whipped Cream (page 856).

Coconut Meringue Pie

MAKES: 6 to 8 servings

TIME: About 1 hour with a prepared crust, plus time to chill

Ⓜ

A twist on classic lemon meringue: Lighter than coconut cream pie, with a rich and creamy filling and a delicate topping. For something even lighter, try the fruit variation, which works for virtually any fruit, including berries.

Other crusts that are good in this recipe: Sweet Piecrust (page 866).

1 recipe Nut Piecrust, preferably made with grated coconut or macadamia nuts (page 867), in a 9- or 10-inch pie plate

$1^3/_4$ cups coconut milk (to make your own, see page 423)

2 cups finely grated or shredded coconut

1 cup sugar

Pinch salt

$^1/_3$ cup cornstarch

4 eggs, separated

2 tablespoons butter, softened

$^1/_4$ cup confectioners' sugar

① Bake the crust (see "Prebaking Pie and Tart Crusts," page 872). Start the filling while the crust is in the oven. When the crust is done, leave the oven at 350°F and cool the crust slightly on a rack.

② Put the coconut milk and $1^3/_4$ cups of the coconut in a blender and purée until smooth; add a little water to help the machine run, but no more than $^1/_4$ cup. (The mixture will still have bits of coconut in it, which is fine.) Put the purée, the sugar, and the salt in a medium saucepan over medium heat. Cook, stirring frequently, until smooth and thick, 10 to 15 minutes.

③ While the filling is cooking, whisk the cornstarch with $^1/_4$ cup water until smooth; beat in the egg yolks. When the coconut mixture is thick, whisk about $^1/_2$ cup of it into the egg yolks. Immediately stir the egg yolk mixture back into the coconut mixture and bring to a boil, whisking constantly. Let it boil for less than a minute, then turn off the heat and add the butter. Let the filling cool a bit before pouring it into the prepared crust.

④ Make the meringue: Beat the egg whites with a pinch of salt, until foamy and turning white. Keep beating, gradually adding the confectioners' sugar, until the mixture is shiny and holds medium-stiff peaks.

⑤ Pour the filling into the crust. Cover with the meringue, making sure the meringue comes in contact with the edges of the crust. Note that the meringue will hold its shape, so you can create swirls and peaks if you like. Sprinkle the top with the remaining coconut. Bake until the meringue is lightly browned, 10 to 15 minutes. Cool on a rack, then refrigerate until set, at least a couple hours.

Apricot (or Virtually Any Fruit) Meringue Pie. Replace the coconut and coconut milk with 2 cups of any fruit purée (see page 862). Combine it with the sugar in the saucepan in Step 2 and proceed with the recipe.

Pineapple (or Almost Any Fruit) Tart

MAKES: 6 to 8 servings

TIME: About 2½ hours, mostly unattended, with a prepared crust

This tart is based on fruit "marinated" in its own juices (see "Macerating and Seasoning Fruit," page 417), which is then slowly baked, so the filling retains some a fresh flavor and texture. The juices that accumulate are boiled down for a few minutes to make a syrup to pass at the table. The results are gorgeous.

You can easily use this recipe for any fruit (or combination of fruits); figure on 5 to 6 cups of chopped fresh fruit or whole berries.

Other crusts you can use: Nut Tart Crust (page 868).

1 pineapple, peeled and cored (see page 435)

1 cup turbinado or other raw cane sugar or packed brown sugar

1 recipe Sweet Tart Crust (page 867) in a 9-inch tart pan

① Halve the pineapple lengthwise, then roughly chop it into ½-inch pieces. Combine the pineapple and sugar in a bowl and toss until mixed; macerate at room temperature for at least an hour or cover and refrigerate for up to 4 hours.

② Bake the crust (see "Prebaking Pie and Tart Crusts," page 872), only stop after you remove the foil and pie weights so the crust is just set but not yet golden. When the crust is done, turn the oven to 350°F and cool the crust slightly on a rack.

③ Drain the pineapple for at least 10 minutes, reserving the juice. Put the fruit in the crust and gently press down to make sure the tart is filled to the edges. Bake, undisturbed, until the crust is firm and browned and the fruit is caramelized and softened, about 1½ hours.

④ While the tart is baking, put the juice in a small pot, turn the heat to medium, and boil, stirring occasionally, until it reduces to a thick syrup, about 15 minutes. Cool and serve the syrup alongside the tart for last-minute saucing.

Grape or Cherry Tart with Port. Use cherries when they're in season; grapes otherwise: Substitute 5 to 6 cups halved (and pitted) cherries or seedless grapes for the pineapple and ½ cup sugar for the full cup; add ⅔ cup ruby port to the fruit in Step 1.

Poached Pear Tart with Dark Chocolate Ganache

MAKES: 6 to 8 servings

TIME: 35 minutes, largely unattended, with a prepared crust and pears

This recipe is all about assembling other recipes, but don't let that discourage you: It's really quite easy and completely impressive, a wonderful end to a fancy dinner or holiday meal.

Ⓕ Fast   Ⓜ Make Ahead   Ⓥ Vegan

The optional Apricot Jam Glaze adds a lovely shine to the tart that makes it look like it's straight from an expensive pastry case; use it if you really want to impress your guests. Also, use the Poached Pears with Asian Spices variation for a more exotic flavor combination.

Other crusts you can use: Nut Tart Crust (especially made with pistachios, page 868), and Chocolate Tart Crust (page 868).

1 recipe Sweet Tart Crust (page 867) in a 9- or 10-inch tart pan

1 recipe Chocolate Ganache (page 860), warmed

1 recipe Poached Pears (page 433)

1 recipe Apricot Jam Glaze (page 858), warmed (optional)

1 teaspoon ground cardamom (optional)

Whipped cream (page 856) for garnish

❶ Bake the crust completely (see "Prebaking Pie and Tart Crusts," page 872) and cool it. Meanwhile, make the ganache.

❷ Pour the ganache into the tart shell to a depth of $^1/_4$ to $^1/_2$ inch and set aside in a cool spot to set. Meanwhile, halve the pears and cut into $^1/_4$-inch-thick slices. Arrange the slices on the set ganache (it can still be a bit soft, but you don't want the pear slices to sink in completely) in overlapping circles. Use a pastry brush to brush the surface of the pears with the apricot glaze if you're using it. Sprinkle with the cardamom if you're using it and chill for at least 15 minutes or store, covered, in the fridge for a day or two. Garnish each serving with whipped cream right before serving.

Fresh Fig Tart. Make this only with the sweetest and juiciest fresh figs, usually available in late summer and early fall: Substitute 1 cup crème fraîche or mascarpone cheese for the ganache; 15 to 20 ripe figs, sliced, for the pears; and 3 tablespoons good-quality honey for the apricot glaze. Omit the cardamom. Spread the crust with a layer of the crème fraîche or mascarpone and arrange the fig slices on top. Drizzle the tart with the honey, chill, and serve.

Strawberry and Cream Cheese Tart. Substitute 1 cup whipped cream cheese for the ganache; and 3 cups or so halved or sliced ripe strawberries for the pears. Omit the cardamom. Spread the crust with a layer of the cream cheese and arrange the strawberries on top. Brush with the apricot glaze, chill, and serve.

Roasted Plum and Pudding Tart. A layer of creamy pudding and richly sweet plums: Use Nut Tart Crust (page 868) if you like. Substitute Vanilla Pudding for the ganache and 6 or 7 ripe sweet plums for the pears. Omit the apricot glaze and cardamom. Halve and pit the plums; brush with butter, and put on a baking sheet cut side up; roast in a 400°F oven until lightly caramelized, about 10 minutes (or broil them). Spread the pudding in the tart shell (no more than an inch deep), arrange the plums on top, chill for at least 2 hours, and serve.

Almond Tart

MAKES: 6 to 8 servings
TIME: 1 hour with a prepared crust

An almond lover's dessert, this is crunchy and slightly chewy, with just the right amount of sweetness. You can make it without the crust if you like; be sure to liberally grease and flour the pan first. And any nuts can be used in place of the almonds: Hazelnuts, walnuts, pecans, macadamias, peanuts, and cashews are all great.

Other crusts you can use: Sweet Tart Crust (page 867).

1 recipe Nut Tart Crust made with almonds (page 868), in a 9-inch tart pan with a removable bottom

2$^1/_2$ cups almonds

6 eggs

1 cup sugar

$^1/_2$ teaspoon ground cinnamon

1 teaspoon grated or finely minced lemon zest

Confectioners' sugar for dusting

1 Prebake the crust as directed (see "Prebaking Pie and Tart Crusts," page 872). Start the filling while the crust is in the oven. When the crust is done, leave the oven at 350°F and cool the crust slightly on a rack.

2 Grind 1$^1/_2$ cups of the almonds to a powder in a food processor or spice mill. Chop the remaining almonds. Beat the eggs and sugar together, preferably in a standing mixer, until thick and light in color (if you are doing this by hand, it will take a good 10 minutes or more). Stir in the cinnamon, lemon zest, and almonds. Pour into the crust.

3 Bake for 30 to 45 minutes, or until a toothpick inserted in the center comes out clean. Cool on a rack, then remove the sides of pan. Dust the top with confectioners' sugar and serve.

Rich Nut Tart. With cream and honey to sweeten: Use any nuts you like; pecans or macadamias make a really rich tart. Substitute $^1/_2$ cup cream for 2 of the eggs and $^1/_2$ cup honey for the sugar.

Rosemary–Pine Nut Tart. Almost savory and terrific with an after-dinner cheese course: Substitute 2 cups pine nuts for the almonds and 1 tablespoon minced rosemary for the cinnamon. Reduce the sugar to $^2/_3$ cup and add up to $^3/_4$ cup golden raisins if you like. Skip grinding the pine nuts—leave them whole.

Granola Tart. Loaded with toasted oats, nuts, and seeds: Substitute 1 cup toasted rolled oats (see page 564), 1 cup chopped nuts, and $^1/_2$ cup pumpkin, sunflower, or sesame seeds for the almonds. Skip grinding the oats, nuts, and seeds.

Ricotta Cheesecake

MAKES: About 12 servings
TIME: 1$^1/_2$ hours, plus time to chill

If you've never made cheesecake with anything but cream cheese, try this. Ricotta makes a creamy, moist, and light cheesecake that's delicious but is much lower in saturated fat (especially if you use part-skim ricotta). The texture is pleasantly grainy (as is ricotta itself); If you want it smoother, whirl the cheese in the food processor first. Like cream cheese, the flavor of ricotta is mild enough to blend with just about any other flavor you like; I start with lemon here, but you can also experiment with other seasonings or extracts. Though turbinado sugar has a more distinctive flavor than granulated or even brown sugar, go ahead and substitute either in a pinch.

Baking in a water bath is the best way to treat cheesecake, which is like a custard. Unfortunately, most springform pans leak water. You have a few options here: Try wrapping the outside of the pan in a large sheet of heavy-duty foil and be careful not to tear or puncture the foil (use two layers for extra protection); this usually works. Or use a solid pan; this, of course works, but it will make getting the cheesecake out of the pan difficult, so I don't like this option. Instead, I get good results by leaving the cheesecake in the oven after turning it off as suggested in the recipe. Or skip both methods and just risk the uneven cooking and cracks.

1 recipe Baked Crumb Crust (pages 868–869)

6 large eggs

1 cup turbinado sugar

1$^1/_2$ pounds (about 3 cups) fresh ricotta cheese

1 tablespoon finely grated lemon zest

2 tablespoons all-purpose flour

1 Press the crust into the bottom of a 9- or 10-inch springform pan and bake as directed, then set aside to cool. Preheat the oven to 325°F.

F Fast **M** Make Ahead **V** Vegan

❷ Use an electric mixer to beat the eggs and sugar until light; add the cheese, zest, and flour and beat until smooth.

❸ Turn the batter into the prepared crust and bake until the cake has separated from the sides of the pan but is still a little jiggly at the center, 45 to 50 minutes. Turn off the oven, but leave the cake inside until cool.

❹ Remove the cake from the oven and cool completely on a rack, cover with plastic wrap, then refrigerate until well chilled before slicing and serving. This will keep in good shape for several days.

Quick Ricotta Pots. With no crust, even easier; this can be done with the main recipe or any of the following variations: Simply pour the batter into greased individual ramekins or into one baking dish and proceed with the recipe. Ramekins will be ready to turn off the oven in 20 to 30 minutes and baking dishes in 30 to 40 minutes, depending on their sizes.

Rum-Raisin Ricotta Cheesecake. Cheesecake for adults: Add 1 cup raisins and $^3/_4$ cup dark rum; reduce the turbinado to $^1/_2$ cup. Soak the raisins in the rum until they are swollen and most of the rum is absorbed. Proceed with the recipe; fold the raisins in after beating the other filling ingredients in Step 2.

Apple Cobbler

MAKES: 6 to 8 servings

TIME: About 1 hour with a prepared topping

An old-fashioned dessert with virtually limitless fruit filling options. Even the biscuit topping can be made with "alternative" flours (see "Substituting Flours in Baking," page 684) and with various spices and other flavorings added; see the variations for some ideas. The filling isn't thickened, so the natural fruit juices melt right into the topping as the cobbler bakes. Serve with ice cream (Buttermilk Ice Cream, page 891, is great) or whipped cream (page 856).

Any of the fruit fillings in the Cherry Crisp (page 878) main recipe and its variations can be used in the cobbler and vice versa.

8 tablespoons (1 stick) cold butter, cut into bits, plus butter for the pan

3 pounds cooking or all-purpose apples

1 cup sugar, or to taste

$^1/_2$ cup all-purpose flour

$^1/_2$ teaspoon baking powder

Pinch salt

1 egg

$^1/_2$ teaspoon vanilla extract

❶ Preheat the oven to 375°F. Grease a 8- or 9-inch square or round baking dish with some butter. Core, peel, and cut the apples into $^1/_2$-inch wedges. (You should have about 6 cups.)

❷ Put the apples in a bowl and toss with half of the sugar. Spread the apples into the prepared dish and let sit while you prepare the biscuit topping.

❸ Combine the flour, baking powder, salt, and remaining $^1/_2$ cup sugar in a food processor and pulse once or twice. Add the butter and process for 10 seconds, until the mixture is well blended. By hand, beat in the egg and vanilla.

❹ Drop this mixture onto the fruit by tablespoonfuls; do not spread it out. Bake until golden yellow and just starting to brown, 35 to 45 minutes. Serve immediately.

Peach-Brandy Cobbler. Nectarines, apricots, and plums work here too: Substitute 3 pounds ripe peaches, pitted, peeled, and chopped, for the apples; and $^1/_4$ cup sour cream or yogurt for half of the butter. Add $^1/_4$ cup brandy and reduce the sugar to $^3/_4$ cup, using $^1/_4$ cup with the peaches and the rest for the topping. Add the brandy along with the sugar to the peaches, and the sour cream along with the butter.

Banana-Date Cobbler. Use speckled ripe bananas for a soft and gooey cobbler or less ripe ones for a chunkier, more textured cobbler: Substitute 2 pounds bananas, peeled and chopped, and $1^1/_2$ cups pitted and chopped dates for the apples. Add to the bananas $^1/_2$ teaspoon grated or finely minced peeled fresh or ground ginger and 1 teaspoon ground cinnamon.

Apple-Rhubarb Cobbler. Slightly pink and tangy: Use 2 pounds of apples and 1 pound of rhubarb. String the rhubarb (see page 284) and cut it into 1-inch chunks.

Cherry Crisp

MAKES: 6 to 8 servings

TIME: 40 minutes with a prepared topping

Fresh tart cherries have a brief season in midsummer, and this is one of the best ways to use them. (After all that pitting, who wants to mess with a piecrust?) But you can use frozen tart cherries throughout the year too. You can also make this crisp with Bing and other cherries, though it won't have as much flavor. I like crisps and cobblers naturally juicy, but if you want to thicken the filling a bit, add 2 tablespoons flour or cornstarch to the sugar you use to toss the fruit in Step 2. Or better still, toss in a handful of dried cherries.

Any of the fruit fillings in the main recipe and its variations can be used in the Apple Cobbler (page 877) and vice versa.

Butter for greasing the dish

3 pounds tart cherries

$^1/_2$ cup sugar, or more to taste

1 recipe uncooked Sweet Crumble Topping or any of its variations (page 870)

1 Preheat the oven to 400°F. Grease an 8- or 9-inch square or round baking dish. Pit the cherries. You should have about 6 cups of fruit.

2 Put the cherries in a bowl and toss with the sugar. Transfer to the prepared dish, crumble on the topping, and bake until golden and just starting to brown, 30 to 40 minutes. Serve immediately, or at least while still warm.

Cranberry-Orange Crisp. Intense flavors, gorgeous color, and a great treat in winter: Substitute 2 pounds oranges (about 6) and 2 cups cranberries for the cherries. Segment the oranges or cut them into wheels (see page 431). Add 1 teaspoon finely peeled and minced fresh ginger.

7 Fruit-and-Topping Crisp Pairings

The Cherry Crisp is the model for making all fruit crisps. Just use 7 to 8 cups of fruit for every recipe of topping, using these pairing suggestions as ideas and inspiration.

1. Figs with Rice-Flour Crumble Topping (page 870)
2. Grapes and peanut butter with Sweet Crumble Topping (page 870)
3. Bananas and chocolate chunks with Rice-Flour Crumble Topping (page 870)
4. Blackberries with Cracked Wheat Crumble Topping (page 870)
5. Peaches or nectarines with Coconut Crumble Topping (page 870)
6. Apricots with Hazelnut or Almond Crumble Topping (page 870)
7. Apples or pears with Citrus-Spice Crumble Topping (page 870)

Phyllo Pastries

Everyone loves phyllo desserts—baklava is the model—and they're usually pretty easy to make, because the phyllo itself is premade; you just buy it. (You *can* make it, but given its thinness, the task takes a certain amount of expertise and a lot of patience.) You'll easily find frozen white flour phyllo in most supermarkets, and even whole wheat phyllo is increasingly available. Both kinds brown and crisp beautifully with almost no effort,

Ⓕ Fast   Ⓜ Make Ahead   Ⓥ Vegan

though whole wheat turns a slightly darker brown, has a subtle nutty flavor, and becomes just as flaky and crisp; it's good stuff.

The Basics of Phyllo

Occasionally you may run across fresh phyllo in Mediterranean markets. If you do, grab it; use it immediately or wrap well and freeze for later. The ultra-thin sheets are made of not much more than flour and water; the dough is stretched out to a huge, impossibly thin sheet that's cut into smaller ones.

There are two little tricks to using frozen phyllo successfully:

1. Don't rush the thawing; it's best to transfer it to the refrigerator at least 24 hours before you plan to use it. Thawing at room temperature makes the sheets stick together.

2. Keep the phyllo from drying out while you work. Simply unroll it and cover the pile of sheets with a piece of plastic wrap and a damp towel. If you handle it carefully, whatever you don't use can be wrapped well and immediately refrozen.

To get that unbelievably crisp crust with phyllo, it's essential to brush each sheet with melted butter (or oil, but butter is *far* superior); this allows the sheets to separate during baking and become crisp and flaky. Taking shortcuts with the butter or trying to reduce fat will yield a flat, raw-looking pastry with little or no flavor; don't try.

The other factor in getting a fantastic phyllo pastry— whether savory or sweet—is using a filling that's flavorful but not too wet. You want *some* moisture in the filling, but not so much that the phyllo gets soggy. Finally, remember that phyllo has a neutral, almost bland flavor; when seasoning your filling, adding a touch more sugar, honey, spices, or what have you is not a bad idea.

HANDLING PHYLLO SHEETS

(STEP 1) Brush the layers of phyllo with butter. Keep the remaining sheets covered with a damp towel (on a plate if you like) until you use them. (STEP 2) Fill, just about to the edges. (STEP 3) Roll carefully, but not too tightly. (STEP 4) Fold over the ends.

Walnut Phyllo "Cigars"

MAKES: 4 to 6 servings
TIME: 40 minutes

A simplified take on baklava, these cigar-shaped pastries are filled with honey-soaked nuts, spices, and a touch of citrus zest. There's nothing complicated about them: just roll up, bake, and cut into "cigars."

$^1/_2$ cup honey

$^1/_2$ cup Sugar Syrup (page 857)

2 cups toasted (page 321) and chopped nuts, any kind or a combination

1 tablespoon ground cinnamon

1 teaspoon ground cardamom

$^1/_4$ teaspoon ground cloves

$^1/_4$ teaspoon freshly grated nutmeg

2 tablespoons minced orange or lemon zest (optional)

16 sheets (about $^1/_2$ pound) phyllo dough, thawed

8 tablespoons (1 stick) butter, melted, or as needed

$^1/_2$ cup granulated or packed brown sugar

1 Preheat the oven to 325°F. Line 2 baking sheets with parchment paper. Mix the honey and syrup with the nuts, spices, and zest if you're using it until the nuts are coated; set aside.

2 Keep the phyllo sheets covered with a piece of plastic and a damp towel over the top to keep them from drying out. Remove one sheet at a time, quickly brush it with the melted butter, and repeat until you have a stack of 4 buttered sheets. Put $^1/_2$ cup of the nut mixture in a line along the narrow edge of the phyllo; sprinkle the phyllo with a couple tablespoons of the sugar and roll it into a long "cigar." Repeat using all the phyllo, nuts, and sugar.

3 Cut the phyllo rolls into 3 or 4 pieces to form the "cigars." Brush them with more butter and put on the prepared baking sheet. Bake until golden brown, about 15 minutes. Let rest for just a couple minutes before removing from the pan. Cool and store, covered at room temperature, for up to 4 days.

Nut and Dried Fruit Phyllo "Cigars." Dried fruit adds sweetness and a slightly chewy texture: Substitute 1 cup finely chopped dried fruit, like raisins, cherries, apples, pears, or apricots, for 1 cup of the nuts.

Banana Strudel

MAKES: 8 servings
TIME: 45 minutes

Just like phyllo, traditional strudel is paper-thin and flaky when baked, so phyllo is a great ready-made substitute. All sorts of fruits will work here, including chopped dried fruit, which can be lightly rehydrated in warm water for added moisture. Whatever filling you use, take care that it's not too wet; strain it first if necessary.

6 tablespoons ($^3/_4$ stick) melted butter, plus more if needed

3 or 4 ripe bananas, peeled and sliced (about $2^1/_2$ cups)

$^1/_3$ cup packed brown sugar

2 tablespoons dark rum (optional)

$^1/_2$ cup chopped pecans or macadamia nuts

$^1/_2$ cup shredded coconut

6 to 8 sheets (about $^1/_4$ pound) phyllo dough, thawed

1 Preheat the oven to 350°F. Line a baking sheet with parchment paper. Put a skillet over medium heat; when it's hot, add 2 tablespoons of the butter, then add the bananas and brown sugar. Add the rum if you're using it. Cook, stirring frequently, until the bananas are just softened, about 2 minutes. Stir in the nuts and coconut. Set aside to cool.

F Fast   M Make Ahead   V Vegan

2 Keep the phyllo sheets covered with a piece of plastic and a damp towel over the top to keep them from drying out. Remove one sheet at a time, put it on the prepared baking sheet, quickly brush it with the melted butter, and repeat until you have a stack of 6 buttered sheets (the extras are available in case sheets rip).

3 Put the banana mixture in a line along the long edge of the phyllo. Roll it into a log, putting the seam side down; tuck in the ends of the log. Brush the strudel with more butter and score the top a few times with a sharp knife. Bake until golden brown, 30 to 40 minutes. Let rest for just a couple minutes or serve at room temperature, cut into 2- to 3-inch-thick slices.

Cherry Strudel. Substitute $2^1/_2$ cups pitted and halved cherries (frozen are fine) for the bananas; 1 cup soft fresh cheese, ricotta, farmer cheese, or drained cottage cheese for the macadamias and coconut; kirsch for the rum if you like; and granulated sugar for the brown sugar. Skip Step 1 and instead toss the cherries with the sugar; drain excess liquid from the cherries if there is more than a couple tablespoons and fold into the cheese. Proceed with the recipe.

Leftover Pound Cake Strudel. Use up those couple-days-old slices of pound cake for a looser but tasty filling; crumble the cake into crumbs: Substitute 2 to 3 cups crumbled pound cake for the bananas, any nuts for the macadamias, and chopped dried fruit for the coconut. Omit the rum and keep the brown sugar if the cake isn't very sweet or if you want a very sweet strudel. Skip Step 1 and proceed with the recipe.

The Basics of Custards, Puddings, and Gelées

These are desserts you generally eat with a spoon. Technically at least, custards contain eggs (and often cream) and can be sauces—like crème Anglaise, or vanilla sauce—or turned into ice cream (page 888) or, on their own, used for familiar things like flan. Puddings are pretty similar but can be made with cornstarch or other thickeners. (Often, pudding is the name given to stove-top versions, while custards are baked, but none of this is ironclad.) Both are mainstays of desserts and have been for centuries, and with good reason: They are simple but rich, sweet, and satisfying and take well to a number of different flavorings.

Cooking custards and puddings can be a bit tricky, especially the first time around, but all it takes is a bit of practice to get the look and feel right. The most common mistakes are either using too-high heat, so the eggs curdle instead of cook slowly to form a smooth, rich dessert, or baking for too long, so they come out rubbery and mealy instead of luxuriously smooth. So: On top of the stove, keep the heat moderate to low. In the oven, use a water bath and remove the custard before you think it's actually done. See "The Basics of Savory Custard, Flan, and Bread Pudding" (page 189) for more information and cooking tips.

Gelled desserts (*gelées* in French) are what Jell-O imitates. Traditionally made with gelatin—an animal-based product—all the recipes here call for the plant-based agar or arrowroot. Because almost any liquid—from fruit juice to tea—can be turned into the base for jelly, you can let your imagination run wild and really experiment with gelées. (Because the ingredients are so inexpensive and the steps so simple, it's no big deal if your experiment goes awry; plenty of mine have, though the ones here are all winners.) And gelées need not only be eaten with a spoon: You can up the thickener to make them stiffer, then cut up and eat out of hand, or dice and add to anything from iced tea (bubble tea style) or juice to dessert soup (pages 903–905).

How to Use Thickeners in Desserts

Thickeners are almost essential in dessert sauces, puddings, pie fillings, and other desserts (they're absolutely critical if you don't eat eggs, which are the most luxuri-

VEGETARIAN THICKENERS AT A GLANCE

THICKENER	WHAT IT IS	PROS	CONS	WHEN TO USE	HOW TO USE
Agar *Agar-agar, kanten*	A form of dehydrated seaweed, frequently used in commercial ice cream	A strong agent; does not require refrigeration to set up	Results are slightly opaque, not clear. May not set when mixed with vinegar or foods high in oxalic acid, like chocolate and rhubarb.	Wherever you would otherwise use gelatin, so not in ice cream or other frozen desserts, even though it's sometimes used that way commercially	Must be heated to dissolve. For powdered agar, start with a straight replacement for plain granular gelatin. For bars, rinse in cold water, wring them out, tear them into small pieces, and add them to the cooking liquid. 1 agar bar = 4 tablespoons flakes = 2 teaspoons powder.
Arrowroot	A starch derived from the rhizome of a West Indian plant; sold as a white powder	The most neutral tasting of all starches, arrowroot withstands heating without breaking down as fast as cornstarch. It also achieves maximum thickening effect at lower temperature than other thickeners and prevents ice crystals from forming in ice cream.	Often you must add it after the liquid is completely cooked because it thickens so quickly. Turns dairy products slimy and makes sauces super-shiny, which makes savory foods strange looking.	For thickening acidic liquids, frozen desserts, or if you haven't had good luck with cornstarch	Make a slurry. Must be heated to activate.
Butter (see "The Dairy Lexicon," page 206)	Butterfat with a varying quantity of water	Delicious; imparts a round, full flavor and gorgeous sheen to sauces	Only moderate thickening capability; does not gel liquids	As often as possible and wherever it makes sense	Swirl small pieces of very cold butter into a hot liquid over low heat until the liquid is emulsified.
Cornstarch	The finely ground white heart of the corn kernel	Neutral tasting, though it may impart a slightly starchy flavor if not cooked long enough; double the thickening power of flour without the pastiness; creates a clear, shiny sauce; produces the smoothest texture of the starch thickeners	Breaks down relatively quickly if overheated, then thins out considerably. Loses potency when mixed with acid; liquids thickened with cornstarch become spongy if frozen.	Whenever you don't have arrowroot handy or to thicken dairy sauces and ice creams	Make a slurry. Overcooking will diminish its thickening properties; it's a good idea to cook part of the fruit filling and cornstarch before baking a pie to make sure you cook out the starchy flavor.

 Fast   Make Ahead   Vegan

THICKENER	WHAT IT IS	PROS	CONS	WHEN TO USE	HOW TO USE
Wheat flours (See "The Basics of Flour," page 680)	White flour is the finely ground endosperm of the wheat kernel; whole wheat flour is the finely ground whole kernel.	Impart a smooth, velvety texture to fruit pie fillings	Liquids thickened with flour become opaque and may thin if overcooked; like all starch thickeners, taste starchy if undercooked. Too much and texture can be pasty.	Whenever you don't have another alternative handy	For sauces, make a slurry or roux (see page 795). For fruit pies, it's best to coat the fruit with flour before filling the crust.
Tapioca	Derived from the cassava root; sold whole pearls, in little white beads as "instant" or "quick-cooking" tapioca or as a fine powder called "tapioca starch"	Imparts a high gloss; neutral in flavor; unlike cornstarch, won't become spongy if frozen; thickens quickly and at a low temperature.	Instant or quick-cooking tapioca is not recommended for one-crust pies—the beads will rehydrate in cooking and show in the finished filling—use tapioca starch instead.	Tapioca pudding (page 885) and in some fruit pies and cobblers, provided it's finely ground	For the powdered variety, it's best to make a slurry; when using beads, soak them for a few hours before adding them to a recipe.

ous thickener). Flour is a common thickener, of course, but agar and cornstarch are better alternatives, simple and reliable; you can find them and others discussed here in specialty markets or natural food stores if they're not in your supermarket (cornstarch certainly is). Almost all come in a convenient powdered or granular form.

The best way to use starch thickeners is to make a "slurry" by combining them with water or a few spoonfuls of the liquid to be thickened. (When used straight from the bag or box, they will clump up.) The idea is to use just enough liquid to dissolve the thickener and smooth out the lumps; so the consistency is like a thin paste. Then you add the slurry to the mixture to be thickened and . . . well, it works!

Usually—but not always—desserts are cooked a bit after a thickener is added, to eliminate some of the raw flavor or to activate the gelling process; some thickeners work better than others in cold liquids. The recipes in this chapter call specifically for one thickener or another and explain how to use it. The chart will help you whenever you need a substitute or want to improvise your own

desserts. It will even help you experiment with thickening savory dishes.

Vanilla Pudding

MAKES: 4 to 6 servings
TIME: 20 minutes, plus time to chill

This pudding, called *blancmange* in Western Europe, is thickened with cornstarch rather than eggs, which makes it less rich (and lower in fat) but just as thick and creamy as regular pudding. If you can't stand the thought of pudding without eggs, see the Traditional Vanilla Pudding variation; all of the other variations will work with the same amount of eggs. You can also make this vegan by using nondairy milk.

2 1/2 cups half-and-half or whole milk

2/3 cup sugar

Pinch salt

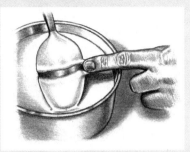

When a custard is ready, it will coat a spoon so that a finger drawn across it leaves a distinct, barely runny line in its wake.

When you're stirring an egg-based custard on top of the stove, this is the easiest way to know when it's done: Dip a large spoon (the larger the spoon, the more surface area you have to judge the coating) into the liquid and drag the tip of your finger across the back of the spoon. If there is a good layer of the liquid clinging to the back of the spoon and a distinct trail from where your finger tip was, it's properly thickened. If the liquid just slides right off the spoon, or your finger trail is covered quickly by runny liquid, keep cooking.

1 vanilla bean or 1 teaspoon vanilla extract

3 tablespoons cornstarch

2 tablespoons unsalted butter, softened (optional)

Whipped cream (page 856) for serving (optional)

1 Put 2 cups of the half-and-half, the sugar, and the salt in a small to medium saucepan over medium-low heat. If you're using a vanilla bean, split it in half length-wise and use a small sharp knife to scrape the seeds into the half-and-half (see page 859); add the pod. Cook just until it begins to steam.

2 Combine the cornstarch and the remaining half-and-half in a bowl and stir to blend; there should be no lumps. Fish the pod out of the steaming milk and add the cornstarch mixture to the pan. Cook, stirring occasion-ally, until the mixture thickens and just starts to boil, about 5 minutes. Reduce the heat to very low and con-tinue to cook, stirring, for another 5 minutes or so. Stir in the butter if you're using it and the vanilla if you're using extract.

3 Pour the mixture into a 1-quart dish or into 4 to 6 small ramekins or bowls. Put plastic wrap directly on top of the pudding to prevent a "skin" from forming (or leave uncovered if you like skin). Refrigerate until chilled and serve within a day, with whipped cream if you like.

Traditional Vanilla Pudding. Sometimes nothing beats a traditional egg-enriched pudding: Substitute 2 eggs and 4 yolks for the cornstarch. In Step 2, whisk or beat the eggs with the sugar and salt; add one-third of the heated half-and-half gradually while whisking constantly, then whisk the egg mixture into the remaining half-and-half. Cook, whisking constantly, until the mixture is thick enough to coat the back of a spoon (see above), about 10 minutes, then stir in the butter and vanilla extract. Proceed with the recipe.

Chocolate Pudding. In Step 2, add 2 ounces chopped bit-tersweet chocolate to the thickened pudding.

Tembleque (Coconut Pudding). A Puerto Rican staple that's easy, delicious, and dairy free: Substitute coconut milk (to make your own, see page 423) for the half-and-half and $1/2$ teaspoon ground cinnamon for the vanilla. Increase the cornstarch to $1/3$ cup. Stir in 2 cups shredded coconut in Step 2.

Real Banana Pudding. Flavored with ripe bananas, this is guaranteed to be the best you've ever made: Use whole milk, reduce the sugar to $1/4$ cup, and add 3 very ripe bananas, peeled and cut into $1/2$-inch pieces. In Step 1, add the bananas and steep them in the warm milk for about 20 minutes. Strain out the

F Fast   **M** Make Ahead   **V** Vegan

bananas and vanilla pod; discard them and return the milk mixture to the pot. Proceed with the recipe.

Apricot or Peach Pudding. You must use ripe and flavorful fruit here or it's not worth the effort: Replace half of the half-and-half with fresh apricot or peach purée (page 862).

Green Tea or Earl Grey Pudding. Omit the vanilla bean and steep a couple tablespoons green or Earl Grey tea in the half-and-half or milk after it steams in Step 1. Strain the liquid and return it to the pot before proceeding

Citrus Tapioca Pudding

MAKES: 4 servings

TIME: 30 minutes, plus time to chill

The combination of orange, lemon, and lime zests gives this tapioca pudding a bright, fruity flavor, the egg yolks enrich it, and the whipped whites make it lighter than any tapioca pudding you've ever had. It's equally fine with coconut or any other nondairy milk.

Note that there are two types of tapioca: pearls and quick-cooking or instant. The round, pearl-shaped variety usually comes in two sizes, small and large; it's less common in supermarkets than the quick-cooking and requires hours of soaking before cooking to become properly tender. Quick-cooking tapioca is broken and parcooked pearl tapioca; it needs no soaking, cooks fast, and is available at most supermarkets.

$1/3$ cup quick-cooking tapioca

$1/2$ cup sugar

1 tablespoon mixed grated orange, lemon, and lime zest

Pinch salt

2 cups milk

2 eggs, separated

$1^1/2$ teaspoons vanilla extract (optional)

 Combine the tapioca, sugar, zest, salt, and milk in a small saucepan and let sit for 5 minutes. Turn the heat to medium, bring to a boil, and cook, stirring, until the tapioca thickens and the tapioca pieces become transparent, about 10 minutes. Remove from the heat, cool for a minute, then beat in the egg yolks. Transfer the mixture to a medium bowl and cool it for a few more minutes before proceeding.

② Beat the egg whites until they hold soft peaks; fold them gently into the tapioca mixture along with the vanilla if you're using it. Spoon into individual serving cups and serve or chill before serving; this keeps well for up to 2 days. Serve with whipped cream (page 856) if you like.

Jasmine-Scented Tapioca Pudding. Get good-quality jasmine tea; that sold loose in Chinese markets is usually pretty good: Substitute 3 tablespoons or so jasmine tea for the zest. Preheat the milk and tea until hot, then remove from the heat and let steep for about 10 minutes; strain and discard the tea. Proceed with the recipe.

Rose Tapioca Pudding. The aroma is as lovely as the flavor: Omit the zest and substitute a teaspoon (or more to taste) rose water for the vanilla extract.

Apple-Cardamom Bread Pudding

MAKES: 6 to 8 servings

TIME: About 1 hour, largely unattended

A great dessert to serve buffet style or—more elegantly—in individual ramekins; top it with a tablespoon of whipped cream (page 856) to melt into each serving. If you reduce the sugar a bit—say, by $1/4$ cup—this becomes a fabulous breakfast or brunch dish to serve with warm maple syrup or Maple Whipped Cream (page 856).

3 cups milk

$1/_2$ cup sugar

Pinch salt

4 tablespoons ($1/_2$ stick) unsalted butter, plus butter for the pan

8 thick slices day-old bread, crusts removed if very thick

3 eggs

2 cups peeled, cored, and chopped apples

$1^1/_2$ teaspoons ground cardamom

❶ Preheat the oven to 350°F. Put the milk, sugar, salt, and butter in a small saucepan over low heat and warm just until the butter melts. Meanwhile, butter a $1^1/_2$-quart or 8-inch square baking dish (glass is nice) and cut or tear the bread into bite-sized pieces—not too small.

❷ Put the bread in the baking dish and pour the hot milk over it. Let it sit for a few minutes, occasionally submerging any pieces of bread that rise to the top. Beat the eggs briefly and stir them into the bread mixture along with the apples and cardamom. Set the baking dish in a larger baking pan and pour enough hot water into the baking pan to come up about an inch from the top of the dish.

❸ Bake for 45 to 60 minutes, or until a thin-bladed knife inserted in the center comes out clean or nearly clean; the center should be just a little wobbly. Run under the broiler for about 30 seconds to brown the top a bit if you like. Serve hot or store, covered, in the refrigerator for up to 2 days. To reheat, cover with foil and heat in a 325°F oven for about 15 minutes; remove the foil and heat for another 5 minutes or so for a crisper crust.

Chocolate Bread Pudding. A favorite; excellent with any ganache (page 860): Add 3 ounces chopped semisweet or bittersweet chocolate and omit the apples and cardamom. Melt the chocolate with the milk in Step 1 or simply stir the chunks into the mixture right before baking.

Prune-Cognac Bread Pudding. Use moist and tender prunes; you want them to start to melt into the bread pudding as it bakes: Substitute pitted prunes (dried plums) for the apples and $1/_2$ cup cognac for $1/_2$ cup of the milk. Proceed with the recipe and serve with Boozy Whipped Cream (page 856).

Spiced Walnut Bread Pudding. Loaded with walnuts and spices, this is like a cross between baklava and bread pudding: Substitute chopped walnuts for the apples and add 2 teaspoons ground cinnamon, 1 teaspoon ground ginger, and $1/_4$ teaspoon each freshly grated nutmeg and cloves. In Step 3, stir in $3/_4$ cup raisins or chopped dates, then proceed with the recipe. Serve with Orange Glaze (page 857) or warm maple syrup.

Vegan Banana–Chocolate Chunk Bread Pudding. The banana not only adds flavor but also serves as an egg replacement, along with the cornstarch: Substitute nondairy milk for the dairy milk and 2 medium ripe bananas for the eggs. Add 1 cup semisweet chocolate chunks. Mash one of the bananas and chop or slice the other one. Stir the bananas and chocolate into the bread in Step 2 where the eggs are added. Proceed with the recipe and serve with Chocolate Glaze (page 861) or Chocolate Ganache (page 860).

Baked Cappuccino Custard

MAKES: 4 to 6 servings
TIME: 45 minutes

Ⓜ

This baked custard has a mellow coffee flavor that makes it perfect after dinner or for breakfast or brunch. Serve it warm or cold with a dollop of Cinnamon or Nutmeg Whipped Cream (page 856). Or turn into a flan (see the first variation); all you have to do is add a bit of caramel to the dish and turn it out before serving.

$1/_4$ cup coffee or espresso beans

2 cups whole milk, half-and-half, cream, or a combination

Ⓕ Fast   Ⓜ Make Ahead   Ⓥ Vegan

2 eggs plus 4 yolks

Pinch salt

$^1/_2$ cup sugar

1 Preheat the oven to 300°F and put a kettle of water on to boil. Use the side of a large knife or a mallet to crack the coffee beans (putting them in a plastic bag first keeps them from flying around). You want mostly large pieces. Put the milk in a small pot with the espresso or coffee. Cook just until it begins to steam; give it a good stir, cover, and set aside.

2 Put the eggs and yolks, salt, and sugar in a medium bowl and whisk or beat until blended. Strain the coffee milk gradually into the egg mixture, whisking constantly. Pour the mixture into a 1-quart dish or into 4 to 6 small ramekins or custard cups.

3 Put the dish or ramekins in a baking pan and pour in hot water to within about 1 inch of the top of the dish or ramekins. Bake until the mixture is not quite set—it should jiggle a bit in the middle—about 20 minutes for the ramekins, 35 to 45 minutes for the dish. Use your judgment; cream sets faster than milk. Serve warm, at room temperature, or cold within a few hours of baking.

Cappuccino Flan. Use this technique with the main recipe or any of the following variations: Put $^1/_2$ cup sugar and $^1/_2$ cup water in a small nonaluminum saucepan over medium heat. Cook without stirring until the sugar liquefies, turns clear, then turns golden brown, 15 to 20 minutes. Remove from the heat and immediately pour the caramel into the bottom of the baking dish or ramekins. Make the custard exactly as directed, pouring it into the prepared dish or cups and baking as directed. Cool completely (until set) on a rack, then serve at room temperature or chill. To remove, dip the dish or cups in boiling water for about 15 seconds, then invert onto a plate or plates. Spoon any caramel remaining in the baking dish over the flan.

Chai Spiced Custard. Simple and unusual: Substitute chai tea for the espresso. Infuse in the hot milk for about 15 minutes, then strain the spices out of the "tea." Proceed with the recipe.

Hazelnut Custard. Or use any nut you like: Substitute hazelnut milk for all or part of the dairy milk if you like and 2 tablespoons of hazelnut butter or finely ground toasted hazelnuts instead of the espresso or coffee beans. Add $^1/_4$ teaspoon ground cinnamon or freshly grated nutmeg if you like. Stir the nuts and spices into the hot milk in Step 2 and proceed with the recipe.

Cinnamon Custard. Substitute a large stick of cinnamon for the espresso or coffee beans.

Gingersnap Custard. Fresh ginger adds a touch of zesty heat; crystallized ginger adds a bit of texture: Substitute 1 teaspoon grated fresh ginger and/or 3 tablespoons finely chopped crystallized ginger for the coffee beans and brown sugar for the white sugar. Add $^1/_2$ teaspoon ground cinnamon and $^1/_4$ teaspoon each freshly grated nutmeg and ground allspice.

Blackberry or Blueberry Custard. A lovely, deep-hued custard: Omit the espresso or coffee beans. Substitute $^1/_2$ cup blackberry or blueberry purée (see page 862) for $^1/_2$ cup of the milk. Add $^1/_2$ teaspoon grated lemon zest if you like. Stir the purée and zest into the hot milk in Step 2 and proceed with the recipe.

Orange Blossom Custard. The delicate flavor of orange blossom water (sold in all Middle Eastern and most Indian food markets) is wonderful: Substitute 1 teaspoon grated orange zest for the espresso or coffee beans. Add 2 teaspoons orange blossom water. Stir in the zest and orange blossom water along with the hot milk in Step 2, then proceed with the recipe.

Lemon-Lime Gelées

MAKES: 4 to 6 servings

TIME: 25 minutes, plus time to chill

Perfect on a summer day or when you want something light, refreshing, and completely nonfat. All sorts of flavors are possible here, from the sweet-tart lemon-lime to coffee to coconut. Experiment on your own with other flavors. Freshly squeezed juice is the best, of course; otherwise, use nectar if it's available. Try unexpected juices like cherry, peach, nectarine, plum, apricot, mango, or passion fruit. To adjust the sweetness of the gelée, replace some of the sugar syrup with water, juice, purée, or other liquid.

Jelly cubes are great for kids: Add another teaspoon of agar, let it set, then—using a small cookie cutter (not larger than about 2 inches across)—cut into cubes, stars, hearts, or other shapes.

2$\frac{1}{2}$ teaspoons agar powder

1 tablespoon mixed grated lemon and lime zest

$\frac{1}{4}$ cup freshly squeezed lemon juice

$\frac{1}{4}$ cup freshly squeezed lime juice

1$\frac{1}{2}$ cups Sugar Syrup (page 857)

1 Put 2 cups water in a small pot and add the agar; let it sit for about 10 minutes, then bring the water to a boil. Combine the remaining ingredients in a small bowl and then stir in the agar water.

2 Strain the liquid into individual ramekins, small bowls, cups, or a single larger dish (keep in mind you probably want the gelée to be at least 1 inch thick). Let the gelée set at room temperature, then refrigerate until chilled and firm, another hour or so.

Raspberry or Any Berry Gelées. Substitute 1$\frac{1}{2}$ cups raspberry or any berry purée (see page 862), strained to removed the seeds, for the zest and lemon and lime juice. Use 1 cup water to dissolve the agar.

Pomegranate Gelées. Drop fresh pomegranate seeds into the cooling gelée if you like: Omit the citrus zest and juice. Use 2$\frac{1}{2}$ cups pomegranate juice to dissolve the agar.

Honey Gelées. Good-quality honey is essential here; don't shy away from some of the bolder-flavored varieties available: Substitute 1$\frac{1}{2}$ cups good-quality and flavorful honey for the sugar syrup. Omit the zest and lemon and lime juice. In Step 1, when the agar water

has boiled, immediately stir in the honey and keep stirring until dissolved.

Coffee Gelées. Omit the citrus zest and juice. Use 1$\frac{1}{2}$ cups freshly brewed coffee or espresso instead of the citrus and zest and dissolve the agar in 1 cup water.

Champagne Gelée with Berries. Pretty with the berries suspended in it; serve it in clear glass: Substitute 3 cups chilled Champagne or sparkling wine. Omit the water. In Step 1, mix the agar in the sugar syrup in the pot and bring it to a boil. Cool it only slightly, about 5 minutes, then carefully stir in the champagne. Transfer to the serving dish(es) and put in the fridge for about 5 minutes so it's just starting to set; drop in the berries (they should suspend in the semiset gelée) and return to the fridge.

The Basics of Ice Cream, Sorbet, and Granita

In the world of ice cream, the reign of vanilla, chocolate, and strawberry is over, and it seems like new flavor combinations—not all of them great ideas—are being invented every day. Grocery store ice cream sections are crammed with everything from double Belgian chocolate to coffee-caramel latte soy milk ice cream to mango sorbet.

Yet still, as is often the case with things you make yourself, homemade ice cream, sorbet, and granita offer even more flavor and ingredient possibilities than anything you can get in your grocery store. Once you learn the base ingredients and techniques for making each, you can create your own flavor combinations and limit the ingredients to those you want instead of those that are convenient for the mass marketers to use.

Though you may not know it, the best ice cream is fresh and has never been frozen hard. So it's best eaten soon after it's made. That's why the ice cream in top

F Fast   **M** Make Ahead   **V** Vegan

restaurants is so good. But if you can make a custard or pudding (see page 881)—and believe me, you can—and you have an ice cream machine, you can make the best ice cream you've ever tasted at home.

The classic base for rich, delicious ice cream is 2 cups milk, half-and-half, or cream; 6 egg yolks; and flavoring—not much else. The base ingredients can be changed too: You can use soy, rice, nut, oat, or dairy milk; you can stir a cup of cream or any liquid into the custard before freezing to lighten it a bit; and you can also use fewer egg yolks (at a minimum 3 or 4) to reduce the fat and calorie content—but don't expect the same richness as you'll get with 6 yolks. Some ice cream recipes—heavy on the cream, light on the eggs (or with no eggs at all), and uncooked—are called either *Philadelphia* or *New York style.* These have their merits and devotees, but they're not as rich and creamy as cooked custard ice cream—and to me, that's what ice cream is about. So when I'm looking to cut calories or fat, I switch to ice milk, sorbet, or granita.

What's incredible, though, is that you can essentially replace the eggs with cornstarch (just as you can make a custard with eggs or cornstarch; see page 883). This produces, a rich, delicious ice cream in which the added flavors really stand out, because they don't compete with the flavors of egg. Try it.

Ice Milk

You can think of ice milk as either the simplest of ice creams or a sorbet with dairy in it; there's no egg and no custard. Ice milk freezes harder and forms larger ice crystals, which makes the texture less smooth and creamy than ice cream; but what you lose in texture and richness you also lose in fat and calories. I think of ice milk as more akin to sorbet than to ice cream and treat it that way.

Sorbet

Typically, though not always, fruit based and dairy and egg free, sorbet is at its core simple and all about the

Ice Creams, Sorbets, and Granitas at Dinner

Omit the sugar in these and they make great additions to Savory Bread Pudding (page 192), savory crêpes (page 196), and cold soups. Or they can be served as a separate course or a savory dessert.

1. Basil or Shiso Ice Cream (page 890)
2. Rum-Chestnut Ice Cream (page 890)
3. Sesame Ice Cream (page 891)
4. Goat Ice Milk (page 892)
5. Orange-Thyme Sorbet (page 892)
6. Fennel-Lemon Sorbet (page 893)
7. Raspberry–Red Wine Sorbet (page 892)
8. Spicy Melon Sorbet (page 892)
9. Pear-Rosemary Sorbet (page 892)
10. Tomato Sorbet (page 892)
11. Pomegranate Granita (page 894)
12. Basil Granita (page 894)
13. Lemongrass-Lime Granita (page 895)
14. Green Tea Granita (page 895)

intensity of flavor. It can be made with just two to three ingredients at a minimum—like a fruit purée (the base), sugar, and sometimes a bit of water. Any fruit, or vegetable for that matter, can be a sorbet base, and beyond that so can chocolate, coffee or espresso, tea, and more. The range is wide, if not a bit overwhelming (take a look at "22 More Sorbet or Ice Milk Flavors," page 892), but there is a flavor for everyone, and there's lots of room for experimentation.

Granita

Granitas have one huge advantage over other frozen desserts: You don't need a machine to make them. But even if you have a machine, the unique texture of granita makes it enormously appealing, at least once in a while. The

MORE ICE CREAM FLAVORS

The base ratio always remains the same: 6 eggs or 2 tablespoons cornstarch with 3 cups total liquid; only the type of liquid and flavorings change. And, remember, cream or dairy milk can always be replaced with nondairy milk.

ICE CREAM	FLAVORING(S)	LIQUID	SWEETENER
Vanilla or Vanilla Cherry Ice Cream	1 vanilla bean, split lengthwise and scraped (see page 859), steeped in hot half-and-half (page 894), or 1 teaspoon vanilla extract; if you like, 1 cup halved pitted fresh or frozen cherries	2 cups half-and-half or milk; 1 cup cream	¹/₂ cup sugar
Strawberry (or Any Berry) Ice Cream	1 cup berry purée, strained (see page 862) and stirred in in Step 4	2 cups half-and-half or milk	¹/₂ cup sugar
Coffee Ice Cream	2 to 3 shots freshly brewed espresso or ¹/₂ cup ground coffee steeped in hot half-and-half for 20 minutes (see page 894)	2 cups half-and-half or milk; 1 cup cream	¹/₂ cup sugar
Coconut Ice Cream	¹/₂ cup shredded coconut, toasted in a dry skillet until lightly browned if you like	2 cups half-and-half or nondairy or dairy milk; 1 cup coconut milk (to make your own, see page 423)	¹/₂ cup sugar
Hot Cinnamon Ice Cream	8 sticks cinnamon (steeped in hot half-and-half, page 894); 1 teaspoon ground cinnamon	2 cups half-and-half or milk; 1 cup cream	¹/₂ cup packed light brown sugar
Real Mint Ice Cream or Real Mint–Chocolate Chip Ice Cream	5 or 6 sprigs fresh mint; ¹/₄ cup very fine chiffonade of mint leaves; ¹/₂ cup finely chopped semisweet chocolate if you like	2 cups half-and-half or milk; 1 cup cream	¹/₂ cup sugar
Chocolate or Chocolate Chile Ice Cream	5 ounces bittersweet or semisweet chocolate, chopped (or use chocolate chips); if you like, steep 2 dried red chiles in the hot half-and-half; add a pinch of ground cinnamon and cloves	2 cups half-and-half or milk; 1 cup cream	¹/₂ cup packed brown sugar
Star Anise–Ginger Ice Cream	2 star anise; 1 teaspoon grated peeled fresh ginger (steeped in hot nut milk, page 894)	2 cups any nut milk; 1 cup cream	¹/₂ cup sugar
Basil or Shiso Ice Cream	¹/₂ cup fresh basil or shiso leaves, blanched, shocked (see page 241), puréed with cream, and strained	2 cups half-and-half or milk; 1 cup cream	¹/₂ cup sugar
Pistachio-Cardamom Ice Cream	¹/₂ cup ground pistachios; 1 teaspoon ground cardamom	3 cups rice milk	¹/₂ cup sugar
Saffron Ice Cream	¹/₂ teaspoon crumbled saffron threads (steeped in hot half-and-half, page 894)	2 cups half-and-half or milk; 1 cup cream	¹/₂ cup sugar
Almond-Peach Ice Cream	¹/₄ cup ground almonds; ¹/₂ cup chopped peeled peach; ¹/₂ cup toasted chopped or sliced almonds	2 cups almond milk; 1 cup peach purée (see page 862)	¹/₂ cup sugar
Rum-Chestnut Ice Cream	³/₄ cup chestnut purée (see page 389); ¹/₄ cup dark rum	1 cup half-and-half or milk; ¹/₂ cup cream	¹/₂ cup maple syrup

     Fast   Ⓜ Make Ahead   Ⓥ Vegan

ICE CREAM	FLAVORING(S)	LIQUID	SWEETENER
Chai Ice Cream	2 teaspoons loose black tea; 3 green cardamom pods, crushed; 2 cloves; 1 stick cinnamon; 2 nickel-size slices of ginger (don't bother to peel); $^1/_2$ star anise, lightly crushed (all steeped with milk, page 894)	3 cups milk	$^3/_4$ cup raw sugar or white sugar
Sesame Ice Cream	3 tablespoons tahini; $^1/_4$ cup toasted black and/or white sesame seeds	3 cups any nut milk or 1 cup half-and-half or milk; $2^1/_2$ cups cream	$^1/_2$ cup sugar

crunchy flakes of intensely flavored ice are made by stirring and scraping a liquid as it freezes, which forms small ice crystals like a good snow cone. Aside from remembering to stir it, there is no special technique to making a granita; it's truly a no-brainer. Even better, you can make it with—literally—any flavored liquid you like; if you can freeze it—even partially—you can turn it into granita.

Buttermilk Ice Cream

MAKES: About 3 cups

TIME: 20 minutes, plus time to chill and freeze

The beauty of ice cream is not only its texture but that it can take on almost any flavor and be made with or without eggs, with either dairy or nondairy milk or cream (which means it can be a vegan "ice cream"). And feel free to adjust the proportion of buttermilk to milk. The most important thing is that the base (the ratio of milks to yolks or cornstarch) remain the same.

This particular flavor is wonderful served with a warm cobbler or crisp, like Apple Cobbler (page 877); the tanginess of the buttermilk pairs perfectly with the fruity sweetness of a cobbler.

2 cups milk or half-and-half

6 egg yolks or 2 tablespoons cornstarch

$^1/_2$ cup sugar

1 cup buttermilk

1 Put the milk in a saucepan over medium-high heat and bring just to a boil, stirring.

2 Meanwhile, beat the yolks and sugar together until thick and slightly lightened in color (you can do this with a whisk or an electric mixer). If you're using cornstarch, mix it with 2 tablespoons or so cold water or milk to make a slurry.

3 For the eggs, stir about $^1/_2$ cup of the milk into the yolk mixture and beat; then stir the warmed egg mixture back into the milk and return to the pan. For the cornstarch slurry, return the milk to the pan and whisk in the slurry and sugar. For both egg and cornstarch mixtures, heat, stirring constantly, until thick. The mixture is ready when it thickly coats the back of a spoon and a line drawn with your finger remains intact (see page 884). (If using cornstarch, strain the mixture before proceeding if you think there might be any lumps.)

4 Cool, then stir in the buttermilk and freeze in an ice cream machine according to the manufacturer's directions.

22 MORE SORBET OR ICE MILK FLAVORS

The Mango or Apricot Sorbet (pages 893–894) and its ice milk variation are the jumping-off points for these variations.

SORBET OR ICE MILK	FLAVORING(S)	LIQUID	SWEETENER
Lemon, Lime, or Yuzu Sorbet	1½ teaspoons each grated lemon and lime zest	1 cup each freshly squeezed lemon and lime juices, or combine with yuzu juice	2 cups Sugar Syrup (page 857)
Frozen Yogurt	¾ cup chopped fresh or dried fruit or 1½ teaspoons grated lemon or orange zest	1¼ cups yogurt (not nonfat); ¾ cup milk	¾ cup superfine sugar or Sugar Syrup (page 857)
Blood Orange or Grapefruit Sorbet	1½ teaspoons blood (or regular) orange zest; ½ teaspoon grated peeled fresh ginger (optional)	2 cups freshly squeezed blood (or regular) orange juice	1 cup superfine sugar or Sugar Syrup (page 857)
Raspberry–Red Wine Sorbet	1 cup raspberries	1 cup red wine (cook all ingredients for 10 minutes and strain)	1 cup Sugar Syrup (page 857)
Espresso Sorbet or Ice Milk	3 to 4 shots freshly brewed espresso; ¼ crushed chocolate-covered espresso beans (optional)	2 cups water or nondairy or dairy milk or cream	1 cup superfine sugar or Sugar Syrup (page 857)
Honey Sorbet		2 cups water (dissolve the honey in hot water)	1 cup good-quality honey
Spicy Melon Sorbet	1 tablespoon minced jalapeño	2 cups any melon purée (see page 862)	¾ cup superfine sugar or Sugar Syrup (page 857)
Goat Ice Milk	1½ teaspoons grated lemon zest	2 cups goat milk	½ cup superfine sugar or Sugar Syrup (page 857)
Tomato Sorbet		2 cups fresh, ripe, peeled red, orange, or yellow tomatoes, pureed and strained; ½ cup water	½ cup superfine sugar or Sugar Syrup (page 857)
Papaya-Lime Sorbet	1½ teaspoons lime zest; 3 tablespoons freshly squeezed lime juice, or to taste	2 cups papaya purée (see page 862)	½ cup superfine sugar or Sugar Syrup (page 857)
Pear-Rosemary Sorbet	1 sprig fresh rosemary (steeped in hot Sugar Syrup, page 857)	2 cups peeled and chopped pear, puréed with lemon juice	¾ cup superfine sugar or Sugar Syrup (page 857)
Orange-Thyme Sorbet	3 sprigs fresh thyme (steeped in hot Sugar Syrup, page 857); ½ teaspoon finely chopped fresh thyme leaves	2 cups freshly squeezed orange juice	¾ cup Sugar Syrup (page 857)
Pineapple-Lavender Sorbet	1 teaspoon lavender buds; ½ cup finely chopped pineapple	2 cups pineapple juice	¾ cup superfine sugar or Sugar Syrup (page 857)
Quince Sorbet	1½ teaspoon grated lemon zest; 2 tablespoons freshly squeezed lemon juice	1 cup quince purée (see page 862), cooked with water and sugar for 20 minutes; ¾ cup water	1 cup superfine sugar or Sugar Syrup (page 857)

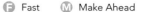 F Fast   M Make Ahead   V Vegan

SORBET OR ICE MILK	FLAVORING(S)	LIQUID	SWEETENER
Chamomile-Tangerine Sorbet	2 tablespoons chamomile buds or tea (steeped in hot Sugar Syrup, page 857)	2 cups freshly squeezed tangerine juice	1 cup Sugar Syrup (page 857)
Cherry-Chocolate Sorbet	$3/4$ cup cocoa powder; 1 cup pitted and halved cherries	2 cups boiling water (mix $1/2$ cup water with the cocoa and sugar; then add remaining ingredients)	$3/4$ cup superfine sugar or Sugar Syrup (page 857)
Fennel-Lemon Sorbet	2 teaspoons grated lemon zest; 2 tablespoons freshly squeezed lemon juice	2 cups shaved fennel, cooked in Sugar Syrup (page 857) until soft, puréed, and strained	1 cup superfine sugar or Sugar Syrup (page 857)
Persimmon Sorbet or Ice Milk	$1/2$ teaspoon ground allspice or cinnamon (optional)	2 cups persimmon purée (see page 862) or 1 cup persimmon purée and 1 cup nondairy or dairy milk or cream	$1/2$ cup honey or Sugar Syrup (page 857)
Horchata Ice Milk	2 cinnamon sticks (steeped in hot rice milk, page 894); 1 teaspoon grated lime zest; 1 tablespoon freshly squeezed lime juice or to taste	2 cups rice milk	1 cup superfine sugar or Sugar Syrup (page 857)
Strawberry–Pink Peppercorn Sorbet or Ice Milk	1 tablespoon crushed pink peppercorns	2 cups strawberry purée (see page 862) or 1 cup strawberry purée and 1 cup nondairy or dairy milk or cream	$1/2$ cup superfine sugar or Sugar Syrup (page 857)
Cucumber-Honey Sorbet		3 cups cucumber purée (see page 390), strained (you should have about 2 cups)	$1/2$ cup honey
Thai Basil Lemon-Lime Sorbet	2 sprigs fresh Thai basil (steeped in hot Sugar Syrup, page 857); 2 tablespoons finely chopped fresh Thai basil leaves; 2 teaspoons grated lemon and lime zest	1 cup freshly squeezed lemon and lime juice	1 cup Sugar Syrup (page 857)

Mango or Apricot Sorbet

MAKES: About 3 cups

TIME: 20 minutes, plus time to churn and chill

This sorbet is so creamy and approaching rich that you may not believe it doesn't contain egg; add some milk or cream (see the variation) and you'll swear it's a proper ice cream.

When you're adding the sugar, remember that the sweetness will be less apparent when the sorbet is frozen, so add a little more when the liquid mixture tastes just right.

4 cups peeled, pitted ripe mango or apricot

1 cup superfine sugar or Sugar Syrup (page 857), or to taste

1 tablespoon freshly squeezed lemon juice, or to taste

① Purée the fruit in a blender with most of the sugar and the lemon juice. Taste and add more of either if nec-

Infusing Liquids with Flavor

Just like steeping tea, you can infuse milk, cream, or any liquid with an ingredient when you want just the flavor and aroma in a dish, not the ingredient itself. It's particularly important when you're making a custard or ice cream where you often want subtle flavors along with a smooth and creamy texture.

Usually the flavoring agent is a spice, herb, or other highly aromatic ingredient, like ginger or lemongrass. When soaked in a hot liquid, ingredients like these release their flavor, aroma, and sometimes color (think of saffron) into the liquid. The steeping and subsequent straining give you the essence of their flavor without any solids.

It really is just like brewing tea: Heat the liquid to boiling (or nearly so for milk), add the flavoring ingredient loose, in a tea ball, or wrapped in cheesecloth, and let it sit for 5 to 20 minutes, depending on the flavoring ingredient and how much flavor you want to infuse; then strain.

essary. If using mango, strain the purée, stirring and pressing the mixture through a strainer with a rubber spatula to leave any fibers behind; be sure to get all the purée from the underside of the strainer.

2 Refrigerate until cool, then churn in an ice cream maker according to the manufacturer's directions.

Mango or Apricot Ice Milk. Thick and creamy: Substitute 1 cup milk (or cream if you want it really rich) for a cup of the fruit. Omit the lemon juice.

Tangerine or Orange Granita

MAKES: About 3 cups
TIME: About 2 hours

Granitas are great, no-special-equipment-needed, minimal-effort desserts that can be made of almost any juice or other liquid imaginable. Their crunchy, icy texture make them unusual, and they're the lightest frozen dessert you can make.

Add a splash or two of vodka or rum to this or any other granita and it becomes a frozen cocktail.

> 2 cups freshly squeezed tangerine or orange juice
>
> Superfine sugar or Sugar Syrup (page 857) to taste
>
> Tangerine or orange zest to taste (optional)

1 Combine all the ingredients, adding enough sugar or syrup to make a nicely sweet blend. Spike with zest if you like.

2 Pour into a shallow glass or ceramic pan and freeze for about 2 hours, stirring to break up the crystals every 30 minutes. It should be slushy and crunchy with ice crystals. If the granita becomes too hard, pulse it (do not purée) in a food processor before serving.

12 Great Granitas

Use these ingredients as your base and sweeten it as you like.

1. Pomegranate Granita: 2 cups bottled or fresh pomegranate juice, a touch of freshly squeezed lemon juice or zest (optional)
2. Strawberry Granita: 3 cups trimmed strawberries, puréed and strained
3. Melon Granita: 2 cups chopped and seeded melon, puréed
4. Green Apple–Lime Granita: 1 cored and chopped Granny Smith apple (peeling is optional) coated with $1/4$ cup freshly squeezed lime juice, $1/2$ teaspoon grated or finely minced lime zest; purée together to minimize browning
5. Tamarind Granita: $1/2$ cup tamarind pulp dissolved in $1 1/2$ cups hot water
6. Basil Granita: $1/2$ cup fresh basil leaves, blanched, shocked, puréed with water, strained; 1 cup water

7. Espresso or Coffee Granita: 3 shots freshly brewed espresso with 2 cups hot water or 2 cups freshly brewed coffee

8. Lemongrass-Lime Granita: $1/2$ cup freshly squeezed lime juice, 2 tablespoons finely minced lemongrass, 1 cup water

9. Guava Granita: 2 cups guava juice, 1 teaspoon grated lemon zest

10. Green Tea Granita: 2 tablespoons green tea

11. Chamomile-Lavender Granita: 2 cups strong chamomile tea brewed with a pinch of lavender buds

12 Zinfandel Granita: $1^1/2$ cups zinfandel wine, $1/2$ cup water

Rice Pudding and Other Sweet Grain Dishes

Just about everyone loves rice pudding, but there's no reason to limit grain-based desserts to white rice. Here I use brown rice, wheat berries, semolina, quinoa, amaranth, couscous, and more, with fabulous results. Although a few of these take a long time to prepare and cook, don't let that discourage you. Much of that time is unattended, nearly mindless baking, and the actual preparation for each takes less than 30 minutes, and in some cases far less than that.

Cinnamon-Nut Rice Pudding

MAKES: 4 servings

TIME: $2^1/2$ hours, largely unattended

Ⓜ Ⓥ

There are dozens of rice puddings, but this is the one I like best. The rice almost melts into the milk, creating a custardlike consistency with a subtle rice flavor. If you prefer a more rice-intense pudding, use the larger quantity of rice.

$1/4$ to $1/3$ cup white rice

$1/3$ to $1/2$ cup sugar, or to taste

Small pinch salt

1 quart nut milk or whole milk

Two 3-inch cinnamon sticks

Ground cinnamon for garnish

Toasted chopped nuts (see page 321) for garnish

❶ Preheat the oven to 325°F. Combine the rice, sugar, salt, milk, and cinnamon sticks in a 3- or 4-quart casserole (an ovenproof saucepan will do), stir a couple of times, and put, uncovered, in the oven. Cook for 2 hours, stirring every 30 minutes.

❷ Now the pudding is almost done. Begin to check the pudding every 10 minutes, stirring gently each time you check. The pudding will be done anywhere from 10 to 30 minutes later, when the rice kernels are very swollen and the pudding is thick but still pourable (it will thicken considerably as it cools). If the mixture is silky-creamy and thick, the rice suspended perfectly in a rich custard, it is overcooked; it will be too hard when it cools (though still quite good to eat). Remember to remove the cinnamon stick while it's cooling.

❸ Serve warm, at room temperature, or cold, garnished with a bit of ground cinnamon and chopped nuts.

Coconut Rice Pudding. Rich: Substitute coconut milk (to make your own, see page 423) for the nut milk, shredded coconut for the nuts. Omit the cinnamon.

Baked Semolina Pudding

MAKES: 9 servings

TIME: 1 hour

Ⓜ

Served warm, this pudding is filling, cakelike, and delicious—perfect for a chilly night. Adding the glaze or cake soak makes it richly sweet and adds wonderful hints of flavor; the soak adds even more moisture. If you prefer a less sweet pudding, skip the glaze or soak; top it with a fruit purée (see page 862) or Chocolate or Vanilla Custard Sauce (page 863).

> 4 tablespoons (¹/₂ stick) butter, plus butter for the pan
>
> ¹/₃ cup almonds or hazelnuts, very finely chopped or ground in a food processor
>
> 1 cup whole-milk yogurt
>
> ³/₄ cup sugar
>
> 1 cup semolina
>
> ¹/₂ teaspoon baking soda
>
> 1 teaspoon vanilla extract
>
> ¹/₂ recipe Rose Water Glaze (page 858) or Vanilla–Brown Sugar Cake Soak (page 859) (optional)
>
> Whipped cream (page 856) for garnish (optional)

1 Preheat the oven to 375°F. Grease an 8- or 9-inch square baking pan. Put the butter in a skillet over medium-high heat. When the foam subsides, add the almonds. Cook, stirring constantly, until they are lightly browned, about 3 minutes.

2 Beat the yogurt and sugar together in a large bowl. Add the almonds and their butter, the semolina, the baking soda, and the vanilla; beat until thoroughly blended. Spread the batter into the prepared pan. Bake until the pudding is lightly browned, about 30 minutes.

3 Pour the glaze or soak over the top (or use none at all). Let rest for a few minutes, then cut into 9 squares and serve warm, with the whipped cream if you like.

Chocolate Semolina Pudding. Omit the nuts if you like. In Step 1, add ¹/₄ cup cocoa powder and ¹/₃ cup (2 ounces) chopped semisweet or bittersweet chocolate to the melted butter. When smooth, stir into the yogurt and sugar in Step 2. Proceed with the recipe. Spread the warm pudding with ¹/₂ recipe of Chocolate Ganache (page 860) or Orange Glaze (page 857).

Indian Cornmeal Pudding

MAKES: 4 servings

TIME: 3¹/₂ hours, largely unattended

A Native American dish that bakes slowly for hours. The results are soft and creamy with subtle spice and deep sweetness from the molasses and sugar. Despite its 3-plus-hours cooking time, it takes minimal effort to make.

> 1 quart whole milk
>
> ¹/₂ cup molasses
>
> ³/₄ cup sugar
>
> ¹/₂ cup cornmeal
>
> 1 teaspoon ground cinnamon
>
> ¹/₂ teaspoon ground ginger
>
> ¹/₂ teaspoon salt
>
> 3 tablespoons butter, plus butter for the pan

1 Put 3¹/₂ cups of the milk in a medium saucepan over medium heat. Stir in the molasses and sugar and, when they are incorporated, turn the heat down to low. Preheat the oven to 300°F.

2 Slowly sprinkle the cornmeal over the warm milk mixture, stirring or whisking all the while; break up any lumps that form. When the mixture thickens—this will take 10 minutes or more—stir in the cinnamon, ginger, salt and 3 tablespoons butter and turn off the heat.

3 Grease an 8- or 9-inch square baking dish or similar-size gratin dish and turn the warm mixture into it; top with the remaining ¹/₂ cup milk; do not stir. Bake for 2¹/₂ to 3 hours, or until the pudding is set. Serve warm, cold, or at room temperature; wrapped well and refrigerated, this keeps for several days.

Vegan Cornmeal Pudding. Just as delicious, especially with hazelnut milk: Substitute nut milk for the dairy milk and omit the butter. Reduce the sugar to ¹/₂ cup. Add ¹/₂ cup chopped nuts or dried fruit (or a combination of the two) if you like.

Sweet Couscous with Pistachios

MAKES: 4 servings

TIME: 15 minutes

A quick, simple, fat-free dessert that really can't go wrong; the couscous is cooked the same way you make it for dinner, but with some sugar in the water. You can dress it up even more by serving it with Almond Custard Sauce (page 863), made with pistachios, or just use warm milk or cream. And you can vary the seasonings any way you like, from the traditional cinnamon-nutmeg combination to ground chiles or fresh ginger.

Cooking the couscous in juice is great way to add loads of flavor and sweetness without adding more sugar.

$^3/_4$ cup sugar

1 cup regular or whole wheat couscous

2 teaspoons grated or finely minced lemon or orange zest

1 cup chopped unsalted pistachios

1 teaspoon ground cardamom

1 or 2 teaspoons rose water (optional)

❶ Put $1^1/_2$ cups water and the sugar in a pot and bring to a boil; add the couscous, zest, pistachios, and cardamom; cover and continue to cook for a minute, then turn off the heat and let sit for 5 minutes.

❷ Fluff the couscous with a fork and sprinkle on the rose water if you're using it. Serve warm or room temperature with a sauce (see headnote) or some milk or cream drizzled over the top.

Sweet Almond Milk Couscous. Almost souplike: Substitute $2^1/_2$ cups almond milk for the water and sliced or chopped almonds for the pistachios.

Sweet Couscous with Dried Fruit. A tablespoon or two of crystallized ginger is a great addition here: Substitute chopped various dried fruit for the pistachios.

Sweet Couscous with Citrus Salad. This is best at room temperature: Use mixed citrus zest and omit the pistachios, cardamom, and rose water. Add 1 cup orange, tangerine, and/or grapefruit segments tossed with 3 tablespoons chopped mint leaves. Proceed with the recipe. Let the couscous cool to room temperature and serve topped with the citrus mix.

Sweet Bulgur with Spices. Good wheaty flavor: Substitute $^1/_2$ cup fine-grind (#1) or medium-grind (#2) bulgur for the couscous, cinnamon for the zest, and raisins for the pistachios. Add $^1/_4$ teaspoon each ground cloves, nutmeg, black pepper, and $^1/_2$ teaspoon ground ginger. Omit the rose water. Proceed with the recipe, letting the bulgur sit for 10 to 20 minutes (depending on the grind) in Step 1.

The Basics of Mousse and Meringue

If cookies are at the crunch end of the dessert spectrum, then mousses and meringues are the fluff, with a light spring and slightly foamy texture that at its best is almost like eating air. One is uncooked, while the other is baked, to form a chewy, almost crackling shell around the outside. For most people, it's love at first bite, but these are both virtually unknown to many people born after 1960. I'm not on a trendy retro kick or anything; they just happen to be perfect desserts, especially after a not-too-heavy meal.

Maybe fear sent mousses and meringues into culinary oblivion. Even though they're really nothing more than whipped cream and egg whites (with a little sweetener and flavor of some kind), the hardest part—which is not hard at all—is whipping or beating the cream and egg whites just right. There's no mystery or even much skill behind it; it's just a matter of knowing when to stop.

For mousse, the cream is whipped to one of two stages, either soft peaks or stiff peaks (see page 856), depending

SEPARATING EGGS

To separate eggs, (STEP 1) break the egg with the back of a knife or on the side of a bowl.

(STEP 2) The simplest way to separate eggs is to use the shell halves, moving the yolk back and forth once or twice so that the white falls into a bowl. Be careful, however, not to allow any of the yolk to mix in with the whites or the whites will not rise no matter how much you beat them.

BEATING EGG WHITES

Soft peak stage: Whites look soft, and when you remove the whisk or beaters, the tops fold over.

Firm peak stage: Whites look stiff, and when you remove the whisk or beaters, the tops make distinct peaks. Do not beat beyond this point.

on whether you're adding egg whites. If egg whites are not being used in the mousse, the cream must provide structure (in addition to a gelling agent, like agar powder), so it must be whipped to the sturdier stiff peaks.

Whipping egg whites is no more complicated than whipping cream, and it provides the base structure for the majority of mousses and all meringues. The whites are whipped to stiff peaks so the softer whipped cream, flavorings, and other additions don't deflate it. See "Beating Egg Whites" (page 899).

Flavoring mousse or meringue is easy; almost anything can be folded into either. Mousse is best with liquid or puréed flavorings as the texture should be soft and smooth. Just be careful that the liquid is at most tepid since warm or hot liquids will deflate the whipped cream or egg whites. It's also important to use a slightly thickened liquid; thicken with egg whites (as in Frozen Honey Mousse, page 900) or a thickening agent like agar powder (as in Blueberry [or Any Berry] Mousse, page 901), or use a naturally thick purée.

 Fast   Make Ahead   Ⓥ Vegan

Whipped egg whites are the essential ingredient in the lightest and fluffiest dishes, including meringues, soufflés, and most mousses. But they're also used in cakes, quick breads, pancake and waffle batters, and more.

Whipping or beating egg whites to a white and fluffy foam is an easy task, especially with an electric mixer. And watching the whites go from clear and slippery to pure white and puffy foam is pretty spectacular, especially since their volume increases by seven or eight times. For simplicity's sake I'll skip the chemistry lesson and just say that whipping egg whites forces air bubbles into them; these get caught in protein molecules that stretch out to hold the molecules together. The process is called *coagulation,* and it's not unlike the reaction that occurs when you cook proteins.

For equipment, at most you'll need a mixer with a whisk attachment and a spotlessly clean metal or glass bowl; at the least a big whisk, the bowl, and a well-rested arm. You've probably seen recipes that tell you to whip your whites in a copper bowl; while it's true that copper will yield a more sturdy foam, really any type of metal or glass bowl will do. The one type of material you want to avoid is plastic because its porous surface can retain fat molecules, which will interfere with the whites' ability to foam.

There are really only a couple of potential pitfalls: The first is getting even the tiniest bit of yolk—or any fat—in the whites; even oil residue clinging to the sides of a bowl will ruin or at least seriously impede your whites' ability to whip up. If a bit of yolk does get in the whites, use the tip of a knife to pluck the yolk out or—much safer—start with a fresh egg.

The other mistake when whipping whites is overbeating them. Just like cream (page 856), egg whites can be whipped to various stages:

Soft peaks: The foam will just make a low peak with a tip that readily folds onto itself.

Medium peaks: A solid peak, still soft, with a tip that folds over but not onto itself.

Stiff or firm peaks: A fairly stiff peak with a tip that hardly bends; dragging your finger through the foam will leave a distinct mark. It should not be clumpy, though (see "Overwhipped").

Overwhipped: The foam will be clumpy, rough looking, and leaking water. There's no fixing overwhipped egg whites; toss 'em.

Adding Sugar, Salt, or Cream of Tartar

Often you'll see recipes calling for cream of tartar (an acid), salt, or sugar to be added to egg whites to make the foam fluffier, more stable, and better tasting (particularly with salt and sugar). Never add more than the tiniest pinch of salt to the eggs; salt does add flavor, but it creates a less stable foam. Many people add cream of tartar in the belief that it helps whip up the eggs; I've found no distinct advantage to adding it, so I always skip it.

Whipping in sugar, on the other hand, has both positives and negatives: the sugar molecules make whipping more difficult (it will take longer for the eggs to foam) and decreases the foam volume a bit; but it also makes for a more stable foam *when cooked.* The sugar helps the egg whites retain moisture while cooking so it's less likely to fall and leak water; this is important for meringues and soufflés in particular. When you do add sugar, use confectioners' sugar, which dissolves more quickly than granulated sugar (undissolved grains of sugar can cause syrupy beads to form on the surface of a meringue), and add it once the whites have formed medium peaks.

(STEP 1) To fold beaten eggs whites into a batter, first lighten the mixture by stirring a couple of spoonfuls of the whites into it.

(STEP 2) Then gently fold the rest of the egg whites in, scooping under the mixture and smoothing over the top. You can use a rubber spatula or your hand, which works equally well.

Meringues, on the other hand, are delicious with chopped or ground nuts, shredded coconut, and the like; the added texture gives the meringue a wonderful chewiness in addition to flavor. Typically you can add a cup of nuts or coconut for every egg white, though it doesn't hurt to add another egg white for posterity.

Frozen Honey Mousse

MAKES: 6 to 8 servings
TIME: 20 minutes, plus time to chill

Mousse is one of those desserts that always impresses people, which I find a bit strange because it's so easy to make. You'll be amazed by the light and airy texture of this mousse—you almost can't tell it's been frozen. You can serve this mousse unfrozen, but it must be served within an hour or two of making it (otherwise it will start leaching water). Be aware that this recipe uses raw eggs; if you want a mousse without raw eggs, see the vegan variation and Blueberry (or Any Berry) Mousse (page 901).

4 egg whites
1/3 cup honey
1/4 cup confectioners' sugar
1 1/2 cups cream

1 Beat the egg whites to soft peaks and beat in the honey and half the confectioners' sugar until they hold stiff peaks, 3 or 4 more minutes (the honey will keep the meringue on the softer side of stiff peaks). Set aside. Beat the cream with the remaining sugar until it holds medium peaks.

2 Thoroughly but gently fold the cream into the whites. Gently transfer the mousse to individual ramekins or cups (it's quicker to chill) or into one dish, cover with plastic, and freeze until firm, 2 to 3 hours. Serve within a few hours or at most a day of making.

Chocolate-Orange Vegan Mousse. Puréed then whipped, this vegan mousse is surprisingly good: Substitute 1 pound silken tofu for the cream, 8 ounces melted bittersweet or semisweet chocolate for the honey, and 3/4 cup Sugar Syrup (page 857) for the confectioners' sugar. Add 1 teaspoon grated or finely minced orange zest. Omit the eggs. Put all the ingredients in a blender and purée until very smooth. Beat with a

F Fast   **M** Make Ahead   **V** Vegan

whisk until aerated and a bit fluffy, about 5 minutes. Chill and serve.

Blueberry (or Any Berry) Mousse

MAKES: 4 servings

TIME: 20 minutes, plus time to chill

Eggless but no less flavorful and rich, although slightly less fluffy. The thickener, agar, provides the base structure to hold the mousse; whipped cream provides airiness.

> 2½ cups cream
>
> ¼ cup confectioners' sugar
>
> 2 cups blueberries or other berries, trimmed as necessary
>
> ½ cup sugar
>
> 2 teaspoons agar powder

1 Put the cream in a bowl and start whipping it; when it's almost stiff, add the confectioners' sugar and finish whipping to stiff peaks. Set aside, in the refrigerator if it's warm.

2 Put the berries and sugar, along with ¼ cup water, in a blender and purée until smooth; strain to remove the seeds. Transfer the purée to a small pot, add the agar, and let sit for 10 minutes. Cook the berry mixture until it comes to a low boil. Remove from the heat, pour into a medium bowl, and stir frequently until it cools and just starts to thicken; this won't take long, about 10 minutes.

3 Stir a couple of spoonfuls of the whipped cream into the berry mixture to lighten it a bit, then fold in the remaining cream gently but thoroughly. Spoon into the serving dish(es) and refrigerate until set and chilled. If you are in a hurry, divide the mousse among 6 cups; it will chill much faster. Serve within a day of making.

Folding Cream or Egg Whites

Folding is an essential technique used to incorporate beaten cream or egg whites into mousses, meringues, soufflés, and other light and airy batters. The idea is to gently add the cream or whites that you've worked hard at making airy without deflating them.

A gentle hand is your best friend here—literally. Though you can use a rubber spatula, I find that using my hand is more effective, because I can actually feel the process as it progresses. You add a bit of the whites or cream to the batter and scoop the batter from the bottom up over it, folding the whites in as gently as you can. Actually, it's done in two or three stages: first you add about a third or so of the whipped ingredient into the base, incorporating pretty fully to lighten the mixture. Then you add the remainder, in one or two stages, folding as gently as possible. Start your folds by scooping from the side to the bottom and folding the ingredients over the top in the middle; continue this folding technique while rotating the bowl slowly.

When the ingredients look mostly incorporated, stop. The most common mistake in folding is overfolding and thus deflating the whipped ingredient. It's okay to have some streaks of whipped cream or egg white in the mixture; you just don't want large clumps of it.

Mango Mousse. Freeze this and it's the perfect dessert after a spicy Indian, Southeast Asian, or Mexican meal: Substitute chopped peeled mango (papaya is good too) for the berries.

Peach or Apricot Mousse. A great summertime mousse when stone fruits are at their best: Substitute chopped peeled peaches or chopped apricots for the berries. No need to strain after puréeing.

Pistachio Meringue

MAKES: About 4 dozen

TIME: About 2¹/₂ hours, plus an hour to cool

Meringues are nearly fat-free treats that can fit any occasion; they can range from tiny, pop-in-your-mouth cookie-sized snacks to containers for purées, ice cream, or sauces (see "Meringues as Edible Containers," below). They can also be flavored with nearly anything you can imagine. For instance, any type of nut can be used in place of or mixed in with the pistachios in the main recipe; see the variations for an eclectic mix of flavors.

4 egg whites, at room temperature

4 pinches cream of tarter

1 teaspoon vanilla extract

Pinch salt

1 cup superfine or regular sugar

¹/₂ cup finely chopped or ground unsalted pistachios

1 teaspoon ground cardamom (optional)

1 Heat the oven to 200°F. Use a standing or hand-held electric mixer to beat the whites and the cream of tarter, vanilla, and salt until they begin to hold peaks. Gradually add the sugar, and beat until the mixture holds stiff peaks. Fold in the pistachios and the cardamom if you like.

2 Line a baking sheet with parchment. Use a pastry bag, a resealable plastic bag with a corner cut out, a spoon, or wet hands to form small mounds of the meringue mixture, each a couple tablespoons (larger if you like); you can put them quite close together since they won't rise.

3 Bake until hard and they release easily, about two hours. Turn off the oven and open the door a bit; let the meringues cool in the oven for another hour or so. These keep well in an airtight container for up to 3 days.

Coconut–Dried Pineapple Macaroons. Slightly chewy with loads of flavor and texture: Substitute ¹/₄ cup shredded coconut and ¹/₄ cup finely chopped dried pineapple for the pistachios and grated or finely minced lime zest for the cardamom if you like, or omit it.

Toasted Oats and Chocolate Chip Macaroons. A bit of brown sugar and any chopped dried fruit is great in these too: Substitute ¹/₂ cup toasted oats and ¹/₂ cup chocolate chunks (¹/₄-inch pieces or smaller) for the pistachios and ground cinnamon for the cardamom. Pulse the oats in a food processor for about 3 seconds to chop lightly.

Meringues as Edible Containers

Meringue batter has a unique fluffy stiffness that holds its shape and then hardens when baked, which makes it great for forming cups or nests for holding purées, ice cream, or fruit.

Making the containers is easy and takes literally seconds to do, though it looks complicated and pretty spectacular. Put the batter in a pastry bag fitted with a plain round or star-shaped tip that's at least ¹/₄ inch in diameter or in a resealable plastic bag with a corner the same diameter cut out. Start by making the bottom of the container: Create a coil, leaving no space between the circles; 3 or 4 inches in diameter is a good single-serving size. Then make the "wall" by piping a ring onto the outermost bottom ring; add another ring if you want a deeper container. Alternatively, you can pipe little dollops of meringue along the outer ring to create a peaked wall. For a really rustic look, make the containers without piping the meringue, simply scooping out the center of a large dollop, leaving a "floor" of meringue.

Bake the meringue containers a bit longer than the cookies to get them hard instead of chewy; 45 to 50 minutes should do it.

Sweet Sesame Meringue. Rich and nutty; sprinkle the tops with black sesame seeds for a striking look: Substitute $^1/_2$ cup toasted sesame seeds for the pistachios and 2 teaspoons grated or finely minced lemon zest for the cardamom. Pulse the sesame seeds with 2 tablespoons of the sugar in the food processor for 4 or 5 seconds to grind them; they will be ground unevenly.

Mocha Meringue. A light blend of chocolate and coffee flavors: Add 1 more egg white. Substitute 3 tablespoons cocoa powder and 1 shot freshly brewed espresso for the pistachios. Omit the cardamom.

The Basics of Dessert Soups

By no means a new concept, soup as dessert doesn't get much attention these days—which is too bad: Dessert soups are a fantastic way to showcase deliciously ripe fruit while ending the meal on the light side.

The soups here are mostly fruit, and since the idea is to capture the fruits' wonderful flavors, the majority are uncooked. But since the fruit is the highlight, getting what's in season and delicious is key; this is no place to compromise on quality or flavor.

Dessert soups, like their savory cousins, can be either brothy, thick, or puréed. All styles are equally easy to make. Here are a few pointers:

- Keep the flavors simple; let the fruit or other base ingredient speak for itself.
- Make the soup no more than a day in advance if not just a couple hours before serving; it will taste fresher.
- In most recipes, you can substitute just about any ripe and flavorful fruit for any other.
- For brothy soups, the flavor of the broth should complement, even highlight, that of the fruit, so use a light hand when seasoning the broth. In general, try to keep the broth crystal clear so you can see the colorful fruit in it (obviously, this doesn't apply to the Sweet Coconut Soup, page 905).

- For puréed soup, the consistency should be like that of heavy cream, neither watery nor overly thick.
- If you like, add a scoop of ice cream, sour cream, crème fraîche, yogurt, sorbet, or granita; it adds another layer of flavor, texture, and temperature.

Watermelon and Mint Soup

MAKES: 4 servings
TIME: 20 minutes

This light and refreshing soup is an ideal summertime dessert—add more rum and turn it into a cocktail you either pour from a glass or eat with a spoon. Cantaloupe, honeydew, and Crenshaw melons work here too, but since they aren't as watery as watermelon you'll have to press the purée more in Step 2 and may have to add a little water to the blender. For a classic berry soup—the kind you'd get at a fancy brunch—try the first variation.

$^1/_2$ cup Sugar Syrup (page 857)

4 stems fresh mint

2 pounds ripe watermelon, rind and seeds removed

3 tablespoons freshly squeezed lemon or lime juice

$^1/_4$ cup rum (optional)

1 teaspoon grated lemon or lime zest

Chopped fresh mint leaves for garnish

1 Put the syrup and mint stems in a small pot and bring to a boil. Turn off the heat and steep for about 10 minutes, then discard the stems and let the mint syrup cool to room temperature.

2 Cut enough of the watermelon into $^1/_2$-inch cubes to measure 2 cups and set aside. Put the remaining watermelon in a blender; add the lemon juice, the rum if you're using it, and the mint syrup. Purée until liquefied. Line a fine-meshed strainer with a clean kitchen towel and set it over a large bowl; strain the watermelon purée, pressing on the pulp to squeeze as much juice out as you can.

❸ Divide the watermelon soup among 4 bowls, add the watermelon cubes and zest and garnish with the chopped mint leaves.

Sparkling Wine with Berries. So simple and lovely: Omit the rum and use lemon juice and zest. Substitute 3 cups mixed berries (whole or sliced as necessary) for the watermelon and add 3¹/₂ cups sparkling white wine; increase the sugar syrup to 1 cup. Skip Step 2. Proceed with the recipe. Pour the mint syrup over the fruit in the bowls, then pour on the sparkling wine.

Vanilla-Apricot Soup. Slice the apricots and float them in the sweet soup or purée together: Use lemon juice and zest and increase the Sugar Syrup to 1 cup. Substitute 1 vanilla bean for the mint stems, ripe apricots for the watermelon, Cointreau or sweet white wine for the rum, and whipped cream or crème fraîche for garnish. Split the vanilla bean in half lengthwise, use a small sharp knife to scrape the seeds into the Sugar Syrup, and add a cup of water and the lemon juice and zest; discard the pod. Skip Step 2; slice the apricots, put in the bowls, and pour the vanilla soup over top. Macerate for up to 2 hours if you have the time.

Persimmon Soup. Creamy and sweet; great for the fall, when persimmons are ripe: Omit the lemon or lime juice and zest. Substitute 2 or more tablespoons honey for the Sugar Syrup, ¹/₂ teaspoon ground cinnamon for the mint stems, ripe peeled hachiya persimmons (see page 434) for the watermelon, and cream for the rum. Put all the ingredients in a blender and purée until smooth, adding more cream or some water if it's too thick; divide between the bowls and serve. Garnish with a sprinkle of ground cinnamon and a dollop of whipped cream or crème fraîche (page 207).

Fruit and Gelée in Ginger Broth. Served cold, gelées add a nice texture; spoon the gelée in or cut into cubes: Omit the lemon or lime juice, rum, and mint leaves and increase the Sugar Syrup to 1 cup. Substi-

tute 1 tablespoon grated or very finely minced peeled fresh ginger for the mint stems and mixed sliced or chopped fruit, like plum, peach, grapes, berries, carambola, or kiwi, for the watermelon. Add 1 recipe fruit or Honey Gelée (page 888). Proceed with Step 1; chill the ginger broth, then strain out the ginger. Skip Step 2. Put 3 or so spoonfuls or cubes of gelée into each bowl, top with fruit, sprinkle with zest, and ladle on the ginger broth.

Rhubarb-Orange Soup

MAKES: 4 servings
TIME: 15 minutes, plus time to chill

Since having this soup in England, where rhubarb is much more popular than in the United States, I can't help making it at the first sight of rhubarb in the market.

1 medium orange

2 pounds rhubarb, trimmed

1 cup sugar

Whipped cream (page 856), sour cream, crème fraîche, or lightly sweetened yogurt for garnish (optional)

❶ Zest the orange and mince the zest; juice the orange. String the rhubarb (see page 284), then cut it into roughly 2-inch lengths.

❷ Combine the rhubarb, sugar, 1 quart water, the orange juice, and half the zest in a saucepan and bring to a boil. (Wrap and refrigerate the remaining zest.) Turn the heat down to medium and cook until the rhubarb begins to fall apart, 10 to 15 minutes.

❸ Chill (if you're in a hurry, pour the mixture into a large bowl and set that bowl in an even larger bowl filled with ice water). When cool, whisk briefly to break up the rhubarb, adding the reserved zest at the same time. Serve cold, garnished with whipped cream if you like.

Cranberry-Orange Soup. Lovely after a filling Thanksgiving or any meal: Substitute 1 pound cranberries for the rhubarb. Thin the soup with more orange juice if necessary.

Quince-Ginger Soup. Another sweet-tart soup: Substitute 2 teaspoons grated or very finely minced peeled fresh ginger for the orange and quince, roughly chopped (skin, core, and all), for the rhubarb. Proceed with the recipe, cooking the quince until the liquid has a pinkish red tinge and the flesh is soft; strain and discard the flesh and chill the soup. Serve chilled with Ginger Whipped Cream (page 856).

Sweet Coconut Soup

MAKES: 4 servings

TIME: 15 minutes with cooked beans

  Ⓥ

Combining jasmine tea and coconut milk makes for an unusual, light, and delicious soup. The beans—not uncommon in Asian desserts—add a mild flavor and texture, but since some people find them too gritty, I make them optional. The fruit adds more layers of flavor, texture, and color; keep the pieces bite-sized for easier eating.

2 teaspoons jasmine tea

1/4 cup sugar, or to taste

2 cups coconut milk (to make your own, see page 423)

1 cup cooked mung or adzuki beans (see page 581; optional)

1 cup sliced or chopped fresh fruit, like mango, kiwi, papaya, melon, lychees, or any tropical fruit

Shaved or shredded coconut, preferably fresh, for garnish

❶ Bring 1 1/2 cups water to a boil and brew the tea for about 5 or 6 minutes (you want it to be strong); discard the tea leaves. Stir in the sugar until it's dissolved; set the tea aside and let it cool (quicker in the fridge). Shake or whisk the coconut milk to blend the thick "cream" with the juice (especially if you're using canned). Chill the

coconut milk as well (to quickly chill the tea and/or coconut milk, put a cup or two of ice in a medium bowl and pour the tea or milk over the top; stir for about 30 seconds, then strain out the ice). Combine the tea and coconut milk.

❷ Divide the beans if you're using them and the fruit among 4 bowls and pour on the coconut-tea mixture. Garnish with the coconut and serve.

Sweet Coconut Soup with Grains or Tapioca. Use cooked grains in place of the beans: Substitute 1 cup cooked pearl couscous, pearled barley, rice, or pearl tapioca for the mung or adzuki beans.

Sweet Coconut Soup with Granita. Based on Indonesian shaved ice desserts, which feature tropical fruits, avocado, and jelly: Omit the tea and add 4 cups or so Tamarind, Basil, Lemongrass-Lime, or Guava Granita (see pages 894–895). Mix the sugar into the coconut milk, stirring until it's dissolved. Assemble the soups with the beans and fruit (add cubes of Lemon-Lime Gelées, page 887, if you like); drizzle on the sweetened coconut milk; top with the granita. Serve immediately.

Sweet Almond Soup. Light and delicious; serve it chilled or warm: Omit the tea and beans. Substitute almond milk for the coconut milk; berries, pomegranate seeds, apricots, or peaches for the fruit; and sliced almonds for the shaved coconut. Add 1 teaspoon almond extract, rose water, or vanilla extract if you like. Mix the sugar and extracts, if you're using any, into the almond milk, stirring until the sugar is dissolved. Chill or warm the almond milk and pour it over the fruit; serve the soup cold or warm.

Candy

Candies can be divided into two types: those that can be made only by professionals (or fanatical amateurs), who have trained for years in the art and science of candy making, and those that can be made by us mortals, in our home kitchens. While the gorgeous, glasslike candy structures you've likely seen on TV are intimidating and virtually impossible to make at home, the brittle and caramels in this section are completely doable; in fact they're downright easy.

It's likely you already have what you'll need; you might want a candy thermometer, but even that isn't essential. Beyond that we're talking a saucepan, a spoon, a pan, maybe some wax paper or plastic wrap, and a bit of patience (specifically for wrapping all the pieces of caramel and taffy; but I used to get my kids to do that part, in exchange for candy of course). The ingredients are as basic as you can get: sugar, milk or cream, butter, and nuts.

I've arranged the recipes here from simplest to trickiest, but neither is truly difficult.

Brittled Popcorn

MAKES: About 12 ounces
TIME: About 20 minutes, plus time to cool

A classic and simple candy that can be whipped up in no time and varied with the addition of different nuts, seeds, and spices (see the list at right). Eat it straight or chop it up and sprinkle it on ice cream. It keeps practically forever.

The brittled popcorn gives you nice clusters of crunchy popcorn, while the nut brittle variations result in the more traditional flat pieces.

Butter or neutral oil for the pan

2 cups sugar

4 cups Buttered Popcorn (page 292) without the butter

Pinch salt

① Grease a large baking pan, preferably one with a low rim, with butter or neutral oil, like grapeseed or corn.

② Put the sugar and $1/3$ cup water in a small deep pot over low heat. Cook, without stirring, until the sugar dis-

solves and starts to color. (If you like, use a brush dipped in water to wash the sugar crystals off the sides of the pot.) Keep cooking until the caramel turns golden but not dark brown, anywhere from 5 to 10 minutes. Put the popcorn in a big heatproof bowl.

③ Drizzle the hot sugar syrup over the popcorn, sprinkle with salt, and toss to coat—you must work quickly so the sugar doesn't harden. While warm, spread the mixture onto the prepared pan, breaking up the large chunks. Let the brittle cool, then break it into pieces or leave it as is. Store in a covered container for several days.

Nut Brittle. The classic, any way you like it: Substitute 2 cups nuts for the popcorn. Roasted or toasted nuts (see page 321) are best (especially hazelnuts and peanuts, which can also be peeled if you like). In Step 3, spread the nuts and sugar syrup mixture into a baking sheet. Cool, then break into pieces. (If you like, you can score the brittle with a knife when it has solidified slightly but not yet turned hard; that way, it will break into even squares.)

Chocolate-Nut Brittle. An excellent holiday treat to give away: Make the preceding Nut Brittle variation. Drizzle the brittle with some melted semisweet, milk, or white chocolate after the brittle has cooled fully but before you break it into pieces. Put it in the refrigerator or freezer to harden, then break up.

6 Other Things to Add to Brittle

Mix and match as you like—sesame seeds with five-spice powder and macadamia with coconut are both good, for example—but keep it simple so the flavors don't muddy.

1. Any other nuts (I like salted nuts in brittle, but you can go either way): peanuts (classic, of course), almonds, walnuts, pecans, macadamia, cashews, or pistachios
2. 1 cup seeds: white and/or black sesame seeds, pumpkin seeds, sunflower seeds, or poppy seeds
3. 2 cups unsweetened shredded coconut
4. 2 cups chopped dried fruit: raisins, dates, cherries, pineapple, or apricots

Ⓕ Fast   Ⓜ Make Ahead   Ⓥ Vegan

5. 1 to 2 teaspoons ground or crushed spices: cinnamon, five-spice powder (to make your own, see page 816), allspice, nutmeg, cardamom, or black or pink peppercorns

6. $^1/_4$ to $^1/_2$ cup crushed espresso beans

Caramels

MAKES: About 50 pieces

TIME: $1^1/_2$ hours (including cooling, cutting, and wrapping the pieces)

These candies take just 30 minutes to cook and cool—it's the wrapping that takes the most time. Recruit some help (this is a good kid project) or wrap them in front of the television, but don't expect to get all 50 pieces in the end (I guarantee you'll wind up sampling a few).

4 tablespoons ($^1/_2$ stick) unsalted butter, plus butter for the pan

$1^1/_2$ cups cream

2 cups sugar

$^1/_2$ cup light corn syrup

Pinch salt

$1^1/_2$ teaspoons vanilla extract (optional)

1 Lightly grease an 8- or 9-inch square baking pan or similar container. Combine all the ingredients except the vanilla in a wide saucepan or deep skillet over medium-low heat. Cook, stirring occasionally, until the sugar dissolves.

2 The mixture will bubble and gradually darken; cook until it's caramel colored and the temperature measures 245°F (a small piece of it will form a firm ball when dropped into a glass of cold water, but the thermometer is an easier and surer test).

3 Stir in the vanilla and pour into the prepared pan. Cool, then remove from the pan in a block and refrigerate, but not for too long: You want the mixture to be cool enough so that it's not too sticky, but not so cold that it's solid; this is the easiest state in which to cut and wrap.

4 Use a sharp knife to cut the caramel into pieces, then wrap each square in wax paper or plastic wrap. These keep for weeks (especially if refrigerated) but are best eaten fresh (and at room temperature).

Coffee Caramels. A great afternoon pick-me-up treat: Substitute 1 cup of strong freshly brewed coffee for 1 cup of the cream or $^1/_2$ cup brewed espresso for $^1/_2$ cup of the cream.

Menus

Breakfasts

Summer Weekend Breakfast
sliced melon
Coffee Cake Muffins   693
Baked Cherry Omelet   179
assorted jams and jellies
iced coffee or tea

Vegan Breakfast
Vegan Breakfast Burritos   175
Minimalist Guacamole   264
Citrus Salsa   752
coffee or tea

Leisurely Sunday Breakfast
fresh orange juice
Fried Eggs with Cheese   168
Crisp Panfried Potatoes   343

Yogurt or Buttermilk Biscuits   694
cappuccino or tea

Autumn Breakfast
Battered Apple "Fries"   249
The Best Scrambled Eggs   167
Pumpkin Ginger Bread
   with Hazelnuts   692
café au lait or tea

Brunches

Spring Brunch
Fava Bean and Mint Salad
   with Asparagus   77
Herbed Cheese Shortbread   696
Green Pea and Parmesan Custard   191
Almond Crêpes   197

909

Macerated strawberries   417
coffee and tea

Fruitful Brunch
Rhubarb-Orange Soup   904
Lemon-Ricotta Pancakes   203
Macerated peaches or nectarines   417
Balsamic Strawberries with Arugula   42
Apricot Mousse   901
assorted fresh-squeezed juices

Winter Brunch
Cheddar Apples with Hazelnuts   402
Endive Salad   44–45
Mushroom Quiche   188
Maple Snaps   841
coffee and tea

Make-Ahead Brunch
Ginger-Molasses Granola   574
mixed fresh berries
Brown Sugar Carrot Bread
    with Almonds   692
Deviled (or Stuffed) Eggs   180
mixed greens with Honey-Garlic
    Vinaigrette   763
coffee and tea

Italian-Style Make-Ahead Brunch
Mushroom Salad, Italian-American Style   62
Broiled Three-Bean Salad, Italian Style   75
Layered Mozzarella with Roasted Peppers
    and Olives   221
Spinach-Cheese Cannelloni   482
Pine Nut Cookies   841
espresso and cappuccino

Southern-Style Buffet Brunch
Celery Rémoulade   47
Lima Bean Purée with Fennel
    and Orange Juice   613
Corn Bread Salad   88
Grits Gratin with Escarole,
    Garlic, and Lemon   551
mixed berries with whipped cream
coffee and iced tea

Lunches

Light Summer Lunch
Yogurt Soup with Cucumber   158
Wheat Berry or Other Whole Grain Salad
    with Roasted Peppers and Zucchini   87
Peaches or Nectarines with Coconut
    Crumble Topping   870

Cool and Spicy Lunch (Vegan)
Cold Tomato Soup with Thai Flavors   158
Pressed Tofu Salad   652
Cold Fiery Noodles   467
Mango or Apricot Sorbet   893

The Updated School Lunchbox
Summer Rolls   743
Sweet Peanut Sauce   796
Scallion-Marinated Cucumbers   47
Coconut-Lime Bars   845

Tailgating Picnic
Egg Salad with Roasted Peppers
    or Sun-Dried Tomatoes   180
Mushroom Pâté   316

Rich Golden Sandwich Bread and store-bought
    hard rolls   715
Quick-Pickled Vegetables   95
Apple Slaw   49
Blondies   844
Whole Grain Apple Spice Cookies   840

Greek-Style Lunch
Orzo Salad, Greek Style   93
Essential Bean Salad, Greek Style   72
Spinach and Feta Pie with Phyllo Crust   408
Date–Olive Oil Cookies   843
Turkish coffee

French Bistro Lunch
More Classic Onion Soup   109
Lyonnaise Salad   38
Baguette with Compound Butter   707, 801
Chocolate Crêpes   197

Spring Lunch
Creamy Watercress, Spinach,
    or Sorrel Soup   132
Lemony Lentil Salad   75
Simplest Asparagus Gratin   383
Strawberry and Cream Cheese Tart   875
tea or coffee

British Pub Lunch
Broiled Tomato and Cheddar Salad
    with Onions   59
Pickled Eggs with Beets
    and Horseradish   182
Garlicky Mashed Potato Pie   351
Traditional Vanilla Pudding   884
brown ale or lager

Vegan Lunch, Indian Style
Rice Salad, Indian Style   82
Red Lentils with Chaat Masala   600
The Simplest Indian-Style Flatbread
    (Chapati)   698
Dried Fruit and Nut Chutney   784
tea

Dinners

Autumn Dinner
Potato and Leek Soup   106
Spicy Autumn Vegetable Burger   665
Caramelized Onion Chutney   786
English Muffins   714
Apple Cobbler   877

Winter Fireside Supper
Roasted Nuts   323
Chili non Carne   607
Corny Corn Bread   688
mixed greens with Chile
    Ranch Dressing   772
Boozy Apple Cake   851
hot chocolate

Italian-Style Summer Dinner
Beer-Battered Squash Blossoms   249
Roasted Pepper Mayonnaise   771
Tomato and Bread Soup
    (Pappa al Pomodoro)   112
Cannellini Beans with Spinach
    and Cavatelli   587
Marinated Garden Vegetables   67
Quick Ricotta Pots   877

Chinese Banquet Dinner (Vegan)
Chinese Marinated Celery   46
Stir-Fried Wide Rice Noodles
    with Pickled Vegetables   472
Stir-Fried Tofu with Scallions
    and Black Beans   646
Spiced Stir-Fried Bean Sprouts   265
Stir-Fried Broccoli with Dried Shiitakes   271
White or Brown Rice   505, 506
Sichuan Peppercorn Cookies   841
fresh pineapple
jasmine tea

Contemporary Asian-Style Dinner (Vegan)
Jean-Georges's Rice Noodle Salad with
    Grapefruit and Peanuts   93
Tofu-Stuffed Wontons   494
Ginger-Scallion Sauce   779
Sea Slaw   55
Avocado Salad with Ginger and Peanuts   51
Champagne Gelée with Berries   888

Provençal-Style Dinner
Green Olive Tapenade   327
Dried Tomato Breadsticks   711
Socca   633
Baked Mixed Vegetables with Olive Oil
    (Tian or Ratatouille)   380
Prune-Cognac Bread Pudding   886

Super-Hearty Dinner
Five-Layer Avocado Salad   51
Jalapeño Deviled Eggs   180
Bean-and-Cheese Burger   661
hamburger buns
Fast, Down-Home Barbecue Sauce   789

salad with "Bleu" Ranch Dressing   772
Double Chocolate Bars   847

Comfort Food Dinner
Seitan and Mushroom Loaf   670
Homemade Ketchup   790
Garlicky Mashed Potatoes   342
Quick-Glazed Carrots   278
Dark Chocolate–Buttermilk Pie   873

A Mostly Grilled Dinner
Grilled Asparagus   261
Grilled or Broiled Radicchio
    with Balsamic Glaze   301
Grilled Watermelon Steak   430
Grilled Polenta   544
Gigantes with Cherry Tomatoes   588
Cherry Crisp   878

Mexican-Style Dinner
Crunchy Corn Guacamole   263
Mexican Cheese Salsa   751
warm tortillas
Grilled Chiles Rellenos   400
Black Beans and Chiles
    with Orange Juice   607
Rice Salad, Mexican Style   79
Coconut Ice Cream with
    Citrus-Mango Sauce   890, 862

South American-Style Carnival Dinner
Brazilian-Style Black Bean Soup   115
Cassava Fritters   394
Chimichurri   769
Rice Baked with Chile, Cheese,
    and Tomatoes   569

Boiled or Steamed Greens   239
Cappuccino Flan   887

Holiday Dinners

New Year's Eve Dinner I
Roasted Artichoke Hearts   259
Fontina and Porcini Fondue   222
Overnight French Bread or Rolls
    for dipping   709
assorted vegetables for dipping
mixed greens with Lemon Vinaigrette   763
Poached Pear Tart with Dark Chocolate
    Ganache   874

New Year's Eve Dinner II
Elegant Lentil Soup   116
Pasta with Chestnut Cream   457
Goat Cheese and Mushroom Tart
    with Potato Crust   227
Green Salad with Caramelized
    Onion-Thyme Dressing   43
Flourless Chocolate Nut Torte   850
Coffee Caramels   907

Valentine's Day Dinner
Beet Crisps   267
Herb and Cheese Soufflé   186
Broiled Cherry Tomatoes with Herbs   374
mixed greens with Mustard Vinaigrette   763
Chocolate Dessert Cups with berries and
    whipped cream or ice cream   844

Mardi Gras Dinner
Fried Okra   324
Garlic Mayonnaise (Aïoli)   771

Black-Eyed Peas with Smoked Tofu   610
Simple Baked Rice with Herbs   515
Sautéed Zucchini or Chayote   362
Vegan Banana–Chocolate Chunk
    Bread Pudding   886

Thanksgiving Day Dinner
Virginian Peanut Soup   134
Sweet Potato Biscuits   695
Creamed Onions   330
Braised and Glazed Brussels Sprouts   272
White Bean and Celery Root Gratin   623
Wild Rice with Chestnuts   567
Cranberry Chutney   785
Chocolate Semolina Pudding with
    Coconut-Pineapple Cake Soak   896, 860
Ginger–Sweet Potato Pie   873

Hanukkah Dinner
Raw Beet Salad with Cabbage
    and Orange   50
Potato "Nik" or Latkes
    (Potato Pancakes)   349, 350
Applesauce   419
Fried Cheese-Stuffed Dumplings   498
Sautéed Eggplant with Onions
    and Honey   296
Honey-Spice Cake with
    Mocha Glaze   854, 858

Christmas Dinner
Gingered Nuts   323
Creamy Fennel Soup   129
Herbed Cheese Shortbread   696
Quinoa and Parsnip Rösti   560
Flageolets with Morels   597
Red Cabbage with Apples   277

Cranberry-Orange Crisp   878
Chocolate-Nut Brittle   906

Summer Southern-Style BBQ Dinner
Egg Pâté with crackers   180
Marinated Tofu with Down-Home
    Barbecue Sauce   653
Grilled Scallions   331
Potato Rémoulade   47
Spicy No-Mayo Coleslaw   49
Coconut Cake   853

Anniversary Celebration Dinner
Cheese Balls and crackers   212
Minestrone   123

Stuffed Artichokes   397
Barley Pilaf   539
Pear and Almond Upside-Down
    Cake   854

Superbowl Buffet Dinner
Parmesan Popcorn   292
Blue Cheese Dip with vegetables
    for dipping   212
Avocado–Red Pepper Salsa   751
Chile-Bean Quesadillas with Salsa Verde
    and sour cream   741, 788
Espresso Black Bean Chili   608
tortilla chips
Peanut-Caramel Bars   845

Recipes by Icon

RECIPE	FAST	MAKE AHEAD	VEGAN
SALADS			
Simple Green Salad	X		X
Chopped Salad	X		X
Greens with Fruit, Cheese, and Nuts	X	X	
Spinach Salad with Warm Dressing and Tofu Croutons		X	X
Spinach Salad with Feta and Nutmeg	X		
Balsamic Strawberries with Arugula	X		X
Parsley and Herb Salad	X		
Tabbouleh			X
Green Salad with Caramelized Onion-Thyme Dressing		X	X

RECIPE	FAST	MAKE AHEAD	VEGAN
Lettuce and Chive Salad, Korean Style	X		X
Endive and Roquefort Salad	X		
Carrot or Celery Salad	X	X	X
Carrot Salad with Cumin	X	X	X
Chinese Marinated Celery		X	X
Celery Rémoulade	X	X	
Waldorf Salad	X		
Cucumber Salad with Sour Cream and Yogurt	X	X	
Cucumber Salad with Soy and Ginger	X		X
Spicy No-Mayo Coleslaw	X	X	X
Raw Beet Salad	X		X

915

RECIPE	FAST	MAKE AHEAD	VEGAN
Jícama Salad with Pineapple and Mint	X		X
Shaved Artichoke Salad	X		
Avocado Salad with Ginger and Peanuts		X	X
Five-Layer Avocado Salad	X		X
Simple Seaweed Salad	X	X	X
Arame and Bean Thread Noodles with Ponzu Dipping Sauce		X	X
Spicy Dulse and Daikon Salad	X		X
Sea Slaw	X	X	
Seaweed Romaine Salad	X	X	
Cherry Tomato Salad with Soy Sauce	X	X	X
Tomato Salad, Ethiopian Style	X		X
Broiled Tomato and Blue Cheese Salad	X		
Heirloom Tomato Salad with Hard-Cooked Eggs	X		
Pan-Seared Tomato Salad	X	X	X
Corn Salad	X	X	X
Corn Salad with Tomatoes, Feta, and Mint	X		
Cauliflower Salad with Olives and Bread Crumbs		X	X
Mushroom Salad, Italian-American Style		X	X
Steamed Mushroom Salad with Coriander		X	X
Grilled Shiitake or Portobello Salad with Soy Vinaigrette			X
Eggplant Salad with Miso	X	X	X
Ratatouille Salad	X	X	X

RECIPE	FAST	MAKE AHEAD	VEGAN
Grilled Eggplant Salad with Garlic and Saffron Mayonnaise		X	
Roasted Onion Salad		X	X
Beet and Avocado Salad	X		X
Greek-Style Cooked Greens	X	X	X
Crisp Okra Salad	X		X
Marinated Garden Vegetables		X	X
Potato Salad		X	X
Roasted Sweet Potato Salad with Red Pepper Vinaigrette			X
Potato Salad with Cream Cheese Dressing	X	X	
Essential Bean Salad		X	X
Warm Chickpea Salad with Arugula	X		
Black Bean and Pan-Roasted Corn Salad	X	X	
Broiled Three-Bean Salad	X	X	X
Lemony Lentil Salad		X	X
Edamame Salad with Seaweed "Mayo"	X	X	X
Two-Mung Salad	X	X	X
Fava Bean and Mint Salad with Asparagus		X	X
Sprouts		X	X
The World of Rice Salads	X	X	
Bulgur and Tomato Salad	X	X	
Quinoa Salad with Lemon, Spinach, and Poppy Seeds	X		X
Quinoa Salad with Tempeh	X	X	X
Sweet Potato and Quinoa Salad		X	X

RECIPE	FAST	MAKE AHEAD	VEGAN
Wheat Berry or Other Whole Grain Salad with Cabbage and Coarse Mustard	X		X
Wheat Berry or Other Whole Grain Salad with Peanuts and Fresh and Dried Fruit	X		X
Wheat Berry or Other Whole Grain Salad with Roasted Peppers	X	X	X
Crouton Salad	X	X	X
Bread Salad, Lebanese Style	X		X
Whole Grain Bread Salad		X	X
Japanese-Style Summertime Pasta Salad	X		
Israeli Couscous Salad	X		X
Couscous Salad with Fennel and Raisins	X		X
Orzo Salad, Greek Style	X		
Jean-George's Rice Noodle Salad with Grapefruit and Peanuts			X
Quick-Pickled Vegetables			X
Spicy Pickles, Asian Style		X	X
Kimchi		X	X
3-Day Pickles		X	X
Kosher Pickles, the Right Way		X	X
Miso-Cured Vegetables		X	X
SOUPS			
Simple, Easy, and Fast Vegetable Stock		X	X
One-Hour Vegetable Stock		X	X
Roasted Vegetable Stock		X	X
Mushroom Stock		X	X

RECIPE	FAST	MAKE AHEAD	VEGAN
Kombu Dashi	X	X	X
Cauliflower Soup, Italian Style			X
Potato and Leek Soup	X	X	
Onion Soup		X	X
Roasted Beet Borscht		X	
Sauerkraut Soup		X	X
Spanish-Style Plantain Stew			X
Tomato and Bread Soup		X	X
Tomato Soup	X	X	X
Wintertime Tomato Soup		X	
Black Bean Soup		X	
Classic Lentil Soup		X	X
Lentil Soup with Coconut			X
Chickpea Soup with Saffron and Almonds		X	X
Smooth Chickpea Soup		X	X
Simplest Split Pea Soup		X	X
Mung Bean Soup		X	X
Bread Soup			X
Minestrone		X	
Mixed Vegetable Soup, Spanish Style		X	X
Peanut Soup, Senegalese Style			X
Southwestern Mixed Vegetable Soup			X
Tortilla Soup		X	
Vegetable Soup, Thai Style	X		X
Mixed Vegetable Soup, Korean Style			X
Creamy Carrot Soup		X	

RECIPE	FAST	MAKE AHEAD	VEGAN
Thai-Style Carrot Soup		X	X
Creamy Cauliflower (or Broccoli) Soup	X	X	
Chile Bisque		X	
Cream of Parsley Soup	X	X	
Creamy Watercress, Spinach, or Sorrel Soup	X	X	
Pumpkin (or Winter Squash) Soup		X	
Curried Coconut Soup with Lemongrass		X	X
Barley Soup with Seasonal Vegetables			X
Mushroom Barley Soup			X
Jook			X
North African Couscous Soup	X		X
Farro Soup		X	
Faux Pho			X
Garlic Fideo Soup	X		X
Persian Noodle Soup		X	
Green Tea Broth with Udon Noodles	X		X
Spaetzle Soup the Easy Way	X		
Whole Wheat Noodles in Curry Broth			X
Kimchi Soup with Tofu	X		X
Korean Mushroom Soup			X
Tofu Skins in Hot Pot			X
Tofu and Bok Choy "Goulash"	X		X
Miso Soup	X		X
Egg "Noodle" Soup with Mushrooms		X	

RECIPE	FAST	MAKE AHEAD	VEGAN
Egg Drop Soup, Eight Ways	X		
Ultra-Fast Avocado Soup	X		
Gazpacho		X	X
Cold Yogurt Soup with Nuts		X	
Cold Cucumber and Seaweed Soup	X		X
EGGS, DAIRY, AND CHEESE			
Soft-Boiled Egg	X		
Medium-Boiled Egg	X		
Hard-Cooked (Hard-Boiled) Egg	X		
Everyday Scrambled Eggs	X		
Fried Eggs, Sunny-Side Up or Over Easy	X		
Baked ("Shirred") Eggs	X		
Poached Eggs	X		
Simplest Omelet	X		
Folded Omelet	X		
Huevos Rancheros		X	
Breakfast Burritos	X		
Japanese Egg Crêpes	X	X	
Chilaquiles	X		
Baked Sweet Omelet	X		
French Toast	X	X	
Egg Salad	X	X	
Deviled (or Stuffed) Eggs	X	X	
Pickled Eggs		X	
Flat Omelet with Cauliflower or Broccoli	X	X	
Pasta Frittata		X	
Cheese Soufflé		X	

RECIPE	FAST	MAKE AHEAD	VEGAN
Pea or Other Vegetable Soufflé		X	
Cheese Quiche		X	
Onion Quiche		X	
Baked Savory Custard		X	
Poblano Custard		X	
Savory Bread Pudding		X	
Eggs au Gratin	X	X	
Hard-Cooked Eggs in Quick Tomato Curry Sauce	X	X	
Crêpes		X	
Cheese Blintzes		X	
Broiled Crêpes or Blintzes	X		
Everyday Pancakes	X	X	
Light and Fluffy Pancakes	X		
Cottage Cheese and Sour Cream Pancakes	X		
Overnight Waffles		X	
Yogurt		X	
Spice-Marinated Feta		X	
Blue Cheese Dip or Spread	X	X	
Cheese Balls	X	X	
Panfried Cheese	X	X	
Fried Fresh Cheese	X		
Grilled Fresh Cheese		X	
Baked Goat Cheese	X	X	
Curried Fresh Cheese	X	X	
Fresh Cheese Scramble	X		
Cheese Crisp with Onions	X		
Cheese "Burger"	X	X	

RECIPE	FAST	MAKE AHEAD	VEGAN
Swiss-Style Cheese Bake		X	
Cheese Fondue	X		
Cheese Enchiladas with Red Mole		X	
Cottage Cheese Patties	X	X	
Baked Phyllo-Wrapped Goat Cheese	X		
Goat Cheese and Mushroom Tart with Potato Crust		X	
Fresh Cheese, the Easy Way		X	
PRODUCE: VEGETABLES AND FRUITS			
Boiled or Steamed Greens	X	X	X
Stir-Fried Vegetables	X		X
Battered and Fried Vegetables, Three Ways	X		
Steamed Artichokes		X	X
Braised Artichoke Hearts		X	X
Asparagus Done Simply	X	X	X
Roasted or Grilled Asparagus	X	X	X
Stir-Fried Asparagus	X		X
Crunchy Corn Guacamole	X	X	X
Spiced Stir-Fried Bean Sprouts	X	X	X
Beets Done Simply		X	X
Beets Baked in Foil		X	X
Beet Crisps	X		X
Beets with Pistachio Butter		X	X
Quick-Cooked Bok Choy	X		X
Stir-Fried Broccoli	X		
Broccoli, Cauliflower, or Just About Anything Else, Roman Style	X	X	X

RECIPE	FAST	MAKE AHEAD	VEGAN
Braised and Glazed Brussels Sprouts	X	X	
Roasted Brussels Sprouts with Garlic		X	X
Sautéed Brussels Sprouts with Hazelnuts	X		
Brussels Sprouts in Coconut Milk	X		X
Quick-Braised Burdock and Carrots	X	X	X
Buttered Cabbage	X		
Red Cabbage with Apples		X	X
Quick-Glazed Carrots	X	X	
Carrots with Dates and Raisins	X	X	X
Basic Steamed Cauliflower	X	X	X
Breaded Sautéed Cauliflower	X		
Roasted Cauliflower with Raisins and Vinaigrette		X	X
Mashed Cauliflower with Cheese	X	X	
Manchurian-Style Cauliflower	X		
Oven-Braised Celery	X	X	X
Chard with Oranges and Shallots	X	X	X
Boiled, Grilled, or Roasted Chestnuts	X	X	X
Steamed Corn on the Cob	X		X
Pan-Grilled Corn with Chile	X		X
Corn on the Cob, Grilled or Roasted	X		
Creamed Corn	X		
Corn Pancakes, Thai Style	X		

RECIPE	FAST	MAKE AHEAD	VEGAN
Corn Fritters	X		
Buttered Popcorn	X		
Dry-Pan Eggplant	X	X	X
Grilled or Broiled Eggplant	X	X	X
Sautéed Eggplant	X		X
Steamed Eggplant	X	X	X
Eggplant Slices with Garlic and Parsley		X	X
Eggplant Parmesan		X	
Eggplant-Tofu Stir-Fry	X		X
Braised Endive, Escarole, or Radicchio		X	X
Grilled or Broiled Radicchio with Balsamic Glaze	X	X	X
Roast Fennel with Orange	X	X	X
Roasted Garlic		X	X
Garlic Braised in Olive Oil		X	X
Green Beans Tossed with Walnut-Miso Sauce	X	X	X
Twice-Fried Green Beans	X		X
Stir-Fried Green Beans and Tofu Skins	X		X
Rolled Kale with Feta and Olives	X		
Leeks Braised in Oil or Butter	X	X	X
Steamed Leeks	X	X	X
Stir-Fried Leeks or Shallots	X		X
Grilled Leeks	X	X	X
Sautéed Mushrooms	X	X	X
Pan-Cooked Mushrooms, Dry Style	X	X	X

RECIPE	FAST	MAKE AHEAD	VEGAN
Mushroom Pâté		X	X
Grilled Mushrooms	X	X	X
Caramelized Spiced Nuts	X	X	X
Fried Okra	X		
Okra Stew with Tomatoes		X	X
Sautéed Olives	X	X	X
Tapenade	X	X	X
Caramelized Onions	X	X	X
Creamed Onions	X		
Roasted Onion Halves		X	X
Grilled Scallions (Green Onions)	X	X	X
Anything-Scented Peas	X	X	
Roasted Red Peppers		X	X
Paprika Peppers	X	X	X
Sautéed Ripe Plantains	X	X	X
Fried Plantain Chips	X	X	X
Baked Potatoes			X
Boiled Potatoes	X	X	X
Mashed Potatoes		X	
Crisp Panfried Potatoes (Home Fries)		X	X
Oven-Roasted Potatoes		X	X
Grilled or Broiled Potatoes		X	X
Braised Potatoes, Nine Ways			X
Potatoes Provençal		X	X
Curried Stir-Fried Potatoes	X		X
Potato "Nik"		X	
Garlicky Mashed Potato Pie		X	

RECIPE	FAST	MAKE AHEAD	VEGAN
French Fries	X	X	X
Potato Croquettes		X	
Braised and Glazed Radishes, Turnips, or Other Root Vegetable	X		
Sea Green and Celery Stir-Fry	X		X
Nori Chips	X	X	X
Spinach with Chiles	X	X	X
Spinach with Currants and Nuts	X	X	X
Spinach with Fresh Cheese and Yogurt	X		
Sautéed Zucchini or Chayote	X		X
Summer Squash and Herbs in Parchment	X		
Butternut Squash, Braised and Glazed	X	X	X
Whole Winter Squash, Cooked Three Ways		X	X
Winter Squash Slices, Roasted		X	
Panfried Pumpkin with Tomato Sauce		X	X
Braised Winter Squash in Caramel Sauce	X	X	X
Spicy Winter Squash Galette		X	
Crisp-Cooked Sunchokes	X		X
Broiled Sunchokes with Garlic or Parmesan		X	
Sweet Potatoes, Simply Cooked			X
Grilled Tomatoes with Basil		X	
Grilled Tomatoes and Scrambled Eggs, Chinese Style	X		

RECIPE	FAST	MAKE AHEAD	VEGAN
Broiled Cherry Tomatoes with Herbs	X		X
Oven-Roasted Fresh Plum Tomatoes		X	X
Tomato Cobbler		X	
Oven-Dried Tomatoes		X	X
Stir-Fried Vegetables, Vietnamese Style	X		X
Quick-Braised Vegetables, Thai Style	X		X
Baked Mixed Vegetables with Olive Oil		X	X
Roasted Vegetables, Thai Style		X	X
Simple Asparagus Gratin	X	X	
Potato and Sunchoke Gratin		X	
Rice Spinach Gratin		X	
Chile Gratin, Mexican Style	X	X	
Essential Vegetable Purée		X	X
Vegetable Pancakes		X	
Crisp Vegetable Pancake, Korean Style		X	
Mushroom Fritters	X	X	
Bread and Herb Stuffing		X	X
Stuffed Onions		X	
Stuffed Artichokes	X	X	
Stuffed Eggplant		X	X
Tomatoes Stuffed with Rice		X	
Chiles Rellenos		X	
Cabbage Stuffed with Lentils and Rice		X	
Blue Cheese Apples		X	
Kale or Chard Pie		X	

RECIPE	FAST	MAKE AHEAD	VEGAN
Layered Vegetable Torte		X	
Applesauce		X	X
Coconut Milk	X	X	X
Preserved Lemons		X	X
Grilled Watermelon Steak	X	X	X
Poached Pears	X	X	
PASTA, NOODLES, AND DUMPLINGS			
Pasta with Garlic and Oil	X		X
Fast Tomato Sauce	X	X	
Linguine with Raw Tomato Sauce	X		
Pasta with Butter and Parmesan	X		
Garlicky Vermicelli or Fideo	X		
Orzo, Risotto Style	X		
Pasta with Broccoli, Cauliflower, or Broccoli Raab	X		X
Pasta with Mushrooms	X		X
Pasta with Lentils or Other Legumes		X	X
Pasta with Almond Butter	X	X	
Pasta with Chestnut Cream	X	X	
Pasta with Walnut Sauce	X		
Baked Ziti		X	
Vegetable Lasagna		X	
Baked Macaroni and Cheese		X	
Creamy Baked Noodles with Eggplant and Cheese		X	
Chinese Egg Noodles in Soy Broth	X		X

RECIPE	FAST	MAKE AHEAD	VEGAN
Cold Sesame or Peanut Noodles	X	X	X
Soba Noodles with Dipping Sauce	X	X	X
Korean-Style Noodles in Cool Bean Broth	X	X	X
Crisp-Fried Noodle Cake	X	X	X
Pad Thai	X	X	
Stir-Fried Wild Rice Noodles with Pickled Vegetables	X	X	X
Rice Cakes with Sweet Soy Sauce	X		X
Fresh Egg Pasta		X	
Eggless Pasta Dough		X	
Herbed Fresh Pasta		X	
Spinach-Ricotta Ravioli		X	
Butternut Squash Tortellini		X	
Ravioli Nudi	X		
Potato Gnocchi			X
Parsnip Gnocchi		X	
Porcini Dumplings		X	
Passatelli in Broth		X	
Spaetzle	X	X	
Dumpling Wrappers		X	X
Steamed Dumplings, Asian Style		X	
Tofu-Stuffed Wontons	X		X
Dumpling Wrappers with Egg		X	
Fresh Egg Noodles with Scallions and Paprika		X	
Fried Potato-Stuffed Dumplings		X	

RECIPE	FAST	MAKE AHEAD	VEGAN
GRAINS			
White Rice	X		X
Brown Rice			X
Steamed Sticky Rice		X	X
Coconut Rice	X		X
Rice with Cheese	X		
Rice with Peas	X		
Rice with Chickpeas	X	X	X
White Rice and Black Beans		X	X
Rice Pilaf, Nine Ways		X	X
Biryani	X		
Rice Cooked in Onions		X	
Yellow Rice, the Best Way	X		
Brown Rice Pilaf with Two Mushrooms			X
Simpler-than-Pilaf Baked Rice	X		
Simplest Fried Rice with Peppers	X		X
Fried Rice, with or without Egg	X		
Paella with Tomatoes	X		X
Sushi Rice			X
Sushi Rolls	X		X
Nigiri Sushi	X		X
Japanese Rice with Edamame and Sea Greens	X	X	X
Rice Balls	X	X	X
Cooking Grains the Easy Way		X	X
Cooked Grains with Butter or Oil	X		
Barley and Mushroom Stew		X	X

RECIPE	FAST	MAKE AHEAD	VEGAN
Barley "Succotash"		X	
Polenta	X		
Pozole with Beans			X
Pozole with Mole		X	X
Polenta "Pizza"		X	
Naked Tamales with Chile Cheese Filling		X	
Grits Gratin with Arugula and Garlic		X	
Pearl Couscous Pilaf with Sun-Dried Tomatoes	X	X	X
Pearl Couscous "Risotto" with Artichoke Hearts	X	X	
Pearl Couscous Tagine		X	X
Whole Wheat Couscous with Cauliflower and Almonds	X	X	X
Pearl Couscous Gratin with Pesto and Goat Cheese		X	
Basic Bulgur	X	X	X
Creamed Bulgur with Spinach	X	X	
Bulgur Pilaf with Vermicelli	X	X	
Bulgur Chili		X	X
Bulgur Croquettes with Walnuts	X	X	
Fluffy Cracked Wheat with Mustard and Tarragon	X	X	
Quinoa with Caramelized Onions		X	X
Quinoa and Parsnip Rösti		X	
Roasted Quinoa with Potatoes and Cheese		X	
Kasha with Golden Brown Onions	X	X	

RECIPE	FAST	MAKE AHEAD	VEGAN
Buckwheat Stew with Tofu and Kale		X	X
Summer Vegetable Stew with Wheat Berries	X	X	X
Millet Mash			X
Autumn Millet Bake		X	X
Rye Berry Gratin with Leeks and Tomatoes		X	
Parmesan Rice Cakes	X		
Griddlecakes Made from Oatmeal (or Other Porridge)	X		
Crunchy Amaranth Griddlecakes	X		
Risotto "Frittata"	X	X	
Oatmeal or Other Creamy Breakfast Cereal	X	X	
Crunchy Granola	X	X	
LEGUMES			
Cooking Beans, the Quick-Soak Way		X	X
Cooking Beans, the No-Soak Way		X	X
Cooking Beans, the Long-Soak Way		X	X
Edamame with Tomatoes and Cilantro	X		X
Quick-Cooked Edamame with Kombu Dashi or Soy Sauce	X		X
Beer-Glazed Black Beans	X	X	
Kidney Beans with Apples and Sherry	X		
Cannellini Beans with Cabbage and Pasta	X		
Gigantes with Brussels Sprouts	X		

RECIPE	FAST	MAKE AHEAD	VEGAN
Briny Black-Eyed Peas	X	X	X
Fried Mung Beans with Sesame	X	X	X
Soybeans with Shiitakes and Sea Greens	X		
Hot and Sour Edamame with Tofu	X		
Fresh Favas with Eggs and Croutons	X		
Twice-Cooked Refreid Beans	X		X
Spicy Red Beans, Indian Style	X	X	X
White Beans, Tuscan Style		X	X
Dried Fruit and Lima Stew		X	
Beans and Greens		X	X
Beans and Mushrooms		X	
Braised Lentils, Spanish Style		X	X
Simplest Dal		X	
Lentils and Potatoes with Curry		X	
Mung Bean Dal with Apples, Coconut, and Mint		X	X
Mixed Whole-Bean Dal with Walnuts		X	
Urad Dal with Poppy Seeds and Cilantro	X	X	X
Stewed Fava Beans with Tahini		X	
Flageolets, French Style		X	
Chickpeas in Their Own Broth, with Crisp Bread Crumbs	X	X	X
Black Beans with Orange Juice	X	X	X
Chile non Carne		X	X
Espresso Black Bean Chili		X	X
Black Soybeans with Soy Sauce		X	X

RECIPE	FAST	MAKE AHEAD	VEGAN
Spicy Soybeans with Kimchi		X	X
Hot, Sweet, and Sour Chickpeas with Eggplant	X	X	X
Black-Eyed Peas with Smoked Tofu		X	X
White Bean Purée	X	X	
Refried Bean Dip	X	X	X
Hummus	X	X	X
Chickpea Fondue	X	X	X
Mashed Favas		X	X
Smashed Edamame and Potatoes with Miso	X		X
Roasted Chickpeas	X		
Baked Beans		X	X
Baked Brazilian Black Beans		X	X
Boulangerie Beans and Potatoes		X	
Baked Lima Beans Parmigiana		X	
Baked Pinto Beans, Enchilada Style		X	
Baked Chickpeas with Fresh Cheese		X	
Winter Bean and Winter Squash Gratin		X	
Pinto Bean Tart with Millet Crust		X	
Falafel		X	
Bean Croquettes	X	X	
Baked White Bean Cakes	X		
Bean Griddlecakes	X		
Mung Bean Pancakes		X	
Crisp-Fried Bean Sprouts	X		X

RECIPE	FAST	MAKE AHEAD	VEGAN
Chickpea Pancake		X	X
Chickpea Fries		X	
TOFU, VEGETABLE BURGERS, AND OTHER HIGH-PROTEIN FOODS			
Poached Tofu	X	X	X
Baked Tofu		X	X
Crispy Panfried Tofu	X	X	X
Grilled or Broiled Tofu	X	X	X
Deep-Fried Tofu	X	X	X
Stir-Fried Tofu with Scallions	X		X
Stir-Fried Tofu with Bell Peppers or Other Vegetables	X		X
Braised Tofu and Peas in Curried Coconut Milk			X
Tofu, Provençal-Style		X	X
Braised Tofu with Eggplant and Shiitakes	X		X
Braised Tofu in Caramel Sauce	X		X
Fast-Braised Tofu with Tempeh	X		X
Spicy Ketchup-Braised Tofu	X		X
Pressed Tofu Salad		X	X
Marinated Tofu			X
Tofu Escabeche		X	X
Tofu Pancakes, Six Ways	X	X	X
Scrambled Tofu with Mushrooms	X		X
Homemade Tofu		X	X
Tofu Croutons		X	X
The Simplest Bean Burgers	X		
Hearty Winter Vegetable Burger		X	

RECIPE	FAST	MAKE AHEAD	VEGAN
Fresh Spring Vegetable Burger		X	
Midsummer Vegetable Burger		X	X
Spicy Autumn Vegetable Burger	X	X	
Tofu Burgers, Asian Style	X	X	X
Fast Nut Burgers	X		
Seitan		X	X
Seitan and Lentil Loaf		X	X
Pan-Seared Seitan	X		X
Grilled or Broiled Seitan	X	X	X
Oven-Roasted Seitan		X	X
Crunchy Crumbled Tempeh	X	X	X
Braised Tempeh, Three Ways	X		X
Tempeh with Rice and Spinach			X
Tempeh Hash		X	X
Tempeh Chili with Black Beans		X	X
BREADS, PIZZAS, SANDWICHES, AND WRAPS			
Corn Bread		X	
Quick Whole Wheat and Molasses Bread		X	
Olive Oil Salt Bread		X	X
Boston Brown Bread		X	
Irish Soda Bread		X	
Banana Bread		X	
Fruit-and-Nut or Vegetable-and-Nut Bread		X	
Muffins, Infinite Ways		X	
Sweet and Rich Muffins		X	
Yogurt or Buttermilk Biscuits		X	
Scones		X	

RECIPE	FAST	MAKE AHEAD	VEGAN
Cheese Shortbread	X	X	
Doughnut Puffs, Sweet or Savory	X		
Crackers	X	X	
The Simplest Indian-Style Flatbread		X	X
Flaky Indian-Style Flatbread		X	
Fast French Bread or Rolls			X
Overnight French Bread or Rolls			X
Breadsticks		X	X
Sandwich Bread, 6 Ways		X	
Rich Golden Bread, 6 Ways		X	
Black Bread		X	X
Pita		X	
Pizza Dough		X	X
White Pizza		X	X
Pizza with Tomato Sauce and Mozzarella		X	
Focaccia		X	X
Calzone		X	
Bruschetta	X		X
Chile-Bean Quesadilla	X		
Egg Rolls		X	X
Summer Rolls			X
Rice and Lentil Crêpes		X	X
Black Lentil Samosas		X	
Bean and Cheese Empanadas		X	
SAUCES, CONDIMENTS, HERBS, AND SPICES			
Fresh Tomato Salsa	X	X	X

RECIPE	FAST	MAKE AHEAD	VEGAN
Fresh Tomatillo Salsa	X	X	X
Papaya and Other Fruit Salsas	X	X	X
Radish Salsa	X	X	X
Flavored Oil	X	X	X
Vinaigrette		X	X
Traditional Pesto	X	X	
Parsley "Pesto" or Parsley Purée	X	X	X
Lighter Cilantro (or Other Herb) "Pesto"	X	X	X
Homemade Mayonnaise	X	X	
Real Ranch Dressing	X	X	
Vegannaise	X	X	X
Seaweed "Mayo"		X	X
The Simplest Yogurt Sauce	X	X	
Grainy Mustard, Many Ways		X	X
Basil Dipping Sauce	X	X	X
Fishless Fish Sauce	X	X	X
Soy and Sesame Dipping Sauce and Marinade, Korean Style	X	X	X
Teriyaki Sauce	X	X	X
Ginger-Scallion Sauce	X	X	X
Dashi Dipping Sauce	X	X	X
Ponzu Sauce	X	X	X
Simple Miso Dipping Sauce	X	X	X
Miso Carrot Sauce with Ginger	X	X	X
Nutty Miso Sauce	X	X	X
Sweet Miso Glaze	X	X	X
Raw Onion Chutney		X	X
Cilantro-Mint Chutney	X	X	X

RECIPE	FAST	MAKE AHEAD	VEGAN
Coconut Chutney	X	X	X
Crunchy Nut Chutney	X	X	X
Pineapple Chutney		X	X
Tomato Chutney	X	X	
Caramelized Onion Chutney		X	X
Salsa Roja		X	X
Cooked Tomatillo Salsa	X	X	X
Fast, Down-Home Barbecue Sauce	X	X	X
Homemade Ketchup		X	X
Mushroom Ketchup		X	X
Grilled Pineapple and Onion Salsa	X	X	X
Smooth Green Chile Sauce, Indian Style	X	X	X
Spicy Indian Tomato Sauce	X	X	
Peanut Sauce, Six Ways		X	
Tahini Sauce	X	X	
Rustic Pine Nut Sauce	X		
Creamy Nut Sauce	X		
Balsamic Syrup	X	X	X
Creamy Bistro Dressing or Sauce	X	X	
Worcestershire Sauce, Hold the Anchovies	X	X	X
Compound Butter	X	X	
Brown Butter	X		
Hollandaise Sauce	X		
Béchamel Sauce, 11 Ways	X		
Fresh Bread Crumbs	X	X	X
Croutons	X	X	X

RECIPE	FAST	MAKE AHEAD	VEGAN
Chili Powder	X	X	X
Chaat Masala	X	X	X
Garam Masala	X	X	X
Hot Curry Powder	X	X	X
Fragrant Curry Powder	X	X	X
Sambar Powder	X	X	X
Five-Spice Powder	X	X	X
Japanese Seven-Spice Mix	X	X	X
Nori "Shake"	X	X	X
Jerk Seasoning	X	X	X
Za'atar	X	X	X
Citrus Sprinkle		X	X
Pickling Spice	X	X	X
Pickled Ginger		X	X
Chile Paste, 8 Ways		X	X
Red Curry Paste	X	X	X
Chile-Garlic Paste	X	X	X
DESSERTS			
Oatmeal Apple Cookies	X	X	
Brown Sugar Cookies with Sea Salt		X	
Maple Snaps		X	
Saffron Olive Oil Cookies		X	
Chewy Almond-Cherry Cookies		X	
Chocolate Tuiles	X	X	
Blondies		X	
Coconut-Lime Bars		X	
Caramel Walnut Bars		X	
No-Bake Granola Bars	X	X	X

RECIPE	FAST	MAKE AHEAD	VEGAN
Double Chocolate Bars		X	
Cornmeal Pound Cake		X	
Almond Cake		X	
Boozy Apple Cake		X	
Olive Oil Cake		X	
Plum-Rosemary Upside-Down Cake		X	
Honey-Spice Cake		X	
Chocolate Vanilla Layer Cake		X	
Sugar Syrup	X	X	X
Orange Glaze	X	X	X
Apricot Jam Glaze	X	X	X
Vanilla Cake Soak	X	X	
Not-Too-Sweet Buttercream Frosting	X	X	
Chocolate Ganache	X	X	
Vanilla-Berry Sauce	X	X	X
Almond Custard Sauce	X	X	X
Sweet Piecrust	X	X	
Sweet Tart Crust	X	X	
Baked Crumb Crust	X	X	
No-Bake Fruit and Nut Crust	X	X	X
Sweet Crumble Topping	X	X	
Buttermilk-Blueberry Pie		X	
Coconut Meringue Pie		X	
Pineapple (or Almost Any Fruit) Tart		X	
Poached Pear Tart with Dark Chocolate Ganache		X	
Almond Tart		X	

RECIPE	FAST	MAKE AHEAD	VEGAN
Ricotta Cheesecake		X	
Apple Cobbler		X	
Cherry Crisp		X	
Walnut Phyllo "Cigars"		X	
Banana Strudel		X	
Vanilla Pudding	X	X	
Citrus Tapioca Pudding	X	X	
Apple-Cardamom Bread Pudding		X	
Baked Cappuccino Custard		X	
Lemon-Lime Gelées	X	X	X
Buttermilk Ice Cream		X	
Mango or Apricot Sorbet	X	X	X
Tangerine or Orange Granita		X	X
Cinnamon-Nut Rice Pudding		X	X
Baked Semolina Pudding		X	
Indian Cornmeal Pudding		X	
Sweet Couscous with Pistachios	X	X	X
Frozen Honey Mousse	X	X	
Blueberry (or Any Berry) Mousse	X	X	
Pistachio Meringue		X	
Watermelon and Mint Soup	X	X	X
Rhubarb-Orange Soup	X	X	X
Sweet Coconut Soup	X	X	X
Brittled Popcorn	X	X	X
Caramels		X	

Sources

Almost all of the ingredients used in this book—probably 98 percent or more—can be found in your local supermarket. In the handful of cases where you'll need a special item, or if you want to explore more unusual varieties of beans, grains, or seasonings (or want to make your own tofu or seitan), you'll probably need to visit natural food stores and international groceries, either in person or online. (The good news is that almost all these foods are pantry items, so you can stock up.)

Though I usually prefer to shop for food in stores, I increasingly find myself turning to on-line and mail order sources. But on-line stores range wildly in service and price, and new ones are opening all the time. So though I make some recommendations here, I urge serious virtual shoppers to use these web sites as a point of comparison for your own Internet foraging.

Everything (virtually, including pizza stones and hard-to-find spices)
Amazon (badly organized, but big)
www.amazon.com

Flour and Whole Grains
Heartland Mill (lovely, comprehensive site)
www.heartlandmill.com
(800) 232–8533
(620) 379–4472

Gluten-Free Cooking and Baking
The Gluten Free Mall
www.glutenfreemall.com
(800) 986–2705

International Foods
Kalustyan's (for teas, grains, legumes, seasonings, dried fruit, you name it)
www.kalustyans.com
(800) 352–3451 (only in the U.S.)
(212) 685–3451

Ethnic Grocer (new site looks good, but as of this printing, no 800 or customer-service number)
www.ethnicgrocer.com

Pantry Items (nuts, beans, flours, vital gluten flour, chiles, etc.)
Barry Farm Foods (good overall source)
www.barryfarm.com
(419) 228–4640

Produce (seasonal and specialty items, including wild mushrooms, chiles, and chestnuts)
Earthly Delights (the best source in the country for dried mushrooms)
www.earthy.com
(800) 367–4709

Salts (every kind possible, from around the world)
Saltworks (pricey, but extensive)
www.saltworks.us
(800) 986–2705

Sea Greens (seaweed)
Maine Coast Sea Vegetables
www.seaveg.com
(207) 565–2907

Soymilk- and Tofu-Making Supplies and Coagulants
Sanlinx, Inc.
www.soymilkmaker.com
(888) 228–3082

Spices
Penzeys Spices (extensive, high quality, and very reasonably priced selection)
www.Penzeys.com
(800) 741–7787

Wild Rice
Native Harvest
www.nativeharvest.com
(888) 274–8318

List of Illustrations

Techniques
Using a Steel   18
Holding a Chef's Knife   19
Chopping   20
Slicing   21
Making Julienne   22
Making Chiffonade   22
Making Dice   23
Using a Paring Knife   23
Measuring Dry Ingredients   23
Ways to Rig a Steamer   25

Salads
The Basics of Preparing Salad Greens   36
Making Sprouts   78

Eggs, Dairy, and Cheese
Folding an Omelet in Half   171
Folding an Omelet in Thirds   171
Folding and Filling a Crêpe   196
Molding and Filling Blintzes   199

Shaving and Grating Parmesan Cheese   209
Wrapping Goat Cheese in Phyllo Dough   227
Finishing Fresh Cheese   229

Produce: Vegetables and Fruit
Trimming Artichokes, Version I   257
Trimming Artichokes, Version II   258
Preparing Asparagus   260
Preparing Avocados   263
Coring and Shredding Cabbage   276
Dicing a Carrot   278
Preparing Cauliflower   280
Preparing Celery   284
Preparing Chestnuts   287
Preparing Corn   288
Preparing Cucumbers   293
Preparing Fennel   302
Peeling Garlic   304
Preparing Leafy Greens with Thick Ribs   308
Preparing Leeks   311
Preparing Onions   328

Flipping Potato "Nik" or Any Large Vegetable
    Pancake   349
Mincing a Shallot   358
Folding Summer Squash in Parchment   362
Peeling Winter Squash   364
Preparing Tomatoes   373Tomato Stuffed with
    Rice   399
Chiles Rellenos   400
Cabbage Stuffed with Lentils and Rice   401
Blue Cheese Apples   402
Coring Apples   419
Preparing Strawberries   421
Skinning and Pitting Mango, Version I   428
Skinning and Pitting Mango, Version II   428
Using a Melon Baller   429
Preparing Citrus   431
Preparing Pineapple   435

Pasta, Noodles, and Dumplings

Making Fresh Pasta Dough   475
Using a Pasta-Rolling Machine   476
Hand-Cutting Broad Noodles   477
Making Ravioli   482
Making Tortellini   484
Making Gnocchi   487
Making Dumpling Wrappers, Egg Roll Wrappers, or
    Wonton Skins   492
Stuffing and Sealing Half Moon–Shaped Dumplings
    (or Ravioli)   494
Sealing Wontons   495

Grains

Rolling and Cutting Maki Sushi   528
Forming Nigiri Sushi   530
Corn Husk Tamales   549

Legumes

Cutting Chickpea Fries   634

Tofu, Vegetable Burgers, and Other High-Protein Foods

Squeezing Tofu with Weights   640
Pressing Homemade Tofu   656
Forming Veggie Burgers   659
Shaping Veggie "Meat"Balls   660
Shaping Vegetarian Cutlets   661
Shaping Seitan   670

Breads, Pizzas, Sandwiches, and Wraps

Shaggy vs. Smooth Dough   703
Kneading Dough   703
Shaping Boules   704
Shaping Rolls   704
Shaping Baguettes   705
Shaping a Sandwich Loaf   712
Forming Coffee Cake   715
Forming Cinnamon Buns   716
Making Challah   717
Shaping Dough for Pizza and Calzones   722
Rolling Burritos   738
Forming Dosa   744
Filling and Forming Samosas   746

Sauces, Condiments, Herbs, and Spices

Preparing Peppers   828

Desserts

Molding Tuiles   844
Handling Vanilla Beans   859
Rolling Pie and Tart Crust Dough   864
Fluting Pie Crusts   865
Making Free-Form Galettes   868
Handling Phyllo Sheets   879
Coating the Back of a Spoon   884
Separating Eggs   898
Beating Egg Whites   898
Folding Egg Whites   900

Index

Page numbers in *italics* indicate illustrations

Acorn squash stuffed with wild rice, 399
Adzuki beans
    about, 578
    croquettes, 628
    and greens, 596
    tofu sesame burger with, 667
Afghan style pickled peaches, 9
Agar, 882, 883
Agedashi tofu, 644
Aïoli (garlic mayonnaise), 771
Alaria, 356
All-cheese quesadilla, 741
Allspice, 811
Almond(s)
    about, 319
    bars, 845
    butter, creamy orzo with, 451
    butter, pasta with, 455–456, 455–457
    butternut squash with saffron and, 365
    cake, 850

with carrot bread, brown sugar, 692
cauliflower, sautéed, with raisins, saffron and, 282
chickpea soup with saffron and, 117–118
cookies, -cherry, chewy, 843
couscous, whole wheat, with cauliflower and, 554
crêpes, 197
crumble topping, 870–871
custard sauce, 863
dal, mixed whole-bean, with cauliflower and, 603
granola, -orange, 574
mascarpone apples with, 402
omelet, baked, 179
onion soup with, Spanish, 109
-peach ice cream, 890
and pear upside-down cake, 854

with potatoes, braised, 347
soup, sweet, 905
stuck-pot rice with sesame seeds, ginger and, 526
tart, 875–876
tomato and brie salad with, broiled, 59
Almond flour, 682
Almond milk couscous, sweet, 897
Aluminum cookware, 9
Amaranth
    about, 478, 536
    griddlecakes, crunchy, 570–571
Amaretto cake, 850
Amchoor, 820
Anadama bread, 713
Anaheim chile, 826
Anasazi beans, 578
Ancho
    about, 828
    -pine nut sauce, 797
Angá (Brazilian polenta), 544

Anise-plum or cherry sauce, 863
Anise seeds, 820
Anjou pears, 433
Annatto, 820
Antioxidants, 754
Anything-scented peas, 333
Appaloosa beans, 578
Apple(s)
    about, 417–419
    battered "fries," 249
    blue cheese, *402*, 402
    bread pudding, -cardamom, 885–886
    cake, boozy, 851–852
    Cheddar, with hazelnuts, 402–403
    and cheese omelet, 172
    cobbler, 877
    cobbler, -rhubarb, 878
    to core, *419*
    granita, 894
    gratin, savory, with coriander, 384

935

Apple(s) *(Continued)*
  -green tomato chutney, 786
  to grill, 413
  kidney beans with red wine
      and, 586
  kidney beans with sherry
      and, 586
  to macerate and season,
      416
  mascarpone, with almonds,
      402
  mung bean dal with
      coconut, mint and,
      602
  oatmeal cookies, 839–840
  oatmeal cookies, vegan,
      840
  red cabbage with, 277–278
  sauce, basil-, 862
  slaw, 49
  spice cookies, whole grain,
      840
  varieties of, 418
  in Waldorf salad, 47–48
Apple butter beans, maple-
    baked, 619
Applesauce, 419–420
Apricot(s)
  about, 420
  dried
      and goat cheese soufflé,
          186
      mung beans and rice
          with, 611–612
      -semolina bars, 845
  ice milk, 894
  jam glaze, 858
  to macerate and season,
      416
  meringue pie, 874
  mousse, 901
  and onion salsa, grilled,
      792
  pudding, 885
  sauce, creamy, 862
  sorbet, 893–894
  soup, vanilla-, 904
Arame
  about, 356
  bean thread noodles with,
      55

and bean thread noodles
    with fermented
    black beans, 55
and bean thread noodles
    with Ponzu dipping
    sauce, 54–55
Arepas, 292
Argentinean pumpkin soup,
    134
Arrowroot, 882
Arrowroot flour, 683
Artichoke(s)
  about, 256–257
  cooking methods, 257–258
  cranberry beans with
      cavatalli and, 587
  to cut, *257–258*
  to grill, 251
  hearts
      braised, 259
      braised, with garlic, lots
          of roasted, 260
      braised, with potatoes,
          260
      braised, vinegar-, 260
      breading and frying,
          246
      couscous, pearl, "risotto"
          with, 552
      roasted, 259–260
  Jerusalem artichoke. *See*
      Sunchoke(s)
  marinated, 68
  marinated, with preserved
      lemons, 68
  salad, shaved, 50–51
  stuffed, 397
Arugula
  about, 35
  balsamic strawberries with,
      42
  balsamic strawberries with
      goat cheese and, 42
  chickpea salad with, warm,
      73–74
  creamy nut sauce with, 798
  grits gratin with garlic and,
      550–551
  grits gratin, smothered,
      with garlic and,
      551

grits gratin with white
    beans, garlic and,
    551
"pesto," 768
Asafetida, 816, 820
Asian barbecue sauce, 790
Asian flavors, sautéed mush-
    rooms with, 315
Asian greens, 268–269
Asian noodles. *See* Noodle(s),
    Asian
Asian pears, 433
Asian spices, poached pears
    with, 434
Asian style
  black beans, beer-glazed,
      586
  dumplings, steamed,
      492–493
  leeks, grilled, 313
  mung bean fritters, 626
  mushroom salad, steamed,
      63
  peppers and onions, pan
      cooked, 334–335
  pickles, spicy, 95–96
  sauces, 777–780
  scallions, roasted, 331
  tofu burgers, 666–667
  tofu pancakes, 654
Asparagus
  about, 260–261
  done simply, 261
  fava bean and mint salad
      with, 77
  gratin, and béchamel,
      383
  gratin, simplest, 383
  to grill, 251
  grilled, 261
  and mushroom pie with
      phyllo crust, 406
  to prepare, *260*, 261
  roasted, 261–262
  soybeans with morels and,
      590
  spread or dip, 264
  stir-fried, 262
  in vegetable burger, fresh
      spring, 664
Autumn millet bake, 566

Autumn millet bake with
    cream, 567
Autumn vegetable torte, 406
Avocado(s)
  about, 262–263
  and beet salad, 66
  and beet salad with citrus,
      66
  and goat cheese dip or
      spread, 264
  to grill, 251
  guacamole
      corn, crunchy, 263–264
      minimalist, 264
      with tomatillos, 264
  "guacasalsa," 264
  to prepare, *263*, 263
  -red pepper salsa, 751
  salad
      five-layer, 51–53
      with ginger and peanuts,
          51
      six-layer, with mangoes,
          53
      six-layer, with queso
          fresco, 53
  soup, ultra-fast, 157
  and tomato, dried, dip or
      spread, 264
  with vegetable soup, mixed,
      southwestern, 126
  yogurt sauce, 774

Babycakes, 853
Baguettes, to shape, 704, *705*
Baked almond or hazelnut
    omelet, 179
Baked beans. *See* Bean(s),
    baked
Baked cappuccino custard,
    886–887
Baked cheese "burgers," 220
Baked cheesy custard, 191
Baked cherry omelet, 179
Baked chickpeas with fresh
    cheese, 622–623
Baked chickpeas with paneer
    and cauliflower,
    622
Baked chickpeas with paneer
    and spinach, 623

Baked crumb crust. *See*
　　Crumb crust, baked
Baked eggs ("shirred"), 169
Baked goat cheese, 217
Baked goat cheese with nuts,
　　217
Baked goat cheese with
　　quinoa, 217
Baked goat cheese with
　　tomato sauce or
　　tomatoes, 217
Baked lentil cakes with
　　Gruyere, 630
Baked lentil samosas,
　　745–746
Baked macaroni and cheese,
　　460–461
Baked mixed vegetables with
　　olive oil, 380
Baked mushroom crepes, 199
Baked phyllo-wrapped goat
　　cheese, 227
Baked potatoes, 339
Baked potato waffles, 206
Baked puffs, 697
Baked rice and red kidney
　　beans, Jamaican
　　style, 510
Baked rice and white beans,
　　Tuscan style, 510
Baked roasted garlic custard,
　　191
Baked savory custard,
　　190–191
Baked semolina pudding,
　　895–896
Baked spinach custard, 191
Baked spinach with fresh
　　cheese and yogurt,
　　361
Baked sweet omelet, 179
Baked sweet omelet with
　　dried fruit, 179
Baked tofu, 641–642
Baked white bean cakes, 629
Baked ziti. *See* Ziti, baked
Baking
　　about, 27
　　bread, 705–706
　　flours in, 680–683, 684
　　leaveners in, 683–686

Baking mixes, gluten-free,
　　683
Baking powder, 683, 685,
　　686
Baking powder biscuits, 695
Baking sheets, 12
Baking soda, 683, 685, 686
Balloon whisk, 14
Balsamic (vinegar)
　　about, 760
　　glaze, grilled or broiled
　　　radicchio with,
　　　301
　　-glazed carrots with garlic,
　　　279
　　mustard, 777
　　onion halves, -roasted, 331
　　seaweed romaine, 57
　　strawberries with arugula,
　　　42
　　strawberries with arugula
　　　and goat cheese, 42
　　syrup, 798–799
　　winter squash, braised, in
　　　caramel sauce with
　　　rosemary and, 368
Bamboo shoots, about,
　　264–265
Bamboo steamers, 25
Banana(s)
　　about, 420
　　bread, 691
　　breading and frying, 246
　　bread pudding, -chocolate
　　　chunk, vegan, 886
　　-butterscotch pie, 873
　　-date cobbler, 878
　　to grill, 413
　　muffins, -nut, 693
　　pancakes, 202
　　pudding, real, 884
　　strudel, 880–881
Barbecue sauce(s)
　　Asian, 790
　　beer, 790
　　bourbon, 790
　　chipotle, 789
　　curry, 789
　　fast, down-home, 789
　　horseradish, 789
　　lighter, 790

　　marinated tofu with, 653
　　mustardy, 789
Barbecue tofu
　　-baked, 642
　　-grilled or broiled, 643
Barbecue utensils, 14
Barley
　　about, 534, 536
　　cucumber salad with wal-
　　　nuts, 83
　　and mushroom stew, 540
　　and mushroom stew,
　　　deeper, 541
　　pea salad, 82
　　pilaf, 539–540
　　salad with cucumber and
　　　yogurt-dill dressing,
　　　82
　　soup
　　　mushroom, 139
　　　with vegetables, roasted
　　　　seasonal, 139
　　　with vegetables, seasonal,
　　　　138–139
　　　with vegetables, summer,
　　　　139
　　"succotash," 541–542
Bars
　　almond, 845
　　blondies, 844–845
　　buttermilk, 846
　　caramel walnut, 846
　　chocolate
　　　cranberry or cherry, 847
　　　double, 847
　　　peppermint, 847
　　　swirl, 847
　　coconut-lime, 845–846
　　dried fruit, 847
　　granola
　　　dried cherry-chocolate,
　　　　847
　　　no-bake, 846–847
　　　nutty, 847
　　　orange-spice, 847
　　　peanut (or any nut) but-
　　　　ter, 847
　　lemon-rosemary, 846
　　mango, 846
　　peanut-caramel, 845
　　semolina-apricot, 845

Bartlett pears, 433
Basic bulgur, 555
Basic fried rice, Thai style,
　　521
Basic fried rice with frozen
　　vegetables, 521
Basic fried rice with lettuce,
　　521
Basic scrambled tofu, 655
Basic steamed cauliflower,
　　281
Basic wild rice, 567
Basil
　　about, 765
　　-apple, pear, or pineapple
　　　sauce, 862
　　bruschetta with tomatoes
　　　and, 735
　　dipping sauce, 777
　　granita, 894
　　ice cream, 890
　　in pesto, 766–767
　　pesto with butter, 768
　　pesto, traditional, 768
　　pumpkin, pan-fried, with
　　　tomato sauce,
　　　Parmesan and, 367
　　purée, 769
　　Thai, mung bean dal with
　　　carrots, cashews
　　　and, 602
　　Thai, sorbet, lemon-lime,
　　　893
　　with tomatoes, grilled,
　　　373–374
Basmati rice, 503
Batter(s)
　　European style, 245, 248,
　　　249
　　Indian style (pakora), 248,
　　　249
　　Japanese style (tempura),
　　　248, 249
Battered apple "fries," 249
Battered and fried vegetables,
　　three ways, 245,
　　248–249
Bay (leaves)
　　about, 765
　　-scented baked potato, 339
　　tomato sauce with, 448

Bean(s), 581–566. *See also*
        Black bean(s);
        Chickpea(s);
        Edamame; Fava
        bean(s), dried;
Fava bean(s), fresh; Green
        bean(s); Legumes;
        Soybeans; White
        bean(s)
additions to cooked beans,
        582
adzuki
    croquettes, 628
    and greens, 598
    tofu sesame burger with,
        667
baked
    618–619, *See also*
        Bean(s), boulan-
        gerie
    black, Brazilian,
        619–620
    black, Brazilian, and rice,
        620
    black, and corn, Enchi-
        lada style, 622
    black, curried, 620
    black, smoky, 620
    buttery, 619
    with cracker crumb
        crust, 619
    curried, 619
    fava, with ricotta and
        Parmesan, 621
    heartier, 619
    lima, Parmigiana, 621
    lima, with ricotta and
        Parmesan, 621
    maple-, apple butter
        beans, 619
    pinto, enchilada style,
        621–622
    pinto, enchilada style,
        and sweet potatoes,
        622
black-eyed peas
    briny, 588–589
    fritters, 626
    with smoked tofu,
        610–611

with smoked tofu and
        mushrooms, 611
    with smoked tofu, sliced,
        611
boulangerie
    and potatoes, 620
    and potatoes, creamy,
        620
    and potatoes, with leeks,
        620
    and potatoes, with Span-
        ish paprika, 621
    and potatoes, tomatoey,
        620
    and sweet potatoes, 621
broth, cool, Korean style
        noodles in, 469
burgers
    -and-cheese, 661–662
    high-protein, 662
    the simplest, 660–661
    -and-spinach, 661
    vegan, simplest, 661
    vegetable, spicy autumn,
        665–666
    -and-veggie, 662
burritos, breakfast,
        174–175
cakes
    black bean, with queso
        fresco, 629–630
    red bean, cheesy, 629
    white bean, baked, 629
cannellini, with cabbage
        and pasta,
        586–587
cannellini, with spinach
        and cavatelli, 587
chili
    black bean, espresso,
        608
    with black beans, tem-
        peh, 677–678
    bulgur with, 558
    chocolate, 608
    con nuts, 608
    smoked tea, 608
    con tempeh, 607
    con tofu, 607
    non carne, 607

cooking methods
    the long-soak way,
        582–583
    the no-soak way,
        581–582
    the quick-soak way, 581
and corn bread, 688
cranberry, with artichokes
        and cavatelli, 587
croquettes, 627
    adzuki, 628
    from leftover dishes, 628
    red, hot and smoky, 628
    sauces for, 628–629
    spicy, 627–628
crumbles, 805
dal
    about, 601
    mixed whole-bean, with
        cabbage and wal-
        nuts, 603
    mixed whole bean, with
        cauliflower and
        almonds, 603
    mixed whole-bean, with
        walnuts, 602–603
    mung bean, with apples,
        coconut, and mint,
        602
    mung bean, with carrots,
        cashews, and Thai
        basil, 602
dip
    cheesy, 614
    creamy, 614
    fast, 614
    refried, 613
    variations, 614
dumplings, steamed, 493
empanadas, and cheese,
        747
flageolets
    with fennel, 605
    French style, 604–605
    with lettuce, 605
    with morels, 597
    with tomatoes, 605
fritters. *See also* Falafel
    black-eyed pea, 626
    mung, Asian style, 626

gigantes
    with Brussels sprouts,
        587–588
    with cherry tomatoes,
        588
    with preserved lemon,
        588
    with shiitakes, 588
and greens, 595
and greens, variations, 596
griddlecakes, 630–631
gumbo, one-pot, 611
kidney
    with apples and red wine,
        586
    with apples and sherry,
        586
    with chipotle and dried
        cherries, hot and
        smoky, 586
    with pears and wine, 586
    with prunes, piquant,
        586
    and rice, baked,
        Jamaican style, 510
lima
    baked, Parmigiana, 621
    baked, with ricotta and
        Parmesan, 621
    pilaf with chickpeas,
        peas and, 512
    purée with fennel and
        orange juice, 613
    stew, dried fruit and,
        594–595
    stuck-pot rice with, 526
mung
    with chile paste, 590
    dal, with apples,
        coconut, and mint,
        602
    dal with carrots, cashews
        and Thai basil, 602
    and fermented black
        beans, 590
    fried, with mung bean
        sprouts, 590
    fried, with sesame, 589
    fritters, Asian style, 626
    pancakes, 631

pancakes, with kimchi,
631
pancake, southeast Asian
style, 631–632
and rice with dried apri-
cots, 611–612
salad, two-mung, 76–77
soup, 121
spiced, and rice with carrots, 612
and mushrooms, 596–597
pasta with, 454–455
pinto
baked, enchilada style,
and sweet potatoes,
622
baked, enchilada style,
621–622
and greens, 596
with red bell pepper, 594
tart with millet crust, 624
tart with millet crust,
cheesy, 624
tart with millet crust,
souffléed, 624–625
pozole with, 544–545
purée(d)
black bean, with chipo-
tles, 613
cheesy, 613
chickpea and eggplant,
613
with garlic, roasted, 613
garlicky, 613
lima bean, with fennel
and orange juice,
613
white, 612–613
white, and celery root,
613
puréed or mashed, 612–617
quesadillas, chile-, 741
quesadillas, chile-, grilled,
741
red, spicy, Indian style, 593
refried, 592
buttery, 592
creamier, 592
dip, 613
flavorings for, 593

and rice
coconut rice with, 508
mung beans with dried
apricots, 611–612
mung beans with spiced
carrots, 612
red kidney beans, baked,
Jamaican style, 510
stuck-pot, with tortilla
crust, 525
white beans, baked, 510
salad(s). See Bean salad(s)
salsa, 751
shell, fresh and frozen, 589
skillet, 583–593
soup(s). See Bean soup(s)
soups with, 136
stews, 593–595
storing cooked beans,
580–581
stuffings, 407
tart
pinto, with millet crust,
624
pinto, with millet crust,
cheesy, 524
pinto, with millet crust,
soufléed, 624–625
white bean and sage with
quinoa crust, 625
texture of cooked beans,
584
yield, 581
yogurt sauce with, 774
Bean salad(s), 71–78
about, 71
bean sprout and dulse,
spicy, 55
black bean and pan-roasted
corn, 74
chickpea, with arugula,
warm, 73–74
chickpea, bulgur, and
tomato, 83
edamame, with seaweed
"mayo," 76
essential, 72–73
Chinese style, 72–73
easiest, 72
French style, 72

Greek style, 72
Indian style, 73
Italian style, 72
Japanese style, 72
fava bean and mint, with
asparagus, 77
lentil, lemony, 75–76
lentil, tangarine, 76
mung, two-, 76–77
three-bean, broiled,
74–75
three-bean, broiled, Italian
style, 75
three-bean, broiled, Spanish style, 75
Bean soup(s), 114–122. See
also Lentil(s), soup
black bean, 115
black bean, Brazilian style,
115
bread, 121–122
chestnut-, 122
chickpea
with olives and oranges,
118
with saffron and
almonds, 117–118
smooth, 118
with spinach, 118
mung bean, 121
and pasta, 123
split pea, simplest,
118–119
split pea, yellow, with
pantry vegetables,
119
white bean, 119–121
Bean sprout(s)
about, 265
crisp-fried, 632
crisp-fried, in lettuce wraps,
632
griddlecakes, 630
to make, 77–78
mung, fried mung beans
with, 590
salad, and dulse, spicy, 55
salad, two-mung, 76–77
stir-fried, spiced, 265
with tofu, scrambled, 655

Bean thread noodles
about, 464
with arame, 55
and arame with fermented
black beans, 55
and arame with Ponzu dip-
ping sauce, 54–55
with coconut milk and
mint, 466
dumplings with, steamed,
vegan, 493–494
egg "noodle" soup with,
154
in two-mung salad, 76–77
Béchamel sauce
and asparagus gratin, 383
11 ways, 803–804
onions, stuffed, 397
Beer
barbecue sauce, 790
batter, European style, 248
-battered squash blossoms,
249
-braised potatoes with
horseradish and
Cheddar, 347–348
with fondue, smoked
cheese, 222
-glazed black beans
Asian style, 586
and chiles, 585, 586
with Thai-style chile
paste, 586
with tamarind, 586
and tomatoes, 585
salsa borracha, 788
Beet(s)
about, 266
baked in foil, 267
borscht, roasted, 109–110
borscht, cold-roasted, 110
cake, with orange glaze, 852
crisps, 267
done simply, 266–267
orange juice with black
beans and, 607
pancakes, 393
in pasta, red, 480
pickled eggs with horseradish and, 182

Beet(s) *(Continued)*
  roasted, and goat cheese
    gratin, 383
  salad
    and avocado, 66
    and avocado, with citrus,
      66
    raw, 49
      raw with cabbage and
        orange, 50
      raw with carrot and
        ginger, 50
      raw with yogurt dress-
        ing, 50
      raw with yogurt sauce,
        66
  in vegetable burger, hearty
    winter, 663
Beet greens, 265–266
Belgian endive. *See also*
    Endive
  about, 34–35, 300
  and Roquefort salad,
    44–45
Bell pepper(s). *See also* Red
    pepper(s)
  about, 829
  eggplant, broiled, with
    onions, yogurt and,
    298–299
  fried rice with, simplest,
    519–520
  to grill, 252
  mixed vegetables with olive
    oil, baked, 381
  and onions, pan cooked,
    Asian style,
    334–335
  and onions, pan cooked,
    with mustard and
    cumin seeds, 335
  and onions, pan cooked,
    my mom's, 334
  paprika, 335
  paprika, smoked, 335
  paprika, with sour cream,
    335
  to prepare, *828*
  roasted
    and cheese empanadas,
      747

    mayonnaise, 771
    tahini sauce, 796
    wheat berry or other
      whole grain salad
      with, 87
  salsa sofrito, 788
  with tofu, stir-fried, 647
  and zucchini, roasted,
    wheat berry or
    other whole grain
    salad with, 87
Berry(ies). *See also specific*
    berries
  about, 420–421
  champagne gelées with,
    888
  gelées, 888
  ice cream, 890
  jam glaze, 858
  mousse, 901
  puréed, 862
  sparkling wine with, 904
  -vanilla sauce, 861–862
Best scrambled eggs, the,
    167
Beurre noisette sauce, 804
Bhide, Monica, 744
Bhutanese rice, 504
Biryani, 512–513
Biscuits
  additions to, 688
  baking powder, 695
  drop ("emergency"), 695
  sweet potato, 695
  yogurt or buttermilk,
    694–695
Bisque, chile, 131
Bistro dressing or sauce,
    creamy, 799
  mustard, 799
  tarragon, 799
Bittersweet chocolate, 837
Black bean(s)
  about, 577
  baked
    Brazilian, 619–620
    Brazilian, and rice, 620
    and corn, Enchilada
      style, 622
    curried, 620
    smoky, 619–620

  beer-glazed, 585
    Asian style, 586
    and chiles, 585
    with tamarind, 586
    and tomatoes, 585
  cakes with queso fresco,
    629–630
  and chile paste, 830
  chili, espresso, 608
  chili with tempeh,
    677–678
  fermented
    arame and bean thread
      noodles with, 55
    bok choy with, 270
    Japanese rice with toma-
      toes and, 532
    kale, rolled, with tofu
      and, 309
    and mung beans, fried,
      590
    rice salad with, 80
    tofu, stir-fried, with scal-
      lions and, 646
  and greens, 596
  ketchup, 791
  with orange juice,
    606–607
    and beets, 607
    and chiles, 607
  purée with chipotles, 613
  and rice, white, 510
  salad, and pan-roasted
    corn, 74
  with shiitakes, dried, 597
  soup, 115
  soup, Brazilian style, 115
  tart with millet crust, Mex-
    ican style, 625
Blackberry(ies)
  about, 421
  custard, 887
Black bread, 716–718
  chocolate, 719
Black butter sauce, 802
Black-eyed peas
  about, 577
  briny, 588–589
  fritters, 626
  with smoked tofu,
    610–611

    with smoked tofu and
      mushrooms, 611
    with smoked tofu, sliced,
      611
Black pepper cookies, 841
Black peppercorns, 809
Black rice, 504
Black soybeans with soy
    sauce, 608–609
Black Thai rice with coconut
    milk and edamame,
    532
Blanching vegetables, 237
Blender, 16
Blender hollandaise, 803
Blintzes
  basics of, 196
  broiled, 199
  cheese, 198
  to fold, *199*
  fruit, 198
  mashed potato, 198
  vegetable and cheese, 198
Blondies, 844–845
Blueberry(ies)
  about, 421
  -buttermilk pie, 871–873
  custard, 887
  mousse (or any berry), 901
  muffins, 693
  -olive oil torte, 853
  pancakes, 202
Blue cheese
  about, 210
  apples, *402*, 402
  dip or spread, 212
  dressing, 774
  dressing, potato salad with,
    71
  fondue, 222
  macaroni and, nutty, 461
  pearl couscous gratin with
    caramelized onions
    and, 555
  shortbread, 696
  tart, and pecan, 228
  and tomato salad, broiled,
    58
  and tomato salad, broiled,
    with fried sage
    leaves, 58

Boiled chestnuts, 287
Boiled dumplings, 497
Boiled vegetables
    greens, 239–240
    potatoes, 340–341
    root, 240
    tender, 240
Boiling technique, 24, 237, 240
Bok choy
    about, 268–269
    with black beans, 270
    Mediterranean style, 270
    quick-cooked, 269–270
    and tofu "goulash," 150–151
Boniato, 377–378
Boozy apple cake, 851–852
Boozy cake soak, 859
Boozy nut sauce, 798
Borscht
    beet or mushroom, cold-roasted, 110
    beet, roasted, 109–110
    consommé, 110
    mushroom, roasted, 110
Bosc pears, 433
Boston brown bread, 690
Boston lettuce
    about, 34
    stuffed, 404
Boulangerie beans and potatoes, 620
    creamy, 620
    with leeks, 620
    with Spanish paprika, 621
    sweet potatoes, 621
    tomatoey, 620
Boule, to shape, 704
Bourbon barbecue sauce, 790
Braeburn apple, 418
Braided rich golden bread, 716
Braised and glazed vegetables
    about, 238
    broccoli, cauliflower, or just about anything else, 271
    Brussels sprouts, 272–273
    butternut squash, 364
    carrots, balsamic-, with garlic, 279

carrots, quick-, 278–279
carrots, quick-, with orange and ginger, 279
radishes, turnips or other root vegetable, 354–355
radishes, turnips or other root vegetables with miso sauce, 355
Braised lentils. See Lentil(s), braised
Braised rice cakes, 474
Braised tempeh, three ways, 675
    hot and sour, 675
    with soy and tomato sauce, 675
Braised tofu
    basics of, 648
    in caramel sauce, 650–651
    with eggplant and shiitakes, 650
    ketchup-, spicy, 651–652
    and peas in coconut milk, curried, 648
    and peas in coconut milk, faster, 648
    and peas in coconut milk, really spicy, 649
    peas, and rice in coconut milk, creamy, 649
    with tempeh, fast-, 651
Braised vegetables
    artichoke hearts, 259
        with garlic, lots of roasted, 260
        with potatoes, 260
        vinegar-, 260
    burdock and carrots, quick-, 274–275
    celery, oven-, 284–285
    endive, escarole, or radicchio, 300–301
    endive, with orange juice, 301
    garlic, in olive oil, 305
    leeks
        with mustard, 311
        in oil or butter, 310
        with olives, 311
        with tomato, 311

olives, with tomatoes, 326
potatoes, 346–347
    with almonds, 347
    beer-, with horseradish and cheddar, 347–348
    cream-, 347
    and garlic, 347
    with miso, 347
    with mustard, 347
    with pineapple in coconut milk, 348
    with sea greens, 347
    soy-, 347
    quick-, Thai style, 379–380
    winter squash in caramel sauce, 368
    winter squash in caramel sauce with balsamic vinegar and rosemary, 368
Braising technique, 27, 238
Bran muffins, 693
Bran and oat sandwich bread, 713
Brazilian black beans, baked, 619–620
    with rice, 620
Brazilian style black bean soup, 115
Brazil nuts, 319
Bread. See also Bread crumbs; Bread(s), quick; Bread(s), yeast; Croutons; Toasts
    for bruschetta, 735
    frittata, 184
    pudding. See Bread pudding
    salad
        corn bread, 88
        crouton, 87–88
        with fresh figs, hearty, 90
        with greens, 88
        grilled, 88
        Lebanese style, 88–89
        whole grain, 89–90
        whole grain, cabbage stuffed with, 401–402
    for sandwiches, 730

soup, 121–122
    pumpkin, -and-water, 134
    tomato and, 112
    stale, using, 719
    storing, 706
    stuffed. See Empanadas; Samosas
    stuffing, and herb, 395–396
Bread(s), quick, 686–701. See also Cheese shortbread; Flatbread(s); Muffins; Puffs
    additions to, 688
    banana, 691
    basics of, 686–687
    biscuits
        baking powder, 695
        drop ("emergency"), 695
        sweet potato, 695
        yogurt or buttermilk, 694–695
    Boston brown, 690
    carrot, brown sugar, with almonds, 692
    corn bread, 687–688
        and bean, 688
        corny, 688
        lighter, richer, 688
        fruit-and-nut or vegetable-and-nut, 691–692
        combinations, 692
        whole grain, 692
    Irish soda, 690–691
    leaveners in, 683, 685
    olive oil salt, 689–690
    olive oil salt, griddled, 690
    pumpkin ginger, with hazelnuts, 692
    scones, 695–696
    whole wheat
        lighter, 689
        and molasses, 689
        with sweet milk, 689
Bread(s), yeast, 726–730. See also Pizza, dough
    additions to, 718
    anadama, 713
    basics of making. See Bread making
    black, 716–718

Bread(s), yeast *(Continued)*
  black, with chocolate, 719
  breadsticks, 711
    herbed, 711
    olive or dried tomato,
      711
    Parmesan, 711
    sesame rice, 711
  buns, cinnamon, 715–716,
    716
  challah, to make, *717*
  coffee cake, streusel pull-
    apart (monkey
    bread), *715*, 715
  egg wash on, 717
  English muffins, 714
  European style breads,
    707–711
  flavoring combos for, 720
  flour substitutions for, 684
  focaccia, 728–729
  French
    fast, 707–708
    more leisurely, 708
    overnight, 709
    whole grain, 708–709
  fruit and nut, saffron, 715
  leaveners in, 683–685
  pita, 719–720
  pita, stuffed, 720–721
  pita, whole wheat, 720
  pumpernickel-raisin,
    718–719
  rich golden, 6 ways,
    714–715
    braided, 716
    cinnamon buns,
      715–716, *716*
    fruit and nut, saffron,
      715
    rolls, 715
    sandwich, 715
  rolls
    dinner, to shape, *704*
    French, whole grain,
      708–709
    French, fast, 707–708
    French, more leisurely,
      708
    French, overnight, 709
    rich golden, 715

sandwich
  about, 711–712
  bran and oat, 713
  half whole-wheat, 713
  rich golden, 715
  to shape, *712*
  white, 712–713
sourdough, 709–711
vegan substitutions, 687
whole grain, about, 713
Bread crumbs
  cauliflower salad with
    capers and, 62
  cauliflower salad with olives
    and, 61–62
  crisp, chickpeas in their
    own broth with,
    605–606
  fresh, 804
  fried, 805
  pasta with, 444
  toasted, 804–805
Breaded vegetables
  about, 246–247
  cauliflower, sautéed, 281
  okra, fried, 324
Bread flour, 680–681
Bread knife, 8
Bread machine, 16
Bread making. *See also*
    Bread(s), yeast
  baking, 705–706
  doneness, 706
  equipment, 701–702
  freezing dough, 706
  gluten development during,
    708
  by hand, 706
  kneading dough, 702,
    703
  mixing dough, 702, *703*,
    706, 707
  pizza dough, 721–723
  rising dough, 702–703
  shaping dough, 703–704
    for baguettes, 704, *705*
    for boule, *704*
    for dinner rolls, *704*
    for sandwich bread, *712*,
      713
  slashing dough, *705*, 705

Bread pudding
  apple-cardamom, 885–886
  banana-chocolate chunk,
    vegan, 886
  chocolate, 886
  prune-cognac, 886
  savory, 192–193
    with Brussels sprouts,
      193
    multigrain, with winter
      squash, 193
    with sun-dried tomatoes
      and mozzarella,
      193
  walnut, spiced, 886
Breadsticks, 711
  herbed, 711
  olive or dried tomato, 711
  Parmesan, 711
  sesame rice, 711
Breakfast burritos, 174–175
Breakfast dishes, with eggs,
    173, 174–179
Breakfast polenta pizza, 547
Brewhouse mustard, 776
Brie
  about, 211
  and tomato salad with
    almonds, broiled,
    59
Brined fresh cheese, 230
Brittle(d)
  additions to, 906–907
  chocolate-nut, 906
  nut, 906
  popcorn, 906
Broccoli
  about, 270
  braised and glazed, 271
  couscous, whole wheat,
    with walnuts and,
    554
  marinated garden vegeta-
    bles, 67–68
  with omelet, flat, 183
  pasta with, 452
  and pesto gratin, 383
  pizza with tomato sauce,
    mozzarella and, 727
  purée, 389
  Roman style, 271

soup, creamy, 130
stir-fried, 270–271
stir-fried, with dried
  shiitakes, 271
stir-fried, with tofu, 647
Broccoli raab
  about, 272
  pasta with, 452
Broiled bruschetta, 735
Broiled cheese, 214
Broiled fruit, 411
Broiled seitan, 672
Broiled tofu, 642
  barbeue-, teriyaki-, or
    ponzu, 643
  miso, 643
Broiled vegetables
  about, 239
  cherry tomatoes with herbs,
    374–375
  cherry tomatoes with
    Parmesan, 375
  eggplant, 295
  eggplant with peppers,
    onions, and yogurt,
    298–299
  potatoes, 346
  potatoes, last-minute, 346
  radicchio with balsamic
    glaze, 301
  sunchokes with garlic or
    Parmesan, 370
  three-bean salad, 74–75
    Italian style, 75
    Spanish style, 75
  tomato
    and blue cheese salad,
      58
    and blue cheese salad
      with fried sage
      leaves, 58
    and brie salad with
      almonds, 59
    and cheddar salad with
      onions, 59
    and feta salad with tape-
      nade, 58–59
    and mozzarella salad
      with pesto, 59
Broiling technique, 28–29,
    239

Broth. *See also* Stock, vegetable
    bean, cool, Korean style
        noodles in, 469
    curry, whole-wheat pasta
        in, 147
    ginger, fruit and gelée in,
        904
    green tea, with udon noo-
        dles, 145–146
    passatelli in, 489
    pasta in, 450–451
    soy, Chinese egg noodles
        in, 465–466
Brown butter, 801–802
Brown lentil(s)
    about, 599
    pancakes, 632
Brown rice, 506–507
    about, 502
    baked, simpler, 515
    and lentil crêpes (dosas),
        745
    pilaf with two mushrooms,
        514–515
    salad, 80
    to substitute for white, 506
    tempeh with spinach and,
        676
Brown rice flour, 682
Brown rice pasta, 443
Brown sauce, 803
Brown sugar
    about, 834
    carrot bread with almonds,
        692
    cookies with sea salt,
        840–841
    -vanilla cake soak, 859
Bruschetta, 735
    broiled, 735
    with tomatoes and basil,
        735
    toppings for, 737
Brushes, 14
Brussels sprouts
    about, 272
    braised and glazed,
        272–273
    bread pudding with, 193
    in coconut milk, 274
    gigantes with, 587–588

roasted, with garlic, 273
sautéed, with hazelnuts, 273
wild rice, 567
Buckwheat
    about, 535
    crêpes, 197
    flour, 478, 682
    groats, about, 535, 539
    noodles, Korean, 465
    pasta, 443
    pizzocheri, 478
    stew with tofu and kale,
        563
Bulgur
    about, 534, 539
    basic, 555
    chili, 557–558
    chili, with beans, 558
    chili, smoky hot, 558
    creamed
        with fennel, 556
        with leeks, 556
        with saffron, 556
        with spinach, 555–556
        with sunchokes, 556
    croquettes
        with mashed potatoes,
            558
        with plantains, 558
        with walnuts, 558
    crust, white bean and veg-
        etable gratin with,
        624
    pilaf
        with cabbage, Lebanese
            style, 557
        with green beans and soy
            sauce, 557
        tomato, with cinnamon,
            556
        with vermicelli, 556
    with spices, sweet, 897
    tabbouleh, 43
    tomato, and chickpea salad,
        83
    and tomato salad, 83
    in vegetable burger, hearty
        winter, 663
Bundt pan, 12
Buns, cinnamon, 715–716,
    716

Burdock (gobo)
    about, 274
    and carrots, quick-braised,
        274–275
Burger(s). *See* Cheese,
        "burger(s)"; Veggie
        burger(s)
Burritos
    basics of, 737–738
    breakfast, 174–175
    breakfast, sauces for, 175
    breakfast, vegan, 175
    fillings and salsas for, 739,
        740
    to roll, *738*, 740
Butter(s)
    about, 207
    beurre noisette sauce, 804
    black, 802
    brown, 801–802
    compound, 801
    compound, basics of, 800
    to cream, 850
    ghee, 601
    grains cooked with, 538
    leeks braised in, 310
    nut. *See* Nut butter(s)
    pasta with cream, Parmesan
        and, 447
    pasta with Parmesan and,
        447
    pasta with pepper, pecorino
        and, 447
    pasta with sage, Parmesan
        and, 447
    pesto with, 78
    precooked vegetables in,
        240–242
    in soup, 136
    substitutes, in vegan cook-
        ing, 29
    as thickener, 882
Buttercream frosting, not-too-
        sweet, 860
    chocolate, 860
    honey, 860
    maple, 860
    parsnip or carrot cake with,
        852
Buttered cabbage, 275–277
Buttered popcorn, 292

Buttermilk
    about, 206–207
    bars, 846
    biscuits, 694–695
    -blueberry pie, 871–873
    in cheese, fresh, the easy
        way, 230
    -dark chocolate pie, 873
    ice cream, 891
    mashed potatoes, 343
    in okra, fried, 324
    pancakes, 202
    in ranch dressing, real, 772
    waffles, everyday, 203–204
Butternut squash
    braised and glazed, 364
    caramelized, pearl couscous
        tagine with, 553
    with coconut milk and
        curry, 365
    couscous, pearl, "risotto,"
        553
    with cream and walnuts,
        365
    grain-fried, 245
    pancakes, and hazelnut,
        393
    and pecorino Romano
        gratin, 385
    with pesto, 364
    purée, 389
    with saffron and almonds,
        365
    with soy, 364
    stuffed, 404
    Thai style, 365
    tortellini, 483–484
    triangles, 484
Butterscotch-banana pie, 873
Buttery baked beans, 619
Buttery lentils and potatoes
        with curry, 602
Buttery oven-roasted potatoes,
        345
Buttery refried beans, 592

Cabbage. *See also* Bok choy;
        Kimchi
    about, 275
    beet salad with orange and,
        50

Cabbage *(Continued)*
bulgur pilaf with, Lebanese
style, 557
buttered, 275–277
cannellini beans with pasta
and, 586–587
and carrot slaw, Mexican
style, 49
chickpeas with pearl couscous and, 587
coleslaw, spicy no-mayo, 49
to core and shred, *276*
dal, mixed whole-bean,
with walnuts and,
603
gratin, 384
pie, 403
quinoa with silky cabbage,
560
red, with apples, 277–278
salted, with sichuan pep-
percorns, 95
in slaw, to salt, 46
in soup, 127
stuffed
with bread salad, whole-
grain, 401–402
with lentils and rice,
401, 401
with lentils and rice in
red wine sauce, 401
Napa, 404
with tofu, stir-fried, 648
with tomatoes and sour
cream, 277
wheat berry or other whole
grain salad with
course mustard
and, 85
Cacao beans, 836
Caesar dressing, vegetarian,
773
Cake(s). *See also* Cake soak
almond, 850
amaretto, 850
apple, boozy, 851–852
babycakes and cupcakes,
853
basics of, 848–949
beet, with orange glaze,
852

blueberry-olive oil torte,
853
cheesecake, ricotta,
876–877
cheesecake, rum-raisin
ricotta, 877
chocolate layer
chocolate nib, 855
cinnamon, 855
ginger, 855
vanilla, 855
chocolate nut torte, flourless, 850–851
coconut, 853
creaming technique, for,
850
dressings and toppings for,
851
fennel, with grapefruit
glaze, 852
ganache coating and filling,
861
honey-spice, 854
molasses-spice, 855
olive oil, 852
parsnip or carrot with not-
too-sweet butter-
cream frosting, 852
pound
cornmeal, 849
ginger, 849
vanilla lime, 849–850
yogurt, 850
raisin or date, 854
upside-down
green tomato, sweet, 854
pear and almond, 854
pineapple, fresh, 854
plum-rosemary,
853–854
Cake flour, 681
Cake pans, 12, 848–849
Cake soak, 851
boozy, 859
coconut-pineapple, 860
coffee cake, spiced, 859
jasmine tea, 860
vanilla, 858–859
vanilla-brown sugar, 859
vanilla milk, 860
California chile, 828

Calzone, 729–730
to shape, *722*
Camembert, 211
Candy
brittle, additions to,
906–907
brittle, chocolate-nut, 906
brittle, nut, 906
caramels, 907
caramels, coffee, 907
popcorn, brittled, 906
Cane vinegar, 761
Canned tomato cobbler,
376–377
Cannellini beans
about, 577
with cabbage and pasta,
586–587
and greens, 596
with spinach and cavatelli,
587
Cannelloni
to make, *483*
spinach-cheese, 482–483
Canola oil, 758
Cantaloupe, to macerate and
season, 416
Caper(s)
cauliflower, sautéed, with
garlic, vinegar and,
281
cauliflower salad with bread
crumbs and, 62
sauce, 804
in tapenade, 326–327
Cappuccino
custard, baked, 886–887
flan, 887
Carambola, 422
Caramel(s), 907
coffee, 907
-peanut bars, 845
sauce
tofu in, braised, 650–651
winter squash in,
braised, 368
winter squash in,
braised, with bal-
samic vinegar and
rosemary, 368
walnut bars, 846

Caramelized carrot chutney,
787
Caramelized fennel chutney,
787
Caramelized French toast,
177
Caramelized melon chutney,
787
Caramelized onions. *See*
Onion(s),
caramelized
Caramelized spiced nuts,
322–323
Caramelized tomato slices,
375
Caraway, 820
Cardamom
about, 811
-apple bread pudding,
885–886
-pistachio cookies, 842
Cardoons, about, 256–258
Carob, 838
Carrot(s)
about, 278
beet salad, raw, with ginger
and, 50
bread, brown sugar, with
almonds, 692
breading and frying, 246
and burdock, quick-
braised, 274–275
and cabbage slaw, Mexican
style, 49
cake with not-too-sweet
buttercream frost-
ing, 852
chutney, caramelized, 787
with dates and raisins,
279–280
to dice, *278*
and dulse salad, spicy, 55
glazed
balsamic-, with garlic,
279
quick-, 278–279
quick-, with orange and
ginger, 279
kasha with, 562
marinated garden vegeta-
bles, 67–68

millet mash with ginger, sesame, and soy, 566

miso sauce with ginger, 781–782

mung bean dal with cashews, Thai basil and, 602

mung beans and rice with, spiced, 612

oatcakes, savory, with peas and, 570

oatmeal cookies, 840

pickled eggs with jalapeños and, 182

purée, 389

and quinoa, rösti, 561

salad, 45
   and celery, 45
   with cumin, 45–46
   rémoulade, 45

soup
   creamy, 129
   glazed, with garlic, tequila, and lime, 105
   glazed, with orange and ginger, 105
   mustard-glazed, 105
   Thai style, 129–130

with walnut butter, 268

Cascabel chile, 827

Cashews
about, 319
mung bean dal with carrots, Thai basil and, 602

Cassava
about, 377–378
fritters, 394
purée, 389

Cassis-orange marmalade glaze, 858

Cast-iron pans
nonreactive, 11
pros and cons, 9
to season and clean, 10

Catalan style chickpeas in their own broth, 606

Cauliflower
about, 280
braised and glazed, 271

chickpeas, baked, with paneer and, 623

couscous, whole-wheat, with almonds and, 554

dal, mixed whole-bean, with almonds and, 603

flatbread, flaky Indian style (paratha), 701

Manchurian style, 283–284

Manchurian style, roasted, 283–284

marinated garden vegetables, 67–68

mashed, with cheese, 282–283

in millet mash, 565–566

with omelet, flat, 183

pasta with, 452

and pesto gratin, 383

and potato gratin with crème fraîche or sour cream, 384

to prepare, 280, 280

purée, 389

roasted, with raisins and vinaigrette, 282

Roman style, 271

salad with capers and bread crumbs, 62

salad with olives and bread crumbs, 61–62

sautéed
   with almonds, raisins, and saffron, 282
   breaded, 281
   with feta and mint, 282
   with garlic, vinegar, and capers, 282
   with onion and olives, 281

soup, creamy, 130

soup, Indian, 130

soup, Italian style, 105–106

steamed, basic, 281

with tofu, stir-fried, 647

Cavatelli
cannellini beans with spinach and, 587

cranberry beans with artichokes and, 587

Cayenne, 826

Celery
about, 284
and carrot salad, 45
Chinese-marinated, 46
and dulse salad, spicy, 55
ginger-marinated, 47
and leek gratin, 385
with lentils, braised, 598
oven-braised, 284–285
rémoulade, 47
salad, 45
and sea green stir-fry, 357
soup, creamy, 129
to string, 284, 284
in Waldorf salad, 47–48

Celery root
about, 285
breading and frying, 246
red lentils with, 600
"schnitzel," 245
and white bean gratin, 623
and white bean gratin, Tuscan style, 623
and white bean purée, 613

Celery seeds, 811

Cellophane noodles with sweet soy sauce, 474

Ceramic cookware, 9

Cereal, breakfast. See also Granola
cooking grains, 572
oatmeal or other creamy cereal, 572–573

Chaat masala, 814–815
red lentils with, 600

Chai
custard, spiced, 887
ice cream, 891

Challah, to make, 717

Chamomile-tangerine sorbet, 893

Champagne gelées with berries, 888

Champagne vinegar, 760

Chanterelles
about, 313
fava beans with, 597

Chapati (flatbread, the simplest Indian style), 698–699
grilled, 699

Chard
about, 285
with oranges and shallots, 286
pie, 403

Charred onion soup, 109

Charred salsa roja, 788

Chayote
about, 361
to grill, 251
rémoulade, 47
sautéed, 362
stuffed, 404

Cheddar
about, 210
apples with hazelnuts, 402–403
dressing, potato salad with, 7
potatoes, beer-braised, with horseradish and, 347–348
and tomato salad, broiled, with onions, 59

Cheese. See also Cheese, fresh
about, 208–209
bake, Swiss style, 220–221
balls, 212–213
basics of cooking, 209–211
bean dip, cheesy, 614
beans, puréed, cheesy, 613
blintzes, 198
blintzes, and vegetable, 198
blue
   apples, 402, 402
   couscous, pearl, gratin with caramelized onions and, 555
   dip or spread, 212
   dressing, 774
   dressing, potato salad with, 71
   fondue, 222
   macaroni and, nutty, 461
   shortbread, 696
   tart, and pecan, 228

Cheese *(Continued)*
  and tomato salad, broiled, 58
  and tomato salad, broiled, with fried sage leaves, 58
  breakfast dishes, 173
  "burger(s)," 220
    baked, 220
    couscous and, 220
    pesto, 220
  cannelloni, spinach-, 482–483
  with cauliflower, mashed, 282–283
  Cheddar
    apples with hazelnuts, 402–403
    dressing, potato salad with, 7
    potatoes, beer-braised, with horseradish and, 347–348
    and tomato salad, broiled, with onions, 59
  chile filling, naked tamales with, 547–549
  with corn, creamed, 291
  corn chowder, cheesy, 135
  cottage cheese
    fresh, 230
    omelet, flat, with rhubarb and, 183
    pancakes, and sour cream, 202–203
    patties, 226
    patties, herbed, 226
    patties, with nuts, 226
    patties, with quinoa, 226–227
    patties, sweet, 227
  cream cheese
    dressing, potato salad with, 70
    maple sauce, pumpkin waffles with, 205–206
    and strawberry tart, 875
    and sweet potato gratin, 384

crisp(s)
  nutty, 220
  with onions, 219
  with potato, 219–220
  simple, 220
custard, baked cheesy, 191
deep-frying, 214
dips and spreads
  blue cheese, 212
  cheeses for, 210–211, 213
  flavorings for, 212, 213
dumplings, 224–225
  fluffy, 225
  goat cheese, 225
  ricotta, 225
  ricotta, panfried, 225
  ricotta, pesto, 226
  ricotta, with quinoa or millet, 225–226
  serving suggestions, 226
and eggplant, creamy noodles with, baked, 462–463
and eggplant, creamy potatoes with, 463
with eggs, fried, 168
with eggs, scrambled, 167
empanadas, bean and, 747
empanadas, corn and, 747
empanadas, roasted peppers and, 747
enchiladas
  garnishes for, 223
  with green enchilada sauce, 224
  hard-cooked egg and, 224
  with red mole, 223–224
  scrambled egg and, 224
  simple, 224
feta
  cauliflower, sautéed, with mint and, 282
  corn salad with tomatoes, mint and, 61
  kale, rolled, with olives and, 308–309
  and olive-stuffed eggs, 181

pea salad with tomatoes, mint and, 61
spice-marinated, 211
spice-marinated patties, quick, 211
and spinach pie with phyllo crust, 408–409
spinach salad with nutmeg and, 41–42
and tomato salad, broiled, with tapenade, 58–59
fondue
  about, 221–222
  blue cheese, 222
  Cheddar, sharp, with red wine, 222
  fontina and porcini, 222
  mustard-, 222
  smoked cheese, with beer, 222
  tomato and chile, 222
  variations, 222–223
goat
  and avocado dip or spread, 264
  baked, 217
  baked, with nuts, 217
  baked phyllo-wrapped, 227
  baked, with quinoa, 217
  baked, with tomato sauce or tomatoes, 217
  and beets, roasted, gratin, 383
  couscous, pearl, gratin with pesto and, 554–555
  dumplings, 225
  macaroni and, with roasted red peppers, 461
  and mushroom tart with potato crust, 227–228
  red peppers stuffed with quinoa and, 399
  soufflé, and dried apricot, 186

strawberries, balsamic, with arugula and, 42
ziti, baked, with olives and, 459
greens with fruit, nuts and, 40
grilling and broiling, 214
Gruyère, with lentil cakes, baked, 630
Gruyère, with potatoes Provençal, 348
hominy baked with chile, tomatoes, and, 569
macaroni and. *See* Macaroni and cheese
manchego and potato gratin, 383
marinated, herb-, 212
marinated, spice-, feta, 211
marinated, spice-, quick, feta patties, 211
marinated, zesty, 212
mascarpone apples with almonds, 402
mashed potato pie with, garlicky, 351
millet mash, cheesy, 566
mornay sauce, 804
mozzarella
  bread pudding with sun-dried tomatoes and, 193
  layered, with roasted peppers and olives, 221
  pizza, margherita, 726
  pizza with tomato sauce and, 726–727
  pizza with tomato sauce, broccoli and, 727
  pizza with tomato sauce and, fresh, 727
  pizza with tomato sauce and, grilled, 727
  and tomato salad, broiled, with pesto, 59
omelet, 172
  and apple, 172
  flat, cheesy, 183

fresh cheese and spinach,
Indian style, 172
panfried, 214–215
Parmesan
breadsticks, 711
"burger," 220
with cherry tomatoes,
broiled, 375
crackers, 698
eggplant, 299
in fettuccine Alfredo, 447
and green pea custard,
191
lima beans, baked,
Parmigiana, 621
lima or fava beans,
baked, with ricotta
and, 621
pasta with butter and,
447
pasta with butter, cream
and, 447
pasta with butter, sage
and, 447
popcorn, 292
potato croquettes with
roasted garlic and,
353
pumpkin, pan-fried,
with tomato sauce,
basil and, 367
rice cakes, 569–570
and ricotta quiche, 188
to serve, *209*
with sunchokes, broiled,
370
pecorino Romano and but-
ternut squash
gratin, 385
pecorino Romano, pasta
with butter, pepper
and, 447
pecorino shortbread, 696
in pesto, 768
in pesto, traditional, 768
pine nut sauce with, rustic,
797
pinto tart, cheesy, with millet crust, 624
potato pancakes, cheesy, 350
puffs, 697

quesadilla(s)
all-cheese, 741
chile-bean, 741
chile-bean, grilled, 741
for one, 741
quiche, 187–188
quinoa with potatoes and,
roasted, 561–562
ravioli, 483
ravioli, mushroom-, 483
red bean cakes, baked,
cheesy, 629
with rice, 508
rice baked with chile,
tomatoes and, 569
ricotta
calzone, 729–730
cheesecake, 876–877
cheesecake, rum-raisin,
877
-chickpea gnocchi,
626–627
dumplings, 225
dumplings, panfried, 225
dumplings, pesto-, 226
dumplings, with quinoa
or millet, 225–226
fresh, 230
lima or fava beans, baked
with Parmesan and,
621
pancakes, lemon, 203
pots, quick, 877
quiche, and Parmesan,
188
ravioli, spinach-,
481–482
with ziti, baked, 459
and zucchini tart with
potato crust, 228
risotto with four cheeses,
418
Roquefort and endive
salad, 44–45
Roquefort and mushroom
gratin, 383
salsa, Mexican, 751
samosas, and spinach, 747
shortbread, 696
blue, 696
herbed, 696

pecorino, 696
spiced, 696
soufflé, 185–186
soufflé, herb and, 186
soups with, 142
substitution in vegan cooking, 30
tomato cobbler with cheesy
topping, 376
tomato sauce, cheesy,
448–449
and tomato tart, 228
vegetable pancakes, cheesy,
393
vegetable torte, cheesy, 406
yogurt, 208
Cheese, fresh
basics of making, 228–229,
229
brined, 230
cottage cheese, 230
curried (paneer masala),
217–218
the easy way, 230
flavorings for, 231
fried, 215
coconut, 215
sauces for, 216
spiced, 215
with spiced yogurt,
215–216
and vegetable pakora,
215
grilled (paneer tikka), 216
mozzarella, pizza with
tomato sauce and,
727
omelet, and spinach,
Indian style, 172
queso fresco, with avocado
salad, six-layer, 53
queso fresco, black bean
cakes with,
629–630
ricotta, 230
scramble, 218–219
with chiles, 219
with eggs, 219
with tomatoes, 219
serving suggestions,
229–230

spinach with yogurt and,
360–361
spinach with yogurt and,
baked, 361
Cheesecake, ricotta, 876–877
rum-raisin, 877
Cheese grater, 13
Chef's knife, 8, 18
to hold, *19*, 19
Cherimoyas, 422
Cherry(ies)
about, 422
-almond cookies, 843
-chipotle salsa, 752
chocolate bars, 847
-chocolate sorbet, 893
crisp, 878
kidney beans with chipotle
and dried cherries,
hot and smoky, 686
to macerate and season, 416
omelet, baked, 179
-port jam glaze, 858
sauce, anise-, 863
sauerkraut soup, 111
strudel, 881
tart with port, 874
Cherry or grape tomato(es)
broiled, with herbs,
374–375
broiled, with Parmesan,
375
gigantes with, 588
oven-dried, 377
salad with soy sauce, 57
Chervil, 765
Chestnut(s)
about, 286–287
-bean soup, 122
boiled, grilled, or roasted,
287
cookies, chewy, 843
cream, pasta with, 457
to grill, 252
pasta, 443
and potato gratin, 384
to prepare, 286, *287*
purée, 389
-rum ice cream, 890
soufflé, 187
wild rice with, 567

Chestnut flour, 682
Chewy almond-cherry
    cookies, 843
Chewy chestnut cookies,
    843
Chewy mocha cookies, 843
Chickpea(s). *See also* Legumes
    about, 577
    baked
        with fresh cheese,
            622–623
        with paneer and cauli-
            flower, 623
        with paneer and spinach,
            623
    with cabbage and pearl
        couscous, 587
    with cremini or shiitake,
        597
    and eggplant purée, 613
    falafel, 625–626
        nutty, 626
        sesame, 626
        with za'atar, 626
    fondue, 615
    fondue, cheesy, 616
    fondue, hummus, 616
    gnocchi, -ricotta, 626–627
    and greens, 596
    hummus, 614–615
    hummus fondue, 616
    with jalapeños, 594
    pasta with, 444
    pilaf with peas, limas and,
        512
    rice with, 509
        almonds and, spiced,
            509–510
        curried, 510
        saffron, 510
    roasted, 618
    roasted, and pistachios, 618
    salad with arugula, warm,
        73–74
    soup
        with olives and oranges,
            118
        with saffron and
            almonds, 117
        smooth, 118
        with spinach, 118

sweet and sour, hot, with
    eggplant, 609–610
sweet and sour, more, with
    eggplant, 610
sweet and sour, with toma-
    toes, 610
in their own broth
    Catalan style, 606
    with crisp bread crumbs,
        605–606
    Cuban style, 606
    nutty, 606
    with sun-dried tomatoes,
        606
    with tahini, 606
tomato, and bulgur salad,
    83
Chickpea flour
    basics of, 633
    blend, 683
    flapjacks, 633–634
    fries, *634*, 634
    fries, peanut and, 634–635
    pancake, 633
    in panissa, 544
    pizza, socca, 633
Chicory, 34–35, 300
Chiffonade technique, 21, *22*
Chilaquiles, 176–177
Chile(s). *See also* Chile paste
    ancho-pine nut sauce, 797
    basics of, 822, 824–825
    bisque, 131
    and black beans, beer-
        glazed, 585
    and black beans with
        orange juice, 607
    in bulgur chili, 557–558
    cheese filling, naked tamales
        with, 547–549
    cheese fondue, and tomato,
        222
    chipotle(s)
        barbecue sauce, 789
        black bean purée with,
            613
        -cherry salsa, 752
        egg hash, 178
        kidney beans with dried
            cherries and, hot
            and smoky, 686

paste, 829
    pumpkin soup with, 133
chutney, hot pepper, 783
cilantro "pesto" with ginger
    and, 770
cookies, -olive oil, 843
with corn, creamed, vegan,
    291
with corn, pan-grilled,
    289–290
dried
    to prepare, 825
    storing, 824
    types of, 827–828
eggplant, broiled, with pep-
    pers, onions, and
    yogurt, 298–299
gratin, Mexican style,
    385–387
to grill, 252
hominy baked with cheese,
    tomatoes and, 569
jalapeño(s)
    chickpeas with, 594
    deviled eggs, 180
    pickled eggs with carrots
        and, 182
lexicon of, 825–828
macaroni and cheese,
    461–462
mayonnaise, 771
mustard, 777
pico de verde, 751
poblano custard, 191
quesadillas, -bean, 741
quesadillas, -bean, grilled,
    741
rellenos, 399–400, *400*
    with corn and pumpkin
        seeds, 400
    with goat cheese and
        walnuts, 400
    grilled, 400
rice baked with cheese,
    tomatoes and, 569
salsa, chipotle-cherry, 752
salsa, -garlic, super-spicy,
    789
salsa, green chile, 789
salsa, pico de verde, 751
salsa roja, 787–788

sauce
    and coconut, 793
    green, smooth, Indian
        style, 792–793
    red, Indian style, 793
    red, North African style,
        793
    -scallion, 780
    -yogurt, 793
with seitan, oven-roasted,
    672
snaps, 842
spinach with, 360
spinach with coconut milk
    and, 360
stuck-pot rice with sour
    cream and, 524
tofu, scrambled, 655
tofu, stir-fried, with scal-
    lions, orange zest
    and, 646
tortillas, scrambled, with
    scallions and,
    176–177
in veggie burgers, 662
vermicelli or fideo with
    tomatoes and, 451
watermelon steak, -rubbed,
    430
Chilean salsa, 750
Chile de Arbol, 826, 827
Chile paste
    and black bean, 830
    chipotle, 829
    eight ways, 828–830
    -garlic, 830
    harissa, 830
    Indian style, 829
    Mexican style, 829
    with mung beans, fried,
        590
    -sesame, beer-glazed black
        beans, Korean style,
        586
    -sesame, smashed edamame
        and potatoes,
        Korean style, 617
    with tempeh, crunchy
        crumbled, 674
    Thai style, 829
    Vietnamese style, 829

Chili
    black bean, espresso, 608
    with black beans, tempeh,
        677–678
    bulgur, 557–558
    bulgur, with beans, 558
    bulgur, smoky hot, 558
    chocolate, 608
    con nuts, 608
    con tempeh, 607
    con tofu, 607
    non carne, 607
    smoked-tea, 608
Chili powder, 814, 824
Chimichurri sauce, 769
Chinese black vinegar, 761
Chinese egg noodles, 464
    in noodle bowls, 468
    in soy broth, 465–466
Chinese marinated celery,
        46–47
Chinese mustard, 775–776
Chinese style
    bean salad, essential, 72–73
    noodles, fresh, 492
    tomatoes, grilled, and
        scrambled eggs, 374
Chinese wheat noodles, 464
Chipotle(s)
    about, 827
    barbecue sauce, 789
    black bean purée with, 613
    -cherry salsa, 752
    egg hash, 178
    kidney beans with dried
        cherries and, hot
        and smoky, 686
    paste, 829
    pumpkin soup with, 133
Chips
    nori, 357
    plantain, fried, 336–337
    potato, 352
Chive(s)
    about, 765
    and lettuce salad, Korean
        style, 44
Chocolate
    bars
        cranberry or cherry, 847
        double, 847

    peppermint, 847
    swirl, 847
    basics of, 836
    black bread, 719
    bread pudding, 886
    bread pudding, banana-
        chocolate chunk,
        vegan, 886
    buttercream frosting, not-
        too-sweet, 860
    -buttermilk pie, dark
        chocolate, 873
    -cherry sorbet, 893
    chili, 608
    to chop, 838, 839
    in cookies, 839
    cookies, cinnamon, 843
    cookies, rice, 844
    cookies, sprinkles for, 844
    cooking with, 838
    crêpes, 197
    custard sauce, 863
    dessert cups, 844
    frosting, 861
    ganache, 860–861
    ganache, dark, poached
        pear tart with,
        874–875
    ganache, uses for, 861
    glaze, 861
    ice cream, 890
    layer cake
        chocolate nib, 855
        cinnamon, 855
        ginger, 855
        vanilla, 855
    mousse, -orange, vegan,
        900–901
    -nut brittle, 906
    nut torte, flourless,
        850–851
    pudding, 884
    semolina pudding, 896
    storing, 838
    tart crust, 868
    truffles, quick, 861
    tuiles, 843–844
    types of, 836–838
Chocolate chip and toasted
        oats macaroons,
        902

Chocolate nib chocolate layer
        cake, 855
Chopped salad, 38–40
Chopping vegetables, 20, 20
Chowder. See Corn chowder
Chow mein noodles, fried,
        465
Choy sum, 269
Churros, 697
Chutney
    carrot, caramelized, 787
    cilantro-mint, 783–784
    cilantro-mint, creamy, 784
    cilantro-mint, long-lasting,
        784
    coconut, 784
    cranberry, 785
    fennel, caramelized, 787
    fruit combinations for, 785
    hot pepper, 783
    melon, caramelized, 787
    nut
        coconut and, 784
        crunchy, 784
        dried fruit and, 784
        real garlicky, 785
        walnut and yogurt, 785
    onion, caramelized, 786
    onion, grilled, 787
    onion, raw, 783
    pineapple, 785
    red pepper, roasted, 787
    tamarind-date, 785
    tomato, 785–786
        green tomato, 786
        green tomato-apple, 786
        grilled, 786
        sweet, 786
Cider vinegar, 761
Cilantro
    about, 765
    dipping sauce, 777
    edamame with tomatoes
        and, 583
    green beans and tofu skins,
        stir-fried, with
        peanuts and, 307
    -mint chutney, 783–784
    -mint chutney, creamy, 784
    -mint chutney, long-lasting,
        784

    "pesto" with ginger and
        chile, 770
    "pesto," lighter, 769–770
    purée, 769
    urad dal with poppy seeds
        and, 603–604
Cinnamon
    about, 811
    bulgur pilaf, tomato with,
        556
    buns, 715–716, 716
    chocolate cookies, 843
    chocolate layer cake, 855
    custard, 887
    eggplant and zucchini salad
        with, 64
    ice cream, hot, 890
    rice pudding, -nut, 895
Citrus. See also specific fruits
    crumble topping, -spice,
        870
    to grill, 413
    to macerate and season,
        416
    -mango sauce, 862
    miso dipping sauce, simple,
        781
    to peel and segment, 431
    -pickled ginger, 822
    ponzu, 780
    rice salad, 82
    salad, sweet couscous with,
        897
    salsa, 752
    sprinkle, 818–819, 823
    tapioca pudding, 885
    vs vinegar, 759
    wheat berry stew with dried
        fruit, nuts and, 565
    to zest, 426
Citrus reamer, 14
Clove(s)
    about, 811
    glaze, 858
Cobbler(s)
    apple, 877
    apple rhubarb, 878
    banana-date, 878
    basics of, 871
    leek, 376
    peach-brandy, 877

Cobbler(s) *(Continued)*
    tomato, 375–376
        canned, 376–377
        with cheesy topping, 376
        with corny topping,
            extra, 376
        with herb topping, 376
        with piecrust topping,
            376
        two-tomato, 376
Cocoa, pan-fried pumpkin
    with tomato sauce,
    pumpkin seeds and,
    367
Cocoa powder, 837
Coco beans, white, 579
Coconut
    about, 422–423
    bars, -lime, 845–846
    cake, 853
    and chile sauce, 793
    chutney, 784
    chutney, and nut, 784
    crêpes, 197
    crumble topping, 870
    crust, no-bake fruit and,
        869
    curry vinaigrette, 763
    fried fresh cheese, 215
    -fried plantains, 245
    fritters, 394
    glaze, 858
    in granola, crunchy, 573
    ice cream, 890
    lentil soup with, 116–117
    macaroons, -dried pineap-
        ple, 902
    mung bean dal with apples,
        mint and, 602
    -pineapple cake soak, 860
    pudding (tembleque), 884
    rice, 507–508
        and beans, 508
        with coconut bits, 508
        pudding, 895
        simpler baked, 516
        spicy, 508
        sweet, 508
    snaps, 842
    soup, curried, with lemon-
        grass, 137–138

soup, sweet, 905
soup, sweet, with grains or
    tapioca, 905
soup, sweet, with granita,
    905
sticky rice with shallots
    and, 507
tahini sauce, 796
Coconut milk, 29
    about, 423
    bean threads with mint
        and, 466
    black Thai rice with
        edamame and, 532
    Brussels sprouts in, 274
    butternut squash with
        curry and, 365
    egg hash with curry and,
        178
    with eggplant, curried,
        296
    potatoes with pineapple
        braised in, 348
    spinach with chiles and,
        360
    sticky rice with soy sauce
        and, 507
    tofu and peas braised in,
        curried, 648
    tofu and peas in, faster, 649
    tofu and peas in, really
        spicy, 649
    tofu, peas, and rice in,
        creamy, 649
Coconut vinegar, 761
Coffee
    cappuccino custard, baked,
        886–887
    cappuccino flan, 887
    espresso black bean chili,
        608
    espresso sorbet or ice milk,
        892
    gelées, 888
    ice cream, 890
Coffee cake
    muffins, 693
    soak, spiced, 859
    streusel pull-apart (monkey
        bread), *715*, 715
Colanders, 13

Cold cucumber and seaweed
    soup, 159–160
Cold fiery noodles, 467
Cold mustard sauce, 771
Cold pressed oils, 754
Cold roasted beet or mush-
    room borscht, 110
Cold sesame or peanut noo-
    dles, 466–467
Cold tomato soup, 158
Cold tomato soup with Thai
    flavors, 158
Coleslaw
    to salt, 46
    spicy no-mayo, 49
Collard greens
    about, 308
    with tofu, stir-fried, 648
Comice pears, 433
Compote, 411
Consommé, borscht, 110
Cooked tomatillo salsa, 788
Cookies. *See also* Bars
    almond-cherry, chewy, 843
    basics of, 838–839
    black pepper, 841
    brown sugar, with sea salt,
        840–841
    cardamom-pistachio, 842
    chestnut, chewy, 843
    chile-olive oil, 843
    chile snaps, 842
    chocolate
        cinnamon, 843
        dessert cups, 844
        rice, 844
        sprinkles for, 844
        tuiles, 843–844
    coconut snaps, 842
    coriander snaps, 842
    date-olive oil, 843
    ginger spice, 841
    improvising tips, 839
    maple snaps, 841–842
    mocha, chewy, 843
    oatmeal
        -apple, 839–840
        -apple, vegan, 840
        carrot or parsnip, 840
        peanut, 840
    pine nut, 841

saffron-olive oil, 842
tuiles, chocolate, 843–844
tuiles, to mold, *844*, 844
whole grain apple spice,
    840
Cookie sheets, 12
Cooking. *See also* Equipment
    and tools; Ingredi-
    ents
    thickeners in, 136, 795,
        881–883
    time for, 4
    vegan substitutions. *See*
        Vegan cooking
    zen of, 4–5
Cooking techniques, 24–29
    cheese, 214
    eggs, 162, 165
    fruit, 410–412
    vegetables, 237–239
Cookware, 9–11
Cool yogurt soup with nuts,
    158
Coriander
    about, 812
    with mushroom salad,
        steamed, 62–63
    with peach or apple gratin,
        savory, 384
    snaps, 842
Corn
    about, 287–288
    arepas, 292
    in barley "succotash,"
        541–542
    and black beans, baked,
        Enchilada style,
        622
    chiles rellenos with
        pumpkin seeds
        and, 400
    chowder, 135
        cheesy, 135
        roasted, 135
        thicker, 135
        with tomatoes, 135
    on the cob
        grilled or roasted, 290
        milk steamed, 289
        steamed, 288–289
    in corn bread, corny, 688

creamed, 290–291
    with cheese, 291
    with chile, vegan, 291
    with onion, 291
dried. *See also* Cornmeal;
        Grits; Hominy;
        Polenta; Popcorn;
        Pozole; Tamale(s)
    lexicon of, 542–543
empanadas, and cheese,
        747
flavorings for, 289
fritters, 292
gratin, hot and smoky,
        387
to grill, 252
guacamole, crunchy,
        263–264
with mole, 546
pancakes, Thai style, 291
pan-grilled, with chile,
        289–290
pan-grilled, with tomatoes,
        290
pan-roasted, and black
        bean salad, 74
and peach salsa, grilled,
        792
to prepare, *288*, 288
purée, 389
salad, 60–61
salad, curried, 61
salad, with tomatoes, feta,
        and mint, 61
salsa, 751
to scrape kernels, *288*
tomato cobber with extra
        corny topping,
        376
with tomato salad, pan-
        seared, 60
in vegetable burger, mid-
        summer, 664–665
Corn bread, 687–688
    and bean, 688
    corny, 688
    lighter, richer, 688
    salad, 88
Corn flour, 543, 681–682
    pasta, 443
Corn husk tamales, *549*, 549

Cornmeal. *See also* Corn
        bread; Grits;
        Polenta
about, 534, 539, 543
in anadama bread, 713
pasta, 443
pizza, Mexican style, 547
pizza, nutty blue, 547
pound cake, 849
pudding, Indian, 896
pudding, vegan, 896
in vegetable burger, mid-
        summer, 664–665
in yeast breads, 681–682
Corn oil, 29, 756
Cornstarch, 882, 883
Corn syrup, 835
Corn tortillas, 738
Cortland apple, 418
Cotija cheese, 210
Cottage cheese
    fresh, 230
    omelet, flat, with rhubarb
        and, 183
    pancakes, and sour cream,
        202–203
    patties, 226
        herbed, 226
        with nuts, 226
        with quinoa, 226–227
        sweet, 227
Couscous
    about, 534
    and cheese "burger," 220
    chickpeas with cabbage and
        pearl couscous, 587
    gratin, pearl
        with caramelized onions
            and blue cheese,
            555
        with pesto and goat
            cheese, 554–555
        with roasted tomatoes,
            555
    pilaf, pearl
        curried, 552
        eggplant, 551–552
        with preserved lemons,
            551
        spicy, 552
        spinach, 552

with sun-dried tomatoes,
            551
    "risotto," pearl
        with artichoke hearts,
            552
        with butternut squash,
            553
        creamy, 552
        alla Milanese, 552
        with tomato, spicy, 553
    salad
        with fennel and raisins,
            92–93
        with hazelnuts, 93
        Israeli, 91–92
        with olives, 93
        soup, North African,
            140–141
    sweet
        almond milk, 897
        with citrus salad, 897
        with dried fruit, 897
        with pistachios, 897
    tagine, pearl, 553
    tagine, pearl, with
            caramelized butter-
            nut squash, 553
    whole wheat, with broccoli
            and walnuts, 554
    whole wheat, with cauli-
            flower and
            almonds, 554
    zucchini stuffed with, 399
Cracked wheat
    about, 535
    crumble topping, 870
    fluffy, with mustard and
            tarragon, 559
    and tomato salad, 83
Cracker crumb crust, baked
            beans with, 619
Crackers, 698
    cream, 698
    Parmesan, 698
Cranberry(ies)
    about, 423
    chocolate bars, 847
    chutney, 785
    muffins, 693
    -nut sauce, creamy, 798
    -orange crisp, 878

-orange soup, 904–905
pumpkin, pan-fried, with
        pistachios and, 367
Cranberry beans
    about, 578
    with artichokes and
        cavatelli, 587
Cream(ed), creamy. *See also*
        Sour cream
about, 207
apricot sauce, 862
bean dip, 614
beans and potatoes,
        boulangerie, 620
to beat, 897–898
bistro dressing, 799
bistro dressing, mustard,
        799
bistro dressing, tarragon,
        799
bulgur
    with fennel, 556
    with leeks, 556
    with saffron, 556
    with spinach, 555–556
    with sunchokes, 556
butternut squash with wal-
        nuts and, 365
chestnut, pasta with, 457
cilantro-mint chutney,
        784
corn, 290–291
    with cheese, 291
    with chile, vegan, 291
    with onion, 291
couscous, pearl, "risotto,"
        552
crackers, 698
crème fraîche, potato and
        cauliflower gratin
        with, 384
to fold, 901
green bean gratin, 386
millet bake, autumn, 567
millet mash, 566
noodles with eggplant and
        cheese, baked,
        462–463
noodles with eggplant and
        tomatoes, sliced,
        463

Cream(ed), creamy
(Continued)
noodles with mushrooms,
463
nut sauce, 797–798
nut sauce, with arugula or
sorrel, 797–798
nut sauce, cranberry-, 798
onion halves, -roasted, 331
onions, 330
orange glaze, 857
orzo with almond butter,
451
parsnip gratin with vanilla,
386
pasta with butter, Parmesan
and, 447
potatoes, -braised, 347
potatoes with eggplant and
cheese, 464
rye berry gratin with leeks
and tomatoes, 568
soup
broccoli, 130
carrot, 129
cauliflower, 130
celery, 129
fennel, 129
Jerusalem artichoke,
130–131
of parsley, 131–132
of parsley, gratinéed, 132
peanut, 125
sauerkraut, 111
sorrel, 132
spinach, 132
of tomato, 113
watercress, 132
spinach, 330
tofu, peas, and rice in
coconut milk, 649
whipped cream, 856–857
Cream cheese
about, 211
dressing, potato salad with,
70
maple sauce, pumpkin waf-
fles with, 205–206
and strawberry tart, 875
and sweet potato gratin,
384

Creamier pozole with mole,
546
Creamier refried beans, 592
Cream puffs, 697
Cream of tartar, 899
Crème fraîche
about, 207
potato and cauliflower
gratin with, 384
Cremini
about, 313
chickpeas with, 597
Creole mustard, 777
Crêpes, 196–197. See also
Blintzes
almond, 197
basics of, 196
broiled, 199
buckwheat, 197
chocolate, 197
coconut, 197
egg, Japanese, 175–176
fillings, sweet and savory,
197
garlic, 197
mushroom, baked, 199
rice and lentil (dosas),
744–745
rice and lentil (dosas),
brown rice, 745
rice and lentil (dosas), to
form, 744
Crisp(s), fruit
basics of, 871
cherry, 878
cranberry-orange, 878
variations, 878
Crisp and buttery panfried
potatoes, 344
Crisp-cooked sunchokes,
369–370
Crisp-fried bean sprouts, 632
Crisp-fried bean sprouts in
lettuce wraps, 632
Crisp-fried noodle cake,
469–470
Crisp-fried noodle soup, 470
Crisp leeks, garlic, or shallots,
312
Crisp marinated tofu, 653
Crisp okra salad, 67

Crisp panfried potatoes,
343–344
Crisp panfried potatoes
(home fries), 343
Crisp panfried potatoes and
eggs, 344
Crisp panfried potatoes with
onions, 344
Crisps. See also Cheese,
crisp(s)
beet, 267
vegetable, seasonings for,
267–268
Crisp shredded hash brown
salad with red pep-
per vinaigrette, 70
Crisp vegetable pancakes,
Korean style,
393–394
Crispy French toast, 177
Crispy kimchi pancake, 394
Crispy panfried tofu, 642
Croquettes
bean, 627
adzuki, 628
from leftover dishes, 628
red, hot and smoky, 628
sauces for, 628–629
spicy, 627–628
bulgur
with mashed potatoes,
558
with plantains, 558
with walnuts, 558
potato, 353
additions to, 353–354
with garlic, roasted, and
Parmesan, 353
Indian style, 353
Japanese style, 353
Crostini, 737
Crouton(s), 806
cubed, 806
dry-baked, 806
fava beans, fresh, with eggs
and, 591–592
fava beans, fresh, with eggs
and, herbed, 592
fava beans, fresh, with tofu
and, 592
herbed, 806

highly seasoned, 806
with olives, sautéed, 326
salad, 87–88
soups with, 106
tofu, 656
tofu, spinach salad with
warm dressing and,
40–41
Crudités
dips to serve with, 89
vegetables for, 88
Crumb crust, baked,
868–869
gingersnap, 869
savory, 869
Crumbles, 805
Crumble topping
citrus-spice, 870
coconut, 870
cracked wheat, 870
hazelnut or almond,
870–871
oat, 870
rice flour, 870
sweet, 870
Crunchier pizza dough, 725
Crunchy amaranth griddle-
cakes, 570–571
Crunchy corn guacamole,
263–264
Crunchy crumbled tempeh,
674
Crunchy crumbled tempeh
with chile paste,
674
Crunchy crumbled tempeh
with fresh herbs,
674
Crunchy crumbled tempeh
with wheat berries,
674
Crunchy granola, 573
Crunchy nut chutney, 784
Crust(s). See also Phyllo;
Piecrust; Tart crust
bulgur, white bean and vegetable gratin with,
624
cracker crumb, baked beans
with, 619
crumb, baked, 868–869

gingersnap, 869
savory, 869
no-bake
to fill, 869–870
fruit and coconut, 869
fruit and nut, 869
pita, stuck-pot rice and
lentils with, 525
potato, stuck-pot rice with,
526
tortilla, stuck-pot rice and
beans with, 525
Crystal sugar, 834
Cuban style
chickpeas in their own
broth, 606
rice salad, 81
Cubed croutons, 806
Cucumber(s)
about, 293
barley salad with walnuts,
83
barley salad with yogurt-dill
dressing and, 82
pickled vegetables, quick-,
95
pickles, kosher, the right
way, 97
pickles, spicy, Asian style,
95–96
pickles, 3–day, 96–97
for pickling, 94
raita, 774
salad Korean style, 49
salad with sour cream or
yogurt, 48
salad with soy and ginger,
48
salsa, Thai style, 753
to salt, 46
scallion-marinated, 47
and seaweed soup, cold,
159–160
to seed, 293, 293
sorbet, -honey, 893
wild rice with yogurt and,
83
yogurt soup with, 158
Cumin (seeds)
about, 812
carrot salad with, 45–46

peppers and onions, pan
cooked, with
mustard and, 335
Cupcakes, 853
Currants
about, 423–424
pilaf with pine nuts and,
511
spinach with nuts and, 360
Curry(ied)
barbecue sauce, 789
beans, baked, 619
black beans, baked, 620
broth, whole wheat pasta
in, 147
butternut squash with
coconut milk and,
365
cheese, fresh (paneer
masala), 217–218
coconut milk, braised tofu
and peas in, 648
coconut soup with lemon-
grass, 137–138
coconut vinaigrette, 763
corn salad, 61
couscous, pearl, pilaf, 552
deviled eggs, 180
egg drop soup, 155
egg hash with coconut milk
and, 178
eggplant with coconut
milk, 296
lentils and potatoes with,
600–601
lentils and potatoes with,
buttery, 602
nuts, wild rice with, 567
oatcakes, 570
peanut sauce, 795
potatoes, stir fried,
348–349
red curry stew, hard-cooked
eggs in, 195
rice, baked with, simpler,
515–516
rice with chickpeas, 510
sauce, 804
with seitan, oven-roasted,
672
tahini sauce, 796

tomato sauce, quick, hard-
cooked eggs in,
194–195
Curry paste
green, 823, 831
red, 823, 830–831
red, smashed edamame and
potatoes with, 617
using, 823
Curry powder
fragrant, 816, 823
hot, 815, 823
smashed edamame and
potatoes with, 617
Custard(s), dessert
basics of, 881
blackberry or blueberry, 887
cappuccino, baked,
886–887
cappuccino flan, 887
chai spiced, 887
cinnamon, 887
doneness, 884, 884
gingersnap, 887
hazelnut, 887
orange blossom, 887
sauce
almond, 863
chocolate, 863
vanilla, 863
Custard(s), savory
baked, 190–191
baked cheesy, 191
basics of, 189–190
bread pudding. See Bread
pudding, savory
green pea and Parmesan,
191
in hot water bath, 190
mushroom, 191
poblano, 191
spinach, 191
vegetables for, 192
vegetable-wrapped, 192
Custard cups, 12
Cutlets, vegetarian, 661, 661
Cutting boards, 13, 30
Cutting techniques, 18–22
artichokes, 257–258
asparagus, 260, 261
cabbage, 276

carrots, 278
chiffonade, 21, 22
chopping, 20, 20
and cooking method, 240
dicing, 21, 23
fennel, 302
julienne, 20–21, 22
leeks, 310, 311
with mandoline, 15, 21
onions, 328
with paring knife, 22, 23
pineapple, 434, 435
raw vegetables, 52
roll (oblique) cut, 21
slicing, 20, 21

Daikon
about, 354
and dulse salad, spicy, 55
purée, 389
Dal
about, 601
mixed whole-bean, with
cabbage and wal-
nuts, 603
mixed whole-bean, with
walnuts, 602–603
mung bean, with apples,
coconut, and mint,
602
mung bean, with carrots,
cashews, and Thai
basil, 602
simplest, 600
urad, with poppy seeds and
cilantro, 603–604
Dandelion greens, 35,
293–294
Dark chocolate, 837
Dark chocolate-buttermilk
pie, 873
Dark simmering liquid for
seitan, 671
Dashi
dipping sauce, 780
kombu, 103
kombu, with edamame,
quick-cooked,
583–584
no-cook, 103
tofu, -boiled, 641

Date(s)
about, 424
-banana cobbler, 878
cake, 854
carrots with raisins and,
279–280
cookies, -olive oil, 843
to macerate and season, 416
-tamarind chutney, 785
Date sugar, 835
Deeper barley and mushroom
stew, 541
Deep-fried cheese, 214
Deep-fried fruit, 411
Deep-fried tofu, 643–644
agedashi, 644
slightly more refined, 644
Deep-fried vegetables
about, 238
battered and fried, three
ways, 245,
248–249
breaded, 246
dipping sauces for, 249
French fries, 352
green beans, twice-fried,
306
okra, 324
potato chips, 352
squash blossoms, beer-
battered, 249
tempura, eggless, 249
Deep-frying technique,
26–27, 238
Deglazing technique, 28
Dehydrator, 416
Desserts, 833–907. *See also*
Bars; Candy; Cook-
ies; Cake(s); Cus-
tard(s), dessert;
Pie(s)
dessert; Pudding(s); Tart(s),
dessert
bulgur, sweet, with spices,
898
cobbler(s)
apple, 877
apple-rhubarb, 878
banana-date, 878
basics of, 871
peach-brandy, 877

couscous, sweet
almond milk, 897
with citrus salad, 897
with dried fruit, 897
with pistachios, 897
crisp(s)
basics of, 871
cherry, 878
cranberry-orange, 878
fruit-and-toppings for,
878
gelée(s)
basics of, 881
champagne, with berries,
888
coffee, 888
honey, 888
lemon-lime, 887–888
pomegranate, 888
raspberry or any berry,
888
grain dishes, sweet,
895–897
granita
basics of, 889, 891
flavors for, 894–895
tangerine or orange, 894
ice cream
basics of, 888–889
buttermilk, 891
flavors for, 891–892
ice milk
basics of, 889
flavors for, 892–893
mango or apricot, 894
macaroons, coconut-dried
pineapple, 902
macaroons, oats, toasted,
and chocolate chip,
902
meringue(s)
mocha, 903
pistachio, 902
sesame, sweet, 903
mousse(s)
basics of, 897–900
blueberry (or any berry),
901
chocolate-orange, vegan,
900–901
honey, frozen, 900

mango, 901
peach or apricot, 901
phyllo pastries
basics of, 878–879, *879*
"cigars," nut and dried
fruit, 880
"cigars," walnut, 880
strudel. *See* Strudel
sauces. *See* Dessert sauce(s)
sorbet
basics of, 889
flavors for, 892–893
mango or apricot,
893–894
soups. *See* Dessert soup(s)
thickeners in, 881–883
Dessert sauce(s)
apple, pear, or pineapple,
basil-, 862
apricot, creamy, 862
berry, vanilla-, 861–862
chocolate ganache,
860–861
citrus-mango, 862
custard, almond, 863
custard, chocolate, 862
custard, vanilla, 862
fruit purées as, 862
plum or cherry, anise-, 863
Dessert soup(s)
almond, sweet, 905
basics of, 903
coconut, sweet, 905
coconut, sweet, with grains
or tapioca, 905
coconut, sweet, with
granita, 905
cranberry-orange, 904–905
fruit and gelée in ginger
broth, 904
persimmon, 904
quince-ginger, 905
rhubarb-orange, 904
sparkling wine with berries,
904
vanilla-apricot, 904
watermelon and mint,
903–904
Deviled eggs. *See* Egg(s),
deviled (stuffed)
Dicing vegetables, 21, *23, 278*

Dijon mustard, about, 775
Dill
about, 765
"pesto," 768
purée, 769
-yogurt dressing, barley
salad with cucum-
ber and, 82
Dill seeds, 812
Dipping sauce(s)
basil, 777
for battered and fried vegetables, 249
chickpea fondue, 615
cilantro, 777
dashi, 780
for dumplings, 496
lemongrass, 778
lime leaf, 778
mint, 778
miso, simple, 781
citrus, 781
herb, 781
soy, 781
ponzu, 780
arame and bean thread
noodles with,
54–55
citrus, 780
lemongrass, 780
soba noodles with,
467–468
soy and sesame marinade
and, Korean style,
778
tahini soy sauce, 778
Thai style, 778
Vietnamese style, 778
Dips and spreads. *See also* Pâté
asparagus, 264
avocado and dried tomato,
264
avocado and goat cheese,
264
bean
cheesy, 614
creamy, 614
fast, 614
refried, 613
variations, 614
blue cheese, 212

cheese dip flavorings, 212, 213
cheeses for, 210–211, 212
for crudités, 89
guacamole
    corn, crunchy, 263–264
    minimalist, 264
    with tomatillos, 264
"guacasalsa," 264
hummus, 614–615
hummus, edamame, 615
hummus, lima, 615
pea, 264
sandwich, 730–735
tapenade, 326–327
tapenade, green olive, 327
tapenade, tomato, dried-, 327
for toasts, 737
tofu, 212
Dosas
    brown rice, 745
    to form, *744*
    rice and lentil, 744–745
Double chocolate bars, 847
Dough, fried
    cheese puffs, 697
    churros, 697
    cream puffs, 697
    doughnut puffs, sweet or savory, 696–697
    doughnuts, savory, 697
    fruit fritters, 697
Doughnut(s)
    puffs, sweet or savory, 696–697
    savory, 697
Dressing(s). *See also* Mayonnaise; Vegannaise; Vinaigrette
    amount of, 37
    bistro, creamy, 799
    bistro, creamy, mustard, 799
    bistro, creamy, tarragon, 799
    blue cheese, 774
    blue cheese, potato salad with, 71
    Caesar, vegetarian, 773
    Cheddar, potato salad with, 70

citrus *vs* vinegar, 759
cream cheese, potato salad with, 70
onion-thyme, caramelized, green salad with, 43–44
ranch, real, 772
for raw vegetable salads, 52
to thin, 36
warm, spinach salad with tofu croutons and, 40–41
yogurt-dill, barley salad with cucumber and, 82
yogurt, raw beet salad with, 50
Dried fruit. *See* Fruit, dried
Dried-tomato tapenade, 327
Drop ("emergency") biscuits, 695
Dry-baked croutons, 806
Dry ingredients, to measure, *23*
Dry-pan eggplant, 294–295
Dulse
    about, 356
    "shake," 818
    spicy
        and bean sprout salad, 55
        and carrot salad, 55
        and celery salad, 55
        and daikon salad, 55
Dumplings. *See also* Gnocchi; Spaetzle
    boiled, 497
    cheese, 224–225
        fluffy, 225
        goat cheese, 225
        ricotta, 225
        ricotta, panfried, 225
        ricotta, pesto, 226
        ricotta, with quinoa or millet, 225–226
        -stuffed, 498
    multigrain and herb, 489
    passatelli in broth, 489
    porcini, 488–489
    potato, 350
    potato gnocchi, 486–487

potato-stuffed, fried, 497–498
pot stickers, about, 494
steamed
    Asian style, 492–493
    bean, 493
    with bean threads, vegan, 493–494
    gyoza with sea greens and edamame, 493
to stuff and seal, *494*
wonton(s), to seal, 495
wonton(s), soup, 495
wonton(s), tofu-stuffed, 494–495
wrappers, 491
    with egg, 395–496
    with egg, whole wheat, 496
    egg roll (wonton skins), 491
    to make, *492*
    store-bought, 493
    whole wheat, 491
    wrapper/stuffing/sauce combos, 496
Durum wheat flour, whole, 478
Dutch oven, 11

Edamame
    about, 578, 585
    black Thai rice with coconut milk and, 532
    with Dijon and wax beans, 583
    with fishless fish sauce, quick-braised, 584
    with green tea, quick-braised, 584
    gyoza, steamed, with sea greens and, 493
    hot and sour, with tofu, 591
    hummus, 615
    with kombu dashi or soy sauce, quick-cooked, 583–584
    ma po, with tofu, 591

with ponzu, quick-braised, 584
and potatoes, smashed
    with curry powder, 617
    with miso, 617
    with red curry paste, 617
    with sesame and soy, 617
rice, Japanese, with sea greens and, 532
rice, sushi style, with shiso and, 532
salad with seaweed "mayo," 70
with sea greens, quick-braised, 584
sweet and sour, with vegetables, 591
with tomatoes and chiles, roasted, 583
with tomatoes and cilantro, 583
with tomatoes and olives, 583
Egg(s), 161–195. *See also* French toast; Meringue(s); Omelet(s); Quiche; Soufflé(s)
    about, 161–165
    baked ("shirred"), 169
    breakfast dishes, 173, 174–179
    burritos, breakfast, 174–175
    cooking techniques, 162, 165
    crêpes
        Japanese, 175–176
        Japanese, with nori, 176
    custard. *See* Custard(s), dessert; Custard(s), savory
    deviled (stuffed), 180
        curried, 180
        feta and olive-, 181
        jalapeño, 180
        miso-, 180–181
        sea greens-, 181
        spring vegetable-, 181
    dumpling wrappers with, 495–496

Egg(s) *(Continued)*
  dumpling wrappers with,
      whole wheat, 496
  fresh cheese scramble with,
      219
  fried
    additions to, 168
    with cheese, 168
    heirloom tomato salad
      with, 59
    pasta with, 447
    sunny-side up or over
      easy, 168
  au gratin, 194
    with fennel, 194
    with onions,
      caramelized, and
      olives, 194
    with spinach, 194
  hard-cooked, 162. *See also*
    Egg(s), deviled
    (stuffed)
    and cheese enchiladas,
      224
    fava beans, fresh, with
      croutons and,
      591–592
    fava beans, fresh, with
      croutons and,
      herbed, 592
    heirloom tomato salad
      with, 59
    in red curry stew, 195
    sauces for, 195
    in tomato curry sauce,
      quick, 194–195
  hash, 178
    with celery and pickles,
      178
    chipotle, 178
    with curry and coconut
      milk, 178
    with rice, 178–179
  huevos rancheros, 174
  huevos rancheros, with red
    mole, 174
  huevos rancheros, simplest,
    174
  Japanese rolls, 176
  Lyonnaise Salad, 38
  main-course dishes, 182

matzo brei, 177
medium-boiled, 165–166
in the nest, 168
"noodles," 176
"noodle" soup with bean
    thread, 154
"noodle" soup with mush-
    rooms, 153–154
"noodle" soup with rice
    cake, 154
paella with, simple, 523
pasta, fresh, 477–478
to peel, 166
pickled, 181
  with beets and horserad-
    ish, 182
  with jalapeños and car-
    rots, 182
  with oranges and warm
    spices, 182
  soy sauce-, 182
poached, 169–170
  heirloom tomato salad
    with, 59
  liquids for poaching, 170
  oven-, 169
  safety of, 163
  sauces for, 170
  soup, 155
  things to serve under,
    170
  in tomato curry sauce,
    195
and potatoes, crisp pan-
    fried, 344
rice, fried, 520–521
safety, 163
salad, 179–180
  pâté, 180
  with roasted red peppers
    or sun-dried toma-
    toes, 180
  tofu "egg" salad, 180
  Waldorf, 180
scrambled
  additions to, 167
  the best, 167
  with cheese, 167
  and cheese enchiladas,
    224
  everyday, 166–167

and tomatoes, grilled,
    Chinese style, 374
to separate, *898*
soft-boiled, 165
soups with, 153, *See also*
    Egg drop soup
  with sun-dried tomatoes
    and garlic, 182
wash, 717
whites, to beat, *898*, 899
whites, to fold, *900*, 901
Egg drop soup, eight ways,
    154–156
  curry, 155
  Italian style, 155
  Mexican style, 155
  poached egg, 155
  with sea greens, 155
  spinach, 155
Eggless pasta dough, 478–479
Eggless tempura, 249
Egg noodles, fresh, 496
  herbed, 496
  with scallions and paprika,
    497
Eggplant
  about, 294
  broiled, 295
  broiled, with peppers,
    onions, and yogurt,
    298–299
  and cheese, creamy noodles
    with, baked,
    462–463
  and cheese, creamy pota-
    toes with, 463
  and chickpea purée, 613
  with chickpeas, sweet and
    sour, hot, 609–610
  with chickpeas, sweet and
    sour, more,
    609–610
  couscous, pearl, pilaf,
    551–552
  curried, with coconut milk,
    296
  dry pan, 294–295
  fritters, and sesame, 395
  gnocchi, 487
  gratin, Greek style, 386
  grilled, 252, 295

layered, with vegetables,
    299
mashed, with honey and
    lemon, 298
mashed, with yogurt and
    mint, spicy, 298
mixed vegetables with olive
    oil, baked, 381
paella with, simple, 523
pan-fried, 244–245
Parmesan, 299
pickled vegetables, quick-,
    95
purée, 389
in ratatouille salad, 64
salad
  grilled, with garlic and
    saffron mayonnaise,
    65
  grilled, with yogurt, 65
  with miso, 63–64
  with miso and tofu, 64
  with soy vinaigrette, 64
  and zucchini, with cin-
    namon, 64
sautéed, 295–296
  with greens, 296
  with onions and honey,
    296
  with tomatoes, 296
sesame-fried, 245
slices with garlic and pars-
    ley, 297–298
steamed, 297
stuffed, *397*, 397–398,
    404
tofu, braised, with shiitakes
    and, 650
-tofu stir-fry, 300
and tomatoes, sliced,
    creamy noodles
    with, 463
Egg rolls, 741–742
  panfried, 742
  smoked tofu and turnip,
    742
  vegetables for, 742–743
Egg roll wrappers (wonton
    skins), 491, 742
Egg substitute, 29
Elegant lentil soup, 116

Elegant wintertime tomato
soup, 114
Empanadas
bean and cheese, 747
corn and cheese, 747
pepper, roasted, and cheese,
747
vegan vegetable, 747
Empire apple, 418
Emulsification process, 762
Enchiladas
cheese
with green enchilada
sauce, 224
hard-cooked egg and,
224
with red mole, 223–224
scrambled egg and, 224
simple, 224
garnishes for, 223
squash, 224
sweet potato, 224
tofu, with red mole, 224
Enchilada sauce
green, 788–789
green, cheese enchiladas
with, 224
red, 788
Enchilada style
black beans and corn,
baked, 622
pinto beans, baked,
621–622
pinto beans and sweet
potatoes, baked,
622
Endive
about, 34–35, 300
braised, 300–301
braised, with orange juice,
301
caramelized, kasha pilaf
with, 563
to grill, 253
and Roquefort salad,
44–45
salad, 38
English muffins, 714
Enoki mushrooms, about,
313
Epazote, 767

Equipment and tools, 7–16
bread making, 701–702
cookware, 9–11
electric appliances/gadgets,
15–16
knives, 8–9
ovenware, 11–12
utensils, 13–15
Escabeche, tofu, 653–654
Escarole
about, 34–35, 300
braised, 300–301
grits gratin with garlic,
lemon and, 551
kasha with, 563
Espresso
black bean chili, 608
sorbet or ice milk, 892
Essential bean salad, 72–73
Essential vegetable purée, 390
Ethiopian style
lentils, braised, 598
tomato salad, 58
European style
batter, 245, 248
yeast breads, 707–711
Everyday buttermilk waffles,
203–204
Everyday pancakes, 200
Everyday scrambled eggs, 166

Falafel, 625–626
crumbles, 805
nutty, 626
sesame, 626
with za'atar, 626
Farmer's cheese, 210
Farro
about, 536, 539
soup, 141
soup, -mushroom, 141
Fast bean dip, 614
Fast-braised tofu with tempeh, 651
Fast, down-home barbecue
sauce, 789
Faster roasted garlic, 304
Faster tofu and peas in
coconut milk, 649
Fast French bread or rolls,
707–708

Fast nut burgers, 667–668
Fast tomato sauce, 445–446
Fats, types of, 754
Faux pho, 143–144
Fava bean(s), dried
about, 577
with chanterelles, 597
mashed, 616–617
with scallions, 594
stewed
with potatoes and spiced
onions, 604
with tahini, 604
tomatoey, 604
with za'atar, 604
Fava bean(s), fresh
about, 577
baked, with ricotta and
Parmesan, 621
with chanterelles, 597
with eggs and croutons,
591–592
with eggs and croutons,
herbed, 592
with feta and croutons,
591–592
and mint salad with asparagus, 77
paella with, 523
with tofu and croutons,
592
Fennel
about, 302
breading and frying, 246
bulgur with, creamed, 556
cake with grapefruit glaze,
852
chutney, caramelized, 787
couscous with raisins and,
92–93
eggs au gratin with, 194
flageolets with, 605
gratin, 384
to grill, 253
-lemon sorbet, 893
lima bean purée with
orange juice and,
613
marinated, with preserved
lemons, 68
to prepare, 302, 302

roast, with orange, 303
soup, creamy, 129
Fennel seeds, 812
Fenugreek, 820
Fermented black beans. See
Black bean(s), fer-
mented
Fermented tofu, 639
Feta
about, 210
cauliflower, sautéed, with
mint and, 282
corn salad with tomatoes,
mint and, 61
kale, rolled, with olives
and, 308–309
and olive-stuffed eggs, 181
pea salad with tomatoes,
mint and, 61
spice-marinated, 211
spice-marinated patties,
quick, 211
and spinach pie with phyllo
crust, 408–409
spinach salad with nutmeg
and, 41–42
and tomato salad, broiled,
with tapenade,
58–59
Fettuccine Alfredo, 447
Fideo
with olives, 450–451
soup, garlic, 144
with tomatoes and chile,
451
Fiery caramelized nuts, 323
Figs
about, 424–425
bread salad with, hearty
fresh, 90
to grill, 413
to macerate and season,
416
tart, fresh, 875
Fishless fish sauce, 778
quick-braised edamame
with, 584
Five spice-pickled eggs with
soy, 182
Five-spice powder, 816–817,
823

Flageolets
    about, 578
    with fennel, 605
    French style, 604–605
    with lettuce, 605
    with morels, 597
    with tomatoes, 605
Flaky Indian style flatbread,
        699–700
Flaky Indian style flatbread
        stuffed with potato,
        700–701
Flan, cappuccino, 887
Flapjacks, chickpea, 633–634
Flatbread(s)
    basics of, 697–698
    crackers, 698
    crackers, cream, 698
    crackers, Parmesan, 698
    flaky Indian style (paratha),
        699–700
    flaky Indian style (paratha),
        spinach, 700
    flaky Indian style (paratha),
        stuffed with potato,
        700–701
    with pizza dough, 727
    simplest Indian style (chap-
        ati), 698–699
    simplest Indian style (chap-
        ati), grilled, 699
Flat omelet. See Omelet, flat
Flavored oil, 758
    about, 756, 758
Flax seeds, 319
Fleur de sel, 808
Flexitarians, ix, x
Flour. See also Chickpea flour
    for bread making, 702
    for cakes, 848
    for cookies, 838–839
    corn, 543, 681–682
    lexicon of, 680–683
    low protein, 708
    to measure, 23
    nonwheat, 478, 680
    substitutions in bread bak-
        ing, 684
    as thickener, 883
Flourless chocolate nut torte,
        850–851

Flour tortillas, 738
Fluffy cheese dumplings, 225
Fluffy cracked wheat with
        mustard and tar-
        ragon, 559
Focaccia, 728–729
Folded omelet, 173
    with grated vegetables, 174
Fondue
    cheese
        about, 221–222
        blue, 222
        Cheddar, sharp, with red
            wine, 222
        fontina and porcini, 222
        mustard-, 222
        smoked, with beer, 222
        tomato and chile, 222
        variations, 222–223
    chickpea, 615
    chickpea, cheesy, 616
    chickpea, hummus, 616
Fontina and porcini fondue,
        222
Food mill, 15, 446
Food processor, 15–16,
        701–702
Food safety, 30
    eggs, 163
Foolproof teff, polenta style,
        544
Forbidden rice, 505
French bread or rolls
    fast, 707–708
    more leisurely, 708
    overnight, 709
    whole grain, 708–709
French fries, 352
French green lentils, 599
French style
    bean salad, essential, 72
    flageolets, 604–605
    green sauce, 771
    lentil soup with sorrel or
        spinach, 116
    rice salad, 81
French toast, 177
    caramelized, 177
    crispy, 177
    nut-crusted, 177
    toppings for, 177–178

Fresh bread crumbs, 804
Fresh cheese. See Cheese, fresh
Fresh egg noodles, 496
Fresh egg noodles with scal-
        lions and paprika,
        497
Fresh egg pasta, 477–478
Fresh favas with eggs and
        croutons, 591–592
Fresh favas with feta and
        croutons, 591–592
Fresh favas with tofu and
        croutons, 591–592
Fresh fig tart, 875
Fresh pineapple upside-down
        cake, 854
Fresh spring vegetable burger,
        664
Fresh tomatillo salsa, 751
Fresh tomato salsa, 750
Fresno chile, 826
Fried bread crumbs, 805
Fried eggs, sunny side up or
        over easy, 168
Fried eggs with cheese, 168
Fried fresh cheese, 215
Fried fresh cheese with
        spiced yogurt,
        215–216
Fried lentil samosas, 746
Fried mung beans with chile
        paste, 590
Fried mung beans with mung
        been sprouts, 590
Fried mung beans with
        sesame, 589
Fried mung and fermented
        black beans, 590
Fried onion rings, stream-
        lined, 245
Fried potato-stuffed
        dumplings,
        497–498
Fried rice with or without
        egg, 520
Fried tofu, 639
Fries
    chickpea, 634, 634
    chickpea, peanut and,
        634–635
    French, 352

oven-roasted cottage "fries,"
        345
oven-roasted cottage "fries,"
        crisp, with garlic,
        345
oven-roasted "fries," 345
    vegetable, 352
Frisée, about, 34–35
Frittata
    basic, 184
    bread, 184
    with grains, 184
    pasta, 184
    potato tortilla, 184
    risotto "frittata," 571–572
Fritters. See also Falafel
    arepas, 292
    basics of, 391–392
    black-eyed pea, 626
    cassava, 394
    coconut, 394
    corn, 292
    eggplant and sesame, 395
    fruit, 697
    mung bean, Asian style,
        626
    mushroom, 394
Frosting. See also Buttercream
        frosting, not-too-
        sweet
    chocolate, 861
Frozen honey mousse, 900
Frozen vegetables, 125, 234,
        235
Fructose, 835
Fruit(s). See also Berry(ies);
        Citrus; Fruit, dried;
        specific fruits
    basics of cooking, 409–412
    blintzes, 198
    buying and handling,
        234–235
    for chutney, 785
    deep-fried, 411
    fritters, 697
    frozen, 234
    and gelée in ginger broth,
        904
    greens with cheese, nuts
        and, 40
    grilled, 411, 412, 413–414

heirloom, 372
lexicon of, 417–437
to macerate and season,
    416, 417
meringue pie, 874
and nut bread, 691–692
    combinations, 692
    dried, 692
    saffron, 715
    whole grain, 692
to oven-dry, 411
panfried, 411
pickling method, 94–95
poached. *See* Poached fruit
puréed, 862
roasted, 411
for salsa, 752
salsas, 751–752
sautéed, 411
storing and preparing, 235
stuffed. *See* Stuffed fruit
wheat berry or other whole
    grain salad with
    peanuts and,
    85–87
Fruit, dried. *See also specific*
    fruit
bars, 847
and coconut crust, no-bake,
    869
couscous with, sweet, 897
drying methods, 412, 415
in granola, crunchy, 573
and lima stew, 594–595
and nut bread, 692
and nut bread, saffron, 715
and nut chutney, 784
and nut crust, no-bake,
    869
and nut pie with phyllo
    crust, 408
with omelet, baked sweet,
    179
to oven-dry, 411, 415–417
phyllo "cigars," nut and,
    880
pilaf with nuts and,
    511–512
to poach, 410
in vegetable burger, hearty
    winter, 663

wheat berry or other whole
    grain salad with
    peanuts and, 85–87
wheat berry stew with cit-
    rus, nuts and, 565
wild rice with, 568
Fuji apple, 418
Funnel, 14

Gai lan, 269
Gala apple, 418
Galette
    free-form crust, *868*
    winter squash, spicy,
        368–369
Ganache, chocolate, 860–861
    dark, poached pear tart
        with, 874–875
    uses for, 861
Garam masala, 815, 823
Garfava flour, 683
Garlic
    about, 303–304
    beans, puréed, garlicky, 613
    braised in olive oil, 305
    with Brussels sprouts,
        roasted, 273
    with carrots, balsamic-
        glazed, 279
    cauliflower, sautéed, with
        vinegar, capers and,
        281
    -chile paste, 830
    -chile salsa, super-spicy, 789
    in chimichurri sauce, 769
    chutney, real garlicky, 785
    with cottage "fries," crisp
        oven-roasted, 345
    crêpes, 197
    crisp, 310
    eggplant slices with parsley
        and, 297–298
    fideo soup, 144
    fresh, 810
    grits gratin
        with arugula and,
            550–551
        with escarole, lemon
            and, 551
        smothered, with arugula
            and, 551

with white beans,
        arugula and, 551
honey-, vinaigrette, 763
mashed potato(es)
    garlicky, 342
    hotcakes, garlicky, 351
    pie, garlicky, 351
    pie, garlicky, with cheese,
        351
mayonnaise (aïoli), 771
in oil, flavored, 758
pasta with oil and,
    443–444
to peel, *304*
and potatoes, braised, 347
roasted, 304
    with artichoke hearts,
        braised, 260
    bean purée with, 613
    custard, baked, 191
    faster, 304
    mustard, 777
    potato croquettes, with
        Parmesan and, 353
    tahini sauce, 796
    teriyaki sauce, 779
and saffron mayonnaise,
    grilled eggplant
    salad with, 65
-scallion sauce, 779
with seitan, oven-roasted,
    672
with sunchokes, broiled,
    370
tomato sauce, garlicky, 448
in veggie burgers, 662
Garlic press, 15
Gazpacho, 157
    spicy, 157–158
Gelée(s)
    basics of, 881
    champagne, with berries,
        888
    coffee, 888
    and fruit in ginger broth,
        904
    honey, 888
    lemon-lime, 887–888
    pomegranate, 888
    raspberry or any berry, 888
German sweet chocolate, 837

Gigantes
    about, 578
    with Brussels sprouts,
        587–588
    with cherry tomatoes, 588
    and greens, 596
    with preserved lemon, 588
    with shiitakes, 588
Ginger(ed)
    about, 812
    avocado salad with peanuts
        and, 51
    basics of, 819, 821
    beet salad, raw, with carrot
        and, 50
    broth, fruit and gelée in,
        904
    carrots, quick-glazed, with
        orange and, 279
    carrot soup, glazed, with
        orange and, 105
    celery, -marinated, 47
    chocolate layer cake, 855
    cilantro "pesto" with chile
        and, 770
    cucumber salad with soy
        and, 48
    millet carrot mash with
        sesame, soy and,
        566
    miso carrot sauce with,
        781–782
    -molasses granola, 574
    nuts, 323
    pickled, 821–822
    pickled, citrus-, 822
    pound cake, 849
    pumpkin bread with hazel-
        nuts, 692
    -quince soup, 905
    -scallion sauce, 779
    with seitan, oven-roasted,
        672
    spice cookies, 841
    stuck-pot rice with
        almonds, sesame
        seeds and, 526
    -sweet potato pie, 873
    vinaigrette, 763
    yogurt sauce, 774
Gingerbread pancakes, 202

Gingersnap
  crumb crust, baked, 869
  custard, 887
Glaze(s)
    apricot jam, 858
  balsamic, grilled or broiled
      radicchio with, 301
  berry jam, 858
  chocolate, 861
  coconut, 858
  grapefruit, fennel cake
      with, 852
  lemon, 858
  lemon-clove, 858
  lime, 858
  marmalade, cassis-orange,
      858
    miso, sweet, 782
  miso, sweet and hot, 782
  mocha, 858
  orange, 857
  orange, beet cake with,
      852
  orange, creamy, 857
  port-cherry jam, 858
  rose water, 858
Glazed and braised technique.
      See Braised and
      glazed vegetables
Glazed carrot soup, 105
  with garlic, tequila, and
      lime, 105
  with orange and ginger,
      105
Gluten
  in bread dough, 708
  in seitan dough, 669
  in whole grain bread, 713
Gluten-free baking mixes, 683
Gluten-free flour, 478, 680
Glutinous rice flour, 682
Gnocchi
  chickpea-ricotta, 626–627
  to make, 486, 487, 488
  parsnip, 487–488
  potato, 486–487
  potato, eggplant, 487
  potato, spinach, 487
  to roast and bake, 489
  sweet potato, 488

Goat cheese
  about, 211
  and avocado dip or spread,
      264
  baked, 217
    with nuts, 217
    phyllo-wrapped, 227
    with quinoa, 217
    with tomato sauce or
        tomatoes, 217
  and beets, roasted, gratin,
      383
  chiles rellenos with walnuts
      and, 400
  couscous, pearl, gratin with
      pesto and ,
      554–555
  dumplings, 225
  macaroni and, with roasted
      red peppers, 461
  and mushroom tart with
      potato crust,
      227–228
  red peppers stuffed with
      quinoa and, 399
  soufflé, and dried apricot,
      186
  strawberries, balsamic, with
      arugula and, 42
  ziti, baked, with olives and,
      459
Goat ice milk, 892
Gobo. See Burdock
Golden delicious apple, 418
Golden simmering liquid for
      seitan, 671
"Goulash" soup
  and bok choy, 150–151
  more traditional, 151
  tempeh, 151
Grains, 499–575. See also
      Grain salad(s);
      specific grains
  additions to, 538, 540
  basics of, 500–501
  breakfast cereals, 572–574
  butternut squash, -fried,
      245
  coconut soup with, sweet,
      905

cooked with butter and oil,
    538
cooking, the easy way,
    537–538
cooking methods, 533, 537
crumbles, 805
frittata with, 184
as garnish, 564
griddlecakes, 569–572
lexicon of, 534–537, 539
precooked
    with nuts or seeds, 539
    with onions, 538
    with onions and mush-
        rooms, 538–539
    with toasted spice, 539
    with vinaigrette, pesto,
        or other sauce, 539
  in soups, 136
  stuffings, 407
  sweet dishes, 895–897
Grain salad(s), 78–93
  barley cucumber, with
      walnuts, 83
  barley, with cucumber and
      yogurt-dill dressing,
      82
  barley pea, 82
  bread
      corn bread, 88
      crouton, 87–88
      with fresh figs, hearty,
          90
      with greens, 88
      grilled, 88
      Lebanese style, 88–89
  bulgur and tomato, 83
  bulgur, tomato, and chick-
      pea, 83
  cooking techniques, 78–79
  cracked wheat and tomato,
      83
  quinoa
      with lemon, spinach,
          and poppy seeds,
          83–84
      and sweet potato, 84–85
      and sweet potato, south-
          western, 85
      with tempeh, 84

rice, 79
  citrus, 82
  Indian style, 8
  Japanese style, 79
  Mexican style, 79, 82
  tomato, 82
  and tomato, 83
  variations, 80–81
  wild rice, with cucumber
      and yogurt, 83
tabbouleh, 43
wheat berry or other whole
    grain
    with cabbage and course
        mustard, 85
    with peanuts and fresh
        and dried fruit,
        85–87
    with roasted peppers, 87
    with roasted peppers and
        zucchini, 87
  whole grain, 89–90
  whole grain, with preserved
      lemons, 92
Grainy mustard, many ways,
    776
Granita
  basics of, 889, 891
  coconut soup with, sweet,
      905
  flavors for, 894–895
  tangerine or orange, 894
Granny Smith apple, 418
Granola
  additions and combos,
      574
  almond-orange, 574
  bars
      cherry, dried, -chocolate,
          847
      no-bake, 846–847
      nutty, 847
      orange-spice, 847
      peanut (or any nut) but-
          ter, 847
  crunchy, 573
  ginger-molasses, 574
  peanut butter, 573–574
  spiced, 574
  tart, 876

tropical, 574
vanilla, real, 574
Grape(s)
 about, 425
 leaves, stuffed, fillings for,
  309
 tart with port, 874
Grapefruit
 about, 425
 glaze, fennel cake with, 852
 rice noodle salad with
  peanuts and, Jean-
  Georges's, 93–94
 sorbet, 892
Grapeseed oil, 29, 756, 770
Gratin(s)
 couscous, pearl
  with onions,
   caramelized, and
   blue cheese, 555
  with pesto and goat
   cheese, 554–555
  with tomatoes, roasted,
   555
 grits
  with arugula, white
   beans, and garlic,
   551
  with arugula and garlic,
   550–551
  with escarole, garlic, and
   lemon, 551
  smothered, with arugula
   and garlic, 551
 mushroom and pumper-
  nickel, 386
 mushroom and Roquefort,
  383
 peach or apple, with
  coriander, savory,
  384
 polenta, 544
 potato(es), 383
  and cauliflower with
   crème fraîche or
   sour cream, 384
  and chestnut, 384
  and manchego, 383
  mashed, 385
  and sunchoke, 383

rye berry, with leeks and
 tomatoes, 568
rye berry, with leeks and
 tomatoes, creamy,
 568
rye berry, with leeks and
 tomatoes, vegan,
 568–569
vegetable. See also
 Gratin(s),
 potato(es)
 asparagus and béchamel,
  383
 asparagus, simplest, 383
 basics of, 382–383
 beets, roasted, and goat
  cheese, 383
 broccoli or cauliflower
  and pesto, 383
 butternut squash and
  pecorino Romano,
  385
 cabbage, 384
 celery and leek, 385
 chile, Mexican style,
  385–387
 corn, hot and smoky,
  387
 eggplant, Greek style,
  386
 fennel, 384
 green bean, creamy, 386
 onion, simplest, 383
 onion, smoky, 385
 parsnip with vanilla,
  creamy, 386
 spinach, rich, 385
 summer squash and
  salsa, 387
 sweet potato and cream
  cheese, 384
 tomato, 386
 vegan curry, 386
white bean
 and celery root, 623
 and celery root, Tuscan
  style, 623
 and tomato, 623–624
 and vegetable with bul-
  gur crust, 624

Gratin dish, 12, 382
Gratinéed cream of parsley
 soup, 132
Great northern beans, 577
Greek salad, 38
Greek style
 bean salad, essential, 72
 eggplant gratin, 386
 greens, cooked, 66–67
 omelet, flat, 184
 orzo salad, 93
 tomato sauce, 449
Green beans
 about, 305
 bulgur pilaf with soy sauce
  and, 557
 gratin, 386
 to grill, 253
 mushroom stew with, 137
 in three-bean salad, 74–75
 and tofu skins, stir-fried,
  306–307
 and tofu skins, stir-fried,
  with peanuts and
  cilantro, 307
 twice-fried, 306
 walnut-miso sauce, tossed
  with, 305–306
Green chile salsa, 789
 Green curry paste, 823,
  831
Green enchilada sauce,
 788–789
Green lentils, 599
Green olive mojo, 769
Green olive tapenade, 327
Green onion(s). See
 Scallion(s)
Green papaya salsa, 753
Green peppercorns, 809
Greens. See also Green
 salad(s); Sea
 green(s); specific
 greens
 Asian, 268–269
 and beans, 595
 and beans, suggestions for
  combos, 596
 boiled or steamed,
  239–240

bread salad with, 88
with eggplant, sautéed,
 296
Greek style cooked, 66–67
pasta with, 452–453
pilaf with, 512
thick ribs, to prepare, 308
with tofu, stir-fried, 648
in vegetable burger, spicy
 autumn, 665–666
Green salad(s), 37–45. See
 also Sea green
 salad(s)
 arugula, balsamic straw-
  berries with, 42
 arugula, balsamic straw-
  berries with goat
  cheese and, 42
 bitter greens, herbs, and
  flowers, 42–45
 chopped, 38–40
 crunchy additions for, 37
 endive, 38
 endive and Roquefort,
  44–45
 Greek, 38
 greens with fruit, cheese,
  and nuts, 40
 lettuce and chive, Korean
  style, 44
 lettuce, with parsley, 43
 Lyonnaise, 38
 with onion-thyme dressing,
  caramelized, 43–44
 parsley and herb, 42–43
 perilla leaves, seasoned, 44
 to prepare greens for, 36,
  36–37
 to salt, 46
 simple, 38
 spinach, with feta and
  nutmeg, 41–42
 spinach, with feta and
  nutmeg, cooked, 42
 spinach, with warm
  dressing and tofu
  croutons, 40–41
 types of greens, 34–36
 variations, 38
 wedge, 37

Green sauce, French style, 771
Green tea
  broth with udon noodles, 145–146
  with edamame, quick-braised, 584
  pudding, 885
Green tomato
  chutney, 786
  chutney, -apple, 786
  ketchup, 790
  pico de verde, 751
  upside-down cake, sweet, 854
Griddlecakes
  amaranth, crunchy, 570–571
  bean, 630–631
  bean sprout, 630
  cornmeal (or other porridge), made from, 570
  oatcakes, curried, 570
  oatcakes, savory, with peas and carrots, 570
  rice cakes, Parmesan, 569–570
  risotto "frittata," 571–572
Griddled olive oil salt bread, 690
Grilled, seitan, 672
Grilled apricot and onion salsa, 792
Grilled bread salad, 88
Grilled chapati, 699
Grilled cheese, 214
  fresh, 216
Grilled chestnuts, 287
Grilled chile-bean quesadillas, 741
Grilled fruit, 411, 412, 413–414
Grilled mushrooms, 316–317
Grilled onion chutney, 787
Grilled peach and corn salsa, 792
Grilled pineapple and onion salsa, 791–792
Grilled pizza, 724

Grilled pizza with tomato sauce and mozzarella, 727
Grilled polenta, 544
Grilled rice balls, 533
Grilled shiitake or portobello salad with soy vinaigrette, 63
Grilled tofu, 642
  barbecue-, teriyaki-, or ponzu, 643
  miso, 643
  rubs and sauces for, 643
  tikka, 216
Grilled tomato chutney, 786
Grilled vegetables
  asparagus, 261
  chiles rellenos, 400
  corn on the cob, 290
  eggplant, 252, 295
  eggplant salad with garlic and saffron mayonnaise, 65
  eggplant salad with yogurt, 65
  leeks, 312–313
  leeks, Asian style, 313
  potatoes, 346
  potatoes, last minute, 346
  radicchio with balsamic glaze, 301
  scallions, 331
  serving suggestions, 249–250
  sweet potato salad with red pepper vinaigrette, 69
  tips, 250, 256
  tomatoes with basil, 373–374
  tomatoes, and scrambled eggs, Chinese style, 374
  tomato sauce, 449
  vegetables for grilling, 239, 251–255
Grilled watermelon steak, 430
Grilling technique, 27–28, 250
Grinder, electric, 16

Grits
  about, 534, 543
  gratin
    with arugula, white beans, and garlic, 551
    with arugula and garlic, 550–551
    with escarole, garlic, and lemon, 551
    smothered, with arugula and garlic, 551
  hominy, 543, 550
Gruyère
  with lentil cakes, baked, 630
  with potatoes Provençal, 348
Guacamole
  corn, crunchy, 263–264
  minimalist, 264
  with tomatillos, 264
"Guacasalsa," 264
Guajillo chile, 827
Gumbo, bean, one-pot, 611
Gyoza, steamed, with sea greens and edamame, 493

Habanero chile, 826, 827
Half-and-half, 207
Half whole wheat sandwich bread, 713
Hard-cooked egg(s). See Egg(s), hard-cooked
Harissa, 830
Hash
  egg, 178
    with celery and pickles, 178
    with chipotle, 178
    with curry and coconut milk, 178
    with rice, 178–179
  tempeh, 676–677
  tempeh, with kimchi, 677
Hash brown(s)
  oven-roasted, 345
  salad, crisp shredded, with red pepper vinaigrette, 70

Hatcho miso, 152
Hazelnut(s)
  about, 320
  Brussels sprouts with, sautéed, 273
  butter, parsnips with, 268
  and butternut squash pancakes, 393
  Cheddar apples with, 402–403
  couscous salad with, 93
  crumble topping, 870–871
  custard, 887
  omelet, 179
  pumpkin ginger bread with, 692
Heartier baked beans, 619
Hearty bread salad with fresh figs, 90
Hearty winter vegetable burger, 663
Heirloom tomato salad with fried eggs, 59
Heirloom tomato salad with hard-cooked eggs, 59
Heirloom tomato salad with poached eggs, 59
Heirloom vegetables, 372
Herb(s), herbed. See also specific herbs
  breadsticks, 711
  and bread stuffing, 395–396
  cheese, -marinated, 212
  cheese shortbread, 696
  cheese soufflé, 186
  with cherry tomatoes, broiled, 374–375
  cottage cheese patties, 226
  croutons, 806
  to cut, 19
  dumplings, multigrain and, 489
  egg noodles, fresh, 496–497
  fava beans, fresh, with eggs and croutons, 591–592
  green sauce, French style, 771

and leek quiche, 188
lettuce salad with mixed
    herbs, 43
lexicon of, 764–766
minestrone, 123
miso dipping sauce, simple,
    781
nuts, roasted, 323
in oil, flavored, 758
and parsley salad, 42–43
pasta, fresh, 479–480
pasta with fresh herbs, 444
pastes, to thin, 769
"pesto," lighter, 769–770
polenta with, 544
popcorn, 292–293
purées, 769
with rice, baked, 515
rice salad, 80
risotto with, 517
risotto with vegetables and,
    517
sauce, 804
spaetzle, 491
stuck-pot rice with lemon
    and, 526
and summer squash in
    parchment, 362
in tabbouleh, 43
tempeh, crunchy crumbled,
    with fresh herbs,
    674
tomato cobbler with herb
    topping, 376
tomato sauce with fresh
    herbs, 448
in veggie burgers, 662
yogurt sauce, 773
High-flavor seaweed romaine,
    57
Highly seasoned croutons, 806
High-protein bean burger, 662
Hijiki (hiziki), 356
Hollandaise sauce, 802–803
    blender, 803
Home fries. See Potato(es),
    panfried, crisp
Homemade ketchup, 790
Homemade mayonnaise, 771
Homemade tofu, *656*,
    656–657

Hominy. *See also* Pozole
    about, 535, 539, 542
    baked with chile, cheese,
        and tomatoes,
        569
    grits, 543
    tamales, naked, with chile
        cheese filling,
        547–549
Honey
    baking with, 835
    buttercream frosting, not-
        too-sweet, 860
    cake, -spice, 854
    eggplant, mashed, with
        lemon and, 298
    eggplant, sautéed, with
        onions and, 296
    -garlic vinaigrette, 763
    gelées, 888
    mousse, frozen, 900
    mustard, 777
    sorbet, 892
    sorbet, cucumber-, 893
Honey substitutes, in vegan
    cooking, 29
Horchata ice milk, 893
Horseradish
    about, 307
    barbecue sauce, 789
    mustard, 777
    potatoes, beer-braised, with
        cheddar and,
        347–348
Hotcakes, garlicky mashed
    potato, 351
Hot curry powder, 815
Hot pepper chutney, 783
Hot pot, tofu skins in,
    149–150
Hot and smoky corn gratin,
    387
Hot and smoky kidney beans
    with chipotle and
    dried cherries, 686
Hot and smoky red bean cro-
    quettes, 628
Hot and sour braised tempeh,
    675
Hot and sour edamame with
    tofu, 591

Hot, sweet and sour chickpeas
    with eggplant,
    609–610
Huevos rancheros, 174
    with red mole, 174
    simplest, 174
Hummus, 614–615
    edamame, 615
    fondue, 616
    lima, 615

Iceberg lettuce, 34
Ice cream
    basics of, 888–889
    buttermilk, 891
    flavors for, 890–891
Ice cream maker, 16
Ice milk
    basics of, 889
    flavors for, 892–893
    mango or apricot, 894
Ida red apple, 418
Indian cauliflower soup, 130
Indian cornmeal pudding,
    896
Indian rice, 535
Indian spices, lentils and
    rhubarb with, 600
Indian style
    batter (pakora), 248, 249
    bean salad, essential, 73
    chile paste, 829
    chile sauce, smooth green,
        792–793
    flatbread, flaky (paratha),
        699–700
    flatbread, flaky (paratha),
        spinach, 700
    flatbread, the simplest (cha-
        pati), 698–699
    flatbread, the simplest (cha-
        pati), grilled, 699
    omelet, fresh cheese and
        spinach, 172
    potato croquettes, 353
    pumpkin soup, 133–134
    red beans, spicy, 593
    red chile sauce, 793
    rice salad, 82
    tofu pancakes, 655
    yogurt sauce, 774

Indian Tomato sauce, spicy,
    793–794
Ingredients
    from local sources, 2–3
    organic, 2
    pantry, 3–4
    quality of, 1–2
Irish soda bread, 690–691
Israeli couscous, 91–92
Italian-American style mush-
    room salad, 62
Italian style
    bean salad, broiled three-
        bean, 75
    bean salad, essential, 72
    cauliflower soup, 105–106
    egg drop soup, 155
    lentil soup with rice, 116

Jalapeño(s)
    about, 826
    chickpeas with, 594
    deviled eggs, 180
    pickled eggs with carrots
        and, 182
Jamaican jerk ketchup,
    790–791
Jamaican style baked rice and
    red kidney beans,
    510
Japanese egg crêpes, 175–176
    with nori, 176
Japanese egg rolls, 176
Japanese flavors, marinated
    tofu with, 653
Japanese rice
    with edamame and sea
        greens, 532
    with tomato and fermented
        black bean, 532
Japanese seven-spice mix, 817,
    823
Japanese style
    batter (tempura), 248, 249
    bean salad, essential, 72
    pasta salad, summertime,
        90–91
    potato croquettes, 353
    rice, mixed, 531–532
    rice salad, 79
Jasmine rice, 503

Jasmine tea
    cake soak, 860
    tapioca pudding, -scented,
        885
Jean-Georges's rice noodle
        salad with grape-
        fruit and peanuts,
        93–94
Jelly-roll pans, 12
Jerk ketchup, Jamaican,
        790–791
Jerk seasoning, 818, 824
Jerusalem artichoke(s). *See*
        Sunchoke(s)
Jícama
    about, 307–308
    to grill, 253
    and orange salad, 50
    salad with pineapple and
        mint, 50
    salsa, 751
Joel Robuchon mashed pota-
        toes, 343
Jonagold apple, 418
Jook, 140
Juicer, electric, 16
Julienne technique, 20–21,
        22
Juniper berries, 820

Kale
    about, 308
    buckwheat stew with tofu
        and, 563
    pie, 403
    rolled, with feta and olives,
        308–309
    rolled, fillings for, 309
    rolled, with tofu and fer-
        mented black
        beans, 308–309
    with tofu, stir-fried, 648
Kalijira rice, 503
Kamut, 478, 537
Kasha
    about, 535
    with carrots, 562
    and mushroom pie, 403
    with mushrooms, 563

with onions, golden brown,
        562
with parsnips, 562
pilaf with caramelized
        endive, 563
with radicchio or escarole,
        563
varnishkes, 562
Ketchup. *See also* Barbecue
        sauce
    black bean, 791
    green, 790
    homemade, 790
    Jamaican jerk, 790–791
    mushroom, 791
    tofu, -braised, spicy,
        651–652
    tomatoless, 791
Kidney beans
    about, 577
    with apples and red wine,
        586
    with apples and sherry, 586
    with chipotle and dried
        cherries, hot and
        smoky, 586
    with pears and wine, 586
    with prunes, piquant, 586
    and rice, baked, Jamaican
        style, 510
Kimchi, 96
    mung bean pancakes with,
        631
    pancake, crispy, 394
    rice, 512
    rice cakes with, 474
    soup with tofu, 148
    soybeans with, spicy, 609
    soybeans with, spicy,
        puréed, 609
    soybeans with, spicy, stir-
        fried tempeh and,
        609
    tofu pancakes with, 654
Kiwis, about, 425–426
Kneading dough, 702, *703*
Knife sharpener, electric, 8, 16
Knives. *See also* Cutting tech-
        niques

to hold, *19*, 19
to sharpen with steel, 8–9,
        18
types of, 8
to wash and store, 8, 30
Kohlrabi, 309–310
Kombu
    about, 356
    -boiled tofu, 641
    dashi, with edamame,
        quick-cooked,
        583–584
Kome-miso, 152
Korean
    buckwheat noodles, 465
    mushroom soup, 148–149
    sweet potato vermicelli,
        465
Korean style
    cabbage, spicy (kimchi), 96
    cucumber salad, 49
    leek and potato soup, 107
    lettuce and chive salad, 44
    noodles in bean broth,
        cool, 469
    potatoes, stir fried, 349
    soy and sesame dipping
        sauce and mari-
        nade, 778
    vegetable pancakes, crisp,
        393–394
    vegetable soup, mixed,
        127–128
Kosher pickles, the right way,
        97
Kosher salt, 807
Kumquats
    about, 426
    to macerate and season,
        416

Lactobacillus bacteria, 683,
        685
Lamb's tongue, 35
Lasagne
    pesto, 460
    vegan, 460
    vegetable, 459–460
    white, 460

Last-minute broiled pota-
        toes, 346
Last-minute crisp panfried
        potatoes (home
        fries), 343
Last-minute grilled potatoes,
        346
Latkes (potato pancakes), 350
Lavash, wraps with, 736
Lavender, 767
Layer cake(s). *See* Cake(s),
        chocolate layer
Layered mozzarella with
        roasted peppers and
        olives, 221
Layered vegetable torte,
        405–406
Leaveners
    substituting, 686
    types of, 683–685
Lebanese style
    bread salad, 88–89
    bulgur pilaf with cabbage,
        557
Leek(s)
    about, 310
    beans and poatoes with,
        boulangerie, 620
    braised
        with mustard, 311
        in oil or butter, 310
        with olives, 311
        with tomato, 311
    bulgur with, creamed, 556
    caramelized, quinoa with,
        560
    cobbler, 376
    crisp, 312
    gratin, and celery, 385
    to grill, 253
    grilled, 312–313
    grilled, Asian style, 313
    and potato soup, 106–107
    and potato soup, Korean
        style, 107
    with potato soup, puréed,
        107
    to prepare, 310, *311*
    quiche, and herb, 188

rye berry gratin with tomatoes and, 568
rye berry gratin with tomatoes and, creamy, 568
rye berry gratin with tomatoes and, vegan, 568–569
steamed, 312
stir-fried, 312
vinaigrette, 310
Leftover pound cake strudel, 881
Leftovers
ideas for, 31
in purées, 391
to reheat, 30, 31–32
"repurposing," 30–31
Legumes, 575–636. *See also* Bean(s); Chickpea(s); Lentil(s); Pea(s), dried
basics of, 576
cooking methods, 579–580
and flatulence, 580
lexicon of, 576–579
main-course dishes, 635
Lemon(s)
about, 426–427
bars, -rosemary, 846
eggplant, mashed, with honey and, 298
gelées, -lime, 887–888
glaze, 858
glaze, -clove, 858
grits gratin with escarole, garlic and, 551
lentil salad, lemony, 75–76
Meyer, 426
orzo, risotto style, 451
pea shoots, -scented, in parchment, 363
pine nut sauce, lemony, 797
with pizza, white, 726
-poppy seed pancakes, 202
preserved
couscous, pearl, pilaf with, 551
fennel or artichoke hearts with, marinated, 68

gigantes with, 588
to make, 427
whole grain salad with, 92
quinoa salad with spinach, poppy seed and, 83–84
-ricotta pancakes, 203
risotto with, 518
sauce, 448
sorbet, 892
sorbet, fennel-, 893
sorbet, -lime, Thai basil, 89
stuck-pot rice with herbs and, 526
vinaigrette, 763
white beans with, 607
zest, paella with spinach and, simple, 523
Lemongrass
about, 767
curried coconut soup with, 137–138
dipping sauce, 778
ponzu, 780
Lentil(s). *See also* Legumes
about, 577
braised
with celery, 598
Ethiopian style, 598
Moroccan style, 598
with parsnips, 598
Spanish style, 598
with winter squash, roasted, 598
cabbage stuffed with rice and, *401*, 401
cabbage stuffed with rice and, in red wine sauce, 401
cakes, baked, with Gruyère, 630
dal, simplest, 600
dal, urad, with poppy seeds and cilantro, 603–604
and greens, 596
pancakes, brown, 632
pancakes, red, spiced, 632
pasta with, 454–455
pâté, 316

and potatoes with curry, 600–601
and potatoes with curry, buttery, 602
red
with celery root, 600
with chaat masala, 600
dal, simplest, 600
pancakes, spiced, 632
with radish, 600
and rhubarb with Indian spices, 600
with tomatoes, fresh, 600
and rice crêpes (dosas), 744–745
and rice crêpes (dosas), brown rice, 745
salad, lemony, 75–76
salad, tangarine, 76
samosas, baked, 745–746
samosas, fried, 746
and seitan loaf, 670–671
soup
classic, 115–116
with coconut, 116–117
elegant, 116
French style with sorrel or spinach, 116
Italian style, with rice, 116
and stuck-pot rice
orange-scented, with pita crust, 525
with pita crust, 525
spicy, 525
varieties of, 599
Lentils du puy, 599
Lettuce(s) *See also* Green salad(s); *specific lettuces*
and chive salad, Korean style, 44
cups and wraps, 39
flageolets with, 605
mixes (mesclun), 35
with rice, fried, basic, 521
salad with mixed herbs, 43
salad with parsley, 43
stuffed, 404
types of, 34

-wrapped custards, 192
wraps, crisp-fried bean sprouts in, 632
Light barbecue sauce, 790
Lighter, richer corn bread, 688
Lighter cilantro (or other herb) "pesto," 769–770
Lighter muffins, 694
Lighter peanut sauce, 796
Lighter whole wheat quick bread, 689
Light and fluffy pancakes, 201
Light tomato sauce, 804
Lima bean(s)
about, 577
baked, Parmigiana, 621
baked, with ricotta and Parmesan, 621
hummus, 615
pilaf with chickpeas, peas and, 512
purée with fennel and orange juice, 613
stew, dried fruit and, 594–595
stuck-pot rice with, 526
Lime(s)
about, 426–427
-coconut bars, 845–846
gelées, lemon-, 887–888
glaze, 858
key lime, 426
pound cake, vanilla-, 849–850
sorbet, 892
sorbet, lemon-, Thai basil, 89
Lime leaf
about, 767
dipping sauce, 778
Linguine
with mushrooms, fresh and dried, 454
with tomato sauce, raw, 446–447
Linseeds, 319
Loaf pan, 12
Loaves. *See* Veggie loaves

Long-lasting cilantro-mint
	chutney, 784
Lupini beans, 579
Lychees
	about, 427
	to macerate and season,
		416
Lyonnaise salad, 38

Macadamia nuts, 320
Macaroni and cheese
	baked, 460–461
	blue cheese, nutty, 461
	chile, 461–462
	goat cheese with roasted
		red peppers, 461
	rich, 461
	simpler, 461
Macaroons
	coconut-dried pineapple,
		902
	toasted oats and chocolate
		chip, 902
Mace, 821
Macerated/seasoned fruit,
	416, 417
Mâche, 35
Macoun apple, 418
Mahogany rice, 504
Maki sushi, 528, 528–530
Malanga (yautia), 377–378
Maldon sea salt, 808
Malt syrup, 835–836
Malt vinegar, 760
Manchego and potato gratin,
	383
Manchurian style cauliflower,
	283–284
	roasted, 284
Mandoline, 15, 21
Mango(es)
	about, 428–429
	with avocado salad, six-
		layer, 53
	bars, 846
	-citrus sauce, 862
	to grill, 413
	ice milk, 894
	mousse, 901
	mustard, 777
	pickled, quick-, 95

to skin and pit, 428, 429
sorbet, 893–894
stuck-pot rice with yogurt
	and, 524
Maple (syrup)
	about, 205
	-baked beans, apple butter,
		619
	buttercream frosting, not-
		too-sweet, 860
	cream cheese sauce, pump-
		kin waffles with,
		205–206
	snaps, 841–842
Maple sugar, 834–835
Ma po edamame with tofu,
	591
Margherita pizza, 726
Marinara pizza, 726
Marinated artichokes, 68
Marinated cheese. See Cheese,
	marinated
Marinated fennel or artichoke
	hearts with pre-
		served lemons, 68
Marinated garden vegetables,
	67–68
Marinated tofu. See Tofu,
	marinated
Marjoram, 765
Marmalade, orange, -cassis
	glaze, 858
Masa, 542
Masa harina, 542
Mascarpone
	about, 211
	apples with almonds,
		402
Mashed cauliflower with
	cheese, 282–283
Mashed eggplant with honey
	and lemon, 298
Mashed favas, 616–617
Mashed potatoes. See
	Potato(es), mashed
Matzo brei, 177
Mayonnaise
	basics of, 770
	chile, 771
	flavorings for, 771–772
	garlic (aïoli), 771

garlic and saffron, grilled
	eggplant salad with,
		65
green sauce, French style,
	771
homemade, 771
mustard sauce, cold, 771
in ranch dressing, real, 772
seaweed "mayo," 773
seaweed "mayo," edamame
	salad with, 76
vegan. See Vegannaise
Meal planning, xi–xii
Measuring techniques, 22–23,
	23
Measuring utensils, 13, 23
Meatballs, vegetarian, 660,
	666
Meatless "meat" sauce, 448
Mediterranean slaw, 301
Mediterranean style
	bok choy, 270
	tofu pancakes, 655
Medium-boiled egg, 165–166
Melon(s). See also Watermelon
	about, 429
	cantaloupe, to macerate
		and season, 416
	chutney, caramelized, 787
	granita, 894
	to grill, 414
	peach tomato salsa, 752
	sorbet, 892
Melon baller, 429
Meringue(s)
	basics of, 897–900
	as edible containers, 892
	egg whites, to beat, 899
	macaroons, coconut-dried
		pineapple, 902
	macaroons, toasted oats
		and chocolate chip,
		902
	mocha, 903
	pie, apricot (or virtually
		any fruit), 874
	pie, coconut, 873–874
	pistachio, 902
	sesame, sweet, 903
Mesclun (salad mixes), about,
	35

Mexican cheese salsa, 751
Mexican rice with vegetables,
	512
Mexican style
	black bean tart with millet
		crust, 625
	cabbage and carrot slaw, 49
	chile gratin, 385–387
	chile paste, 829
	cornmeal pizza, 547
	egg drop soup, 155
	omelet, flat, 183
	pickled vegetables, quick-,
		95
	rice salad, 79, 82
Microwaving
	about, 16
	asparagus, 261
	beets, 266–267
	fruit, 411
	polenta, 544
	rice, white, 505
	sweet potatoes, 371
	vegetables, 237
Midsummer vegetable burger,
	664–665
Milk. See also Coconut milk
	fat content of, 206
	to sour, 207
	sour, pancakes, 202
	-steamed corn on the cob,
		289
	UHT, 207
Milk chocolate, 837
Milk products
	storage of, 206
	types of, 206–207
Milk substitutes, 29, 132, 136
Milled grains, 500
Millet
	about, 535
	bake, autumn, 566
	bake, autumn, with cream,
		567
	crust, pinto bean tart with,
		624
	mash, 565–566
		carrot, with ginger,
			sesame, and soy,
			566
		cheesy, 566

creamy, 566
miso, 566
tahini, 566
ricotta dumplings, 225–226
soufflé, 187
Mincing vegetables, *20*, 20, 358
Minestrone, 123
herbed, 123
Minimalist guacamole, 264
Mint
about, 765
bean threads with coconut milk and, 466
cauliflower, sautéed, with feta and, 282
-cilantro chutney, 783–784
-cilantro chutney, creamy, 784
-cilantro chutney, long-lasting, 784
corn salad with tomatoes, feta and, 61
dipping sauce, 778
eggplant, spicy mashed, with yogurt and, 298
and fava bean salad with asparagus, 77
ice cream, real, 890
jícama salad with pineapple and, 50
mung bean dal with apples, coconut and, 602
pea salad with tomatoes, feta and, 61
"pesto," 768
with pizza, white, 726
pumpkin, pan-fried, with tomato sauce, yogurt and, 367
purée, 769
in tabbouleh, 43
tahini sauce, minty, 796
and watermelon soup, 903–904
Mirliton. *See* Chayote
Miso
basics of, 151–152
dipping sauce, simple, 781

citrus, 781
herb, 781
soy, 781
with edamame and potatoes, smashed, 617
eggplant salad with, 63–64
glaze, sweet, 782
millet mash, 566
potatoes with, braised, 347
sauce
carrot, with ginger, 781–782
nutty, 782
with radishes, turnips or other root vegetables, braised and glazed, 355
tahini, 782
tomato, 449
-walnut, green beans tossed with, 305–306
soup, 152–153
soybeans with shiitakes and, 590–591
-stuffed eggs, 180
tofu, -baked, 641–642
tofu, grilled, 643
tofu, scrambled, 655
types of, 152
vegetables, -cured, 98
in veggie burgers, 662
Mixed rice, Japanese style, 531–532
Mixed whole-bean dal with cabbage and walnuts, 603
Mixed whole-bean dal with cauliflower and almonds, 603
Mixed whole-bean dal with walnuts, 602–603
Mixer, electric, 16, 707, 899
Mixing bowls, 13, 14
Mizuna, 35
Mocha
cookies, chewy, 843
glaze, 858
meringue, 903
Modified Atmosphere Packaging (MAP), 35

Molasses
about, 835
-ginger granola, 574
mustard, 777
-spice cake, 855
and whole wheat bread, quick, 689
Mole
corn with, 546
pozole with, 545–546
pozole with, creamier, 546
red, cheese enchiladas with, 223–224
red, tofu enchiladas with, 224
vegetable, 546
Monkey bread (streusel pull-apart coffee cake), *715*, 715
Monterey Jack, 210
More classic onion soup, 109
More leisurely French bread or rolls, 708
Morels
about, 313
flageolets with, 597
soybeans with asparagus and, 590
Mornay sauce, 804
Moroccan style braised lentils, 598
Mousse(s)
basics of, 897–900
blueberry (or any berry), 901
chocolate-orange, vegan, 900–901
honey, frozen, 900
mango, 901
peach or apricot, 901
Mozzarella
about, 210
bread pudding with sun-dried tomatoes and, 193
layered, with roasted peppers and olives, 221
pizza
margherita, 726
with tomato sauce and, 726–727

with tomato sauce, broccoli and, 727
with tomato sauce and fresh mozzarella, 727
with tomato sauce and, grilled, 727
and tomato salad, broiled, with pesto, 59
Muffins
additions to, 688
banana-nut, 693
basics of, 686–687
blueberry, 693
bran, 693
coffee cake, 693
cranberry, 693
English, 714
fruit-and-nut or vegetable-and-nut, 691
infinite ways, 692–693
lighter, 694
savory, 694
sour cream, 693
spice, 693
sweet and rich, 694
yogurt, 693
Muffin tins, 12
Mugi-miso, 152
Multigrain bread pudding with winter squash, 193
Multigrain and herb dumplings, 48
Mung bean(s)
about, 579
with apples, coconut, and mint, 602
dal with apples, coconut, and mint, 602
dal with carrots, cashews and Thai basil, 602
fried
with chile paste, 590
and fermented black beans, 590
with mung bean sprouts, 590
with sesame, 589
pancakes, 631
pancakes, with kimchi, 631

Mung bean(s) *(Continued)*
  pancake, southeast Asian
      style, 631–632
  and rice with apricots,
      dried, 611–612
  and rice with carrots,
      spiced, 612
  salad, two-mung, 76–77
  soup, 121
Mung bean sprouts
  fried mung beans with,
      590
  to make, 77–78
Mushroom(s)
  about, 314
  and asparagus pie with
      phyllo crust, 406
  and barley stew, 540
  and barley stew, deeper,
      541
  and beans, 596–597
  black-eyed peas with
      smoked tofu and,
      611
  borscht, cold-roasted, 110
  borscht, roasted, 110
  breading and frying, 246
  brown rice pilaf with two
      mushrooms,
      514–515
  chanterelles, fava beans
      with, 597
  cremini, chickpeas with,
      597
  crêpes, baked, 199
  custard, 191
  dried
      linguine with, 454
      to reconstitute, 317
      risotto with, fresh mush-
          rooms and,
          518–520
      shiitakes, black beans
          with, 597
      shiitakes, stir-fried broc-
          coli with, 271
  egg "noodle" soup with,
      153–154
  in endive and roquefort
      salad, 44–45
  fritters, 394

and goat cheese tart with
      potato crust,
      227–228
grains, precooked, with
      onions and,
      538–539
gratin, and pumpernickel,
      386
gratin, and Roquefort, 383
to grill, 253
grilled, 316–317
grilled shiitake or porto-
      bello salad with soy
      vinaigrette, 63
with kasha, 563
and kasha pie, 403
ketchup, 791
linguine with fresh and
      dried mushrooms,
      454
morels, flageolets with, 597
morels, soybeans with
      asparagus and, 590
noodles with, creamy, 463
paella with mushroom
      caps, simple, 523
pan cooked, dry style,
      315–316
pasta with, 454
pâté, 316
with pizza, white, 726
porcini dumplings,
      488–489
porcini and fontina fondue,
      222
quiche, 188–189
ravioli, -cheese, 483
risotto with, dried and
      fresh mushrooms,
      518–520
salad
      grilled shiitake or porto-
          bello, with soy
          vinaigrette, 63
      Italian-American style,
          62
      shaved, 51
      steamed, Asian style, 63
      steamed, with coriander,
          62–63
sauce, 448

sauce, béchamel, 804
sauerkraut soup, 111
sautéed, 314–315
sautéed, with Asian flavors,
      315
scrambled tofu with, 655
and sea green stir-fry, 357
and seitan loaf, 670–671
shiitake(s)
      chickpeas with, 597
      dried, stir-fried broccoli
          with, 271
      dried, black beans with,
          597
      gigantes with, 588
      in parchment, 363
      salad, grilled, with soy
          vinaigrette, 63
      soybeans with miso and,
          590–591
      soybeans with sea greens
          and, 590
      tofu, braised, with egg-
          plant and, 650
      with tofu, stir-fried, 647
soup
      barley, 139
      -farro, 141
      Korean, 148–149
stew, 137
stew, with green beans, 137
stock, 102–103
stuffed, 397
tempeh with rice and, 676
teriyaki sauce, 779
varieties of, 313–314
wild rice with, 568
Muskmelon, 429
Mustard
  barbecue sauce, mustardy,
      789
  bistro dressing, creamy, 799
  brewhouse, 776
  -cheese fondue, 222
  course, wheat berry salad
      with cabbage and,
      85
  cracked wheat, fluffy, with
      tarragon and, 559
  forms of, 775–776
  -glazed carrot soup, 105

grainy, additions to,
      776–777
grainy, many ways, 776
with leeks, braised, 311
peppers and onions, pan-
      cooked, with cumin
      seeds and, 335
port wine, 776
potatoes with, braised, 347
relish, 776
sauce, 804
sauce, cold, 771
vinaigrette, 763
Mustard greens, about,
      317–318
Mustard seeds, 775
My mom's pan-cooked pepper
      and onions, 334

Naked tamale loaf, pie, or
      cake, 549–550
Naked tamales with chile
      cheese filling,
      547–549
Napa cabbage, stuffed, 404
Navy beans
  about, 577
  and greens, 596
Nectarines
  about, 432
  to grill, 414
  to macerate and season,
      416
  stuffed, 405
New Mexico chile, 826, 827
Nigiri sushi, *530*, 530–531
Nixtamal
  about, 539, 542
  in tamales, naked, with
      chile cheese filling,
      547–549
No-bake fruit and coconut
      crust, 869
No-bake fruit and nut crust,
      869
No-bake granola bars,
      846–847
Nondairy creams and milks,
      29, 132, 136
Nonstick coatings, cookware
      with, 9

Noodle(s)
creamy, with eggplant and cheese, baked, 462–463
creamy, with eggplant and tomatoes, sliced, 462–463
creamy, with mushrooms, 462–463
crumbles, 805
egg, fresh, 496
egg, fresh, herbed, 496–497
egg, fresh, with scallions and paprika, 197
and sea green stir-fry, 357
soup, 143–147
crisp-fried, 470
fideo, garlic, 144
Persian, 144–145
pho, faux, 143–144
spaetzle, the easy way, 146
udon, with green tea broth, 145
whole wheat noodles in curry broth, 147
in soups, 142–143
Noodle(s), Asian
in bean broth, cool, Korean style, 469
bean thread(s)
with arame, 55
and arame with fermented black beans, 55
and arame with Ponzu dipping sauce, 54–55
with coconut milk and mint, 466
dumplings with, steamed, vegan, 493–494
egg "noodle" soup with, 154
in two-mung salad, 76–77
bowls, to make, 466, 468
cake, crisp-fried, 469–470
cellophane, with sweet soy sauce, 474

egg, in soy broth, Chinese, 465–466
fiery, cold, 467
fresh, Chinese style, 492
lexicon of, 463–465
pad Thai, 470–472
panfried dishes, 469–472
ramen, vastly improved store-bought, 466
rice
brown, stir-fried, with pickled vegetables, 472–473
salad with grapefruit and peanuts, Jean-Georges's, 93–94
with sweet soy sauce, 474
wide, stir-fried, with pickled vegetables, 472–473
rice cakes
braised, 474
egg "noodle" soup with, 154
with kimchi, 474
with Shaoxing wine, 474
with sweet soy sauce, 473
with sweet soy sauce and vegetables, 473–474
sesame or peanut, cold, 466–467
soba, with dipping sauce, 467–468
soup, crisp-fried, 470
udon, with green tea broth, 145–146
vegetable dishes for stir-frying with, 471
Nori
about, 356
chips, 357
Japanese egg crêpes with, 176
in maki sushi (rolls), 528, 529–530
in nigiri sushi, 530, 531
"shake," 817–818
soy mustard, 777

North African couscous soup, 140–141
North African style red chile sauce, 793
Not-too-sweet buttercream frosting. See Buttercream frosting, not-too-sweet
Nut(s). See also Nut butter(s); specific nuts
about, 318
to blanch, 322
bread
and dried fruit, 692
fruit-and-, or vegetable-and-, 691–692
fruit-and-, or vegetable-and-, whole grain, 692
and fruit, saffron, 715
and fruit or vegetable combinations, 692
brittle, 906
brittle, chocolate-, 906
burgers
fast, 667–668
nuttier, 668
-and-seed, 668
vegan, 668
caramelized, fiery, 323
caramelized, spiced, 322–323
cheese crisp, nutty, 220
chickpeas in their own broth, nutty, 606
chili con, 608
chocolate torte, flourless, 850–851
chutney
coconut and, 784
crunchy, 784
dried fruit and, 784
real garlicky, 785
walnut and yogurt, 785
in cookies, 839
cottage cheese pancakes with, 226
crumbles, 805
crust, and fruit, no-bake, 869
curried, wild rice with, 567

falafel, nutty, 626
French toast, -crusted, 177
gingered, 323
with goat cheese, baked, 217
with grains, precooked, 539
in granola, crunchy, 573
granola bars, nutty, 847
greens with fruit, cheese and, 40
to grind, 322
lexicon of, 319–320
macaroni and blue cheese, nutty, 461
miso sauce, nutty, 782
muffins, banana-, 693
pasta with ground nuts, 444
in pesto, 767
in pesto, traditional, 768
phyllo "cigars," and dried fruit, 880
piecrust, 867
pilaf with fruit and, 511–512
pizza, blue cornmeal, nutty, 547
rice pudding, cinnamon-, 895
risotto with, 418
roasted, 323
roasted, herbed, 323
to roast and toast, 318, 321
sauce
béchamel, 804
boozy, 798
chestnut cream, pasta with, 457
cranberry-, creamy, 798
creamy, 797–798
creamy, with arugula or sorrel, 798
peanut. See Peanut(s), sauce
pine nut. See Pine nut(s), sauce
walnut, pasta with, 458
walnut, rich, pasta with, 458
to shell, 318

Nut(s) *(Continued)*
in soups, 136
spinach with currants and,
360
tart, rich, 876
tart crust, 868
wheat berry stew with citrus, dried fruit and,
565
yogurt soup with, cool, 158
ziti, baked, nutty, 459
Nut butter(s)
almond, creamy orzo with,
451
almond, pasta with,
455–457
flavorings for, 322
granola bars, 847
hazelnut, parsnips with,
268
to make, 322
pancakes, 202
-pasta combinations, 457
peanut, granola, 573–574
peanut, granola bars, 847
pistachio, beets with, 268
walnut, carrots with, 268
Nut flours, 682
Nutmeg, 812
Nut milks, 29
Nut oils, 29, 757

Oat(s)
about, 534, 535
and bran sandwich bread,
713
crumble topping, 870
in granola, crunchy, 573
piecrust, 867
toasted, and chocolate chip
macaroons, 902
Oatcakes
curried, 570
savory, with peas and carrots, 570
Oat flour, 682–683
Oatmeal
breakfast cereal, 572–573
cookies
-apple, 839–840
-apple, vegan, 840

carrot or parsnip, 840
peanut, 840
griddlecakes made from,
570
Oil(s). *See also* Olive oil
extracting process in making, 753–754
fats, about, 754
flavored, 758
flavored, about, 756, 758
grains cooked with, 538
leeks braised in, 310
lexicon of, 755–758
in mayonnaise, 770
in pesto, 767
precooked vegetables in,
240–242
smoke point, 755–756
storing, 754–755
in vegan baking, 29
for vinaigrette, 762
Okra
about, 323–324
fried, 324
to grill, 254
salad, crisp, 67
stew with roux, 324–325
stew with tomatoes,
324–325
Olive(s)
about, 325
braised, with tomatoes,
326
breadsticks, 711
cauliflower salad with bread
crumbs and,
61–62
cauliflower, sautéed, with
onion and, 281
chickpea soup with oranges
and, 118
couscous salad with, 93
edamame with tomatoes
and, 583
eggs au gratin with
caramelized onions
and, 194
and feta stuffed-eggs, 181
kale, rolled, with feta and,
308–309
with leeks, braised, 311

mojo, green olive, 769
paella with oranges, saffron
and, simple, 523
rice salad with, 80
sauce, fried, 448
sautéed, 326
sautéed, with croutons, 326
tapenade, 326–327
tapenade, green olive, 327
varieties of, 325–326
vermicelli or fideo with,
450
ziti, baked, with goat
cheese and, 459
Olive oil
advantages of, 759
-blueberry torte, 853
cake, 852
cookies
chile-, 843
date-, 843
saffron-, 842
extra virgin, 754, 756
garlic braised in, 305
mixed vegetables with,
baked, 380–381
mixed vegetables with,
stovetop, 381
pasta with garlic and,
443–444
"pure," 757
salt bread, 689–690
salt bread, griddled, 690
Omega 3 fatty acids, 754
Omelet(s)
almond or hazelnut, baked,
179
basics of, 171
cheese, 172
cheese and apple, 172
cheese, fresh, and spinach,
Indian style, 172
cherry, baked, 179
fillings for, 172–173
flat. *See also* Frittata
about, 182–183
with cauliflower or broc-
coli, 183
cheesy, 183
fillings for, 184–185
Greek style, 184

Mexican style, 183
with rhubarb and
cottage cheese, 185
with rutabaga (frozen),
183
to fold, *171*
folded, 173
folded, with grated vegetables, 174
mashed potato, 172
simplest, 171–172
Spanish, 172
sweet, baked, 179
sweet, with dried fruit,
baked, 179
Omnivore's Dilemma, The
(Pollan), 2
One-hour vegetable stock,
101–102
One-pot bean gumbo, 611
Onion(s). *See also* Scallion(s);
Shallots
about, 327–329
and apricot salsa, grilled,
792
breading and frying, 246
caramelized, 329
chutney, 786–787
eggs au gratin with olives
and, 194
pasta with, 453
pasta with, savory, 453
pearl couscous gratin
with blue cheese
and, 555
pizza, white, with vine-
gar and, 726
quinoa with, 559–560
sweeter, 329
teriyaki sauce, 779
-thyme dressing, green
salad with,
43–44
uses for, 329
cheese crisp with, 219
chutney, caramelized, 786
chutney, grilled, 787
chutney, raw, 783
creamed, 330
creamed, vegan, 330
to cut, *328*

favas, stewed, with potatoes and spiced onions, 604
golden brown, kasha with, 562
grains, precooked with, 538
grains, precooked with mushrooms and, 538–539
gratin, simplest, 383
gratin, smoky, 385
to grill, 254
to pan cook, 329
and peppers, pan cooked Asian style, 334
with mustard and cumin seeds, 335
my mom's, 334
and pineapple salsa, grilled, 791–792
potatoes, crisp panfried, with, 344
quiche, 188
raw, to salt, 46
rice cooked in (soubise), 514
rice, fried, the simplest, 519–520
rings, fried, streamlined, 245
roasted halves, 330–331
roasted halves, balsamic-, 331
roasted halves, cream-, 331
salad, roasted, 65–66
soup, 108
with almonds, Spanish, 109
charred, 109
more classic, 109
stuffed, 396–397
stuffed, béchamel, 397
with tofu, scrambled, smoky, 655
yogurt sauce, 774
Orange(s). See also Tangerine(s)
about, 430–431
beet salad with cabbage and, 50

chard with shallots and, 286
chickpea soup with olives and, 118
-chocolate mousse, vegan, 900–901
-cranberry crisp, 878
-cranberry soup, 904–905
with fennel, roast, 303
glaze(d), 857
beet cake with, 852
carrots with ginger and, quick-, 279
carrot soup with ginger and, 105
creamy, 857
marmalade-cassis, 858
granita, 894
granola, -almond, 574
granola bars, -spice, 847
and jícama salad, 50
juice
black beans with, 606–607
black beans with, and beets, 6073007
black beans with, and chiles, 607
with endive, braised, 301
lima bean purée with fennel and, 613
paella with olives, saffron and, simple, 523
pickled eggs with warm spices and, 182
-rhubarb soup, 904
sorbet, blood orange, 892
sorbet, -thyme, 892
stuck-pot rice and lentils, -scented, with pita crust, 525
zest, stir-fried tofu with scallions, chiles and, 646
Orange blossom custard, 887
Oregano, 766
Organic food, 2
Orzo
creamy, with almond butter, 451
risotto style, 451

risotto style, lemon, 451
salad, Greek style, 93
Oven-braised celery, 284–285
Oven-dried fruit, 411, 415–417
Oven-dried tomatoes, 377
cherry or grape tomato, 377
Oven-poached eggs, 169
Oven-roasted potatoes. See Potato(es), oven-roasted
Oven-roasted seitan. See Seitan, oven-roasted
Oven-roasted tomatoes. See Tomato(es), oven-roasted
Oven timer, 13
Ovenware, 11–12
Overnight French bread or rolls, 709
Oyster mushrooms, about, 313

Packham pears, 433
Pad Thai, 470–472
Paella
basics of, 522
with eggplant, simple, 523
with eggs, simple, 523
with fava beans, simple, 523
with mushroom caps, simple, 523
with oranges, olives, and saffron, simple, 523
with prunes, simple, 523
rices for, 504
with spinach and lemon zest, simple, 523
with tomatoes, 522–523
Pakora
batter, 248
dipping sauces for, 249
Palm syrup, 836
Pancake(s). See also Crêpes; Griddlecakes; Waffles
banana, 202
basics of, 200
blueberry, 202

buttermilk, yogurt, or sour milk, 202
chickpea, 633
cottage cheese and sour cream, 202–203
everyday, 200
gingerbread, 202
lemon-poppy seed, 202
lemon-ricotta, 203
lentil, brown, 632
lentil, red, spiced, 632
light and fluffy, 201
mung bean, 631
mung bean, with kimchi, 631
mung bean, southeast Asian style, 631–632
nut butter, 202
potato
cheesy, 350
garnishes for, 350–351
latkes, 350
"Nik," 349–350
for purists, 350
sourdough, 201
tofu, six ways, 654–655
Asian style, 654
Indian style, 655
with kimchi, 654
Mediterranean style, 655
Thai style, 654–655
variations, 201–202
vegan, 201
vegetable, 392–393. See also Fritters; Pancake(s), potato
basics of, 391–392
beet, 393
butternut squash and hazelnut, 393
carrot and quinoa rösti, 561
cheesy, 393
corn, Thai style, 291
crisp, Korean style, 393–394
to flip, 349
kimchi, crispy, 394
parsnip and quinoa rösti, 560–561

Pancake(s) *(Continued)*
    purées as base for, 392
    zucchini-pesto, 393
  wheatless, 202
  whole grain, 202
Pan-cooked mushrooms, dry style, 315–316
Pan-cooked peppers and onions, Asian style, 334–335
Pan-cooked peppers and onions with mustard and cumin seeds, 335
Paneer
  and cauliflower, baked chickpeas with, 623
  and spinach, baked chickpeas with, 623
Panfried cheese, 214–215
Panfried dumplings, ricotta, 225
Panfried egg rolls, 742
Panfried fruit, 411
Panfried noodles, Asian, 469–472
Panfried polenta, 544
Panfried tofu, crispy, 642
Panfried vegetables
  about, 238
  breading and frying, 246–247
  butternut squash, grain-fried, 245
  celery root "schnitzel," 245
  eggplant (or other vegetable), 244–245
  onion rings, fried, streamlined, 245
  plantain chips, fried, 336–337
  plantains, coconut-fried, 245
  potatoes, , crisp, seasonings for, 344
  potatoes, crisp, 343
    and buttery, 344
    and eggs, 344
    last-minute, 343–344
    with onions, 344

pumpkin
  with cranberries and pistachios, 367
  with tomato sauce, 366–367
  with tomato sauce, cocoa, and pumpkin seeds, 367
  with tomato sauce, Parmesan, and basil, 367
  with tomato sauce, yogurt, and mint, 367
Panfrying technique, 25–26, 238
Pan-grilled corn with chile, 289–290
Pan-grilled corn with tomatoes, 290
Panissa, 544
Pan-seared seitan, 671
Pan-seared tomato salad, 59–60
Pan-seared tomato salad with corn, 60
Pantry, vegetarian, 3–4
Papaya(s)
  about, 431–432
  to grill, 414
  pickled, quick-, 95
  salsa, 751–752
  salsa, green, Thai style, 753
  sorbet, -lime, 892
Paprika
  about, 813
  egg noodles, fresh, with scallions and, 497
  Spanish, boulangerie beans and potatoes with, 621
Paprika chile, 828
Paprika peppers, 335
  smoked, 335
  with sour cream, 335
Paratha (flatbread, flaky Indian style), 699–700
  cauliflower, 701
  spinach, 700
  stuffed with potato, 700–701

Parboiling, 24, 237
Parchment
  lemon-scented pea shoots in, 363
  shiitakes in, 363
  summer squash and herbs in, 362
Paring knife, 8, 18
  techniques, 22, *23*
Parmesan
  about, 209
  breadsticks, 711
  "burger," cheese, 220
  with cherry tomatoes, broiled, 375
  crackers, 698
  eggplant, 299
  in fettuccine Alfredo, 447
  and green pea custard, 191
  lima beans, baked, Parmigiana, 621
  lima or fava beans, baked, with ricotta and, 621
  pasta with butter and, 447
  pasta with butter, cream and, 447
  pasta with butter, sage and, 447
  popcorn, 292
  potato croquettes with roasted garlic and, 353
  pumpkin, pan-fried, with tomato sauce, basil and, 367
  rice cakes, 569–570
  and ricotta quiche, 188
  to serve, *209*
  with sunchokes, broiled, 370
Parsley
  about, 766
  in chimichurri sauce, 769
  and herb salad, 42–43
  lettuce salad with, 43
  purée (pesto), 768–769
  soup, cream of, 131–132
  soup, cream of, gratinéed, 132
  in tabbouleh, 43

Parsnip(s)
  about, 331–332
  breading and frying, 246
  cake with not-too-sweet buttercream frosting, 852
  gnocchi, 487–488
  gratin with vanilla, 386
  with hazelnut butter, 268
  kasha with, 562
  with lentils, braised, 598
  oatmeal cookies, 840
  purée, 389
  and quinoa rösti, 560–561
  and white bean purée, 613
Pasilla chile, 828
Passatelli in broth, 489
Passion fruit, 432
Pasta. *See also* Noodle(s); Noodle(s), Asian; Noodle soup(s); Pasta, fresh; Pasta salad(s)
  with almond butter, 455–457
  baked, 458–463
  basics of, 440–441
  and bean soup, 123
  with bread crumbs, 444
  with broccoli, cauliflower, or broccoli raab, 452
  in broth, 450–451
  with butter, cream, and Parmesan, 447
  with butter and Parmesan, 447
  with butter, pepper, and pecorino, 447
  with butter, sage, and Parmesan, 447
  cannellini beans with cabbage and, 586–587
  cavatelli, cannellini beans with spinach and, 587
  cavatelli, cranberry beans with artichokes and, 587
  with chestnut cream, 457

with chickpeas, 444
in dairy-based sauces, 447,
450
with eggs, fried, 447
fettuccine Alfredo, 447
fideo
with olives, 450–451
soup, garlic, 144
with tomatoes and chile,
451
frittata, 184
with garlic and oil,
443–444
with greens, 452–453
with herbs, fresh, 444
kasha varnishkes, 562
lasagne
pesto, 460
vegan, 460
vegetable, 459–460
white, 460
legume dishes that can be
tossed with, 456
with legumes and vegeta-
bles, 451–455
with lentils or other
legumes, 454–455
lexicon of, 441–442
linguine, with mushrooms,
fresh and dried,
454
linguine with tomato sauce,
raw, 446–447
macaroni and cheese
baked, 460–461
blue cheese, nutty, 461
chile, 461–462
goat cheese with roasted
red peppers, 461
nutty, 461
rich, 461
simpler, 461
with mushrooms, 454
-nut butter combinations,
457
with nuts, ground, 444
with nut sauces, 455–458
with onions, caramelized,
453
with onions, caramelized,
savory, 453

orzo
creamy, with almond
butter, 451
risotto style, 451
risotto style, lemon, 451
salad, Greek style, 93
to sauce, 440–441
with seeds, toasted, 444
serving size, 440
shapes, 441
in soups, 136
in tomato-based sauces,
445–447, 448–449
toppings for, 444
vegetable dishes that can be
tossed with, 456
with vegetables and
legumes, 451–455
vermicelli
bulgur pilaf with, 556
with olives, 450–451
pilaf, 512
rice, about, 464
sweet potato, Korean,
465
with tomatoes and chile,
451
with walnut sauce, 458
with walnut sauce, rich,
458
wheatless varieties,
442–443
whole wheat, 442
ziti, baked, 458–459
with goat cheese and
olives, 459
nutty, 459
with ricotta, 459
Pasta, fresh, 474–498. See also
Dumplings; Gnoc-
chi
about, 474–475
canneloni, to make, 483
canneloni, spinach-cheese,
482–483
to cut, 476–477, 477
egg, 477–478
eggless, 478–479
to flavor dough, 480
free-form, 490
herbed, 479–480

to make, 475, 475–476,
476
nonwheat flours in, 478
noodles, Chinese style,
492
pinci, 479
pizzocheri, 478
ravioli
cheese, 483
to make, 482
mushroom-cheese, 483
spinach, 483
spinach-ricotta, 481–482
to stuff and seal, 494
red, 480
to sauce, 480–481
spaetzle, 490–491
spaetzle, herb, 491
spinach, 480
stuffed, 481–486
stuffing, dishes for, 485
tortellini
butternut squash,
483–484
to make, 484
potato, 484
sweet potato, 484
triangles, butternut squash,
484
Pasta salad(s)
couscous
with fennel and raisins,
92–93
with hazelnuts, 93
Israeli, 91–92
with olives, 93
orzo, Greek style, 93
rice noodle, with grapefruit
and peanuts, Jean-
Georges's, 93–94
at room temperature, 90
storage of, 90
summertime, Japanese
style, 90–91
Pasta machine, 15, 476, 476
Pastry flour, 681
whole wheat, 681
Pâté
egg salad, 180
lentil, 316
mushroom, 316

tofu, 180
walnut, 316
Pea(s), dried. See also Legumes
about, 577
and samp, 545
split pea soup, simplest,
118–119
split pea soup, yellow, with
pantry vegetables,
119
split yellow, and rice with
prunes, 612
Pea(s), green
about, 332–333
anything-scented, 333
barley salad, 82
dip or spread, 264
oatcakes, savory, with carrots and, 570
and Parmesan custard, 191
pilaf with chickpeas, limas
and, 512
and potato samosas, 746
purée, 390
rice with, 509
salad with tomatoes, feta,
and mint, 61
shoots, about, 332
shorts, lemon-scented, in
parchment, 363
snap peas or snow peas
with tofu, stir-fried,
647
soufflé, 186
to string, 332
tempeh with rice and, 676
and tofu, braised, in curried coconut milk,
648
and tofu, braised, in curried coconut milk,
faster, 649
with tofu, stir-fried, 647
in vegetable burger, fresh
spring, 664
yogurt soup with fresh
peas, 159
Peach(es)
about, 432
-almond ice cream, 890
cobbler, -brandy, 877

Peach(es) *(Continued)*
  and corn salsa, grilled, 792
  gratin, savory, with corian-
    der, 384
  to grill, 414
  to macerate and season,
    416
  melon tomato salsa, 752
  mousse, 901
  mustard, 777
  pickled, Afghan style, 97
  pudding, 885
  stuffed, 405
Peanut(s)
  about, 320, 577
  avocado salad with ginger
    and, 51
  butter granola, 573–574
  butter granola bars, 847
  -caramel bars, 845
  green beans and tofu skins,
    stir-fried, with
    cilantro and, 307
  noodles, cold, 466–467
  oatmeal cookies, 840
  rice noodle salad with
    grapefruit and,
    Jean-Georges's,
    93–94
  sauce, six ways, 794–796
    curry, 795
    lighter, 796
    simpler, 796
    southern style, 796
    sweet, 796
  soup
    creamy, 125
    Senegalese style,
     124–125
    Virginian, 134–135
    Virginian, vegan, 135
  sticky rice with shallots
    and, 507
  tomato sauce, 449
  wheat berry or other whole
    grain salad with
    fresh and dried fruit
    and, 85–87
Peanut flour, and chickpea
    fries, 634–635
Peanut oil, 756

Pear(s)
  about, 432–433
  kidney beans with wine
    and, 586
  to macerate and season,
    416
  poached, 433–434
  poached, with Asian spices,
    434
  sauce, basil-, 862
  sorbet, rosemary, 892
  stuffed, 405
  tart, poached, with dark
    chocolate ganache,
    874–875
  upside-down cake, and
    almond, 854
  varieties of, 433
  watercress soup, with pota-
    toes and, 133
Pearl couscous. *See* Couscous
Pecan and blue cheese tart,
    228
Pecorino Romano
  and butternut squash
    gratin, 385
  pasta with butter, pepper
    and, 447
  shortbread, 696
Peeler, 13
Peeling vegetables, 18
Pepita pico de verde, 751
Peppermint chocolate bars,
    847
Pepper, peppercorns
  basics of, 808
  black pepper cookies, 841
  to grind, 808–809
  lexicon of, 809
  pasta with butter, pecorino
    and, 447
  sichuan, with cabbage,
    salted, 95
  sichuan, cookies, 841
Peppers, chile. *See* Chile(s);
    Chile paste
Peppers, sweet, 829. *See also*
    Bell pepper(s); Red
    pepper(s)
Perilla leaves, seasoned, 44
Persian noodle soup, 144–145

Persian style rice salad, 81
Persimmon(s)
  about, 434
  to macerate and season,
    416
  salsa, 752
  sorbet or ice milk, 893
  soup, 904
Pesto
  about, 766–768
  arugula "pesto," 768
  with butter, 768
  butternut squash with, 364
  and cauliflower gratin, 383
  cheese "burger," 220
  cilantro (or other herb)
    "pesto," lighter,
    769–770
  cilantro "pesto" with ginger
    and chile, 770
  couscous, pearl, gratin with
    goat cheese and,
    554–555
  with grains, precooked,
    539
  lasagne, 460
  mint or dill "pesto," 768
  parsley "pesto," 768–769
  quiche, 188
  rice salad with, 80
  -ricotta dumplings, 226
  soufflé, 186
  with tomato and mozzarella
    salad, broiled, 59
  tomato sauce, 449
  traditional, 768
  -zucchini pancakes, 393
Pho, faux, 143–144
Phyllo
  basics of, 878–879
  "cigars," nut and dried
    fruit, 880
  "cigars," walnut, 880
  crust
    fillings for pies, 409
    to make, 406
    spinach and feta pie
     with, 408–409
  goat cheese, -wrapped,
    baked, 227
  to handle, *879,* 879

strudel
  banana, 880–881
  cherry, 881
  pound cake, leftover,
    881
Pickles, pickled
  basics of pickling, 94–95
  cabbage, salted, with
    sichuan pepper-
    corns, 95
  eggs, 181
    with beets and horserad-
     ish, 182
    with jalapeños and car-
     rots, 182
    with oranges and warm
     spices, 182
    soy sauce-, 182
  ginger, 821–822
  ginger, citrus-, 822
  kimchi (spicy Korean style
    cabbage), 96
  kosher, the right way, 97
  mango or papaya, quick-,
    95
  miso-cured vegetables, 98
  peaches, Afghan style, 97
  spicy, Asian style, 95–96
  3–day, 96–97
  tofu (fermented), 639
  vegetables
    quick-, 95
    quick-, Mexican style, 95
    stir-fried brown rice
     noodles with, 473
    stir-fried wide rice noo-
     dles with, 472–473
Pickling spice, 94, 819, 824
Pie(s), dessert
  apricot (or virtually any
    fruit) meringue,
    874
  banana-butterscotch, 873
  basics of, 871
  buttermilk-blueberry,
    871–873
  chocolate, dark, -butter-
    milk, 873
  coconut meringue,
    873–874
  ginger-sweet potato, 873

Pie(s), savory. *See also* Torte, vegetable
  cabbage, 403
  dried fruit and nut, with phyllo crust, 408
  kale or chard, 403
  mashed potato, garlicky, 351
  mashed potato, garlicky, with cheese, 351
  mushroom and kasha, 403
  with phyllo crust, 406, 408
    mushroom and asparagus, 406
    parsnips and wheat berry, 408
    spinach and feta, 408–409
  vegetable, basics of, 403
  winter squash galette, spicy, 368–369
Piecrust. *See also* Crust(s)
  additions to, 871
  to bake, 866
  basics of, 863–864
  edges of dough, *865*, 866
  nut, 867
  oat, 867
  phyllo, spinach and feta pie with, 408–409
  to prebake, 872
  to roll dough, *864*, 864–865
  savory, 867
  sweet, 866–867
  wheat, 867
Pie plate, 12
Pierogi (fried potato-stuffed dumplings), 497–498
Pigeon peas, 578
Pilaf
  barley, 539–540
  bulgur
    with cabbage, Lebanese style, 557
    with green beans and soy sauce, 557
    tomato, with cinnamon, 556
    with vermicelli, 556

couscous, pearl
  curried, 552
  eggplant, 551–552
  with preserved lemons, 551
  spicy, 552
  spinach, 552
  with sun-dried tomatoes, 551
kasha, with caramelized endive, 563
rice, nine ways, 511–515
  brown, with two mushrooms, 514–515
  with chickpeas, peas, limas, or other beans, 512
  with currants and pine nuts, 511
  with fruit and nuts, 511–512
  red or green rice, 511
  with spinach or other greens, 512
  with vegetables, Mexican, 512
  vermicelli, 512
Pinci, 479
Pineapple
  about, 434
  chutney, 785
  -coconut cake soak, 860
  to cut, 434, *435*
  dried, -coconut macaroons, 902
  fried rice, 521
  to grill, 414
  jícama salad with mint and, 50
  to macerate and season, 416
  potatoes with, braised, in coconut milk, 348
  salsa, and onion, grilled, 791–792
  sauce, basil-, 862
  sorbet, -lavender, 892
  tart, 874
  upside-down cake, fresh, 854
  yogurt soup with, 159

Pine nut(s)
  about, 320
  cookies, 841
  in pesto, traditional, 768
  pilaf with currants and, 511
  sauce
    ancho-, 797
    lemony, 797
    puréed, 797
    rustic, 796–797
    rustic, with cheese, 797
    with tomatoes, 797
  tart, -rosemary, 876
Pink beans, 578
Pink lady apple, 418
Pink peppercorns, 809
Pinto beans
  baked, enchilada style, 621–622
  baked, enchilada style, and sweet potatoes, 622
  and greens, 596
  with red bell pepper, 594
  tart with millet crust, 624
  tart with millet crust, cheesy, 624
  tart with millet crust, souffléed, 624–625
Piquant kidney beans with prunes, 586
Piquin chile, 827
Pistachio(s)
  about, 320
  butter, beets with, 268
  -cardamom ice cream, 890
  chickpeas and, roasted, 618
  cookies, cardamom-, 842
  couscous with, sweet, 897
  meringue, 902
  pumpkin, pan-fried, with cranberries and, 367
Pistou, 123
Pita, 719–720
  crust, stuck-pot rice and lentils with, orange-scented, 525
  crust, stuck-pot rice and lentils with, 525

stuffed, 720–721
whole wheat, 720
Pizza, 721–730
  basics of making, 721–724
  calzone, 729–730
  calzone, to shape, *722*
  cornmeal "pizza," Mexican style, 547
  cornmeal "pizza," nutty blue, 547
  crusts, alternative, 728
  dough
    basic recipe, 724–725
    crunchier, 725
    flatbread with, 727
    preparing, 721
    shaping, 721–723, *722*
    whole wheat, 725
  to grill, 724
  margherita, 726
  marinara, 726
  polenta "pizza," 547
  polenta "pizza," breakfast, 547
  socca, 633
  with tomato sauce and mozzarella, 726–727
  with tomato sauce, mozzarella, and broccoli, 727
  with tomato sauce and mozzarella, fresh, 727
  with tomato sauce and mozzarella, grilled, 727
  toppings for, 723, 727–728
  vegan toppings, 728
  white, 725–726
    with lemon, 726
    with mint, 726
    with mushrooms, 726
    with onions, caramelized, and vinegar, 726
Pizza stone, 702, 723
Pizzocheri, 478
Plantain(s)
  about, 335–336
  breading and frying, 246
  bulgur croquettes with, 558

Plantain(s) *(Continued)*
 chips, fried, 336–337
 coconut-fried, 245
 to grill, 254
 sautéed ripe, 336
 stew, Spanish style, 111
Plum(s)
 about, 435
 to grill, 414
 roasted, and pudding tart, 875
 sauce, anise-, 863
 upside-down cake, -rosemary, 853–854
Plum vinegar, 761
Poached eggs. *See* Egg(s), poached
Poached fruit
 about, 410–411
 dried, 410
 pears, 434
 pears, with Asian spices, 434
 pear tart with dark chocolate ganache, 874–875
Poached tofu, 641
Poblano
 about, 826
 custard, 191
Polenta, 543–544
 about, 543
 angá (Brazilian), 544
 gratin, 544
 grilled or fried, 544
 with herbs, 544
 microwave, 544
 panissa, 544
 "pizza," 547
 "pizza," breakfast, 547
 soufflé, 187
Polenta style teff, foolproof, 544
Pollan, Michael, 2
Pomegranate(s)
 about, 436
 gelées, 888
 granita, 894
Ponzu sauce, 780
 arame and bean thread noodles with, 54–55

citrus, 780
 with edamame, quick-braised, 584
 lemongrass, 780
 tofu, -baked, 642
 tofu, -grilled or broiled, 643
Popcorn
 about, 543
 brittled, 906
 buttered, 292
 flavorings for, 293
 herb, 292–293
 Parmesan, 292
 salty-sweet, 292
Poppy seed(s)
 about, 821
 -lemon pancakes, 202
 quinoa salad with lemon, spinach and, 83–84
 urad dal with cilantro and, 603–604
Porcini
 about, 313–314
 dumplings, 488–489
 and fontina fondue, 222
Port
 -cherry jam glaze, 858
 grape or cherry tart with, 874
 mustard, 776
Portobello
 about, 314
 salad, grilled, with soy vinaigrette, 63
Potato(es)
 about, 337, 339
 artichoke hearts with, braised, 260
 baked, 339
  bay- or rosemary-scented, 339
  mashed, 341–342
  salted, 339
  toppings for, 339–340
  waffles, 206
 boiled, 340–341
 boulangerie beans and, 620
 creamy, 620
 with leeks, 620

with Spanish paprika, 621
 tomatoey, 620
braised, 346–347
 with almonds, 347
 beer-, with horseradish and Cheddar, 347–348
 cream-, 347
 and garlic, 347
 with miso, 347
 with mustard, 347
 with pineapple in coconut milk, 348
 with sea greens, 347
 soy-, 347
breading and frying, 247
broiled, 346
broiled, last-minute, 346
cheese crisp with, 219
chips, 352
creamy, with eggplant and cheese, 464
croquettes, 353
 additions to, 353–354
 with garlic, roasted, and Parmesan, 353
 Indian style, 353
 Japanese style, 353
crust, goat cheese and mushroom tart with, 227–228
crust, ricotta cheese and zucchini tart with, 228
crust, stuck-pot rice with, 526
dumplings, 350
dumplings, -stuffed, fried, 497–498
and edamame, smashed
 with curry powder, 617
 with miso, 617
 with red curry paste, 617
 with sesame and soy, 617
in egg hash, 178
favas, stewed, with spiced onions and, 604
flatbread, flaky Indian style, stuffed with, 700–701

gnocchi, 486–487
gnocchi, eggplant, 487
gnocchi, spinach, 487
gratin, 384
 and cauliflower, with crème fraîche or sour cream, 384
 and chestnut, 384
 and manchego, 383
 mashed, 385
 and sunchoke, 384
to grill, 254
grilled, 346
grilled, last-minute, 346
hash, tempeh, 676–677
and lentils with curry, 600–601
and lentils with curry, buttery, 602
mashed, 341
 baked, 341–342
 blintzes, 198
 bulgur croquettes with, 558
 buttermilk, 343
 flavorings and garnishes, 342
 garlicky, 342
 gratin, 385
 hotcakes, garlicky, 351
 Joel Robuchon, 343
 omelet, 172
 pie, garlicky, 351
 pie, garlicky, with cheese, 351
 vegan, 342–343
 vegetable additions, 343
oven-roasted, 344–345
 buttery, 345
 cottage "fries," 345
 cottage "fries," crisp, with garlic, 345
 "fries," 345
 hash browns, 345
 seasonings for, 344
pancakes
 cheesy, 350
 to flip, *349*
 garnishes for, 350–351
 latkes, 350

"Nik," 349–350
  for purists, 350
  panfried, crisp, 343
    and buttery, 344
    and eggs, 344
    last-minute, 343–344
    with onions, 344
    seasonings for, 344
  Provençal, 348
  Provençal, with Gruyère, 348
  quinoa with cheese and, roasted, 561–562
  salad, 68–69
    with blue cheese dressing, 71
    with Cheddar dressing, 70
    with cream cheese dressing, 70
    grilled, 69
    hash brown, crisp shredded, with red pepper vinaigrette, 70
    potatoes for, 70
    rémoulade, 47
  samosas, and pea, 746
  skin crumbles, 805
  "smashed," 342
  soup
    and leek, 106–107
    and leek, Korean style, 107
    with leeks, puréed, 107
    selecting potato for, 108
    vichyssoise, 107
    vichyssoise, vegan, 107
  soups with, 136
  steamed, 341
  stir fried, curried, 348–349
  stir fried, Korean style, 349
  tortellini, 484
  tortilla, 184
  twice-baked, fillings for, 338
  types of, 337, 340
  in vegetable burger, fresh spring, 664
  watercress soup, with pears and, 133
Potato flour, 683

Pot holders and mitts, 13
Pots and pans, 9–11
Pot stickers, 494
Pound cake
  cornmeal, 849
  ginger, 849
  strudel, leftover, 881
  vanilla-lime, 849–850
  yogurt, 850
Powdered sugar, 834
Pozole
  about, 542
  with beans, 544–545
  with mole, 545–546
  with mole, creamier, 546
  samp and peas, 545
Precooked grains. *See* Grains, precooked
Preserved lemon. *See* Lemon(s), preserved
Pressed tofu, 639, *656*
  salad, 652
Pressure cooker, 16
Provençal potatoes, 348
  with Gruyère, 348
Provençal style tofu, 649–650
Prune(s)
  -cognac bread pudding, 886
  kidney beans with, piquant, 586
  to macerate and season, 416
  paella with, simple, 523
  split yellow peas and rice with, 612
Pudding(s)
  apricot or peach, 885
  banana, real, 884
  basics of, 881
  bread. *See* Bread pudding
  chocolate, 884
  cornmeal, Indian, 896
  cornmeal, vegan, 896
  green tea or Earl Grey, 885
  rice, cinnamon-nut, 895
  rice, coconut, 895
  semolina, baked, 895–896
  semolina, chocolate, 896

  tapioca, citrus, 885
  tapioca, jasmine-scented, 885
  tapioca, rose, 885
  tembleque (coconut), 884
  vanilla, 883–884
  vanilla, traditional, 884
Puffs. *See also* Shortbread, cheese
  baked, 697
  cheese, 697
  cream, 697
  doughnut, sweet or savory, 696–697
Pumpernickel-raisin bread, 718–719
Pumpkin
  bread, ginger, with hazelnuts, 692
  pan-fried
    with cranberries and pistachios, 367
    with tomato sauce, 366–367
    with tomato sauce, cocoa, and pumpkin seeds, 367
    with tomato sauce, Parmesan, and basil, 367
    with tomato sauce, yogurt, and mint, 367
  soup, 133
    Argentinean, 134
    bread-and-water, 134
    with chipotle, 133
    Indian style, 133–134
    rustic, 134
  waffles with maple cream cheese sauce, 205–206
Pumpkin seed(s)
  about, 321
  chiles rellenos with corn and, 400
  pumpkin, pan-fried, with tomato sauce, cocoa and, 367
  sauce, 789
Puntarella, 34–35

Purée(s). *See also* Pesto
  bean. *See* Bean(s), puréed
  fruit, 862
  green olive mojo, 769
  herb, 769
  parsley, 768–769
  to thicken sauce, 795
  tofu, 640
  vegetable. *See* Puréed vegetables
Puréed pine nut sauce, 797
Puréed potato soup with leeks, 107
Puréed salsa fresca, 750
Puréed spicy soybeans with kimchi, 609
Puréed tomato sauce, 449
Puréed tomato soup, 113
Puréed vegetables
  basics of, 387–388, 390
  essential purée, 390
  in griddle cakes and fritters, 392
  leftovers, 391
  rich purée, 390
  suggestions for, 388–389
  vegetables for, 388
Puttanesca sauce, 449
Puy lentils, 599

Quesadilla(s)
  all-cheese, 741
  chile-bean, 741
  chile-bean, grilled, 741
  for one, 741
Queso fresco
  about, 210
  avocado salad with, six-layer, 53
  black bean cakes with, 629–630
Quiche
  basics of, 187
  cheese, 187–188
  leftovers in, 189
  "Lorraine," 188
  mushroom(s), 188–189
  onion, 188
  pesto, 188
  ricotta and Parmesan, 188
  vegetables for, 189

Quick-braised burdock and
carrots, 274–275
Quick-braised edamame with
fishless fish sauce,
584
Quick-braised edamame with
green tea, 584
Quick-braised edamame with
ponzu, 584
Quick-braised edamame with
sea greens, 584
Quick-braised vegetables, Thai
style, 379–380
Quick bread(s). *See* Bread(s),
quick
Quick-cooked bok choy,
269–270
Quick-cooked edamame with
kombu dashi or soy
sauce, 583–584
Quickest easiest waffles, 204
Quick-glazed carrots,
278–279
Quick-glazed carrots with
orange and ginger,
279
Quick pickled mango or
papaya, 95
Quick-pickled vegetables, 95
Quick-pickled vegetables,
Mexican style, 95
Quick ricotta pots, 877
Quick spice-marinated feta
patties, 211
Quick wheat berry stew with
citrus, dried fruit,
and nuts, 565
Quick wheat berry stew with
fall vegetables, 565
Quick wheat berry stew with
spring vegetables,
565
Quince
about, 436
-ginger soup, 905
sorbet, 892
Quinoa
about, 534, 535
with cabbage, silky, 560
cottage cheese pancakes
with, 226–227

crust, white bean and sage
tart with, 625
with goat cheese, baked,
217
with leeks, caramelized, 560
with onions, caramelized,
559–560
with potatoes and cheese,
roasted, 561–562
red peppers stuffed with
goat cheese and,
399
ricotta dumplings, 225–226
rösti, and carrot, 561
rösti, and parsnip, 560–561
salad with lemon, spinach,
and poppy seeds,
83–84
salad with tempeh, 84
and sweet potato salad,
84–85
and sweet potato salad,
southwestern, 85
Quinoa flour, 478
Quinoa pasta, 443

Radicchio
about, 34–35, 300
braised, 300–301
to grill, 253
grilled or broiled with balsamic glaze, 301
kasha with, 563
slaw, Mediterranean, 301
Radish(es)
about, 354
braised and glazed,
354–355
braised and glazed, with
miso sauce, 355
daikon and dulse salad,
spicy, 55
daikon purée, 389
red lentils with, 600
salsa, 752–753
to salt, 46
yogurt soup with, 159
Raisin(s)
cake, 854
carrots with dates and,
279–280

cauliflower, roasted, with
vinaigrette and, 282
cauliflower, sautéed, with
almonds, saffron
and, 282
couscous with fennel and,
92–93
to macerate and season,
416
-pumpernickel bread,
718–719
rum-, ricotta cheesecake,
877
Raita, 774
Ramekins, 12
Ramen noodles
about, 464–465
vastly improved store-
bought, 466
Ranch dressing, real, 772
Raspberry(ies)
about, 421
gelées, 888
-red wine sorbet, 892
vinegar, 761
Ratatouille
baked mixed vegetables
with olive oil,
380–381
salad, 64
stovetop mixed vegetables
with olive oil, 381
Ravioli
cheese, 483
to make, *482*
mushroom-cheese, 483
nudi, 485–486
spinach, 483
spinach-ricotta, 481–482
to stuff and seal, *494*
Raw onion chutney, 783
Raw sugar, 834
Real banana pudding, 884
Real garlicky nut chutney,
785
Really spicy tofu and peas in
coconut milk, 649
Real ranch dressing, 772
Real vanilla granola, 574
Red cabbage with apples,
277–278

Red chile sauce Indian style,
793
Red chile sauce North African
style, 793
Red curry paste, 823,
830–831
smashed edamame and
potatoes with, 617
Red delicious apple, 418
Red enchilada sauce, 788
Red lentils
about, 599
with celery root, 600
with chaat masala, 600
dal, simplest, 600
with radish, 600
and rhubarb with Indian
spices, 600
with tomatoes, fresh, 600
Red pasta, 480
Red pepper(s)
-avocado salsa, 751
pinto beans with, 594
roasted, 333–334
chutney, 787
egg salad with, 180
layered mozzarella with
olives and, 221
macaroni and goat
cheese with, 461
in pasta, red, 480
stuffed with quinoa and
goat cheese, 399
and tomato sauce, 449
vinaigrette
hash brown salad with,
crisp shredded, 70
sweet potato salad with,
grilled, 69
sweet potato salad with,
roasted, 69
Red pepper flakes, hot, 825,
827
Red rice, 503, 504
Reduction sauce, 795
Red wine. *See* Wine, red
Red wine vinegar, 760
Refried beans. *See* Bean(s),
refried
Refrigeration, 30
Reheating food, 30, 31–32

Relish, mustard, 776
Rémoulade
    carrot, 45
    celery, 47
    chayote (mirilton), 47
    potato, 47
Rhubarb
    about, 436–437
    -apple cobbler, 878
    and lentils with Indian
        spices, 600
    omelet, flat, with cottage
        cheese and, 183
    -orange soup, 904
Rice. *See also* Brown rice; Rice
        cakes; Wild rice
    baked
        with chile, cheese, and
            tomatoes, 569
        and red kidney beans,
            Jamaican style,
            510
        and white beans, Tuscan
            style, 510
    baked, simpler-than-pilaf,
        515
        brown rice, 515
        with coconut, 516
        with herbs, 515
        with tomato, 516
    balls, 532–533
    balls, grilled, 533
    balls, with sesame, 533
    bean gumbo, one-pot,
        611
    biryani, 512–513
    black beans and, Brazilian,
        620
    in black-eyed peas with
        smoked tofu,
        610–611
    black Thai, with coconut
        milk and edamame,
        532
    cabbage stuffed with lentils
        and, *401*, 401
    cabbage stuffed with lentils
        and, in red wine
        sauce, 401
    cakes, Parmesan, 569–570
    with cheese, 508

with chickpeas, 509
with chickpeas and
    almonds, spiced,
    509–510
with chickpeas, curried,
    510
coconut, 507–508
    and beans, 508
    with coconut bits, 508
    spicy, 508
    sweet, 508
egg hash with, 178–179
flavorings for, 505–506
fried
    additions to, 521–522
    with egg, or without,
        520–521
    with lettuce, basic, 521
    with onions, simplest,
        520
    with peppers, simplest,
        519–520
    pineapple, 521
    Thai style, basic, 521
    tips, 519
    with vegetables, frozen,
        basic, 521
Japanese, with edamame
    and sea greens,
    532
Japanese, with tomatoes
    and fermented
    black beans, 532
Japanese style, mixed,
    531–532
jook, 140
jook with vegetables, 140
kimchi, 512
and lentil crêpes (dosas),
    744–745
and lentil crêpes (dosas),
    brown rice, 745
lexicon of, 501–505
long-grain, 502–503
microwaving, 505
and mung beans with apri-
    cots, dried,
    611–612
and mung beans with car-
    rots, spiced, 612
paella. *See* Paella

pilaf. *See* Pilaf, rice
pudding, cinnamon-nut,
    895
pudding, coconut, 895
risotto. *See* Risotto
salad, 79
    citrus, 82
    Indian style, 82
    Japanese style, 79
    Mexican style, 79, 82
    tomato, 82, 83
    variations, 80–81
    wild rice, with cucumber
        and yogurt, 83
short-grain, 504–505
soubise (cooked in onions),
    514
and split yellow peas with
    prunes, 612
sticky
    about, 502
    long-grain, 503
    with shallots and
        peanuts or coconut,
        507
    short-grain, 504
    with soy sauce and
        coconut milk, 507
    steamed, 507
    with vegetable filling,
        507
storage of, 501
stuck-pot. *See* Stuck-pot
    rice
stuffings, 407
sushi, 527
sushi style, with edamame
    and shiso, 532
tempeh
    with brown rice and
        spinach, 676
    with mushrooms and,
        676
    with peas and, 676
    with spinach and,
        675–676
tofu, and peas in coconut
    milk, creamy, 649
tomatoes stuffed with,
    398–399, *399*
white, 505

white, and black beans,
    510
yellow, the best way,
    513–514
yellow, the fast way, 514
Rice cakes
    braised, 474
    egg "noodle" soup with,
        154
    with kimchi, 474
    with Shaoxing wine, 474
    with sweet soy sauce,
        473
    with sweet soy sauce and
        vegetables,
        473–474
Rice flour, 682
    crumble topping, 870
Rice noodle(s)
    brown, stir-fried, with
        pickled vegetables,
        473
    salad with grapefruit and
        peanuts, Jean-
        Georges's, 93–94
    with sweet soy sauce, 474
    wide, stir-fried, with pick-
        led vegetables,
        472–473
Rice paper wrappers
    about, 465
    for egg rolls, 742
    for summer rolls, 743
Ricer, 15
Rice sticks
    about, 464
    in noodle bowls, 468
Rice syrup, 835
Rice vermicelli, 464
Rice vinegar, 760
Rich golden bread, 6 ways,
    714–715
Rich golden rolls, 715
Rich golden sandwich bread,
    715
Rich macaroni and cheese,
    461
Rich nut tart, 876
Rich spinach gratin, 385
Rich vegetable purée, 390
Rich zucchini soup, 156

Ricotta
in calzone, 729–730
cheesecake, 876–877
cheesecake, rum-raisin, 877
-chickpea gnocchi,
626–627
dumplings, 225
panfried, 225
pesto-, 226
with quinoa or millet,
225–226
fresh, 230
lima or fava beans, baked
with Parmesan and,
621
pancakes, lemon, 203
pots, quick, 877
quiche, and Parmesan, 188
ravioli, spinach-, 481–482
ziti, baked, with, 459
and zucchini tart with
potato crust, 228
Ricotta salata, 210
Risotto
basics of, 516–517
with four cheeses, 418
"frittata," 571–572
with herbs, 517
with lemon, 518
with mushrooms, dried and
fresh, 518–520
with nuts, 418
with red wine, 518
rices for, 504
simple, 517
with vegetables and herbs,
517–518
"Risotto," pearl couscous
with artichoke hearts, 552
with butternut squash,
553
creamy, 552
alla Milanese, 552
with tomato, spicy, 553
Risotto style orzo, 451
lemon, 451
Roasted chestnuts, 287
Roasted chickpeas, 618
Roasted chickpeas and pistachios, 618
Roasted fruit, 411

Roasted garlic teriyaki sauce,
779
Roasted mushroom borscht,
110
Roasted nuts, 318, 321, 323
herbed, 323
Roasted pepper mayonnaise,
771
Roasted peppers and cheese
empanadas, 747
Roasted quinoa with potatoes
and cheese,
561–562
Roasted red pepper chutney,
787
Roasted seeds, 318, 321
Roasted vegetables
about, 238–239
artichoke hearts, 259–260
asparagus, 261–262
beet borscht, 109–110
beets, and goat cheese
gratin, 383
Brussels sprouts with garlic,
273
cauliflower, Manchurian
style, 283–284
cauliflower, with raisins and
vinaigrette, 282
corn chowder, 135
corn on the cob, 290
fennel with orange, 303
garlic, 304
garlic, faster, 304
onion halves, 330–331
onion halves, balsamic-,
331
onion halves, cream-, 331
onion salad, 65–66
potatoes, oven-, 344–345
buttery, 345
cottage "fries," 345
cottage "fries," crisp,
with garlic, 345
"fries," 345
hash browns, 345
red peppers, 333–334
scallions, 331
scallions, Asian style, 331
squash, winter, pieces in
the shell, 366

squash, winter, slices, 366
stock, 102
sweet potato salad with red
pepper vinaigrette,
69
Thai style, 381–382
tomatoes, oven-
canned plum, 375
everyday, 375
fresh plum, 375
Roasting pans, 12
Roasting technique, 27,
238–239
Rock salt, 808
Roll (oblique) cut, 21
Rolled kale with feta and
olives, 308–309
Rolled kale with tofu and fermented black
beans, 308–309
Rolling pin, 14
Rolls, bread
dinner, to shape, 704
French
fast, 707–708
more leisurely, 708
overnight, 709
whole grain, 708–709
rich golden, 715
Rolls, egg. See Egg rolls
Rolls, summer, 743–744
Romaine
about, 34
seaweed, balsamic, 57
seaweed, high-flavor, 57
seaweed salad, 56–57
Roman style broccoli, cauliflower, or just
about anything else,
271
Rome apple, 418
Root vegetables. See Veg-
etable(s), root; spe-
cific vegetables
Roquefort
and endive salad, 44–45
and mushroom gratin, 383
Rosemary
about, 766
baked potato, -scented,
339

-lemon bars, 846
-pine nut tart, 876
-plum upside-down cake,
853–854
winter squash, braised, in
caramel sauce with
balsamic vinegar
and, 368
Rose water
glaze, 858
tapioca pudding, 885
Rösti
quinoa and carrot, spicy,
561
quinoa and parsnip,
560–561
Roux, 795
Rum-raisin ricotta cheesecake,
877
Rustic pine nut sauce,
796–797
Rustic pine nut sauce with
cheese, 797
Rustic pumpkin soup, 134
Rutabaga
flat omelet with, 184
purée, 390
Rye berry(ies)
about, 539
gratin with leeks and tomatoes, 568
gratin with leeks and tomatoes, creamy, 568
gratin with leeks and tomatoes, vegan,
568–569
Rye flour, 478, 681

Saffron
about, 813
bulgur with, creamed, 556
butternut squash with
almonds and, 365
cauliflower, sautéed, with
almonds, raisins
and, 282
chickpea soup with
almonds and,
117–118
cookies, -olive oil, 842
fruit and nut bread, 715

and garlic mayonnaise,
    grilled eggplant
    salad with, 65
ice cream, 890
paella with oranges, olives
    and, simple, 523
rice with chickpeas, 510
Sage
    about, 766
    leaves, fried, broiled tomato
        and blue cheese
        salad with, 58
    pasta with butter, Parmesan
        and, 447
    and white bean tart with
        quinoa crust, 625
Saimin noodles, 464–465
Salad(s)
    bean. *See* Bean salad(s)
    egg. *See* Egg(s), salad
    grain. *See* Grain salad(s)
    green. *See* Green salad(s);
        Sea greens salad(s)
    main course, 86
    make-ahead, 71
    pressed tofu, 652
    seaweed sprinkles in, 56
    serving suggestions, 37
    vegetable. *See* Slaw(s);
        Tomato salad(s);
        Vegetable salad(s),
        cooked; Vegetable
        salad(s), raw
Salad bowl and servers, 14
Salad dressing(s). *See* Dress-
    ing(s)
Salad mixes (mesclun), 35
Salad spinner, 13–14, *36*
Salsa(s)
    apricot and onion, grilled,
        792
    borracha, 788
    for burritos and tacos, 739,
        740
    chile-garlic, super-spicy,
        789
    chile pico de verde, 751
    chipotle-cherry, 752
    citrus, 752
    corn, 751
    cucumber, Thai style, 753

fresh, about, 750
fruit, 751–752
green chile, 789
jícama, 751
papaya, 751–752
papaya, green, Thai style,
    753
peach and corn, grilled,
    792
peach melon tomato, 752
pepita pico de verde, 751
persimmon, 752
pineapple and onion,
    grilled, 791–792
radish, 752–753
roja, 787–788
    charred, 788
    smoky and hot, 788
sea green, 753
sofrito, 788
and summer squash gratin,
    387
tomatillo, cooked, 788
tomatillo, fresh, 751
tomato, cooked. *See* Salsa,
    roja
tomato, fresh
    avocado-red pepper, 751
    bean, 751
    cheese, Mexican, 750
    Chilean, 750
    cruda, 751
    green tomato pico de
        verde, 751
    peach melon, 752
    puréed, 750
    salsa fresca, 750
Salsify, 355
Salt
    basics of, 806–807
    lexicon of, 807–808
    pickling, 94
Salted baked potato, 339
Salted cabbage with sichuan
    peppercorns, 95
Salty-sweet popcorn, 292
Sambar powder, 816, 823
Samosas
    to fill and form, *746*, 746
    fillings for, 747
    lentil, baked, 745–746

lentil, fried, 746
potato and pea, 746
spinach and cheese, 747
Samp
    about, 542–543
    and peas, 545
Sandwich(es), 730–737. *See
    also* Toasts
    breads for, 730
    cheeses for, 210
    cold, 731–732
    fillings and spreads,
        730–735
    hot, 732–734
    keeping fresh, 735
    wraps, 736
Sandwich bread
    about, 711–712
    bran and oat, 713
    half whole wheat, 713
    rich golden, 715
    to shape, *712*
    white, 712–713
Saran, Suvir, 283, 744
Sauce(s). *See also* Mayonnaise;
        Mole; Pesto; Nut
        butter(s); Salsa(s);
        Vinaigrette
    Asian style, 777–780
    balsamic syrup, 798–799
    barbecue
        Asian, 790
        beer, 790
        bourbon, 790
        chipotle, 789
        curry, 789
        fast, down-home, 789
        horseradish, 789
        lighter, 790
        marinated tofu with,
            553
        mustardy, 789
    béchamel
        and asparagus gratin,
            383
        11 ways, 803–804
        onions, stuffed, 397
    bistro, creamy, 799
        mustard, 799
        tarragon, 799
    brown, 803

butter(s)
    beurre noisette, 804
    black, 802
    brown, 801–802
    compound, 800–801
caper, 804
caramel
    tofu in, braised,
        650–651
    winter squash in,
        braised, 368
    winter squash in,
        braised, with bal-
        samic vinegar and
        rosemary, 368
chile
    and coconut, 793
    green, smooth, Indian
        style, 792–793
    red, Indian style, 793
    red, North African style,
        793
    -scallion, 780
    -yogurt, 793
chimichurri, 769
curry, 804
deglazing pan, 28
dessert. *See* Dessert sauce(s)
dipping. *See* Dipping
    sauce(s)
enchilada, green, 788–789
enchilada, green, cheese
    enchiladas with,
    224
enchilada, red, 788
fishless fish, 778
fishless fish, quick-braised
    edamame with,
    584
garlic-scallion, 779
ginger-scallion, 779
with grains, precooked,
    539
herb, 804
herb purées, 769
hollandaise, 802–803
hollandaise, blender, 803
lemon, 804
maple cream cheese, pump-
    kin waffles with,
    205–206

Sauce(s) *(Continued)*
  miso
    carrot, with ginger,
      781–782
    nutty, 782
    with radishes, turnips or
      other root vegeta-
      bles, braised and
      glazed, 355
    tahini, 782
    walnut-, green beans
      tossed with,
      305–306
  mojo, green olive, 769
  mornay (cheese), 804
  mushroom, 448
  mushroom, béchamel, 804
  mustard, 804
  mustard, cold, 771
  nut. *See also* Sauce(s),
      peanut; pine nut;
      walnut
    béchamel, 804
    boozy, 798
    cranberry-, creamy, 798
    creamy, 797–798
    creamy, with arugula or
      sorrel, 798
  peanut, six ways, 794–796
    curry, 795
    lighter, 796
    simpler, 796
    southern style, 796
    sweet, 796
  pine nut
    ancho-, 797
    lemony, 797
    puréed, 797
    rustic, 796–797
    rustic, with cheese, 797
    with tomatoes, 797
  pumpkin seed, 789
  red wine, cabbage stuffed
      with lentils and rice
      in, 401
  shallot, 803
  tahini
    coconut, 796
    curry, 796
    garlic, roasted, 796
    minty, 796

  pepper, roasted, 796
  yogurt, 796
  teriyaki, 779
    garlic, roasted, 779
    mushroom, 779
    onion, caramelized, 779
    tropical, 779
  to thicken, 795
  tomato. *See* Tomato sauce(s)
  vinegar-based, 798–800
  walnut
    -miso, green beans tossed
      with, 305–306
    pasta with, rich, 458
    pasta with, 458
  Worcestershire, hold the
      anchovies, 799–800
  yogurt
    about, 773–774
    beet salad with, 66
    chile-, 793
    the simplest, 774–775
    uses for, 775
    variations, 774
Sauerkraut soup, 110–111
  cherry, 111
  creamy, 111
  mushroom, 111
Sautéed fruit, 411
Sautéed mushrooms, 314–315
  with Asian flavors, 315
Sautéed vegetables
  about, 237–238
  Brussels sprouts with hazel-
      nuts, 273
  cauliflower
    with almonds, raisins,
      and saffron, 282
    breaded, 281
    with feta and mint, 282
    with garlic, vinegar, and
      capers, 282
    with onion and olives,
      281
  eggplant, 295–296
    with greens, 296
    with onions and honey,
      296
    with tomatoes, 296
  olives, 326
  olives with croutons, 326

  peppers and onions, pan
      cooked, my mom's,
      34
  plantains, ripe, 336
  zucchini or chayote, 362
Sautéing technique, 25–26
Savory doughnuts, 697
Savory muffins, 694
Savory oatcakes with peas and
      carrots, 570
Savory peach or apple gratin
      with coriander, 384
Savory piecrust, 867
Savory tart crust, 868
Scale, kitchen, 14
Scallion(s)
  about, 327
  -chile sauce, 780
  cucumbers, -marinated, 47
  egg noodles, fresh, with
      paprika and, 497
  favas with, 594
  -garlic sauce, 779
  -ginger sauce, 779
  to grill, 254
  grilled, 331
  in oil, flavored, 758
  roasted, 331
  roasted, Asian style, 331
  with tofu, stir-fried,
      645–646
    and black beans, 646
    and orange zest and
      chiles, 646
    and walnuts, 646
Scissors, kitchen, 14
Scones, 688, 695–696
Scramble, cheese. *See* Cheese,
      fresh, scramble
Scrambled eggs. *See* Egg(s),
      scrambled
Scrambled tofu. *See* Tofu,
      scrambled
Scrambled tortillas, 176
  with scallions and chiles,
      176–177
Sea beans, 356
Sea green(s)
  about, 355–356
  and cucumber soup, cold,
      159–160

  dulse "shake," 818
  with edamame, quick-
      braised, 584
  egg drop soup with, 155
  in fishless fish sauce, 778
  gyoza, steamed, with
      edamame and,
      493
  Japanese rice with
      edamame and,
      532
  lexicon of, 356
  "mayo," seaweed, 773
  "mayo," seaweed, edamame
      salad with, 76
  nori chips, 357
  nori, Japanese egg crêpes
      with, 176
  nori "shake," 817–818
  in ponzu sauce, 780
  potatoes with, braised,
      347
  to rehydrate, 53
  salsa, 753
  soybeans with shiitakes
      and, 590
  sprinkles, in salads, 56
  stir-fry
    and celery, 357
    and mushroom, 357
    and noodle, 357
  -stuffed eggs, 181
Sea greens salad(s), 53–57
  about, 53
  arame
    bean thread noodles
      with, 55
    and bean thread noodles
      with fermented
      black beans, 55
    and bean thread noodles
      with Ponzu dipping
      sauce, 54–55
  dulse, spicy
    and bean sprout, 55
    and carrot, 55
    and celery, 55
    and daikon, 55
  romaine, 56–57
  romaine, balsamic, 57
  romaine, high-flavor, 57

simple, 53–54
slaw, 55–56
Sea salt
about, 807–808
brown sugar cookies with, 840–841
Sea slaw, 55–56
Seasoned crumbled tempeh, 674
Seaweed. *See* Sea green(s); Sea greens salad(s)
Seckel pears, 433
Seeds. *See also specific seeds*
about, 318, 321–322
in cookies, 839
grains, precooked, with, 539
in granola, crunchy, 573
lexicon of, 319–320
-and-nut burgers, 668
to roast and toast, 318, 321
sauces, 794–798
toasted, pasta with, 444
Seitan
basics of, 668–669
grilled or broiled, 672
and lentil loaf, 670
to make, 669–670, *670*
and mushroom loaf, 670–671
oven-roasted, 672
with chile, 672–673
with curry, 672–673
with garlic, 672–673
with ginger, 672–673
sauces for, 672–673
pan-seared, 671
simmering liquid for, dark, 671
simmering liquid for, golden, 671
Self-rising flour, 681
Semolina
bars, -apricot, 845
pudding, baked, 895–896
pudding, chocolate, 896
Semolina flour, 478
Senegalese style peanut soup, 124–125
Serrano chile, 826

Sesame (seeds). *See also* Tahini
about, 813
-chile paste, beer-glazed black beans, Korean style, 586
-chile paste, smashed edamame and potatoes, Korean style, 617
edamame and potatoes, smashed, with soy and, 617
eggplant, -fried, 245
and eggplant fritters, 395
falafel, 626
ice cream, 891
meringue, sweet, 903
millet carrot mash with ginger, soy and, 566
with mung beans, fried, 589
noodles, cold, 466–467
rice balls with, 533
rice breadsticks, 711
and soy dipping sauce and marinade, Korean style, 778
stuck-pot rice with almonds, ginger and, 526
tofu burger with adzuki beans, 667
Sesame oil
dark, 756
light, 757
Seven-spice mix, Japanese, 817, 823
Shallots
about, 358
chard with oranges and, 286
crisp, 312
to mince, *358*
in oil, flavored, 758
sauce, 803
sticky rice with peanuts or coconut and, 507
stir-fried, 312
Shallow frying, 25–26

Sharp cheddar fondue with red wine, 222
Shaved artichoke salad, 50–51
Shaved mushroom salad, 51
Sherry, kidney beans with apples and, 586
Sherry vinegar, 760
Shiitake(s)
about, 314
chickpeas with, 597
dried, stir-fried broccoli with, 271
gigantes with, 588
in parchment, 363
salad, grilled, with soy vinaigrette, 63
soybeans with miso and, 590–591
soybeans with sea greens and, 590
tofu, braised, with eggplant and, 650
with tofu, stir-fried, 647
white beans with, 597
Shiso
about, 767
rice, sushi style, with edamame and, 532
Shocking vegetables, 236, 241
Shortbread, cheese, 696
blue, 696
herbed, 696
pecorino, 696
spiced, 696
Sichuan peppercorn(s)
about, 809
with cabbage, salted, 95
cookies, 841
Silicone mat, 15
Silken tofu, 639
Simmering technique, 24
Simple, easy and fast vegetable stock, 101
Simple cheese crisps, 220
Simple cheese enchiladas, 224
Simple green salad, 38
Simple miso citrus dipping sauce, 781
Simple miso dipping sauce, 781

Simple miso herb dipping sauce, 781
Simple miso soy dipping sauce, 781
Simple paella with eggplant, 523
Simple paella with eggs, 523
Simple paella with fava beans, 523
Simple paella with mushroom caps, 523
Simple paella with oranges, olives, and saffron, 523
Simple paella with prunes, 523
Simple paella with spinach and lemon zest, 523
Simple risotto, 517
Simpler macaroni and cheese, 461
Simpler peanut sauce, 796
Simpler-than-pilaf baked rice, 515–516
Simple seaweed salad, 53–54
Simplest asparagus gratin, 383
Simplest dal, 600
Simplest fried rice with onions, 519–520
Simplest fried rice with peppers, 519–520
Simplest huevos rancheros, 174
Simplest Indian style flatbread (chapati), 698–699
Simplest omelet, 171–172
Simplest onion gratin, 383
Simplest scrambled tofu, 656
Simplest split pea soup, 118–119
Simplest vegan bean burgers, 661
Simplest yogurt sauce, 774–775
Simple syrup, 857
Six-layer avocado salad with mangoes, 53
Six-layer avocado salad with queso fresco, 53
Skewers, 14

Skillets, 11
Skimmers and "spiders,"
        Asian, 14
Slaw(s)
    apple, 49
    cabbage and carrot, Mexi-
        can style, 49
    coleslaw, spicy no-mayo,
        49
    Mediterranean, 301
    to salt cabbage, 46
    sea, 55–56
Slicing vegetables, 20, *21*
Slightly more refined deep-
        fried tofu, 644
Slurry, 795, 883
Smashed edamame and pota-
        toes. *See* Edamame,
        and potatoes,
        smashed
"Smashed" potatoes, 342
Smoked cheese fondue with
        beer, 222
Smoked paprika peppers, 335
Smoked-tea chili, 608
Smoked tofu and turnip egg
        rolls, 742
Smoke point, 755–756
Smoky baked black beans,
        620
Smoky and hot bulgur chili,
        558
Smoky and hot salsa roja, 788
Smoky onion gratin, 385
Smoky scrambled tofu, 655
Smooth chickpea soup, 118
Smothered grits gratin with
        arugula and garlic,
        551
Snap peas with tofu, stir-fried,
        647
Snow peas with tofu, stir-
        fried, 647
Soak, cake. *See* Cake soak
Soba noodles
    about, 464
    with dipping sauce,
        467–468
    in noodle bowls, 468
Socca pizza, 633
Soft-boiled egg, 165

Somen noodles
    about, 464
    in noodle bowls, 468
Sorbet
    basics of, 889
    flavors for, 892–893
    mango or apricot, 893–894
Sorghum, 836
Sorrel
    about, 358–359
    nut sauce with, creamy,
        798
    soup, creamy, 132
Soufflé(s)
    basics of, 185
    cheese, 185–186
    cheese, herb and, 186
    chestnut, 187
    goat cheese and dried apri-
        cot, 186
    pea or other vegetable, 186
    pesto, 186
    polenta or millet, 187
    spinach, 187
Soufflé dish, 12
Souffléed pinto bean tart with
        millet crust,
        624–625
Soup(s), 99–160. *See also*
        Broth; Stock, veg-
        etable
    avocado, ultra-fast, 157
    barley
        mushroom, 139
        with roasted seasonal
            vegetables, 139
        with seasonal vegetables,
            138–139
        with summer vegetables,
            139
    bean. *See* Bean soup(s)
    borscht
        beet, roasted, 109–110
        beet or mushroom, cold-
            roasted, 110
        consommé, 110
        mushroom, roasted, 110
    bread, 121–122
    bread, and tomato, 112
    broccoli, creamy, 130
    cabbage in, 127

carrot
    creamy, 129
    glazed, 105
    glazed, with garlic,
        tequila, and lime,
        105
    glazed, with orange and
        ginger, 105
    mustard-glazed, 105
    Thai style, 129–130
cauliflower
    creamy, 130
    Indian, 130
    Italian style, 105–106
celery, creamy, 129
with cheese, 142
chile bisque, 131
coconut, curried, with
        lemongrass,
        137–138
cold soups, 156–160
condiments for, 131
corn chowder, 135
    cheesy, 135
    roasted, 135
    thicker, 135
    with tomatoes, 135
couscous, North African,
        140–141
creamy soups, 128–138
with croutons, 106
cucumber and seaweed,
        cold, 159–160
dessert. *See* Dessert soup(s)
egg drop, eight ways,
        154–156
    curry, 155
    Italian style, 155
    Mexican style, 155
    poached egg, 155
    with sea greens, 155
    with spinach, 155
egg "noodle"
    with bean thread, 154
    with mushrooms,
        153–154
    with rice cake, 154
with eggs, 152
farro, 141
farro, -mushroom, 141
fennel, creamy, 129

to flavor, 100
to freeze, 104
frozen vegetables in, 125
"goulash"
    and bok choy, 150–151
    more traditional, 151
    tempeh, 151
    improvising ingredients for,
        107
Jerusalem artichoke,
        creamy, 130–131
jook, 140
jook with vegetables, 140
main dish soups, 120
minestrone, 123
minestrone, herbed, 123
miso, 152–153
mixed vegetable soups,
        122–128
with nondairy creams and
        milks, 132, 136
noodle, 143–147
    fideo, garlic, 144
    Persian, 144–145
    pho, faux, 143–144
    spaetzle, the easy way,
        146
    udon, with green tea
        broth, 145
    whole wheat noodles in
        curry broth, 147
with noodles, 142–143
onion, 108
    with almonds, Spanish,
        109
    charred, 109
    more classic, 109
parsley, cream of, 131–132
parsley, cream of, gratinéed,
        132
pasta and bean, 123
peanut
    creamy, 125
    Senegalese style,
        124–125
    Virginian, 134–135
    Virginian, vegan, 135
with potatoes, 108
potato and leek, 106–107
potato and leek, Korean
        style, 107

potato with leeks, puréed, 107
pumpkin, 133
   Argentinean, 134
   bread-and-water, 134
   with chipotle, 133
   Indian style, 133–134
   rustic, 134
sauerkraut, 110–111
   cherry, 111
   creamy, 111
   mushroom, 111
single-vegetable soups, 104–105
thickeners, 136
with tofu, 147–151
   "goulash," and bok choy, 150–151
   "goulash," more traditional, 151
   hot pot, tofu skins in, 149–150
   kimchi, 148
   mushroom, Korean, 148–149
   types of tofu, 147–148
tomato. See Tomato soup(s)
with tomatoes, 113
tortilla, 126–127
vegetable, mixed, southwestern, 125–126
vegetable, mixed, Spanish style, 124
vegetable, mixed, Thai style, 127–128
vegetable, Thai style, 127
vichyssoise, 107
vichyssoise, vegan, 107
watercress, with potatoes and pears, 133
watercress, spinach or sorrel, creamy, 132
wonton, 495
yogurt
   with cucumber, 158
   with nuts, 158
   with peas, fresh, 159
   with pineapple, 159
   with radish, 159

   with strawberry, 159
   with tomato, 158–159
   zucchini, rich, 156
Sour cream
   about, 207
   cabbage with tomatoes and, 277
   and cottage cheese pancakes, 202–203
   cucumber salad with, 48
   muffins, 693
   paprika peppers with, 335
   potato and cauliflower gratin with, 384
   stuck-pot rice with chiles and, 524
Sourdough bread, 709–711
Sourdough pancakes, 201
Sourdough starter, 683, 685, 710
Sour milk
   to make, 207
   pancakes, 202
Southeast Asian style mung bean pancake, 631–632
Southern style peanut sauce, 796
Southwestern
   sweet potato and quinoa salad, 85
   vegetable soup, mixed, 125–126
   vegetable soup, mixed, with avocado, 126
Soy (sauce)
   bulgur pilaf with green beans and, 557
   butternut squash with, 364
   cherry tomato salad with, 57
   cucumber salad with ginger and, 48
   edamame, quick-cooked, with, 583–584
   edamane and potatoes, smashed, with sesame and, 617
   millet carrot mash with ginger, sesame and, 566

miso dipping sauce, simple, 781
-pickled eggs, 182
potatoes, -braised, 347
and sesame dipping sauce and marinade, Korean style, 778
with soybeans, black, 608–609
sticky rice with coconut milk and, 507
sweet, rice cakes with vegetables and, 473–474
sweet, rice or cellophane noodles with, 474
tahini, 778
tempeh, braised, with tomato sauce and, 675
tofu, baked, 641
in veggie burgers, 662
vinaigrette, 763
   eggplant salad with, 64
   shiitake or portobello salad with, grilled, 63
Soybean oil, 758
Soybeans. See also Edamame
about, 578
black, with soy sauce, 608–609
and greens, 596
with kimchi, spicy, 509
with kimchi, spicy, puréed, 609
with kimchi, spicy, and stir-fried tempeh, 609
with morels and asparagus, 590
with shiitakes and miso, 590–591
with shiitakes and sea greens, 590
Soy flour, 682
Soy milk, 29
Soy nuts, 321
Soy pasta, 443
Soy protein isolate, 673

Spaetzle, 490–491
   herb, 491
   soup the easy way, 146
Spanikopita (spinach and feta pie with phyllo crust), 408–409
Spanish flavors, marinated tofu with, 653
Spanish omelet, 172
Spanish onion soup with almonds, 109
Spanish style
   lentils, braised, 598
   plantain stew, 111
   rice salad, 81
   three-bean salad, broiled, 75
   vegetable soup, mixed, 124
Sparkling wine with berries, 904
Spatula, offset, 15
Spelt, 478, 536
Spelt flour, 682
Spice(s). See also specific spices
   Asian, poached pears with, 434
   basics of, 809–810
   cake, honey-, 854
   cake, molasses-, 855
   chile paste. See Chile paste
   cookies, ginger, 841
   cookies, whole grain apple, 840
   feta, -marinated, 211
   grinder for, 16, 810
   Indian, lentils and rhubarb with, 600
   lexicon of, 810, 811–814, 820–821
   mixtures, 810, 814–818
      chaat masala, 814–815
      chili powder, 814
      citrus sprinkle, 818–819
      curry powder, fragrant, 816
      curry powder, hot, 815
      dulse "shake," 818
      five-spice powder, 816–817
      garam masala, 815
      jerk seasoning, 818

Spice(s) *(Continued)*
    nori "shake," 817–818
    sambar powder, 816
    seven-spice, Japanese, 817
    using, 823–824
    za'atar, 818
  muffins, 693
  pickling, 94, 819, 824
Spiced cheese shortbread, 696
Spiced coffee cake soak, 859
Spiced fried fresh cheese, 215
Spiced granola, 574
Spiced mung beans and rice with carrots, 612
Spiced red lentil pancakes, 632
Spiced rice with chickpeas and almonds, 509–510
Spiced stir-fried bean sprouts, 265
Spiced tomato sauce, 449
Spiced walnut bread pudding, 886
Spicy autumn vegetable burger, 665–666
Spicy bean croquettes, 627–628
Spicy bean sprout and dulse salad, 55
Spicy carrot and quinoa rösti, 561
Spicy coconut rice, 508
Spicy dulse and carrot salad, 55
Spicy dulse and daikon salad, 55
Spicy gazpacho, 157–158
Spicy Indian tomato sauce, 793–794
Spicy ketchup-braised tofu, 651–652
Spicy Korean style cabbage (kimchi), 96
Spicy mashed eggplant with yogurt and mint, 298
Spicy no-mayo coleslaw, 49
Spicy pearl couscous pilaf, 552
Spicy pickles, Asian style, 95–96

Spicy red beans, Indian style, 593
Spicy soybeans with kimchi, 609
Spicy soybeans with kimchi and stir-fried tempeh, 609
Spicy tomato pearl couscous "risotto," 553
Spicy winter squash galette, 368–369
Spinach
  about, 359
  -and-bean burgers, 662
  bulgur with, creamed, 555–556
  cannellini beans with cavatelli and, 587
  cannelloni, -cheese, 482–483
  with cheese, fresh, and yogurt, 360–361
  with cheese, fresh, and yogurt, baked, 361
  chickpeas, baked, with paneer and, 623
  chickpea soup with, 118
  with chiles, 359–360
  with chiles and coconut milk, 360
  couscous, pearl, pilaf, 552
  creamed, 330
  creamed, vegan, 330
  with currants and nuts, 360
  custard, baked, 191
  egg drop soup with, 155
  eggs au gratin with, 194
  and feta pie with phyllo crust, 408–409
  flatbread, flaky Indian style (paratha), 700
  gnocchi, 487
  gratin, rich, 385
  omelet, fresh cheese and, Indian style, 172
  pasta, 480
  pilaf with, 512
  quinoa salad with lemon, poppy seed and, 83–84
  ravioli, 483

  ravioli, -ricotta, 481–482
  salad
    with feta and nutmeg, 41–42
    with feta and nutmeg, cooked, 42
    with warm dressing and tofu croutons, 40–41
  samosas, and cheese, 747
  soufflé, 187
  soup, creamy, 132
  tempeh with brown rice and, 676
  tempeh with rice and, 675–676
Split pea soup
  simplest, 118–119
  yellow, with pantry vegetables, 119
Split yellow peas and rice with prunes, 612
Sponge (biga, poolish), 685
Spoons, 13
Spreads. *See* Dips and spreads
Springform pan, 12
Spring vegetable-stuffed eggs, 181
Sprouts. *See* Bean sprout(s)
Squash, summer. *See also* Chayote; Zucchini
  about, 361
  breading and frying, 247
  to grill, 255
  in parchment, to fold, *362*
  in parchment, and herbs, 362
  and salsa gratin, 387
Squash, winter. *See also* Butternut squash; Pumpkin
  about, 363–364
  acorn, stuffed with wild rice, 399
  braised, in caramel sauce, 368
  braised, in caramel sauce with balsamic vinegar and rosemary, 368
  breading and frying, 247

  with bread pudding, multigrain, 193
  enchiladas, 224
  galette, spicy, 368–369
  to grill, 255
  in millet bake, autumn, 566
  to peel, *364*
  roasted
    with lentils, braised, 598
    pieces in the shell, 366
    slices, 366
    wild rice with, 567
  whole, cooked three ways, 365–366
    steamed, 366
    pieces in the shell, roasted, 366
Squash blossoms
  beer-battered, 249
  breading and frying, 247
Squash seeds, 321
Stainless steel cookware, 9, 11
Star anise, 813
  -ginger ice cream, 890
Star fruit, 422
Steamed dumplings. *See* Dumplings, steamed
Steamed sticky rice, 507
Steamed vegetables, 237
  artichokes, 258–259
  cauliflower, basic, 281
  corn on the cob, 288–289
  corn on the cob, milk-, 289
  eggplant, 297
  greens, 239–240
  leeks, 312
  potatoes, 341
  root, 240
  tender, 240
  winter squash, whole, 366
Steaming basket, 14–15, *25*, 237
Steaming technique, 24–25
Steel, sharpening knives with, 8–9, *18*
Stevia, 835
Stew(s)
  barley and mushroom, 540
  barley and mushroom, deeper, 541

buckwheat, with tofu and
kale, 563
fava beans, stewed, with
potatoes and spiced
onions, 604
fava beans, stewed, with
tahini, 604
fava beans, stewed, with
za'atar, 604
fruit, dried, and lima,
594–595
mushroom, 137
mushroom, with green
beans, 137
okra, with roux, 324–325
okra, with tomatoes,
324–325
plantain, Spanish style,
111
red curry, hard-cooked eggs
in, 195
vegetable, summer, with
wheat berries,
564–565
wheat berry, with citrus,
dried fruit, and
nuts, quick, 565
wheat berry, with fall
vegetables, quick,
565
wheat berry, with spring
vegetables, quick,
565
Sticky rice. *See* Rice, sticky
Stir-fried rice noodles
brown, with pickled vegetables, 473
wide, with pickled vegetables, 472–473
Stir-fried tofu
basics of, 644–645
with bell peppers or
other vegetables,
647
with broccoli or cauliflower,
647
with cabbage, kale, collards,
or other greens,
648
with peas, snow peas, or
snap peas, 647

with scallions, 645–646
and black beans, 646
orange zest, and chiles,
646
and walnuts, 646
with shiitake mushrooms,
647
to thicken with cornstarch,
645
Stir-fried vegetables, 242–243
about, 242
additions to, 243, 244
asparagus, 262
bean sprouts, spiced, 265
broccoli, 270–271
broccoli, with dried shi-
itakes, 271
eggplant-tofu, 300
green beans and tofu skins,
306–307
green beans and tofu skins
with peanuts and
cilantro, 307
leeks or shallots, 312
peppers and onions, pan-
cooked, Asian style,
334–335
potatoes, curried, 348–349
potatoes, Korean style, 349
sea green and celery, 357
sea green and mushroom,
357
sea green and noodle, 357
seasonings for, 244
tofu with bell peppers or
other vegetables,
647–648
Vietnamese style, 379
Stir-frying technique, 26,
242, 646
Stock, vegetable
additions to, 103–104
dashi, kombu, 103
dashi, no-cook, 103
vs meat stock, 100
mushroom, 102–103
one-hour, 101–102
roasted, 102
simple, easy and fast, 101
storing, 100–101
Stockpots, 11

Stovetop mixed vegetables
with olive oil, 381
Strawberry(ies)
about, 421
balsamic, with arugula, 42
balsamic, with arugula and
goat cheese, 42
granita, 894
ice cream, 890
to macerate and season,
416
to prepare, *421*
sorbet or ice milk, -pink
peppercorn, 893
tart, and cream cheese, 875
yogurt soup with, 159
Streusel. *See also* Crumble
topping
coffee cake, pull-apart
(monkey bread),
715, 715
Strudel
banana, 880–881
cherry, 881
pound cake, leftover, 881
Stuck-pot rice
basics of, 523–524
and beans with tortilla
crust, 525
and lentils with pita crust,
525
and lentils with pita crust,
orange-scented,
525
and lentils, spicy, 525
with potato crust, 526
with almonds, sesame
seeds, and ginger,
526
with aromatic vegetables,
526
with lemon and herbs,
526
with lima beans, 526
with sour cream and chiles,
524
with yogurt and mango,
524
with yogurt and spices, 524
Stuffed eggs. *See* Egg(s),
deviled (stuffed)

Stuffed fruit
apples, blue cheese, *402,*
402
apples, Cheddar, with
hazelnuts, 402–403
apples, mascarpone, with
almonds, 403
peaches or nectarines, 405
pears, 405
Stuffed pasta, 481–486
Stuffed vegetables
acorn squash, with wild
rice, 399
artichokes, 397
basics of, 395
butternut squash, 404
cabbage with bread salad,
whole-grain,
401–402
cabbage with lentils and
rice, 400–401, *401*
cabbage with lentils and
rice in red wine
sauce, 401
cabbage, Napa, 404
chayote, 404
chiles rellenos, 399–400,
400
with corn and pumpkin
seeds, 400
with goat cheese and
walnuts, 400
grilled, 400
dishes for stuffing, 407
eggplant, *397*, 397–398,
404
mushrooms, 397
onions, 396–397
onions, béchamel, 397
red peppers, with quinoa
and goat cheese,
399
suggestions for, 404–405
tomatoes, with rice,
398–399, *399*
zucchini, with couscous,
399
Stuffing
bread and herb, 395–396
dishes for stuffing pasta,
485

Stuffing (Continued)
dishes for stuffing vegetables, 407
for pasta, 481
"Succotash," barley, 541–542
Sugar. See also Brown sugar
beating into egg whites, 899
types of, 834–835
Sugar syrup, 857
Sumac, 821
Summer rolls, 743–744
Summer squash. See Squash,
summer
Summer vegetable stew with
wheat berries,
564–565
Sunchoke(s)
about, 369
broiled, with garlic or
Parmesan, 370
bulgur with, creamed, 556
crisp-cooked, 369–370
pasta, 443
and potato gratin, 384
salad, 51
soup, creamy, 130–131
Sun-dried tomato(es)
and avocado dip or spread,
264
bread pudding with moz-
zarella and, 193
breadsticks, 711
chickpeas in their own
broth with, 606
egg salad with, 180
pearl couscous pilaf with,
551
pickled eggs with garlic
and, 182
sauce, 449
tapenade, 327
Sunflower seeds, about, 321
Superfine sugar, 834
Super-spicy chile-garlic salsa,
789
Sushi
basics of, 527
bowls, 527–528, 529
nigiri, 530, 530–531
rice, 527
rolls (maki), 528, 528–530

Sushi style rice with edamame
and shiso, 532
Sweating technique, 26
Sweet almond milk couscous,
897
Sweet almond soup, 905
Sweet bulgur with spices, 897
Sweet coconut rice, 508
Sweet coconut soup, 905
Sweet coconut soup with
grains or tapioca,
905
Sweet coconut soup with
granita, 905
Sweet cottage cheese pancakes,
227
Sweet couscous with citrus
salad, 897
Sweet couscous with dried
fruit, 897
Sweet couscous with pistachios, 897
Sweet crumble topping, 870
Sweeteners
basics of, 833–834
granulated, 834–835
liquid, 835–836
Sweeter caramelized onions,
329
Sweeter vegannaise, salad
dressing style, 773
Sweet green tomato upside-
down cake, 854
Sweet and hot miso glaze, 782
Sweet miso glaze, 782
Sweet peanut sauce, 796
Sweet piecrust, 866–867
Sweet potato(es)
about, 370–371
and beans, boulangerie,
621
biscuits, 695
breading and frying, 247
and cream cheese gratin,
384
gnocchi, 488
to grill, 255
pie, ginger-, 873
and pinto beans, baked,
enchilada style, 622
and quinoa salad, 84

and quinoa salad, south-
western, 85
salad, grilled, with red pepper vinaigrette, 69
salad, roasted, with red
pepper vinaigrette,
69
simply cooked, 371
tortellini, 484
in vegetable burger, spicy
autumn, 665–666
vermicelli, Korean, 465
waffles, 206
Sweet and rich muffins, 694
Sweet sesame meringue, 903
Sweet and sour
chickpeas, hot, with egg-
plant, 609–610
chickpeas, more, with
eggplant, 610
chickpeas with tomatoes,
610
edamame with vegetables,
591
Sweet tart crust, 867–868
Sweet tomato chutney, 786
Swiss chard. See Chard
Swiss style cheese, 209–210
bake, 220–221
Syrup
balsamic, 798–799
sugar (simple), 857

Tabbouleh, 43
Table salt, 808
Tacos
basics of, 737–738
fillings and salsas for, 739,
740
Tagine, pearl couscous, 553
with caramelized butternut
squash, 553
Tahini
chickpeas in their own
broth with, 606
in hummus, 614–615
edamame, 615
fondue, 616
lime, 615
millet mash, 566
miso sauce, 782

sauce, 796
coconut, 796
curry, 796
garlic, roasted, 796
minty, 796
pepper, roasted, 796
yogurt, 796
soy sauce, 778
Tamale(s)
corn husk, 549, 549
dishes for fillings, 550
naked, with chile cheese
filling, 547–549
naked, loaf, pie, or cake,
549–550
Tamarind
with black beans, beer-
glazed, 586
-date chutney, 785
granita, 894
Tangerine(s)
about, 430–431
granita, 894
lentil salad, 76
sorbet, -chamomile, 893
Tapenade, 326–327
green olive, 327
tomato, dried-, 327
with tomato and feta salad,
broiled, 58–59
Tapioca
about, 883
coconut soup with, sweet,
905
pudding, citrus, 885
pudding, jasmine-scented,
885
pudding, rose, 885
Tapioca flour, 683
Tarbaises, 579
Taro, 377–378
Tarragon
about, 766
bistro dressing, creamy, 799
cracked wheat, fluffy, with
mustard and, 559
mustard, 777
Tart(s), dessert
almond, 875–876
basics of, 871
fig, fresh, 875

granola, 876

grape or cherry, with port, 874

nut, rich, 876

pear, poached, with dark chocolate ganache, 874–875

pineapple (or almost any fruit), 874

plum, roasted, and pudding, 875

rosemary-pine nut, 876

strawberry and cream cheese, 875

Tart(s), savory. *See also* Galette

black bean, with millet crust, Mexican style, 625

blue cheese and pecan, 228

cheese and tomato, 228

goat cheese and mushroom, with potato crust, 227–228

pinto bean, with millet crust, 624

pinto bean, with millet crust, cheesy, 624

pinto bean, with millet crust, souffléed, 624

ricotta cheese and zucchini with potato crust, 228

white bean and sage, with quinoa crust, 625

Tart crust

additions to, 871

to bake, 866

basics of, 863–864

chocolate, 868

edges of dough, *865*, 865

free-form, *868*, 868

millet, pinto bean tart with, 624

nut, 868

potato, goat cheese and mushroom tart with, 227–228

potato, ricotta cheese and zucchini tart with, 228

to prebake, 872

quinoa, white bean and sage tart with, 625

to roll dough, *864*, 864–865

savory, 868

sweet, 867–868

Tart pan, 12

Tatsoi, 35, 269

Tea

chai custard, spiced, 887

chai ice cream, 891

chamomile-tangerine sorbet, 893

green tea broth with udon noodles, 145–146

green tea or Earl Grey pudding, 885

green tea with edamame, quick-braised, 584

jasmine-scented tapioca pudding, 885

jasmine tea cake soak, 860

smoked-tea chili, 608

Teff

about, 536

polenta style, foolproof, 544

Tembleque (coconut pudding), 884

Tempeh

basics of, 673–674

braised, three ways, 675

hot and sour, 675

with soy and tomato sauce, 675

chili with black beans, 677–678

chili con, 607

crumbled, crunchy, 674

with chili paste, 674

with herbs, fresh, 674

with wheat berries, 674

crumbled, seasoned, 674

"goulash" soup, 151

hash, 676–677

hash with kimchi, 677

quinoa salad with, 84

with rice

brown, and spinach, 676

and mushrooms, 676

and peas, 676

and spinach, 675–676

stir-fried, spicy soybeans with kimchi and, 609

with tofu, fast-braised, 651

-tofu burger, 667

Tempura

batter, 248

dipping sauces for, 249

eggless, 249

Teriyaki sauce, 779

garlic, roasted, 779

mushroom, 779

onion, caramelized, 779

tropical, 779

Teriyaki tofu

-baked, 642

-grilled or broiled, 643

Textured soy protein (TSP), 673

Textured vegetable protein (TVP), 673

Thai basil

mung bean dal with carrots, cashews and, 602

sorbet, lemon-lime, 893

Thai black rice with coconut milk and edamame, 532

Thai chile, 826, 827

Thai style

butternut squash, 365

black beans, beer-glazed with chile paste, 586

carrot soup, 129–130

chile paste, 829

corn pancakes, 291

cucumber salsa, 753

dipping sauce, 778

edamame and potatoes, smashed, with chile paste, 617

green papaya salsa, 753

rice, fried, basic, 521

tofu pancakes, 654–655

tomato soup, cold, 158

vegetable soup, 127

vegetables, quick-braised, 379–380

vegetables, roasted, 381–382

Thermometer, instant-read, 13, 702

Thickeners

in desserts, 881–883

in sauces, 795

in soups, 136

in stir-fry, 645

Thicker vegannaise, 773

3–day pickles, 96–97

Thyme

about, 766

-onion dressing, caramelized, green salad with, 43–44

Tian, 380–381

Toasted bread crumbs, 804–805

Toasted oats and chocolate chip macaroons, 902

Toasts

bruschetta, 735

broiled, 735

with tomatoes and basil, 735

toppings, 737

crostini, 737

French toast, 177

caramelized, 177

crispy, 177

nut-crusted, 177

toppings for, 177–178

spreads for, 737

Tofu

about, 638

baked, 641

barbecue-, teriyaki-, or ponzu-, 642

miso-, 641–642

soy-, 641

braised

basics of, 648

in caramel sauce, 650–651

with eggplant and shiitakes, 650

ketchup-, spicy, 651–652

and peas in coconut milk, curried, 648

and peas in coconut milk, faster, 648

Tofu *(Continued)*
  and peas in coconut
    milk, really spicy,
    649
  peas, and rice in coconut
    milk, creamy, 649
  with tempeh, fast-, 651
  broiled, 642
    barbecue-, teriyaki-, or
      ponzu, 643
    miso, 643
  buckwheat stew with kale
    and, 563
  burger(s)
    Asian style, 666–667
    sesame, with adzuki
      beans, 667
    -tempeh, 667
    -walnut, 667
  to buy and store, 640
  as cheese substitute, 30
  chili con, 607
  coagulants in, 657
  croutons, 656
  croutons, spinach salad
    with warm dressing
    and, 40–41
  dashi- or kombu-boiled,
    641
  deep-fried, 643–644
    agedashi, 644
    slightly more refined,
      644
  dip or spread, 212
  in dumplings, steamed,
    Asian style,
    492–493
  edamame with, hot and
    sour, 591
  edamame with, ma po, 591
  eggplant salad with miso
    and, 64
  -eggplant stir-fry, 300
  in egg rolls, 742
  egg rolls, smoked tofu and
    turnip, 742
  "egg" salad, 180
  enchiladas with red mole,
    224
  escabeche, 653–654

  grilled, 642
    barbecue-, teriyaki-, or
      ponzu, 643
    miso, 643
    rubs and sauces for, 643
  homemade, 656, 656–657
  kale, rolled, with fermented
    black beans and,
    308–309
  lexicon of, 638–640
  marinated, 652–653
    with barbecue sauce,
      653
    crisp, 653
    with Japanese flavors,
      653
    with Spanish flavors,
      653
  pancakes, six ways,
    654–655
    Asian style, 654
    Indian style, 655
    with kimchi, 654
    Mediterranean style, 655
    Thai style, 654–655
  panfried, crispy, 642
  pâté, 180
  poached, 641
  to prepare, *640*, 640–641
  Provençal style, 649–650
  quiche "Lorraine," 188
  rice, fried, without egg,
    520–521
  salad, pressed, 652
  scrambled
    basic, 655
    with beans sprouts, 655
    chile, 655
    miso, 655
    with mushrooms, 655
    the simplest, 656
    smoky, with onions, 655
  smoked
    black-eyed peas with
      mushrooms and,
      611
    black-eyed peas with,
      sliced, 611
    black-eyed peas with,
      610–611

    scrambled with onions,
      smoky, 655
    and turnip egg rolls, 742
  soup(s), 147–151
    "goulash," and bok choy,
      150–151
    "goulash," more tradi-
      tional, 151
    hot pot, tofu skins in,
      149–150
    kimchi, with tofu, 148
    mushroom, Korean,
      148–149
    types of tofu, 147–148
  stir-fried
    basics of, 644–645
    with bell peppers or
      other vegetables,
      647
    with broccoli or cauli-
      flower, 647
    with cabbage, kale, col-
      lards, or other
      greens, 648
    with peas, snow peas, or
      snap peas, 647
    with scallions, 645–646
    with scallions and black
      beans, 646
    with scallions, orange
      zest, and chiles, 646
    with scallions and wal-
      nuts, 646
    with shiitake mush-
      rooms, 647
    to thicken with corn-
      starch, 645
  tikka, grilled, 216
  in vegannaise, 772–773
  to wash, 18
  wontons, -stuffed, 494–495
Tofu noodles, 465
Tofu skins
  about, 640
  and green beans, stir-fried,
    306–307
  and green beans, stir-fried,
    with peanuts and
    cilantro, 307
  in hot pot, 149–150

Tomatillo(s)
  about, 371
  guacamole with, 264
  salsa, cooked, 788
  salsa, fresh, 751
Tomato(es). *See also* Tomato
    salad(s); Tomato
    sauce(s); Tomato
    soup(s)
  about, 371–372
  beans and potatoes,
    boulangerie, toma-
    toey, 620
  and black beans, beer-
    glazed, 585
  breading and frying, 247
  bruschetta with basil and,
    735
  bulgur pilaf with cinna-
    mon, 556
  and bulgur salad, 83
  cabbage with sour cream
    and, 277
  caramelized slices, 375
  cheese fondue, and chile,
    222
  with cheese scramble, fresh,
    219
  and cheese tart, 228
  cherry or grape. *See* Cherry
    or grape tomato(es)
  with chickpeas, sweet and
    sour, 610
  chutney, 785–786
    green tomato, 786
    green tomato-apple, 786
    grilled, 786
    sweet, 786
  cobbler, 375–376
    canned tomato,
      376–377
    with cheesy topping,
      376
    with extra corny top-
      ping, 376
    with herb topping, 376
    with piecrust topping,
      376
    two-tomato, 376
  with corn, pan-grilled, 290

corn salad with feta, mint and, 61
and cracked wheat salad, 83
in crouton salad, 87–88
edamame with cilantro and, 583
edamame with olives and, 583
edamame with roasted chiles and, 583
with eggplant, sautéed, 296
and eggplant, sliced, creamy noodles with, 463
favas, stewed, tomatoey, 604
flageolets with, 605
with goat cheese, baked, 217
gratin, 386
green. See Green tomato
to grill, 255
grilled, with basil, 373–374
grilled, and scrambled eggs, Chinese style, 374
hominy baked with chile, cheese and, 569
ketchup
   black bean, 791
   green, 790
   homemade, 790
   Jamaican jerk, 790–791
with leeks, braised, 311
to macerate and season, 416
mixed vegetables with olive oil, baked, 381
mustard, 777
okra stew with, 324–325
with olives, braised, 326
oven-dried, 377
oven-dried cherry or grape tomatoes, 377
oven-roasted
   canned plum, 375
   everyday, 375
   fresh plum, 375
   sauce, 449
paella with, 522–523

pearl couscous "risotto," spicy, 553
pea salad with feta, mint and, 61
to peel, core, and seed, 372, 373
pine nut sauce with, 797
pizza, margherita, 726
pizza, marinara, 726
to purée, 446
in ratatouille salad, 64
red lentils with fresh tomatoes, 600
rice baked with chile, cheese and, 569
with rice, baked, simplest, 516
rice, Japanese, with fermented black beans and, 532
and rice salad, 82, 83
roasted, pearl couscous gratin with, 555
rye berry gratin with leeks and, 568
rye berry gratin with leeks and, creamy, 568
rye berry gratin with leeks and, vegan, 568–569
salsa, fresh
   avocado-red pepper, 751
   bean, 751
   cheese, Mexican, 750
   Chilean, 750
   cruda, 751
   green tomato pico de verde, 751
   peach melon, 752
   puréed, 750
   salsa fresca, 750
salsa roja, 787–788
   charred, 788
   smoky and hot, 788
sorbet, 892
stuffed, with rice, 398–399, 399
sun-dried. See Sun-dried tomato(es)

vermicelli or fideo with chile and, 451
and white bean gratin, 623–624
yogurt soup with, 158
Tomato salad(s), 57–60
broiled
   and blue cheese, 58
   and blue cheese, with fried sage leaves, 58
   and brie, with almonds, 59
   and Cheddar, with onions, 59
   and feta, with tapenade, 58–59
   and mozzarella, with pesto, 59
cherry tomato, with soy sauce, 57
Ethiopian style, 58
heirloom
   with fried eggs, 59
   with hard-cooked eggs, 59
   with poached eggs, 59
pan-seared, 59–60
pan-seared, with corn, 60
to salt, 46
Tomato sauce(s)
   with aromatic vegetables, 448
   basics of, 445
   with bay leaves, 448
   cheesy, 448–449
   curry, quick, hard-cooked eggs in, 194–195
   enchilada, red, 788
   fast, 445–446
   fresh, 448
   garlicky, 448
   goat cheese, baked, with, 217
   Greek style, 449
   grilled, 449
   with herbs, fresh, 448
   Indian, spicy, 793–794
   light, 804
   meatless "meat," 448
   miso, 449

mushroom, 448
olive, fried, 448
oven-roasted, 449
peanut, 449
pesto, 449
pizza
   with mozzarella, broccoli and, 727
   with mozzarella and, 726–727
   with mozzarella, fresh, and, 727
   with mozzarella and, grilled, 727
   pumpkin, pan-fried with , 366–367
   with cocoa, pumpkin seeds and, 367
   with Parmesan, basil and, 367
   with yogurt, mint and, 367
puréed, 449
puttanesca, 449
raw, linguine with, 446–447
and red pepper, 449
salsa. See Salsa, tomato, fresh; Salsa, roja
spiced, 449
spicy, 448
sun-dried tomato, 449
tempeh, braised, with soy and, 675
thicker, more intense, 449
vegetable, 449
vodka, creamy, 449
walnut-, pasta with, 458
wine, 448
Tomato soup(s), 112–113
about, 111
bread and, 112
cold, 158
cold, with Thai flavors, 158
cream of, 113
gazpacho, 157
gazpacho, spicy, 157–158
puréed, 113
and rice, wintertime, 114
types of tomatoes for, 113

Tomato soup(s) *(Continued)*
    wintertime, 113–114
    wintertime, elegant, 114
Tongs, 13
Toppings. *See also* Bread
        crumbs; Croutons;
        Crumble topping
    crumbles, 805
Torte
    blueberry-olive oil, 853
    chocolate nut, flourless,
        850–851
    vegetable
        autumn, 406
        cheesy, 406
        layered, 405–406
Tortellini
    butternut squash, 483–484
    to make, *484*
    potato, 484
    sweet potato, 484
Tortilla, potato, 184
Tortilla(s)
    burritos
        basics of, 737–738
        breakfast, 174–175
        breakfast, sauces for,
            175
        breakfast, vegan, 175
        fillings and salsas for,
            739, 740
        to roll, *738*, 740
    to cook, 738
    corn and flour, 738
    crust, stuck-pot rice and
        beans with, 525
    quesadilla(s)
        all-cheese, 741
        chile-bean, 741
        chile-bean, grilled, 741
        for one, 741
    scrambled, 176
    scrambled, with scallions
        and chiles, 176
    soft, to cook, 738
    soup, 126–127
    tacos, basics of, 737–738
    tacos, fillings and salsas for,
        739, 740
    wraps with, 736
Traditional pesto, 768

Traditional vanilla pudding,
    884
Trans fats, 754
Treacle, 836
Triangles, butternut squash,
    484
Triticale, 537
Tropical granola, 574
Tropical rice salad, 81
Tropical teriyaki sauce, 779
Truffles, quick, 861
Tube pan, 12
Tubers, tropical
    about, 377–378
    breading and frying, 247
    cassava fritters, 394
    cassava purée, 389
Tuiles
    chocolate, 843–844
    to mold, *844*, 844
Turmeric, 821
Turnip(s)
    about, 378
    braised and glazed,
        354–355
    braised and glazed, with
        miso sauce, 355
    purée, 390
    and smoked tofu egg rolls,
        742
Turnip greens, 317–318
Turnovers. *See* Empanadas
Tuscan style
    rice and white beans, baked,
        510
    white bean and celery root
        gratin, 623
    white beans, 594
Twice-baked potatoes, fillings
    for, 338
Twice-cooked beans. *See*
    Refried beans
Twice-fried green beans, 306
Two-mung salad, 76–77
Two-tomato cobbler, 376

Udon noodles
    about, 464
    with green tea broth,
        145–146
    in noodle bowls, 468

Ultra-fast avocado soup, 157
Unsweetened chocolate, 837
Upside-down cake
    green tomato, sweet, 854
    pear and almond, 854
    pineapple, fresh, 854
    plum-rosemary, 853–854
Urad dal, 579
    with poppy seeds and
        cilantro, 603–604
Utensils, small, 13–15

Vanilla
    -apricot soup, 904
    -berry sauce, 861–862
    cake soak, 858–859
    cake soak, -brown sugar,
        859
    cake soak, milk, 860
    chocolate layer cake, 855
    custard sauce, 863
    granola, real, 574
    ice cream, 890
    pound cake, -lime,
        849–850
    pudding, 883–884
    pudding, traditional, 884
Vanilla beans, 814, *859*, 860
Vastly improved store-bought
    ramen, 466
Vegan cooking
    basic substitutions in,
        29–30
    pizza toppings, 728
    purées, 388
    yeast breads, 687
Vegan dishes
    bean burgers, simplest, 661
    bread pudding, banana-
        chocolate, 886
    burritos, breakfast, 175
    cookies, oatmeal apple, 840
    corn, creamed, with chile,
        291
    cornmeal pudding, 896
    curry gratin, 386
    dumplings with bean
        threads, steamed,
        493–494
    empanadas, vegetable, 747
    lasagne, 460

mashed potatoes, 342–343
mayonnaise substitute. *See*
    Vegannaise
mousse(s), chocolate-
    orange, 900–901
nut burgers, 668
onions, creamed, 330
pancakes, 201
peanut soup, Virginian, 135
rye berry gratin with leeks
    and tomatoes,
    568–569
spinach, creamed, 330
vichyssoise, 107
Vegannaise, 770, 772–773
    salad dressing style, sweeter,
        773
    thicker, 773
Vegetable(s). *See also specific
        vegetables*
    aromatic, stuck-pot rice
        with, 526
    basics of cooking, 235–239
    blintzes, and cheese, 198
    boiled. *See* Boiled vegetables
    braised. *See* Braised vegeta-
        bles; Braised and
        glazed vegetables
    broiled. *See* Broiled vegeta-
        bles
    burger(s). *See* Veggie
        burger(s), vegetable
    buying and handling,
        234–235
    in chopped salad, 39–40
    cooking methods, 237–239
    crisps, beet, 267
    crisps, seasonings for,
        267–268
    crisp-tender, 239
    crudités, 88, 89
    for custards, 192
    custards, -wrapped, 192
    to cut. *See* Cutting tech-
        niques
    doneness, 236
    edamame with, sweet and
        sour, 591
    egg, stuffed, -spring
        vegetable, 181
    in egg rolls, 742–743

empanadas, vegan, 747
fried. *See* Deep-fried vegetables; Panfried vegetables
fries, 352
fritters. *See* Fritters
frozen, 125, 234, 235
gratin(s). *See* Gratin(s), vegetable
grilled. *See* Grilled vegetables
heirloom, 372
holiday and celebration dishes, 408
jook with, 140
lasagne, 459–460
miso-cured, 98
mixed
    with olive oil, baked, 380–381
    with olive oil, stovetop, 380–381
    quick-braised Thai style, 379–380
    roasted, Thai style, 381–382
    stir-fried, Vietnamese style, 379
    very simple, 381
mole, 546
-and-nut bread, 691–692
-and-nut bread, whole grain, 692
nutrients in cooking, 236
omelet, folded, with grated vegetables, 174
pancakes. *See* Pancake(s), vegetable
in parchment, 363
pasta with, 451–455, 456
pickles, pickled
    basics of pickling, 94–95
    quick-, 95
    quick-, Mexican style, 95
pies. *See* Pie(s), savory; Torte, vegetable
precooked, in butter or oil, 240–242
puréed. *See* Puréed vegetables
for quiches, 189

rice with, Mexican, 512
risotto with herbs and, 517–518
roasted. *See* Roasted vegetables
Roman style, broccoli, cauliflower, or just about anything else, 271
root. *See also specific vegetables*
    boiled or steamed, 240
    braised and glazed, 354–355
    braised and glazed with miso sauce, 355
salad(s). *See* Vegetable salad(s), raw; Vegetable salad(s), cooked
sautéed. *See* Sautéed vegetables
to shock, 236, 241
soufflé, 186
for soufflés, 187
soup(s). *See* Vegetable soup(s), mixed
steamed. *See* Steamed vegetables
stew, summer, wheat berries with, 564–565
stir fried. *See* Stir-fried vegetables
stock. *See* Stock, vegetable
storing, 235
stuffed. *See* Stuffed vegetables
for summer rolls, 743–744
to wash, peel and trim, 18, 234
wheat berry stew with fall vegetables, quick, 565
wheat berry stew with spring vegetables, quick, 565
Vegetable salad(s), cooked, 60–68. *See also* Bean salad(s)
beet and avocado, 66

beet and avocado, with citrus, 66
beet, with yogurt sauce, 66
cauliflower, with capers and bread crumbs, 62
cauliflower, with olives and bread crumbs, 61–62
corn, 60–61
corn, curried, 61
corn with tomatoes, feta, and mint, 61
eggplant
    grilled, with garlic and saffron mayonnaise, 65
    grilled, with yogurt, 65
    with miso, 63–64
    with miso and tofu, 64
    with soy vinaigrette, 64
    and zucchini, with cinnamon, 64
greens, Greek style cooked, 66–67
marinated artichokes, 68
marinated fennel or artichoke hearts with preserved lemons, 68
marinated garden vegetables, 67–68
mushroom
    grilled shiitake or portabello, with soy vinaigrette, 63
    Italian-American style, 62
    steamed, with coriander, 62–63
    steamed, Asian style, 63
okra, crisp, 67
onion, roasted, 65–66
pea, with tomatoes, feta, and mint, 61
potato, 68–69
    with blue cheese dressing, 71
    with cheddar dressing, 70
    with cream cheese dressing, 70

grilled, 69
hash brown, crisp shredded, with red pepper vinaigrette, 70
potatoes for, 70
rémoulade, 47
ratatouille, 64
sweet potato, grilled, with red pepper vinaigrette, 69
sweet potato, roasted, with red pepper vinaigrette, 69
Vegetable salad(s), raw, 45–53. *See also* Slaw(s)
artichoke, shaved, 50–51
avocado
    five-layer, 51–52
    with ginger and peanuts, 51
    six-layer, with mangoes, 53
    six-layer, with queso fresco, 53
beet, 49–50
    with cabbage and orange, 50
    with carrot and ginger, 50
    with yogurt dressing, 50
carrot, 45
    and celery, 45
    with cumin, 45–46
    rémoulade, 45
celery, 45
    and carrot, 45
    Chinese-marinated, 46–47
    ginger-marinated, 47
    rémoulade, 47
chayote (mirliton) rémoulade, 47
cucumber(s)
    Korean style, 49
    scallion-marinated, 47
    with sour cream or yogurt, 48
    with soy and ginger, 48
cutting techniques, 52
dressings for, 52

Vegetable salad(s), raw
    (*Continued*)
  ingredients, 52
  jícama and orange, 50
  jícama, with pineapple and
      mint, 50
  mushroom, shaved, 51
  to salt, 46
  sunchoke (Jerusalem arti-
      choke), 51
  Waldorf, 47–48
Vegetable soup(s), mixed,
    122–128
  barley, with seasonal veg-
      etables, 138–139
  Korean style, 127–128
  minestrone, 123
  minestrone, herbed, 123
  pasta and bean, 123
  peanut, Senegalese,
      124–125
  peanut, creamy, 125
  pistou, 123
  southwestern, 125–126
  southwestern, with avo-
      cado, 126
  Spanish style, 124
  Thai style, 127
  tortilla, 126–127
Vegetable steamer, 14–15, *25*,
    237
Vegetarian caesar dressing,
    773
Vegetarian diet
  food sources for, xii-xiii
  health benefits of, xii
  meal planning, xiii-xiv
  umami (savory-ness) in,
      638
Veggie burger(s)
  to bake or broil, 660
  bean
      -and-cheese, 661–662
      high-protein, 662
      the simplest, 660–661
      -and-spinach, 661
      vegan, simplest, 661
      vegetable burger, spicy
          autumn, 665–666
      -and-veggie, 662
  binders for, 658

ingredients and flavorings,
    657–658, 662–663
to make ahead, 659
mix
  in cutlets, 661
  as ground "meat," 662
  in loaves, 664
nut
  fast, 667–668
  nuttier, 668
  -and-seed, 668
  vegan, 668
serving suggestions,
    659–660
to shape, 658–659, *659*
  cutlets, *661*
  "meat" balls, *660*
tofu
  Asian style, 666–667
  sesame, with adzuki
      beans, 667
  -tempeh, 667
  -walnut, 667
vegetable
  autumn, spicy,
      665–666
  bean-and-, 662
  midsummer, 664–665
  spring, fresh, 664
  summer, fresh, with
      cheese, 665
  winter, hearty, 663
Veggie loaves
  burger mix in, 664
  seitan and lentil, 670
  seitan and mushroom,
      670–671
Vereniki (fried potato-stuffed
    dumplings),
    497–498
Verjuice (verjus), 761
Vermicelli
  bulgur pilaf with, 556
  with olives, 450–451
  pilaf, 512
  rice, about, 464
  sweet potato, Korean, 465
  with tomatoes and chile,
      451
Very simple mixed vegetables,
    381

Vichyssoise, 107
  vegan, 107
Vietnamese style
  chile paste, 829
  dipping sauce, 778
  vegetables, stir-fried, 379
Vietnamese summer rolls,
    743–744
Vinaigrette, 762–763
  about, 759, 761–762
  additions to, 763–764
  cauliflower, roasted, with
      raisins and, 282
  coconut curry, 763
  ginger, 763
  with grains, precooked,
      539
  honey-garlic, 763
  leeks, 310
  lemon, 763
  mustard, 763
  red pepper
      hash brown salad with,
          crisp shredded, 70
      sweet potato salad with,
          roasted, 69
      sweet potato salad with,
          grilled, 69
  soy, 763
      eggplant salad with, 64
      shiitake or portobello
          salad with, grilled,
          63
Vinegar
  artichoke hearts, -braised,
      260
  balsamic. *See* Balsamic
      (vinegar)
  basics of, 759
  cauliflower, sautéed, with
      garlic, capers and,
      281
  vs citrus, 759
  in mayonnaise, 770
  in sauces, 798–800
  types of, 760–761
  for vinaigrette, 762
Virginian peanut soup,
    134–135
  vegan, 135
Vodka sauce, creamy, 449

Waffles
  basics of, 203
  buttermilk, everyday,
      203–204
  overnight, 204–205
  potato, baked, 206
  pumpkin, with maple
      cream cheese sauce,
      205–206
  the quickest, easiest, 204
  sweet potato, 206
  variations, 204
  wheatless, 204
  whole grain, 204
Wakame, 53, 356
Waldorf egg salad, 180
Waldorf salad, 47–48
Walnut(s)
  about, 321
  barley cucumber salad
      with, 83
  bread pudding, spiced, 886
  bulgur croquettes with, 558
  butter, carrots with, 268
  butternut squash with
      cream and, 365
  caramel bars, 846
  chiles rellenos with goat
      cheese and, 400
  chutney, and yogurt, 785
  couscous, whole wheat,
      with broccoli and,
      554
  with dal, mixed whole-
      bean, 602–603
  dal, mixed whole-bean, with
      cabbage and, 603
  pâté, 316
  in pesto, traditional, 768
  phyllo "cigars," 880
  sauce
      -miso, green beans tossed
          with, 305–306
      pasta with, rich, 458
      pasta with, 458
  -tofu burger, 667
  tofu, stir-fried, with scal-
      lions and, 646
  tomato sauce, pasta with,
      458
  in Waldorf salad, 47–48

Warm chickpea salad with
arugula, 73–74
Wasabi, 776
Washing vegetables, 18
Water bath, hot, 190
Water chestnuts, 378–379
Watercress
about, 35
soup, creamy, 132
soup, with potatoes and
pears, 133
Watermelon
about, 429
soup, and mint, 903–904
steak, chile-rubbed, 430
steak, grilled, 430
Wax beans, edamame with
Dijon and, 583
Wheat berry(ies)
about, 535, 539
salad
with cabbage and course
mustard, 85
with peanuts and fresh
and dried fruit,
85–87
with roasted peppers,
87
with roasted peppers and
zucchini, 87
stew
with citrus, dried fruit,
and nuts, quick,
565
with fall vegetables,
quick, 565
with spring vegetables,
quick, 565
with tempeh, crunchy
crumbled, 674
with vegetable stew,
summer, 564–565
Wheatless pancakes, 202
Wheatless waffles, 204
Whipped cream, 856–857
White bean(s)
cakes, baked, 629
gratin
and celery root, 623
and celery root, Tuscan
style, 623

grits, with arugula, garlic
and, 551
and tomato, 623–624
and vegetable with bul-
gur crust, 624
with lemon, 607
purée, 612–613
purée, and celery root or
parsnip, 613
and rice, baked, 510
and sage tart with quinoa
crust, 625
with shiitakes, 597
soup, 119–121
Tuscan style, 594
White chocolate, 837–838
White flours, 680–681
White lasagne, 460
White pizza. See Pizza, white
White rice, 505
White rice and black beans,
510
White rice in microwave, 505
White sugar, 834
White wine vinegar, 760
Whole grain
bread, about, 713
bread salad, 89–90
cookies, apple spice, 840
French bread or rolls,
708–709
fruit-and-nut or vegetable-
and-nut bread,
692
pancakes, 202
salad with preserved lemon,
92
waffles, 204
Whole rye, 536
Whole wheat
about, 535
bread, quick, with sweet
milk, 689
bread, quick, lighter, 689
bread, quick, and molasses,
689
couscous with broccoli and
walnuts, 554
couscous with cauliflower
and almonds, 554
dumpling wrappers, 491

dumpling wrappers with
egg, 496
pasta, 442
pasta, in curry broth, 147
piecrust, 867
pita, 720
pizza dough, 725
sandwich bread, half, 713
Whole wheat flour, 478, 681,
848
Whole winter squash cooked
three ways,
365–366
Whole winter squash,
steamed, 366
Wild rice, 567
about, 535
acorn squash stuffed with,
399
with Brussels sprouts, 567
with chestnuts, 567
with curried nuts, 567
with dried fruit, 568
with mushrooms, 568
salad, 81
salad with cucumber and
yogurt, 83
with winter squash,
roasted, 567
Wine
champagne gelées with
berries, 888
and pears, kidney beans
with, 586
port
-cherry jam glaze, 858
grape or cherry tart with,
874
mustard, 776
red
and apples, kidney beans
with, 586
cheddar fondue with,
sharp, 222
-raspberry sorbet, 892
risotto with, 518
sauce, cabbage stuffed
with lentils and rice
in, 401
Shaoxing, rice cakes with,
474

sparkling, with berries, 904
tomato sauce with, 448
Wine vinegar, 760
Winter squash. See Squash,
winter
Wintertime tomato soup,
113–114
Wire racks, 14
Wonton(s)
to seal, 495
soup, 495
tofu-stuffed, 494–495
Wonton noodles, 465
Wonton skins (egg roll wrappers), 491
Worcestershire sauce, hold
the anchovies,
799–800
Wrappers. See Dumplings,
wrappers; Rice
paper wrappers
Wraps, 736
lettuce, 39

Yams
about, 370
breading and frying, 247
Yeast
active dry, 684–685, 686
fresh, 684
instant, 683–684
Yeast bread(s). See Bread(s),
yeast
Yellow rice
the best way, 513–514
the fast way, 514
Yellow split pea soup with
pantry vegetables,
119
Yellow squash. See Squash,
summer
Yogurt
about, 207
biscuits, 694–695
cheese, 208
cucumber salad with, 48
dressing, -dill, barley salad
with cucumber
and, 82
dressing, raw beet salad
with, 50

Yogurt (*Continued*)
  eggplant, broiled, with peppers, onions and, 298–299
  with eggplant salad, grilled, 65
  eggplant, spicy mashed, with mint and, 298
  flavorings for, 208
  frozen, 892
  to make, 207–208
  muffins, 693
  pancakes, 202
  pound cake, 850
  pumpkin, pan-fried, with tomato sauce, mint and, 367
  sauce
    about, 773–774
    beet salad with, 66
    chile-, 793
    simplest, 774–775
    simplest, variations, 774
    uses for, 775
  soup
    with cucumber, 158
    with nuts, 158
    with peas, fresh, 159
    with pineapple, 159
    with radish, 159
    with strawberry, 159
    with tomato, 158–159
  spiced, fried fresh cheese with, 215–216
  spinach with fresh cheese and, 360–361
  spinach with fresh cheese and, baked, 361
  stuck-pot rice with mango and, 524
  stuck-pot rice with spices and, 524

tahini sauce, 796
and walnut chutney, 785
wild rice with cucumber and, 83

Za'atar, 818, 823
  falafel with, 626
  fava beans with, 604
Zester, 15
Zesting citrus fruit, 426
Zesty marinated cheese, 212
Ziti, baked, 458–459
  with goat cheese and olives, 459
  nutty, 459
  with ricotta, 459
Zucchini
  about, 361
  breading and frying, 247
  and eggplant, salad with cinnamon, 64
  to grill, 255
  marinated garden vegetables, 67–68
  mixed vegetables with olive oil, baked, 381
  pancakes, -pesto, 393
  and peppers, roasted, wheat berry or other whole grain salad with, 87
  pickled vegetables, quick-, 95
  in ratatouille salad, 64
  and ricotta tart with potato crust, 228
  sautéed, 362
  soup, rich, 156
  stuffed with couscous, 399
  in vegetable burger, midsummer, 664–665

20 Essential Vegetarian Dishes

1. The World of Rice Salads   79
2. Simple, Easy, and Fast Vegetable Stock   101
3. Wintertime Tomato Soup   113
4. Baked Savory Custard   190
5. Fresh Cheese, the Easy Way   230
6. Stir-Fried Vegetables   242
7. Dry-Pan Eggplant   294
8. Caramelized Spiced Nuts   322
9. Vegetable Pancakes   392
10. Pasta with Walnut Sauce   458
11. Cooking Grains, the Easy Way   537
12. Cooking Beans, the Quick-Soak Way   581
13. Crispy Panfried Tofu   642
14. The Simplest Bean Burgers   660
15. Quick Whole Wheat and Molasses Bread   689
16. White Pizza   725
17. The Simplest Yogurt Sauce, Unleashed   774
18. Chile Paste, 8 Ways   828
19. Oatmeal Apple Cookies   839
20. Frozen Honey Mousse   900

20 Essential Charts

1. Breading and Frying Other Vegetables   246–247
2. Grilling Everyday Vegetables   251–255
3. The Nut and Seed Lexicon   319–321
4. Grilling Everyday Fruits   413–414
5. Everyday Grains   534–535
6. Grains for Enthusiasts   536–537
7. Everyday Legumes   577–578
8. Legumes for Enthusiasts   578–579
9. Cold Sandwiches   731–732
10. Hot Sandwiches   732–734
11. Everyday Oils   755
12. Oils for Enthusiasts   757
13. Types of Vinegar   760–761
14. Everyday Herbs   765–766
15. Specialty Herbs for Enthusiasts   767
16. Everyday Spices   811–814
17. Spices for Enthusiasts   820–821
18. Everyday Fresh Chiles   826
19. Everyday Dried Chiles   827–828
20. Mild or Sweet Peppers   829